D0687769

TRANSLATOR AND EDITOR:
Rabbi Israel V. Berman

MANAGING EDITOR:
Baruch Goldberg

ASSOCIATE EDITOR:
Rabbi Moshe Sober

ASSOCIATE TRANSLATORS AND EDITORS:
Dr. Jeffrey M. Green
Rabbi Eli Touger

COPY EDITORS:
Gershon Gale
Alec Israel
Michael Plotkin

PRODUCTION MANAGER:
Meir Hanegbi

BOOK DESIGNER:
Ben Gasner

GRAPHIC ARTIST:
Michael Etkin

TECHNICAL STAFF:
Moshe Greenvald
Chana Lawrence

Random House Staff

PRODUCTION MANAGER:
Linda Kaye

ART DIRECTOR:
Bernard Klein

CHIEF COPY EDITOR:
Mitchell Ivers

THE TALMUD
THE STEINSALTZ EDITION

VOLUME II

TRACTATE BAVA METZIA

PART II

VOLUME II
TRACTATE BAVA METZIA
PART II

RANDOM HOUSE
NEW YORK

THE TALMUD

תלמוד בבלי

THE STEINSALTZ EDITION

Commentary by Rabbi Adin Steinsaltz

 Published in the United States by Random House, Inc., New York, and simultaneously in Canada by Random House of Canada Limited, Toronto.

This work was originally published in Hebrew by The Israel Institute for Talmudic Publications, Jerusalem.

Library of Congress Cataloging-in-Publication Data

Talmud. English.
The Talmud : the Steinsaltz edition / the Talmud with commentary by
Adin Steinsaltz
p. cm.
ISBN 0-394-58233-0 (v. II)
I. Talmud—Commentaries I. Steinsaltz, Adin. II. Title.
BM499.5.E4 1989 296.1'250521—dc20 89-42911

Manufactured in the United States of America
98765432

כרך זה מוקדש ע״י
ישראל קלבין
לזכר הוריו
זאב קדישביץ קלבין ז״ל
ורחל האס קלבין ז״ל

ולזכר הורי־הוריו:
ישראל ופיגא קדישביץ ז״ל
ואברהם ומרים האס ז״ל

Dedicated by
Israel Klabin

in memory of his parents
Wolff Kadishewitz Klabin
and Rose Haas Klabin

and his grandparents
Israel and Fanny Kadishewitz
and Arthur and Matilde Haas

The Steinsaltz Talmud in English

The English edition of the Steinsaltz Talmud is a translation and adaptation of the Hebrew edition. It includes most of the additions and improvements that characterize the Hebrew version, but it has been adapted and expanded especially for the English reader. This edition has been designed to meet the needs of advanced students capable of studying from standard Talmud editions, as well as of beginners, who know little or no Hebrew and have had no prior training in studying the Talmud.

The overall structure of the page is similar to that of the traditional pages in the standard printed editions. The text is placed in the center of the page, and alongside it are the main auxiliary commentaries. At the bottom of the page and in the margins are additions and supplements.

The original Hebrew-Aramaic text, which is framed in the center of each page, is exactly the same as that in the traditional Talmud (although material that was removed by non-Jewish censors has been restored on the basis of manuscripts and old printed editions). The main innovation is that this Hebrew-Aramaic text has been completely vocalized and punctuated, and all the terms usually abbreviated have been fully spelled out. In order to retain the connection with the page numbers of the standard editions, these are indicated at the head of every page.

We have placed a *Literal Translation* on the right-hand side of the page, and its punctuation has been introduced into the Talmud text, further helping the student to orientate himself. The *Literal Translation* is intended to help the student to learn the meaning of specific Hebrew and Aramaic words. By comparing the original text with this translation, the reader develops an understanding of the Talmudic text and can follow the words and sentences in the original. Occasionally, however, it has not been possible to present an exact literal translation of the original text, because it is so different in structure from English. Therefore we have added certain auxiliary words, which are indicated in square brackets. In other cases it would make no sense to offer a literal translation of a Talmudic idiom, so we have provided a close English equivalent of the original meaning, while a note, marked "lit.," explaining the literal meaning of the words, appears in parentheses. Our purpose in presenting this literal translation was to give the student an appreciation of the terse and enigmatic nature of the Talmud itself, before the arguments are opened up by interpretation.

Nevertheless, no one can study the Talmud without the assistance of commentaries. The main aid to understanding the Talmud provided by this edition is the *Translation and Commentary,* appearing on the left side of the page. This is Rabbi Adin Steinsaltz's highly regarded Hebrew interpretation of the Talmud, translated into English, adapted and expanded.

This commentary is not merely an explanation of difficult passages. It is an integrated exposition of the entire text. It includes a full translation of the Talmud text, combined with explanatory remarks. Where the translation in the commentary reflects the literal translation, it has been set off in bold type. It has also been given the same reference numbers that are found both in the original text and in the literal translation. Moreover, each section of the commentary begins with a few words of the Hebrew-Aramaic text. These reference numbers and paragraph headings allow the reader to move from one part of the page to another with ease.

There are some slight variations between the literal translation and the words in bold face appearing in the *Translation and Commentary.* These variations are meant to enhance understanding, for a juxtaposition of the literal translation and the sometimes freer translation in the commentary will give the reader a firmer grasp of the meaning.

The expanded *Translation and Commentary* in the left-hand column is intended to provide a conceptual understanding of the arguments of the Talmud, their form, content, context, and significance. The commentary also brings out the logic of the questions asked by the Sages and the assumptions they made.

Rashi's traditional commentary has been included in the right-hand column, under the *Literal Translation.* We have left this commentary in the traditional "Rashi script," but all quotations of the Talmud text appear in standard square type, the abbreviated expressions have all been printed in full, and Rashi's commentary is fully punctuated.

Since the *Translation and Commentary* cannot remain cogent and still encompass all the complex issues that arise in the Talmudic discussion, we have included a number of other features, which are also found in Rabbi Steinsaltz's Hebrew edition.

At the bottom of the page, under the *Translation and Commentary,* is the *Notes* section, containing additional material on issues raised in the text. These notes deepen understanding of the Talmud in various ways. Some provide a deeper and more profound analysis of the issues discussed in the text, with regard to individual points and to the development of the entire discussion. Others explain Halakhic concepts and the terms of Talmudic discourse.

The *Notes* contain brief summaries of the opinions of many of the major commentators on the Talmud, from the period after the completion of the Talmud to the present. Frequently the *Notes* offer interpretations different from that presented in the commentary, illustrating the richness and depth of Rabbinic thought.

The *Halakhah* section appears below the *Notes.* This provides references to the authoritative legal decisions reached over the centuries by the Rabbis in their discussions of the matters dealt with in the Talmud. It explains what reasons led to these Halakhic decisions and the close connection between the Halakhah today and the Talmud and its various interpreters. It should be noted that the summary of the Halakhah presented here is not meant to serve as a reference source for actual religious practice but to introduce the reader to Halakhic conclusions drawn from the Talmudic text.

English commentary and expanded translation of the text, making it readable and comprehensible

Hebrew/Aramaic text of the Talmud, fully vocalized, and punctuated

Literal translation of the Talmud text into English

REALIA

קַלְתָּה **Her basket.** The source of this word is the Greek κάλαθος, kalathos, and it means a basket with a narrow base.

Illustration from a Greek drawing depicting such a basket of fruit.

CONCEPTS

פֵּאָה ***Pe'ah.*** **One of the presents left for the poor** (מַתְּנוֹת עֲנִיִּים). The Torah forbids harvesting "the corners of your field," so that the produce left standing may be harvested and kept by the poor (Leviticus 19:9).

The Torah did not specify a minimum amount of produce to be left as *pe'ah*. But the Sages stipulated that it must be at least one-sixtieth of the crop.

Pe'ah is set aside only from crops that ripen at one time and are harvested at one time. The poor are allowed to use their own initiative to reap the *pe'ah* left in the fields. But the owner of an orchard must see to it that each of the poor gets a fixed share of the *pe'ah* from places that are difficult to reach. The poor come to collect *pe'ah* three times a day. The laws of *pe'ah* are discussed in detail in tractate *Pe'ah*.

Marginal notes provide essential background information

TRANSLATION AND COMMENTARY

[1]**and her husband threw her a bill of divorce into her lap or into her basket**, which she was carrying on her head, [2]would you say **here, too,** that **she would not be divorced**? Surely we know that the law is that she *is* divorced in such a case, as the Mishnah (*Gittin* 77a) states explicitly!

אֲמַר לֵיהּ [3]Rav Ashi **said** in reply to Ravina: The woman's **basket is** considered to be **at rest, and it is she who walks beneath it.** Thus the basket is considered to be a "stationary courtyard," and the woman acquires whatever is thrown into it.

MISHNAH הָיָה רוֹכֵב [4]If a **person was riding on an animal and he saw an ownerless object** lying on the ground, **and he said to another person** standing nearby, **"Give that object to me,"** [5]if **the other person took** the ownerless object **and said, "I have acquired it for myself,"** [6]he has **acquired it** by lifting it up, even though he was not the first to see it, and the rider has no claim to it. [7]But **if, after he gave** the object to the rider, the person who picked it up **said, "I acquired** the object **first,"** [8]**he** in fact **said nothing.** His words are of no effect, and the rider may keep it. Since the person walking showed no intention of acquiring the object when he originally picked it up, he is not now believed when he claims that he acquired it first. Indeed, even if we maintain that when a person picks up an ownerless object on behalf of someone else, the latter does *not* acquire it automatically, here, by *giving* the object to the rider, he makes a gift of it to the rider.

GEMARA תְּנַן הָתָם [9]**We have learned elsewhere** in a Mishnah in tractate *Pe'ah* (4:9): **"Someone who gathered** ***pe'ah*** — produce which by Torah law [Leviticus 23:22] is left unharvested in the corner of a field by the owner of the field, to be gleaned by the poor — **and said, 'Behold, this** *pe'ah* which I have gleaned **is** intended **for so-and-so the poor man,'** [10]**Rabbi Eliezer says:** The person who gathered the *pe'ah* **has acquired it**

בִּרְשׁוּת הָרַבִּים [1]וְזָרַק לָהּ גֵּט לְתוֹךְ חֵיקָהּ אוֹ לְתוֹךְ קַלְתָּהּ — [2]הָכָא נַמִי דְּלָא מִגָּרְשָׁה? [3]אֲמַר לֵיהּ: קַלְתָּהּ מֵינָח נַיְיחָא, וְאִיהִי דְּקָא מְסַגְּיָא מִתּוּתָהּ.

משנה [4]הָיָה רוֹכֵב עַל גַּבֵּי בְהֵמָה וְרָאָה אֶת הַמְּצִיאָה, וְאָמַר לַחֲבֵירוֹ "תְּנָה לִי", [5]נְטָלָהּ וְאָמַר, "אֲנִי זָכִיתִי בָּהּ", [6]זָכָה בָּהּ. [7]אִם, מִשֶּׁנְּתָנָהּ לוֹ, אָמַר, "אֲנִי זָכִיתִי בָּהּ תְּחִלָּה", [8]לֹא אָמַר כְּלוּם.

גמרא [9]תְּנַן הָתָם: "מִי שֶׁלִּיקֵּט אֶת הַפֵּאָה וְאָמַר, 'הֲרֵי זוֹ לִפְלוֹנִי עָנִי', [10]רַבִּי אֱלִיעֶזֶר

LITERAL TRANSLATION

in a public thoroughfare [1]and [her husband] threw her a bill of divorce into her lap or into her basket, [2]here, too, would she not be divorced? [3]He said to him: Her basket is at rest, and it is she who walks beneath it.

MISHNAH [4][If a person] was riding on an animal and he saw a found object, and he said to another person, "Give it to me," [5][and the other person] took it and said, "I have acquired it," [6]he has acquired it. [7]If, after he gave it to him, he said, "I acquired it first," [8]he said nothing.

GEMARA [9]We have learned there: "Someone who gathered *pe'ah* and said, 'Behold this is for so-and-so the poor man,' [10]Rabbi Eliezer says:

RASHI

קלתה – סל שעל ראשה, שנותנת בה כלי מלאכתה וטווי שלה. הכי נמי דלא הוי גיטא – והאנן תנן במסכת גיטין (עז,א): זרק לה גיטה לתוך חיקה או לתוך קלתה – הרי זו מגורשת!

משנה לא אמר כלום – דאפילו אמרינן המגביה מציאה לחבירו לא קנה חבירו, כיון דיהבה ליה – קנייה ממה נפשך. אי קנייה קמא דלא מתכוין להקנות לחבירו – הא יהבה ניהליה במתנה. ואי לא קנייה קמא משום דלא היה מתכוין לקנות – הויא ליה הפקר עד דמטא לידיה דהאי, וקנייה האי בגבהה דעקרה מידיה דקמא לשם קנייה.

גמרא מי שליקט את הפאה – אדם בעלמא שאינו בעל שדה. דאי בבעל שדה – לא אמר רבי אליעזר זכה. דליכא למימר "מגו דזכי לנפשיה", דאפילו הוא עני מוזהר הוא שלא ללקט פאה משדה שלו, כדאמר בשחיטת חולין (קלא,ב). "לא תלקט לעני" – להזהיר עני על שלו.

Hebrew commentary of Rashi, the classic explanation that accompanies all editions of the Talmud

Numbers link the three main sections of the page and allow readers to refer rapidly from one to the other

NOTES

מִי שֶׁלִּיקֵּט אֶת הַפֵּאָה **If a person gathered *pe'ah*.** According to *Rashi*, the Mishnah must be referring to someone other than the owner of the field. By Torah law the owner of a field is required to separate part of his field as *pe'ah*, even if he himself is poor, and he may not take the *pe'ah* for himself. Therefore the "since" (מִגּוֹ) argument

Notes highlight points of interest in the text and expand the discussion by quoting other classical commentaries

HALAKHAH

קַלְתָּה **A woman's basket.** "If a man throws a bill of divorce into a container that his wife is holding, she thereby acquires the bill of divorce and the divorce takes effect." (*Shulḥan Arukh, Even HaEzer* 139:10.)

הַמְלַקֵּט פֵּאָה עֲבוּר אַחֵר **A person who gathered *pe'ah* for someone else.** "If a poor person, who is himself entitled to collect *pe'ah*, gathered *pe'ah* for another poor person, and said, 'This *pe'ah* is for X, the poor person,' he acquires the *pe'ah* on behalf of that other poor person. But if the person who collected the *peah* was wealthy, he does not acquire the *pe'ah* on behalf of the poor person. He must give it instead to the first poor person who appears in the field," following the opinion of the Sages, as explained by Rabbi Yehoshua ben Levi. (*Rambam, Sefer Zeraim, Hilkhot Mattenot Aniyyim* 2:19.)

On the outer margin of the page, factual information clarifying the meaning of the Talmudic discussion is presented. Entries under the heading *Language* explain unusual terms, often borrowed from Greek, Latin, or Persian. *Sages* gives brief biographies of the major figures whose opinions are presented in the Talmud. *Terminology* explains the terms used in the Talmudic discussion. *Concepts* gives information about fundamental Halakhic principles. *Background* provides historical, geographical, and other information needed to understand the text. *Realia* explains the artifacts mentioned in the text. These notes are sometimes accompanied by illustrations.

The best way of studying the Talmud is the way in which the Talmud itself evolved – a combination of frontal teaching and continuous interaction between teacher and pupil, and between pupils themselves.

This edition is meant for a broad spectrum of users, from those who have considerable prior background and who know how to study the Talmud from any standard edition to those who have never studied the Talmud and do not even know Hebrew.

The division of the page into various sections is designed to enable students of every kind to derive the greatest possible benefit from it.

For those who know how to study the Talmud, the book is intended to be a written Gemara lesson, so that, either alone, with partners, or in groups, they can have the sense of studying with a teacher who explains the difficult passages and deepens their understanding both of the development of the dialectic and also of the various approaches that have been taken by the Rabbis over the centuries in interpreting the material. A student of this kind can start with the Hebrew-Aramaic text, examine Rashi's commentary, and pass on from there to the expanded commentary. Afterwards the student can turn to the Notes section. Study of the *Halakhah* section will clarify the conclusions reached in the course of establishing the Halakhah, and the other items in the margins will be helpful whenever the need arises to clarify a concept or a word or to understand the background of the discussion.

For those who do not possess sufficient knowledge to be able to use a standard edition of the Talmud, but who know how to read Hebrew, a different method is proposed. Such students can begin by reading the Hebrew-Aramaic text and comparing it immediately to the *Literal Translation*. They can then move over to the *Translation and Commentary*, which refers both to the original text and to the *Literal Translation*. Such students would also do well to read through the *Notes* and choose those that explain matters at greater length. They will benefit, too, from the terms explained in the side margins.

The beginner who does not know Hebrew well enough to grapple with the original can start with the *Translation and Commentary*. The inclusion of a translation within the commentary permits the student to ignore the *Literal Translation*, since the commentary includes both the Talmudic text and an interpretation of it. The beginner can also benefit from the *Notes*, and it is important for him to go over the marginal notes on the concepts to improve his awareness of the juridical background and the methods of study characteristic of this text.

Apart from its use as study material, this book can also be useful to those well versed in the Talmud, as a source of additional knowledge in various areas, both for understanding the historical and archeological background and also for an explanation of words and concepts. The general reader, too, who might not plan to study the book from beginning to end, can find a great deal of interesting material in it regarding both the spiritual world of Judaism, practical Jewish law, and the life and customs of the Jewish people during the thousand years (500 B.C.E.–500 C.E.) of the Talmudic period.

Contents

The Talmud

The Steinsaltz Edition

Volume II

Tractate Bava Metzia

Part II

Introduction to Chapter Two

אֵלּוּ מְצִיאוֹת

"If you meet your enemy's ox or his ass going astray, you shall surely bring it to him again." (Exodus 23:4.)

"You shall not see your brother's ox or his sheep go astray and hide yourself from them: you shall surely bring them back to your brother. And if your brother is not near to you, or if you do not know him, then you shall bring it to your own house, and it shall be with you until your brother seeks after it, and you shall restore it to him again. And so shall you do for his ass, and so shall you do for his garment, and so shall you do for every lost thing of your brother's, which he has lost, and you have found. You may not hide yourself." (Deuteronomy 22:1-3.)

"If you see the ass of him that hates you lying under its burden, and you would forbear from helping him, you shall surely help with him." (Exodus 23:5).

"You shall not see your brother's ass or his ox fall down by the way, and hide yourself from them: you shall surely lift them with him." (Deuteronomy 22:4.)

The laws governing the return of lost articles are set forth quite explicitly in the Torah. However, the Torah does not tell us what to do when it is impossible (momentarily or permanently) to locate the owner of a lost article, or what the rights and duties of the finder are while the article is in his possession. Likewise, the Torah does not indicate under what circumstances the finder of a lost article is permitted to keep it. These questions are the principal theme of this chapter.

When it is clear who the rightful owner of a lost object is, and he can be found and the article returned to him, the Torah's instructions can be followed without difficulty. However, things seldom transpire just this way. Sometimes, when a person announces that he has found something, someone may claim that the lost object belongs to him, yet it may not. It remains to be seen what is considered adequate proof of ownership (e.g., witnesses or identifying marks). Additional and more basic questions arise when it is impossible to determine who the owner of the lost article is. Generally, it is assumed that if it is impossible to find the owner of a lost item, the finder may keep it. This too is a central theme of our chapter.

A fundamental problem here is determining the conditions under which it may be assumed that there is no possibility of returning the lost object to its rightful owner. The theoretical issue at stake here is how to define the legal situation in which ownership of the lost object lapses and is transferred to the person who finds it. The determining factor in such cases is "the giving up of hope on the part of the owner." When the owner of a lost object gives up hope of recovering it, we regard him as if he has formally rendered it ownerless, and thus whoever finds the lost object is permitted to keep it. Hence, it is necessary to determine under what circumstances and from what point in time the owner of a lost object gives up hope of recovering it. The question is related to that of the Halakhic status of identifying marks on a lost object, when and how compelling they are as proof of ownership, among other issues.

Another problem discussed in this chapter arises when the finder is not permitted to keep the lost item: What are his duties and responsibilities regarding the lost object? May he use it, and if so, under what circumstances?

There appears to be a conceptual similarity between the laws concerning assistance to a fallen animal and the laws of returning lost objects (as implied also by their juxtaposition in the Torah). However, while the basic aspects of these laws are explicitly set forth in the Torah, many of the particulars still require clarification. Under what circumstances and upon whom does the obligation to assist a fallen animal devolve? Are there any exemptions from it? Is this obligation merely a variation on the law of returning lost property, or does it also reflect specific concern for the animal's suffering? These questions, and others deriving from them, are discussed in detail in the later pages of the chapter.

אֵלּוּ

[1]מְצִיאוֹת שֶׁלּוֹ, וְאֵלּוּ חַיָּיב לְהַכְרִיז?
[2]אֵלּוּ מְצִיאוֹת שֶׁלּוֹ: מָצָא פֵּירוֹת מְפוּזָּרִין, מָעוֹת מְפוּזָּרוֹת, כְּרִיכוֹת בִּרְשׁוּת הָרַבִּים, [3]וְעִגּוּלֵי דְבֵילָה, כִּכָּרוֹת שֶׁל נַחְתּוֹם, מַחֲרוֹזוֹת שֶׁל דָּגִים, וַחֲתִיכוֹת שֶׁל בָּשָׂר, [4]וְגִיזֵּי צֶמֶר הַלְּקוּחִין מִמְּדִינָתָן, וַאֲנִיצֵי פִשְׁתָּן, וּלְשׁוֹנוֹת שֶׁל אַרְגָּמָן — [5]הֲרֵי אֵלּוּ שֶׁלּוֹ. [6]דִּבְרֵי רַבִּי מֵאִיר.

LITERAL TRANSLATION

MISHNAH [1]Which found objects are his, and which is he obliged to announce?
[2]These found objects are his: [If] he found scattered fruit, scattered coins, small sheaves in the public domain, [3]or round cakes of pressed figs, loaves of a baker, strings of fish, or pieces of meat, [4]or fleeces of wool that have been brought from the (lit., "their") country, or stalks of flax, or strips of purple wool, [5]these are his. [6][These are] the words of Rabbi Meir.

RASHI

משנה **אלו מציאות. מצא פירות מפוזרין** — נתייאשו הבעלים מהן, כדאמר בגמרא, והפקר הן. **מעות מפוזרות** — הואיל ואין להם סימן ניכר — אייאושי מיאש והוו להו הפקר, וזהו טעם כולם. **כריכות** — עומרים קטנים; כמו "מאלמים אלומים", ומתרגמינן בירושלמי: מכרכן כריכן (בראשית לז). **ברשות הרבים** — שהכל דשין עלייהו, ואם היה סימן נקשר עליהן — הרי הוא נשחת. **של נחתום** — כל ככרות הנחתומין שוין, אבל ככרות של בעל הבית יש בהן סימן. **ממדינתן** — כמות שהן גזוזות כשאר כל גיזת המדינה, לאפוקי הבאות מבית האומן, כדקתני סיפא. **אניצי פשתן** — *ריסט"א בלשון אשכנז, ובמקומינו **פופי"ר. **ולשון של ארגמן** — צמר סרוק ומשוך כמין לשון, וצבוע ארגמן, ומלויין הן.

TRANSLATION AND COMMENTARY

MISHNAH אֵלּוּ מְצִיאוֹת שֶׁלּוֹ [1]**Which found objects are the finder's, and which is he obliged to announce** publicly, so that the owner can come and identify them?

אֵלּוּ מְצִיאוֹת שֶׁלּוֹ [2]**The following found objects are his** to keep: items without identifying marks, such as **scattered fruit,** or **scattered coins,** or **small sheaves in the public domain,** where any identifying mark on them can be assumed to have been obliterated by passersby, [3]**or** standardized items like **round cakes of** dried, **pressed figs, loaves of a** commercial **baker, strings of fish, or pieces of meat,** [4]**or fleeces of wool that have been brought from the country** after shearing but have not yet been processed, **or stalks of flax** in bundles, **or strips of purple wool.** [5]All **these** articles **are** the finder's to keep, because they appear identical to others of the same kind and bear no distinguishing marks by means of which their owners can identify them. We therefore assume that their owners have given up hope of getting them back and have abandoned them. [6]The above is the opinion **of Rabbi Meir.**

NOTES

אֵלּוּ מְצִיאוֹת שֶׁלּוֹ, וְאֵלּוּ חַיָּיב לְהַכְרִיז **Which found objects are the finder's and which is he obliged to announce?** The Torah (Deuteronomy 22:1-3) requires that people who find lost property return it to its rightful owner. The Mishnah (below, 27a) deduces from the detailed list of types of lost property mentioned in the verses — ox, lamb, ass, clothing — that not all items need be returned. On the contrary, this positive commandment applies only if the owner of the lost property expects to get it back — if he plans to look for it and is confident that he will be able to identify it. But if the finder has compelling reasons to assume that the owner has given up hope of recovering the lost object, it is considered ownerless and the finder may keep it.

There is a Halakhic difference of opinion as to whether the concept of giving up hope of recovering one's property (יֵאוּשׁ) applies to other areas of law, notably to cases of theft. If a thief steals an object he must return it. If, after the theft, the owner's title to the object were nullified in some way, the thief need not return the object itself, but must pay for it instead. There is a difference of opinion as to whether giving up hope is itself sufficient to nullify an owner's title and allow the thief to keep the object and merely reimburse the owner for its value. Nevertheless, all agree that giving up hope is effective in nullifying the owner's title to a lost object.

אֵלּוּ מְצִיאוֹת שֶׁלּוֹ **Which found objects are the finder's?** The Mishnah asks: "Which found objects are the finder's?" rather than: "Which found objects is he *not* obliged to announce?" in conformity with the style of the next clause — "Which is he obliged to announce?" — in order to teach us an additional law, that the finder has an absolute claim to such items. Not only is the finder not obliged to seek out the owner, but even if the owner comes forward of his own accord and proves his ownership, the finder may still keep what he has found. Since the objects have no identifying marks, we may assume with certainty that the owners despaired of recovering them and relinquished their rights, rendering them ownerless (*Ritva*).

וְגִיזֵּי צֶמֶר הַלְּקוּחִין מִמְּדִינָתָן **Fleeces of wool that come from the country.** The translation here follows *Rashi. Rosh,*

HALAKHAH

אֵלּוּ מְצִיאוֹת שֶׁלּוֹ **These found objects are his.** "A found object may be kept by its finder even if it contains an identifying mark, provided that its owner has clearly given up hope of recovering it. Items without identifying marks, of whose loss the owner can reasonably be expected to have been aware, may be kept by their finder." (*Shulḥan Arukh, Ḥoshen Mishpat* 262:5-6, following the Mishnah and the conclusion of the Gemara.)

פֵּירוֹת מְפוּזָּרִין **Scattered fruit.** "If a person finds scattered fruit which appears to have been put there intentionally, he

BACKGROUND

פֵּירוֹת מְפוּזָּרִין **Scattered fruit.** The term "fruit" is used broadly here to include both the fruit of a tree and all sorts of produce and seeds.
As explained in the Gemara, fruit may be scattered either because it has fallen (out of a bundle, a sack, or a loaded wagon) or because it was left where it was by its owners, who did not wish to gather it or were unable to do so while they were gathering the rest of their produce.

מַחֲרוֹזוֹת שֶׁל דָּגִים **Strings of fish.** In order to sell their catch more easily, fishermen used to string fish on cords by the gills, and buyers would take a whole string of fish or part of it, as required. The Gemara explains that such strings were often of standard length, each one containing the same number of fish, so that they did not have any particular identifying mark.

הַלְּקוּחִין מִמְּדִינָתָן **Brought from the country.** After sheep were sheared, in the first stage of the marketing of the wool, the packages of raw wool were transported to market without being sorted. There the wool was sold to private buyers or to wool merchants. Since these fleeces had not yet undergone any processing or sorting, it was impossible to tell one fleece from another.

אֲנִיצֵי פִשְׁתָּן **Stalks of flax.** These are the linen fibers which have been completely removed from the stems and combed, so that they are ready to be spun into thread. The stalks of flax are at the equivalent stage of processing as the fleeces of wool.

SAGES

רַבִּי מֵאִיר **Rabbi Meir.** A Tanna of the generation before the completion of the Mishnah. See *Bava Metzia,* Part I, pp. 28-29.

LANGUAGE (RASHI)

*ריסט"א From the Old French *ristes* — and the Old German *risten* — bundles of untreated flax.

**פופי"ר The correct reading is פופיד"ש, from the Old French *popedes* — bundles of untreated flax.

LITERAL TRANSLATION

[1]Rabbi Yehudah says: Anything in which there is something different he is obliged to announce. [2]How so? [3][If] he found a round cake [of figs] and inside it a potsherd, [or] a loaf and inside it coins.

[4]Rabbi Shimon ben Elazar says: All *anporya* vessels he is not obliged to announce.

GEMARA [5]"[If] he found scattered fruit." And how much? [6]Rabbi Yitzḥak said: A *kav* in four cubits.

[7]What is it like? [8]If [the fruit was lying] in a manner [indicating that] it had fallen, even more also! [9]And if [it was lying] in a manner [indicating that] it had been put down, [10]even less than this also should not [belong to the finder]!

[1]רַבִּי יְהוּדָה אוֹמֵר: כָּל שֶׁיֵּשׁ בּוֹ שִׁינּוּי חַיָּיב לְהַכְרִיז. [2]כֵּיצַד? [3]מָצָא עִגּוּל וּבְתוֹכוֹ חֶרֶס, כִּכָּר וּבְתוֹכוֹ מָעוֹת.

[4]רַבִּי שִׁמְעוֹן בֶּן אֶלְעָזָר אוֹמֵר: כָּל כְּלֵי אַנְפּוּרְיָא אֵין חַיָּיב לְהַכְרִיז.

גמרא [5]״מָצָא פֵּירוֹת מְפוּזָּרִין״. וְכַמָּה? [6]אָמַר רַבִּי יִצְחָק: קַב בְּאַרְבַּע אַמּוֹת.

[7]הֵיכִי דָּמֵי? [8]אִי דֶּרֶךְ נְפִילָה, אֲפִילּוּ טוּבָא נַמִי! [9]וְאִי דֶּרֶךְ הִינּוּחַ, [10]אֲפִילּוּ בְּצִיר מֵהָכִי נַמִי לָא!

TRANSLATION AND COMMENTARY

רַבִּי יְהוּדָה אוֹמֵר [1]But **Rabbi Yehudah says: Anything,** even one of the above articles, **that has something different about it,** distinguishing it from other articles of its kind, **must be announced.** [2]**How so?** [3]**If he found a round cake of figs with a potsherd inside it, or a loaf** of bread **with coins inside it,** he must announce that he has found them, because the original owner may have put the potsherd or the money in them deliberately. Thus he may be able to identify them, and he will not necessarily have given up hope of getting them back.

רַבִּי שִׁמְעוֹן בֶּן אֶלְעָזָר אוֹמֵר [4]**Rabbi Shimon ben Elazar says: All *anporya* vessels,** i.e., new items of merchandise, which have just arrived from the marketplace and have not yet been used, **do not have to be announced** by the finder, because they appear identical and do not yet have any identifying marks.

GEMARA מָצָא פֵּירוֹת מְפוּזָּרִין [5]The Mishnah states: **"If he found scattered fruit."** Since the expression "scattered" is not precisely defined by the Mishnah, the Gemara asks: **How much** is considered "scattered"? What quantity of fruit scattered over what area comes under the category of "scattered" fruit?

אָמַר רַבִּי יִצְחָק [6]**Rabbi Yitzḥak said** in reply: The fruit is considered "scattered" if there was **a *kav*** of it scattered **in** an area of **four cubits** by four cubits. (A *kav* is a measure of volume, the equivalent of about two liters; a cubit is about half a meter long.)

הֵיכִי דָּמֵי [7]The Gemara now proceeds to clarify Rabbi Yitzḥak's statement and asks: **How is this to be visualized?** [8]**If the fruit was lying in a manner indicating that it had fallen** and had not been placed there intentionally, **even more** than a *kav* lying in this manner should **also** belong to the finder. Since the fruit has no identifying mark, there is no way for the original owner to identify it, and he presumably gave up hope of recovering it. [9]**And if** the fruit **was lying in a manner indicating that it had been put down** there intentionally to be collected later, [10]then **even** if **less than** a *kav* was scattered over four cubits square, it **should also not belong to the finder,** since the rightful owner clearly plans to come back and collect his fruit!

RASHI

מצא עיגול — של דבילה. **אנפוריא** — בגמרא מפרש.

גמרא וכמה — חשוב פיזור? **קב** — מפוזר בארבע אמות, אבל בשלש אמות לא הוי פיזור, וטעמא מפרש ואזיל. **אי דרך נפילה** — אם מנאם דרך נפילה, שיש לדעת שלא הונחו שם מדעת, אלא נפלו. **אפילו טובא** — מקב נמי, דכיון דאין בהן סימן איאושי מיאש. **ואי דרך הינוח וכו׳** — עתיד לחזור וליטלן.

LANGUAGE

אַנְפּוּרְיָא New vessels. This word is derived from the Greek ἐμπορία, *emporia,* which means "merchandise."

SAGES

רַבִּי יְהוּדָה Rabbi Yehudah. When the Mishnah speaks of Rabbi Yehudah without any further details, it is referring to Rabbi Yehudah son of Rabbi Il'ai, one of the greatest Tannaim of the fourth generation. He was one of the last five of Rabbi Akiva's disciples, and his father, Rabbi Il'ai, had been a disciple of Rabbi Eliezer. Rabbi Yehudah learned Rabbi Eliezer's teachings from his father. In his youth he studied with Rabbi Tarfon, and he transmits teachings in his name as well as in the names of the other Sages of Yavneh: Rabbi Eliezer, Rabbi Yehoshua, Rabban Gamliel, Rabbi Elazar ben Azaryah, Rabbi Yishmael, and Rabbi Yose HaGelili. But Rabbi Yehudah's main teacher was Rabbi Akiva, according to whose teachings he laid the foundations for the Halakhic exegesis of Leviticus in a work known as the *Sifra* (or *Torat Kohanim*). According to tradition, an unattributed statement in the *Sifra* is a teaching of Rabbi Yehudah. He was ordained by Rabbi Yehudah ben Bava and is frequently quoted in Aggadic exegesis together with Rabbi Neḥemyah. In differences of opinion between Rabbi Yehudah and Rabbi Meir, or between Rabbi Yehudah and Rabbi Shimon, the Halakhah follows Rabbi Yehudah. Among his disciples were Rabbi Elazar son of Rabbi Shimon, Rabbi Yishmael son of Rabbi Yose, and Rabbi Yehudah HaNasi. His son, Rabbi Yose son of Rabbi Yehudah, was also a famous Sage.

רַבִּי שִׁמְעוֹן בֶּן אֶלְעָזָר Rabbi Shimon ben Elazar. One of the Sages of the Mishnah during the last generation of Tannaim. See *Bava Metzia,* Part I, p. 37.

רַבִּי יִצְחָק Rabbi Yitzḥak. A prominent Palestinian Amora of the second and third generations, Rabbi Yitzḥak's full name is Rabbi Yitzḥak Nappaḥa. He was a disciple of Rabbi Yoḥanan and often presents teachings in the

NOTES

however, understands the word מְדִינָה to mean "bundle" (cf. the Aramaic expression מְדָאנֵי אָסָא "bundles of myrtle"), and explains מִמְּדִינָתָם as meaning "from their bundle," in other words, untied or loose. Hence, the Mishnah would read "loose fleeces of wool."

וְכַמָּה? אָמַר רַבִּי יִצְחָק And how much? Rabbi Yitzḥak said. *Tosafot* (see "וכמה") establishes that this is not a question asked by the Sages of the Talmud and answered by Rabbi Yitzḥak, but must rather be regarded as a single statement in which Rabbi Yitzḥak himself asked and then answered the question as to the criteria for determining whether fruit is scattered. Rabbi Yitzḥak defines fruit narrowly, as grain, and specifically, grains of wheat. According to *Tosafot* the statement of Rav Ukva bar Ḥama below (21a, p. 5) is in explanation of Rabbi Yitzḥak's point of view, and leaves open the question of how the law would be applied to other kinds of fruit.

HALAKHAH

may not touch it; but if the fruit appears to have fallen accidentally, the finder may keep it. (*Shulḥan Arukh, Ḥoshen Mishpat* 262:7.)

כָּל שֶׁיֵּשׁ בּוֹ שִׁינּוּי Anything that has something different about it. "If a person found a fig cake containing a potsherd, or a loaf of bread with coins inside it, he must announce that he has found them, since such things are unusual, even though the potsherd or the money may have fallen into the

LITERAL TRANSLATION

[1] Rav Ukva bar Ḥama said: We are dealing with the gathering [of grain] on the threshing floor: [2] [If] a *kav* is [spread] over four cubits, where the effort [to collect it] is great, [3] a person does not make the effort and does not come back and collect it; [4] [hence, we may assume that] he has abandoned it. [5] [But if the *kav* is spread over a] smaller [area] than this, [6] he makes the effort and comes back and collects it, and he does not abandon it.

[7] Rabbi Yirmeyah asked: What about half a *kav* in two cubits? [8] What is the reason [why people abandon] a *kav* in four cubits? [9] [Is it] because the effort [to collect it] is great, [10] [and in that case] half a *kav* in two cubits, since the effort [involved] is not great, one would not abandon it?

[1] אֲמַר רַב עוּקְבָא בַּר חָמָא: בְּמַכְנַשְׁתָּא דְבֵי דָרֵי עָסְקִינַן: [2] קַב בְּאַרְבַּע אַמּוֹת, דְּנָפֵישׁ טִרְחַיְיהוּ, [3] לָא טָרַח אִינִישׁ וְלָא הָדַר אָתֵי וְשָׁקֵיל לְהוּ; [4] אַפְקוּרֵי מַפְקַר לְהוּ. [5] בְּצִיר מֵהָכִי, [6] טָרַח וְהָדַר אָתֵי וְשָׁקֵיל לְהוּ, וְלָא מַפְקַר לְהוּ.

[7] בָּעֵי רַבִּי יִרְמְיָה: חֲצִי קַב בִּשְׁתֵּי אַמּוֹת מַהוּ? [8] קַב בְּאַרְבַּע אַמּוֹת טַעְמָא מַאי? [9] מִשּׁוּם דְּנָפֵישׁ טִרְחַיְיהוּ, [10] חֲצִי קַב בִּשְׁתֵּי אַמּוֹת, כֵּיוָן דְּלָא נָפֵישׁ טִרְחַיְיהוּ, לָא מַפְקַר לְהוּ?

RASHI

במכנשתא דבי דרי — בשעת אסיפת גרנות, וכאן דשן בעליהן ונשאו את העיקר ונותרו אלו. **נפיש טרחייהו** — לקבצן. **בציר מהכי** — אם היה פזורן בפחות מכן.

TRANSLATION AND COMMENTARY

אֲמַר רַב עוּקְבָא בַּר חָמָא [1] **Rav Ukva bar Ḥama said** in reply: We are not dealing here with a situation where the fruit fell by accident, or where the owner left it there with the intention of collecting it later. **We are dealing with the gathering of grain** kernels **on the threshing floor.** The owner of the grain threshed it and took most of it away, leaving only a small quantity behind. This small quantity is the "scattered fruit" referred to in the Mishnah. [2] Rabbi Yitzḥak's explanation can now be understood as follows: **If a** *kav* of grain **is spread over** an area of **four cubits** square, **where the effort** involved **in collecting it is great** for a relatively small return, [3] **a person would not make the effort to come back and collect it.** [4] **Hence, we may assume that** the owner **has abandoned it,** and the finder may keep it. [5] **But if the** *kav* **is spread over a smaller area than this,** [6] the owner presumably planned to **make the effort to come back and collect it, and has not abandoned it.** Therefore, the finder should not take it, and if he does so he must announce what he has found.

בָּעֵי רַבִּי יִרְמְיָה [7] In order to clarify Rabbi Yitzḥak's view further, a number of practical problems in applying it are now raised. They all revolve around the question: What is the main motive in the owner's decision to abandon part of his crop? Rabbi Yitzḥak has explained that the owner was prepared to abandon part of his crop because the effort involved in collecting it was too great for such a small return. But the question remains: Which of these factors is the primary one — the effort or the return? Would the owner make the effort if the return were slightly greater? Would he accept the original return if the effort required were slightly reduced? Addressing these questions, **Rabbi Yirmeyah asked:** (1) **What about half a** *kav* scattered **over** an area of **two cubits** by four cubits? I.e., what is the law if half the quantity were scattered over half the area? [8] The basis of the problem is as follows: **What is the reason why people abandon a** *kav* of wheat which they have left scattered **over four cubits** by four? [9] **Is it because the effort to collect it is** too **great?** [10] **In that case would one not abandon half a** *kav* **in two cubits** by four, **where the effort involved** in collecting it **is not great,** because two

NOTES

מַכְנַשְׁתָּא דְּבֵי דָרֵי **The gathering of grain on the threshing floor.** The translation and explanation here follow *Rashi. Rabbenu Ḥananel* explains this expression slightly differently: The grain that accumulates when the threshing floor is swept and cleaned.

חֲצִי קַב בִּשְׁתֵּי אַמּוֹת מַהוּ **What about half a** ***kav*** **in two cubits?** Cubits are a measurement of length. When the Gemara uses the expression "four cubits" as a measurement of area, it normally means "four cubits by four." What, then, is meant here by "two cubits"?

Tosafot explains that the Gemara means "two cubits by two," a quarter of the area previously mentioned.

HALAKHAH

fig cake or loaf of bread by accident. *Rema,* however, following *Rosh,* maintains that the finder need not announce that he has found such an item." (Ibid., 262:15.) This dispute is rooted in a textual problem: If we read "these are the words of Rabbi Meir" in the Mishnah (as in our text), the Halakhah in general follows Rabbi Yehudah's view rather than Rabbi Meir's, and this explains the ruling in the *Shulḥan Arukh.* However, if we do not read "these are the words of Rabbi Meir" (as was the reading of many of the classical commentators), Rabbi Yehudah's view is not followed, since it opposes that of the anonymous Mishnah.

בְּמַכְנַשְׁתָּא דְּבֵי דָרֵי **The gathering of grain on the threshing floor.** "If a person found grain scattered on the threshing floor, he may keep it, provided that a *kav* (or less)

latter's name. He also spent part of his life in Babylonia, where he was an important source of information about the teachings and customs of Eretz Israel.

BACKGROUND

מַכְנַשְׁתָּא דְּבֵי דָרֵי **The gathering of grain on the threshing floor.** This refers to threshing floors where wheat was scattered. In this context it appears that such places were not on a single person's private property, and were used by several different people successively.

SAGES

רַבִּי יִרְמְיָה **Rabbi Yirmeyah.** Born in Babylonia, Rabbi Yirmeyah was one of the leading Amoraim of the third and fourth generations. He studied in Babylonia in his youth but soon thereafter immigrated to Eretz Israel. There, he was a disciple of the greatest Sages of the generation, the students of Rabbi Yoḥanan (Rabbi Zera and Rabbi Abbahu). Rabbi Yirmeyah had a special dialectical method of great acuity, and he used to ask provocative questions of his teachers and colleagues. Since these questions may have given the impression that Rabbi Yirmeyah was seeking to undermine the accepted rules of Halakhic dialectic, he was even punished and removed from the House of Study for a limited period. Rabbi Yirmeyah's teachings are quoted extensively in both the Babylonian and the Jerusalem Talmud, so much so that in Babylonia his teachings are often simply referred to as "They say in the West" (i.e., in Eretz Israel).

TERMINOLOGY

בָּעֵי **He asked.** Generally a בָּעֲיָא — "problem" — arises from a given Halakhic ruling and raises a specific case or possibility which cannot be resolved by the existing ruling. A problem generally has two sides: i.e., someone asks a question (or the Gemara explains the questioner's position) showing that, in the given situation, two different solutions are possible. Frequently a problem (בָּעֲיָא) is raised with the purpose of

sharpening the definitions and distinctions used in formulating the existing Halakhic decision.
The Jerusalem Talmud uses this term in a different sense.

BACKGROUND

שׁוּמְשׁוּם Sesame. The sesame (*sesamus orientale*) is an annual plant and a member of the *pedaliaceae* family.

The sesame plant is hairy, and has pink or white flowers. It produces a follicle that opens, releasing many tiny seeds, each approximately three millimeters in size, which are used as a spice for various foods, and as a source of fine oil. The residue is used for animal and human consumption.
Sesame plants were cultivated by ancient civilizations as far back as Biblical times. While sesame seeds were obviously much more expensive than grain, as already noted, they are small and difficult to gather.

TRANSLATION AND COMMENTARY

cubits by four is a small area? [1]**Or, perhaps,** a person who leaves a *kav* of wheat scattered over four cubits square abandons it primarily **because it is not** an **important** enough quantity to justify going back. [2]In that case **half a *kav*** scattered **over two cubits** by four, **which is even less important, would** surely **be abandoned.**

קַבַּיִים בִּשְׁמוֹנֶה אַמּוֹת [3]On the basis of the question just raised, a further question now arises: (2) **What about two *kavs*** scattered **over** an area of **eight cubits** by four? I.e., what is the law if twice the quantity were scattered over twice the area? [4]The basis of this problem is as follows: **What is the reason why people abandon a *kav*** of wheat which they have left scattered **over four cubits** by four? [5]**Is it because the effort to collect it is** too **great?** [6]**In that case it would be even more so with two *kavs*** scattered **over eight cubits** by four, **and since the effort involved is even greater,** because they are spread over a larger area, **they** too **would be abandoned.** [7]**Or, perhaps, is it** primarily **because** one *kav* scattered over four cubits by four **is not** an **important** enough quantity to justify going back? [8]In that case **two *kavs*** scattered **over eight cubits** by four **are** an **important** quantity, and **would not be abandoned** by their owner.

קַב שׁוּמְשְׁמִין בְּאַרְבַּע אַמּוֹת [9]Another question is now raised: (3) **What about a *kav* of sesame seeds** scattered **over four cubits** by four? The basis of this problem is as follows: Sesame seeds, although smaller than wheat kernels and more difficult to collect, are far more valuable. [10]Now **what is the reason why people abandon a *kav*** of wheat which they have left scattered **over four cubits** square? [11]**Is it because it is not** an **important** enough quantity to justify going back? [12]**In that case a *kav* of sesame seeds, which is** an **important** quantity, **would not be abandoned** by the owner. [13]**Or** do people **perhaps** abandon a *kav* of wheat, primarily **because**

[1]אוֹ דִּלְמָא, מִשּׁוּם דְּלָא חֲשִׁיבִי, [2]וַחֲצִי קַב בִּשְׁתֵּי אַמּוֹת, כֵּיוָן דְּלָא חֲשִׁיבִי, מַפְקַר לְהוּ. [3]קַבַּיִים בִּשְׁמוֹנֶה אַמּוֹת מַהוּ? [4]קַב בְּאַרְבַּע אַמּוֹת טַעְמָא מַאי? [5]מִשּׁוּם דְּנָפֵישׁ טִרְחַיְיהוּ, [6]וְכָל שֶׁכֵּן קַבַּיִים בִּשְׁמוֹנֶה אַמּוֹת, כֵּיוָן דִּנְפִישָׁא טִרְחַיְיהוּ טְפֵי, מַפְקַר לְהוּ? [7]אוֹ דִּלְמָא, מִשּׁוּם דְּלָא חֲשִׁיבִי, [8]וְקַבַּיִים בִּשְׁמוֹנֶה אַמּוֹת, כֵּיוָן דַּחֲשִׁיבִי, לָא מַפְקַר לְהוּ?

[9]קַב שׁוּמְשְׁמִין בְּאַרְבַּע אַמּוֹת מַהוּ? [10]קַב בְּאַרְבַּע אַמּוֹת טַעְמָא מַאי? [11]מִשּׁוּם דְּלָא חֲשִׁיבִי, [12]וְשׁוּמְשְׁמִין, כֵּיוָן דַּחֲשִׁיבִי, לָא מַפְקַר לְהוּ? [13]אוֹ דִּלְמָא, מִשּׁוּם דְּנָפֵישׁ טִרְחַיְיהוּ,

LITERAL TRANSLATION

[1]Or, perhaps, [is it] because it is not important, [2]and half a *kav* in two cubits, because it is not important, one would abandon it?
[3]What about two *kavs* in eight cubits? [4]What is the reason [why people abandon] a *kav* in four cubits? [5][Is it] because the effort [to collect it] is great, [6]and [in that case it would be] even more so [with] two *kavs* in eight cubits, [and] since the effort [involved] is even greater, one would abandon them? [7]Or, perhaps, [is it] because it is not important, [8]and two *kavs* in eight cubits, because they are important, one would not abandon them?
[9]What about a *kav* of sesame seeds in four cubits? [10]What is the reason [why people abandon] a *kav* in four cubits? [11][Is it] because it is not important [12]and [in that case a *kav* of] sesame seeds, because they are important, one would not abandon them? [13]Or, perhaps, [is it] because the effort [to collect it] is great,

RASHI

משום דלא חשיבי – עליה קב פירות לטרוח עליהן טורח קיבוץ של ארבע אמות. **שומשמין** – דקין מאד, ויש טורח בקיבוצן יותר מחטין, אבל דמיהן יקרין.

NOTES

Accordingly, Rabbi Yirmeyah's question relates to a situation where a relatively unimportant quantity of grain is concentrated in a particularly convenient, small area.

Rashba and *Ritva,* however, feel that Rabbi Yirmeyah is clearly decreasing the area and the quantity by the same proportions, and that "two cubits" here must mean "two cubits by four." This interpretation is followed here in the commentary.

HALAKHAH

of grain was scattered in an area of at least four cubits by four cubits. The reason is that we presume that the owner abandoned the grain because he did not want to take the trouble to go back and collect it. But if half a *kav* was scattered over two cubits by four, or two *kavs* were scattered over eight cubits by four, or if the scattered produce was a combination of dates, pomegranates, or sesame seeds, it is not clear what the law is; therefore, the finder should not pick up the fruit, but if he does so, he may keep it." (*Shulḥan Arukh, Ḥoshen Mishpat* 260:7.)

TRANSLATION AND COMMENTARY

collecting a *kav* of scattered wheat **requires great effort?** [1]**In that case it would be even more so with** a *kav* of **sesame seeds** scattered over four cubits square, [2]**and since the effort involved is even greater,** as they are extremely small, **they would be abandoned** by their owner!

קַב תַּמְרֵי בְּאַרְבַּע אַמּוֹת [3]Another question is now raised: (4) **What about a *kav* of dates or a *kav* of pomegranates** scattered **over four cubits** square? The basis of this problem is the reverse of the previous one regarding sesame seeds. Here there is no special difficulty in picking up the scattered dates or pomegranates, because they are large. On the other hand, they are cheap. [4]Now **what is the reason why people abandon a *kav*** of wheat which they have left scattered **over four cubits** square? [5]**Is it because it is not** an **important** enough quantity to justify going back for it? [6]**In that case, a *kav* of dates** scattered **over four cubits** square, **or a *kav* of pomegranates** scattered **over four** cubits square, [7]**which are** also inexpensive and thus **not** an **important** quantity, **would be abandoned** by their owner! [8]**Or** do people perhaps abandon a *kav* of wheat primarily **because collecting** a *kav* of wheat scattered over four cubits **requires great effort?** [9]**In that case, a *kav* of dates** scattered **over four cubits** square, **or a *kav* of pomegranates** scattered **over four cubits** square, [10]**would not be abandoned** by their owner, **since collecting** them **does not require great effort!** [11]**What is the law** regarding all these questions?

תֵּיקוּ [12]The Gemara replies: **The** series of **questions** raised by Rabbi Yirmeyah **remains undecided.**

[1]וְכָל שֶׁכֵּן שׁוּמְשְׁמִין, [2]כֵּיוָן דִּנְפִישׁ טִרְחַיְיהוּ טְפֵי, מַפְקַר לְהוּ? [3]קַב תַּמְרֵי בְּאַרְבַּע אַמּוֹת, קַב רִמּוֹנֵי בְּאַרְבַּע אַמּוֹת, מַהוּ? [4]קַב בְּאַרְבַּע אַמּוֹת טַעְמָא מַאי? [5]מִשּׁוּם דְּלָא חֲשִׁיבֵי, [6]קַב תַּמְרֵי בְּאַרְבַּע אַמּוֹת, קַב רִמּוֹנֵי בְּאַרְבַּע אַמּוֹת נַמִי, [7]כֵּיוָן דְּלָא חֲשִׁיבֵי, מַפְקַר לְהוּ? [8]אוֹ דִּלְמָא, מִשּׁוּם דִּנְפִישָׁא טִרְחַיְיהוּ, [9]וְקַב תַּמְרֵי בְּאַרְבַּע אַמּוֹת וְקַב רִמּוֹנֵי בְּאַרְבַּע אַמּוֹת, [10]כֵּיוָן דְּלָא נְפִישׁ טִרְחַיְיהוּ, לָא מַפְקַר לְהוּ? [11]מַאי? [12]תֵּיקוּ.

LITERAL TRANSLATION

[1]and [in that case it would be] even more so [with] sesame seeds, [2][and] since the effort [involved] is even greater, one would abandon them?

[3]What about a *kav* of dates [or] a *kav* of pomegranates in four cubits? [4]What is the reason [why people abandon] a *kav* in four cubits? [5][Is it] because it is not important, [6][and in that case] a *kav* of dates in four cubits, [or] a *kav* of pomegranates in four cubits, [7]since they are not important, one would also abandon them? [8]Or, perhaps, [is it] because the effort [to collect it] is great, [9]and [in that case] a *kav* of dates in four cubits or a *kav* of pomegranates in four cubits, [10]since the effort [to collect them] is not great, one would not abandon them? [11]What [is the law]?

[12]Let [the questions] remain [undecided].

RASHI

תמרים ורמונין — גסים הן, ואין טורח בקבולן.

TERMINOLOGY

תֵּיקוּ Lit., **let it stand,** i.e., the question raised in the previous passage remains unresolved ("standing"), because we do not possess sources enabling us to resolve this problem, and there is also no logical proof tending towards one or another solution. From a theoretical standpoint, therefore, the question remains "standing" in its place. However, in Halakhic decision-making there are various principles as to what action is to be taken in such cases. If the unresolved problem relates to a prohibition found in the Torah, the decision leans toward stringency. If the unresolved problem refers to a Rabbinical decree, the decision leans toward leniency. In matters of civil law, where absolute degrees of stringency or leniency have no place, the decision is to leave the existing situation in place. In the case of a lost object, the finder may be forbidden to take it, but if he has already done so, the court does not remove it from his possession.

Until this point in the discussion the Gemara has been dealing with situations in which the owner of a lost object becomes aware of his loss before someone else finds the object. Since the owner realizes that he has no way of identifying the object, he is considered to have given up hope of recovering it. The object becomes ownerless and its finder is entitled to keep it, since he is considered to have acquired it legitimately (בְּהֶיתֵּר). This giving up of hope by the owner is called יֵאוּשׁ מִדַּעַת — "conscious *ye'ush*." Situations can, however, arise in which the finder takes possession of an object without identifiable features before its owner has become aware of its loss. As soon as the owner realizes that he has lost the object he will give up hope of recovering it, because he has no means of identifying it. But the finder took possession of it before the owner realized that he had lost it and before he gave up hope of recovering it. Thus the finder's claim to the object rests on potential rather than actual *ye'ush*. The Gemara now begins a long and complicated analysis of the

NOTES

שׁוּמְשְׁמֵי, תַּמְרֵי, רִמּוֹנֵי Sesame seeds, dates, pomegranates. The commentators were puzzled by the seemingly unnecessary variations contained in these problems, all of which revolve around the same fundamental issue. Indeed, it seems that *Rambam* had a different reading in his text of the Gemara, in which all the fruits are included in a single problem: "If a *kav* of mixed sesame seeds, dates, and pomegranates were found in a storehouse, may the finder keep them, since some of the fruits are expensive and some cheap, and some are easy to collect and others not?"

To defend the reading found in our text of the Gemara, *Rashba* suggests that these problems may not have been raised at the same time; rather, they were posed in different academies, and were later gathered together and presented as a single unit. But *Rashba* also notes that certain differences can be detected between the problems. Each case presents a different combination of the effort involved in recovery as compared with the anticipated return. Thus the sesame seeds are very expensive and very difficult to recover, while the pomegranates are very inexpensive and quite easy to recover, etc.

[1]אִיתְּמַר: [21B] יֵאוּשׁ שֶׁלֹּא מִדַּעַת, [2]אַבַּיֵי אֲמַר: לָא הָוֵי יֵאוּשׁ. וְרָבָא אֲמַר: הָוֵי יֵאוּשׁ. [3]בְּדָבָר שֶׁיֵּשׁ בּוֹ סִימָן, כּוּלֵּי עָלְמָא לָא פְּלִיגִי דְּלָא הָוֵי יֵאוּשׁ. [4]וְאַף עַל גַּב דְּשְׁמָעִינֵיהּ דִּמְיָאֵשׁ לַסּוֹף, לָא הָוֵי יֵאוּשׁ, [5]דְּכִי אֲתָא לִידֵיהּ, בְּאִיסּוּרָא הוּא דַּאֲתָא לִידֵיהּ. [6]דִּלְכִי יָדַע דִּנְפַל מִינֵּיהּ, לָא מְיָאֵשׁ. [7]מֵימַר אֲמַר: "סִימָנָא אִית לִי בְּגַוֵּיהּ. יָהֲבְנָא סִימָנָא, וְשָׁקֵילְנָא לֵיהּ".

LITERAL TRANSLATION

[1]It was said: [21B] [Regarding] anticipated *ye'ush* (lit., "unconscious despair"), [2]Abaye said: It is not [considered] *ye'ush*. But Rava said: It is *ye'ush*. [3]Regarding an object that has an [identifying] mark, all agree (lit., "the whole world does not differ") that it is not *ye'ush*. [4]And even though we hear him giving up hope in the end, it is not *ye'ush*, [5]for when it came into [the finder's] hand, it was in [a time of] prohibition that it came into his hand. [6]For when he knows that it has fallen from him, he does not give up hope. [7]He surely says: "I have an [identifying] mark on it. I will give the [identifying] mark, and I will take it?"

TRANSLATION AND COMMENTARY

question whether such יֵאוּשׁ שֶׁלֹּא מִדַּעַת — "potential or anticipated *ye'ush*" — is effective. In other words, is the assumption that the owner will give up hope when he realizes his loss enough to enable the finder to become the legal owner of the object, even before the owner has become aware of his loss?

אִיתְּמַר [1]**It was said** [21B] that there is a dispute between Amoraim regarding this problem: In a situation where an object has been found before its owner is aware of its loss, there is a difference of opinion between Abaye and Rava regarding such an owner's **anticipated *ye'ush*** ("giving up hope") of recovering it. In certain cases, it is assumed that the owner of a lost object will give up hope of recovering it as soon as he becomes aware of his loss. For example, if a lost object has no identifying marks, then with the best will in the world the finder will not be able to return it, and it is assumed that the owner will give up hope as soon as he realizes that he has lost it. But what is the law if the object is found before the owner realizes that he has lost it? What is the legal status of potential *ye'ush* that has not yet been expressed? Does the owner's forfeiture of his rights take effect at the time of the loss, or only when he realizes that he has lost the object? On this point Abaye and Rava disagree. [2]**Abaye said:** Anticipated *ye'ush* **is not considered *ye'ush***, and the finder is not entitled to keep the lost object. **Rava said: It is** considered ***ye'ush***, and the finder is entitled to keep the object.

בְּדָבָר שֶׁיֵּשׁ בּוֹ סִימָן [3]The Gemara now attempts to delimit the dispute: **Regarding an object that has an identifying mark, all agree that** anticipated *ye'ush* **is not** considered ***ye'ush***, and the finder must return the object. [4]**And even though in the end,** after the lost object has been found but before it has been returned, **we hear the owner giving up hope** of recovering it, even Rava would agree that at this late stage such *ye'ush* **is not** considered ***ye'ush*** at all, and the finder is still obliged to return the object. [5]**For when the object entered the finder's possession, it did so at a time when it was prohibited** for him to keep it, as the Gemara now explains: [6]**For when** the owner **realizes that** an identifiable lost object **has fallen from** his possession, **he does not** immediately **give up hope** of its recovery. [7]Rather, **he says** to himself: "**I have an identifying mark on it. I will** track down the finder and **give** him a clear description of **the identifying mark and recover** the object." Now, since the original owner has not yet given up hope of recovering the lost object when it was found, the object has not become ownerless, and the finder is obliged, by Torah law, to return it as soon as possible. Indeed, the finder becomes, in a sense, the owner's bailee, and even if the owner later gives up hope of recovering the object, this *ye'ush* is of no effect. The finder is forbidden to keep the object for himself, and if he does so he is considered a thief.

RASHI

יאוש דלא מדעת — דבר שסתמו יאוש לכשידע שנפל ממנו, וכשמצאו עדיין לא ידעו הבעלים שנפל מהן. **לא הוי יאוש** — לקמיה מפרש פלוגתייהו. **דמיאש לבסוף** — לאחר שמצאו זה. וכללא דיאוש, כגון דאמר: "ווי ליה לחסרון כיס", דגלי דעתיה שנואש מהן. **באיסורא אתא לידיה** — דדבר שאינו עשוי להתיאש הוא.

NOTES

יֵאוּשׁ שֶׁלֹּא מִדַּעַת **Anticipated *ye'ush*.** In connection with this principle *Ra'avad* comments: In many places elsewhere in the Talmud there is a difference of opinion among Tannaim as to whether the outcome of an action can be considered to have taken effect retroactively (בְּרֵירָה — "retroactive designation"), and it would appear, at first glance, that Abaye and Rava are essentially arguing over the same point. *Ra'avad* states that it is possible to distinguish between the issues, but does not elaborate. Various explanations of the distinction have been offered by Aḥaronim: *Or Same'aḥ* points out that in tractate *Eruvin* 82a the Gemara distinguishes between indecision and lack of information. If a person is undecided as to what to do, and "decides" to behave in accordance with some event that has

BACKGROUND

יֵאוּשׁ שֶׁלֹּא מִדַּעַת **Anticipated *ye'ush*.** The passage that deals with the issue of anticipated *ye'ush* regarding the recovery of a lost object is long and well constructed. It deals mainly with a single problem: To what degree does the owner's giving up of hope, which will certainly occur in time, take effect from the moment of the loss itself (before the owner has become aware of it)?

Although this is a specific problem, it is connected to a much more general and complex issue: To what degree can one apply Halakhic principles retroactively? In other words, to what extent may one consider events that are certain to take place as if they have already occurred? In various ways this question applies not only to civil and criminal law, but also to ritual law. The problem has a great many variants, such as the distinction between something that will happen of its own accord and something that will be effected by human agency, or the distinction between something that is initially defined as a condition and something that has not been so defined. Aspects of this question are also connected to many controversies connected with the principle of בְּרֵירָה — "retroactive designation" (see note): Can a doubtful situation that is later clarified be considered as though it has been so defined from the outset? There are many other examples. The passage here does not restrict itself to the question as it is defined, but instead seeks proofs in broader areas of the Halakhah in order to reach a solution.

TERMINOLOGY

בְּ... כּוּלֵּי עָלְמָא לָא פְּלִיגִי, כִּי פְּלִיגִי בְּ... **Everyone agrees [lit., does not disagree] about A; where they disagree, is about B.** Sometimes the Gemara attempts to delimit an issue in dispute by first stating which points are agreed upon by both sides: "Everyone agrees [i.e., both parties agree] that the law in case A is such-and-such; the disputants differ about case B...."

TRANSLATION AND COMMENTARY

בְּזוּטוֹ שֶׁל יָם [1]On the other hand, **in the case of an object washed up by the rising sea or by an overflowing river,** [2]even though the lost item has **an identifying mark,** [3]**the Torah permitted** the finder to keep **it,** regardless of whether it came into his possession before the owner became aware of his loss, and even if the owner never gave up hope of its recovery, **as we shall have occasion to explain below** (22b).

כִּי פְּלִיגִי [4]**Where** Abaye and Rava **disagree is in the case of an object without an identifying mark,** which was lost in an ordinary way, as the Gemara now explains: [5]**Abaye says:** Anticipated *ye'ush* **is not** considered *ye'ush,* **because** at the time when the finder came into possession of the object **the owner did not** yet **know that he had dropped it,** and he had not yet given up hope of recovering it. Even later on, when the owner does learn of his loss and does give up hope, the finder is not permitted to keep the object, because he took possession of it at a time when its owner had not yet given up hope. [6]But **Rava says:** Anticipated *ye'ush* **is** considered *ye'ush,* **for when** the owner **realizes that he has dropped** the object, **he will** at once **give up hope** of recovering it. [7]For **he will say.** "**I have no identifying mark on it** and no chance of getting it back." [8]**Therefore** we consider it as if **he has** effectively **given up hope** of recovering it **from now,** the moment when the loss took place.

סִימָן [9]The Gemara now cites a series of Tannaitic sources in an attempt to resolve the difference of opinion between Abaye and Rava. The sequence of cases mentioned is summarized by the following **mnemonic:** פמג״ש ממקגט״י ככסע״ז (see notes below).

[1]בְּזוּטוֹ שֶׁל יָם וּבִשְׁלוּלִיתוֹ שֶׁל נָהָר, [2]אַף עַל גַּב דְּאִית בֵּיהּ סִימָן, [3]רַחֲמָנָא שַׁרְיֵיהּ, כְּדִבְעֵינַן לְמֵימַר לְקַמָּן.

[4]כִּי פְּלִיגִי בְּדָבָר שֶׁאֵין בּוֹ סִימָן. [5]אַבַּיֵי אֲמַר: לָא הָוֵי יֵאוּשׁ, דְּהָא לָא יָדַע דְּנְפַל מִינֵּיהּ. [6]רָבָא אֲמַר: הָוֵי יֵאוּשׁ, דִּלְכִי יָדַע דִּנְפַל מִינֵּיהּ, מְיָאֵשׁ. [7]מֵימַר אָמַר: ״סִימָנָא לֵית לִי בְּגַוֵּיהּ״. [8]מֵהָשְׁתָּא הוּא דְּמְיָאֵשׁ.

[9](סִימָן: פמג״ש ממקגט״י ככסע״ז).

LITERAL TRANSLATION

[1][In the case of an object washed up] by the rising sea or by an overflowing river, [2]even though there is an identifying mark on it, [3]the Torah (lit., "the Merciful One") permitted it, as we shall have [occasion] to say below.

[4]Where they disagree is in [the case of] an object without an [identifying] mark. [5]Abaye says: It is not *ye'ush,* for surely he does not know that it has fallen from him. [6]Rava says: It is *ye'ush,* for when he knows that it has fallen from him, he gives up hope. [7]He surely says: "I do not have an [identifying] mark on it." [8][Therefore] it is from now that he gives up hope.

[9]Mnemonic: פמג״ש ממקג״י ככסע״ז.

RASHI

זוטו של ים — מקומות בשפת הים שדרך הים לחזור לאחוריו עשר פרסאות או חמשה עשר פרסאות פעמיים ביום, ושוטף מה שמוצא שם והולך. **זוטו** — לשון גודל ושירוע בלשון יווני, כמו שכתבו הזקנים לתלמי המלך: ״ואל אצילי״ — ואל זאטוטי (מגילה ט,א). **ושלוליתו של נהר** — כשהוא גדל ויוצא חוץ לגדותיו, ושולל שלל ושוטף הנמצא. **רחמנא שרייה** — ואפילו באת ליד המוצא לפני יאוש. **לקמן** — בשמעתין; מנין לאבידה ששטפה נהר כו׳. **מהשתא הוי יאוש** — שהרי נפל. וכשיודע, שוב אין דעתו עליו.

LANGUAGE

זוטו Neither the source of this word nor its meaning has been well established. In the opinion of *Rashi* and others **זוטו** is a word in its own right, meaning the tidal area at the edge of the sea, but other commentators read it as connected to the word **זוט**, which means the bottom or the lower part of a vessel.

SAGES

אַבַּיֵי Abaye. One of the greatest Sages of the Talmud, Abaye was a member of the fourth generation of Babylonian Amoraim. He was left an orphan and was raised in the home of his uncle, Rabbah. Although Rabbah was a priest and the head of a yeshivah, he and Abaye lived in poverty. Abaye was also the student of Rav Yosef, and after Rav Yosef's death Abaye became the head of the Pumbedita Yeshivah.

Apart from his eminence as a Torah scholar, Abaye was considered outstanding in his piety and acts of charity.

Halakhic discussions between him and Rabbah, and even more so between him and Rav Yosef, are found throughout the Talmud. But his most important discussions are with his colleague, Rava. These are considered examples of the most profound and creative Halakhic dialectic, and form an important element in the structure of the Babylonian Talmud. Though the intellectual approaches of these two Sages are similar, Abaye's is generally more formalistic.

In Halakhic decision-making the general principle is that in disputes between Abaye and Rava the opinion of Rava is accepted, except in a small number of cases (יע״ל קג״ם). Abaye's son, Bibi bar Abaye, was also a well-known Sage.

רָבָא Rava. A great Babylonian Amora of the fourth generation, Rava was a colleague of Abaye. His father, Rav Yosef bar Ḥama, was also a famous Sage. Rava's outstanding teacher was Rav Naḥman bar Ya'akov, and he was also a student of Rav Ḥisda, with whom he studied together with his colleague Rami bar Ḥama. Rav Ḥisda's daughter married Rami bar Ḥama, and when Rami bar

NOTES

זוטו שֶׁל יָם An object washed up by the rising sea. Our translation and commentary follows *Rashi*, who translates זוטו שֶׁל יָם as "tidal area." *Rabbenu Ḥananel* renders it "the seabed," while *Ramakh* suggests that it is the place where a river flows into the sea, where the waters are particularly violent.

סִימָן פמג״ש וכו׳ Mnemonic. This is a mnemonic for the "come and hear" proofs presented in this passage. Mnemonics of this kind are found frequently in the Talmud. They were meant to make it easier to memorize groups of Halakhot or groups of problems in a given passage. Often the mnemonic is a group of words connected together to form a single idea which can be memorized, or else initials which form a meaningful word. The letters of these mnemonics do not always correspond to the first letters of the key words. This is the case with the present mnemonic: פ=פֵּירוֹת מְפוּזָּרִין; מ=מָעוֹת מְפוּזָּרוֹת; ג=עִיגּוּלֵי דְבֵילָה; ש=לְשׁוֹנוֹת שֶׁל אַרְגָּמָן; מ=מָעוֹת; מ=מֵאֵימָתַי כָּל אָדָם; ק=קְצִיעוֹת; ג=הַגַּנָּב; ט=שָׁטַף נָהָר; י=יָרַד; כ=כֵּיצַד אָמְרוּ; כ=כַּלֵּךְ; ס=כְּסִיפוּתָא; ע=עוֹדֵהוּ הַטַּל; ז=יָצְאתָה זוֹ.

not yet taken place, we have a case of בְּרֵירָה. But if a person would have no trouble deciding what to do, but simply does not know until it is too late that he must make a decision, as in our case, where the owner does not realize that he has lost the object and that he is expected to give up hope of its recovery, then בְּרֵירָה does not apply.

Others explain that in a case of בְּרֵירָה we base present action upon something that will be determined only later, and the problem is that the future is unpredictable. In the case of *ye'ush*, however, there is no doubt as to what will happen later — the owner will give up hope. The problem is that he has not yet done so. Hence, Abaye maintains that anticipated *ye'ush* is not effective, since the finder is obligated to return the object immediately. Subsequently, when the owner does give up hope, it will be too late for the finder to acquire the object, since it came into his possession at a time when it was prohibited. Rava, by contrast, maintains that anticipated *ye'ush* is effective, and even if the owner were never to realize that he has lost the object, the finder has already acquired it (*Rabbi Zvi Ḥayyot*).

TRANSLATION AND COMMENTARY

תָּא שְׁמַע [1](1) The Gemara's first suggestion is as follows: **Come and hear** a refutation of Abaye's viewpoint from our Mishnah. The Mishnah states: **"Scattered fruit is the finder's."** But, argues the Gemara, **surely** it is possible that at the time the fruit was found the owner of the fruit **did not** yet **realize that it had fallen from him**, and had not yet given up hope of recovering it. Nevertheless, the Mishnah rules that the finder is entitled to keep it, implying that anticipated *ye'ush* is indeed considered effective.

הָא אֲמַר רַב עוּקְבָא בַּר חָמָא [2]The Gemara rejects this argument: **Surely Rav Ukva bar Hama** has already **said** (above, 21a): **Here,** where the Mishnah speaks of "scattered fruit," **we are dealing with the gathering of grain on the threshing floor, which** does not come under the category of property whose loss is unknown to its owner but **is** in fact **an intentional loss,** for the owner is aware that he left the wheat there and intentionally rendered it ownerless. Thus, it is not a case of anticipated *ye'ush* and no proof can be adduced from it.

תָּא שְׁמַע [3](2) **Come and hear** another refutation of Abaye's viewpoint from our Mishnah, which states: **"Scattered coins belong to the finder."** [4]**Why,** asks the Gemara, should this be so? **Surely** it is possible that at the time the coins were found their owner **did not** yet **realize that he had dropped them,** and he had not yet given up hope of their recovery. And even so, the finder is still permitted to keep them. This surely implies that anticipated *ye'ush* is considered effective.

הָתָם נַמִי כִּדְרַבִּי יִצְחָק [5]The Gemara answers: **There, too, the Mishnah** can be understood as not contradicting Abaye's viewpoint. It **can be explained in accordance with** the view of **Rabbi Yitzhak, who said** elsewhere: **A person is likely to feel for what is in his moneybag at all times.** [6]**Here, too, we can say that a person is likely to feel for what is in his moneybag at all times.** Therefore, we can assume that the owner became aware of his loss immediately, and gave up hope of recovering the money before the coins were found. Thus, this case in no way involves the question of anticipated *ye'ush.*

[1]תָּא שְׁמַע: ״פֵּירוֹת מְפוּזָּרִין״. הָא לָא יָדַע דְּנָפַל מִינֵּיהּ!
[2]הָא אֲמַר רַב עוּקְבָא בַּר חָמָא: הָכָא בְּמַכְנִשְׁתָּא דְבֵיזְרֵי עָסְקִינַן, דַּאֲבֵידָה מִדַּעַת הִיא.
[3]תָּא שְׁמַע: ״מָעוֹת מְפוּזָּרוֹת — הֲרֵי אֵלּוּ שֶׁלּוֹ״. [4]אַמַּאי? הָא לָא יָדַע דְּנָפַל מִינֵּיהּ!
[5]הָתָם נַמִי כִּדְרַבִּי יִצְחָק, דְּאָמַר: אָדָם עָשׂוּי לְמַשְׁמֵשׁ בְּכִיסוֹ בְּכָל שָׁעָה וְשָׁעָה. [6]הָכָא נַמִי, אָדָם עָשׂוּי לְמַשְׁמֵשׁ בְּכִיסוֹ בְּכָל שָׁעָה וְשָׁעָה.

LITERAL TRANSLATION

[1]Come [and] hear: "Scattered fruit [is the finder's]." Surely he did not know that it fell from him!

[2]Surely Rav Ukva bar Hama said: Here we are dealing with the gathering [of grain] on the threshing floor, which is an intentional loss.

[3]Come [and] hear: "Scattered coins — these are his." [4]Why? Surely he did not know that [they] fell from him!

[5]There, too, [the Mishnah can be explained] according to Rabbi Yitzhak, who said: A person is likely to feel for [what is in] his moneybag at all times. [6]Here, too, a person is likely to feel for [what is in] his moneybag at all times.

RASHI

דאבידה מדעת היא — שלא נפלו ממנו, ומדעת הניחם הפקר. **עשוי למשמש** — וקודם שמצאו זה נודע לבעלים שנפלו, ונואשו.

NOTES

תָּא שְׁמַע...תָּא שְׁמַע... Come and hear... come and hear.... Even though the answers to many of these objections are essentially identical, the Gemara still raised them all. This is a common practice in the Talmud when an answer appears forced. Often the Halakhah rejects a particular viewpoint, against which no single decisive argument has been advanced, simply because of the cumulative difficulty of applying a somewhat implausible answer in several instances (*Hokhmat Manoah*).

כִּדְרַבִּי יִצְחָק In accordance with what Rabbi Yitzhak said. *Tosafot* asks: It is clear from the Gemara's language that Rabbi Yitzhak's comment was originally directed toward the Baraita about money found in public places. Why did he not comment directly on our Mishnah?

Tosafot answers that the Mishnah merely tells us that scattered coins have no distinguishing mark, whereas the Baraita seems to give as a reason the fact that the objects were lost in public places, even though the owner was unaware of his loss. Therefore Rabbi Yitzhak preferred to link his comment to the Baraita.

HALAKHAH

אָדָם עָשׂוּי לְמַשְׁמֵשׁ בְּכִיסוֹ A person is likely to feel for what is in his moneybag. "One who finds scattered coins or coins lying in a public place may keep them. This is because the original owner presumably became aware of his loss immediately after it occurred, since people normally check their money frequently. Hence we may assume that he gave up hope of recovering the coins. Similarly, one who finds round cakes of figs or bakers' loaves may keep them, since because of their weight the original owner presumably became aware of his loss immediately after it occurred, and gave up hope of recovering them." (*Shulhan Arukh, Hoshen Mishpat* 262: 3,6,11.)

Hama died, she married Rava. Rava also studied with Rav Yosef. He founded a yeshivah in Mehoza. In all the many Halakhic controversies between him and Abaye the Halakhah follows him, except for six cases (יע״ל קג״ם). After Abaye's death, Rava was appointed head of the Pumbedita Yeshivah, which he transferred to his home city of Mehoza. Among his students were Rav Pappa and Rav Huna the son of Rav Yehoshua. A great number of Sages transmit teachings in his name: Rav Zevid, Mar the son of Rav Yosef, Rav Mesharshiya, Rav Pappi, Ravina, and others. After his death the yeshivah of Mehoza split in two, and Rav Nahman bar Yitzhak filled his place as the head of the Pumbedita Yeshiva, while Rav Pappa established a yeshivah of his own in Neresh.

TERMINOLOGY

תָּא שְׁמַע Come and hear. An expression used to introduce a source (usually Tannaitic, but sometimes Biblical or Amoraic) which will be used to support an opinion, prove a point, raise an objection, or resolve a problem. Where תָּא שְׁמַע introduces a suggested solution to a problem, if the solution is rejected, another solution is often introduced by the same expression. When a solution is finally accepted, the concluding expression שְׁמַע מִינָּהּ — "Prove it from this" — is often used.

BACKGROUND

אָדָם עָשׂוּי לְמַשְׁמֵשׁ בְּכִיסוֹ A person is likely to feel for what is in his moneybag. Since in those days pockets were not sewn into garments, this expression refers to a wallet or moneybag held in a person's hand containing valuables. Since the moneybag held valuables, and was always at hand, it was assumed that a person would frequently check that its contents were in place.

TRANSLATION AND COMMENTARY

תָּא שְׁמַע [1](3) **Come and hear** another refutation of Abaye's viewpoint from our Mishnah, which states: **"Round cakes of pressed figs and loaves of a** commercial **baker belong to the finder."** [2]**Why,** asks the Gemara, should this be so? **Surely** it is possible that at the time these items were found their owner **did not** yet **realize that they had fallen from** his possession, and he had not yet given up hope of their recovery. Nevertheless, according to the Mishnah, the finder is permitted to keep them. This surely implies that anticipated *ye'ush* is effective.

הָתָם נַמִּי [3]The Gemara answers: **There, too,** we can explain the Mishnah as not contradicting Abaye's viewpoint: **Since** the fig cakes and loaves **are heavy,** their owner **surely realizes** immediately after they have fallen that he has lost them, and he at once gives up hope of recovering them.

תָּא שְׁמַע [4](4) **Come and hear** another refutation of Abaye's viewpoint from our Mishnah, which states: **"Strips of purple wool belong to the finder."** [5]**But why,** asks the Gemara, should this be so? **Surely** it is possible that at the time the strips of wool were found their owner **did not** yet **realize that they had fallen from** his possession, and had not yet given up hope of their recovery. Nevertheless, according to the Mishnah, the finder is permitted to keep them. This surely implies that anticipated *ye'ush* is effective.

הָתָם נַמִּי [6]The Gemara answers: **There, too,** we can explain the Mishnah as not contradicting Abaye's viewpoint: **Since** the strips of wool **are important** and expensive, their owner continually **feels for them,** discovers their loss immediately, and gives up hope of recovering them, **as Rabbi Yitzḥak said** regarding money.

תָּא שְׁמַע [7](5) **Come and hear** another refutation of Abaye's viewpoint from the following Baraita: **"One who finds coins in synagogues, or in houses of study, or in any place where many people are found —** [8]**they belong to him, because the owners give up hope of recovering them."** [9]**But surely,** argues the Gemara, it is possible that at the time the coins were found, their owner **did not** yet **realize that he had dropped them,** and had not yet given up hope of their recovery. Nevertheless, according to the Baraita, the finder is permitted to keep them. This surely implies that anticipated *ye'ush* is effective.

אָמַר רַבִּי יִצְחָק [10]The Gemara answers: **Rabbi Yitzḥak said** in relation to this case: **A person is likely to feel for what is in his moneybag at all times.** The owner of the coins discovers his loss immediately and gives up hope of getting them back. Thus this Baraita does not contradict Abaye's viewpoint.

[1]תָּא שְׁמַע: ״עִיגּוּלֵי דְבֵילָה וְכִכָּרוֹת שֶׁל נַחְתּוֹם — הֲרֵי אֵלּוּ שֶׁלּוֹ״. [2]אַמַּאי? וְהָא לָא יָדַע דְּנָפַל מִינֵּיהּ!

[3]הָתָם נַמִּי, אַגַּב דְּיַקִּירֵי, מֵידַע יָדַע בְּהוּ.

[4]תָּא שְׁמַע: ״וּלְשׁוֹנוֹת שֶׁל אַרְגָּמָן — הֲרֵי אֵלּוּ שֶׁלּוֹ״. [5]וְאַמַּאי? הָא לָא יָדַע דְּנָפַל מִינֵּיהּ!

[6]הָתָם נַמִּי, אַגַּב דַּחֲשִׁיבִי, מַשְׁמוּשֵׁי מְמַשְׁמֵשׁ בְּהוּ, וְכִדְרַבִּי יִצְחָק.

[7]תָּא שְׁמַע: ״הַמּוֹצֵא מָעוֹת בְּבָתֵּי כְנֵסִיּוֹת, וּבְבָתֵּי מִדְרָשׁוֹת, וּבְכָל מָקוֹם שֶׁהָרַבִּים מְצוּיִין שָׁם — [8]הֲרֵי אֵלּוּ שֶׁלּוֹ, מִפְּנֵי שֶׁהַבְּעָלִים מִתְיָאֲשִׁין מֵהֶן״. [9]וְהָא לָא יָדַע דְּנָפַל מִינֵּיהּ!

[10]אָמַר רַבִּי יִצְחָק: אָדָם עָשׂוּי לְמַשְׁמֵשׁ בְּכִיסוֹ בְּכָל שָׁעָה.

LITERAL TRANSLATION

[1]Come [and] hear: "Round cakes of pressed figs and loaves of a baker — these are his." [2]Why? But surely he did not know that [they] fell from him!

[3]There, too, since they are heavy, he surely knows about them.

[4]Come [and] hear: "Or strips of purple wool — these are his." [5]But why? Surely he did not know that [they] fell from him!

[6]There, too, since they are important, he surely feels for them, as Rabbi Yitzḥak [said].

[7]Come [and] hear: "One who finds coins in synagogues, or in houses of study, or in any place where many people are found — [8]they are his, because the owners give up hope of [recovering] them." [9]But surely he did not know that they fell from him!

[10]Rabbi Yitzḥak said: A person usually feels for [what is in] his moneybag at all times.

RASHI

דיקירי — ככד מסא.

BACKGROUND

לְשׁוֹנוֹת שֶׁל אַרְגָּמָן Strips of purple wool, skeins of wool which, after washing and initial processing, were combed into long "tongues" before being spun into thread. These tongues came in a fixed size and shape, and they owed their high price to the purple dye used to color them. The dye was extracted from the special secretions of a rare murex (the *ḥillazon*), and was produced by a complicated and secret process. Accordingly, purple clothing was traditionally considered a sign of social prominence and authority.

NOTES

עִיגּוּלֵי דְבֵילָה Round cakes of figs. The commentators ask why the Talmud did not raise an objection from the clauses in the Mishnah that mention strings of fish, pieces of meat, fleeces of wool, and bundles of flax. They answer that these objects, too, are heavy, just like the fig cakes (*Ramban, Ran*).

Rosh asks: Concerning the cakes of figs etc., why does the Gemara not answer that food is important and people check for it, in accordance with its explanation later on in the passage concerning individual figs? He answers that the Gemara took advantage of the opportunity to introduce the idea of weight, so as to cover the cases of wool and flax as well.

TRANSLATION AND COMMENTARY

תָּא שְׁמַע [1](6) **Come and hear** another refutation of Abaye's viewpoint from a Mishnah in tractate *Pe'ah* (8:1). Gleanings of individual stalks of corn left in the field after the harvest belong only to the poor (Leviticus 19:9-10 and 23:22). But once the poor have stopped being interested in gleaning or have given up hope of finding anything there worth gleaning, whatever is left in the field is permitted to everyone, including the rich. In relation to such a situation the Mishnah asks: **"From what stage is anyone,** and not just the poor, **permitted to collect** for himself **gleanings** of grain left over in the field after the harvest?" The Mishnah answers: **"After the** ***namoshot*** **[נָמוֹשׁוֹת] have passed through** the field."

וְאָמְרִינַן מַאי נָמוֹשׁוֹת [2]The Gemara now clarifies the meaning of *namoshot*: We know that **we have said** elsewhere, in a discussion of this Mishnah: **What is meant by the** term ***namoshot?*** [3]**And** in reply **Rabbi Yoḥanan said:** The word *namoshot* means **"old men who walk leaning on a staff."** [4]**And Resh Lakish said:** The word *namoshot* means **"people who glean after the** first **gleaners** have finished gleaning." According to both explanations, the implication of the Mishnah is that, after these *namoshot* have finished gleaning, we may assume there is hardly any grain remaining in the field, and hence the poor give up hope of collecting any additional gleanings. But the question arises: [5]**Why,** even after the poor have given up hope, should the remaining gleanings be permitted to people who are not poor? **Granted that the poor who live here may have given up hope** of collecting additional gleanings, since they have seen that the *namoshot* have already passed through the field, [6]**but there are** still **poor** people **in other places who have not given up hope,** since they do not know that the *namoshot* have passed through the field. As far as they are concerned, this is a situation of anticipated *ye'ush.* When the poor from other places eventually learn that the *namoshot* have already passed through the field here, they will give up hope, retroactively making the gleanings ownerless now. This, surely, is a refutation of Abaye's viewpoint.

אָמְרִי [7]The Gemara answers: **We** can **say** in reply: **Since there are poor** people **here,** [8]the poor people in other places **give up hope from the outset** of collecting the gleanings remaining in the field here, irrespective of whether the *namoshot* have yet visited the field. [9]**They say** to themselves: **"The poor** people **who are there will** doubtless **collect** all the gleanings first." As far as the poor of other places are concerned, they gave up hope from the beginning that they would have any share in the gleanings of the fields here, and yielded the right to glean to the local poor.

[1]תָּא שְׁמַע: ״מֵאֵימָתַי כָּל אָדָם מוּתָּרִים בְּלֶקֶט? מִשֶּׁיֵּלְכוּ בָּהּ הַנָּמוֹשׁוֹת״.
[2]וְאָמְרִינַן: מַאי ״נָמוֹשׁוֹת״? [3]וַאֲמַר רַבִּי יוֹחָנָן: סָבֵי דְּאָזְלֵי אַתִּיגְרָא. [4]רֵישׁ לָקִישׁ אֲמַר: לָקוֹטֵי בָּתַר לָקוֹטֵי. [5]וְאַמַּאי? נְהִי דַּעֲנִיִּים דְּהָכָא מְיָאֲשִׁי, [6]אִיכָּא עֲנִיִּים בְּדוּכְתָּא אַחֲרִיתָא דְּלָא מְיָאֲשִׁי!
[7]אָמְרִי: כֵּיוָן דְּאִיכָּא עֲנִיִּים הָכָא, [8]הָנָךְ מֵעִיקָּרָא אַיאוּשֵׁי מְיָאַשׁ [9]וְאָמְרִי: ״עֲנִיִּים דְּהָתָם מְלַקְּטִי לֵיהּ״.

LITERAL TRANSLATION

[1]Come [and] hear: "From when is every man permitted [to collect] gleanings? After the *namoshot* have passed through it."

[2]And we have said: What [is meant by] "the *namoshot*"? [3]And Rabbi Yoḥanan said: Old men who walk [leaning] on a staff. [4][And] Resh Lakish said: Gleaners after gleaners. [5]But why? Granted that the poor who are here give up hope, [6][but] there are poor in other places who do not give up hope!

[7]We say: Since there are poor here, [8]the others from the outset give up hope [9]and say: "The poor who are there will collect it."

RASHI

סבי דאזלי אתיגרא — זקנים עניים הולכים על משענתם בנחת, ורואין כל שבולת ושבולת. ולשון נמושות כמו ״לא ימושו״ (ישעיהו נט), שממשמשין והולכים. לקוטי בתר לקוטי — לשון נמושות כמו ״לא ימיש״ (שמות יג), שנוטלין ומשין הכל מלפניהם. ואמאי — אי יאוש שלא מדעת לאו יאוש הוא. נהי — דלגבי עניים דהכא הוי יאוש מדעת, שראו שהלכו בה הנמושות ונתיאשו, אלא עניים דעיר אחרת עדיין לא ידעי, והיאך מותרין בו, אלא משום כיון דלכי ידעי מיאשי, הוי יאוש משעה שהלכו בו, ובהיתר באו ליד זה.

NOTES

סָבֵי דְּאָזְלֵי אַתִּיגְרָא Old men who walk leaning on a staff. The Geonim read אַתִּיגְדָּא. *Arukh* explains that this word also means "staff," but others suggest that it means "boundaries." According to this explanation, the Gemara here is referring to "old people who walk around the boundaries of the field."

HALAKHAH

מֵאֵימָתַי כָּל אָדָם מוּתָּרִים בְּלֶקֶט From when is everyone permitted to collect gleanings? *Rambam* rules that everyone is permitted to glean after the first and second groups of gleaners have finished geaning. This ruling seems

CONCEPTS

לֶקֶט Gleanings. One of the obligatory agricultural gifts given to the poor. The Torah prohibits the owner of a field from gleaning individual stalks that have fallen during the harvest (Leviticus 19:9). Less than three stalks that have fallen in one place are deemed לֶקֶט and considered the property of the poor. The owner of the field is forbidden to take them for his own use.

LANGUAGE

נָמוֹשׁוֹת ***Namoshot.*** Scholars of Hebrew etymology have debated the source of this word. Some maintain that there is a verb *namash* (נמש) similar in meaning to *emesh* (אֶמֶשׁ) — "yesterday evening" — and that it means "to be late." Therefore the *namoshot* would be latecomers. Other authorities maintain that the real root of the word is *mashash* — "to grope" — and that, in a common exchange of consonants, a *nun* (נ) has replaced the *mem* (מ). Others have connected this word with various words in Arabic and other ancient Semitic languages.

אַתִּיגְרָא On a staff. Most manuscripts of the Talmud read אַתִּיגְדָּא, which is the Aramaic word for a staff or rod. The word derives from the root גדד, meaning "to cut," i.e., a branch cut from a tree and used as a staff.

SAGES

רַבִּי יוֹחָנָן Rabbi Yoḥanan. See *Bava Metzia*, Part 1, pp. 19-20.

רֵישׁ לָקִישׁ Resh Lakish. Rabbi Shimon ben Lakish, commonly known as Resh Lakish, was one of the greatest of the Palestinian Amoraim. He was a student, colleague, and brother-in-law of Rabbi Yoḥanan.

As a youth Resh Lakish studied Torah and showed great talent. However, apparently constrained by dire poverty, he sold himself as a gladiator in the Roman arena. Many stories are told of his exceptional courage and physical strength. In time, following a meeting with Rabbi Yoḥanan, he returned to the world of Torah, beginning as Rabbi Yoḥanan's student and then becoming his colleague and marrying his sister.

TRANSLATION AND COMMENTARY

תָּא שְׁמַע [1] After six attempts to refute Abaye's viewpoint have failed, the Gemara now seeks to refute Rava's viewpoint. (7) **Come and hear:** a refutation of Rava's viewpoint from the following Mishnah (*Ma'aserot* 3:4): **"If one found cut,** drying, **figs** without an identifying mark **on the road, or even** if one found them **at the side of a field which is used for drying cut figs, [2] and similarly if a fig tree** whose roots and trunk were in private property **had branches growing above the road, and one found figs under them, [3] the figs are permitted** to be taken and are not forbidden **because of** the prohibition against **robbery.** Since the figs have no identifying mark on them, it is assumed that their owners have given up hope of recovering them, and the finder may keep them for himself. For the same reason the figs **are exempt from being tithed** by the finder, because ownerless produce need not be tithed. [4] **But with regard to olives and carobs** found under such circumstances, **it is forbidden for the finder to take them."**

At first glance there appears to be an internal contradiction in this Mishnah. In the first clause it states that the finder of the fruit is permitted to keep it, although the owners may not yet be aware of their loss, and so by definition may not have given up hope of recovering it. This would imply that anticipated *ye'ush* is effective, and would support Rava's viewpoint. On the other hand, in the last clause the Mishnah states that the finder of olives and carobs is forbidden to take them, presumably because the owners have not yet given up hope of recovering the fruit. This would imply that anticipated *ye'ush* is not effective, and would support Abaye's viewpoint.

[1] תָּא שְׁמַע: "קְצִיעוֹת בַּדֶּרֶךְ, וַאֲפִילּוּ בְּצַד שְׂדֵה קְצִיעוֹת, [2] וְכֵן תְּאֵנָה הַנּוֹטָה לַדֶּרֶךְ, וּמָצָא תְּאֵנִים תַּחְתֶּיהָ, [3] מוּתָּרוֹת מִשּׁוּם גֶּזֶל, וּפְטוּרוֹת מִן הַמַּעֲשֵׂר. [4] בְּזֵיתִים וּבְחָרוּבִים, אָסוּר".

LITERAL TRANSLATION

[1] Come [and] hear: "[If one found] cut figs on the road, or even at the side of a field [which is used to dry] cut figs, [2] and similarly [if] a fig tree [was] leaning over the road, and one found figs underneath it, [3] they are permitted because [in these cases there is no prohibition] of robbery, and they are exempt from [being] tithed. [4] [But] with regard to olives and with regard to carobs, it is forbidden [for the finder to take them]."

RASHI

קציעות – תאנים שקוצצין אותם באיזמל, ומוהל שלהן זב, ושוטחן בשדה ליבש. **ואפילו בצד שדה קציעות** – שדה ששוטחים בה קציעות, דידע דמהכא אתו. **מותרות משום גזל** – אף על גב דכי נפל לא ידע, כיון דלכי ידע מיאש, מהשתא הוי יאוש, כרבא. **ופטורות מן המעשר** – כדין הפקר, דהפקר פטור מן המעשר. **בזיתים ובחרובים אסור** – כאביי.

NOTES

קְצִיעוֹת **Cut figs.** Most Rishonim agree that קְצִיעוֹת are figs left out to dry, but they disagree over the etymology of the word. *Rashi* derives it from the word לְקַצֵּץ — "to cut" — since the figs have to be cut open before they can be dried. *Rash*, basing himself on a Mishnah in tractate *Shevi'it*, suggests that the tool used to cut the figs is called מוּקְצֶה, possibly from the same root. *Ra'avad* agrees that the source of the word is מוּקְצֶה, but maintains that the מוּקְצֶה is the field in which the figs are dried, from the root קצה — "boundary." *Radbaz*, however, in his commentary on the *Rambam's Mishneh Torah*, understands קְצִיעוֹת to mean simply "loose," as opposed to "growing on the tree."

וּפְטוּרוֹת מִן הַמַּעֲשֵׂר **And they are exempt from being tithed.** The Rishonim offer various explanations as to why the figs need not be tithed. Our commentary follows *Rashi*, who explained that ownerless produce is generally exempt from being tithed.

Ritva, however, objects to this explanation, on the grounds that produce that was made ownerless after harvest is normally not exempt. He argues instead that the figs are exempt because they have not yet been fully processed. Produce that is set aside to be dried need not be tithed until after the drying is complete, and in the meantime one may eat from it without tithing.

Rashba combines these two explanations and states that figs which were set aside to be dried, and were made ownerless when they were not yet subject to tithing, remain exempt even after the processing is complete.

HALAKHAH

to follow the view of Resh Lakish, even though we usually do not decide in accordance with his viewpoint when he is in conflict with Rabbi Yohanan. *Radbaz*, following *Rambam's* own commentary on the Mishnah, suggests that Resh Lakish was not disagreeing with Rabbi Yohanan but merely explaining that "old men with staffs" are the second group of gleaners. *Kesef Mishneh* suggests, in the name of *Rashba*, that Rabbi Yoḥanan and Resh Lakish were not in disagreement about the Halakhah. Both would agree that the presence either of old people or of a second group of gleaners signals the end of the gleaning period. Rather, they are merely disagreeing about the meaning of the word *namoshot*. (*Rambam, Sefer Zeraim, Hilkhot Mattenot Aniyyim* 1:11.)

קְצִיעוֹת **Cut figs.** "One who finds cut figs on the road, even if they were lying next to a field of loose figs, need not tithe them," following the Mishnah. (Ibid., *Hilkhot Ma'aser* 3:21.)

בְּזֵיתִים וּבְחָרוּבִים, אָסוּר **But with regard to olives and carobs, it is forbidden.** "One who finds olives under an olive tree or carobs under a carob tree must tithe them. However, if one finds figs under a fig tree, it is not certain whether they need be tithed. Therefore, they must be treated in accordance with the procedure for doubtfully tithed produce." (Ibid., 3:24; see also *Radbaz* and *Kesef Mishneh*.)

Rabbi Yoḥanan and Resh Lakish had many Halakhic differences of opinion. However, in great measure Resh Lakish's intention was not to disagree with Rabbi Yoḥanan, but rather to clarify and elucidate matters by means of dialectical argumentation. Rabbi Yoḥanan regarded him with great respect and used to say, "My equal disagrees with me."

Resh Lakish was famous for his piety and rigor, and it was said that one could lend money without witnesses to a person with whom Resh Lakish spoke in public, for he spoke only to people of unblemished character. When he died he left a son who was notable for his talents and genius.

BACKGROUND

קְצִיעוֹת וְעִיגּוּלֵי דְבֵילָה **Cut figs and round cakes of dried figs.** The use of figs was widespread during the Mishnaic and Talmudic periods. Only a small amount of figs were eaten fresh, while most of the harvest was dried in various ways. Generally, after the fruit was picked, the stalks were cut off and the figs were laid out to dry in the sun. At that stage the figs were called קְצִיעוֹת or קְצוּצוֹת — "beheaded." Figs which were dried, but underwent no further processing, were called גְּרוֹגְרוֹת. They were occasionally stored in barrels in that condition, or were threaded on strings. However, a significant portion of the dried figs underwent further processing, being pressed in barrels or round vessels. These pressed figs were known as דְּבֵלִים. After being pressed and completely dried, the cakes of figs would be removed from their container and people would cut pieces from them as needed.

CONCEPTS

מַעֲשֵׂר **Tithe.** Certain portions of agricultural produce designated by Torah law for special purposes. According to most opinions, only grain, wine, and olive oil are required by Torah law to be tithed. By Rabbinic decree, however, any food that grows from the ground must be tithed. There are three main types of tithes: מַעֲשֵׂר רִאשׁוֹן

TRANSLATION AND COMMENTARY

בִּשְׁלָמָא רֵישָׁא לְאַבַּיֵי [1]The Gemara now explains: We can take it for **granted that the first clause poses no difficulty for Abaye,** as he can explain it as follows: [2]**Since** the cut figs **are important,** the owner frequently **checks that they are there,** and hence he very soon becomes aware of their loss and gives up hope of recovering them. [3]Similarly, **regarding** the overhanging branches of **a fig tree,** the owner **knows** very well **that fruit tends to fall.** Thus he gives up hope of recovering them in advance. We see, therefore, that the first part of the Mishnah can be satisfactorily explained according to Abaye's viewpoint that anticipated *ye'ush* is not effective. [4]**But the last clause** of the Mishnah **is difficult** to reconcile with the viewpoint of **Rava, for it states: "With regard to olives and carobs** found under such circumstances, **it is forbidden for the finder to take them."** Now, if the laws governing olives and carobs are different from those governing figs, it must presumably be because olives and carobs tend not to fall from the tree when ripe, and there is no reason to assume that their owners gave up hope of recovering them in advance. Thus, even though they give up hope when they find out that the fruit fell, this does not retroactively give the finder permission to take the fruit *now.* This would seem to prove that anticipated *ye'ush* is not effective, in contradiction to Rava's viewpoint.

אָמַר רַבִּי אַבָּהוּ [5]**Rabbi Abbahu said** in reply: The objection against Rava may be answered as follows: **An olive is different, because its appearance proves** who owns it and from which tree it fell. Thus the owner will not give up hope of recovering the fruit, because he will assume that any honest passerby will recognize that the fallen olives belong to the owner of the tree, and it is as if they have a clear identifying mark on them. [6]**And,** continues Rabbi Abbahu, since each fallen olive specifically resembles those olives remaining on the tree nearby, **even though olives fall from trees just as figs do, it is well known** to everyone **that** if fallen olives are found **in a certain person's place, that person is their owner.**

אִי הָכִי [7]The Gemara objects: **If so,** if fallen fruit can be linked by its appearance to a specific tree and to a specific owner, **the same** principle **should also apply to the first clause** of the Mishnah dealing with fallen figs, and the figs should belong to their owner rather than to the finder, because the owner will not have given up hope of recovering them since they can be identified.

אָמַר רַב פַּפָּא [8]**Rav Pappa said** in reply: There is a difference between olives and figs. When olives fall from a tree they retain their appearance and are not disfigured. By contrast, **a fig** is disfigured and damaged **when it falls** and **becomes repellent.** Hence the owner has no interest in keeping fallen figs, even though he

[1]בִּשְׁלָמָא רֵישָׁא לְאַבַּיֵי לָא קַשְׁיָא: [2]אַגַּב דַּחֲשִׁיבִי, מְמַשְׁמֵשׁ בְּהוּ; [3]תְּאֵנָה נַמִי, מֵידַע יְדִיעַ דְּנָתְרָא. [4]אֶלָּא סֵיפָא לְרָבָא קַשְׁיָא, דְּקָתָנֵי: ״בְּזֵיתִים וּבֶחָרוּבִים אָסוּר״!

[5]אָמַר רַבִּי אַבָּהוּ: שָׁאנֵי זַיִת, הוֹאִיל וַחֲזוּתוֹ מוֹכִיחַ עָלָיו, [6]וְאַף עַל גַּב דְּנָתְרִין זֵיתֵי, מֵידַע יְדִיעַ דּוּכְתָּא דְּאִינִישׁ אִינִישׁ הוּא.

[7]אִי הָכִי, אֲפִילּוּ רֵישָׁא נַמִי!

[8]אָמַר רַב פַּפָּא: תְּאֵנָה עִם נְפִילָתָהּ נִמְאֶסֶת.

LITERAL TRANSLATION

[1]Granted that the first clause is not difficult for Abaye: [2]Since they are important, one feels for them; [3][and regarding] a fig tree, too, it is known that [the fruit] falls. [4]But the last clause is difficult for Rava, for it teaches: "With regard to olives and with regard to carobs, it is forbidden [for the finder to take them"!

[5]Rabbi Abbahu said: An olive is different, because its appearance proves about it, [6]and even though olives fall, it is well known [that] a person's place [belongs to] that person.

[7]If so, [the same should apply] even [in] the first clause too!

[8]Rav Pappa said: A fig, when it falls, becomes repellent.

RASHI

בשלמא רישא לאביי — מצי לתרוצי דמעיקרא ידע ואייאש, כדמפרש ואזיל. **דקתני בזיתים ובחרובין אסור** — וסלקא דעתך משום דלא עבידי דנתרי, וליכא למימר ידע דאייאש, ואף על גב דלכי ידע מייאש — לא הוי יאוש מהשתא. **חזותו מוכיח עליו** — מראיתו ניכר של מי הוא, הלכך מריה לכי ידע דנפיל לא מייאש, דמימר אמר: כולי עלמא ידעי דדידי נינהו ולא הפקר הן, ולא שקלי להו. **עם נפילתה נמאסת** — הלכך: כיון דידיע דנתרא — מעיקרא מייאש משום מאיסותא, דמכי נפלה — לא חשיבא עליה ומפקר לה. **לא ידיע** — לא גרסינן, ופירוש היה משובש בספרים.

— "first tithe"; מַעֲשֵׂר שֵׁנִי — "second tithe"; and מַעֲשַׂר עָנִי — "poor man's tithe." These tithes are set aside from foods after they have ripened and been brought into the house. Ownerless food is exempt from tithes, and hence no tithes are taken during the Sabbatical Year, when all food growing from the ground is deemed ownerless. Similarly, food eaten in the course of an אֲכִילַת עֲרַאי — "an incidental meal" (e.g., fruit eaten straight from the tree) — need not be tithed. Most of the laws of tithes appear in tractate *Ma'aserot.*

TERMINOLOGY

בִּשְׁלָמָא Lit., **in peace,** meaning, "granted that...." This term introduces a question in which the element that is understood and acceptable is placed first and the difficulty is placed second. In the example cited here, one Halakhah is understandable according to Abaye's viewpoint, but another Halakhah is difficult to understand according to Rava's viewpoint.

SAGES

רַבִּי אַבָּהוּ Rabbi Abbahu. See *Bava Metzia,* Part I, p. 100.

רַב פַּפָּא Rav Pappa. See *Bava Metzia,* Part I, p. 131.

BACKGROUND

חֲזוּתוֹ מוֹכִיחַ עָלָיו Its appearance proves from which tree it fell. There are many different strains of olives, and already in Mishnaic and Talmudic times detailed knowledge existed of the strains found in Eretz Israel. The types of olives are distinguished from each other according to various characteristics, such as the time of their ripening, their oil content, etc. Each strain of olive also has its own characteristic shape, and its pits also have different shapes. It is, therefore, possible to determine from which tree a fallen olive has come.

תְּאֵנָה עִם נְפִילָתָהּ נִמְאֶסֶת A fig, when it falls, becomes repellent. A fig that falls to the ground is far less likely to be still edible than an olive that has fallen. Although olives full of oil may occasionally fall and become

NOTES

הוֹאִיל וַחֲזוּתוֹ מוֹכִיחַ עָלָיו Because its appearance proves from which tree it fell. Our commentary follows most Rishonim, who explain that the olives on the ground resemble in appearance those on the tree. However, other explanations are offered, involving slightly different versions of the text. A notable example is that of *Meiri,* who reads חֲזִיתַיְיהוּ instead of חֲזוּתוֹ and translates it as "boundary," from the root חזית. According to this explanation, the Gemara simply means that the olives' location, within the general bounds of the tree, is itself a valid proof of ownership.

תְּאֵנָה עִם נְפִילָתָהּ נִמְאֶסֶת A fig, when it falls, becomes

TRANSLATION AND COMMENTARY

could identify them if he wished, since they are presumably no longer fit for consumption. Therefore, he gives up his right of ownership of such fallen fruit in advance. Thus we see that the various cases cited in the Mishnah from tractate *Ma'aserot* can be reconciled with the viewpoints of both Abaye and Rava.

תָּא שְׁמַע [1](8) Up to this point in the discussion all the cases cited by the Gemara have dealt with situations where property was lost in an ordinary way, and its owner did or did not give up hope of its recovery. In the next case we are introduced to a situation where the property was lost as a result of theft, robbery, or natural disaster. **Come and hear** another refutation of Abaye's viewpoint from the following Tosefta (*Ketubot* 8:3): **"A thief who took** something **from one** person **and gave** it **to another,** [2]**and similarly a robber who took** something **from one** person **and gave it to another,** [22A] [3]**and similarly, if the Jordan** or any other **river swept** something away **from one** person **and gave** it **to another**, in all these cases [4]**what was taken** by the thief, robber, or river **was taken** effectively, **and what was given** to a third party by the thief, robber, or river **was given** effectively." In other words, whoever receives an article from a thief, robber, or river can legitimately keep it, because we presume that the original owner has given up hope of its recovery. [5]Now, says the Gemara, we can take it for **granted** that **in the case of a robber and of the Jordan, where** the owner actually **sees them** taking the object from his possession **and gives up hope** of recovering it, the recipient may keep the item he has been given by the robber or recovered from the river. In both cases the owner of the article is deprived of it openly, and the article comes into the possession of the recipient after the owner has given up hope of recovering it. [6]**However, in the case of a thief**, who deprives the owner of his property by stealth, **does** the owner actually **see** the thief taking the object, **so that he gives up hope** of its recovery? In all likelihood, the owner does not immediately realize that the item has been stolen, and he will give up hope of recovering it only later, after the thief has already transferred it to the third party. Yet the Tosefta rules that the recipient may keep the object, implying that anticipated *ye'ush* is effective. This is surely a refutation of Abaye's viewpoint.

[1]תָּא שְׁמַע: ״הַגַּנָּב שֶׁנָּטַל מִזֶּה וְנָתַן לָזֶה, [2]וְכֵן גַּזְלָן שֶׁנָּטַל מִזֶּה וְנָתַן לָזֶה, [22A] [3]וְכֵן יַרְדֵּן שֶׁנָּטַל מִזֶּה וְנָתַן לָזֶה, [4]מַה שֶּׁנָּטַל נָטַל, וּמַה שֶּׁנָּתַן נָתַן״. [5]בִּשְׁלָמָא גַּזְלָן וְיַרְדֵּן, דְּקָא חָזֵי לְהוּ וּמְיָאֵשׁ. [6]אֶלָּא גַּנָּב, מִי קָא חָזֵי לֵיהּ דְּמִיָּאֵשׁ?

LITERAL TRANSLATION

[1]Come [and] hear: "A thief who took from this one and gave to that one, [2]and similarly a robber who took from this one and gave to that one, [22A] [3]and similarly, [if] the Jordan [River] took from this one and gave to that one, [4]what it took it took, and what it gave it gave." [5]Granted [in the cases of] a robber and the Jordan, for he sees them and gives up hope. [6]However, [in the case of] a thief, does he see him so that he gives up hope?

RASHI

ירדן — וכן שאר נהרות. ותנא זה על יד הירדן היה יושב.

NOTES

repellent. This statement poses a number of problems, and there are many different readings of the text here. *Rashi*'s explanation, followed by our commentary, is that fallen figs are barely edible; hence the owner readily relinquishes his rights to them, even though he could, if he wanted, identify and recover them. According to this viewpoint, even if the figs are in the farmer's field they are ownerless and may be taken. Other commentators, however, have readings that suggest that the figs may still be valuable, but the issue is the usual one of the lack of identifying marks. Since figs usually become damaged when they fall, they are no longer distinguishable, and the owner gives up hope of recovering them. According to Rava, they are then ownerless by virtue of anticipated *ye'ush*. According to Abaye, actual *ye'ush* is involved, since the owner knows that fig trees shed their fruit and gives up hope in advance. According to this interpretation, only figs found in the public domain may be taken, as those found in the farmer's field are not ownerless (*Tosafot, Rosh*, and others).

וְכֵן יַרְדֵּן **And similarly the Jordan River.** According to *Rashi*, followed by our commentary, the law cited here applies to any river and not just the Jordan; and the reason why the Jordan is mentioned here is that the Sage who taught this Tosefta happened to live near that particular river. However, most commentators (*Ramban, Rashba, Rosh, Ran*) do not accept this interpretation. They follow the interpretation found in the Jerusalem Talmud, that the Tosefta is not referring to the Jordan taking property from one person and giving it to another, but to its altering the borders of Eretz Israel. For certain Halakhic purposes, the Jordan River constitutes the eastern boundary of Eretz Israel. Since its course changes from time to time, this Tosefta teaches us that no matter where the Jordan flows, it forms the boundary: if, because of changes in the river's course, a field becomes situated on the east bank, it loses its holy status, just as an owner loses his rights to an object that was stolen from him and given to another.

Alternatively, *Ritva* suggests an entirely different explanation of the Hebrew word יַרְדֵּן. By changing the vowels he arrives at יַרְדָּן, *yardan*, meaning "squatter," instead of יַרְדֵּן, *yarden*, meaning "Jordan," and he understands the text as referring to another category of thief.

dirty or misshapen, in any event most olives are meant to be crushed for their oil, and are not irreparably damaged by falling. By contrast, figs generally become inedible when they fall. Moreover, although strains of figs do differ from each other, and the fruit may be distinguishable by its color, shape, or size, it is nevertheless likely — because of its softness — to lose its shape completely once it has fallen from the tree.

CONCEPTS

גַּנָּב וְגַזְלָן **A thief and a robber.** A thief (גַּנָּב) and a robber (גַּזְלָן) are similar, in that they both take property that is not their own. However, a thief takes things by stealth and does not want his victim to know his identity. By contrast, a robber forcibly takes from people in their presence, without attempting to conceal himself. The Halakhah differentiates between the two with regard to the restoration of the goods taken. The robber must return the value of the property he took. (Under certain circumstances he must pay a fine of one-fifth of its value.) If there are witnesses to the theft, the thief must pay double (and if he has stolen animals, he must occasionally pay four or five times their value, depending on the kind of livestock). The distinction between robbers and thieves is discussed below (22a), and further on the tractate discusses the whole subject of misappropriation of possessions, including fraud and refusal to pay a proper return for goods or services.

יַרְדֵּן **The Jordan River.** Especially in the section between the Sea of Galilee and the Dead Sea, the Jordan flows for more than sixty miles down a very gradual slope. Because of the plentiful supply of loam in the Jordan Valley, and because the river does not contain a lot of water, it flows in meandering fashion (its actual length is more than twice the distance, as the crow flies, from one end to the other). Increases in the flow of the river in winter and spring and the accumulation of mud along the

¹תִּרְגְּמָהּ רַב פַּפָּא בְּלִסְטִים מְזוּיָּן.
²אִי הָכִי, הַיְינוּ גַּזְלָן!
³תְּרֵי גַּוְונֵי גַּזְלָן.
⁴תָּא שְׁמַע: "שָׁטַף נָהָר קוֹרָיו עֵצָיו וַאֲבָנָיו, וּנְתָנוֹ בְּתוֹךְ שְׂדֵה חֲבֵירוֹ, ⁵הֲרֵי אֵלּוּ שֶׁלּוֹ, מִפְּנֵי שֶׁנִּתְיָאֲשׁוּ הַבְּעָלִים".

LITERAL TRANSLATION

[1] Rav Pappa explained [the Tosefta] as referring to an armed bandit.

[2] If so, that is the same as a robber!

[3] [The Tosefta is describing] two kinds of robbers.

[4] Come [and] hear: "If a river washed away his beams, wood, or stones, and deposited them within his fellow's field, [5] they are his, because the owner has given up hope."

TRANSLATION AND COMMENTARY

תִּרְגְּמָהּ רַב פַּפָּא [1] The Gemara answers: **Rav Pappa explained** the expression "thief" in **the Tosefta as referring** not to an ordinary thief but **to an armed bandit**, who seeks to carry out his crime by stealth, but is prepared to resort to force if he encounters resistance, and then goes into hiding once more. The victim in such a case is thus immediately aware of his loss and gives up hope of recovering it.

אִי הָכִי [2] But the Gemara now objects: **If** this is **so**, and the Tosefta is using the expression "thief" to refer to an armed bandit, such a "thief" **is the same as a robber.** What difference is there between this "thief" and the "robber" also mentioned in the Tosefta?

תְּרֵי גַּוְונֵי גַּזְלָן [3] The Gemara answers: **The Tosefta is** indeed merely **describing two kinds of robbers.** The one, referred to by the Tosefta as a "robber," is an ordinary robber who openly seizes property from its rightful owner. The other, referred to by the Tosefta as a "thief," is an armed bandit who prefers to avoid detection and to achieve his purpose by stealth, but who is armed and will resort to force if resisted — and then go into hiding once more. In both cases the injured party is at once aware of what is happening, and immediately gives up hope of recovering his property.

תָּא שְׁמַע [4] (9) **Come and hear** a refutation of Rava's view from the following Tosefta, which is a continuation of the one cited in the last quotation (*Ketubot* 8:3): **"If a river washed away** a person's **beams, wood, or stones, and deposited them within someone else's field, [5] they belong to the finder, because the owner** demonstrates by his inactivity that he **has given up hope** of recovering them." This case is different from one where property is lost בְּשִׁלּוּלִיתוֹ שֶׁל נָהָר — "in an overflowing river" (above, 21b). In that case the lost property is considered irretrievable. Hence no distinction is made between identifiable and unidentifiable objects. By contrast, in the case discussed here, the objects were washed downstream into another field, and are no different from any other lost objects. The Gemara initially assumes, from the fact that the finder is entitled to keep the objects, that they were unidentifiable. Nevertheless, the owner could have recovered them if he had made immediate efforts to do so. The Tosefta treats the fact that he did not make the effort as an indication that he has given up hope of recovering them. (See notes below.)

RASHI

בלסטים מזוין — ובחזקה נטלה הימנו, ומעיקרא ידע ומייאש. **שטף נהר קוריו** — של זה ומצאן אחר. **הרי אלו כו'** — הכי גרסינן: **הרי אלו שלו מפני שנתיאשו הבעלים**, דכל שטיפת נהר כקורות עצים ואבנים, הבעלים ידעו בה מיד, דיש לה קול.

riverbed cause flooding for brief periods which inundates the Jordan Valley and alters the course of the river. Therefore it often happens that the Jordan "takes from one person and gives to another," by a shift in the riverbed or a flood.

LANGUAGE

לִסְטִים **Bandit, robber.** This word is derived from the Greek ληστής, *lestes,* meaning a robber or pirate. The form לִיסְטִים (rather than לִסְטִים) owes its origin to an ancient spelling error (interchange between the letters ם and ס, which look alike), and this form eventually became standard.

NOTES

שָׁטַף נָהָר קוֹרָיו **If a river washed away his beams.** According to *Rashi's* interpretation of this Tosefta, the case here involves the flooding river described above (21b), which automatically renders objects ownerless, regardless of the owner's attitude. Moreover, the issue here is not one of giving up hope (יֵאוּשׁ), but the related one of deliberate renunciation of property (הֶפְקֵר). According to *Rashi,* the Gemara initially assumed that the beams were rendered ownerless in accordance with the law applying to objects that were irretrievably lost upon being swept away by a flood. It is irrelevant whether the beams were identifiable or not; in either case they are comparable to ordinary lost objects *without distinguishing marks.* In other words, the owner is considered to have given up hope of recovering them the moment he heard of their loss, which in the case of a natural disaster was probably almost immediately. The Tosefta states that the objects are the finder's "*because* the owner gave up hope of recovering them." This clearly implies that awareness of loss is essential for *ye'ush* to be effective, in apparent support of Abaye's view. In order to explain the Tosefta according to Rava, the Gemara first suggests that the flood here is not the one described above (21b). In this case, the beams can still be saved, and therefore they are not automatically rendered ownerless. They are thus comparable to lost objects *with distinguishing marks,* which must be returned unless the owner actually gives up hope of recovering them before they are found. At this point the Gemara points out that, if this suggestion were right, the beams should only be ownerless if the owner expressly makes them so, but the language of the Tosefta would seem to indicate that, on the contrary, they are automatically ownerless unless the owner makes a strenuous effort to recover them. The Gemara then modifies its answer and says that we are indeed talking about a

HALAKHAH

שָׁטַף נָהָר קוֹרָיו **If a river washed away his beams.** "Property washed away by a river may be kept by the finder, even if the original owner argues vehemently that he never gave up hope of recovering it." (*Shulḥan Arukh, Ḥoshen*

TRANSLATION AND COMMENTARY

טַעְמָא דִּנְתְיָאֲשׁוּ הַבְּעָלִים [1]The Gemara now draws an inference from the wording of this Tosefta: **The reason** given by the Tosefta for the ruling that the finder may keep these items **is that the owner** manifestly **gave up hope** of recovering them when he saw what was happening and did not try to retrieve them. [2]**But,** by implication, **ordinarily** if the owner was not nearby and did not become aware of his loss immediately, **this would not be the case.** We would not permit the finder to keep the objects in such circumstances, even though they are not identifiable, because the owner has not yet had the opportunity to give up hope. And even though when he ultimately discovers his loss he will give up hope, because the objects do not contain any identifying marks, nevertheless at present this is merely a case of anticipated *ye'ush.* This would imply that anticipated *ye'ush* is not effective, in contradiction to Rava's viewpoint.

הָכָא בְּמַאי עָסְקִינַן [3]The Gemara answers: **With what are we dealing here?** [4]We are dealing with a case **where** the owner still has a chance **to save the lost items,** and therefore does not relinquish his ownership unless he specifically expresses his *ye'ush.* This case is similar to one where the object lost has an identifying mark, and the concept of anticipated *ye'ush* is inapplicable.

אִי הָכִי אֵימָא סֵיפָא [5]The Gemara objects: **If so, consider** what is stated in **the last clause** of the Tosefta: [6]"**If the owner was** present at the time and was **running after the lost item, the finder must return it** to him." This is because the attempt by the owner to retrieve his property is an indication that he has not given up hope, and therefore the finder must return the property to him. [7]**Now, if** this clause in the Tosefta is referring to a case where the owner **can save the lost item, why does it speak of** the owner **"running after"** it? [8]**Even if** the owner **was not running after** the lost item, **the same ruling should also apply.** The finder should have to return it, because the owner has the ability to retrieve it and thus has not yet given up hope of recovering it.

[1]טַעְמָא דִּנְתְיָאֲשׁוּ הַבְּעָלִים, [2]הָא סְתָמָא לָא!
[3]הָכָא בְּמַאי עָסְקִינַן? [4]כְּשֶׁיָּכוֹל לְהַצִּיל.
[5]אִי הָכִי, אֵימָא סֵיפָא: [6]"אִם הָיוּ הַבְּעָלִים מְרַדְּפִין אַחֲרֵיהֶם, חַיָּיב לְהַחֲזִיר". [7]אִי בִּיכוֹלִין לְהַצִּיל, מַאי אִרְיָא מְרַדְּפִין? [8]אֲפִילּוּ אֵין מְרַדְּפִין נַמִי!

LITERAL TRANSLATION

[1]The reason is that the owner has given up hope, [2]but ordinarily [this would] not [be the case]. [3]With what are we dealing here? [4]Where he is able to save [the lost items].

[5]If so, consider (lit., "say") the last clause: [6]If the owner was running after them [the lost items, the finder] must return [them]." [7][Now,] if he can save [the lost items], why does it speak of (lit., "deal with") "running after"? [8]Even if he was not running after [them, the same ruling should] also [apply].

RASHI

הא סתמא — הא אם היתה אבידה אחרת שאין לנו לומר שידעו הבעלים — לא הויא של מוצאה, קשיא לרבא! **כשיכול להציל** — ודכוותה במציאה אחרת, דבר שיש בו סימן, דיכול ליתן סימן וליטול — מודינא בה דחייב להחזיר. **אפילו אין מרדפין נמי** — דסמכי אהצלה דלמחר וליומא אוחרא ולא מייאשי.

TERMINOLOGY

הָכָא בְּמַאי עָסְקִינַן What we are dealing with here is..., i.e., the case that we are referring to here is.... This expression is used by the Gemara to introduce an אוּקִימְתָּא — an explanation whose purpose is usually to answer a previously raised objection, and to limit the application of the Mishnah or Baraita under discussion to one particular set of circumstances.

מַאי אִרְיָא Why [this] discussion? As a rule, statements in a Mishnah or a Baraita are framed to include all relevant cases. If, therefore, a Mishnah or a Baraita links a law to a particular, unusual, set of circumstances when it could have chosen a more common situation, the Talmud may object: "Why [this] discussion?" In other words, "Why was it necessary to specify this particular situation, since the same law would also apply in other cases?"

NOTES

regular flood, which can render objects ownerless automatically. However, this particular flood has not yet irretrievably washed away the beams. Therefore, if the owner immediately sets off to retrieve them, the beams must be returned, even if they were recovered by someone else, since they were not yet ownerless when found. But if the owner does not attempt to recover them, then the person who recovers them may keep them — even if he recovers them before they are washed away and automatically become ownerless. That is because, under the circumstances, the owner's considered failure to take action amounts to deliberate renunciation (הֶפְקֵר).

Most Rishonim do not accept *Rashi's* interpretation largely because the Tosefta unmistakably uses the expression "giving up hope" (יֵאוּשׁ) and not "renunciation" (הֶפְקֵר), and also because of other textual problems with *Rashi's* reading. Therefore, they explain (and this explanation is followed in the commentary here) that the Gemara never thought that the flood described in the Tosefta was of the type that automatically renders an object ownerless. In such a flood, the river overflows with such force that it sweeps everything in its path into the sea, whereas here the river merely took the beams and deposited them in the next field. Therefore, the finder may keep the beams only if the owner gave up hope of recovering them — consciously, for Abaye, and even potentially, according to Rava. However, the language of the Tosefta is problematic for Rava, since it specifically mentions that the owner "gave up hope" and also that he "ran after" the beams, whereas according to Rava potential *ye'ush* is sufficient. Hence, Rava explains the Tosefta's mention of conscious giving up of hope by saying that the beam had an identifying mark and could have been recovered, if the owner had not given up hope. He explains the need for the owner to attempt to recover his property by pointing to the increased difficulty in saving the beam if not done immediately. Thus, failure to pursue immediately on hearing of the loss is an indication of *ye'ush* (*Tosafot*, *Ramban*, *Rashba*, *Rosh*, *Ran*, and others).

HALAKHAH

Mishpat 259:7.) However, if the owner could have saved the property, even with difficulty, and was either taking steps to try to save it, or was not present at the time and someone else recovered it immediately, the finder must return the lost

[1] הָכָא בְּמַאי עָסְקִינַן? [2] בִּיכוֹלִין לְהַצִּיל עַל יְדֵי הַדְּחָק. [3] מְרַדְּפִין, לָא אַיְיאוּשׁ. [4] אֵין מְרַדְּפִין, אַיְיאוּשֵׁי מְיַאַשׁ.

[5] תָּא שְׁמַע: ״כֵּיצַד אָמְרוּ: הַתּוֹרֵם שֶׁלֹּא מִדַּעַת, תְּרוּמָתוֹ תְּרוּמָה? [6] הֲרֵי שֶׁיָּרַד לְתוֹךְ שְׂדֵה חֲבֵירוֹ וְלִיקֵּט וְתָרַם שֶׁלֹּא בִּרְשׁוּת, [7] אִם חוֹשֵׁשׁ מִשּׁוּם גָּזֵל, אֵין תְּרוּמָתוֹ תְּרוּמָה, [8] וְאִם לָאו, תְּרוּמָתוֹ תְּרוּמָה.

LITERAL TRANSLATION

[1] With what are we dealing here? [2] With [a case where the owner] can save [the lost items only] with difficulty. [3] If he runs after [them], he has not given up hope. [4] If he does not run after [them], he has surely given up hope.

[5] Come [and] hear: "In what circumstances did [the Sages] say: 'One who separates terumah without [the owner's] knowledge, his terumah is terumah'? [6] If he went down into his fellow's field and gathered [produce] and separated terumah [from it] without permission, [7] if [the owner] is concerned about [it being] robbery, his terumah is not terumah, [8] but if not, his terumah is terumah.

TRANSLATION AND COMMENTARY

הָכָא בְּמַאי עָסְקִינַן [1] The Gemara answers: **With what are we dealing here?** [2] We are dealing **with a case where the owner can save the lost item only with difficulty.** Recovery is possible even if he does not take immediate steps, but his task will be much more difficult. Hence, [3] **if he runs after** the lost item, this is a clear indication that **he has not given up hope** of recovering it, and the finder is obliged to return it. [4] But **if he** is present and **does not run after** the lost item immediately, this is a clear indication that **he has surely given up hope** of recovering it. On the other hand, if the owner was not present at the time of the loss and knew nothing about it, the finder must return the object, because even when the owner finds out he will not give up hope, since the object has identifying marks on it and there is no reason to imagine that the owner has given up hope of retrieving it.

תָּא שְׁמַע [5] (10) **Come and hear.** The Gemara now attempts to refute Abaye's view contradicting a Tosefta on another subject (*Terumot,* chapter 1). All Israelite farmers in Eretz Israel were obliged by Torah law to separate a portion of their harvest and give it to the priests. The produce thus separated is called terumah (תְּרוּמָה). In general the separation of terumah had to be performed by the farmer himself or by his agent. The Tosefta from which the Gemara now seeks to draw an inference on the subject of *ye'ush* describes a situation where the act of separating terumah was performed by a third party acting without the farmer's knowledge: **"In what circumstances did the Sages say** that if a person **separates terumah** from a farmer's produce **without the owner's knowledge, his** separation of the **terumah is** nevertheless considered effective and the produce acquires the status of **terumah?** Such separation is valid in the following circumstances: [6] **If** someone **went down into another person's field, gathered produce** for the owner, **and separated terumah from it without** the owner's **permission.** In such a case the validity of the third party's unsolicited action is determined by the farmer's first, spontaneous, reaction to it. [7] **If the owner** demonstrates by his **concern** that, in his opinion, the person who separated the terumah was guilty of **robbery,** the third party's act of separating the **terumah is not** considered effective, and the **terumah** is not valid, since he separated the terumah against the owner's will. [8] **But if** the owner did **not** give any indication that he considered the person who separated the terumah guilty of robbery, then **his terumah is**

RASHI

על ידי הדחק – ואם לא ימהר להציל לא יצילו, הלכך אין מרדפין – אפקורי אפקרינהו, דהא ידעו ולא הצילו. **שלא מדעת** – בעלים. **וליקט** – לצורך בעל הבית. **ואם חושש** – בעל הבית, ומקפיד על מה שעשה זה. **משום גזל** – שתרם תרומתו בלא רשותו.

CONCEPTS

תְּרוּמָה, תְּרוּמָה גְּדוֹלָה Terumah, the great terumah. Whenever the term תְּרוּמָה appears without qualification, it refers to this offering, תְּרוּמָה גְּדוֹלָה. Deuteronomy 18:4 commands that "the first fruit of your corn, of your wine, and of your oil" be given to the priest (see also Numbers 18:12). The Sages extended the scope of this commandment to include all produce. This mitzvah applies only in Eretz Israel. After the בִּיכּוּרִים — the first fruits — have been separated, a certain portion of the produce must be set aside for priests. The Torah does not specify the amount of terumah that must be set aside; one may theoretically fulfill one's obligation by giving even a single kernel of grain from an entire crop. The Sages established a measure: one-fortieth for a generous gift, one-fiftieth for an average gift, and one-sixtieth for a miserly gift. A person should not set aside other tithes until he has set aside terumah. This is considered holy and may only be eaten by a priest and his household while they are in a state of ritual purity (see Leviticus 22:9-15). To emphasize that state of ritual purity, the Sages obligated the priests to wash their hands before partaking of the terumah. This is the source of the practice of נְטִילַת יָדַיִם — "the ritual washing of hands." A ritually impure priest — or a non-priest — who eats terumah is subject to the penalty of death at the hand of Heaven (מִיתָה בִּידֵי שָׁמַיִם). If terumah contracts ritual impurity, it may no longer be eaten and must be burned. Nevertheless, it remains the property of the priest and he may benefit from its being burned. Nowadays, terumah is not given to the priests because they have no definite proof of their priestly lineage. Nevertheless, the obligation to separate terumah still remains; but only a small portion of the produce is separated.

NOTES

וְלִיקֵּט וְתָרַם **Someone who gathered another person's produce and separated terumah from it.** The Gemara is not referring to a case of theft, but rather to one where the person who gathered the produce knew that the owner would not object to his doing so for himself. Therefore, he assumed that he would also not object to his separating terumah for the owner (*Ketzot HaḤoshen,* following *Shakh*).

HALAKHAH

item (*Tur* and *Rema*; see also *Rambam, Sefer Nezikin, Hilkhot Gezelah Va'Avedah* 6:1).

הַתּוֹרֵם שֶׁלֹּא מִדַּעַת **One who separates terumah without the owner's permission.** "A person who separates terumah for the owner without his permission, or a person who goes into another person's field without the owner's permission and gathers produce for himself and separates terumah from it — in both of these cases, if, when the owner found him, he said, 'You should have gone to choice-quality produce,' then, if better produce was available, the terumah is valid; otherwise it is not valid. However, if the owner came and separated additional produce as terumah, then in either case the terumah that had already been separated is valid." This ruling is not in accordance with the Gemara's explanation of the Tosefta as referring only to an appointed agent. According to some commentators, that answer was

TRANSLATION AND COMMENTARY

considered valid **terumah.** [1]**And how does** the person who separated the terumah **know whether the owner is concerned about robbery or not?** [2]The way to judge the owner's reaction is as follows: **If the owner came and found him** separating terumah from the produce, **and said to him,** 'What a pity you separated the terumah from this produce. **You should have gone to the choicest produce** in the field, and separated the terumah from there,' [3]then, if in fact **choicer produce than** that selected **could be found** in the field, **the terumah** separated **is** considered valid **terumah.** For the owner's remarks indicate that he consented after the event to the separation of the terumah by the other person, and it is as if the latter acted with the knowledge and consent of the owner. [4]**But if no** better produce was available, **the terumah** he separated **is not** considered valid **terumah.** In this case we assume that the owner's remark, 'You should have gone to the choicest produce,' was meant sarcastically, as an expression of anger toward the person who had separated the terumah without permission. [5]**If,** however, when **the owner** came to the field, he **gathered** additional **produce and added it to the terumah already separated,** [6]then **in either case,** whether or not better produce was found, **the terumah is** considered valid **terumah."** For the owner, by adding to the terumah already separated, is indicating his unreserved agreement with the action of the person he found in his field, and it is as if the latter had acted with the owner's knowledge and consent.

וְכִי נִמְצְאוּ יָפוֹת [7]The Gemara now proceeds to present its suggested refutation of the viewpoint of Abaye: The Tosefta states that "**if in fact choicer produce was available, the terumah** separated is considered valid **terumah.**" [8]But **why** is this so? **Surely at the time that** the other person **separated the terumah, the owner did not know** about it! Thus, we may infer from the Tosefta that even though the owner indicated his approval only later, it took effect retroactively. Similarly, in the case of *ye'ush*, once the owner of the property becomes aware of his loss, he gives up hope, and this anticipated *ye'ush* should also take effect retroactively from the time of the actual loss. This would imply that anticipated *ye'ush* is effective, and thus Abaye's viewpoint is refuted.

[1]וּמְנַיִן הוּא יוֹדֵעַ אִם חוֹשֵׁשׁ מִשּׁוּם גָּזֵל וְאִם לָאו? [2]הֲרֵי שֶׁבָּא בַּעַל הַבַּיִת וּמְצָאוֹ, וְאָמַר לוֹ: ׳כַּלֵּךְ אֵצֶל יָפוֹת׳, [3]אִם נִמְצְאוּ יָפוֹת מֵהֶן, תְּרוּמָתוֹ תְּרוּמָה, [4]וְאִם לָאו, אֵין תְּרוּמָתוֹ תְּרוּמָה. [5]לִיקְּטוּ הַבְּעָלִים וְהוֹסִיפוּ עֲלֵיהֶן, [6]בֵּין כָּךְ וּבֵין כָּךְ תְּרוּמָתוֹ תְּרוּמָה.״

[7]וְכִי נִמְצְאוּ יָפוֹת מֵהֶן תְּרוּמָתוֹ תְּרוּמָה? [8]אַמַּאי? בְּעִידָּנָא דְּתָרַם, הָא לָא הֲוָה יָדַע!

LITERAL TRANSLATION

[1]And how does he know whether [the owner] is concerned about robbery or not? [2]If the owner came and found him, and said to him, 'You should have gone to choice (lit., "beautiful") [fruits],' [3]if choicer [fruits] than these were found, his terumah is terumah, [4]but if not, his terumah is not terumah. [5]If the owner gathered [fruits] and added [them] to [the terumah already separated], [6]in either case his terumah is terumah."

[7]And if choicer [fruits] than these were found, his terumah is terumah? [8]Why? Surely at the time that he separated the terumah, he [the owner] did not know.

RASHI

כלך אצל יפות – היה לך לילך אלל יפות לתת מהן לכהן. **לא הוה ידע** – אלמא כיון דלכי ידע דניחא ליה – אמרינן מעיקרא נמי ניחא ליה, ולענין יאוש נמי, כיון דלכי ידע מייאש, מעיקרא נמי הוי יאוש.

LANGUAGE

כַּלֵּךְ אֵצֶל יָפוֹת You should have gone to choice produce. The Sages frequently used the word כַּלֵּךְ, though its derivation is not clear. Generally it is explained as an abbreviation of לְכָה לְךָ — "go away" — or of כַּלֵּה וָלֵךְ — "finish and go away." In any event, its meaning is not simply "go," but rather, "forget about it," or "get on to something else," and it is often used concretely and literally, mainly in the context of calling for the abandonment of a certain subject or debate.

NOTES

שִׁעוּרֵי תְּרוּמָה Statutory quantities of terumah. According to Torah law, there is no fixed minimum quantity that one is required to set aside as terumah, and even one kernel of wheat, from an entire pile of grain, is sufficient in order to fulfill the mitzvah. However, the Rabbis ordained that farmers should separate between one-fortieth and one-sixtieth of their produce, the precise proportion depending on their generosity. Thus, a generous person would give one-fortieth, an average person one-fiftieth, and an ungenerous person one-sixtieth. Moreover, all these figures are considered proper, so that an agent has complete discretion in determining the owner's generosity. It follows from this that an owner cannot invalidate the action of his agent who has separated one-fortieth, for example, even if the owner ordinarily separates only one-sixtieth. Accordingly, *Tosafot* asks: How can the owner in our Gemara invalidate the agent's separation of terumah on the grounds that he selected choice-quality produce instead of medium-quality produce? Why does the agent not have discretionary powers here as well? *Tosafot* answers that these regulations apply only to quantity, but as far as quality is concerned, all people ordinarily separate terumah from produce of medium quality. If the owner wishes to be unusually generous, he may, of course, act in that way, but an agent has no discretion in the matter (see also the explanation of *Hokhmat Manoah*).

HALAKHAH

rejected at the end of the passage, where Rava distinguishes between religious obligations and ordinary gifts (*Rambam, Sefer Zeraim, Hilkhot Terumot* 4:3; *Kesef Mishneh; Shulhan Arukh, Yoreh De'ah* 331:31; see also *Gra* there and his marginal note on *Bava Metzia* 22a).

TERMINOLOGY

הָכִי נַמִּי מִסְתַּבְּרָא So, too, it is reasonable, i.e., indeed, what has just been stated makes sense (because...). Arguments introduced by this expression are usually considered conclusive.

TRANSLATION AND COMMENTARY

תִּרְגְּמָה רָבָא אַלִּיבָּא דְּאַבַּיֵּי [1]The Gemara answers: **Rava** himself suggested a way to **explain** the Tosefta **according to Abaye:** Perhaps the Tosefta is not referring to a case where the other person acted without the owner's consent. Perhaps it is referring to a case **where** the owner **appointed** the other person **as his agent,** and authorized him in advance to separate the terumah on his behalf. In such a case, if the agent had followed his instructions, there would have been no question about the validity of his act. The problem arose because the agent deviated slightly from his instructions, as the Gemara will explain, and under the circumstances we are not certain if the owner would have approved. Hence the validity of the agent's selection depends on the owner indicating his approval of the way in which the separation was carried out (see note). Thus this Tosefta has no bearing on the difference of opinion between Rava and Abaye concerning anticipated *ye'ush.*

הָכִי נַמִּי מִסְתַּבְּרָא [2]Before going on to explain Rava's answer, the Gemara first provides additional support for his suggestion that the Tosefta is referring to a situation where the owner had appointed the other person as his agent: **This** interpretation of the Tosefta **also stands to reason. For if it should enter your mind** to think **that** the owner **did not appoint** the other person **as his agent,** and the latter acted entirely on his own initiative, [3]**would his** act of separating **terumah be** considered effective, and would the **terumah** be valid even if the owner approved after the event? [4]**But surely** in the verse dealing with the separation of terumah (Numbers 18:28) **the Torah did not merely say, "You** shall offer up the terumah of the Lord," **but, "You also** shall offer up," etc. The word "also" is used **to include your agent.** The word "also" is superfluous here, and the

[1]תִּרְגְּמָה רָבָא אַלִּיבָּא דְּאַבַּיֵּי: דְּשַׁוְּיֵהּ שָׁלִיחַ. [2]הָכִי נַמִּי מִסְתַּבְּרָא, דְּאִי סָלְקָא דַּעְתָּךְ דְּלָא שַׁוְּיֵהּ שָׁלִיחַ, [3]מִי הָוְיָא תְּרוּמָתוֹ תְּרוּמָה? [4]וְהָא "אַתֶּם" "גַּם אַתֶּם" אָמַר רַחֲמָנָא,

LITERAL TRANSLATION

[1]Rava explained it according to Abaye: Where he appointed him [as his] agent.

[2]This also stands to reason, for if it should enter your mind that he did not appoint him [as his] agent, [3]would his terumah be terumah? [4]But surely the Torah said [not merely] "you" [but] "you also,"

RASHI

אתם גם אתם – "כן תרימו גם אתם", מהכא נפקא לן שלוחו של אדם כמותו לתרומה, שהשליח שתרם תרומתו תרומה, וכיון דשליחות מהכא נפקא לן, על כרחך שלוחכם דומיא ד"אתם" בעינן.

NOTES

תִּרְגְּמָה רָבָא אַלִּיבָּא דְּאַבַּיֵּי Rava explained it according to Abaye. Throughout the Talmud we find that Sages interpret or explain matters or resolve difficulties by using the approach of other Sages. The term תִּרְגְּמָה, in such cases, means "to explain or account for," generally by viewing the case appearing in the written source as a specific instance rather than a general case.

The present example is somewhat unusual in that Rava, who disagreed with Abaye on this subject, nevertheless took the trouble of finding a solution to the challenge posed to Abaye, although that challenge actually supported Rava's own position. Rava did so because the controversy between the Sages was not personal, but rather a method by which both sides were attempting to discover the truth. Therefore it is not particularly surprising to find one Sage setting out to clarify a fundamental problem by using the approach of a Sage who disagrees with him. In any event, the Sage does not seek personal victory but rather to establish the truth.

אַתֶּם גַּם אַתֶּם "You," "you also." The principle behind this interpretation is that the word "also" (גַּם), wherever it appears, is an expression of increment. In other words, its use shows that something must be added to what is explicitly stated in the text of the Torah. Since this expression of increment is regarded as though it were explicitly stated in Scripture, we now read the verse as though it said explicitly: "You or your agent separate terumah." Therefore, the rest of the interpretation is based on an analogy: Since a person and his agent are equivalent to each other, this equivalence must be regarded as total in every respect (according to the principle אֵין הֶקֵּשׁ לְמֶחֱצָה — "there are no half measures in analogy"), and the laws applying to the owner apply to the agent as well.

שָׁלִיחַ An agent. The present ruling regarding the separation of terumah is one of the most important sources in the Talmud for the general laws governing agency. In many contexts the Halakhic rule is שְׁלוּחוֹ שֶׁל אָדָם כְּמוֹתוֹ — "a person's agent is like himself." Hence the agent has the legal authority to do whatever the person who has appointed him has the legal authority to do. However, the phrase underlying the discussion here, אַתֶּם גַּם אַתֶּם, which, on the one hand, defines the agent as taking the place of the person who has appointed him, also serves, on the other hand, as the basis for the ruling that no one may serve as an agent unless he is the Halakhic equivalent of the person who appoints him. For that reason, only a mentally competent Jew may serve as an agent.

HALAKHAH

אַתֶּם גַּם אַתֶּם "You," "you also." "One may appoint an agent to separate terumah and tithes on one's behalf." This ruling follows the Scriptural derivation cited in the Gemara (*Rambam*, ibid., 4:1; *Shulḥan Arukh, Yoreh De'ah* 331:29).

LITERAL TRANSLATION

to include your agent. [1]Just as you [can separate terumah only] with your knowledge, [2]so too your agent [must separate terumah only] with your knowledge.

[3]Rather, with what are we dealing here? [4]For example, [with a case] where he appointed him [as his] agent, and said to him: "Go [and] separate terumah," [5]but did not say to him: "Separate terumah from these [fruits]." [6]Now, ordinarily, when an owner separates terumah, he separates terumah from medium-quality [fruits]. [7]But this one went and separated terumah from choice-quality [fruits]. [8]And the owner came and found him, and said to him: [9]"You should have gone to choice [fruits]." [10]If choicer [fruits] than these were found, his terumah is terumah, [11]but if not, his terumah is not terumah.

לְרַבּוֹת שְׁלוּחֲכֶם. [1]מָה אַתֶּם לְדַעְתְּכֶם, [2]אַף שְׁלוּחֲכֶם לְדַעְתְּכֶם.

[3]אֶלָּא, הָכָא בְּמַאי עָסְקִינַן? [4]כְּגוֹן דְּשַׁוְּיֵהּ שָׁלִיחַ, וַאֲמַר לֵיהּ: "זִיל תְּרוֹם", [5]וְלָא אֲמַר לֵיהּ: "תְּרוֹם מֵהָנֵי". [6]וּסְתָמֵיהּ דְּבַעַל הַבַּיִת כִּי תְּרוֹם, מִבֵּינוֹנִית הוּא תְּרוֹם. [7]וַאֲזַל אִיהוּ וְתָרַם מִיָּפוֹת. [8]וּבָא בַּעַל הַבַּיִת וּמְצָאוֹ, וְאָמַר לֵיהּ: [9]"כַּלֵּךְ אֵצֶל יָפוֹת". [10]אִם נִמְצְאוּ יָפוֹת מֵהֶן, תְּרוּמָתוֹ תְּרוּמָה, [11]וְאִם לָאו, אֵין תְּרוּמָתוֹ תְּרוּמָה.

RASHI

אף שלוחכם לדעתכם — שהבעלים מינוהו שליח.

TRANSLATION AND COMMENTARY

Rabbis interpreted its inclusion as indicating that not only the owner but "also" his agent is permitted to separate the owner's terumah. [1]Now, since the basis for the law that it is permitted for an agent to separate terumah on behalf of the owner of the produce is the superfluous word "also," and since the word "also" appears in juxtaposition to the word "you," the Sages inferred that the comparison between owner and agent should be extended further: **Just as you**, the owner, **can separate terumah only with your** own **knowledge** and approval, [2]**so too must your agent separate terumah only with your knowledge** and approval. Thus it follows that one person cannot separate terumah on behalf of another unless he has been appointed by that person as his agent.

אֶלָּא הָכָא בְּמַאי עָסְקִינַן [3]Having presented logical support for the suggestion that the Tosefta quoted above is referring to a situation where the farmer's agent separated terumah on his behalf, the Gemara now resumes its explanation of the Tosefta: **Rather, with what** particular case of agency **are we dealing here** in the Tosefta? [4]**For example, with a case where** the owner **appointed** the other person **as his agent** to separate terumah for him, **and said to him: "Go and separate terumah** for me," [5]**but did not say to him: "Separate terumah from this** particular **produce."** In other words, the owner did not give the agent specific instructions as to what quality of produce he should separate as terumah. [6]**Now, ordinarily, when a** property **owner separates terumah** from his own produce, **he separates terumah from produce of medium quality,** and not from produce of choice quality. [7]**But** in our case the agent **went and separated terumah from choice-quality** produce. The question now arises as to whether the agent has deviated from his instructions by separating the terumah from choice-quality produce. [8]When **the owner came and found him, he said to him:** [9]**"You should have gone to** separate terumah from **choice produce."** We must analyze the significance of this remark. [10]**If choicer produce than that** selected by the agent **was to be found, his** act of separating **terumah is** effective, and the terumah is considered valid **terumah,** because it is clear that the owner wanted to give terumah generously, as the agent did, and his only criticism of his agent was that the latter could have been even more generous. [11]**But if** there was **no** better produce available, **the terumah** separated by the agent **is not** considered valid **terumah,** because the owner's sarcastic remark indicates that it was not his intention to separate terumah from anything better than medium-quality produce. By separating choice-quality produce, the agent deviated from his instructions and his action does not obligate the owner.

NOTES

כְּגוֹן דְּשַׁוְּיֵהּ שָׁלִיחַ **For example, where he appointed him as his agent.** *Tosafot* asks why this interpretation is any less difficult for Abaye than the previous one. The owner still does not know in advance that the agent plans to separate terumah generously, and even if he agrees to it after the event, it should still be invalid, in accordance with Abaye's view that anticipated *ye'ush* is not effective *ye'ush*. *Tosafot* answers that in this case the owner's present generous attitude towards mitzvot is considered indicative of his previous attitude as well. *Rabbi Zvi Ḥayyot* answers, following *Ra'avad*, that according to the first interpretation of the Tosefta, the owner did not know that the other person was separating terumah at all, and hence could in no sense be considered as having given permission in advance. Therefore, if approval after the event is effective, we are forced to conclude that anticipated *ye'ush* is also effective. But according to the second interpretation, the owner expressly asked the other person to separate the

TRANSLATION AND COMMENTARY

אֲמֵימָר וּמָר זוּטְרָא וְרַב אַשִׁי [1]In connection with the previous discussion, the Gemara now relates the following incident: **Amemar, Mar Zutra, and Rav Ashi happened to be at Mari bar Isak's orchard.** Mari bar Isak was not present, but his sharecropper was. [2]**The sharecropper brought dates and pomegranates and set them before** the Rabbis. [3]**Amemar and Rav Ashi ate** the fruit, but **Mar Zutra did not eat**, because he was afraid that it had been taken by the sharecropper and given to the Rabbis without Mari bar Isak's permission. [4]**Meanwhile, Mari bar Isak came and found** the Rabbis eating, **and said to his sharecropper:** [5]**"Why did you not bring the Rabbis some of these fine fruits?"** pointing to some particularly fine produce. [6]**Amemar and Rav Ashi said to Mar Zutra: "Why does the Master** [Mar Zutra] **not eat now?** [7]**Surely it has been taught** in a Tosefta: **'If choicer produce than this was found, the terumah is** considered valid **terumah'!"** Since the other produce really was better, Mari bar Isak's remark was certainly not meant sarcastically. Hence his remark, like that of the owner of the produce with regard to the separation of terumah carried out on his behalf, must indicate that Mari bar Isak approved of his sharecropper's actions. [8]Mar Zutra **said** in reply **to** Amemar and Rav Ashi: "There is no comparison between the two cases. With regard to the ruling in the Tosefta concerning the separation of terumah, **Rava stated as follows:** [9]**The Sages said** that the expression, **'You should have gone to choice produce,'** indicates that the owner approves of his agent's actions **only with regard to terumah, because it is a commandment** to separate terumah. Therefore it stands to reason that the owner **is pleased** that it has been fulfilled in a generous manner. Thus, it is only in the case of the separation of terumah that we are justified in interpreting the words of the owner as indicating satisfaction with what his agent has done. [10]**But here,** in the case of Mari bar Isak's fruit, although it is true that Mari bar Isak was not being sarcastic, **it may** only **have been because he was embarrassed** to appear ungenerous to his guests **that he said** what he said, and not because he actually approved of the sharecropper's actions."

[1]אֲמֵימָר וּמָר זוּטְרָא וְרַב אַשִׁי אִקְלְעוּ לְבוּסְתָּנָא דְּמָרִי בַּר אִיסַק. [2]אַיְיתֵי אֲרִיסֵיהּ תַּמְרֵי וְרִימּוֹנֵי וּשְׁדָא קַמַּיְיהוּ. [3]אֲמֵימָר וְרַב אַשִׁי אָכְלֵי; מָר זוּטְרָא לָא אָכֵיל. [4]אַדְּהָכִי, אֲתָא מָרִי בַּר אִיסַק אַשְׁכַּחִינְהוּ, וַאֲמַר לֵיהּ לַאֲרִיסֵיהּ: [5]"אַמַּאי לָא אַיְיתִית לְהוּ לְרַבָּנַן מֵהָנָךְ שַׁפִּירָתָא?" [6]אֲמַרוּ לֵיהּ אֲמֵימָר וְרַב אַשִׁי לְמָר זוּטְרָא: "הַשְׁתָּא אַמַּאי לָא אָכֵיל מָר? [7]וְהָתַנְיָא: 'אִם נִמְצְאוּ יָפוֹת מֵהֶן, תְּרוּמָתוֹ תְּרוּמָה'!" [8]אֲמַר לְהוּ: "הָכִי אֲמַר רָבָא: [9]לֹא אָמְרוּ, 'כַּלֵּךְ אֵצֶל יָפוֹת', אֶלָּא לְעִנְיַן תְּרוּמָה בִּלְבַד, מִשּׁוּם דְּמִצְוָה הוּא, וְנִיחָא לֵיהּ. [10]אֲבָל הָכָא מִשּׁוּם כְּסִיפוּתָא הוּא דַּאֲמַר הָכִי".

LITERAL TRANSLATION

[1]Amemar and Mar Zutra and Rav Ashi happened to be at Mari bar Isak's orchard. [2]His sharecropper brought dates and pomegranates and set [them] before them. [3]Amemar and Rav Ashi ate; Mar Zutra did not eat. [4]Meanwhile, Mari bar Isak came [and] found them, and said to his sharecropper: [5]"Why did you not bring the Rabbis some of these fine [fruits]?" [6]Amemar and Rav Ashi said to Mar Zutra: "Now why does the Master not eat? [7]Surely it has been taught: 'If choicer [fruits] than these were found, his terumah is terumah'!" [8]He said to them: "Rava said as follows: [9][The Sages] did not say, 'You should have gone to choice [fruits],' except with regard to terumah alone, because it is a commandment, and he is pleased. [10]But here it is because of embarrassment that he said this."

RASHI

לבוסתנא – פרדס. **לא אכל** – דגזל ניהו, שהבעלים לא ידעו. **אם נמצאו יפות כו׳** – אלמא גלי דעתיה דניחא ליה, הכא נמי גלי דעתיה דניחא ליה במה שנתן לנו. **לא אמרו כלך אצל יפות** – דהוי גלוי דעת, אלא לענין תרומה.

LANGUAGE

בּוּסְתָּנָא Orchard. This term is derived from the Persian *bostan* (lit., "fragrant place"), which means orchard or garden.

BACKGROUND

מָרִי בַּר אִיסַק Mari bar Isak. He is mentioned in several places in the Talmud. Some authorities claim that there were two people of this name. However, it is possible that there was only one man, and that he lived to a great age. Mari bar Isak was wealthy, and various Sages used to frequent his home. Nonetheless, the Sages believed that he misused his wealth, and for that reason they reversed the laws of evidence to his disadvantage (see *Ketubot* 27b). They also regarded his generosity with a degree of suspicion.

SAGES

אֲמֵימָר Amemar. One of the greatest Babylonian Amoraim of the fifth and sixth generations. See *Bava Metzia*, Part I, p. 197.

מָר זוּטְרָא Mar Zutra. A colleague of Rav Ashi, Mar Zutra was one of the leading Sages of his generation, and his teachers, Rav Pappa and Rav Naḥman bar Yitzḥak, accepted him as their equal. Apart from his greatness in Torah, Halakhah, and Aggadah, Mar Zutra was noted as a preacher, and his sermons are cited throughout the Talmud. He apparently held an official position as scholar-in-residence and preacher in the Exilarch's house. In his old age, he was appointed head of the Pumbedita Yeshivah. Meetings between Mar Zutra, Amemar, and Rav Ashi are frequently mentioned in the Talmud, and some of these meetings may well have been formal conferences of the leaders of Babylonian Jewry of that generation.

רַב אַשִׁי Rav Ashi. Born in the year that Rava died, he became one of the greatest Amoraim of Babylonia during the sixth generation. He edited the Babylonian Talmud and headed the yeshivah of Mata Meḥasya for sixty years. His main teacher was Rabbi Kahana of Pum Nahara. Rav Ashi's father-in-law was Rami

NOTES

terumah on his behalf, and we may assume that the owner allowed the agent a reasonable degree of discretion. The only remaining question is this: Was the agent's judgment reasonable? And even Abaye would agree that, for that purpose, the owner's behavior after the event can serve as an indication.

שִׁיטַת מָר זוּטְרָא Mar Zutra's viewpoint. The Rishonim explain the dispute between Amemar and Rav Ashi and Mar Zutra as follows: Since an אָרִיס — "a sharecropper" — has a certain share in the produce, the fruit he set before the Rabbis need not have been stolen. It could have been his own. However, since the produce of the field had not yet been divided between the owner and the sharecropper, Mar Zutra was concerned lest the sharecropper forget to compensate Mari bar Isak for the produce he had given away (*Tosafot, Ramban, Rashba, Rosh*).

אֶלָּא לְעִנְיַן תְּרוּמָה בִּלְבַד, מִשּׁוּם דְּמִצְוָה הוּא Except with regard to terumah alone, because it is a commandment. According to some commentators, Amemar and Rav Ashi were equally aware that the separation of terumah is a religious duty, but felt that honoring Torah Sages is a religious duty of similar importance (*Shittah Mekubbetzet*).

LITERAL TRANSLATION

[1] Come [and] hear: "[If] the dew was still upon them, and he was pleased, [2] this [case] is [included] in [the principle of] 'if [water] is put.' [3] [If] they had dried, even though he was pleased, [22B] they are not [included] in [the principle of] 'if [water] is put.'"

[4] What is the reason? [5] Is it not that we do not say: Since it has become clear that now he is pleased, from the outset he was also pleased?

[1] תָּא שְׁמַע: "עוֹדֵהוּ הַטַּל עֲלֵיהֶן, וְשָׂמַח, [2] הֲרֵי זֶה בְּ'כִי יוּתַּן'. [3] נִגְבּוּ, אַף עַל פִּי שֶׁשָּׂמַח, [22B] אֵינָן בְּ'כִי יוּתַּן'".

[4] טַעְמָא מַאי? [5] לָאו מִשּׁוּם דְּלָא אָמְרִינַן: כֵּיוָן דְּאִיגְלָאִי מִילְּתָא דְּהַשְׁתָּא נִיחָא לֵיהּ, מֵעִיקָּרָא נַמִי נִיחָא לֵיהּ?

RASHI

עודהו הטל עליהן — המעלה פירותיו לגג, וירד עליהן הטל. **ושמח** — בטל שירד עליהן. **הרי זה בכי יותן** — והוכשרו לטומאה מעתה ועד עולם. **נגבו** — עד שלא מלאן. **אף על פי ששמח** — עכשיו בטל שירד עליהן. **אינן בכי יותן** — ולא אמרינן, כיון דהשתא ניחא, מהני האי דעתא למעיקרא, ותיהוי הכשר, וקשיא לרבא!

TRANSLATION AND COMMENTARY

תָּא שְׁמַע [1] (11) **Come and hear** an attempt to refute Rava's view, as being in contradiction to a Tosefta on another subject (*Makhshirin* 3). According to Torah law (Leviticus 11:34-38), fruit or any other food cannot become ritually impure, even if it has come into contact with a ritually impure object, unless previously, between the time it was harvested and the time it touched the ritually impure object, it was moistened by water, dew, or certain other liquids. In addition, the water or other liquids must have been intentionally placed on the harvested produce by the owner, or at least with his approval. The Tosefta now seeks to define what constitutes the owner's "approval": "If the owner placed freshly harvested fruit on his roof and dew fell on it, and **if the dew was still on** the fruit when the owner noticed it **and he was pleased,** then the fruit became susceptible to ritual impurity from that point, even after the dew evaporated, [2] as **this case is included within the principle** derived from the Biblical verse, 'But **if** any **water is put** [כִּי יוּתַּן] upon the seed, and any part of their carcass fall upon it, it shall be unclean to you.'" (Leviticus 11:38.) In other words, the satisfaction expressed by the owner at the fact that his fruit has been moistened by the dew is evidence of his approval, and it is as if he himself had consciously and willingly placed the liquid on the fruit. [3] The Tosefta continues: "But **if** the fruit **had already dried** and the dew had evaporated by the time the owner noticed it, then **even though** the owner **was pleased** that the dew had moistened the fruit, [22B] it has not become susceptible to ritual impurity, as this case **is not included within the principle** derived from the verse **'if water is put.'"** The reason why the fruit has not become susceptible to ritual impurity in this case is because the owner was not present to express his approval of the moistening of the fruit by the dew at the time that this occurred.

טַעְמָא מַאי [4] The Gemara now goes on to explain how this Tosefta contradicts the viewpoint of Rava and supports that of Abaye: **What is the reason** why the owner's approval is ineffective in the second case, where the dew has already evaporated? [5] **Is it not that** Abaye is correct, and **we do not use** the following argument based on Rava's reasoning: **Since it has become clear that now,** having learned about the dew, **the owner is pleased** that it fell on the fruit, his attitude has a retroactive effect, and it is as if **from the outset he was also pleased!** If we were to accept this argument, the fruit should be susceptible to ritual impurity from the moment it was moistened, provided that the owner eventually approved of its having been moistened, regardless of when he heard about it. But since the Tosefta rules that the owner's satisfaction after the dew has evaporated has no retroactive effect, it is clear that this argument is unacceptable, and the same should apply to anticipated *ye'ush*. Accordingly, the giving up of hope for a lost object some time after the loss has occurred should likewise have no effect retroactively. This would contradict Rava's ruling that anticipated *ye'ush* is effective.

bar Abba, and his son, Mar bar Rav Ashi, inherited his position. Another of his sons, Rav Sama, was also a Sage.

BACKGROUND

עוֹדֵהוּ הַטַּל עֲלֵיהֶן If the dew was still upon them. In many cases fresh fruit was spread out on a roof or some other exposed surface to prevent it from becoming moldy. Because the fruit or vegetables would dry in the sun, the owner was often pleased when dew fell on them, thus adding to their freshness. Moreover, since the produce lost some of its weight when it was dried, and had its original weight restored when it was moistened, this was important for those who wished to sell the fruit.

NOTES

By contrast, *Ritva,* in explaining Mar Zutra's point of view, dismisses this comparison. He quotes *Rashi* who expains in tractate *Kiddushin* (52b) that the significance of the fact that terumah is a mitzvah lies in it being obligatory in any case, and because it makes no difference financially to the owner whether he or someone else performs it. Hence there is little reason for the owner to be put out by the other person separating terumah for him. If he expresses approval, it may be taken as being sincere. On the other hand, there is no obligation to spend money to honor the Sages.

הֶכְשֵׁר לְטוּמְאָה Rendering foodstuffs susceptible to ritual impurity. Food or produce cannot contract ritual impurity until (1) it has been severed from its place of growth; and (2) it has come into contact with a liquid, either directly

HALAKHAH

כִּי יוּתַּן If water is put. "If water, dew, milk, honey, wine, olive oil, or blood come into contact with any kind of food with the owner's approval, the food becomes susceptible to ritual impurity, and remains so even after the water, or other liquid, has dried." (*Rambam, Sefer Tohorah, Hilkhot Tum'at Okhalin* 1:1-2.)

TERMINOLOGY

אִי הָכִי If so. An expression introducing an objection to a previous explanation or response: "If what was just said is in fact so, then the following objection can be raised."

רָמֵי Raised a contradiction (lit., "cast," "threw"). This expression is used to introduce a contradiction between two equally authoritative sources. Such a question does not challenge either statement, but indicates that a contradiction exists which must be resolved, either by showing that the two sources deal with different subjects or by finding a solution suitable to both sources. In the context here the question focuses on the apparent contradiction between the word יתן as it is written in the text of the Torah and as it is traditionally pronounced.

TRANSLATION AND COMMENTARY

שָׁאנֵי הָתָם [1]The Gemara answers: **It is different there** in the case of ritual impurity. The laws governing susceptibility to ritual impurity differ from those regarding anticipated *ye'ush*. **For it is written** in the Torah (Leviticus 11:38) concerning ritual impurity: **"If he puts** water upon the seed." This implies that the fruit does not become susceptible to ritual impurity **unless he puts** the water on the fruit **himself.** The Gemara is here using a hermeneutical rule called קְרִי—כְּתִיב, in which laws are derived from a comparison between the way a word is written in the Torah and the way it is traditionally pronounced. In the present instance, the text is read "If water is put on seed." But the Hebrew word for "is put" (יוּתַּן) is spelled in the text without the letter *vav*, as if it were an active form: יִתֵּן — "he puts." As part of the קְרִי—כְּתִיב interpretation, the Gemara initially reads and interprets the verse in accordance with the spelling (כְּתִיב), taking it to mean that the food is rendered susceptible to ritual impurity only if the owner himself actually poured the water on it.

אִי הָכִי [2]Continuing the קְרִי—כְּתִיב interpretation, the Gemara now objects: **If so,** if we are to follow the spelling and the owner of the food himself must put the liquid on the food to render it susceptible to ritual impurity, **this should be so in the first clause** of the Tosefta **as well,** where the owner did not put the dew on the fruit but merely expressed his satisfaction that it had fallen there. In the first clause, too, the fruit should not have been rendered susceptible to ritual impurity.

הָתָם כִּדְרַב פַּפָּא [3]The Gemara answers: **There** the matter can be explained **in accordance with the interpretation of Rav Pappa,** who originally provided the קְרִי—כְּתִיב interpretation of this verse. [4]**For Rav Pappa raised a contradiction** between the spelling and vocalization of the word יתן in the verse (Leviticus 11:38) dealing with the manner in which liquids render food susceptible to ritual impurity. As we have seen, the word יתן **is written** in the text of the Torah as if its meaning were **"if he puts"** (כִּי יִתֵּן), implying that the owner of the fruit must himself place liquid on the fruit in order to render it susceptible to ritual impurity. [5]**But we read** the word differently, vocalizing it as יוּתַּן, as if its meaning were **"if it is put"** (כִּי יוּתַּן), implying that the liquid does not need to be placed on the fruit by its owner, but may be placed there by a third party or may even fall on the fruit naturally, without any human intervention. [6]Now, **how is this** contradiction between the spelling of the text and its traditional vocalization **to be resolved?** Rav Pappa suggests that the two elements should be combined: We do indeed interpret the text in accordance with its traditional vocalization, and there is no requirement that the owner of the fruit must himself place the liquid upon it. Nevertheless, we interpret the vocalized word as far as possible in accordance with its spelling. [7]Thus **we require** that the expression **"if it is put" must be** as **similar** in meaning as possible **to "if he puts." Just as** the procedure described by the consonantal text, [8]"if **he puts,**" namely, that the owner must himself place the liquid on the fruit, can only **be done with** the owner's **knowledge** and approval, [9]**so too** the procedure described by the vocalized text, **"if it is put," must also be** interpreted as being done **with the** owner's **knowledge and approval.** Hence, if a liquid, such as dew, fell on fruit by accident, the fruit can become susceptible to ritual impurity only if the owner was present and expressed approval while the fruit was still wet. Thus, the laws governing the susceptibility of liquids to ritual impurity are special ones derived directly from the text of the Torah, and no parallels may be drawn between such laws and those of anticipated *ye'ush*.

[1]שָׁאנֵי הָתָם, דִּכְתִיב: "כִּי יִתֵּן" — עַד שֶׁיִּתֵּן.
[2]אִי הָכִי, רֵישָׁא נָמֵי.
[3]הָתָם כִּדְרַב פַּפָּא. [4]דְּרַב פַּפָּא רָמֵי: כְּתִיב: "כִּי יִתֵּן" [5]וְקָרֵינַן: "כִּי יוּתַּן". [6]הָא כֵּיצַד? [7]בָּעֵינַן "כִּי יוּתַּן" דּוּמְיָא דְּ"כִי יִתֵּן": [8]מָה "יִתֵּן" לְדַעַת, [9]אַף "כִּי יוּתַּן" נָמֵי לְדַעַת.

LITERAL TRANSLATION

[1]It is different there, for it is written: "If he puts" — until he [himself] puts.

[2]If so, [this should be so in] the first clause as well.

[3]There [it is] in accordance with [the interpretation] of Rav Pappa. [4]For Rav Pappa raised a contradiction (lit., "threw"): It is written: "If he puts" (כִּי יִתֵּן), [5]but we read: "If it is put" (כִּי יוּתַּן). [6]How is this [to be resolved]? [7]We require "if it is put" [to be] similar to "if he puts": [8]Just as "he puts" [must be] with [his] knowledge, [9]so too "if it is put" [must] also [be] with [his] knowledge.

RASHI

כתיב כי יתן — ולא כתיב "כי יותן". **לדעת** — שידע בנתינה והוכשר בעיניו, ועודהו הטל עליהן עדיין הן בנתינתו.

NOTES

through the action of its owner, or without his direct intervention but nevertheless with his approval. (See Leviticus 11:34-38.) There are seven liquids that make foodstuffs liable to contract ritual impurity: water, wine, honey, olive oil, milk, dew, and blood.

TRANSLATION AND COMMENTARY

תָּא שְׁמַע [1](12) **Come and hear** another objection to Rava's viewpoint, based on a Baraita: **For Rabbi Yoḥanan said in the name of Rabbi Shimon ben Yehotzadak:** [2]**"From where** in the Torah **do we know that a lost object** of any kind, even one containing an identifying mark, **that was swept away by a river is** always **permitted to** be kept by **the finder,** regardless of the owner's attitude? [3]**As it is written** (Deuteronomy 22:3) regarding the obligation to return a lost object to its owner: **'And so shall you do with his ass, and so shall you do with his garment, and so shall you do with every lost thing of your brother's, which is lost from him and which you have found.'** [4]From the presence of the seemingly superfluous word מִמֶּנּוּ — 'from him' — the Rabbis drew the following conclusion: **Only that which is lost 'from him'** — i.e., as far as its owner alone is concerned — **but is available to everyone** else **must be returned.** [5]By inference, **this excludes** an item that was swept away by a river, since **this object** is not only **lost to** its owner, **but is** also **not available to anyone** else, since the river is likely to carry it away altogether, and it is only by extraordinary luck that it will be found at all. Accordingly, such an object is deemed ownerless by decree of the Torah, and the finder may keep it." [6]**And** from this ruling, says the Gemara, we may make a further inference: The circumstances in which lost objects **are forbidden to** be kept by **the finder must be** Halakhically **similar to** the circumstances

[1]תָּא שְׁמַע: דְּאָמַר רַבִּי יוֹחָנָן מִשּׁוּם רַבִּי שִׁמְעוֹן בֶּן יְהוֹצָדָק: [2]מִנַּיִן לַאֲבֵידָה שֶׁשְּׁטָפָהּ נָהָר שֶׁהִיא מוּתֶּרֶת? [3]דִּכְתִיב: "וְכֵן תַּעֲשֶׂה לַחֲמוֹרוֹ, וְכֵן תַּעֲשֶׂה לְשִׂמְלָתוֹ, וְכֵן תַּעֲשֶׂה לְכָל אֲבֵידַת אָחִיךָ, אֲשֶׁר תֹּאבַד מִמֶּנּוּ וּמְצָאתָהּ". [4]מִי שֶׁאֲבוּדָה הֵימֶנּוּ וּמְצוּיָה אֵצֶל כָּל אָדָם. [5]יָצְאתָה זוֹ, שֶׁאֲבוּדָה מִמֶּנּוּ וְאֵינָהּ מְצוּיָה אֵצֶל כָּל אָדָם. [6]וְאִיסּוּרָא דּוּמְיָא

LITERAL TRANSLATION

[1]Come [and] hear: For Rabbi Yoḥanan said in the name of Rabbi Shimon ben Yehotzadak: [2]From where [do we know] that a lost object that was swept away by a river is permitted [to the finder]? [3]As it is written: "And so shall you do with his ass, and so shall you do with his garment, and so shall you do with every lost thing of your brother's, which is lost from him and which you have found." [4][Only] that which is lost from him but is available to every man [must be returned]. [5]This is excluded, which is lost from him and is not available to every man. [6]And what is forbidden [to the finder] is similar to what

RASHI

ממנו — קרא יתירא הוא לאשמועינן שאינו אבוד אלא הימנו. **ואיסורא דומיא דהיתירא** — כיון דמחד קרא ילפינן, מלויה אלא לכל אדם שיחזור, ושאינה מלויה יזכה בה, איתקושי אתקוש להדדי, זו לאיסורא וזו להיתירא.

SAGES

רַבִּי שִׁמְעוֹן בֶּן יְהוֹצָדָק **Rabbi Shimon ben Yehotzadak.** A first generation Palestinian Amora, Rabbi Shimon ben Yehotzadak was a teacher of Rabbi Yoḥanan. Most of his teachings — some of which were given the status of Baraitot — are transmitted by Rabbi Yoḥanan. He was a priest and died in Lod (Lydda).

NOTES

אֲבֵידָה שֶׁשְּׁטָפָהּ נָהָר **A lost object that was swept away by a river.** This Halakhic exegesis by Rabbi Shimon ben Yehotzadak is in fact a brief definition of the Halakhic category of a "lost object." According to this definition, the criterion that makes an object "lost" in the Halakhic sense (meaning that its finder has a Halakhic obligation to attempt to restore it to its owner) is subjective: An object has been mislaid because its owner has forgotten it or because of some small error, and the owner cannot locate it. In such cases, the presence or absence of identifying marks is an important consideration, as is the question whether the owner has given up hope of recovering it. However, when an object has been removed from its owner's possession through an accident of nature and is not under any person's control, it is no longer someone's lost object. The event itself has caused the owner to forfeit any right to it, and it becomes ownerless, as if it had never been anyone's property at all. Such an event, regarded as *force majeure,* nullifies ownership and property rights, and the object reverts, as it were, to raw nature, losing its former characteristics.

וְאִיסּוּרָא דּוּמְיָא דְּהֶיתֵּירָא **And what is forbidden to the finder is like what is permitted to the finder.** The Rishonim had considerable difficulty with this sentence. Why is it obvious that the same rules that apply to objects swept away by floods should apply to lost objects as well? *Rashi* explains that the Gemara is deriving the analogy between "forbidden" and "permitted" from a hermeneutical rule called *hekesh* (הֶקֵּשׁ) — "juxtaposition." When the Torah juxtaposes two laws in a way that suggests that they are analogous, we can infer that the regulations governing the laws are identical. Thus, since the Torah teaches the law about objects swept away by floods in juxtaposition to the law about returning ordinary lost objects, we can infer that just as all objects swept away by floods are *permitted* to the finder, irrespective of whether they possess identifying marks, so too are all ordinary lost objects *forbidden* to the finder, irrespective of whether they possess identifying marks.

Most of the Rishonim, however, did not agree that the verse in the Torah is to be understood as presenting a *hekesh.* Therefore, *Ba'al HaMa'or* suggests that the clause linking the forbidden and the permitted is not the Gemara's inference from the verse cited by Rabbi Yoḥanan, but is the

HALAKHAH

שֶׁאֲבוּדָה מִכָּל אָדָם **An object that is lost to everyone.** "If someone saves an object from a lion or a bear, or retrieves an object swept away by the tide or by an overflowing river, he may keep it, even if the owner of the object is present at the time and protests." *Rema* notes that it is nevertheless praiseworthy for the finder to return the object to its original owner. (*Shulḥan Arukh, Ḥoshen Mishpat* 259:7.)

LITERAL TRANSLATION

is permitted [to the finder]: [1]Just as what is permitted is permitted whether it has an identifying mark on it, or whether it does not have an identifying mark on it, [2]so too what is forbidden is forbidden whether it has an identifying mark on it, or whether it does not have an identifying mark on it.

[3]The refutation of Rava is a [conclusive] refutation. [4]And the Halakhah is in accordance with Abaye in יע״ל קג״ם.

דְּהֶיתֵּירָא: [1]מַה הֶיתֵּירָא בֵּין דְּאִית בָּהּ סִימָן, וּבֵין דְּלֵית בָּהּ סִימָן שָׁרָא, [2]אַף אִיסּוּרָא בֵּין דְּאִית בָּהּ סִימָן, וּבֵין דְּלֵית בָּהּ סִימָן אֲסוּרָה.

[3]תְּיוּבְתָּא דְּרָבָא תְּיוּבְתָּא.

[4]וְהִלְכְתָא כְּוָותֵיהּ דְּאַבַּיֵי בְּיע״ל קג״ם.

RASHI

מה היתירא – שאינה מצויה, לא חילק בין שיש בה סימן לשאין בה סימן. **אף איסורא** – דמצויה אצל כל אדם, לא חילק בין אין סימן דכי ידע מיאש ליש סימן דלכי ידע לא מיאש, וכי היכי דיש סימן אסירה, כי אין סימן נמי אסירה היכא דאיכא למימר לא ידע דנפלה קודם שבאת ליד זה. **יע״ל קג״ם** – סימני הלכות הן: ׳יאוש שלא מדעת׳ דהכא, ׳עד זומם למפרע הוא נפסל׳ בסנהדרין (כז,א), ׳לחי העומד מאליו׳ בעירובין (טו,א), ׳קדושין שלא נמסרו לביאה׳ בקדושין (נא,א), ׳גלוי דעתא בגיטא׳ בגיטין (לד,א), ׳מומר אוכל נבילות להכעיס פסול לענין עדות׳ בסנהדרין (כז,א).

TRANSLATION AND COMMENTARY

in which lost objects are **permitted to** be kept by **the finder** (see note). [1]**Just as what** the Torah **permitted** to everyone — i.e., an object carried away in a flood — **is permitted** to be kept by the finder **whether it has an identifying mark on it or not,** [2]**so too what** the Torah **forbade** to be kept by the finder **is forbidden** by the Torah **whether it has an identifying mark on it or not,** as the Torah does not render objects ownerless against the owner's will, except in the case of objects carried away in a flood. Thus the finder must return any object lost in the ordinary way, unless the owner consciously gives up hope of recovering it and thus himself renders it ownerless. Hence, according to this Baraita, even an unidentifiable object that will be given up as lost by its owner as soon as he learns of its loss must be returned by the finder, if the owner was unaware of his loss at the time the finder came into possession of the object. This, argues the Gemara, constitutes a refutation of Rava's viewpoint.

תְּיוּבְתָּא דְּרָבָא תְּיוּבְתָּא [3]The Gemara concludes that **the refutation of Rava's view is,** indeed, **a conclusive refutation.** [4]**And** even though the Halakhah is usually in accordance with the viewpoint of Rava in his differences of opinion with Abaye, nevertheless **the Halakhah is in accordance with Abaye** here in the case of *ye'ush* and **in** those six cases represented by the mnemonic יע״ל קג״ם. The six cases referred to are: (1) יֵאוּשׁ שֶׁלֹּא מִדַּעַת (*Bava Metzia* 21a-22b), (2) עֵד זוֹמֵם (*Sanhedrin* 27a), (3) לֶחִי הָעוֹמֵד מֵאֵלָיו (*Eruvin* 15a), (4) קִידּוּשִׁין שֶׁאֵינָן מְסוּרִין לְבִיאָה (*Kiddushin* 51a), (5) גִּילּוּי דַּעַת בְּגֵט (*Gittin* 34a), (6) מוּמָר אוֹכֵל נְבֵלוֹת לְהַכְעִיס (*Sanhedrin* 27a).

TERMINOLOGY

תְּיוּבְתָּא דְּרָבָא תְּיוּבְתָּא The refutation of Rava is a conclusive refutation. A תְּיוּבְתָּא — "refutation" — establishes the error of an Amoraic statement, usually on the basis of a Tannaitic source which contradicts the Amora's remarks. The תְּיוּבְתָּא is generally followed by an explanation rejecting it and showing that the Amora's teaching does not actually contradict the Mishnah or the Baraita in question. However, the explanation occasionally fails to resolve the difficulty, and then the argument is summed up with the remark: תְּיוּבְתָּא דְּר׳ פְּלוֹנִי תְּיוּבְתָּא — "the refutation of the viewpoint of Rabbi X is a conclusive refutation." This means that the refutation of the Sage's words (in the present case, those of Rava) is a conclusive one, and this particular teaching of his is therefore rejected from the Halakhah. Very rarely, a Sage's approach is refuted in this fashion but is nevertheless given Halakhic validity, and in such cases astonishment is expressed: תְּיוּבְתָּא וְהִלְכְתָא? — "A refutation and it is the Halakhah?"

NOTES

conclusion of Rabbi Yoḥanan's statement. Thus, it was Rabbi Yoḥanan himself who explicitly supported Abaye and argued that "what is prohibited is like...," and the refutation of Rava derives from an early authority, Rabbi Yoḥanan, who rejected his view.

Most of the Rishonim, however, reject *Ba'al HaMa'or's* interpretation (see *Ra'avad* and *Ramban*). They feel that the passage should be amended to remove the offending sentence. Hence it should read: "This is excluded, which is lost to him and is not available to everyone. The refutation of Rava's view...." Accordingly, the Gemara should be explained as follows: Ordinarily, a person who knows that his property has been swept away in a flood gives up hope of recovering it. Therefore, if Rava were correct, there would be no need for the Torah to permit such items, since they are in any case ownerless. But according to Abaye, the Torah had to specifically permit the finder to keep property that was swept away in a flood without the owner being aware of it, since otherwise it would be a case of anticipated *ye'ush*. Hence, the extra word מִמֶּנּוּ in the verse is there to teach us that even though anticipated *ye'ush* is normally ineffective, in the case of a flood it is effective (see *Ramban*, *Rashba*, *Rosh*, and others).

תְּיוּבְתָּא דְּרָבָא תְּיוּבְתָּא The refutation of Rava is a conclusive refutation. The refutation of Rava's approach to anticipated *ye'ush* was accomplished through a proof based on a Tannaitic source. This proof did not, however, provide the essential, inherent foundation for generalizations regarding the retroactive validity of actions or decisions. The question of the effectiveness of בְּרֵירָה — "retroactive designation" — has been left open, because the effort to produce a more general proof (from the laws governing terumah or from those that deal with making seeds susceptible to ritual impurity) was unsuccessful. Even the convincing proof produced regarding lost objects themselves is merely a "decree of Scripture" that the finder of a lost object is not permitted to keep it unless it is clear that the owner has explicitly expressed forfeiture of his ownership by giving up hope of recovering it.

יע״ל קג״ם Our commentary follows *Rashi* in interpreting this mnemonic. But *Rabbenu Tam* explains that the letter ל refers not to לֶחִי הָעוֹמֵד מֵאֵלָיו but to יְמֵי לֵידָה שֶׁאֵינָהּ רוֹאָה בָּהֶן (*Niddah* 37a; see *Tosafot*), and the Rabbis of Narbonne suggest that it refers to לֹא אֶפְשָׁר וּמִתְכַּוֵּן (*Pesaḥim* 25b).

TRANSLATION AND COMMENTARY

אָמַר לֵיהּ רַב אַחָא [1]**Rav Aḥa, the son of Rava, said to Rav Ashi: "Now that Rava has been refuted,** and it has shown that anticipated *ye'ush* is not effective, [2]**how can we** be permitted to **eat those dates that the wind blows** from the palm trees, since the owner of the fruit may not yet have become aware of his loss?"

אָמַר לֵיהּ [3]Rav Ashi **said to him** in reply: "**Since** the owner of the fruit is aware that **there are vermin and creeping animals that eat** windfall dates, [4]**he has surely given up hope of** recovering **them from the outset,** even before they fell from the tree, and hence whoever finds them is permitted to keep them.

[1]אָמַר לֵיהּ רַב אַחָא בְּרֵיהּ דְּרָבָא לְרַב אַשִׁי: "וְכִי מֵאַחַר דְּאִיתּוֹתַב רָבָא, [2]הָנֵי תַּמְרֵי דְּזִיקָא הֵיכִי אָכְלִינַן לְהוּ?" [3]אָמַר לֵיהּ: "כֵּיוָן דְּאִיכָּא שְׁקָצִים וּרְמָשִׂים דְּקָא אָכְלֵי לְהוּ, [4]מֵעִיקָּרָא יָאוּשֵׁי מְיָאֵשׁ מִנַּיְיהוּ".

LITERAL TRANSLATION

[1]Rav Aḥa, the son of Rava, said to Rav Ashi: "But now that Rava has been refuted, [2]how can we eat those dates that the wind [blows away]?"

[3]He said to him: "Since there are vermin and creeping animals that eat them, [4]from the outset he surely gives up hope of them."

RASHI

הני תמרי דזיקא — שהרוח משיר. **היכי אכלינן להו** — הא לא מיאש, והא דנקט למיבעי בעית מאחר דאיתותב רבא קשיא לי, דהלא איתותב רבא איכא למיבעי, דהא מודה רבא בכל דבר שמזומו מוכיח עליו, חוץ מן התאנה מפני שנמאסת עם נפילתה, ונראה בעיני דלא נקט לה אלא להרבות בחומר איסור, כלומר, מאחר דאיתותב אפילו בדבר שאין בו סימן, כל שכן שאלו אסורין שיש בהן סימן. **מעיקרא** — מקודם נפילתו. **יאושי מיאש** — דיודע הוא שהרוח משיר מהן והשקצים מזומנים לאוכלן.

SAGES

רַב אַחָא בְּרֵיהּ דְּרָבָא Rav Aḥa the son of Rava. A Baylonian Amora of the sixth generation (not related to the famous Amora, Rava), Rav Aḥa, the son of Rava, was a colleague of Rav Ashi and of Ravina. Like them, he was a disciple of Rav Kahana. Rav Aḥa, the son of Rava, is cited frequently in the Talmud in discussion with Rav Ashi and Ravina. Wherever the Talmud states that "Rav Aḥa" disagrees with Ravina, the commentators assume that it is Rav Aḥa the son of Rava.

BACKGROUND

שְׁקָצִים וּרְמָשִׂים Vermin and creeping animals. These expressions do not have precise zoological meaning but are general terms for small animals (usually non-kosher ones) which crawl on the ground. They include reptiles, insects, and worms of all kinds.

NOTES

מאחר דְּאִיתּוֹתַב רָבָא Now that Rava has been refuted. *Rashi* asks: From the Gemara's question it would appear that the well-established custom of allowing passersby to eat fallen dates is problematic according to Abaye, but not according to Rava. But the Gemara earlier (above, 21b) considered a similar problem involving figs and olives, and resolved it according to the views of both Rava and Abaye. How does this case differ from that one? *Tosafot* adds that it is clear from the Gemara's answer here that dates frequently fall, as do figs. Otherwise, there could be no resolution of the problem based on "giving up hope from the outset." Hence, the owner must be fully aware from the outset of everything that will eventually happen to the dates, and there should be no difference at all between Abaye and Rava on this matter.

Rashi suggests that Rav Aḥa's objection may indeed be equally valid according to Rava, but he prefers to strengthen it by pointing out that the Halakhah follows the strict opinion of Abaye.

Tosafot suggests that the dates were not merely blown off the tree by the wind but were blown far away, and explains the Gemara as follows: Dates, like olives, are readily identifiable, and are not seriously damaged by their fall from the tree. Hence, Rav Aḥa felt that the owner of the palm tree would not abandon them in advance. Therefore, the basis for the custom of allowing passersby to eat fallen dates must be the fact that they were blown far away by an unusually strong wind, to the point where the owner would not bother trying to recover them. But the owner may not know that his dates have been blown far away. Hence, the basis for the custom must be anticipated *ye'ush*, which poses a problem for Abaye. In response, the Gemara explains that even though dates are not damaged by their fall from the tree, they are subject to attack by vermin. Hence, their status is effectively the same as that of figs, and the owner abandons them in advance.

Ritva adds that this may be the reason why Rav Aḥa asked his question about dates: Palm trees are very tall, and a strong wind can easily blow the fruit far away.

הָנֵי תַּמְרֵי דְּזִיקָא Those dates that the wind blows away. The question asked by Rav Aḥa, the son of Rava, is actually an attempt to point out a contradiction between the Halakhic conclusion regarding anticipated *ye'ush* and accepted, common practice — that people who observe the Halakhah do eat dates that the wind has blown down from trees. This practice seems to confirm Rava's approach and to show that the Halakhah does not follow Abaye, despite the explicit ruling on this matter.

Rav Ashi explains that the custom does not contradict the Halakhah, and that one must indeed determine the Halakhah according to Abbaye.

כֵּיוָן דְּאִיכָּא שְׁקָצִים וּרְמָשִׂים Since there are vermin and creeping animals. Several commentators understand the Gemara's answer to apply only to dates and not to other fruits, because dates are unusually sweet and tend to attract animals. This interpretation is especially apt according to those Rishonim who read "animals" instead of "vermin and creeping animals" in our Gemara. (*Shulḥan Arukh, Ḥoshen Mishpat* 260:6.)

שְׁקָצִים וּרְמָשִׂים Vermin and creeping animals. Our commentary follows *Rashi* and other Rishonim who explain that animals will probably eat most of the dates after they fall, and the owner, knowing this, gives up hope of recovering them. This interpretation is consistent with the view of those Rishonim who read animals" instead of "vermin and creeping animals" in our Gemara. *Rashba, Ritva,*

HALAKHAH

תַּמְרֵי דְּזִיקָא Dates that the wind blows away. "A person who finds dates that the wind has blown from a tree may keep them, since the owner presumably gave up hope of recovering them. However, if the dates belonged to orphans, or if the tree was surrounded by a fence to prevent the dates from being lost, they are forbidden to the finder." (*Shulḥan Arukh, Ḥoshen Mishpat,* 260:6.)

[1] ״יַתְמֵי, דְּלָאו בְּנֵי מְחִילָה נִינְהוּ, [2] מַאי?״
[3] אֲמַר לֵיהּ: ״בָּאגָא בְּאַרְעָא דְּיַתְמֵי לָא מַחְזְקִינַן״.
[4] ״מוּחְזַק וְעוֹמֵד, מַאי? [5] כְּרַכְתָּא, מַאי?״
[6] אֲמַר לֵיהּ: ״אֲסִירָן״.

LITERAL TRANSLATION

[1] "[If they belong to] orphans, who cannot waive [their rights] (lit., 'are not sons of waiving'), [2] what [is the law]?"

[3] He said to him: "We do not presume [that] a valley is the land of orphans."

[4] "[If the field] is known to be (lit., 'presumed and standing') [orphans' property], what [is the law]? [5] [If the palm trees were surrounded by] walls, what [is the law]?"

[6] He said to him: "They are forbidden."

RASHI

יתמי – קטנים, שאין הפקירן הפקר. **באגא בארעא דיתמי לא מחזקינן** – אין עלינו להחזיק כל הבקעה בחזקת הקרקע של יתומין ולאסור כל התמרים משום ספק קרקע של יתומים, אלא הולכין אחר הרוב. **מוחזק ועומד מאי** – קרקע עצמה של יתומין מאי? **כרכתא מאי** – דקלים הכרוכין ומוקפין בגדר של אבנים סביב, שאין שקלים ורמשים נכנסין שם.

TRANSLATION AND COMMENTARY

יַתְמֵי [1] In response to this answer by Rav Ashi, Rav Aḥa now asks a further question: "But **if** the date palms **belong to orphans, who are** minors and are thus **not** legally **competent to waive their rights** to their property, [2] **what is the law** in such a case?" Why is the finder permitted to eat fruit that has fallen from trees belonging to orphans? Even if the orphans have given up hope of recovering the fruit, such *ye'ush* does not render the fruit Halakhically ownerless.

אֲמַר לֵיהּ [3] Rav Ashi **said to** Rav Aḥa in reply: **"We do not presume that a whole valley is the property of orphans."** It is unreasonable to forbid finders from benefiting from fallen fruit throughout an entire agricultural area, on the grounds that some of the trees may belong to orphans who are minors. Even if orphans do own some of the trees in the neighborhood, this is outweighed by the fact that most of the trees belong to adults.

מוּחְזַק וְעוֹמֵד [4] Rav Aḥa now asks two further questions: "But **if the field** where the dates are located **is known to be orphans' property, what is the law?** [5] Similarly, even if the field were not orphans' property, **if the palm trees were surrounded by a wall** to prevent animals from reaching and eating the dates, **what would the law be** if a few dates fell outside the wall, without the owner being aware of the fact?"

אֲמַר לֵיהּ אֲסִירָן [6] Rav Ashi **said to** Rav Aḥa: "The dates **would be forbidden** in such cases."

NOTES

and *Meiri* suggest an alternative explanation, in accordance with our reading: Fruit that is blown away by the wind is probably worthless anyway, seeing that it generally falls because insects damaged it while it was still on the tree. Therefore, the owner consciously abandons all fruit blown away by the wind.

יַתְמֵי דְּלָאו בְּנֵי מְחִילָה נִינְהוּ Orphans who cannot waive their rights. Earlier, we reached the conclusion that *ye'ush* cannot be defined objectively as a specific situation in which a reasonable man is liable to give up hope of recovering an object he has lost. Rather, in accordance with Abaye's viewpoint, *ye'ush* is an inner decision as the result of which a person forfeits (only against his will and under the pressure of circumstances) property that belongs to him. Only through that act of *ye'ush* does the property become ownerless. This forfeiture of ownership (מְחִילָה is the term the Talmud uses here) is thus a conscious act, dependent on the owner's awareness. Therefore, if the owners are not mentally competent (the most common case would be orphans who are minors, who are not considered legally competent to transfer ownership or to waive it), they have no legal possibility of giving up ownership, and even if they say that they have given up hope, their utterance has no legal force.

בָּאגָא בְּאַרְעָא דְּיַתְמֵי לָא מַחְזְקִינַן We do not presume that a valley is the land of orphans. The problem raised by Rav Aḥa, the son of Rava, was as follows: Since, according to Abaye's viewpoint, the expression of *ye'ush* must be voluntary and conscious, should we not refrain from eating all dates blown down by the wind? It could well be that those dates belonged to someone who did not give up in advance all hope of recovering them.

Rav Ashi responds that we have no proof that these dates belong to orphans, and we may presume that palms ordinarily belong to legally competent people. We cannot be stringent simply because of an unfounded doubt. In other words, not only do most fields not belong to orphans, but also, so long as it is not clear to us that there were orphans in that particular valley, we need not take their hypothetical existence into account.

כְּרַכְתָּא Surrounded by walls. Our commentary follows *Rashi*. Other commentators suggest that the tree was surrounded by mats, which the owner had placed to catch the falling dates (*Shittah Mekubbetzet*). *Rabbenu Ḥananel* had a reading in our Gemara of "animals," instead of "vermin and creeping animals." Accordingly, he explains that כְּרַכְתָּא means "a city," where animals are not likely to be found. *Ritva* explains that the "vermin" mentioned by the Gemara damaged the dates before they fell, thus rendering them unfit for consumption (see previous note). Accordingly, he explains that כְּרַכְתָּא means "branches"; where entire branches fell, there is no reason to assume that the dates had themselves been affected, and the owner would not abandon them in advance.

LITERAL TRANSLATION

[1] "Small sheaves in the public domain... these are his." [2] Rabbah said: And even in [the case of] an object that has an identifying mark on it. [3] Thus Rabbah is of the opinion [that] an identifying mark that is liable to be trampled on is not a [valid] identifying mark. [4] Rava said: [The Sages] did not teach [this] except in [the case of] an object that does not have an identifying mark on it. [5] But in [the case of] an object that does have an identifying mark on it, he must announce [it]. [6] Thus Rava is of the opinion [that] an identifying mark that is liable to be trampled on is a [valid] identifying mark.

[1] ״כְּרִיכוֹת בִּרְשׁוּת הָרַבִּים... הֲרֵי אֵלּוּ שֶׁלּוֹ״. [2] אָמַר רַבָּה: וַאֲפִילּוּ בְּדָבָר שֶׁיֵּשׁ בּוֹ סִימָן. [3] אַלְמָא קָסָבַר רַבָּה: סִימָן הֶעָשׂוּי לִידָּרֵס לָא הָוֵי סִימָן. [4] רָבָא אָמַר: לֹא שָׁנוּ אֶלָּא בְּדָבָר שֶׁאֵין בּוֹ סִימָן. [5] אֲבָל בְּדָבָר שֶׁיֵּשׁ בּוֹ סִימָן, חַיָּיב לְהַכְרִיז. [6] אַלְמָא קָסָבַר רָבָא: סִימָן הֶעָשׂוּי לִידָּרֵס הָוֵי סִימָן.

TRANSLATION AND COMMENTARY

כְּרִיכוֹת בִּרְשׁוּת הָרַבִּים [1] After completing its discussion on the subject of anticipated *ye'ush,* the Gemara now returns to its analysis of the text of the Mishnah: **We have learned** in the Mishnah that **"small sheaves in the public domain belong to the finder."** [2] In connection with this section of the Mishnah, **Rabbah said: And** this law applies to any **object** lying in the street, **even if it has an identifying mark on it.** Even if the small sheaves contain an identifying mark, the finder is entitled to keep them because they are lying in the street and their owner will have given up hope of recovering them as soon as he learned of their loss. [3] The Gemara now makes the following inference from Rabbah's statement: **Thus** we may infer from the significance that Rabbah attaches to the fact that an object is lying in the street that **Rabbah is of the opinion that an identifying mark** on an object **that is liable to be trampled on is not** considered **a valid identifying mark,** since the mark will probably be defaced. The owner, realizing this, knows that he cannot rely on the identifying mark. The finder may therefore assume that the owner has given up hope of recovering the lost sheaves, as if they contained no identifying mark at all, and even if the mark was not in fact defaced the finder is permitted to keep the sheaves.

רָבָא אָמַר [4] By contrast **Rava said: The Sages did not teach** the law in our Mishnah, that someone who finds such objects as small sheaves in the street may keep them, **except in the case of an object that does not have an identifying mark on it,** which the owner could never have identified in any event. [5] **But in the case of an object that does have an identifying mark on it,** the finder **must announce** that he has found **it,** although he found it in the street. [6] The Gemara now makes the following inference from Rava's statement: **Thus,** from the fact that Rava attaches no significance to an unidentifiable object's lying in the street and applies the regular law to it, we may infer that **Rava is of the opinion that an identifying mark** on an object **that is liable to be trampled on is** still considered **a valid identifying mark.** According to Rava, the owners of small sheaves place reliance on such identifying marks as the sheaves contain, and take into account the natural tendency of passersby to pick up objects in the street and not trample on them indiscriminately. Even if they do not go to the trouble of picking up such objects, they will walk round them and not step on them. Hence the finder may not assume that the owner gave up hope of recovering the lost sheaves, and must announce his discovery.

RASHI

העשוי לידרס — שהמקום שהוא שם רגיל בדריסת בני אדם, והחפץ נמוך ונוח לידרס. **לא הוי סימן** — שאין בעליו סומך לתת בו סימן, מימר אמר: נשחת הסימן בדריסת הרגלים.

BACKGROUND

רְשׁוּת הַיָּחִיד וּרְשׁוּת הָרַבִּים A private domain and the public domain. The significance and definition of these terms depend on their context. In laws governing the Sabbath, a private domain is defined as a place surrounded by a fence; in laws of ritual impurity a private domain is a place where there is, at a given moment, only one person; in civil and commercial law, a private domain may be a certain person's private property, but sometimes it is simply a place that is not public.

TERMINOLOGY

אַלְמָא Thus, therefore. A sentence beginning with אַלְמָא is not simply a summary of earlier remarks. It draws a conclusion that derives logically from what has been said: "Since one thing has been established, we can reach a further conclusion...." Though this conclusion has not been explicitly stated, it is necessarily implied in the preceding remarks.

NOTES

כְּרִיכוֹת בִּרְשׁוּת הָרַבִּים Small sheaves in the public domain. This passage begins as a difference of opinion between the Amoraim Rabbah and Rava regarding the interpretation of our Mishnah. But it develops into the clarification of three other general problems, which had remained unresolved until their generation. The questions were: (1) Is an identifying mark that is liable to be trampled upon and defaced considered valid? (2) Is the place where an object is found a valid identifying mark? (3) Is it permissible to pass by food without picking it up? These three problems are not intrinsically connected with each other, but in the course of the discussion the Sages attempt to show that the difference of opinion over the interpretation of the Mishnah was in fact a result of differences of opinion in principle regarding these more fundamental questions.

סִימָן הֶעָשׂוּי לִידָּרֵס An identifying mark that is liable to be defaced. *Ramban* asks: If we are to disregard an identifying mark, merely because it is liable to be obliterated by passing traffic, why does the Mishnah (below, 24b) state that one is required to return a pile of fruit or coins? How can the fact that something is arranged in a pile serve as an identifying mark, when the pile is likely to collapse under the weight of traffic? He answers: Rabbah, who is the author of this opinion, also believes that it is forbidden to leave food lying around and neglected. Therefore, since the pile of fruit is food, it will be picked up promptly and saved without being damaged. The same applies to money, which people notice and tend to pick up quickly. Therefore, the pile of coins will soon be picked up and saved.

TERMINOLOGY

וְאִיכָּא דְּמַתְנֵי לְהָא שְׁמַעְתָּא And there are some who teach this Amoraic discussion.... This expression means that a certain Halakhic discussion or a difference of opinion among Amoraim appears in several versions. After presenting one account of the saying, another one is also cited. In certain cases the second version differs with regard to the Sages involved in the discussion, and in some instances the subject of the discussion is different. When the Gemara says וְאִיכָּא דְּמַתְנֵי לְהָא שְׁמַעְתָּא בְּאַנְפֵּי נַפְשָׁהּ — "And there are some who teach this Amoraic discussion independently" — it means that the subject presented was discussed on its own, without regard for any particular Tannaitic source.

SAGES

רַבָּה Rabbah. One of the greatest Babylonian Amoraim of the third generation. See *Bava Metzia*, Part I, p. 25.

TRANSLATION AND COMMENTARY

וְאִיכָּא דְּמַתְנֵי לְהָא שְׁמַעְתָּא [1]The Gemara adds: **There are some** authorities **who transmit this Amoraic discussion independently,** not in connection with the interpretation of our Mishnah, but as a separate, independent controversy: [2]**Regarding an identifying mark** on an object **that is liable to be trampled on, Rabbah said: It is not** considered **a valid identifying mark,** even if it was not in fact trampled on. [3]**But Rava said: It is** considered **a valid identifying mark.**

תְּנַן כְּרִיכוֹת בִּרְשׁוּת הָרַבִּים [4]The Gemara now raises an objection to Rava's viewpoint from the text of our Mishnah. The objection is based on two clauses in the Mishnah, one on page 21a and the other on page 24b. These clauses, read together, clearly imply that the fact that an object is lying in the street is highly significant. **We have learned** in the Mishnah (above, 21a) that **"small sheaves in the public domain belong to the finder."** [5]But, continues the Mishnah (below, 24b), "if he finds them **in a private domain, he takes them and announces** that he has found them." [6]The Gemara now proceeds to clarify its objection: **How is the case** described in the Mishnah **to be visualized?** [7]**If** we assume that the sheaves **have no identifying mark on them, what can the finder announce,** even **if he found them in a private domain?** Surely the owner has no way of identifying them. [8]**Rather, is** the Mishnah **not** referring in both places to **a case where** the sheaves **have an identifying mark, and** nevertheless the Mishnah **teaches: "In the public domain, the sheaves belong to the finder"?** Surely this can only be because the owner believes that the identifying mark is ineffective, and therefore gives up hope of recovery. [9]**Thus,** concludes the Gemara, we can infer that **an identifying mark** on an object **that is liable to be trampled on is not** considered **a valid identifying mark.** [10]**Does this not** constitute **a refutation of Rava?**

אָמַר לָךְ [11]The Gemara answers: **Rava can reply to you: In fact,** we can explain that the Mishnah is referring only to **a case where** the sheaves **do not have an identifying mark on them.** Thus the text presents no contradiction of Rava's viewpoint. [12]**And regarding** the point that the Gemara had found objectionable in this

[1]וְאִיכָּא דְּמַתְנֵי לְהָא שְׁמַעְתָּא בְּאַנְפֵּי נַפְשָׁהּ: [2]סִימָן הֶעָשׂוּי לִידָּרֵס, רַבָּה אָמַר: לָא הָוֵי סִימָן. [3]וְרָבָא אָמַר: הָוֵי סִימָן. [4]תְּנַן: ״כְּרִיכוֹת בִּרְשׁוּת הָרַבִּים... הֲרֵי אֵלּוּ שֶׁלּוֹ. [5]בִּרְשׁוּת הַיָּחִיד, נוֹטֵל וּמַכְרִיז״. [6]הֵיכִי דָּמֵי? [7]אִי דְּלֵית בְּהוּ סִימָן, בִּרְשׁוּת הַיָּחִיד, מַאי מַכְרִיז? [8]אֶלָּא לָאו דְּאִית בְּהוּ סִימָן, וְקָתָנֵי: ״בִּרְשׁוּת הָרַבִּים הֲרֵי אֵלּוּ שֶׁלּוֹ״. [9]אַלְמָא, סִימָן הֶעָשׂוּי לִידָּרֵס לָא הָוֵי סִימָן. [10]תְּיוּבְתָּא דְּרָבָא! [11]אָמַר לָךְ רָבָא: לְעוֹלָם, דְּלֵית בְּהוּ סִימָן, [12]וּדְקָא אָמְרַתְּ:

LITERAL TRANSLATION

[1]And there are some who teach this Amoraic discussion independently: [2][Regarding] an identifying mark that is liable to be trampled on, Rabbah said: It is not a [valid] identifying mark. [3]But Rava said: It is a [valid] identifying mark.

[4]We have learned: "Small sheaves in the public domain... these are his. [5]In a private domain, he takes [them] and announces [them]." [6]What is it like? [7]If they do not have an identifying mark on them, [if he found them] in a private domain, what does he announce? [8]Rather, is it not [a case] where they have an identifying mark, and it teaches: "In the public domain they are his." [9]Thus, an identifying mark that is liable to be trampled on is not a [valid] identifying mark. [10][Is this not] a refutation of Rava?

[11]Rava can say to you: In fact, [it is a case] where they do not have an identifying mark on them, [12]and [regarding] what you said:

RASHI

ברשות היחיד — כגון בשדה זרועה, שאין רוב בני אדם דורכין בה, ויש מיעוט שהולכין בה. **הכי גרסינן: אי דלית בהו סימן ברשות היחיד מאי מכריז** — כלומר, כי מכריז זה מצא אבידה מאי מכריז שיוכל ליתן האובד סימן בה?

NOTES

בִּרְשׁוּת הַיָּחִיד In a private domain. The Mishnah could not be referring to a truly private domain, in the usual sense of the word, since outsiders would not enter such a place without permission, and it would be easy to establish who could possibly have lost the object there, even without an identifying mark. Rather, the Mishnah must be referring to a location that is open to the public, but is not frequently visited. *Rashi* suggests that it refers to a field where crops are growing. *Rabbenu Yehonatan* suggests that it refers to the remains of what was once a building. Similarly, the public domain referred to in the Mishnah is not a usual public thoroughfare. It may, in fact, be the interior of a building, if it is a public building that is frequently visited.

TRANSLATION AND COMMENTARY

interpretation, namely the question raised previously [1]("If the sheaves are unmarked, **what can** the finder **announce,** even **if he found them in a private domain?**"), this poses no difficulty according to Rava. For what the Mishnah means is that the finder **announces the place** where he found the sheaves, without specifying what he has found. Accordingly, if the owner left the sheaves there, he will be able to identify them by indicating that the objects he lost were sheaves. Hence, even unmarked sheaves can be identified, provided that they were found in a secluded place. But unmarked sheaves in the street cannot be identified at all (see below). On the other hand, marked sheaves must be announced, wherever they are found, in accordance with Rava's viewpoint. Thus the Mishnah presents no problem to Rava.

״בִּרְשׁוּת הַיָּחִיד, [1]מַאי מַכְרִיז?״ — מַכְרִיז מָקוֹם.
[2]וְרַבָּה אָמַר: מָקוֹם לָא הָוֵי סִימָן. [3]דְּאִיתְּמַר: מָקוֹם, [4]רַבָּה אָמַר: לָא הָוֵי סִימָן. [5]וְרָבָא אָמַר: הָוֵי סִימָן.
[6]תָּא שְׁמַע: ״כְּרִיכוֹת בִּרְשׁוּת הָרַבִּים — הֲרֵי אֵלּוּ שֶׁלּוֹ. [7]בִּרְשׁוּת הַיָּחִיד, נוֹטֵל וּמַכְרִיז. [8]וְהָאֲלוּמוֹת, בֵּין בִּרְשׁוּת הָרַבִּים בֵּין בִּרְשׁוּת הַיָּחִיד, נוֹטֵל

LITERAL TRANSLATION

"[If he found them] in a private domain, [1]what does he announce?" — he announces the place.
[2]But Rabbah says: Place is not a [valid] identifying mark. [3]For it has been said: [Regarding] place, [4]Rabbah says: It is not a [valid] identifying mark. [5]But Rava says: It is a [valid] identifying mark.
[6]Come [and] hear: "Small sheaves in the public domain, these are his. [7]In a private domain, he takes [them] and announces [them]. [8]But large sheaves, whether in the public domain [or] whether in a private domain, he takes [them]

RASHI

מכריז מקום — ואינו מכריז שם האבידה אלא שם המקום, מי שאבדה ממנו אבידה במקום פלוני יבא ויאמר מה איבד, וזה בא ואומר: אבדתי שם חפץ פלוני. **והאלומות** — עומרים גדולים.

וְרַבָּה אָמַר [2]The Gemara now observes: **But Rabbah says** that as a general rule the **place** where an item was left **is not a valid identifying mark.** Thus, even if someone accurately names the object said to have been found in a particular place, this is not considered sufficient identification to justify returning it to him. [3]**For it has been said** that there was a dispute among the same Amoraim, Rabbah and Rava, concerning this very matter. **Regarding** the **place** where a lost item was found, [4]**Rabbah says:** A lost object's place **is not** considered **a valid identifying mark,** [5]**but Rava says: It is** considered **a valid identifying mark.** Thus we see that Rabbah's and Rava's opinions in these two disputes are interrelated. According to Rava, a marked object must be announced even if it was found in the street, because a mark that may be trampled beyond recognition is nevertheless valid. Rava also maintains that an unmarked object must be announced, provided it was found in a secluded place, because he is of the opinion that location is a valid means of identification. By contrast, according to Rabbah unmarked objects need never be announced, because he is of the opinion that location is not a valid means of identification. Rabbah also maintains that even marked objects need not be announced, if they were found in the street, because, according to him, a mark that may be trampled beyond recognition is also not valid. Thus both Rava and Rabbah can accept the Mishnah's distinction between private and public places, but Rabbah explains the Mishnah as referring to marked objects, whereas Rava explains it as referring to unmarked objects.

תָּא שְׁמַע [6]**Come and hear** objections against the viewpoints of both Rabbah and Rava from the following Baraita: **"Small sheaves in the public domain belong to the finder.** [7]But if he finds them **in a private domain, he takes them and announces** that he has found **them.** [8]**But** if he finds **large sheaves, whether in the public domain or in a private domain, he takes them and announces** that he has found **them."** The first part of this Baraita, in which a distinction is made between small sheaves in a secluded place and those in the street, is the same as our Mishnah. Rabbah can explain it as referring to marked sheaves, because an identifying mark on sheaves is useless in the street, where it can easily be obliterated. On the other hand, Rava can explain it as referring to unmarked sheaves, which can be identified on the basis of location, provided that they were found in a

NOTES

מַכְרִיז מָקוֹם Announcing the place where the object was found. Our commentary follows *Rashi*, who says that the finder must announce that he found a lost object in a certain place, and the owner must identify the object. *Tosafot*, however, suggests that the finder must announce what he has found, and the owner must identify the place where it was lost. Others explain that the finder must indicate what he has found, and also in general terms where he found it, while the owner must pinpoint the exact location (*Shittah Mekubbetzet*).

וּמַכְרִיז״. [1] רַבָּה הֵיכִי מְתָרֵץ לָהּ, [2] וְרָבָא הֵיכִי מְתָרֵץ לָהּ? [3] רַבָּה מְתָרֵץ לְטַעְמֵיהּ — בְּסִימָן. [4] וְרָבָא מְתָרֵץ לְטַעְמֵיהּ — בְּמָקוֹם.

[5] רַבָּה מְתָרֵץ לְטַעְמֵיהּ — בְּסִימָן: [6] ״כְּרִיכוֹת בִּרְשׁוּת הָרַבִּים — הֲרֵי אֵלּוּ שֶׁלּוֹ״, מִשּׁוּם [23A] דְּמִדְרְסָא. [7] ״בִּרְשׁוּת הַיָּחִיד, נוֹטֵל וּמַכְרִיז״, דְּלָא מִדְרְסָא. [8] ״וְהָאֲלוּמּוֹת, בֵּין בִּרְשׁוּת הָרַבִּים וּבֵין בִּרְשׁוּת הַיָּחִיד, נוֹטֵל וּמַכְרִיז״ — [9] כֵּיוָן דְּגְבִיהָן, לָא מִדְרְסָא.

[10] וְרָבָא מְתָרֵץ לְטַעְמֵיהּ — [11] בְּמָקוֹם: ״כְּרִיכוֹת בִּרְשׁוּת הָרַבִּים, הֲרֵי אֵלּוּ שֶׁלּוֹ״,

LITERAL TRANSLATION

and announces [them].'' [1] How does Rabbah explain it, [2] and how does Rava explain it?

[3] Rabbah explains [it] in accordance with his viewpoint — by an identifying mark. [4] And Rava explains [it] in accordance with his viewpoint — by the place.

[5] Rabbah explains [it] in accordance with his viewpoint by an identifying mark: [6] "Small sheaves in the public domain — these are his," because [23A] they are trampled upon. [7] In a private domain, he takes [them] and announces [them]," because they are not trampled upon. [8] "But large sheaves, whether in the public domain or in a private domain, he takes and announces" — [9] since they are tall, they are not trampled upon.

[10] And Rava explains [it] in accordance with his viewpoint [11] by the place: "Small sheaves in the public domain, these are his,"

TRANSLATION AND COMMENTARY

secluded place. The new feature contained in this Baraita is that large sheaves, as distinct from small ones, must be announced by the finder, even if they are found in the public domain. [1] On this point the Gemara asks: **How does Rabbah explain** the Baraita's ruling that large sheaves are identifiable even in the street, in the light of his opinion that identifying marks on sheaves are useless in the street? [2] **And,** similarly, **how does Rava explain** the Baraita's ruling that large sheaves are identifiable even in the street, in the light of his explanation that the Baraita's ruling about small sheaves applies only where the sheaves are unmarked? If the small sheaves are unmarked, the large sheaves must also be unmarked, and just as an owner cannot identify unmarked small sheaves found in the street, he cannot identify unmarked large sheaves found in the street either.

רַבָּה מְתָרֵץ לְטַעְמֵיהּ [3] The Gemara answers: **Rabbah can explain** the Baraita **in accordance with his viewpoint** as referring specifically to sheaves that have **an identifying mark.** [4] **And Rava can explain it in accordance with his viewpoint by** maintaining that **the place** where the sheaves were found can serve as identification.

רַבָּה מְתָרֵץ לְטַעְמֵיהּ [5] The Gemara now elaborates: **Rabbah can explain** the Baraita **in accordance with his viewpoint,** maintaining that it refers specifically to sheaves that have **an identifying mark,** as follows: [6] **"Small sheaves in the public domain belong to the finder," because** [23A] **they are trampled upon** there. Their identifying mark is defaced, and the owner gives up hope of recovering them. [7] But if the small sheaves were lost **"in a private domain,** the finder **takes them and announces** that he has found **them," because they are not** likely to be **trampled upon** in a private domain. The identifying marks on them will remain intact, and the owner does not give up hope of recovering them. [8] **"But** if a person finds **large sheaves, whether in the public domain or in a private domain,** in either case **he takes** them **and announces** that he has found them," [9] because **since they are tall, they are not trampled upon.** Even if they are not picked up by passersby, they are at least avoided, their identifying marks remain intact, and their owner does not give up hope of recovering them.

וְרָבָא מְתָרֵץ לְטַעְמֵיהּ [10] On the other hand, **Rava can explain** the Baraita **in accordance with his viewpoint,** that the small sheaves do not have identifying marks, [11] and it is **the place** where they were found that is their identifying mark. He can explain the Baraita as follows: **"Small sheaves in the public domain belong to the finder," because they** tend **to be moved** away from the place where they were left as they are trampled by passersby and animals. Hence even if the owner of the sheaves knew precisely where he lost them, he would assume

RASHI

רבה היכי מתרץ לה — רבה דאמר טעמא דרשות הרבים משום דנדרס, מאי שנא אלומות? ורבא — דמוקים לכריכות כשאין בו סימן, מאי שנא כריכות ומאי שנא אלומות?! **רבה מתרץ לטעמיה** — דטעמא דרשות הרבים דכריכות משום סימן, ובדבר שיש בה סימן. **במקום** — טעמא דכריכות ברשות הרבים משום מקום, ובדבר שאין בו סימן. **דמדרסא** — וסימן העשוי לידרס הוא.

HALAKHAH

כְּרִיכוֹת **Small sheaves.** "One may keep small sheaves of grain found in the public domain, and also those found in a private domain that seem to have fallen by chance. But small sheaves found in a private domain that seem to have been left there intentionally must be returned to their owner, since an object's location can serve as identification

דְּמִינַשְׁתְּפָא. [1]״בִּרְשׁוּת הַיָּחִיד, חַיָּיב לְהַכְרִיז״, דְּלָא מִינַשְׁתְּפָא. [2]״וְהָאֲלוּמּוֹת, בֵּין בִּרְשׁוּת הָרַבִּים וּבֵין בִּרְשׁוּת הַיָּחִיד, [3]נוֹטֵל וּמַכְרִיז״ — כֵּיוָן דְּיַקִּירִי, לָא מִינַשְׁתְּפָא.

[4]תָּא שְׁמַע: ״כִּכָּרוֹת שֶׁל נַחְתּוֹם — הֲרֵי אֵלּוּ שֶׁלּוֹ״. [5]הָא שֶׁל בַּעַל הַבַּיִת חַיָּיב לְהַכְרִיז. [6]שֶׁל בַּעַל הַבַּיִת מַאי טַעְמָא? [7]כֵּיוָן דְּאִית בְּהוּ סִימָן, דְּמֵידַע יְדִיעַ רִפְתָּא דְּאִינִישׁ אִינִישׁ הוּא. [8]וְלָא שְׁנָא רְשׁוּת הָרַבִּים וְלָא שְׁנָא רְשׁוּת הַיָּחִיד. נוֹטֵל וּמַכְרִיז. [9]אַלְמָא, סִימָן הֶעָשׂוּי לִידָּרֵס הָוֵי סִימָן. [10]תְּיוּבְתָּא דְּרַבָּה.

LITERAL TRANSLATION

because they are moved about. [1]"In a private domain, he is obliged to announce [them]," because they are not moved about. [2]"But large sheaves, whether in the public domain or whether in a private domain, [3]he takes and announces" — since they are heavy, they are not moved about.

[4]Come [and] hear: "Loaves of a baker — these are his." [5]Whereas [those that are] homemade (lit., "of the owner of the house") he is obliged to announce. [6]Homemade [loaves], what is the reason [why he must announce]? [7]Because they [all] have an identifying mark, for it is surely known that each person's loaf [belongs to] that person. [8]And there is no difference [in] the public domain and there is no difference [in] a private domain. He takes [them] and announces [them]. [9]Thus, an identifying mark that is likely to be trampled on is a [valid] identifying mark. [10][Is this not] a refutation of Rabbah.

TRANSLATION AND COMMENTARY

that they had been moved and would give up hope of recovering them. [1]But if the small sheaves were lost **"in a private domain,** the finder **is obliged to announce** that he has found **them," because** in a private domain **they are not moved about** by passersby or animals, and the owner does not give up hope of recovering them. [2]**But,** by contrast, if a person finds **large sheaves, whether in the public domain or in a private domain,** [3]in either case **he takes** them **and announces** that he has found them," because **since they are heavy, they are not** easily **moved about.** Their owner expects to claim them by citing their location, and does not give up hope of recovering them. Thus both Rabbah and Rava can reconcile their respective viewpoints with this Baraita, as large heavy sheaves tend not to be moved or trampled, and it makes no difference whether they are found in the street or in a private place.

תָּא שְׁמַע [4]The Gemara now returns to another clause in our Mishnah in a further attempt to resolve the difference of opinion between Rabbah and Rava: **Come and hear: "Loaves of a** commercial **baker belong to the finder."** [5]From this statement, says the Gemara, we can make the following inference: If someone finds the **homemade loaves, he must announce** that he has found them. [6]Now, continues the Gemara, **what is the reason why** the finder of **homemade loaves must announce** that he has found them? [7]It must surely be **because** people who are not commercial bakers bake their loaves in their own particular way, so that the loaves **all have identifying marks.** Thus **it is known that each person's loaf belongs to that person.** [8]The Gemara now continues its analysis of the Mishnah: Since the Mishnah did not qualify its statement in any way with respect to where the loaves were found, it follows that **there is no difference** between homemade loaves found in **the public domain and** those found in **a private domain.** In either case the finder must **take** the loaves **and announce** that he has found **them.** But loaves lost in the street are liable to be trampled on. [9]**Thus** we may infer that **an identifying mark** on an object **that is liable to be trampled on is** still considered **a valid identifying mark.** [10]**Is this not** clearly **a refutation of Rabbah?**

RASHI

דמינשתפא — מתגלגל ברגלי אדם ובהמה, ואינה נמצאת במקום שנפלה תחילה. **דיקירי** – כבידות. **הא של בעל בית חייב להכריז** — ואף על גב דבהדיא תני לה במתניתין, איידי דנקט לאותיה מרישא כריכות ברשות הרבים דאותיב מינה לרבא, נקט נמי לאותוביה לרבה מדוקיא דרישא.

NOTES

הָא שֶׁל בַּעַל הַבַּיִת Whereas those that are homemade.... *Rashi* and other Rishonim were puzzled as to why the Gemara here resorts to an argument based on inference, since the Mishnah (below, 25a) explicitly states that homemade loaves must be returned. Why did the Gemara not simply ask how Rabbah interprets this Mishnah?

Ramban explains that the Gemara wanted to prove that the homemade loaves must be returned, whether found in

HALAKHAH

[following Rava's view]. Someone who found, in either domain, large sheaves which are not easily moved from place to place, must take them and announce that he has found them." (*Shulḥan Arukh, Ḥoshen Mishpat* 262:9.)

LANGUAGE

מִינַשְׁתְּפָא They are moved about. The root of this word is apparently נפש in Aramaic, meaning "to move" or "to shift from place to place."

REALIA

כִּכָּרוֹת שֶׁל נַחְתּוֹם Bakers' loaves during the Mishnaic period.

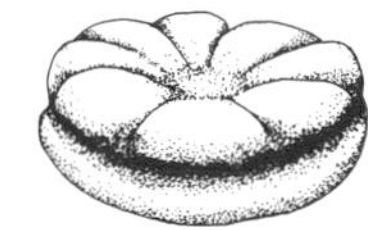

(Found in Pompeii)

The dough from which such bread was baked was placed in molds, thereby producing loaves of uniform size and shape. However, ordinary people baked loaves of whatever size and shape they wished.

TRANSLATION AND COMMENTARY

אָמַר לָךְ רַבָּה [1]The Gemara answers: **Rabbah can say to you:** An identifying mark that is liable to be defaced is in fact not valid. And as for your question concerning why it is necessary to announce the finding of homemade loaves in the public domain, **the reason is that** the loaves are not liable to be trampled on, [2]because the Halakhah says that **we are not permitted to pass by food** left unattended. According to the Halakhah, it is prohibited to leave food lying on the ground. Instead, out of respect, we are required to pick it up. The owner can therefore assume that the loaves were not trampled underfoot, since the first person who found them would have picked them up. Hence the owner will not have given up hope of recovering them.

וְהָא אִיכָּא נָכְרִים [3]The Gemara objects further: **But surely there are non-Jews,** who are not under the Halakhic obligation to pick up food left unattended. Is it not possible that the loaves may have been trampled underfoot by non-Jews before a Jew could come and pick them up? And will not the owner, realizing this, immediately give up hope of recovering them?

נָכְרִים חָיְישֵׁי לִכְשָׁפִים [4]The Gemara answers: **Non-Jews** who see food lying on the ground **are afraid** that it may have been left there for the purposes of **witchcraft,** and hence for superstitious reasons they too will avoid treading on it.

וְהָאִיכָּא בְּהֵמָה וּכְלָבִים [5]Again the Gemara objects: **But surely there are cattle and dogs** that tread on food. They are liable to deface any identifying mark that the food may contain.

בְּאַתְרָא דְּלָא שְׁכִיחִי [6]The Gemara answers: **The case refers to a place where cattle and dogs are not common.**

[1]אָמַר לָךְ רַבָּה: הָתָם הַיְינוּ טַעְמָא: [2]מִשּׁוּם דְּאֵין מַעֲבִירִין עַל הָאוֹכָלִין.
[3]וְהָא אִיכָּא נָכְרִים.
[4]נָכְרִים חָיְישֵׁי לִכְשָׁפִים.
[5]וְהָאִיכָּא בְּהֵמָה וּכְלָבִים.
[6]בְּאַתְרָא דְּלָא שְׁכִיחִי בְּהֵמָה וּכְלָבִים.

LITERAL TRANSLATION

[1]Rabbah can say to you: There this is the reason: [2]Because we may not pass by food. [3]But surely there are non-Jews. [4]Non-Jews are afraid of witchcraft. [5]But surely there are cattle and dogs. [6][The case refers] to a place where cattle and dogs are not common.

RASHI

אין מעבירין על האוכלין — המוצא אוכלין בדרך אין רשאי לעבור עליהם ולהניחם שם, הלכך לא נדרסו, שמי שמצאן ראשון הגביהן. **אין מעבירין על האוכלין** — לאו לשון דריסה הוא, אלא כמו "אין מעבירין על המצות" (יומא לג,א). **חיישי לכשפים** — סבורים שמחמת כשפים הונחו לשם כדי להכשיל הדורסים עליהן, והוי נמי דאין מגביהין אותם, מיהו לא דרסי עליהן משום כשפים.

BACKGROUND

חָיְישֵׁי לִכְשָׁפִים Are afraid of witchcraft. In many places in the ancient world people used to cast malicious magic spells on various foods. Because non-Jews were extremely apprehensive about such spells, they were careful not to take food left in public places, and they would not even touch it.

בְּהֵמָה וּכְלָבִים Cattle and dogs. Even people in urban settlements used to keep animals in the Talmudic period, and these animals would often roam freely in the city streets on their way to and from the pasture and the barn in the owner's courtyard. Although it was uncommon to keep dogs at home, many dogs used to wander the streets of cities in the Near East. They were tolerated by the residents of the towns because they ate refuse and destroyed various kinds of vermin.

NOTES

a secluded place or in the street. Had it not been for the comparison with bakery loaves in the first Mishnah, one might try to explain away the second Mishnah as referring specifically to a private domain. Therefore, the Gemara preferred to resort to inference here. However, *Ramban* also noted that the Gemara often resorts to the use of arguments based on an inference, even when explicit rulings can be found in the sources.

אֵין מַעֲבִירִין עַל הָאוֹכָלִין It is forbidden to pass by food. This prohibition is part of a general prohibition against בִּיזּוּי אוֹכָלִין — the disrespectful treatment of food, which should only be used for nutritional purposes. The central idea underlying the prohibition is that food is God's gift to man, and one must treat it with respect. Tractate *Derekh Eretz,* which, among other subjects, discusses customs connected with eating, contains many instructions and laws relating to the respectful treatment of food. *Ritva* and *Meiri* interpret the word מַעֲבִירִין as "to walk over" or "to tread upon," meaning that it is forbidden to step on food. But most commentators believe that the word מַעֲבִירִין here has a broader meaning — that it is forbidden to pass by food lying on the ground without picking it up and placing it elsewhere.

וְהָא אִיכָּא נָכְרִים But surely there are non-Jews. The basis of the Gemara's question is that since the owner assumes that his loaves will be trampled upon by non-Jews before a Jew can find them, he gives up hope of recovering them. The loaves are, therefore, to be treated as ownerless, even if they were not in fact trampled on and were found by a Jew. However, the commentators point out that if most of the residents in the area were non-Jews, the loaves should have been permitted to the finder in any case, as explained below (24a), because the person who lost them would assume that a non-Jew would find them and keep them, whether or not they had identifying marks. Hence, the owner would give up hope of recovering them, and the loaves should have been treated as ownerless, even if a Jew found them. Accordingly, the Gemara must have been referring to an area where non-Jews were a minority. However, in that case, why should the owner have imagined that non-Jews would trample on his loaves before they could be found by a Jew?

Rashba responds that a distinction is to be drawn between an owner assuming that a non-Jew will find an

HALAKHAH

אֵין מַעֲבִירִין עַל הָאוֹכָלִין We may not pass by food. "One who sees food on the ground should not leave it there; instead, he should pick it up and put it where it will not be stepped on" (following Rabbah's view). (*Magen Avraham, Shulḥan Arukh, Oraḥ Ḥayyim* 171:1.) Although the Halakhah generally follows Rava's opinion, we still follow Rabbah on this question. (*Rivash, Rashba.*)

TRANSLATION AND COMMENTARY

לֵימָא כְּתַנָּאֵי [1] Up to this point in the discussion the difference of opinion between Rabbah and Rava has remained unresolved, and each Amora has been able to explain the sources cited according to his own point of view. Now the Gemara seeks to suggest that their difference of opinion in fact reflects a Tannaitic dispute between Rabbi Meir, the first Tanna in our Mishnah, and Rabbi Yehudah: **Shall we say that this dispute** between Rabbah and Rava **is the same as the difference of opinion between Tannaim** recorded in our Mishnah: **"Rabbi Yehudah says:** [2] **Anything that has something different in it must be announced** by the finder. [3] **How so? If he found a round fig cake and inside it a potsherd, or a loaf and inside it coins."** [4] **This** statement by Rabbi Yehudah **proves by implication that the first Tanna,** Rabbi Meir, the author of the first part of the Mishnah, with whom Rabbi Yehudah is presumably disagreeing, **is of the opinion that these objects** belong to the finder and **are his** to keep. [5] In order to clarify the connection between this Mishnah and the difference of opinion between Rabbah and Rava, the Gemara notes: When the Rabbis studying this Mishnah suggested this connection, they initially **assumed that according to everyone** — both Rabbi Yehudah and Rabbi Meir — **an identifying mark that** may have **come about of itself is** considered **a valid identifying mark.** The cases cited in our Mishnah of a cake of figs with a potsherd in it and a loaf containing coins are unusual. By far the simplest explanation for their occurrence is that some kind of accident happened while the fig cake or bread was being prepared. But it is also possible that they were inserted deliberately as an identifying mark. Hence the Gemara is now assuming that both Rabbi Meir and Rabbi Yehudah consider this to be a real possibility, and that they maintain that such marks are valid identification marks. [6] **And,** moreover, the Rabbis also assumed that both Rabbi Meir and Rabbi Yehudah were in agreement **that it is permissible to pass by food** without picking it up. From this assumption it would follow that the sign on the food is, in fact, liable to be defaced. [7] Having made these preliminary assumptions the Gemara continues: **Is it not** reasonable to conclude **that** the Tannaim in the Mishnah **disagree about** the validity of **an identifying mark** on an object **that**

[1] לֵימָא כְּתַנָּאֵי: ״רַבִּי יְהוּדָה אוֹמֵר: [2] כָּל דָּבָר שֶׁיֵּשׁ בּוֹ שִׁינּוּי, חַיָּיב לְהַכְרִיז. [3] כֵּיצַד? מָצָא עִיגּוּל וּבְתוֹכוֹ חֶרֶס, כִּכָּר וּבְתוֹכוֹ מָעוֹת״. [4] מִכְּלָל דְּתַנָּא קַמָּא סָבַר: הֲרֵי אֵלּוּ שֶׁלּוֹ. [5] סַבְרוּהָ דְּכוּלֵּי עָלְמָא סִימָן הַבָּא מֵאֵילָיו הָוֵי סִימָן, [6] וּמַעֲבִירִין עַל הָאוֹכָלִין. [7] מַאי לָאו בְּסִימָן הֶעָשׂוּי לִידָּרֵס קָא מִיפַּלְגִי?

LITERAL TRANSLATION

[1] Shall we say [that this dispute is the same] as [the following dispute between] Tannaim: "Rabbi Yehudah says: [2] Anything that has something different in it, he is obliged to announce. [3] How so? [If] he found a round [cake of figs] and inside it a potsherd, [or] a loaf and inside it coins." [4] [This proves] by implication that the first Tanna is of the opinion [that] these [objects] are his. [5] They assumed that [according to] everyone (lit., "the whole world") an identifying mark that comes about of itself is a [valid] identifying mark, [6] and [that] we may pass by food. [7] Is it not that they disagree about an identifying mark that is liable to be trampled on?

RASHI

לימא כתנאי — פלוגתא דרבה ורבא. **הבא מאיליו** — הראוי לבא מאליו, כגון חרס פעמים שנופל בעיגול. **הוי סימן** — דאמרינן לשם סימן נתנו שם ולא נפל מאליו, ודבר שיש בו סימן הוא. ואפילו הכי פליגי רבנן ואמרי: הרי אלו שלו, משום דקסברי מעבירין על האוכלין והוה ליה סימן העשוי לידרס.

TERMINOLOGY

לֵימָא כְּתַנָּאֵי Shall we say that this dispute is the same as the following dispute between Tannaim? Sometimes, in an attempt to understand an Amoraic controversy, the Gemara may suggest that each of the Amoraic viewpoints parallels a corresponding Tannaitic viewpoint. This suggestion is usually rejected by the Gemara, which proceeds to show that the Amoraim are in fact discussing a previously unconsidered aspect of law. The expression לֵימָא — "shall we say" — generally introduces a proposition which is rejected at the end of the discussion. In any event, presenting a difference of opinion between Amoraim as an exact parallel to an earlier difference of opinion among Tannaim entails a difficulty, for even if the Amoraim are divided in their opinion as to which of the Tannaim they support, they each ought to have stated initially, "I agree with Rabbi X (or Y)," and they should not have presented their difference of opinion as though it were a new one.

...מִכְּלָל דְּ [This proves] by implication that.... When the Gemara presents an argument for a Halakhic ruling based on an authoritative source (either a Biblical text, a Tannaitic statement, an accepted tradition, or an established legal principle), it often introduces the inference with this expression.

סַבְרוּהָ They thought, they assumed [that].... This term introduces an assumption proposed at the beginning of a discussion, but later found to be erroneous.

NOTES

object first, which applies only where non-Jews are in the majority, and an owner assuming that his loaves will be stepped on, which applies as long as there is a significant minority of careless people, or even animals, in the area.

סִימָן הַבָּא מֵאֵילָיו An identifying mark that comes about of itself. Whenever an object bears a mark of which the owner is clearly aware, that mark is a means of identification. In the Gemara's discussion here a question arises with regard to a distinguishing characteristic which may have come about on its own, by chance, without the owner's knowledge. The example presented by the Mishnah, the presence of money in a loaf of bread, may have been accidental. The money may have fallen from the hand of the person who was kneading the flour and may have remained in the dough without his knowledge. However, it is also possible that the baker purposely placed the coins in the dough — to hide them, for example. Similarly, since figs are dried in a field, there may have been a piece of broken pottery in the field which stuck to the figs and was later inserted in the cake without the owner's knowledge. On the other hand, that piece of pottery may have been purposely placed in the fig cake because its owner wished to mark a particular characteristic or quality possessed by that fig cake. The difference of opinion regarding "an identifying mark that comes about of itself" concerns mainly the degree of likelihood that the person who lost the object knew of the presence of the identifying mark in it.

סִימָן הַבָּא מֵאֵילָיו An identifying mark that comes about of itself. The view of the first Tanna in our Mishnah is clearly that coins are never put into a loaf intentionally. Hence there is no reason to assume that the owner knows that they are there. But the view of Rabbi Yehudah is the subject of a difference of opinion among the Rishonim. Our commentary follows *Rashi,* who explains that Rabbi Yehudah was of the

[1]מָר סָבַר: לָא הָוֵי סִימָן, [2]וּמָר סָבַר: הָוֵי סִימָן.

[3]אֲמַר רַב זְבִיד מִשְּׁמֵיהּ דְּרָבָא: [4]אִי סָלְקָא דַּעְתָּךְ דְּקָא סָבַר תַּנָּא קַמָּא סִימָן הֶעָשׂוּי לִידָּרֵס לָא הָוֵי סִימָן, וּמַעֲבִירִין עַל הָאוֹכָלִין, [5]כִּכָּרוֹת שֶׁל בַּעַל הַבַּיִת בִּרְשׁוּת הָרַבִּים אַמַּאי מַכְרִיז?

[6]אֶלָּא אֲמַר רַב זְבִיד מִשְּׁמֵיהּ דְּרָבָא: [7]דְּכוּלֵּי עָלְמָא סָבְרִי סִימָן הֶעָשׂוּי לִידָּרֵס הָוֵי סִימָן, [8]וּמַעֲבִירִין עַל הָאוֹכָלִין. [9]וְהָכָא בְּסִימָן הַבָּא מֵאֵילָיו קָא מִיפַּלְגִי. [10]דְּתַנָּא קַמָּא סָבַר:

LITERAL TRANSLATION

[1][One] Sage maintains [that] it is not a [valid] identifying mark, [2]and [the other] Sage maintains [that] it is a [valid] identifying mark.

[3]Rav Zevid said in the name of Rava: [4]If it should enter your mind that the first Tanna maintains [that] an identifying mark that is liable to be trampled on is not a [valid] identifying mark, and [that] we may pass by food, [5][then] why does he announce homemade loaves [found] in the public domain?

[6]Rather, Rav Zevid said in the name of Rava: [7]Everyone maintains [that] an identifying mark that is liable to be trampled on is a [valid] identifying mark, [8]and [that] we may pass by food. [9]But here they disagree about an identifying mark that comes about of itself. [10]For the first Tanna maintains

TRANSLATION AND COMMENTARY

is liable to be trampled on? [1]**One Sage,** Rabbi Meir, **maintains that it is not** considered **a valid identifying mark.** Although the fig cake and the loaf are properly marked, since we have assumed that an identifying mark which may have come about of itself is valid, nevertheless in this case the identification mark is useless because the objects were found in the street and were likely to be trampled on. [2]By contrast, **the other Sage,** Rabbi Yehudah, **maintains that** a mark on such an object **is** considered **a valid identifying mark,** despite the fact that it is liable to be defaced by passersby. Therefore, since by assumption the fig cake and the loaf are properly marked, a person finding such an object must announce it. We see, therefore, that the difference of opinion between Rabbah and Rava regarding an identifying mark which is liable to be defaced has already been recorded in the Mishnah. Rabbah seems to be in agreement with Rabbi Meir, and Rava with Rabbi Yehudah.

אֲמַר רַב זְבִיד [3]The preceding analysis was based on two assumptions. The Gemara now challenges these assumptions: **Rav Zevid said in the name of Rava:** [4]**If it should enter your mind** to think **that** Rabbi Meir, **the first Tanna, maintains that an identifying mark** on an object **that is liable to be trampled on is not** considered **a valid identifying mark,** as we assumed above, **and that we are permitted to pass by food,** as we assumed above, [5]**why then** in the case of **homemade loaves** found **in the public domain does** the first part of the Mishnah, attributed to Rabbi Meir, require the finder to **announce** what he has found? Even if the loaves did contain an identifying mark, it would probably have been obliterated by the passersby, and the owner would have given up hope of recovering them. Thus it is obvious that Rabbi Meir must either agree with Rava that an identifying mark on an object that is liable to be trampled on is still valid, and disagree with Rabbi Yehudah about something else, or he must agree with Rabbah that one is not permitted to leave food lying on the ground. Thus our initial assumption must be wrong.

אֶלָּא אֲמַר רַב זְבִיד [6]**Rather,** each of the two Amoraim will now explain the difference of opinion between Rabbi Meir and Rabbi Yehudah in accordance with his own opinion: **Rav Zevid said in the name of Rava:** The difference of opinion between the Tannaim should be explained as follows: [7]**Everyone,** both Rabbi Meir and Rabbi Yehudah, **maintains that an identifying mark** on an object **that is liable to be trampled on is** nevertheless considered **a valid identifying mark,** in accordance with Rava's viewpoint. [8]Moreover, both Rabbi Meir and Rabbi Yehudah agree **that we are permitted to pass by food** without picking it up. [9]**But here** Rabbi Meir and Rabbi Yehudah **disagree about** whether **the identifying marks** in the cake of figs or in the loaf are valid, inasmuch as they may have **come about of themselves.** [10]**For** Rabbi Meir, **the first Tanna, maintains that**

RASHI

ורבי יהודה סבר הוי סימן — ואף על פי שזה עשוי לידרס נמי הוי סימן. **ומעבירין על האוכלין** — ואפילו הכי ככרות של בעל הבית חייב להכריז, דסימן העשוי לידרס הוי סימן. **ועיגול היינו טעמא** — דסימן הבא מאיליו לאו סימן הוא, ורבי יהודה סבר הוי סימן.

SAGES

רַב זְבִיד Rav Zevid. A fifth generation Babylonian Amora, Rav Zevid was an outstanding disciple of Abaye and Rava, and he frequently cited their teachings. Rav Zevid often engaged in discussions with the leading Amoraim of his generation, and was noted as an expounder of Baraitot from the school of Rabbi Hoshaya (see below, 92b).
Rava's yeshivah divided after his death, and Rav Zevid replaced him as head of the Pumbedita Yeshivah for about ten years.

NOTES

opinion that the coins had indeed been put in the bread intentionally, precisely in order to serve as an identifying mark, in the event that the loaf was lost. *Tosafot* and others explain that Rabbi Yehudah agrees that the coins got into the bread by accident. But it is still quite likely that the owner was aware of the loaf's peculiarity, and is relying on using it as an identifying mark.

TRANSLATION AND COMMENTARY

an identifying mark that may have **come about of itself is not** considered **a valid identifying mark,** and thus if a person finds a cake of figs in which there is a potsherd he is not obliged to announce it and may keep it for himself. [1]**But Rabbi Yehudah maintains that it is** considered **a valid identifying mark,** and the finder must announce that he has found it, even if he found it in the street, since both Rabbi Meir and Rabbi Yehudah agree that an identifying mark that is liable to be defaced is nevertheless a valid one.

וְרַבָּה אָמַר לָךְ [2]Rav Zevid has so far explained the difference of opinion in our Mishnah in accordance with Rava's viewpoint. The Gemara now offers an explanation of this dispute that is in accordance with Rabbah's viewpoint: **But Rabbah can say to you** that the difference between the Tannaim can be explained as follows: **Everyone** — both Rabbi Meir and Rabbi Yehudah — **agrees that an identifying mark** on an object **that is liable to be trampled on is not** considered **a valid identifying mark,** in accordance with Rabbah's viewpoint. Thus, if a person lost in the street an ordinary object containing an identifying mark liable to be defaced, he would surely give up hope of recovering it. [3]But here we are dealing with a loaf of bread or a cake of figs **and** the law in such a case is different, because both Rabbi Meir and Rabbi Yehudah agree **that we are not permitted to pass by food** without picking it up. Hence, if the cake of figs or the loaf were properly marked, both Tannaim would agree that it should be announced. [4]**But here** the Tannaim **disagree about** whether **the identifying marks** in the cake of figs or in the loaf are valid, inasmuch as they may have **come about of themselves.** [5]Rabbi Meir, **the first Tanna, maintains that** such a mark **is not** considered **a valid identifying mark,** and thus if a person finds a cake of figs in which there is a potsherd he is not obliged to announce it and may keep it for himself. [6]**But Rabbi Yehudah maintains that it is** considered **a valid identifying mark,** and the finder must announce that he has found it, since the objects in question are food and are not likely to be trampled on.

אִיכָּא דְּאָמְרִי [7]**There are some** scholars **who report** a slightly different version of the previous passage. According to this second version, the Rabbis studying our Mishnah initially **assumed that according to everyone** — both Rabbi Yehudah and Rabbi Meir — **an identifying mark that** may have **come about of itself is** considered **a valid identifying mark.** This assumption is the same as in the first version. [8]In the second version, however, instead of assuming that the Tannaim agree that it is permissible to leave food lying on the ground, the Rabbis instead assumed that both Rabbi Meir and Rabbi Yehudah were in agreement **that an identifying mark** on an object **that is liable to be trampled on is not** considered **a valid identifying mark.** [9]Having made these preliminary assumptions the Gemara continues: **Is it not** reasonable to conclude **that** Rabbi Meir and Rabbi Yehudah **disagree about whether we are permitted to pass by food** and not pick it up? [10]**One Sage,** Rabbi Meir, **maintains that we are permitted to pass by** food without picking it up. [11]**And the other Sage,** Rabbi Yehudah, **maintains that we are not permitted to pass by** food without being required to pick it up. Thus, since the identifying mark on the food remains intact, the finder is required to announce what he found.

סִימָן הַבָּא מֵאֵילָיו לָא הָוֵי סִימָן, [1]וְרַבִּי יְהוּדָה סָבַר: הָוֵי סִימָן. [2]וְרַבָּה אֲמַר לָךְ: דְּכוּלֵּי עָלְמָא סִימָן הֶעָשׂוּי לִידָּרֵס לָא הָוֵי סִימָן, [3]וְאֵין מַעֲבִירִין עַל הָאוֹכָלִין. [4]וְהָכָא בְּסִימָן הַבָּא מֵאֵילָיו קָמִיפַּלְגִי. [5]תַּנָּא קַמָּא סָבַר: לָא הָוֵי סִימָן, [6]וְרַבִּי יְהוּדָה סָבַר: הָוֵי סִימָן.

[7]אִיכָּא דְּאָמְרִי: סַבְרוּהָ דְּכוּלֵּי עָלְמָא סִימָן הַבָּא מֵאֵילָיו הָוֵי סִימָן, [8]וְסִימָן הֶעָשׂוּי לִידָּרֵס לָא הָוֵי סִימָן. [9]מַאי לָאו בְּמַעֲבִירִין עַל הָאוֹכָלִין קָא מִיפַּלְגִי? [10]דְּמָר סָבַר: מַעֲבִירִין, [11]וּמָר סָבַר: אֵין מַעֲבִירִין.

LITERAL TRANSLATION

[that] an identifying mark that comes about of itself is not a [valid] identifying mark, [1]and Rabbi Yehudah maintains [that] it is a [valid] identifying mark.

[2]But Rabbah can say to you: Everyone [agrees that] an identifying mark that is liable to be trampled on is not a [valid] identifying mark, [3]and [that] we may not pass by food. [4]But here they disagree about an identifying mark that comes about of itself. [5]The first Tanna maintains [that] it is not a [valid] identifying mark, [6]and Rabbi Yehudah maintains [that] it is a [valid] identifying mark.

[7]There are some who say: They assumed that [according to] everyone an identifying mark that comes about of itself is a [valid] identifying mark, [8]and [that] an identifying mark that is liable to be trampled on is not a [valid] identifying mark. [9]Is it not that they disagree about [whether] we may pass by food? [10]For [one] Sage maintains [that] we may pass by, [11]and [the other] Sage maintains [that] we may not pass by.

RASHI

ורבה אמר לך כו׳ — והכא היינו טעמא דרבי יהודה, משום דאין מעבירין על האוכלין. ותנא קמא הכי נמי אית ליה אין מעבירין, ומשום הכי ככרות של בעל הבית חייב להכריז, וטעמייהו בעיגול — משום דסימן הבא מאליו הוא, ורבי יהודה סבר הוי סימן. **איכא דאמרי סברוה כו׳** — וכי אתמר לימא כתנאי דאין מעבירין על האוכלין אתמר.

[1] אֲמַר רַב זְבִיד מִשְּׁמֵיהּ דְּרָבָא: [2] אִי סָלְקָא דַּעְתָּךְ סָבַר תַּנָּא קַמָּא סִימָן הֶעָשׂוּי לִידָּרֵס לָא הָוֵי סִימָן, וּמַעֲבִירִין עַל הָאוֹכָלִין, [3] כִּכָּרוֹת שֶׁל בַּעַל הַבַּיִת בִּרְשׁוּת הָרַבִּים אַמַּאי מַכְרִיז?
[4] אֶלָּא אֲמַר רַב זְבִיד מִשְּׁמֵיהּ דְּרָבָא: דְּכוּלֵּי עָלְמָא סָבְרִי סִימָן הֶעָשׂוּי לִידָּרֵס הָוֵי סִימָן, [5] וּמַעֲבִירִין עַל הָאוֹכָלִין. [6] וְהָכָא בְּסִימָן הַבָּא מֵאֵילָיו קָא מִיפַּלְגִי. [7] דְּתַנָּא קַמָּא סָבַר: סִימָן הַבָּא מֵאֵילָיו לָא הָוֵי סִימָן, [8] וְרַבִּי יְהוּדָה סָבַר: הָוֵי סִימָן.
[9] וְרַבָּה אֲמַר לָךְ: דְּכוּלֵּי עָלְמָא סִימָן הֶעָשׂוּי לִידָּרֵס לָא הָוֵי סִימָן, [10] וְאֵין מַעֲבִירִין עַל הָאוֹכָלִין. [11] וְהָכָא בְּסִימָן הַבָּא מֵאֵילָיו קָא מִיפַּלְגִי. [12] תַּנָּא קַמָּא סָבַר: סִימָן הַבָּא מֵאֵילָיו לָא הָוֵי סִימָן, [13] וְרַבִּי יְהוּדָה סָבַר: הָוֵי סִימָן.

LITERAL TRANSLATION

[1] Rav Zevid said in the name of Rava: [2] If it should enter your mind [that] the first Tanna maintains [that] an identifying mark that is liable to be trampled on is not a [valid] identifying mark, and [that] we may pass by food, [3] [then] why does he announce homemade loaves [found] in the public domain?

[4] Rather, Rav Zevid said in the name of Rava: Everyone maintains [that] an identifying mark that is liable to be trampled on is a [valid] identifying mark, [5] and [that] we may pass by food. [6] But here they disagree about an identifying mark that comes about of itself. [7] For the first Tanna maintains [that] it is not a [valid] identifying mark, [8] and Rabbi Yehudah maintains [that] it is a [valid] identifying mark.

[9] But Rabbah can say to you: Everyone [agrees that] an identifying mark that is liable to be trampled on is not a [valid] identifying mark, [10] and [that] we may not pass by food. [11] But here they disagree about an identifying mark that comes about of itself. [12] The first Tanna maintains [that] an identifying mark that comes about of itself is not a [valid] identifying mark, [13] and Rabbi Yehudah maintains [that] it is a [valid] identifying mark.

TRANSLATION AND COMMENTARY

אֲמַר רַב זְבִיד מִשְּׁמֵיהּ דְּרָבָא [1] The Gemara now rejects this analysis: **Rav Zevid said in the name of Rava:** [2] **If it should enter your mind** to think **that** Rabbi Meir, **the first Tanna, maintains that an identifying mark** on an object **that is liable to be trampled on is not** considered **a valid identifying mark and that we are permitted to pass by food,** [3] **then,** in the case of **homemade loaves** found **in the public domain, why does** Rabbi Meir require the finder to **announce** what he has found? For, according to the explanation just given, any identifying marks on the bread will have been defaced, and in the absence of any other identification, there is no point in announcing the discovery of the loaves. Hence, another explanation of the dispute must be sought, as it is obvious that Rabbi Meir must either agree with Rava that an identification mark on an object that is likely to be trampled on is still valid, thus refuting our initial assumption, or he must agree with Rabbah that one is not permitted to leave food lying on the ground, and disagree with Rabbi Yehudah about something else.

אֶלָּא אֲמַר רַב זְבִיד [4] **Rather,** each of the two Amoraim will now explain the difference of opinion between Rabbi Meir and Rabbi Yehudah in accordance with his own opinion. This explanation is identical to that given in the first version: **Rav Zevid said in the name of Rava:** The difference of opinion between the Tannaim should be explained as follows: **Everyone,** both Rabbi Meir and Rabbi Yehudah, **maintains that an identifying mark** on an object **that is liable to be trampled on is** nevertheless considered **a valid identifying mark,** in accordance with Rava's viewpoint. [5] Moreover, both Rabbi Meir and Rabbi Yehudah agree **that we are permitted to pass by food** without picking it up. [6] **But here** Rabbi Meir and Rabbi Yehudah **disagree about** whether **the identifying marks** in the cake of figs or in the loaf are valid, inasmuch as they may have **come about of themselves.** [7] **For** Rabbi Meir, **the first Tanna, maintains that** an identifying mark that may have come about of itself **is not** considered **a valid identifying mark.** [8] **But Rabbi Yehudah maintains that it is** considered **a valid identifying mark.**

וְרַבָּה אֲמַר לָךְ [9] Rav Zevid has so far explained the difference of opinion in our Mishnah in accordance with Rava's viewpoint. The Gemara now offers an explanation of this difference of opinion that is in accordance with Rabbah's viewpoint: **But Rabbah can say to you** that the dispute between the Tannaim can be explained as follows: **Everyone** — both Rabbi Meir and Rabbi Yehudah — **agrees that an identifying mark** on an object **that is liable to be trampled on is not** considered **a valid identifying mark,** and this would be in accordance with Rabbah's opinion. [10] **And** both Rabbi Meir and Rabbi Yehudah agree **that we are not permitted to pass by food** and leave it on the ground. [11] **But here** the Tannaim **disagree** about whether the **identifying marks** in the cake of figs or in the loaf are valid, inasmuch as they may have **come about of themselves.** [12] Rabbi Meir, **the first Tanna, maintains that** such a mark **is not** considered **a valid identifying mark.** [13] **But Rabbi Yehudah maintains that it is** considered **a valid identifying mark.**

LITERAL TRANSLATION

[1] Rav Zevid said in the name of Rava: A general principle concerning lost objects is: [2] If he has said: "Alas for the loss [out of my] pocket!" he has given up hope of it.

[3] And Rav Zevid also said in the name of Rava: [4] The Halakhah is: Small sheaves in the public domain — these are his. [5] In a private domain, if [they were found lying] in a manner [indicating that they had] fallen, they are his; [6] if [they were found lying] in a manner [indicating that they had been] laid down,

[1] אָמַר רַב זְבִיד מִשְּׁמֵיהּ דְּרָבָא: כְּלָלָא דַּאֲבֵידְתָּא: [2] כֵּיוָן דְּאָמַר "וַוי לָהּ לְחֶסְרוֹן כִּיס", מְיָאֵשׁ לֵיהּ מִינָּהּ.

[3] וְאָמַר רַב זְבִיד מִשְּׁמֵיהּ דְּרָבָא: [4] הִלְכְתָא: כְּרִיכוֹת בִּרְשׁוּת הָרַבִּים — הֲרֵי אֵלּוּ שֶׁלּוֹ. [5] בִּרְשׁוּת הַיָּחִיד, אִי דֶּרֶךְ נְפִילָה, הֲרֵי אֵלּוּ שֶׁלּוֹ; [6] אִי דֶּרֶךְ הַנָּחָה,

TRANSLATION AND COMMENTARY

Two further statements by Rav Zevid in the name of Rava now follow, in which the Gemara presents in summary form a number of rulings connected with the previous discussion. These rulings revolve around two main points: (1) The responses of an owner of property, from which one may infer that he has given up hope of recovering something he has lost. (2) A summary of the difference of opinion between Rabbah and Rava, and the final Halakhic decision in the matter.

אָמַר רַב זְבִיד מִשְּׁמֵיהּ דְּרָבָא [1] **Rav Zevid said in the name of Rava: There is a general principle concerning the laws of lost objects:** [2] **Once** we have heard the owner of a lost object **say: "Alas for the loss of money** I have incurred" (or words to that effect), this means that **he has given up hope of** recovering the lost object, even if the object was marked and identifiable, and anyone who finds it after that point may keep it.

וְאָמַר רַב זְבִיד מִשְּׁמֵיהּ דְּרָבָא [3] **And Rav Zevid also said in the name of Rava:** [4] **The Halakhah is:** Unmarked **small sheaves in the public domain belong to the finder,** because in the street the location of an unmarked found object cannot serve as a means of identifying it. Hence, in the case of small sheaves, which are liable to be moved about by passersby, the finder has no obligation to announce his find and the owner no means of identifying it. [5] However, **in a private domain,** where location is significant, only **if** the sheaves **were found lying in a manner indicating that they had fallen** by chance, without the owner's knowledge, **do they belong to the finder,** as it is quite unlikely that the owner will know the precise location where he lost them. [6] But **if they were found lying in a manner indicating that they had been laid down** intentionally by the owner, and if

RASHI

הלכתא כריכות ברשות הרבים כו׳ — כדמוקי לה, בשאין בו סימן. **ברשות היחיד אי דרך נפילה הרי אלו שלו** — דליכא למימר מקום הוי סימן, דהא לא ידע היכא נפיל מיניה. **אי דרך הינוח נוטל ומכריז** — מקום, ולא יניחם שם, שמא ימלאם נכרי ויטלם, ושמא שכחום הבעלים.

NOTES

וַוי לָהּ לְחֶסְרוֹן כִּיס Alas for the loss out of my pocket. This definition of giving up hope is meant to show that there is no need for an explicit statement on the part of the person who has lost property to indicate that he has given up hope of recovering it. He certainly does not need to say explicitly that he has waived any claim to the property which he has lost. It seems that a general statement, such as, "What a shame I lost that money," is enough to indicate that the owner has given up hope in the full Halakhic sense of the term.

אָמַר רַב זְבִיד מִשְּׁמֵיהּ דְּרָבָא הִלְכְתָא Rav Zevid said in the name of Rava: The Halakhah is.... The Rishonim ask: How could Rava issue a Halakhic decision regarding an issue in which he himself was one of the disputants? Because of this question, *Tosefot Rid* amended the text to remove the reference to Rava. *Ritva* suggests that Rava was not issuing a ruling, but merely noting the fact that the accepted ruling was in accordance with his own view. *Rif* chooses to prove from other sources that Rava's view was accepted. *Ramban,* in his commentary on *Rif,* explains that Rav Zevid was not giving a ruling; he was merely reiterating Rava's known position. However, the Halakhah is, in fact, in accordance with Rava, as *Rif* proves from the other sources.

כְּרִיכוֹת בִּרְשׁוּת הָרַבִּים Small sheaves in the public domain. The Gemara ruled (above, 22b) that anticipated *ye'ush* is not effective, and an object does not become ownerless until the owner learns of its loss and gives up hope of recovering it. How, then, can we permit the finder to keep small sheaves that he found in the public domain, since it is possible that the owner does not yet know he has lost them?

It is possible to answer, along the lines suggested by the Gemara (above, 21b), that the sheaves are heavy, so that the owner notices their loss immediately. Even though in our discussion Rava (23a) explains that small sheaves are light and can be moved easily, they still weigh enough to make the owner notice their loss within a very short time (*Ritva*).

אִי דֶּרֶךְ הַנָּחָה If they were found lying in a manner indicating that they had been laid down. The Rishonim

HALAKHAH

וַוי לָהּ לְחֶסְרוֹן כִּיס Alas for the loss out of my pocket. "If someone finds a lost object, even one that has an identifying mark, and knows that before it was found the original owner expressly indicated that he had given up hope of recovering it, he may keep it. The same applies if the lost item has obviously been lying around for a very long time,

BACKGROUND

בְּקִטְרָא דְּצַיָּידָא With a hunter's knot. Throughout the world there are various standard ways of tying knots, and such knots have names, such as the English terms a bowline hitch, a square knot, etc. Similarly, the term קִטְרָא דְּצַיָּידָא mentioned here is the name of a specific kind of knot, though we do not know exactly what it was. The Talmud also mentions a "camel" knot and other types of knots. As noted, the knot in question here is a hunter's knot and was apparently quite common, so it could not serve as an identifying mark. In contrast to standard knots, there are unusual knots or knots of a particular design invented by an individual, and for that reason such knots *can* serve as an identifying mark.

TRANSLATION AND COMMENTARY

they appear to have been forgotten by the owner or in danger of being stolen, the finder must **take them and announce** that he has found **them,** using the location as the means of identification, in accordance with Rava's viewpoint. [1] Moreover, both of **these rules apply** only **to an object which does not have an identifying mark on it.** [2] **But in the case of an object which does have an identifying mark on it,** [3] **there is no difference whether it was found in the public domain or in a private domain,** [4] **whether** it lay **in a manner indicating that it had fallen or in a manner indicating that it had been laid down** intentionally. [5] In all circumstances the finder **must announce** that he has found **it,** since the owner does not despair of recovering items that he knows have an identifying mark, and an identifying mark that is liable to be defaced is still a valid means of identification, in accordance with Rava's viewpoint. Thus the Halakhah follows Rava — that an identifying mark in danger of being defaced is a valid identifying mark, and that location is a valid means of identification.

נוֹטֵל וּמַכְרִיז. [1] וְזֶה וְזֶה בְּדָבָר שֶׁאֵין בּוֹ סִימָן. [2] אֲבָל בְּדָבָר שֶׁיֵּשׁ בּוֹ סִימָן, [3] לָא שְׁנָא בִּרְשׁוּת הָרַבִּים וְלָא שְׁנָא בִּרְשׁוּת הַיָּחִיד, [4] בֵּין דֶּרֶךְ נְפִילָה וּבֵין דֶּרֶךְ הַנָּחָה, [5] חַיָּיב לְהַכְרִיז.

[23B] [6] ״וּמַחֲרוֹזוֹת שֶׁל דָּגִים״. [7] אַמַּאי? לֶהֱוֵי קֶשֶׁר סִימָן! [8] בְּקִטְרָא דְּצַיָּידָא, דְּכוּלֵּי עָלְמָא הָכִי מְקַטְרִי.

LITERAL TRANSLATION

he takes [them] and announces [them]. [1] This [rule] and that [rule apply] to an object which does not have an identifying mark on it. [2] But in [the case of] an object which does have an identifying mark on it, [3] there is no difference [whether it was] in the public domain and there is no difference [whether it was] in a private domain, [4] whether in a manner [indicating that it had] fallen or whether in a manner [indicating that it had been] laid down, [5] he is obliged to announce [it].

[23B] [6] "And strings of fish." [7] Why? Let the knot be an identifying mark.

[8] [The fish were tied] with a hunter's knot, for everyone ties [fish] in this manner.

RASHI

אבל בדבר שיש בו סימן כו׳ — רבא לטעמיה, דאמר: סימן העשוי לידרס הוי סימן.

וּמַחֲרוֹזוֹת שֶׁל דָּגִים [23B] [6] The Gemara now turns to consider the next clause of the Mishnah, which states that **"strings of fish**... belong to the finder." [7] With reference to this the Gemara asks: **Why** should they belong to the finder? In the absence of an identifying mark on the fish, **let the knot** with which they were tied together **be** considered **an identifying mark.** Surely the knots on the strings of fish are individual to their owners, who will rely on their ability to identify their property by means of the knot, and will not give up hope of recovering the property.

בְּקִטְרָא דְּצַיָּידָא [8] The Gemara answers: The Mishnah is referring to a situation where **the fish were tied with the** standard **hunter's knot** used by all fishermen, and since **everyone ties fish in this manner,** such a knot is not a distinctive means of identification.

NOTES

ask: Why is the finder allowed to pick up something that was intentionally left there by the owner? On the contrary, the Gemara (below, 25b) says that if there is even a possibility that an object was left intentionally, it must not be touched. Our commentary follows *Rashi* and other Rishonim, who explain that the Gemara here is referring to a case where the owner clearly forgot the object, or where the object is in an unsafe place. Alternatively, *Ritva* points out that the Gemara (below, 25b) explicitly refers to a case where there was no identifying mark on the object, whereas the Gemara here is referring to a case where the sheaves' location can serve as an identifying mark.

לֶהֱוֵי קֶשֶׁר סִימָן Let the knot be an identifying mark. The Rishonim ask: In an earlier discussion in the first chapter (above, 20b), the Gemara asked: "Can we infer from here that a knot is a valid means of identification?" Thus it would appear that the Gemara there initially assumed that a knot cannot serve as a valid identifying mark, whereas the Gemara here seems to assume that it can. *Ramban* and others explain that it is not possible to use the language of a question in order to prove conclusively what the Halakhah is. Questions are raised as part of the Talmudic debate and are often phrased in deceptively decisive language. The Rishonim do, however, agree that, in fact, the Halakhah is that a knot *can* serve as an identifying mark.

HALAKHAH

since the original owner must eventually have given up hope of recovering it, even though it had an identifying mark." (*Shulhan Arukh, Hoshen Mishpat* 262:5.)

קֶשֶׁר מִדָּה וּמִנְיָן Knots, dimensions, and number. "The dimensions of a lost object, its weight, its location, or the number of items lost are considered definitive identifying marks (סִימָן מוּבְהָק). A knot is also considered a valid form of identification," following the Gemara's conclusion. (Ibid., 262:3; 267:7.)

[1] וְלֶהֱוֵי מִנְיָן סִימָן! [2] בְּמִנְיָנָא דְשָׁוִין. [3] בָּעוּ מִינֵּיהּ מֵרַב שֵׁשֶׁת: [מִנְיָן] הָוֵי סִימָן, אוֹ לָא הָוֵי סִימָן? [4] אֲמַר לְהוּ רַב שֵׁשֶׁת: תְּנִיתוּהָ: [5] ״מָצָא כְּלֵי כֶסֶף וּכְלֵי נְחוֹשֶׁת, גַּסְטְרוֹן שֶׁל אֲבָר, וְכָל כְּלֵי מַתָּכוֹת, [6] הֲרֵי זֶה לֹא יַחֲזִיר עַד שֶׁיִּתֵּן אוֹת אוֹ עַד שֶׁיְּכַוֵּין מִשְׁקְלוֹתָיו״. [7] וּמִדְּמִשְׁקָל הָוֵי סִימָן, [8] מִדָּה וּמִנְיָן נַמִי הָוֵי סִימָן. [9] ״וַחֲתִיכוֹת שֶׁל בָּשָׂר וכו׳״. [10] אַמַּאי? לֶהֱוֵי מִשְׁקְלָא סִימָן! [11] בְּמִשְׁקְלָא דְשָׁוִין.

LITERAL TRANSLATION

[1] But let the number [of fish] be an identifying mark. [2] When the number [of fish on each string] is standard. [3] They asked Rav Sheshet: Is number a [valid] identifying mark, or is it not a [valid] identifying mark?

[4] Rav Sheshet said to them: You have learned it: [5] "[If] he found silver utensils or copper utensils, pieces of lead, or any [other] metal utensils, [6] he should not return [them] unless [the claimant] can give a sign or unless he can state their exact weight." [7] And since weight is a [valid] identifying mark, [8] dimensions and number are also a [valid] identifying mark.

[9] "And pieces of meat...."

[10] Why? Let weight be an identifying mark!

[11] When the weight is standard.

TRANSLATION AND COMMENTARY

וְלֶהֱוֵי מִנְיָן סִימָן [1] The Gemara asks: **But** although the knot used in tying the strings of fish is uniform, **let the number** of fish on the string **be** used as **an identifying mark.**

בְּמִנְיָנָא דְשָׁוִין [2] The Gemara answers: The Mishnah is referring to a situation **where the number of fish on each string was uniform.** Thus, since the number of fish on each string and the manner in which they were tied present no means of identification, the person who finds such a string of fish may keep it.

בָּעוּ מִינֵּיהּ מֵרַב שֵׁשֶׁת [3] In this last question and answer there was an underlying assumption that "number" (מִנְיָן) can serve as a means of identification. This assumption is now questioned. The Rabbis **asked Rav Sheshet: Is** the **number** of items found together considered **a valid** means of **identification, or not?** I.e., if several objects without identification were found together, can the person claiming such items use their number as a means of identifying them?

אֲמַר לְהוּ רַב שֵׁשֶׁת [4] **Rav Sheshet said to them: You have** already **learned** the answer to this question in the following Baraita: [5] **"If one found silver utensils or copper utensils, pieces of lead, or any other metal utensils,** [6] **he is not obliged to return them** to the putative owner **unless the claimant can describe a distinguishing sign** on the utensil, thereby identifying it, **or can state its exact weight."** [7] From this Baraita Rav Sheshet draws the following conclusion: **Since weight is** considered **a valid** means of **identification,** [8] we can infer that the **dimensions** of a lost object **and** the **number** of items found **are also** considered **valid** means of **identification,** even though there is no specific identifying mark on the lost object itself.

וַחֲתִיכוֹת שֶׁל בָּשָׂר [9] The Gemara continues its analysis of the Mishnah by quoting the next clause: **"And pieces of meat...** belong to the finder." [10] With reference to this the Gemara asks: **Why** should they belong to the finder? In the absence of an identifying mark on the meat itself, **let the weight** of the pieces **serve as** a means of **identification.** I.e., let the finder announce that he has found "pieces of meat," and let the owner come and identify them by weight.

בְּמִשְׁקְלָא דְשָׁוִין [11] The Gemara answers: The Mishnah is referring to a place where the butchers cut meat in a uniform manner and **the weight** of the pieces **is uniform.**

RASHI

במנינא דשוין — כבר נהגו הציידין לחרוז כמנין הזה בחרוז אחד. **וגסטרון של אבר** = שברי חתיכות של אבר. **שיכוין משקלותיו** — שיאמר משקלו ויכוין האמת. **במתקלא דשוין** — שנהגו הטבחים לעשות החתיכות במשקל הזה.

SAGES

רַב שֵׁשֶׁת **Rav Sheshet.** A Babylonian Amora of the third and fourth generations. See *Bava Metzia*, Part I, p. 36.

LANGUAGE

גַּסְטְרוֹן **Pieces of lead.** This word is apparently derived from the Greek κασσίτερος, *kassiteros*, which means "tin," and might also have been used to refer to a mixture of lead and tin.

NOTES

מִשְׁקָל מִדָּה וּמִנְיָן **Weight, dimension and number.** Up to now the term "mark" has been used to indicate some unusual feature found on or in the object, such as a stain, a tear, or a flaw, or else something attached to the object, such as a tag or a knot. In these examples the mark distinguishes a certain object from all others. By contrast, weight, number, or dimension are characteristics associated with an object but do not distinguish it from all others in the world. If we accept these qualities as an identifying mark, this implies that a claim of ownership of lost property on that basis is valid. However, a specific identifying mark found on an object or attached to it is regarded as a "definitive identifying mark," whereas other characteristics are not "definitive marks" (see below, 27b, for a discussion of this problem).

חֲתִיכוֹת שֶׁל בָּשָׂר **Pieces of meat.** Why does the Gemara not suggest that the *number* of pieces of meat should serve as identification as it did in the case of fish? *Ritva* explains that number is a valid means of identification only when the objects are attached to each other in some way, as in the case of the fish, which were strung together. But pieces of meat are not customarily strung together. Moreover, even if we were to interpret the Mishnah as referring to strings of pieces of meat, we could answer the same way as we did in the case of strings of fish, by suggesting that the number found on each string was uniform.

¹וְתֶהֱוֵי חֲתִיכָה גּוּפָהּ סִימָן — ²אוֹ דְּדַפְקָא אוֹ דְּאַטְמָא? ³מִי לָא תַּנְיָא: ״מָצָא חֲתִיכוֹת דָּגִים וְדָג נָשׁוּךְ, חַיָּיב לְהַכְרִיז; ⁴חָבִיּוֹת שֶׁל יַיִן, וְשֶׁל שֶׁמֶן, וְשֶׁל תְּבוּאָה, וְשֶׁל גְּרוֹגָרוֹת, וְשֶׁל זֵיתִים, הֲרֵי אֵלּוּ שֶׁלּוֹ״. ⁵הָכָא בְּמַאי עָסְקִינַן? ⁶בְּדְאִיכָּא סִימָנָא בְּפַסְקָא, ⁷כִּי הָא דְּרַבָּה בַּר רַב הוּנָא מְחַתֵּיךְ לֵיהּ אַתְּלָתָא קַרְנָתָא.

LITERAL TRANSLATION

[1]But let the cut itself be an identifying mark — [2]either from the neck or from the thigh. [3]Has it not been taught: "[If] he found pieces of fish or a fish that had been bitten, he must announce [them; [4]but if he found] jars of wine, or of oil, or of grain, or of dried figs, or of olives, they are his." [5]With what are we dealing here? [6]Where there is an identifying mark in the cut, [7]like that of Rabbah bar Rav Huna, [who] cut [meat] into triangles (lit., "on three corners").

TRANSLATION AND COMMENTARY

וְתֶהֱוֵי חֲתִיכָה גּוּפָהּ סִימָן [1]The Gemara asks: **But** even if we accept that under the circumstances weight alone cannot serve as a valid means of identification, **let the cut** from which the meat was taken **be** considered a **valid** means of **identification,** [2]and let the claimant tell us from which part of the animal the meat was taken — **whether from the neck,** for example, **or from the thigh.** [3]The Gemara now reinforces its question with a quotation: **Has it not been taught** in a Baraita: **"If one found pieces of fish or a fish that had been bitten, he must announce** his discovery"? In the case of the fish that was bitten, that fact itself is the means of identification. In the case of the pieces of fish, the means of identification is understood by the Gemara to be the part of the fish from which the pieces come — the head, for example, or the tail. [4]The Baraita continues: **"But if he found jars of wine, or of oil, or of grain, or of dried figs, or of olives, they are his,** beause the jars are of a standard size without distinguishing characteristics." Thus, from this Baraita it would appear that ordinary pieces of fish are treated as if they had an identifying mark, and the reason for this must surely be because we can ask the claimant from which part of the fish they were cut. The same should also apply to pieces of meat.

הָכָא בְּמַאי עָסְקִינַן [5]The Gemara refutes this argument: **With what are we dealing here** in this Baraita, when it states that "pieces of fish" must be announced? [6]**Where there is an identifying mark in the** *way* the fish was **cut,** i.e., where it was cut in an unusual way, [7]**as in the case of Rabbah bar Rav Huna, who would cut meat into triangles.** When Rabbah bar Rav Huna sent meat to his wife by non-Jewish messenger, he was concerned that it might be exchanged for non-kosher meat during the journey. To enable his household to identify the meat as coming from him, he would cut it in an unusual way. From this anecdote the Gemara proves that an unusual way of cutting meat can serve as a valid means of identification.

RASHI

חתיכה גופה סימן — יאמר מאבר פלוני היה. **או דדפקא** — צואר, שמעתי. ומשום רבי יצחק ברבי מנחם שמעתי דדפקא = *פלנק"ן, מקום שדופק כשהוא יגע. **חתיכות דג חייב להכריז** — קא סלקא דעתך כשאין בהן סימן והחתיכה גופה סימן, או מאצל הראש או מן הזנב. **ודג נשוך** — זהו סימן שלו. **הכא במאי עסקינן** — דקתני חתיכות דג חייב להכריז. **בדאיכא סימנא בפסקא** — שלא נחתכה כדרך החותכין. **כי הא דרבה** — כשהיה שולח בשר לאשתו ביד נכרי. **מחתך לה אתלת קרנתא** — עושה החתיכה בת שלש קרנות, כזה

SAGES

רַבָּה בַּר רַב הוּנָא Rabbah bar Rav Huna. The son of Rav Huna, Rabbah was a student of Rav's and his deputy, but received most of his Halakhic education from his father, Rav Huna. He was also closely connected with Rav Ḥisda and was his student and colleague. He discussed Halakhic questions with most of the Sages of his generation. Rabbah bar Rav Huna had close relations with the Exilarch, and we frequently hear of him visiting his house, though he did not regard himself as subject to the Exilarch's authority, and defended his own independence. Rabbah bar Rav Huna was known for being extremely humble, and he spoke of his colleagues with respect, even of the most junior of them. He also had close relations with Rabbah bar Rav Naḥman, and the harsh things he said of him were only said because at the time he did not know Rabbah's true identity. Rabbah bar Rav Huna died in Babylonia and was buried in Eretz Israel. A lament recited to eulogize him at his funeral has been preserved. He had a son, Rava, who was one of the Amoraim of the following generation.

LANGUAGE (RASHI)

פלנק"ן* From the Old French *flanche,* meaning "thigh" or "flank" of an animal.

NOTES

דַּפְקָא The neck. The translation here follows *Rashi*'s first interpretation. He also suggests that the word may mean "flank." Others read רַפְקָא here. This could also mean "neck," through a transposition of the letters in the word מַפְרֶקֶת — "neck bone." Alternatively, it could refer to the foreleg, from the word מַרְפֵּק — "elbow."

רַבָּה בַּר רַב הוּנָא מְחַתֵּיךְ לֵיהּ אַתְּלָתָא קַרְנָתָא Rabbah bar Rav Huna cut meat into triangles. This passage appears in three places in the Talmud. Here and in *Betzah* 28a, *Rashi* explains that Rabbah used a non-Jewish messenger to send meat to his household. Therefore, he cut the meat in this distinctive manner to avoid any danger of non-kosher meat being substituted for his meat. In *Ḥullin* 95b, however, *Rashi* explains that Rabbah cut the meat in this way precisely in order to establish an identifying mark and prevent people from stealing his meat.

HALAKHAH

חֲתִיכוֹת בָּשָׂר וְדָג נָשׁוּךְ Pieces of meat and a fish that has been bitten. "If someone finds pieces of meat cut in a distinctive manner, or a fish that has been bitten, or the like, he must announce his discovery, as such objects are considered to have an identifying mark. But someone who finds pieces of meat cut in the regular fashion may keep them. Even if the claimant can identify the meat as being cut from the neck or the flank or the like, this is not considered valid identification." (*Shulḥan Arukh, Ḥoshen Mishpat,* 262:15.)

LITERAL TRANSLATION

[1][This] is also accurate, for [the Baraita] teaches ["pieces of fish" as being] similar to "a fish that had been bitten." [2]Conclude from this [that this interpretation is correct].

[3]The master said: "[If he found] jars of wine, or of oil, or of grain, or of dried figs, or of olives, they are his." [4]But surely we have learned: "[If he found] jars of wine or jars of oil, he must announce [them]."

[5]Rabbi Zera said in the name of Rav: Our Mishnah [refers] to a sealed [jar].

[6][This] implies that the Baraita [refers] to an open [jar]. [7][But] if [it refers] to an open [jar], it is an intentional loss.

[1]דַּיְקָא נַמִי, דְּקָתָנֵי דּוּמְיָא דְּדָג נָשׁוּךְ. [2]שְׁמַע מִינָּהּ.

[3]אָמַר מָר: ״חָבִיּוֹת שֶׁל יַיִן, וְשֶׁל שֶׁמֶן, וְשֶׁל תְּבוּאָה, וְשֶׁל גְּרוֹגָרוֹת, וְשֶׁל זֵיתִים, הֲרֵי אֵלּוּ שֶׁלּוֹ.״ [4]וְהָא תְּנַן: ״כַּדֵּי יַיִן וְכַדֵּי שֶׁמֶן, חַיָּיב לְהַכְרִיז״!

[5]אָמַר רַבִּי זֵירָא אָמַר רַב: מַתְנִיתִין בְּרָשׁוּם.

[6]מִכְּלָל דְּבָרַיְיתָא בְּפָתוּחַ. [7]אִי בְּפָתוּחַ, אֲבֵידָה מִדַּעַת הִיא!

RASHI

דומיא דדג נשוך — דיש בו סימן. **מתניתין** — דחייב להכריז. **ברשום** — חביותיהם של חרס היו, וגפין אותם במגופת חרס, וטורקין טיט סביב לדבק המגופה שלא יצא ריח היין, ובימי שבט או ניסן שמוכרין בעלי בתים חביות לחנווני כעשר או כחמש עשרה יחד, נוטלין מגופותיהם וטועמין את היין וחוזר וסותמו, וטח בו טיט סביב המגופה, והוא קרוי רושם, ונושאן החנווני לביתו. ומתניתין בחבית רשומה — והיינו סימן, שיש רושמין ויש שנושאין אותה פתוחה למוכרה מיד. **ופרכינן מכלל דברייתא** — דקתני "הרי אלו שלו" — בפתוחה קתני? בתמיה — פשיטא, דהא אבידה מדעת היא, שהניחה פתוחה וכל שקצים ורמשים ונחשים שותים הימנה.

TRANSLATION AND COMMENTARY

דַּיְקָא נַמִי [1]The Gemara now goes on to observe: **This** interpretation **also** has independent support from the language of the Baraita itself, which proves it to be **accurate**. It is clear that the "pieces of fish" referred to in the Baraita were cut in an unusual way, **because the Baraita teaches "pieces of fish" as being similar to "a fish which was bitten"** in a manner suggesting a comparison between the two. Now, since a bite on a fish is certainly very distinctive in appearance and is therefore a particularly convincing means of identification, we can infer that the "pieces of fish" mentioned in this Baraita were cut in an equally distinctive manner. [2]The Gemara now sums up: It is possible to **conclude from this that this interpretation** of the Baraita **is correct**, and that the "pieces of fish" mentioned in the Baraita are in a different category from the "pieces of meat" mentioned in our Mishnah. The latter have no distinguishing characteristics other than the part of the animal from which they were cut, and need not be announced by the finder, as such vague identifying marks are unacceptable.

אָמַר מָר [3]The Gemara now turns to consider in detail the second half of the Baraita just cited: **The author** of the Baraita **said** in the second sentence of the Baraita: **"If he found jars of wine, or of oil, or of grain, or of dried figs, or of olives, they are his."** [4]The Gemara objects: **But surely we have learned** the opposite in the following Mishnah (below, 25a): **"If one found jars of wine or jars of oil, he must announce** that he has found **them."** How can this contradiction be resolved? Surely in both cases we are dealing with utensils lacking any unique features that could serve as a means of identification!

אָמַר רַבִּי זֵירָא [5]In reply **Rabbi Zera said in the name of Rav: The Mishnah,** which requires the finder to announce his discovery, **is referring to a sealed jar.** In the days of the Mishnah, wine producers brought their wine to the wine merchants in standard jars. The merchants then inspected the wine and sealed the jars for transportation to their customers. Since every merchant sealed his jars differently, the Mishnah considered the seals to be distinctive identifying marks.

מִכְּלָל דְּבָרַיְיתָא בְּפָתוּחַ [6]The Gemara now challenges this solution: **This** explanation **implies that the Baraita,** which permits the finder to keep the jar, **is referring to an open jar.** [7]**But if it is referring to an open jar, it is** surely obvious that the finder should be entitled to keep it. What the owner has done in leaving his jar of wine open amounts to nothing less than **an intentional loss.** Leaving wine in an open jar will attract insects, and rodents, and the like, and the wine will soon be spoiled. Thus it was superfluous for the Baraita to state that the jar need not be returned to the owner.

HALAKHAH

חָבִיּוֹת שֶׁל יַיִן וְשֶׁל שֶׁמֶן Jars of wine and oil. "If someone finds sealed jars of wine, oil, or the like before the storehouses have been opened, he must announce his discovery, because the seals on the jars are considered valid identifying marks. But he may keep the jars if he found them after the storehouses were opened. If the jars were not full, the finder must announce his discovery, even if he found them after the storehouses were opened, since the quantity they contain can serve as identification." (Ibid., 262:9, in *Rema*'s gloss.)

TERMINOLOGY

דַּיְקָא נַמִי, דְּקָתָנֵי Lit., it is also precise, for it teaches.... An expression introducing a proof in support of the view previously stated, based on a precise examination of the wording of a Mishnah or a Baraita.

אָמַר מָר It was said above (lit., "the master said"). A term used to cite a passage from a Mishnah or a Baraita previously mentioned, which will now be elucidated at greater length by the Talmud (usually as a continuation of the previous discussion).

וְהָא תְּנַן (וְהָתְנַן) But surely we have learned. This expression usually introduces an objection based on a Mishnah: "But surely we have learned differently in the following Mishnah...?"

BACKGROUND

כַּדִּים וְחָבִיּוֹת Jars. The Amoraim themselves proved that the terms כַּד — "pitcher," in modern Hebrew — and חָבִית — "barrel" or "keg" — are actually synonymous, referring to various sorts of pottery containers which are mainly used to hold liquids. Aside from these general terms we find many others meant to specify vessels of various sizes and shapes, such as פִּיטָס "pythos" — which refers to a very large container, and חֲבִיוֹנָה — "small flask." When the Sages refer to a jar of wine, they generally mean an amphora, a long vessel with two handles and a pointed bottom which could be laid on its side or stood up in special holes made for that purpose.

SAGES

רַבִּי זֵירָא Rabbi Zera. One of the greatest of the third generation of Babylonian Amoraim, he belonged essentially to the Babylonian tradition, and he studied mainly with the disciples of Rav and Shmuel. After some time he immigrated to Eretz Israel, where he studied under Rabbi Yoḥanan and was a colleague of Rabbi Yoḥanan's greatest disciples. When Rabbi Zera reached Eretz Israel he was extremely impressed by the method of learning used there and decided to accept it in full. Accordingly, he undertook 100 fasts in order to forget the Babylonian method of learning. He also fasted so that the fire of Gehinnom should not rule over him, and as he did so the calves of his legs were burned. Because of this event he became known as the "short man with the scorched calves." Rabbi Zera was famous for his great piety, for his modesty, and for being affable and accommodating, and all the members of his generation greatly loved and honored him. He had many disciples throughout Eretz Israel, and quotations of his teachings are plentiful in both the Babylonian and the Jerusalem Talmud. He had a son who was also a Sage, Rabbi Ahavah.

BACKGROUND

רָשׁוּם וּמֵצִיף **Sealed and stoppered.** The covers of vessels were generally separate from them and not tightly fastened (except in the case of vessels that did not have actual covers but were closed with a layer of mud). This practice made it easier to open the vessel to pour from it and also permitted the fermentation of the wine to be completed. The kind of cover that was merely placed on top of a jar but was not firmly attached to it was known as a מֵצִיף. Afterwards, however, particularly when vessels were transported from the winery to the customer's house, the vessel would be tightly sealed (רָשׁוּם) with a layer of mud.

חָבִית רְשׁוּמָה **A sealed jar.**

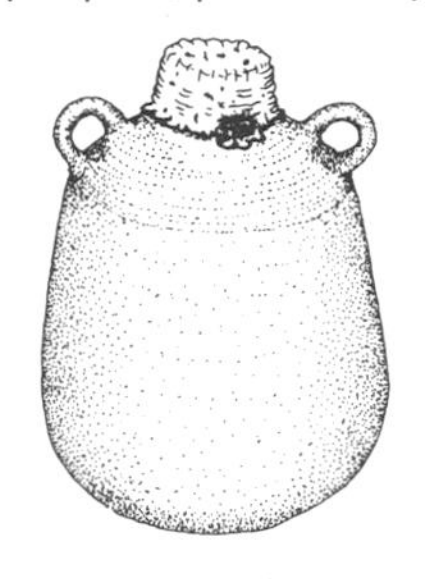

The חָבִית was a large earthenware container used to store different types of liquids, especially wine. Ordinarily, it was closed with an earthenware lid (the מְגוּפָה). But since this lid did not seal the jar completely, it could be

TRANSLATION AND COMMENTARY

אָמַר רַב הוֹשַׁעְיָא [1]Rav Hoshaya said in reply: The Baraita **is referring to a stoppered** but not sealed **jar.** Thus it cannot be considered that the owner has deliberately abandoned the jar; but on the other hand it does not have a distinctive, identifiable seal.

אַבַּיֵי אָמַר [2]**Abaye** explained the apparent contradiction between the Mishnah and the Baraita in a different way and **said: You may even say that both** the Mishnah and the Baraita **refer to sealed jars, and there is** still **no difficulty** in resolving the seeming contradiction between them: [3]**Here,** in the case of the Mishnah, jars must be returned, because **it is** referring to a situation where the jars were found **before** the season when **the storehouses were opened** to the public. Thus, the jars must have been lost by a wine merchant, and the seals on the jars are an excellent way of identifying which wine cellar sealed them. [4]But **here,** in the case of the Baraita, the finder may keep the lost jars, because **it is** referring to a situation where the jars were found **after** the date when **the storehouses were opened,** and the wine merchants had begun selling jars to retailers and to the general public. Thus, the person who sealed the jar originally might already have sold the wine, and since the jar may have passed through the hands of more than one owner, the seal is no longer a valid proof of ownership.

כִּי הָא דְּרַב יַעֲקֹב בַּר אַבָּא [5]The Gemara now quotes an incident in which Abaye gave a practical legal decision in accordance with the distinction he had made between jars of wine found before and those found after the opening of the storehouses: Abaye's viewpoint is illustrated by **the case where Rav Ya'akov bar Abba found a jar of wine after the storehouses had been opened.** [6]**He came before** his teacher, **Abaye,** to ask him what he should do with the jar, whether he could keep it for himself or whether he was obliged to announce that he had found it. Abaye **said to him: "Go and take it for yourself.** There is no need to announce that you found the jar." This incident shows that Abaye was not concerned to find out whether the jar was sealed. According to him, once the storehouses were opened, the seal on a jar was no longer an effective means of identification.

בְּעָא מִינֵּיהּ רַב בִּיבִי [7]**Rav Bivi asked Rav Naḥman:** If someone finds a lost object that does not have on it any means of identification, and there is reason to suppose that the putative owner will know the precise location where the object was found, **is the place** where the object was found considered **a valid identifying mark or not?**

אָמַר לֵיהּ [8]Rav Naḥman **said to him** in reply: **You have** already **learned** the answer to this question in the

[1]אָמַר רַב הוֹשַׁעְיָא: בְּמֵצִיף.
[2]אַבַּיֵי אָמַר: אֲפִילּוּ תֵּימָא אִידֵי וְאִידֵי בְּרָשׁוּם, וְלָא קַשְׁיָא:
[3]כָּאן קוֹדֶם שֶׁנִּפְתְּחוּ הָאוֹצָרוֹת;
[4]כָּאן לְאַחַר שֶׁנִּפְתְּחוּ הָאוֹצָרוֹת.
[5]כִּי הָא דְּרַב יַעֲקֹב בַּר אַבָּא אַשְׁכַּח חָבִיתָא דְּחַמְרָא לְאַחַר שֶׁנִּפְתְּחוּ הָאוֹצָרוֹת. [6]אֲתָא לְקַמֵּיהּ דְּאַבַּיֵי. אָמַר לֵיהּ: "זִיל, שְׁקוֹל לְנַפְשָׁךְ".
[7]בְּעָא מִינֵּיהּ רַב בִּיבִי מֵרַב נַחְמָן: מָקוֹם הָוֵי סִימָן, אוֹ לָא הָוֵי סִימָן?
[8]אָמַר לֵיהּ: תְּנֵיתוּהָ: "מָצָא חָבִיּוֹת שֶׁל יַיִן, וְשֶׁל שֶׁמֶן,

LITERAL TRANSLATION

[1]Rav Hoshaya said: [It refers] to a stoppered [jar].
[2]Abaye said: You may even say that this and that [both refer] to a sealed [jar], and there is no difficulty: [3]Here [it is] before the storehouses were opened; [4]here [it is] after the storehouses were opened.
[5]Like that [case] where Rav Ya'akov bar Abba found a jar of wine after the storehouses had been opened. [6]He came before Abaye. He said to him: "Go, take [it] for yourself."
[7]Rav Bivi asked Rav Naḥman: Is the place a [valid] identifying mark, or is it not a [valid] identifying mark?
[8]He said to him: You have learned it: "[If] he found jars of wine, or of oil,

RASHI

במציף — שהניח מגופה עליה ולא שרקה בטיט. סימן ליכא, ואבידה מדעת נמי ליכא. קודם שנפתחו האוצרות — שעדיין לא הגיע זמן מוכרי החביות, ויחיד בעלמא הוא דעביד — הוי רושם סימן.

NOTES

רָשׁוּם וְנִפְתְּחוּ הָאוֹצָרוֹת **Sealed jars and open storehouses.** The commentary here follows *Tosafot* and others, who explain that according to Rabbi Zera sealed jars could always be identified, because each wine producer had a distinctive seal, whereas according to Abaye this was true only before the wine season. *Rashi,* however, explains that the very presence of the seal, rather than its specific appearance, served as an identifying mark, according to Rabbi Zera. This is because not all jars were sealed, as some were selected for immediate use. Abaye, on the other hand, felt that the presence of a seal could serve as an identifying mark only before the wine season, when very few jars were sold.

TRANSLATION AND COMMENTARY

following Baraita: **"If one found jars of wine, or of oil, [1]or of grain, or of dried figs, or of olives, they are his,"** because the jars are of a standard size without distinguishing characteristics, and the owner gives up hope of recovering them. [2]From this Baraita Rav Naḥman draws the following conclusion: **Now if it should enter your mind** to think **that the place** where a lost object was found **is** considered **a valid identifying mark,** the question arises: Why should the jars belong to the finder? **Let** the finder **announce the place** where he found the lost item, and let the owner specify which item he lost in that place, and claim the item on the basis of this method of identification. The fact that the Baraita discounts such a possibility indicates that location is not a valid means of identification.

אָמַר רַב זְבִיד [3]**Rav Zevid**, who ruled above (23a) that location is a valid means of identification, was not convinced by Rav Naḥman's argument. He **said:** No conclusions can be drawn from this Baraita as to whether, in general, location is a valid means of identification. The case dealt with in the Baraita is a special one, for **with what are we dealing here?** [4]**With** a case where the **jars** were **found on the bank of a river,** where boats carrying merchandise anchor. This particular area on the riverbank was used for the unloading of merchandise, and from here the merchandise would be taken to its destination. It sometimes happened that an owner would forget part of the cargo on the riverbank and it would remain unclaimed. In such circumstances, the location would not be a valid means of identification.

אָמַר רַב מָרִי [5]**Rav Mari** provided an additional explanation of why a location such as the storage area on a riverbank was not considered a valid means of identification and **said: What is the reason why the Rabbis said that the bank of a river is not** considered **a valid identification mark**? I.e., if the finder says: "I found something on the riverbank," and the putative owner identifies the object correctly, why should it not be returned to him? [6]It is **because we say to him: "Just as it happened to you** that you forgot your jars there on the riverbank, **so too it** is possible that it **happened to another person** that he forgot his jars there. It is a public place, used as a temporary storage area by many people." Hence, merely describing one's merchandise in general terms, without citing an identifying mark on the object itself, does not prove that an object found on the riverbank belongs to the claimant.

אִיכָּא דְּאָמְרִי [7]**There are some who report** a somewhat different version of Rav Mari's statement: **Rav Mari said: What is the reason why the Rabbis said that** even **the** precise **location** where an object was found **is not** considered **a valid** identifying mark if the object was found on a riverbank? [8]It is **because we say to** the

[1]וְשֶׁל תְּבוּאָה, וְשֶׁל גְּרוֹגָרוֹת, וְשֶׁל זֵיתִים, הֲרֵי אֵלּוּ שֶׁלּוֹ". [2]וְאִי סָלְקָא דַּעְתָּךְ דְּמָקוֹם הָוֵי סִימָן, לִכְרוֹז מָקוֹם!

[3]אָמַר רַב זְבִיד: הָכָא בְּמַאי עָסְקִינַן? [4]בְּרַקְתָּא דְּנַהֲרָא.

[5]אָמַר רַב מָרִי: מַאי טַעְמָא אָמְרוּ רַבָּנַן רַקְתָּא דְּנַהֲרָא לָא הָוֵי סִימָן? [6]דְּאָמְרִינַן לֵיהּ: "כִּי הֵיכִי דְּאִתְרְמִי לְדִידָךְ, אִתְרְמִי נַמִי לְחַבְרָךְ".

[7]אִיכָּא דְּאָמְרִי: אָמַר רַב מָרִי: מַאי טַעְמָא אָמְרוּ רַבָּנַן מָקוֹם לָא הָוֵי סִימָן? [8]דְּאָמְרִינַן לֵיהּ:

LITERAL TRANSLATION

[1]or of grain, or of dried figs, or of olives, they are his." [2]Now if it should enter your mind that the place is a [valid] identifying mark, let him announce the place.

[3]Rav Zevid said: With what are we dealing here? [4][With jars found] on the bank of a river.

[5]Rav Mari said: What is the reason [why] the Rabbis said that the bank of a river is not a [valid] identifying mark? [6]Because we say to him: "Just as it happened to you, so too it happened to your fellow."

[7]There are some who say: Rav Mari said: What is the reason [why] the Rabbis said that place is not a [valid] identifying mark? [8]Because we say to him:

RASHI

ברקתא דנהרא — והיין בא לעיר בספינה, והלוקחין מפנין הספינה ומניחו על שפת הנהר, ונושאין אחת אחת, ופעמים ששוכח. **איבא דאמרי כו'** — נפקא מינה דאפילו כוון ואמר מקום מוכרח מסוים — לא הוי סימן.

opened at any time. Hence mud was applied around the lid to seal the jar (referred to by the Talmud as רישום — "a seal"). Occasionally people would make marks on the seal or write on it. Unlike the jars, which were of a standard size and shape, the seals were distinctive in appearance, being made individually.

רַקְתָּא דְּנַהֲרָא On the bank of a river. This term is particularly applicable to Babylonia, which has two very large rivers, the Tigris and the Euphrates, as well as many smaller rivers and irrigation canals, some of which are as large as rivers. This extensive irrigation network was also used to transport merchandise, so that the riverbank often served as a dock where merchandise was loaded and unloaded.

NOTES

מַאי טַעְמָא אָמְרוּ רַבָּנַן מָקוֹם לָא הָוֵי סִימָן What is the reason why the Rabbis said that place is not a valid means of identification? Taken literally, Rav Mari appears to be ruling that any claim based on location is invalid, in support of Rav Naḥman, and in opposition to Rav Zevid. Therefore, since no one disputes Rav Mari's reasoning, and since Rav Naḥman's rulings are in any case normally authoritative, the Halakhah should, presumably, follow this opinion. But in fact the

HALAKHAH

רַקְתָּא דְּנַהֲרָא A riverbank. "Ordinarily, the place where an object was found serves as a valid identifying mark. But this does not apply to places where everyone leaves possessions, such as that part of the riverbank where people unload cargo from their boats." (*Shulḥan Arukh, Ḥoshen Mishpat* 262:9, in *Rema*.)

״כִּי הֵיכִי דְּאִתְרְמֵי לְדִידָךְ הַאי מָקוֹם, אִתְרְמֵי נַמִּי לְחַבְרָךְ הַאי מָקוֹם״.
[1]הַהוּא גַּבְרָא דְּאַשְׁכַּח כּוּפְרָא בֵּי מַעֲצַרְתָּא. [2]אֲתָא לְקַמֵּיהּ דְּרַב. אֲמַר לֵיהּ: ״זִיל, שְׁקוֹל לְנַפְשָׁךְ״. [3]חַזְיֵיהּ דַּהֲוָה קָא מְחַסֵּם. [4]אֲמַר לֵיהּ: ״זִיל, פְּלוֹג לֵיהּ לְחִיָּיא בְּרִי מִינֵּיהּ״.
[5]לֵימָא קָא סָבַר רַב מָקוֹם לָא הָוֵי סִימָן?
[6]אָמַר רַבִּי אַבָּא: מִשּׁוּם יֵאוּשׁ בְּעָלִים נָגְעוּ בָּהּ, [7]דַּחֲזָא דְּקָדְחִי בֵּיהּ חִלְפֵי.

LITERAL TRANSLATION

"Just as it happened to you [in] this place, so too it happened to your fellow [in] this place."

[1]A certain person found pitch by a winepress. [2]He came before Rav. He said to him: "Go, take [it] for yourself." [3]He saw that he was hesitating. [4]He said to him: "Go, share part of it with my son Ḥiyya."

[5]Shall we say [that] Rav was of the opinion [that] the place is not a [valid] identifying mark?

[6]Rabbi Abba said: [It was] because of the giving up of hope by the owners [that] they dealt with (lit., "touched") it [in this way], [7]for he saw that weeds had grown on it.

TRANSLATION AND COMMENTARY

putative owner: **"Just as it happened to you** that you forgot your property **in this place, so too** it is possible that **it happened to another person** that he forgot his property precisely **in this place."** The difference between the two versions of Rav Mari's statement is that, according to the second, the bank of a river is of no value as a means of identification, even if the claimant cites the precise location where he left his property.

הַהוּא גַּבְרָא דְּאַשְׁכַּח כּוּפְרָא [1]The Gemara now relates a story to illustrate the points raised in this discussion: **A certain person found pitch by a winepress.** [2]**He came before Rav** to ask him what to do with it, as it contained no identifying mark. Rav **said to him: "Go** and **take it for yourself,** since it has no identifying mark." [3]Rav **saw that the man was hesitating** because he felt it might not be permissible to keep the pitch. [4]Rav then **said to him:** "You have a perfect right to keep the pitch for yourself, but if you prefer, **go** and **share part of it with my son Ḥiyya.** In this way you will realize how certain I am about this ruling, for I am even willing to risk my own son's reputation by allowing him to benefit from the lost pitch."

לֵימָא קָא סָבַר רַב [5]In relation to this decision of Rav, the Gemara now asks: **Shall we say that Rav was of the opinion that the place where a lost object is found is not** considered **a valid identifying mark?** For otherwise he would have decided that the finder of the pitch should announce only the location where it was found, and the owner could have claimed it by identifying the object as pitch.

אָמַר רַבִּי אַבָּא [6]**Rabbi Abba said:** Rav's decision permitting the finder to keep the pitch had nothing to do with the issue of whether location is a valid means of identification or not. Rather, **it was because of the** evident **giving up of hope** of recovering it **on the part of the owner that Rav dealt with** the case **in this way.** [7]**For** Rav **saw that weeds had grown on** the pitch. Rav reasoned that the pitch had been left there for such a long time that the original owner had certainly given up hope of recovering it, and in such a case even an object containing an identifying mark would belong to the finder.

RASHI

כופרא — זפת, דבר שאין בו סימן הוה. **מחסם** — לשון "לא תחסום" (דברים כה) — מגמגם בדבר ולבו נוקפו. **דקדחו ביה חלפי** — *אורטי"א בלעז, גדלו עליה. שמע מינה מימים רבים היה שם, וכבר נואשו הבעלים.

NOTES

Rishonim generally ruled against Rav Naḥman and in favor of Rav Zevid, and declared that location is indeed a valid means of identification. The reason for this unusual ruling is that this question has already been discussed above (22b-23a). In that passage, it was Rabbah who maintained the position of Rav Naḥman (that location is not a valid identification mark), whereas Rava maintained the position of Rav Zevid (that it is valid). The question, however, arises: Why should we rule in favor of Rava and Rav Zevid rather than in favor of Rabbah and Rav Naḥman? *Ba'al HaMa'or* points out that at the end of the passage above (23b), the Gemara expressly ruled that location is indeed a valid means of identification. Other Rishonim, however, are not satisfied, as the Gemara's decision in favor of Rav Zevid and Rava was actually given in the names of Rav Zevid and Rava themselves, and it is impossible to determine whether it was really a decision or whether it was merely a restatement of their position (*Ramban*). *Rif* points out that there is yet another passage (below, 25b) that appears to support the argument that location is valid, thus tilting the scales in its favor. In order to simplify the problem somewhat, the Rishonim explain that Rav Mari's question — "Why did the Rabbis say that location is not valid?" — refers only to a location on a riverbank (*Shittah Mekubbetzet*, explaining *Rashi*). Even though this is obviously a forced interpretation, it has been followed in our commentary, as most Rishonim support it.

פְּלוֹג לֵיהּ לְחִיָּיא בְּרִי מִינֵּיהּ **Share part of it with my son**

HALAKHAH

דְּקָדְחִי בֵּיהּ חִלְפֵי **That weeds had grown on it.** "If someone finds a lost object that has obviously been lying in its present

LANGUAGE

מְחַסֵּם **Hesitating.** There are many variants of this word in manuscripts of the Talmud and in other sources. The three main variants are: מְחַסֵּם; מְהַסֵּם; and מְהַסֵּס. The last mentioned is the one that has entered modern Hebrew, though there are grounds for preferring the others. It is not clear whether this usage of the root "חסם" has a special sense — "to be uncertain" — or whether it is connected to other senses of the root, meaning "to gain strength" or "to overcome."

LANGUAGE (RASHI)

אורטי"א* From the Old French *ortie,* meaning "nettle."

BACKGROUND

כּוּפְרָא Pitch. This is tar or pitch, which was widely used as a sealant in ancient times. In various places tar was distilled from the sap of trees, though in Babylonia local petroleum tar was also used. Here the term refers to tar that has hardened into a solid mass. Such pieces of tar were sometimes left in the open for a long time so that they became cracked, and various plants began to grow in them.

זִיל, פְּלוֹג לֵיהּ לְחִיָּיא בְּרִי מִינֵּיהּ Go, share part of it with my son, Ḥiyya. Rav's son, Ḥiyya, followed in his father's footsteps and also devoted his life to Torah. Because Ḥiyya did so and was not, apparently, a wealthy man, Rav thought that the gift of the found tar would both be helpful to him and convince the finder that it was certainly not forbidden to keep it, since a scholar such as Ḥiyya bar Rav was permitted to derive benefit from it.

SAGES

רַב חִיָּיא בַּר רַב Rav Ḥiyya bar Rav. A Babylonian Amora, Rav's son. Although Rav had other children, only Rav Ḥiyya bar Rav also became a Sage. We know that during Rav's life, and also after his death, Rav's greatest students took care of Rav Ḥiyya, and Rav's friend, Shmuel, showed affection towards him because of his

TRANSLATION AND COMMENTARY

רַבִּי שִׁמְעוֹן בֶּן אֶלְעָזָר [1]The Gemara now turns to consider the next clause of the Mishnah, which states: **"Rabbi Shimon ben Elazar says** that one who finds *anporya* vessels is not required to announce his discovery." The Gemara asks: **What are "*anporya* vessels"?**

אָמַר רַב יְהוּדָה [2]**Rav Yehudah said in the name of Shmuel:** They are **new utensils with which the eye** of the owner **has not yet become familiar.** Such vessels need not be announced, according to Rabbi Shimon ben Elazar, but by implication vessels with which the owner is familiar must be announced.

הֵיכִי דָּמֵי [3]On this point the Gemara now asks: **How is the case** of *anporya* vessels **to be visualized?** [4]**If** these utensils **have an identifying mark** on them, **what difference** does it make **if the eye** of the owner **has not yet become familiar with them?** Surely the owner can identify them by their identifying mark? [5]And **if they do not have an identifying mark** on them, but appear like any other new merchandise, **what difference** would it make **if the eye** of the owner **had become familiar with them?** In this case the owner has no mark by which to identify them. Such utensils are surely no better than used utensils without identifying marks, which the finder is not obliged to announce, because their owner is presumed to have given up hope of recovering them.

לְעוֹלָם [6]The Gemara answers: **In fact,** any marked utensil must be announced, even according to Rabbi Shimon ben Elazar, and even if the owner has not yet become familiar with it. Now, since Rabbi Shimon ben Elazar permitted the finder to keep the *anporya* utensils mentioned here, it is clear that **they do not have an identifying mark** on them. But there is still a Halakhically significant difference between utensils with which the owner has not yet become familiar by sight and utensils with which he is familiar, because there are certain circumstances in which even unmarked lost property is returned on the basis of the claimant's word

[1]"רַבִּי שִׁמְעוֹן בֶּן אֶלְעָזָר אוֹמֵר וכו׳". מַאי "אַנְפּוֹרְיָא"? [2]אָמַר רַב יְהוּדָה אָמַר שְׁמוּאֵל: כֵּלִים חֲדָשִׁים שֶׁלֹּא שְׂבָעָתָן הָעַיִן. [3]הֵיכִי דָּמֵי? [4]אִי אִית בְּהוּ סִימָן, כִּי לָא שְׂבָעָתָן הָעַיִן מַאי הָוֵי? [5]אִי דְּלֵית בְּהוּ סִימָן, כִּי שְׂבָעָתָן הָעַיִן מַאי הָוֵי? [6]לְעוֹלָם, דְּלֵית בְּהוּ סִימָן,

LITERAL TRANSLATION

[1]"Rabbi Shimon ben Elazar says, etc." What are "*anporya* [utensils]"?

[2]Rav Yehudah said in the name of Shmuel: New utensils with which the eye has not [yet] become familiar (lit., "satiated").

[3]What is it like? [4]If they have an identifying mark, what [difference] is there if the eye has not become familiar with them? [5]If they do not have an identifying mark, what [difference] is there if the eye has become familiar with them?

[6]In fact, they do not have an identifying mark,

RASHI

שלא שבעתן — עדיין לא הורגל בראייתן ותשמישן שיהא מכירן יפה. ולשון 'אנפוריא' נוטריקון: אין פה ראיה.

NOTES

Ḥiyya. Obviously it is forbidden for a Rabbi to benefit materially from his own ruling. However, in this case, Rav was not ordering the man to give his son the pitch. He was merely suggesting a way of dispelling his doubts. Technically it might even have been permissible for Rav himself to take the pitch, but he did not do so, in order not to appear to be acting in a manner that might seem improper to the beholder (*Rabbi Ya'akov Emden*).

HALAKHAH

position for a very long time, he may keep it, since the original owner must have given up hope of recovering it. This applies even if the object has a distinguishing mark." (*Shulḥan Arukh, Ḥoshen Mishpat* 262:5.)

כֵּלִים חֲדָשִׁים וּטְבִיעַת עַיִן New utensils and recognition by sight. "One who finds a utensil of a standard type may keep it if the utensil is brand new. But if the utensil is used, the finder must announce his discovery, because it may belong to a Rabbinic scholar who could recognize it by sight. Only those Rabbinic scholars who never lie — except with regard to those matters which the Talmud permitted — are considered Rabbinic scholars for the purposes of this law." (Ibid., 262:21, following our Gemara.) The requirement to announce the discovery of standard utensils applies only in a place frequented by Rabbinic scholars, such as a synagogue. (*Rema*, based on *Ra'avad* and *Ramban*.) If such an object was found elsewhere, it is not necessary to announce it. But if a Rabbinic scholar recognizes it, many opinions hold that it is necessary to return it to him. (*Kesef Mishneh* on *Rambam, Hilkhot Gezelah Va'Avedah* 14:13.) Even though most Talmudic regulations regarding Rabbinic scholars are not applicable today, this law still applies. (*Taz* on the passage in *Shulḥan Arukh*.)

father. Rav had a particular love for this son and derived pleasure from his wisdom, even as a child; he also took care to give him much advice and strengthened him, since his health was delicate. Rav Ḥiyya's son, Rav Shimi bar Rav Ḥiyya, was one of the most brilliant Amoraim of the following generation.

LANGUAGE

אַנְפּוֹרְיָא New vessels. This word is derived from the Greek ἐμπορία, *emporia*, which means "merchandise." *Anporya* vessels were manufactured and sold commercially. They were not handmade for a specific purpose but were meant for general sale.

SAGES

רַב יְהוּדָה (בַּר יְחֶזְקֵאל) Rav Yehudah (bar Yeḥezkel). The name Rav Yehudah without any patronymic in the Gemara refers to Rav Yehudah bar Yeḥezkel, one of the greatest Babylonian Amoraim of the second generation. He was the founder of the Pumbedita Yeshivah. According to tradition he was born on the day Rabbi Yehudah HaNasi died (*Kiddushin* 72b). His father, Rav Yeḥezkel, was an Amora of the first generation, and Rami bar Yeḥezkel was his brother. He studied under Rav and Shmuel, and Shmuel used to call him שִׁינָנָא — "the sharp-witted one." Rav Sheshet was his colleague, and among his students were Rabbah, Rav Yosef, Rabbi Zera and others. Eretz Israel was very dear to him, but he nevertheless strongly opposed the immigration of his students to Eretz Israel. The Hebrew language was also very dear to him, and he used it frequently.

BACKGROUND

שְׂבָעָתָן הָעַיִן With which the eye has become familiar. In ancient times, when manufacturing was not completely mechanized, even standard vessels, while not having a specific identifying mark, were different from each other in some way, so

[1]נָפְקָא מִינָּהּ לְאַהֲדוּרֵי לְצוּרְבָא מֵרַבָּנַן בִּטְבִיעוּת עֵינָא. [2]שְׁבָעָתָן הָעַיִן, [3]קִים לֵיהּ בְּגַוַּיְיהוּ, וּמְהַדְּרִינַן לֵיהּ. [4]כִּי לָא שְׁבָעָתָן הָעַיִן, [5]לָא קִים לֵיהּ בְּגַוַּיְיהוּ, וְלָא מְהַדְּרִינַן לֵיהּ.

[6]דַּאֲמַר רַב יְהוּדָה אֲמַר שְׁמוּאֵל: [7]בְּהָנֵי תְּלָת מִילֵּי עָבִידִי רַבָּנַן דִּמְשַׁנּוּ בְּמִלַּיְיהוּ:

LITERAL TRANSLATION

[1] [and] the practical difference (lit., "it comes out from it") is with regard to returning [them] to a scholar on [the basis of] recognition (lit., "imprinting") by sight. [2] [If] the eye has become familiar with them, [3] he is certain about them, and we return [them] to him. [4] If the eye has not become familiar with them, [5] he is not certain about them, and we do not return [them] to him.

[6] For Rav Yehudah said in the name of Shmuel: [7] In these three matters Rabbis are liable to alter their words:

TRANSLATION AND COMMENTARY

alone. [1] **The practical difference** concerning whether or not the owner is familiar with the utensils **is with regard to returning them to a scholar on the basis of** his **recognition** of them **by sight.** Sometimes the owner of an item which does not have any distinctive marks on it will recognize it, even though he cannot describe any unique features that the item possesses. [2] Accordingly, if a Rabbinic scholar, who is presumed to be honest and whose word is trusted without additional external proof, identifies a utensil as his own through visual recognition but without citing an identifying mark, and **if** the utensils have been in his possession long enough for **his eye to have become familiar with them,** [3] so that **he will be certain about** his identification of them, then **we return them to him** on the basis of his recognition by sight and of his word alone. [4] But **if** the utensils are very new and have **not** been in his possession long enough for **his eye** to have **become familiar with them,** such utensils are called *anporya.* [5] The scholar **will not be certain about** his identification of the lost utensils, **and** in such circumstances **we do not return them to him,** even though he is scrupulously honest, as it is possible that he is making a mistake. Thus, the statement of Rabbi Shimon ben Elazar in our Mishnah is intended to teach us that new utensils need not be returned even if they are claimed by a Rabbinic scholar, since the scholar was presumably not yet familiar enough with them to recognize them by sight.

דַּאֲמַר רַב יְהוּדָה אֲמַר שְׁמוּאֵל [6] The Gemara now brings support for its interpretation by quoting an authoritative statement of Rav Yehudah himself: **For Rav Yehudah said in the name of Shmuel:** [7] A Rabbi always tells the truth. **In** the following **three matters** alone **Rabbis are liable to alter their words,** and the accuracy of

RASHI

נפקא מינה כו׳ — וכגון דזה התובען צורבא מרבנן הוא.

NOTES

לְאַהֲדוּרֵי לְצוּרְבָא מֵרַבָּנַן Returning them to a Rabbinic scholar. It would appear from the Gemara here that the finder is only obliged to announce the discovery of standard merchandise that is not brand new if it belongs to a Rabbinic scholar. But the announcement is made precisely because the finder does not know who the owner is. So how is he supposed to know whether or not the object he found belongs to such a scholar? *Ra'avad* suggests that announcements be posted only in synagogues and study houses, and if there is no response after a few days, it may be assumed that the object was not lost by a scholar. Others explain that an announcement need be made only if the object was found in a place frequented by Rabbinic scholars (*Ramban*). Others explain that the Gemara is referring only to those lost objects that ordinarily belong to Rabbinic scholars, such as holy books and so on (*Rash Vidash*).

לְאַהֲדוּרֵי לְצוּרְבָא מֵרַבָּנַן Returning lost objects to a scholar. A Torah scholar is not merely someone who has studied and who knows the Torah, but rather someone who applies what he has learned. Moreover, a Torah scholar is called upon not only to fulfill all the obligations incumbent on any Jew, but also to be particularly scrupulous in his actions, and to be stricter with himself than an ordinary person would be. The privileges of a Torah scholar depend upon the many particular obligations he takes upon himself, and if he does not live up to these obligations, he does not belong in the category of Torah scholars. The trustworthiness of a Torah scholar derives from the assumption that he is more scrupulous than other people in speaking nothing but the truth, and would not claim something that did not belong to him.

בִּטְבִיעוּת עֵינָא On the basis of recognition by sight. "Recognition by sight" is the ability to identify a familiar person or object by his/its general appearance, rather than by a specific identifying mark that can be described in words. Recognition by sight is actually superior to an identifying mark as a means of identification. For example, a person may be able to pick out his friend in a crowd from a considerable distance, and still not be able to describe him to other people. Recognition by sight is a universal human capability, and is obviously not restricted to Rabbinic scholars. But because it cannot be verified, it can only be relied upon when claimed by people known to be scrupulously honest (see *Tosafot, Bava Metzia* 19a, under אבל).

דִּמְשַׁנּוּ בְּמִלַּיְיהוּ To alter their words. *Tosafot* and other commentators point out that the list given here of things regarding which a Torah scholar may alter the truth is not exhaustive, for there are things about which anyone, including a Torah scholar, may tell untruths for reasons of common courtesy, such as in professing to admire something which someone else has acquired. Nor, of course, does this list include instances where it is permissible, even obligatory, to lie, such as in order to restore good relations between two people, especially a married couple.

that it was possible to recognize each individual vessel. However, before a person could recognize an object that lacked a specific identifying mark, he had to have had contact with it for a certain time, and that period was known as שְׂבִיעַת הָעַיִן — "letting the eye get its fill of it."

LANGUAGE

צוּרְבָא מֵרַבָּנַן A Rabbinical scholar. This is a common term for a scholar (usually a young scholar) in the Talmud, though its source and precise significance are not clear. Some suggest that it derives from the root צרב, meaning something hot, burning with the fire of Torah. Others suggest that it is derived from the Arabic word meaning hard or strong, for indeed a צוּרְבָא מֵרַבָּנַן has a sharp and powerful mind (*Rav Hai Gaon*).

CONCEPTS

טְבִיעוּת עֵינָא Recognizing something by sight. The ability to recognize or identify something even though it does not have any distinguishing marks (i.e., the ability to recognize an article or a person by its or his general appearance). טְבִיעוּת עֵינָא literally means the "imprinting of the eye," i.e., the ability to recognize things imprinted on the memory by sight.

SAGES

שְׁמוּאֵל Shmuel. One of the greatest of the Babylonian Amoraim of the first generation, Shmuel was Rav's colleague. His father, Abba bar Abba, was a Sage of the city of Neharde'a. In addition to his prominence as a Torah scholar, Shmuel became a great expert in medicine and astronomy, and was especially famous as an eye doctor. Because of his knowledge of astronomy he was known as שְׁמוּאֵל יַרְחִינָאָה — "Shmuel the expert in months." Because of his profound knowledge in civil matters, the Halakhah follows him in that area. Among his students were Rav Naḥman, who inherited his position as head of the yeshivah in Neharde'a, and Rav Yehudah (bar Yeḥezkel), who founded the Pumbedita Yeshivah.

TRANSLATION AND COMMENTARY

their statements is not to be relied upon: [1](1) **With regard to a tractate.** If a Rabbinic scholar is asked whether he has studied a particular tractate, he may answer, out of modesty, that he has not, even if in fact he has studied it. [2](2) **And** similarly **with regard to a bed.** If a Rabbinic scholar is asked whether he has slept on a particular bed, he may reply that he has not, so as to spare himself unnecessary embarrassment. [24A] [3](3) **And** similarly **with regard to a guesthouse.** If a Rabbinic scholar is asked about the hospitality he received in a certain place, he may reply somewhat less enthusiastically than the facts would warrant. His purpose in doing this is to save his host from being exploited by unscrupulous people who might abuse his hospitality and cause him serious financial loss.

[1]בְּמַסֶּכֶת, [2]וּבְפוּרְיָא, [24A] [3]וּבְאוּשְׁפִּיזָא.
[4]מַאי נָפְקָא מִינָּהּ?
[5]אֲמַר מָר זוּטְרָא: לְאַהֲדוּרֵי לֵיהּ אֲבֵידְתָא בְּטְבִיעוּת עֵינָא. [6]אִי יָדְעִינַן בֵּיהּ דְּלָא מְשַׁנֵּי אֶלָּא בְּהָנֵי תְּלָת, [7]מְהַדְּרִינַן לֵיהּ. [8]וְאִי מְשַׁנֵּי בְּמִילֵּי אַחֲרִינֵי, [9]לָא מְהַדְּרִינַן לֵיהּ.

LITERAL TRANSLATION

[1]With regard to a tractate, [2]and with regard to a bed, [24A] [3]and with regard to a guesthouse.
[4]What [practical] difference does it make?
[5]Mar Zutra said: To return a lost article to him on [the basis of] recognition by sight. [6]If we know about him that he does not alter [the truth] except in these three [matters], [7]we return [it] to him. [8]But if he alters [the truth] in other matters, [9]we do not return [it] to him.

RASHI

במסכת — יש בידך מסכת פלוני סדורה בגירסא או לאו? ואף על גב שסדורה היא לו — יאמר לו לאו. ומדת ענוה היא. **בפוריא** — שימשת מטתך? יאמר לאו, מדת צניעות הוא. **באושפיזא** — שאלוהו על אושפיזו אם קבלו בסבר פנים יפות, ואמר לאו — מדה טובה היא, כדי שלא יקפצו בו בני אדם שאינן מהוגנין לבא תמיד עליו ויכלו את ממונו.

מַאי נָפְקָא מִינָּהּ [4]The Amoraim studying Rav Yehudah's statement asked: **What practical difference does it make?** What Halakhic relevance does this statement of Rav Yehudah in the name of Shmuel have?

אֲמַר מָר זוּטְרָא [5]**Mar Zutra said** in reply: It has a bearing on the following problem that we have been discussing: Whether **to return a lost article to** its owner **on the basis of recognition by sight** alone, without recourse to formal means of identification. [6]**If we know that** the Rabbinic scholar claiming a lost article **does not alter the truth except in these three matters,** while in all other matters he scrupulously avoids uttering a falsehood, [7]**we return** the lost object **to him** if he claims to recognize it by sight, as his honesty is above suspicion. [8]**But if he alters the truth in** regard to **other matters** apart from those three mentioned above, [9]**we do not return** the lost object **to him** on the basis of his claim that he recognizes it by sight, because he may be lying. In such a case a Rabbinic scholar is treated no differently from anyone else, and must either produce evidence supporting his claim or a convincing identifying mark.

NOTES

בְּמַסֶּכֶת With regard to a tractate. The commentary here follows *Rashi*'s interpretation. *Rambam*, however, understood the Gemara as follows: A Rabbinic scholar is permitted to speak untruthfully about which tractate he is learning, so as to avoid being questioned on a particular subject. Since the Torah requires scholars to answer questions, *Rambam* must be referring to a situation where it would not be appropriate for the scholar to answer the question, either because he has not yet attained sufficient proficiency in the subject (*Leḥem Mishneh*), or because an expert on the subject is available nearby and the question should be addressed to him (*Be'er HaGolah*).

בְּמַסֶּכֶת With regard to a tractate. *Tosafot* explains that there is a difference between (1) someone who is asked something for the purpose of information, in which case it is not fitting for a Torah scholar to say he does not know, but must instead give a full answer, and (2) a case where people wish to determine whether a certain person is a great scholar. In the latter case, for the sake of modesty, the person asked may alter the truth and say he has not studied something, or that he is not well versed in it.

וּבְפוּרְיָא And with regard to a bed. In our commentary we have used the second interpretation found in *Tosafot*, giving the literal translation of פּוּרְיָא as a bed. *Rashi*, however, believes the term is meant as a euphemism for sexual relations with a woman, and that it is not fitting for a Torah scholar to say he has had such relations. *Tosafot* comments that such a question is not common among polite people, and proposes a different interpretation: If a Torah scholar was absent from the House of Study because he was with his wife and had to immerse himself in a ritual bath afterwards and therefore could not come to the House of Study on time, it would not be fitting for him to give the real reason, and he is permitted to invent some other explanation.

וּבְאוּשְׁפִּיזָא And with regard to a guesthouse. The commentary here follows the interpretation of most of the Rishonim, who explain that a scholar is allowed to describe the way his host treated him in less than glowing terms, so that the host will not be overwhelmed with unwanted guests. *Rambam* (*Hilkhot Gezelah Va'Avedah* 14:13), however, explains that the scholar is permitted to claim that he had lodged with a person other than his real host.

וְאִי מְשַׁנֵּי בְּמִילֵּי אַחֲרִינֵי Altering the truth in other matters. The Rishonim ask: It is stated elsewhere (*Yevamot* 65b) that it is proper to tell a lie for the sake of maintaining peace between people. Why, then, is this case not listed here as well? *Tosafot* answers: All three examples mentioned here

LANGUAGE

אוּשְׁפִּיזָא Guesthouse. The source of this word is the Persian *ispanj,* which means "hotel."

BACKGROUND

אוּשְׁפִּיזָא Guesthouse. In Talmudic times very few Houses of Study arranged to feed and lodge their students, and those who came to study, especially during the twice-yearly study sessions lasting a month (יַרְחֵי כַּלָּה), generally took lodgings in private homes. Occasionally people volunteered to take in students without charge, and the man of the house would join in the studies. However, even when the owner of the house received money for the lodgings, he would not take the normal fee, but rather give a reduction in order to contribute to the study of Torah. Information about the generosity of a certain host, whether in giving free lodgings or in providing particularly polite service, might cause too many people to come and exploit his generosity, thus causing him considerable monetary loss.

TERMINOLOGY

מַאי נָפְקָא מִינָּהּ What difference does it make? I.e., what practical consequences does it have? This expression is used when a problem raised by the Gemara seems to be merely academic.

LITERAL TRANSLATION

[1] A silver cup was stolen from the host of Mar Zutra the Pious. [2] He saw one of the students who was washing his hands and drying [them] on the cloak of his fellow. [3] He said: "This is the one, for he does not care about the property of his fellow." [4] He tied him up and he confessed.

[5] It was taught: "Rabbi Shimon ben Elazar agrees about new utensils with which the eye has become familiar that he must announce [them]. [6] And the following are new utensils with which the eye has not [yet] become familiar that he is not obliged to announce: [7] For example, poles (lit., "branches") of needles, and knitting needles,

[1] מָר זוּטְרָא חֲסִידָא אִגְּנֵיב לֵיהּ כָּסָא דְּכַסְפָּא מֵאוּשְׁפִּיזָא. [2] חַזְיָא לְהַהוּא בַּר בֵּי רַב דְּמָשֵׁי יָדֵיהּ וְנָגֵיב בִּגְלִימָא דְּחַבְרֵיהּ. [3] אֲמַר: "הַיְינוּ הַאי, דְּלָא אִיכְפַּת לֵיהּ אַמָּמוֹנָא דְּחַבְרֵיהּ". [4] כְּפָתֵיהּ וְאוֹדִי.

[5] תַּנְיָא: "מוֹדֶה רַבִּי שִׁמְעוֹן בֶּן אֶלְעָזָר בְּכֵלִים חֲדָשִׁים שֶׁשְּׂבָעָתָן הָעַיִן שֶׁחַיָּיב לְהַכְרִיז. [6] וְאֵלּוּ הֵן כֵּלִים חֲדָשִׁים שֶׁלֹּא שְׂבָעָתָן הָעַיִן שֶׁאֵינוֹ חַיָּיב לְהַכְרִיז: [7] כְּגוֹן, בַּדֵּי מְחָטִין, וְצִינּוֹרִיּוֹת,

RASHI

אגניב ליה כסא דכספא — כלי של אושפיזו היה. **בדי מחטין וצינוריות** — לקמיה מפרש: בדי מחטין — שתולין בו מחטין. **וצינוריות** — מזלגות קטנים שטוות בו זהב.

TRANSLATION AND COMMENTARY

מָר זוּטְרָא חֲסִידָא [1] Continuing the previous discussion regarding the strict moral demands made of Rabbinic scholars, the Gemara relates: **A silver cup was stolen from the host of Mar Zutra the Pious,** and they did not know the identity of the thief. [2] Then Mar Zutra **saw one of the students washing his hands and drying them on someone else's cloak.** [3] Mar Zutra **said: "This is the** thief, **for he** has shown that he **does not care about other people's property,** and such a person is capable of theft." [4] Mar Zutra **tied** the student **up** and interrogated him, **and he confessed** that he had stolen the cup.

תַּנְיָא [5] The Gemara now proceeds to examine Rabbi Shimon ben Elazar's point of view in greater detail: **It was taught** in a Tosefta (*Bava Metzia* 2:1): "**Rabbi Shimon ben Elazar agrees** with the opinion of the first Tanna in our Mishnah **with regard to new utensils with which the eye has become familiar, that** the finder **must announce** that he has found such articles." He disagrees with the first Tanna only with regard to *anporya* utensils — new utensils with which the eye has not yet become familiar. [6] The Tosefta continues: "**And the following are new utensils with which the eye has not yet become familiar,** and which, according to Rabbi Shimon ben Elazar, the finder **is not obliged to announce:** [7] **For example, poles of needles, and knitting needles, and strings of axes,** which are all articles that are difficult to identify with any certainty when they are brand new." The Tosefta singles out the above items

BACKGROUND

בַּר בֵּי רַב Student. The literal meaning of this expression is someone who frequents a Sage's house, i.e., someone who studies Torah, a scholar. Generally, בַּר בֵּי רַב refers to a young student who has just begun his studies. An older scholar, who has already gained a considerable degree of knowledge, is called צוּרְבָא מֵרַבָּנָן, and someone who has learned even more is called simply חַד מֵרַבָּנָן, one of the Sages.

צִינּוֹרִיּוֹת Knitting needles. In this context the word refers to a piece of metal which, depending on its size, could be used for a number of purposes. Small צִינּוֹרִיּוֹת were used as knitting needles and also to clean lantern wicks. Larger צִינּוֹרִיּוֹת were used as pokers in fireplaces or to remove objects from the fire.

NOTES

are special cases of the "for the sake of maintaining peace" rule. They were mentioned because they are the most common examples.

אִגְּנֵיב לֵיהּ כָּסָא דְּכַסְפָּא A silver cup was stolen. *Rashi* emphasizes that the cup belonged to the host, not to Mar Zutra. *Rabbi Ya'akov Emden* asks: Surely this point is obvious from the Gemara itself? Why does *Rashi* need to emphasize it? He explains: Even though it is permitted to take the law into one's own hands in the manner described in our passage, it is not considered behavior befitting a scholar, and the story is being brought precisely as an example of Mar Zutra's piety. Therefore, it is important to remember that the cup did not belong to Mar Zutra, and that it is forbidden to be over-scrupulous in one's behavior if someone else (the rightful owner of the cup) will suffer loss as a result.

חַזְיָא לְהַהוּא בַּר בֵּי רַב He saw one of the students. It seems that the connection between this story and the previous passage can be explained as follows: A person who has no respect for other people's property should be presumed to be dishonest, even if he is a Rabbinic scholar who would ordinarily be considered trustworthy. It is permissible to treat him with suspicion, and to accuse him of committing theft, even without concrete evidence (*Meiri*).

כְּפָתֵיהּ וְאוֹדִי He tied him up and he confessed. The translation and commentary follow some of the Rishonim. Others explain that he pressured him to confess by threatening to excommunicate him, others that he used force in the interrogation (*Shittah Mekubbetzet*).

מוֹדֶה רַבִּי שִׁמְעוֹן בֶּן אֶלְעָזָר Rabbi Shimon ben Elazar agrees. The difference of opinion between Rabbi Shimon ben Elazar and the first Tanna in our Mishnah can be summarized as follows: Rabbi Shimon ben Elazar maintains that a lost new utensil with which the owner has not yet had time to become familiar, and which has no identifying marks, does not need to be announced, because the owner would not yet have been sufficiently familiar with the object to be able to recognize it by sight. But a lost new object with which the owner *has* had time to become familiar must be announced, even if it bears no identifying marks, if it was found in a place frequented by Rabbinic scholars, because it is possible that it was lost by a scholar who still hopes to recover it through his ability to recognize it by sight. The first Tanna maintains, however, that even a lost new utensil with which the owner has not yet had time to become familiar must be announced, if it was found in a place frequented by such scholars. But if a lost new utensil was found in a place not frequented by such scholars, both the first Tanna and Rabbi Shimon ben Elazar agree that it belongs to the finder, even if the owner has had sufficient time to become familiar with it (*Tosafot*).

בַּדֵּי מְחָטִין Bundles of needles. Rabbi Shimon ben Elazar

TRANSLATION AND COMMENTARY

because these specific items and others like them cannot be recognized by sight when they are new. Other new articles, however, can be recognized by sight. [1]The Tosefta continues: **"All those** objects **that were mentioned** in this list, and that the finder is not obliged to announce, **when are they permitted** to be retained by the finder? [2]**When he found them** singly, i.e., **one** set of needles or **one** string of axes. [3]**But if he found them in twos,** or in greater numbers, **he must announce** that he has found **them,** since the number of objects found can serve as a means of identification."

מַאי בַּדֵּי [4]The Gemara asks parenthetically: **What** does the term *baddei* (בַּדֵּי) mean literally? [5]The Gemara answers: Wooden **branches.**

וְאַמַּאי קָרוּ לֵיהּ בַּדֵּי [6]The Gemara asks: **And why do** people **call them "branches"?** [7]The Gemara answers: **Something on which people hang things is called a branch** (בַּד). [8]The Gemara now provides a Talmudic source in support of this answer: The use of the word "branch" here is **like** the usage **stated elsewhere** (*Sukkah,* 44b), in connection with the laws of the willow branch: "A willow from which some of its leaves have fallen is valid for use in the mitzvah of 'taking the willow' on the Festival of Sukkot, [9]even if **one leaf** is still attached to **one branch** [בַּד]."

וְכֵן הָיָה רַבִּי שִׁמְעוֹן בֶּן אֶלְעָזָר [10]The Gemara now considers the next clause of the Tosefta just cited: **"And similarly, Rabbi Shimon ben Elazar used to say: [11]Someone who rescues an article from a lion, or from a bear, or from a leopard, or from a panther, [12]or from a rising sea, or from an overflowing river,** may keep it, as it is

וּמַחֲרוֹזוֹת שֶׁל קַרְדּוּמּוֹת. [1]כָּל אֵלּוּ שֶׁאָמְרוּ, אֵימָתַי מוּתָּרִים? [2]בִּזְמַן שֶׁמְּצָאָן אֶחָד אֶחָד. [3]אֲבָל מְצָאָן שְׁנַיִם שְׁנַיִם, חַיָּיב לְהַכְרִיז". [4]מַאי בַּדֵּי? [5]שׁוֹכֵי. [6]וְאַמַּאי קָרוּ לֵיהּ בַּדֵּי? [7]דָּבָר דְּתָלוּ בֵּיהּ מִידֵּי, בַּד קָרוּ לֵיהּ; [8]כִּי הַהוּא דִּתְנַן הָתָם: [9]"עָלֶה אֶחָד בְּבַד אֶחָד". [10]"וְכֵן הָיָה רַבִּי שִׁמְעוֹן בֶּן אֶלְעָזָר אוֹמֵר: [11]הַמַּצִּיל מִן הָאֲרִי, וּמִן הַדּוֹב, וּמִן הַנָּמֵר, וּמִן הַבַּרְדְּלָס, [12]וּמִן זוּטוֹ שֶׁל יָם, וּמִשְּׁלוּלִיתוֹ שֶׁל נָהָר;

LITERAL TRANSLATION

and strings of axes. [1]All these that they mentioned, when are they permitted? [2]When he found them one [by] one. [3]But [if] he found them two [by] two, he must announce [them]."

[4]What are *"baddei"* (בַּדֵּי)?

[5]Branches.

[6]And why do they call them "branches" (בַּדֵּי)? [7]Something on which [people] hang things, they call a branch (בַּד); [8]like that which was stated elsewhere: [9]"One leaf on one branch [בַּד]."

[10]"And Rabbi Shimon ben Elazar also used to say: [11]Someone who rescues [an article] from a lion, or from a bear, or from a leopard, or from a panther, [12]or from a rising sea, or from an overflowing river;

RASHI

אחת אחת – כד אחת ומחרוז אחד. **חייב להכריז** – דמנין הוי סימן. **שוכי** – ענפים של אילן. **עלה אחד בבד אחד** – במסכת סוכה (מד,ב), גבי ערבה שנשרו מקצת עליה ונשתיירו בה שלשה עלין לחין, ואיכא דאמרי אפילו עלה אחד בבד אחד כשירה. **ברדלס** – צבוע. ויש אומרים: *פוטיא״ש, ודרך להרוג אווזים ותרנגולים.

LANGUAGE

בַּרְדְּלֵס Panther. This word is derived from the Greek πάρδαλις, *pardalis,* which means "leopard" or "panther." It is also used in an extended sense to mean various animals or objects containing stripes or speckles.

LANGUAGE (RASHI)

פוטיא״ש* From the Old French *puteis,* meaning "marten," "weasel."

BACKGROUND

בַּרְדְּלֵס Panther. In the Talmud, the word בַּרְדְּלֵס, commonly translated as "panther," refers not to one type of animal but to at least three different animals. One type of בַּרְדְּלֵס is a small animal similar to a marten (see *Rashi*). Another בַּרְדְּלֵס is a hyena, and some authorities maintain that the Gemara is referring to such a בַּרְדְּלֵס here. Still others maintain that the Gemara refers here to the cheetah, a spotted member of the cat family, *acinonyx jubatus,* which is found in Asia and Africa. This animal can reach up to 180 centimeters in length (including its tail); its color is yellowish brown, and it has dark spots.

NOTES

admits that even brand-new items can be identified by their owner if they are intended for personal use, e.g., cups and plates. But the brand-new items in our passage are arranged in sets, and thus are clearly intended for sale, and there is no reason to imagine that the owner will be able to identify them separately (*Tosefot Rid*).

הַמַּצִּיל מִן הָאֲרִי One who rescues an article from a lion... because the owners give up hope. The Rishonim ask: Why does Rabbi Shimon ben Elazar explain that the reason why the finder is permitted to keep such items is that the owner gives up hope of recovering them, when in fact the law permitting objects lost as a result of floods or wild animals to be kept is derived from a Biblical verse? (See above, 22b.)

Rashba answers that the clause, "because the owners give up hope...," refers only to the last cases in the list — the various public places. Alternatively, even though the application of the Biblical law is not dependent on the owner's giving up hope, it is not unrelated to it, since the rationale behind the law is that owners do not normally expect to recover objects seized by lions or washed away in floods.

HALAKHAH

מְצָאָן שְׁנַיִם שְׁנַיִם But if he found them in twos. "If a person finds needles, nails and the like, he may keep them, provided that he found each individually. But if he found two or more, he must announce his discovery." (*Shulḥan Arukh, Ḥoshen Mishpat* 262:16.)

...הַמַּצִּיל מִן הָאֲרִי One who rescues an article from a lion.... "If a person rescues an object from a lion or a bear, from a rising sea or from an overflowing river, he may keep it." *Rema* adds that it is nevertheless praiseworthy and proper to return the object. (Ibid., 259:7.)

[1]הַמּוֹצֵא בִּסְרַטְיָא וּפְלַטְיָא גְּדוֹלָה, וּבְכָל מָקוֹם שֶׁהָרַבִּים מְצוּיִין שָׁם — [2]הֲרֵי אֵלּוּ שֶׁלּוֹ, מִפְּנֵי שֶׁהַבְּעָלִים מִתְיָאֲשִׁין מֵהֶן״.

[3]אִיבַּעְיָא לְהוּ: כִּי קָאָמַר רַבִּי שִׁמְעוֹן בֶּן אֶלְעָזָר, [4]בְּרוֹב נָכְרִים, [5]אֲבָל בְּרוֹב יִשְׂרָאֵל, לֹא? [6]אוֹ דִּלְמָא אֲפִילּוּ בְּרוֹב יִשְׂרָאֵל נַמִי אָמַר?

[7]אִם תִּמְצָא לוֹמַר אֲפִילּוּ בְּרוֹב יִשְׂרָאֵל נַמִי אָמַר, [8]פְּלִיגִי רַבָּנַן עֲלֵיהּ אוֹ לָא פְּלִיגִי?

LITERAL TRANSLATION

[1]someone who finds [an article] on a highway or a large public square, or in any place where many [people] are found — [2]these are his, because the owners give up hope of them."

[3]It was asked of them: When Rabbi Shimon ben Elazar said [this], [4][was the case] where the majority are non-Jews, [5]but where the majority are Jews, not? [6]Or perhaps he also said [this] even where the majority are Jews?

[7]If you can say [that] he also said [this] even where the majority are Jews, [8]do the Sages disagree with him or do they not disagree?

TRANSLATION AND COMMENTARY

automatically rendered ownerless. [1]**Someone who finds an article on a highway or in a large public square, or in any place where many people are found** — [2]in all these cases, **the person** who rescues or retrieves the article **is entitled to keep it,** even if it has an identifying mark on it, **because the owners have given up hope of recovering it.**" Since it was lost in a public place and was not immediately returned, the owners assume that it has been picked up by someone who has no intention of returning it. Therefore, even if it was not picked up immediately and subsequently an honest person picked it up, he need not return it, as it became ownerless when its owner gave up hope of recovering it.

אִיבַּעְיָא לְהוּ [3]In connection with the last part of the Tosefta just cited, the following series of interrelated questions **was asked of** the Sages in the Academy: (1) **When Rabbi Shimon ben Elazar** made **this** statement, permitting articles found in public places to be kept by the finder, [4]**was** he referring only to a **case** where the object was lost in a place **where the majority of the population were non-Jews?** Since the owner will assume that a non-Jew will find it and not return it, the owner will give up hope and relinquish his rights to it, even if, in fact, it was found by a Jew. [5]**But where the majority** of the local population **are Jews,** would Rabbi Shimon ben Elazar maintain that the finder is **not** permitted to keep the lost object, since the owner will assume that it will be found by a Jew and returned to him? [6]**Or** do we say **perhaps** that Rabbi Shimon **also said** that **this** ruling applies **even where the majority of the population are Jews,** since the owner will give up hope of recovering an object lost in an area frequented by so many people?

אִם תִּמְצָא לוֹמַר [7]On the basis of this question the Gemara now continues to ask: (2) **If you say** that Rabbi Shimon ben Elazar also said that the finder is entitled to keep the lost object even where the majority of the population are Jews, [8]a further problem arises: **Do the Sages disagree with him** in both cases, and maintain that irrespective of whether the majority of the population is Jewish or non-Jewish the finder of the lost object must announce it; **or do they not disagree** with him at all, and maintain that in both cases the finder is entitled to keep the lost object?

RASHI

וכל מקום שהרבים כו׳ — ואפילו דבר שיש בו סימן. **פליגי רבנן עליה** — בתרוייהו.

NOTES

וּבְכָל מָקוֹם שֶׁהָרַבִּים מְצוּיִין שָׁם Or in any place where many people are found. Rabbi Shimon ben Elazar's view, that when people lose something in a place frequented by many people, they give up hope of recovering it, is based on the assumption (at least according to the view that he is also referring to places where the majority are Jews) that in any place frequented by many people there will always be at least some dishonest people who would not return a lost object even though Halakhah requires them to do so. Rabbi Shimon ben Elazar is convinced that in any place frequented by many people the chance of recovering a lost object is so small that the person who has lost it will not even check to see whether someone is attempting to return it, and, since he has given up hope, the lost object belongs to the finder in any event.

בְּרוֹב נָכְרִים Where the majority are non-Jews. Returning a lost object is not regarded in principle as a monetary obligation like repaying a loan. From the juridical point of view, a lost object becomes ownerless. That was the position taken by the law in Talmudic times, and to a certain degree that law still applies today. For example, when buried treasure is discovered, the state appropriates it without making any effort to locate the owners or their heirs. This approach derives from the assumption that lost property has left the ownership of its owner, either becoming ownerless or else reverting to the state. The commandment to return lost property as written in the Torah is, like certain other Halakhot, a form of good deed, a particular obligation falling upon a Jew with regard to his fellow-Jews, a special act performed within the framework of the family of Judaism. This commandment, as explained below (27b), also implies a feeling of mutuality, in that the finder returns lost property under the assumption that if he should lose something, he too will have it returned. However, in the Talmudic period when non-Jews were not at all accustomed to returning lost objects, there was no place for such reciprocity. Nevertheless,

LANGUAGE

סְרַטְיָא Highway. The source of this word is the Latin *strata,* which means "paved highway."

פְּלַטְיָא Large public square. The source of this word is the Greek πλατεῖα, *plateia,* which means "wide road" or "large area."

BACKGROUND

פְּלַטְיָא Large public square.

The forum in Pompeii, in Mishnaic times.

The פְּלַטְיָא was the city thoroughfare through which people passed and where they gathered. It is an excellent example of a public domain, as it fulfills all the Halakhic requirements of such a domain.

בְּרוֹב נָכְרִים Where the majority are non-Jews. The Gemara assumes that an object lost in a place where the majority are non-Jews would not be returned because at that time non-Jews did not believe in a religion which required them to return lost objects, nor was that their custom, and whatever they found they would keep for themselves. Moreover, in several states it was then the law that a found object belonged to the authorities and, therefore, either people did not trouble to pick things up at all, for they received only a small compensation, if any, for doing so, or else they concealed the object from the authorities and kept it for themselves. Only in a place where the majority were Jews, who were obligated by the Torah to return lost objects, was there a possibility that an article might be returned to its owner.

TERMINOLOGY

אִם תִּמְצָא לוֹמַר If you say.... This expression occasionally means, "If you say," or "If you assume." But its precise meaning is "If you follow this through to the end," i.e., "if you pursue this line of thought and try to draw all the conclusions that follow

LITERAL TRANSLATION

[1]And if you can say [that] they disagree, [2]where the majority are Jews they certainly disagree, [3][but] where the majority are non-Jews, do they disagree or do they not disagree?

[4]And if you can say [that] they disagree even where the majority are non-Jews, [5]is the Halakhah in accordance with him or is the Halakhah not in accordance with him?

[6]If you can say [that] the Halakhah is in accordance with him, [7][is this] only where the majority are non-Jews, [8]or even where the majority are Jews?

[9]Come [and] hear: "Someone who finds coins in synagogues, or in houses of study, or in any place where many [people] are found, [10]these are his, because the owners give up hope of [recovering] them." [11]Of whom have you heard that he goes after the majority? Rabbi Shimon ben Elazar.

[1]וְאִם תִּמְצָא לוֹמַר פְּלִיגִי, [2]בְּרוֹב יִשְׂרָאֵל וַדַּאי פְּלִיגִי, [3]בְּרוֹב נָכְרִים, פְּלִיגִי אוֹ לָא פְּלִיגִי?
[4]וְאִם תִּמְצָא לוֹמַר פְּלִיגִי אֲפִילּוּ בְּרוֹב נָכְרִים, [5]הֲלָכָה כְּמוֹתוֹ אוֹ אֵין הֲלָכָה כְּמוֹתוֹ?
[6]אִם תִּמְצָא לוֹמַר הֲלָכָה כְּמוֹתוֹ, [7]דַּוְקָא בְּרוֹב נָכְרִים, [8]אוֹ אֲפִילּוּ בְּרוֹב יִשְׂרָאֵל?
[9]תָּא שְׁמַע: "הַמּוֹצֵא מָעוֹת בְּבָתֵּי כְנֵסִיּוֹת, וּבְבָתֵּי מִדְרָשׁוֹת, וּבְכָל מָקוֹם שֶׁהָרַבִּים מְצוּיִין שָׁם, [10]הֲרֵי אֵלּוּ שֶׁלּוֹ, מִפְּנֵי שֶׁהַבְּעָלִים מִתְיָאֲשִׁין מֵהֶן. [11]מַאן שָׁמְעַתְּ לֵיהּ דְּאָזֵיל בָּתַר רוּבָּא? רַבִּי שִׁמְעוֹן בֶּן אֶלְעָזָר!

RASHI

המוצא מעות — קא סלקא דעתך לצורי מעות דקתני מתניתין חייב להכריז והכא הואיל ורבים מצויין שם — הרי אלו שלו, שנתייאשו הבעלים. **דאזיל בתר רובא** — כלומר, שהולך בדין מציאה אחר טעם "רבים מצויים שם".

TRANSLATION AND COMMENTARY

וְאִם תִּמְצָא לוֹמַר [1](3) **And if you say that** the Sages and Rabbi Shimon ben Elazar **disagree,** what exactly is their point of disagreement? It is reasonable to assume that [2]**where the majority** of the population **are Jews they certainly disagree,** with the Sages maintaining that in such a case the finder of a lost object must announce that he has found it. But it is by no means certain that they disagree where the majority of the population are non-Jews. [3]The question still remains: **Do they disagree** with Rabbi Shimon ben Elazar even **where the majority** of the population **are non-Jews,** insisting that the finder must announce the lost object because of the minority of Jews among the population, **or do they not disagree** with him on this point?

וְאִם תִּמְצָא לוֹמַר [4](4) **And if you say that** the Sages and Rabbi Shimon ben Elazar **disagree even where the majority** of the population **are non-Jews,** [5]a further question arises: **Is the Halakhah in accordance with** Rabbi Shimon ben Elazar's view **or not?**

אִם תִּמְצָא לוֹמַר [6](5) **And if you say that the Halakhah is in accordance with** Rabbi Shimon ben Elazar's view, and the lost object belongs to the finder, [7]a further question arises: **Does this apply only where the majority** of the population **are non-Jews,** since it would be reasonable to assume that the object was lost by a non-Jew, [8]**or** does it apply **even where the majority** of the population **are Jews,** because the owner will give up hope of recovering his property even in such a situation?

תָּא שְׁמַע [9]In order to resolve this series of interrelated problems, the Gemara presents a Baraita (also quoted above, 21b): **Come and hear: "Someone who finds coins in synagogues, or in houses of study, or in any place that the public frequents —** [10]**they belong to him, because the owners give up hope of recovering them."** In quoting this Baraita the Gemara is making two assumptions: (1) That the place where the object is found contains a majority of Jews. (2) That the money found is tied together in some way and not scattered, because if it were scattered it would bear no means of identification and would belong to the finder even if found in a place not frequented by the public. [11]Now the Gemara reasons: **Of which** Sage **have you heard that,** in deciding the ownership of lost property, **he uses the argument** that the object was found **"in a place that the public frequents"?** I.e., which Sage maintains that the presence of many people is a significant factor in deciding what the finder of lost property should do? Surely it was **Rabbi Shimon ben Elazar** who expressed this opinion in the Tosefta quoted above concerning articles found "on a highway or in a large public square."

NOTES

certain great Sages used to return objects to anyone who had lost them, including non-Jews, either because of a deep moral conviction or else because they wished to forge peaceful and friendly relations with their non-Jewish neighbors, and therefore went beyond the strict limits of their legal obligations.

from it regarding aspects that are not mentioned in connection with the basic Halakhah, but which derive from it."

BACKGROUND

הֲלָכָה כְּמוֹתוֹ Is the Halakhah in accordance with him? This question is not a common one in Talmudic debate. However, in the present case, the Sages knew that, although Rabbi Shimon ben Elazar's opinion was presented as an individual view, Halakhic rulings tended to follow his opinion. Nevertheless, there were doubts concerning the application of Rabbi Shimon ben Elazar's opinion, both with regard to the limits of its Halakhic scope and also regarding his general approach. See the next page (24b), where we find that many Sages did indeed rule according to him, either completely or in part.

בָּתֵּי כְּנֵסִיּוֹת Synagogues. The literal meaning of this expression is a place where people gather. Indeed, for many generations, synagogues served not only as places of worship but also as places where the people assembled to deal with various communal and social concerns, so that in some cases the synagogue was called בֵּית הָעָם — "the house of the people." The original meaning of the Greek word from which the term "synagogue" is derived also includes a gathering place. It was a long time before the term came to be used specifically to refer to a Jewish house of worship in Hebrew and in Greek. In the writings of the Sages we also find the term used in its general, secular sense, as in the phrase בָּתֵּי כְנֵסִיּוֹת שֶׁל עַמֵּי הָאֲרָצוֹת — "the meeting places of the ignorant."

TERMINOLOGY

מַאי אִרְיָא Why [this] discussion? As a rule, statements in a Mishnah or a Baraita are framed to include all relevant cases. If, therefore, a Mishnah or a Baraita links a law to a particular, unusual, set of circumstances when it could have chosen a more common situation, the Talmud may object: "Why [this] discussion?" In other words: "Why was it necessary to specify this particular situation, since the same law would also apply in other cases?"

LITERAL TRANSLATION

[1] Conclude from here [that he says so] even where the majority are Jews.

[2] With what are we dealing here? With scattered [coins].

[3] If [we are dealing] with scattered [coins], why discuss a place where many [people] are found? [4] [It should apply] even where many [people] are not found.

[5] Rather, in fact [the Baraita is dealing] with [coins] tied in bundles. [6] And with what are we dealing here? With houses of assembly of non-Jews.

[7] [About] "houses of study" what is there to say?

[8] [It is referring to] our houses of study in which non-Jews are staying.

[1] שְׁמַעְתְּ מִינָּהּ אֲפִילּוּ בְּרוֹב יִשְׂרָאֵל נַמִי.

[2] הָכָא בְּמַאי עָסְקִינַן? בִּמְפוּזָּרִין.

[3] אִי בִּמְפוּזָּרִין, מַאי אִרְיָא מָקוֹם שֶׁהָרַבִּים מְצוּיִין שָׁם? [4] אֲפִילּוּ אֵין הָרַבִּים מְצוּיִין שָׁם!

[5] אֶלָּא, לְעוֹלָם בִּצְרוּרִין. [6] וְהָכָא בְּמַאי עָסְקִינַן? בְּבָתֵּי כְנֵסִיּוֹת שֶׁל נָכְרִים.

[7] בָּתֵּי מִדְרָשׁוֹת מַאי אִיכָּא לְמֵימַר?

[8] בָּתֵּי מִדְרָשׁוֹת דִּידָן, דְּיָתְבִי בְּהוּ נָכְרִים.

RASHI

ברוב ישראל — דסתם בתי כנסיות — ישראל בהן. **במפוזרים** — ורבנן היא דמודו במפוזרין, דתנן: מעות מפוזרין הרי אלו שלו. **כנסיות** — אסיפת מקום, שמתכנסים שם להתיעץ ולהוועד. **דיתבי בהו נכרים** — שהן חוץ לעיר, ומושיבין בה נכרים לשמור.

TRANSLATION AND COMMENTARY

[1] Now if the Baraita is an expression of Rabbi Shimon ben Elazar's views, it should be possible to **conclude from here that** Rabbi Shimon also intended his statement to apply **even where the majority of the population are Jews,** since the items mentioned in our Baraita were lost in synagogues or houses of study, which are specifically frequented by Jews. If this conclusion is valid, a solution has been found to the first of the series of questions raised in the Academy.

הָכָא בְּמַאי עָסְקִינַן [2] The Gemara rejects this interpretation by denying the second of its assumptions — that the money found was tied together in some way: **With what are we dealing here? With** a case where he found **scattered coins** that cannot be identified by their owner. All agree that in this case such coins need not be returned, regardless of where they were found (see above, 21a). But it is possible that even Rabbi Shimon ben Elazar agrees that a lost object containing an identifying mark and found in a place that the public frequents does have to be announced.

אִי בִּמְפוּזָּרִין [3] The Gemara objects, supporting its original assumption: **If we are dealing with scattered coins, why** does the Baraita **refer specifically to a place that the public frequents?** [4] The same law **should apply even** if the coins were found in **a place that the public does not frequent,** and the finder should be permitted to keep them, since all agree that scattered coins belong to the finder, wherever they were found, because they lack any means of identification.

אֶלָּא לְעוֹלָם בִּצְרוּרִין [5] **Rather,** says the Gemara, this interpretation is untenable; the original assumption is still valid, and **in fact the Baraita is dealing with** a case where **coins** were found **tied in bundles**, and are thus identifiable. Nevertheless, we still cannot solve our problem, because there is no proof that the Baraita's ruling applies to places frequented primarily by Jews, as there is another way of interpreting it. [6] **With what are we dealing here? With houses of assembly of non-Jews.** The term used in the Baraita is *batei khenessiyot* (בָּתֵּי כְנֵסִיּוֹת), and even though its usual meaning is "synagogues," it literally means "houses of assembly." Thus the Gemara can explain that the *batei khenessiyot* mentioned in the Baraita were not synagogues at all, but rather houses of assembly used by non-Jews. Thus the Baraita is not referring to a situation in which an article was found in a place where the majority of the population is Jewish.

בָּתֵּי מִדְרָשׁוֹת מַאי אִיכָּא לְמֵימַר [7] But the Gemara objects: It is possible to interpret the words *batei khenessiyot* as referring to non-Jewish houses of assembly. But **about** the expression **"houses of study," what is there to say?** The term "houses of study" (בָּתֵּי מִדְרָשׁוֹת) can only mean places of Jewish religious and Talmudic study, which are frequented only by Jews. What possible connection can such places have with the non-Jewish world?

בָּתֵּי מִדְרָשׁוֹת דִּידָן [8] The Gemara answers: **It** is possible that the Baraita **is referring to our,** Jewish, **houses of study in which non-Jews are staying** as guards and attendants, because the buildings are located outside the city.

NOTES

דְּיָתְבִי בְּהוּ נָכְרִים Houses of study in which non-Jews are staying. Even though non-Jewish caretakers are not normally the majority of the occupants of a study house, they do tend to notice objects lying about, since for them the study house is a kind of home. By contrast, the Jews come in and out to study and pay little attention to objects left lying about. Therefore, the situation is comparable to a place where the majority of those present are non-Jews (*Rashba*).

הָשְׁתָּא דְּאָתֵית לְהָכִי [1]Now that you have come to this, [2]the synagogues may also be ours, in which non-Jews are staying. [3]Come [and] hear: "[If] he found a lost object there, [4]if the majority are Jews, he must announce [it, [5]but] if the majority are non-Jews, he is not obliged to announce [it]." [6]Of whom have you heard that he said that we go after the majority? [7]Rabbi Shimon ben Elazar. [8]Conclude from here [that] when Rabbi Shimon ben Elazar said [this, [9]he meant] where the majority are non-Jews, [10]but where the majority are Jews, not.

[11]Whose [view] is this? It is [that of] the Sages.

[12][Then] you can conclude from it that the Sages agree with Rabbi Shimon ben Elazar where the majority are non-Jews.

TRANSLATION AND COMMENTARY

הָשְׁתָּא דְּאָתֵית לְהָכִי [1]The Gemara notes: **Now that you have come to this** way of explaining the Baraita, [2]you can also explain that **the** word **"synagogues"** mentioned in the Baraita **may also be** referring to **our** synagogues, **in which non-Jews are staying.** Accordingly, no conclusions regarding the series of problems raised above can be drawn from this Baraita.

תָּא שְׁמַע [3]**Come and hear** another attempt to clarify the issue, based on a Mishnah (*Makhshirin* 2:8): **If he found a lost object there,** in a city inhabited by both Jews and non-Jews, [4]the following rules apply: **If the majority** of the population **are Jews, he must announce** his discovery, [5]**but if the majority are non-Jews, he is not obliged to announce** his discovery." [6]On the basis of this Mishnah the Gemara now asks: **Of which** Sage **have you heard that**, in deciding the ownership of lost property, **he says that we use the argument** that what is done with lost property depends on the nature of **the majority** of a city's population? [7]Surely it is **Rabbi Shimon ben Elazar.** [8]Now if the Mishnah is an expression of Rabbi Shimon ben Elazar's views, it should be possible to **conclude from here that when Rabbi Shimon ben Elazar said** that an object found in a public place belongs to the finder, [9]he was referring only to a situation **where the majority of the population are non-Jews;** [10]**but where the majority are Jews,** this ruling does **not** apply. If this argument is correct, it provides the solution to the first of the questions raised in the Academy.

הָא מַנִּי [11]The Gemara rejects this argument: It is possible to interpret the Mishnah differently: **Whose view is** being expressed in the Mishnah? Not that of Rabbi Shimon ben Elazar, but **that of the Sages** who disagree with him. It is thus possible that Rabbi Shimon ben Elazar would maintain that property lost in a public place is permitted to the finder, even if the majority of the population are Jews.

תִּפְשׁוֹט מִינָּהּ [12]The Gemara now suggests: If the view expressed in the Mishnah in tractate *Makhshirin* represents the opinion of the Sages, **you can resolve by means of it** at least one of the problems raised earlier. It is clear from this interpretation **that the Sages agree with Rabbi Shimon ben Elazar where the majority are non-Jews,** and allow the finder to keep the lost article in such circumstances. It is only where the majority of the population are Jews that the Sages disagree with Rabbi Shimon ben Elazar and insist that the finder must announce his discovery. This interpretation would enable us to resolve the second of the questions raised in the Academy.

[1]הָשְׁתָּא דְּאָתֵית לְהָכִי, [2]בָּתֵּי כְנֵסִיּוֹת נַמִי דִּידָן, דְּיָתְבִי בְּהוּ נָכְרִים.

[3]תָּא שְׁמַע: "מָצָא בָּהּ אֲבֵידָה, [4]אִם רוֹב יִשְׂרָאֵל, חַיָּיב לְהַכְרִיז, [5]אִם רוֹב נָכְרִים, אֵינוֹ חַיָּיב לְהַכְרִיז". [6]מַאן שָׁמְעַתְּ לֵיהּ דְּאָמַר אָזְלִינַן בָּתַר רוּבָּא? [7]רַבִּי שִׁמְעוֹן בֶּן אֶלְעָזָר! [8]שָׁמְעַתְּ מִינָּהּ: כִּי קָאָמַר רַבִּי שִׁמְעוֹן בֶּן אֶלְעָזָר, [9]בְּרוֹב נָכְרִים, [10]אֲבָל בְּרוֹב יִשְׂרָאֵל, לָא.

[11]הָא מַנִּי? רַבָּנַן הִיא.

[12]תִּפְשׁוֹט מִינָּהּ דְּמוֹדוּ לֵיהּ רַבָּנַן לְרַבִּי שִׁמְעוֹן בֶּן אֶלְעָזָר בְּרוֹב נָכְרִים!

RASHI

מצא בה אבידה — משנה היא בסדר טהרות, בעיר שישראל ונכרים דרים בה, במסכת מכשירין. **ותפשוט מיהא** — מקצת משאלותיך, דמודו רבנן ברוב נכרים ופליגי ברוב ישראל.

TERMINOLOGY

הָשְׁתָּא דְּאָתֵית לְהָכִי Now that you have come to this. Sometimes the Rabbis raise a series of objections to a certain viewpoint, and each objection is given a different answer; then a new objection is raised, and someone suggests an answer which resolves not only the new objection but also the previous ones. At that point the Talmud uses this expression, proposing a revision of the solutions first advanced.

NOTES

תִּפְשׁוֹט מִינָּהּ דְּמוֹדוּ לֵיהּ רַבָּנַן Conclude from this Mishnah that the Sages agree with Rabbi Shimon ben Elazar. The Rishonim ask: How is it possible to prove anything from this Mishnah? There are two possible interpretations of it, one in accordance with Rabbi Shimon ben Elazar, and one in accordance with the Sages. If we interpret it in accordance with Rabbi Shimon ben Elazar, we must accept that he distinguishes between Jews and non-Jews, but we learn nothing about the Sages' view. If we interpret it in accordance with the Sages, we must accept that the Sages distinguish between Jews and non-Jews, but we learn nothing about Rabbi Shimon ben Elazar's view. Since both interpretations are equally plausible, we cannot with any certainty prove anything at all about either view.

They answer: One of the possibilities we entertained at the beginning of the passage was that Rabbi Shimon ben Elazar permits the object to be kept by the finder even if the majority of the population are Jews, and the Sages

TRANSLATION AND COMMENTARY

אֶלָּא [1]The Gemara now rejects the conclusion just suggested and offers a different explanation of the Mishnah. **Rather**, the Mishnah **is, in fact,** in accordance with **the view of Rabbi Shimon ben Elazar,** as originally suggested. Nevertheless it offers no solution to the questions raised in the Academy. [2]It is possible that Rabbi Shimon ben Elazar's view — that the finder can keep the object for himself — **applies even where the majority** of the population **are Jews,** in cases other than the one discussed in the Mishnah in *Makhshirin*. [3]**But** this case is an exception. **With what are we dealing here?** With a case **where** the object found **had been** deliberately **hidden** there by its owner and had accidentally been discovered by the finder. Since the object had been hidden there, it cannot be considered "lost" at all, and there is no question of the owner giving up hope of recovering it. Therefore, if the object was found in a place where the majority of the population are Jews, it must be returned.

אִי בְּטָמוּן [4]The Gemara now asks: **If the case** concerns an object that was deliberately **hidden, what is it doing in** the finder's **possession?** According to what authority is he allowed to pick it up at all? The fact that it was hidden indicates that it was placed there intentionally, and that the owner plans to come to recover it. [5]**For surely we have learned** in a Mishnah (below, 25b): **"If he found a utensil in a heap of refuse,** where useless things are thrown away, [6]**if it is covered, he may not touch it,** for it was surely hidden there intentionally. [7]**But if it is uncovered, he takes it and announces** that he has found **it."** Thus we see that hidden items must not be picked up at all, even if they are hidden in a heap of refuse.

כִּדְאָמַר רַב פַּפָּא [8]The Gemara answers: The problem posed by the Mishnah in *Makhshirin* can be explained in accordance with the interpretation offered by **Rav Pappa** in connection with the Mishnah (below, 25b) just quoted: Where the Mishnah says the finder may not touch the object hidden in the heap of refuse, **this refers to a heap of refuse that is not usually cleared away**, but is left undisturbed for some time. **But** in fact **its owner changed his mind about it and decided to clear it away.** As a result the hidden object came to light. In such a case the finder must announce his discovery. He may neither keep it nor throw it away with the rest of the refuse. But if the object had been found in an ordinary heap of refuse, the finder would be entitled to assume that the owner had abandoned it. [9]The Gemara reasons that **here too,** in the Mishnah in *Makhshirin,* we can explain that the Mishnah **is referring to a heap of refuse that is not usually cleared away,** [10]**but its owner changed his mind about it and decided to clear it away** and in the process a valuable article was found. In such circumstances the decision as to what to do with the article depends on the status of the majority of the city's inhabitants. If the majority are Jewish, the discovery must be announced, as the object probably belongs to a Jew who has not given up hope of recovering it, since it was hidden rather than lost. If the majority are non-Jews, it need not be announced, even though the owner expects to recover it, as according to Rabbi Shimon ben Elazar ownership can be determined on the basis of a statistical majority, and there is no Halakhic

[1]אֶלָּא, לְעוֹלָם רַבִּי שִׁמְעוֹן בֶּן אֶלְעָזָר הִיא, [2]וַאֲפִילּוּ בְּרוֹב יִשְׂרָאֵל נַמִי. [3]וְהָכָא בְּמַאי עָסְקִינַן? בְּטָמוּן.
[4]אִי בְּטָמוּן, מַאי עֲבִידְתֵּיהּ גַּבֵּיהּ? [5]וְהָתְנַן: "מָצָא כְּלִי בְּאַשְׁפָּה, [6]מְכוּסֶּה, לֹא יִגַּע בּוֹ, [7]מְגוּלֶּה, נוֹטֵל וּמַכְרִיז!". [8]כִּדְאָמַר רַב פַּפָּא: בְּאַשְׁפָּה שֶׁאֵינָהּ עֲשׂוּיָה לְפַנּוֹת, וְנִמְלַךְ עָלֶיהָ לְפַנּוֹתָהּ. [9]הָכָא נַמִי בְּאַשְׁפָּה שֶׁאֵינָהּ עֲשׂוּיָה לְפַנּוֹת, [10]וְנִמְלַךְ עָלֶיהָ לְפַנּוֹתָהּ.

LITERAL TRANSLATION

[1]Rather, it is in fact [the view of] Rabbi Shimon ben Elazar, [2]and [applies] even where the majority are Jews. [3]But with what are we dealing here? Where it was concealed.

[4]If [the case is] where it was concealed, what is it doing in his possession? [5]For surely we have learned: "[If] he found a utensil in a heap of refuse, [6][if] it is covered, he may not touch it, [7][but if] it is uncovered, he takes [it] and announces [it]." [8][It is] as Rav Pappa said: [This refers] to a heap of refuse that is not usually cleared away, but [its owner] changed his mind about it [and decided] to clear it away. [9]Here too [this refers] to a heap of refuse that is not usually cleared away, [10]but [its owner] changed his mind about it [and decided] to clear it away.

RASHI

בטמון — דכיון דטמנו לאו אבידה היא, הלכך ברוב ישראל יכריז. **שאינה עשויה לפנות** — רגילים היו בעלים להניחה ימים רבים, ולא לפנותה מיד. **ונמלך עליה לפנותה** — מיד, ועל כרחו, או יטלנו או יהא הפקר. להכי נקט שאינה עשויה לפנות, דאי עשויה לפנות אבידה מדעת היא, שהיה לו לחוש שמא יפנה.

TERMINOLOGY

אֶלָּא, לְעוֹלָם Rather, in fact. This phrase expresses rejection of the previous explanation and offers a new one. Occasionally we may return to an even earlier explanation which, for various reasons, had previously been rejected. In any event, we determine that "in fact," i.e., as a general principle and not just in this specific case, one must understand that....

BACKGROUND

אַשְׁפָּה Refuse heap. The אַשְׁפָּה in question here and elsewhere in the Talmud was not a place where garbage of all kinds was discarded, but rather a place where discarded objects and things not wanted for use by their owners were thrown away. Occasionally such a refuse heap might be in a private domain (although many people would commonly throw their things away there). As noted here, there were heaps of refuse which no one intended to remove, and there were places from which the owners or the residents of the city did clear away the accumulated refuse.

NOTES

prohibit it even if the majority are non-Jews. That position, at least, is now untenable, as it is clear from this Mishnah that one authority distinguishes between Jews and non-Jews (*Tosafot* and others).

TRANSLATION AND COMMENTARY

obligation to return found objects to non-Jews. At all events, this Mishnah has no bearing on the problems we have been discussing, for it does not refer to lost objects.

[24B] וְאִיבָּעֵית אֵימָא [1]Now that the Gemara has shown that the Mishnah from *Makhshirin* can be ascribed to the viewpoint of Rabbi Shimon ben Elazar and yet cannot be used as a source to solve the series of problems raised above, it goes back to its earlier suggestion that the Mishnah represents the viewpoint of the Sages who disagree with Rabbi Shimon ben Elazar. The Gemara says: **And if you wish** you can **say** that, **in fact,** the Mishnah represents the viewpoint of **the Sages,** as we attempted to say earlier, and there is no need to interpret it as referring to the highly unusual case of an object that was hidden. Nevertheless it does not prove that the Sages agree with Rabbi Shimon ben Elazar that where the majority are non-Jews the finder of the lost article can keep it for himself. [2]For consider the language of the Mishnah. **Does the Mishnah say** that, where a person finds lost objects in a city where the majority of the population are non-Jews, **"they are his"** and the finder has an absolute right to keep them for himself? It says no such thing. [3]**It** merely **says: "He is not obliged to announce** that he has found them." There is a big difference between these two expressions. The author of the Mishnah specifically chose the second expression to indicate that the finder does not need to announce his find, because of the non-Jewish majority in the city, but it does not say that he has a legal right to keep it for himself. The reason why the Sages of the Mishnah are not willing to allow the finder to keep the article is because in monetary matters they maintain that a statistical majority of the local population is not sufficient to establish ownership. [4]What, then, does the author of the Mishnah require the finder to do? In the meantime **he should leave** the found article **in his possession** without making use of it until **a Jew comes and describes an identifying mark on it and takes it.** Thus, according to this explanation, too, the Mishnah cannot throw any light on the problems raised above (24a).

תָּא שְׁמַע [5]**Come and hear** an authoritative ruling by an early Amora which may throw light on the viewpoints of Rabbi Shimon ben Elazar and the Sages and help solve the problems raised earlier with regard to their interpretation: **Rav Assi said: If** a Jew **found a jar of wine in a city in which the majority of the population are non-Jews,** [6]**it is permitted with respect to the laws of found objects,** and the finder is under no obligation to announce that he has found it, for the likelihood is that it was lost by a non-Jew; and even if it was lost by a Jew we assume that the owner has given up hope of recovering it, because the majority of the city's population are non-Jews. [7]**But he is forbidden to benefit from it,** for he is forbidden to benefit from the wine of non-Jews. [8]**If a Jew comes and describes an identifying mark on it,** thus proving that it belonged to him, [9]the wine **is permitted to be drunk by its finder,** as we accept the mark as evidence that this Jew lost the wine. Nevertheless the wine need not be returned to the claimant, as we assume that he has already given up hope of recovering it, in accordance with Rabbi Shimon ben Elazar's reasoning, in the light of the fact that the

[24B] [1]וְאִיבָּעֵית אֵימָא: לְעוֹלָם רַבָּנַן. [2]מִי קָתָנֵי: ״הֵן שֶׁלּוֹ״? [3]״אֵינוֹ חַיָּיב לְהַכְרִיז״ קָתָנֵי. [4]וְיַנִּיחַ וְיֵיתֵי יִשְׂרָאֵל וְיָהֵיב בֵּיהּ סִימָנָא וְשָׁקֵיל.

[5]תָּא שְׁמַע: דְּאָמַר רַב אַסִי: מָצָא חָבִית יַיִן בְּעִיר שֶׁרוּבָּהּ נָכְרִים, [6]מוּתֶּרֶת מִשּׁוּם מְצִיאָה, [7]וַאֲסוּרָה בַּהֲנָאָה. [8]בָּא יִשְׂרָאֵל וְנָתַן בָּהּ סִימָן, [9]מוּתֶּרֶת בִּשְׁתִיָּה

LITERAL TRANSLATION

[24B] [1]And if you wish, say: In fact, [it is] the Sages. [2]Does it teach: "They are his"? [3]It teaches: "He is not obliged to announce." [4]And he should leave it [in his possession] and a Jew will come and give an identifying mark on it and take [it].

[5]Come [and] hear: For Rav Assi said: [If] he found a jar of wine in a city in which the majority are non-Jews, [6]it is permitted with respect to [the laws of] a found object, [7]but it is forbidden to benefit [from it]. [8][If] a Jew came and gave an identifying mark on it, [9]it is permitted to be drunk by its

RASHI

ואיבעית אימא לעולם רבנן – ובשאינה טמון, ולא תפשוט מינה דמודו ליה ברוב נכרים. **מי קתני כו׳ אינו חייב להכריז קתני** – דכיון דרובא נכרים דלמא דנכרים הוא, ושלו נמי לא הויא, דלא אזלי רבנן בתר רובא בממונא. **מותרת משום מציאה** – דאינו חייב להכריז. **ואסורה בהנאה** – ולקמיה פריך: אם כן מה היתר יש במציאתה? **בא ישראל ונתן סימן** – יצאת מספק יין נכרים ומותרת בשתיה למוצאה דכיון דרובא נכרים נתייאשו הבעלים.

HALAKHAH

מָצָא חָבִית יַיִן If he found a jar of wine. "If a person finds a jar of wine in a city where the majority of the population are non-Jews, he may not benefit from the wine itself, but may keep the jar for his own use. If a Jew comes and identifies the jar, the finder may drink the wine, since he can assume that the Jew was the original owner. And he need not return the jar, since he can assume that the owner has already given up hope of recovering the jar," following the ruling of Rav Assi here. (*Shulḥan Arukh, Ḥoshen Mishpat* 259:4.)

TERMINOLOGY

(וְ)אִיבָּעֵית אֵימָא If you wish, say.... This expression is used to introduce an additional answer to a question previously asked, or an additional explanation of a problem previously raised.

יַיִן שֶׁל נָכְרִים Wine of non-Jews. In ancient times, as noted in Daniel 1:8, Jews refrained from drinking wine made by non-Jews. It was forbidden to benefit from this wine, and there were also grounds to fear that it was used for idolatry (יֵין נֶסֶךְ), the prohibition of which precludes benefiting from any statues, symbols and other objects associated with idol worship. The reason for extending this suspicion beyond wine clearly consecrated to idolatry lay in the Greek custom of pouring out a small oblation to the gods before drinking wine. For that reason, all the wine (and not only the portion that was poured out) was considered יֵין נֶסֶךְ. Halakhic rulings were made in the Talmudic period that it was permitted to benefit from wine produced by non-Jews who did not practice that custom.

לְמוֹצְאָה. [1]כְּמַאן? כְּרַבִּי שִׁמְעוֹן בֶּן אֶלְעָזָר. [2]שְׁמַע מִינָּהּ: כִּי קָאָמַר רַבִּי שִׁמְעוֹן בֶּן אֶלְעָזָר, [3]בְּרוֹב נָכְרִים, אֲבָל בְּרוֹב יִשְׂרָאֵל, לֹא.

[4]לְעוֹלָם, אֵימָא לָךְ רַבִּי שִׁמְעוֹן בֶּן אֶלְעָזָר אֲפִילּוּ בְּרוֹב יִשְׂרָאֵל נַמִי קָאָמַר, [5]וְרַב אַסִי סָבַר לָהּ כְּוָותֵיהּ בַּחֲדָא [6]וּפָלֵיג עֲלֵיהּ בַּחֲדָא.

[7]וְכִי מֵאַחַר דַּאֲסִירָא בַּהֲנָאָה, [8]מוּתֶּרֶת מִשּׁוּם מְצִיאָה לְמַאי הִלְכְתָא?

[9]אֲמַר רַב אַשִׁי: לְקַנְקַנָּהּ.

[10]הַהוּא גַּבְרָא דְּאַשְׁכַּח אַרְבָּעָה זוּזֵי דְּצַיְּירֵי בִּסְדִינָא וּשְׁדוּ בִּנְהַר בִּירָן. [11]אֲתָא לְקַמֵּיהּ דְּרַב יְהוּדָה. אֲמַר לֵיהּ: ״זִיל אַכְרִיז״.

[12]וְהָא זוּטוֹ שֶׁל יָם הוּא!

LITERAL TRANSLATION

finder. [1]In accordance with whom [is this statement]? In accordance with Rabbi Shimon ben Elazar. [2]Conclude from here [that] when Rabbi Shimon ben Elazar said [this], [3][it was] where the majority are non-Jews, but not where the majority are Jews.

[4]In fact, I can say to you [that] Rabbi Shimon ben Elazar also said [this] even where the majority are Jews, [5]but Rav Assi agrees with him in one [case] [6]and disagrees with him in one.

[7]But since it is forbidden to benefit [from it], [8]for what [purpose] is the Halakhah [that] it is permitted with respect to [the laws of] a found object?

[9]Rav Ashi said: For its vessel.

[10]A certain man found four zuzim that were tied up in a cloth and thrown into the river Biran. [11]He came before Rav Yehudah. He said to him: "Go [and] announce [it]."

[12]But surely, this is [a case of] the rising sea.

TRANSLATION AND COMMENTARY

majority of the local population are non-Jews. The finder has thus taken an ownerless object legally. [1]The Gemara now analyzes Rav Assi's statement: **In accordance with whose** view **is** Rav Assi's **statement?** Clearly it is **in accordance with** the viewpoint of **Rabbi Shimon ben Elazar,** who maintains that if the wine was lost in a public place where the majority of the population are non-Jews, we may assume that the owner of the wine has given up hope of recovering it. [2]**Conclude,** then, **from here that when Rabbi Shimon ben Elazar** made his statement, [3]he was referring only to a case **where the majority of the population are non-Jews; but where the majority are Jews,** his statement does **not** apply. For Rav Assi specified that his ruling applied only in a city populated mostly by non-Jews. From Rav Assi's statement it would seem that we can solve the first of the problems raised earlier (above, 24a).

לְעוֹלָם אֵימָא לָךְ [4]The Gemara rejects this argument: **In fact,** says the Gemara, **I can say to you that Rabbi Shimon ben Elazar** may also have made his statement **even where the majority are Jews,** [5]**but** the ruling under discussion was made by Rav Assi, and it is possible that **Rav Assi agrees with** Rabbi Shimon ben Elazar **in one** case, where the majority in the city are non-Jews, [6]**and disagrees with him in another** case, where the majority are Jews, and maintains that in the latter case the finder must announce his find. Thus Rav Assi's ruling proves nothing about Rabbi Shimon ben Elazar's position.

וְכִי מֵאַחַר דַּאֲסִירָא בַּהֲנָאָה [7]Parenthetically, the Gemara now questions the logic of Rav Assi's ruling: **But since** Rav Assi ruled that the finder **is forbidden to benefit from** the wine, [8]**for what** practical **purpose does the Halakhah** state **that** the wine **is permitted with respect to the laws of found objects?** Why should the finder want to keep it? Of what value is it to him?

אֲמַר רַב אַשִׁי [9]**Rav Ashi said** in reply: Even if the wine is forbidden, it is worth keeping **for its container.**

הַהוּא גַּבְרָא [10]The Gemara now mentions an actual incident, and seeks by means of the ruling laid down in connection with it to solve one of the problems raised above (24a): **There was a certain man who found four zuzim,** silver coins, **that had been tied up in a cloth and thrown into the Biran River.** [11]**He came before Rav Yehudah** to ask him what he should do with the coins, whether he was entitled to keep them or whether he should announce that he had found them. Rav Yehudah **said to him: "Go and announce** the find, so that the rightful owner can have the opportunity to come and identify it."

וְהָא זוּטוֹ שֶׁל יָם הוּא [12]In connection with this Halakhic ruling the Gemara asks: Why should the finder of the coins have to announce his find? **Surely this** case **is** essentially similar to **the case** where someone retrieves a lost object from the tidal area **of the rising sea,** or from a flooding river, concerning which we

TERMINOLOGY

סָבַר לָהּ כְּוָותֵיהּ בַּחֲדָא וּפָלֵיג עֲלֵיהּ בַּחֲדָא **He agrees with him in one [case] and disagrees with him in another [case].** An expression used by the Gemara to describe a situation where Rabbi A made a statement involving two elements, and Rabbi B accepted Rabbi A's ruling in one part but not in the other, maintaining that there was no fundamental logical connection between the two.

הַהוּא גַּבְרָא **A certain man.** This expression is often used by the Gemara to introduce an incident in which an individual claimant appeared before a scholar or before a Rabbinical Court to receive a decision on a point of law.

BACKGROUND

נְהַר בִּירָן **The Biran River.** From the context it appears that the Biran River was close to Pumbedita. It is not clear whether this was a natural river or a large canal like the Malkha River and others, which brought water from the great natural rivers. In any event, since large areas of Babylonia were flat, the water flowed slowly, and a great deal of mud was swept into the river, blocking it from time to time. Therefore in Talmudic times it had to be dredged and the banks cleared to keep the water flowing. The work of clearing the canals and rivers was occasionally done by local residents, though larger rivers were apparently dredged by special laborers appointed for that task, and, as explained here, in the area of the Biran River most of these laborers were Jews.

RASHI

ושדו בנהר בירן – ומושלכין בנהר בירן.

HALAKHAH

נְהַר בִּירָן **The Biran River.** "If an object is found in a river containing a dam or some other obstruction, so that anything washed away by the river will probably get caught, it is not treated like an object lost in a flood but like a regular lost object. It cannot be assumed that the owner gave up hope of recovering it; and therefore, if the object can be identified, it must be returned." (*Shulḥan Arukh, Ḥoshen Mishpat* 259:7.)

LITERAL TRANSLATION

[1]The river Biran is different. [2]Since there are obstacles, he does not give up hope.
[3]But surely the majority are non-Jews. [4]Conclude from this [that] the Halakhah is not in accordance with Rabbi Shimon ben Elazar even where the majority are non-Jews.
[5]The river Biran is different, for Jews dam it up, and Jews dredge it. [6]Since Jews dam it, one may say [that] it fell from a Jew, [7]and since Jews dredge it, he does not give up hope.
[8]Rav Yehudah was following after Mar Shmuel in the cereal market. [9]He said to him: "[If someone] found a moneybag here, what is [the law]?"
[10]He said to him: "They belong to him."

[1]שָׁאנֵי נְהַר בִּירָן. [2]כֵּיוָן דְּמִתְקִיל, לָא מְיָאֵשׁ.
[3]וְהָא רוּבָּא נָכְרִים נִינְהוּ! [4]שְׁמַע מִינָּהּ אֵין הֲלָכָה כְּרַבִּי שִׁמְעוֹן בֶּן אֶלְעָזָר אֲפִילּוּ בְּרוֹב נָכְרִים!
[5]שָׁאנֵי נְהַר בִּירָן, דְּיִשְׂרָאֵל סָכְרוּ לֵיהּ, וְיִשְׂרָאֵל כָּרוּ לֵיהּ. [6]כֵּיוָן דְּיִשְׂרָאֵל סָכְרוּ לֵיהּ, אֵימוֹר מִיִּשְׂרָאֵל נְפַל, [7]וְכֵיוָן דְּיִשְׂרָאֵל כָּרוּ לֵיהּ, לָא מְיָאֵשׁ.
[8]רַב יְהוּדָה הֲוָה שָׁקֵיל וְאָזֵיל בָּתְרֵיהּ דְּמָר שְׁמוּאֵל בְּשׁוּקָא דְּבֵי דַּיְסָא. [9]אֲמַר לֵיהּ: "מָצָא כָּאן אַרְנָקִי, מַהוּ?"
[10]אֲמַר לֵיהּ: "הֲרֵי אֵלּוּ שֶׁלּוֹ".

RASHI

דמתקיל — יש בו מכשולים, אבנים וסתימת גדר שעושין לדגים, ולא מיאש, סבר לא יוכל הנהר להוליכם חוץ למכשולים, ורגילים היו לסוכרו ולנקותו ולכרותו שיטפו מימיו, וסומך שימצאם כשיסכרו אותו וינקוש. סכרו ליה — סקורין *נשנ״ש בלעז, כמו עושי סכר אגמי נפש (ישעיה יט). אימא מישראל נפיל — לפיכך חייב להכריז, ולא אמרינן יניח כדאמרינן לעיל ברוב נכרים לרבנן. לא מיאש — שהכורה ימצאם. דבי דיסא — שמוכרים שם חטים כתושין לדייסא, ורבים מצויין שם.

TRANSLATION AND COMMENTARY

learned above (21b) that the object may be kept by the finder in all cases, since the owner is considered by the Torah to have given up hope of recovering it.

שָׁאנֵי נְהַר בִּירָן [1]The Gemara replies: The situation where an object is found in **the Biran River is different** from the situation where an object is found in the tidal area of the rising sea or retrieved from an overflowing river. [2]**Since there are obstacles** and dams on the Biran River, the owner will hope to find what he has lost on one of the obstacles, or when the flow of the stream is stopped in order to clean out the channel. Hence, **he does not give up hope** of recovering the coins.

וְהָא רוּבָּא נָכְרִים נִינְהוּ [3]The Gemara raises another question: What difference does it make that the owner has not given up hope? **Surely the majority** of the local population **are non-Jews.** [4]If the finder of the coins is obliged to announce his find, are we not entitled to **conclude from this that the Halakhah is not in accordance with Rabbi Shimon ben Elazar even where the majority of the population are non-Jews?**

שָׁאנֵי נְהַר בִּירָן [5]The Gemara answers: The case of **the Biran River is different, for** it is **Jews** who **dam it up, and** it is **Jews** who **dredge it** to clean out and deepen the stream. [6]Therefore, **since** it is **Jews** who **dam it up, one may** reasonably **assume that** the coins **fell from a Jew** while he was taking part in the construction work to dam the stream, [7]**and since** it is **Jews** who **dredge** the river and clean out and repair the channel, the owner of the coins **does not give up hope,** since he expects a fellow Jew to find them and return them. Therefore the finder of the coins is obliged to announce his find.

רַב יְהוּדָה [8]The Gemara now relates another incident: **Rav Yehudah was once following** his teacher, **Mar Shmuel, in the cereal market,** a place frequented by many people, the majority of whom were non-Jews. [9]Rav Yehudah **asked** Shmuel: **"If someone found** an identifiable object, such as **a moneybag, here** or in a place like it, **what would the law be?** Would the finder have to announce his discovery or would it belong to him?"

אֲמַר לֵיהּ [10]Shmuel **said to him** in reply: "It would **belong to him,** because the owner can be assumed to have given up hope of recovering it, in accordance with Rabbi Shimon ben Elazar's reasoning."

NOTES

כֵּיוָן דְּמִתְקִיל **Since there are obstacles.** *Ra'avad* explains that the Biran River had a tendency to silt up, and it was frequently necessary to dredge it to afford clear passage. Therefore, it cannot be compared to the case of an overflowing river.

HALAKHAH

מָצָא מְצִיאָה בַּשּׁוּק **An object found in the marketplace.** "If a person finds an object in a place where the majority of the people are non-Jews, he is not obliged to return it, even if a Jew identifies it as having belonged to him, since the owner may be presumed to have given up hope of recovering it. Though the strict letter of the law does not require it, it is good and proper behavior to return the object to the person who has identified it as his." *Rema* adds that since returning the article is an act not required by the law, if the finder was poor and the loser rich, the finder need not go beyond the letter of the law and may keep the object for himself. (Ibid., 259:5.)

SAGES

מָר שְׁמוּאֵל **Mar Shmuel.** See *Bava Metzia,* Part I, p. 161.

BACKGROUND

שָׁקֵיל וְאָזֵיל בָּתְרֵיהּ **He was following after him.** This is a description of a disciple attending his master on his way, either to honor him by not letting him travel on his own, or to help him in other ways. In such a case the disciple not only enjoyed the privilege of fulfilling the commandment to serve Sages, but also had the opportunity of inquiring about various Halakhic subjects that had occurred to him but which could not always be clarified in a formal lesson in the House of Study.

שׁוּקָא דְּבֵי דַּיְסָא **The cereal market.** In the cities of Babylonia, as in many oriental cities, certain streets, known as "markets," were devoted to commerce and small-scale manufacturing. Each of these markets was usually a commercial center in its own right, with everyone working in a certain occupation. Just as there were food markets (שׁוּקָא דְּבֵי דַּיְסָא), there were also markets specializing in other commodities such as leather (שׁוּקָא דְּגִלְדָּאֵי) or metal. The market, more than a small street, was a place frequented by many people, both the owners of the stores and their customers.

LANGUAGE

אַרְנָקִי **Moneybag.** The source of this word is the Greek ἀρνακίς, *arnakis,* meaning a pouch or bag into which money is put.

LANGUAGE (RASHI)

*נשנ״ש (correct reading: אשקלושנ״ט). From the Old French *esclusent,* it means the blocking of the flow of a river in order to build a dam.

TERMINOLOGY

תַּרְתֵּי **Both?!** An expression indicating, in this context, astonishment at an internal contradiction within a source.

CONCEPTS

לִפְנִים מְשׁוּרַת הַדִּין Lit., **inside the line of justice.** The forgoing of a legal right. This concept is applied in civil law, when the letter of the law would grant a litigant certain rights, but he forgoes them as an act of generosity to the other person. Though the Sages could not always compel someone to go לִפְנִים מְשׁוּרַת הַדִּין — "beyond the requirement of the law" — they strongly advised it. Indeed, the Talmud says that Jerusalem was destroyed only because its inhabitants conducted their affairs according to the strict rules of the law (see below, 30b).

BACKGROUND

שׁוּקָא דְּרַבָּנַן **The market of the Rabbis.** This market apparently got its name because scholars frequented it, either because it was close to the House of Study or because other scholars owned stores there and the market was named after them.

TRANSLATION AND COMMENTARY

בָּא יִשְׂרָאֵל [1]Rav Yehudah asked again: **"If a Jew came and** accurately **described an identifying mark on it,** establishing conclusively that he was its owner, **what would the law be** in such a case?"

אֲמַר לֵיהּ [2]Shmuel **said to him** in reply: "In such a case **he would be obliged to return** the moneybag."

תַּרְתֵּי [3]In reaction to Shmuel's second answer Rav Yehudah asked in amazement: "How can you say **both** things? Your two answers appear contradictory. If the moneybag belongs to the finder, because the owner has given up hope, why should the finder return it if the owner comes and identifies it?"

אֲמַר לֵיהּ [4]Shmuel **said to him** in reply: "In the second case, although the finder has a valid legal title to the moneybag, he should nevertheless return it, and in so doing he goes **beyond the** strict **requirement of the law.** According to the letter of the law, the moneybag belongs to the finder and he need not go to the trouble of announcing that he has found it. But since the identity of the owner is now known to him, it would be proper to return it anyway.

כִּי הָא דַּאֲבוּהּ דִּשְׁמוּאֵל [5]The Gemara now illustrates the principle laid down by Shmuel by telling the following story involving Shmuel's father: It is **like that incident where Shmuel's father found some asses in the desert** [6]and returned **them to their owner after twelve months had passed** from the time they were lost. [7]In acting this way, Shmuel's father went **beyond the** strict **requirement of the law,** because the owner of the animals had certainly given up hope of recovering them after such a long time.

רָבָא הֲוָה שָׁקֵיל [8]The Gemara now relates another incident which bears on the present discussion: **Rava was once following after** his teacher, **Rav Naḥman, in the market of the leather workers,** [9]**and some say that it was in the market of the Rabbis,** a market which the Sages frequented. (According to both versions, the majority of the people in the place were non-Jews.) [10]Rava **asked** Rav Naḥman: **"If someone found** an identifiable object, such as **a moneybag here** or in a place like it, **what would the law be?"**

[1]״בָּא יִשְׂרָאֵל וְנָתַן בָּהּ סִימָן, מַהוּ?״

[2]אֲמַר לֵיהּ: ״חַיָּיב לְהַחֲזִיר״.

[3]״תַּרְתֵּי?!״

[4]אֲמַר לֵיהּ: ״לִפְנִים מְשׁוּרַת הַדִּין״.

[5]כִּי הָא דַּאֲבוּהּ דִּשְׁמוּאֵל אַשְׁכַּח הָנָךְ חֲמָרֵי בְּמַדְבְּרָא, [6]וְאַהַדְרִינְהוּ לְמָרַיְיהוּ לְבָתַר תְּרֵיסַר יַרְחֵי שַׁתָּא, [7]לִפְנִים מְשׁוּרַת הַדִּין.

[8]רָבָא הֲוָה שָׁקֵיל וְאָזֵיל בָּתְרֵיהּ דְּרַב נַחְמָן בְּשׁוּקָא דְּגִלְדָּאֵי, [9]וְאָמְרִי לַהּ בְּשׁוּקָא דְּרַבָּנַן. [10]אֲמַר לֵיהּ: ״מָצָא כָּאן אַרְנָקִי, מַהוּ?״

LITERAL TRANSLATION

[1]"[If] a Jew came and gave an identifying mark on it, what is [the law]?"

[2]He said to him: "He is obliged to return [it]."

[3]"Both?!"

[4]He said to him: "Beyond the requirement of the law (lit., 'inside the line of justice')."

[5]As when Shmuel's father found some asses in the desert, [6]and he returned them to their owner after twelve months of the year [had passed], [7]beyond the requirement of the law.

[8]Rava was following after Rav Naḥman in the market of leather workers, [9]and some say, in the market of the Rabbis.

[10]He said to him: "[If someone] found a moneybag here, what is [the law]?"

RASHI

בתר תריסר ירחי שתא — מלאם.

דגלדאי — רלענים.

NOTES

אַהַדְרִינְהוּ לְמָרַיְיהוּ לְבָתַר תְּרֵיסַר יַרְחֵי שַׁתָּא **He returned them after twelve months.** The commentary here follows *Rashi,* who explained that Shmuel's father found the asses twelve months after they had been lost. *Rashi* (*Berakhot* 58b) maintains that, after twelve months have elapsed, it may be assumed that the owner has given up hope of recovering property he has lost. He bases his argument on the Talmud's use of the Biblical verse (Psalms 31:13), "I am forgotten as a dead man out of mind; I am like a lost vessel," to prove that after twelve months a deceased person is no longer mourned. In the same way, a lost article is forgotten after twelve months and the owner has given up hope of recovering it. (*Shittah Mekubbetzet.*)

Ra'avad and *Ritva* add that it is possible that Shmuel's father knew that a year had passed, because he had noticed the asses in the desert a year before, and a year later he noticed them again and caught them.

Tosafot (and *Rosh* and *Ran*) reject the idea that the passage of time alone is proof that the owner has given up hope. They explain that Shmuel's father found the asses immediately after they were lost, and then cared for them for a year before their owner was located. Accordingly, he was not entitled to ownership of the asses, as they came into his custody before the owner gave up hope of recovering them. But after caring for them for a year he became entitled to keep the asses and return their monetary value (see below, 28b); yet, as an act of piety, he returned the asses themselves.

TRANSLATION AND COMMENTARY

אָמַר לֵיהּ [1]Rav Naḥman **said to him** in reply: **"It would belong to him,** in accordance with Rabbi Shimon ben Elazar's reasoning."

בָּא יִשְׂרָאֵל [2]Rava continued to ask: **"If a Jew came and described an identifying mark on it,** establishing conclusively that he had lost it, **what would the law be** in such a case?"

אָמַר לֵיהּ [3]Rav Naḥman **said to him** in reply: **"It would** still **belong to** the finder." By giving up hope of recovering the moneybag, the owner has renounced his ownership of it, and the finder has become the legal owner by picking it up.

וַהֲלֹא עוֹמֵד וְצוֹוֵחַ [4]Rava then asked: **"But is** the owner **not standing** there **shouting?"** He has identified the object, and is protesting that he is the real owner.

נַעֲשָׂה כְּצוֹוֵחַ [5]Rav Naḥman replied: **"He is like someone who is shouting** and complaining bitterly **about his house that has collapsed or about his boat that has sunk in the sea."** Since there is a legal presumption that he gave up hope of recovering his loss at the time he became aware of it, no amount of protest now can reverse his abandonment of legal ownership.

הַהוּא דַּיּוֹ דְּשָׁקֵיל בִּשְׂרָא בְּשׁוּקָא [6]The Gemara now relates another incident and again attempts to solve one of the problems raised above (24a): **There was a vulture that seized meat in the market and dropped it among the palm trees in Bar Marion's estate.** [7]Bar Marion **came before Abaye** to ask whether he could keep the meat for himself or whether he was obliged to announce that he had found it. [8]Abaye **said to him: "Go and take it for yourself,"** but did not give a reason for his ruling.

וְהָא רוּבָּא דְּיִשְׂרָאֵל נִינְהוּ [9]The Gemara now assumes that Abaye's ruling was based on the argument used by Rabbi Shimon ben Elazar, that the meat was lost in a public marketplace. Hence the Gemara now asks: **But surely the majority** of the local population **are Jews,** and nevertheless Abaye allowed the finder to keep the meat. [10]May we not **conclude from here that** according to Abaye **the Halakhah is in accordance with** the viewpoint of **Rabbi Shimon ben Elazar even where the majority** of the population **are Jews?**

[1]אָמַר לֵיהּ: "הֲרֵי אֵלּוּ שֶׁלּוֹ".
[2]"בָּא יִשְׂרָאֵל וְנָתַן בָּהּ סִימָן, מַהוּ?"
[3]אָמַר לֵיהּ: "הֲרֵי אֵלּוּ שֶׁלּוֹ".
[4]"וַהֲלֹא עוֹמֵד וְצוֹוֵחַ?"
[5]"נַעֲשָׂה כְּצוֹוֵחַ עַל בֵּיתוֹ שֶׁנָּפַל, וְעַל סְפִינָתוֹ שֶׁטָּבְעָה בַּיָּם".
[6]הַהוּא דַּיּוֹ דְּשָׁקֵיל בִּשְׂרָא בְּשׁוּקָא וְשַׁדְיֵהּ בְּצִנְּיָיתָא דְּבֵי בַּר מָרְיוֹן. [7]אֲתָא לְקַמֵּיהּ דְּאַבָּיֵי. [8]אֲמַר לֵיהּ: "זִיל שְׁקוֹל לְנַפְשָׁךְ".
[9]וְהָא רוּבָּא דְּיִשְׂרָאֵל נִינְהוּ! [10]שְׁמַעַתְּ מִינָּהּ: הֲלָכָה כְּרַבִּי שִׁמְעוֹן בֶּן אֶלְעָזָר אֲפִילּוּ בְּרוֹב יִשְׂרָאֵל!

LITERAL TRANSLATION

[1]He said to him: "They belong to him."

[2]"[If] a Jew came and gave an identifying mark on it, what is [the law]?"

[3]He said to him: "They belong to him."

[4]"But is he not standing and shouting?"

[5]"He is like someone who shouts about his house that collapsed or about his boat that sank in the sea."

[6]A vulture seized meat in the market and dropped it among the palm trees in Bar Marion's estate. [7]He came before Abaye. [8]He said to him: "Go, take [it] for yourself."

[9]But surely the majority are Jews. [10]Conclude from here [that] the Halakhah is in accordance with Rabbi Shimon ben Elazar even where the majority are Jews.

RASHI

דיו – עוף שקורין *אולטו"ר, והוא לשון דיה. ושדיה בצנייתא דבי בר מריון – השליכתו בין דקלים של בר מריון.

REALIA

דַּיּוֹ **Vulture, kite.**

This is the bird known in modern Hebrew as דַּיָּה, the vulture or kite (probably the common kite, *milvus migrans*), a bird of prey found almost everywhere in the world, including Eretz Israel and Babylonia. The דַּיּוֹ is about 55 cm. in length and brownish black in color. It has long wings, a long, forked tail, and short legs. It feeds on small animals and carrion, and generally nests in tall trees. It tends to live near human habitations, and may boldly catch small fowl or snatch pieces of meat.

LANGUAGE (RASHI)

אולטור"* (correct reading: וולטור") From the Old French *voltur,* vulture.

BACKGROUND

בַּר מָרְיוֹן **Bar Marion.** This was apparently the name of a wealthy family whose affluence lasted for several generations. The source of the name may be the Greek μόριον, *morion,* meaning a member of society, and the like.

NOTES

וַהֲלֹא עוֹמֵד וְצוֹוֵחַ **But is he not standing and shouting?** It is proper to go beyond the requirement of the law, and to return lost property to its original owner even though a strict legal obligation to do so does not exist. If Rav Naḥman himself had actually found a moneybag, he would certainly have returned it. But he was asked the question in his capacity as a judge, and he responded according to the letter of the law. There are people who are not required to go beyond the letter of the law, such as poor people (*Rema* in *Shulḥan Arukh, Ḥoshen Mishpat* 259:5). Moreover, according to some authorities, it is only important people who are expected to go beyond the letter of the law, whereas ordinary people are not required to do so (*Rabbenu Yehonatan*).

HALAKHAH

צִפּוֹר שֶׁחָטְפָה בָּשָׂר **A bird that seized meat.** "Meat that was seized in one place by a bird and dropped elsewhere may be kept by the finder, even if a majority of the local population are Jews, since the owner must certainly have given up hope of recovering the meat." (*Shulḥan Arukh, Ḥoshen Mishpat* 259:6.)

BACKGROUND

בֵּין טְבֶרְיָא לְצִיפּוֹרִי **Between Tiberias and Sepphoris.** These two cities were the regional capitals of upper and lower Galilee respectively. They were apparently populated mainly by Jews. However, at the time these incidents took place (the third and fourth centuries C.E.), there were already many non-Jewish settlements in Galilee, so that it was appropriate to raise the question whether there was still a Jewish majority in the region.

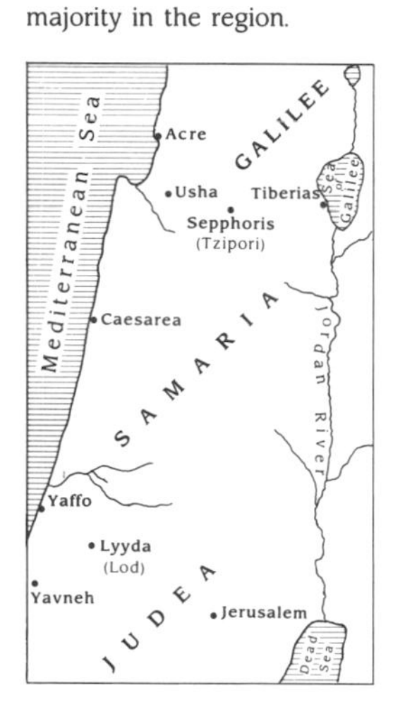

LITERAL TRANSLATION

[1] A vulture is different, in that it is like the rising sea. [2] But surely Rav said [that] meat that has disappeared from the eye is forbidden. [3] Where he was standing and watching it.

[4] Rabbi Ḥanina found a ritually slaughtered young goat between Tiberias and Sepphoris and they permitted it to him. [5] Rabbi Ammi said: They permitted it to him with respect to [the laws of] a found object, in accordance with Rabbi Shimon ben Elazar, [6] [and] with respect to ritual slaughter, in accordance with Rabbi Ḥananya, the son of Rabbi Yose HaGelili.

[1] שָׁאנֵי דַּיּוֹ, דִּכְזוּטוֹ שֶׁל יָם דָּמֵי. [2] וְהָא אָמַר רַב: בָּשָׂר שֶׁנִּתְעַלֵּם מִן הָעַיִן אָסוּר! [3] בְּעוֹמֵד וְרוֹאֵהוּ.
[4] רַבִּי חֲנִינָא מָצָא גְּדִי שָׁחוּט בֵּין טְבֶרְיָא לְצִיפּוֹרִי וְהִתִּירוּהוּ לוֹ. [5] אָמַר רַבִּי אַמִּי: הִתִּירוּהוּ לוֹ מִשּׁוּם מְצִיאָה, כְּרַבִּי שִׁמְעוֹן בֶּן אֶלְעָזָר, [6] מִשּׁוּם שְׁחִיטָה, כְּרַבִּי חֲנַנְיָא בְּנוֹ שֶׁל רַבִּי יוֹסֵי הַגְּלִילִי.

RASHI

אסור – שמא נתחלף בנבילה. **ורואהו** – משנטלו עד שהשליכו.

TRANSLATION AND COMMENTARY

שָׁאנֵי דַּיּוֹ [1] The Gemara rejects this argument: It is still possible to argue that in a place where the majority of the population are Jews the Halakhah is not in accordance with Rabbi Shimon ben Elazar, and the finder of lost property is obliged to announce his discovery. But the reasoning of Abaye in **the case of the vulture is different** from what we originally thought, **in that** meat seized by a vulture **is like** an object cast up by **the rising sea** (above, 21b). Items that cannot be recovered through ordinary human effort are considered ownerless by Torah decree, and need not be returned, even if they are successfully salvaged. We thus see that the case of the vulture has no bearing on the disposition of lost property whether the majority of the population of a certain place are Jews or non-Jews.

וְהָא אָמַר רַב [2] The Gemara now asks a parenthetical question on Abaye's ruling: The fact that Abaye ruled that Bar Marion could keep the meat would seem to indicate that the meat was considered by Abaye to be fit to be eaten, because it came from a place where the majority of the people were Jews. On this point the Gemara asks: **But surely Rav said** (*Ḥullin* 95a) **that** kosher **meat that** has not been under constant supervision but **has disappeared from the eye is forbidden** to be eaten, in case it was exchanged for another piece of possibly non-kosher meat. Perhaps the meat dropped by the bird was not the same meat it seized in the market. How, then, could Abaye permit it?

בְּעוֹמֵד וְרוֹאֵהוּ [3] The Gemara answers: **In the case** in which Abaye gave his ruling Bar Marion **was standing** there **and watching** the vulture from the moment it took the meat until it dropped it, and there was thus no danger that the meat was exchanged.

רַבִּי חֲנִינָא מָצָא גְּדִי שָׁחוּט [4] The Gemara now describes another related incident: **Rabbi Ḥanina found a ritually slaughtered young goat** on the road **between Tiberias and Sepphoris and** the Sages **permitted him** to keep it and eat it.

אָמַר רַבִּי אַמִּי [5] In interpreting this decision, **Rabbi Ammi said: They permitted it to him with respect to the laws of found objects, in accordance with** the ruling of **Rabbi Shimon ben Elazar,** who maintains (above, 24a) that if a lost object is found in a place where many people are found, it belongs to the finder. The highway between two major population centers certainly comes into this category. [6] **And with respect to** the laws of **ritual slaughter,** they allowed him to eat it, **in accordance with** the ruling of **Rabbi Ḥananya, the son of Rabbi**

NOTES

וְהָא אָמַר רַב בָּשָׂר שֶׁנִּתְעַלֵּם מִן הָעַיִן אָסוּר **Rav said: Meat that has disappeared from the eye is forbidden.** Rav's ruling was in dispute in Talmudic times, and remains so to this day. Some Rishonim argue that although our Gemara asks a question based on Rav's opinion, this is not a conclusive proof on which a practical Halakhic decision is to be made (see *Rashba* and others). Rav's reasoning is that a piece of meat that was left unwatched might have been exchanged for a similar piece of non-kosher meat, unless it was clearly marked and can be identified (see *Ḥullin* 95a).

HALAKHAH

בָּשָׂר שֶׁנִּתְעַלֵּם מִן הָעַיִן **Meat that has disappeared from the eye.** "Meat that is found, whether in the market or in the hands of a non-Jew, may not be eaten, even if all the slaughterers and butchers in the area are Jewish. Moreover, even if a person buys meat and leaves it in his house, he is forbidden to eat it if he lost sight of it, unless the meat has a sign by which it can be identified, or the owner recognizes it by sight, or it was packed and sealed with an identifiable seal." This is the ruling of the *Shulḥan Arukh* (*Yoreh De'ah* 63:1-2), in accordance with *Rif* and *Rambam,* following the viewpoint of Rav in our Gemara. *Rema* rules (ibid.), in accordance with *Tosafot, Rosh,* and *Mordekhai,* that such meat is permitted if it is found in the same place as it was left. This ruling follows the view of Levi who disagrees with Rav in *Ḥullin* 95a.

מָצָא גְּדִי שָׁחוּט **Finding a slaughtered animal.** "If a slaughtered animal is found in a place where the majority of the population are non-Jews, but the majority of butchers

LITERAL TRANSLATION

[1] For it has been taught: "If he lost his young goats or his chickens [and then] he went and found them ritually slaughtered, [2] Rabbi Yehudah forbids [them], [3] and Rabbi Ḥananya, the son of Rabbi Yose HaGelili, permits [them]. [4] Rabbi said: The words of Rabbi Yehudah appear [correct] where he found them on a heap of refuse, [5] and the words of Rabbi Ḥananya, the son of Rabbi Yose HaGelili, [appear correct] where he found them in a house." [6] Since they permitted it to him with respect to ritual slaughter, [7] the majority must have been Jews. [8] Conclude from here [that] the Halakhah is in accordance with Rabbi Shimon ben Elazar, even where the majority are Jews.

[1] דְּתַנְיָא: ״הֲרֵי שֶׁאָבְדוּ לוֹ גְּדָיָיו וְתַרְנְגוֹלָיו, הָלַךְ וּמְצָאָן שְׁחוּטִין, [2] רַבִּי יְהוּדָה אוֹסֵר, [3] וְרַבִּי חֲנַנְיָא בְּנוֹ שֶׁל רַבִּי יוֹסֵי הַגְּלִילִי מַתִּיר. [4] אָמַר רַבִּי: נִרְאִין דִּבְרֵי רַבִּי יְהוּדָה כְּשֶׁמְּצָאָן בְּאַשְׁפָּה, [5] וְדִבְרֵי רַבִּי חֲנַנְיָא בְּנוֹ שֶׁל רַבִּי יוֹסֵי הַגְּלִילִי כְּשֶׁמְּצָאָן בַּבַּיִת״. [6] מִדְּהִתִּירוּהוּ לוֹ מִשּׁוּם שְׁחִיטָה, [7] רוּבָּא יִשְׂרָאֵל נִינְהוּ. [8] שָׁמְעַתְּ מִינַּהּ הֲלָכָה כְּרַבִּי שִׁמְעוֹן בֶּן אֶלְעָזָר אֲפִילּוּ בְּרוֹב יִשְׂרָאֵל!

RASHI

כשמצאו באשפה – שדרך נבילה להשליכה לאשפה.

TRANSLATION AND COMMENTARY

Yose HaGelili, [1] **as it has been taught** in the following Baraita (*Ḥullin* 12a): **"If a person lost his young goats or his chickens, and then he went and found them ritually slaughtered,** and there is a doubt as to whether they were properly slaughtered, [2] **Rabbi Yehudah forbids them** to be eaten, in case they were slaughtered improperly, [3] **and Rabbi Ḥananya, the son of Rabbi Yose HaGelili, permits them** to be eaten, since they were presumbaly slaughtered in a proper manner. [4] In explaining this difference of opinion, **Rabbi** Yehudah HaNasi **said:** It is the place where they were found that is critical. **Rabbi Yehudah's statement appears correct** specifically **where** the finder of the goats or chickens **found them on a heap of refuse.** The fact that they were discarded indicates that they were slaughtered improperly. [5] **And the statement of Rabbi Ḥananya, the son of Rabbi Yose HaGelili, appears correct where** the finder of the goats or chickens **found them in a house."** This Baraita, as interpreted by Rabbi Yehudah HaNasi, lends support to the explanation given above by Rabbi Ammi that the Sages permitted Rabbi Ḥanina to eat the young goat that he found on the main road between Tiberias and Sepphoris, because they agreed with the viewpoint of Rabbi Ḥananya, the son of Rabbi Yose HaGelili. Just as the latter permitted goats or chickens "found in a house," so the Sages permitted Rabbi Ḥanina to eat the goat "found on the main road."

מִדְּהִתִּירוּהוּ לוֹ מִשּׁוּם שְׁחִיטָה [6] The Gemara now argues: **Since** the Sages **permitted** the young goat **to** Rabbi Ḥanina **with respect to** the laws of **ritual slaughter,** and did not take into account the possibility that the animal had been slaughtered in an improper manner, [7] we may assume that **the majority** of the local population where the young goat was found **must have been Jews,** since otherwise the meat would have been presumed to be non-kosher. However, the Sages still allowed Rabbi Ḥanina to keep the goat and did not oblige him to announce that he had found it, in accordance with Rabbi Shimon ben Elazar's reasoning. [8] We can surely **conclude from here that the Halakhah is in accordance with** the viewpoint of **Rabbi Shimon ben Elazar, even where the majority** of the population **are Jews.**

BACKGROUND

נִרְאִין **Appear correct.** Sometimes one Sage will say of another's words that they "appear correct" to him. This is not an absolute Halakhic judgment that the other Sage's opinion is authoritative, but merely a statement that his view is logical. Therefore such an opinion is occasionally not followed in the Halakhah. But since the opinion "appears" well grounded, action taken in accordance with it is not reversed.

מִדְּהִתִּירוּהוּ לוֹ מִשּׁוּם שְׁחִיטָה **They permitted it to him with respect to ritual slaughter.** Although one can detect by its appearance whether an animal has been slaughtered according to Jewish ritual law, there are a number of reasons why an act of ritual slaughter might not have been according to the Halakhah. For example, the knife used or the manner in which the animal was slaughtered may not have been proper. In many cases it is impossible to tell after the fact whether the act of slaughter was flawed in some way. Generally, one does not suspect that the slaughter was flawed, for one assumes that most of the people who perform ritual slaughter are experts at it and do their jobs correctly. But it can happen that the slaughterer is not qualified to carry out the task. He may, for example, not be mentally competent.

NOTES

וּמְצָאָן שְׁחוּטִין **And found them ritually slaughtered.** In the parallel passage in *Ḥullin* 12a, the Talmud concludes that both Rabbi Yehudah and Rabbi Ḥanina agree that most Jews who ritually slaughter animals are competent slaughterers. Therefore an animal found slaughtered in a house is presumed to be kosher. Conversely, they would both also agree that an animal found discarded on a public refuse heap must be presumed to be non-kosher. Their difference of opinion is restricted to the case of a slaughtered animal found in a heap of refuse near a house, or to a slaughtered animal found in the street, but not in a heap of refuse (see *Tosafot* and *Meiri*).

HALAKHAH

and slaughterers are Jews, it may be eaten, and it belongs to its finder." (*Shulḥan Arukh, Ḥoshen Mishpat* 259:6.) It is, however, subject to the prohibitions relating to meat that disappeared from sight (*Sma,* see previous entry).

אָבְדוּ לוֹ גְּדָיָיו וּמְצָאָן שְׁחוּטִין **A person who lost his animals and found them slaughtered.** "If a person lost his goats or chickens (or they were stolen), and he later found them ritually slaughtered, then, if the majority of the local population are Jews, he may eat them, even if he found them in the market or in a heap of refuse near someone's home. But if he found them in a heap of refuse in the market, they are forbidden, as it would appear that they were slaughtered improperly." This follows Rabbi's ruling, in accordance with the Gemara's clarification in *Ḥullin* 12a, and Rabbi Ammi's ruling in our passage. (*Shulḥan Arukh, Yoreh De'ah* 1:4.)

TRANSLATION AND COMMENTARY

אָמַר רָבָא רוֹב נָכְרִים [1]Rava rejected this argument and said: **The majority** of the population **were non-Jews, but the majority of the** ritual **slaughterers were Jews.** The reason why the Sages permitted Rabbi Ḥanina to keep the goat was because the majority of the people in the area were non-Jews. This decision was in accordance with the viewpoint of Rabbi Shimon ben Elazar. But if the majority of the people in the area had been Jews, it is possible that the Sages would have decided differently, and that the Halakhah is not in accordance with Rabbi Shimon ben Elazar in such a situation. As to why the Sages permitted Rabbi Ḥanina to eat the goat when it was found — as has been said — in a place where the majority of the people were non-Jews, the answer is that the majority of those responsible for the slaughter of animals in the area where the goat was found were Jews.

רַבִּי אַמִי אַשְׁכַּח פַּרְגִּיּוֹת [2]The Gemara continues with another related incident: **Rabbi Ammi found ritually slaughtered chicks** on the road **between Tiberias and Sepphoris.** [3]**He came before Rabbi Assi** to ask him what he should do. [4]**And some say** that he came **before Rabbi Yoḥanan, and some say** that he came **to the study hall** to ask what he should do. [5]**And they said to him: "Go and take them for yourself."**

רַבִּי יִצְחָק נַפָּחָא [6]Similarly, **Rabbi Yitzḥak Nappaḥa found a bundle of string from which nets were woven.** This occurred in a place frequented by many people. [7]**He came before Rabbi Yoḥanan, and some say** that he came

[1]אָמַר רָבָא: רוֹב נָכְרִים, וְרוֹב טַבָּחֵי יִשְׂרָאֵל.
[2]רַבִּי אַמִי אַשְׁכַּח פַּרְגִּיּוֹת שְׁחוּטוֹת בֵּין טְבֶרְיָא לְצִיפּוֹרִי. [3]אֲתָא לְקַמֵּיהּ דְּרַבִּי אַסִי, [4]וְאָמְרִי לַהּ לְקַמֵּיהּ דְּרַבִּי יוֹחָנָן, וְאָמְרִי לַהּ בֵּי מִדְרְשָׁא. [5]וַאֲמַרוּ לֵיהּ: "זִיל, שְׁקוֹל לְנַפְשָׁךְ".
[6]רַבִּי יִצְחָק נַפָּחָא אַשְׁכַּח קִיבּוּרָא דְּאָזְלִי בֵּיהּ אַזְלוּיֵי. [7]אֲתָא לְקַמֵּיהּ דְּרַבִּי יוֹחָנָן, וְאָמְרִי לַהּ בְּבֵי מִדְרְשָׁא,

LITERAL TRANSLATION

[1]Rava said: The majority [of the population] were non-Jews, but the majority of the slaughterers were Jews.

[2]Rabbi Ammi found ritually slaughtered chicks between Tiberias and Sepphoris. [3]He came before Rabbi Assi, [4]and some say before Rabbi Yoḥanan, and some say to the study hall. [5]And they said to him: "Go, take [them] for yourself."

[6]Rabbi Yitzḥak Nappaḥa found a bundle of string from which nets were woven. [7]He came before Rabbi Yoḥanan, and some say to the house of study,

RASHI

פרגיות – גוזלות. **אשכח קיבורי דאזלי ביה אזלויי** – מלא פקעיות של טווי למכמורות ורשתות במקום שהציידין מצויין. **אזלוי** – ציידים העושים מכמורות.

BACKGROUND

מָצָא גְּדִי... אַשְׁכַּח פַּרְגִּיּוֹת He found a young goat... he found chicks. The purpose of presenting this series of examples was to prove that there is a certain Halakhic tradition regarding objects found in places frequented by many people, and the various views are brought together in order to present a single Halakhic conclusion. However, since those who were of the opinion that it is permissible to keep the lost object did not publicly state an explicit Halakhic conclusion, and because they did not explain the reasoning behind each of the decisions they reached, it was necessary to attempt to deduce a uniform conclusion from these many examples.

LANGUAGE

פַּרְגִּיּוֹת Chicks. This word is etymologically close to the Arabic فرخ, meaning "fledglings," "young birds."

NOTES

רַבִּי אַמִי אַשְׁכַּח פַּרְגִּיּוֹת שְׁחוּטוֹת Rabbi Ammi found ritually slaughtered chicks. This story appears to be a mere repetition of the principle established in the previous stories, that the Halakhah follows Rabbi Shimon ben Elazar where the majority of the local population is non-Jewish, but not where it is Jewish. This is especially likely, in view of the fact that the story about the chicks is almost identical with the story about the goat. Both occurred on the same road between Tiberias and Sepphoris, and Rabbi Ammi is mentioned in both cases. Moreover, in the story about the chicks it is Rabbi Assi who issues the ruling, and the Gemara has already established, in the case of the wine above, that Rabbi Assi's own view is indeed that the Halakhah follows Rabbi Shimon ben Elazar where the majority is non-Jewish, but not where it is Jewish. Similarly, it is possible to explain that the following story about Rabbi Yitzḥak Nappaḥa finding a bundle of string occurred in a place where the majority of the population was non-Jewish.

But the Rishonim find this explanation of the story of the chicks difficult to accept: Granted that the population along the road between Tiberias and Sepphoris was mainly non-Jewish, and granted that the slaughterers in the area where mainly Jewish, it is still not clear why Rabbi Ammi was permitted to eat the chicks, because small birds were not usually brought to a slaughterer to be killed, but were killed at home, both by Jews and especially by non-Jews. Hence, if the birds were permitted, it could only have been because the demography of the area changed, and the Tiberias-Sepphoris road came to have a Jewish majority!

Because of this objection, *Ra'avad* decided that in telling these last stories, the Gemara was reversing its previous position and ruling in favor of Rabbi Shimon ben Elazar, even in a place where the majority of the population is Jewish. But the other Rishonim are reluctant to accept that the Gemara was making such a radical change without saying so explicitly. Accordingly, they insist that the population along the Tiberias-Sepphoris road was still mainly non-Jewish, and suggest that perhaps most bird trappers in the area were Jewish, or perhaps the permission granted Rabbi Ammi was not to eat the chicks, but to make use of them as he would his own non-kosher meat (*Rashba, Ran*).

אֲתָא לְקַמֵּיהּ דְּרַבִּי אַסִי He came before Rabbi Assi. The Rishonim note that from other passages it would appear that Rabbi Ammi was a Sage of greater stature than Rabbi Assi. Why, then, did Rabbi Ammi ask for Rabbi Assi's opinion?

Tosafot point out that although Rabbi Ammi may have

TRANSLATION AND COMMENTARY

to the study hall to ask what he should do. [1]**They said to him: "Go and take it for yourself."** Thus we see that the Gemara was unable to establish with any certainty whether or not Rabbi Shimon ben Elazar intended his reasoning to apply to Jews as well as non-Jews, and it was likewise unable to establish the viewpoint of the other Sages. But the Gemara *has* established that for practical purposes the Halakhah follows Rabbi Shimon ben Elazar's reasoning where the majority of the population are non-Jews, but not where the majority are Jews.

MISHNAH וְאֵלּוּ חַיָּיב לְהַכְרִיז [2]The following Mishnah is a continuation of the first Mishnah of this chapter (above, 21a). In the first Mishnah the subject under discussion was lost property which the finder is entitled to keep. In the following Mishnah the subject is those items of lost property that must be returned, i.e., objects containing identifying marks, which their owners have not given up hope of recovering: **And these** are the lost articles whose discovery the finder **is obliged to announce:** [3]**If he found fruit in a utensil, or a utensil by itself,** [4]if he found **money in a moneybag, or a moneybag by itself,** he is obliged to announce them, since utensils and moneybags can usually be identified by their owners. [5]If he found **heaps of fruit** or **heaps of money,** he is obliged to announce them, because in both cases the way in which the objects are lying is an indication that they did not fall but were placed where they were later found. It is thus possible that their owner will respond to an announcement by the finder and identify them, either by citing the number of fruits or coins found, or by citing the place where he left them.

שְׁלֹשָׁה מַטְבְּעוֹת [25A] [6]If he found **three coins** resting **one on top of the other,** he must announce them, because they were evidently placed this way intentionally, showing that their owner intended to come back and collect them but forgot to do so. Thus the finder must announce them, to give their owner the opportunity to identify and reclaim them. [7]If the finder came upon **small sheaves** of grain **in a private domain,** he must announce them, because the place where they were found (assuming they were left there deliberately) can serve as a means of identifying them. [8]If he found **home-baked loaves** of bread, he must announce them, because they are prepared according to each private baker's style and can be identified by their owner. [9]If he found **fleeces of wool taken from the craftsman's workplace,** he must announce them, because each wool processor

[1]וַאֲמַרוּ לֵיהּ: ״זִיל, שְׁקוֹל לְנַפְשָׁךְ״.

מִשְׁנָה [2]וְאֵלּוּ חַיָּיב לְהַכְרִיז: [3]מָצָא פֵּירוֹת בִּכְלִי, אוֹ כְּלִי כְּמוֹת שֶׁהוּא, [4]מָעוֹת בְּכִיס, אוֹ כִּיס כְּמוֹת שֶׁהוּא, [5]צִבּוּרֵי פֵּירוֹת, צִבּוּרֵי מָעוֹת, [25A] [6]שְׁלֹשָׁה מַטְבְּעוֹת זֶה עַל גַּב זֶה, [7]כְּרִיכוֹת בִּרְשׁוּת הַיָּחִיד, [8]וְכִכָּרוֹת שֶׁל בַּעַל הַבַּיִת, [9]וְגִיזֵּי צֶמֶר הַלְּקוּחִין מִבֵּית הָאוּמָּן,

LITERAL TRANSLATION

[1]and they said to him: "Go, take [it] for yourself."

MISHNAH [2]And these he is obliged to announce: [3][If] he found fruit in a vessel, or a vessel by itself, [4]money in a moneybag, or a moneybag by itself, [5]heaps of fruit, heaps of money, [25A] [6]three coins, one on top of the other, [7]small sheaves in a private domain, [8]and home-baked loaves (lit., "loaves of a householder"), [9]and fleeces of wool taken from the craftsman's workplace,

RASHI

משנה מצא פירות בכלי — וקמה כלי יש בו סימן. כמות שהוא — ריקן. כיס — יש בו סימן לבעלים. צבורי פירות — בגמרא מפרש סימנייהו, או מנין או מקום. שלשה מטבעות זו על גב זו — בגמרא מפרש סימנייהו.

BACKGROUND

כְּרִיכוֹת בִּרְשׁוּת הַיָּחִיד Small sheaves in a private domain. The reasons given by the Gemara as to why small sheaves in the public domain are awarded to the finder are the following: If they had an identifying mark, it would probably have been trampled by passersby, and if the sheaves were left in a specific place, they would probably have been moved by passersby. By contrast, in a private domain, where few people are present, one may assume that passersby will step over the small sheaves, neither trampling nor moving them.

כִּכָּרוֹת שֶׁל בַּעַל הַבַּיִת Homemade loaves. A private householder who bakes bread for himself does not use a standard design, nor does he make certain that the loaves he bakes are of a certain, regular size. Therefore he will be able to recognize the loaves he has baked according to the particular way in which he alone is accustomed to bake them.

NOTES

been of greater Rabbinic stature than Rabbi Assi, the two were colleagues, and it was therefore appropriate that Rabbi Ammi seek out Rabbi Assi's opinion.

כְּלִי וְכִיס כְּמוֹת שֶׁהוּא A vessel or a moneybag by itself. *Ritva* asks: Why did the Mishnah repeat itself and say: "If he found a vessel (or a moneybag) by itself." The only reason why he needs to announce the fruit or the money is that they were found in an identifiable utensil or moneybag. What difference does it make if the utensil or the moneybag was full or empty?

He answers that a full utensil or moneybag need not be returned specifically on the basis of identifying marks. The owner can also identify them by saying which fruits and which coins were in them. Therefore, the Mishnah needs to tell us that utensils and moneybags are themselves normally distinguishable, even when empty.

HALAKHAH

כְּרִיכוֹת בִּרְשׁוּת הַיָּחִיד Small sheaves in a private domain. "If a person finds small sheaves in a private domain, and if they appear to have fallen, they may be kept by the finder. But if they appear to have been placed there intentionally, the finder must pick them up and announce his discovery." (*Shulḥan Arukh, Ḥoshen Mishpat* 262:9.)

כִּכָּרוֹת וְגִיזֵּי צֶמֶר Loaves and fleeces of wool. "Home-baked loaves and processed fleeces of wool have an individualized appearance which can serve as an identifying mark. Therefore their discovery must be announced," following the Mishnah. (Ibid., 262:8.)

LITERAL TRANSLATION

[1] jars of wine and jars of oil — [2] these he is obliged to announce.

GEMARA [3] The reason is because he found fruit in a vessel or money in a moneybag. [4] But a vessel and in front of it fruit, [5] [or] a moneybag and in front of it money, [6] these would be his.

[7] We have learned that which our Rabbis taught: [8] "[If someone] found a vessel, and in front of it fruit, [9] [or] a moneybag, and in front of it money, [10] they are his. [11] [If] some of them are in the vessel and some of them on the ground, [12] [or if] some of them are in the moneybag and some of them are on the ground, [13] he is obliged to announce [his find]."

[1] כַּדֵּי יַיִן וְכַדֵּי שֶׁמֶן — [2] הֲרֵי אֵלּוּ חַיָּיב לְהַכְרִיז.

גמרא [3] טַעְמָא דְּמָצָא פֵּירוֹת בַּכְּלִי וּמָעוֹת בַּכִּיס. [4] הָא כְּלִי וּלְפָנָיו פֵּירוֹת, [5] כִּיס וּלְפָנָיו מָעוֹת — [6] הֲרֵי אֵלּוּ שֶׁלּוֹ.

[7] תָּנֵינָא לְהָא דְּתָנוּ רַבָּנַן: [8] "מָצָא כְּלִי וּלְפָנָיו פֵּירוֹת, [9] כִּיס וּלְפָנָיו מָעוֹת, [10] הֲרֵי אֵלּוּ שֶׁלּוֹ. [11] מִקְצָתָן בַּכְּלִי וּמִקְצָתָן עַל גַּבֵּי קַרְקַע, [12] מִקְצָתָן בַּכִּיס וּמִקְצָתָן עַל גַּבֵּי קַרְקַע, [13] חַיָּיב לְהַכְרִיז".

RASHI

גמרא טעמא דמצא כו׳ — התם הוא דאמר שהפירות לבעל הכלי. **הא כלי ולפניו פירות** — הרי אלו הפירות של מוצאן, ואף על פי שהכלי לבעל הסימן — את הכלי יחזיר ואת הפירות יעכב לו, ולא אמרינן מהאי מנא נפל. **מקצתן בכלי כו׳** — הדבר מוכיח, דהנך דעל גבי קרקע דהנך הוא, וחייב להחזירם למי שיתן סימן בכלי, וכן מעות לבעל הכיס.

TRANSLATION AND COMMENTARY

processes his raw material in a different way and will be able to identify it. [1] If he found **jars of wine or jars of oil,** he must announce them, because the owner may be able to identify them by the special seal he placed on them. [2] All **these** examples mentioned in this Mishnah **must be announced** by their finder, because they are identifiable, and since the owner can identify them he has not given up hope of recovering them.

GEMARA טַעְמָא דְּמָצָא פֵּירוֹת בַּכְּלִי [3] The Gemara begins its analysis of the Mishnah by examining the particular terminology used in the examples given: The Mishnah specifies that the finder is obliged to make an announcement when he finds fruit in a utensil, or money in a moneybag. **The reason** why he must make this announcement **is because he found the fruit inside the utensil or the money inside the moneybag.** In such a case the Mishnah assumes that the contents of the container belong to the owner of the container. [4] **But** if someone were to find **an empty utensil and fruit** lying **in front of it,** [5] **or an** empty **moneybag and money** lying **in front of it,** [6] in such circumstances the fruit or the money **would belong to the finder.** Even though the finder would be required to return the utensil or the moneybag, he would be entitled to keep the fruit or the money, because we assume that there is no necessary connection between the utensil and the fruit or between the moneybag and the money.

תָּנֵינָא לְהָא דְּתָנוּ רַבָּנַן [7] On the basis of this analysis the Gemara concludes that **we have learned** implicitly in our Mishnah the same principle that **the Rabbis taught** explicitly in the following Baraita: [8] **"If someone found a utensil, and in front of it fruit,** [9] **or a moneybag, and in front of it money,** [10] the fruit or the money **is his** to keep, and he need not search for its owner. He does, however, have to announce that he has found the utensil or the moneybag. [11] But **if some of** the fruit **is** found still **in the utensil and some of it** is already lying **on the ground, or,** [12] similarly, **if some of** the money **is** found still **in the moneybag and some of it** is already lying **on the ground,** [13] **he is obliged to announce** everything he has found, and must return the fruit together with the utensil or the money together with the moneybag to the person who can identify the utensil or the moneybag as his, as it is obvious from the way the fruit or the money fell that it came from the utensil or the moneybag." The Baraita just quoted states explicitly what the Gemara deduced implicitly from our Mishnah: that fruit found near an empty fruit container or money found near an empty moneybag belongs to the finder.

BACKGROUND

כְּלִי וּלְפָנָיו פֵּירוֹת A vessel and in front of it fruit. As explained below in the Gemara, an identifying mark is not necessarily one that is found on the lost object itself, but rather any sign attached to or associated with the object (such as the saddle on an animal). The problem here is that the fruit, which bears no identifying mark, and the container, which could be expected to have an identifying mark, are not actually touching each other. The question under discussion concerns what is reasonable or likely: When and how can one reasonably assume that the fruit has fallen out of the container, and when can one say that there is no proof of any connection between the two?

TERMINOLOGY

תָּנֵינָא לְהָא דְּתָנוּ רַבָּנַן We have learned that which our Rabbis taught.... An expression used to introduce a Baraita in support of the previous statement, usually a Mishnah or an Amoraic elucidation of a Mishnah.

HALAKHAH

כְּלִי וּלְפָנָיו פֵּירוֹת A vessel and in front of it fruit. "If a person finds a utensil with fruit lying nearby, the utensil must be announced by the finder, but the fruit may be kept by him. But if it appears likely that the utensil and the fruit belong to the same person, the fruit must also be announced. For example, if the utensil faces away from the fruit, the finder may keep the fruit. If the mouth of the utensil is facing towards the fruit, the finder must announce the fruit, unless the utensil has an inner rim, in which case he need only announce the fruit if a trace of it remains in the utensil," following Rav Pappa's interpretation. (*Shulḥan Arukh, Ḥoshen Mishpat* 262:19.) According to *Rosh* and *Tur,* this ruling applies only to ordinary fruit, but in a case of a barrel of flax, the law is different, and follows Rav Zevid's explanation. *Rambam,* however, interprets Rav Pappa as disagreeing with Rav Zevid's distinction between flax and other produce, and rules according to Rav Pappa (see *Sma* and *Gra* on above-mentioned passage in the *Shulḥan Arukh*).

LITERAL TRANSLATION

[1]But there is a contradiction to this (lit., "cast them [against each other]"): [2]"[If someone] found something that does not have an identifying mark next to something that does have an identifying mark, [3]he is obliged to announce [his find]. [4][If] the owner of an identifying mark came and took what was his, [5]the other is entitled to the item that does not have an identifying mark."

[6]Rav Zevid said: There is no difficulty. [7]This [refers] to a barrel and flax, [8][and] that [refers] to a basket and fruit.

[1]וּרְמִינְהוּ: [2]"מָצָא דָּבָר שֶׁאֵין בּוֹ סִימָן בְּצַד דָּבָר שֶׁיֵּשׁ בּוֹ סִימָן, [3]חַיָּיב לְהַכְרִיז. [4]בָּא בַּעַל סִימָן וְנָטַל אֶת שֶׁלּוֹ, [5]זָכָה הַלָּה בְּדָבָר שֶׁאֵין בּוֹ סִימָן".

[6]אָמַר רַב זְבִיד: לָא קַשְׁיָא. [7]הָא בְּכוּבָא וְכִיתָּנָא, [8]הָא בְּצַנָּא וּפֵירֵי.

TRANSLATION AND COMMENTARY

וּרְמִינְהוּ [1]The Gemara now challenges the principle that it has just established: **But there is a contradiction** between the following Tosefta (*Bava Metzia* 2:9) and the Baraita that has just been quoted and, by implication, our Mishnah: [2]**"If a person found something that does not have an identifying mark** (like fruit) lying **next to something that does have an identifying mark** (like a utensil), [3]**he is obliged to announce his discovery** of both items. [4]**If the owner of** the item possessing **the identifying mark** then **comes and takes** the item **that is his,** admitting that the rest of what was found does not belong to him, [5]**the other one,** the finder, **is entitled to the item that does not have an identifying mark."** The first clause of this Tosefta contradicts the Baraita quoted earlier, and also contradicts our Mishnah. According to our Mishnah and the Baraita, if a person finds a utensil and fruit near it, he is entitled to keep the fruit. According to the first clause of the Tosefta, he must announce his discovery of the fruit. How, asks the Gemara, can this contradiction be resolved?

The Gemara now gives four responses to the contradiction raised:

אָמַר רַב זְבִיד [6](1) **Rav Zevid said** in reply: **There is no difficulty** in reconciling this seeming contradiction. [7]The Tosefta **is referring** specifically **to a barrel** lying next to a bundle of **flax** and to similar cases, where it is reasonable to suppose that the flax had been in the barrel and fell out without leaving a trace. [8]From the language of the Mishnah and the Baraita, on the other hand, it is clear that they **are referring to a basket** lying next to a pile of **fruit.** If the basket shows no traces of having once contained the fruit, it is unlikely to have fallen out of it, and the fruit's location next to it is most probably a coincidence.

RASHI

הכי גרסינן: מצא דבר שאין בו סימן בצד דבר שיש בו סימן – כגון מעות לפני כיס. **חייב להכריז** – על הכל, ויתנו המעות לבעל הכיס. **בא בעל סימן ונטל את שלו** – את הכיס, ואמר אין המעות שלי, זכה הלה במעות. **הא** – דקתני הרי אלו שלו. **בכובא וכיתנא** – גיגית מוטלת ופשתן לפניה, דודאי האי פשתן לאו מכובא נפל, דאי מינה נפל – הוה משתייר בה, והוא הדין לכיס ולפניו מעות מהאי טעמא, והא דקתני חייב – בצנא ופירי, דעבידי דשרקי ונפלי מיניה כולהו.

BACKGROUND

בְּכוּבָא וְכִיתָּנָא A barrel and flax. A כּוּבָא was apparently a large bowl with a very wide mouth used mainly to hold liquids. According to *Rashi* the flax was scattered, and in such a case, if there had originally been any flax in the vessel, it would be almost impossible for none to remain in it. But, according to *Tosafot,* the flax was in a bundle, so that if it had fallen from the vessel, all of it would have fallen at once.

בְּצַנָּא וּפֵירֵי A basket and fruit. A צַנָּא is a basket, generally woven of palm fronds or willow branches, sometimes with one or two handles. Baskets of this kind were woven in many forms: simple shapes with wide mouths, or more rigid shapes with narrower openings and rims to prevent objects from falling out.

NOTES

דָּבָר שֶׁאֵין בּוֹ סִימָן בְּצַד דָּבָר שֶׁיֵּשׁ בּוֹ סִימָן Something that does not have an identifying mark next to something that does have an identifying mark. The Aharonim (see commentators on *Shulhan Arukh, Hoshen Mishpat* 262:19) raise the following problem: The Gemara seems to be assuming that the fruit belongs to the owner of the container merely because the container and the fruit are near each other. Now, it is true that "proximity" is an argument that can be used in this way. But there is an established Talmudic principle that this consideration is overridden by an argument of "majority" (רוֹב וְקָרוֹב רוֹב עָדִיף). In other words, since there are many places from which the fruit could have come, we ought to assume that it came from one of those places and not from the marked container near which it is lying.

Ketzot HaHoshen answers, based on an interpretation of *Ramban,* that a distinction must be made between objects that are merely close to each other and those that are right next to each other. *Hatam Sofer* and *Netivot HaMishpat* explain that, in our case, even though the fruit itself is unmarked, the owner of the container is expected to stipulate the kind of fruit that was in his container. The fact that the owner can give this information, added to the "proximity" argument, overrides the "majority" argument.

הָא בְּכוּבָא וְכִיתָּנָא This text is referring to a barrel and flax. *Rashi,* whose explanation is followed in the commentary here, explains that according to Rav Zevid, the Mishnah and the Baraita are referring to flax, since, in certain unusual contexts, flax is called a "fruit." Thus the finder is allowed to keep the "fruit" lying next to the container and the money lying next to the moneybag because the "fruit" being described is fibrous flax, which does not tend to fall out entirely without leaving a trace, and the same is true of coins falling out of a moneybag. The Tosefta, by contrast, refers to actual fruit, which does tend to fall out without leaving any behind. Rav Pappa then points out that even fruit does not normally fall from a basket without leaving a trace, since baskets usually have an inner rim.

Tosafot, however, and most of the Rishonim (see *Rashba, Ran, Ritva*) explain that, according to Rav Zevid, the Tosefta is referring to flax, while the Baraita and the Mishnah indisputably refer to fruit.

In practice, there is no difference between *Rashi*'s and *Tosafot*'s versions of Rav Pappa's conclusions about fruit. But they do disagree about the case of flax in a barrel, according to Rav Zevid, and this may have implications for the far more important case of money in a moneybag (according to *Rashi,* it is like flax; according to *Tosafot,* it is

REALIA

אוֹגְנִין Rims.

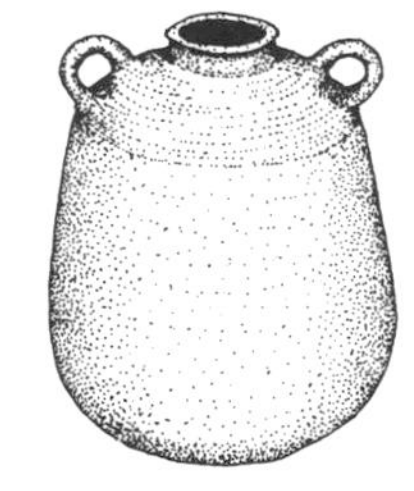

TRANSLATION AND COMMENTARY

רַב פַּפָּא אֲמַר [1](2) **Rav Pappa** offered an alternative explanation and **said: Both** the Tosefta, on the one hand, **and** the Mishnah and the Baraita on the other, **are referring to a basket and fruit, and there is** nevertheless **no difficulty** in reconciling them, because the sources refer to different circumstances. [2]The ruling of the Tosefta, stating that if a person finds an item without an identifying mark next to an item with an identifying mark he is obliged to announce both items, **applies where something remains in** the utensil — in this case, some fruit in the basket. Thus it is reasonable to assume that the fruit near the basket fell from it. [3]By contrast, the ruling in the Mishnah and the Baraita permitting the finder to keep the fruit and only announce his discovery of the basket **applies** specifically **where nothing remains in** the basket. Since most baskets have an inner rim, it is likely that some fruit would have remained in the basket after it was disturbed. The fact that the basket was found completely empty indicates that the fruit nearby did not fall from it.

וְאִיבָּעֵית אֵימָא [4](3) The Gemara now gives another alternative explanation, based on the explanation offered by Rav Pappa: **If you wish, you can say** that the seemingly contradictory sources are both referring to a case where fruit is found near a basket, as Rav Pappa explained. **Both are referring to a case where no** fruit **remains** in the basket, [5]**and there is** nevertheless **no difficulty** in reconciling them. [6]The ruling of the Tosefta **applies where** the basket's **opening is turned towards the fruit,** indicating that the fruit had fallen out of that basket. Thus the finder announces that he has found a basket and fruit, and the owner of the basket identifies the basket and claims both the basket and the fruit. [7]By contrast, the clause in the Baraita (and the ruling in our Mishnah) permitting the finder to keep the fruit **applies** specifically **where the opening** of the basket **is not turned towards the fruit.** In such a case it is reasonable to assume that there is no connection between the empty basket and the fruit nearby.

וְאִיבָּעֵית אֵימָא [8](4) The Gemara now gives yet another alternative explanation, based on Rav Pappa's explanation that the contradictory sources are both referring to a case in which fruit was found near a basket, and also based on the third answer just given, that no fruit remains in the basket: **If you wish, you can say** that both sources **are referring to a case where the opening** of the basket **is turned towards the fruit,** [9]**and there is** nevertheless **no difficulty** in reconciling them. [10]The ruling of our Mishnah and of the Baraita, permitting the finder to keep the fruit, **applies where the basket has rims** curving inwards, so that it is almost impossible that the contents spilled out without leaving something behind. In such a situation we assume that the fruit did not belong to the owner of the empty basket, and the finder is allowed to keep the fruit for himself. [11]By contrast, the ruling of the Tosefta **applies** specifically **where the basket does not have rims.** In such a case we interpret the basket's position, facing the fruit, as indicating that the fruit spilled from it, and disregard

[1]רַב פַּפָּא אֲמַר: הָא וְהָא בְּצַנָּא וּפֵירֵי, וְלָא קַשְׁיָא. [2]הָא דְּאִשְׁתַּיַּיר בָּהּ מִידֵי, [3]הָא דְּלָא אִשְׁתַּיַּיר בָּהּ מִידֵי.

[4]וְאִיבָּעֵית אֵימָא: הָא וְהָא דְּלָא אִשְׁתַּיַּיר בָּהּ מִידֵי, [5]וְלָא קַשְׁיָא. [6]הָא דִּמְהַדְּרִי אַפֵּיהּ לְגַבֵּי פֵּירֵי, [7]הָא דְּלָא מְהַדְּרִי אַפֵּיהּ לְגַבֵּי פֵּירֵי.

[8]וְאִיבָּעֵית אֵימָא: הָא וְהָא דִּמְהַדְּרִי אַפֵּיהּ לְגַבֵּי פֵּירֵי, [9]וְלָא קַשְׁיָא. [10]הָא דְּאִית לָהּ אוֹגָנִין לְצַנָּא, [11]הָא דְּלֵית לָהּ אוֹגָנִין לְצַנָּא.

LITERAL TRANSLATION

[1]Rav Pappa said: This and that [refer] to a basket and fruit, and there is no difficulty. [2]This [applies] where something remains in it, [3][and] that [applies] where nothing remains in it.

[4]And if you wish, say: This and that [apply] where nothing remains in it, [5]and there is no difficulty. [6]This [applies] where its opening (lit., "face") is turned towards the fruit, [7][and] that [applies] where its opening is not turned towards the fruit.

[8]And if you wish, say: This and that [apply] where its opening is turned towards the fruit, [9]and there is no difficulty. [10]This [applies] where the basket has rims, [11][and] that [applies] where the basket does not have rims.

RASHI

הא דקתני חייב בדאשתייר — ואיכא למימר הנך דאבראי מיניה נפל. **והא דלא אשתייר** — כיון דסתם צנא יש לו אוגנין כפולים לתוכו, אי מתוכו נפל הוה משתייר ביה דאוגנין מעכבי ליה. הכי גרסינן: הא והא דלא אשתייר ביה מידי. **הא דאית ליה אוגנין** — לאו מיניה נפל, דאי מיניה נפל — הוה משתייר ביה מידי.

NOTES

like fruit). The main objections to *Rashi*'s interpretation are the unusual definition of "fruit" in the Mishnah, and the fact that Rav Pappa appears to be contesting Rav Zevid's familiarity with the common construction of baskets and the normal effects of spillage, rather than suggesting possible additional distinctions between the two Tannaitic sources.

TRANSLATION AND COMMENTARY

the fact that no fruit remains in the basket. In such a case the finder must announce that he has found both the basket and the fruit, and if the owner of the basket can identify it the fruit is returned as well.

צִבּוּרֵי פֵּירוֹת וְצִבּוּרֵי מָעוֹת [1]The Gemara now considers the next clause in the Mishnah: A person who finds **"heaps of fruit** or **heaps of money"** must announce his discovery, because they contain some means of identification. The Gemara now examines the nature of this means of identification, [2]attempting to **conclude from** the plural form used in **this** clause of the Mishnah that it is the number of heaps of fruit or money found that provides the means of identification. If this is so, our Mishnah can be used to prove **that,** in general, if one finds a number of similar items lying near each other, their **number is a valid identifying mark** and the finder is obliged to announce his discovery.

תְּנִי צִבּוּר פֵּירוֹת [3]The Gemara replies that such a conclusion cannot be drawn from our Mishnah, as we are not certain of the exact text. It is possible that the Mishnah should be amended to **read: "A single heap of fruit."** This proposed reading would imply that the means of identification is that the fruit was piled up intentionally in a certain place and then forgotten. The finder would thus announce his find, and the owner would describe the place where he left the fruit as the means of identifying it.

שָׁמְעַתְּ מִינָּהּ [4]In response to this answer the Gemara remarks: But if the reading in our Mishnah is "a heap of fruit," it should be possible to **conclude from this that** in general the **place** where an item is found **is a valid identifying mark.**

תְּנִי צִבּוּרֵי פֵּירוֹת [5]The Gemara replies that we cannot necessarily draw this conclusion either. Since we are not certain of the exact text of the Mishnah, it may well be that the Mishnah should **read "heaps of fruit,"** in the plural. In that case "number" and not "place" is a valid means of identification. Thus, since the exact text is not certain, there is no way of arriving at a definite conclusion.

שְׁלֹשָׁה מַטְבְּעוֹת [6]The Gemara now considers the next clause in the Mishnah: "If a person finds **three coins, one on top of the other,** he must announce his discovery," as it is clear that they did not fall by accident but were placed there intentionally by their owner and then forgotten. [7]**Rabbi Yitzḥak of Migdal said: This** law **applies only where** coins **are** found **arranged** in an orderly pile **like towers.** In other words, the largest coin

[1]״צִבּוּרֵי פֵּירוֹת וְצִבּוּרֵי מָעוֹת״. [2]שָׁמְעַתְּ מִינָּהּ מִנְיָן הָוֵי סִימָן! [3]תְּנִי: ״צִבּוּר פֵּירוֹת״. [4]שָׁמְעַתְּ מִינָּהּ מָקוֹם הָוֵי סִימָן! [5]תְּנִי: ״צִבּוּרֵי פֵּירוֹת״. [6]״שְׁלֹשָׁה מַטְבְּעוֹת זֶה עַל גַּב זֶה״. [7]אָמַר רַבִּי יִצְחָק מִגְדְּלָאָה: וְהוּא שֶׁעֲשׂוּיִין כְּמִגְדָּלִין.

LITERAL TRANSLATION

[1]"Heaps of fruit, and heaps of money." [2]Conclude from this [that] number is a [valid] identifying mark.
[3]Read (lit., "teach"): "A heap of fruit."
[4]Conclude from this [that] place is a [valid] identifying mark.
[5]Read: "Heaps of fruit."
[6]"Three coins, one on top of the other." [7]Rabbi Yitzḥak the Midgdalite said: And this [applies only] where they are arranged like towers.

RASHI

שמע מינה מנין הוי סימן — דאי לאו הכי, מאי סימן איכא? **תני צבור פירות** — דאין כאן מנין, מאי סימניה? מקום, דכיון דלצבורין הינוח הוה, ויהיב סימנא: במקום פלוני הנחתים. **תני צבורי פירות** — סימני מנין, דהוי מדחי ליה: לא הא תפשוט ולא הא תפשוט. **והוא שעשוין כמגדלין** — לקמיה מפרש שסדרן רחבין זה מזה, ומניח מלמטה את הרחב ועליו את הבינוני, ועליון הוא הקצר שבכולן, כמגדל זה העשוי היסוד רחב ומקצר ועולה, וכי מנחי הכי — לאו דרך נפילה הוה אלא דרך הינוח, והיה דעתו לחזור וליטלן ושכח, הלכך נוטל ומכריז, וזה בא ונותן סימן, ואומר: מגדלין היו עשוין.

NOTES

צִבּוּרֵי פֵּירוֹת Heaps of fruit. *Rosh* asks: The Gemara's argument revolves around the use of the plural form צִבּוּרֵי rather than the singular צִבּוּר. But all the examples given in this entire chapter of the Mishnah are given in the plural form ("sheaves... loaves... jars...") and no significance is attached to this perfectly conventional choice of style. He answers that the question revolves around the Mishnah's use of the plural of the word "heap." Instead of using the expression "heaps of fruit" (צִבּוּרֵי פֵּירוֹת), it should have read "fruits heaped up" (פֵּירוֹת צְבוּרִין), which would have fitted the convention even better, being an exact parallel to the expression "scattered fruit" (פֵּירוֹת מְפוּזָּרִין) used in the Mishnah.

Ritva adds that it is possible that the Gemara was not actually seeking to amend the text when it said that it should read: "A single heap of fruit" (תְּנִי צִבּוּר פֵּירוֹת). Rather,

HALAKHAH

צִבּוּרֵי פֵּירוֹת וְצִבּוּרֵי מָעוֹת Heaps of fruit and heaps of money. "If a person finds even a single neat heap of money or fruit, it must be announced. But if he finds money or fruit scattered about, even if some of the coins or fruit are resting one on top of the other, they may be kept by the finder." (*Shulḥan Arukh, Ḥoshen Mishpat,* 262:11; see *Gra.*)

כְּמִגְדָּלִין Like towers. "If a person finds at least three coins, one on top of the other, in the form of a tower, or in the

TERMINOLOGY

תְּנִי... תְּנִי Read... read.... The argumentation here is an example of what the Talmud (*Mo'ed Katan* 15b) calls זִיל הָכָא קָא מַדְחֵי וְזִיל הָכָא קָא מַדְחֵי לֵיהּ (lit., "go here and he rejects it, go here and he rejects it"), meaning that the Gemara has not reached a clear conclusion on the subject. Thus a slight change in the wording can be used only in order to reject any absolute proof in one direction or the other, the main conclusion being that one cannot rely on precision in the wording in order to reach significant Halakhic conclusions here.

SAGES

רַבִּי יִצְחָק מִגְדְּלָאָה Rabbi Yitzḥak the Migdalite. A Sage belonging to the first generation of Amoraim in Eretz Israel, he is mentioned in several places in the Talmud and the Midrashim. In some cases he gives interpretations of unclear expressions used in the Mishnah. The simple sense of his name seems to indicate that he came from the city of Migdal, near the Sea of Galilee, a place mentioned in the Talmud and other sources (see below).

LANGUAGE

רַבִּי יִצְחָק מִגְדְּלָאָה Rabbi Yitzḥak the Migdalite. This rather odd name can be understood as "Rabbi Yitzḥak of the town of Migdal," but "migdal" means "tower," so his name may be "Rabbi Yitzḥak of the towers." *Rabbi Zvi Ḥayyot* explains that Sages whose names appear infrequently in the Talmud are sometimes nicknamed after their most famous statement — in this case, "Rabbi Yitzḥak of the towers."

BACKGROUND

עֲשׂוּיִין כְּמִגְדָּלִים Like towers.

מְשַׁלְחֲפֵי שַׁלְחוּפֵי Overlapping.

TERMINOLOGY

תַּנְיָא נַמִּי הָכִי It was also taught thus. A term used to introduce a Baraita which supports the previous statement by the Gemara or by an individual Amora.

אֵימָא סֵיפָא Consider the last clause, i.e., read the last clause in the source under discussion, and then you will realize that your interpretation of the first clause is incorrect.

BACKGROUND

שְׁלֹשָׁה מְלָכִים... מֶלֶךְ אֶחָד Three kings... one king. Generally, each king would mint new coins upon his accession to the throne, for the minting of coins was regarded as a powerful expression of the power and legitimacy of the regime. Most coins of that time bore the likeness of a king, either the Roman emperor or the king of Persia, stamped on one face of the coin. Usually coins of the current ruler were the most widely used, and occasionally the authorities even issued decrees requiring this. Hence, where coins fell in the same place it was likely that they would be of the same kind. But even coins minted by a single king were of various denominations, and therefore, especially at times when the value of a coin was connected with the value of the metal from which it was minted, they were also of different sizes. Hence the Gemara concludes here that the coins need not actually have been minted by different kings, but that they must be of different sizes.

TRANSLATION AND COMMENTARY

was at the bottom of the pile, the next largest on top of it, and the smallest on top of that.

תַּנְיָא נַמִּי הָכִי [1]In support of this statement by Rabbi Yitzḥak of Migdal, the Gemara notes: **This** same principle **has also been taught** in the following Baraita: **"If someone found scattered coins, they are his.** [2]But **if** the coins **are** found **arranged like towers,** the finder **is obliged to announce his discovery.** [3]**And the following is** what is meant by the expression, **'arranged like towers'**: [4]it means **three coins, one on top of the other."**

הָא גּוּפָא קַשְׁיָא [5]The Gemara now raises a problem concerning the meaning of the Baraita just quoted: **This** Baraita **is itself difficult** to understand, because it contains a hidden internal contradiction between its two clauses. [6]On the one hand **you have said** in the first clause: **"If someone finds scattered coins, they are his."** [7]This implies that **if** the coins **are overlapping, he is obliged to announce his find,** as the position of the coins indicates that they did not fall by chance. [8]But, says the Gemara, **consider the last clause** of the Baraita: **"If** the coins **are arranged like towers, he is obliged to announce his find."** [9]This implies that the finder must announce his discovery only if the coins are lying in an orderly fashion, one on top of the other. But **if** the coins **are** merely **overlapping, they belong to the finder.** Thus the implications of the two clauses of this Baraita appear to contradict each other.

תָּנָא [10]The Gemara answers: **The Tanna** who is the author of this Baraita **refers to as "scattered" all coins that are not arranged like towers.** In other words, the Tanna defines "arranged like towers" very strictly and "scattered coins" very broadly, and includes the situation of "overlapping coins" in his definition of "scattered coins." Thus there is no contradiction between the two clauses in the Baraita, and if someone finds coins overlapping each other, he does not need to announce them, as they are assumed to have fallen that way by chance.

אָמַר רַבִּי חֲנִינָא [11]**Rabbi Ḥanina said:** When **the Mishnah** states that if a person finds three coins, one on top of the other, he is obliged to announce his find, it **refers only to** a case where he found **coins of three kings,** i.e., different currencies, [12]**but** if all the coins are **coins of one king, he is not obliged to announce** his discovery.

[1]תַּנְיָא נַמִּי הָכִי: ״מָצָא מָעוֹת מְפוּזָּרוֹת, הֲרֵי אֵלּוּ שֶׁלּוֹ. [2]עֲשׂוּיִין כְּמִגְדָּלִים, חַיָּיב לְהַכְרִיז. [3]וְאֵלּוּ הֵן עֲשׂוּיִין כְּמִגְדָּלִים — [4]שְׁלֹשָׁה מַטְבְּעִין, זֶה עַל גַּב זֶה.

[5]הָא גּוּפָא קַשְׁיָא. [6]אָמְרַתְּ: ״מָצָא מָעוֹת מְפוּזָּרוֹת, הֲרֵי אֵלּוּ שֶׁלּוֹ״. [7]הָא מְשַׁלְחֲפֵי שַׁלְחוּפֵי, חַיָּיב לְהַכְרִיז. [8]אֵימָא סֵיפָא: ״עֲשׂוּיִין כְּמִגְדָּלִין, חַיָּיב לְהַכְרִיז״. [9]הָא מְשַׁלְחֲפֵי שַׁלְחוּפֵי, הֲרֵי אֵלּוּ שֶׁלּוֹ!

[10]תָּנָא כָּל שֶׁאֵין עֲשׂוּיִין כְּמִגְדָּלִין ״מְפוּזָּרוֹת״ קָרֵי לְהוּ.

[11]אָמַר רַבִּי חֲנִינָא: לֹא שָׁנוּ אֶלָּא שֶׁל שְׁלֹשָׁה מְלָכִים, [12]אֲבָל שֶׁל מֶלֶךְ אֶחָד אֵינוֹ חַיָּיב לְהַכְרִיז.

LITERAL TRANSLATION

[1]It was also taught thus: "[If] he found scattered coins, these are his. [2][If] they are arranged like towers, he is obliged to announce [his find]. [3]And these are the ones that are arranged like towers — [4]three coins, one on top of the other."

[5]This itself is difficult. [6]You have said: "[If someone] found scattered coins, these are his." [7][So, if] they were overlapping, he is obliged to announce [his find]. [8]Consider (lit., "say") the last clause: "[If] they are arranged like towers, he is obliged to announce [his find]." [9][So, if] they were overlapping, they are his.

[10]The Tanna calls "scattered" all [coins] that are not arranged like towers.

[11]Rabbi Ḥanina said: They only taught [concerning coins] of three kings, [12]but [coins] of one king he is not obliged to announce.

RASHI

שלוש מטבעות — שאין דומות זו לזו ברחבן. **משלחפי שלחופי** — מקצת זו על חבירתה, ומקצת על גבי קרקע. **חייב להכריז** — אלמא: כי האי גוונא לאו דרך נפילה הוא. **של שלשה מלכים** — קא סלקא דעתך שלא היו צורותיהם שוות, שכל מלך כותב שמו וצורתו על מטבע שלו.

NOTES

the debate is over whether any significance should be attached to the plural form, or whether it should be treated as a mere matter of literary style and convention.

HALAKHAH

form of a staircase, he must announce his discovery." (*Shulḥan Arukh, Ḥoshen Mishpat* 262:12.) *Rema* adds that the "tower" rule applies only if the coins were of different size, with the widest at the bottom and the smallest at the top, following Rabbi Ḥanina. *Gra,* in his commentary on the Talmud, explains that the *Shulḥan Arukh* omits this condition, because it rules in accordance with Rabbi Yoḥanan, following *Rif* and *Rambam.*

[1]הֵיכִי דָּמֵי? [2]אִי דַּעֲשׂוּיִין כְּמִגְדָּלִין, [3]אֲפִילּוּ שֶׁל מֶלֶךְ אֶחָד נַמִי. [4]וְאִי דְּאֵין עֲשׂוּיִין כְּמִגְדָּלִין, [5]אֲפִילּוּ שֶׁל שְׁלֹשָׁה מְלָכִים נַמִי לָא!

[6]אֶלָּא, אִי אִתְּמַר, הָכִי אִתְּמַר: [7]לֹא שָׁנוּ אֶלָּא שֶׁל מֶלֶךְ אֶחָד כְּעֵין שְׁלֹשָׁה מְלָכִים. [8](אֲבָל שֶׁל מֶלֶךְ אֶחָד אֵינוֹ חַיָּיב לְהַכְרִיז). [9]וְהֵיכִי דָּמֵי? [10]דַּעֲשׂוּיִין כְּמִגְדָּלִים — רְוִיחָא תַּתָּאָה, וּמְצִיעָא עִילָּוֵיהּ, וְזוּטָא עִילָּוֵיהּ מְצִיעָא. [11]דְּאָמְרִינַן: אַנּוּחֵי אַנְחִינְהוּ. [12]אֲבָל שֶׁל מֶלֶךְ אֶחָד, דְּכוּלְּהוּ כִּי הֲדָדֵי נִינְהוּ, [13]אַף עַל גַּב דְּמַנְחִי אַהֲדָדֵי, הֲרֵי אֵלּוּ שֶׁלּוֹ. [14]אֵימַר אִתְרַמּוּיֵי אִתְרְמֵי, וּבַהֲדֵי הֲדָדֵי נְפוּל.

[15]וְרַבִּי יוֹחָנָן אָמַר: אֲפִילּוּ שֶׁל מֶלֶךְ אֶחָד נַמִי מַכְרִיז.

LITERAL TRANSLATION

[1]What is it like? [2]If they are arranged like towers, [3][then] even [coins] of one king also. [4]And if they are not arranged like towers, [5][then] even [coins] of three kings also not.

[6]Rather, if it was said, it was said as follows: [7]They only taught [concerning coins] of one king [yet] like [coins of] three kings. [8]But [coins] of one king he is not obliged to announce. [9]And how are we to visualize this? [10]Where they are arranged like towers — the wide one at the bottom, and the medium one on top of it, and the small one on top of the medium one. [11]For we say: [Someone] surely placed them [this way]. [12]But [coins] of one king, where all of them are equal, [13]even though they are resting on each other, they are his. [14]Say [that] it happened by chance, and they fell together.

[15]But Rabbi Yohanan said: Even [coins] of one king he also announces.

RASHI

אי דעשויין כמגדלין — שאין שוין ברחבן, ומונחים כמו שפירשית. **אפילו של מלך אחד** — שצורת שלשתן שוות. **של מלך אחד כעין שלשה מלכים** — כלומר, אפילו הן של מלך אחד — שצורת שלשתן שוה, והן כעין שלשה מלכים — שחלוקין ברחבן, ודומין לשלשה מטבעות. **הכי גרסינן: והיכי דמי כגון שעשויין כמגדלין חייב להכריז. דכולהו כי הדדי נינהו** — שוין ברחבן. **אף על גב דכי הדדי מנחי** — זה על זה ולאו משלחפי. **אימור [אתרמויי] אתרמי** — דהכי נפל, ואין זה הינוח, וסימן אין לו בהם, ואפילו מקום, דלא ידע היכן נפל. **אפילו של מלך אחד מכריז** — הואיל ומטבעות הוו זו על גב זו — יש כאן סימן, דלא אתרמי דנפול הכי.

TRANSLATION AND COMMENTARY

הֵיכִי דָּמֵי [1]From this statement of Rabbi Ḥanina it is not clear whether the difference between coins of one king or of three different kings is in their appearance or in their size. On this point the Gemara now asks: **How are we to visualize** the cases to which Rabbi Ḥanina is referring? [2]**If** the coins were of different sizes and **were found arranged like towers,** [3]**then even** if the **coins** were all minted by **one king,** the finder should **also** be required to announce them; for since their sizes are different, they were clearly placed there intentionally. [4]**And if** the coins **are not arranged like towers,** but are of equal size, lying one on top of the other, [5]**then even** if the **coins** had been minted by **three** different **kings,** he should **also** be allowed to keep them, and **not** be required to announce his discovery, since it is possible that the coins were lost by some passerby and by chance fell one upon the other.

The Gemara answers: The decisive element underlying Rabbi Ḥanina's statement is the size of the coins, not their appearance, and it makes no real difference whether the coins were of one king or several. His statement needs to be amended.

אֶלָּא, אִי אִתְּמַר [6]**Rather,** says the Gemara, **if the** statement of Rabbi Ḥanina **was made, it was made in the following form:** [7]When the Mishnah states that if a person finds three coins, one on top of the other, he is obliged to announce his find, it may even be **referring to coins of one king,** but only if the coins differ from each other in size in a manner **analogous to coins of three** different **kings.** [8]**But he is not obliged to announce** identical-sized **coins of one king,** even if they are lying one on top of the other. [9]**And how are we to visualize** a situation where a person who finds coins is obliged to announce them? [10]**Where they are** of different sizes and **arranged like towers: the widest one at the bottom, and the medium-sized one on top of it, and the smallest one on top of the medium-sized one.** Only if the coins are found lying in such a position is the finder obliged to announce them. [11]**For** in such a case **we say** that **someone surely placed them in that way** intentionally. [12]**But** if all the **coins** he found were **minted by one king, where all of them are** of **identical** size, [13]then, **even though they are resting on each other** in a neat pile, **they are** nevertheless **his** to keep. [14]For in such a case we **say** that the coins came to be lying **that way by chance, and they fell together** in that way. Thus, since there was no conscious plan behind the arrangement of the coins and they lack any means of identification, the finder is entitled to keep them.

וְרַבִּי יוֹחָנָן אָמַר [15]**But Rabbi Yoḥanan** disagreed with Rabbi Ḥanina's statement and his interpretation of the Mishnah. He **said: Even** if the **coins** in the "tower" were minted by **one king,** and are identical in size, **he must announce** his discovery. Since the coins are piled neatly on top of each other, it is not at all likely that

TERMINOLOGY

אֶלָּא, אִי אִתְּמַר, הָכִי אִתְּמַר **Rather, if it was said, it was said as follows.** Sometimes, when an objection has been raised against an Amoraic statement, the Talmud resolves this objection by suggesting that the Amora's remark was reported incorrectly, and hence it must be emended: "If such a statement was made, it was made in the following form."

SAGES

רָבִינָא **Ravina.** A Babylonian Amora of the fifth and sixth generations, Ravina apparently came from Mata Meḥasya, though some authorities claim that he came from Eretz Israel. He was among Rava's students. The Gemara records Halakhic discussions between the two and, more frequently, between Ravina and various other students of Rava. Although Ravina was older than Rav Ashi, he accepted Rav Ashi as his teacher and became his student and colleague. He was apparently also an active participant in the editing of the Babylonian Talmud, which was accomplished by Rav Ashi. We have little information about his private life, though the Talmud implies that he had children. Rav Ashi's sons were students of Ravina. He also had many other students, the most important of whom was Ravina the Younger (רָבִינָא זוּטֵי), his sister's son, who completed the main burden of the final editing of the Talmud.

[1]מַאי מַכְרִיז? מִנְיָן. [2]מַאי אִירְיָא תְּלָתָא? אֲפִילּוּ תְּרֵין נַמִּי! [3]אָמַר רָבִינָא: "טִבְעָא מַכְרִיז". [4]בָּעֵי רַבִּי יִרְמְיָה: כְּשִׁיר מַהוּ? [5]כְּשׁוּרָה מַהוּ? [6]כַּחֲצוּבָה מַהוּ? [7]כְּסוּלָּם מַהוּ?

TRANSLATION AND COMMENTARY

this occurred by chance. Their arrangement is itself a means of identification and the finder cannot keep them for himself. We see, therefore, that in the Gemara there are two conflicting interpretations of the expression in our Mishnah: "Three coins, one on top of the other." Rabbi Yitzḥak of Migdal and Rabbi Ḥanina are of the opinion that it is only where the coins are arranged in the form of a "tower" or pyramid that the finder must announce them, whereas Rabbi Yoḥanan is of the opinion that as long as the coins are lying one on top of the other the finder must announce them.

מַאי מַכְרִיז [1]The Gemara now asks: Where the coins are found lying one on top of the other, **what does** the finder **announce?** If we assume that the coins were not dropped, but were left there intentionally and then forgotten, there are two possible means of identifying them — by their number or by their arrangement. Which should the finder use? The Gemara answers: The finder announces **the number** of coins he has found, and the owner identifies them by describing their arrangement.

מַאי אִירְיָא תְּלָתָא [2]The Gemara now asks: In that case, **why** does the Mishnah **specifically** mention the number **"three"? Even** if there were only **two coins** involved, the same procedure should **also** be followed. Since you have said that no importance is attached to the number of coins as a means of identification, but that their arrangement is crucial, what difference does it make if there were three coins or only two?

אָמַר רָבִינָא [3]**Ravina said** in reply: The finder **announces** that he has found **"coins,"** without specifying their number, and the owner has to provide two pieces of information: the number of coins and their arrangement. Now if there were only two coins, the plural word in the announcement would be too revealing. Therefore, it is possible to announce the discovery of an orderly pile only if it consists of at least three coins.

בָּעֵי רַבִּי יִרְמְיָה [4]**Rabbi Yirmeyah** now posed a series of related problems and **asked: If the coins were** found arranged in a circle **like a bracelet, what is the law?** Does the finder have to announce them or is he entitled to keep them? [5]If they were lying **in a** straight **line, what is the law?** [6]If they were lying **in** the form of **a triangle, what is the law?** [7]If they were found arranged **like a ladder** or a set of stairs, with each coin resting mainly on the coin below it and partially suspended in the air, **what is the law?** Rabbi Yirmeyah's examples are all part of a general problem: Do these arrangements indicate that the coins were left intentionally, in the

LITERAL TRANSLATION

[1]What does he announce? The number.

[2]Why does he discuss three? Even two also!

[3]Ravina said: He announces "coins."

[4]Rabbi Yirmeyah asked: If they were like a bracelet, what is [the law]? [5]Like a line, what is [the law]? [6]Like a triangle, what is [the law]? [7]Like a ladder, what is [the law]?

RASHI

ופרכינן מאי מכריז מנין — קן וקן מטבעות מלאתי, וזה בא ונתן סימן: זו על גב זו מלאתים. טבעא מכריז — מטבעות מלאתי, הלכך תרי לאו סימנא הוא, דמיעוט מטבעות שתים. כשיר — מוטלין בעגול כאצעדה. כשורה — זו אצל זו. כחצובה — כשלשה רגלי קנקן, כל אחד כנגד אויר של שני, כזה. כסולם — רוב אמצעי על התחתון, ורוב העליון על האמצעי, כמו מעלות שקורין *אשקולינו"ש.

BACKGROUND

בָּעֵי רַבִּי יִרְמְיָה **Rabbi Yirmeyah asked.** Common to many of Rabbi Yirmeyah's questions is the aim of clarifying the boundaries of Halakhah. Here, too, the questions are meant to ascertain whether the expression "scattered coins" specifically means coins lying in an arrangement which is clearly random, indicating that they were dropped. If this is so, we may assume that coins lying in an orderly arrangement of any kind were placed that way intentionally. Conversely, "piles of coins" could be interpreted as coins specifically placed one upon the other, so that any other arrangement of coins must be viewed as random, a sign that the coins fell and were scattered without any intentional arrangement.

כְּשִׁיר **Like a bracelet.**

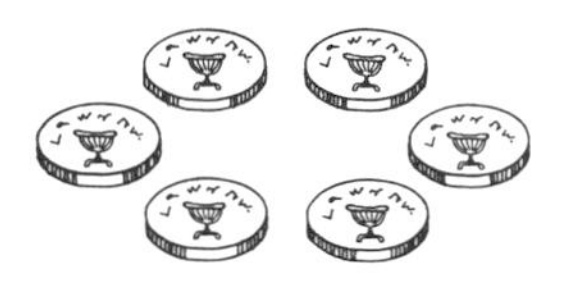

כְּשׁוּרָה **Like a line.**

כַּחֲצוּבָה **Like a triangle.**

כְּסוּלָּם **Like a ladder.**

LANGUAGE (RASHI)

אשקולינו"ש* From the Old French *eschelons,* meaning the rungs of a ladder.

NOTES

טִבְעָא מַכְרִיז **He announces "coins."** *Rashi,* whose interpretation is followed in the commentary here, explains that the tower arrangement is itself the means of identification. The Gemara is merely asking what language the finder should use in his announcement. At first the Gemara answers that he should announce the number of coins he found, so that the owner can give the tower arrangement as a means of identification. But in that case there would be no significance to the number "three." Therefore, Ravina rejects this answer and says the finder must announce that he found "coins." The owner must then cite both the number and the arrangement.

Most of the other Rishonim explain that the tower arrangement is not a sufficient means of identification in itself, at least according to Rabbi Yoḥanan, who does not require a true tower, and possibly even according to Rabbi Ḥanina. Rather, the tower merely serves as an indication that the coins were not dropped accidentally, but were placed there intentionally and then forgotten. Accordingly, the Gemara asks how the owner can possibly identify the coins, since they are not marked, and answers, "by number," provided that there are at least three. According to this explanation, מַאי מַכְרִיז? מִנְיָן cannot be translated literally, "he announces the number," but rather, "the finder announces that he found the coins, and the owner cites the number." Thus, when Ravina says the finder announces "coins," he is explaining, not disputing, the previous statement that the finder announces "number."

כְּסוּלָּם **Like a ladder.** On the face of it, this possibility is difficult to understand. The Gemara has already established

HALAKHAH

כְּשִׁיר וּכְשׁוּרָה **Coins lying like a bracelet or in a line.** "If a person finds coins lying in the pattern of a bracelet, or in a straight line, or in the form of a triangle, it is doubtful whether he is obliged to announce them. Therefore, they

TRANSLATION AND COMMENTARY

same way as the "tower" arrangement? In this case the owner can come and use the arrangement of the coins as a means of identification. Or did they fall into one of these patterns by chance?

פְּשׁוֹט מֵהָא חֲדָא [1]The Gemara notes: It is at least possible to **resolve one** of the above problems **by** applying **the following** statement: **For Rav Naḥman said in the name of Rabbah bar Avuha:** [2]**Whenever** one finds a pile of coins, **if** it is possible to **insert a splinter of wood among them and lift them** all **up together,** [3]this is an indication that they were placed there intentionally and the finder **is obliged to announce his find.** This statement of Rav Naḥman provides a solution to one of the problems raised by Rabbi Yirmeyah — the case of coins found arranged like a set of stairs. By inserting a splinter of wood under or between them, all those above the splinter can be lifted together, and this indicates that they were placed that way intentionally.

[1]פְּשׁוֹט מֵהָא חֲדָא: דְּאָמַר רַב נַחְמָן אָמַר רַבָּה בַּר אֲבוּהּ: [2]כָּל שֶׁאִילּוּ מַכְנִיס לָהּ קֵיסָם בֵּינֵיהֶן וְנוֹטְלָם בְּבַת אַחַת, [3]חַיָּיב לְהַכְרִיז.

[4]בָּעֵי רַב אַשִׁי: [25B] [5]כְּאַבְנֵי בֵּית קוּלִיס מַהוּ?

[6]תָּא שְׁמַע, דְּתַנְיָא: [7]"מָצָא מָעוֹת מְפוּזָּרוֹת, הֲרֵי אֵלּוּ שֶׁלּוֹ. [8]כְּאַבְנֵי בֵּית קוּלִיס, חַיָּיב לְהַכְרִיז. [9]וְאֵלּוּ הֵן אַבְנֵי בֵּית קוּלִיס: [10]אַחַת מִכָּאן וְאַחַת מִכָּאן וְאַחַת עַל גַּבֵּיהֶן".

LITERAL TRANSLATION

[1]Resolve one from the following: For Rav Naḥman said in the name of Rabbah bar Avuha: [2]Wherever if he inserts a splinter among them, he can lift them together, [3]he is obliged to announce [his find].

[4]Rav Ashi asked: [25B] [5][If coins were lying] like the stones of the house [of the idol] Culis, what is [the law]?

[6]Come [and] hear, for it has been taught: [7]"[If] he found scattered coins, they are his. [8][But if they were lying] like the stones of the house of Culis, he must announce [his find]. [9]And these are the stones of the house of Culis: [10]One on this side and one on that side and one on top of them."

RASHI

פשוט מהא — דרב נחמן חדא. **כל שאילו מכניס כו׳** — וכי הוו כסולם — ניטלים בבת אחת. **כאבני בית קוליס** — מרקולים, והיא שם עבודה זרה. ולקמיה מפרש היכי עבדי. **אחת מכאן ואחת מכאן והשלישית** — תליה על זה ותליה על זה.

BACKGROUND

בֵּית קוּלִיס The house of Culis. "Culis" is a corruption of the name of the Roman god Mercury (parallel to the Greek god Hermes). Among other things, he was the god of commerce and roads. For that reason people used to erect statues or various symbols of him along the roads. One way in which he was worshipped was through the placement of stones in a special arrangement, primarily two stones placed slightly apart with a third stone bridging them. This was called an altar of Culis.

כְּאַבְנֵי בֵּית קוּלִיס Like the stones of the house of Culis.

בָּעֵי רַב אַשִׁי [4]**Rav Ashi** posed a similar problem and **asked:** [25B] [5]**If** someone found **coins lying** in an arrangement **like** that of **the stones** set up at the place of worship **of the idol Culis,** which was worshipped in rituals involving stones [see background note], **what is the law** in such a case? Is the peculiar arrangement of the coins an indication that they were placed there intentionally, thus obliging the finder to announce his discovery? Or should the arrangement of the coins be considered random, thus allowing the finder to keep them for himself?

תָּא שְׁמַע [6]The Gemara answers: **Come and hear** a solution to this problem from **what has been taught** in the following Baraita: [7]**"If a person finds scattered coins, they belong to him.** [8]**But if they are lying like the stones of the house of Culis, he must announce his find.** [9]**And this is the way the stones of the house of Culis are arranged:** [10]**One on this side and one on that side and one on top of** the two of **them."** It is clear from this Baraita that the same law applies to an arrangement of two coins on the ground with a third resting on top of them as applies to coins found in the form of a tower mentioned earlier, and anyone who finds such coins must assume that they were placed that way deliberately and announce his discovery. Thus Rav Ashi's question is resolved by this unambiguous Baraita.

NOTES

that "overlapping" coins are considered scattered. What, then, is the difference between coins that "overlap" and coins arranged "like a ladder"? The Rishonim answer that coins "like a ladder" are carefully arranged with the upper coin only slightly off the center of the lower, whereas "overlapping" coins merely touch each other or are raised slightly at one end (*Ritva* and others).

HALAKHAH

should be left lying there, in accordance with the procedure for doubtful objects," following the conclusion of the Gemara, which does not resolve these three problems raised by Rabbi Yirmeyah. (*Shulḥan Arukh, Ḥoshen Mishpat* 262:12.)

כְּאַבְנֵי בֵּית קוּלִיס Coins lying like the stones of the place of worship of Culis. "If the coins were arranged one on this side and one on that side and one on top of the two, the finder must announce his discovery." (Ibid.; see also *Gra's* comment.)

[1]תָּנוּ רַבָּנַן: ״הַמּוֹצֵא סֶלַע בַּשּׁוּק, וּמְצָאוֹ חֲבֵירוֹ וְאָמַר: [2]׳שֶׁלִּי הִיא, חֲדָשָׁה הִיא, נֵירוֹנִית הִיא, שֶׁל מֶלֶךְ פְּלוֹנִי הִיא׳, [3]לֹא אָמַר כְּלוּם. [4]וְלֹא עוֹד, אֶלָּא אֲפִילּוּ שְׁמוֹ כָּתוּב עָלֶיהָ, [5]לֹא אָמַר כְּלוּם, לְפִי שֶׁאֵין סִימָן לַמַּטְבֵּעַ״, [6]דְּאָמַר: דִּלְמָא אַפּוּקֵי אַפְּקָהּ, וּמֵאִינִישׁ אַחֲרִינָא נָפַל.

LITERAL TRANSLATION

[1]Our Rabbis taught: "One who finds a sela in the marketplace, and his fellow found him and said: [2]'It is mine, it is new, it is Neronian, it is of King A,' [3]he has not said anything. [4]And furthermore, even [if] his name is written on it, [5]he has not said anything, because there is no identifying mark for a coin," [6]for one [can] say: Perhaps he spent it, and it fell from another person.

RASHI

נירונית היא — נירון קיסר כתוב עליה.

TRANSLATION AND COMMENTARY

תָּנוּ רַבָּנַן [1]Until this point in the discussion the Gemara has been dealing with cases where a number of individually unidentifiable coins have been found, either scattered or in some sort of order. Their number or their arrangement has been the only way of identifying them. The Gemara now considers a situation where only one coin is involved. **Our Rabbis taught** the following Baraita (see Tosefta *Bava Metzia* 2:10): **"If one finds a sela,** a large coin, **in the marketplace, and another person finds him** picking it up **and says,** [2]**'It is my coin.** I lost it, and I can prove my ownership of it because I can identify it. **It is** a **new** coin in mint condition'; or: **'It is** a coin bearing a likeness **of** the Emperor **Nero'**; or: **'It is** a coin stamped with the image **of King A,'** even if the putative owner successfully identifies the coin in this way, [3]it is as if **he has not said anything."** His claim is rejected and the finder may keep the coin, because all these means of identification are invalid, as the Gemara will shortly explain. [4]The Baraita continues: "**Furthermore, even if** the claimant's own **name is written on** the coin, proving conclusively that the coin did once belong to him, [5]**he has** still **not said anything,** and the coin need not be returned to him, **because there is no identifying mark on a coin** that can conclusively prove ownership." [6]The Gemara now explains: The reason why an individual coin cannot be positively identified is because money changes hands frequently. Hence, it is possible to **say** that the coin did **perhaps** once belong to this man, and he went so far as to inscribe his name on it. But afterwards **he spent it, and it was lost by another person.** Moreover, even if the claimant really did lose the coin, since he knew he could never prove it was his, he gave up hope of recovering it from the outset, and thus lost his rights to it immediately.

NOTES

לְפִי שֶׁאֵין סִימָן לַמַּטְבֵּעַ Because there is no identifying mark for a coin. The Rishonim interpret this passage in two ways. The commentary here follows the first explanation (*Ritva*, probably *Rif* and *Rambam, Shulḥan Arukh*): The reason why money cannot be identified is because it is designed to be spent and transferred constantly from one person to another. Thus, even if someone recognizes a coin and correctly identifies it, this does not constitute proof that he was the one who lost it. It is possible that someone else, with whom the claimant had done business, lost the coin, and the claimant may be lying in an attempt to recover a coin that he has already handed over to someone else. The difficulty with this explanation is that if we suspect claimants of lying in order to recover property they once owned, we should be equally suspicious of claims regarding any object that is commonly bought and sold. In response to this objection, *Ritva* argues that we are more suspicious in a case of money, because money is constantly spent and never generates a presumption of ownership, whereas other objects are presumed to belong to their original owner unless they are known to have been sold.

Because of this difficulty, *Ramban* and others explain that we do not suspect the claimant of lying, but rather believe he made an honest mistake. He may indeed have lost a coin just like the one found here, but someone else may also have done so. There are many coins with this king's likeness on them, and there may even be many coins with the claimant's name inscribed on them, some of which may have entered circulation as a result of his business transactions. Therefore, such marks and inscriptions cannot serve as valid means of identification. But if the coin is marked in a truly unique way, such as by a crack or some other defect, the owner would be believed according to this view.

HALAKHAH

הַמּוֹצֵא סֶלַע One who finds a sela. "A single coin need not be returned to its owner, even if he comes forward and cites an identifying mark, such as the king whose likeness appears on it, or even if the name of the claimant was written on it." (*Shulḥan Arukh, Ḥoshen Mishpat* 262:13.) However, *Rema* rules, following *Ramban,* that if the coin was cracked, the crack is a valid identifying mark (see notes).

REALIA

סֶלַע Sela.

The word סֶלַע, which means "rock" or "stone" in Hebrew, refers to a coin, a usage which is probably connected to use of the word סֶלַע as a unit of weight (cf. the British use of the word "stone," which, however, refers to a much heavier weight). A סֶלַע, the largest silver coin in circulation, was worth four dinars. This sum was a full day's wages for a simple laborer.

נֵירוֹנִית Neronian.

The use of the term "Neronian" did not apparently depend on the form of the coin ("of a specific king") but rather on its value. After many years, during which the coins were kept at a stable weight and value, Nero introduced a substantial devaluation. Therefore "Neronian" coins, which entered circulation for a certain period, weighed less than the coins that had previously been in circulation.

TRANSLATION AND COMMENTARY

MISHNAH מָצָא אַחַר הַגַּפָּה [1]If a person found one of the lost objects mentioned in the previous Mishnayot, he was obliged to pick it up, and the fundamental question was whether he was entitled to keep it for himself or whether he was required to announce his discovery. The present Mishnah deals with a different situation — where a person finds an object and it is forbidden to touch it. He must, instead, leave it where it is, on the assumption that its rightful owner will come back and collect it: If a person **finds tied young birds behind a** wooden **fence, or behind a** stone **wall, or on paths in the fields,** [2]**he must not touch them.** He must leave them where they are, because we assume that their owner has left them there deliberately and intends to return and collect them.

מָצָא כְּלִי בְּאַשְׁפָּה [3]If a person **finds a utensil in a heap of refuse,** and **if** the utensil **is** completely **covered** by refuse, **he may not touch it,** even if it contains an identifying mark, because it is clear that someone buried it there deliberately. Since the utensil is well protected against chance discovery, it does not come under the category of a lost object. [4]**But if** the utensil **is uncovered,** the finder is required to **take it and announce** that he has found **it**. In this case we assume that the object has been lost, and the finder is Halakhically obliged to return it to its owner.

משנה [1]מָצָא אַחַר הַגַּפָּה אוֹ אַחַר הַגָּדֵר גּוֹזָלוֹת מְקוּשָּׁרִים, אוֹ בִּשְׁבִילִין שֶׁבִּשְׂדוֹת, [2]הֲרֵי זֶה לֹא יִגַּע בָּהֶן.
[3]מָצָא כְּלִי בְּאַשְׁפָּה, אִם מְכוּסֶּה, לֹא יִגַּע בּוֹ. [4]אִם מְגוּלֶּה, נוֹטֵל וּמַכְרִיז.

LITERAL TRANSLATION

MISHNAH [1][If] he found tied young birds behind a fence, or behind a wall, or on the paths in the fields, [2]he must not touch them.

[3][If] he found a utensil in a heap of refuse, if it is covered, he may not touch it, [4][but] if it is uncovered, he takes [it] and announces [it].

RASHI

משנה מצא אחר הגפה [או אחר הגדר] גוזלות מקושרין — גפה — סתימת כותל של עץ או של קנים. גדר — של אבנים. לא יגע בהן — טעמא מפרש בגמרא. מכוסה לא יגע בו — דאין זו אבידה שיהא מוזהר עליה ב״לא תוכל להתעלם״, דמשתמר הוא.

LANGUAGE

גַּפָּה Fence. Most commentators explain this word in accordance with the view of *Rivmats* and *Rash* (*Pe'ah* 6:2), that a גַּפָּה is a kind of dry stone wall made without mortar, as opposed to a regular wall made of masonry and secured with mortar. *Rashi's* interpretation here, which is followed by *Bertinoro*, is that a גַּפָּה is a fence made of wood or cane. However, *Rambam* in his commentary on the Mishnah writes that a גַּפָּה is a kind of gate, from the expression in Neḥemiah (7:3): יָגִיפוּ הַדְּלָתוֹת — "let them shut the doors." In his commentary on tractate *Eduyyot*, *Ra'avad's* interpretation of the word seems to be similar.

BACKGROUND

לֹא יִגַּע בּוֹ He may not touch it. This strong expression, forbidding one even to touch an object that was presumably not lost but rather left in its place by its owner, can be explained as follows: In the case of certain found objects the Gemara rules that if one so much as touches or moves them, one has the immediate responsibility of looking after them and seeing that they are returned. Therefore, when a person does not have the intention or the ability to return a lost object, it is preferable for him not to touch it at all.

NOTES

גַּפָּה A fence. The translation here follows *Rashi*. *Rash*, however, explains that a wall made of rough stones without mortar is called a גַּפָּה.

מָצָא אַחַר הַגַּפָּה... גּוֹזָלוֹת מְקוּשָּׁרִים, אוֹ בִּשְׁבִילִין שֶׁבִּשְׂדוֹת If he found behind a fence... tied young birds, or on the paths in the fields. In the translation of the Mishnah the order of these phrases was altered for the sake of clarity, but in the original Hebrew they appear as in the title of this note, with the young birds placed in the middle of the list of possible places where they might have been found. This syntax, while grammatically correct, is rather unusual.

Tiferet Yisrael explains that, by using this language, the Mishnah is seeking to emphasize that there are two necessary conditions for the law to be applied: (1) The object must be one about which there is a doubt as to whether it was placed where it was found or came to be there by chance, such as tied birds; and (2) the object must be found in a place that is secluded but not completely protected, such as next to a fence. If the wording of the Mishnah had followed a more normal order, we might erroneously have thought that the law is the same for objects clearly left near the fence deliberately, such as work tools, as for objects, such as tied birds, that are found in other places.

Avnei Kodesh explains that by inserting the phrase "tied young birds" after the words "fence" and "wall," and before "paths in the fields," the Mishnah is seeking to indicate that the former are generally considered secure locations, but not for tied young birds. Paths, by contrast, where people occasionally walk, are considered semi-protected areas for all objects — including tied young birds.

מָצָא אַחַר הַגַּפָּה If he found behind a fence. It appears from the Gemara that the birds must be left where they were found only because they contain no means of identification. From this it follows that if they did contain a valid identifying mark (for instance, if they were tied in such a way that they could not hop, so that their location could serve as an identifying mark), the finder would be required to take them home and announce his discovery, even though it is clear

HALAKHAH

מָצָא אַחַר הַגַּפָּה If he found behind a fence. "If someone finds an object, such as a work tool, which clearly was deliberately left in the place where it was found, he should not touch it, regardless of whether or not it is marked. In most cases, even if he picked it up, he should return it to the place where he found it. If, however, it is an object which only gives the appearance of having been placed there deliberately, such as a tied young bird, the finder should also not touch it; but if he erred and took it, then, if it was marked, he must not return it to the place where he found it, but must announce his discovery in the usual way." (Ibid., 260:9-10, following the Gemara.) If the object was unmarked, the *Shulḥan Arukh*, following *Rambam*, rules that the finder may keep it for himself, whereas *Rema*, following *Ra'avad* and others, rules that he must take care of it indefinitely. *Rema* further rules that any marked object found in a place that is not completely protected should be announced and not left there, even if it looks as if it may have been placed there deliberately. If the object is unmarked, the finder should not take it; but if he took it, then even if he only picked it up but did not take it into his home, he should not return it, since the place where he found it is not completely protected. (See also *Sma* and *Shakh*.)

מָצָא כְּלִי בְּאַשְׁפָּה If he found a utensil in a heap of refuse. "Should a person find a utensil in a heap of refuse, if the

TRANSLATION AND COMMENTARY

GEMARA מַאי טַעְמָא [1]The Gemara asks: **What is the reason** why a person who finds tied young birds must not touch them?

דְּאָמְרִינַן [2]The Gemara answers: **Because we say: Someone must have hidden** these young birds, since they are tied together and have been left in a place where people are unlikely to stumble upon them. Their owner is presumably planning to come back and retrieve them later. [3]Thus, **if** the finder **takes them** and announces that he has found them, **their owner** may well not be able to get them back and will suffer financial loss, as he **does not have any identifying mark on them.** [4]**Therefore,** the best thing the finder can do is to **leave them** where he found them **until their owner comes and takes them.** If the young birds had some means of identification, the finder would be obliged to take them and announce that he had found them. But in this case, since they are not identifiable by their owner, it is in his interest that the finder leave them where they are.

וְאַמַּאי [5]The Gemara now asks: **But why** should the finder not take the young birds and announce his discovery? Surely the birds are tied together, and when the putative owner comes to claim them, **the knot** with which the birds were tied **can serve as an identifying mark.**

אָמַר רַבִּי אַבָּא בַּר זַבְדָּא [6]In reply, **Rabbi Abba bar Zavda said in the name of Rav:** The Mishnah is **referring to** a case where the **birds** were **tied** to each other **by their wings**, not by string. [7]Such a knot cannot serve as a means of identification, **because everyone ties** young birds **this way.**

וְלֶהֱוֵי מָקוֹם סִימָן [8]The Gemara again asks: **But let the location** where the birds were found **be an identifying mark.** Let the finder announce what he has found, and let the owner identify the birds by stating the place where he left them.

אָמַר רַב עוּקְבָא בַּר חָמָא [9]**Rav Ukva bar Ḥama said** in reply: The Mishnah is **referring to** a case where the **birds were hopping** about from place to place. They could not fly because their wings were tied, but they could still move about by hopping, and it is impossible to tell precisely where they were originally placed.

גמרא [1]מַאי טַעְמָא? [2]דְּאָמְרִינַן: הָנֵי אֱינָשׁ אַצְנְעִינְהוּ, [3]וְאִי שָׁקֵיל לְהוּ, לֵית לְהוּ לְמָרַיְיהוּ סִימָנָא בְּגַוַּויְיהוּ. [4]הִלְכָּךְ, לִשְׁבְקִינְהוּ עַד דְּאָתֵי מָרַיְיהוּ וְשָׁקֵיל לְהוּ. [5]וְאַמַּאי? לֶיהֱוֵי קֶשֶׁר סִימָנָא! [6]אָמַר רַבִּי אַבָּא בַּר זַבְדָּא אָמַר רַב: בִּמְקוּשָּׁרִין בִּכְנְפֵיהֶן, [7]דְּכוּלֵּי עָלְמָא הָכִי מְקַטְרִי לְהוּ. [8]וְלֶהֱוֵי מָקוֹם סִימָן! [9]אָמַר רַב עוּקְבָא בַּר חָמָא: בִּמְדַדִּין.

LITERAL TRANSLATION

GEMARA [1]What is the reason?

[2]Because we say: A person hid them, [3]and if he takes them, their owner does not have an identifying mark on them. [4]Therefore, let him leave them until their owner comes and takes them.

[5]But why? Let the knot be an identifying mark.

[6]Rabbi Abba bar Zavda said in the name of Rav: [It refers] to [birds] tied by their wings, [7]for everyone (lit., "the whole world") ties them this way.

[8]But let the place be an identifying mark.

[9]Rav Ukva bar Ḥama said: [It refers] to [birds that] were hopping.

RASHI

גמרא במדדין – ממקום למקום.

BACKGROUND

בִּמְקוּשָּׁרִין בִּכְנְפֵיהֶן It refers to birds tied by their wings. The young birds in question are young doves and not chickens. To prevent them from flying away it was customary to tie their wings together by turning them inside out. Since their wings were bound and because they were young, they could not move far away; but because their legs were not tied, they could hop a little from place to place. If they were left for a long time, they could move a considerable distance, so their owners would not know where they had gone.

NOTES

that the owner put them there deliberately and is presumably not interested in the finder's help!

The Rishonim (*Tosafot, Ran*, and others) explain that this passage refers only to places that are partially protected, such as the shadow of a wall or a path in a field. But if the birds had been left out in the open, they would be treated like ordinary lost objects — they should be taken and announced, if marked, and may be kept by the finder, if unmarked. If they were found in a fully protected place, they should be left there, regardless of whether they contain identifying marks. But if the birds were found in a place that is only protected for a short period of time, as in the case in our Mishnah, then the fact that the owner is nowhere to be seen must be taken as an indication that the birds have been forgotten and are in danger of being lost to their owner forever. Therefore, if they are marked, they must be taken home and their discovery announced. But if they are not marked, they should be left where they were found, because this is the only hope the owner has of recovering them.

HALAKHAH

utensil was covered by refuse, he may not touch it." (*Shulḥan Arukh, Ḥoshen Mishpat* 260:11.) *Rema* adds that if it was a heap of refuse that is regularly cleared away, the utensil may be assumed to have been discarded, and may be kept by the finder.

TRANSLATION AND COMMENTARY

אִי בִּמְדַדִּין [1]The Gemara now asks: But if the Mishnah **is referring to** a case where the **birds** were **hopping** about from place to place, it is possible that **they came from elsewhere, and are permitted** to be kept by the person who finds them. They may not have been deliberately placed where the finder came upon them, but may have moved some distance from where they were originally left. Their owner will be unable to retrieve them, and since there is no means of identifying them he may long since have given up hope of recovering them.

אִיכָּא לְמֵימַר מֵעָלְמָא אָתוּ [2]The Gemara answers: **It is,** as you claim, **possible to say that** the birds **came from elsewhere, but** on the other hand [3]**it is also possible to say that someone hid them** here deliberately, because the place where they were found is to some extent protected from chance discovery. [4]**It is,** therefore, **a case where we are in doubt** as to **whether** the owner deliberately **placed** them where they were ultimately found or whether they were lost and ended up behind the fence or wall by chance. [5]**And Rabbi Abba bar Zavda said in the name of Rav: In any case where we are in doubt** as to **whether** something without an identifying mark was deliberately **placed** where it was found or was lost by its owner, [6]**in the first instance** the finder **should not take** the object at all. It is preferable that he leave it where he found it, giving the owner the opportunity to recover it for himself. [7]**But if** the finder **did take it** for himself, **he should not return it,** because there is nobody who can identify it.

מָצָא כְּלִי בְּאַשְׁפָּה [8]The Gemara now considers the next clause of the Mishnah: "**If a person finds a utensil in a heap of refuse,** and if the utensil is completely **covered** by refuse, **he may not touch it,** [9]**but if it is uncovered, he must take it and announce** that he has found it." [10]**But,** says the Gemara, **there is a contradiction** between this Mishnah and the following Baraita: "**If a person finds a utensil hidden in a heap of refuse, he should take it and announce** his find in the normal way, and not leave it there for the owner to retrieve later.

[1]אִי בִּמְדַדִּין, מֵעָלְמָא אָתוּ, וּמוּתָּרִין!
[2]אִיכָּא לְמֵימַר מֵעָלְמָא אָתוּ, [3]וְאִיכָּא לְמֵימַר אֱינָשׁ אַצְנְעִינְהוּ, [4]וַהֲוָה לֵיהּ סְפֵק הִינּוּחַ, [5]וְאָמַר רַבִּי אַבָּא בַּר זַבְדָּא אָמַר רַב: כָּל סְפֵק הִינּוּחַ, [6]לְכַתְחִילָּה לֹא יִטּוֹל, [7]וְאִם נָטַל, לֹא יַחֲזִיר.
[8]"מָצָא כְּלִי בְּאַשְׁפָּה, מְכוּסֶּה, לֹא יִגַּע בּוֹ, [9]מְגוּלֶּה, נוֹטֵל וּמַכְרִיז". [10]וּרְמִינְהוּ: "מָצָא כְּלִי טָמוּן בְּאַשְׁפָּה, נוֹטֵל וּמַכְרִיז,

LITERAL TRANSLATION

[1]If [it refers] to [birds that] were hopping, they came from elsewhere and are permitted.

[2]It is possible to say [that] they came from elsewhere, [3]but it is possible to say [that] someone hid them, [4]and it is [a case of] doubtful placing, [5]and Rabbi Abba bar Zavda said in the name of Rav: [In] any [case of] doubtful placing, [6]in the first instance he should not take [it], [7]but if he took [it], he should not return [it].

[8]"[If] he found a utensil in a heap of refuse, [and if it is] covered, he may not touch it, [9][but if] it is uncovered, he takes [it] and announces [it]."

[10]But raise them [as contradictory] (lit., "cast them [against each other]"): "[If] he found a utensil hidden in a heap of refuse, he takes [it] and announces [it],

RASHI

מעלמא אתו — ואין זה הינוח, וכיון דאין בהן סימן — נימא הרי אלו שלו. **ואיכא למימר איניש אצנעינהו** — הואיל ומקושרין. **ספק הינוח** — בדבר שאין בו סימן, וכל שכן ודאי הינוח. **לכתחילה לא יטול** — דאי שקלת לה, ליכא למרייהו סימנין למיתב בהו ויפסיד, הלכך לא יטול, והבעלים יזכרו ויבאו ויטלום. **ואם נטל לא יחזיר** — דהא ליכא דיהיב סימנא.

BACKGROUND

סְפֵק הִינּוּחַ Doubtful placing. To take an object which was undoubtedly put in a specific place by its owner would be theft, and a person who takes it must make every possible effort to restore it to its owner. In such a case, even if the object bears no identifying mark, the finder is not permitted to make any use of it.

SAGES

רַבִּי אַבָּא בַּר זַבְדָּא Rabbi Abba bar Zavda. A Palestinian Amora of the second and third generations. See *Bava Metzia*, Part I, p. 192.

NOTES

וְאָמַר רַבִּי אַבָּא בַּר זַבְדָּא אָמַר רַב And Rabbi Abba bar Zavda said in the name of Rav.... In the Jerusalem Talmud, this ruling is the conclusion of a story. Rabbi Abba bar Zavda found such an object and picked it up in the hope of returning it to its rightful owner. He then asked Rav what to do and received this answer.

וְאִם נָטַל לֹא יַחֲזִיר But if he took it, he should not return it. The commentary here follows *Rashi,* who explains that the expression "he should not return it" means: "He should not return the object to its rightful owner." According to this view, there is no distinction between cases where it is certain that the object was deliberately left in the place where it was found and cases where this is a matter of doubt, and the Gemara's ruling applies only to unmarked objects. Someone who finds such an object must leave it where he found it. If he took it, he may not return it to any claimant, since it lacks an identifying mark. Marked objects, of course, should be taken and announced in the usual way. *Rashi* does not say what should ultimately be done with an unmarked object that was taken by the finder and cannot be returned to its owner. According to *Rambam,* the finder may keep the object for himself, as is the law with any other unmarked object. *Ra'avad* disagrees: Since the owner had not yet given up hope of recovering the object when it was picked up, the finder can never acquire ownership of it. Therefore, he is obliged to take care of the object indefinitely, or until witnesses come forward and conclusively prove who owns it.

Most of the Rishonim disagree with *Rashi* and explain that the expression "he should not return it" means "he should not return the object to the place where he found it," as this is not an adequate way of fulfilling his obligation to return

[1] שֶׁכֵּן דֶּרֶךְ אַשְׁפָּה לְפַנּוֹת״. [2] אָמַר רַב זְבִיד: לָא קַשְׁיָא. [3] הָא בְּכוּבֵי וְכָסֵי, [4] הָא בְּסַכִּינֵי וְהַמְנִיק. [5] בְּכוּבֵי וְכָסֵי, לָא יִגַּע; [6] בְּסַכִּינֵי וְהַמְנִיק, נוֹטֵל וּמַכְרִיז. [7] רַב פַּפָּא אֲמַר: הָא וְהָא בְּכוּבֵי וְכָסֵי, [8] וְלָא קַשְׁיָא. [9] כָּאן בְּאַשְׁפָּה הָעֲשׂוּיָה לְפַנּוֹת; [10] כָּאן בְּאַשְׁפָּה שֶׁאֵינָהּ עֲשׂוּיָה לְפַנּוֹת.

LITERAL TRANSLATION

[1] for it is [in] the nature of a heap of refuse to be cleared away."

[2] Rav Zevid said: There is no difficulty. [3] This [refers] to barrels and cups, [4] [and] that [refers] to knives and forks. [5] In [the case of] barrels and cups, he must not touch [them]; [6] in [the case of] knives and forks, he takes and announces.

[7] Rav Pappa said: This and that [refer] to barrels and cups, [8] and there is no difficulty. [9] Here [it refers] to a heap of refuse that is usually cleared away; [10] here [it is referring] to a heap of refuse that is not usually cleared away.

TRANSLATION AND COMMENTARY

The finder should not assume that the owner hid the utensil in the heap of refuse for safekeeping, [1] **for it is in the nature of heaps of refuse to be cleared away."** If the finder does not take the object immediately and announce it, there is a danger that it will be noticed when the refuse is cleared away and that it will be taken by some unscrupulous person and not announced. Since the object is lost property, the finder has a Halakhic responsibility to look after it and attempt to restore it to its rightful owner. Thus there is a clear contradiction between the Mishnah, which states that the finder of an article covered by refuse must not touch it, and the Baraita, which states that he must take it and announce that he has found it.

אָמַר רַב זְבִיד [2] **Rav Zevid said** in reply: **There is no difficulty** in reconciling this seeming contradiction. [3] **The** Mishnah's **ruling**, forbidding the finder to touch a utensil that he finds covered in a heap of refuse, **is referring to barrels and cups** and similarly large items which have clearly been placed there deliberately and thus do not constitute lost property. Such objects must be left where they are. [4] By contrast, **the** Baraita's **ruling**, requiring the finder to take and announce an object that he finds hidden in a heap of refuse, **is referring to knives and forks** and the like, which are small and may well have fallen into the refuse by accident and been lost there. [5] **In the case of barrels and cups,** the finder **must not touch them,** as they are too large to have fallen there by accident and must therefore have been deliberately buried in the refuse for safekeeping in spite of the risks involved. [6] But **in the case of knives and forks,** the finder **should take** them **and announce** them, as they probably fell there by accident.

רַב פַּפָּא אֲמַר [7] **Rav Pappa** did not accept Rav Zevid's distinction between large and small utensils, and said: **The Mishnah and the Baraita** may well both **be referring to barrels and cups** that were deliberately hidden in the heap of refuse, [8] **and there is** still **no difficulty** in reconciling the seeming contradiction between them. The difference is not between two kinds of utensils but between two kinds of refuse heaps. [9] The Baraita **is referring to a heap of refuse that is usually cleared away** from time to time. When the refuse is cleared away, the utensils will be discovered. Since it is not customary to deliberately place utensils in such a place, they come under the category of lost property and the finder is obliged to try to restore them to their owner. [10] By contrast, the Mishnah **is referring to a heap of refuse that is not usually cleared way**. Utensils found there were deliberately placed there by their owner. They are likely to remain there undisturbed, and the finder should not move them.

RASHI

שכן דרך אשפה ליפנות — ואי לא שקיל ליה האי השתא לכשיפנה יטלנה נכרי או ישראל חשוד, הלכך אבידה היא ומוזהר עליה. **כובי וכסי** — טמונים מדעת הוא, ולא יגע בהן. **סכיני והמניק** — שהן כלים קטנים — אבדה הן, שהשליכם שם עם האשפה שהוציאם מן הבית, ולקמן פריך: מאי שכן דרך אשפה לפנות?

LANGUAGE

הַמְנִיק Fork. The manuscripts contain many versions of this word, and its source has not been ascertained. The *Arukh*, following the Geonim, defines it as a kind of two-pronged fork used by the Persians.

BACKGROUND

אַשְׁפָּה Refuse heap. The refuse to which the Talmud refers here is a heap of objects that people have discarded and removed from their homes. Such a refuse heap may contain things like remains of food, broken utensils, or unwanted stones and dirt. If the refuse heap is a certain distance from the city, or there is a large refuse dump where residents of a city or of a certain neighborhood always throw whatever they no longer need, this ordinarily comes under the category of refuse that is not removed. But a person may occasionally accumulate a pile of refuse within his courtyard, and after this heap grows to a certain size he will clear it away and move it to the permanent refuse dump outside the city.

NOTES

a lost object to its rightful owner. Rather, he must take it home and announce his discovery, if the object is marked, or keep it indefinitely, if it is unmarked. This explanation is also supported by the parallel passage in the Jerusalem Talmud. According to this view, a question arises: Does the prohibition against returning an object to the place where it was found apply only if the finder took it home, since it is possible that the owner passed by in the meantime and noticed that the object was not where he had left it, or does it apply even if the finder merely picked it up, since he is now personally obliged to take care of it? In analyzing this point, the Rishonim distinguish between marked and unmarked objects, between deliberate and "doubtful" placings, and between totally protected places and places that are less than totally protected (see *Tosafot, Ramban, Rashba, Rosh,* etc.).

TRANSLATION AND COMMENTARY

אַשְׁפָּה הָעֲשׂוּיָה לְפַנּוֹת [1]The Gemara now expresses surprise at this distinction and asks: **But surely** an object buried in **a heap of refuse that is usually cleared away** from time to time must be considered to have been **deliberately abandoned**. The owner must have known that the refuse would soon be cleared away and the utensils discovered. Thus it is clear that he gave up hope of recovering them. Why, then, should the finder go to the trouble of trying to restore them to him?

אֶלָּא [2]**Rather,** explains the Gemara, the Baraita, like the Mishnah, **is referring to a heap of refuse that is not usually cleared away**. Thus the utensils' owner had reason to believe that it was safe to bury his utensils there. [3]**But** in the meantime **the owner** of the heap of refuse **changed his mind about it and decided to clear** all the refuse **away**. Thus the owner of the utensils cannot be said to have deliberately abandoned them, and the finder is obliged to announce his discovery and do his best to restore the utensils to their rightful owner.

בִּשְׁלָמָא לְרַב פַּפָּא [4]The Gemara now remarks: The resolution of the seeming contradiction between the Mishnah and the Baraita proposed by **Rav Pappa fits well** with the plain meaning of the text, because it is supported by the words of the Baraita itself. [5]**The reason why** the Baraita **states, "For it is in the nature of a heap of refuse to be cleared away,"** at a moment's notice, at the whim of its owner, is precisely to make Rav Pappa's point that there are two different kinds of heaps of refuse — permanent (as in the case of the Mishnah) and temporary (as in the case of the Baraita). [6]**But,** asks the Gemara, **according to Rav Zevid's** explanation, which stresses the distinction between large and small utensils, **what is the meaning of** the expression used by the Baraita, **"For it is in the nature of a heap of refuse to be cleared away"?** According to this view, the nature of a heap of refuse is utterly irrelevant to the Baraita's reasoning.

שֶׁכֵּן דֶּרֶךְ אַשְׁפָּה [7]The Gemara explains: This is how the clause is to be read according to Rav Zevid: "The finder should take the object and announce his find, **for it is in the nature of a heap of refuse that** people **clear away small utensils into it"** even without the knowledge of the utensils' owners. Thus the finder of such small objects is obliged to do his best to restore them to their rightful owner.

MISHNAH מָצָא בְּגַל וּבְכוֹתֶל יָשָׁן [8]**If a person found objects** hidden **in a heap of stones, or in** a cavity in **an old wall** that is still standing, **they are his** to keep. This ruling applies even to objects that contain identifying marks, as the Gemara will explain below.

[1]אַשְׁפָּה הָעֲשׂוּיָה לְפַנּוֹת אֲבֵידָה מִדַּעַת הִיא! [2]אֶלָּא, בְּאַשְׁפָּה שֶׁאֵינָהּ עֲשׂוּיָה לְפַנּוֹת, [3]וְנִמְלַךְ עָלֶיהָ לְפַנּוֹתָהּ. [4]בִּשְׁלָמָא לְרַב פַּפָּא: [5]הַיְינוּ דְּקָתָנֵי: "שֶׁכֵּן דֶּרֶךְ אַשְׁפָּה לְפַנּוֹת". [6]אֶלָּא לְרַב זְבִיד, מַאי: "שֶׁכֵּן דֶּרֶךְ אַשְׁפָּה לְפַנּוֹת?" [7]"שֶׁכֵּן דֶּרֶךְ אַשְׁפָּה לְפַנּוֹת לָהּ כֵּלִים קְטַנִּים".

משנה [8]מָצָא בְּגַל וּבְכוֹתֶל יָשָׁן, הֲרֵי אֵלּוּ שֶׁלּוֹ.

LITERAL TRANSLATION

[1][But surely] a heap of refuse that is usually cleared away is [a case of] deliberate loss.

[2]Rather, [it refers] to a heap of refuse that is not usually cleared away, [3]but [its owner] changed his mind about it [and decided] to clear it away.

[4]It is well according to Rav Pappa: [5]This is why it teaches: "For it is [in] the nature of a heap of refuse to be cleared away." [6]But according to Rav Zevid, what is [the meaning of]: "For it is [in] the nature of a heap of refuse to be cleared away"?

[7]"For it is [in] the nature of a heap of refuse to clear away into it small utensils."

MISHNAH [8][If] he found [objects] in a heap of stones or in an old wall, they are his.

RASHI

אבידה מדעת היא — דהוה ליה לאסוקי אדעתיה שיפנוה. **היינו דקתני שכן דרך אשפה לפנות** — שהבעלים נמלכים לפנות. **לפנות לה כלים קטנים** — מן הבית שלא מדעת.

משנה מצא בגל — גל אבנים מחומה שנפלה. **הרי אלו שלו** — בגמרא מפרש.

NOTES

בְּגַל וּבְכוֹתֶל יָשָׁן **In a heap of stones or in an old wall.** The Rishonim ask: Even if the object did not originally belong to the owner of the wall or of the heap of stones, it should have become his by courtyard-acquisition by virtue of the fact that it was left on his property, even if he was unaware of its presence. *Tosafot, Rosh,* and others explain that courtyard-acquisition is effective only in the case of objects that can readily be found, but objects buried in someone's

HALAKHAH

מָצָא בְּגַל וּבְכוֹתֶל יָשָׁן... מָצָא בְּכוֹתֶל חָדָשׁ **If he found objects in a heap of stones or in an old wall.... If he found them in a new wall....** "If a person finds an object in a heap of stones or in an ancient wall which has been in existence since time immemorial, he may keep it, provided that the object is so rusty that it is reasonable to assume it was left by the ancient tribes who inhabited the area, and provided that it was found hidden deep within the pile of

[1]מָצָא בְּכוֹתֶל חָדָשׁ, מֵחֶצְיוֹ וְלַחוּץ, שֶׁלּוֹ; [2]מֵחֶצְיוֹ וְלִפְנִים, שֶׁל בַּעַל הַבַּיִת. [3]אִם הָיָה מַשְׂכִּירוֹ לַאֲחֵרִים, [4]אֲפִילּוּ בְּתוֹךְ הַבַּיִת, הֲרֵי אֵלּוּ שֶׁלּוֹ.

גמרא [5]תָּנָא: ״מִפְּנֵי שֶׁיָּכוֹל לוֹמַר לוֹ: ׳שֶׁל אֱמוֹרִיִּים הֵן׳״.

LITERAL TRANSLATION

[1][If] he found [them] in a new wall, [2]from half of its [thickness] and outwards, [they are] his; from half of its [thickness] inwards, [they] belong to the owner of the house. [3]If he was renting it to others, [4]even within the house, they are his.

GEMARA [5]He taught: "Because he can say to him: 'They belonged to the Amorites.'"

TRANSLATION AND COMMENTARY

מָצָא בְּכוֹתֶל חָדָשׁ [1]**If he found them in** a cavity of **a new wall** adjoining the public domain, their position within the wall is significant: If he found them buried **from half of** the wall's **thickness and outwards,** i.e., in a cavity in the outer half of the thickness of the wall, **they are his** to keep, even if they contain identifying marks, as they were presumably left there by someone passing by in the street outside and forgotten. When their owner later remembered that he had left them there, he would have given up hope of recovering them because he left them unprotected in a public place. [2]But if the finder found them buried **from half of its thickness and inwards,** i.e., in a cavity in the inner side of the wall, **they belong to the owner of the house,** because it is normal for people to hide things in the walls of their home even for an extended period. This ruling applies if the owner of the house is in fact living there. [3]But **if he was** in the habit of **renting** his house **to other people,** and several tenants had already lived there, [4]then **even if** someone **found the objects within the house** itself **they are the finder's** to keep, as we do not know which of the former tenants left them there and assume that their original owner has given up hope of recovering them.

GEMARA תָּנָא [5]The first clause in the Mishnah briefly stated that an object found in a heap of stones or in an old wall belongs to the finder. The Gemara now cites a Tosefta (*Bava Metzia* 2:12) which provides the reason for the Mishnah's ruling: A Tanna **stated** in the following Tosefta: "The reason why the Mishnah gives a person the right to keep an object he finds in a heap of stones or in an old wall, and does not recognize the claim of the owner of the stones or of the wall that the object belongs to him, is **because** the finder **can say to the owner** of the stones or of the wall: 'The objects I found do not belong to you. **They** originally **belonged to the Amorites,** one of the ancient Canaanite tribes.'" In other words, the finder can claim that they were buried in this spot since time immemorial, perhaps even from the period before the Israelites conquered the land of Canaan, and whoever finds them is entitled to keep them.

RASHI

מחציו ולחוץ — באחד מחורי כותל הסמוכים לרשות הרבים מצאה, מחצי עוביו של כותל ולחוץ — שלו, דאמרינן אחד מבני רשות הרבים נתנו שם ושכח, דאף על גב דאמרן לעיל ספק הינוח לא יטול, והאי ודאי הינוח הוא — הא מוקמינן למתניתין בגמרא דשתיך טפי, דאיכא יאוש בעלים. **ואפילו מצא בתוך הבית כו׳** — דלא ידוע דמאן ניהו, ובעליו נואשו.

גמרא תנא — גבי גל וכותל ישן. **שיכול לומר לו** — לבעל הגל או לבעל הכותל. **של אמוריים** — שהורישו אבותינו היו.

NOTES

property are not acquired by anyone until they are found. *Rambam* explains that objects which are buried and forgotten, so that nobody can easily find them, have the same status as objects which were washed out to sea. Such objects were declared ownerless by the Torah.

Ra'avad argues against the analogy with an object that was washed out to sea. He maintains that in the case mentioned in the Mishnah, courtyard-acquisition is not effective because we are dealing here with a situation in which the courtyard does not protect the object exclusively for its owner. In such a case it is necessary for the owner to physically stand by the courtyard and declare that the courtyard is acquiring the object on his behalf.

שֶׁל אֱמוֹרִיִּים הֵן **They belonged to the Amorites.** *Rashba* explains that property left by the ancient Canaanites belongs to the Jewish people as a whole, and not to any particular person. Since the Jewish people "lost" this particular object, and obviously "gave up hope of recovering it," it belongs to whoever discovers it first. The status of the wall in which the object was hidden is analogous to that of a finder who picks up an object before its owner has given up hope of recovering it. Just as such a finder cannot acquire the object even after the owner does give up hope, so too the wall cannot acquire by the laws of courtyard-acquisition, even after the Jewish people "have given up hope."

HALAKHAH

stones or the wall. But if the object looks as if it was placed there recently, he may not touch it (and it must be treated like an object deliberately hidden in a heap of refuse — *Sma*). If the object was found in a wall of recent origin which was built by its present owner or by his forebears, then, if the object was found in the outer half of the wall facing the street, it may be kept by the finder, provided that it appears to have been left there for a long time, so that its original owner gave up hope of recovering it. But if it was found in the inner half of the wall, it belongs to the owner of the wall, as we presume that he is its rightful owner." (*Shulḥan Arukh, Ḥoshen Mishpat* 260:1-3.)

TERMINOLOGY

תָּנָא (occasionally תָּאנָא) Lit., **he taught**, a term used to introduce Baraitot and Toseftot. Usually the Baraitot introduced by this expression are very short (one or two sentences), and they clarify, supplement or limit statements in the Mishnah.

BACKGROUND

שֶׁל אֱמוֹרִיִּים הֵן **They belonged to the Amorites.** Property owned by Jews can only be relinquished if a specific act is performed. It has to be sold, given away or abandoned (the owner's giving up hope of recovering lost property is a form of abandonment). Property is also transferred by inheritance, and it makes no difference how many generations have passed since the original owner acquired it. Since farmers in general and Jewish farmers in Eretz Israel in particular inherited their holdings, one's initial assumption ought to be that a found object originally belonged to one of the Jewish owners of the place, and was subsequently passed on to his heirs. However, the finder of a very old object can claim that it never belonged to the owner of the place, but rather to the nations that previously inhabited the land, all of whose possessions became the property of all the Jews.

TRANSLATION AND COMMENTARY

אַטּוּ אֱמוֹרִים מַצְנְעֵי [1]The Gemara expresses surprise at this explanation: **But were Amorites the only people to hide things? Do Jews not hide things?** Surely the person most likely to have hidden the object is the wall's present owner, particularly if the object was found in a cavity in the inner half of the wall. How can a finder be permitted to claim ownership of an object on the basis of such a fanciful claim?

לָא. צְרִיכָא [2]The Gemara answers: **No!** The ruling of the Mishnah as amplified by the Tosefta **is necessary** in the following specific case: [26A] **where** the object found in the heap of stones or in the wall **was very rusty,** clearly indicating that it had been put there in the distant past.

בְּכוֹתֶל חָדָשׁ [3]The Gemara now considers the next clause of the Mishnah: "If a person found objects buried **in** a cavity of **a new wall from half of** the wall's **thickness and outwards, they are his** to keep. [4]But if he found them buried in a cavity **from half of** the wall's **thickness and inwards, they belong to the owner of the house."** [5]In connection with this statement in the Mishnah **Rav Ashi said:** If **a knife** or a moneybag is found concealed in a cavity in a wall, the ownership of the knife **is determined by** the position of **its handle,** [6]**and** that of **the moneybag by** the position of **its laces,** by which it is tied. These objects possess means of identification enabling us to determine whether they were placed in the cavity by the owner of the house or a member of his household, or by someone passing in the street outside. If the handle of the knife or the laces of the moneybag point inwards, the entire knife or moneybag belongs to the owner of the house, as he is presumably the one who put it there. If they point outwards, the entire knife or moneybag belongs to the finder, as it was presumably left there by a passerby. In such a case, according to Rav Ashi, it makes no difference where in the wall the object is found.

[1]אַטּוּ אֱמוֹרִים מַצְנְעֵי? יִשְׂרָאֵל לָא מַצְנְעֵי?!
[2]לָא. צְרִיכָא [26A] דִּשְׁתִיךְ טְפֵי.
[3]״בְּכוֹתֶל חָדָשׁ, מֶחֶצְיוֹ וְלַחוּץ, שֶׁלּוֹ; [4]מֶחֶצְיוֹ וְלִפְנִים, שֶׁל בַּעַל הַבַּיִת״. [5]אָמַר רַב אַשִׁי: סַכִּינָא בָּתַר קַתָּא, [6]וְכִיסָא בָּתַר שְׁנָצֵיהּ.

LITERAL TRANSLATION

[1]But do [only] Amorites hide [things]? Do Jews not hide [things]?
[2]No. It is necessary [26A] where it was very rusty.
[3]"In a new wall, from half of its [thickness] and outwards, [they are] his; [4]from half of its [thickness] and inwards, [they] belong to the owner of the house." [5]Rav Ashi said: A knife [goes] after [its] handle, [6]and a moneybag after its laces.

RASHI

ישראל לא מצנעי — ומחציו ולפנים אמאי שלו הרי בעל הבית זה משתמש בה זה כמה שנים. **דשתיך טפי** — העלו חלודה רבה, דלוי האי לא שביק להו. **סכינא** — הנמצא באחד מחורי הכותל. **בתר קתא** — אזיל, אי קתיה לגיו — בני הבית נתנוהו שם, אי קתא לבר — בני רשות הרבים נתנוהו שם, שכן דרך אחיזתו. וכן כיסא בתר שנציה — *אשטדל״א בלעז.

NOTES

דִּשְׁתִיךְ טְפֵי **Where it was very rusty.** The Talmud is not necessarily implying that it is possible, on the basis of corrosion alone, to determine that an article must be thousands of years old. What it means is that the article is so old that we can safely conclude that even if it had once belonged to a Jew, he must already have given up hope of recovering it (*Ritva* and others).

Gra suggests that *Rambam* had a different reading in the Talmudic text — דִּשְׁתִית, meaning "where the item was embedded deeply." In other words, the object was found deep inside the wall or under the heap of stones, and not near the surface, where one would have expected it to be found had it been buried there in recent times. Hence it is clearly very old.

בְּכוֹתֶל חָדָשׁ **In a new wall.** The Rishonim ask: The article was certainly not placed in the wall by accident. It must have been put there deliberately. Why is the finder allowed to take it?

Some commentators answer: The Talmud's previous response — "it was very rusty" — was intended to apply to this case as well. Here, too, we are referring to a case where it is obvious that the owner of the article long ago gave up any hope of recovering it (*Tosafot, Rosh*).

HALAKHAH

הַמּוֹצֵא חֲפָצִים בְּכוֹתֶל חָדָשׁ **If a person finds objects in a new wall.** "If one finds an object in a wall of recent origin, which was built by its present owner or his forebears, then, if the object was found in the outer half of the wall, facing the street, it may be kept by the finder. But if it was found in the inner half of the wall, it belongs to the owner of the house. If the object (e.g., coins) filled the entire width of the wall, then it must be divided between the finder and the owner of the house, even if the cavity in the wall was sloping in such a way as to suggest that the coins may have rolled down the incline from one side. If the object has a handle, for example, a knife or a moneybag, then it belongs to the one in whose direction the handle was pointing when it was found. All of the above applies only if the owner of the house claims the object is his, or at least argues that it may have belonged to his ancestors. But if he admits that it was left by some stranger, it belongs exclusively to the finder." (Ibid., 260:1-3.)

BACKGROUND

דִּשְׁתִיךְ טְפֵי **Where it was very rusty.** Although most metal objects corrode if left unprotected for any length of time, there is a difference between the amount of corrosion accumulated on a metal object over a few years and the thick layer of corrosion that is found on a very ancient object. This is especially noticeable in the case of an object that was not left exposed to the elements but under a pile of stones or in a wall, for such an object corrodes at a constant rate.

סַכִּינָא בָּתַר קַתָּא **A knife goes after its handle.** This explanation is based on the assumption that a person normally grasps things in the ordinary way. Generally a person does not hold a knife by the blade, to avoid cutting himself. Similarly, a person holds a moneybag with its mouth towards him, to prevent the money from spilling out of it. We assume that whoever hid the object was holding it in the ordinary way. Consequently, we can tell on which side of the wall he was standing, by looking at the direction in which the part of the object that is normally grasped is facing. The examples of the knife and the moneybag are extreme. In general one grasps objects by handles placed on them for that purpose. It is only when an object has no specific or well-defined handles that one cannot determine on which side of the wall the person holding it was standing.

REALIA

כִּיסָא **A moneybag.**

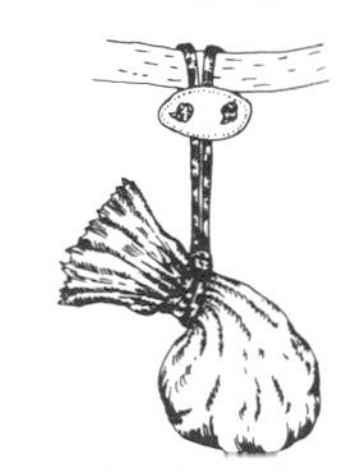

A moneybag from the time of Bar Kokhba. The bag was tied to a beam by the laces with which it was tied.

LANGUAGE (RASHI)

אשטדל״א* (correct reading: אשטרל״ש) From the Old French *esterles,* meaning the straps or laces by which a moneybag was tied.

TRANSLATION AND COMMENTARY

וְאֶלָּא מַתְנִיתִין [1]The Gemara now objects to Rav Ashi's ruling and asks: **But then** how do we reconcile Rav Ashi's ruling with **our Mishnah, which says** that if a person finds objects concealed in a cavity of a new wall, **"from half of the** wall's **thickness and outwards, they are his** to keep, [2]**from half of** the wall's **thickness and inwards, they belong to the owner of the house."** Why does the Mishnah make this distinction? [3]For, if we find a knife in a wall, all **we** have to do is **see if the handle is pointing inwards or outwards.** [4]And if we find a moneybag, all we have to do is see **if its laces are pointing inwards or outwards.**

מַתְנִיתִין בְּאוּדְרָא וְנִסְכָּא [5]The Gemara replies: **Our Mishnah is referring** not to articles or utensils but (a) **to** various sorts of **stuffing material**, such as cotton wool, **and** (b) to **pieces of metal,** which do not have handles and do not need to be held in a special way. It is only in the case of such things that the distinction between the inner and the outer part of a cavity in a wall is significant.

תָּנָא [6]Up to this point we have been considering situations in which an object is found in a cavity of a wall, either on its inner or its outer side. The question now arises: What if there is an opening that extends right through the wall and an object or material is found filling the entire cavity? To answer this question the Gemara now quotes an authoritative Tannaitic source: **A Tanna taught** in a Baraita: **"If** the cavity extends right through the wall, and this cavity in **the wall is filled with** articles the ownership of which is undetermined, the finder and the owner of the wall have equal claims and **divide** the articles between them," in accordance with the principle that property of doubtful ownership is divided equally between the claimants.

פְּשִׁיטָא [7]With reference to this ruling the Gemara asks: Surely **this is obvious!** Why did the author of the Baraita find it necessary to make this statement, and what new information does it provide?

לָא [8]The Gemara answers: **No!** The statement in the Baraita **is necessary,** as without it we would not know how to decide in a case **where** the cavity in the wall **is sloping to one side,** i.e., where the floor of the cavity is not level. [9]**You might** mistakenly **have said** that **the article** found in the wall was originally concealed at the upper end of the cavity and only later **rolled down** towards the lower end. Hence, it should be awarded to whoever owns the upper end of the cavity. [10]Therefore, the author of the Baraita **informs us that this is not so,** and we assess ownership on the basis of the situation at the time the article was found.

אִם הָיָה מַשְׂכִּירוֹ לַאֲחֵרִים [11]The Gemara now considers the next clause of the Mishnah: **"If** the owner of the house **was renting it to others,** [12]then **even if** someone **finds objects** lying around **within the house,** while it is temporarily vacant, **they are his** to keep," as it is impossible to determine which of the former tenants left them there. [13]On this point the Gemara asks: **But why** should we award the objects to the finder? Would it not be better to **go after the last tenant,** and assume that he is the owner of the object, since he is by far the

[1]וְאֶלָּא מַתְנִיתִין, דְּקָתָנֵי: "מֶחֶצְיוֹ וְלַחוּץ, שֶׁלּוֹ; [2]מֶחֶצְיוֹ וְלִפְנִים, שֶׁל בַּעַל הַבַּיִת", [3]וְלֶחֱזֵי אִי קַתָּא לְגָאו אִי קַתָּא לְבַר; [4]אִי שְׁנָצֵיהּ לְגָאו אִי שְׁנָצֵיהּ לְבַר!

[5]מַתְנִיתִין בְּאוּדְרָא וְנִסְכָּא.

[6]תָּנָא: "אִם הָיָה כּוֹתֶל מְמוּלָּא מֵהֶן, חוֹלְקִין". [7]פְּשִׁיטָא!

[8]לָא. צְרִיכָא דְּמְשַׁפַּע בְּחַד גִּיסָא. [9]מַהוּ דְּתֵימָא: אִשְׁתַּפּוּכֵי אִישְׁתַּפּוּךְ. [10]קָא מַשְׁמַע לָן.

[11]"אִם הָיָה מַשְׂכִּירוֹ לַאֲחֵרִים, [12]אֲפִילּוּ מָצָא בְּתוֹךְ הַבַּיִת, הֲרֵי אֵלּוּ שֶׁלּוֹ". [13]וְאַמַּאי? לֵיזִיל בָּתַר בַּתְרָא!

LITERAL TRANSLATION

[1]But then, [regarding] our Mishnah, which teaches: "From half of its [thickness] and outwards, [they are] his; [2]from half of its [thickness] and inwards, [they] belong to the owner of the house," [3]let us see if the handle is [pointing] inwards [or] if the handle is [pointing] outwards; [4]if its laces are [pointing] inwards [or] if its laces are [pointing] outwards.

[5]Our Mishnah [refers] to stuffing material and a piece of metal.

[6][A Tanna] taught: "If the wall was filled with them, they divide."

[7]This is obvious.

[8]No. It is necessary where it is sloping to one side. [9]You might have said: They rolled down. [10]He informs us [that this is not so].

[11]"If he was renting it to others, [12]even [if] he found [the objects] within the house, they are his." [13]But why? Let us go after the last [tenant].

RASHI

באודרא — מוכין. נסכא — *פלט"א של כסף. ממולא — מן החפץ, שמחזיק כל רוחב הכותל. לא צריכא דמשפע — הכותל לחד גיסא. מהו דתימא — בצד הגובה היה תחילה, ואשתפוכי אשתפוך לצד הנמוך, קמשמע לן.

LANGUAGE (RASHI)

פלט"א* From the Old French *plate,* it means a chunk or a solid piece of something.

BACKGROUND

אִשְׁתַּפּוּכֵי אִישְׁתַּפּוּךְ They rolled down. This argument appears to be reasonable, though we must understand, as the Jerusalem Talmud explains, that we are not dealing with a case in which there was only a hole in one side of the wall, but rather an opening extending all the way through the wall. Since the whole interior of the wall is filled with objects, it is clear that whoever hid them intended to push in everything he was holding, and he was just as likely to have pushed the objects upwards as downwards. Therefore the doubt is unresolved, and the found objects are divided.

HALAKHAH

אִם הָיָה מַשְׂכִּירוֹ לַאֲחֵרִים If he was renting the house out to others. "If a house is rented out, anything found in it is presumed to have been left by the most recent tenant and must be returned to him. If the house is rented to three

LITERAL TRANSLATION

[1] Have we not learned: "Coins that were found in front of cattle dealers are always [treated as] tithe [money];

[1] מִי לָא תְּנַן: ״מָעוֹת שֶׁנִּמְצְאוּ לִפְנֵי סוֹחֲרֵי בְהֵמָה לְעוֹלָם מַעֲשֵׂר;

RASHI

לפני סוחרי בהמה – בירושלים. לעולם – בין בשעת הרגל בין שלא בשעת הרגל. מעשר – שרוב בשר הנאכל בירושלים מעשר, לפי שאין אדם שוהה בירושלים עד שיאכל כל מעשרותיו, ונותן מעות מעשר לעניי העיר או לאוהביו יושבי העיר, ורוב הולאות מעשר לוקחין בהן בהמות לשלמים, כדגמר שם שם מעשר משלמים, במסכת מנחות (פב,א).

TRANSLATION AND COMMENTARY

most likely person to have lost it. If the article had belonged to the owner, it would surely have been found by one of the succession of tenants. Each of the occupants would in turn have given up hope of recovering the object, except for the last tenant, who may still be hoping that it will be found.

מִי לָא תְּנַן [1] The Gemara now strengthens its question by quoting a Mishnah which bears on the issue of who presumably lost money, based on the time and place where the money is found: **Have we not learned** in a Mishnah in a different context (*Shekalim* 7:2): **"Coins that were found** on the ground in Jerusalem in the cattle market **in front of cattle dealers are always treated as** second-**tithe money."** Money used to redeem produce of second tithe (see note) took on the sanctity of the second tithe itself and could only be used to buy food products in Jerusalem and, in particular, animals to be offered as sacrifices. Since very large numbers of people throughout Eretz Israel took their second-tithe money to Jerusalem at the time of the Pilgrim Festivals, there tended to be a surfeit of such money, and it tended to remain in circulation all year round, even during the periods between the Festivals when there were few visitors in Jerusalem. Thus it was unusual for anyone to buy sacrificial animals with ordinary, unconsecrated money. Hence, since this money was clearly dropped by a customer who had come to buy an animal, it is presumed to be tithe money, irrespective of the time of year in which it was found, and it is governed by the restrictions that apply to such money. This ruling applies specifically to money found near the cattle dealers' market.

TERMINOLOGY

מִי לָא תְּנַן **Have we not learned in a Mishnah?** An expression used to introduce a proof or supporting statement (usually by analogy) from a Mishnah.

CONCEPTS

פִּדְיוֹן מַעֲשֵׂר שֵׁנִי **The redemption of the second tithe.** The Torah says (Deuteronomy 14:25) that if it is difficult to bring the second tithe itself to Jerusalem, one may redeem (מְחַלְּלִים) it with money (minted coins only, not paper money, bullion, or any other commodity), and then the produce itself is no longer consecrated. The money, however, takes on the sanctity of the second tithe, and must be brought to Jerusalem, where it is used to buy food and drink. The money then loses its sanctity, and the purchased food becomes consecrated as though it itself was second-tithe produce, and must be eaten in Jerusalem. When the owner is the one who redeems the tithed produce, he must add a fifth to its price.

NOTES

מָעוֹת מַעֲשֵׂר **Tithe money.** The tithe referred to here is second tithe (מַעֲשֵׂר שֵׁנִי), which was set aside by the farmers after the priestly dues (תְּרוּמָה) had been given to the priests and the first tithe (מַעֲשֵׂר רִאשׁוֹן) had been given to the Levites. The second tithe was given in the first, second, fourth and fifth years of the Sabbatical cycle. It had to be taken to Jerusalem at the first opportunity and eaten there in a state of ritual purity. The second tithe was forbidden to be eaten anywhere else. Since it was clearly not practical for all the farmers throughout Eretz Israel to bring their produce in this form to Jerusalem, the Torah (Deuteronomy 14:25) allowed the farmer to redeem his second-tithe produce for its value. After the redemption, the produce itself became ordinary, unconsecrated produce, but the money became sanctified, and had to be taken to Jerusalem to buy food products, or animals for peace-offerings. After the purchase, the money lost its sanctity, but the purchased food became sanctified and had to be eaten in Jerusalem in a state of ritual purity.

The second tithe, or its equivalent, could be consumed at any convenient time until Passover of the fourth or seventh year of the Sabbatical cycle. There was no fixed time for bringing it to Jerusalem. But the usual practice was for pilgrims going to Jerusalem for the three Pilgrim Festivals to use the opportunity to take their second-tithe produce or money and to use it to pay for any food or sacrifices they might need during their stay. Thus they had little need for ordinary, unconsecrated money on these visits, and during the Festival season there tended to be far more second-tithe money in circulation in Jerusalem than ordinary money. In fact, it was normal for pilgrims to leave behind in Jerusalem the second-tithe money they had not spent during the Festival, for the year-round use of the residents of Jerusalem. Hence, even during the rest of the year, sacrificial animals bought by the residents of Jerusalem tended to be paid for with remaining second-tithe money, though outside the area of the cattle market itself ordinary, unconsecrated money usually predominated.

Therefore, the Mishnah from tractate *Shekalim* tells us that money dropped by customers in the cattle market could be presumed to be second-tithe money all year round; money found on the Temple Mount — which did not require to be swept frequently — could be presumed to be ordinary money dropped by a Jerusalem resident during the course of the year; and money found elsewhere in Jerusalem — where the public places and streets were swept regularly — could be presumed to have been dropped very recently and hence to be second-tithe money during the Festivals, and ordinary money during the rest of the year.

מָעוֹת שֶׁנִּמְצְאוּ לִפְנֵי סוֹחֲרֵי בְהֵמָה **Coins that were found in front of cattle dealers.** The Rishonim ask: The Mishnah is assuming that the money was lost by a customer on his

HALAKHAH

non-Jews, it is considered an inn, and the finder may keep whatever he finds," following the Gemara's interpretation of the Mishnah, in accordance with the views of *Rif* and *Rambam* who maintain that Rav Naḥman's reasoning is contradicted by Rava's authoritative ruling further on in the passage. (*Shulḥan Arukh, Ḥoshen Mishpat* 260:3.)

מָעוֹת שֶׁנִּמְצְאוּ בִּירוּשָׁלַיִם **Coins found in Jerusalem.** "Money found in Jerusalem in Temple times could be presumed to be unconsecrated, since the streets were swept daily and money tended to be found on the day it was lost. During the Festival season, it was presumed to be second-tithe money, for the same reason. Money found near the cattle

TRANSLATION AND COMMENTARY

[1]The Mishnah continues: "By contrast, money found **on the Temple Mount** itself, whether at the time of the Pilgrim Festivals or during the rest of the year, is treated **as unconsecrated money."** This second ruling is based on the assumption that money found on the Temple Mount was not lost there during the limited period of the Festival (when most money in the possession of pilgrims is second-tithe money), but rather during the rest of the year (when most of the money in circulation in the city is unconsecrated). [2]The Mishnah continues: **"But** if the money was found **elsewhere in Jerusalem,** neither in the cattle market nor on the Temple Mount, its status depends on the time of year in which it was found: If it was found **during the rest of the year,** not during the Festival period, it is treated **as unconsecrated money** and is presumed to have been lost by one of the residents of the city. [3]But if it was found **during the Pilgrim Festival season,** when most people in the city are pilgrims and thus most of the money in circulation is second-tithe money, **it is all treated as** second-**tithe money** lost by a pilgrim." [4]Having quoted this Mishnah from tractate *Shekalim,* the Gemara continues to develop its question by noting that in connection with this Mishnah **Rav Shemayah bar Ze'era** made the following clarification. He **said: What is the reason** why the Mishnah makes a distinction between (1) money found on the Temple Mount during the Festival season, which we assume was lost before the Festival by a Jerusalem resident even if it was found during the Festival, and is therefore treated as unconsecrated, and (2) money found in the streets of Jerusalem during the Festival season, where we ignore this possibility and assume that it must have been lost recently by a pilgrim?

[1]בְּהַר הַבַּיִת, חוּלִּין; [2]וּבִירוּשָׁלַיִם, בִּשְׁאָר יְמוֹת הַשָּׁנָה, חוּלִּין, [3]בִּשְׁעַת הָרֶגֶל, הַכֹּל מַעֲשֵׂר." [4]וְאָמַר רַב שְׁמַעְיָה בַּר זְעֵירָא: מַאי טַעְמָא?

LITERAL TRANSLATION

[1]on the Temple Mount, [as] unconsecrated [money]; [2]and [elsewhere] in Jerusalem, on the other days of the year, [as] unconsecrated [money], [3]during the Pilgrim Festival season (lit., 'in the hour of the Pilgrim Festival'), it is all [treated as] tithe [money]." [4]And Rav Shemayah bar Ze'era said: What is the reason?

RASHI

ובהר הבית חולין — ואפילו בשעת הרגל, ואף על פי שרוב מעות שבעיר מעשר, שעולי רגלים מביאין מעות מעשרותיהן לאכלם, לא שבקינן רובא דשתא ואזלינן בתר רגל, אלא אמרינן מלפני הרגל נפלו כאן וחולין הן. **ובירושלים** — בשאר שווקים שבה. **בשאר ימות השנה חולין** — דרוב מעות שבעיר חולין. **ובשעת הרגל מעשר** — שרוב מעות העיר מעשר. **ואמר רב שמעיה בר זעירא מאי טעם** — בירושלים בשעת הרגל מעשר, ולא אמרינן מלפני הרגל נפלו, כדאמרן בהר הבית.

CONCEPTS

שָׁלֹשׁ רְגָלִים The three Pilgrim Festivals. Pesaḥ, Shavuot, and Sukkot. On these three Festivals Jewish men were obligated to appear in the Temple (Deuteronomy 16:16). All sacrifices previously pledged to the Temple were also brought on these Festivals, so as not to violate the prohibition against delaying sacrifices that one had pledged.

SAGES

רַב שְׁמַעְיָה בַּר זְעֵירָא Rav Shemayah bar Ze'era. A Babylonian Amora of the fifth generation, Rav Shemayah bar Ze'era is mentioned by the Talmud as a student of Abaye and of Rava, to whom he addresses various questions.

NOTES

way to buy a sacrificial animal, but it could equally well have been lost by the cattle dealer himself after he had received the money for the sale of the animal. Now, second-tithe money loses its sanctity as soon as it has been used to purchase an animal. Thus any money lost by the cattle dealer would be unconsecrated. Why is the Mishnah not concerned about this possibility?

Tosafot and others answer that there are many customers for every individual vendor. Hence we follow the majority and assume that the money was lost by a customer.

בְּהַר הַבַּיִת, חוּלִּין Coins found on the Temple Mount are treated as unconsecrated money. Our commentary follows *Rashi,* who explains that the money is assumed to be ordinary money lost by a Jerusalemite who happened to be visiting the Temple Mount. The Rishonim object to this explanation, since it is forbidden to carry money up to the Temple Mount out of respect for the sanctity of the place. *Tosafot* suggests that this prohibition applies only to money carried in an obvious way. However, *Rambam* and others reject *Rashi*'s viewpoint and explain that we assume the money was lost by the Temple treasurer after it had been used to buy sacrificial animals.

Ketzot HaḤoshen asks: Even if the money that was lost was originally unconsecrated, why does the Temple treasury not acquire it automatically, even without being aware of its presence, by virtue of courtyard-acquisition, since it was found on the Temple Mount? Among the answers offered are the following: (1) The law of courtyard-acquisition does not apply to the Temple treasury (*Magen Avraham, Shulḥan Arukh, Oraḥ Ḥayyim* 154:23). (2) The law of courtyard-acquisition applies automatically, even without awareness on the part of its owner, only if the courtyard is protected and under its owner's control. But the Temple Mount is usually crowded and not protected at all (*Ḥatam Sofer* and others).

HALAKHAH

dealers' stalls was presumed to be second-tithe money throughout the year. Money found on the Temple Mount was always presumed to be unconsecrated, even during the Festival season," following the Mishnah quoted by the Gemara. (*Rambam, Sefer Zeraim, Hilkhot Ma'aser Sheni* 6:9-10.)

[1] הוֹאִיל וְשׁוּקֵי יְרוּשָׁלַיִם עֲשׂוּיִין לְהִתְכַּבֵּד בְּכָל יוֹם. [2] אַלְמָא אָמְרִינַן: קַמָּאֵי קַמָּאֵי אָזְלוּ, וְהָנֵי אַחֲרִינֵי נִינְהוּ. [3] הָכָא נַמִי, קַמָּא קַמָּא אָזַל, וְהָנֵי דְּבַתְרָא הוּא! [4] אָמַר רֵישׁ לָקִישׁ מִשּׁוּם בַּר קַפָּרָא: כְּגוֹן שֶׁעֲשָׂאוֹ פּוּנְדָּק לִשְׁלֹשָׁה יִשְׂרָאֵל. [5] שְׁמַע מִינָּהּ: הֲלָכָה כְּרַבִּי שִׁמְעוֹן בֶּן אֶלְעָזָר אֲפִילּוּ בְּרוֹב יִשְׂרָאֵל!

LITERAL TRANSLATION

[1] Because the markets of Jerusalem were swept every day. [2] Hence we say: The first ones (lit., "the first, the first") have gone, and these are others. [3] Here, too, the first one (lit., "the first, the first") has gone, and these belong to the last [tenant].

[4] Resh Lakish said in the name of Bar Kappara: For example, where he made it an inn for three Jews.

[5] Conclude from here: The Halakhah is in accordance with Rabbi Shimon ben Elazar even where the majority are Jews.

TRANSLATION AND COMMENTARY

[1] The reason for this seeming contradiction, says Rav Shemayah bar Ze'era, is **because the markets** and streets **of Jerusalem were swept** thoroughly **every day,** and lost money would not normally remain undiscovered for more than one day. Therefore, if money was found there during the Festival, it must have been lost during the Festival, and was treated as second-tithe money. By contrast, the Temple Mount was constantly kept meticulously clean, because of the special regulations regarding the appearance and clothing of all who visited it. Thus there was no need to sweep the Temple Mount every day, and any money found there during the Festival was assumed to have been lost before the Festival and was treated as unconsecrated, because the majority of money in circulation in Jerusalem outside the Festival period was unconsecrated. On the basis of the Mishnah and the explanation given by Rav Shemayah bar Ze'era, the Gemara now returns to the subject of objects found in a wall, and draws a conclusion that seems to contradict the ruling in our own Mishnah: Money found in a place that is regularly swept and kept tidy is assumed in the Mishnah in tractate *Shekalim* to have been lost just before it was found. [2] **Hence we say** that in such cases any money lost **previously,** before the last cleanup, has already been found and **has** long since **gone.** Thus any money found now, during the Festival, must be **other** money lost recently. [3] **In our case, too,** says the Gemara, we should be able to argue in the same way: Any article left in a house by mistake by **a previous** tenant would have been found immediately by the next tenant. Thus any article found there now can only be **the property of the last tenant.** Therefore, even in a rented house, there is a good chance of finding the owner of objects found there, and there is no reason why the finder should not be obligated to return them in the usual manner. Why, then, does our Mishnah state that such objects belong to the finder?

אָמַר רֵישׁ לָקִישׁ [4] The Gemara now gives two answers to this question: (1) **Resh Lakish said in the name of Bar Kappara:** Our Mishnah is referring, **for example,** to a situation where the owner of the house **made** his house **an inn for three** or more **Jews,** who would stay there at the same time. It is true, says Resh Lakish, that where one tenant takes over occupancy from another we should assume that property found by the new tenant in all probability belongs to the previous one. But the situation here is that there are three (or more) tenants involved simultaneously, and in such a case the person who lost the property will have given up hope of recovering it because he does not know from whom to claim.

שְׁמַע מִינָּהּ [5] The underlying assumption behind Resh Lakish's response is that our Mishnah is referring to a situation where an object is lost in a place where the majority of the population are Jews, and that in such a situation the lost property belongs to the finder. But this assumption was itself the subject of a Tannaitic dispute and an unresolved Talmudic debate earlier in this chapter (above, 24a-b). The Gemara now asks: If Resh Lakish is correct in his interpretation, we should be able to **conclude from** our Mishnah that **the Halakhah is in accordance with** the view of **Rabbi Shimon ben Elazar,** who maintains that where an object is found in a place frequented by many people, it belongs to the finder, **even where the majority are Jews.** If Resh Lakish's explanation were correct, the Gemara would have been able to resolve the question of whether Rabbi Shimon ben Elazar's viewpoint was accepted as Halakhah from our Mishnah here. The fact that the Gemara did not

RASHI

ושוקי ירושלים עשויין להתכבד בכל יום — ואם נפלו שם לפני הרגל — כבר מצאום מכבדי השוק, אבל הר הבית אין צריך להתכבד בכל יום, שאין טיט ועפר קולט שם מתוך שהוא משופע, ועוד, שאין אדם נכנס שם במנעל ובאבק שעל רגליו. **אלמא** — בדבר שעשוי להתכבד אמרינן קמאי קמאי אזלו והני אחריני נינהו. **הכא נמי** — סתם שוכר בית, כשהוא יוצא — מחפש כל זויותיו ונוטל את שלו ויוצא, ונימא האחרונים שכחוהו שאילו הראשונים שכחוהו — כבר מצאו האחרונים. **לשלשה ישראל** — בבת אחת, וכל שכן אם היו נכרים, ומי שנפל ממנו מיאש, דלא ידע ממאן נבעי. **פונדק** — מקום שעוברים ושבים לנים לילה אחד ושנים. **ואפילו ברוב ישראל** — דעביד דמייאש, ולא סמיך דליהדרו ניהליה, דלא מפלגי בין דבר שיש בו סימן לאין בו סימן.

LANGUAGE

פּוּנְדָּק Inn. This word is derived from the Greek πανδοκεῖον, *pandokeion,* which means "lodging-house" or "inn."

SAGES

בַּר קַפָּרָא Bar Kappara. This Sage was one of the last of the Tannaim and a very close disciple of Rabbi Yehudah HaNasi. He was a colleague of Rabbi Shimon ben Rabbi and of Rabbi Ḥiyya. It is not certain what his first name was, but some authorities claim that he was the posthumous son of Rabbi Elazar HaKappar and was given the name Elazar as well.

Bar Kappara was one of the greatest Halakhic authorities of his generation, and he also edited a collection of Baraitot known as מִשְׁנַת בַּר קַפָּרָא, which the Talmud quotes several times. Bar Kappara was also famous as a preacher and an eloquent speaker, and many sayings and fables are presented in his name, as well as prayers which he composed.

Almost all the important Amoraim of the first generation of Amoraim in Eretz Israel were among his students, and one important Amora, Rabbi Yehudah bar Pedayah (bar Pada), was his nephew.

SAGES

רַב מְנַשְׁיָא בַּר יַעֲקֹב Rav Menashya bar Ya'akov. A Babylonian Amora of the third generation, and a colleague of Rav Naḥman.

רַבָּה בַּר אֲבוּהּ Rabbah bar Avuha. A Babylonian Amora of the second generation, Rabbah bar Avuha was a disciple of Rav, and transmitted many teachings in Rav's name. He was the teacher and father-in-law of Rav Naḥman bar Ya'akov, who transmitted almost all his teachings. He belonged to the family of the Exilarch and lived in Meḥoza, where he was one of the leading judges. His daughter, Yalta, who married Rav Naḥman, was a famous personality in her own right, and is quoted on a number of occasions in the Talmud.

TRANSLATION AND COMMENTARY

do so indicates that Resh Lakish's explanation is incorrect.

אֶלָּא אָמַר רַב מְנַשְׁיָא בַּר יַעֲקֹב [1](2) **Rather, Rav Menashya bar Ya'akov said:** There is another possible interpretation of our Mishnah which would avoid not only the problem posed by the Mishnah from tractate *Shekalim*, but also the difference of opinion between Rabbi Shimon ben Elazar and the Sages: Our Mishnah may be referring, **for example,** to a situation **where** the owner of the house **made it an inn for three non-Jews.** Hence we may assume that the object was lost by a non-Jew and need not be returned. If Rav Menashya bar Ya'akov's explanation is accepted, no difficulty arises with regard to the discussion earlier in the Gemara (above, 24a-b) regarding Rabbi Shimon ben Elazar's viewpoint.

רַב נַחְמָן אָמַר רַבָּה בַּר אֲבוּהּ [2]**Rav Naḥman said in the name of Rabbah bar Avuha:** It is not necessary to reject Resh Lakish's explanation. **You can even say,** as Resh Lakish said earlier, **that** our Mishnah is referring to a case in which the owner of the house **turned it** into **an inn for three Jews.** Nevertheless, the case in our Mishnah offers no way of solving the problem regarding Rabbi Shimon ben Elazar, because there is a fundamental difference between the situation described in our Mishnah and that described by Rabbi Shimon ben Elazar. Rav Naḥman goes on to explain: In the case described by Rabbi Shimon ben Elazar, where an object is lost in a place frequented by many people, the owner of the lost property believes it will be found by an honest person who will announce it, so that the owner can claim it. For this reason, the Sages disagree with Rabbi Shimon ben Elazar, who says that the object belongs to the finder, and they maintain that the finder must announce it, because the owner has not given up hope. [3]This argument, says Rav Naḥman, does not apply to the case in our Mishnah. **What is the reason** why the finder is allowed to keep the object he found in this inn? It is because in this case the finder is entitled to assume that **the person who lost the object has** already **given up hope** of recovering it. [4]**He surely says** to himself: **"Since no other person, apart from these two** men, **was with me** in the inn when I lost the article, it is obvious to me that one of them must have taken it. [5]**I said to them a number of times that they should return it to me, but they** denied any knowledge of it and **did not return it.** I do not believe them, but what is the use of persisting? [6]**Will they now** suddenly have a change of heart and decide to **return it?** [7]**If their intention had been to return it, they would have returned it to me** long ago. [8]**The fact that they have not returned it** until now **shows that it is their intention to steal it."** Hence, in the case in our Mishnah the owner gives up hope of ever recovering his lost article. Therefore, the Mishnah rules that the finder of such an article may keep it.

[1]אֶלָּא אָמַר רַב מְנַשְׁיָא בַּר יַעֲקֹב: כְּגוֹן שֶׁעֲשָׂאוֹ פּוּנְדָק לִשְׁלֹשָׁה נָכְרִים.
[2]רַב נַחְמָן אָמַר רַבָּה בַּר אֲבוּהּ: אֲפִילּוּ תֵּימָא לִשְׁלֹשָׁה יִשְׂרָאֵל. [3]מַאי טַעְמָא? הַהוּא דִּנְפַל מִינֵּיהּ מְיָאֵשׁ. [4]מֵימַר אָמַר: "מִכְּדֵי אִינִישׁ אַחֲרִינָא לָא הֲוָה בַּהֲדַי אֶלָּא הָנֵי, [5]אֲמַרִי קַמַּיְיהוּ כַּמָּה זִמְנֵי לִיהַדְרוּ לִי, וְלָא הַדְרוּ לִי. [6]וְהַשְׁתָּא לִיהַדְרוּ?! [7]אִי דַּעְתַּיְיהוּ לְאַהֲדוּרַהּ, אַהַדְרוּהּ נִיהֲלִי; [8]וְהַאי דְּלָא אַהַדְרוּהּ לִי בְּדַעְתַּיְיהוּ לְמִיגְזְלַהּ".

LITERAL TRANSLATION

[1]Rather, Rav Menashya bar Ya'akov said: For example, where he made it an inn for three non-Jews.

[2]Rav Naḥman said [in the name of] Rabbah bar Avuha: You can even say [that he made it an inn] for three Jews. [3]What is the reason? The one from whom it fell gives up hope. [4]He surely says: "Now, since no other person was with me apart from these men, [5]I said to them a number of times that they should return [it] to me, but they did not return [it] to me. [6]And now they will return [it]? [7]If their intention had been to return it, they would have returned it to me; [8]and the fact that they did not return it to me [shows that] it is their intention to steal it."

RASHI

שלשה נכרים – אידי דנקט שלשה גבי ישראל נקט נמי גבי נכרים, והוא הדין חד וכלבד שיהא אחרון. **אפילו תימא לשלשה ישראל** – ולא תפשוט דהלכה כרבי שמעון בן אלעזר, דכי פליגי רבנן עליה – היכא דנפלה במקום שהרבים מצויין דלא ידע להו לכולהו, דסבר האובד ומימר אמר ההוא דאשכחה לא ידע ממי נפלה, ולכשיגיע הרגל יכריז עליה ואתן סימן ואטול, אבל הכא דידע להו לכולהו ותבעינהו ולא אודו – מיאושי מיאוש, מימר אמר כו'. **אמרי קמייהו** – אמרתי לפניהם. **והשתא ליהדרו** – בתמיה!

NOTES

פּוּנְדָק לִשְׁלֹשָׁה נָכְרִים An inn for three non-Jews. *Rashi* and others explain that the reasoning of Rav Menashya bar Ya'akov is that the object was lost by a non-Jew and need not be returned. Accordingly, the house need not have been turned into an inn, nor was it necessarily ever rented to more than one non-Jew. Rather, Rav Menashya bar Ya'akov's use of the number "three" is merely a convention designed to parallel the choice of language used by Resh Lakish.

Ra'avad and *Meiri* explain that "three non-Jews" means

TRANSLATION AND COMMENTARY

And this ruling would be acceptable to both Rabbi Shimon ben Elazar and the Sages who disagree with him (above, 24a-b).

וְאָזְדָא רַב נַחְמָן לְטַעְמֵיהּ [1]The Gemara now notes that, in offering this explanation of our Mishnah, **Rav Naḥman is following his regular line of argument** as expressed by him elsewhere. **For Rav Naḥman said:** [2]**If someone saw a sela,** a coin, [26B] **fall from** the possession of one of **two people,** and then saw them looking for it together, **he is obliged to return it,** despite the fact that a sela is an object without a means of identification. [3]Rav Naḥman continues: **What is the reason** for this ruling? It is because **the person from whom** the money **fell does not give up hope** of recovering it, even though as of now he has not succeeded in finding it. [4]For **he will surely say** to himself: **"Since no other person was with me** when I lost the money **apart from this person,** it is obvious that he must have taken it. [5]Therefore, all **I will** need to do is to **take hold of him and say to him: 'You are the one who took it!'"** Hence, even though his companion did not actually take it, his mistaken impression prevents the one who dropped the coin from giving up hope. Thus the finder took possession of the money before *ye'ush* occurred, and cannot keep it for himself. Even if the owner of the money ultimately does give up hope, the finder may not keep it, because the Halakhah is in accordance with the viewpoint of Abaye that anticipated *ye'ush* is not valid. (See note.)

[1]וְאָזְדָא רַב נַחְמָן לְטַעְמֵיהּ, [2]דְּאָמַר רַב נַחְמָן: רָאָה סֶלַע [26B] שֶׁנָּפַל מִשְּׁנַיִם, חַיָּיב לְהַחֲזִיר. [3]מַאי טַעְמָא? הַהוּא דִּנְפַל מִינֵּיהּ לָא מְיָאֵשׁ. [4]מֵימַר אָמַר: ״מִכְּדִי אִינִישׁ אַחֲרִינָא לָא הֲוָה בַּהֲדַאי אֶלָּא הַאי, [5]נָקֵיטְנָא לֵיהּ וְאָמִינָא לֵיהּ: ׳אַתְּ הוּא דִּשְׁקַלְתֵּיהּ!׳״

LITERAL TRANSLATION

[1]And Rav Naḥman is following his [own] argument, for Rav Naḥman said: [2][If] he saw a sela [26B] that fell from two [people], he is obliged to return [it]. [3]What is the reason? The one from whom it fell does not give up hope. [4]He will surely say: "Since another person was not with me except this one, [5]I will take hold of him and say to him: 'You are the one who took it!'"

RASHI

נקיטנא ליה כו׳ — משבעגא ליה שבועת היסת, ולא נתייאש מיד כשמשמש ולא מצא, ונמצא שבא ליד זה לפני יאוש, והלכה כאביי.

TERMINOLOGY

אָזְדָא לְטַעְמֵיהּ He follows his [regular line of] argument. The Talmud uses this expression when pointing out that a scholar's statement in the case at hand follows the same principle or line of reasoning that he employs elsewhere.

NOTES

"three people, at least two of whom must be non-Jews." Accordingly, Rav Menashya bar Ya'akov is informing us that if the object was found in an inn inhabited mainly by Jews, it had to be returned, but if the majority of tenants were non-Jews, it could be kept.

Tosafot explains that the owner of the house is living in the inn with his three tenants, and he himself is the most likely person to have lost the article. Accordingly, the object must be returned to the owner of the house, unless the inn is frequented by many non-Jews (in this context, three or more), in which case we may assume that the owner gave up hope of recovering the object.

הַהוּא דִּנְפַל מִינֵּיהּ לָא מְיָאֵשׁ The person from whom the money fell does not give up hope. The underlying assumption of this passage, and of Rava's summary of the laws of lost coins below, is the fundamental difference between the obligations of a finder of lost property before the owner gives up hope of recovering it and his obligations afterwards. If the owner has not yet given up hope, even if only because he is under a mistaken impression, the finder must return the lost coins to him, and he violates three commandments if he takes them for himself. But after the owner finds out that the coins have really been lost and gives up hope, the finder is free to keep them for himself.

Rashi points out that this assumption is the subject of the difference of opinion between Abaye and Rava (above, 21b-22b). According to Rava, potential *ye'ush* is effective *ye'ush*, and a person who will ultimately give up hope when he becomes fully informed is considered as though he gave up hope from the moment the object was lost. *Rashi* explains that our Gemara is in accordance with the Halakhah as it was ultimately decided, which is in accordance with Abaye's opinion. The difficulty with this explanation is the fact that Rava himself is the author of several of the statements cited in this passage, and it is unreasonable to assume that he retracted his opinion to conform with that of Abaye.

Some Rishonim go so far as to amend the text, substituting Rabbah for Rava throughout (*Ramban* and others). Others suggest that in our case the loser may in fact never give up hope, because he may cling to the (mistaken) belief that one of his companions took the money, no matter how much time passes or how many searches are conducted. Hence, Rava would agree that in our case potential *ye'ush* is not effective because the owner may never in fact give up hope (*Tosafot* and others).

Other Rishonim argue that our passage is referring only to money that has an identifying mark, such as money in a wallet (*Ritva* and others).

According to these explanations, Rava's summary below of the laws of lost coins and the applicability of the three commandments would be relevant only in the case where the money was lost by one of three people, or where the money was identifiable.

נָקֵיטְנָא לֵיהּ I will take hold of him. According to *Rashi*, this expression means that the owner intends taking the person

HALAKHAH

מַטְבֵּעַ שֶׁנָּפְלָה מֵאֲנָשִׁים רַבִּים A coin that fell from among a group of people. "A person is not required to return a lost object that is worth less than one perutah, or even a more expensive object owned jointly by several people, such that

TRANSLATION AND COMMENTARY

בִּשְׁלֹשָׁה אֵינוֹ חַיָּיב לְהַחֲזִיר [1] Rav Naḥman continues: But if there were **three** people together, and one of them lost a sela in the presence of the other two and another person took it, the finder **is not obliged to return it,** even if it contains a means of identification. [2] **What is the reason** for this ruling? It is because **the person from whom** the money **fell certainly gives up hope** of recovering it as soon as he becomes aware of his loss. [3] **He will surely say** to himself: "**Since two** other people **were with me,** I have no way of finding out which of them took the money. [4] **If I take hold of this one** and demand the money back from him, **he will** simply **say: 'I did not take it,'** [5] **and if I take hold of the other one** and demand the money back from him, **he** too **will say: 'I did not take it.'**" Hence, even though neither of these two people actually took the money, the owner's mistaken impression makes him give up hope of recovering it. The finder takes possession of the money after the owner has given up hope of recovering it, hence he is entitled to keep it. Thus we see that Rav Naḥman's resolution of the apparent disagreement between our Mishnah and the Mishnah in tractate *Shekalim* is consistent with his known view that under certain circumstances a person immediately gives up hope of recovering his property, and this permits the finder to keep the property for himself.

אָמַר רָבָא [6] Qualifying Rav Naḥman's ruling, **Rava said: The ruling that you gave** — that if the money was

[1] בִּשְׁלֹשָׁה אֵינוֹ חַיָּיב לְהַחֲזִיר. [2] מַאי טַעְמָא? הַהוּא דִּנְפַל מִינֵּיהּ וַדַּאי מְיָאֵשׁ. [3] מֵימַר אָמַר: "מִכְּדִי תְּרֵי הָווּ בַּהֲדַאי, [4] אִי נָקֵיטְנָא לְהַאי, אָמַר: 'לָא שְׁקַלְתֵּיהּ,' [5] וְאִי נָקֵיטְנָא לְהַאי, אָמַר: 'לָא שְׁקַלְתֵּיהּ.'" [6] אָמַר רָבָא: הַאי דְּאָמְרַתְּ "בִּשְׁלֹשָׁה אֵינוֹ חַיָּיב לְהַחֲזִיר",

LITERAL TRANSLATION

[1] With three he is not obliged to return [it]. [2] What is the reason? The one from whom it fell certainly gives up hope. [3] He will surely say: "Since two were with me, [4] if I take hold of this one, he will say: 'I did not take it,' [5] and if I take hold of that one, he will say: 'I did not take it.'"

[6] Rava said: That which you said: "With three he is not obliged to return [it],"

RASHI

אי נקיטנא וכו׳ — ואינו יכול להשביעו בטענת שמא, שאין נשבעין בטענת שמא אלא אותן השנויין במשנה: ואלו נשבעים שלא בטענה כו׳ (שבועות מה,א), ואם תאמר, הא מקמי יאוש אתי לידיה, ואוקימנא הלכתא כאביי ביע״ל קג״ם, הא אמרן דמעות מידע ידיע מיד, כרבי יצחק, דאמר אדם עשוי למשמש בכיסו כו׳ (בבא מציעא כא,ב).

NOTES

he suspects to court and forcing him to take an "oath of inducement" (שְׁבוּעַת הֵיסֵּת). This oath is imposed only if the plaintiff is certain of his claim, as in the case where he lost his property while in the company of one person, but not if he is in doubt, as in the case where he lost his property while in the company of two or more people. In the latter case, as the plaintiff has no redress, he gives up hope.

The Rishonim (*Tosafot, Ritva,* and others) raise several objections to this explanation. Firstly, even if the owner was accompanied by one person when he lost his property, his assumption that his companion is guilty cannot easily be taken as a legal certainty. Secondly, while Rav Naḥman was certainly prepared as a judge to invoke the "oath of inducement," and while he may indeed have been the Rabbinic authority who instituted this oath, nevertheless in our passage he is explaining the words of Resh Lakish and Bar Kappara who lived before the date when this oath was instituted (see *Torat Ḥayyim*).

Hence, some Rishonim explain that the owner of the property is so convinced of his companion's guilt that an oath taken by the latter is futile. The plaintiff will simply not believe it (*Rosh*). Alternatively, it may not even be applicable, in the absence of legal certainty (*Ritva*). These authorities understand the expression "I will take hold of him" as meaning "I will harass him and embarrass him until he confesses" (*Tosafot, Rosh, Ritva,* and others).

HALAKHAH

each one's share is worth less than one perutah, provided that it is clear that it is owned jointly. However, if a person sees an object worth less than three perutot fall from among a group of three people, he must consider the possibility that it is owned by only two of them," following Rava's explanation. (*Shulḥan Arukh, Ḥoshen Mishpat* 262:2.)

מִצְוַת הֲשָׁבַת אֲבֵידָה The commandment to return lost property. "Someone who finds an object lost by a Jew must pick it up and take care of it, in order to return it to its owner, as the verse says: 'You shall surely return them.' If he picked it up before the owner gave up hope of recovering it, with the intention of robbing the owner of it, he violates this commandment, as well as those which state that 'you shall not rob,' and 'you may not hide yourself.' Even if he returns the object later, he has still violated the prohibition against ignoring it. If he picked it up with the intention of returning it and changed his mind and decided to keep it for himself, he has still violated the commandment to return it. And if he left it lying there until the owner gave up hope and then picked it up, he has still violated the prohibition against ignoring it." (Ibid., 259:1.)

TRANSLATION AND COMMENTARY

lost by one of **three** people the finder **is not obliged to return it** — [1]**is only applicable where** the total amount lost **was less than the equivalent of one perutah,** the smallest unit of currency, **for each one** of the people present, i.e., the value of the coin was less than three perutot, and if it were divided between the three people, each would receive less than a perutah, and something worth less than a perutah is of no Halakhic significance. [2]**But if** the amount lost was greater than this, and would provide at least **the equivalent of one perutah for each one** of the people present, the finder **is obliged to return it** to its rightful owner. [3]**What is the reason** for this ruling? It is because it is possible to **argue** that the three companions **are** actually **partners,** each with a share in the lost money, and do not suspect each other of stealing. Hence, when one of the three loses the money, he imagines that one of his partners has picked it up with the intention of returning it later, **and he does not give up hope** of recovering it. Even though his partners give no indication of having found the money, this does not cause the owner to give up hope of recovering it, for they could merely be teasing him. But if the sum involved is less than three perutot, the finder need not return it, since if the three are partners each one has a share of less than one perutah in the money, and there is no Halakhic requirement to return such an insignificant amount. Nevertheless, if the three are not partners, the owner gives up hope of recovering the money, as explained above, and the finder has no obligation to return it.

אִיכָּא דְּאָמְרִי [4]The Gemara now cites another version of Rava's statement quoted above: [5]**There are some who say** that **Rava's statement** was in the following form: In a situation where one of three people lost money, **even if** the money **is only the equivalent of two perutot** in value, the finder **is** still **obliged to return it,** even though each would receive less than a perutah if the money were divided between the three people. [6]**What is the reason** for this ruling? It is because it is possible to **argue that** the three **were** indeed **partners,** [7]**but one of them has renounced his share in favor of his colleagues,** thus leaving each remaining partner with a one-perutah share in the money. The implication of this for the finder is that he is now obliged to return the money, and furthermore, since the partners trust each other, the owner of the money has not given up hope of recovering it. Thus, according to this version of Rava's statement, the finder must return the money even if its total value is less than three perutot and the loss involves three people, and in this Rava disagrees with Rav Naḥman.

וְאָמַר רָבָא [8]The Talmud now quotes another statement by Rava, summarizing the laws concerning lost coins and describing three possible situations. **Rava also said:** (1) **If a person saw a sela fall** from someone's possession, and **picked it up before** the owner **gave up hope** of recovering it, then if the finder

[1]לָא אֲמָרַן אֶלָּא דְּלֵית בֵּיהּ שָׁוֶה פְּרוּטָה לְכָל חַד וְחַד. [2]אֲבָל אִית בֵּיהּ שָׁוֶה פְּרוּטָה לְכָל חַד וְחַד, חַיָּיב לְהַחֲזִיר. [3]מַאי טַעְמָא? אֵימוּר שׁוּתָּפֵי נִינְהוּ וְלָא מְיָאֲשׁוּ.

[4]אִיכָּא דְּאָמְרִי: [5]אָמַר רָבָא: אַף עַל גַּב דְּלֵית בֵּיהּ אֶלָּא שָׁוֶה שְׁתֵּי פְּרוּטוֹת, חַיָּיב לְהַחֲזִיר. [6]מַאי טַעְמָא? אֵימוּר שׁוּתָּפֵי נִינְהוּ, [7]וְחַד מִנַּיְיהוּ אַחוּלֵי אַחְלֵיהּ לְמְנָתֵיהּ גַּבֵּי חַבְרֵיהּ.

[8]וְאָמַר רָבָא: רָאָה סֶלַע שֶׁנָּפְלָה, נְטָלָהּ לִפְנֵי יֵאוּשׁ

LITERAL TRANSLATION

[1]we do not say so except where there is not in it a perutah's worth for each one. [2]But [if] there is in it a perutah's worth for each one, he is obliged to return [it]. [3]What is the reason? Say [that] they are partners and do not give up hope.

[4]There are some who say: [5]Rava said: Even though there is not in it except two perutot worth, he is obliged to return [it]. [6]What is the reason? Say [that] they are partners, [7]and one of them renounced his share in favor of his fellow.

[8]Rava also said: [If] he saw a sela that fell, [if] he took it before *ye'ush*

RASHI

אימור שותפי נינהו — בסלע זו, ונאמנים זה על זה, ואין האחד חושד את חבירו בחלקו, ולכי מישמש בכיסו ולא מצאה לא אייאש, מימר אמר: אחד מן השותפים מצאה ולצערני הוא שותק. ונמצא, כשבאת ליד זה — לפני יאוש באת לידו, והא אוקמיה כאביי, הלכך אף על גב דסלע דבר שאין בו סימן הוא — חייב להחזיר, אבל כי אין בו שלש פרוטות, מה נפשך? אי שותפין הן בו — אין כאן משום השבת אבידה, ואם של אחד מהם הוא או של השנים — נואשו ואמרו חברנו זה גנב הוא והרי משמט ואמר "לא לקחתיו", אחד מכם לקחו וגנבו מחבירו. **אימור שותפי נינהו** — ומהימני אהדדי, ואין חושדין זה את זה, ונמצאת שבאת ליד זה לפני יאוש. **ראה סלע שנפלה** — ולא גרסינן משנים. **נטלה לפני יאוש** — שלא שהה כדי למשמש זה בכיסו.

BACKGROUND

דְּלֵית בֵּיהּ שָׁוֶה פְּרוּטָה When there is not in it a perutah's worth. According to this explanation, the sela referred to above is not the valuable silver coin of that name, which was worth four dinarim (nearly 800 perutot), nor can it even be the סֶלַע מְדִינָה — "the state sela" — which was worth half a dinar. The value of a perutah was set at one-eighth of an Italian isar, and half a dinar was worth close to 100 perutot. Reference here is to a small coin worth far less than a true sela.

שָׁוֶה פְּרוּטָה A perutah's worth. The perutah was the smallest coin in circulation, and in the Halakhah it is particularly meaningful. The perutah is considered the smallest monetary unit with any Halakhic significance; anything worth less than a perutah is not regarded as being worth money at all, and none of the commandments concerning money apply to it. Naturally, something worth less than a perutah does have some value, for the value of a perutah can be made up of many tiny objects. However, so long as their total value does not reach that basic amount, one may have moral responsibility for the objects but they are not recognized as having monetary value.

NOTES

שָׁוֶה שְׁתֵּי פְּרוּטוֹת The equivalent of two perutot. Although it is logically possible that a coin worth a single perutah may also be owned jointly by three partners, and that two of them may have renounced their share in favor of the third, this possibility is too remote to be considered seriously (*Tur* and others).

עַל מְנָת לְגוֹזְלָהּ, [1]עוֹבֵר בְּכוּלָּן: [2]מִשּׁוּם "לֹא תִגְזוֹל", [3]וּמִשּׁוּם "הָשֵׁב תְּשִׁיבֵם", [4]וּמִשּׁוּם "לֹא תוּכַל לְהִתְעַלֵּם". [5]וְאַף עַל גַּב דְּהָדְרָה לְאַחַר יֵאוּשׁ, [6]מַתָּנָה הוּא דְּיָהֵיב לֵיהּ, וְאִיסּוּרָא דַּעֲבַד, עֲבַד.

[7]נְטָלָהּ לִפְנֵי יֵאוּשׁ עַל מְנָת לְהַחֲזִירָהּ, וּלְאַחַר יֵאוּשׁ נִתְכַּוֵּין לְגוֹזְלָהּ, [8]עוֹבֵר מִשּׁוּם "הָשֵׁב תְּשִׁיבֵם".

LITERAL TRANSLATION

with the intention of robbing [the owner of] it, [1]he transgresses them all:

[2]Because of "you shall not rob," [3]and because of "you shall surely return them," [4]and because of "you may not hide yourself."

[5]And even though he returned it after *ye'ush*, [6]it is a gift that he gives him, and the transgression (lit., "prohibition") that he committed, he has committed.

[7][If] he took it before *ye'ush* in order to return it, and after *ye'ush* intended to rob [the owner of] it, [8]he transgresses because of "you shall surely return them."

TRANSLATION AND COMMENTARY

picked it up **with the** deliberate **intention of robbing the owner of it** and not returning it, [1]**he has transgressed all** of the following Torah laws: [2](a) the general prohibition **"you shall not rob"** (Leviticus 19:13), [3](b) the positive commandment **"you shall surely return them** [lost objects]**"** (Deuteronomy 22:1), [4]and (c) the negative commandment **"you may not hide yourself"** (Deuteronomy 22:3). The finder has transgressed the prohibition against robbery by taking the lost coin before the owner gave up hope of recovering it, even though he did not seize the object from its owner by force. By taking the lost coin with the intention of keeping it for himself, he has transgressed the positive commandment to restore lost property to its rightful owner. [5]By acting deliberately to frustrate the express purpose of the prohibition by taking the object for himself, he has transgressed the prohibition against being indifferent to the fate of the lost object "you may not hide yourself." Moreover, **even if** the finder later has a change of heart and **returns** the coin to its owner **after** the latter has **given up hope**, he does not thereby correct all his transgressions. When the owner gave up hope of recovering the coin, he effectively renounced ownership of it. [6]Therefore, legally, the coin the finder is returning **is** merely **a gift that he is giving him, and the transgression that** the finder **committed, he has committed.** In other words, the failure to fulfill the positive commandment to restore lost property and the transgression of the negative commandment "you may not hide yourself" are not cancelled out by the finder's change of heart. These commandments came into force immediately the owner lost the coin. Once the owner gave up hope of recovering his property, it left his ownership completely, and the finder is now making him a present of something else. By contrast, the prohibition against robbery is in a special category: There is a specific positive commandment — "and he shall restore that which he took away by robbery" (Leviticus 5:23) — to correct and cancel out the prohibition against robbery. By restoring the coin to its rightful owner, even after the latter has given up hope of recovering it, the finder has at least corrected his transgression of the prohibition against robbery.

נְטָלָהּ לִפְנֵי יֵאוּשׁ [7](2) If the finder **picked up** the lost coin **before** the owner **gave up hope** of recovering it, **with the intention of returning it** to its owner, **but** some time later, **after** the owner had already **given up hope**, the finder changed his mind and **decided** not to return it but **to rob the owner of it**, [8]**he transgresses** the positive commandment **"you shall surely return them,"** but not the other two commandments. Since his act of picking the object up was itself lawful, he did not violate the prohibition "you shall not rob," and by the

BACKGROUND

עַל מְנָת לְגוֹזְלָהּ With the intention of robbing the owner of it. The Halakhic meaning of the physical act of picking up the coin is defined by the finder's intention. If the finder intends to keep the coin for himself, then he is performing a certain act of acquisition by picking it up. Once the action has been completed and the finder has thus transferred the found object into his possession, it's as if the object has become his property. This means that he is liable for its misappropriation under the category of theft or robbery, and must bring a sacrifice to atone for his sin. It also means that he has accepted responsibility for it. By contrast, if he picked up the object with the intention of returning it, this was not an act of acquisition. As long as he has no intention of becoming its owner, he is merely the custodian of the lost object.

RASHI

עובר משום השב תשיבם — "לא תגזול" לא שייך אלא בשעת נטילה כמו "ויגזול את החנית מיד המצרי" (שמואל ב' כג), כדאמר בבבא קמא (עט,א). "לא תוכל להתעלם" אינה אזהרה אלא לכובש את עיניו ונמנע מלהציל, הלכך הנוטלה על מנת להחזיר ולאחר יאוש נתכוין לגוזלה — אין כאן מתעלם, אבל "השב תשיבם" איכא משנטל עד שישיבנה.

NOTES

וְאַף עַל גַּב דְּהָדְרָה לְאַחַר יֵאוּשׁ And even though he returned it after *ye'ush*. This clause is found in most, but not all, versions of the Gemara. There is a tradition that it was an addition made by the post-Talmudic authority *Rav Yehudai Gaon*. The Rishonim (*Tosafot, Ba'al HaMaor,* and others) ask: The Gemara (*Ḥullin* 141a) explains that the prohibition "you shall not rob" (Leviticus 19:13) is a negative commandment whose violation can and must be corrected by fulfilling the positive commandment (Leviticus 5:23): "And he shall restore that which he took away by robbery." Why then is the finder in our Gemara not able to correct his sin in the same way as a true robber? Indeed, because of this difficulty, *Ra'avad* eliminated this sentence from his text of the Talmud.

Some Rishonim (followed here in the commentary) explain that it is only the prohibition "you may not hide yourself" (*Tosafot*), and possibly also "you shall surely return them" (*Rashba*), that cannot be corrected. "You shall not rob" is indeed corrected by returning the lost money.

Ramban explains that a "finder-robber" who takes a lost object for himself before its owner has given up hope of recovering it is neither a true robber nor an ordinary finder.

TRANSLATION AND COMMENTARY

time he changed his mind the owner had already given up hope and renounced ownership of the object. Furthermore, since he did not hesitate to pick up the object originally and intended initially to restore it to its owner, he did not violate the prohibition "you may not hide yourself." By contrast, since he failed to take any action to return the lost object to its owner, he did violate the positive commandment "you shall surely return them."

הַמְתִּין לָהּ [1](3) **If,** when the finder first saw the coin fall, **he waited** and did not touch **it until** it was clear that **the owners had given up hope and** only then **picked it up,** [2]**he has only transgressed** the negative commandment **"you may not hide yourself."** During the period before the owners gave up hope of recovering the object, the finder did "hide himself" from his obligation to restore the owner's property. On the other hand, he has not transgressed the prohibition against robbery, because he took the object after the owner had given up hope and renounced his ownership. Likewise, he has not transgressed the positive commandment to restore lost property, because at the time he took it was no longer in the category of "lost property" and had been renounced by its owner. Indeed, the concept of "restoring lost property" can only be applied to something that belongs to someone but is not in his possession.

אֲמַר רָבָא [3]The Talmud now quotes another statement by Rava concerning the discovery of coins: **Rava also said: A person who sees money fall from someone's** possession **among the sand dunes, and finds it and picks it up,** [4]**is not obliged to return it,** even if he knows who the owner is, and even if the money contains some means of identification.

[1]הַמְתִּין לָהּ עַד שֶׁנִּתְיָאֲשׁוּ הַבְּעָלִים, וּנְטָלָהּ, [2]אֵינוֹ עוֹבֵר אֶלָּא מִשּׁוּם ״לֹא תוּכַל לְהִתְעַלֵּם״ בִּלְבַד.

[3]אֲמַר רָבָא: הַאי מַאן דְּחָזֵי דְּנָפַל זוּזֵי מֵחַבְרֵיהּ בֵּי חָלְתָא, וְאַשְׁכְּחֵיהּ וּשְׁקָלֵיהּ, [4]לָא מִיחַיַּיב לְאַהֲדוּרֵי לֵיהּ.

LITERAL TRANSLATION

[1][If] he waited for it until the owners gave up hope, and took it, [2]he does not transgress except because of "you may not hide yourself" alone.

[3]Rava [also] said: This [person] who saw that a zuz fell from his fellow in the sands, and he found it and took it, [4]is not obliged to return it to him.

RASHI

המתין לה כו׳ — נשעה שרלה לוטה, ולא נטלה להחזירה. **עובר בלא תוכל להתעלם** — שהרי העלים עיניו. **בי חלתא** — בין החולות.

BACKGROUND

בֵּי חָלְתָא **In the sands.** In sand dunes a person gives up hope of finding what he has lost, both because objects sink into the sand and disappear and also because the wind blows sand over the spot where the object fell and covers it. Furthermore, sand dunes generally have no landmarks, and even if a person realizes that he has lost money there, it is difficult to locate the exact place where it happened, and a search throughout an entire area of sand dunes is considered to be beyond human capability.

NOTES

By decree of the Torah, a true robber must return an object even after its owner has given up hope of recovering it. An ordinary finder who picks up an object with the intent of returning it becomes the legal guardian (bailee) of the object and must return it even after the owner has given up hope of recovering it. But any finder who is not a bailee can acquire full ownership the moment the original owner gives up hope. Hence the "finder-robber" here is not obliged to return the object after its owner gives up hope (see also *Radbaz*).

Other commentators (*Talmid Rabbenu Peretz, Leḥem Mishneh*) explain that the Gemara's use of the word "gift" does not imply that the finder is without obligation to return the object. Rather, the point of the Gemara is to distinguish between an ordinary finder, whose picking up of another person's property is completely blameless, indeed praiseworthy, provided he returns it later, and the "finder-robber" here who has committed a crime by picking it up. Even though he, like any other robber, can expiate his sin by returning the object, he has still committed a criminal act as the object is no longer "returnable," in the sense of a lost object, but merely "givable," in the sense of monetary compensation for damage inflicted.

אֵינוֹ עוֹבֵר אֶלָּא מִשּׁוּם ״לֹא תוּכַל לְהִתְעַלֵּם״ בִּלְבַד **He does not transgress except under the category of "you may not hide yourself."** The commentary here follows *Rashi* and most Rishonim (see particularly *Ra'avad*), who explain that the negative commandment not to ignore a lost object applies only at the time the finder first comes across the object. After that point there is only a positive commandment to return it.

Ba'al HaMa'or deduces from Rava's choice of language that, while it is possible to violate the negative commandment not to ignore the object, without violating the positive commandment to return it, since the obligation to return the object applies only after it is picked up, the converse is not the case, and failure to return an object is always considered a form of ignoring it. Hence, the finder who changes his mind violates both the positive and the negative commands.

זוּזֵי בֵּי חָלְתָא **A zuz lost in the sand.** The Rishonim ask: Since the owner is clearly searching, how can we assume he has given up hope? *Rivash* answers that, since the object is not marked and need not normally be returned, even a relatively weak argument suffices in order to consider it ownerless. Therefore, the finder is entitled to assume that

HALAKHAH

חֵפֶץ שֶׁנָּפַל בַּחוֹל **An object that fell in the sand.** "If someone sees that another person has dropped an object or a coin in the sand, he may take it for himself, as the owner must certainly have given up hope of recovering it. Even if he sees the owner searching in the sand with a sieve, it makes no difference," following Rava here. (*Shulḥan Arukh, Ḥoshen Mishpat* 262:14.)

TRANSLATION AND COMMENTARY

[1]**What is the reason** for this ruling? It is because of the very serious difficulty involved in finding a coin lost in sand. Thus **the person who dropped it gives up hope** of ever recovering his coin, and the finder is entitled to keep it. [2]Moreover, **even if** the finder **sees that** the owner **brings a sieve and** starts **sifting** the sand, thereby displaying determination to recover what he has lost, nevertheless the finder may still presume that the owner has given up hope. [3]**He is surely saying** to himself: **"Just as my** coin **fell from me** in the sand and was lost, [4]**so too** a similar coin or something else may have **fallen from another person, and I** may yet **find something."** Thus his actions do not prove that he has not given up hope.

MISHNAH מָצָא בַּחֲנוּת [5]**If** a person **finds an** unmarked **lost article in** the front part of **a shop, it is his** to keep, as shops are frequented by many people and the owner of the object has certainly already given up hope of recovering it. [6]If he found it **between the counter and the shopkeeper**, the lost article is presumed to have been lost by **the shopkeeper**, since other people do not go to that part of the shop.

לִפְנֵי שׁוּלְחָנִי [7]Similarly, if a person **finds money in front of a money changer** in the area occupied by the customers, **it is his** to keep, because the money changer's stool stands between the money changer and the money, and if he had lost the money, it would have fallen between him and the stool. [8]But if a person finds money **between the** money changer's **stool and the money changer, it is the money changer's.**

[1]מַאי טַעְמָא? הַהוּא דִּנְפַל מִינֵּיהּ מְיָאֵשׁ הוּא. [2]אַף עַל גַּב דְּחַזְיֵיהּ דְּאַיְיתֵי אַרְבְּלָא וְקָא מַרְבֵּל, [3]מֵימַר אָמַר: "כִּי הֵיכִי דִּנְפוּל מִינַּאי דִּידִי, [4]הָכִי נְפוּל מֵאִינִישׁ אַחֲרִינָא, וּמַשְׁכַּחְנָא מִידֵּי".

משנה [5]מָצָא בַּחֲנוּת, הֲרֵי אֵלּוּ שֶׁלּוֹ. [6]בֵּין הַתֵּיבָה וְלַחֶנְוָנִי, שֶׁל חֶנְוָנִי. [7]לִפְנֵי שׁוּלְחָנִי, הֲרֵי אֵלּוּ שֶׁלּוֹ. [8]בֵּין הַכִּסֵּא וְלַשּׁוּלְחָנִי, הֲרֵי אֵלּוּ שֶׁל שׁוּלְחָנִי.

LITERAL TRANSLATION

[1]What is the reason? The one from whom it fell gives up hope. [2]Even though he sees him bring a sieve and sift, [3]he is surely saying: "Just as mine fell from me, [4]so too [another] fell from another person, and I will find something."

MISHNAH [5][If] he found [lost articles] in a shop, these are his. [6]Between the counter and the shopkeeper, [they are] the shopkeeper's. [7][If he found coins] in front of a money changer, they are his. [8]Between the stool and the money changer, they are the money changer's.

RASHI

ארבלא – כברה.

משנה מצא בחנות הרי אלו שלו – בדבר שאין בו סימן קאי, דההוא דנפל מיניה מיאש, שהכל נכנסים לשם. **בין התיבה** – שהחנוני יושב לפניה, ותמיד נוטל ממנה ונותן לפניו ומוכר, ומעות שנותנין לו נותן לתיבה, ולא נפל שום דבר אלא מיד חנוני. **שולחני** – מחליף מעות, ונותן מטבעותיו בשולחן שלפניו, והבאין להחליף אף הן נותנין שם מעותיהן. **הרי אלו שלו** – דאמרינן מן הבאין נפלו, שהרי השולחן מפסיק בין שולחני למעות שנמצאו, ואם מן השולחני נפלו, היה להם להמצא בינו לכסא שהשולחן מונח עליו.

LANGUAGE

אַרְבְּלָא A sieve. Some scholars are of the opinion that this word and especially the verb כרבל, meaning to shake things within a sieve — is derived from the Latin *cribrum*, or sieve. However, the root ערבל is also found in Arabic to describe the action of sifting.

BACKGROUND

שׁוּלְחָנִי Money changer. In ancient times money changers had to be experts in evaluating coins (in some places this is true to this day), since their profession was to exchange large coins for small, and foreign currency for local coinage. Hence they acted as expert assessors who evaluated coins brought before them.

NOTES

the owner is looking for something else, unless he expressly stipulates that he is searching for his lost coin.

Ritva explains that a coin lost in the sand is comparable to an object lost in the rising sea (see above, 22b). Since it is very difficult for anyone to recover it, the Torah declared it ownerless, regardless of the owner's feelings.

מָצָא בַּחֲנוּת If he found lost articles in a shop. The Rishonim ask: Even assuming that the article was lost by a customer, why does the shopkeeper not acquire it automatically, by virtue of courtyard-acquisition (קִנְיַן חָצֵר), since it was left within the bounds of his courtyard?

Rashba answers that courtyard-acquisition is effective automatically only when the courtyard is secure, that is, when objects found in it are under the courtyard-owner's control. But in our case the shop is full of people, and they are even more likely to find the article than is the owner of the shop. Therefore courtyard-acquisition cannot be automatically effective here. Alternatively: A shop that is open to all who wish to enter has the status of a public thoroughfare, and courtyard-acquisition is not effective in it.

HALAKHAH

מְצִיאָה בַּחֲנוּת וְאֵצֶל שׁוּלְחָנִי Lost articles found in a shop or at a money changer's. "If someone finds a lost article at a money changer's, in front of or even on his table, the finder may keep it for himself. But anything found behind the table belongs to the money changer. Similarly, if someone finds a lost article in a shop in front of the counter, he may keep it; if it is behind the counter, he must give it to the shopkeeper." If he finds it on the counter itself, the *Shulḥan Arukh* rules that he may keep it, whereas *Rema* rules, in the name of *Tur*, that he must give it to the shopkeeper. (*Shulḥan Arukh, Ḥoshen Mishpat* 260:5.)

TRANSLATION AND COMMENTARY

הַלּוֹקֵחַ פֵּירוֹת מֵחֲבֵירוֹ [1]If a person **buys fruit from someone,** or if **the latter sent him fruit** as a gift, **and he found among** the fruit loose **money,** the money **is his** to keep, as it certainly came to be there by accident, and its owner has surely given up hope of recovering it. (The Gemara [below, 27a] explains this case in greater detail.) [2]But **if** the money **was tied up** in a bundle, **he must take it and announce** his discovery, as the money is identifiable and the owner will not have given up hope of recovering it.

GEMARA **אָמַר רַבִּי אֶלְעָזָר** [3]The Gemara begins its analysis of the Mishnah by considering the clause: "If he found coins in front of a money changer, they are his." What is meant by the words "in front of a money changer"? On this point **Rabbi Elazar said: Even if** the money **was** found **lying on top of the** money-changing **table** itself, the finder may keep it, because both the money changer and his customers place their money there. Thus, according to Rabbi Elazar, whether the money was found on the floor or on the table, it belongs to the finder.

תְּנַן [4]But, the Gemara objects, surely **we have learned** in the Mishnah: "If he found coins **in front of a money changer, they are his.**" [5]From the Mishnah's restrictive language, "in front of a money changer," we should be able to infer that, by contrast, if the money was found **on top of the** money-changing **table, it belongs to the money changer.** Thus the inference from our Mishnah seems to contradict the ruling of Rabbi Elazar.

אֵימָא סֵיפָא [6]The Gemara responds by **considering a later clause** of the Mishnah, and applying the same reasoning: The Mishnah states: "If he found money **between the** money changer's **stool and the money changer, it is the money changer's.**" [7]From the Mishnah's restrictive language, "between the stool and the money changer," we should be able to infer that, by contrast, if the money was found **on top of the table, it is** the finder's to keep. This, of course, is precisely the opposite inference from the previous one, and supports the ruling of Rabbi Elazar. [8]**Rather,** concludes the Gemara, **from** the contradictory inferences drawn from our Mishnah **it is impossible** to deduce any further laws, as the phraseology of the Mishnah does not lend itself to unequivocal conclusions.

וְרַבִּי אֶלְעָזָר [9]The Gemara now reverts to its previous question and asks: **But what** then **is the source for Rabbi Elazar's** ruling that money found on a money changer's table belongs to the finder? This question is pertinent because we have just seen that our Mishnah cannot be used to provide a logical basis for Rabbi Elazar's ruling.

[1]הַלּוֹקֵחַ פֵּירוֹת מֵחֲבֵירוֹ, אוֹ שֶׁשִּׁילַּח לוֹ חֲבֵירוֹ פֵּירוֹת, וּמָצָא בָּהֶן מָעוֹת, הֲרֵי אֵלּוּ שֶׁלּוֹ. [2]אִם הָיוּ צְרוּרִין, נוֹטֵל וּמַכְרִיז.

גמרא [3]אָמַר רַבִּי אֶלְעָזָר: אֲפִילּוּ מוּנָּחִין עַל גַּבֵּי שׁוּלְחָן. [4]תְּנַן: "לִפְנֵי שׁוּלְחָנִי, הֲרֵי אֵלּוּ שֶׁלּוֹ". [5]הָא עַל גַּבֵּי שׁוּלְחָן, דְּשׁוּלְחָנִי. [6]אֵימָא סֵיפָא: "בֵּין הַכִּסֵּא וְלַשּׁוּלְחָנִי, שֶׁל שׁוּלְחָנִי". [7]הָא עַל גַּבֵּי שׁוּלְחָן, שֶׁלּוֹ! [8]אֶלָּא, מֵהָא לֵיכָּא לְמִשְׁמַע מִינָּהּ. [9]וְרַבִּי אֶלְעָזָר, הָא מְנָא לֵיהּ?

LITERAL TRANSLATION

[1]One who buys fruit from his fellow, or whose fellow has sent him fruit, and he found coins among them, they are his. [2]If they were tied up, he takes [them] and announces.

GEMARA [3]Rabbi Elazar said: Even if they are lying on top of the table.

[4]We have learned: "In front of a money changer, they are his." [5]But on top of the table, [they belong] to the money changer.

[6]Consider (lit., "say") the last clause: "Between the stool and the money changer, [they are] the money changer's." [7]But on top of the table, [they are] his.

[8]Rather, from this, it is impossible to learn from it [anything].

[9]But Rabbi Elazar, from where does he [know] this?

RASHI

הלוקח פירות מחבירו — מפרש בגמרא. **ואם היו צרורין** — הוי סימן או קשר או מנין שבהם.

גמרא אמר רבי אלעזר אפילו מונחין על גבי שולחן — נראה בעיני דלא גרסינן צרורין. **לפני** — משמע על גבי קרקע.

NOTES

אֲפִילּוּ מוּנָּחִין עַל גַּבֵּי שׁוּלְחָן Even if they were lying on top of the table. The translation here follows *Rashi*'s version of the Gemara, according to which the finder found only loose, unmarked money which need not be announced, and the only remaining question is whether the money changer himself left it there. Several Rishonim, however, have a reading of צְרוּרִין — "tied up" — as well as מוּנָּחִין — "lying." According to this reading, Rabbi Elazar is saying that even marked objects left on the money changer's table need not be announced, either because the money changer has many non-Jewish customers (*Tosafot, Rambam*) or because the owner will assume that the money changer took his money and will give up hope of recovering it (*Rashba*).

Ra'avad goes even further. He argues that *only* tied-up money may be kept by the finder, as it presumably was lost by customers, whereas loose money must be presumed to have been left on the table by the money changer himself, even according to Rabbi Elazar.

TERMINOLOGY

אֶלָּא מֵהָא לֵיכָּא לְמִשְׁמַע מִינָּהּ Rather, from this, it is impossible to learn from it. This expression is generally used after a failed attempt to prove a point using the method of דִּיּוּק — the precise examination of the wording of a Tannaitic statement. The essence of this method is that one subjects the wording of a Tannaitic statement to precise analysis, showing that everything not contained within the narrow definition of the source is subject to a different ruling. Proofs using this method of דִּיּוּק are often accepted, but they are sometimes refuted when it can be shown that application of the very same method of close analysis to another portion of the same Mishnah or Baraita leads to the opposite conclusion. In such cases the argument is summed up with the phrase אֶלָּא מֵהָא לֵיכָּא לְמִשְׁמַע מִינָּהּ, meaning that one cannot reach conclusions from this source by using the method of precise analysis, since we would thus draw inferences that are mutually contradictory.

SAGES

רַבִּי אֶלְעָזָר Rabbi Elazar. Rabbi Elazar ben Pedat was one of the greatest of the Palestinian Amoraim. He came originally from Babylonia and studied there with Rav and Shmuel. But it seems that he immigrated to Eretz Israel as a young man and married there. In Eretz Israel he became the main disciple of Rabbi Yoḥanan. The spiritual affinity between Rabbi Elazar and Rabbi Yoḥanan was so close that occasionally an objection is raised to an argument presented in the name of one of them because it conflicts with the other's teachings, since they are assumed to have adopted the same approach to Halakhah. Rabbi Elazar venerated his teacher Rabbi Yoḥanan and in time the bond between them grew so strong that Rabbi Yoḥanan said of him: "Have you seen the son of Pedat, who sits and expounds the Torah like Moses from the very mouth of the Almighty?" Rabbi Elazar was a priest. He was very poor for most of his

LITERAL TRANSLATION

[1] Rava said: Our Mishnah was difficult for him. [2] Why did it particularly teach: "Between the stool and the money changer, [they are] the money changer's"?

[3] Let it teach: "On the table." [4] Alternatively: "[If] he found [it] on [a money changer's] tables" as it teaches [in] the first clause: "[If] he found [it] in a shop, [it is] his." [5] Rather, conclude from it: Even if they are lying on top of the table, they are his.

[6] "One who buys fruit from his fellow, etc." [7] Resh Lakish said in the name of Rabbi Yannai: They only taught [this] [27A] in [the case of] one who buys from a merchant, [8] but in [the case of] one who buys from a private person (lit., "the owner of a house") — he is obliged to return [it].

[1] אֲמַר רָבָא: מַתְנִיתִין קָשִׁיתֵיהּ. [2] מַאי אִרְיָא דְּתָנֵי: ״בֵּין הַכִּסֵּא לַשּׁוּלְחָנִי, שֶׁל שׁוּלְחָנִי״? [3] לִיתְנֵי: ״עַל שׁוּלְחָן״. [4] אִי נַמִּי: ״מָצָא בַּשּׁוּלְחָנוֹת״, כִּדְקָתָנֵי רֵישָׁא: ״מָצָא בַּחֲנוּת, שֶׁלּוֹ״. [5] אֶלָּא, שְׁמַע מִינָּהּ: אֲפִילּוּ מוּנָּחִין עַל גַּבֵּי שׁוּלְחָן, הֲרֵי אֵלּוּ שֶׁלּוֹ.

[6] ״הַלּוֹקֵחַ פֵּירוֹת מֵחֲבֵירוֹ וכו׳״. [7] אָמַר רֵישׁ לָקִישׁ מִשּׁוּם רַבִּי יַנַּאי: לֹא שָׁנוּ אֶלָּא [27A] בְּלוֹקֵחַ מִן הַתַּגָּר, [8] אֲבָל בְּלוֹקֵחַ מִבַּעַל הַבַּיִת חַיָּיב לְהַחֲזִיר.

TRANSLATION AND COMMENTARY

אֲמַר רָבָא [1] **Rava said** in reply: The language used in **our Mishnah posed a difficulty for** Rabbi Elazar, and in resolving this difficulty, he arrived at his ruling. He wanted to know what the law would be regarding money found on a money changer's table. [2] He came to the conclusion that the language of the Mishnah implied that such money belongs to the finder, because if it were to be argued that the money belongs to the money changer, the following difficulty arises: **Why did the Mishnah use the particular words:** "If he found money **between the** money changer's **stool and the money changer, it is the money changer's**"?

לִיתְנֵי [3] **Let** the Mishnah **say** instead: "If he found money **on the** money changer's **table,** it belongs to the money changer." Then it would be obvious that money found between the money changer's stool and the money changer belongs to the money changer. [4] **Alternatively,** instead of using the words: "If he found money in front of a money changer, it is his to keep," the Mishnah could have said: **"If he found** money **at the money changer's**, it is his to keep," which would be **just like** the language used by the Mishnah **in the first clause: "If he found a lost article in a shop, it is his** to keep." [5] **Rather**, because the Mishnah chose not to use these expressions and used the phrase "in front of the money changer, it is the finder's," we can **conclude** that **even if** the money **was** found **lying on top of the** money-changing **table, it is** the finder's to keep, as money changers place their money in drawers, and do not leave it lying on the table. Hence this money must have been forgotten by one of the customers, and has the same status as money lying in front of the table.

הַלּוֹקֵחַ פֵּירוֹת [6] The Gemara now considers the next clause in the Mishnah: "If a person **buys fruit from someone** and finds among the fruit loose money, the money is his to keep." [7] **Resh Lakish said in the name of Rabbi Yannai: The Mishnah stated this law only** [27A] **in the case of someone who bought** the fruit **from a merchant,** who himself had bought the fruit from several people. The Mishnah's ruling is only applicable in this case since it is impossible to tell who actually lost the money. The fruit has passed through many hands, and the finder cannot announce his discovery because the coins contain no specific identifying mark. [8] **But in the case of someone who bought** the fruit directly **from a private person,** i.e., from a farmer, and found money among the fruit, the Mishnah's ruling does not apply and **he is obliged to return** even loose money. Since the farmer sold the fruit directly to the buyer, he will not have given up hope of recovering the money he accidentally left in the fruit. He knows from whom to claim it, and the buyer must return it.

RASHI

לתני על גבי שולחן — של שולחני, וכל שכן בין הכסא ולשולחני. **אי נמי** — ניתני ברישא מצא בשולחנות, כדקתני רישא מצא בחנות, מדנקט ״לפני השולחני״ אף על השולחן במשמע. **בלוקח מן התגר** — שאף הוא לקח תבואה זו מאנשים הרבה ולא ידיע דמאן ניניהו, וכיון דלית בהו סימן נתייאשו הבעלים.

HALAKHAH

הַלּוֹקֵחַ פֵּירוֹת מֵחֲבֵירוֹ One who buys fruit from his fellow. "A person who buys produce, or receives a gift of produce, from another person and finds a bundle of money concealed in it, must announce his discovery. If the money was loose, he may keep it for himself, provided he received the produce from a merchant. But if he received the produce directly from a farmer who harvested and processed the produce without any assistance (except from his Canaanite slaves), he must return the money to him," following the Mishnah and Rav Naḥman's interpretation. (*Shulḥan Arukh, Ḥoshen Mishpat* 262:17.)

life, and his material situation apparently did not improve until his latter years, when he was one of the leaders of the nation.

After Rabbi Yoḥanan's death Rabbi Elazar was one of the most important scholars in Eretz Israel. He was also one of the Sages who participated in setting the Hebrew calendar, and he would send Halakhic directives from Eretz Israel to Babylonia, where they were regarded as authoritative and binding.

Many stories are told of Rabbi Elazar's great love for the Torah, and he is presented as the model of a person entirely immersed in the study of Torah.

Because of his greatness he was known as מָרָא דְּאַרְעָא דְּיִשְׂרָאֵל — "Master of Eretz Israel." Almost all of the Amoraim of the third generation in Eretz Israel were his students. His son, Rabbi Pedat, was also a Sage.

BACKGROUND

מַתְנִיתִין קָשִׁיתֵיהּ Our Mishnah was difficult for him. Sometimes a linguistic or logical difficulty within the Mishnah itself leads a Sage to restrict its application to a particular instance or to limit the conclusions that can be drawn from it. The difficulty causes him to attribute a special explanation to the Mishnah in order to resolve the problem or explain its style. In the present instance, the change between the language of the first section — "he found in a shop" — and that of the second section — "he found in front of a money changer" — necessitates an explanation. Hence Rabbi Elazar reaches the Halakhic conclusion that the expression "before a money changer" must be understood to include everything found before the money changer, including his table.

LANGUAGE

תַּגָּר Merchant. This word is found in sources from the Second Temple period, and is apparently taken from the Assyrian, although some authorities maintain that its original source is Hebrew. תַּגָּר means a merchant, but the term is generally used with

LITERAL TRANSLATION

[1] A Tanna taught likewise before Rav Naḥman: [2] "They only taught [this] in [the case of] one who buys from a merchant, [3] but in [the case of] one who buys from a private person, he is obliged to return [it]." [4] Rav Naḥman said to him: "But did the private person himself thresh them?"

[5] He said to him: "Shall I delete it?"

[6] He said to him: "No, explain the Baraita [as referring], [7] for example, to where he had them threshed by his Canaanite slave and maidservant."

MISHNAH [8] The garment, too,

[1] וְכֵן תָּנֵי תַּנָּא קַמֵּיהּ דְּרַב נַחְמָן: [2] "לֹא שָׁנוּ אֶלָּא בְּלוֹקֵחַ מִן הַתַּגָּר, [3] אֲבָל בְּלוֹקֵחַ מִבַּעַל הַבַּיִת חַיָּיב לְהַחֲזִיר". [4] אֲמַר לֵיהּ רַב נַחְמָן: "וְכִי בַּעַל הַבַּיִת בְּעַצְמוֹ דָּשָׁן?" [5] אֲמַר לֵיהּ: "אִיסְמְיֵהּ?" [6] אֲמַר לֵיהּ: "לָא, תְּתַרְגֵּם מַתְנִיתָא [7] כְּגוֹן שֶׁדְּשָׁן עַל יְדֵי עַבְדּוֹ וְשִׁפְחָתוֹ הַכְּנַעֲנִים".

מִשְׁנָה [8] אַף הַשִּׂמְלָה הָיְתָה

RASHI

דשן — וכי הוא עצמו דש את התבואה הזאת, הלא פועלים הרבה דשו אותה. **איסמייה** — אסיר ברייתא זו מגרסתי? **אמר ליה לא** תסמי תתרגם מתניתין כו׳.

TRANSLATION AND COMMENTARY

וְכֵן תָּנֵי תַּנָּא [1] The Talmud relates: **A Tanna** (an expert in the oral transmission of Baraitot) **quoted a similar Baraita before Rav Naḥman:** [2] **"The Mishnah stated this** law only **in the case of someone who bought** the fruit **from a merchant,** [3] **but in the case of someone who bought** the fruit directly **from a private person, he is obliged to return** the money. [4] Concerning this Baraita, **Rav Naḥman said to** the Tanna: "**But did the private person himself thresh** the grain or pick and pack the fruit?" (The Gemara assumes that the word "fruit" in the Mishnah includes grain — a common use of the word.) Surely the farmer has several employees working in his field, and any one of them might have lost the money. Therefore, since it is impossible to tell who lost it, the finder should be allowed to keep the money.

אֲמַר לֵיהּ [5] Recognizing the validity of Rav Naḥman's remark, the Tanna **said to him: "Shall I delete** this Baraita from my list of authorized Baraitot, since it is obviously incorrect?"

אֲמַר לֵיהּ [6] Rav Naḥman **said to him** in reply: **No,** it is not necessary to reject the Baraita altogether, provided that you **explain the Baraita as referring** to a particular case: [7] **For example, where** the farmer **had** the grain **threshed by his Canaanite slaves and maidservants** — who lack the legal capacity to own property of their own. Thus the money belongs to the farmer regardless of who lost it.

MISHNAH אַף הַשִּׂמְלָה [8] The Mishnah is an excerpt from a Halakhic Midrash (Sifrei, *Tetze* 224), a Tannaitic exegesis of the legal portions of the Torah. The Sifrei is commenting on Deuteronomy 22:1-3, where the Torah outlines the obligation to return lost objects. The passage reads as follows: "[1] You shall not see your brother's ox or his lamb go astray, and hide yourself from them. You shall surely return them to your brother. [2] And if your brother is not near to you, or you do not know him, then you shall bring it into your house, and it shall be with you until your brother seeks after it, and you shall return it to him. [3] And so shall you do with his ass, and so shall you do with his garment, and so shall you do with every lost thing of your brother's, which is lost from him and which you have found. You may not hide yourself." In this passage, the Torah says that a finder must return "every lost thing of your brother's," but it also singles out for special mention

the distinct sense of a small trader who buys locally from a number of people and sells to individuals, whereas a סוֹחֵר travels to distant places and deals with merchandise on a larger scale.

TERMINOLOGY

תָּנֵי תַּנָּא קַמֵּיהּ דְּ... The Tanna taught [a Baraita] before.... This expression describes the situation in which a Baraita was recited in the presence of the head of the Academy, and the latter offered his comments on it.

תְּתַרְגֵּם מַתְנִיתָא Explain the Baraita. The verb לְתַרְגֵּם — usually meaning "to translate" — here means "to explain." When this term is applied to the wording of a Mishnah or a Baraita, it usually introduces an interpretation in which the Tannaitic source is applied to a specific case rather than being understood as a general ruling.

NOTES

אִיסְמְיֵהּ Shall I remove it? The word תַּנָּא — "Tanna" — has two very different meanings in the Talmud. The first refers to one of the early Rabbinic scholars whose statements are quoted in the Mishnah and in Baraitot. The second meaning, found here, is that of an expert in the oral transmission of Baraitot, an assistant to an Amora, whose responsibility it was to research the Mishnah and the Baraitot and to establish an accurate text. During the Amoraic period (c. 200 C.E.-500 C.E.) it was not customary to work from a written text, and each Talmudic school would have a Baraita reviewer whose job it was to memorize the texts and then act as a reference source for the other students.

The accuracy of the texts of the Baraitot quoted by the assistants to the Amoraim varied considerably. Some Tannaitic material was well known and commonly studied in all the Talmudic academies. Included in this category were the Tosefta, and to a lesser degree the Tannaitic commentaries on the Torah. This material tended to have an accepted text with precise language, from which inferences could reasonably be drawn. The texts of other Baraitot, however, were less clear, and some were too riddled with transmission errors to be worth retaining. It was the reviewer's responsibility to maintain as complete and accurate a body of Baraita material as possible for the students' use. The Amora, in this case Rav Naḥman, would tell the reviewer which Baraitot to retain, which to remove, and which to retain with minor corrections.

אַף הַשִּׂמְלָה הָיְתָה בִּכְלַל כָּל אֵלּוּ The garment, too, was included among all these. The Mishnah here uses Midrashic exegetic technique to derive a law from its source in the Torah. The text of the Mishnah appears to employ rule eight of Rabbi Yishmael's thirteen rules of Biblical exegesis: "Something that was included in a generalization, but was explicitly specified to teach something, was

TRANSLATION AND COMMENTARY

a lost ox, ass, lamb, and garment. The Mishnah now quotes the *Sifrei*'s question: Since **the garment is** obviously merely a particular example which is already **included in** the Torah's general command to return **all** lost property, [1] **why was it singled out** and mentioned explicitly? [2] The Mishnah, again quoting from the *Sifrei,* answers that lost garments were singled out to illustrate a point, **to** make us **compare** garments with other lost objects. The Torah is **saying to us:** Only objects that are similar to garments must be returned. [3] **A garment is special in that there are identifying marks on it and** as a result **it has claimants.** It is a man-made object in which its owner has made some investment, thus he will not give up hope of recovering it. [4] **So, too, must everything that has identifying marks on it and has claimants be announced.** But lost articles that are not marked or are not likely to be claimed need not be returned, because their owner will have given up hope of recovering them. This is the source in the Torah of the concept of *ye'ush* mentioned many times in this chapter, and it is from this Midrashic explanation that we derive the law that if a person gives up hope of recovering property he has lost, he divests himself of the legal ownership of that property. It thereby becomes ownerless (הֶפְקֵר), and whoever takes possession of it first becomes its owner.

GEMARA מַאי בִּכְלַל כָּל אֵלּוּ [5] The Gemara begins its investigation of the Mishnah by asking: **What is the meaning of** the expression **"included among all these"** used by the Mishnah? The Mishnah is obviously referring to some general category not mentioned here. In what general category is the garment included?

אֲמַר רָבָא [6] **Rava said** in reply: The Mishnah is referring to the passage (Deuteronomy 22:1-3) dealing with the laws of lost articles: "You shall not see your brother's ox or his lamb go astray... you shall surely return them to your brother.... And so shall you do with his ass, and so shall you do with his garment, and so shall you do with every lost thing of your brother's." The garment is **included in the category of "every lost thing of your brother's"** mentioned towards the end of verse 3. Hence, the Mishnah asks why the garment was singled out for special mention, and answers that it was intended to serve as an example from which general legal principles could be derived.

אֲמַר רָבָא [7] In connection with this passage, **Rava** further **said:** What additional information about lost articles is conveyed by the series of examples given in these verses? **Why does the Torah need to write** about an **ox,** an **ass,** a **lamb, and** a **garment?** Granted that one example was needed, for the reason stated in our Mishnah, but what was the reason for specifying the other three examples?

בִּכְלַל כָּל אֵלּוּ. [1] וְלָמָּה יָצָאת? [2] לְהַקִּישׁ אֵלֶיהָ, לוֹמַר לְךָ: [3] מַה שִּׂמְלָה מְיוּחֶדֶת, שֶׁיֵּשׁ בָּהּ סִימָנִין וְיֵשׁ לָהּ תּוֹבְעִין, [4] אַף כָּל דָּבָר שֶׁיֵּשׁ בּוֹ סִימָנִין וְיֵשׁ לוֹ תּוֹבְעִים חַיָּיב לְהַכְרִיז.

גמרא [5] מַאי "בִּכְלַל כָּל אֵלּוּ"?

[6] אֲמַר רָבָא: בִּכְלַל "כָּל אֲבֵדַת אָחִיךָ".

[7] אֲמַר רָבָא: לָמָּה לִי דִּכְתַב רַחֲמָנָא "שׁוֹר חֲמוֹר שֶׂה וְשִׂמְלָה"?

LITERAL TRANSLATION

was included among all these. [1] And why was it singled out? [2] To compare to it, to say to you: [3] Just as a garment is special, in that it has identifying marks on it and it has claimants, [4] so too everything that has identifying marks on it and has claimants he is obliged to announce.

GEMARA [5] What is [the meaning of] "included among all these"?

[6] Rava said: Included among "every lost thing of your brother."

[7] Rava said: For what do I need that the Torah wrote "ox, ass, lamb, and garment"?

RASHI

משנה בכלל כל אלו – בגמרא מפרש לה. למה יצאתה – וכן תעשה לשמלתו, סתם שמלה יש בה סימן, וכל שמלה יש לה בעלים תובעין אותה שלא נעשית אלא בידי אדם ולא באת מן ההפקר. אף כל שיש לו תובעין – למעוטי מידי דידעינן ביה דמיאש.

גמרא שור וחמור שה ושמלה – "לא תראה את שור אחיך או שיו" "וכן תעשה לחמורו וכן תעשה לשמלתו".

NOTES

intended to teach not just about itself but about the entire generalization." However, it is also possible that the Mishnah is employing rule six, namely: "When a generalization in the Torah is followed by one or more details, and they, in turn, are followed by another generalization, application of the law under discussion is limited to items that resemble the detail." (See *Ra'avad.*)

HALAKHAH

סִימָנִין וְתוֹבְעִין Identifying marks and claimants. "Any object that has an identifying mark and is likely to have claimants must be returned." (*Rambam, Sefer Nezikin, Hilkhot Gezelah Va'Avedah* 14:1.)

BACKGROUND

מַה שִּׂמְלָה מְיוּחֶדֶת Just as a garment is special. A garment is not only special because it is presented as a particular example or detail within the general ruling about "every lost thing of your brother's," but it is also distinct from the other examples mentioned in the verse (ox, ass, and lamb) because it is man-made. Thus it must have had owners at some time, and cannot originally have been ownerless. Moreover, especially at a time when clothing was not mass-produced, a garment was likely to have some particular feature which its owner could cite as an identifying mark, or by which it could be recognized by witnesses, who could then locate its owner.

CONCEPTS

מִדְרַשׁ הֲלָכָה Halakhic Midrash. In general, Halakhic Midrash is the exegetical method by which the particular details of the Oral Law are derived from the wording of Scripture. The assumption underlying the exegetical method used in Halakhic Midrash is that nothing in the Torah is imprecise or insignificant. Thus any apparently superfluous word, or any unusual form of a word in the sources, permits us to derive special Halakhic rulings from it.

Halakhic Midrash is governed by a large number of rules which define and restrict the way in which it is applied. These are the hermeneutic principles (הַמִּדּוֹת שֶׁהַתּוֹרָה נִדְרֶשֶׁת בָּהֶן). Among the best-known presentations of these are the thirteen principles of Rabbi Yishmael, which are regarded as so important that they are included in Jewish prayerbooks and are part of the daily liturgy. In addition to that listing, however, there are many other standard principles, some of which were accepted by all the Sages, whereas others (such as the method of רִיבּוּי וּמִיעוּט — amplification and restriction — and סְמִיכַת הַפְּסוּקִים — the juxtaposition of verses) — were studied only in particular academies.

The Talmud contains many

TRANSLATION AND COMMENTARY

צְרִיכִי [1]Rava proceeds to answer his own question: **They are all necessary,** because each one has a special characteristic that can be applied to the general laws of returning lost property. **For if the Torah had used** only **"garment"** as an example of lost property that must be returned to its owner, and had not mentioned the other examples, [2]**I would have thought that** the obligation to return lost objects **applies only where** the claimant can produce **witnesses** who recognize **the lost article itself** and know its owner, **or** where the claimant can cite **identifying marks on the lost article itself.** [3]**But in the case of an ass** with a saddle on its back, I might argue differently. An ass is quite difficult to identify, but usually wears a distinctive saddle. Hence, the claimant might not be able to produce witnesses capable of identifying it directly. However, he should be able to produce **witnesses** capable of **identifying the saddle or** the claimant may well be able to cite **identifying marks on the saddle.** [4]Thus **I might think** that the finder **should not return** the ass **to** the claimant, but only the saddle. [5]**Therefore the Torah** included the additional example of an **ass, to teach us that even an ass** and property like it **should be returned,** even though the owner's claim is **based only on the identifying marks on the saddle.**

שׁוֹר וְשֶׂה [6]Rava now continues his explanation of the verse: So far we have considered the Torah's use of the examples of an ass and a garment, and we have shown what additional principles in the laws concerning the return of lost property can be derived from them. But **why does the Torah need** to include the examples of an **ox** and a **lamb?** What extra information is conveyed by these?

שׁוֹר דַּאֲפִילּוּ לְגִיזַּת זְנָבוֹ [7]Rava answered: By mentioning the example of the **ox,** the Torah **teaches** us **that** if the finder shears the ox's tail, **he must return even those shearings** to the ox's owner. In other words, the seemingly superfluous example of the ox informs us that a finder is obliged to return a lost object in the condition in which he found it. Even something as trivial as the shearings of an ox's tail cannot be withheld, and must be returned to the owner. [8]Rava continues: The example of the **lamb is mentioned** by the Torah to inform us that **its shearings** must be returned to the owner together with the lamb itself. This concludes Rava's statement.

[1]צְרִיכִי. דְּאִי כְּתַב רַחֲמָנָא "שִׂמְלָה", [2]הֲוָה אָמֵינָא: הָנֵי מִילֵּי בְּעֵדִים דְּגוּפָהּ וְסִימָנִין דְּגוּפָהּ. [3]אֲבָל חֲמוֹר בְּעֵדִים דְּאוּכָּף וְסִימָנִין דְּאוּכָּף, [4]אֵימָא לָא מְהַדְּרִינַן לֵיהּ. [5]כְּתַב רַחֲמָנָא "חֲמוֹר", דַּאֲפִילּוּ חֲמוֹר בְּסִימָנֵי הָאוּכָּף.

[6]"שׁוֹר וְשֶׂה" דִּכְתַב רַחֲמָנָא לָמָּה לִי?

[7]"שׁוֹר" דַּאֲפִילּוּ לְגִיזַּת זְנָבוֹ; [8]וְ"שֶׂה" לְגִיזּוֹתָיו.

LITERAL TRANSLATION

[1][They are all] necessary. For if the Torah had written "garment," [2]I would have said [that] these words [apply] only where [there are] witnesses to [the lost article] itself or identifying marks on [the lost article] itself. [3]But [in the case of] an ass where [there are] witnesses to [identify] the saddle or identifying marks on the saddle, [4][I would] say they should not return [it] to him. [5][Therefore] the Torah wrote "ass," [to teach us] that even an ass [is returned] on the basis of identifying marks on the saddle. [6]For what do I need [the words] "ox" and "lamb" that the Torah wrote?

[7]"Ox" [teaches] that even the shearing of its tail [must be returned]; [8]and "lamb" [is mentioned] for its shearings.

RASHI

בסימני אוכף — אם אין לו סימן בחמור ויש לו סימן באוכף שעליו. **כתב רחמנא חמור** — קרא יתירא לדרשה. **לגיזת זנבו** — שאפילו שער שבסוף הזנב יחזיר.

NOTES

שׁוֹר דַּאֲפִילּוּ לְגִיזַּת זְנָבוֹ "Ox" teaches that even the shearing of its tail must be returned. *Tosafot* asks: The Gemara will later quote a Baraita which rules that only lost objects worth at least one perutah need to be returned. Hence, if the shearings of the ox's tail are worth a perutah, they must obviously be returned, and if not, not. What, then, is the Gemara deducing here from the word "ox"?

Tosafot (see also *Rashba*) answers that the Torah is telling us that the finder is required to shear the ox's tail, even though the actual shearings are worth less than a perutah. The reason is that a finder is required to care for a lost object and to preserve its value.

Ritva answers that the shearings are deemed to be part of the ox and must be returned together with the ox, even if they themselves are worth less than a perutah.

HALAKHAH

חֲמוֹר בְּסִימָנֵי הָאוּכָּף An ass is returned on the basis of identifying marks on the saddle. "Even if there are no identifying marks on the saddle, but there are identifying marks on the saddle itself, the finder must return them both." (*Shulḥan Arukh, Ḥoshen Mishpat* 262:18.)

גִּיזַּת אֲבֵידָה The shearing of a lost animal. "As long as a

discussions on the precise rules according to which each of these principles is to be applied, and Sages throughout the generations have written widely on the limits and details of these hermeneutic principles. The Rishonim discuss to what extent these interpretations are to be viewed as the *source* of the Halakhah, both in general and with regard to particular cases, and whether some of them are merely adduced as particular cases or as support (אַסְמַכְתָּא) for an already commonly accepted Halakhah.

Since the Mishnah is primarily a compilation of Halakhic rulings, it contains few examples of Halakhic Midrash in its primary form, and these examples are mainly used to provide general and comprehensive definitions of individual Halakhic subjects. By contrast, there are exhaustive compilations of Halakhic Midrash on the books of Exodus, Leviticus, Numbers, and Deuteronomy, and these compilations (Mekhilta, Sifra, Sifrei) were edited by leading Tannaitic scholars.

BACKGROUND

שׁוֹר וְשֶׂה...לָמָּה לִי For what do I need the words "ox" and "lamb"? The four specific examples presented in these verses are meant to explain, and, to some degree (according to the hermeneutic principles), to restrict the general term "every lost thing of your brother's." Therefore, something specific must be inferred from each example which cannot be inferred from the other examples. And, as far as possible, whatever is derived from the specific example should distinguish that example from the others. For example, an ass generally wears a saddle and bridle, hence identifying marks are attached to it. By contrast, an ox only wears a yoke while it is being worked, and otherwise may not be marked with special signs. Therefore a different detail is deduced from the example of the ox — that occasionally the hair of its tail is sheared.

BACKGROUND

שׁוֹר דַּאֲפִילּוּ לְגִיזַּת זְנָבוֹ "Ox" teaches that even the shearing of its tail must be returned. Although the hair of ox and horse tails was used for stringed instruments and the like, in general the tails were clipped for the benefit of the animals themselves, since a long tail was liable to become tangled in thorns. To spare the animal suffering, the hair of its tail would be cut short.

חֲמוֹר דְּבוֹר The word "ass" in connection with the laws of a pit. The Torah states: "And if a man shall open a pit, or if a man shall dig a pit, and not cover it, and an ox or an ass fall into it, the owner of the pit shall make it good, and give money to the owner of them...." (Exodus 21:33-34.) The Sages disagree regarding the details of the Halakhah: The anonymous viewpoint of the majority of the Sages maintains that this law requires the owner of the pit to pay for damage caused only to *animals* that fall into it, whereas if other things fall into it and are damaged, the owner of the pit is not required to pay compensation. They interpret the words "an ox or an ass" to mean specifically "an ox — and not a man," "an ass — and not utensils." However, in Rabbi Yehudah's opinion, the word "ass" in this verse is brought merely as an example, and nothing is to be inferred from it.

גְּלָלִים אַפְקוּרֵי מַפְקַר לְהוּ Dung the owner abandons. Dung has monetary value, for it is widely used for fertilizer, and in some places it is burned as fuel. Animals are kept in special stalls to make it possible to gather their dung, and even today care is taken not to let it go to waste. However, dung is only worth collecting if it is available in large quantities, such as the dung of an entire herd. The dung of a single animal is not worth the labor required to gather it.

TRANSLATION AND COMMENTARY

וְלִכְתּוֹב רַחֲמָנָא שׁוֹר [1]**But,** asks the Gemara, why is it necessary for the text to mention the example of the lamb? **Let the Torah** merely **write, "ox," to teach that even the shearings of** an ox's **tail must be returned.** [2]Since even the shearings of an ox's tail must be returned, **we can** surely **infer, even more so,** that **the shearings of a lamb** must be returned together with the lamb. After all, the shearings of an ox's tail are of little value to its owner, whereas the shearings of a lamb are its main value as property.

אֶלָּא אָמַר רָבָא [3]**Rather, Rava said:** I concede that the argument just presented is convincing. Indeed it is one of two cases in the Torah where the text includes an example that seems to add nothing to our understanding of the subject under discussion. The two cases are: (1) **The word "ass,"** which appears in the Torah **in connection with the laws of** damages pertaining to an animal falling into **a pit** (Exodus 21:33). This word is difficult to explain and superfluous in its context **according to** the opinion of **Rabbi Yehudah,** who does not accept the law derived by other Sages from that word (see *Bava Kamma* 54a and note below). [4](2) **The word "lamb,"** which, as we have seen, appears in the Torah **in connection with the laws of lost property.** [5]This word **is difficult** to explain and superfluous in its context **according to everyone's opinion.** We know of no adequate explanation for these two seemingly superfluous words.

וְאֵימָא לִגְלָלִים הוּא דַּאֲתָא [6]**But,** the Gemara suggests, let us perhaps **say that** the extra word "lamb" **comes to teach** us **that** the finder of a lamb **must return** even its **dung.** Perhaps the inclusion of "ox" as an example was intended to show that something of minor value, such as the shearings of an ox's tail, must be returned, and the inclusion of "lamb" as an example was intended to show that even something to which people attach no value at all, such as a lamb's dung, must also be returned.

גְּלָלִים אַפְקוּרֵי מַפְקַר לְהוּ [7]The Gemara answers: **The** lamb's **owner** surely **abandons its dung,** as it is customary for owners to give their animals' dung to the person who is taking care of them — in this case, the finder. Hence, the Torah could not be telling us to return the dung of lost animals, since the dung of an individual animal has so little value that it has no claimant.

וְדִילְמָא לְסִימָנִין [8]**But,** the Gemara suggests, **perhaps** the extra word "lamb" **comes to teach** us that even if there are no witnesses to confirm the claimant's plea, the Torah requires us to return lost objects on

[1]וְלִכְתּוֹב רַחֲמָנָא "שׁוֹר", דַּאֲפִילּוּ לְגִיזַּת זְנָבוֹ, [2]וְכָל שֶׁכֵּן שֶׂה לְגִיזּוֹתָיו!

[3]אֶלָּא אָמַר רָבָא: "חֲמוֹר" דְּבוֹר, לְרַבִּי יְהוּדָה, [4]וְ"שֶׂה" דַּאֲבֵידָה, לְדִבְרֵי הַכֹּל, [5]קַשְׁיָא.

[6]וְאֵימָא לִגְלָלִים הוּא דַּאֲתָא!

[7]גְּלָלִים אַפְקוּרֵי מַפְקַר לְהוּ.

[8]וְדִילְמָא לְסִימָנִין הוּא דַּאֲתָא?

LITERAL TRANSLATION

[1]But let the Torah write "ox," [to teach] that even the shearing of its tail [must be returned], [2]and [we can infer that] how much more so a lamb for its shearings.

[3]Rather, Rava said: [The word] "ass" in connection with [the laws of] a pit, according to Rabbi Yehudah, [4]and [the word] "lamb" in connection with [the laws of] lost property, according to everyone, [5]are difficult.

[6]But say that it comes to [teach that] dung [must be returned]!

[7]Dung [the owner] abandons.

[8]But perhaps it comes to [teach] identifying marks?

RASHI

חמור דבור לרבי יהודה — דמחייב על נזקי כלים בבור, קשיא לן למאי אתא, דאילו לרבנן מבעי להו: שור ולא אדם חמור ולא כלים. **לגללים** — להחזיר את גלליו, דאי כתב שור הוה אמינא: כי אתא לגיזת זנבו אתא, אבל גללים לא חשיבי ולא ליהדר, כתב רחמנא קרא יתירא לאתויי גללים. **אפקורי מפקר להו** — למי שטרח בו, ולא אתא קרא לרבויינהו, דאין לו תובעין הוא. **לסימנין אתא** — לאשמועינן דליהדריה בסימנין בלא עדים, דקמיבעיא לן לקמן סימנין דאורייתא או דרבנן, ובעינן למפשט ממתניתין דיליף להו מ"שמלה", ודחינן ואמר: תנא תובעין אצטריכא ליה, סימנין כדי נסבה, נפשוט מקרא יתירא ד"שה" לסימנין אתא וסימנין דאורייתא.

NOTES

חֲמוֹר דְּבוֹר The word "ass" in connection with the laws of a pit. *Tosafot* notes that there are other examples of Biblical verses containing seemingly superfluous expressions that could have been cited by the Talmud. However, the Talmud mentioned only those that deal with animals.

HALAKHAH

lost object is in the finder's possession, he must care for it, preserve it against deterioration, and even improve it. For example, lost sheep must be sheared, and even lost oxen must have their tails sheared, even though the value of the shearings is very small." (*Shulḥan Arukh, Ḥoshen Mishpat* 267:17.)

TRANSLATION AND COMMENTARY

the basis of **identifying marks** alone? [1]**For** later in this passage the Gemara **raises the following problem: Are identifying marks,** without witnesses, **valid by Torah law or** merely **by Rabbinic decree?** [2]Perhaps we can argue, in answer to this question, that **the Torah wrote** the apparently superfluous word **"lamb"** for this very purpose — **to teach** us **that** the Torah requires us to **return a lost object**, **even** when it is identified only **by means of identifying marks,** and not by witnesses. [3]**Thus** we can infer that **identifying marks are** indeed **valid by Torah law.**

אָמְרִי מִדְּקָתָנֵי לְהוּ תַּנָּא [4]The Gemara dismisses this argument. **We can say** in reply **that the Tanna** in our Mishnah **mentioned identifying marks in connection with** the word **"garment,"** not with the word "lamb." [5]**For he says** in the Mishnah: **"Just as a garment is special, in that it has identifying marks and claimants, thus obliging** the finder **to announce it,** [6]**so too** must **everything that has identifying marks and claimants be announced."** [7]Hence we may **conclude from** the Tanna's choice of words **that the word "lamb" did not come to teach** us about **identifying marks.** This concept can only be derived from the word "garment." Rather, the word "lamb" was written in the Torah to teach us something else, but unfortunately we do not know what.

תָּנוּ רַבָּנַן [8]The Gemara now brings another passage from the Sifrei dealing with the same verse (Deuteronomy 22:3): **Our Rabbis taught:** "'And so shall you do with every lost thing of your brother's, which shall be lost from him and you have found it.' What can we learn from the expression, **'Which shall be lost'?** We learn that the Torah uses this expression **to exclude** from the obligation to return lost property **a lost object that is not worth a perutah.** Since such a lost object is worth less than a perutah, it is considered Halakhically of no monetary value. Thus it does not come into the category of lost property at all, and is not subject to the commandment to return lost property. [9]**Rabbi Yehudah says:** We learn this law from the expression, **'And you have found it,'** which the Torah uses in order **to exclude a lost object worth less than a perutah** from the obligation to return found objects. Since the lost object is considered worthless, it is not in the category of something 'you have found,' and is not subject to the commandment to return lost property."

[1]דְּאִיבַּעְיָא לָן: סִימָנִין דְּאוֹרַיְיתָא אוֹ דְּרַבָּנַן? [2]כָּתַב רַחֲמָנָא "שֶׂה" דַּאֲפִילּוּ בְּסִימָנִין מְהַדְּרִינַן, [3]וְסִימָנִין דְּאוֹרַיְיתָא.

[4]אָמְרִי מִדְּקָתָנֵי לְהוּ תַּנָּא לְסִימָנִין גַּבֵּי "שִׂמְלָה" — דְּקָתָנֵי: [5]"מַה שִּׂמְלָה מְיוּחֶדֶת, שֶׁיֵּשׁ בָּהּ סִימָנִין וְיֵשׁ לָהּ תּוֹבְעִין, חַיָּיב לְהַכְרִיז, [6]אַף כָּל דָּבָר שֶׁיֵּשׁ בּוֹ סִימָנִין וְיֵשׁ לוֹ תּוֹבְעִין חַיָּיב לְהַכְרִיז" — [7]שְׁמַע מִינַּהּ דְּ"שֶׂה" לָאו לְסִימָנִין הוּא דַּאֲתָא.

[8]תָּנוּ רַבָּנַן: "'אֲשֶׁר תֹּאבַד' — פְּרָט לַאֲבֵידָה שֶׁאֵין בָּהּ שָׁוֶה פְּרוּטָה. [9]רַבִּי יְהוּדָה אוֹמֵר: 'וּמְצָאתָהּ' פְּרָט לַאֲבֵידָה שֶׁאֵין בָּהּ שָׁוֶה פְּרוּטָה".

LITERAL TRANSLATION

[1]For [the following] has been asked of us: Are identifying marks [valid] by Torah [law] or by Rabbinic [decree]? [2][Therefore] the Torah wrote "lamb" [to teach] that even by means of identifying marks we return [a lost object], [3]and [thus] identifying marks are [valid] by Torah law.

[4][We can] say [that] since the Tanna taught identifying marks in connection with "garment" — [5]for he teaches: "Just as a garment is special, in that it has identifying marks on it and it has claimants, [and therefore] he is obliged to announce [it], [6]so too everything that has identifying marks on it and has claimants he is obliged to announce" — [7]conclude from this that [the word] "lamb" did not come to [teach] identifying marks.

[8]Our Rabbis taught: "'Which shall be lost' — to exclude a lost object that is not worth a perutah. [9]Rabbi Yehudah says: 'And you have found it' — to exclude a lost object that is not worth a perutah."

RASHI

אמרי מדנקט תנא — במתניתין למילף סימנין מ"שמלה" בהדי תובעין — פשיטא ליה ד"שה" למלתא אחריתי אתא, ולאו הוא דלא ידעינן, משום הכי לא פשיטא ליה לקמן סימנין מ"שה", הלכך קשיא לן למאי אתא. **אשר תאבד** — שתהא קרויה אבידה. **ומצאתה** — שתהא קרויה מציאה.

BACKGROUND

כָּתַב רַחֲמָנָא "שֶׂה" דַּאֲפִילּוּ בְּסִימָנִין מְהַדְּרִינַן The Torah wrote "lamb" to teach that even by means of identifying marks we return a lost object. The basic logic behind the suggestion that the ruling about identifying marks is derived from the word "lamb" written in the Torah is as follows: The word appears to be superfluous, since it does not teach any specific Halakhah; therefore it may have been intended to emphasize something not stated explicitly in the previous examples: that a lost object must be returned on the basis of identifying marks. Although the main justification for this inference is the apparent superfluity of the word, there are also grounds for it in real life. Shepherds commonly paint marks on sheep, and this is further justification for using the word "sheep" as the basis for inferring that a lost object must also be returned on the basis of identifying marks alone.

דְּ"שֶׂה" לָאו לְסִימָנִין הוּא דַּאֲתָא That the word "lamb" did not come to teach identifying marks. Although the Gemara will explain below (27b) that the mention of identifying marks on a garment does not prove that the ruling that one must return lost objects on the basis of such marks is derived from the Torah, nevertheless, the fact that the Tanna connects the subject of identifying marks with the word "garment" mentioned in the Torah proves that the ruling regarding identifying marks, whether it is of Torah origin or only a Rabbinical decree, cannot be inferred from any *other* component of this verse. According to this view, the word "lamb" still remains without a sufficient explanation.

HALAKHAH

שִׁיעוּר פְּרוּטָה בַּאֲבֵידָה A lost object must have a minimum value of one perutah. "An object that was worth less than one perutah when it was lost need not be returned even if it was worth a perutah when it was found. Likewise, an object that was not worth one perutah when it was found need not be returned even if it was worth a perutah when it was lost. However, as long as an article was worth a perutah both at the time it was lost and at the time it was found, it must be returned, regardless of any fluctuations in its value in the interim." (Ibid., 262:1.)

TERMINOLOGY

מַאי בֵּינַיְיהוּ What is the difference between them? Where the Gemara records a difference of opinion about the reason for a law or the definition of a legal concept, it often asks: "What practical difference is there between the reasons or definitions cited in the previous passage?" The answer to this question is introduced by the expression אִיכָּא בֵּינַיְיהוּ — "The difference between them is...."

CONCEPTS

מַשְׁמָעוּת דּוֹרְשִׁין אִיכָּא בֵּינַיְיהוּ The appropriateness of the texts for the law they derive is the difference between them. This expression has been interpreted in various ways. Some authorities maintain that it means there is really no Halakhic difference between the two interpretations, and that the Sages merely differ concerning the specific Biblical verse which should be taken as the source of this particular Halakhah, with one Sage citing one verse and the other citing a different one.
However, other authorities maintain that although the difference between the two Halakhic Midrashim here may have no explicit effect on the Halakhah at present under discussion, nevertheless there is a potential difference regarding other Halakhot. Since each Sage used a different Biblical verse to prove his point, the verse that he did *not* cite remains available for further Halakhic Midrash. It is possible that one of these remaining sources may lead the Sages to different conclusions regarding other Halakhot.

TRANSLATION AND COMMENTARY

מַאי בֵּינַיְיהוּ [1]This Baraita raises two questions: (1) Since the first Tanna and Rabbi Yehudah both agree that lost property worth less than a perutah need not be returned, what is the difference of opinion between them? (2) Why do the two Tannaim derive this principle from different expressions used by the Torah? To clarify these questions the Gemara now asks: **What is the** practical **difference between** the first Tanna and Rabbi Yehudah? Surely they both agree that an object worth less than a perutah need not be returned.

אָמַר אַבָּיֵי [2]In answer to this question the Gemara states: **Abaye said:** There is no practical difference between these two opinions. **The difference between them is** with regard to **the appropriateness of the** respective **texts for the law they derive.** [3]**The first Sage derives** the perutah rule **from** the expression **"which shall be lost,"** [4]**and the other Sage,** Rabbi Yehudah, **derives it from** the expression **"and you have found it."**

וּלְמַאן דְּנָפְקָא לֵיהּ [5]The Gemara asks: **But according to the first Sage, who derived** the perutah rule **from** the expression **"which shall be lost,"** [6]**what does he do with the** superfluous **expression "and you have found it"?** What further information does he derive from the latter phrase?

הַהוּא מִיבָּעֵי לֵיהּ לִכְדְרַבְּנַאי [7]The Gemara answers: The first Sage **needs that expression for** the derivation of another law, **which** the Amora **Rabbenai** is known to have **stated.** [8]**For Rabbenai said:** The expression **"and you have found it" means that** the lost object has not only been discovered by the finder, but **has** actually **reached his hand.** Even though the Torah expressly forbids the finder of a lost object to ignore it, and this prohibition applies from the moment the object is seen, there are Halakhic distinctions between an object that has been picked up and one that has merely been discovered. Rabbenai's primary purpose is to inform us that the exemptions from the law that lost objects must be returned apply not only to objects that were merely discovered, but even to those that were physically picked up. At all events, since the first Tanna needed the expression "and you have found it" for the teaching later enunciated by the Amora Rabbenai, he was forced to derive the principle that a perutah was the minimum value of a lost object requiring to be returned from the expression "which shall be lost."

וּלְמַאן דְּנָפְקָא לֵיהּ מִוּמְצָאתָהּ [9]**But,** the Gemara further asks, **according to** Rabbi Yehudah, **who derives** the perutah rule **from** the expression "and you have found it," [10]**what does he do with the** superfluous **expression "which shall be lost"?** What further information does he derive from it?

מִבָּעֵי לֵיהּ לִכְדְרַבִּי יוֹחָנָן [11]The Gemara answers: Rabbi Yehudah **needs** that expression for the derivation of

[1]מַאי בֵּינַיְיהוּ? [2]אָמַר אַבָּיֵי: מַשְׁמָעוּת דּוֹרְשִׁין אִיכָּא בֵּינַיְיהוּ. [3]מָר נָפְקָא לֵיהּ מֵ״אֲשֶׁר תֹּאבַד״, [4]וּמָר נָפְקָא לֵיהּ מִ״וּמְצָאתָהּ״. [5]וּלְמַאן דְּנָפְקָא לֵיהּ מֵ״אֲשֶׁר תֹּאבַד״, [6]הַאי ״וּמְצָאתָהּ״ מַאי עָבֵיד לֵיהּ? [7]הַהוּא מִיבָּעֵי לֵיהּ לִכְדְרַבְּנַאי. [8]דַּאֲמַר רַבְּנַאי: ״וּמְצָאתָהּ״ דַּאֲתָאי לִידֵיהּ מַשְׁמַע. [9]וּלְמַאן דְּנָפְקָא לֵיהּ מִ״וּמְצָאתָהּ״, [10]הַאי ״אֲשֶׁר תֹּאבַד״ מַאי עָבֵיד לֵיהּ? [11]מִבָּעֵי לֵיהּ לִכְדְרַבִּי יוֹחָנָן.

LITERAL TRANSLATION

[1]What is [the difference] between them?

[2]Abaye said: The appropriateness [of the texts for the law] they derive is [the difference] between them. [3]One Sage derives it from "which shall be lost," [4]and the other Sage derives it from "and you have found it."

[5]But according to the one who derives it from "which shall be lost," [6]this [expression] "and you have found it," what does he do with it?

[7]He needs that [expression] for that which Rabbenai [stated]. [8]For Rabbenai said: "And you have found it" means that it has reached his hand.

[9]But according to the one who derives it from "and you have found it," [10]this [expression] "which shall be lost," what does he do with it?

[11]He needs it for that which Rabbi Yoḥanan [stated].

RASHI

דאתא לידיה משמע — ואפילו הכי אחיך ולא נכרי ולמדך שאבידת נכרים מותרת, ולא תימא כי אמעוט אבידת נכרי — מלטרוח אחריה אמעוט, אבל אי נקטה — חייב לאהדורה.

NOTES

נָפְקָא לֵיהּ מִ״וּמְצָאתָהּ״ He derives it from "and you have found it." *Tosafot* (*Sanhedrin* 14a) points out that there is no standard rule about deriving additional Halakhic information from a conjunction. A Tanna will sometimes make such a derivation, when he considers it appropriate, and will sometimes refrain from doing so. Thus, Rabbi Yehudah, who here derives Rabbenai's rule from the conjunction "and" in "and you have found it," is described in tractate *Temurah* (2b) as not deriving anything from a conjunction.

[1] דְּאָמַר רַבִּי יוֹחָנָן מִשּׁוּם רַבִּי שִׁמְעוֹן בֶּן יוֹחַאי: [2] מִנַּיִין לַאֲבֵידָה שֶׁשְּׁטָפָהּ נָהָר שֶׁהִיא מוּתֶּרֶת? [3] שֶׁנֶּאֱמַר: ״כֵּן תַּעֲשֶׂה לְכָל אֲבֵדַת אָחִיךָ, אֲשֶׁר תֹּאבַד מִמֶּנּוּ וּמְצָאתָהּ״. [4] מִי שֶׁאֲבוּדָה הֵימֶנּוּ וּמְצוּיָה אֵצֶל כָּל אָדָם. [5] יָצְתָה זוֹ, שֶׁאֲבוּדָה הֵימֶנּוּ וְאֵינָהּ מְצוּיָה אֵצֶל כָּל אָדָם. [6] וְאִידָךְ, הָא דְּרַבְּנַאי מְנָא לֵיהּ? [7] נָפְקָא לֵיהּ מִ״וּמְצָאתָהּ״. [8] וְאִידָךְ, הָא דְּרַבִּי יוֹחָנָן מְנָא לֵיהּ? [9] נָפְקָא לֵיהּ ״מִמֶּנּוּ״. [10] וְאִידָךְ? [11] ״מִמֶּנּוּ״ לֹא מַשְׁמַע לֵיהּ.

LITERAL TRANSLATION

[1] For Rabbi Yoḥanan said in the name of Rabbi Shimon ben Yoḥai: [2] From where [do we know] that a lost object that was swept away by a river is permitted [to the finder]? [3] As it is said: "So shall you do with every lost thing of your brother's, which is lost from him and which you have found." [4] [Only] that which is lost from him but is available to every man [must be returned]. [5] This is excluded, which is lost from him and is not available to every man.

[6] But the other [Sage], from where does he [derive] this [law] of Rabbenai?

[7] He derives it from "and you have found it."

[8] But the other [Sage], from where does he [derive] this [law] of Rabbi Yoḥanan?

[9] He derives it [from] "from him."

[10] And the other [Sage]?

[11] "From him" is not significant for him.

TRANSLATION AND COMMENTARY

another law **which** the Amora, **Rabbi Yoḥanan,** is known to have **stated.** [1] **For Rabbi Yoḥanan said in the name of Rabbi Shimon ben Yoḥai:** [2] **"From where** in the Torah **do we know that a lost object** of any kind, even one containing an identifying mark, **that was swept away by a river is** always **permitted to** be kept by **the finder** and need not be returned to its original owner? [3] **As it is said: 'So shall you do with every lost thing of your brother's, which is lost from him and which you have found.'** [4] From the presence of the seemingly superfluous word מִמֶּנּוּ — 'from him' — the Rabbis drew the following conclusion: **Only that which is lost 'from him'** — i.e., as far as its owner alone is concerned — **but is available to everyone** else **must be returned.** [5] By inference, **this excludes** an item which was swept away by a river — **which is** not only **lost to** its owner, **but is not available to anyone** else either, since the river is likely to carry it away altogether. Accordingly, the Torah declared such objects to be ownerless, and they need not be returned, even if their original ownership is not in dispute (see above, 22b)." Because the word מִמֶּנּוּ — "from him" — needed to be included in the text for this particular derivation, the additional words אֲשֶׁר תֹּאבַד — "which is lost" — were also necessary in the context.

וְאִידָךְ [6] The Gemara asks: **But from where does the other Sage,** Rabbi Yehudah, who derived the perutah rule from the expression "and you have found it," **derive the law of Rabbenai** who made use of this expression for his derivation?

נָפְקָא לֵיהּ מוּמְצָאתָהּ [7] The Gemara answers: **He derives it from** the conjunction "and" in the expression "**and you have found it,"** meaning that the text is referring to an object that "you have already found, that is already in your possession." The conjunction is needed to derive this additional law.

וְאִידָךְ [8] The Gemara now asks a similar question regarding the position of the first Sage: **And from where does the first Sage,** who derived the perutah rule from the expression "which shall be lost from him," **derive the law of Rabbi Yoḥanan** concerning an object swept away by a river?

נָפְקָא לֵיהּ מִמֶּנּוּ [9] The Gemara answers: **He derives it from** the expression **"from him,"** which was not required for the perutah law. "From him" implies lost to him alone and not to anyone else. Thus the expression "which shall be lost from him" can be used for the derivation of two laws: (a) the first part of the phrase teaches that the obligation to return lost property applies only if the object is worth at least a perutah, and (b) the second part of the phrase teaches that only an object which is lost as far as its owner is concerned but is available for others to find places the finder under an obligation to return it.

וְאִידָךְ [10] The Gemara asks: **And the other Sage,** Rabbi Yehudah, who derives Rabbi Yoḥanan's law from the entire expression, "which shall be lost from him," does he derive something else from the expression "from him"?

מִמֶּנּוּ [11] The Gemara answers: According to Rabbi Yehudah, the phrase "**from him**" in the clause "which shall be lost from him" is an integral and necessary part of the complete expression. It **is not meaningful** in isolation from the rest of the phrase, and nothing further can be learned from it. This concludes the discussion of Abaye's reply to the Gemara's original question.

TERMINOLOGY

וְאִידָךְ And the other Sage? i.e., what does the scholar holding the conflicting opinion say to this argument? This expression is used to clarify differences of opinion between scholars, with the Gemara asking each in turn how he will answer the argument brought by the other.

RASHI

מי שאבודה ממנו — ולאיידי דכתב "ממנו" כתב "אשר תאבד".
ומצאתה — הוי"ו יתירה, משמע ומצאתה כבר.

[1] רָבָא אֲמַר: פְּרוּטָה שֶׁהוּזְלָה אִיכָּא בֵּינַיְיהוּ. [2] מַאן דְּאָמַר מֵ"אֲשֶׁר תֹּאבַד" אִיכָּא, [3] וּמַאן דְּאָמַר מִ"וּמְצָאתָהּ" לֵיכָּא.
[4] וּלְמַאן דְּאָמַר "אֲשֶׁר תֹּאבַד", [5] הָא בָּעֵינַן "וּמְצָאתָהּ" וְלֵיכָּא!
[6] אֶלָּא, פְּרוּטָה שֶׁהוּקְרָה אִיכָּא בֵּינַיְיהוּ. [7] מַאן דְּאָמַר "וּמְצָאתָהּ" אִיכָּא, [8] וּמַאן דְּאָמַר "אֲשֶׁר תֹּאבַד" לֵיכָּא.
[9] וּלְמַאן דְּאָמַר "וּמְצָאתָהּ", [10] הָא בָּעֵינַן "אֲשֶׁר תֹּאבַד", וְלֵיכָּא!
[11] אֶלָּא, פְּרוּטָה שֶׁהוּקְרָה וְהוּזְלָה וְחָזְרָה וְהוּקְרָה אִיכָּא בֵּינַיְיהוּ.

LITERAL TRANSLATION

[1] Rava said: [An object worth] a perutah that depreciated is [the difference] between them. [2] The one who said [that we derive this law] from "which shall be *lost*" [would rule that] there is here [the loss of a perutah], [3] and the one who said [that we derive this law] from "and you have *found it*" [would rule that] there is not [here the finding of a perutah].

[4] But according to the one who says "which shall be lost," [5] surely we require "and you have found it," and it is not [the case]?

[6] Rather, [an object worth less than] a perutah that has appreciated is [the difference] between them. [7] The one who said [that we derive this law from] "and you have *found it*" [would rule that] there is here [the finding of a perutah], [8] and the one who said [that we derive this law from] "which shall be *lost*" [would rule that] there is not here [the loss of a perutah].

[9] But according to the one who says "and you have found it," [10] surely we require "which shall be lost," and it is not [the case].

[11] Rather, [an object worth] a perutah that appreciated and depreciated and again appreciated is [the difference] between them.

TRANSLATION AND COMMENTARY

רָבָא אֲמַר [1] The Gemara now offers a second answer to the question raised earlier as to why the first Tanna and Rabbi Yehudah used different sources to derive the law that lost property must be worth at least a perutah in order for the finder to be obliged to return it: **Rava said: There is a** practical **difference between** the views of the first Sage and of Rabbi Yehudah, and the difference is not, as Abaye claims, merely that they disagree as to the source in the Torah for the law that an object must be worth at least a perutah for it to come under the category of lost property that has to be returned. This practical difference, says Rava, can be seen in the case of **a** lost **object** that was **worth a perutah** when it was lost **but depreciated** in value in the meantime and was no longer worth a perutah when it was found. [2] **The** first Sage, **who said that we derive** the perutah **law from** the expression, **"which shall be *lost*," would rule that** in such a case **there is an** actual ***loss*** of something worth **a perutah** for the purposes of this law, since the object was, in fact, worth a perutah when it was *lost*. [3] On the other hand, Rabbi Yehudah, **who said that we derive** the perutah **law from** the expression **"and you have *found* it," would rule that** in such a case **there is no** actual ***finding* of** something worth **a perutah** for the purposes of this law, since the object was not worth a perutah when it was *found*.

וּלְמַאן דְּאָמַר אֲשֶׁר תֹּאבַד [4] **But,** asks the Gemara, even **according to the one who says** that we derive the perutah law from the expression **"which shall be lost,"** [5] **surely we** also **require** a fulfillment of the expression **"and you have found it," and** finding an object worth less than a perutah **is not** considered "finding" at all.

אֶלָּא [6] **Rather,** suggests the Gemara, perhaps the opposite is true. **The** practical **difference between** the first Sage and Rabbi Yehudah concerns **an object** which was **worth less than a perutah** when lost, but **which appreciated** in value and was worth a perutah or more when found. [7] Rabbi Yehudah, **who said that we derive** the perutah **law from** the expression, **"and you have *found* it," would rule that** in such a case **there is an** actual ***finding* of** something worth a **perutah** for the purposes of this law, since the object was, in fact, worth a perutah when it was found. [8] On the other hand, the first Sage, **who said that we derive** the perutah **law from** the expression **"which shall be *lost*," would rule that** in such a case **there is no** actual ***loss* of** something worth **a perutah** for the purposes of this law, since the object was not worth a perutah when it was lost.

וּלְמַאן דְּאָמַר וּמְצָאתָהּ [9] But, asks the Gemara, even **according to the one who says** that we derive the perutah law from the expression **"and you have found it,"** [10] **surely we** also **require** a fulfillment of the expression **"which shall be lost," and** losing an object worth less than a perutah **is not** considered "losing" at all.

אֶלָּא [11] **Rather,** suggests the Gemara, **the** practical **difference between** the first Sage and Rabbi Yehudah concerns **an object worth a perutah that appreciated,** i.e., that was worth a perutah when it was lost, **and depreciated** in the interim until it was worth less than a perutah, **and again appreciated** before it was found

RASHI

שהוזלה — דבשעת אבידה שוה פרוטה, ובשעת מציאה הוזלה.

BACKGROUND

פְּרוּטָה שֶׁהוּזְלָה An object worth a perutah that depreciated. These questions apply in real life to objects worth almost exactly a perutah. Even a very small decrease in the market value of such objects transfers them from the category of property with monetary value into the category of things that are without monetary value. Under certain circumstances the market may be very volatile, as after the lifting of a siege or the end of a famine, when the price of foodstuffs may fall sharply within a very short time (see II Kings, 7). Hence there might be a significant difference between the value of an object at the time it was lost and its value when it was recovered.

The Gemara explains the distinctions drawn here, regarding something worth a perutah which increased in value and decreased in value, as a question of timing. Which moment determines when the laws of lost and found property first apply? Is the decisive moment the one when the object was lost, so that if it was then worth a perutah, it comes into the category of a lost object regardless of any further developments? Or is the determining moment the one when it was found? The Gemara concludes that the controversy concerns whether the lost object must be worth at least a perutah during the entire period that it was lost, or whether it is sufficient to take only certain moments into account — the moment it was lost and the moment it was found.

LITERAL TRANSLATION

[1]The one who said [that we derive this law from] "which shall be lost" [would rule that] there is here [the loss of a perutah], [2]and the one who said [that we derive this law from] "and you have found it" [would rule that] we require [an object] that has the value of a found object from the time of loss until the time of discovery. [3]It was asked of them: Are identifying marks [valid] by Torah law or by Rabbinic decree? [4]What difference does it make (lit., "what comes out from it")?

[27B] [5]To return a woman's bill of divorce on the basis of identifying marks. [6]If you say [that they are valid] by Torah law, we return [it]. [7]But if you say [that they are valid] by Rabbinic decree [we do not].

[1]מַאן דְּאָמַר ״אֲשֶׁר תֹּאבַד״ אִיכָּא, [2]וּמַאן דְּאָמַר ״וּמְצָאתָהּ״ בָּעֵינַן דְּאִית בָּהּ שִׁיעוּר מְצִיאָה מִשְּׁעַת אֲבֵידָה וְעַד שְׁעַת מְצִיאָה.

[3]אִיבַּעְיָא לְהוּ: סִימָנִין דְּאוֹרָיְיתָא אוֹ דְּרַבָּנַן? [4]מַאי נָפְקָא מִינָּהּ?

[27B] [5]לְאַהֲדוּרֵי גֵּט אִשָּׁה בְּסִימָנִים. [6]אִי אָמְרַתְּ דְּאוֹרָיְיתָא, מְהַדְרִינַן. [7]וְאִי אָמְרַתְּ דְּרַבָּנַן,

RASHI

לאהדורי גט — שאבד מן השליח המביאו קודם שנתן לה.

TRANSLATION AND COMMENTARY

until it was worth a perutah once more. [1]The first Sage **who said** that **we derive** the perutah **law from** the expression, **"which shall be lost," would rule that** in such a case **there is an** actual **loss of a perutah** for the purposes of this law, since the object was worth a perutah both when lost and when found. [2]On the other hand, Rabbi Yehudah, **who said that we derive** the perutah **law from** the expression, "**and you have found it**," **would rule that** the object is considered not to be worth a perutah for the purposes of this law, since he would maintain that **we require an object to have the** minimum **value of a found object** — i.e., a perutah — constantly **from the time of loss until the time of discovery;** in this case, since the object was worth less than a perutah at some time between the moment it was lost and the moment it was found, it need not be returned.

אִיבַּעְיָא לְהוּ [3]A problem mentioned in passing in the previous passage is now analyzed in detail: The scholars in the Academy **posed the following problem: Are identifying marks** unsupported by witnesses **valid by Torah law or** only **by Rabbinic decree?** [4]The Gemara presents various aspects of the problem: No one disputes that a lost object must be returned if the owner can cite an identifying mark on it. So **what** practical **difference does it make** if the source of this law is a verse in the Torah or a Rabbinic decree?

לְאַהֲדוּרֵי גֵּט אִשָּׁה בְּסִימָנִים [27B] [5]The Gemara answers: The difference is whether a finder is required **to return a** lost **bill of divorce on the basis of identifying marks** or not. The case discussed here concerns an agent sent by a husband to deliver a bill of divorce to his wife. The agent lost the bill of divorce before delivering it, and it was found by someone else. The agent cannot produce witnesses to prove that the bill of divorce which was found is in fact the one he lost, but he is able to identify the document by citing specific definitive features it contains. The question is whether identification by the agent is sufficient. [6]**If you say that** returning lost property on the basis of identifying marks **is valid by Torah law, we** should allow the finder to **return** the bill of divorce to the agent who claims to have lost it, since the Torah has decreed that such identifying marks are acceptable. [7]**But if you say that** identifying marks **are valid** only **by Rabbinic decree, we should not** allow the finder to return the bill of divorce to the agent on the basis of his identification, even though such

BACKGROUND

לְאַהֲדוּרֵי גֵּט אִשָּׁה בְּסִימָנִים **To return a woman's bill of divorce on the basis of identifying marks.** A bill of divorce severs the connection between husband and wife from the moment the wife receives the bill of divorce from her husband or from his agent.

A bill of divorce that has been lost by the agent and found by someone else cannot be delivered to the wife because doubt exists as to whether it is the same document that was originally written for that particular woman. Although the names of the husband and wife are the same, this is not sufficient proof, for there is a possibility that this bill of divorce happened to be written by another man of the same name for a woman of the same name.

Although the chances of this occurring are very remote, the prohibition against sexual relations with a married woman is extremely severe, and she is not permitted to remarry unless it has been proved beyond doubt that her previous marriage has been terminated.

NOTES

סִימָנִים **Identifying marks.** The Rishonim, basing themselves on various Talmudic sources, define three categories of identifying marks: (1) סִימָנִים מוּבְהָקִים בְּיוֹתֵר — "completely definitive identifying marks" — e.g., the presence of a hole next to a letter on the parchment of a bill of divorce, or the presence of a sixth finger on a hand. Identifying marks of this nature are accepted in all cases. (2) סִימָנִים אֶמְצָעִיִּים — "intermediate identifying marks" — such as a hole in a document or a mole on a person. Ordinarily, when the Talmud uses the word סִימָנִים alone, it refers to marks of this kind. They are effective as the basis for returning a lost article. However, their acceptability as the basis for returning a lost bill of divorce or providing conclusive identification of a corpse is the subject of an unresolved problem in the Gemara — whether these marks are valid by Torah law or by Rabbinic decree. (The term סִימָנִים מוּבְהָקִים may be used either for marks in this category or for the definitive marks in the first category, depending on the author and context.) (3) סִימָנִים גְּרוּעִים — "inferior signs" — e.g., a person's rough height or the color of clothing. These are of no value as means of identification.

HALAKHAH

סִימָנִים דְּאוֹרָיְיתָא **Are identifying marks valid by Torah law?** "Completely definitive identifying marks (סִימָנִים מוּבְהָקִים בְּיוֹתֵר), for example, a hole next to a particular letter on the parchment of a bill of divorce, or a sixth finger on a corpse's hand, constitute valid proof of identity by Torah law, and can be used to identify a bill of divorce or a corpse

TRANSLATION AND COMMENTARY

identification would be acceptable for other lost property. [1]The distinction is as follows: **When the Rabbis made the enactment** permitting the return of lost property on the basis of identifying marks, **they did so** only in connection with ordinary lost property, which is purely a **monetary matter**, and the Rabbinical Court has the power to make decisions changing the legal ownership of property. [2]**But** where the case involves the possible violation of **ritual prohibitions,** such as a case concerning a lost bill of divorce, which has the power to dissolve a marriage and allow a woman to remarry, **the Rabbis did not** have the authority to **make the enactment** permitting a bill of divorce to be returned to the agent on the basis of identifying marks, because the Rabbis cannot make an enactment superseding a Torah prohibition. According to the argument that identifying marks are valid only by Rabbinic decree, a lost bill of divorce can thus only be returned on the basis of testimony by witnesses.

תָּא שְׁמַע [3]Having stated the problem, the Gemara now makes a series of attempts to resolve it: **Come and hear** a proof from our Mishnah (above, 27a): "Since **a garment is** already **included in** the Torah's general command to return **all** lost property, [4]**why was it singled out** and mentioned explicitly? [5]**To** make us **compare** garments with other lost objects **and to say to you:** [6]**Just as a garment is special, in that there are identifying marks on it and it has claimants, and therefore** the finder **is obliged to announce it,** [7]**so too must everything that has identifying marks on it and has claimants be announced."** The Mishnah states that the word "garment" was specifically mentioned in the Torah because of two characteristics it possesses — identification marks and claimants. Thus it would appear obvious that identifying marks are accepted by the Torah as a basis for the restoration of lost property.

תַּנָּא תּוֹבְעִין אִצְטְרִיכָא לֵיהּ [8]The Gemara answers: This proof is not conclusive. **The Tanna** in our Mishnah **needed** primarily **to teach** us that lost property must only be announced when there are **claimants** to it. Where the owners have given up hope of recovering their property, the finder has no obligation to announce it, and is permitted to keep it. [9]The subject of **identifying marks was included** in the Mishnah incidentally, **for no special reason.** Since they too can be used as the basis of a claim, they are included in the Mishnah, but their validity is by Rabbinic decree only.

[1]כִּי עֲבוּד רַבָּנַן תַּקַּנְתָּא, בְּמָמוֹנָא, [2]אֲבָל בְּאִיסּוּרָא לָא עֲבוּד רַבָּנַן תַּקַּנְתָּא.
[3]תָּא שְׁמַע: "אַף הַשִּׂמְלָה הָיְתָה בִּכְלַל כָּל אֵלּוּ. [4]וְלָמָּה יָצְאת? [5]לְהַקִּישׁ אֵלֶיהָ, וְלוֹמַר לָךְ: [6]מָה שִׂמְלָה מְיוּחֶדֶת, שֶׁיֵּשׁ לָהּ סִימָנִין וְיֵשׁ לָהּ תּוֹבְעִין, חַיָּיב לְהַכְרִיז, [7]אַף כָּל דָּבָר שֶׁיֵּשׁ לוֹ סִימָנִין וְיֵשׁ לוֹ תּוֹבְעִין חַיָּיב לְהַכְרִיז"!
[8]תַּנָּא תּוֹבְעִין אִצְטְרִיכָא לֵיהּ; [9]סִימָנִין כְּדִי נָסְבָא.

LITERAL TRANSLATION

[1]When the Rabbis made the enactment, [they made it] regarding monetary matters, [2]but regarding [ritual] prohibitions the Rabbis did not make the enactment.

[3]Come [and] hear: "The garment, too, was included among all these. [4]And why was it singled out? [5]To compare to it, and to say to you: [6]Just as a garment is special, in that it has identifying marks on it and it has claimants, [and therefore] he is obliged to announce [it], [7]so too anything that has identifying marks on it and has claimants he is obliged to announce."

[8]The Tanna needed [to teach about] claimants; [9]identifying marks he brought for no [special] reason.

RASHI

תקנתא — לקמן בשמעתין מפרש מאי היא. **בממונא** — דהפקר בית דין הפקר. **תובעין אצטריכא ליה** — קרא לתובעין אתא, ולמעוטי מידי דליאוש ומפקריה. **כדי נסבה** — בלא מקרא, אלא אסמכינהו אקרא בעלמא.

NOTES

סִימָנִין כְּדִי נָסְבָא Identifying marks he brought without special reason. The verse really teaches us that only a lost object that is likely to be claimed must be announced, and that it is to be returned to its owner only after he has proved his ownership. The principle of "identifying marks" is not derived from the exegesis of the verse, but was connected to the verse by the Mishnah so that its exposition would include the practical guidelines of Rabbinic law (*Rashi, Rashba*).

HALAKHAH

to permit a woman to remarry. Intermediate identifying marks (סִימָנִים אֶמְצָעִיִּים), offering compelling but not conclusive evidence of identity (e.g., a hole somewhere in a bill of divorce or a mole somewhere on a corpse's hand), are the subject of an unresolved problem in the Gemara, and it is unclear whether they meet the standards of proof the Torah demands to permit a woman to remarry. Hence, a woman may not remarry on the basis of such evidence. However, if she does remarry, many opinions do not require her to be divorced (*Rabbenu Yeruḥam* and others, quoted

BACKGROUND

כִּי עֲבוּד רַבָּנַן תַּקַּנְתָּא, בְּמָמוֹנָא When the Rabbis made the enactment, they made it regarding monetary matters. If we assume that identifying marks are not sufficient proof of ownership according to Torah law, then the return of lost property on the basis of such marks is merely a regulation ordained by the Sages for the public good.
The reasoning here must be understood as follows: It is true that the citation of identifying marks is not absolute proof of ownership, and doubt will always persist as to whether the claimant who received the lost object was actually its owner. But, with regard to civil law, the Sages are empowered to institute regulations such as these, for a court has the right to impound a person's property and deliver it to someone else. The recipient of a lost object on the basis of identifying marks thus receives it on the basis of an ordinance and directive of the court. Other laws, however, which do not concern property, do not depend upon the authority of the court to impound property, and a court cannot ordain laws in these other areas if they are not consistent with the laws of the Torah. If proof of ownership on the basis of identifying marks is not considered sufficient according to Torah law, the court cannot institute a Rabbinic regulation dissolving a marriage.

TERMINOLOGY

כְּדִי נָסְבָא He brought for no special reason. The meaning of כְּדִי is "incidentally" or "for nothing." Thus the meaning of the phrase כְּדִי נָסְבָא is that a certain expression in a Mishnah or a Baraita should not be viewed as a Halakhic ruling central to the matter under discussion, but rather as something stated parenthetically. In the present instance, the matter of identifying marks was introduced merely in order to complete treatment of the practical consequences of the subject under discussion, but is not integral to the Halakhic Midrash.

TRANSLATION AND COMMENTARY

תָּא שְׁמַע [1]**Come and hear** another proof from a Baraita (quoted above, 27a): "The Torah used the additional example of an ass to teach us that **an ass should be returned** even though the owner's claim is **based** only **on the identifying marks on the saddle.**" The Gemara established above that this law was derived from the word "ass" appearing in the verse (Deuteronomy 22:3). Hence it would seem that identifying marks are valid by Torah law.

אֵימָא [2]The Gemara answers: The text of this Baraita is not certain. It should be amended to **say:** "An ass should be returned **on the basis of** the evidence of **witnesses** who testify **to the ownership of the saddle.**" In other words, if there are witnesses who recognize the saddle and know to whom it belongs, the ass too can be returned on the basis of their testimony. Thus this Baraita, in its amended form, offers no solution to our problem.

תָּא שְׁמַע [3]**Come and hear** a proof from another Baraita (Sifrei, *Tetze* 223): "The Torah says (Deuteronomy 22:2): **'And it** [a lost article being looked after by its finder] **shall be with you until your brother seeks after it.'** The plain meaning of this verse would seem to be that the finder must look after lost property until its owner comes to claim it. [4]On this the Sages comment: **But would it enter your mind that** the finder **should give it to** the owner **before he claims it?** How is the finder supposed to know to whom to give it? [5]**Rather,** we must interpret this verse differently, since the verb used here, *lidrosh* (לִדְרוֹשׁ), has several meanings. Even though it appears to mean 'to claim' in this verse, we should understand it **as meaning** 'to examine.' Thus the Torah is instructing the finder not to accept a claim at face value, but rather to **examine** the claimant **to see if he is a fraud or not."** Thus the Baraita understands the verse as saying that the finder must examine the credibility of the claimant, but it does not specify how this examination should be conducted. [6]The Gemara now analyzes the Baraita: How should this examination by the finder be carried out? **Is** the Torah **not** insisting that the examination of the claimant's veracity be carried out **by** his citing **identifying marks** on the article he claims is his? If this interpretation by the Baraita of the Torah text is correct, it provides a clear source for the validity of identifying marks by Torah law.

לֹא בְּעֵדִים [7]The Gemara answers: **No,** the Baraita is referring to an examination of the claimant **by means of witnesses.** It is possible that by Torah law the finder is not permitted to return a lost object solely on the basis of identifying marks cited by the claimant, but must insist that witnesses testify to the claimant's ownership. Thus the validity of identifying marks may be only of Rabbinic authority.

[1]תָּא שְׁמַע: ״חֲמוֹר בְּסִימָנֵי אוּכָּף״!
[2]אֵימָא: ״בְּעֵדֵי אוּכָּף״.
[3]תָּא שְׁמַע: ״׳וְהָיָה עִמְּךָ עַד דְּרֹשׁ אָחִיךָ אֹתוֹ׳. [4]וְכִי תַּעֲלֶה עַל דַּעְתְּךָ שֶׁיִּתְּנֶנּוּ לוֹ קוֹדֶם שֶׁיִּדְרְשֶׁנּוּ? [5]אֶלָּא, דָּרְשֵׁהוּ אִם רַמַּאי הוּא אוֹ אֵינוֹ רַמַּאי״.
[6]מַאי לָאו בְּסִימָנִין?
[7]לֹא, בְּעֵדִים.

LITERAL TRANSLATION

[1]Come [and] hear: "An ass [is returned] on the basis of identifying marks on the saddle."

[2]Say: "On the basis of witnesses [to the ownership] of the saddle."

[3]Come [and] hear: "'And it shall be with you until your brother seeks after it.' [4]But would it enter your mind that he should give it to him before he seeks after it? [5]Rather, [it means:] examine him [to see] if he is a fraud or not a fraud."

[6]Is this not by means of identifying marks?

[7]No, by means of witnesses.

RASHI

תא שמע – דאוקמינן לעיל ״חמור״ לסימני אוכף אתא. **אימא בעדי אוכף** – אם יש עדים המכירין בטביעות עין לאוכף שהוא שלו – מחזירין לו את החמור. **דרשהו** – והכי משמע ״עד דרוש אחיך אותו״ – עד דרשך את אחיך. **בעדים** – שיבא עדים שהוא שלו.

BACKGROUND

אֵימָא בְּעֵדֵי אוּכָּף Say: On the basis of witnesses to the ownership of the saddle. Since the main idea of the Halakhic Midrash is that it is permitted to rely not only upon identification of the lost object itself, but also upon the identification of something associated with the object or attached to it (in the way that a saddle is attached to an ass), identifying marks on the saddle are certainly sufficient evidence for returning both the saddle and the ass, according to the ordinance of the Sages. But for the purpose of absolutely positive identification, witnesses are needed.

NOTES

דָּרְשֵׁהוּ אִם רַמַּאי הוּא Examine him to see if he is a fraud. This does not mean that the Torah requires the claimant to bring character witnesses. Rather, it means that the finder should not accept at face value a claim to ownership of the article he has found. He should insist on some kind of proof — identifying marks or witnesses. The investigation of the claimant's character (see below, 28b) is only a Rabbinic institution (*Rid, Rosh*).

לֹא בְּעֵדִים No, by means of witnesses. Our commentary follows *Rashi*, who explains that, if it were not for the word דרש, interpreted here as "to examine," we might have thought that a finder should surrender the lost object to

HALAKHAH

by *Bet Shmuel*). Inferior identifying marks (סִימָנִים גְּרוּעִים), suggesting identity but not proving it (e.g., a claim that a bill of divorce or corpse was larger or smaller than average), are of no value in determining whether or not to permit a woman to remarry. If her decision to remarry was based on such evidence, she must be divorced." (Based on *Shulḥan Arukh, Even HaEzer* 17:24; 132:4.)

TRANSLATION AND COMMENTARY

תָּא שְׁמַע [1]**Come and hear** a proof from a Mishnah (*Yevamot* 120a) which deals with the identification by witnesses of a corpse. Conclusive identification of a woman's deceased husband is necessary in order to grant her permission to remarry. The Mishnah rules as follows: **"Witnesses may testify** that they definitely know that a man is dead **only if they have seen the entire face with the nose** intact and have recognized it. But if the witnesses cannot identify the face, their testimony cannot be accepted as conclusive identification, **even though** they do recognize **identifying marks on** the corpse's **body or on his clothes."** [2]The Gemara now suggests that we can **conclude from this that identifying marks are not valid by Torah law,** since we see that we do not rely on them in order to release a woman from the prohibition against her remarrying.

אָמְרִי [3]The Gemara answers that the point of the Mishnah in *Yevamot* is to distinguish between vague identifying marks and definitive ones, not to disqualify all identifying marks: **We can say:** Definitive identifying marks are a valid means of identification by Torah law, but the Mishnah in *Yevamot* is referring only to vague, inconclusive marks which are not acceptable. Thus, when the Mishnah refuses to accept the witnesses' testimony **regarding** identifying marks on **the body,** it is referring to such general **identifying marks** as **tall or short.** Such descriptions are not specific enough to be considered valid means of identifying a corpse.

[1]תָּא שְׁמַע: ״אֵין מְעִידִין אֶלָּא עַל פַּרְצוּף הַפָּנִים עִם הַחוֹטֶם, אַף עַל פִּי שֶׁיֵּשׁ סִימָנִין בְּגוּפוֹ וּבְכֵלָיו״. [2]שְׁמַע מִינָּהּ: סִימָנִין לָאו דְּאוֹרַיְיתָא. [3]אָמְרִי: גּוּפוֹ, דְּאָרוֹךְ וְגוּץ.

LITERAL TRANSLATION

[1]Come [and] hear: "[Witnesses] may not testify except on [their having seen] the [entire] face with the nose, even though there are identifying marks on his body or on his clothes." [2]Conclude from this [that] identifying marks are not [valid] by Torah law.

[3]We can say: [Regarding] his body, [the identifying marks were] that he was tall or short.

RASHI

אין מעידין – על אדם שמת להשיא את אשתו אלא אם כן ראו פרצוף פניו שהוא עם החוטם. דארוך או גוץ – שאין זה סימן שהרבה ארוכין וגוצים יש.

BACKGROUND

אֶלָּא עַל פַּרְצוּף הַפָּנִים **Except on their having seen the entire face....** People do not recognize each other because of specific identifying marks, but rather on the basis of general recognition (טְבִיעוּת עַיִן), which depends on many particulars that a person cannot define with certainty. Positive identification of a person is made on the basis of his face, and for that purpose the Sages determined that one must be able to see the entire face, including the nose, because the nose is a very important feature in recognizing a person. If someone's nose is changed or destroyed, his whole face is changed, and he can no longer be identified with absolute certainty.

NOTES

anyone claiming to be its owner, and not concern himself with precise verification. The Torah, therefore, instructs the finder to investigate the claim of the putative owner. The Gemara suggests that the verse may be a Scriptural source for the acceptability of identifying marks, but notes that it is also possible that the Torah requires the finder to demand witnesses to the claimant's ownership before surrendering what he has found.

Other Rishonim reject this interpretation, considering it obvious that a finder cannot discharge himself of his responsibilities without being reasonably certain of the veracity of the putative owner's claim. If it were not for the word דְּרשׁ, interpreted as "to examine," we might have thought that a finder should not surrender the lost object to anyone without insisting that he bring witnesses in support of his claim. But by the inclusion of the word דְּרשׁ the Torah authorizes the finder to accept a less exacting standard of proof. The verse would appear to be a Scriptural source for the acceptability of identifying marks, but the Gemara notes that it is also possible that the Torah is authorizing the finder to accept less precise evidence on the part of witnesses.

Ba'al HaMaor suggests that the Gemara is referring to character witnesses, who testify that the claimant is a Talmudic Sage whose word is accepted if he claims to recognize the article.

Ramban suggests that the Gemara is referring to witnesses who testify that the claimant purchased or made the lost article, but do not know whether it still belonged to him at the time of the loss.

אֵין מְעִידִין אֶלָּא עַל פַּרְצוּף הַפָּנִים עִם הַחוֹטֶם **Witnesses may not testify except on their having seen the entire face with the nose.** The Aharonim have devoted much discussion to the attempt to discover inherent differences between ritual and monetary matters. One suggestion is that higher standards are demanded to disprove an established legal presumption (חֲזָקָה) than to resolve a question which is entirely in doubt. To use the present examples, the legal presumption is that a married woman is not divorced, and a living person is not dead, until proven otherwise. Hence, the standard of proof required to reverse that presumption must have the full weight of Torah law. By contrast, we have no legal presumptions regarding the ownership of a found article, and the less exacting standards demanded by the Rabbis are sufficient to resolve the issue (*Noda BiYehudah* and others).

HALAKHAH

פַּרְצוּף הַפָּנִים וְחוֹטֶם **An entire face including the nose.** "If a corpse of man is found with the face, including the nose, intact, and witnesses recognize it and identify it positively, they can testify that the man is dead, and this testimony is sufficient to permit the widow to remarry." (*Shulhan Arukh, Even HaEzer* 17:24.)

סִימָנִים בִּבְגָדִים **Identifying marks on clothes.** "If the witnesses cannot positively identify the corpse itself, because the face is no longer recognizable, but are able to identify the clothes on the corpse beyond the shadow of a doubt, they cannot testify that the wife's husband is dead, because we take into account the possibility that the deceased may have borrowed these clothes from the woman's husband." (Ibid.)

TRANSLATION AND COMMENTARY

[1]When the Mishnah refuses to accept witnesses' testimony **regarding** the corpse's **clothes, it is because** even unmistakable marks on clothing are no proof of the corpse's identity, since **we are concerned about** the possibility that the dead man may have **borrowed** the clothes and that they did not belong to him at all. Thus, even if identifying marks are valid by Torah law, and we accept the evidence of the witnesses that these clothes belonged to the deceased, we do not permit the widow to remarry on the basis of this evidence, because it is possible that the husband lent the clothes to someone else and that the other person is the deceased.

אִי חָיְישִׁינַן לִשְׁאֵלָה [2]The Gemara now objects to this argument: **If we** reject identifying marks on clothes and the like because we **are concerned about** the possibility **that they were borrowed, how can we return an ass on the basis of identifying marks on the saddle?** We assumed earlier that the owner of the saddle was definitely the owner of the ass. Is it not possible that the owner of the saddle lent his saddle to the owner of the ass? The ass and the saddle were lost, and now the owner of the saddle, who clearly recognizes it, is taking advantage of the situation to claim the ass as well.

אָמְרִי [3]The Gemara answers: **We can say:** The case of a **saddle is different. People do not borrow saddles, because** saddles are individually made to fit a specific animal, and a borrowed saddle tends to **lacerate the ass's back.**

אִיבָּעֵית אֵימָא [4]The Gemara now offers an alternative explanation as to why identifying marks on clothes are not conclusive proof of a corpse's identity: **If you wish,** you can **say** as follows: We do not need to use the argument that we suspect the clothes were borrowed. There is a different reason why the marks on the clothes were not a valid means of identification. It is because they were vague and inconclusive. Thus, when the Mishnah refuses to accept the witnesses' testimony **regarding** the corpse's **clothes,** it is because **the identification** was very vague and merely **referred to** the clothes being **white or red.** Since it is possible that other people wore clothes of the same color, these means of identification are not specific enough to be valid.

אֶלָּא הָא דְּתַנְיָא [5]The Gemara now returns to the question whether we reject marks on articles of clothing as a means of identification, because we suspect that they were borrowed, and asks: **But what about the** statement made in the **following Baraita** (*Yevamot* 120a): **"If** the husband's agent lost a bill of divorce that he was instructed to deliver to the husband's wife, and subsequently **found it tied to his pouch or to his moneybag,**

[1]כֵּלָיו, דְּחָיְישִׁינַן לִשְׁאֵלָה.
[2]אִי חָיְישִׁינַן לִשְׁאֵלָה, חֲמוֹר בְּסִימָנֵי אוּכָּף הֵיכִי מְהַדְּרִינַן?
[3]אָמְרִי: אוּכָּף, לָא שְׁאוּלֵי אֱינָשֵׁי אוּכָּפָא, מִשּׁוּם דְּמְסַקֵּב לֵיהּ לַחֲמָרָא.
[4]אִיבָּעֵית אֵימָא: כֵּלָיו, בְּחִיוָּרֵי וּבְסוּמָקֵי.
[5]אֶלָּא הָא דְּתַנְיָא: "מְצָאוֹ קָשׁוּר בְּכִיס אוֹ בְּאַרְנָקִי וּבְטַבַּעַת,

LITERAL TRANSLATION

[1][Regarding] his clothes, [it is] because we are concerned about borrowing.

[2]If we are concerned about borrowing, how can we return an ass on the basis of identifying marks on the saddle?

[3]We can say: A saddle [is different]. People do not borrow a saddle, because it lacerates the ass's [back].

[4]If you wish, say: [Regarding] his clothes, [the identification referred] to white or red.

[5]But [what about] this that has been taught: "[If] he found it tied to a pouch, or to a moneybag, or to a ring,

RASHI

כליו – בגדיו. **חיישינן** – שמא השאילם לאחר, ואותו אחר הוא שמת. **מסקב** – *דורוי״ש בלע״ז. **חיורי או סומקי** – אין זה סימן, שהרבה כאלה יש. **מצאו קשור בכיס שלו או בארנקי כו׳** – שליח המביא גט ואבד הימנו, לאחר זמן מצאו קשור בכיס שלו או בארנקי כו׳.

LANGUAGE

מִשּׁוּם דִּמְסַקֵּב לֵיהּ לַחֲמָרָא Because it lacerates the ass's back. The root סקב is an Aramaic one which may be connected with the Hebrew root סגף — "to mortify" — although some scholars have suggested that it is related to the Latin verb *scabo*, to scratch or rub. The verb סקב means to wound by scraping and pressure. An animal's saddle must fit its back well, for if it is too narrow or too wide, it scrapes the animal's skin, leading to saddle-sores.

LANGUAGE (RASHI)

***דורוויי״ש** From the Old French *redoisier*, meaning "causing sores by friction."

REALIA

טַבַּעַת Ring.

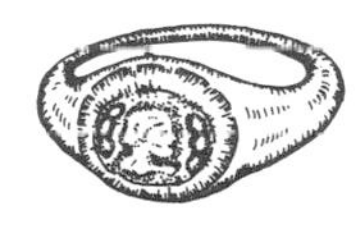

A gold ring with a jewel seal on it, from Pompeii during the Mishnaic period.

In antiquity, most rings contained seals, which were used by their owners to ratify various documents. It was uncommon for a person to lend his seal to anyone else, since to do so was tantamount to granting power of attorney (see Esther 3:10).

NOTES

חָיְישִׁינַן לִשְׁאֵלָה We suspect borrowing. The Rishonim ask: If we accept this principle, how can any lost article ever be returned? Should we not suspect that it was borrowed and the borrower is claiming to be the owner? They explain that in practice we are not concerned with this rather remote possibility, except in the realm of ritual law, where a higher standard of certainty is required. (In fact, the Halakhic literature deals extensively with this problem in relation to the identification of corpses.) For the purposes of deciding monetary questions, we can allay this concern with the argument that only the person who lost the article will know that it was lost and seek to claim it. Furthermore, it is unlikely that the borrower of an article will know the signs with which it can be identified (*Ramban, Rashba* and others).

חֲמוֹר בְּסִימָנֵי אוּכָּף Returning an ass on the basis of identifying marks on the saddle. The Rishonim ask: Why does the Gemara base the question about returning an unmarked object attached to a marked object on the case of the ass and the saddle, which is not expressly mentioned

HALAKHAH

קָשׁוּר בְּכִיס אוֹ בְּאַרְנָקִי Tied to a pouch or to a moneybag. "If someone finds a lost bill of divorce tied to an object that can be positively identified, this is considered positive identification of the bill of divorce, provided that the object is of a type never lent to other people. Such a bill of divorce is considered valid." (Ibid., 132:4.)

TRANSLATION AND COMMENTARY

or to his ring, [1]or if he found it among his articles at home, even if he found it a long time after he lost it, the bill of divorce is valid. We do not suspect that the bill of divorce was exchanged by mistake for another one containing the same details, and thus that the one found was not written expressly for this couple. [2]But, the Gemara asks, if it should enter your mind that we are concerned about the possibility that an article may have been borrowed, then why is the bill of divorce valid when the agent found it tied to his pouch or some other object belonging to him? [3]Surely we should be concerned about the possibility that the pouch or other object had been borrowed by someone else, that the borrower may have tied this bill of divorce to it, and that both of them were returned together by mistake to the agent.

אָמְרִי [4]The Gemara answers: In reply to this objection we can say that pouches, moneybags and rings are exceptions, because people do not generally lend them out. [5]The reasons for this are as follows: (1) A pouch and a moneybag are not usually lent by people because they are superstitious. In Talmudic times there was a prevalent superstition that if a person gave or lent his moneybag to someone else, it was as if he was giving away his luck. [6](2) A person does not lend his signet ring to anyone, because of the danger that the other person may use it to forge his personal seal.

לֵימָא כְּתַנָּאֵי [7]Until this point in the discussion, the Gemara has been unable to reach a conclusion as to whether identifying marks are valid by Torah law or by Rabbinic decree. It now suggests that this question was already the subject of a difference of opinion during the Tannaitic period: Shall we say that this problem concerning identifying marks is in fact the same as the dispute between Tannaim recorded in a Baraita (*Yevamot* 120a), in connection with the laws concerning identification of corpses? The Baraita is as follows: "Witnesses may not testify to a man's death if their identification is based solely on a mole that they recognized on the corpse, because such evidence is not definitive enough to establish the man's identity and to permit his wife to remarry. [8]But Elazar ben Mehavai says: Witnesses may testify to a man's death, even if their identification

[1]אוֹ שֶׁמְּצָאוֹ בֵּין כֵּלָיו, אֲפִילּוּ לִזְמַן מְרוּבֶּה, כָּשֵׁר. [2]וְאִי סָלְקָא דַּעְתָּךְ חָיְישִׁינַן לִשְׁאֵלָה, כִּי מְצָאוֹ קָשׁוּר בְּכִיס, אַמַּאי כָּשֵׁר? [3]נֵיחוּשׁ לִשְׁאֵלָה! [4]אָמְרִי: כִּיס וְאַרְנְקִי וְטַבַּעַת לָא מַשְׁאֲלִי אֱינָשֵׁי. [5]כִּיס וְאַרְנְקִי, מִשּׁוּם דִּמְסַמְּנִי, [6]וְטַבַּעַת, מִשּׁוּם דִּמְזַיֵּיף. [7]לֵימָא כְּתַנָּאֵי: "אֵין מְעִידִין עַל הַשּׁוּמָא. [8]וְאֶלְעָזָר בֶּן מַהֲבַאי אוֹמֵר: מְעִידִין עַל הַשּׁוּמָא".

LITERAL TRANSLATION

[1]or if he found it among his articles, even after a long time, it is valid." [2]But if it should enter your mind [that] we are concerned about borrowing, when he found it tied to a pouch, why is it valid? [3]Let us be concerned about borrowing!

[4]We can say: A pouch and a moneybag and a ring — people do not lend. [5]A pouch and a moneybag, because they are superstitious, [6]and a ring, because one can forge [with it]. [7]Shall we say [this problem is] like [the following dispute between] Tannaim: "[Witnesses] may not testify on [the basis of] a mole. [8]But Elazar ben Mehavai says: [Witnesses] may testify on [the basis of] a mole."

RASHI

בין כליו — כלי תשמישו שבביתו. אפילו לזמן מרובה — אף על גב דתנן (גיטין כז,א): המביא גט ואבד הימנו מצאו לזמן מרובה — פסול, הכא כשר. ניחוש לשאלה — שמא השאיל כיסו לאחר, והוא קשרו בו. דמסמני — מנחשי, ואומר סימן לאדם שמשאיל כיסו שמוכר לו מזלו. דמזייף — שהיה לכל איש חותם ניכר בטבעתו, וכשאלת שום דבר סתום מכסהו וחותמו בטבעתו, לפיכך אינו משאיל טבעתו, שמא יעשה זה חותם כנגד חותמו ויזייף בו את שליחותיו. אין מעידין על השומא — המעידין על האשה להשיאה, ואמרו: סימן היה בו, שומא באבר פלוני. שומא — *וורוא״ה בלעז.

BACKGROUND

אֵין מְעִידִין עַל הַשּׁוּמָא **Witnesses may not testify on the basis of a mole.** The discussion as to whether a mole in a certain place on a person's body or face may be regarded as a definitive identifying mark is not pursued in all its details here. Without doubt, certain moles look so distinctive that they may well be regarded as definitive identifying marks. But an ordinary mole is not so uncommon, and if one is found in a particular place on a person's body, it is nevertheless not regarded as a definitive identifying mark.

LANGUAGE (RASHI)

וורוא״ה* From the Old French *vorrue,* meaning "mole" or "wart."

NOTES

anywhere in the primary Tannaitic sources? Why does it not ask this question in connection with the Mishnah (above, 24b) which rules that unmarked fruit in a marked container is to be returned, even though a fruit container is far more likely to have been borrowed than a saddle?

Rashba and others answer: The suspicion of borrowing is farfetched, and there is no doubt that it is to be ignored in practice, at least by Rabbinic decree. Hence, the Mishnah may simply be reflecting the practical Halakhah, and may not be relevant to the question of whether this Halakhah is Scriptural or Rabbinic in origin. The case of the ass's saddle, by contrast, is based on the exegesis of a Biblical verse and clearly shows that the Torah itself dismissed the suspicion of the saddle having been borrowed.

HALAKHAH

שׁוּמָא **A mole.** "A mole is not a definitive identifying mark leaving no room for doubt, and cannot be used to identify a body and permit a wife to remarry." (*Shulḥan Arukh, Even HaEzer* 17:24.) It is, however, a valid ordinary mark. (*Bet Shmuel,* following *Rambam.*)

[1] מַאי לָאו בְּהָא קָמִיפַּלְגִי: [2] דְּתַנָּא קַמָּא סָבַר: סִימָנִין דְּרַבָּנַן, [3] וְאֶלְעָזָר בֶּן מְהַבַאי סָבַר: סִימָנִין דְּאוֹרַיְיתָא? [4] אֲמַר רָבָא: דְּכוּלֵּי עָלְמָא סִימָנִין דְּאוֹרַיְיתָא, [5] וְהָכָא בְּשׁוּמָא מְצוּיָה בְּבֶן גִּילוֹ קָמִיפַּלְגִי. [6] מָר סָבַר: שׁוּמָא מְצוּיָה בְּבֶן גִּילוֹ. [7] וּמָר סָבַר: שׁוּמָא אֵינָהּ מְצוּיָה בְּבֶן גִּילוֹ. [8] אִיבָּעֵית אֵימָא: דְּכוּלֵּי עָלְמָא שׁוּמָא אֵינָהּ מְצוּיָה בְּבֶן גִּילוֹ. [9] וְהָכָא בְּסִימָנִין הָעֲשׂוּיִן לְהִשְׁתַּנּוֹת לְאַחַר מִיתָה קָמִיפַּלְגִי. [10] מָר סָבַר: סִימָנִין עֲשׂוּיִם לְהִשְׁתַּנּוֹת לְאַחַר מִיתָה. [11] וּמָר סָבַר: סִימָנִין אֵין עֲשׂוּיִם לְהִשְׁתַּנּוֹת לְאַחַר מִיתָה.

LITERAL TRANSLATION

[1] Is it not that they disagree about this: [2] That the first Tanna is of the opinion [that] identifying marks are [valid] by Rabbinic decree, [3] and Elazar ben Mehavai is of the opinion [that] identifying marks are [valid] by Torah law?

[4] Rava said: It is [the view] of everyone [that] identifying marks are [valid] by Torah law, [5] but here they differ about [whether a similar] mole [could be] found on another person born under the same star (lit., "a son of his circle"). [6] [One] Sage is of the opinion [that a similar] mole [could be] found on another person born under the same star. [7] And [the other] Sage is of the opinion [that a similar] mole is not [likely to be] found on another person born under the same star.

[8] If you wish, say: It is [the view] of everyone [that a similar] mole is not [likely to be] found on another person born under the same star, [9] but here they differ about [whether] identifying marks are liable to change after death. [10] [One] Sage is of the opinion [that] identifying marks are liable to change after death. [11] And [the other] Sage is of the opinion [that] identifying marks are not liable to change after death.

TRANSLATION AND COMMENTARY

is based solely **on a mole** that they recognized on the corpse." [1] The Gemara now elaborates the arguments of the two parties to the dispute: **Is it not** the case **that** the two Tannaim **are in disagreement about the following** issue? [2] **The first Tanna is of the opinion that** moles cannot be used as a means of identifying a corpse, because **identifying marks are valid** only **by Rabbinic decree.** Such marks can, therefore, be used in deciding monetary matters, but not in matters involving Torah prohibitions. [3] On the other hand, **Elazar ben Mehavai is of the opinion that identifying marks are valid by Torah law** and can be used as evidence in all cases.

אֲמַר רָבָא [4] The Gemara now rejects this attempt to interpret the dispute between the first Tanna and Elazar ben Mehavai as being based on the question of whether identifying marks are valid by Torah law or not. It gives three alternative answers: (1) **Rava said:** There is another way to interpret the Baraita. It is possible that **everyone** — both the first Tanna and Elazar ben Mehavai — **agrees that identifying marks are valid by Torah law** and can be used as evidence even in cases like this one, involving serious problems of personal status. [5] **But here,** where the identifying mark is a mole, the Tannaim **differ over whether** or not we should be concerned about the widely held belief that **a similar mole is likely to be found on another person born under the same star** as the dead man. [6] The first **Sage is of the opinion that a similar mole is likely to be found on another person born under the same star** as the dead man. Hence moles cannot be relied on as a valid means of identification. [7] Whereas **the other Sage,** Elazar ben Mehavai, **is of the opinion that a similar mole is not likely to be found on another person born under the same star** as the dead man. In his view, such a possibility is remote and need not be taken into consideration, and thus moles can be relied on as a valid means of identification.

אִיבָּעֵית אֵימָא [8] The Gemara now offers another possible explanation: (2) **If you wish,** you can **say** that it is possible that **everyone** — both the first Tanna and Elazar ben Mehavai — **agrees that a similar mole is not likely to be found on another person born under the same star** as the dead man, and that everyone also agrees that moles, like all other identifying marks, are perfectly valid as evidence of identity even by Torah law. [9] **But here,** where the problem is the identification of a corpse, the Tannaim **differ over whether** or not we should be concerned about the possibility that moles and other similar **identifying marks are liable to change** in appearance **after death.** [10] The first **Sage is of the opinion that identifying marks are liable to change after death** and cannot therefore serve as the basis for identifying a corpse. [11] However, **the other Sage,** Elazar ben Mehavai, **is of the opinion that identifying marks are not liable to change after death** to the point where they are no longer recognizable. Hence moles may be relied on as a means of identification.

RASHI

סימנין דרבנן – וגבי אשת איש, דאיסור דאורייתא הוא – לא סמכינן עלייהו. בבן גילו – הנולד בשעתו, שנולדו במזל אחד. בסימנין העשוין כו' – אם עשוין להשתנות או אינן עשוין להשתנות, אם בחייו היתה שומא שחורה – במותו נעשית לבנה, או איפוך.

BACKGROUND

בֶּן גִּילוֹ Born under the same star. This phrase, which literally means someone of the same age, refers to two people born under the same astrological sign, at exactly the same moment, who are extremely similar to each other. In various areas of the Halakhah, two people born under the same astrological sign are regarded as being very similar, indeed almost identical, to each other. The question raised here is whether the similarity between two people born under the same star is merely a general similarity or whether one can assume that it also includes small details such as the presence of a mole. Relatives often have moles in exactly the same place on their bodies, and two people born under the same star are considered, to a certain degree, to be doubles, similar in almost every detail.

LITERAL TRANSLATION

[1]If you wish, say: It is [the view] of everyone [that] a mole is not liable to change after death, [2]and identifying marks are [valid only] by Rabbinic decree, [3]but here they differ about [whether] a mole is a definitive identifying mark. [4][One] Sage is of the opinion [that] a mole is a definitive identifying mark. [5]And [the other] Sage is of the opinion [that] a mole is not a definitive identifying mark.

[6]Rava said: If you say [that] identifying marks are not [valid] by Torah law, [7]how [can we] return a lost object on the basis of identifying marks? [8]Because it is advantageous to the finder of a lost object that he return [it] on the basis of identifying marks, [9]so that when he himself loses [something], they will also return [it] to him on the basis of identifying marks.

[10]Rav Safra said to Rava: But may a person do himself a favor with money that is not his?

[11]Rather, it is advantageous to the owner of a lost object

[1]אִיבָּעֵית אֵימָא: דְּכוּלֵּי עָלְמָא שׁוּמָא אֵינָהּ עֲשׂוּיָה לְהִשְׁתַּנּוֹת לְאַחַר מִיתָה, [2]וְסִימָנִין דְּרַבָּנַן, [3]וְהָכָא בְּשׁוּמָא סִימָן מוּבְהָק הוּא קָמִיפַּלְגִי. [4]מָר סָבַר: שׁוּמָא סִימָן מוּבְהָק הוּא. [5]וּמָר סָבַר: שׁוּמָא לָאו סִימָן מוּבְהָק הוּא.

[6]אָמַר רָבָא: אִם תִּמְצֵי לוֹמַר סִימָנִין לָאו דְּאוֹרַיְיתָא, [7]הֵיכִי מְהַדְּרִינַן אֲבֵידְתָא בְּסִימָנִין? [8]דְּנִיחָא לֵיהּ לְמוֹצֵא אֲבֵידָה דְּנֶהֱדַר בְּסִימָנִין, [9]כִּי הֵיכִי דְּכִי אָבְדָה לֵיהּ לְדִידֵיהּ, נַמִי נֶהֶדְרוּ לֵיהּ בְּסִימָנִין.

[10]אֲמַר לֵיהּ רַב סָפְרָא לְרָבָא: וְכִי אָדָם עוֹשֶׂה טוֹבָה לְעַצְמוֹ בְּמָמוֹן שֶׁאֵינוֹ שֶׁלּוֹ?

[11]אֶלָּא, נִיחָא לֵיהּ לְבַעַל אֲבֵידָה

RASHI

מובהק – ואפילו סימנין דרבנן, יש לסמוך על זה. היכי מהדרינן – כלומר, מה תקנה ראו חכמים בדבר ליכנס בספק להחזיר ממון למי שאינו שלו? אלא – לא גרסינן. וכי אדם עושה – ובניחותא דמולא מאי איכפת לן, אם מי שאבדה ממנו לא ניחא ליה. אלא – אמר רבא: כל אובדי אבידה ניחא להו שתהא דת זו בישראל

TRANSLATION AND COMMENTARY

אִיבָּעֵית אֵימָא [1]The Gemara's first two explanations have been based on the assumption that both Tannaim accept the validity of identifying marks by Torah law. It now offers a third possible explanation, based on the opposite assumption: (3) **If you wish,** you can **say** that it is possible that **everyone** — both the first Tanna and Elazar ben Mehavai — **agrees that** an identifying mark such as a **mole is not liable to change after death,** [2]**and** that **identifying marks** in general **are valid only by Rabbinic decree.** [3]**But here,** where the identifying mark is a mole, the Tannaim **differ over whether** or not **a mole is a definitive identifying mark,** which is relied upon even in matters involving Torah prohibitions. [4]**One Sage,** Elazar ben Mehavai, **is of the opinion that a mole is a definitive identifying mark,** and no one disputes that we may rely on definitive identifying marks, even in matters involving Torah prohibitions, and even if the validity of ordinary marks is not of Scriptural origin. [5]However, **the first Sage is of the opinion that a mole is not a definitive identifying mark,** and, like other ordinary marks, cannot be relied upon in matters involving Torah prohibitions, such as the laws of personal status.

אָמַר רָבָא [6]The problem of whether identifying marks have Torah validity or not has still not been solved by the Gemara, and the suggestion that this problem is itself the subject of dispute among the Tannaim has been rejected. Continuing the discussion on the status of identifying marks, **Rava** now asks himself the following rhetorical question: **If you assume that identifying marks are not valid by Torah law** and maintain that by Torah law witnesses are required in order to prove ownership, [7]**how can** the Sages have decided that **we** are permitted to **return a lost object on the basis of identifying marks** to a person who is not necessarily its owner? It is true that the Sages had the authority to accept the validity of identifying marks, but surely they would not — without very good reason — use their authority to institute a practice that carried with it the danger of a miscarriage of justice. [8]Rava answers his own question: In instituting this practice, the Sages were promoting the welfare of the parties involved, **because it is to the advantage of the finder of a lost object** that we take it away from him and insist **that he return it** to the person who claims to be its owner **on the basis of identifying marks.** [9]The advantage to the finder lies in the fact **that if he himself** ever **loses something, it will also be returned to *him* on the basis of identifying marks.**

אֲמַר לֵיהּ [10]**Rav Safra** disagreed with this argument, and **said to Rava: But may a person do himself a favor with property that is not his?** The finder of the lost object may indeed be satisfied with this arrangement, but his views are immaterial since the article is not his. Surely we should be equally concerned for the welfare of the owner of the property, and he may not be satisfied with this arrangement.

אֶלָּא [11]**Rather,** says Rava, it is necessary to modify the explanation I have just given: **It is to the advantage of the owner of a lost object to** accept the Sages' decree that whoever can **cite identifying marks** is entitled **to**

SAGES

רַב סָפְרָא **Rav Safra.** A Babylonian Amora of the third and fourth generations. See *Bava Metzia*, Part I, p. 244.

BACKGROUND

שׁוּמָא אֵינָהּ עֲשׂוּיָה לְהִשְׁתַּנּוֹת לְאַחַר מִיתָה **A mole is not liable to change after death.** Problems of identifying bodies generally arise when a corpse is found which has undergone change because of things that have happened to it (wounds, burns, and the like). There is also a natural process of change which takes place when parts of the body decay. In such cases doubt arises as to whether the color and shape of a mole remain constant, and to what degree one may attribute its appearance to changes that have taken place after death.

דְּנִיחָא לֵיהּ לְמוֹצֵא אֲבֵידָה **Because it is advantageous to the finder of a lost object....** If we assume that the return of a lost object on the basis of identifying marks is a Rabbinic ordinance, this ordinance must be based on the general benefit it confers on the public. Rava's explanation is based on the assumption that people generally agree to accept inconclusive proof because to do so is ultimately beneficial to everyone. Indeed, in various areas of the Halakhah the Sages base their ordinances upon commonly accepted mutual agreement among residents of a certain place or members of a certain profession.

וְכִי אָדָם עוֹשֶׂה טוֹבָה לְעַצְמוֹ בְּמָמוֹן שֶׁאֵינוֹ שֶׁלּוֹ **But may a person do himself a favor with money that is not his?** Rava's first explanation is that the Rabbinical ordinance regarding identifying marks is based on general agreement among people who find things: a finder is prepared to waive his right to acquire the object (since, were it not for the identifying marks, the object would belong to him) in order to benefit from this kind of inconclusive proof himself when the time comes. Rabbi Safra argues against this that the agreement of the finder cannot be the reason

לְמֵיהַב סִימָנִין וּלְמִשְׁקְלֵיהּ. [1]מֵידַע יָדַע דְּעֵדִים לֵית לֵיהּ, [2]וּמֵימַר אָמַר: ״כּוּלֵּי עָלְמָא לָא יָדְעִי סִימָנִין מוּבְהָקִים דִּידָהּ, [3]וַאֲנָא יָהֵיבְנָא סִימָנִין מוּבְהָקִים דִּידָהּ וּשְׁקַלְנָא לָהּ״.

[4]אֶלָּא הָא דִּתְנַן: ״רַבָּן שִׁמְעוֹן בֶּן גַּמְלִיאֵל אוֹמֵר: [5]אֶחָד הַלֹּוֶה מִשְּׁלֹשָׁה, יַחֲזִיר לַלֹּוֶה; [6]שְׁלֹשָׁה שֶׁלָּווּ מִן הָאֶחָד, יַחֲזִיר לַמַּלְוֶה״. [7]נִיחָא לֵיהּ לַלֹּוֶה לְאַהֲדוּרֵי לֵיהּ לַמַּלְוֶה?

LITERAL TRANSLATION

to cite identifying marks and to take it. [1]He knows very well that he does not have witnesses, [2]and he surely says: "Everyone does not know its definitive identifying marks, [3]but I can cite its definitive identifying marks and take it."

[4]But [what about] this that we have learned: "Rabban Shimon ben Gamliel said: [5]One who borrowed from three [lenders, the finder] should return [the documents] to the borrower; [6]three who borrowed from one [lender, the finder] should return [the documents] to the lender." [7]Is it advantageous to the borrower that they return [the documents] to the lender?

TRANSLATION AND COMMENTARY

take the lost article without further proof. [1]The advantage to the owner lies in the fact that **he knows very well that** circumstances can easily arise where **he does not have witnesses** available to testify to his ownership, and his only realistic chance of recovering his property is by citing identifying marks. [2]Moreover, the owner of the lost object **surely says** to himself: **"Nobody** else **knows the definitive identifying marks** on the article I have lost, and the finder is unlikely to be fooled into giving my property away to a false claimant. [3]By contrast, I am the only person who **can cite its definitive identifying marks,** since I know it so well, **and take it** back. Therefore, the Sages' decree is to my advantage, since it affords me the best possible chance of recovering my property."

אֶלָּא הָא דִּתְנַן [4]Rava's explanation, as amended by Rav Safra, is that the law requiring a finder to return a lost article on the basis of identifying marks is based on the presumption that this procedure is advantageous to the owner of the article. The Gemara now attacks this explanation by quoting cases where it is to the disadvantage of owners that their lost property be restored, but the Sages nevertheless insisted that this procedure be followed: **But what about** the ruling **that we have learned** in a Mishnah (above, 20a), which states: **"Rabban Shimon ben Gamliel said:** [5]In a case where a person finds three lost promissory notes tied together, if they all record loans drawn up by **one** borrower **who borrowed from three** separate **lenders, the finder should return** all three **documents to the borrower,** since it is reasonable to assume that it was he who lost them. [6]Conversely, if the lost documents record loans drawn up by **three** separate borrowers **who** all **borrowed from one lender, the finder should return** all three **documents to the lender,** since it is reasonable to assume that it was he who lost them." [7]With reference to the second part of this Mishnah, which states that promissory notes must be returned to the lender, the Gemara asks: **Is it to the advantage of the borrower that the promissory note** he has written **be returned to the lender** on the basis of identifying marks? After all, if the borrower has already repaid the loan, then as long as the note is in the possession of the finder, it is worthless. But if we insist that the promissory note is to be returned on the basis of identifying marks, it is possible that the lender may be able to identify it, receive it back, and use it to collect his debt a second time.

RASHI

למיתב סימנין, וכל הבא ונותנו יטלנה, מאי טעמא? מידע ידע דעדים לית ליה, פעמים שאין לו עדים עליה, ואם יזקיקוהו לעדים לא תבא לעולם לידו, ומימר אמר: טוב לי שיחזירוה לכל האומר סימניה, דלא שכיחא דנימא סימנין דידה אלא אנא, דכולי עלמא לא ידעי כו'. **אלא הא דתנן כו'** — ואמרו להחזיר לו למלוה בלא עדים — בסימן זה שאומר שלשה היו, ומשלשה לוים, ואם מן הלוה נפלו שכבר פרעם, מי ניחא ליה בתקנה זו שיתנם המוצאם לכל הבא ונותן סימניהם, והלא טוב לו שיהו מונחים ביד המוצאם עולמית, דכל זמן שהם בידו ולא יחזירם למלוה הרי הם כשרופים, ולא ניחא דליהדר להו בסימנין דלמא מיתרמי דידע מלוה בסימניהן.

NOTES

וַאֲנָא יָהֵיבְנָא סִימָנִין מוּבְהָקִים דִּידָהּ **But I can cite its definitive identifying marks.** The Rishonim note that the expression סִימָנִים מוּבְהָקִים — "definitive identifying marks" — used here does not refer to the highest category of identifying marks (see note, p. 103), as it does in the discussion about the mole. *Rashba* points out that if it were true that owners, and only owners, were able to cite definitve identifying marks, it would be in the interest of the owner that all other marks be invalidated. Rather, the expression must be understood here as referring to ordinary marks. *Rashba* adds that, in fact, most owners are not able to cite definitive identifying marks. *Tosafot* explains that the term "definitive" as used here is a relative one. The owner is confident that even if someone else succeeds in correctly citing one ordinary identifying mark, he, the owner, will be able to cite more and better marks and will convince the finder that he is telling the truth.

here, because the finder does not own the object, and even though the object may ultimately remain in his possession if no proof of ownership is brought, he cannot be viewed as its owner. Rather, he is merely responsible for it until its ownership is determined. Indeed, the view that someone who has lost an object without any identifying marks will give up hope of recovering it presumes that there is an obligation to return lost objects where identifying marks *are* found on them. The finder's agreement to waive continued possession of the object in order to derive some future profit is therefore illegal, and it is certainly not moral, for he may well be depriving the true owner of his property. Therefore, in his revised explanation, Rava states that the general agreement to the ordinance is actually that of the true owners of the lost object. The loser is prepared to take the risk that the finder may deliver it to someone else who is able to cite the correct identifying marks, because in general it will be difficult for the owner to find witnesses to identify the object positively, whereas on the basis of identifying marks he has a good chance of recovering it. Because the loser, the owner of the object, has an interest in maintaining this ordinance, the ordinance may be regarded as reflecting general agreement.

נִיחָא לֵיהּ לַלֹּוֶה **Is it advantageous to the borrower...?** In the light of Rava's explanation that the restoration of a lost object on the basis of its identifying marks is based on the agreement in principle of the person who has lost it, the Gemara now considers cases in which a lost object may be returned even against the wishes of the person who has lost it. In the case of an ordinary lost object the owner is prepared to take the risk that someone else may try to claim it, for his own chances of recovering it are greater than those of anyone else. However, when a borrower loses a promissory note for a loan that has already been repaid, not only does he not have better knowledge of its identifying marks than the lender, who held the note in his possession for a long time, but he is also liable to incur significant loss by its return, for he will have to pay the debt again. If indeed the returning of a lost object on the basis of its identifying marks is based on the agreement of the person who has lost it, in cases like those involving promissory notes he would certainly not agree to it.

[1] אֲמַר לֵיהּ: הָתָם, סְבָרָא הוּא: [2] אֶחָד הַלֹּוֶה מִשְּׁלֹשָׁה, יַחֲזִיר לַלֹּוֶה, [3] דְּגַבֵּי לֹוֶה שְׁכִיחִי, גַּבֵּי מַלְוֶה לָא שְׁכִיחִי. [4] שְׁמַע מִינָּהּ מִלֹּוֶה נְפוּל. [5] שְׁלֹשָׁה שֶׁלָּווּ מֵאֶחָד, יַחֲזִיר לַמַּלְוֶה, [6] דְּגַבֵּי מַלְוֶה שְׁכִיחִי, גַּבֵּי לֹוֶה לָא שְׁכִיחִי.

[28A] [7] אֶלָּא הָא דִּתְנַן: ״מָצָא תַּכְרִיךְ שֶׁל שְׁטָרוֹת אוֹ אֲגוּדָּה שֶׁל שְׁטָרוֹת, הֲרֵי זֶה יַחֲזִיר״. [8] הָכִי נַמִי דְּנִיחָא לֵיהּ לַלֹּוֶה לַאֲהַדּוּרֵי לֵיהּ לַמַּלְוֶה?

[9] אֶלָּא אֲמַר רָבָא: סִימָנִין דְּאוֹרַיְיתָא, [10] דִּכְתִיב: ״וְהָיָה

LITERAL TRANSLATION

[1] He said to him: There, it is a commonsense argument: [2] [In the case of] one who borrowed from three, he should return [them] to the borrower, [3] for they are likely [to be] with the borrower, [and] they are not likely [to be] with the lender. [4] Conclude from this [that] it fell from the borrower. [5] [In the case of] three who borrowed from one, he should return [them] to the lender, [6] for they are likely [to be] with the lender, [and] they are not likely [to be] with the borrower.

[28A] [7] But [what about] this that we have learned: "[If] he found a roll of documents or a bundle of documents, he should return [them]." [8] Here, too, is it advantageous to the borrower that they return [the documents] to the lender?

[9] Rather, Rava said: Identifying marks are [valid] by Torah law, [10] as it is written: "And it shall be

TRANSLATION AND COMMENTARY

אֲמַר לֵיהּ [1] Rava **said** in reply **to** his questioner: **There,** in the case described in the Mishnah, there **is a commonsense argument** why the finder must return the notes to the lender, in addition to the factor of the identifying marks he can cite on the documents. [2] The reasoning in the two parts of the Mishnah is as follows: **In the** first **case,** where the finder found three promissory notes drawn up by **one** borrower **who** had **borrowed from three** separate lenders, **he should return them** all **to the borrower.** [3] **For the likelihood is** that the three notes were lost together by **the borrower** after he had repaid the loans and received the promissory notes back from the lenders, **and it is** most **unlikely** that three such notes were lost at the same time in the same place by **the** three different **lenders** mentioned in them. [4] Hence, it is logical to **conclude that they were lost by the borrower.** [5] On the other hand, **in the** second **case,** where the finder found three promissory notes drawn up by **three** different borrowers **who** had **borrowed from one** lender, **he should return them** all **to the lender,** [6] **for the likelihood is** that the three notes were lost together by **the lender,** whereas **it is** most **unlikely** that three such notes were lost at the same time in the same place by **the** three different **borrowers.** Therefore, common sense dictates that the notes be returned to the lender.

[28A] אֶלָּא הָא דִּתְנַן [7] The Gemara now continues to attack Rava's explanation that the law requiring a finder to return lost property on the basis of identifying marks is based on the presumption that this procedure is advantageous to the owner of the article: **But,** the Gemara asks, **what about** the following ruling **that we have learned** in the same Mishnah (above, 20a) as was just quoted, which states: **"If** a person **found a roll of documents or a bundle of documents, he should return them** to whichever party accurately identifies them." Thus, if it is the lender who is able to identify the documents, they are returned to him. [8] Now, asks the Gemara, will Rava argue that **here, too, it is to the advantage of the borrower that the documents be returned to the lender** on the basis of identifying marks? Surely such an action must be to the borrower's disadvantage, because he may already have repaid the loan. The lender may be able to identify the promissory notes, and may then claim repayment of the loan a second time. In a situation such as this it is obvious that the borrower would prefer to have the promissory notes remain in the possession of the finder indefinitely.

אֶלָּא אֲמַר רָבָא [9] In reply to this objection **Rava** retracted and **said:** The objection is convincing, and I cannot find a logical basis for the argument that identifying marks were instituted by the Rabbis. I am therefore led to the conclusion that **identifying marks are valid by Torah law,** [10] and the source in the Torah from which this

RASHI

התם — בסימנין כי האי לא איכפת לן בניחותא דלוה, דודאי לאו מיניה נפיל, דהנך שטרי אחריני מאי בעו גביה. **אלא הא דתנן מצא תכריך** — דמשום סימנא מהדרינן, ואם נתן מלוה סימן — מחזירין לו, ואי נפול מיניה דלוה מי ניחא ליה דתהוי הך תקנתא דניהדרה בסימן, והא ניחא ליה דנהוו ביד המוצא לעולם.

NOTES

סִימָנִין דְּאוֹרַיְיתָא, דִּכְתִיב **Identifying marks are valid by Torah law, as it is written....** Rava's repetition of the proof from the Sifrei, as well as the Gemara's parenthetical question and answer later on ("If you say?! Surely... as we answered above") present many problems to the commentators. As the Gemara has explained (above, 27b), the proof from the Sifrei is far from conclusive, since it can be explained in two ways: (1) The Sifrei is referring to identifying marks, and such marks are of Torah origin. (2) The Sifrei is referring to witnesses, and identifying marks are a Rabbinic decree. The reason why Rava rejected the idea that identifying marks are a Rabbinic decree was because

עִמְּךָ עַד דְּרֹשׁ אָחִיךָ אֹתוֹ״. [1]וְכִי תַעֲלֶה עַל דַּעְתְּךָ שֶׁיִּתְּנֶנּוּ קוֹדֶם שֶׁיִּדְרְשֶׁנּוּ? [2]אֶלָּא, דָּרְשֵׁהוּ אִם רַמַּאי הוּא אוֹ אֵינוֹ רַמַּאי. [3]לָאו בְּסִימָנִין? [4]שְׁמַע מִינָּהּ.

[5]אֲמַר רָבָא: אִם תִּמְצֵי לוֹמַר סִימָנִין דְּאוֹרַיְיתָא....

[6]״אִם תִּמְצֵי לוֹמַר״?! [7]הָא פָּשֵׁיט לֵיהּ סִימָנִין דְּאוֹרַיְיתָא!

[8]מִשּׁוּם דְּאִיכָּא לְמֵימַר כִּדְשַׁנֵּינָן.

LITERAL TRANSLATION

with you until your brother seeks after it." [1]But would it enter your mind that he should give it [to him] before he seeks after it? [2]Rather, [it means:] examine him [to see] if he is a fraud or not a fraud. [3][Is this] not by means of identifying marks? [4]Conclude from this [that this is so].

[5]Rava said: If you say [that] identifying marks are [valid] by Torah law....

[6]"If you say"?! [7]Surely he has proved [that] identifying marks are [valid] by Torah law.

[8]Because it is possible to say as we answered [above].

TRANSLATION AND COMMENTARY

principle is derived is the verse (Deuteronomy 22:2) where **it is written: "And it shall be with you until your brother seeks after it."** [1]On this the Sages (Sifrei, *Tetze* 223; see above, 27b) comment: **But would it enter your mind that** the finder **should give it to** the owner **before he claims it?** [2]**Rather,** we must interpret this verse **as meaning "examine** the claimant, **to see if he is a fraud or not."** [3]Rava now notes: By what means do the Sages expect the finder to examine the claimant? **Is it not by means of identifying marks?** From the Sages' interpretation of this verse as authorizing the use of identifying marks in restoring lost property to its rightful owner, [4]Rava **draws the conclusion** that identifying marks are valid even by Torah law.

אֲמַר רָבָא [5]The Gemara now continues with a further statement by Rava: **Rava said: If you say that identifying marks are valid by Torah law....**

אִם תִּמְצֵי לוֹמַר [6]At this point the Gemara interrupts Rava's statement, astonished at his opening words: What does Rava mean by saying, **"If you say** that..."?! Is Rava in doubt as to whether identifying marks are valid by Torah law? [7]**Surely he** himself **has** just **proved that identifying marks are valid by Torah law!**

מִשּׁוּם דְּאִיכָּא לְמֵימַר כִּדְשַׁנֵּינָן [8]The Gemara answers its objection: The issue is not quite settled **because it is** still **possible to say** that the inference from the Sifrei is not conclusive. **As we explained above** (27b), the Sifrei may mean that the Torah requires the claimant to produce witnesses, and not merely cite identifying marks, before allowing the finder to surrender the lost object. Now, even though Rava does not find this alternative explanation convincing, he prefers to leave the question formally open, as the rulings he is about to give are not dependent on the resolution of this problem and are also consistent with the opinion that identifying marks are Rabbinic in origin. Thus, Rava's opening words should be interpreted as follows: "Even on the assumption that identifying marks are valid by Torah law, there are circumstances in which they are not accepted as conclusive proof of ownership."

RASHI

כדשנינן — בעדים. **אם תימצי לומר סימנים דאורייתא** — רבותא נקט, דאפילו אמרינן דאורייתא, אפילו הכי עדים עדיפי, כדמפרש ואזיל: סימנין ועדים — ינתן לבעל עדים.

NOTES

of the difficulties he had in explaining the Mishnah (above, 20a), not because of any new insight into the Sifrei.

Rava's restatement of the Sifrei proof should therefore be understood as follows: Since we have proved from the Mishnah (20a) that it is untenable to argue that identifying marks are only a Rabbinic decree, we must read the Sifrei as referring to identifying marks and not to witnesses. However, the essential starting point, according to Rava, is still the Mishnah, not the Sifrei, and the Gemara's parenthetical explanation that Rava used the expression, "if you say," because he had doubts about the correct interpretation of the Sifrei, is difficult to understand (*Ran* and others). Indeed, many Rishonim consider the parenthetical remark to be an addition to the Talmud made by Rav Yehudai Gaon (see *Ritva* and others).

Rava's use of the expression, "if you say," should be understood as leaving an open mind to the possibility that someone may find an answer to the objection raised by Rava from the Mishnah (*Ritva*).

Alternatively, it may not be an expression of doubt at all. It may be a way of emphasizing the point that Rava is about to make in the series of rulings that follows: Identifying marks are an imprecise method of identification. Rava may simply be telling us that this is accepted even by the strongest proponents of the idea that the acceptability of such marks is of Torah origin (*Rashi* and others).

אִם תִּמְצֵי לוֹמַר סִימָנִין דְּאוֹרַיְיתָא If you say that identifying marks are valid by Torah law. Rava's purpose in laying down the various Halakhot regarding the use of identifying marks for the return of lost objects was to define the limitations on their use. Even if we assume that the use of identifying marks as the basis for returning a lost object is grounded on Torah law, Rava seems to wish to emphasize that, in any event, identifying marks provide an indication of ownership which is likely but not absolutely certain. In itself, the ability to cite identifying marks is not proof of ownership, but an indication by means of which the finder can assess the plausibility of the claimant's case. However, since this assessment is based on probabilities, one must consider each case carefully before accepting identifying marks as proof of ownership. Take, for example, the case of witnesses to the weaving of a garment and witnesses that a certain

TRANSLATION AND COMMENTARY

סִימָנִין וְסִימָנִין יַנִּיחַ [1]This observation leads to a series of rulings by Rava, describing situations in which there are two claimants to the same lost article: (1) If two different people both claim to own a lost object, the finder must of course insist that each cite identifying marks. **If both claimants** successfully **cite identifying marks, the finder** must not give the object to either claimant. Rather, he **must leave it** in his possession, pending further investigation.

סִימָנִין וְעֵדִים [2](2) If one claimant successfully cites the object's **identifying marks, and** the other brings **witnesses** that the object belongs to him, the object **must be given to the one who has witnesses,** for there is no dispute that witnesses constitute much better proof of ownership than identifying marks, even if identifying marks are valid by Torah law.

סִימָנִין וְסִימָנִין וְעֵד אֶחָד [3](3) If both claimants successfully cite the object's **identifying marks, and** one also brings **one witness** to support his claim, [4]the **one witness is** considered from a legal point of view **as someone who does not exist,** because the Torah declared that all matters are to be determined by the testimony of at least two witnesses (Deuteronomy 19:15). Hence, this case reverts to being one where both claimants cite identifying marks, **and** here, too, **the finder must retain custody of** the object pending further investigation.

[1]סִימָנִין וְסִימָנִין, יַנִּיחַ. [2]סִימָנִין וְעֵדִים, יִנָּתֵן לְבַעַל הָעֵדִים. [3]סִימָנִין וְסִימָנִין וְעֵד אֶחָד, [4]עֵד אֶחָד כְּמַאן דְּלֵיתֵיהּ דָּמֵי, וְיַנִּיחַ.

LITERAL TRANSLATION

[1][If two claimants cite] identifying marks and identifying marks, [the finder] must leave [it].

[2]Identifying marks and witnesses, it must be given to the one who has witnesses.

[3]Identifying marks and identifying marks and one witness, [4]one witness is as someone who does not exist, and [the finder] must leave [it].

RASHI

סימנין וסימנין – כאו שנים ונתנו סימניה. **יניח** – עד שיבא אליהו.

NOTES

person dropped it, which appears to be an exception to this general rule. Although it seems that each claimant has valid witnesses, this case should not be viewed as one where testimony by two groups of witnesses is contradictory, but one must instead weigh the respective significance of each group's testimony. Thus witnesses to the weaving of the garment, although they testify that it was once owned by a certain person, do not contradict the witnesses who saw someone else drop it. Similarly, with regard to identifying marks of various kinds, one must weigh the degree to which each claim is reliable.

סִימָנִין וְסִימָנִין יַנִּיחַ If both claimants cite identifying marks, the finder must leave it. According to some Rishonim, some identifying marks are more conclusive than others, even according to the opinion that identifying marks are valid by Torah law. Hence, if one claimant cites the article's dimensions, for example, and the other its weight, the finder must give it to the one who who cited the weight. The rule that the finder must continue to keep the article and look after it applies only if the two identifying marks are of equal significance (*Rashba*).

Other Rishonim maintain that if we accept that identifying marks are recognized by the Torah, there is no difference in the validity of one mark over another. Even if one claimant were to cite a definitive mark, such as a hole next to a certain letter in a document, and the other claimant were to cite an ordinary identifying mark, the rule would still be that the finder must keep the article in his possession. According to this view, the later rulings mentioned in the passage, which compare the validity of different marks (e.g., where one claimant knows the dimensions and the other the weight), follow the opinion that identification by marks is a Rabbinic institution (*Ra'avad*).

סִימָנִין וְסִימָנִין וְעֵד אֶחָד Identifying marks versus identifying marks and one witness. There is a dispute among the Rishonim (above, 2b) as to whether the evidence of one witness is sufficient to exempt a claimant from taking an oath. *Mordekhai,* who supports this idea, is troubled by the statement of the Gemara here (28a) that an individual witness "is like someone who does not exist." He asks: Why is the evidence of a single witness not effective in our case, as it would be, for example, if the two claimants were both holding on to the article? There the law is that they must both take an oath and divide the article, unless one of them has the support of a single witness.

He answers that the support of a single witness is effective to exempt a claimant from taking an oath, but not to decide a monetary matter where no oaths are involved. By way of

HALAKHAH

סִימָנִין וְסִימָנִין Identifying marks versus identifying marks. "If two claimants both successfully identify a lost article by citing identifying marks, the article must remain in the care of the finder until one claimant acknowledges the other's claim or the two claimants reach a compromise." (*Shulḥan Arukh, Ḥoshen Mishpat* 267:8.)

סִימָנִין וְעֵדִים Identifying marks versus witnesses. "If one claimant cites identifying marks and the other brings witnesses, the article must be given to the one who brought the witnesses." (Ibid., 267:9.) *Shakh* argues, based on *Rosh,* that this applies even when the one claimant cited definitive identifying marks.

סִימָנִין וְסִימָנִין וְעֵד אֶחָד Identifying marks versus identifying marks and one witness. "If one claimant cites identifying marks and the other cites identifying marks and brings a single witness, the article must remain in the

[1] עֵדֵי אֲרִיגָה וְעֵדֵי נְפִילָה, [2] תִּנָּתֵן לְעֵדֵי נְפִילָה, [3] דְּאָמְרִינַן: זַבּוּנֵי זַבְּנָהּ, וּמֵאִינִישׁ אַחֲרִינָא נְפַל.

[4] מִדַּת אָרְכּוֹ וּמִדַּת רָחְבּוֹ, [5] תִּנָּתֵן לְמִדַּת אָרְכּוֹ, [6] דְּמִדַּת רָחְבּוֹ שְׁעוּרֵי קָא מְשַׁעֵר לָהּ כַּד מְכַסֵּי לָהּ מָרָהּ וְקָאֵי, [7] וּמִדַּת אָרְכּוֹ לָא מִשְׁתַּעֵר לָהּ.

[8] מִדַּת אָרְכּוֹ וּמִדַּת רָחְבּוֹ [9] וּמִדַּת גַּמָּיו, [10] יִנָּתֵן לְמִדַּת אָרְכּוֹ וְרָחְבּוֹ.

TRANSLATION AND COMMENTARY

עֵדֵי אֲרִיגָה וְעֵדֵי נְפִילָה [1] (4) If one claimant brings **witnesses that he wove** the lost garment, **and** the other brings **witnesses that** the lost garment was in his possession when **it fell,** [2] **it must be given to the one who has witnesses that** it was in his possession when **it fell.** [3] **For** if it is at all possible, **we** prefer to **say** that both pairs of witnesses are telling the truth, and their testimony can be reconciled as follows: The first claimant indeed wove the garment. But then **he sold it** to someone else, **and that other person lost it.**

מִדַּת אָרְכּוֹ וּמִדַּת רָחְבּוֹ [4] (5) If each claimant cites a different identifying mark, the finder must judge which identifying mark is more convincing. Thus, **if one cites** the garment's **length, and the other cites its width,** [5] **it must be given to the one who cited its length.** [6] Length is a more convincing means of identification than width, **because it is possible** even at a distance **to estimate** a garment's **width** by simply observing it **while its owner is standing wearing it,** [7] **but length cannot be estimated** so easily. Thus the claim based on identification of length is preferred.

מִדַּת אָרְכּוֹ וּמִדַּת רָחְבּוֹ וּמִדַּת גַּמָּיו [8] (6) **If one** claimant **cites** both **the length and width** of a lost article, [9] **and the other can** only **cite the combined sum of its length and width,** without being able to specify the length and the width as separate measurements, [10] **it must be given to the one who cited** both **its length and its width,** because his identification is more convincing.

LITERAL TRANSLATION

[1] Witnesses of weaving and witnesses of falling, [2] it must be given to [the one who has] witnesses of falling, [3] for we say: He sold it, and it fell from another person.

[4] [If one cites] the measure of its length and [the other cites] the measure of its width, [5] it must be given to [the one who cited] the measure of its length, [6] because he can estimate the measure of its width when its owner is wearing it and standing, [7] but he cannot estimate the measure of its length.

[8] [If one cites] the measure of its length and the measure of its width, [9] and [the other cites] the combined measure [of its length and width], [10] it must be given to [the one who cited] the measure of its length and width.

RASHI

מדת ארכו כו׳ — זה אומר מדת ארכו וזה נותן מדת רחבו. **שעורי משער לה** — אם ראה אותה ביד הבעלים שיערה כשהיה בעלה מכוסה בה, אם טלית היא. **מדת ארכו ורחבו ומדת גמיו** — זה אומר: כך ארכו וכך רחבה, וזה אומר: ארכה ורחבה כך וכך אמות בין הכל, אבל אינו יודע כמה באורך וכמה ברוחב. **גמיו** — גאם יוונית, עשויה כמין ד׳ שלנו, להכי קרי אורך ורוחב יחד גמיו.

BACKGROUND

מִדַּת גַּמָּיו The combined measure of its length and width. In this case the garment is awarded to the claimant who presents the most precise details. A claimant may be able to guess a garment's combined dimensions, which can be made up of various lengths and widths. However, someone who states the specific length and width separately is offering a more precise and unequivocal criterion for identifying the garment.

LANGUAGE

גַּמָּיו Its combined length and width. The source of the word is the Greek letter *gamma,* which in capital form is written in the shape of two sides of a rectangle.

Γ

In Hebrew, the word גַּמָּא thus has two meanings: (1) The Greek letter *gamma.* (2) The combined length and width of a rectangle.

NOTES

example he points out that a contradiction between two sets of identifying marks is analogous to a contradiction between two pairs of witnesses, and an additional witness is of no value in resolving a contradiction between two pairs of witnesses.

Commenting on our passage, *Mordekhai* uses the same analogy between identifying marks and witnesses to answer a different question: Even on the assumption that identifying marks are valid by Torah law, how can they be used to determine a question of marriage and divorce? We have a principle that we cannot deduce anything about a ritual law from a monetary law (אִיסּוּרָא מִמָּמוֹנָא לָא יָלְפִינַן).

He answers that once the Torah established that identifying marks are valid, they became a method of determining facts, analogous to witnesses; just as witnesses are valid in all cases, so too are identifying marks. But in his comment earlier in the tractate (above, 2b) he adds that even according to this argument identifying marks are still not nearly as effective as witnesses.

HALAKHAH

custody of the finder." (*Shulḥan Arukh, Ḥoshen Mishpat* 267:10.) *Rema,* following *Rosh,* rules that the one whose claim is not supported by the witness must take an oath to support his claim. Otherwise, the article is given to the claimant whose claim is supported by the witness.

עֵדֵי אֲרִיגָה וְעֵדֵי נְפִילָה Witnesses of weaving versus witnesses of falling. "If one claimant brings witnesses that he wove the article and the other brings witnesses that he lost the article, it must be given to the one who brought witnesses that he lost it." (Ibid., 267:11.)

מִדַּת אָרְכּוֹ וּמִדַּת רָחְבּוֹ Length versus width. "If one claimant cites the length of an article and the other its width, it must be given to the one who cited its length, as its width can easily be estimated." (Ibid., 267:12.)

אָרְכּוֹ וְרָחְבּוֹ וְגַמָּיו Length and width versus combined length and width. "If one claimant cites an article's length and width separately, and the other cites its combined length and width, it must be given to the one who cited its length and width separately." (Ibid., 267:14.)

TRANSLATION AND COMMENTARY

מִדַּת אָרְכּוֹ וּמִדַּת רָחְבּוֹ וּמִדַּת מִשְׁקְלוֹתָיו [1](7) **If one** claimant **cites** both **the length and the width** of a lost article, [2]**and the other cites its weight,** [3]**it must be given to the one who cited its weight,** as an object's weight is much more difficult to estimate than its linear dimensions.

הוּא אוֹמֵר סִימָנֵי הַגֵּט [4](8) If someone finds a lost bill of divorce, and both the husband and the wife claim it, the decision as to whom it is to be returned also determines the status of the marriage. If the husband lost it, it cannot yet have been delivered, and thus the couple are still married; whereas if the wife lost it, it can only have been in her possession as a result of her having been divorced by means of it. In this case, as in the previous ones, the finder must demand that the husband and the wife cite convincing identifying marks on the bill of divorce. **If the husband and the wife** both **cite identifying marks on the bill of divorce,** the rule applied in the cases discussed above does not apply, and the finder does not retain the bill in his custody. [5] Rather, the finder **must give** the bill **to the wife.** The reason is as follows: The husband's familiarity with the bill of divorce means very little, since he drew it up, but the wife's familiarity means a great deal, since she could not have seen it and examined it in detail unless it was delivered to her.

בְּמַאי [6]The Gemara now asks: **To what identifying marks are we referring** in this ruling? [7]**If we say** that we are referring **to the length and the width** of the bill of divorce, how can we be certain that it has already been delivered to the wife? [8]**Perhaps** the wife **saw it** on some occasion **while he was holding it** in his hand, and that is how she became familiar with the bill's dimensions. [9]**Rather,** says the Gemara, we cannot be referring to a case where the claimants cite nonspecific identifying marks such as dimension. We must be referring in this ruling **to** a case **where** the husband and the wife both cite definitive identifying marks on the document, such as **a hole in** the parchment of the bill of divorce **next to a certain letter.** The reason why the bill of divorce is returned to the wife in such a situation is because the only way she could have known about such a hole is if the bill had actually been delivered to her and she had had time to examine it closely.

הוּא אוֹמֵר סִימָנֵי הַחוּט [10](9) **If the husband and the wife both cite the identifying marks of the string** with which the bill of divorce was tied, [11]the bill of divorce **must be given to her,** since here, too, her familiarity means much more than his.

[1]מִדַּת אָרְכּוֹ וּמִדַּת רָחְבּוֹ [2]וּמִדַּת מִשְׁקְלוֹתָיו, [3]יִנָּתֵן לְמִדַּת מִשְׁקְלוֹתָיו.

[4]הוּא אוֹמֵר סִימָנֵי הַגֵּט וְהִיא אוֹמֶרֶת סִימָנֵי הַגֵּט, [5]יִנָּתֵן לָהּ.

[6]בְּמַאי? [7]אִילֵימָא בְּמִדַּת אָרְכּוֹ וְרָחְבּוֹ, [8]דִּלְמָא בַּהֲדֵי דְּנָקִיט לֵיהּ חֲזִיתֵיהּ. [9]אֶלָּא, נֶקֶב יֵשׁ בּוֹ בְּצַד אוֹת פְּלוֹנִי.

[10]הוּא אוֹמֵר סִימָנֵי הַחוּט וְהִיא אוֹמֶרֶת סִמָּנֵי הַחוּט, [11]יִנָּתֵן לָהּ.

LITERAL TRANSLATION

[1][If one cites] the measure of its length and the measure of its width [2]and [the other cites] the measure of its weight, [3]it must be given to [the one who cited] the measure of its weight.

[4][If] he cites the identifying marks of the bill of divorce and she cites the identifying marks of the bill of divorce, [5]it must be given to her.

[6]To what [identifying marks are we referring]? [7]If we say: to the measure of its length and width, [8]perhaps while he was holding it she saw it. [9]Rather, [to where] there is a hole in it next to a certain letter.

[10][If] he cites the identifying marks of the string and she cites the identifying marks of the string, [11]it must be given to her.

RASHI

הוא אומר סימני הגט — ואומר: ממני נפל, שנמלכתי שלא ליתן. **והיא אומרת סימני הגט** — וממני נפל, שנתנו לי וגרשתני. **ינתן לה** — שהוא נתנו וידע סימנין, אבל היא, אם לא נתנו לה — מהיכן ידעה. **סימני החוט** — שהגט קשור בו.

BACKGROUND

סִימָנֵי הַחוּט The identifying marks of the string. A bill of divorce, which is generally written on parchment or paper, is a document which must be preserved for some time because the woman is likely to need it, for instance when she wishes to remarry. Therefore it was rolled up and tied with thread.

HALAKHAH

אוֹרֶךְ רוֹחַב וּמִשְׁקָל Length and width versus weight. "If one claimant cites an article's length and width, and the other cites its weight, it must be given to the one who cited its weight." (*Shulḥan Arukh, Ḥoshen Mishpat* 267:13.)

בַּעַל וְאִשְׁתּוֹ בְּסִימָנֵי גֵּט A husband and wife and identifying marks on a bill of divorce. "If a bill of divorce is found in the marketplace, and the wife claims that she already received the bill of divorce and subsequently lost it, and the husband claims that he decided not to divorce his wife and himself lost the bill, then, if the wife can cite identifying marks, it must be given to her, regardless of whether or not the husband can also cite identifying marks. But if she cannot cite identifying marks on it, it must not be given to her." (Ibid., *Even HaEzer* 153:1.) The question of whether or not the bill of divorce is given to the husband if the wife cannot cite identifying marks depends on the locality. In a place where a separate ketubah is customarily not written and the bill of divorce itself serves as a ketubah, it must not be given to the husband, but rather left in the custody of the court pending further investigation, because the bill of divorce attests to monetary rights and obligations. But in other places it may be given to the husband (*Bet Shmuel*). For the purposes of this law, "identifying marks" mean definitive identifying marks that leave no room for doubt, according to *Rif* and *Rambam,* and intermediate, but not inferior, identifying marks, according to *Rosh.*

TRANSLATION AND COMMENTARY

בְּמַאי [1]The Gemara now asks: **To what identifying marks are we referring** in this ruling? [2]**If we say** that we are referring **to the color** of the string, and the claim is, for example, that it is **white or red,** how can we be certain that the bill of divorce has already been delivered to the wife? [3]**Perhaps** it was never delivered, **but** the wife **saw it** on some occasion **while** the husband **was holding it** in his hand. [4]**Rather,** says the Gemara, we must be referring **to the length** of the string with which the bill of divorce was tied. The wife's knowledge of the string's exact length could only have been gained after the bill of divorce was delivered to her.

הוּא אוֹמֵר בַּחֲפִיסָה [5](10) **If** in seeking to provide identification of a lost bill of divorce **the husband says** that the bill **was in a small bag and the wife** also **says it was in a small bag,** [6]the bill **must be given to him,** because in this case his familiarity means much more than hers. [7]**What is the reason? She knows very well that he places all his documents in** this **small bag.** Therefore, she can guess that this is where he left the bill of divorce as well.

[1]בְּמַאי? [2]אִילֵימָא בְּחִיוּוָרָא וּבְסוּמָּקָא, [3]וְדִלְמָא בַּהֲדֵי דְּנָקֵיט לֵיהּ חֲזִיתֵיהּ? [4]אֶלָּא, בְּמִדַּת אָרְכּוֹ.

[5]הוּא אוֹמֵר בַּחֲפִיסָה וְהִיא אוֹמֶרֶת בַּחֲפִיסָה, [6]יִנָּתֵן לוֹ. [7]מַאי טַעְמָא? מֵידַע יָדְעָה דְּכָל מַה דְּאִית לֵיהּ בַּחֲפִיסָה הוּא דְּמַנַּח לֵיהּ.

מִשְׁנָה [8]וְעַד מָתַי חַיָּיב לְהַכְרִיז? [9]עַד כְּדֵי שֶׁיֵּדְעוּ בּוֹ שְׁכֵנָיו: דִּבְרֵי רַבִּי מֵאִיר. [10]רַבִּי יְהוּדָה אוֹמֵר: שָׁלֹשׁ רְגָלִים, וְאַחַר הָרֶגֶל הָאַחֲרוֹן שִׁבְעָה יָמִים, [11]כְּדֵי שֶׁיֵּלֵךְ לְבֵיתוֹ שְׁלֹשָׁה וְיַחֲזוֹר שְׁלֹשָׁה וְיַכְרִיז יוֹם אֶחָד.

LITERAL TRANSLATION

[1]To what [identifying marks are we referring]? [2]If we say: to [the colors] white or red, [3]but perhaps while he was holding it she saw it. [4]Rather, to the measure of its length.

[5][If] he says [it was] in a small bag and she says [it was] in a small bag, [6]it must be given to him. [7]What is the reason? She knows very well that all [documents] that he has he places in a small bag.

MISHNAH [8]And until when is he obliged to announce? [9]Until its neighbors will know about it: [these are] the words of Rabbi Meir. [10]Rabbi Yehudah says: Three Pilgrim Festivals, and after the last Pilgrim Festival seven days, [11]so that he may go to his home three [days], and return three [days], and announce one day.

RASHI

בחפיסה — מלאת אותו.

משנה שכיניו — מפרש בגמרא.

כדי שילך — כל אחד לביתו. **שלשה** — משישמע ההכרזה, וידע אם אבד לו כלום, ואם יבין שאבד — יחזור שלשה. **ויכריז יום אחד** — אני אבדתי ואלו סימניה, ובגמרא פריך: דבשלשה ימים אין שהות לחזור לסוף ארץ ישראל.

MISHNAH וְעַד מָתַי [8]The Mishnah asks: **And until when is** the finder of a lost article **obliged to announce** it? In other words, for how long or on how many occasions must the finder bring the fact that he has found something to the attention of the public? [9]The Mishnah gives the answers of two Tannaim to this question: (1) **Until** enough time has passed that **its neighbors** (explained below in the Gemara) **will know about it. These are the words of Rabbi Meir.** [10](2) **Rabbi Yehudah says:** He must make his announcement in Jerusalem at each of the next **three Pilgrim Festivals, and after the last Pilgrim Festival** he must continue making the announcement **for seven** more **days.** [11]This period will give the article's owner enough time **to go home** and check whether he has, in fact, lost anything. The journey home from Jerusalem can take up to **three days,** and the journey **back** to Jerusalem another **three days,** leaving the claimant **one day to** make contact with the finder and **announce** that he is the owner of the lost object.

NOTES

וְיַכְרִיז יוֹם אֶחָד And announce one day. Our commentary follows *Rashi,* who explains that this clause in the Mishnah refers to the owner, who must announce his claim. *Rambam* states that this clause in the Mishnah refers to the finder, who is required to announce the article for the last time on the seventh day after the Festival, so that the owner who may have been traveling for six days can find him. *Rabbenu Tam* explains that the word "announce" in this context must be interpreted as meaning "search." Thus the owner is given one day to go through his possessions, between the three days he spends traveling home and the three days he spends returning to Jerusalem.

HALAKHAH

מַכְרִיז שָׁלֹשׁ רְגָלִים He makes his announcement on three Pilgrim Festivals. "In Temple times, anyone who found a lost object would announce his discovery on the three Pilgrim Festivals. On the first one he would say 'first,' on the second one 'second,' and on the third one he would make his announcement without specifying on how many Festivals he had previously done so. During the seven days after the third Festival, he made his announcement for the

TRANSLATION AND COMMENTARY

GEMARA **תָּנָא** [1]The Mishnah uses the expression "Until enough time has passed that its neighbors know about it." There is an authoritative Baraita in which **a Tanna** briefly elaborated on the expression "its neighbors" used in the Mishnah, and **said:** "The expression 'its neighbors' means **'the neighbors of the lost article.'"**

מַאי שְׁכֵנֵי אֲבֵידָה [2]The explanation provided by the Baraita is itself extremely cryptic, and leads the Gemara to ask: **What is the meaning of** the expression used by the Baraita, **"the neighbors of the lost article"?** To which neighbors is it referring? [3]**If we say** that it means **"the neighbors of the owner of the lost article,"** this would imply that the finder already knows the identity of the owner; and **if he knows him, he should** simply **go and return** the object **to him,** without bothering with announcements. [4]**Rather,** says the Gemara, the expression "the neighbors of the lost article" must **mean "the neighbors** living near **the place where the lost article was found."** It is for their benefit that the finder must make his announcement, because it is among them that the owner of the lost article is most likely to be found.

גמרא [1]תָּנָא: ״שְׁכֵנֵי אֲבֵידָה״. [2]מַאי ״שְׁכֵנֵי אֲבֵידָה״? אִילֵימָא ״שְׁכֵינִים דְּבַעַל אֲבֵידָה״, [3]אִי יָדַע לֵיהּ, לֵיזוּל וּלְהַדְּרֵיהּ נְהֲלֵיהּ! [4]אֶלָּא: ״שְׁכֵנֵי מָקוֹם שֶׁנִּמְצֵאת בּוֹ אֲבֵידָה״.

[5]״רַבִּי יְהוּדָה אוֹמֵר כו׳״. [6]וּרְמִינְהוּ: ״בִּשְׁלֹשָׁה בְּמַרְחֶשְׁוָן, שׁוֹאֲלִין אֶת הַגְּשָׁמִים. [7]רַבָּן גַּמְלִיאֵל אוֹמֵר: בְּשִׁבְעָה בּוֹ, שֶׁהוּא חֲמִישָּׁה עָשָׂר יוֹם אַחַר הֶחָג, [8]כְּדֵי שֶׁיַּגִּיעַ אַחֲרוֹן שֶׁבְּאֶרֶץ יִשְׂרָאֵל לִנְהַר פְּרָת״.

[9]אָמַר רַב יוֹסֵף: לָא קַשְׁיָא. [10]כָּאן בְּמִקְדָּשׁ רִאשׁוֹן,

LITERAL TRANSLATION

GEMARA [1][A Tanna] taught: "The neighbors of the loss."

[2]What is [the meaning of] "the neighbors of the loss"? [3]If we say "the neighbors of the owner of the lost article," [but] if he knows him, let him go and return it to him. [4]Rather, [it means] "the neighbors of the place where the lost article was found."

[5]"Rabbi Yehudah says...." [6]But there is a contradiction to this (lit., "cast them [against each other]"): "On the third of Marḥeshvan, we [begin] requesting rain. [7]Rabban Gamliel says: On the seventh of [Marḥeshvan], which is fifteen days after the Festival, [8]so that the last [pilgrim] in Eretz Israel can reach the Euphrates River."

[9]Rav Yosef said: There is no difficulty.

[10]Here [it refers] to the First Temple;

RASHI

גמרא שכני מקום שנמצא בו אבידה – שמא שלהן היא. כדי שיגיע כו׳ – ולא ידביקוהו הגשמים, אלמא כולי האי בעינן, ומתניתין תני שלשה.

רַבִּי יְהוּדָה אוֹמֵר [5]The Gemara now turns to the next clause of the Mishnah: **"Rabbi Yehudah says:** Three Pilgrim Festivals plus one week." Rabbi Yehudah's opinion is based on the calculation that it takes no more than three days for a pilgrim to return home from Jerusalem. [6]**But a contradiction can be raised** against this from the following Mishnah (*Ta'anit* 10a): **"On the third** day of the month **of Marḥeshvan, we begin** inserting in our daily prayers **a** special **request for rain,** for this is when the rainy season begins in Eretz Israel. [7]**Rabban Gamliel says:** We wait until **the seventh of Marḥeshvan, which is fifteen days after the** conclusion of the Sukkot **Festival,** [8]in order to give **the last pilgrim from** the farthest corner of **Eretz Israel** time enough **to reach the Euphrates River** before the rains overtake him." Thus it appears from this Mishnah that it takes up to fifteen days, not three, to return home from Jerusalem.

אָמַר רַב יוֹסֵף [9]To reconcile Rabbi Yehudah's view in our Mishnah with the Mishnah in tractate *Ta'anit,* the Gemara now brings the opinions of three Amoraim. (1) **Rav Yosef said: There is no difficulty** in resolving this apparent contradiction: [10]**Here,** in the Mishnah in *Ta'anit,* where the journey home from Jerusalem by the pilgrims is described as taking as much as fifteen days, **it is referring to the First Temple** period;

NOTES

כָּאן בְּמִקְדָּשׁ רִאשׁוֹן Here it is referring to the First Temple. Although Rabban Gamliel, the author of the ruling in the Mishnah in tractate *Ta'anit,* did not live in the First Temple period, he transmitted this Halakhah from that period. He himself was the head of the Jewish community in Eretz Israel after the destruction of the Second Temple (*Rabbi Ya'akov Emden*).

HALAKHAH

fourth and last time," in accordance with the viewpoint of Rabbi Yehudah and the Baraita. (*Rambam, Sefer Nezikin, Hilkhot Gezelah Va'Avedah* 13:8.)

זְמַן שְׁאֵלַת גְּשָׁמִים The time from which the prayer requesting rain is made. "In Eretz Israel, the period each year during which a prayer requesting rain (the expression וְתֵן טַל וּמָטָר — "and give dew and rain") is added to the ninth blessing of the Amidah (בִּרְכַּת הַשָּׁנִים) begins on the seventh

BACKGROUND

לִנְהַר פְּרָת To the Euphrates River. The obligation to make the pilgrimage to Jerusalem in Temple times was incumbent upon the Jewish inhabitants of Eretz Israel itself, but not on people who lived in the Diaspora. The Euphrates was the final boundary with regard to this Halakhah; beyond it the territory was not part of Eretz Israel. Therefore only those who had to travel as far as the Euphrates were taken into account, though there were certainly people from other countries who occasionally made the pilgrimage.

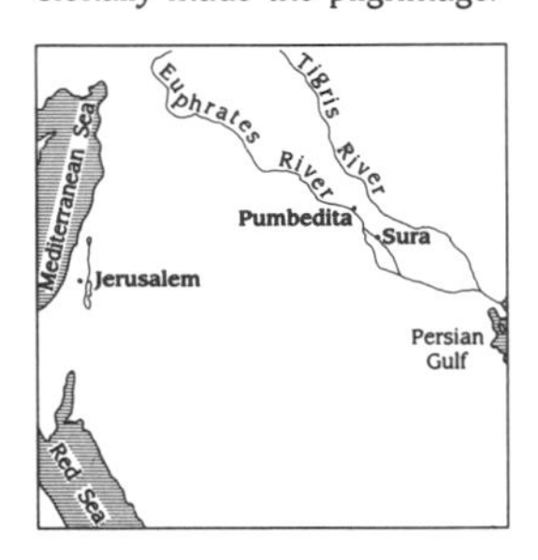

CONCEPTS

שְׁאֵלַת גְּשָׁמִים The request for rain. During the season when it normally rains in Eretz Israel, a request for rain is added in the Amidah prayer in the blessing (בִּרְכַּת הַשָּׁנִים) thanking God for the produce of the fields. In Eretz Israel, this addition is made from the 7th of Ḥeshvan (Marḥeshvan) until the Pesaḥ Festival. In the Diaspora, the addition is generally made from the sixtieth day after the autumnal equinox until Pesaḥ. However, in certain countries, if the rainy season falls after Pesaḥ, different laws may apply. שְׁאֵלַת גְּשָׁמִים is not to be confused with הַזְכָּרַת גְּשָׁמִים — "mentioning rain" — which is the term used to describe the phrase מַשִּׁיב הָרוּחַ וּמוֹרִיד הַגֶּשֶׁם — "who causes the wind to blow and the rain to fall" — that is added to the second blessing of the Amidah prayer between Shemini Atzeret and Pesaḥ.

SAGES

רַב יוֹסֵף Rav Yosef. The son of Ḥiyya, Rav Yosef was one of the greatest Amoraim of Babylonia during the third generation. He was a disciple of Rav Yehudah and a colleague of Rabbah, and was

TRANSLATION AND COMMENTARY

[1]whereas **here,** in our Mishnah, where the same journey home is described as taking three days, **it is referring to the Second Temple** period. [2]Rav Yosef now goes on to explain: **During the First Temple period, the Jewish population** of Eretz Israel **was very numerous,** [3]**as it is written** (I Kings 4:20, describing the reign of King Solomon): **"Judah and Israel were many, as the sand which is by the sea in multitude."** [4]Therefore, a pilgrim might have **needed all that time** to return home, as the area of Jewish settlement in Eretz Israel was very extensive during that period. [5]On the other hand, **during the Second Temple period the Jewish population** of Eretz Israel **was not very numerous,** [6]**as it is written** (Ezra 2:64, which gives the number of Jews who returned to Eretz Israel from Babylonia after Cyrus' proclamation): **"The whole congregation together was forty-two thousand three hundred and sixty."** [7]Therefore, a pilgrim would **not have needed all that time** to return home, and three days would have been sufficient to reach all areas of Jewish settlement in Eretz Israel.

אֲמַר לֵיהּ אַבַּיֵי [8](2) **Abaye said to** Rav Yosef: [9]**But surely** the following verse also describes the return to Eretz Israel from Babylonia in the time of Cyrus, and paints a different picture. **It is written** (Ezra 2:70): "And the priests, and the Levites, and some of the people, **and the singers, and the gatekeepers,** and the Netinim in their cities **and all Israel dwelt in their cities."** This verse means, according to Abaye, that the returning Jews settled in *all* the places where they had traditionally lived. Thus the area of Jewish settlement in Eretz Israel was no less extensive during the Second Temple period than during the First. [10]Now, continues Abaye, **since this is so, it is more reasonable** to resolve the contradiction in **the opposite** way from that proposed by Rav Yosef, and to explain that our Mishnah is referring to the First Temple period, and the Mishnah in *Ta'anit* is referring to the Second Temple period. [11]Abaye now proceeds to develop his argument: **During the First Temple period, when the Jewish population** of Eretz Israel **was very numerous,** [12]**when people were closely linked** to each other geographically and socially, transportation between the various parts of the country was highly developed, [13]**and caravans were** readily **available that would travel both by day and by night.** [14]Therefore, a pilgrim **did not need all the time** specified in

[1]כָּאן בְּמִקְדָּשׁ שֵׁנִי. [2]בְּמִקְדָּשׁ רִאשׁוֹן, דִּנְפִישִׁי יִשְׂרָאֵל טוּבָא — [3]דִּכְתִיב בְּהוּ: ״יְהוּדָה וְיִשְׂרָאֵל רַבִּים כַּחוֹל אֲשֶׁר עַל הַיָּם לָרֹב״ — [4]בָּעֵינַן כּוּלֵּי הַאי. [5]בְּמִקְדָּשׁ שֵׁנִי, דְּלָא נְפִישִׁי יִשְׂרָאֵל טוּבָא — [6]דִּכְתִיב בְּהוּ: ״כָּל הַקָּהָל כְּאֶחָד אַרְבַּע רִבּוֹא אַלְפַּיִם שְׁלֹשׁ מֵאוֹת שִׁשִּׁים״ — [7]לָא בָּעֵינַן כּוּלֵּי הַאי.
[8]אֲמַר לֵיהּ אַבַּיֵי: [9]וְהָא כְּתִיב: ״וַיֵּשְׁבוּ הַכֹּהֲנִים וְהַלְוִיִּם וגו׳ וְהַמְשֹׁרְרִים וְהַשּׁוֹעֲרִים... וְכָל יִשְׂרָאֵל בְּעָרֵיהֶם״. [10]וְכֵיוָן דְּהָכִי הוּא, אִפְּכָא מִסְתַּבְּרָא: [11]מִקְדָּשׁ רִאשׁוֹן, דִּנְפִישִׁי יִשְׂרָאֵל טוּבָא, [12]דִּמְצָווֹת עָלְמָא, [13]וּמִשְׁתַּכְּחִי שַׁיַּירְתָּא דְּאָזְלִי בֵּין בִּימָמָא וּבֵין בְּלֵילְיָא, [14]לָא בָּעֵינַן כּוּלֵּי הַאי,

LITERAL TRANSLATION

[1]here [it refers] to the Second Temple. [2]During the First Temple [period], when the Israelites were very numerous — [3]as it is written about them: "Judah and Israel were many, as the sand which is by the sea in multitude" — [4]we need all that [time]. [5]During the Second Temple [period], when the Israelites were not very numerous — [6]as it is written about them: "The whole congregation together was forty-two thousand three hundred and sixty" — [7]we do not need all that [time].
[8]Abaye said to him: [9]But surely it is written: "And the priests and the Levites... and the singers and the gatekeepers... and all Israel dwelt in their cities." [10]And since this is so, the opposite is more reasonable: [11][During] the First Temple [period], when the Israelites were very numerous, [12]when people (lit., "the world") joined together, [13]and caravans were available that would travel both by day and by night, [14]we did not need all that [time],

RASHI

והכתיב וישבו כל ישראל בעריהם — ואף על גב דפורתא הוו — בכל עריהן היו מפוזרים, ויש רחוקים מירושלים כבתחילה. הכי **גרסינן** — וכיון דהכי הוא איפכא מסתברא. **דמצות עלמא** — לוות יש לו, טובים השנים.

the head of the Pumbedita Yeshivah for two-and-a-half years. He was known as "Sinai" because of his expert knowledge of Baraitot and oral traditions of the Bible, and of its translation. His most important students were Abaye and Rava. An illness caused him to forget all his learning, but Abaye helped restore it to him. Rav Yosef also became blind. After his death, Abaye succeeded him as head of the Pumbedita Yeshivah.

BACKGROUND

וְכָל יִשְׂרָאֵל בְּעָרֵיהֶם "And all Israel dwelt in their cities." Abaye was of the opinion that, although the dense area of Jewish settlement after the return of the Babylonian exiles was in Judea, members of other tribes also returned and settled in their ancient locations. In fact, as we see from the Book of Maccabees, there was also a Jewish settlement in Galilee, though that region was not at all part of the "Jewish" district of the Persian Empire. Hence pilgrims also used to come from places very distant from Jerusalem.

דִּמְצָווֹת עָלְמָא When people joined together. The caravans to distant places passed through desert areas plagued by many robbers. When the caravan consisted of many travelers, they could defend themselves and continue on their way night and day. However, when the travelers were few, the leaders of the caravans were cautious and advanced only by day, camping at fixed stopping places every night. These stopovers consumed a lot of time, because the stopping places were not all exactly a full day's journey apart, so that a small and vulnerable caravan might take twice as long as a large one to reach its destination.

TERMINOLOGY

אִפְּכָא מִסְתַּבְּרָא The opposite [of what was just stated] is more reasonable! An expression of astonishment concerning a statement, the opposite of which appears to be more reasonable.

HALAKHAH

day of Marḥeshvan. In the Diaspora the addition is made from the sixtieth day after the autumnal equinox (i.e., from the 5th or 6th of December). Both in Eretz Israel and in the Diaspora the period during which this request for rain is made ends on the eve of Passover." (*Shulḥan Arukh, Oraḥ Ḥayyim* 117:1.)

וְסַגֵּי בִּתְלָתָא יוֹמָא. [1] מִקְדָּשׁ שֵׁנִי, דְּלָא נְפִישִׁי יִשְׂרָאֵל טוּבָא, [2] וְלָא מִצְוַות עָלְמָא, [3] וְלָא מִשְׁתַּכְּחִי שַׁיָּירָתָא דְּאָזְלִי בֵּין בִּימָמָא וּבֵין בְּלֵילְיָא, [4] בָּעֵינַן כּוּלֵּי הַאי.

[5] רָבָא אָמַר: לָא שְׁנָא בְּמִקְדָּשׁ רִאשׁוֹן וְלָא שְׁנָא בְּמִקְדָּשׁ שֵׁנִי: [6] לֹא הִטְרִיחוּ רַבָּנַן בַּאֲבֵדָה יוֹתֵר מִדַּאי.

[7] אֲמַר רָבִינָא: שְׁמַע מִינָּהּ כִּי מַכְרִיז, ״גְּלִימָא״ מַכְרִיז. [8] דְּאִי סָלְקָא דַּעְתָּךְ ״אֲבֵידְתָא״ מַכְרִיז, [9] בָּעֵינַן לְמַטְפֵּי לֵיהּ חַד יוֹמָא לְעִיּוּנֵי בְּמָאנֵיהּ.

LITERAL TRANSLATION

and three days were enough. [1] [During] the Second Temple [period], when Israelites were not very numerous, [2] and people were not joined together, [3] and caravans were not available that would travel both by day and by night, [4] we needed all that [time].

[5] Rava said: There is no difference in the First Temple [period] and there is no difference in the Second Temple [period]: [6] the Sages did not trouble [people] too much in [returning] lost property.

[7] Ravina said: Conclude from this [Mishnah that] when he announces, he announces, "[I have found] a cloak." [8] For if it were to enter your mind [that] he announces, "[I have found] a lost article," [9] we would need to add for him [the owner] one [extra] day to examine his possessions.

TRANSLATION AND COMMENTARY

the Mishnah in *Ta'anit,* **and the three days** mentioned in our Mishnah **were enough** to reach all areas of Jewish settlement in Eretz Israel. [1] On the other hand, **during the Second Temple period, when the Jewish population** of Eretz Israel **was not very numerous,** [2] **people were not closely linked** to each other, [3] **and caravans were not** readily **available that would travel both by day and by night.** [4] Therefore travel became much more difficult, and pilgrims **needed all that time** — a full fifteen days — to reach destinations that in the First Temple period required a journey of only three days.

רָבָא אָמַר [5] (3) **Rava** offered a different reply to the seeming contradiction between the two Mishnayot, and **said: There is no difference** in law **between the First Temple period and the Second Temple period.** In both periods it could take up to fifteen days to reach the Euphrates River from Jerusalem. [6] But the reason finders of lost objects were required to make announcements for a period of only seven days after the last Festival was because **the Sages did not** wish to **make people go to more trouble than necessary in returning lost property.** The finder of lost property derived no material benefit from his attempts to locate the property's rightful owner. Thus, a week after the third Pilgrim Festival was considered the maximum period that a finder could be expected to wait in Jerusalem for the rightful owner to appear to claim his property. After this time, the Sages placed no further obligations on the finder.

אֲמַר רָבִינָא [7] The Gemara seeks to prove from our Mishnah that the announcement made by the finder must be sufficiently specific for the owner not to have to engage in a lengthy search of his possessions to find out what is missing: **Ravina said:** It is possible to **draw the conclusion from our Mishnah that when** a person **announces** that he has found a lost article, **he** must **announce** the type of article he found, e.g., **"I have found a cloak,"** and the owner must then identify the article by citing specific identifying marks. Clearly, the more information the finder provides as to the nature of the object he has found, the easier it becomes for a dishonest person to obtain it. Conversely, the more specific the finder is as to the nature of the found object, the higher the standards for accepting identifying marks will become, to the inconvenience of the true owner. (See below, 28b, for a complete discussion of this issue.) At all events, says Ravina, it is clear from our Mishnah that in his announcement the finder does reveal specific information about the nature of the object he has found. [8] **For if it were to enter your mind that he** simply **announces: "I have found a lost article,"** without any further specification, [9] the Mishnah **would need to add** at least **one extra day** beyond the week provided in the Mishnah **for the owner to examine** all **his possessions** and see what is missing.

RASHI

שמע מינה — מדלא יהבי ליה לרבנן שהות אלא הליכה וחזרה. **גלימא מכריז** — זה שמוצא מכריז שם חפץ: ״טלית מצאתי״ ולכך לא הוצרכו ליתן שהות יום אחד לעיין בכליו מה אבד, שהאדם יודע כמה טליתות יש לו, וכשהוא בביתו בודק אם ימצאנה, ואין צריך שהות. **דאי סלקא דעתך אבידתא מכריז** — ואינו מזכיר שם החפץ, ליתבו ליה לכל חד וחד אכתי טפי יומא לעיוני במאניה, אם כל כליו בידו, ופלוגתא היא בהא לקמן.

HALAKHAH

כֵּיצַד מַכְרִיז הַמּוֹצֵא **How does the finder make his announcement?** "The finder describes in a general way what he has found, e.g., coins or clothing or an animal. The owner must then cite specific identifying marks," in accordance with the viewpoint of Ravina, who was a late and authoritative Amora. (*Shulḥan Arukh, Ḥoshen Mishpat* 267:4.)

TRANSLATION AND COMMENTARY

[1]**Rather,** says Ravina, we can **conclude from this Mishnah that** the finder **announces: "I have found a cloak,"** so that people can quickly check whether they have lost such an article. [2]Ravina is of the opinion that we can indeed **conclude from this** Mishnah that the wording of the announcement must be specific.

רָבָא אָמַר [3]**Rava,** however, disagreed and **said:** Your inference is not conclusive, and **you can even say that** the finder **announces: "I have found a lost article,"** without specifying what kind, because, as Rava himself stated above, there is another possible explanation for the short period of time allotted to the owner to examine his possessions: [4]**The Sages did not** wish to **make people go to more trouble than necessary in returning lost property.**

תָּנוּ רַבָּנַן [5]The Gemara now cites a Baraita which sets out the form of announcement to be made on each of the Festivals: **Our Sages taught** the following Baraita: "The finder of a lost article must announce it on each of the three Pilgrim Festivals following his discovery. **On the first Festival he says: 'This is the first Festival** on which I am making this announcement.' [6]**On the second Festival he says: 'This is the second Festival** on which I am making this announcement. [7]But **on the third Festival he simply says that he has found something,** without mentioning how many times he has previously made the announcement. In this way the owner will know that he has only seven more days after the Festival to claim the object."

וְאַמַּאי [8]On this point the Gemara asks: **But why** should he deliberately refrain from announcing that this is the third Festival on which he is making the announcement? **Let him** specifically **say: "This is the third festival,"** and thus avoid any possible misunderstanding.

דְּלָא אָתֵי לְאַחְלוּפֵי בְּשֵׁנִי [9]The Gemara answers: The mention of the third Festival is omitted **so that people should not come to mistake it for the second.** The listeners may not hear the announcement clearly and may think that the finder said: "This is the second Festival." Hence, they will not check their possessions promptly.

שֵׁנִי נַמִי [10]The Gemara now asks: But if we are to take the possibility of error into consideration, the finder should not use the expression "This is **the second** Festival" **either.** [28B] Surely there is a danger that people **may come to mistake it for the first.** The listeners may think that the finder said: "This is the first Festival."

הָא קָא אָתֵי רֶגֶל שְׁלִישִׁי [11]The Gemara answers: It is true that an error may occur, but this is not an important consideration during the second Festival, because **the third Festival is** still **to come,** and the claimant has the opportunity to identify his property then.

תָּנוּ רַבָּנַן [12]The Gemara now quotes a Tannaitic source describing changes in the practice of announcing the finding of lost property that took place during the Second Temple period, and during the centuries after its destruction, when Eretz Israel was under Roman rule. **Our Sages taught** the following Baraita: "**At first,** in Temple times, **anyone who found a lost object would announce** his discovery in Jerusalem **at** each

[1]אֶלָּא, שְׁמַע מִינָּהּ "גְּלִימָא" מַכְרִיז. [2]שְׁמַע מִינָּהּ.
[3]רָבָא אָמַר: אֲפִילּוּ תֵּימָא "אֲבֵידְתָא" מַכְרִיז: [4]לֹא הִטְרִיחוּ רַבָּנַן בַּאֲבֵידָה יוֹתֵר מִדַּאי.
[5]תָּנוּ רַבָּנַן: "רֶגֶל רִאשׁוֹן אוֹמֵר: 'רֶגֶל רִאשׁוֹן'. [6]רֶגֶל שֵׁנִי אוֹמֵר: 'רֶגֶל שֵׁנִי'. [7]רֶגֶל שְׁלִישִׁי אוֹמֵר סְתָם".
[8]וְאַמַּאי? לֵימָא: "רֶגֶל שְׁלִישִׁי".
[9]דְּלָא אָתֵי לְאַחְלוּפֵי בְּשֵׁנִי.
[10]שֵׁנִי נַמִי, [28B] אָתְיָא לְאַחְלוּפֵי בְּרִאשׁוֹן!
[11]הָא קָא אָתֵי רֶגֶל שְׁלִישִׁי.
[12]תָּנוּ רַבָּנַן: "בָּרִאשׁוֹנָה, כָּל מִי שֶׁמָּצָא אֲבֵידָה הָיָה מַכְרִיז עָלֶיהָ

LITERAL TRANSLATION

[1]Rather, conclude from this [Mishnah that] he announces, "[I have found] a cloak." [2]Conclude from this.

[3]Rava said: You may even say [that] he announces, "[I have found] a lost article": [4]The Sages did not make [people] go to more trouble than necessary in [returning] lost property.

[5]Our Sages taught: "[On] the first Festival he says: '[This is] the first Festival.' [6][On] the second Festival he says: '[This is] the second Festival.' [7][On] the third Festival he simply says [that he has found something]."

[8]But why? Let him say: "[This is] the third Festival."

[9]So that one should not come to mistake [it] for the second.

[10]The second, too, [28B] one might come to mistake for the first.

[11]Surely the third Festival is coming.

[12]Our Sages taught: "At first, anyone who found a lost object would announce about it [on]

RASHI

לא הטריחו — זה שיהא שוהא יותר משבעה ימים. **רגל ראשון** — שהוא מכריז. **אומר** — בהכרזתו "זהו רגל ראשון", שלא להטריח את האובד לחזור, וכשיבא רגל שני יעלה לרגל ויתן סימניה. **שלישי אומר סתם** — "אבידה מצאתי", ואינו אומר איזה רגל הוא למציאתה, כדי שלא יסמוך האובד על רגל הבא, ויבין שזהו רגל האחרון. (אתי לאחלופי בשני שמא יש שהוא סבור שאמר רגל שני.)

BACKGROUND

לֹא הִטְרִיחוּ רַבָּנַן בַּאֲבֵידָה **The Sages did not trouble people too much in returning lost property.** Although the obligation to return a lost object is a Torah commandment, the duty of announcing that one has found something is a Rabbinical ordinance instituted to help the owner recover his property. Since, by law, the finder received no payment for returning the object (though in certain places it was common to offer a reward), his obligation to announce that he had found something and the necessity to wait for a period after the Festival was in itself a considerable nuisance. Therefore, in order not to cause people to violate commandments of the Torah, the Sages were careful not to cause undue trouble to the finder. They assumed that most pilgrims lived relatively close to Jerusalem, so that it would take them no longer than a week to return home, take an inventory of their possessions, and then go back to Jerusalem to recover what they had lost.

BACKGROUND

וּמִשֶּׁרַבּוּ הָאַנָּסִים But when the men of violence multiplied. These אַנָּסִים — robbers, lit., "forcers" — may have been officials of the foreign authorities or their associates, who used to transfer lost property to the royal treasury. The Gemara uses this term for them because they forced people to violate laws of the Torah. However, there were undoubtedly others who used the imperial law in order to extort money from people who found property, by threatening to deliver it all to the authorities.

אֲבֵידְתָא לְמַלְכָּא Today (as in antiquity), local laws vary regarding the disposition of lost objects. In many countries a treasure buried in the ground belongs entirely to the state, and in the case of found objects the finder receives half and the state receives half. In contrast, according to Roman law the found object belonged wholly to the finder. Rabbi Ammi, who came from Babylonia, which was under Persian rule, knew the laws of the state there, but in Eretz Israel, which was under Roman rule, the lost object belonged to the finder.

TRANSLATION AND COMMENTARY

of the next **three Pilgrim Festivals,** [1]**and after the last Pilgrim Festival** he would continue making the announcement for **seven more days.** [2]This period gave the article's owner enough time **to go** home to check whether he had, in fact, lost anything. The journey home from Jerusalem could take up to **three days.** And then he had enough time **to return** to Jerusalem within another **three days.** This left him **one day to** make contact with the finder and **announce** that he was the owner of the lost article. [3]**After the Temple was destroyed — may it be rebuilt speedily in our days —** [4]**the Sages** had to change the established procedure, and they **instituted that finders** of lost property **should make the** necessary **announcement in synagogues and in houses of study,** since there was now no longer any single place where all Jews gathered. [5]**But when the men of violence proliferated** (this expression will be explained by the Gemara below), and people were afraid to give too much publicity to the fact that they had found articles of value, [6]**the Sages** had to change the procedure again, and **instituted that a finder should** restrict himself to **informing his neighbors and acquaintances, and that was** considered **sufficient."**

שְׁלֹשָׁה רְגָלִים, [1]וְאַחַר רֶגֶל אַחֲרוֹן שִׁבְעַת יָמִים, [2]כְּדֵי שֶׁיֵּלֵךְ שְׁלֹשָׁה, וְיַחֲזוֹר שְׁלֹשָׁה, וְיַכְרִיז יוֹם אֶחָד. [3]מִשֶּׁחָרַב בֵּית הַמִּקְדָּשׁ — שֶׁיִּבָּנֶה בִּמְהֵרָה בְיָמֵינוּ — [4]הִתְקִינוּ שֶׁיְּהוּ מַכְרִיזִים בְּבָתֵּי כְנֵסִיּוֹת וּבְבָתֵּי מִדְרָשׁוֹת. [5]וּמִשֶּׁרַבּוּ הָאַנָּסִים, [6]הִתְקִינוּ שֶׁיְּהוּ מוֹדִיעִין לִשְׁכֵינָיו וְלִמְיוּדָּעָיו, וְדַיּוֹ".

[7]מַאי "מִשֶּׁרַבּוּ הָאַנָּסִין"? [8]דְּאָמְרִי: אֲבֵידְתָא לְמַלְכָּא. [9]רַבִּי אַמִי אַשְׁכַּח אוּדְיָא דְּדִינָרֵי. [10]חַזְיֵיהּ הַהוּא רוֹמָאָה דְּקָא מִירְתַת. [11]אֲמַר לֵיהּ: "זִיל, שְׁקוֹל לְנַפְשָׁךְ, [12]דְּלָאו פַּרְסָאֵי אֲנַן דְּאָמְרִי: אֲבֵידְתָא לְמַלְכָּא". [13]תָּנוּ רַבָּנַן: "אֶבֶן טוֹעַן הָיְתָה

LITERAL TRANSLATION

three Pilgrim Festivals, [1]and after the last Pilgrim Festival seven [more] days, [2]so that he could go three [days], and return three [days], and announce one day. [3]After the Temple was destroyed — may it be rebuilt speedily in our days — [4]they [the Sages] instituted that [finders] should announce in synagogues and in houses of study. [5]But when the men of violence multiplied, [6]they [the Sages] instituted that [a finder] should inform his neighbors and acquaintances, and [that would be] sufficient."

[7]What is [the meaning of] "when the men of violence multiplied"?

[8][Those] who say: Lost objects [belong] to the king.

[9]Rabbi Ammi found a vessel [full] of gold coins. [10]A certain Roman saw that he was frightened. [11]He said to him: "Go, take [it] for yourself, [12]for we are not Persians who say: Lost objects [belong] to the king."

[13]Our Sages taught: "There was a [stone called] *even to'an* (lit., 'stone of claims')

RASHI

אודיא דדינרי — כלי מלא זהובים.

מַאי מִשֶּׁרַבּוּ הָאַנָּסִין [7]On this Baraita the Gemara now asks: **What is the meaning of** the expression, **"When the men of violence proliferated"?** What sort of people were they?

דְּאָמְרִי אֲבֵידְתָא לְמַלְכָּא [8]The Gemara answers: The expression refers to **those** people **who say** that according to the laws of the country all **lost objects belong to the king.** In the light of this changed situation, the Sages were concerned lest these "men of violence" see a person publicly announcing that he had found lost property, and force him to hand it over to the government.

רַבִּי אַמִי [9]The Gemara illustrates this point with a story: **Rabbi Ammi found a vessel full of gold coins.** [10]**A certain Roman saw that** Rabbi Ammi **was frightened** that he would inform against him to the authorities. [11]The Roman reassured Rabbi Ammi and **said to him: "Go** and **take it for yourself.** I have no intention of informing the authorities about this, [12]**for we** Romans **are not** like the **Persians, who say** that all **lost objects belong to the king."**

תָּנוּ רַבָּנַן [13]The Gemara now quotes another Tannaitic source describing the place in Jerusalem that served in Temple times as the center for announcements regarding lost property. **Our Sages taught** the following

NOTES

אֶבֶן הַטּוֹעַן The *even to'an*. According to most Rishonim, the stone was called אֶבֶן הַטּוֹעַן, literally "the claiming stone," because it marked the place in Jerusalem where claims and counterclaims were made. In the version of this story found in tractate *Ta'anit* 19a, the stone was called אֶבֶן הַטּוֹעִין — "the error stone" — or, according to some, אֶבֶן הַתּוֹעִין —

HALAKHAH

הַכְרָזָה בִּזְמַן הַזֶּה Announcing the finding of lost property nowadays. "After the destruction of the Second Temple, the Rabbis decreed that people who found lost property should announce their finds in synagogues and houses of study.

TRANSLATION AND COMMENTARY

Baraita: **"There was a stone called the *even to'an* (אֶבֶן טוֹעַן) in Jerusalem.** [1]Its function was as follows: **Anyone who lost an article would go there, and anyone who found a lost article would go** there, because this was the place where all announcements regarding the finding of lost property were made. [2]The person who had found a lost article **would stand and make his announcement,** and the owner of the article **would stand and cite identifying marks and take** back his property. [3]**And this is the stone we learned about** in a different context in the following Mishnah (*Ta'anit* 19a), where the story is told of how in a year of drought Ḥoni HaMe'agel once prayed for rain. When a large amount of rain had fallen as a result of his prayers, the Jerusalemites asked him to pray that the rain should cease. Ḥoni replied: **'Go out and see if the *even to'an* is covered,** and if it is I will pray for the rain to cease.'"

MISHNAH אָמַר אֶת הָאֲבֵידָה [4]**If** the claimant **described what the lost object was, but was not able to describe its identifying marks,** the finder **must not give** the object **to him,** because the claimant has not provided sufficient information to prove that he is the real owner. [5]Moreover, if **the** claimant is a person suspected of being a **fraud,** the finder **must not give** the object **to him, even though he described its identifying marks.** [6]This latter rule is derived from a verse in the Torah, **as it is said** (Deuteronomy 22:2): "And it shall be with you **until your brother seeks after it."** The authoritative interpretation of this verse, based on understanding the word *drosh* (דְּרֹשׁ) as meaning "to examine" rather than "to seek after" (see above, 27b), is: [7]The object you have found shall remain with you **until you examine your brother, to ascertain whether or not he is a fraud.**

GEMARA אִתְּמַר [8]The Gemara begins its analysis of the Mishnah by citing a difference of opinion between Amoraim as to the way in which the finder announces what he has found: **It was said: Rav Yehudah said:** When a person **announces** that he has found a lost article, he merely says: **"I have found a lost article,"** without specifying what kind. [9]**But Rav Naḥman said:** When a person announces that he has found a lost article, **he** must **announce** the type of object he has found, saying, for example, **"I have found a cloak."**

בִּירוּשָׁלַיִם. [1]כָּל מִי שֶׁאָבְדָה לוֹ אֲבֵידָה נִפְנֶה לְשָׁם, וְכָל מִי שֶׁמּוֹצֵא אֲבֵידָה נִפְנֶה לְשָׁם. [2]זֶה עוֹמֵד וּמַכְרִיז, וְזֶה עוֹמֵד וְנוֹתֵן סִימָנִין וְנוֹטְלָהּ. [3]וְזוֹ הִיא שֶׁשָּׁנִינוּ: 'צְאוּ וּרְאוּ אִם נִמְחֵת אֶבֶן הַטּוֹעַן'".

משנה [4]אָמַר אֶת הָאֲבֵידָה, וְלֹא אָמַר סִימָנֶיהָ, לֹא יִתֵּן לוֹ. [5]וְהָרַמַּאי, אַף עַל פִּי שֶׁאָמַר סִימָנֶיהָ, לֹא יִתֵּן לוֹ, [6]שֶׁנֶּאֱמַר: "עַד דְּרֹשׁ אָחִיךָ אֹתוֹ" — [7]עַד שֶׁתִּדְרוֹשׁ אֶת אָחִיךָ אִם רַמַּאי הוּא אִם אֵינוֹ רַמַּאי.

גמרא [8]אִתְּמַר: רַב יְהוּדָה אָמַר: "אֲבֵידְתָא" מַכְרִיז. [9]וְרַב נַחְמָן אָמַר: "גְּלִימָא" מַכְרִיז.

LITERAL TRANSLATION

in Jerusalem. [1]Everyone who lost an article turned to there, and everyone who found a lost article turned to there. [2]This one stands and announces, and this one stands and gives identifying marks and takes it. [3]And this is [the stone about] which we have learned: 'Go out and see if the *even to'an* is covered.'"

MISHNAH [4][If] he said [what] the lost object [was], but did not say its identifying marks, he must not give [it] to him. [5]And the deceiver, even though he said its identifying marks, he must not give [it] to him, [6]as it is said: "Until your brother seeks after it" — [7]until you examine your brother [to see] if he is a deceiver [or] if he is not a deceiver.

GEMARA [8]It was said: Rav Yehudah said: He announces, "[I have found] a lost article." [9]But Rav Naḥman said: He announces, "[I have found] a cloak."

RASHI

וזו היא ששנינו — במסכת תענית (יט,א) בחוני המעגל. **צאו וראו אם נמחת אבן טוען** — אם נכסת בגשמים, שגבהו הגשמים למעלה הימנו — יש גשמים יותר מדאי ואתפלל עליהם שילכו.

BACKGROUND

אֶבֶן הַטּוֹעַן The *even to'an*. This was apparently a large boulder or a very tall stone column. The expression used by Ḥoni HaMe'agel was certainly an exaggeration, since he spoke of a flood so severe that it not only penetrated low-lying houses, but also covered the whole area with deep water.

גְּלִימָא A cloak. This was an outer cloak worn over other garments. It was wide and open and considered a formal garment to be worn in public places or on ceremonial occasions.

NOTES

literally "the wanderers' stone" — since it marked the place where people would recover their strayed animals.

אִם נִמְחֵת אֶבֶן הַטּוֹעַן If the *even to'an* is covered. Our translation follows *Rashi*, who explains that when this stone was covered with water, it was time to cease praying for rain, as this level of water indicated that abundant rain, sufficient for the coming dry summer, had already fallen. It is, however, an unusual translation of the root מחה, although *Rosh* finds support for this usage. *Tosafot*, however, quotes the Jerusalem Talmud, which translates מחה in the usual

HALAKHAH

When the men of violence increased in number, the Rabbis instituted that people who found lost property should inform their neighbors and acquaintances, and that would be sufficient." (*Rambam, Hilkhot Gezelah Va'Avedah* 13:9.)

אֶבֶן הַטּוֹעַן The *even to'an*. "There was a large stone outside Jerusalem where people used to make announcements about lost articles." (Ibid., 13:1. According to some other commentators, the stone was in Jerusalem.)

רַב יְהוּדָה אֲמַר: ״אֲבֵידְתָא״ מַכְרִיז, דְּאִי אָמְרַתְּ ״גְּלִימָא״ מַכְרִיז, חָיְישִׁינַן לְרַמַּאי.

רַב נַחְמָן אֲמַר: ״גְּלִימָא״ מַכְרִיז. לְרַמַּאי לָא חָיְישִׁינַן, דְּאִם כֵּן, אֵין לַדָּבָר סוֹף.

תְּנַן: ״אָמַר אֶת הָאֲבֵידָה, וְלֹא אָמַר אֶת סִימָנֶיהָ, הֲרֵי זֶה לֹא יִתֵּן לוֹ״. אִי אָמְרַתְּ בִּשְׁלָמָא ״אֲבֵידְתָא״ מַכְרִיז, הָא קָא מַשְׁמַע לָן: אַף עַל גַּב דַּאֲמַר גְּלִימָא, כִּי לֹא אֲמַר סִימָנִין, לָא מְהַדְּרִינַן לֵיהּ. אֶלָּא אִי אָמְרַתְּ ״גְּלִימָא״ מַכְרִיז, אֲמַר אִיהוּ ״גְּלִימָא״ וַאֲמַר אִיהוּ ״גְּלִימָא״. צְרִיכָא לְמֵימַר כִּי לֹא אֲמַר סִימָנִין, לָא מְהַדְּרִינַן לֵיהּ?!

LITERAL TRANSLATION

[1] Rav Yehudah said: He announces, "[I have found] a lost article," [2] for if you say [that] he announces, "[I have found] a cloak," [3] we suspect [that the claimant is] a deceiver.

[4] Rav Naḥman said: He announces, "[I have found] a cloak." [5] We do not suspect [that the claimant is] a deceiver, for if so, there is no end to the matter.

[6] We have learned: "[If] he said [what] the lost object [was], but did not say its identifying marks, then this one must not give [it] to him." [7] It is well if you say [that] he announces, "[I have found] a lost article," [8] [for then] he is telling us this: [that] although he said [that it was] a cloak, [9] since he did not say [its] identifying marks, we do not return [it] to him. [10] But if you say [that] he announces, "[I have found] a cloak," [11] he [the finder] said "cloak" and he [the claimant] said "cloak." [12] Does it need to say that if he did not say [its] identifying marks, we do not return [it] to him?

TRANSLATION AND COMMENTARY

רַב יְהוּדָה אֲמַר [1] The Gemara now explains the reasoning underlying the difference of opinion between the Amoraim. **Rav Yehudah said: He announces, "I have found a lost article,"** and says nothing more, [2] **for if you say that** the finder must let everyone know what kind of article he has found by **announcing,** for example, **"I have found a cloak,"** you open yourself to the possibility that a dishonest person, knowing that a neighbor of his has lost a certain cloak, may come forward to claim it and cite identifying marks. [3] Thus, if the finder specifies in his announcement the nature of the article he has found, we are placed in the position of **suspecting that** every **claimant is a fraud,** thus defeating the entire purpose of the law.

רַב נַחְמָן אֲמַר [4] **Rav Naḥman,** by contrast, is of the opinion that we must make every effort to facilitate the return of lost property to its rightful owner. He dismisses Rav Yehudah's concern and **says: He announces, "I have found a cloak,"** and asks any claimant to cite identifying marks on the article. [5] According to this view, **we do not suspect that the claimant is a fraud, for if** we were to try to achieve perfect certainty, **there would be no end to the matter.** Even if the finder were merely to say he found a lost article, without specifying what kind, a dishonest neighbor could still come forward, guess which article it was and cite its identifying marks.

תְּנַן [6] The Gemara now seeks to prove the correctness of Rav Yehudah's viewpoint from our Mishnah: **We have learned** in the Mishnah: **"If** the claimant **described what the lost object was, but was not able to describe its identifying marks, then** the finder **must not give** the object **to him."** [7] **This** Mishnah **can be** perfectly **well** understood, **if you say,** as Rav Yehudah does, **that** the finder only **announces that he has found a lost article.** [8] According to this view, the Mishnah **is telling us the following: Although** the claimant **has** accurately **described** the lost object in general terms, saying **that it was a cloak,** and we therefore have some confidence that he is the true owner, [9] **we** still **do not return** the cloak **to him since he cannot say** what **its identifying marks** are. [10] **But if you say,** as Rav Naḥman does, **that** the finder explicitly **announces that he has found a cloak,** the Mishnah becomes difficult to understand. [11] If **the finder says,** "I have found a **cloak, and the claimant** can **say** no more than "I have lost a **cloak,"** without citing any identifying marks on it, [12] **does** the Mishnah **need to state** that **if** the claimant **does not cite** the cloak's **identifying marks we do not return** it **to** him?

RASHI

חיישינן לרמאי — שמא שמע האובד מתאונן בין שכניו "טליתי נאבדה", וזה יודע את סימניה, וכשישמע את מוצאה מכריז "טלית מצאתי" — יקום ויתן סימניה, הלכך אבידתא מכריז, ואינו נותן לב לומר "טלית זו אבדתי ואלו סימניה". **אין לדבר סוף** — דהשתא נמי מסיק אדעתיה ואמר: אם טלית היא שמצאת — אלו סימניה. **אי אמרת בשלמא אבידתא מכריז** — ולא מזכיר שם החפץ, אצטריך תנא לאשמועינן דאף על גב דאמר האי "טלית אבדתי" — צריך ליתן סימנין.

BACKGROUND

רַמַּאי A deceiver, a fraud. In general the Halakhah assumes a person is honest until the opposite is proven. However, since citing the identifying marks of an object is not in itself proof of ownership, there is a possibility of fraud in any assertion of ownership of a lost object made on this basis. When it became common practice for people to abuse knowledge they had in order to claim other people's property, the Sages found it necessary to institute this unusual ordinance. They introduced a similar decree regarding testimony about the new moon. Once they knew that a certain group of people were interested in bringing false witnesses, they required witnesses to bring proof of their own reliability.

NOTES

sense of "to obliterate." According to this interpretation, Ḥoni HaMe'agel was using hyperbole to inform his listeners: "In the same way as water cannot wash away the *even to'an,* I cannot annul the blessed arrival of the rain."

TRANSLATION AND COMMENTARY

Surely this is obvious, and the Mishnah had no need to mention it.

אָמַר רַב סָפְרָא [1]**Rav Safra said** in reply: This argument from our Mishnah against Rav Naḥman's viewpoint is not conclusive. **In fact,** it is possible that Rav Naḥman's viewpoint is correct and the finder does **announce that he has found a cloak.** [2]Thus **the finder** in the Mishnah **says,** "I have found a **cloak," and the claimant** then **describes its identifying marks.** [3]But, continues Rav Safra, if the claimant does cite identifying marks on the article, **what is the meaning of** the next clause of the Mishnah, which says that the claimant **"did not** in fact **describe its identifying marks"?** [4]It means that **he did not describe its definitive identifying marks.** If the claimant cannot cite definitive identifying marks, but only inferior means of identification, such as, "It is a large cloak," or the like, the finder must not give it to him, for fear that he is not the true owner.

וְהָרַמַּאי [5]The Gemara now considers the next clause of the Mishnah: "Moreover, if **the** claimant is a person suspected of being a **fraud,** the finder **must not give** the object **to him, even though he described its identifying marks."** The Gemara quotes a Tannaitic source explaining and elaborating on this clause: [6]**Our Sages taught** the following Baraita: **"At first, anyone who lost an article would cite** its **identifying marks, and** if they were found to be satisfactory he would **take it.** [7]But **when dishonest people increased in number,** and many incidents took place in which, despite all precautions, untrustworthy people successfully cited identifying marks on other people's objects, and received them from those who had found them, the Sages stopped relying on identifying marks alone. [8]**They decreed that** the court **should say to** any claimant who successfully cited the object's identifying marks: [9]**'Go out and bring witnesses** to testify before us **that you are not a fraud, and** we will then permit you to **take** the object on the basis of your identification of it.'"

כִּי הָא דַּאֲבוּהּ דְּרַב פַּפָּא [10]The Gemara now illustrates the ruling of this Baraita with the following story: **An incident** took place **in which Rav Pappa's father lost an ass and other people found it.**

[1]אָמַר רַב סָפְרָא: לְעוֹלָם ״גְּלִימָא״ מַכְרִיז. [2]אָמַר אִיהוּ ״גְּלִימָא״, וְאָמַר אִיהוּ סִימָנִין. [3]וּמַאי ״לֹא אָמַר אֶת סִימָנֶיהָ״? [4]לֹא אָמַר סִימָנִין מוּבְהָקִין דִּידָהּ.

[5]״וְהָרַמַּאי, אַף עַל פִּי שֶׁאָמַר אֶת סִימָנֶיהָ, הֲרֵי זֶה לֹא יִתֵּן לוֹ״. [6]תָּנוּ רַבָּנַן: ״בָּרִאשׁוֹנָה, כָּל מִי שֶׁאָבְדָה לוֹ אֲבֵידָה הָיָה נוֹתֵן סִימָנִין וְנוֹטְלָהּ. [7]מִשֶּׁרַבּוּ הָרַמָּאִין, [8]הִתְקִינוּ שֶׁיְּהוּ אוֹמְרִים לוֹ: [9]׳צֵא וְהָבֵא עֵדִים דְּלָאו רַמַּאי אַתְּ, וְטוֹל׳״.

[10]כִּי הָא דַּאֲבוּהּ דְּרַב פַּפָּא אִירְכַּס לֵיהּ חֲמָרָא וְאַשְׁכְּחוּהּ.

LITERAL TRANSLATION

[1]Rav Safra said: In fact, he announces, "[I have found] a cloak." [2]He [the finder] says "cloak" and he [the claimant] says [its] identifying marks. [3]And what is [the meaning of] "he did not say [its] identifying marks"? [4]He did not say its definitive identifying marks.

[5]"And the deceiver, even though he said its identifying marks, he must not give [it] to him." [6]Our Sages taught: "At first, everyone who lost an article would give identifying marks and take it. [7]When the deceivers multiplied [in number], [8]they decreed that they should say to him: [9]'Go out and bring witnesses that you are not a deceiver, and take.'"

[10]Like this [incident] in which the father of Rav Pappa lost an ass and [others] found it.

BACKGROUND

לֹא אָמַר סִימָנִין מוּבְהָקִין דִּידָהּ **He did not cite its definitive identifying marks.** In any instance when a person does not cite positive identifying marks one suspects that the object may not be his, and that he is guessing or mentioning what he saw when the object was in someone else's possession. In the case of a cloak which has a definitive identifying mark (such as a stain in a certain place), the fact that the claimant does not mention it would seem to be proof that the object is not his.

NOTES

מִשֶּׁרַבּוּ הָרַמָּאִין **When the deceivers multiplied.** Originally, claimants of lost property were believed if they could cite the identifying marks of the article claimed; their characters were not questioned unless there were grounds for suspicion. However, after the number of fraudulent claims increased, the Rabbis instituted that everyone should be treated as though he were suspect, unless he could prove his good character (*Rambam*).

HALAKHAH

סִימָן לֹא מוּבְהָק וְרַמַּאי **Inferior identifying marks and dishonest people.** If a person claims a lost object and cites nonspecific identifying marks, we do not return it to him. Moreover, a dishonest person is not believed even if he cites convincing identifying marks. He must produce witnesses." (*Shulḥan Arukh, Ḥoshen Mishpat* 267:5.)

מָה מַכְרִיז **What information does the finder include in his announcement?** "The finder should describe, in a general way, what kind of article he has found," following Rav Naḥman, whose rulings are normally authoritative on monetary questions, and following Ravina's similar ruling (above, 28a). (Ibid., 267:4.)

עֵדִים שֶׁאֵינוֹ רַמַּאי **Character witnesses.** "When the number of dishonest people increased, the Rabbis decreed that claimants were required to bring witnesses to testify to their good character before they could receive their lost property back." (Ibid., 267:6.) *Rema* rules, following *Tur,* that a definitive identifying mark is acceptable without character

TRANSLATION AND COMMENTARY

[1] **He came before Rabbah bar Rav Huna,** and requested that the court permit him to recover his animal on the basis of identifying marks that he was able to provide. [2] Rabbah bar Rav Huna **said to him: "Go and bring witnesses that you are not a fraud and** we will then permit you to **take** your ass, since you have successfully described its identifying marks." [3] Rav Pappa's father **went and brought witnesses.** [4] Rabbah bar Rav Huna **said to them: "Do you know that** Rav Pappa's father **is a fraud?"** [5] **They said to him: "Yes."** Rav Pappa's father **said to them** in astonishment: **"I? Am I a fraud?"** [6] **They said to him** in reply: **"We meant to say that you are not a fraud,** but we were confused by the unusual way Rabbah bar Rav Huna phrased his question, and we answered 'yes,' thinking that he had asked us to confirm that you are completely honest." [7] **Rabbah bar Rav Huna** was now faced with the problem of whether to consider the second statement made by the witnesses as an explanation of their original testimony or as a retraction of it. He **said:** Even though witnesses are not normally permitted to retract or alter their testimony, in this case we may accept the claim that the witnesses were confused, because **it stands to reason that a person does not bring** witnesses to testify to his **disadvantage.** Thus the witnesses did not retract their earlier testimony. They merely explained how their confusion had arisen.

MISHNAH כָּל דָּבָר שֶׁעוֹשֶׂה וְאוֹכֵל [8] **Every** lost animal **that can work and** thus cover the expense of the food it **eats should work** for the finder **and** thus cover the expense of the food it **eats.** [9] **But** an animal **that cannot work but** nevertheless **eats** and thus does not cover the expenses of its upkeep **should be sold** by its finder after a reasonable amount of time has passed. It should not remain indefinitely in the finder's possession,

[1] אֲתָא לְקַמֵּיהּ דְּרַבָּה בַּר רַב הוּנָא. [2] אֲמַר לֵיהּ: "זִיל אַיְיתִי סַהֲדֵי דְּלָאו רַמַּאי אַתְּ, וְטוֹל". [3] אֲזַל אַיְיתִי סַהֲדֵי. [4] אֲמַר לְהוּ: "יְדַעִיתוּן בֵּיהּ דְּרַמַּאי הוּא?" [5] אֲמַרוּ לֵיהּ: "אִין". אֲמַר לְהוּ: "אֲנָא, רַמָּאָה אֲנָא?!" [6] אֲמַרוּ לֵיהּ: "אֲנַן לָאו רַמַּאי אַתְּ קָאָמְרִינַן". [7] אֲמַר רַבָּה בַּר רַב הוּנָא: "מִסְתַּבְּרָא לָא מַיְיתֵי אִינִישׁ חוּבְתָא לְנַפְשֵׁיהּ".

משנה [8] כָּל דָּבָר שֶׁעוֹשֶׂה וְאוֹכֵל יַעֲשֶׂה וְיֹאכַל. [9] וְדָבָר שֶׁאֵין עוֹשֶׂה וְאוֹכֵל יִמָּכֵר,

LITERAL TRANSLATION

[1] He came before Rabbah bar Rav Huna. [2] He said to him: "Go [and] bring witnesses that you are not a deceiver, and take."

[3] He went [and] brought witnesses. [4] He said to them: "Do you know about him that he is a deceiver?" [5] They said to him: "Yes." He said to them: "I, am I a deceiver?" [6] They said to him: "We said [that] you are not a deceiver." [7] Rabbah bar Rav Huna said: "It stands to reason that a person does not bring disadvantage to himself."

MISHNAH [8] Everything that works and eats should work and eat. [9] But a thing that does not work but eats should be sold,

RASHI

אמרו ליה אין – כסבורין שאמר להן "ידעיתון ביה דלאו רמאי הוא", שכך היה לו לשואלן. **מסתברא** – שזה היה דעתן מתחילה, ואין כאן משום מגיד וחוזר ומגיד. **לא מייתי איניש חובה לנפשיה** – וכשהביאן לבית דין – בטוח היה שלא יעידו חובתו.

משנה כל דבר שעושה ואוכל – אם אבידה זו דבר שיכולין להאכילו את שכר מעשיו, כגון שור וחמור – יעשה ויאכל, ולא ימכור אותו המוצא אם שהו בעליו מלדרשו, שכל אדם נוח לו בבהמתו, שהכירה בו כבר ולימדה לרצונו.

BACKGROUND

אֲמַרוּ לֵיהּ אִין They said to him: "Yes." The reason for this error is simple. Generally, when one inquires as to whether someone is trustworthy, one asks the witnesses whether they know the man to be honest; and since they were sure that the inquiry would be put in that manner, they answered "yes," without paying close attention to the actual wording of the question.

לָא מַיְיתֵי אִינִישׁ חוּבְתָא לְנַפְשֵׁיהּ A person does not bring disadvantage to himself. The normal assumption is that no one would bring proof against himself in court. If a claimant does not think he has a right to something, he can admit as much or withdraw his claim. Since Rav Pappa's father took the trouble to bring witnesses, it is reasonable to assume that he thought they would testify in his favor. Therefore, when Rabbah bar Rav Huna himself realized that he had asked the question in a misleading manner, he accepted the corrected testimony — not as a change in the previous testimony, but rather as a correction to a slip of the tongue.

וְדָבָר שֶׁאֵין עוֹשֶׂה וְאוֹכֵל But a thing that does not work but eats. Generally, animals that do not work are worth more when sold (for meat or the like) than it costs to keep them. However, this only applies where someone raises such animals professionally. By contrast, the finder of such an animal may submit a much higher bill for expenses for food and for the time he has spent taking care of the animal, and this sum may be greater than the market value of the animal.

NOTES

לָא מַיְיתֵי אִינִישׁ חוּבְתָא לְנַפְשֵׁיהּ A person does not bring disadvantage to himself. There is a general rule in the laws of evidence that כֵּיוָן שֶׁהִגִּיד שׁוּב אֵינוֹ חוֹזֵר וּמַגִּיד — "Once witnesses have completed their testimony, they may not retract or alter it," even if they insist that their original testimony was untrue. In the case of Rav Pappa's father, this rule would appear to be especially applicable because the witnesses' retraction came at the behest of the claimant, who threatened them. Thus it appears that they should not have been allowed to alter their testimony, even if they did so immediately, within the normal time allowed for changes caused by an initial slip of the tongue (*Ritva*). Nevertheless, Rabbah bar Rav Huna ruled that where it is clear that the witnesses' original testimony was given unintentionally, as a result of a misunderstanding, they may correct their words even in a case like ours (*Meiri*).

יַעֲשֶׂה וְיֹאכַל... יִמָּכֵר An animal's working for its keep versus its being sold. The Aḥaronim point out that whether the animal is capable of working for its keep or not, the law is essentially the same. The animals must be kept and fed

HALAKHAH

witnesses, even after the Rabbinic requirement of character witnesses was implemented.

הַמּוֹצֵא בַּעֲלֵי חַיִּים One who finds a lost animal. "If a person finds a lost domestic animal that works for its keep, he should keep it and work it for twelve months. If necessary, he should hire it out. He should then deduct the expenses of caring for the animal from the income the animal has provided and set the entire remainder aside for the owner, when he appears. This law applies to cows, asses, egg-laying hens, and the like. After twelve months, the finder should continue working the animal and not sell it, but he is entitled from then on to treat it like a regular animal placed in his

TRANSLATION AND COMMENTARY

generating no income and costing the finder money, [1]**as it is said** (Deuteronomy 22:2): **"And you shall restore it to him,"** [2]which teaches us, among other things, that the finder should **see how to restore** the lost object **to** its owner in such a way that the owner will benefit in real terms from the finder's fulfillment of the commandment to restore lost property. If the animal spends a long time in the care of the finder, the owner will get nothing of value when it is returned to him, since he will have to reimburse the finder for all his expenses.

מַה יְהֵא בַּדָּמִים [3]If the owner does not come forward and the finder is forced to sell the animal, **what should be done with the money** the finder receives in exchange for the lost animal? Is the finder permitted to make use of the proceeds of the sale or not? [4]**Rabbi Tarfon says:** The finder **may use it** for his own purposes, as long as he does not know to whom the money rightfully belongs. [5]**Therefore, if** the money **is lost** while in the finder's possession, **he is responsible for it,** as he has the benefit of its use (see below, 29a-b). [6] **Rabbi Akiva says:** The money must remain untouched in the finder's care until it is claimed by the owner of the animal. The finder **may not use it** for his own purposes. [7]**Therefore,** since the finder receives no benefit from the money, **if it is lost** the finder **is not responsible for it** and is not required to replace it — in the same way as he is not required to replace the lost object itself if it is lost while in his care.

GEMARA וּלְעוֹלָם [8]The Mishnah ruled that any found animal that can work should do so in order to pay for its keep while in the custody of the finder. But, the Gemara asks, is the finder required to be responsible for looking after it **forever?** What happens if years go by without the owner appearing?

אָמַר רַב נַחְמָן [9]**Rav Naḥman replied in the name of Shmuel:** The finder is required to look after the animal **up to** a maximum of **twelve months** from the time he found it. From then on, he is permitted to sell it.

[1]שֶׁנֶּאֱמַר: "וַהֲשֵׁבֹתוֹ לוֹ" — [2]רְאֵה הֵיאַךְ תְּשִׁיבֶנּוּ לוֹ. [3]מַה יְּהֵא בַּדָּמִים? [4]רַבִּי טַרְפוֹן אוֹמֵר: יִשְׁתַּמֵּשׁ בָּהֶן. [5]לְפִיכָךְ, אִם אָבְדוּ, חַיָּיב בְּאַחֲרָיוּתָן. [6]רַבִּי עֲקִיבָא אוֹמֵר: לֹא יִשְׁתַּמֵּשׁ בָּהֶן. [7]לְפִיכָךְ, אִם אָבְדוּ, אֵין חַיָּיב בְּאַחֲרָיוּתָן.

גמרא [8]וּלְעוֹלָם? [9]אָמַר רַב נַחְמָן אָמַר שְׁמוּאֵל: עַד שְׁנֵים עָשָׂר חֹדֶשׁ.

LITERAL TRANSLATION

[1]as it is said: "And you shall restore it to him" — [2]see how you should restore it to him.

[3]What should be [done] with the money? [4]Rabbi Tarfon says: He may use it. [5]Therefore, if it is lost, he is responsible for it. [6]Rabbi Akiva says: He may not use it. [7]Therefore, if it is lost, he is not responsible for it.

GEMARA [8]And forever?

[9]Rav Naḥman said in the name of Shmuel: Up to twelve months.

RASHI

ראה היאך תשיבנו לו — שלא תאכילנו תלי דמיו, שאם כן אין זו השבה. **לפיכך** — מפרש בגמרא.

גמרא ולעולם — וכי עד עולם זקוק זה לטפל בטורח שמירה.

NOTES

for a period of time and then sold. However, there is still a basic difference between the cases: It is permitted to sell a working animal after the stated period of time has passed, but it is not obligatory to do so. The finder may, if he wishes, continue to work the animal indefinitely to cover expenses. By contrast, non-working animals must be sold after the stated period of time has passed, since the owner is losing money with each passing day (*Maharam Schiff, Torat Ḥayyim*).

וַהֲשֵׁבֹתוֹ לוֹ **"And you shall restore it to him."** There is an important Halakhic principle, derived from the Biblical verse (Proverbs 3:17): "Her ways are ways of pleasantness," that, whenever possible, Scriptural commands are to be interpreted in a manner that is manifestly benevolent. In the case under discussion, the Torah requires a finder to return lost animals to their owner. If this commandment cannot be fulfilled immediately, the finder must either spend his own money to do someone else a favor, or starve the animals, or seek reimbursement from the owner. It is clear that the last course of action is the only one that is benevolent to both the finder and the owner. However, if the owner is ultimately compelled to pay an exorbitant amount for expenses incurred by the finder, he will be getting nothing, and thus the express purpose of the law will be defeated. Hence, the only benevolent way to explain the Torah's command is to say that when the finder will incur expense in looking after the owner's property, the Torah expects the finder to sell the property and return its value (*Rabbenu Yehonatan*).

HALAKHAH

care. The rule is that he must assess the value of the animal at the time, and from then on keep a record of profits, losses, and expenses. When the owner appears, the two parties divide the total profit or loss equally," following *Rambam*'s interpretation of the Gemara here. (*Shulḥan Arukh, Ḥoshen Mishpat* 267:22.)

TRANSLATION AND COMMENTARY

תַּנְיָא נַמִי הָכִי [1]The Gemara now notes that there is **also** a Baraita in which **this** ruling of Rav Naḥman **is taught: "All** lost animals **that can work and** thus cover the expense of the food they **eat — for example, cows** or **asses,** which are profitable enough to cover their expenses easily — [2]**must be taken care of** by the finder for **up to twelve months.** [3]**From then on,** the finder is entitled to **assess their value,** sell them, **and set the money aside.** [4]**Calves and young asses,** which do no work but are not very expensive or time-consuming to keep, **must be taken care of** by the finder **for three months.** [5]**From then on,** the finder is entitled to **assess their value,** sell them, **and set the money aside.** [6]**Geese and cocks,** which do no work and are very expensive and time-consuming to keep, **must be taken care of for thirty days.** [7]But **from then on,** the finder is entitled to **assess their value,** sell them, **and set the money aside."** This Baraita supports the ruling of Rav Naḥman that the finder's responsibility to look after animals that work for their keep lasts for a maximum period of twelve months.

אָמַר רַב נַחְמָן בַּר יִצְחָק [8]**Rav Naḥman bar Yitzḥak said: An** egg-laying **hen is like a large domestic animal** such as a cow or an ass. The fact that a hen lays eggs, and that the eggs generate enough profit to cover her upkeep, places a hen in the same category as a large domestic animal, and the finder must therefore look after a hen for a maximum of twelve months.

תַּנְיָא נַמִי הָכִי [9]The Gemara now notes that there is **also** a Baraita in which **this** ruling of Rav Naḥman bar Yitzḥak **is taught: "Hens and large** domestic **animals must be taken care of** by the finder **for** up to **twelve months.** [10]**From then on,** the finder is entitled to **assess their value,** sell them, **and set the money aside.** [11]**Calves and young asses must be taken care of** by the finder **for thirty days.** [12]**From then on,** the finder is entitled to

[1]תַּנְיָא נַמִי הָכִי: ״כָּל דָּבָר שֶׁעוֹשֶׂה וְאוֹכֵל — כְּגוֹן פָּרָה וַחֲמוֹר — [2]מְטַפֵּל בָּהֶן עַד שְׁנֵים עָשָׂר חֹדֶשׁ. [3]מִכָּאן וְאֵילָךְ, שָׁם דְּמֵיהֶן וּמַנִּיחָן. [4]עֲגָלִים וּסְיָיחִין, מְטַפֵּל בָּהֶן שְׁלֹשָׁה חֳדָשִׁים. [5]מִכָּאן וְאֵילָךְ, שָׁם דְּמֵיהֶן וּמַנִּיחָן. [6]אַוָּזִין וְתַרְנְגוֹלִין, מְטַפֵּל בָּהֶם שְׁלֹשִׁים יוֹם. [7]מִכָּאן וְאֵילָךְ, שָׁם דְּמֵיהֶן וּמַנִּיחָן״.
[8]אָמַר רַב נַחְמָן בַּר יִצְחָק: תַּרְנְגוֹלֶת כִּבְהֵמָה גַּסָּה.
[9]תַּנְיָא נַמִי הָכִי: ״תַּרְנְגוֹלֶת וּבְהֵמָה גַּסָּה, מְטַפֵּל בָּהֶן שְׁנֵים עָשָׂר חוֹדֶשׁ. [10]מִכָּאן וְאֵילָךְ, שָׁם דְּמֵיהֶן וּמַנִּיחָן. [11]עֲגָלִים וּסְיָיחִין, מְטַפֵּל בָּהֶן שְׁלֹשִׁים יוֹם. [12]מִכָּאן וְאֵילָךְ, שָׁם דְּמֵיהֶן וּמַנִּיחָן.

LITERAL TRANSLATION

[1]It was also taught thus: "Everything that works and eats — for example, a cow or an ass — [2]he takes care of them up to twelve months. [3]From here on, he assesses their value and sets [the money] aside. [4]Calves and young asses, he takes care of them [for] three months. [5]From here on, he assesses their value and sets [the money] aside. [6]Geese and roosters, he takes care of them [for] thirty days. [7]From here on, he assesses their value and sets [the money] aside."

[8]Rav Naḥman bar Yitzḥak said: A hen is like a large domestic animal.

[9]It was also taught thus: "A hen and a large domestic animal, he takes care of them [for] twelve months. [10]From here on, he assesses their value and sets [the money] aside. [11]Calves and young asses, he takes care of them [for] thirty days. [12]From here on, he assesses their value and sets [the money] aside.

RASHI

שם דמיהן — מוכרן, ומניח הדמים אצלו. **עגלים וסייחין** — דקין, שאין עושין מלאכה. **תרנגולין** — זכרים, שאין מטילין בלים. **בבהמה גסה** — שעושה ואוכלת, ומטפל בה שנים עשר חדש, דיכול להאכילה דמי בלים. **מטפל** — *אנשמיטר״א בלעז.

BACKGROUND

עֲגָלִים וּסְיָיחִין אַוָּזִין וְתַרְנְגוֹלִין Calves and young asses, geese and roosters. The difference between the various rulings here derives from the greater difficulty involved in taking care of certain kinds of animals. It is not very difficult to take care of animals which can be kept in a courtyard or sent out to pasture. However, geese and chickens must be watched carefully, to prevent them from escaping; they also need a special coop, or else they will dirty the place where they are kept. Because the Sages did not wish to make the returning of lost objects too burdensome, they set a time limit for the care of those animals that are difficult to tend.

LANGUAGE (RASHI)

אנשמיטר״א* From the Old French *entremetre,* meaning "to occupy oneself with," "to care for."

NOTES

שָׁם דְּמֵיהֶן He assesses their value. The normal meaning of שׁם is "to assess," i.e., to appraise the value of an object. If we read the word in this way, the finder is entitled to keep the animal for himself, as long as he has appraised the animal at its fair market value and has set the money aside pending the owner's appearance. *Ramban* and other Rishonim do, in fact, interpret the Gemara this way. *Rashi,* however, rules that the finder must sell the animal to another person. (Some commentators, troubled by *Rashi*'s unusual usage of the word שָׂם, have suggested translating it as "to place" rather than "to assess.")

Rif goes even further than *Rashi*, and rules that the finder

HALAKHAH

מָצָא עֲגָלִים וּסְיָיחִין One who finds a lost calf or young ass. "If a person finds a lost calf or young ass and the animal is capable of grazing in the field, he should care for it for three months. But if the animal must be fed by the finder, he should care for it for one month only," following the conclusion of the Gemara here. (*Shulḥan Arukh, Ḥoshen Mishpat* 267:23.)

מָצָא אַוָּזִין וְתַרְנְגוֹלִין One who finds a lost goose or rooster. "If a person finds a lost goose or a male chicken, and the bird is mature, he should care for it for thirty days;

TRANSLATION AND COMMENTARY

assess their value, sell them, **and set the money aside.** [1]**Geese and roosters and anything the cost of whose keep is greater than their profit must be taken care of** by the finder **for three days.** [2]**From then on,** the finder is entitled to **assess their value,** sell them, **and set the money** aside." This Baraita supports the ruling of Rav Naḥman bar Yitzḥak that an egg-laying hen comes under the same category as a large domestic animal and must be looked after by the finder for a maximum of twelve months. Thus two Baraitot have been cited, one in support of the ruling of Rav Naḥman bar Ya'akov and the other in support of the ruling by Rav Naḥman bar Yitzḥak.

קַשְׁיָא עֲגָלִים וּסְיָיחִין [3]The Gemara now remarks: This second Baraita certainly supports Rav Naḥman bar Yitzḥak's ruling comparing hens to large domestic animals. But **there is a contradiction between the ruling about calves and young asses** in the first Baraita, **and the ruling about calves and young asses** in the second Baraita. In the first Baraita the maximum time allotted for their care was three months, but in the second only thirty days. [4]Similarly, there is a contradiction **between the ruling about geese and roosters** in the first Baraita **and the ruling about geese and roosters** in the second Baraita. In the first Baraita the maximum time allotted for their care was thirty days, but in the second only three days.

עֲגָלִים וּסְיָיחִין [5]The Gemara answers: **There is no difficulty in reconciling the ruling** in the first Baraita **about calves and young asses with the ruling** in the second Baraita **about calves and young asses.** [6]**The first** Baraita's **ruling refers to** a situation where the calves and young asses can be fed at little expense by putting them out to **pasture.** Hence, the time allotted is three months. **The second** Baraita's **ruling refers to** a situation where there is no pasture available, so the calves and young asses have to be **fattened** at considerable expenditure of money and time by using feed from the finder's own supplies. Hence, the time allotted is only thirty days.

אֲוָוזִין וְתַרְנְגוֹלִין [7]Similarly, says the Gemara, **there is no difficulty in reconciling the ruling** in the first Baraita **about geese and roosters with the ruling** in the second Baraita **about geese and roosters.** [8]**The first** Baraita's **ruling refers to** a situation where the geese and roosters are **large,** and can seek out their own sources of food. Hence,

[1]אֲוָוזִין וְתַרְנְגוֹלִין וְכָל דָּבָר שֶׁטִּיפּוּלוֹ מְרוּבֶּה מִשְּׂכָרוֹ, מְטַפֵּל בָּהֶן שְׁלֹשָׁה יָמִים. [2]מִכָּאן וְאֵילָךְ, שָׁם דְּמֵיהֶן וּמַנִּיחָן". [3]קַשְׁיָא עֲגָלִים וּסְיָיחִין אַעֲגָלִים וּסְיָיחִין, [4]אֲוָוזִין וְתַרְנְגוֹלִין אַאֲוָוזִין וְתַרְנְגוֹלִין! [5]עֲגָלִים וּסְיָיחִין אַעֲגָלִים וּסְיָיחִין לָא קַשְׁיָא. [6]הָא דִּרְעָיָא, וְהָא דִּפְטוּמָא. [7]אֲוָוזִין וְתַרְנְגוֹלִין אַאֲוָוזִין וְתַרְנְגוֹלִין נַמִי לָא קַשְׁיָא. [8]הָא בְּרַבְרְבֵי, הָא בְּזוּטְרֵי.

LITERAL TRANSLATION

[1]Geese and roosters and everything [the cost of] whose care is greater than its profit, he takes care of them [for] three days. [2]From here on, he assesses their value and sets [the money] aside."

[3]There is a contradiction [between one ruling about] calves and young asses and [the other ruling about] calves and young asses, [4][and between one ruling about] geese and roosters and [the other ruling about] geese and roosters.

[5]There is no difficulty [in reconciling the one ruling about] calves and young asses with [the other ruling about] calves and young asses. [6]This [ruling refers] to pasture, and that [ruling refers] to fattening. [7]There is also no difficulty [in reconciling the one ruling about] geese and roosters with [the other ruling about] geese and roosters. [8]This [ruling refers] to large ones, that [ruling refers] to small ones.

RASHI

הא דרעיא הא דפטומא — הא דקתני שלשה [חדשים] — באורך מרעה וזמן הדשאים, שאין טיפולו מרובה, והא דקתני שלשים [יום] — בזמן שאין מרעה וצריך לפטמה על אבוסה ממה שבבית, שדמיה יקרים. **רברבי** — אוכלין הרבה, הלכך שלשה ימים, דהא אוקימנא בזכרים.

BACKGROUND

שְׁלֹשָׁה יָמִים Three days. Rather than state that an animal could be sold immediately, the Rabbis apparently set this period of time because the owner might come and claim it in the meantime, and it was assumed that he would prefer to receive the animal rather than its monetary value.

בְּרַבְרְבֵי... בְּזוּטְרֵי To large ones... to small ones. Large fowl can find their own food, or are satisfied with readily available food (seeds and the like). However, chicks cannot eat a great variety of food, especially when they are not with their mothers, so special feed has to be prepared for them. This, of course, involves expense and time for the person tending them.

NOTES

must sell the animal to another person in the presence of a court. *Maharal* explains that, since the finder is in a hurry to sell the animal before expenses accumulate, he is unlikely to get the best price for it. Hence, the court is required in order to ensure that the price is reasonable under the circumstances. For *Rambam*'s interpretation, see entry in Halakhah section (pp. 126-127).

HALAKHAH

but if it is very young, so that its care is quite costly, he should care for it only three days. This latter law applies equally to any animal whose care costs more than it is worth. After the period of time has elapsed, the finder should sell the animal in court." (Ibid., 267:24.) *Rema* rules, in the name of *Rosh,* that the sale need not take place in the presence of the court. Moreover, the finder can appraise the animal at its fair market value and take it for himself, setting aside the value of the animal for the owner.

[1]״וְשֶׁאֵינוֹ עוֹשֶׂה וְאוֹכֵל״. [2]תָּנוּ רַבָּנַן: ״׳וַהֲשֵׁבֹתוֹ לוֹ׳ — [3]רְאֵה הֵיאַךְ תְּשִׁיבֶנּוּ לוֹ, שֶׁלֹּא יַאֲכִיל עֵגֶל לָעֲגָלִים, [4]וּסְיָח לִסְיָיחִין, אַוְוזָא לְאַוָּוזִין, וְתַרְנְגוֹל לְתַרְנְגוֹלִין״.

[5]״מַה יְּהֵא בַּדָּמִים? [6]רַבִּי טַרְפוֹן אוֹמֵר: יִשְׁתַּמֵּשׁ וכו׳״. [7]עַד כָּאן לָא פְּלִיגִי [29A] אֶלָּא כְּשֶׁנִּשְׁתַּמֵּשׁ בָּהֶן. [8]אֲבָל לֹא נִשְׁתַּמֵּשׁ בָּהֶן, אִם אָבְדוּ, פָּטוּר. [9]לֵימָא תֶּיהֱוֵי תְּיוּבְתָּא דְּרַב יוֹסֵף. [10]דְּאִתְּמַר: שׁוֹמֵר אֲבֵידָה:

LITERAL TRANSLATION

[1]"But one that does not work but eats." [2]Our Sages taught: "'And you shall restore it to him' — [3]see how you should restore it to him, so that he should not feed a calf to calves, [4]or a young ass to young asses, [or] a goose to geese, or a rooster to roosters."

[5]"What should be [done] with the money? [6]Rabbi Tarfon says: He may use it, etc." [7]Up to here they do not differ [29A] except when he has used it. [8]But [if] he has not used it, [then] if it is lost, he is exempt. [9]Shall we say that this will be a refutation of Rav Yosef. [10]For it was said: A guardian of a lost object:

TRANSLATION AND COMMENTARY

their upkeep is less costly, and the time allotted is thirty days. **The second** Baraita's **ruling refers to** a situation where the geese and roosters are **small,** and have to be fed by the finder from his own supplies. Hence their upkeep is more costly, and the time allotted is only three days.

שֶׁאֵינוֹ עוֹשֶׂה וְאוֹכֵל [1]The Gemara now considers the following clause in our Mishnah: **"But** an animal **that cannot work but** nevertheless **eats** and thus does not cover the expenses of its upkeep **should be sold."** [2]In relation to this, the Gemara notes: **Our Sages taught** the following Baraita, elaborating on this Mishnah: "The Biblical verse (Deuteronomy 22:2) says: **'And you shall restore it to him.'** On this the Sages comment: **See how to restore** the lost object **to** its owner in such a way that he will benefit in real terms from receiving it back. [3]The finder **should not feed** the value of **a calf to calves.** In other words, he should not spend so much on the calf's upkeep that it approaches the value of the calf itself, because in the end, after reimbursing the finder for his expenses, the owner will be left with nothing. [4]Similarly, the finder should not feed the value of **a young ass to young asses** in his care, **or** the value of **a goose to geese** in his care, or the value of **a rooster** to **roosters** in his care." In all these cases the finder is enjoined to consider the ultimate benefit to the owner of the lost animal. Where it is to the benefit of the owner that the animal be sold rather than kept in the finder's possession, the finder must sell the animal and keep the proceeds of the sale for the owner.

מַה יְּהֵא בַּדָּמִים [5]The Gemara now goes on to consider the second half of our Mishnah, which discusses the situation that arises if the finder sells the animal he has found. The Mishnah said: "If the owner does not come forward and the finder is forced to sell the animal, **what should be done with the money** the finder receives in exchange for the lost animal? [6]**Rabbi Tarfon says:** The finder **may use it** for his own purposes until its owner comes to claim his property, whereas Rabbi Akiva disagrees." [7]The Gemara notes: **Rabbi Tarfon and Rabbi Akiva** only **differ** [29A] with regard to the finder's responsibility for the money, on the question of **whether** the finder **has** permission to **make use of the money** or not. Rabbi Tarfon says that, since he is permitted to use it, he is in the category of a paid bailee and is responsible for it; whereas Rabbi Akiva says that since he is not permitted to use it, he is in the category of an unpaid bailee and is exempt from liability. [8]**But if** it is accepted that **he is not** permitted **to use** the money, **then** even Rabbi Tarfon would agree that **if** the money **was lost, he would be exempt** from liability.

לֵימָא תֶּיהֱוֵי תְּיוּבְתָּא [9]The Gemara now suggests: **Shall we say that this** Mishnah **is a refutation of** the opinion of **Rav Yosef?** [10]**For it was said** that there is a difference of opinion between Amoraim on the question of the legal status of **someone who** has found and **is looking after a lost object** until the owner comes to claim it.

RASHI

שלא יאכיל עגל לעגלים — מן העגלים שנמצא לא יאכיל לו דמי עגל. **עד כאן לא פליגי** — לענין להתחייב באבידתו. **אלא** — משום שכר שימוש מעות, אבל שכר שמירת מצוה, דנימא מגו דלא בעי למיתב ריפתא לעניא, דהעוסק במצוה פטור מן המצוה — לא מחייבינן ליה. **בשנשתמש** — לאו דוקא, אלא משום שכר שימוש קאמר, מפני שמותר להשתמש בהן.

TERMINOLOGY

...לֵימָא תֶּיהֱוֵי תְּיוּבְתָּא דְ Shall we say that this will be a refutation of...? The Talmud uses this expression to suggest that a Mishnah contradicts a particular Amora's view, usually rejecting that idea later in the discussion.

NOTES

אֶלָּא כְּשֶׁנִּשְׁתַּמֵּשׁ בָּהֶן Except when he has used it. The commentary here follows *Rashi* and *Tosafot,* who explain that the issue is not whether the finder actually used the money, but rather whether he was *permitted* to use it. Even according to Rabbi Akiva, if the finder actually used the money he would be required to replace it if it were lost, in accordance with the law regarding a person who illegally uses someone else's property. Rabbi Akiva and Rabbi Tarfon disagree about a situation in which he did not actually use the money. The Gemara explains later that if Rabbi Tarfon

LITERAL TRANSLATION

[1] Rabbah said: He is like an unpaid bailee. [2] Rav Yosef said: He is like a paid bailee.
[3] Rav Yosef can say to you: In [a case of] theft or loss, everyone agrees (lit., "the whole world does not disagree") that he is responsible. [4] Where they disagree, [it is] about [unavoidable] accidents, where a borrower [is responsible]. [5] Rabbi Tarfon is of the opinion [that] the Sages permitted him to use it,

[1] רַבָּה אָמַר: כְּשׁוֹמֵר חִנָּם. [2] רַב יוֹסֵף אָמַר: כְּשׁוֹמֵר שָׂכָר. [3] אָמַר לָךְ רַב יוֹסֵף: בִּגְנֵיבָה וַאֲבֵידָה, דְּכוּלֵּי עָלְמָא לָא פְּלִיגִי דְּחַיָּיב. [4] כִּי פְּלִיגִי, בְּאוֹנָסִין דְּשׁוֹאֵל. [5] רַבִּי טַרְפוֹן סָבַר: שָׁרוּ לֵיהּ רַבָּנַן לְאִשְׁתַּמּוּשֵׁי בְּגַוַּיְיהוּ,

RASHI

כשומר חנם — ולינו חייב אלא בפשיעה. **כשומר שכר** — וחייב בגניבה ואבידה, דשומר שכר מלוה הוא, דהעוסק במלוה פטור מן המלוה. **כולי עלמא לא פליגי דמחייב** — כדין שומר שכר.

TRANSLATION AND COMMENTARY

[1] **Rabbah said** that someone looking after a lost object until the owner comes to claim it **is like an unpaid bailee,** and is not liable if the object is lost or stolen while in his care. The reason for this, according to Rabbah, is that the finder will not receive payment from the owner for looking after the object; nor has the finder any right to make use of the object for his own purposes. His responsibilities are thus those of an unpaid bailee, who is only responsible for damage caused to an object in his care if he is negligent in looking after it. [2] On the other hand, **Rav Yosef said** that **he is like a paid bailee,** and is liable if the object is lost or stolen while in his care. The reason for this, according to Rav Yosef, is that a finder does receive certain benefits for looking after the object, in that while caring for it he is exempt from performing other acts of kindness such as giving charity, in accordance with the principle that someone engaged in the performance of a religious duty (in this case, looking after someone's lost property) is exempt from other religious duties. Therefore, he has the status of a paid bailee, and is liable if the object is stolen or lost. But, says the Gemara, from our Mishnah it would appear that: (1) If the finder is not permitted to use money from the sale of the lost animal, he is exempt from responsibility for theft or loss, like an unpaid bailee. (2) If the finder *is* permitted to use money from the sale of the lost animal, it is this permission that makes him a paid bailee, and responsible in the event of theft or loss; his benefit is not that he is exempt from the performance of other acts of kindness while looking after the lost property. Thus our Mishnah would appear to contradict Rav Yosef's opinion.

אָמַר לָךְ רַב יוֹסֵף [3] The Gemara answers: The assumption upon which this question is based is that Rabbi Akiva and Rabbi Tarfon differ as to whether the finder of lost property is in the category of an unpaid bailee, and thus exempt from liability for theft or loss, or in the category of a paid bailee, and thus liable for theft and loss. This assumption, says the Gemara, is without foundation. In fact, **Rav Yosef can say to you:** As regards the finder's responsibility **in a case of theft or loss, everyone,** even Rabbi Akiva, **agrees that** a finder **is responsible** like a paid bailee, even when he is not permitted to use the lost object, because he has the benefit of being exempt from performing other religious duties while looking after it. [4] **What** Rabbi Tarfon and Rabbi Akiva do **disagree about is** whether the finder should be held responsible if the object being looked after by him was lost in an **unavoidable accident.** If the finder *is* held responsible in such a case, he would belong to the category of **a borrower,** who **is responsible** even in such circumstances. The decision as to whether the finder is in the category of a borrower depends on whether or not he has the right to make use of money from the sale of the lost object. [5] **Rabbi Tarfon is of the opinion that** in this case **the Sages permitted** the finder **to use** the money.

CONCEPTS

שׁוֹמְרִים Bailees. The Halakhah recognizes four types of guardians or bailees: (1) an unpaid bailee (שׁוֹמֵר חִנָּם); (2) a paid bailee (שׁוֹמֵר שָׂכָר); (3) a hirer (שׂוֹכֵר); and (4) a borrower (שׁוֹאֵל). These four types fall into three separate categories (there is a Tannaitic dispute as to whether the hirer is considered like an unpaid bailee or a paid bailee, but in practice the Halakhah rules that he has the obligations of a paid bailee). An unpaid bailee receives no remuneration for looking after the object placed in his care, and is obliged to take reasonable care of it. If the object is stolen or lost, he is not required to pay for it. He is only liable if he is criminally negligent or if he takes the article for himself. A paid bailee receives payment, either in money or in some other tangible benefit, for looking after the object, and must reimburse the owner if the object is lost or stolen. A borrower, who has permission to use the object without having to pay for its use, is not only obliged to pay for it if it is lost or stolen, but is also liable if something happens to it in circumstances entirely beyond his control. The borrower is only exempt from paying for the object if it is destroyed during normal use by him, or if the lender was employed by the borrower at the time the article was borrowed.
The guardian of a lost object who uses the money received from its sale is regarded as if he has borrowed the money from the object's owner, and thus has full responsibility to return it if it is lost under any circumstances.

NOTES

is correct and the finder is allowed to use the money, he becomes responsible for it immediately, even if he does not in fact use it. On the other hand, if Rabbi Akiva is correct, the finder is not responsible for it so long as he has not actually used it illegally. (See *Torat Ḥayyim* and *Me'orot Natan*.)

רַב יוֹסֵף אָמַר כְּשׁוֹמֵר שָׂכָר **Rav Yosef said: He is like a paid bailee.** This whole question is discussed more fully in tractate *Bava Kamma* (56b), where the Gemara explains the reasoning behind the positions taken by Rabbah and Rav Yosef. It is clear that the guardian of a lost object is performing a religious duty which in itself is not of benefit to him. In general, the fulfillment of the commandments is not regarded as conveying benefit, but rather as being an obligation, since the reward which one will receive in the world to come is not taken into account.

Two explanations are offered for Rav Yosef's opinion that the guardian of a lost object is nevertheless benefiting by

HALAKHAH

דִּין שׁוֹמֵר אֲבֵידָה **The law regarding a person who looks after a lost object.** "If a lost object was lost by the finder or stolen from him, he is responsible for it and must replace it, in accordance with the law for paid bailees," following the opinions of *Rif* and *Rambam* and others, who ruled in accordance with the viewpoint of Rav Yosef and the line of

TRANSLATION AND COMMENTARY

[1]Therefore **he is a borrower**, as he enjoys the benefits of making use of the money, and is thus liable to pay even for loss caused by forces beyond his control. [2]**Whereas Rabbi Akiva is of the opinion that the Sages did not permit** the finder **to use** the money. [3]**Therefore, he is not a borrower** but a paid bailee; he is responsible for loss and theft, but not for unavoidable accidents.

אִי הָכִי [4]The Gemara now asks: **If so,** if Rabbi Akiva is of the opinion that the finder is not permitted to use money from the sale of the animal he found, **why do I need** the whole clause beginning with the word **"therefore" that Rabbi Akiva** included in his ruling? Is there any necessity to stress the point that if the finder is not allowed to use the money, he need not pay for damage caused by forces beyond his control? Surely it is obvious that if he cannot use the money, he can in no way be considered a borrower. [5]The Gemara now goes on to elaborate the difficulty in Rav Yosef's explanation: The point of Rabbi Akiva's ruling **is well** taken **if you say,** as does Rabbah, **that the difference of opinion** between Rabbi Akiva and Rabbi Tarfon **is** whether or not to make the finder liable for **theft or loss** like a paid bailee. [6]**Then this** explains **why** the Mishnah uses the expression: **"Rabbi Akiva says: He may not use** the money. **Therefore if it is lost, he is not responsible for it."** [7]This sentence is necessary, **for** otherwise **you might assume that** even though the finder is not permitted to use the money, **he is** nevertheless considered to be **a paid bailee, in accordance with** the viewpoint of **Rav Yosef,** who maintains that the mere fact that the finder is exempt from other religious duties while looking after the lost object (or its monetary value) for its owner makes him a paid bailee. [8]Thus the finder **is responsible for theft and loss,** even though he is not permitted to use the money. [9]**Hence** the clause beginning with the word **"therefore"** in the Mishnah **informs us that now that**

[1]וַהֲוָה לֵיהּ שׁוֹאֵל עֲלַיְיהוּ. [2]וְרַבִּי עֲקִיבָא סָבַר: לָא שָׁרוּ לֵיהּ רַבָּנַן לְאִשְׁתַּמּוּשֵׁי בְּגַוַּיְיהוּ. [3]הִלְכָּךְ לָא הָוֵי שׁוֹאֵל עֲלַיְיהוּ.

[4]אִי הָכִי, ״לְפִיכָךְ״ דְּאָמַר רַבִּי עֲקִיבָא לָמָּה לִי? [5]אִי אָמְרַתְּ בִּשְׁלָמָא בִּגְנֵיבָה וַאֲבֵידָה הוּא דִּפְלִיגִי. [6]הַיְינוּ דְּקָתָנֵי: ״רַבִּי עֲקִיבָא אוֹמֵר: לֹא יִשְׁתַּמֵּשׁ בָּהֶן. לְפִיכָךְ, אִם אָבְדוּ, אֵינוֹ חַיָּיב בְּאַחֲרָיוּתָן״. [7]סָלְקָא דַּעְתָּךְ אָמֵינָא שׁוֹמֵר שָׂכָר הָוֵי, כְּדְרַב יוֹסֵף, [8]וּבִגְנֵיבָה וַאֲבֵידָה מִחַיֵּיב. [9]קָא מַשְׁמַע לָן ״לְפִיכָךְ״:

LITERAL TRANSLATION

[1]and he is a borrower of it. [2]But Rabbi Akiva is of the opinion [that] the Sages did not permit him to use it. [3]Therefore, he is not a borrower of it.

[4]If so, for what do I need "therefore..." that Rabbi Akiva said? [5]It is well if you say that it is regarding theft and loss that they disagree. [6][Then] this is why it teaches: "Rabbi Akiva says: He may not use it. Therefore, if it is lost, he is not responsible for it." [7][For] you might say (lit., "it arises in your mind to say") [that] he is a paid bailee, in accordance with Rav Yosef, [8]and he is responsible for theft and loss. [9][Hence], "therefore..." informs us [that]

NOTES

doing so. The first explanation (which *Rashi* uses in our passage) is that, since the guardian of a lost object is fulfilling a commandment, he is exempt, according to Halakhic principle, from fulfilling another commandment at the same time, and this exemption may be to the guardian's financial advantage. Rav Yosef does not maintain that the finder of a lost object is actively fulfilling a commandment during the entire time the lost object is in his care, but only while he is actually engaged in tending the object (which is part of the commandment of returning lost objects). At that time, if a poor person asks him for charity, he may refrain from giving charity, because at that moment he is engaged in fulfilling another commandment, which exempts him from the obligation to give charity. Thus the person engaged in tending a lost object could have a certain financial benefit — the perutah which he would otherwise have had to give the poor person, and which the Talmud calls "Rav Yosef's perutah" (פְּרוּטָה דְּרַב יוֹסֵף).

Rabbah's response to this argument is that it is very unlikely that at the very moment one is tending a lost object a poor person would come to ask for charity, and such an uncommon coincidence need not be considered.

The second explanation offered in support of Rav Yosef's opinion is that the finder of a lost object is like a paid bailee because the Torah *obligates* him to tend the lost object. This is not a voluntary action on his part, like being an unpaid bailee, but is a guardianship with responsibilities similar to those of a paid bailee, who also has a responsibility — in his case, because he accepts payment. Rabbah believes that as long as there is no actual payment involved in the guardianship, the finder does not have the obligations of a paid bailee.

HALAKHAH

argument presented by our Gemara." (*Shulḥan Arukh, Ḥoshen Mishpat* 267:16.) *Rema* rules, following *Tosafot* and *Rosh,* that the law is in accordance with the viewpoint of Rabbah, as it generally is when he differs with Rav Yosef, and a finder has the status of an unpaid bailee, who is not held responsible for articles stolen or lost while in his possession.

הָשְׁתָּא דְּאָמְרַתְּ לֹא יִשְׁתַּמֵּשׁ בָּהֶן, [1] שׁוֹמֵר שָׂכָר לָא הָוֵי, וְלָא מְחַיֵּיב בִּגְנֵיבָה וַאֲבֵידָה. [2] אֶלָּא אִי אָמְרַתְּ בִּגְנֵיבָה וַאֲבֵידָה דְּכוּלֵּי עָלְמָא לָא פְּלִיגֵי דְּחַיָּיב, [3] כִּי פְּלִיגֵי, בְּאוֹנָסִין דְּשׁוֹאֵל, [4] מַאי ״לְפִיכָךְ״ דְּרַבִּי עֲקִיבָא? [5] הָכִי מִבָּעֵי לֵיהּ לְמִתְנָא: ״רַבִּי עֲקִיבָא אוֹמֵר: לֹא יִשְׁתַּמֵּשׁ בָּהֶן״, [6] וַאֲנָא יָדַעְנָא דְּכֵיוָן דְּלָא יִשְׁתַּמֵּשׁ בָּהֶן, לָאו שׁוֹאֵל הָוֵי, וְאֵינוֹ חַיָּיב בְּאַחֲרָיוּתָן. [7] ״לְפִיכָךְ״ דְּרַבִּי עֲקִיבָא לָמָּה לִי?

[8] מִשּׁוּם, ״לְפִיכָךְ״ דְּרַבִּי טַרְפוֹן. [9] וּ״לְפִיכָךְ״ דְּרַבִּי טַרְפוֹן לָמָּה לִי?

[10] הָכִי קָאָמַר: כֵּיוָן דְּשָׁרוּ לֵיהּ רַבָּנַן לְאִשְׁתַּמּוּשֵׁי בְּגַוַּיְיהוּ, [11] כְּמַאן דְּאִישְׁתַּמֵּשׁ בְּגַוַּיְיהוּ דָּמֵי, וְחַיָּיב בְּאַחֲרָיוּתָן.

LITERAL TRANSLATION

now that you say [that] he may not make use of them, [1] he is not a paid bailee, and is not responsible for theft or loss. [2] But if you say [that] in [a case of] theft or loss everyone agrees that he is responsible, [3] [and] when they disagree, [it is] about [unavoidable] accidents, where a borrower [is responsible], [4] what is [the need for] "therefore..." [used] by Rabbi Akiva? [5] This is what [the Tanna] should have taught: "Rabbi Akiva says: He may not use it," [6] and I would know that since he may not use it, he is not a borrower, and is not responsible for it. [7] For what do I need "therefore..." [used] by Rabbi Akiva?

[8] Because of [the word] "therefore..." [used] by Rabbi Tarfon. [9] And for what do I need "therefore..." [used] by Rabbi Tarfon?

[10] This is what he is saying: Since the Sages permitted him to use it, [11] he is like someone who has [already] used it, and he is responsible for it.

RASHI

מאי לפיכך דרבי עקיבא – כיון דאמר לא ישתמש, מהיכא תיסק אדעתין לחיוביה, דאיצטריך למימר אינו חייב?

TRANSLATION AND COMMENTARY

Rabbi Akiva **says that** the finder **is not permitted to make use of** the money, [1] **he is not** considered to be **a paid bailee, and he is not responsible for theft or loss.** In other words, Rabbi Akiva is informing us by the second part of the sentence that the finder should only be held responsible for theft or loss if he is entitled to make use of the object or money. If he is not entitled to make use of it, he is not held responsible, even though he has the benefit that he is exempt from other religious duties. [2] **But if you say,** as does Rav Yosef, **that** both Rabbi Akiva and Rabbi Tarfon **agree that** a finder *is* **responsible in a case of theft or loss,** [3] **and that their disagreement is over** whether to hold him responsible in the case of **an unavoidable accident like a borrower who is** held **responsible** in such circumstances, [4] then **what is the need for** the clause beginning with **"therefore" used by Rabbi Akiva?** [5] It is surely obvious that according to him the finder cannot be placed in the category of a borrower, and **this is what the Mishnah should have said: "Rabbi Akiva says: He may not use** the money," and nothing further, [6] **and I would know that since he is not permitted to use it, he is not** considered **a borrower, and he is not responsible for it** if it is lost because of circumstances beyond his control. [7] **Why,** then, **do I need** the whole clause beginning with **"therefore" used by Rabbi Akiva?**

מִשּׁוּם [8] The Gemara answers: This clause is in fact superfluous, but was included for stylistic reasons, **because** it balances the clause beginning with **"therefore" used by Rabbi Tarfon.**

וּלְפִיכָךְ [9] **But,** the Gemara asks, **why do I need** the clause beginning with **"therefore" used by Rabbi Tarfon?** Surely it is obvious that if a finder is permitted to make use of the object or the money in his care he must be held responsible for it.

הָכִי קָאָמַר [10] The Gemara answers: **This is what** Rabbi Tarfon **is** in fact **saying: Since the Sages permitted** the finder **to make use of** the money, [11] **he is** immediately considered **like someone who has already made use of it,** even before he actually does so. **And** if, in fact, it is lost due to forces beyond his control before he has a chance to use it, **he is** nevertheless **responsible for it.**

NOTES

כְּמַאן דְּאִישְׁתַּמֵּשׁ בְּגַוַּיְיהוּ דָּמֵי **He is like someone who has already used it.** The Gemara here appears to conclude that there is no difference between the finder being permitted to use money from the sale of the object he found and his actual use of it. In both cases the finder becomes a borrower, subject to all the laws which that status involves. The Rishonim raise the following problem: There is a Mishnah (below, 43a) which reads: "If someone deposits loose money with a money changer, the latter may use it. Therefore, if it is lost, he is responsible for it." The conclusion of the Gemara there is that if the money changer did not actually use the money, he has the status of a paid bailee. Thus, if the loose money was lost as a result of forces beyond his control, he is not responsible for it. Hence we see that a person does not become a borrower merely by being *permitted* to use money. He becomes a borrower only if he *actually* uses it! (Note continued in outer margin.)

TERMINOLOGY

הָכִי קָאָמַר **This is what he is saying.** I.e., his statement should be interpreted as explained below. This term is used to introduce a new explanation or a textual emendation of a difficult passage in a Mishnah or a Baraita, usually proposed in order to resolve a problem raised by the Gemara regarding this passage.

NOTES (Continued)

Several Rishonim accept the explanation of *Rabbenu Efra'im,* who says that a money changer who is not permitted to use money placed in his care is an unpaid bailee. Therefore, in circumstances where he *is* permitted to use the money, he is raised to the level of a paid bailee, until he actually uses it. Then he becomes a borrower. A finder, however, is already a paid bailee, according to Rav Yosef. Therefore, when he is permitted to use the lost property, he is immediately raised to the level of a borrower, whether or not he actually uses it. According to this explanation, our Gemara's ruling applies only according to Rav Yosef.

Other Rishonim prefer the interpretation of *Ra'avad.* He argues that a person cannot become a borrower without agreeing to borrow. Hence, a money changer does not become a borrower unless he actually chooses to use the money. If he prefers to hold on to the money for a while, in the expectation that the owner will soon come to collect it, he remains a paid bailee, since permission to use the money is equivalent to remuneration. In the case of a finder, however, the two parties did not agree to anything, since the owner and the finder have had no contact with each other. It was the Sages who assessed the finder's state of mind, and they decided that most finders would prefer to borrow the money and treat it like their own, rather than keep it idefinitely in a safe place. Hence, the finder is bound by this assessment, even if he in fact feels otherwise and chooses not to use the money. According to this explanation, our Gemara's ruling is independent of the

TRANSLATION AND COMMENTARY

וְהָא אָבְדוּ קָתָנֵי [1]The Gemara now continues to question Rav Yosef's opinion: **But surely** the Mishnah **uses the expression: "If it is lost,"** and does not say: "If it is lost due to forces beyond his control." (In Hebrew the two terms are entirely different.) Does this not indicate that the issue in dispute in the Mishnah is the responsibility of a paid bailee, not that of a borrower?

כְּדְרַבָּה [2][29B] The Gemara answers: Our Mishnah's use of the word "lost" **can be** compared to the use of the word "lost" in another Mishnah (*Shekalim* 2:1) and can be **interpreted in accordance with the interpretation** given to it **by Rabbah** (below, 58a). **For Rabbah said** that when the Mishnah in tractate *Shekalim* used the words "stolen" and "lost," it was not using them in their usual meaning. [3]Rather, the expression **"they were stolen"** used there **means** "stolen by **armed robbers,"** and the expression **"they were lost"** used there **means that his ship sank in the sea.** The Mishnah in *Shekalim* deals with a case where the annual contributions to the Temple service from a particular city were entrusted to an agent to be taken to Jerusalem and handed over to the Temple treasury. On the way to Jerusalem the money was lost or stolen from the agent. During the course of the discussion of this Mishnah in *Shekalim* in the Gemara (below, 58a), Rabbah explains that the usage in the Mishnah is unusual. Even though the cases in the Mishnah may be described as cases in which money was "stolen" or "lost," they are really cases of loss due to forces beyond the agent's control. Thus, says the Gemara here, Rav Yosef can explain the use of the word "lost" in our Mishnah the same way, and can explain the difference of opinion between Rabbi Akiva and Rabbi Tarfon as being limited to whether or not the finder should be regarded as a borrower.

אָמַר רַב יְהוּדָה [4]**Rav Yehudah said in the name of Shmuel: The Halakhah is in accordance with** the opinion of **Rabbi Tarfon.** The finder is permitted to use the money he receives when he sells the lost object. He has the legal status of a borrower of this money, and is responsible for its safekeeping even if it is lost as a result of circumstances beyond his control.

בְּיַד רַחֲבָה [5]The Gemara illustrates an application of this ruling in the following story: The Babylonian Amora, **Rahavah, had in his care certain money belonging to orphans who were minors.** [6]**He came before Rav Yosef and asked him: "What is the law regarding my making use of** this money? Am I allowed to use it, or must I put it away in a safe place, like ordinary objects placed in my care?"

אָמַר לֵיהּ [7]Rav Yosef **said to him** in reply: **"This is what Rav Yehudah said in the name of Shmuel:** [8]**The Halakhah is in accordance with** the opinion of **Rabbi Tarfon,** that the finder of lost property who sells it is entitled to make use of the money he receives as a result of the sale. In my opinion, the orphans' money in your care comes into the same category, and you are permitted to make use of it."

[1]וְהָא "אָבְדוּ" קָתָנֵי!
[29B] [2]כְּדְרַבָּה, דְּאָמַר רַבָּה: "נִגְנְבוּ" — בְּלִסְטִים מְזוּיָּין; [3]"אָבְדוּ" — שֶׁטָּבְעָה סְפִינָתוֹ בַּיָּם.
[4]אָמַר רַב יְהוּדָה אָמַר שְׁמוּאֵל: הֲלָכָה כְּרַבִּי טַרְפוֹן.
[5]בְּיַד רַחֲבָה הֲוָה לֵיהּ הָנְהוּ זוּזֵי דְיָתְמֵי. [6]אֲתָא לְקַמֵּיהּ דְּרַב יוֹסֵף. אֲמַר לֵיהּ: "מַהוּ לְאִשְׁתַּמּוּשֵׁי בְּגַוַּיְיהוּ?"
[7]אֲמַר לֵיהּ: "הָכִי אָמַר רַב יְהוּדָה אָמַר שְׁמוּאֵל: [8]הֲלָכָה כְּרַבִּי טַרְפוֹן".

LITERAL TRANSLATION

[1]But surely he teaches: "[If] it is lost."

[2][29B] [This can be interpreted] in accordance with [the interpretation of] Rabbah, for Rabbah said: "They were stolen" [means stolen] by armed robbers; [3]"they were lost" [means] that his ship sank in the sea.

[4]Rav Yehudah said in the name of Shmuel: The Halakhah is in accordance with Rabbi Tarfon.

[5]In Rahavah's care (lit., "hand") there were [deposited] certain coins of orphans. [6]He came before Rav Yosef. He asked him: "What about making use of them?"

[7]He said to him: "This is what Rav Yehudah said in the name of Shmuel: [8]The Halakhah is in accordance with Rabbi Tarfon."

RASHI

כדרבה — בפרק הזהב (בבא מציעא נח,א) גבי בני העיר ששלחו את שקליהן.

SAGES

dispute between Rabbah and Rav Yosef.

רַחֲבָה Rahavah. A Babylonian Amora of the third generation, Rahavah was a disciple of Rav Yehudah and reported many Halakhic teachings in his name. We also find him quoted in the Talmud in discussions with other Sages of his generation. Rahavah was famous for the precision with which he reported teachings, so that when the Sages wished to express praise for someone's precision they would say he was as accurate and precise as "Rahavah of Pumbedita." His two sons, Efah and Avimi, were famous Sages, known as "the חֲרִיפֵי דְּפוּמְבְּדִיתָא — sharp-witted scholars of Pumbedita."

NOTES

הָנְהוּ זוּזֵי דְיָתְמֵי Coins belonging to orphans. The commentators raise the following problem: It would appear that Rahavah was asked to look after these coins by their owners. He did not find them. But the entire question of whether to allow someone to make use of money in his care only applies to finders of lost property. Everyone agrees that ordinary bailees have no right to use property placed in their care, unless they receive the owner's permission.

Ra'avad answers that the money was originally placed in Rahavah's care by the father of the orphans, to be looked after by him until such time as the orphans grew up. Hence, it was a long-term deposit, which would not be claimed for some time, and it could well have been in everyone's interest to allow Rahavah to make use of the money.

Nimmukei Yosef explains that the money was indeed lost and Rahavah found it. He then happened to discover that it

TRANSLATION AND COMMENTARY

אָמַר לֵיהּ אַבָּיֵי [1]**Abaye said to** Rav Yosef: Surely there is a difference between the two cases. **Was there not** an Amoraic statement **about** our Mishnah which narrows the application of the ruling by Rav Yehudah in the name of Shmuel that the Halakhah is in accordance with Rabbi Tarfon? Did not **Rabbi Ḥelbo say in the name of Rav Huna:** [2]**The Mishnah only stated this ruling** of Rabbi Tarfon, permitting the finder to make use of unclaimed money in his care, **with reference to money received** by the finder **in exchange for** selling **a lost object.** Only in this case did Rabbi Tarfon permit the finder to make use of the money, **since he took trouble** in looking after the animal he found for a considerable period of time before he sold it. [3]**But** if someone simply found **lost money, for which he did not** have to **go to** any **trouble,** he is **not** permitted to make use of it and must treat it like any other lost object. [4]Now, concludes Abaye, these coins belonging to orphans that Raḥavah has in his care **are** considered **like lost money,** and not like money received in exchange for the sale of a lost object, since they were deposited in his care in the form of cash, and he went to no special trouble in looking after them. Hence, Raḥavah should not be allowed to make use of them.

אָמַר לֵיהּ [5]As a result of Abaye's intervention and his explanation of the difference between the case in our Mishnah and that of Raḥavah, Rav Yosef **said to** Raḥavah: "Go. **They do not allow me to give you permission** to use the orphans' money, for Abaye's argument is correct."

MISHNAH מָצָא סְפָרִים [6]**If** a person **finds** lost **books** (written in the form of scrolls), **he must read them once every thirty days** to air the books and prevent them from becoming moldy. [7]**If** the finder **does not know how to read, he must** nevertheless **roll them** through from end to end to air them. [8]**But** where the finder reads the contents of the book in order to air them, **he is not permitted to learn from them some topic** that he is studying **for the first time,** because it is possible that he may damage the books during the course of extended reading. [9]Similarly, **someone else is not permitted to read** the book together **with him,** in case one pulls in one direction and the other in the opposite direction, and they thus tear the book.

[1]אָמַר לֵיהּ אַבָּיֵי: ״וְלָאו אִתְּמַר עֲלַהּ: אָמַר רַבִּי חֶלְבּוֹ אָמַר רַב הוּנָא: [2]לֹא שָׁנוּ אֶלָּא בִּדְמֵי אֲבֵידָה, הוֹאִיל וְטָרַח בָּהּ, [3]אֲבָל מָעוֹת אֲבֵידָה, דְּלָא טָרַח בְּהוּ, לָא. [4]וְהָנֵי כְּמָעוֹת אֲבֵידָה דָּמוּ״. [5]אֲמַר לֵיהּ: ״זִיל. לָא שְׁבָקוּ לִי דְּאִשְׁרֵי לָךְ״.

משנה [6]מָצָא סְפָרִים, קוֹרֵא בָּהֶן אֶחָד לִשְׁלֹשִׁים יוֹם, [7]וְאִם אֵינוֹ יוֹדֵעַ לִקְרוֹת, גּוֹלְלָן. [8]אֲבָל לֹא יִלְמוֹד בָּהֶן בַּתְּחִילָּה, [9]וְלֹא יִקְרָא אַחֵר עִמּוֹ.

LITERAL TRANSLATION

[1]Abaye said to him: "But was it not said about it: Rabbi Ḥelbo said in the name of Rav Huna: [2]They did not teach [this ruling] except with reference to payment for a lost object, since he took trouble for it, [3]but lost money, for which he did not take trouble, not. [4]And these [coins] are like lost money."

[5]He said to him: "Go. They did not allow me to give you permission [to use it]."

MISHNAH [6][If] he found books, he reads them once in thirty days, [7]and if he does not know [how] to read, he rolls them. [8]But he may not learn from them for the first time, [9]and someone else may not read with him.

RASHI

בדמי אבידה – שמכרה לאחר שנטפל בה, כמו שאמרו חכמים. **אבל מעות אבידה** – כגון שמלא מעות בכיס, או שלש מטבעות עשוין כמגדלין.

משנה אחת לשלשים יום – שמתעפשין כששוהים מלפותחן, וכל ספרים שלהן היו עשוין בגליון. **גוללן** – מתחילתן לסופן שיכנס בהן האויר. **בתחלה** – מה שלא למד, מפני שצריך להשהותו לפניו. **ולא יקרא אחר עמו** – לפי שזה מושך אצלו וזה מושך אצלו, ונקרע.

BACKGROUND

סְפָרִים **Books.** In Talmudic times and in later generations, the term סֵפֶר referred to books written in the form of scrolls. Important and expensive books were written on parchment, and others were written on paper. Relatively short scrolls were wound at one end, but long scrolls, such as a Torah scroll, were rolled from both ends on two poles. Because tightly rolled scrolls, especially new ones from which all the moisture had not yet been removed, might become moldy, the Sages recommended that people unroll scrolls from time to time to ventilate them.

NOTES

belonged to orphans, and he agreed to look after it until they were old enough to look after it themselves.

Maharam Schiff suggests that the case was one where the orphans' father lost an animal and Raḥavah found it and eventually sold it. Raḥavah was then entitled to use the money, but before he could do so the owner of the animal died and the ownership of the money passed to his heirs, the orphans. According to this explanation, the Gemara is telling us that in relation to the new owner — the orphans — the money must be treated like lost money and not like money received by the finder as a result of selling an object he has found. This is why Raḥavah may not use it.

HALAKHAH

דְּמֵי אֲבֵידָה **The money received by the finder for his sale of a lost article.** "Money received by the finder when he sells an unclaimed lost object may be used by him for his own purposes. Therefore, he is considered a borrower of this money and is responsible for any loss that occurs, even if such a loss was caused by forces beyond his control. But if he simply found lost money, the same rule does not apply. He may not use such money for his own purposes, and he

TRANSLATION AND COMMENTARY

מָצָא כְּסוּת [1]If a person **finds a** lost **garment, he must shake it out once every thirty days,** [2]**and he must spread it out** or hang it up to air, provided that this is solely **for its benefit and not for his** own **honor** (to display the fact that he possesses fine garments).

כְּלֵי כֶסֶף וּכְלֵי נְחוֹשֶׁת [3]If a person finds **vessels of silver or vessels of copper,** he places them in the earth for safekeeping. **He may** take them out and **use them** occasionally **for their benefit,** so that they do not corrode, **but** may **not** use them to such an extent **that he wears them away.**

כְּלֵי זָהָב וּכְלֵי זְכוּכִית [4]If a person finds **vessels of gold or vessels of glass,** he places them in the earth for safekeeping. But since gold does not corrode and glass is fragile, he must leave them in the earth and **he may not touch them until Elijah** the Prophet **comes** and tells us to whom they belong.

מָצָא שַׂק אוֹ קוּפָּה [5]The Mishnah now moves on to a different subject: **If** a person of high social standing **found a sack or a basket or anything which it would not be his practice to handle or carry,** even if it were his, **then he is not** under any obligation to **take it** and look after it until the owner comes to claim it. He does not violate the prohibition against ignoring lost objects by simply leaving it where he found it, since the Torah did not require people to humiliate themselves or act in a manner inappropriate to their social status in order to return a lost object.

GEMARA אָמַר שְׁמוּאֵל [6]**Shmuel said: Someone who finds tefillin in the marketplace** is not required to look after them for an extended period. **He** is **immediately** permitted to **assess their value,** sell them, **and set aside the money** for the owner when he comes. (See note.)

[1]מָצָא כְּסוּת, מְנַעֲרָהּ אֶחָד לִשְׁלֹשִׁים יוֹם, [2]וְשׁוֹטְחָהּ לְצָרְכָּהּ, אֲבָל לֹא לִכְבוֹדוֹ.

[3]כְּלֵי כֶסֶף וּכְלֵי נְחוֹשֶׁת, מִשְׁתַּמֵּשׁ בָּהֶן לְצָרְכָּן, אֲבָל לֹא לְשָׁחֲקָן.

[4]כְּלֵי זָהָב וּכְלֵי זְכוּכִית, לֹא יִגַּע בָּהֶן עַד שֶׁיָּבוֹא אֵלִיָּהוּ.

[5]מָצָא שַׂק אוֹ קוּפָּה וְכָל דָּבָר שֶׁאֵין דַּרְכּוֹ לִיטּוֹל, הֲרֵי זֶה לֹא יִטּוֹל.

גמרא [6]אָמַר שְׁמוּאֵל: הַמּוֹצֵא תְּפִילִּין בַּשּׁוּק שָׁם דְּמֵיהֶן וּמַנִּיחָן לְאַלְתַּר.

LITERAL TRANSLATION

[1][If] he found a garment, he shakes it out once in thirty days, [2]and spreads it out for its benefit, but not for his honor.

[3]Vessels of silver or vessels of copper, he uses them for their benefit, but not so as to wear them away.

[4]Vessels of gold or vessels of glass, he may not touch them until Elijah comes.

[5][If] he found a sack or a basket or anything which it is not his practice to take, then he need not take [it].

GEMARA [6]Shmuel said: Someone who finds tefillin in the marketplace assesses their value and sets [the money] aside immediately.

RASHI

שוטחה לצרכה — לשלוט בה אויר שלא תכלה ולא תאכלנה עש. **לצרכן** — שמתעפשים בקרקע, שצריך לתתן בקרקע, כדאמרינן לקמן שזו היא שמירתן, ולפיכך משתמש בהם לפרקים. **אבל לא לשחקן** — לא ישתמש בהן זמן ארוך שישחקן, *אוזי״ר. **לא יגע בהן** — זהב אינו מתעפש בארץ, וזכוכית שמא ישבר. **שאין דרכו ליטול** — דבר שגנאי הוא לו, שאדם חשוב הוא ואין דרכו ליטול קופה שלו להכניסה מן החוץ לבית שמור — לא יטול, ופטור מהשבת אבידה, דילפינן מ״והתעלמת״.

BACKGROUND

כְּלֵי כֶסֶף Vessels of silver.... Copper vessels are liable to corrode if they are not cared for, as are silver vessels (even those made of pure silver). Only vessels of gold or glass are immune to such damage.

שָׁם דְּמֵיהֶן וּמַנִּיחָן לְאַלְתַּר He assesses their value and sets the money aside immediately. The word וּמַנִּיחָן has two meanings, both of which are possible here: (1) "To put something on" — in which case the word refers to the pair of tefillin: "He puts them on immediately" (*Rambam*, and certain versions of *Rashi*; see also Halakhah section). (2) "To set something aside" — in which case the word refers to the money from the sale of the lost tefillin (*Ramban* and others). Our commentary interprets the passage according to the second meaning. The difficulty with the first meaning is that the same word has been used above (28b) in connection with many other kinds of lost property which clearly cannot be worn. The difficulty with the second meaning is that Shmuel himself ruled above that the Halakhah is in accordance with the viewpoint of Rabbi Tarfon, who declared that money obtained in exchange for a lost object need not be set aside, but can be treated by the finder as a loan (see *Rosh*, 28b).

LANGUAGE (RASHI)

אוזי״ר* From the Old French *user,* meaning "to make use of," or "to wear out something by using it."

NOTES

הַמּוֹצֵא תְּפִילִּין Someone who finds tefillin. The commentators ask: Since the finder must set aside the money from the sale of the tefillin, it is clear that they are identifiable and returnable. Why, then, is the finder not required to look after the tefillin and return them intact to the owner when he claims them, as would be the case with any other object, even one that is readily available on the market? Even geese, which cost more to keep than they are worth, must be looked after by the finder for three days. Surely lost tefillin, which require no special care, should be looked after by the finder indefinitely.

Shittah Mekubbetzet answers in the name of *Ritva* that the finder is allowed to keep the tefillin for himself, or sell them to someone else and set aside their value for the owner to recover, because the owner is happy to have a commandment fulfilled with his property. Later on in the passage, the Gemara uses similar reasoning in connection with lost Torah scrolls, and even though the Gemara rejects this argument there, *Ritva* argues that a distinction is to be made between a scroll — which an owner is unwilling to give up because it cannot be replaced — and tefillin, which an owner has no trouble giving up because they are readily available in the market. According to this reasoning, people are generally willing to let other people take their property to fulfill a commandment, provided that they will have no difficulty in replacing it later.

Rambam and *Rosh* answer that tefillin can only be used to fulfill commandments, and people do not have the same

HALAKHAH

הַמּוֹצֵא תְּפִילִּין Someone who finds tefillin. "If a person finds a pair of tefillin, he may assess their value and put them on immediately, if he so wishes," following the opinion of Shmuel. (Ibid., 267:21.)

is not considered a borrower. He is, rather, a paid bailee, according to the *Shulḥan Arukh,* or an unpaid bailee, according to *Rema.*" (*Shulḥan Arukh, Ḥoshen Mishpat* 267:25.)

TRANSLATION AND COMMENTARY

מְתִיב רָבִינָא [1]Ravina objected: Our Mishnah says that **"if a person finds lost books, he must read them once every thirty days, [2]and if he does not know how to read, he must roll them."** [3]Now, says Ravina, the implication of the Mishnah is that **he is permitted to roll them** but **is not permitted to assess their value,** sell them, **and set the money aside.** Why then should the law be different for tefillin? Why should the finder of tefillin be permitted to sell them at once?

אָמַר אַבָּיֵי [4]**Abaye said** in reply: **Tefillin can readily be found at the house of Bar Ḥavu** (a major tefillin manufacturer of the time). Hence, the owner will not object to the finder selling his original pair, as he will easily be able to buy another pair. [5]By contrast, **books are not** nearly so **common,** and are individually copied. Thus the owner may not find it easy to replace them. Therefore the finder is obliged to look after them and restore them to their rightful owner.

תָּנוּ רַבָּנַן [6]**Our Sages taught** the following Baraita which elaborates on the law in our Mishnah: **"Someone who borrows a Torah scroll from another person may not lend it to someone else.** [7]**He may open it and read it, provided that he does not** use it to **learn** some topic that he is just beginning to study **for the first time,** because he may thereby damage it. [8]Similarly, he must **not** allow **someone else to read** it together **with him,** in case they tear it by so doing. [9]**Likewise if someone deposits a Torah scroll with another person, the latter must roll it** from beginning to end once **every twelve months.** [10]**He may open it and read it, but is forbidden to open it** just **for himself.** [11]**Summakhos says: He must roll a new scroll once every thirty days,** as new scrolls are still rather damp and need frequent ventilation. In this, Summakhos disagrees with the first Tanna, who makes no distinction between old and new scrolls. [12]But Summakhos agrees with the first Tanna that **an old scroll** must be rolled **once every twelve months.** [13]**Rabbi Eliezer ben Ya'akov says: In both cases,** whether the scroll is old or new, he must roll it **once every twelve months,** an opinion which appears to be precisely that of the first Tanna."

[1]מְתִיב רָבִינָא: ״מָצָא סְפָרִים, קוֹרֵא בָּהֶן אֶחָד לִשְׁלֹשִׁים יוֹם, [2]וְאִם אֵינוֹ יוֹדֵעַ לִקְרוֹת, גּוֹלְלָן״. [3]גּוֹלְלָן — אִין. שָׁם דְּמֵיהֶן וּמַנִּיחָן — לָא!

[4]אָמַר אַבָּיֵי: תְּפִילִּין בֵּי בַּר חָבוּ מִשְׁכַּח שְׁכִיחִי; [5]סְפָרִים לָא שְׁכִיחִי.

[6]תָּנוּ רַבָּנַן: ״הַשּׁוֹאֵל סֵפֶר תּוֹרָה מֵחֲבֵירוֹ הֲרֵי זֶה לֹא יַשְׁאִילֶנּוּ לְאַחֵר. [7]פּוֹתְחוֹ וְקוֹרֵא בּוֹ, וּבִלְבַד שֶׁלֹּא יִלְמוֹד בּוֹ בַּתְּחִילָּה, [8]וְלֹא יִקְרָא אַחֵר עִמּוֹ. [9]וְכֵן הַמַּפְקִיד סֵפֶר תּוֹרָה אֵצֶל חֲבֵירוֹ, גּוֹלְלוֹ כָּל שְׁנֵים עָשָׂר חֹדֶשׁ. [10]פּוֹתְחוֹ וְקוֹרֵא בּוֹ. אִם בִּשְׁבִילוֹ פְּתָחוֹ, אָסוּר. [11]סוּמְכוֹס אוֹמֵר: בְּחָדָשׁ שְׁלֹשִׁים יוֹם; [12]בְּיָשָׁן שְׁנֵים עָשָׂר חֹדֶשׁ. [13]רַבִּי אֱלִיעֶזֶר בֶּן יַעֲקֹב אוֹמֵר: אֶחָד זֶה וְאֶחָד זֶה, שְׁנֵים עָשָׂר חֹדֶשׁ״.

LITERAL TRANSLATION

[1]Ravina objected: "[If] he found books, he reads them once in thirty days, [2]and if he does not know [how] to read, he rolls them." [3]Rolls them — yes. Assesses their value and sets [the money] aside — no!

[4]Abaye said: Tefillin are readily found at the house of Bar Ḥavu; [5]books are not found.

[6]Our Sages taught: "Someone who borrows a Torah scroll from his fellow may not lend it to someone else. [7]He opens it and reads it, provided that he does not learn from it for the first time, [8]and someone else may not read with him. [9]And likewise someone who deposits a Torah scroll with his fellow, [the bailee] rolls it every twelve months. [10]He opens it and reads it. [But] if he opened it for himself, it is forbidden. [11]Summakhos says: With a new [scroll] thirty days; [12]with an old [scroll] twelve months. [13]Rabbi Eliezer ben Ya'akov says: In both cases (lit., 'one this and one that'), twelve months."

RASHI

גמרא בי בר חבו — בבית פלוני העוסק תפילין, מלוין לימכר, ויחזור ויקנה מן הדמים. **גוללו** — בכל שנים עשר חדש פעם אחת. **אם בשבילו פתחו** — כולה מפרש לקמיה.

BACKGROUND

בֵּי בַּר חָבוּ The house of Bar Ḥavu. This was a large family factory for the production of tefillin and mezuzot situated in the city of Meḥoza. The workers in this factory are also mentioned in other Talmudic sources as being renowned for their expert craftsmanship. Once such a factory and others like it existed, tefillin and mezuzot were no longer rare items, and there was no need for each individual to find a scribe especially for his own needs.

סְפָרִים לָא שְׁכִיחִי Books are not found. Before the invention of printing, all books were copied by scribes. The labor and writing materials were expensive, making books both valuable and scarce. Only a few extremely popular books were widely copied. Hence it is clear why the Sages assumed that a person would not be satisfied with the monetary value of his book rather than the book itself, for it was not at all certain that the book could be replaced.

SAGES

סוּמְכוֹס Summakhos. A Tanna of the fifth generation. See *Bava Metzia,* Part I, p. 15.

רַבִּי אֱלִיעֶזֶר בֶּן יַעֲקֹב Rabbi Eliezer ben Ya'akov. There were two Tannaim of this name. The first belonged to the second generation of Tannaim and lived when the Second Temple was still standing. The second belonged to the fourth generation. He was a student of Rabbi Akiva and a colleague of Rabbi Akiva's disciples. He is found in various passages in the Talmud discussing the Halakhah with them. Since in this passage we find Rabbi Eliezer ben Ya'akov in disagreement with Summakhos, who was Rabbi Meir's closest disciple, the reference must be to the second Rabbi Eliezer ben Ya'akov, who seems to have outlived his colleague, Rabbi Meir.

NOTES

sentimental attachment to ritual objects that they have to other property. One object may be preferred for subjective reasons over another of equal value, but one pair of tefillin is exactly like another. Hence, the finder may take the tefillin for himself, provided he can replace them without delay when the owner appears.

HALAKHAH

הַשּׁוֹאֵל סֵפֶר תּוֹרָה Someone who borrows a Torah scroll. "The borrower of any article is not allowed to lend it to someone else. This applies even to a Torah scroll, where the use of such a scroll is a religious duty." (Ibid., 342:1.)

TRANSLATION AND COMMENTARY

אָמַר מָר [1]The Gemara now considers the various clauses of the Baraita in detail: **The author** of the Baraita **said**, above: **"Someone who borrows a Torah scroll from another person may not lend it to someone else."** [2]Challenging this sentence of the Baraita, the Gemara asks: **Why does** the Baraita **specifically mention a Torah scroll?** Surely the law **also** applies to **everything,** and not just to a Torah scroll. Surely it is always forbidden for a borrower to lend a borrowed object to someone else without the owner's permission. [3]**For Rabbi Shimon ben Lakish said** in a comment on a Mishnah in tractate *Gittin* (29a): **Here,** in this Mishnah, **Rabbi Yehudah HaNasi** parenthetically **taught** the law **that a borrower is not permitted to lend** something he has borrowed to someone else, [4]**and a hirer is not permitted to rehire** the object hired to someone else, without the owner's permission. Why, then, did the Baraita quoted above single out the case of a Torah scroll, when the same law applies to any borrowed object?

סֵפֶר תּוֹרָה אִיצְטְרִיכָא לֵיהּ [5]The Gemara answers: The Mishnah **needed to mention** the law that a borrower is not permitted to lend out what he has borrowed specifically in connection with **a Torah scroll** [6]because otherwise **you might have said** that the borrower could assume that **a person is pleased** to allow **a commandment to be fulfilled with his property,** so that a Torah scroll would be an exception to the rule. [7]**Therefore** the Mishnah expressly **informs us that this is not so,** and that even a Torah scroll may not be lent out by a borrower without the owner's express permission.

פּוֹתְחוֹ וְקוֹרֵא בּוֹ [8]The Gemara now considers the next clause of the Baraita: "The borrower of a Torah scroll **may open it and read it."** [9]On this the Gemara remarks: Surely **this is obvious. For what** other purpose **did he borrow it from him?** Surely his purpose in borrowing it was precisely so that he could read it.

סֵיפָא אִיצְטְרִיכָא לֵיהּ [10]The Gemara answers: This particular clause was not strictly necessary in its own right, but **needed** to be included in the Baraita in order to introduce the next clause: **"Provided that he does not** use it to **learn some topic** that he is just beginning to study **for the first time."** Thus, the Baraita is informing us that a borrower of a Torah scroll may not assume that he has permission to use it to study new material.

[1]אָמַר מָר: ״הַשּׁוֹאֵל סֵפֶר תּוֹרָה מֵחֲבֵירוֹ הֲרֵי לֹא יַשְׁאִילֶנּוּ לְאַחֵר״. [2]מַאי אִרְיָא סֵפֶר תּוֹרָה? אֲפִילּוּ כָּל מִילֵּי נַמִי! [3]דְּאָמַר רַבִּי שִׁמְעוֹן בֶּן לָקִישׁ: כָּאן שָׁנָה רַבִּי שֶׁאֵין הַשּׁוֹאֵל רַשַּׁאי לְהַשְׁאִיל, [4]וְאֵין הַשּׂוֹכֵר רַשַּׁאי לְהַשְׂכִּיר.

[5]סֵפֶר תּוֹרָה אִיצְטְרִיכָא לֵיהּ. [6]מַהוּ דְּתֵימָא: נִיחָא לֵיהּ לְאִינִישׁ דְּתִיעֲבִיד מִצְוָה בְּמָמוֹנֵיהּ. [7]קָא מַשְׁמַע לָן.

[8]״פּוֹתְחוֹ וְקוֹרֵא בּוֹ״. [9]פְּשִׁיטָא! וְאֶלָּא לְמַאי שַׁיְּילֵיהּ מִינֵּיהּ? [10]סֵיפָא אִיצְטְרִיכָא לֵיהּ: ״וּבִלְבַד שֶׁלֹּא יִלְמוֹד בּוֹ בַּתְּחִלָּה״.

LITERAL TRANSLATION

[1]The master said: "Someone who borrows a Torah scroll from his fellow may not lend it to someone else." [2]Why [this] discussion [specifically about] a Torah scroll? Even everything also. [3]For Rabbi Shimon ben Lakish said: Here Rabbi [Yehudah HaNasi] taught that a borrower is not permitted to lend, [4]and a hirer is not permitted to rehire.

[5]He needed [to mention] a Torah scroll. [6]You might have said: A person is pleased that a commandment should be fulfilled with his property. [7][Therefore] it tells us [that this is not so].

[8]"He opens it and reads it." [9]This is obvious. For what [else] did he borrow it from him? [10]He needed it for the latter clause: "Provided that he does not learn from it for the first time."

RASHI

מאי אריא ספר — שהוא נוח להתקלקל בטשטוש וקריעה. **כאן שנה רבי** — במסכת גיטין (כט,א) תנן: השולח גט בארץ ישראל, הרי זה משלחו ביד אחר. ואם אמר לו ״טול חפץ פלוני הימנה״ — לא ישלחנו ביד אחר, שאין רצונו שיהא פקדונו ביד אחר, ואמר ריש לקיש עלה: כאן שנה רבי, במשנה זו למדנו רבי שסתם המשניות אין השואל כו׳, דבכולהו שייך למימר אין רצונו שיהא פקדונו ביד אחר.

BACKGROUND

כָּאן שָׁנָה רַבִּי Here Rabbi (Yehudah HaNasi) taught. This is a reference to something written in the Mishnah, edited by Rabbi Yehudah HaNasi. The expression does not refer to a ruling mentioned in the Mishnah, but rather to a parenthetical remark appearing in the Mishnah. Despite the parenthetical nature of the remark in the original source, it is nevertheless possible to derive an important Halakhic principle from it.

נִיחָא לֵיהּ לְאִינִישׁ דְּתִיעֲבִיד מִצְוָה בְּמָמוֹנֵיהּ A person is pleased that a commandment should be fulfilled with his property. Although in general we assume that no one wants another person to use his property without explicit permission, our assumption is different where the performance of a commandment is involved. We assume that, on the contrary, anyone would be interested in having his property used to fulfill a commandment, and would view it as a privilege to have helped someone keep the commandments, for this would also be a token of respect to himself. Therefore, wherever the use of an object to perform a commandment occasions no loss to its owner, one assumes that the owner would not object.

NOTES

דְּתִיעֲבִיד מִצְוָה בְּמָמוֹנֵיהּ That a commandment should be fulfilled with his property. The conclusion of the Gemara here appears to be that this principle is not accepted. The commentators ask: In other Talmudic passages (e.g., *Pesaḥim* 4b), the Gemara states that we assume that a person is pleased when his property is used to fulfill a commandment.

Ritva explains that it is a matter of weighing loss against gain: We can assume that a person will accept a small loss in order to fulfill a commandment, but we cannot assume

HALAKHAH

וְאֵין הַשּׂוֹכֵר רַשַּׁאי לְהַשְׂכִּיר And a hirer is not permitted to rehire. "Someone who hires an animal or other movable property from another person is not allowed to rehire it to someone else." (*Shulḥan Arukh, Ḥoshen Mishpat* 307:4.)

TRANSLATION AND COMMENTARY

וְכֵן הַמַּפְקִיד סֵפֶר תּוֹרָה [1]The Gemara now considers the next clause of the Baraita: **"Likewise if someone deposits a Torah scroll with another person,** [2]**the latter must roll it** from beginning to end once **every twelve months. He may open it and read it."** [3]Regarding this the Gemara asks: **What business has he got to be using it?** It was not lent to him to be used. It was deposited with him for safekeeping. [4]**And furthermore,** says the Gemara, there is another problem with this passage: The Baraita contradicts itself in the next line: **"But he is forbidden to open it for himself."** [5]**Surely** the Baraita **has** just **said** that **"he may open it and read it."**

הָכִי קָאָמַר [6]The Gemara answers: **This is what** the Baraita **is saying:** The person to whom the Torah scroll is entrusted must roll it once every twelve months. **If, while he is rolling it** in order to air it, he avails himself of the opportunity **to open it and read it, it is permitted,** even though he is looking after the scroll for its owner and has not borrowed it for the purpose of using it. [7]But **he is forbidden to open it** just for **himself.**

סוּמָכוֹס אוֹמֵר [8]The Gemara now considers the next clause of the Baraita: **"Summakhos says: He must roll a new scroll once every thirty days,** but **an old scroll** must be rolled **once every twelve months.** [9]**Rabbi Eliezer ben Ya'akov says: In both cases,** whether the scroll is old or new, he must roll it **once every twelve months."** [10]On this the Gemara asks: Surely **Rabbi Eliezer ben Ya'akov's** opinion **is the same as** that of **the first Tanna,** who also ruled that both old and new scrolls must be aired once a year. Why, then, is it stated as a separate opinion?

[1]״וְכֵן הַמַּפְקִיד סֵפֶר תּוֹרָה אֵצֶל חֲבֵירוֹ, [2]גּוֹלְלוֹ כָּל שְׁנֵים עָשָׂר חֹדֶשׁ. פּוֹתְחוֹ וְקוֹרֵא בּוֹ״. [3]מַאי עֲבִידְתֵּיהּ גַּבֵּיהּ? [4]וְתוּ: ״אִם בִּשְׁבִילוֹ פְּתָחוֹ, אָסוּר״. [5]הָא אָמְרַתְּ: ״פּוֹתְחוֹ וְקוֹרֵא בּוֹ״! [6]הָכִי קָאָמַר: אִם, כְּשֶׁהוּא גּוֹלְלוֹ, פּוֹתְחוֹ וְקוֹרֵא בּוֹ, מוּתָּר. [7]אִם בִּשְׁבִילוֹ פְּתָחוֹ, אָסוּר. [8]״סוּמָכוֹס אוֹמֵר: בְּחָדָשׁ שְׁלֹשִׁים יוֹם; בְּיָשָׁן שְׁנֵים עָשָׂר חֹדֶשׁ. [9]רַבִּי אֱלִיעֶזֶר בֶּן יַעֲקֹב אוֹמֵר: אֶחָד זֶה וְאֶחָד זֶה, שְׁנֵים עָשָׂר חֹדֶשׁ״. [10]רַבִּי אֱלִיעֶזֶר בֶּן יַעֲקֹב הַיְינוּ תַּנָּא קַמָּא!

LITERAL TRANSLATION

[1]"And likewise someone who deposits a Torah scroll with his fellow, [2][the latter] rolls it every twelve months. He opens it and reads it." [3]What is his business with it? [4]And furthermore: "If he opened it for himself, it is forbidden." [5]Surely you have said: "He opens it and reads it." [6]This is what he says: If, while he is rolling it, he opens it and reads it, it is permitted. [7]If he opened it for himself, it is forbidden.

[8]"Summakhos says: With a new [scroll] thirty days; with an old [scroll] twelve months. [9]Rabbi Eliezer ben Ya'akov says: In both cases, twelve months." [10]Rabbi Eliezer ben Ya'akov is the same as the first Tanna.

RASHI

מאי עבידתיה גביה — קא סלקא דעתך לצורכו קאמר, ולא לצורך ספר תורה, דהא לצורך ספר תורה תנא ליה גוללו כל שנים עשר חדש, להכי פרכינן מאי עבידתיה דהאי, גבי ספר תורה לקרות בו לצורך עצמו? **אם כשהוא גוללו** — להנאת ספר תורה, פתחו וקרא בו — מותר. **בחדש שלשים יום** — החדש ממהר להתעפש מן הישן.

NOTES

that he will accept a high risk of damage to his precious Torah scroll.

Sefer HaOrah explains that a person is prepared to sustain a financial loss in order to fulfill one commandment, but we cannot assume that he will lend his property out indefinitely while there is a commandment to be fulfilled. Thus, in our case, the owner of the scroll has already fulfilled a commandment by lending it to one person, and we cannot assume that he is prepared to lend it to everyone else.

מַאי עֲבִידְתֵּיהּ גַּבֵּיהּ **What is his business with it?** Our translation and commentary follow *Rashi. Rashba,* however, is not convinced by *Rashi*'s explanation that the Gemara is essentially asking the same question in two different ways, and considers the Gemara's answer — that the person with whom the scroll was deposited is allowed to read the scroll while airing it out — to be obvious. Hence he gives the following explanation. The Gemara's first question is: Why is the person with whom the scroll is deposited required to roll it? Surely it is the owner's responsibility to take care of his property. The second question is: Why does the Baraita use the expression "he may open it and read it, but he is forbidden to open it for himself"? If the Baraita means no more than the Mishnah, which also rules that the finder

HALAKHAH

הַמַּפְקִיד סֵפֶר תּוֹרָה **Someone who deposits a Torah scroll.** "Someone with whom a Torah scroll is deposited must roll it through once every twelve months. While rolling it, he may read it, but he may not open it and read it for his own benefit alone." (Ibid., 292:20.)

TRANSLATION AND COMMENTARY

אֶלָּא אֵימָא [1]**Rather,** answers the Gemara, it is necessary to emend the text of the Baraita and **say instead: "Rabbi Eliezer ben Ya'akov says: 'In both cases,** whether the scroll is old or new, he must roll it **once every thirty days,'"** because in his opinion even an old Torah scroll must be aired frequently. As a result of this emendation of the text of the Baraita, Rabbi Eliezer ben Ya'akov's opinion is distinct from both that of Summakhos and that of the first Tanna. The first Tanna requires both old and new Torah scrolls to be rolled every twelve months. Summakhos requires an old scroll to be rolled every twelve months and a new scroll every month. Rabbi Eliezer ben Ya'akov requires both old and new scrolls to be rolled every month. In fact, Rabbi Eliezer ben Ya'akov's opinion corresponds to the opinion expressed in our Mishnah (see above), which also rules that all scrolls need to be aired once every month. This concludes the discussion of the Baraita.

אֲבָל לֹא יִלְמוֹד [2]The Gemara now considers the next clause of our Mishnah: **"But he is not permitted to** use the scroll that he has found to **learn some topic** that he is studying **for the first time, and someone else is not permitted to read** the scroll together **with him."** [3]The Gemara now asks: **But a contradiction can be raised** between this section of our Mishnah and the parallel passage in the Tosefta (*Bava Metzia* 2:21) which states: "The finder of a lost scroll **is not permitted to read a passage and repeat it.** [4]**Nor is he permitted to read a passage and translate it,** as these procedures take too much time and could damage the scroll. [5]**Nor is he permitted to open it** to a width of **more than three columns,** as the scroll might roll off the table and tear. [6]**Nor are three people permitted to read it at the same time,** in case they pull it in different directions and tear it." [7]The statement in the Tosefta, that three people are not permitted to read a found Torah scroll together, leads the Gemara to conclude: **Thus** *two* people **are permitted to read** the scroll at the same time. This surely contradicts our Mishnah.

אָמַר אַבַּיֵי [8]**Abaye said** in reply: **There is no difficulty** in reconciling the Mishnah and the Tosefta. The Tosefta, which forbids three people to read a found scroll together but permits two, **is referring to** a number of people studying **one subject** together. In such a situation it is safe for two people, though not for three, to study together. [9]By contrast, the Mishnah, which forbids two people to read a found scroll together, **is referring to** two people studying **two** separate **subjects.** Since the readers are paying no attention to each other, they are likely to pull the scroll in different directions and damage it.

[1]אֶלָּא אֵימָא: ״רַבִּי אֱלִיעֶזֶר בֶּן יַעֲקֹב אוֹמֵר: אֶחָד זֶה וְאֶחָד זֶה, שְׁלֹשִׁים יוֹם״.
[2]״אֲבָל לֹא יִלְמוֹד בּוֹ בַּתְּחִלָּה, וְלֹא יִקְרָא אַחֵר עִמּוֹ״.
[3]וּרְמִינְהוּ: ״לֹא יִקְרָא פָּרָשָׁה וְיִשְׁנֶה, [4]וְלֹא יִקְרָא בּוֹ פָּרָשָׁה וִיתַרְגֵּם, [5]וְלֹא יִפְתַּח בּוֹ יוֹתֵר מִשְּׁלֹשָׁה דַפִּין, [6]וְלֹא יִקְרְאוּ בוֹ שְׁלֹשָׁה בְנֵי אָדָם בְּכֶרֶךְ אֶחָד״.
[7]הָא שְׁנַיִם קוֹרִין!
[8]אֲמַר אַבַּיֵי: לָא קַשְׁיָא. כָּאן בְּעִנְיָן אֶחָד, [9]כָּאן בִּשְׁנֵי עִנְיָנִים.

LITERAL TRANSLATION

[1]Rather say: "Rabbi Eliezer ben Ya'akov says: In both cases, thirty days."

[2]"But he may not learn from it for the first time, and someone else may not read with him." [3]But a contradiction can be raised (lit., "and cast them"): "He may not read a passage and repeat [it], [4]and he may not read a passage in it and translate [it], [5]and he may not open in it more than three columns, [6]and three people may not read in one volume." [7]Thus two may read.

[8]Abaye said: There is no difficulty. [9]Here [it refers] to one subject, here to two subjects.

RASHI

אימא אחד זה ואחד זה שלשים יום — ומתניתין נמי דקתני קורא בהן אחת לשלשים יום, ולא מפליג בין ישן לחדש — רבי אליעזר בן יעקב היא. **בענין אחד** — בפרשה אחת אין קורין. **בשני ענינים** — זה בדף זה וזה בדף זה קורין, דלא אתי לשמוטי מהדדי.

BACKGROUND

כָּאן בְּעִנְיָן אֶחָד... Here it refers to one subject.... In our commentary we have followed *Rambam,* who explains that two people reading a single topic together pay attention to each other and will not pull the scroll until it tears. However, if each of them is studying something different, and each is reading a different part of the scroll, they each might unwittingly pull it towards himself until it tears. *Rashi,* by contrast, explains this point in the opposite way: When two people are studying a single topic, since both are eager to read the same passage, each pulls the scroll in his own direction. However, if they are dealing with two separate subjects in different parts of the scroll, each is busy with his own concerns, and the scroll is open wide enough so as not to be damaged.

NOTES

of a lost scroll may read it only in the course of airing it out, it should use the Mishnah's brief wording.

According to this view, the Gemara answers that the person with whom the scroll is deposited is not required to air the scroll, but may do so as a favor to the owner, and may read the scroll while doing so. But he may not use this as an excuse to read the scroll when it does not need airing.

HALAKHAH

אֲבָל לֹא יִלְמוֹד **But he may not learn.** "Someone who finds lost scrolls must read them once a month. If he does not know how to read, he must roll them. He must be careful not to do the following things which tend to damage scrolls: he must not use them to study a topic that he has not studied before, nor may he study a passage and repeat it or study a passage and translate it. He must not open a scroll to a width of more than three columns. Two people

TRANSLATION AND COMMENTARY

מָצָא כְּסוּת [1]The Gemara now considers the next clause of the Mishnah: **"If a person finds a** lost **garment, he must shake it out once every thirty days."** [2]On this the Gemara asks: **Do you mean to say that shaking out** a garment **is beneficial to it?** In other words, since the Sages insist that the finder of a garment shake it out monthly, they must think that such an action is of benefit to it. [3]**But surely Rabbi Yohanan** gave a piece of practical advice on this subject and **said** sarcastically: **Only someone who has a professional weaver** living permanently **in his house** to repair his garments **can** allow himself the luxury of **shaking garments out every day.** From this piece of practical advice offered by Rabbi Yohanan we can see that shaking out a garment tends to damage it, which contradicts the ruling in our Mishnah.

אָמְרֵי [4]The Gemara now gives four alternative answers to this question: (1) **We can say:** Shaking out a garment **every day is bad for it,** as Rabbi Yohanan says, [5]but **shaking it out once in thirty days is beneficial to it.**

אִיבָּעֵית אֵימָא [6](2) **If you wish,** you can **say: There is no difficulty** in reconciling our Mishnah with Rabbi Yohanan's statement: [7]The Mishnah **is referring to one** person shaking out the garment, and Rabbi Yohanan **is referring to two** people shaking out the garment together. The act of shaking out a garment is not in itself harmful to the garment, but when two people do it together, they are quite likely to tear it.

אִיבָּעֵית אֵימָא [8](3) **If you wish,** you can **say: There is no difficulty.** [9]The Mishnah **is referring to** a person **shaking out** a garment **by hand, and** Rabbi Yohanan **is referring to** a person **beating** a garment **with a stick.**

אִיבָּעֵית אֵימָא [10](4) **If you wish,** you can **say: There is no difficulty.** [11]The Mishnah **is referring to a woolen** garment, which benefits from being shaken out, whereas Rabbi Yohanan is **referring to a linen** garment, which is damaged by being shaken out.

אֲמַר רַבִּי יוֹחָנָן [12]Since the Gemara has introduced a piece of practical advice given by Rabbi Yohanan, it now quotes some other statements of a similar kind by the same Sage: **Rabbi Yohanan said:** It is better to risk drinking from **a sorcerers' cup rather than** from **a cup of lukewarm water,** because lukewarm water is extremely unhealthy. [13]Rabbi Yohanan's statement is now qualified: **This only applies to** drinking lukewarm water from **metal vessels,** [14]**but as far as** drinking such water from **earthenware vessels is concerned,** there is **no** reason

[1]״מָצָא כְּסוּת, מְנַעֲרָהּ אֶחָד לִשְׁלֹשִׁים יוֹם״. [2]לְמֵימְרָא דְּנִיעוּר מַעֲלֵי לָהּ? [3]וְהָאָמַר רַבִּי יוֹחָנָן: מִי שֶׁיֵּשׁ לוֹ גַּרְדִּי אוּמָּן בְּתוֹךְ בֵּיתוֹ יְנַעֵר כְּסוּתוֹ בְּכָל יוֹם!

[4]אָמְרִי: בְּכָל יוֹם קָשֵׁי לָהּ; [5]אֶחָד לִשְׁלֹשִׁים יוֹם מַעֲלֵי לָהּ.

[6]אִיבָּעֵית אֵימָא: לָא קַשְׁיָא. [7]הָא בְּחַד, וְהָא בִּתְרֵי.

[8]אִיבָּעֵית אֵימָא: לָא קַשְׁיָא. [9]הָא בִּידָא, וְהָא בְּחוּטְרָא.

[10]אִיבָּעֵית אֵימָא: לָא קַשְׁיָא. [11]הָא בְּדַעֲמְרָא; הָא בִּדְכִיתָּנָא.

[12]אֲמַר רַבִּי יוֹחָנָן: כָּסָא דְחָרָשִׁין וְלָא כָּסָא דְּפוֹשְׁרִין. [13]וְלָא אֲמַרַן אֶלָּא בִּכְלֵי מַתָּכוֹת, [14]אֲבָל בִּכְלֵי חֶרֶשׂ לֵית לָן בָּהּ.

LITERAL TRANSLATION

[1]"[If] he found a garment, he shakes it out once in thirty days." [2][Do you mean] to say that shaking out is beneficial to it? [3]But surely Rabbi Yohanan said: [Only] someone who has a weaver in his household may shake his garment out every day.

[4][We can] say: Every day is bad for it; [5]once in thirty days is beneficial to it.

[6]If you wish, say: There is no difficulty. [7]This [refers] to one, and that [refers] to two.

[8]If you wish, say: There is no difficulty. [9]This [refers to shaking out] by hand, and that [refers to beating] with a stick.

[10]If you wish, say: There is no difficulty. [11]This [refers] to wool; that [refers] to linen.

[12]Rabbi Yohanan said: A cup of sorcerers and not a cup of lukewarm water. [13]And we only said [this] with reference to metal vessels, [14]but regarding earthenware vessels we have no [concern] about it.

RASHI

מי שיש לו גרדי אומן בביתו — שיארוג לו טליתות חדשות תמיד. **ינער כסותו בכל יום** — ולמדנו דרך ארץ דניעור קשה לה. **בחד** — כשאדם אחד אין ניעורו קורעה. **שנים** — האוחזין בשני ראשיה ומנערין ממתחין אותה יותר מדאי, וקשה לה. **דעמרא** — קשה לה שנמתחת ונקרעת. **כסא דחרשין** — נוח לשתות כוס של מכשפות מכוס של מים פושרין, והאי דאיירי במילי דרבי יוחנן בהלכות דרך ארץ נקט הני שמעתא.

HALAKHAH

may study a single passage together, but they may not study two separate passages at the same time, and under no circumstances may three people use a scroll at the same time." (*Shulhan Arukh, Hoshen Mishpat* 267:20.)

מָצָא כְּסוּת מְנַעֲרָהּ **If a person finds a garment, he must shake it out.** "Someone who finds a woolen garment must shake it out once a month. He should not shake it out together with another person, nor should he beat it with a stick. He may spread it out over a bed provided he is doing so strictly for the benefit of the garment, but not so as to decorate his own house." (Ibid., 267:18.)

LANGUAGE

גַּרְדִּי **Weaver.** The source of the word is the Greek word γερδιός, *gerdios,* or γέρδις, *gerdis,* meaning "weaver."

BACKGROUND

מִי שֶׁיֵּשׁ לוֹ גַּרְדִּי **Only someone who has a weaver....** This piece of advice, like the other practical matters cited in the name of Rabbi Yohanan here, is offered in sardonic style to make it more memorable. Generally, remarks of this kind were made during a sermon. Preachers wanted to reach an audience consisting not only of advanced scholars but also of the general public, for whom they wished to provide guidance. Therefore they spoke in a provocative style so that people would heed and remember their teachings.

יְנַעֵר כְּסוּתוֹ **He may shake his garment out.** One mainly shakes out garments to remove dust, to prevent moths and other pests from damaging the cloth, and also to keep garments and bedding from becoming permanently wrinkled. In our commentary we have followed *Rif* and *Rambam,* who state that shaking damages linen garments and is beneficial to woolen garments (although *Rashi* states the opposite). This may be dependent on climate, for woolen fibers generally absorb more moisture than linen, and in a relatively dry climate shaking is good for wool, but not for linen.

וְלָא כָּסָא דְּפוֹשְׁרִין **And not a cup of lukewarm water.** Rabbi Yohanan anticipated modern science here. Centuries were to pass before the microscope was invented and it was discovered that lukewarm water is an environment in which microbes proliferate very quickly, unless, as Rabbi Yohanan's statement is explained below, the water has previously been boiled. The difference between a clay vessel and a metal one is that the latter gives the water a metallic aftertaste. Both that taste and some microorganisms are neutralized when certain spices are added to the drink.

TERMINOLOGY

לֵית לָן בָּהּ Lit., **we have nothing in it.** An expression limiting the applications of a statement made earlier: "The prohibition, law or ruling stated earlier in general terms does not apply in this case, and it poses no problem for us."

BACKGROUND

בְּכִיתָּנָא רוּמִיתָא Refers to Roman linen. The fibers of different types of linen vary considerably in thickness and strength. The linen known as Roman linen could apparently be spun very fine, but the threads were not strong. Garments made of Roman linen were extremely expensive (see *Yoma* 34b), and wore out very quickly, so that anyone who wore them frequently was liable to spend a great deal of money on clothing.

בְּזוּגִיתָא חִיוָּרְתָא Refers to white glass. White glass, apparently glass which was entirely transparent, was more difficult to manufacture than colored glass, mainly because the raw materials had to be chosen with care and kept free of any admixture. "White" glass vessels were also more delicate and fragile, and their use was equated with wasting money.

TRANSLATION AND COMMENTARY

to worry about it. [1] **And** drinking lukewarm water from **metal vessels** is not always dangerous. The recommendation not to do so **only applies where** the water **has not been boiled,** [2] **but where** the water in the metal vessel **has been boiled,** there is **no** reason to **worry about** drinking **it.** [3] **And** drinking lukewarm water that has not previously been boiled from metal vessels is not always dangerous. The recommendation not to do so **only applies where spice wood has not been thrown into** the lukewarm water, [4] **but where spice wood has been thrown into** the water, there is **no** reason **to worry about** drinking **it.**

וְאָמַר רַבִּי יוֹחָנָן [5] The Gemara now quotes another piece of practical advice offered in an ironic tone by Rabbi Yoḥanan: **Rabbi Yoḥanan further said: Someone whose father left him a lot of money and who wishes to lose it should** engage in the following wasteful practices: [6] He should **wear linen garments,** which wear out quickly; **use glass vessels,** which break easily; **and hire laborers and not sit with them** to supervise what they are doing, because in this way he will give them the best opportunity to cheat him. [7] The Gemara now qualifies Rabbi Yoḥanan's statement: **"He should wear linen garments" refers** specifically **to Roman linen,** which is particularly expensive and delicate. [8] **"He should use glass vessels" refers** specifically **to white glass,** which is very expensive and brittle. [9] **"He should hire laborers and not sit with them" was explained** [30A] **as referring to** laborers working with the owner's **oxen** in the field. Rabbi Yoḥanan is warning the owner of the oxen that **the losses** that can be **caused by** oxen handled by workers who are not supervised with the utmost care **can be** very **great.** In Talmudic times, oxen were used for many purposes besides plowing, and serious damage could be caused to both crops and animals by unsupervised workers who casually allowed oxen to trample through a field full of crops.

[1]וּבְכְלֵי מַתָּכוֹת נַמִי, לָא אֲמָרַן אֶלָּא דְּלָא צְוִיץ, [2]אֲבָל דִּצְוִיץ לֵית לָן בָּהּ. [3]וְלָא אֲמָרַן אֶלָּא דְּלָא שְׁדָא בֵּיהּ צִיבְיָא, [4]אֲבָל שְׁדָא בֵּיהּ צִיבְיָא לֵית לָן בָּהּ.

[5]וְאָמַר רַבִּי יוֹחָנָן: מִי שֶׁהִנִּיחַ לוֹ אָבִיו מָעוֹת הַרְבֵּה וְרוֹצֶה לְאַבְּדָן [6]יִלְבַּשׁ בִּגְדֵי פִשְׁתָּן, וְיִשְׁתַּמֵּשׁ בִּכְלֵי זְכוּכִית, וְיִשְׂכּוֹר פּוֹעֲלִים וְאַל יֵשֵׁב עִמָּהֶן. [7]״יִלְבַּשׁ בִּגְדֵי פִשְׁתָּן״ בְּכִיתָּנָא רוּמִיתָא. [8]״וְיִשְׁתַּמֵּשׁ בִּכְלֵי זְכוּכִית״ בְּזוּגִיתָא חִיוָּרְתָא. [9]״וְיִשְׂכּוֹר פּוֹעֲלִים וְאַל יֵשֵׁב עִמָּהֶן״ תַּרְגּוּמָא [30A] בְּתוֹרֵי, דְּנָפִישׁ פְּסֵידַיְיהוּ.

LITERAL TRANSLATION

[1] And also regarding metal vessels, we only said [this] where it had not boiled, [2] but where it has boiled we have no [concern] about it. [3] And we only said [this] where he did not throw [spice] wood into it, [4] but [where] he did throw [spice] wood into it we have no [concern] about it.

[5] And Rabbi Yoḥanan further said: Someone whose father left him a lot of money and wishes to lose it [6] should wear linen garments, and should use glass vessels, and should hire laborers and not sit with them. [7] "He should wear linen garments" [refers] to Roman linen. [8] "He should use glass vessels" [refers] to white glass. [9] "He should hire laborers and not sit with them" is explained [30A] [as referring] to oxen, the loss [caused] by which is great.

RASHI

צויץ — רותח. **ציביא** — כל דבר שנותנין לתוך המשקה, או עשבים או תבלין או עקרי בשמים, קרי ליביא. **ורוצה לאבדן** — ללמדנו בא שלא ירגיל אדם בכך, שהעושה אלה מאבד מהר הון רב. **כתנא רומיתא** — דמיהם יקרין וממהרין לכלות. **תרגמה** — להך שכירות דפועלים. **בתורי** — בפועלים המנהיגים בשוורי בעל הבית. **דנפיש פסידייהו** — שרוב עבודת קרקעות שלהן בשוורים היתה, אף חרישת הכרמים ובצירתם מנהיגים כלי המחרישה בעגלה בין שורות הכרם עם הבוצרים ונותנין שם הענבים, לפיכך אם אין הבעלים עליהם יש הפסד גדול, שאין דרך הפועלים לחוס על הכרם ועל השוורים, ומנהיגים אותן על הגפנים ועל הנטיעות, והם מתקלקלין, והשוורין נסמכין ונשברים.

NOTES

מָעוֹת הַרְבֵּה A lot of money. Some Rishonim have a different version, מָעוֹת רִבִּית — "money obtained through usury." According to this version, Rabbi Yoḥanan is not necessarily being ironic at all. The law is that there are many cases where money illegally obtained through usury need not be returned. In particular, the heirs of the usurer need not return such money if they inherit it. However, if a person inherits such tainted money, he might, out of piety, not wish to retain it. In such circumstances, the best course for the usurer's heirs is to return the money or give it to charity. But if for some reason they prefer to find another way to avoid benefiting from their father's estate, they can take Rabbi Yoḥanan's advice.

בְּתוֹרֵי As referring to oxen. Our commentary follows *Rashi*. *Rabbenu Ḥananel* has a slightly different reading here: תַּוָּרֵי — "drivers of oxen." According to this interpretation, it is especially important for an employer to supervise the plowing of his fields by his workers, for if the workers are not supervised and act in an irresponsible way at that stage, this can lead to the loss of an entire crop (*Tosafot*).

An alternative interpretation of *Rabbenu Ḥananel* explains the word תַּוָּרֵי as meaning "small oxen," which are not

TRANSLATION AND COMMENTARY

שׁוֹטְחָהּ לְצוֹרְכָּהּ [1]The Gemara now goes on to consider the next clause of the Mishnah: "The finder of a lost garment **must spread it out** to air it, provided that this is **for its benefit,** but not for his own honor." [2]The scholars in the Academy **posed the following problem: If** the finder **spreads out** the garment both **for his** own **benefit and for the benefit of the garment, what is the law?** Is such an act permitted or forbidden?

תָּא שְׁמַע [3]The Gemara now makes a series of attempts to answer this question by quoting Tannaitic sources that may be able to throw light on its solution: (1) **Come and hear** an inference from the language of our Mishnah itself: "The finder of a lost garment must spread it out **for its benefit."** [4]From the emphasis on the expression "for its benefit," says the Gemara, we can infer that only if he spreads it out **for *its* benefit is he permitted** to spread it out at all; **but** if he wanted to spread it out both **for his** own **benefit *and* for its benefit,** he would **not** be permitted to do so.

אֵימָא סֵיפָא [5]The Gemara now responds by **considering the next clause** in the Mishnah and applying the same reasoning. The Mishnah states: **"But** he may **not** spread it out **for his own honor."** [6]Applying the same reasoning used above, we should argue as follows: **It is** only **for his** own **honor that he is not permitted to spread it out.** [7]**But** it would seem that if he spread out the garment both **for its benefit *and* for his benefit, it would be perfectly acceptable.** This, of course, is precisely the opposite of the previous inference, and results in a contradiction between the first and second parts of the same sentence in the Mishnah.

אֶלָּא [8]**Rather,** concludes the Gemara, **from this** method of inference **it is impossible to deduce any** further laws from our Mishnah, one way or the other, as the phraseology of the Mishnah does not lend itself to such inferences.

תָּא שְׁמַע [9](2) Come and hear another solution of the problem from the following Baraita (*Pesaḥim* 26b): "The finder of a lost garment **may not spread it out on a bed or on a** clothes **hanger for his** own **benefit,** [10]**but he may spread it out on a bed or on a** clothes **hanger for** the **benefit** of the garment, to air it and clean it. [11]But **if guests happened to visit him, he may not spread** the garment **out on a bed or on a** clothes **hanger** under any circumstances, [12]regardless of **whether** he wishes to do so **for his** own **benefit** to impress his guests, **or** if he wishes to do so specifically **for its benefit,** as it needs airing." From this Baraita, argues the Gemara, it would seem that he is not permitted to spread out a lost garment both for his own benefit and for that of the garment.

[1]״שׁוֹטְחָהּ לְצוֹרְכָּהּ, אֲבָל לֹא לִכְבוֹדוֹ וכו׳״. [2]אִיבַּעְיָא לְהוּ: לְצוֹרְכּוֹ וּלְצוֹרְכָּהּ, מַאי? [3]תָּא שְׁמַע: ״שׁוֹטְחָהּ לְצוֹרְכָּהּ״. [4]לְצוֹרְכָּהּ — אִין; הָא לְצוֹרְכּוֹ וּלְצוֹרְכָּהּ — לָא. [5]אֵימָא סֵיפָא: ״אֲבָל לֹא לִכְבוֹדוֹ״. [6]לִכְבוֹדוֹ הוּא דְּלָא; [7]הָא לְצוֹרְכָּהּ וּלְצוֹרְכּוֹ, שַׁפִּיר דָּמֵי! [8]אֶלָּא, מֵהָא לֵיכָּא לְמִשְׁמַע מִינָּהּ. [9]תָּא שְׁמַע: ״לֹא יִשְׁטְחֶנָּה, לֹא עַל גַּבֵּי מִטָּה וְלֹא עַל גַּבֵּי מָגוֹד, לְצָרְכּוֹ; [10]אֲבָל יִשְׁטְחֶנָּה עַל גַּבֵּי מִטָּה וְעַל גַּבֵּי מָגוֹד לְצָרְכָּהּ. [11]נִזְדַּמְּנוּ לוֹ אוֹרְחִים, לֹא יִשְׁטְחֶנָּה, לֹא עַל גַּבֵּי מִטָּה וְלֹא עַל גַּבֵּי מָגוֹד, [12]בֵּין לְצוֹרְכּוֹ בֵּין לְצוֹרְכָּהּ״!

LITERAL TRANSLATION

[1]"He spreads it out for its benefit, but not for his honor, etc." [2]It was asked of them: [If he spread it out] for his benefit and for its benefit, what is [the law]?

[3]Come [and] hear: "He spreads it out for its benefit." [4]For *its* benefit — yes; for his benefit *and* for its benefit — no.

[5]Say the latter clause: "But not for his honor." [6]It is for his honor that he may not [spread it out]; [7]but for its benefit *and* for his benefit, it is well.

[8]Rather, from this it is impossible to learn [anything] from it.

[9]Come [and] hear: "He may not spread it out, not on a bed and not on a hanger, for his benefit; [10]but he may spread it out on a bed or on a hanger for its benefit. [11]If guests happened to [visit] him, he may not spread it out, not on a bed and not on a hanger, [12]whether for his benefit [or] whether for its benefit."

RASHI

מגוד — *קביל״א בלעז. **נזדמנו לו אורחים** — קא סלקא דעתך טעמא משום דמתכבד בהם ואיכא לצורכה ולצרכו.

BACKGROUND

לְצוֹרְכּוֹ וּלְצוֹרְכָּהּ **For his benefit and for its benefit.** Clearly, someone who finds an object may not use it for his own needs, for it is not permitted to use another person's property without his knowledge and permission. The problem discussed here arises when the finder does something for the benefit of the object he has found — an action not only permitted but obligatory — while, at the same time, he himself derives some benefit from so doing. It may seem surprising that this should be a problem, since the Halakhah stipulates that if A can benefit from B's property without causing B any loss thereby, to prevent A from doing so would be to behave according to "the ethical standards of Sodom." Moreover, even regarding found objects we know that a person is permitted to read a scroll which he has found, because in any event the scroll must be rolled and aired (see above, 29b). Therefore *Tosafot* explain that the cases being discussed here are those where there is some ground for suspicion that in permitting a person to use the object for its own benefit we may encourage the finder to use it more than is necessary, and thus damage it.

LANGUAGE (RASHI)

קביל״א* From the Old French *cheile,* meaning a wooden stake or frame.

NOTES

mature or strong enough to plow a field efficiently (*Maharshal*). Compare also parallel passages: *Bava Metzia* 73a and *Ḥullin* 84b, and see *Tosafot* on all three passages.

HALAKHAH

לְצוֹרְכּוֹ וּלְצוֹרְכָּהּ **Both for his benefit and for its benefit.** "The finder of a lost garment must spread it out for its benefit, but not for his own honor. Nor may he spread it out with both purposes in mind. When guests are visiting, he

TRANSLATION AND COMMENTARY

שָׁאנֵי הָתָם [1]The Gemara now rejects this argument: The case discussed **there,** in the last clause of the Baraita, **is different**. The reason why the finder is not permitted to spread out the garment in the presence of guests has no connection with the problem that the Gemara is seeking to solve. [2]By exposing the garment to the gaze of his guests, the finder is, as it were, **burning it**, actively destroying it, **either because** such an action exposes the garment to **the evil eye, or because** the more people who know about its presence in his house, the more likely it is to attract the attention **of thieves.**

תָּא שְׁמַע [3](3) **Come and hear** another resolution of the problem posed above from a Baraita (*Pesaḥim* 26a/b) dealing with the laws of "the heifer whose neck is broken" (עֶגְלָה עֲרוּפָה): The Torah (Deuteronomy 21:1-9) relates that if a murdered person's body is found between two towns and the identity of the murderer is not known, a heifer must be taken to an untilled riverbed and have its neck broken in a ceremony of atonement. Only a heifer that has never been used for any work and has never been brought under a yoke is fit for this purpose. The Baraita explains this regulation: "If on some previous occasion the farmer **brought** the heifer **into the** ox **team** for some reason unconnected with farm work, **and**, without the farmer's approval, **it threshed** the farmer's grain together with the other animals, **it is** still **fit** to serve as the heifer in the atonement ceremony, because work of this kind is not considered intentional. [4]**But** if he brought the heifer into the team with two purposes in mind — firstly, for the benefit of the heifer itself, **in order that it should suck** from its mother who happened to be in the team; **and** secondly, for his benefit, in order that it **thresh** his grain — then the heifer is forever rendered unfit to serve in the atonement ceremony, because the work done by the heifer resulted from a conscious decision by its owner." [5]**But surely,** argues the Gemara, in the case described **here**, in the last sentence of the Baraita, the action taken by the owner — leading the calf into the team — was taken both **for his benefit and for the benefit of the heifer, and nevertheless** the Baraita **teaches** that the heifer **is unfit.** Hence we see that an action taken both for his benefit and for its benefit is considered to have been taken for his benefit alone. Thus it would appear that we can solve the problem regarding a lost object from this Baraita, and where an action is for the benefit of both the finder and the object, it is forbidden.

[1]שָׁאנֵי הָתָם, דְּמִקְלָא קָלֵי לָהּ, [2]אִי מִשּׁוּם עֵינָא, אִי מִשּׁוּם גַּנָּבֵי.

[3]תָּא שְׁמַע: ״הִכְנִיסָהּ לִרְבֵקָה וְדָשָׁה, כְּשֵׁירָה, [4]בִּשְׁבִיל שֶׁתִּינַק וְתָדוּשׁ, פְּסוּלָה״. [5]וְהָא הָכָא דִּלְצוֹרְכּוֹ וּלְצוֹרְכָּהּ הוּא, וְקָתָנֵי פְּסוּלָה!

LITERAL TRANSLATION

[1]It is different there, for he surely burns it, [2]either because of [the evil] eye, or because of thieves.

[3]Come [and] hear: "[If] he brought it into a team and it threshed, it is fit, [4][but] in order that it should suck and thresh, it is unfit." [5]But surely here it is for his benefit and for its benefit, and [yet] it teaches [that] it is unfit.

RASHI

שאני התם דקא קלי לה — בשטיחה זו הוא שורפה, ומה הוא שריפתה. **אי משום עינא** — שתשלוט בה עין רע של אורחין. **אי משום גנבי** — פן יגנבוה האורחים. **הכניסה לרבקה** — בעגלה ערופה קאי. רבקה — *קופל״ה בלעז, שמדבקים שלש בהמות או ארבעה בצואריהן, זו אצל זו, ודשים הדישה. **כשירה** — הואיל ולא נתכוון שתדוש. **ואם בשביל שתינק ותידוש** — שהיתה אמה דשה והכניס את הבת לשם שתינק, ואף נתכוון שתדוש, פסולה.

BACKGROUND

אִי מִשּׁוּם עֵינָא Either because of the evil eye. The Sages of the Mishnah and the Talmud greatly feared the "evil eye," believing that the look of someone filled with thoughts of envy or hatred could cause direct damage even in the world of visible reality. They also believed that the "evil eye" was capable of indirectly provoking events that could cause damage to an object in some other way, such as by fire, accident, or the like.

CONCEPTS

עֶגְלָה עֲרוּפָה A heifer whose neck is broken. When a murdered person's body is found outside a town and it is not known who caused his death, the following procedure takes place (see Deuteronomy 21:1-9). First, judges from the Great Sanhedrin (סַנְהֶדְרִין גְּדוֹלָה) come to measure the distance between the corpse and the nearest town, to determine which town must perform the rite of the עֶגְלָה עֲרוּפָה. This measurement is carried out even if it is clear beyond any doubt which town is closest to the corpse. Afterwards, the elders of that town must bring a heifer that has never been worked and break its neck in a riverbed that is not tilled. The elders wash their hands and make a statement absolving themselves from guilt. If the murderer is discovered before the heifer has been killed, the rite of עֶגְלָה עֲרוּפָה is not performed.

LANGUAGE

רְבֵקָה A team. *Rashi* and others explain that רְבֵקָה is a pair or team of animals tied together, and there is an Arabic word, رِبْقَة, with that meaning. Others claim that it derives from the Biblical word מַרְבֵּק, and has the sense of stabling and giving fodder.

LANGUAGE (RASHI)

קופל״ה* From the Old French *cople,* meaning a yoke of oxen.

NOTES

הִכְנִיסָהּ לִרְבֵקָה If he brought it into the team. Our translation follows *Rashi. Rabbenu Ḥananel* and other Rishonim translate רְבֵקָה as the stall where animals are fed, from the word מַרְבֵּק (I Samuel 28:24). Thus, the owner brought the heifer to the stall in order to feed it, and in the course of its feeding it threshed some grain, without the owner intending it to do so.

וְהָא הָכָא דִּלְצוֹרְכּוֹ וּלְצוֹרְכָּהּ הוּא But surely here it is for his benefit and for its benefit. *Radbaz* asks: The case of the lost garment is an example of monetary law. The cases of the heifer whose neck is to be broken and the Red Heifer are examples of ritual law. In general, rules governing monetary law cannot be derived from rules governing ritual law (מָמוֹנָא מֵאִיסּוּרָא לָא יָלְפִינַן). Thus, even if it is accepted that for the purposes of ritual law action taken both for his benefit and for its benefit is always considered to be for his benefit, this ought not to serve as a precedent for the case of the lost garment.

Radbaz answers that our case is not an example of monetary law at all. There is no dispute about the garment's

HALAKHAH

may not spread it out at all, even for its benefit alone," following *Rambam* and *Rosh,* who rule stringently in situations where a problem raised by the Gemara has failed to be resolved. (*Shulḥan Arukh, Ḥoshen Mishpat* 267:18.)

הִכְנִיסָהּ לִרְבֵקָה, שָׁכַן עָלֶיהָ עוֹף Bringing into a team a heifer whose neck is to be broken.... If a bird rested on a Red Heifer.... "A Red Heifer becomes unfit if it performs any work with its owner's approval. If the owner used it in any way for his own or someone else's benefit, it is disqualified; for the heifer's benefit alone, it is still fit; both for its benefit and

TRANSLATION AND COMMENTARY

שָׁאנֵי הָתָם [1]The Gemara answers: The case of the heifer whose neck is to be broken **is different** from other cases, **for the verse** in the Torah (Deuteronomy 21:3) uses the expression "a heifer **which has not been put to work** [אֲשֶׁר לֹא עֻבַּד בָּהּ]" — an expression of the most general kind — to describe the kind of work that renders the heifer unfit. From the fact that the Torah uses the passive voice — "has not been put to work" — the Gemara infers that in the case of the heifer whose neck is to be broken the Torah forbids work **of any kind.** This, then, is a special case, and cannot be used to decide what the law should be if the finder of a lost object performs some action with it which is both to his benefit and to the benefit of the object itself.

[1]שָׁאנֵי הָתָם, דְּאָמַר קְרָא: ״אֲשֶׁר לֹא עֻבַּד בָּהּ״ — מִכָּל מָקוֹם. [2]אִי הָכִי, אֲפִילּוּ רֵישָׁא נַמִּי! [3]הָא לָא דָּמְיָא אֶלָּא לְהָא דִּתְנַן: ״שָׁכַן עָלֶיהָ עוֹף, כְּשֵׁירָה; [4]עָלָה עָלֶיהָ זָכָר, פְּסוּלָה״. [5]מַאי טַעְמָא? כִּדְרַב פַּפָּא.

LITERAL TRANSLATION

[1]It is different there, for the verse says: "Which has not been put to work" — of any kind (lit., "from every place").

[2]If so, even the first clause too.

[3]This only resembles that which we have learned: "[If] a bird rested on it, it is fit; [4][if] a male mounted it, it is unfit."

[5]What is the reason? As Rav Pappa [explained].

RASHI

הא לא דמיא — מירוצא היא. **שכן עליה עוף** — בפרה אדומה קאי. **עלה עליה זכר פסולה** — שנאמר ״אשר לא עלה עליה עול״, ותניא: עול אין לי אלא עול כו׳, במסכת סוטה (מו,א), והאי הכניסה לרבקה ודשה דלא ניחא ליה בה דמיא לשכן עליה עוף.

אִי הָכִי [2]But, objects the Gemara, **if** we accept the argument just presented, that work of any kind performed by the heifer renders it unfit to serve in the atonement ceremony, the same law should apply **even** to **the first clause too,** and the act of threshing performed by the heifer without the intent of the owner should also be included in the generalized definition of work given above.

הָא לָא דָּמְיָא [3]The Gemara answers that the difference between the rulings in the two clauses in the Baraita derives from an additional factor — the intention of the owner and his satisfaction with the work done. **This** case of the heifer, says the Gemara, **can only be compared to** the case of the Red Heifer (Numbers 19), which is also disqualified by any form of work, and in particular the bearing of any burden. Concerning the Red Heifer, **we have learned** in the following Mishnah (*Parah* 2:4): **"If,** without the knowledge of the owner of the Red Heifer, **a bird rested on it, it is** still **fit** and can be used for the ceremony of purification, because the owner did not derive any satisfaction from it. [4]But **if a bull mounted it, it is** forever rendered **unfit**, because the owner doubtless approves of the heifer being made pregnant." In citing this Mishnah the Gemara is seeking to compare the first clause of the Baraita, where the heifer threshes without the owner intending that it do so, with the first clause of the Mishnah, where a bird comes to rest on the Red Heifer. In both cases the heifers would normally be disqualified if they performed any work, and in both cases the Baraita and the Mishnah state that what occurred did not disqualify them. The factor common to both cases is that the owner did not intend the "act of work" to take place, and this, argues the Gemara, is why in both cases the animals remain fit for their respective ceremonies.

מַאי טַעְמָא [5]The Gemara now asks: **What is the reason** for the distinction between the case of the bird and the case of the bull in this Mishnah? The Gemara answers: The reason is **as Rav Pappa explained.** In the passage dealing with the heifer whose neck is to be broken, where the Torah says that work performed by the heifer disqualifies it, it uses the passive voice *ubad* (עֻבַּד) — "was put to work" — which is spelled consonantally exactly like the parallel form in the active voice — *avad* (עָבַד) — meaning "he worked it." The difference in meaning between the active and the passive is, of course, that in the former case the owner

NOTES

ownership. The issue is the proper behavior of the person looking after the garment. He does not want to violate the commandments of the Torah by misusing another person's property. Hence, it is in essence a ritual question.

שָׁכַן עָלֶיהָ עוֹף If a bird rested on it. The Rishonim point out that the Mishnah in tractate *Parah* is dealing with the Red Heifer, whereas Rav Pappa's explanation is based on a word appearing in a passage in the Talmud dealing with the

HALAKHAH

for his, it is disqualified. If the heifer did work of its own volition, if the owner approves, it is disqualified; if he does not approve, it is still fit. Thus, if he led it into a team of oxen and it threshed some grain of its own volition, it is still fit; if he led it into the team both in order that it should suck *and* in order that it should thresh, it is disqualified. If a bird rested on it, it is still fit; if a bull mounted it, it is disqualified." (*Rambam, Sefer Tohorah, Hilkhot Parah Adumah* 1:7.) The same laws apply to the heifer whose neck is to be broken. (*Rambam, Sefer Nezikin, Hilkhot Rotze'aḥ* 10:3.)

TRANSLATION AND COMMENTARY

himself caused the animal to work, whereas in the latter case the animal was worked by others or acted on its own initiative. It is only through the traditional pronunciation that we know that the word is to be read in the passive form. This generates a form of hermeneutical rule called קרי—כתיב, whereby we derive information both from the spelling of a word as it appears in the Torah text and from its traditional pronunciation. [1]**For Rav Pappa said: If**, when the Torah disqualified from the ceremony of atonement a heifer that had borne a burden, **it** had spelled the word using the passive voice and **had written** ***ubad*** (עוּבַּד) — **"it was worked"** — **and** if **we** also **read** the word, in the same way, **as** ***ubad*** (עוּבַּד) — **"it was worked"** — [2]then **I would have said that** the heifer **is unfit even if it worked of its own volition** without the owner's approval. [3]**And if** the Torah had spelled the word using the active voice and **had written** ***avad*** (עָבַד) — **"he worked it"** — **and** if **we** also **read** the word, in the same way, **as** ***avad*** (עָבַד) — **"he worked it"** — [4]then **I would have said:** The heifer **is fit unless** the owner **worked it himself** intentionally. [5]But **now that** the Torah has spelled the word using the active voice and **has written** it as *avad* (עָבַד) — **"he worked it" — and we** nevertheless **read it as** the passive voice ***ubad*** (עוּבַּד) — **"it was worked"** — we combine the information contained in both forms of the word and interpret the Torah as teaching us a previously unstated principle: [6]In order for the heifer to be disqualified, **we require** only a passive kind of work, suitable to the description **"it was worked,"** but we require it **to be comparable** to the active kind of work justifying the term **"he worked it."** [7]**Just as** the expression **"he worked it" implies that** the owner **approved** of the work, and that it was done according to his wishes, [8]**so too** does the expression **"it was worked" imply that he approved** of the work, even though he did not actually order it done. Rav Pappa interprets the words used by the Torah with reference to the heifer whose neck was to be broken, but applies his interpretation to the case of the Red Heifer as well, because in both cases work done by the animal disqualifies it. Hence, the fact that the Red Heifer bore a bird on its back is not considered work, as the owner has no interest in it; but the fact that a bull mounted the Red Heifer is considered an act of work, even though it happened without the owner intending it, as the owner doubtless approves of the Red Heifer being made pregnant. Hence the Red Heifer is disqualified. Similarly, in the case of the heifer whose neck is to be broken, if the owner brought the heifer to the threshing team for some other reason, it is assumed that he does not approve of its threshing, as he already has sufficient oxen in the team. But if he brought the heifer to the team with the intention of having it thresh, even if his primary purpose was to let it receive milk from its mother, the heifer is disqualified. But in cases other than those involving a Red Heifer and a heifer whose neck is to be broken, it is still possible that action taken both for one's own benefit and also for the benefit of an object in one's keeping is considered to have been taken mainly for the latter's benefit. Thus, after three attempts, the Gemara has not found a solution to the problem raised above — whether a person is permitted to make use of a found object if his action is both for his own benefit and for that of the found object.

[1]דְּאָמַר רַב פַּפָּא: אִי כְּתִיב "עוּבַּד" וְקָרֵינַן "עוּבַּד", [2]הֲוָה אָמִינָא אֲפִילּוּ מִמֵּילָא. [3]וְאִי כְּתִיב "עָבַד" וְקָרֵינַן "עָבַד", [4]הֲוָה אָמִינָא עַד דְּעָבַד בָּהּ אִיהוּ. [5]הַשְׁתָּא דִּכְתִיב "עָבַד" וְקָרֵינַן "עוּבַּד", [6]בָּעֵינַן "עוּבַּד" דּוּמְיָא דְּ"עָבַד". [7]מָה "עָבַד" דְּנִיחָא לֵיהּ, [8]אַף "עוּבַּד" דְּנִיחָא לֵיהּ.

LITERAL TRANSLATION

[1]For Rav Pappa said: If it had been written *ubad* — "it was worked" — and we read [it as] *ubad* — "it was worked" — [2]I would have said [that it is unfit] even [if it worked] of its own volition. [3]And if it had been written *avad* — "he worked [it]" — and we read [it as] *avad* — "he worked [it]" — [4]I would have said [that it is fit] unless he worked it himself. [5]Now that it is written *avad* — "he worked [it]" — and we read [it as] *ubad* — "it was worked" — [6]we require [that] "it was worked" be comparable to "he worked [it]." [7]Just as "he worked [it]" [implies] that it was agreeable to him, [8]so too "it was worked" [implies] that it was agreeable to him.

NOTES

heifer whose neck is to be broken. *Ramban* and *Rashba* explain that the laws governing the prohibition against working the Red Heifer and against working the heifer whose neck is to be broken are identical, and are, in fact, derived from each other. Hence, for the purposes of his explanation, Rav Pappa treated them as though they were one and the same.

דְּנִיחָא לֵיהּ **That he approved.** The Rishonim ask: A Red Heifer is very rare and hence very valuable. Why, then, would its owner ever approve of any work the heifer might do? Whatever profit he may derive from the heifer's work would be dwarfed by the depreciation in its value caused by its being disqualified.

Rosh answers that the assessment regarding which kinds of work the owner approves of is not based on the actual approval of this particular owner, but is a legal presumption

[1] ״כְּלֵי כֶסֶף וּכְלֵי נְחוֹשֶׁת, מִשְׁתַּמֵּשׁ בָּהֶן וכו׳״. [2] תָּנוּ רַבָּנַן: ״הַמּוֹצֵא כְּלֵי עֵץ מִשְׁתַּמֵּשׁ בָּהֶן בִּשְׁבִיל שֶׁלֹּא יֵרָקְבוּ. [3] כְּלֵי נְחוֹשֶׁת, מִשְׁתַּמֵּשׁ בָּהֶן בְּחַמִּין אֲבָל לֹא עַל יְדֵי הָאוּר, מִפְּנֵי שֶׁמַּשְׁחִיקָן. [4] כְּלֵי כֶסֶף, מִשְׁתַּמֵּשׁ בָּהֶן בְּצוֹנֵן אֲבָל לֹא בְּחַמִּין, מִפְּנֵי שֶׁמַּשְׁחִירָן. [5] מַגְרֵיפוֹת וְקַרְדּוּמוֹת, מִשְׁתַּמֵּשׁ בָּהֶן בְּרַךְ אֲבָל לֹא בְּקָשֶׁה, מִפְּנֵי שֶׁמַּפְחִיתָן. [6] כְּלֵי זָהָב וּכְלֵי זְכוּכִית, לֹא יִגַּע בָּהֶן עַד שֶׁיָּבֹא אֵלִיָּהוּ. [7] כְּדֶרֶךְ שֶׁאָמְרוּ בַּאֲבֵידָה, כָּךְ אָמְרוּ בְּפִקָּדוֹן״. [8] פִּקָּדוֹן? מַאי עֲבִידְתֵּיהּ גַּבֵּיהּ? [9] אָמַר רַב אַדָּא בַּר חָמָא אָמַר רַב שֵׁשֶׁת: בְּפִקָּדוֹן שֶׁהָלְכוּ בַּעֲלֵיהֶן לִמְדִינַת הַיָּם.

LITERAL TRANSLATION

[1] "Vessels of silver or vessels of copper, he uses them, etc." [2] Our Sages taught: "Someone who finds vessels of wood uses them so that they do not rot. [3] Vessels of copper, he uses them with hot [water] but not over a fire, because it wears them away. [4] Vessels of silver, he uses them with cold [water] but not with hot [water], because it makes them black. [5] Shovels and spades, he uses them on soft but not on hard [substances], because it damages them. [6] Vessels of gold or vessels of glass, he may not touch them until Elijah comes. [7] Just as they said about a lost object, so did they say about a deposit."

[8] A deposit? What is his business with it?

[9] Rav Ada bar Ḥama said in the name of Rav Sheshet: [It refers] to a deposit whose owner has gone overseas (lit., "to a country of the sea").

RASHI

משתמש בהן בחמין – וכל שכן בצונן. **אבל לא על ידי האור** – לא יתן הכלי על האור. **מגריפות** – *וודיל״ש, עשויין לגרוף הכירות או להפריש תאנים המדובקים. **שמפחיתן** – פוגמן. **מאי עבידתיה גביה** – מה לו להשתמש בו יבא בעליו וישתמש בו.

TRANSLATION AND COMMENTARY

כְּלֵי כֶסֶף וּכְלֵי נְחוֹשֶׁת [1] The Gemara now goes on to consider the next clause of the Mishnah: "If a person finds **vessels of silver or vessels of copper he may use them** occasionally for their benefit, taking care that they are not damaged.

[2] **"Our Sages taught** the following Baraita which elaborates on our Mishnah: **"Someone who finds vessels** made **of wood may use them** from time to time **so that they do not rot** from disuse. [3] Similarly, someone who finds **vessels** made **of copper may use them with hot water, but not** directly **over a fire, because** direct exposure to fire **wears them away.** [4] Similarly, someone who finds **silver vessels may use them with cold water, but not with hot water, because** hot water tarnishes them and **makes them black.** [5] Similarly, someone who finds **shovels and spades may use them on soft** substances, **but not on hard substances, because** hard substances can **damage them.** [6] On the other hand, someone who finds **gold vessels or glass vessels may not touch them** at all, **until Elijah** the Prophet **comes** and tells us to whom they belong. [7] **All** the rules **that** the Sages **laid down with regard to** the care of **lost objects, they also laid down with regard to deposits,** and a person with whom one of the objects listed above is deposited should use the vessels in his charge in accordance with the material from which the vessels are made."

פִּקָּדוֹן [8] On the last sentence of the Baraita the Gemara asks: **A deposit? What business has** the person looking after the deposit **with it?** Why is he allowed to make any use at all of vessels placed in his care? They are the owner's responsibility, not his, and the owner himself can come and use them from time to time so that they do not deteriorate.

אָמַר רַב אַדָּא בַּר חָמָא [9] **Rav Ada bar Ḥama said** in reply **in the name of Rav Sheshet:** The Baraita **is referring to a deposit whose owner has gone overseas** for an extended period of time. The responsible thing for the person looking after the owner's possessions to do is to behave in a manner analogous to that of a finder of

NOTES

based upon owners and cows in general. Work that would ordinarily be approved by an owner if performed by an ordinary cow is deemed to be approved by this owner as well.

HALAKHAH

שִׁימּוּשׁ בִּכְלֵי אֲבֵידָה **Using lost objects.** "The finder of a lost vessel may use it, if it would otherwise deteriorate from disuse. A wooden vessel may be used occasionally, so that it does not rot. A copper vessel may be used with hot water, but may not be placed directly on a fire. A silver vessel may be used with cold water only. A shovel and a spade may be used with soft substances, but not with hard substances. Gold and glass vessels, and linen garments, may not be touched at all." (*Shulḥan Arukh, Ḥoshen Mishpat* 267:19.)

שִׁימּוּשׁ בִּכְלֵי פִּקָּדוֹן **Using objects deposited in one's care.** "If the owner leaves his vessels in someone's care and goes abroad for an extended period, the person with whom the vessels have been deposited should treat them in the same way he would treat lost objects, so that they do not

BACKGROUND

מִפְּנֵי שֶׁמַּשְׁחִירָן **Because it makes them black.** Silver articles become tarnished over time. Tarnish is a layer of silver sulfate (Ag_2S) caused by the presence of a small amount of sulfuric acid (H_2SO_4) in the air. Silver tarnishes less if it is used. However, the application of heat increases the chemical activity and the rate of tarnishing.

מַגְרֵיפוֹת וְקַרְדּוּמוֹת...מִשְׁתַּמֵּשׁ בָּהֶן בְּרַךְ **He uses them on soft substances.** The metal blades of agricultural tools will rust if they are not scraped clean, and the proper way to scrape them is to use them for work. However, care must be taken not to wear out the tools, and they must be kept sharp and intact.

כָּךְ אָמְרוּ בְּפִקָּדוֹן **So did they say about a deposit.** In principle, the law requiring the return of lost property does not apply only to objects found in the street, but has also been expanded into a general imperative regarding what a person must do to prevent monetary loss to someone else. Anything that a person can do for another in order to prevent damage to the latter's property is included in the category of returning lost objects. Therefore, someone who is looking after another person's property, and knows that its owner cannot tend to it, is required by the laws concerning the return of lost objects to make sure that no damage befalls the object placed in his care.

SAGES

רַב אַדָּא בַּר חָמָא **Rav Ada bar Ḥama.** A Babylonian Amora of the third generation, he was a disciple of Rav Sheshet and transmitted rulings in the name of his teacher. Variant readings give his name as Rav Yosef bar Ḥama, and if the latter reading is correct he was the father of the famous Amora, Rava. He lived in Meḥoza.

LANGUAGE (RASHI)

וודיל״ש* From the Old French *vadils*, meaning shovels for removing ashes from a fire.

TERMINOLOGY

מְנָהָנֵי מִילֵּי From where are these things derived? i.e., what verse in the Torah is the source of the statement just made? This question by the Gemara is usually followed either by a specific Biblical text or, as in this case, by a Midrashic interpretation of Biblical verses from which the Halakhic ruling is derived.

BACKGROUND

הָיָה כֹּהֵן וְהִיא בְּבֵית הַקְּבָרוֹת If he was a priest and it was in a cemetery. Since a priest is forbidden to contract ritual impurity conveyed by a corpse (except in the case of his closest relatives), he is forbidden to enter a cemetery. For even if he does not actually touch a corpse, he can hardly avoid touching or leaning over a grave, and the Torah (Numbers 19:18) says that a grave conveys ritual impurity in the same way as a corpse.

TRANSLATION AND COMMENTARY

a lost object, and to act in the best interests of the absent owner.

מָצָא שַׂק אוֹ קוּפָּה [1]The Gemara now goes on to consider the next clause of the Mishnah: **"If a person found a sack or a basket or anything which it would not be his practice to handle** or carry, even if it were his, **then he is not** under any obligation **to take it** and look after it until the owner comes to claim it." The Mishnah lays down the principle that in such cases a finder is allowed to leave the object where he found it, and does not thereby violate the Torah's prohibition, "You may not hide yourself" (Deuteronomy 22:3).

מְנָהָנֵי מִילֵּי [2]Regarding this the Gemara asks: **From where** in the Torah **is** the law laid down in the Mishnah **derived?**

דְּתָנוּ רַבָּנַן [3]The Gemara answers: This law is derived from the interpretation of the Biblical text which **our Sages taught** in the following Baraita (Sifrei, *Tetze* 222, 225): "The Torah says (Deuteronomy 22:1): 'You shall not see your brother's ox or his lamb go astray, **and hide yourself** from (i.e., ignore) them. You shall surely bring them back to your brother.'" The word וְהִתְעַלַּמְתָּ can be interpreted as descriptive, as in the simple meaning of the verse given above, or as a positive injunction — "and *you shall* hide yourself from them." [4]Following the latter interpretation, the Sifrei rules: **"Sometimes you** are permitted to **hide yourself** from a lost object and are not obliged to fulfill the commandment of restoring lost property to its rightful owner, whereas **sometimes you** are **not** permitted to **hide yourself** from it." In other words, even though the main purpose of the Torah is to inform us that we are obliged to return lost objects, it nevertheless hints, through its ambiguous use of the word וְהִתְעַלַּמְתָּ, that there are exceptions to this law. [5]The Sifrei goes on to elaborate: **"How so?** What are these exceptions? (1) **If** the finder **is a priest,** who is forbidden by Torah law to have any contact with or to go near a dead body (Leviticus 21:1), **and** the lost object **is in a cemetery,** then the priest should not enter the cemetery. He should ignore ('hide himself from') the lost object and proceed on his way. [6](2) Similarly, **if** the finder **is an elder, and it is not in keeping with his honor** to pick up a lost sack or basket, take it home, and set about the task of finding the rightful owner, then he too should ignore ('hide himself from') it and proceed on his way. [7](3) Similarly, **if** the finder's **own work is greater than that of the other person** — i.e., if the financial loss that would be incurred by the finder, were he to take time off from his work to pick up the lost object and look after it, is greater than the value of the object itself — then he too should ignore ('hide himself from') it and proceed on his way, [8]because it was **for this** reason **that** the Torah **said: 'And you shall hide yourself from them.'"** Thus this Baraita indicates the Biblical source for the ruling in our Mishnah that if a person who finds a lost object is of superior social standing and it does not accord with his dignity to busy himself with restoring lost property to its rightful owner, he is not obliged to do so.

[1]"מָצָא שַׂק אוֹ קוּפָּה [וְכָל דָּבָר] שֶׁאֵין דַּרְכּוֹ לִיטוֹל, הֲרֵי זֶה לֹא יִטּוֹל".

[2]מְנָהָנֵי מִילֵּי?

[3]דְּתָנוּ רַבָּנַן: "'וְהִתְעַלַּמְתָּ'. פְּעָמִים שֶׁאַתָּה מִתְעַלֵּם, [4]וּפְעָמִים שֶׁאִי אַתָּה מִתְעַלֵּם. [5]הָא כֵּיצַד? הָיָה כֹּהֵן וְהִיא בְּבֵית הַקְּבָרוֹת, [6]אוֹ שֶׁהָיָה זָקֵן וְאֵינָהּ לְפִי כְּבוֹדוֹ, [7]אוֹ שֶׁהָיְתָה מְלַאכְתּוֹ שֶׁלּוֹ מְרוּבָּה מִשֶּׁל חֲבֵירוֹ. [8]לְכָךְ נֶאֱמַר: 'וְהִתְעַלַּמְתָּ מֵהֶם'".

LITERAL TRANSLATION

[1]"[If] he found a sack or a basket or anything which it is not his practice to take, then he need not take [it]."

[2]From where are these things [derived]?

[3]For our Sages taught: "'And you shall hide yourself.' [4]Sometimes you hide yourself, and sometimes you do not hide yourself. [5]How so? [If] he was a priest and it was in a cemetery, [6]or [if] he was an elder and it was not in keeping with his honor, [7]or [if] his own work was more than that of his fellow. [8]For this it was said: 'And you shall hide yourself from them.'"

RASHI

והתעלמת מהם — וללמדך בא שמותר להתעלם. **ופעמים שאי אתה מתעלם** — דכתיב "לא תוכל להתעלם". **והיא בבית הקברות** — האבידה בבית הקברות. **ואינה לפי כבודו** — שישינה. **או שהיה בטל ממלאכה שלו** — שיבטל בהשבתה, מרובה על דמי האבידה.

HALAKHAH

deteriorate. But if the owner is in the country, the person with whom the vessels have been deposited may not use them, regardless of how much they deteriorate." (*Shulḥan Arukh, Ḥoshen Mishpat* 292:21-22.)

כֹּהֵן וְזָקֵן A priest and an elder. "A priest who sees a beast of burden in need of assistance in a cemetery is not allowed to contract ritual impurity in order to help it." (Ibid., 272:2.) "Similarly, if a lost object is found by an elder or a scholar, who would not ordinarily concern himself with objects like the one he has found, he need not pick it up to return it to its owner." (Ibid., 263:1.)

TRANSLATION AND COMMENTARY

לְמַאי אִיצְטְרִיךְ קְרָא [1]On this Baraita the Gemara now asks: **For which case** of the three mentioned in the Baraita **was the verse** actually needed, in order to give the finder specific permission to ignore the object? Surely some of these exceptions are covered by other laws of the Torah. [2]The Gemara goes on to explain: **If we say** that the Torah needed to inform us that **a priest** passing near a cemetery is entitled to ignore a lost object he sees lying **in the cemetery**, this surely cannot be correct, because this exception **is obvious** for two other reasons: [3](1) The commandment to return lost objects — "You shall surely return them" (Deuteronomy 22:1) — **is a positive commandment,** whereas the prohibition against a priest entering a cemetery is both **a negative commandment** — "He shall not defile himself" (Leviticus 21:1) — **and a positive commandment** — "They shall be holy" (Leviticus 21:6). [4]**And** the rule is that **a positive commandment cannot supersede a negative commandment and a positive commandment** on the same subject. Thus in any case the priest is not permitted to pick up and return the object lost in the cemetery, and the specific mention of the word וְהִתְעַלַּמְתָּ

[1]לְמַאי אִיצְטְרִיךְ קְרָא? [2]אִילֵימָא לְכֹהֵן וְהִיא בְּבֵית הַקְּבָרוֹת, פְּשִׁיטָא. [3]הַאי עֲשֵׂה, וְהַאי לֹא תַעֲשֶׂה וַעֲשֵׂה; [4]וְלֹא אָתֵי עֲשֵׂה וְדָחֵי אֶת לֹא תַעֲשֶׂה וַעֲשֵׂה.

LITERAL TRANSLATION

[1]For which [case] is the verse needed? [2]If we say for the priest where it is in the cemetery, it is obvious. [3]This is a positive commandment, and that is a negative commandment and a positive commandment; [4]and a positive commandment does not come and supersede a negative commandment and a positive commandment.

RASHI

האי עשה — "השב תשיבם", ואף על גב דלא תעשה נמי איכא, אין לא תעשה מועיל לדחות לא תעשה, אלא עשה הוא דקא דחי ליה, כדאמרינן ביבמות (כא,א). **לא תעשה ועשה** — "לנפש לא יטמא" "קדושים יהיו".

NOTES

הַאי עֲשֵׂה, וְהַאי לֹא תַעֲשֶׂה וַעֲשֵׂה **This is a positive commandment, and that is a negative commandment and a positive commandment.** The Rishonim point out several difficulties with regard to the Gemara's first question. (1) Returning a lost object is *also* both a positive and a negative commandment (see above, 26b). (2) The positive commandment supporting the prohibition against a priest contracting ritual impurity is not recognized as such in other passages in the Gemara. Moreover, both the positive and the negative versions of this prohibition are of the type called אֵינוֹ שָׁוֶה בַּכֹּל — "prohibitions that are not equally applicable to all" — because it is a prohibition applying specifically to priests, and it is doubtful whether the regular rules of עֲשֵׂה דּוֹחֶה לֹא תַעֲשֶׂה — "a positive commandment supersedes a negative commandment" — apply in such cases. (3) The Gemara (above, 26b) has established that when a person ignores a lost object and fails to pick it up, he violates a negative commandment but not a positive commandment. (4) The rules of עֲשֵׂה דּוֹחֶה לֹא תַעֲשֶׂה apply only when *the same action* is both prohibited and commanded; but in this case, the priest must enter the cemetery and thus violate the prohibition *before* he can begin to fulfill the commandment of restoring the lost object.

Answers are given by the Rishonim to each of these objections, but several Rishonim argue that the primary issue raised by the Gemara here is the conflict between monetary and ritual law, and that the discussion of overlapping religious obligations was not intended to be decisive. (See *Ramban, Rashba, Rosh, Ritva.*)

עֲשֵׂה דָּחֵי לֹא תַעֲשֶׂה **A positive commandment supersedes a negative commandment.** *Rambam* defines this principle in the following way: If a person encounters a positive commandment and a negative commandment, and can fulfill both of them, he does so, but if he cannot fulfill them both, the positive commandment supersedes the negative commandment (*Hilkhot Nezirut* 7:15).

Among the details of this regulation are: (1) The defining characteristic of a positive or a negative commandment is the way in which the commandment is phrased in the Torah — "you shall..." or "you shall not..." — and not whether the immediate action called for is active or passive (שֵׁב וְאַל תַּעֲשֶׂה/קוּם וַעֲשֵׂה). (2) Only those negative commandments that the Torah did not strengthen in some way can be superseded by a positive commandment. Negative commandments whose violation leads to severe penalties such as excision (כָּרֵת) cannot be superseded (*Yevamot* 3b). Commandments that were phrased both negatively and positively, like the example in our Gemara, cannot be set aside. The Rishonim (see *Tosafot, Yevamot* 3b; *Rashba, Yevamot* 8a) disagree as to whether actions prohibited by two independent negative commandments can be superseded. (3) This regulation is not to be confused with those cases where the Torah specifically commands behavior at odds with the normal Torah rules, such as the Torah's commandment that priests wear clothes made of a mixture of wool and linen, or the Torah's commandment that a brother-in-law perform a levirate marriage with the widow of his childless deceased brother (*Tosafot, Yevamot* 4a). This regulation applies only where the positive and the negative commandments exist independently, but happen to conflict because of unusual circumstances. (4) This regulation applies only when the same action is both commanded and prohibited, not when a law of the Torah must be transgressed *now* in order to perform a positive commandment *later* (*Tosafot, Yevamot* 6a). (5) For all practical purposes, this regulation applies only to those specific circumstances considered by the Sages. It is not a normative principle to be applied in daily life. (See also next note.)

TRANSLATION AND COMMENTARY

— "and you shall hide yourself" — is thus not needed for this case. [1] (2) **And furthermore** the rule is that **we do not set aside a ritual prohibition**, such as the one forbidding priests from entering cemeteries, **on account of a monetary law,** such as the one requiring finders to return lost objects. Hence, for this reason also, the priest is not permitted to return the lost object. [2] **But,** continues the Gemara, **if we say that the expression** "you shall hide yourself" **is needed for the case where his own work was greater than that of the other person,** this exception, too, is obvious for other reasons. [3] The Gemara goes on to explain: **That case is derived from what Rav Yehudah said in the name of Rav.** [4] **For Rav Yehudah said in the name of Rav:** The Torah says (Deuteronomy 15:4): **"Except that** [30B] **there shall be no poor among you."** The word בְּךָ — "in you," "among you" — appears superfluous in this sentence, and Rav uses it as the source for his ruling that we have a responsibility to see to it that we do not ourselves become paupers. [5] Hence, says Rav, **your** financial needs **come before those of all** other **men,** and you are not required to suffer severe financial loss merely in order that others can make a profit. Thus, from this analysis of the Baraita quoted above, the Gemara has shown that neither the first case (the priest and cemetery) nor the last case (financial loss to the finder) requires as its basis the expression "and you shall hide yourself from them" in the verse quoted in the Baraita. For what case, then, was this expression needed? [6] **Rather,** concludes the Gemara, **the expression** "and you shall hide yourself from them" **is needed** in the case of **an elder, where** picking up and taking care of the lost object **is not in keeping with his honor,** and it informs us that he is permitted to ignore such an object and proceed on his way.

אָמַר רַבָּה [7] Although an elder who finds a lost object which it is beneath his dignity to handle and take care of is absolved from the responsibility of returning it to its owner, sometimes even such a dignified person is obliged to accept this responsibility. On this point **Rabbah said:** The elder's exemption from the obligation to return lost objects applies only if he stands on his dignity and makes no effort whatsoever to return it to its rightful owner. But **if,** for example, he found a lost animal and **he struck it** even once, in the manner of a person driving an animal, he forfeits his exemption as an elder; and from that moment **he is obliged to take care of it** just like anyone else until its owner can be found.

[1] וְתוּ, לָא דָּחֵינַן אִיסּוּרָא מִקַּמֵּי מָמוֹנָא. [2] אֶלָּא לְשֶׁלּוֹ מְרוּבָּה מִשֶּׁל חֲבֵירוֹ, [3] מִדְּרַב יְהוּדָה אָמַר רַב נָפְקָא, [4] דְּאָמַר רַב יְהוּדָה אָמַר רַב: "אֶפֶס כִּי [30B] לֹא יִהְיֶה בְּךָ אֶבְיוֹן" — [5] שֶׁלְּךָ קוֹדֵם לְשֶׁל כָּל אָדָם. [6] אֶלָּא, לְזָקֵן, וְאֵינוֹ לְפִי כְּבוֹדוֹ.

[7] אָמַר רַבָּה: הִכִּישָׁהּ, חַיָּיב בָּהּ.

LITERAL TRANSLATION

[1] And furthermore, we do not set aside a ritual prohibition on account of a monetary [matter]. [2] But [if we say that the verse is needed] for [the case where] his own [work] was greater than that of his fellow, [3] that is derived from what Rav Yehudah said in the name of Rav, [4] for Rav Yehudah said in the name of Rav: "Except that [30B] there shall be no poor among you" — [5] yours comes before that of every man. [6] Rather, [the expression is needed] for an elder, and [where] it is not in keeping with his honor.

[7] Rabbah said: [If] he struck it, he is obliged with regard to it.

RASHI

לא יהיה בך אביון — לא תביא עצמך לידי עניות. **הכישה** — זה שאינו לפי כבודו, אם הכישה הכאה אחת להסיבה — נתחייב בה להחזירה הואיל והתחיל.

BACKGROUND

אֶפֶס כִּי לֹא יִהְיֶה בְּךָ אֶבְיוֹן "Except that there shall be no poor among you." In its context the plain meaning of this verse is a promise to the Jewish people that if they keep the laws of the Torah, none among them will need loans or other forms of support. However, the Sages interpreted this verse to mean that poverty itself is a reprehensible condition, and that a person must not merely rely on the mercy of Heaven to prevent him from lapsing into poverty, but must actively strive not to let himself become impoverished. Although this was not stated in the Torah as a commandment, the Sages stressed that avoidance of poverty should be viewed as a kind of religious duty.

In consequence, the Halakhah stipulates that there must be a limit to the financial demands involved in the fulfillment of a commandment, so that a person does not become poor by fulfilling it. A person must first provide for himself (just as he is required to perform any commandment that comes his way), and his own needs take precedence over those of others.

NOTES

לָא דָּחֵינַן אִיסּוּרָא מִקַּמֵּי מָמוֹנָא We do not set aside a ritual prohibition on account of a monetary law. The Gemara asserts this regulation without source or explanation, apparently because it is obvious. *Ramban* explains: Any action that would be forbidden if carried out for oneself is forbidden even if performed as an act of kindness to someone else, because all Jews are obligated first and foremost by their duty to God, and are required to refuse to perform acts of kindness if these involve transgressions. Thus, if the priest himself lost an object in the cemetery, he could not recover it himself. Moreover, if the owner of the lost object told the priest that he did not want him to return the object to him, there would no longer be a positive commandment to do so. Hence, the commandment ultimately depends on the wishes of the owner, and the owner, like the priest himself, is bound by the laws of the Torah.

הִכִּישָׁהּ חַיָּיב בָּהּ If he struck it, he is obliged with regard to it. Our commentary follows *Rashi* and *Rambam,* who say that this rule applies to all lost objects, and that the choice

HALAKHAH

הִכִּישָׁהּ חַיָּיב בָּהּ If he struck it, he is obliged with regard to it. "If an elderly man or a scholar finds a lost animal and strikes it to make it move, he thereby becomes obligated to return it to its owner, since he has begun to perform the commandment." (*Shulḥan Arukh, Ḥoshen Mishpat* 263:2.) *Sma* adds that most commentators agree that this law applies only to lost animals, but not to inanimate lost objects.

LITERAL TRANSLATION

[1] Abaye was sitting before Rabbah. [2] He saw some goats that were standing. He took a pebble and threw it at them. [3] He said to him: "You have obligated yourself with regard to them. [4] Get up [and] return them."

[5] It was asked of them: [If] it is his practice to return [a lost object] in the field but it is not his practice to return [a lost object] in the city, what is [the law]? [6] Do we say: We require a proper [act of] returning, [7] and since it is not his practice to return [lost objects] in the city, he is not obliged? [8] Or perhaps: It is in the field, at all events, that he has obligated himself, [9] and since he has obligated himself in the field, he has obligated himself in the city?

[10] Let [the question] stand [undecided].

LANGUAGE (RASHI)

מרט״א* (correct reading: מוט״א). From the Old French *mote,* meaning "clod of earth."

[1] אַבַּיֵי הֲוָה יָתֵיב קַמֵּיהּ דְּרַבָּה. [2] חֲזָא לְהָנָךְ עִיזֵּי דְּקָיְימוּ. שְׁקַל קָלָא וּשְׁדָא בְּהוּ. [3] אֲמַר לֵיהּ: "אִיחַיְּיבַת בְּהוּ. [4] קוּם אַהַדְרִינְהוּ".

[5] אִיבַּעְיָא לְהוּ: דַּרְכּוֹ לְהַחֲזִיר בַּשָּׂדֶה וְאֵין דַּרְכּוֹ לְהַחֲזִיר בָּעִיר, מַהוּ? [6] מִי אָמְרִינַן: הֲשָׁבָה מְעַלְיָא בָּעֵינַן, [7] וְכֵיוָן דְּלָאו דַּרְכֵּיהּ לְהַחֲזִיר בָּעִיר, לָא לִחַיֵּיב? [8] אוֹ דִּלְמָא: בַּשָּׂדֶה מִיהַת הוּא דְּאִיחַיַּיב לֵיהּ, [9] וְכֵיוָן דְּאִיחַיַּיב לֵיהּ בַּשָּׂדֶה, אִיחַיַּיב לֵיהּ בָּעִיר?

[10] תֵּיקוּ.

RASHI

קלא — *מרט״א. דרכו להחזיר בשדה — שאין שם רואים כל כך ואינו בוש. ואין דרכו בעיר — שהוא בוש משכיניו והוא מלא בשדה. מהו — שיתחייב להשיבה. לא מיחייב — להתחיל בהשבתה בשדה. וכיון דאיחייב — שהזיזה ממקומה, חייב אף בעיר.

TRANSLATION AND COMMENTARY

אַבַּיֵי הֲוָה יָתֵיב קַמֵּיהּ דְּרַבָּה [1] To illustrate this ruling by Rabbah, the Gemara now tells a story in which Rabbah acted in accordance with his ruling: Once the great scholar **Abaye was sitting before** his teacher, **Rabbah.** [2] Abaye **caught sight of some** stray **goats that were standing** nearby. **He took a pebble and threw it at** them to make them start returning home. [3] At this point Rabbah **said to him**: "Now by your action **you have obligated yourself to take care of them,** and you have forfeited your exemption as an eminent scholar. [4] **Get up** and complete what you have begun **and return** the goats to their rightful owners."

אִיבַּעְיָא לְהוּ [5] The scholars in the Academy **posed the following problem: If it is the practice** of an elder **to return a lost object** that he finds **in the field,** because in the informal setting of the countryside with few people around he does not stand on his dignity, **but it is not his practice to return such an object** if he finds it **in the city,** because the presence of his relatives and friends inhibits him, **what is the law** if such a person finds a lost animal in the field in circumstances that will entail his entering the city to return it to its rightful owner? [6] **Do we say that we** always **require a proper**, complete, **act of returning** in order to fulfill the commandment of restoring a lost object to its owner? [7] **And,** therefore, **since it is not his practice to return lost objects in the city, he is not obliged** even to begin the fulfillment of the commandment by taking care of the animal while it is in the field. [8] **Or** do we **perhaps** say: **In the field, at all events, he is obliged** to fulfill the commandment of restoring lost property; [9] **and once he does undertake the obligation** while he is **in the field,** by performing some action beginning the process of restoring the lost animal, **he is obliged** to continue taking care of the animal and to restore it to its owner (as Rabbah ruled above) even when he returns **to the city.**

תֵּיקוּ [10] The Gemara answers: **The question remains undecided.**

NOTES

of an animal was made purely for the purposes of illustration. The Aḥaronim discuss the question: Why, in fact, is the elder obliged to return the object if he picks it up or throws something at it? They suggest that this is an application of the Talmudic principle that when a person has begun to fulfill a commandment, he has to continue and finish it.

An alternative answer is that the Gemara distinguished between a person who simply ignores a lost object and a person who picks it up and fails to return it. The former only violates the commandment, "you may not hide yourself," from which elders were specifically exempted by the Torah, while the latter also violates the commandment, "you shall surely return them," from which elders enjoy no exemption. (See *Mat'amei Yitzḥak* and *Even HaAzel.*)

Other Rishonim, however, basing themselves on a passage in tractate *Bava Batra* (88a), understand Rabbah to be referring only to animals. An elder is exempt from returning inanimate lost objects, even if he picks them up, but he must return an animal that he has struck. This is because an animal that has been struck is liable to wander further, and the elder will be responsible for having prevented the owner from finding it. Hence, the elder becomes responsible for the animal and must return it (*Rosh, Ran,* and others).

HALAKHAH

דַּרְכּוֹ לְהַחֲזִיר בַּשָּׂדֶה וְאֵין דַּרְכּוֹ לְהַחֲזִיר בָּעִיר **If it is his practice to return a lost object in the field but not in the city.** "In the case of an elder who finds a lost object that he would not pick up in town but would pick up in the country, if he found it in town, he need not pick it up. If he found it in the country, he must return it to the owner, even within

[1]אָמַר רָבָא: כָּל שֶׁבְּשֶׁלּוֹ מַחֲזִיר, בְּשֶׁל חֲבֵירוֹ נַמִּי מַחֲזִיר. [2]וְכָל שֶׁבְּשֶׁלּוֹ פּוֹרֵק וְטוֹעֵן, בְּשֶׁל חֲבֵירוֹ נַמִּי פּוֹרֵק וְטוֹעֵן.

[3]רַבִּי יִשְׁמָעֵאל בְּרַבִּי יוֹסֵי הֲוָה קָאָזֵיל בְּאוֹרְחָא. [4]פָּגַע בֵּיהּ הַהוּא גַּבְרָא. הֲוָה דָּרֵי פַּתְכָא דְּאוּפֵי. [5]אוֹתְבִינְהוּ וְקָא מִיתְפַּח. אֲמַר לֵיהּ: "דְּלִי לִי". [6]אֲמַר לֵיהּ: "כַּמָּה שָׁוִין?" אֲמַר לֵיהּ: "פַּלְגָּא דְּזוּזָא". [7]יָהֵיב לֵיהּ פַּלְגָּא דְּזוּזָא וְאַפְקְרָהּ. הֲדַר זָכָה בְּהוּ. [8]הֲדַר יָהֵיב לֵיהּ פַּלְגָּא דְּזוּזָא וְאַפְקְרָהּ. [9]חַזְיֵיהּ דַּהֲוָה קָא בָּעֵי לְמִיהֲדַר לְמִזְכֵּיהּ בְּהוּ. [10]אֲמַר לֵיהּ: "לְכוּלֵּי עָלְמָא אַפְקְרַנְהוּ, [11]וְלָךְ לָא אַפְקְרַנְהוּ".

LITERAL TRANSLATION

[1]Rava said: Anything that if it were his he would bring back, he must also bring back [if] it is his fellow's. [2]And anything that if it were his he would unload and load, he must also unload and load [if] it is his fellow's.

[3]Rabbi Yishmael the son of Rabbi Yose was walking on a road. [4]A certain man met him. He was carrying a bundle of branches. [5]He put them down and rested. He said to him: "Lift [them] up onto me." [6]He said to him: "How much are they worth?" He said to him: "Half a zuz." [7]He gave him half a zuz and renounced ownership of it [the bundle]. He acquired them again. [8]He again gave him half a zuz and renounced ownership of it. [9]He saw that he wanted to acquire them [yet] again. [10]He said to him: "I renounced ownership of them to everyone (lit., 'the whole world'), [11]but to you I did not renounce ownership of them."

TRANSLATION AND COMMENTARY

אָמַר רָבָא [1]Rava now lays down a general principle governing the conduct of an elder (a) with regard to restoring lost property, and (b) with regard to the commandment to assist one's fellow man in loading and unloading his animals. **Rava said:** The principle is: **Anything that** an elder **would** pick up, look after, and **bring back** to his home **if it were his, he must also bring back** and restore to its rightful owner. [2]Furthermore, says Rava, there is a similar exemption for elders in the case of the Torah's commandment to assist other people in loading and unloading their animals (Exodus 23:5, Deuteronomy 22:4), **and** here, too, **anything that he would unload and load if it were his, he must also unload and load if it is another person's.**

רַבִּי יִשְׁמָעֵאל בְּרַבִּי יוֹסֵי [3]The Gemara now tells a story to show how an illustrious scholar became involved in a situation where he had to decide what was the correct behaviour demanded of him by the law regarding helping another person load or unload what he was carrying: **Rabbi Yishmael the son of Rabbi Yose was walking along a road.** [4]**A certain man met him, carrying a bundle of branches.** [5]The man **put** the bundle of branches **down and caught his breath.** After resting, the man **said to** Rabbi Yishmael the son of Rabbi Yose: "Please help **lift** the bundle of branches **up onto** my back." Rabbi Yishmael the son of Rabbi Yose felt reluctant to do such undignified labor, but did not wish to refuse the request. [6]Therefore, **he said to** the man: "**How much are** the branches **worth?"** The man **said to him: "Half a zuz."** Rabbi Yishmael the son of Rabbi Yose **gave** the man **half a zuz,** thus becoming the owner of the bundle of branches, [7]**and he** then **renounced** his **ownership of the bundle.** At this point, the man **acquired** the now ownerless branches **again**, and once again requested Rabbi Yishmael the son of Rabbi Yose to help him load the bundle onto his back. [8]The latter **again gave him half a zuz and renounced ownership of** the bundle. [9]At this point **he saw that** the man **intended to acquire** the branches **yet again.** [10]**He** then **said to** the man: When **I renounced my ownership of** the bundle of branches, I renounced it **to everyone,** [11]**but** with one exception — **I did not renounce ownership of them to you.** Therefore, you have no right to take them."

RASHI

פורק וטוען — פורק משא מן החמור וטוען עליו, דכתיב "עזוב תעזוב", "הקם תקים". **פתכא דאופי** — משאוי של עצים. **וקא מיתפח** — עומד לפוש. **דלי לי** — הטעינני. **הדר זכה בהו** — חזר האיש ההוא והחזיק בהן מן ההפקר.

NOTES

פַּתְכָא דְּאוּפֵי A bundle of branches. Our translation follows *Rashi.* The Geonim say that this expression refers to a kind of mat made from the ends of palm fronds, for use as decoration or as a kind of lifebelt.

HALAKHAH

the city." (*Shulḥan Arukh, Ḥoshen Mishpat* 263:2, following *Rambam.*) *Rema* rules, in the name of *Rosh,* that he must bring it only as far as the gates of the city. There is also an opinion expressed by some Rishonim that he need not return it at all.

כָּל שֶׁבְּשֶׁלּוֹ מַחֲזִיר Anything that if it were his he would

BACKGROUND

כָּל שֶׁבְּשֶׁלּוֹ מַחֲזִיר Anything that if it were his he would bring back. In general a person takes care of his own property and does certain things to preserve it which he would not do for the property of others. However, Rava's principle establishes a different criterion where the fulfillment of commandments is involved: In such a situation, the property of one's fellowman must be as dear to one as one's own. Thus the criterion regarding things which are beneath a person's dignity is not set by his practice towards other people but rather by that towards his own property. If his dignity would prevent him from dealing with one of his own possessions, he need not lower himself by dealing with it for the purpose of fulfilling this commandment. But if he would take the trouble to preserve his own property, he must also do so for someone else when the fulfillment of a commandment is involved.

SAGES

רַבִּי יִשְׁמָעֵאל בְּרַבִּי יוֹסֵי Rabbi Yishmael the son of Rabbi Yose. He was a Tanna of the last generation of Tannaim, and a disciple of the compiler of the Mishnah, Rabbi Yehudah HaNasi. Rabbi Yishmael was the eldest son of the Tanna, Rabbi Yose bar Ḥalafta, studied under his guidance, and became his successor in Sepphoris. He was also privileged to know and study under many of the greatest scholars of the earlier generations.

Rabbi Yishmael the son of Rabbi Yose was regarded as his father's successor in scholarly authority. Nevertheless he accepted the authority of Rabbi Yehudah HaNasi and became his disciple, constantly attending his yeshivah and discussing the Halakhah with Rabbi Shimon the son of Rabbi, and with Rabbi Ḥiyya. In addition to his greatness as a Torah scholar, Rabbi Yishmael was famous for his sagacity and brilliant conversation, and applied his sharp mind to every area of life.

Almost all the disciples of Rabbi Yehudah HaNasi also

TRANSLATION AND COMMENTARY

וּמִי הָוֵי הֶפְקֵר [1]The Gemara now examines this story and asks: **But is it a valid renunciation of ownership to do so in this manner?** [2]**Surely we have learned in a Mishnah** (*Pe'ah* 6:11): **"Bet Shammai say: Renunciation of ownership to the poor** alone, and not to the rich, **is a valid** form of **renunciation of ownership,** and any poor person finding the abandoned object is entitled to take it. [3]**But Bet Hillel say: It is not a valid renunciation of ownership unless it is a renunciation of ownership** to everyone, **to the poor and to the rich, as** is the case with **Sabbatical Year produce,** where the Torah declared all crops to be ownerless." From this Mishnah we see that according to Bet Hillel — and the Halakhah follows their opinion — renunciation of ownership is not effective if it contains exceptions. Thus the device used by Rabbi Yishmael the son of Rabbi Yose achieved no purpose.

אֶלָּא [4]**Rather,** answers the Gemara, **Rabbi Yishmael the son of Rabbi Yose** in fact **renounced ownership of** the bundle of branches **to everyone,** including this man, **and he was holding him back with mere words** to stop him from acquiring the bundle yet again.

וְהָא רַבִּי יִשְׁמָעֵאל בְּרַבִּי יוֹסֵי [5]The Gemara now asks another question related to the incident in which Rabbi Yishmael the son of Rabbi Yose was involved: **But surely Rabbi Yishmael the son of Rabbi Yose was a** distinguished scholar and **elder for whom** loading a bundle of branches onto someone's back **was not in keeping with his honor** and dignity. Why did he need to buy the bundle and then renounce ownership of it? He surely would have been within his rights simply to refuse the man's request.

[1]וּמִי הָוֵי הֶפְקֵר כִּי הַאי גַּוְונָא? [2]וְהָתְנַן: בֵּית שַׁמַּאי אוֹמְרִים: הֶפְקֵר לַעֲנִיִּים הֶפְקֵר. [3]וּבֵית הִלֵּל אוֹמְרִים: אֵינוֹ הֶפְקֵר עַד שֶׁיְּהֵא הֶפְקֵר לַעֲנִיִּים וְלָעֲשִׁירִים, כַּשְּׁמִיטָּה".

[4]אֶלָּא רַבִּי יִשְׁמָעֵאל בְּרַבִּי יוֹסֵי לְכוּלֵּי עָלְמָא אַפְקְרִינְהוּ, וּבְמִלְּתָא בְּעָלְמָא הוּא דְּאוֹקְמֵיהּ.

[5]וְהָא רַבִּי יִשְׁמָעֵאל בְּרַבִּי יוֹסֵי זָקֵן וְאֵינוֹ לְפִי כְּבוֹדוֹ הֲוָה!

LITERAL TRANSLATION

[1]But is it a [valid] renunciation of ownership [to do so] in this manner? [2]But surely we have learned: "Bet Shammai say: Renunciation of ownership to the poor is [valid] renunciation of ownership. [3]But Bet Hillel say: It is not a [valid] renunciation of ownership unless it is a renunciation of ownership to the poor and to the rich, like Sabbatical Year [produce]."

[4]Rather, Rabbi Yishmael the son of Rabbi Yose renounced ownership of them to everyone, and it was with a mere word that he was holding him [back].

[5]But surely Rabbi Yishmael the son of Rabbi Yose was an elder and it was not in keeping with his honor.

RASHI

הפקר לעניים הוי הפקר – אף על גב שלא הפקירו אלא לעניים הוי הפקר למפטר מן המעשר.

NOTES

וּמִי הָוֵי הֶפְקֵר כִּי הַאי גַּוְונָא **But is it a valid renunciation of ownership to do so in this manner?** The Gemara objects to the renunciation of ownership because it was not universal. *Tosafot* has another objection: In this story, only two people were present, Rabbi Yishmael the son of Rabbi Yose and the man with the bundle of branches. But the Gemara (*Nedarim* 45a) rules that renunciation of ownership can only be effected in the presence of three people (in addition to the person making the renunciation).

Tosafot and *Rosh* suggest that there may have been two other Sages accompanying Rabbi Yishmael the son of Rabbi Yose, and these other Sages were not mentioned in the story. Alternatively, *Tosafot* and *Rosh* point out that the requirement that three people be present is merely a Rabbinic enactment; by Torah law renunciation of ownership is valid even if performed by the owner without anyone else being present. The only reason why Rabbi Yishmael the son of Rabbi Yose had formally to renounce his ownership of the bundle of branches was in order to save an innocent bystander from inadvertently "stealing" from him, and for this purpose renunciation of ownership as required by Torah law was sufficient.

Ritva explains that the Rabbinic requirement that three people be present applies only when there is some doubt as to the declarer's sincerity in renouncing ownership of his property, but in a case such as ours, where the interest of Rabbi Yishmael the son of Rabbi Yose in renouncing his ownership is all too plain, the renunciation is valid even if nobody else is present.

HALAKHAH

bring back. "Any object that a person would care for, if it were his, he must return if it belongs to another person." (Ibid., 263:1.) The law is similar with regard to assisting with loading and unloading an animal. (Ibid., 272:3.)

הֶפְקֵר לַעֲנִיִּים **Renunciation of ownership to the poor.** "Someone who renounces ownership of his property to poor people but not to rich people has not effectively renounced ownership of his property. He must renounce ownership to everyone, without reservations or exceptions," following the opinion of Bet Hillel. (Ibid., 273:5.)

learned from Rabbi Yishmael and transmitted teachings in his name. Even Rabbi Yehudah HaNasi learned certain ancient traditions from him, especially those transmitted in the name of his father, Rabbi Yose. Rabbi Yishmael was apparently a wealthy man, a property owner and a merchant, but we know almost nothing about his private life or his family.

BACKGROUND

הֶפְקֵר לַעֲנִיִּים **Renunciation of ownership to the poor.** The controversy between Bet Shammai and Bet Hillel concerns the definition of ownerless property (הֶפְקֵר). According to Bet Hillel, property is abandoned only when a person renounces all ownership of it. Therefore, if he states that the property is not renounced in favor of everyone, he retains some degree of ownership over it, and such conditional renunciation must be viewed as a kind of gift. By contrast, according to Bet Shammai, since the owner is not transferring his property to a specific person but is merely excluding people of a certain type from those eligible to receive it, the property is not a gift but ownerless.

A more important consequence relates to the laws of tithes. The Sages decreed that ownerless property is not subject to tithes, whereas someone who receives a gift must give the appropriate tithes from it. Therefore, if a person states that he is renouncing ownership of his field or vineyard in favor of poor people only, this is not a valid renunciation of ownership, but rather a gift to the poor, and they are required to give tithes from it.

וּבְמִלְּתָא בְּעָלְמָא **And it was with a mere word.** In other words, if the man whom Rabbi Yishmael the son of Rabbi Yose encountered had been well versed in the Halakhah, he would have known that Rabbi Yishmael's words were ineffective. Rabbi Yishmael made a statement devoid of Halakhic significance in order to prevent the man from exploiting the situation.

TRANSLATION AND COMMENTARY

רַבִּי יִשְׁמָעֵאל בְּרַבִּי יוֹסֵי [1]The Gemara answers: **Rabbi Yishmael the son of Rabbi Yose was acting beyond the** strict **requirements of the law.** Even though he had no legal obligation to help the man, he did so out of a sense of moral duty. [2]**For** in this connection **Rav Yosef quoted** a Baraita explaining the verse (Exodus 18:20) in which Jethro tells Moses how to guide the Children of Israel in their social and moral behavior. Jethro says: "And you shall teach them the statutes and the laws, and you shall show them the way in which they shall walk, and the deeds that they shall do." Ignoring the first clause, which is self-explanatory, the Baraita takes up each phrase in this verse and shows that it contains an essential requirement in Jewish religious life: **"'And you shall show them' — this means 'the house of their life,'** an expression that refers to learning a trade by which to live. [3]**'The way' — this means acts of kindness.** [4]**'Which they shall walk' — this means** the commandment **to visit the sick.** [5]**'In it'** — this expression **hints at** the commandment **to bury** the dead. [6]**'And the deed' — this means obedience to the law** as enforced by the courts. [7]**'That they shall do' — this means** going **beyond the requirements of the law."**

אָמַר מָר [8]The Gemara now questions certain problematic clauses in this Baraita: **It was said above** in the Baraita: **"'Which they shall walk' — this means** the commandment **to visit the sick."** [9]But **surely,** asks the Gemara, the commandment to visit the sick **comes under the heading of acts of kindness,** which has already been mentioned by the Baraita. Visiting the sick is simply one of the many ways in which one can show kindness to one's fellow man.

לֹא נִצְרְכָה [10]The Gemara answers: The expression explained by the Baraita as specifically referring to visiting the sick **is needed only for** the case of **someone born under the same star** as the sick person.

[1]רַבִּי יִשְׁמָעֵאל בְּרַבִּי יוֹסֵי לִפְנִים מִשּׁוּרַת הַדִּין הוּא דַּעֲבַד. [2]דְּתָנֵי רַב יוֹסֵף: "'וְהוֹדַעְתָּ לָהֶם' — זֶה בֵּית חַיֵּיהֶם. [3]'אֶת הַדֶּרֶךְ' — זוֹ גְּמִילוּת חֲסָדִים. [4]'אֲשֶׁר יֵלְכוּ' — זֶה בִּיקּוּר חוֹלִים. [5]'בָהּ' — זוֹ קְבוּרָה. [6]'וְאֶת הַמַּעֲשֶׂה' — זֶה הַדִּין. [7]'אֲשֶׁר יַעֲשׂוּן' — זוֹ לִפְנִים מִשּׁוּרַת הַדִּין".
[8]אָמַר מָר: "'אֲשֶׁר יֵלְכוּ' — זֶה בִּיקּוּר חוֹלִים". [9]הַיְינוּ גְּמִילוּת חֲסָדִים!
[10]לֹא נִצְרְכָה אֶלָּא לְבֶן גִּילוֹ.

LITERAL TRANSLATION

[1]Rabbi Yishmael the son of Rabbi Yose was acting beyond the requirements of the law (lit., "inside the line of justice"). [2]For Rav Yosef taught: "'And you shall show them' — this [means] the house of their life. [3]'The way' — this [means] acts of kindness. [4]'Which they shall walk' — this [means] visiting the sick. [5]'In it' — this [means] burial. [6]'And the work' — this [means] the law. [7]'That they shall do' — this [means] beyond the requirements of the law."
[8]The master said: "'Which they shall walk' — this means visiting the sick." [9]Surely this is the same as acts of kindness.
[10]It is not necessary except for someone born under the same star.

RASHI

זה בית חייהם — ללמוד להם אומנות להתפרנס בו, חוקות ותורות כמיני ברישיה דקרא.

NOTES

זֶה בֵּית חַיֵּיהֶם This means the house of their life. Our commentary follows *Rashi* here. But in tractate *Bava Kamma* (100a) *Rashi* explains this phrase as referring to Torah study.

בֶּן גִּילוֹ Someone born under the same star. The translation and commentary here follow most of the Rishonim, who explain that this refers to a person born at the same moment, under the same star as the sick person (see *Rosh* and *Ran, Nedarim* 39b). *Rashi,* however (*Nedarim* 39b), explains the phrase literally, and says that it refers to anyone of the same age as the sick person.

HALAKHAH

לִפְנִים מִשּׁוּרַת הַדִּין בַּאֲבֵידָה Acting beyond the requirements of the law regarding lost objects. "An elder is not required to return a lost object. But it is proper for him to go beyond the strict requirements of the law, to forgo the honor to which he is entitled, and to care for and return the lost object." (*Shulḥan Arukh, Ḥoshen Mishpat* 263:3.) *Rema* disagrees, being of the opinion that it is wrong for an elder to behave in an undignified fashion, as he too must respect his own Torah knowledge. According to *Rema,* what the Gemara means is that it is praiseworthy to act beyond the strict requirements of the law and to pay for the owner's loss, as did Rabbi Yishmael the son of Rabbi Yose.

בִּיקּוּר חוֹלִים קְבוּרָה וכו׳ Visiting the sick, burying the dead, etc. "There is a positive Rabbinic commandment to visit the sick and to console mourners, to accompany the dead to their final resting place, and to do all that is necessary in arranging their burial, to arrange weddings, and to participate in the joy of bridegrooms and brides. All of the above are considered acts of kindness to be performed by a person himself, and there are no fixed limits to their fulfillment. They all come under the general heading of the Torah commandment: 'And you shall love your neighbor as yourself' (Leviticus 19:18)." (*Rambam, Sefer Shoftim, Hilkhot Evel* 14:10.)

CONCEPTS

לִפְנִים מִשּׁוּרַת הַדִּין Beyond the requirements of the law. The strict "line" or letter of the law (שׁוּרַת הַדִּין) is the limit to a person's obligations as set by the Halakhah. "Beyond the requirements of the law" (לִפְנִים מִשּׁוּרַת הַדִּין) implies the exercise of restraint in claiming one's due, so as to fulfill a religious commandment.
In the context of a person's duty to God, such conduct is generally called הידור מִצְוָה — "the beautification of a commandment" — and usually involves carrying it out with extra scrupulousness. But in commercial relationships the expression "beyond the requirements of the law" is used to describe a situation where one person does a favor for another although he is not strictly obliged to do so by the Halakhah. Generally the Sages are of the opinion that, the greater a person is, the more he is morally obliged to behave "beyond the requirements of the law" and to exact less than the full rights to which he is legally entitled.

BACKGROUND

וְהוֹדַעְתָּ לָהֶם "And you shall show them." The general idea behind this homiletic passage is that Moses was commanded to not only teach and admonish the Israelites about the laws, teachings and commandments incumbent upon them, but also to inform them, through the Oral Law, that there are additional obligations, not all of which are defined specifically by the Halakhah, but which come under the category of acts of devotion to God. The details of the interpretation are based on an exhaustive exegesis of the language used in the text. The expression "which they shall walk" (אֲשֶׁר יֵלְכוּ) is understood as referring to visiting the sick, a commandment fulfilled by *going to* the sick person and providing for all his needs. The expression "in it" (בָהּ) is understood as referring to burial, placing a dead body *in the ground.* And if the expression "the deed" (הַמַּעֲשֶׂה) refers in a general sense to the law — that which is specifically obligatory — there

LITERAL TRANSLATION

[1] For the master said: Someone who was born under the same star takes away one-sixtieth of his illness, [2] but even so he is required to go to him.
[3] "'In it' — this [means] burial." [4] Surely this is the same as acts of kindness.
[5] It is not necessary except for an elder, and [where] it is not in accordance with his honor.
[6] "'That they shall do' — this [means] beyond the requirements of the law. [7] For Rabbi Yoḥanan said: Jerusalem was destroyed only because they judged in it [according to] the law of the Torah.
[8] Should they rather have judged [according to] the laws of arbitrary tribunals?
[9] But say [instead]: Because they based their judgments on the [strict] law of the Torah, [10] and they did not act beyond the requirements of the law.
MISHNAH [11] What is a lost object?

[1] דְּאָמַר מָר: בֶּן גִּילוֹ נוֹטֵל אֶחָד מִשִּׁשִּׁים בְּחָלְיוֹ, [2] וַאֲפִילּוּ הָכִי מִבָּעֵי לֵיהּ לְמֵיזַל לְגַבֵּיהּ.
[3] "'בָּהּ' — זוֹ קְבוּרָה". [4] הַיְינוּ גְּמִילוּת חֲסָדִים!
[5] לֹא נִצְרְכָה אֶלָּא לְזָקֵן וְאֵינוֹ לְפִי כְּבוֹדוֹ.
[6] "'אֲשֶׁר יַעֲשׂוּן' — זוֹ לִפְנִים מִשּׁוּרַת הַדִּין". [7] דְּאָמַר רַבִּי יוֹחָנָן: לֹא חָרְבָה יְרוּשָׁלַיִם אֶלָּא עַל שֶׁדָּנוּ בָּהּ דִּין תּוֹרָה.
[8] אֶלָּא דִּינֵי דִּמְגִיזְתָא לְדַיְינוּ?!
[9] אֶלָּא אֵימָא: שֶׁהֶעֱמִידוּ דִּינֵיהֶם עַל דִּין תּוֹרָה, [10] וְלֹא עָבְדוּ לִפְנִים מִשּׁוּרַת הַדִּין.
מִשְׁנָה [11] אֵי זוֹ הִיא אֲבֵידָה?

RASHI

דיני דמגיזתא לדיינו — בתמיה, דמגיזתא גוזלי, הדנין ביסורים ובחזקה, ותכירו בבבא קמא (קיד,א): דדייני בגזותא.
משנה איזו היא אבידה — בגמרא מפרש.

TRANSLATION AND COMMENTARY

[1] **For we have been informed elsewhere** (*Nedarim* 39b): A visitor who was **born under the same star** as the sick person **takes away one-sixtieth of his illness** and takes it upon himself. Hence, visiting the sick may be dangerous to a person born under the same star, [2] **but even so** such a person **is required to go to** visit the sick person.

בָּהּ זוֹ קְבוּרָה [3] The Gemara continues its analysis of the Baraita by quoting the next clause: "**'In it' — this** expression **hints at** the commandment to **bury** the dead." [4] But **surely**, asks the Gemara, the commandment to bury the dead **comes under the heading of acts of kindness,** which has already been mentioned by the Baraita.

לֹא נִצְרְכָה [5] The Gemara answers: The expression explained by the Baraita as specifically referring to burying the dead **is needed only for** the case of **an elder, where it was not in keeping with his honor.** The verse teaches us that even though such people are exempt from many deeds of kindness, they are not exempt from the commandment to bury the dead, and must perform it when appropriate, without regard for their dignity.

אֲשֶׁר יַעֲשׂוּן [6] The Gemara concludes its analysis of the Baraita by quoting its final clause: "**'That they shall do' — this means** going **beyond the requirements of the law.**" [7] This clause of the Baraita, says the Gemara, is supported by a statement of Rabbi Yoḥanan. **For Rabbi Yoḥanan said: Jerusalem was destroyed only because** people **judged in it according to the law of the Torah.**

אֶלָּא דִּינֵי דִּמְגִיזְתָא לְדַיְינוּ [8] On this cryptic statement of Rabbi Yoḥanan the Gemara immediately asks: By what other law should they have judged? **Should they rather have judged according to the laws of** arbitrary tribunals, instead of in accordance with Torah law?

אֶלָּא אֵימָא [9] The Gemara explains: What Rabbi Yoḥanan means to **say** is that Jerusalem was destroyed **because** the courts **based their judgments on the strict law of the Torah,** [10] **and they did not act beyond the requirements of the law.** Since, says Rabbi Yoḥanan, no one was prepared to compromise or to forgo any of his rights under Torah law, Jerusalem was destroyed.

MISHNAH אֵי זוֹ הִיא אֲבֵידָה [11] The Mishnah begins by asking a general question: **What** comes under the category of **a lost object,** which must be returned by the finder, and what comes under the category of an object intentionally left by its owner, with which the finder has no right to meddle?

NOTES

נוֹטֵל אֶחָד מִשִּׁשִּׁים **Takes away one-sixtieth.** The number sixty need not necessarily be taken literally. It may have been selected because one part in sixty is, in many Halakhic contexts, a proportion that is deemed negligible. Hence it is possible to interpret the Gemara as saying that the visitor takes away so small a portion of the illness that the

HALAKHAH

בִּיקּוּר חוֹלִים בְּבֶן גִּילוֹ **Visiting a sick person born under the same star.** "It is a positive commandment to visit the sick, provided that the visit is not a burden to the sick person. Even someone born under the same star as the sick person must visit him." (*Shulḥan Arukh, Yoreh De'ah* 335:2).

is an additional message in the expression "that they shall do" (אֲשֶׁר יַעֲשׂוּן), implying that, rather than insist on one's rights according to the letter of the law, one must act "beyond the requirements of the law."

בֶּן גִּילוֹ **Someone who was born under the same star.** Two people of exactly the same age were held to be extremely close to each other, as if there were some deep resonance between them, a sense of empathy. Thus the Talmud stresses that if someone visits a sick person of exactly his own age, he takes upon himself a certain part of the patient's illness. However, even though a person of exactly the same age suffers more than someone else by visiting the sick, he may not on that account refrain from fulfilling this commandment.

אֶלָּא עַל שֶׁדָּנוּ בָּהּ דִּין תּוֹרָה **Only because they judged in it according to the law of the Torah.** This saying of Rabbi Yoḥanan is one of a series of sayings dealing with the question of why the Second Temple was destroyed, even though most of the Jews of Jerusalem in that period kept the commandments. The Sages also said that Jerusalem was destroyed because of שִׂנְאַת חִנָּם — unjustified hatred — and because the citizens were not flexible enough to forgo some of what they held to be their due. This inability to accept less than their due in every single case is what brought about the destruction of Jerusalem, both by human forces and as punishment from heaven. Similarly, the Sages state that the destruction of Sodom came about because the people there attempted to create a society in which the laws were devoid of the concept of mercy and compassion.

LANGUAGE

מְגִיזְתָא **Arbitrary tribunals.** Several explanations have been offered as to the meaning of this word, and attempts have been made to find its origin in a number of different languages. Rabbi Benjamin Musafia and other scholars are of the opinion that the origin of the word lies in the

[1] מָצָא חֲמוֹר אוֹ פָּרָה רוֹעִין בַּדֶּרֶךְ, אֵין זוֹ אֲבֵידָה. [2] חֲמוֹר וְכֵלָיו הֲפוּכִין, פָּרָה רָצָה בֵּין הַכְּרָמִים — הֲרֵי זוֹ אֲבֵידָה.

[3] הֶחֱזִירָהּ וּבָרְחָה, הֶחֱזִירָהּ וּבָרְחָה, [4] אֲפִילוּ אַרְבָּעָה וַחֲמִישָּׁה פְּעָמִים, חַיָּיב לְהַחֲזִירָהּ, [5] שֶׁנֶּאֱמַר: ״הָשֵׁב תְּשִׁיבֵם״.

[6] הָיָה בָּטֵל מִסֶּלַע, לֹא יֹאמַר לוֹ: ״תֵּן לִי סֶלַע״, [7] אֶלָּא נוֹתֵן לוֹ שְׂכָרוֹ כְּפוֹעֵל. [8] אִם יֵשׁ שָׁם בֵּית דִּין, מַתְנֶה בִּפְנֵי בֵּית דִּין. [9] אִם אֵין שָׁם בֵּית דִּין, בִּפְנֵי מִי יַתְנֶה? [10] שֶׁלּוֹ קוֹדֵם.

גמרא [11] אַטּוּ כָּל הָנֵי דְּאָמְרִינַן לָאו אֲבֵידָה הָווּ?! [12] אָמַר רַב יְהוּדָה: הָכִי קָאָמַר:

LITERAL TRANSLATION

[1] [If] he found an ass or a cow grazing by the road, this is not a lost object. [2] [But] an ass with its trappings overturned [or] a cow running among the vineyards — this is a lost object.

[3] [If] he returned it and it ran away, he returned it again and it ran away, [4] even four or five times, he is obliged to return it, [5] as it is said: "You shall surely return them."

[6] [If] he wasted [time worth] a sela, he may not say to him: "Give me a sela," [7] but he gives him wages as a laborer. [8] If there is a court there, he may stipulate before the court. [9] If there is no court there, before whom shall he stipulate? [10] His own takes precedence.

GEMARA [11] Were all these that we have said [in fact] not lost property?

[12] Rav Yehudah said: He says thus:

TRANSLATION AND COMMENTARY

[1] The Mishnah answers: **If** a person **finds an ass or a cow grazing by the road,** he may assume that **it is not a lost object** and that its owner has left it there deliberately and will return to collect it. [2] **But** if he finds **an ass with its trappings overturned** and in disarray, **or a cow running among the vineyards** and not quietly grazing, then he must assume that **it is a lost object** and he is under an obligation to look after it and restore it to its owner.

הֶחֱזִירָהּ וּבָרְחָה [3] The Mishnah now turns to a different question: **If** the finder **returned** a lost animal to its owner **and it ran away** again, and **he returned it** again, **and** again **it ran away,** [4] **even** if this happened **four or five times, he is obliged to return it** each time he finds it. The reason why the finder is obliged to perform the commandment repeatedly and to keep restoring the same item of lost property to its rightful owner is that the Torah used a specially emphatic expression to describe the finder's obligation, [5] **as it is said: "You shall surely return** them," in which a double verb — הָשֵׁב תְּשִׁיבֵם — was used for emphasis.

הָיָה בָּטֵל מִסֶּלַע [6] The Mishnah now turns to a different question: **If** the finder **wasted a sela's worth of his work time** recovering the lost object, he is entitled to compensation from the owner of the object. But **he may not say to** the owner: **"Give me the** full **sela** that I lost as a result of my efforts on your behalf." [7] **Instead,** the owner **must give him his wages as** if he were **an** unemployed **laborer** — a significantly smaller sum. [8] If the finder realizes that his fulfillment of the commandment to restore lost property will be costly for him, there is another course of action open to him: **If there are** three people **there** who could constitute **a court, he may stipulate before the court** that he is recovering the object on condition that he be compensated in full for his lost time. [9] But, the Mishnah asks, **if there is no court there, before whom can he stipulate?** What course of action should be taken? [10] The Mishnah answers that in such a situation the finder's **own interests take precedence**, and if the compensation paid an unemployed laborer is too little to offset his loss, he need not pick up the object.

GEMARA אַטּוּ כָּל הָנֵי דְּאָמְרִינַן [11] The Gemara begins its analysis of the Mishnah by challenging the language of the question with which the Mishnah begins. This question — "What is a lost object?" — seems to imply that the Mishnah is only now introducing the concept of a lost article. On this the Gemara asks: **Were all those** cases **mentioned** in the **earlier** Mishnayot of this chapter **not really** cases of **lost property?**

אָמַר רַב יְהוּדָה [12] **Rav Yehudah said** in reply: **This is what** the Mishnah **means** to say: In many cases there

RASHI

אין זו אבידה — ואינו חייב להחזיר, שמדעת הניחוה שם. **רצה בין הכרמים** — דמסתכנא. **לא יאמר לו תן לי סלע** — שבטלתי ממלאכתי, שיאמר לו: אם עשית מלאכתך היית מרבה טורח, עכשיו לפי מה שטרחת טול. **כפועל** — בגמרא מפרש. **אם יש שם בית דין** — אם נוח לו לטרוח יותר כדי להרבות שכר ואינו חפץ ליבטל ממלאכתו, מה יעשה? אם יש שם שלשה בני אדם — יתנה בפניהם ויאמר: ראו שאני משתכר כך וכך, ואי איפשי ליבטל ליטול שכר מועט, אני אשיב אם תאמרו שאטול שכר משלם.

Greek μεγιστᾶνες, *megistanes,* meaning "courtiers," "nobles." In this context it would therefore mean: "Should they rather have judged according to the laws of the gentiles and their leaders?"

BACKGROUND

אֲפִילוּ אַרְבָּעָה וַחֲמִישָּׁה פְּעָמִים Even four or five times. "Four or five times" is merely meant as an example. As will be explained below (31a), there is no limit to the number of times a person must attempt to return a lost object. The numbers are cited merely to show that the law does not refer to a one-time occurrence, but rather to something that may need to be done with a certain frequency, more than three times, while the obligation nevertheless continues to remain in force.

אִם יֵשׁ שָׁם בֵּית דִּין If there is a court there. This need not be an official court, composed of experts; a lay court (בֵּית דִּין שֶׁל הֶדְיוֹטוֹת) composed of any three worthy Jews is sufficient for this purpose. By stating his condition in an appropriate announcement before a court, the finder removes it from the status of a one-sided decision, and, with the court's approval, it becomes a claim which the owner of the object cannot refuse to pay. Although the court has limited power to exercise its own discretion, it can determine whether it is appropriate for the owner of the property to pay a relatively large sum to recover it.

TERMINOLOGY

הָכִי קָאָמַר He says thus — i.e., his statement should be interpreted as explained below. This term is used to introduce a new explanation or a textual emendation of a difficult passage in a Mishnah or a Baraita, usually proposed in order to resolve a problem raised by the Gemara regarding the passage.

NOTES

patient may not be significantly affected by it. In other words, the visitor is endangering himself while accomplishing very little, but even so is obliged to visit the sick (*Torat Ḥayyim*).

TRANSLATION AND COMMENTARY

may be doubt as to whether or not an object has actually been lost. [1]Hence the Mishnah seeks to establish **which is the general rule regarding lost property for which** a finder is **responsible**, and how it can be distinguished from a case where the owner of the property has deliberately left it and intends to come back and collect it. [2]To this question the Mishnah replies: The answer depends on the circumstances. If a person **finds an ass or a cow grazing by the road,** he may assume that **it is not lost,** [3]**and he is not obliged** to take any action **with regard to it.** [4]**But** if he finds **an ass with its trappings overturned or a cow running among the vineyards,** [5]then he must assume that **this is a lost object and he is obliged** to return it.

וּלְעוֹלָם [6]Continuing its analysis of the clause which states that an ass or a cow grazing by the road is not considered lost, the Gemara asks: Does this apply **forever?** If the animals remain by the road for a very long time, are we still to assume that the owner knows where they are? Why has he not collected them?

אָמַר רַב יְהוּדָה אָמַר רַב [7]In reply to this question, **Rav Yehudah said in the name of Rav:** The rule mentioned in the Mishnah applies only for a period of **up to three days.** After three days, they are assumed to be lost and must be returned.

הֵיכִי דָּמֵי [8]On this the Gemara asks: **How is** Rav Yehudah's explanation **to be visualized?** When precisely were the animals seen? [9]**If** the finder saw them there **at night,** why should he have to wait three days before taking action? The presence of animals by the side of the road at night for **even one hour** shows that they are lost, since people do not normally leave their animals by the road at night. [10]On the other hand, **if** the finder saw the animals by the road on three consecutive days, but only **during the day,** this too is an implausible explanation, because if the animals were only there during the day, **even more** than three days is **also not** an indication that they are lost: the owner may be sending the animals out to the same pasture every morning and collecting them every evening.

לָא [11]The Gemara answers: **No!** Rav Yehudah's statement **was necessary** to describe a situation **where** the finder **saw** the animals **in the early morning,** before dawn, **or at dusk** — before and after the hours when animals are normally sent out to pasture. [12]**For three days we say that it just happened** that for some reason known to the owner the animal **went out** a little early or stayed out a little late. [13]But if the animal is out at such an hour for more than three consecutive days, we say that it is certainly lost, as the owner would not have let it

[1]אֵי זוֹ הִיא כְּלָל אֲבֵידָה שֶׁהוּא חַיָּיב בָּהּ? [2]מָצָא חֲמוֹר וּפָרָה רוֹעִין בַּדֶּרֶךְ, [3]אֵין זוֹ אֲבֵידָה, וְלֹא מִיחַיַּיב בָּהּ. [4]חֲמוֹר וְכֵלָיו הֲפוּכִים, פָּרָה וְרָצָה בֵּין הַכְּרָמִים — [5]הֲרֵי זוֹ אֲבֵידָה, וּמִיחַיַּיב בָּהּ.

[6]וּלְעוֹלָם?

[7]אָמַר רַב יְהוּדָה אָמַר רַב: עַד שְׁלֹשָׁה יָמִים.

[8]הֵיכִי דָּמֵי? [9]אִי בְּלֵילְוָתָא, אֲפִילּוּ חֲדָא שַׁעְתָּא נַמִי. [10]אִי בִּימָמָא, אֲפִילּוּ טוּבָא נַמִי לָא.

[11]לָא. צְרִיכָא דַּהֲוָה חָזֵי לָהּ בְּקַדְמְתָא וּבַחֲשֵׁכְתָּא. [12]תְּלָתָא יוֹמֵי אָמְרִינַן: אִיתְרַמוּיֵי אִתְרְמֵי לָהּ וְנָפְקָא. [13]טְפֵי, וַדַּאי אֲבֵידָה הִיא.

LITERAL TRANSLATION

[1]Which is the general rule of lost property for which he is responsible? [2][If] he found an ass or a cow grazing by the road, [3]this is not a lost object, and he is not obliged with regard to it. [4][But] an ass with its trappings overturned [or] a cow running among the vineyards — [5]this is a lost object, and he is obliged with regard to it.

[6]And forever?

[7]Rav Yehudah said in the name of Rav: Up to three days.

[8]How is this to be visualized (lit., "how is it like")? [9]If at night, even one hour also. [10]If during the day, even more also not.

[11]No. It is necessary where he saw it in the early morning or at dusk. [12][For] three days we say [that] it just happened that it went out. [13][For] more, it is certainly a lost object.

RASHI

גמרא כלל — סתם אבידה שמוכחת שהיא שם שלא מדעת בעלים. **ולעולם** — בתמיה: וכי אף אם ימצאנה שם לעולם — נאמר מדעת היא, וכי דרך שלא להכניס? **בקדמותא** — לפני עלות השחר. **חשכתא** — שחשכה ערבית.

BACKGROUND

עַד שְׁלֹשָׁה יָמִים Up to three days. According to the Halakhah, a period of three days (or an action or occurrence repeated three times) creates a legal presumption (חֲזָקָה) in many situations. In other words, the matter is no longer a chance occurrence but has become something regular. The presence of the ass or cow grazing alone at twilight may be explained as a matter of chance if it happens once or twice, but if it occurs on three consecutive days it can no longer be viewed as a chance event and indicates that the animal is lost.

NOTES

לְעוֹלָם? אָמַר רַב יְהוּדָה And forever? Rav Yehudah said.... Some Rishonim explain that the question "Forever?" was asked by Rav Yehudah himself, as a way of introducing his ruling that the maximum period during which the animal is

HALAKHAH

דֶּרֶךְ אֲבֵידָה בִּבְהֵמָה Indications that an animal is lost. "If a person finds a cow or an ass grazing by the road during the day, he may assume that it is not lost. If he finds one or the other of them at night, or if the trappings on the ass are

TRANSLATION AND COMMENTARY

out at such an odd hour so frequently.

תַּנְיָא נַמִּי הָכִי [1]The Gemara notes: **There is a Baraita in which the same** point as that mentioned by Rav Yehudah **is taught: "If** a person **finds a garment or a spade** [31A] **on a main road, or a cow running among the vineyards** and not quietly grazing, then he must assume that **they are lost objects.** [2]**But** if he finds **a garment by the side of a fence,** or **a spade by the side of a fence, or a cow grazing among the vineyards,** he may assume that **they are not lost objects.** He is forbidden to touch them, even if they have identifying marks, because their owner may have left them there deliberately with the intention of returning and collecting them later. [3]**But** if he sees the same objects on **three consecutive days,** then he must assume that **they are lost objects.** [4]**If** a person **sees** flood **waters approaching** someone else's field, **he must make a barrier** or a dam **before them,** so as to prevent damage to his neighbor's property." This preventive action, says the Baraita, comes under the category of the restoration of lost property to its rightful owner.

אָמַר רָבָא [5]The Gemara now cites a statement of Rava in which the concept of the restoration of lost property is extended beyond the area of movable property, such as animals and utensils, to include the restoration of land itself. **Rava said:** The passage in the Torah dealing with the law of restoring lost property contains the following verse (Deuteronomy 22:3): "And so shall you do with his ass; and so shall you do with his garment; and so shall you do with every lost thing of your brother's." The purpose of the words "**with every lost thing of your brother's,"** and specifically the word "every," **is to include loss of land** as a loss of property which we are required to prevent. Even though for many purposes the Halakhah treats immovable property differently from movable property, in this case the Torah included immovable property by using the word "every."

אָמַר לֵיהּ רַב חֲנַנְיָה לְרָבָא [6]**Rav Ḥananyah said to Rava: There is a statement in a Baraita** (the one quoted above) **that supports you:** [7]**"If** a person **sees flood waters approaching** someone else's field, **he must make a barrier** or a dam **before them."** This Baraita, says Rav Ḥananyah, provides support for your contention that prevention of damage to someone's field comes under the category of the restoration of lost property.

[1]תַּנְיָא נַמִּי הָכִי: "מָצָא טַלִּית וְקַרְדּוֹם [31A] בְּאִסְרַטְיָא, וּפָרָה רָצָה בֵּין הַכְּרָמִים, הֲרֵי זוֹ אֲבֵידָה. [2]טַלִּית בְּצַד גָּדֵר, קַרְדּוֹם בְּצַד גָּדֵר, וּפָרָה רוֹעָה בֵּין הַכְּרָמִים — אֵין זוֹ אֲבֵידָה. [3]שְׁלֹשָׁה יָמִים זֶה אַחַר זֶה — הֲרֵי זוֹ אֲבֵידָה. [4]רָאָה מַיִם שֶׁשּׁוֹטְפִין וּבָאִין, הֲרֵי זֶה גּוֹדֵר בִּפְנֵיהֶם".

[5]אָמַר רָבָא: "לְכָל אֲבֵידַת אָחִיךָ" לְרַבּוֹת אֲבֵידַת קַרְקַע.

[6]אָמַר לֵיהּ רַב חֲנַנְיָה לְרָבָא: תַּנְיָא דִּמְסַיֵּיעַ לָךְ: [7]"רָאָה מַיִם שֶׁשּׁוֹטְפִין וּבָאִין, הֲרֵי זֶה גּוֹדֵר בִּפְנֵיהֶם".

LITERAL TRANSLATION

[1]It was also taught thus: "[If] he found a garment or a spade [31A] on a main road, or a cow running among the vineyards, this is a lost object. [2][But] a garment by the side of a fence, a spade by the side of a fence, or a cow grazing among the vineyards — this is not a lost object. [3][But] three days, one after the other — this is a lost object. [4][If] he saw waters that were flooding and coming [nearer], this person must make a barrier before them."

[5]Rava said: "With every lost thing of your brother's" [comes] to include the loss of land.

[6]Rav Ḥananyah said to Rava: [What] was taught supports you: [7]"[If] he saw waters that were flooding and coming [nearer], this person must make a barrier before them."

RASHI

אסרטיא — דרך כבושה לרבים. **ששוטפין ובאין** — לשדה חבירו. **אמר רבא לכל אבידה כו׳** — מילתא באפיה נפשיה היא, דאמרה רבא בבי מדרשא.

LANGUAGE

בְּאִסְרַטְיָא On a main road. See above, p.52, under סְרַטְיָא.

BACKGROUND

רָאָה מַיִם שֶׁשּׁוֹטְפִין If he saw waters that were flooding. Flash floods are common in Eretz Israel in winter, and streams sometimes overflow their banks and threaten to flood distant fields. In Babylonia this can occur in summer, while sheaves are drying in the field, if the banks of an irrigation canal collapse. Such a flood can cause damage by washing away objects or animals. It can also damage the soil of the field itself, since valuable topsoil may be washed away, troughs may be formed in the ground, sand may be washed up and cover the plowed soil, etc.

אֲבֵידַת קַרְקַע The loss of land. The need to emphasize the loss of land, as in the quotation from the Baraita here, depends on the principles of Halakhic Midrashim. It is clear that in real life serious damage can be caused to someone through loss of land, when the soil is eroded or when water or other elements damage it. However, the Halakhic problem here is whether land is to be included in the formal definition of a lost object. The list in the Biblical verse (ox, sheep, ass, garment) includes only movable objects, not land or anything attached to the ground. Rava wished to say that the emphatic form of the verse, "every lost thing of your brother's," and especially the word "every," is meant to make it so comprehensive that it even covers things not at all similar to the items specified in the verse.

TERMINOLOGY

תַּנְיָא דִּמְסַיֵּיעַ לָךְ What was taught supports you. A term used by one Amora to introduce a Baraita which supports the view of another Amora.

NOTES

שְׁלֹשָׁה יָמִים Three days. According to *Rashba,* the three-day law applies not only to animals found a little late or a little

assumed to have been deliberately left is three days (*Tosafot,* above, 21a, *Tosefot HaRosh*).

HALAKHAH

טַלִּית בְּצַד גָּדֵר A garment by the side of a fence. "Any object that appears to have been left intentionally by its owner must not be touched — for example, a garment or a spade left by the side of a fence." (*Shulḥan Arukh, Ḥoshen Mishpat* 260:9-10.)

אֲבֵידַת קַרְקַע Loss of land. "There is a positive obligation to save one's neighbor's landed property from loss, just as

overturned, he must assume the animal to be lost. If he finds it at dawn or at dusk on three consecutive occasions, he must assume it to be lost." (*Shulḥan Arukh, Ḥoshen Mishpat* 261:1.) *Arukh HaShulḥan* adds that determining whether an animal is lost is subject to local custom. Only behavior significantly different from local custom is an indication of loss.

TRANSLATION AND COMMENTARY

אָמַר לֵיהּ [1]In reply, Rava **said to** Rav Ḥananyah: **If your argument supporting** my ruling **is based only on** that Baraita, **it is inconclusive,** since the Baraita is referring to a different situation and can be understood even on the assumption that there is no requirement to protect someone else from loss to his landed property. [2]For it can be argued: **With what are we dealing here in the Baraita? With a case where there are** harvested **sheaves** lying in the field, that will be destroyed by the flood if it reaches them. The Baraita informs us that someone who sees the flood approaching must take steps to protect his neighbor's sheaves.

אִי דְּאִיכָּא עוֹמָרִין [3]Rav Ḥananyah replied: **If** we are dealing with **a case where there are sheaves** in the field, **what** need **was there** for the Baraita **to say** anything? Surely it is obvious that sheaves need protecting just like any other movable property.

לָא [4]Rava replied: **No.** The Baraita's ruling **is necessary** for a case **where there are sheaves** in the field **that** still **need the soil.** In other words, the sheaves are still not quite dry enough to be taken from the field, though they are already harvested. Such grain is considered to belong to an intermediate category between immovable and movable property. [5]**You might have said,** had it not been for the Baraita, that **since** the sheaves still **need the soil, they are like the soil itself,** and are not subject to the law requiring us to protect our neighbor's movable property. [6]**Therefore,** the Baraita **tells us that this is not so,** and the sheaves are to be treated like any other movable property. Thus, the Baraita can be explained as being unconnected with Rava's ruling, and Rava's ruling stands on its own as an independent, unsupported statement.

מָצָא חֲמוֹר וּפָרָה [7]The Gemara now goes on to consider the first part of the Mishnah in its entirety: **"If a** person **finds an ass or a cow...."** [8]The Gemara asks: This whole first part of the Mishnah, classifying what does and what does not constitute lost property, **is difficult** to understand because the two clauses in it lead to opposite logical conclusions. [9]On the one hand **the Mishnah says: "If a** person **finds an ass or a cow grazing by the road,** he may assume that **it is not a lost object."** [10]This sentence implies that **it is** only **if** the ass or cow is ***grazing* by the *road* that it is not** considered to be **a lost object;** [11]**but if the animal is *running* by the road or grazing among the *vineyards*, it is** considered to be **a lost object.** [12]Now let us **consider the next clause** in the Mishnah: **"But** if he finds **an ass with its trappings overturned, or a cow running among the vineyards,** then he

[1]אָמַר לֵיהּ: אִי מִשּׁוּם הָא, לָא תְּסַיְּיעֵי. [2]הָכָא בְּמַאי עָסְקִינַן? בִּדְאִיכָּא עוֹמָרִין.
[3]אִי דְּאִיכָּא עוֹמָרִין, מַאי לְמֵימְרָא?!
[4]לָא! צְרִיכָא דְּאִית בָּהּ עוֹמָרִין דִּצְרִיכֵי לְאַרְעָא. [5]מַהוּ דְּתֵימָא: כֵּיוָן דִּצְרִיכֵי לְאַרְעָא, כִּי גּוּפַהּ דְּאַרְעָא דָּמְיָין. [6]קָא מַשְׁמַע לָן.
[7]״מָצָא חֲמוֹר וּפָרָה וכו׳״. [8]הָא גּוּפָהּ קַשְׁיָא! [9]אָמְרַתְּ: ״מָצָא חֲמוֹר וּפָרָה רוֹעִין בַּדֶּרֶךְ, אֵין זוֹ אֲבֵידָה״. [10]רוֹעִין בַּדֶּרֶךְ הוּא דְּלָא הָווּ אֲבֵידָה, [11]הָא רָצָה בַּדֶּרֶךְ וְרוֹעָה בֵּין הַכְּרָמִים, הָוְיָא אֲבֵידָה! [12]אֵימָא סֵיפָא: ״חֲמוֹר וְכֵלָיו הֲפוּכִים, וּפָרָה רָצָה בֵּין הַכְּרָמִים — הֲרֵי זוֹ אֲבֵידָה״.

LITERAL TRANSLATION

[1]He said to him: If [you argue] on the basis of this, you will not support me. [2]With what are we dealing here? With [a case] where there are sheaves.

[3]If [it means] where there are sheaves, what is there to say?

[4]No. It is necessary where there are in it sheaves that need the soil. [5]You might have said: Since they need the soil, they are like the soil itself. [6][Therefore] it tells us [that this is not so].

[7]"[If] he found an ass or a cow...." [8]This itself is difficult. [9]You said: "[If] he found an ass or a cow grazing by the road, this is not a lost object." [10]It is [if] they are *grazing* by the *road* that they are not a lost object, [11]but [if the animal] is *running* by the road or grazing among the *vineyards,* it is a lost object. [12]Say the latter clause: [But] an ass with its trappings overturned, or a cow running among the vineyards — this is a lost object."

RASHI

מאי למימרא — ותיפוק ליה משום עומרין שישנן בכלל אבידה דדמו לפרטא דשה ושלמה, ולמה לי לכל לרבויניהו?

BACKGROUND

אִי מִשּׁוּם הָא, לָא תְּסַיְּיעֵי If you argue on the basis of this, you will not support me. This is one example among many in the Talmud (see above, 22a — תַּרְגְּמָה רָבָא אַלִּיבָּא דְּאַבָּיֵי) where a Sage who has advanced a certain opinion offers support for a contrary view, or shows that the proofs in support of his own approach are incomplete. Since the primary aim of the Sages is to reach the truth, they do not necessarily support their own views rather than those of someone else.

עוֹמָרִין דִּצְרִיכֵי לְאַרְעָא Sheaves that need the soil. Normally, after sheaves have been cut, they are viewed as ordinary movable property, and the laws governing the restoration of lost property apply to them. But sometimes sheaves still "need" the soil — for example, when their owners wish to leave them in the field for a certain additional time to dry more completely. In such a case one can say that, although the sheaves have been physically severed from the earth, they are nevertheless attached to it to some degree. According to the Halakhah, as long as they are physically attached to the ground, whether or not they "need" to be left there, they can be considered part of the land.

NOTES

early on three consecutive days outside their regular protected environment, but to all lost objects. If a person sees an object lying unattended for three days in a place where it is somewhat unusual to leave it, he must assume it to be lost and return it to its owner.

HALAKHAH

there is a positive obligation to return his lost movable property. Thus, if one sees that another person's field is about to be flooded, one is obliged to make a barrier to protect the field from damage." (Ibid., 259:9.)

TRANSLATION AND COMMENTARY

must assume that **it is a lost object.**" [1]From this sentence we can infer that **it is** only **if** the cow **is *running* among the *vineyards* that it is** considered to be **a lost object;** [2]**but if the animal is running by the *road*** or ***grazing* among the vineyards, it is not** considered to be **a lost object.** Thus the inferences drawn from the two clauses appear to contradict each other: According to the first clause, "running by the road" or "grazing among the vineyards" is an indication that the animal is lost. According to the second clause, "running by the road" or "grazing among the vineyards" is an indication that the animal is not lost.

אָמַר אַבַּיֵי [3]**Abaye said** in reply: We must apply here the rule of interpretation poetically known as **"his companion will tell about him,"** after a verse in Job (36:33). According to this rule, the two clauses of the Mishnah complement each other. Neither is complete, and each supplies details the other lacks. Abaye goes on to explain: The fundamental difference between the two clauses of the Mishnah is the difference between "running" and "grazing." The place where these activities take place is secondary. [4]The way to understand the Mishnah is as follows: **The Mishnah teaches** in the first clause **that "grazing by the *road*" is not** an indication that an animal is **a lost object,** [5]**and the same applies to grazing among the *vineyards.*** [6]Similarly, in the second clause **the Mishnah teaches that "running among the *vineyards*"** is an indication that an animal is **a lost object,** [7]**and the same applies to running by the *road.*** Thus, according to Abaye, the two clauses of the Mishnah are in harmony, the one complementing the other.

אָמַר לֵיהּ רָבָא [8]**Rava said to** Abaye: I cannot accept the logic of your argument. **If** the Mishnah had been written in the style called **"his companion will tell about him,"** as you maintain, it would have used a different example. If, as you maintain, every case of "running" is an indication that the animal is lost, and every case of "grazing" is an indication that the animal is not lost, [9]**let the Mishnah teach the lenient case and** leave out the severe case, and we can infer that the ruling applies **all the more so to the severe case.** [10]Rava now goes on to explain his objection in detail: **Let** the Mishnah **teach** in the second clause **that if the animal is running by the *road,*** this is an indication that the animal **is a lost object,** [11]**and** we would be able to infer **how much more so** the animal is lost **if it is running among the *vineyards.*** [12]Similarly, **let** the Mishnah **teach** in the first clause **that if** the animal **is grazing among the *vineyards,*** this **is not** an indication that the

[1]רָצָה בֵּין הַכְּרָמִים הוּא דְּהָוְיָא אֲבֵידָה, [2]הָא רָצָה בַּדֶּרֶךְ וְרוֹעָה בֵּין הַכְּרָמִים, אֵין זוֹ אֲבֵידָה!
[3]אָמַר אַבַּיֵי: "יַגִּיד עָלָיו רֵעוֹ". [4]תָּנָא "רוֹעָה בַּדֶּרֶךְ", דְּלָא הָוְיָא אֲבֵידָה, [5]וְהוּא הַדִּין לְרוֹעָה בֵּין הַכְּרָמִים. [6]תָּנָא "רָצָה בֵּין הַכְּרָמִים", דְּהָוְיָא אֲבֵידָה, [7]וְהוּא הַדִּין לְרָצָה בַּדֶּרֶךְ.
[8]אָמַר לֵיהּ רָבָא: אִי "יַגִּיד עָלָיו רֵעוֹ", [9]לִיתְנֵי קִילְּתָא וְכׇל שֶׁכֵּן חֲמִירְתָּא: [10]לִיתְנֵי רָצָה בַּדֶּרֶךְ, דְּהָוְיָא אֲבֵידָה, [11]וְכׇל שֶׁכֵּן רָצָה בֵּין הַכְּרָמִים, [12]וְלִתְנֵי רוֹעָה בֵּין הַכְּרָמִים, דְּלָא הָוְיָא אֲבֵידָה,

LITERAL TRANSLATION

[1]It is [if] it is *running* among the vineyards that it is a lost object, [2]but [if the animal] is running by the *road* or *grazing* among the vineyards, this is not a lost object.

[3]Abaye said: "His companion will tell about him." [4][The Mishnah] teaches "grazing by the *road,*" that it is not a lost object, [5]and the same is the law regarding grazing among the *vineyards.* [6][The Mishnah] teaches "running among the *vineyards,*" that it is a lost object, [7]and the same is the law regarding running by the *road.*

[8]Rava said to him: If "his companion will tell about him," [9]let [the Mishnah] teach the lenient case and how much more so the severe case. [10]Let it teach [that if the animal is] running by the *road,* it is a lost object, [11]and how much more so [if it is] running among the *vineyards,* [12]and let [it teach] that [if it is] grazing among the *vineyards,* it is not a lost object,

RASHI

רועה בדרך — איכא תרתי למעליותא: חדא דרועה, ועוד, דאפילו רצה לא מסתכנא. רצה בין הכרמים איכא תרתי לגריעותא: חדא דרצה, ועוד דכרמים מסכני לה, רצה בדרך איכא חדא לגריעותא: דרצה ומתקלקלת בריצתה, אי נמי תלך למרחקים. רועה בין הכרמים חדא לגריעותא: דזימנין דמסתכנא.

BACKGROUND

יַגִּיד עָלָיו רֵעוֹ "His companion will tell about him." The difficulty in interpreting the Mishnah derives from the contradiction that emerges when its various clauses are closely analyzed.

In other situations the Sages might have been content to state that the Mishnah is not worded in a way which permits us to draw logical inferences from it. However, a cow running along a road or grazing in a vineyard is not in a far-fetched intermediate category. It is no less common in reality than the cases actually mentioned in the Mishnah, and a practical decision is required as to how one should act.

For this reason Abaye argues that the Mishnah should not be interpreted using the method of precise analysis, but the detailed cases it presents should be merely viewed as examples. According to him, the main distinction is between a grazing animal (which is not lost) and a running animal (which is probably lost), and he offers an unusual explanation for the style of the Mishnah — "his companion will tell about him." This picturesque quotation from the Book of Job means that the Mishnah presented the examples and details only to provide a more vivid picture of the cases, and did not imply that logical inferences could be drawn from them.

Rava does not accept this explanation because, in his opinion, the examples presented in the Mishnah are not straightforward ones. According to him, they represent extraordinary cases. Therefore he interprets the Mishnah differently.

HALAKHAH

אֲבֵידַת פָּרָה A lost cow. "If one finds a cow running along a road towards town, it may be presumed not to be lost. If it is running away from town, it must be presumed to be lost. If it is found grazing in a vineyard, it must be returned to its owner, not because it is lost, but because of the damage to the vineyard. If the vineyard is owned by an idolater, the cow need not be returned. But if the cow is itself in danger — for example, where the idolater is liable to kill it if he finds it in his vineyard, or where the cow's owner is liable to be fined for allowing his cow to graze in the vineyard (*Rema*) — the cow must be returned." (*Shulḥan Arukh, Ḥoshen Mishpat* 261:2.)

TRANSLATION AND COMMENTARY

animal is **a lost object,** [1]**and** we would be able to infer **how much more so** the animal is not lost **if it is grazing by the *road*.** Hence, the Mishnah cannot be explained in the way advocated by Abaye, and another explanation of its seeming self-contradiction must be found.

אֶלָּא אֲמַר רָבָא [2]**Rather, Rava said: There is no difficulty** in resolving the contradiction between "running" and "running" in the two clauses of the Mishnah: When in the first clause the Mishnah implies that "running" is an indication that the animal is lost, [3]**it is** referring to **a case where** the animal's **face is towards the fields** and away from the town, indicating that it is running away from its owner, and when in the second clause the Mishnah implies that "running" is *not* an indication that the animal is lost, [4]**it is** referring to **a case where** the animal's **face is towards the town,** indicating that it is on its way back to its owner. [5]Similarly, explained Rava, **there is no difficulty** in resolving the contradiction **between "grazing" and "grazing"** in the two clauses of the Mishnah: [6]In the one case **it refers to the loss of the animal itself,** [7]and in the other case **it refers to the loss of the land.** [8]Rava goes on to explain: **When** in the first clause the Mishnah **teaches that grazing by the road is not** an indication that the animal is **a lost object —** [9]**thus implying that grazing among the vineyards** is an indication that **it *is* a lost object — it is referring to the damage caused to the land** by the animal's grazing in the wrong place, not to damage caused to the animal. [10]**And when** in the second clause the Mishnah **teaches that running among the vineyards is** an indication that the animal is **a lost object —** [11]**thus implying that grazing among the vineyards is not** an indication that the animal is **a lost object —** [12]**it is referring to the damage caused to the animal itself,** [13]**because** an animal **running among the vineyards can** easily **be injured,** [14]**whereas** an animal quietly **grazing among** the **vineyards is not injured** thereby. Thus, according to Rava, there is no contradiction between the two clauses of the Mishnah, because the circumstances in each case are different.

וְרוֹעָה בֵּין הַכְּרָמִים [15]**But,** asks the Gemara, **granted that** by **grazing among the vineyards** the animal **is not injured,** [16]the finder should nevertheless still be required to return it to its owner, as his obligation can equally well **be derived from the damage caused to the land** by the animal's presence among the vines!

בְּדְנָכְרִי [17]The Gemara answers: The case discussed by the Mishnah is **where** the animal, though owned by a Jew, **was** found in **the field of a non-Jew.** The relations between Jew and non-Jew were strained during the Talmudic period, and there was no formal Halakhic obligation to protect a non-Jew's property. Hence, if the animal itself is lost or in danger, it must be returned, but if the animal is in no danger, it need not be returned merely to protect a non-Jew's vineyard.

[1]וְכָל שֶׁכֵּן רוֹעָה בַּדֶּרֶךְ. [2]אֶלָּא אֲמַר רָבָא: ״רָצָה״ אַ״רָצָה״ לָא קַשְׁיָא: [3]הָא דְּאַפָּהּ לְגַבֵּי דַּבְרָא, [4]הָא דְּאַפָּהּ לְגַבֵּי מָתָא. [5]״רוֹעָה״ אַ״רוֹעָה״ נַמִי לָא קַשְׁיָא: [6]כָּאן בַּאֲבֵידַת גּוּפָהּ, [7]כָּאן בַּאֲבֵידַת קַרְקַע. [8]כִּי קָתָנֵי רוֹעָה בַּדֶּרֶךְ לָא הָוְיָא אֲבֵידָה — [9]הָא רוֹעָה בֵּין הַכְּרָמִים הָוְיָא אֲבֵידָה — בַּאֲבֵידַת קַרְקַע. [10]וְכִי קָתָנֵי רָצָה בֵּין הַכְּרָמִים הָוְיָא אֲבֵידָה — [11]הָא רוֹעָה בֵּין הַכְּרָמִים לָא הָוְיָא אֲבֵידָה — [12]בַּאֲבֵידַת גּוּפָהּ; [13]דְּרָצָה בֵּין הַכְּרָמִים, מִסַּקְבָא, [14]וְרוֹעָה בֵּין הַכְּרָמִים, לָא מִסַּקְבָא.

[15]וְרוֹעָה בֵּין הַכְּרָמִים, נְהִי דְּלָא מִסַּקְבָא, [16]תֵּיפוֹק לֵיהּ מִשּׁוּם אֲבֵידַת קַרְקַע?

[17]בִּדְנָכְרִי.

LITERAL TRANSLATION

[1]and how much more so [if it is] grazing by the *road*. [2]Rather, Rava said: There is no difficulty [between] "running" and "running": [3]This [case] is where its face is towards the field, [4]that [case] is where its face is towards the town. [5]There is also no difficulty [between] "grazing" and "grazing": [6]Here [it refers] to the loss of [the animal] itself, [7]here [it refers] to the loss of the land. [8]When it teaches [that] grazing by the road it is not a lost object — [9]thus [implying that] grazing among the vineyards it is a lost object — [it refers] to the loss of the land. [10]And when it teaches that running among the vineyards it is a lost object — [11]thus [implying that] grazing among the vineyards it is not a lost object — [12][it refers] to the loss of [the animal] itself, [13]for running among the vineyards, it is injured, [14]but grazing among the vineyards, it is not injured.

[15]But grazing among the vineyards, granted that it is not injured, [16]let him derive it because of the loss of the land.

[17][Where it was] in [the field] of a non-Jew.

RASHI

והא באבידת גופה כו׳ — מפרש ואזיל לה. **באבידת קרקע** — וחייב להוציאה משום הפסד כרמים.

TRANSLATION AND COMMENTARY

וְתֵיפּוֹק לֵיהּ מִשּׁוּם [1]**But,** continues the Gemara, even if the animal was in a non-Jew's vineyard, the finder should still be required to return it to its owner, as his obligation can now be **derived from the loss of the animal itself! For** if the non-Jew finds the animal grazing in his vineyard, **there is a possibility that he will kill it.** Hence, the finder should be obliged to save the animal and return it to its owner.

בְּאַתְרָא דְּמַתְרוּ [2]The Gemara answers: The Mishnah **refers to** a case where the animal was found in a non-Jew's vineyard in **a place where** people **warn** the owner of an animal that his animal is causing damage, **and then kill** the animal if **it** causes damage a second time.

וְדִלְמָא אַתְרוּ בָּהּ [3]**But,** suggests the Gemara, **perhaps** this is the second time the animal has entered the non-Jew's vineyard, and the non-Jew **has** already **warned** the owner **about it.** The animal is thus in immediate danger, and there should be an obligation on the finder to restore it to its owner.

אִי אַתְרוּ בָּהּ [4]The Gemara answers: Whichever way you look at it, the finder is not obliged to look after the animal. If the non-Jew has not warned its owner about the animal's presence in his vineyard, the animal is in no danger. And **if** the non-Jew **has warned** the owner **about** his animal **and he has not been careful about** looking after **it, it clearly** comes under the category of **an intentional loss,** because it is certain that the non-Jew will kill it. The owner has acted irresponsibly in allowing the animal to enter the non-Jew's vineyard, so it does not come under the category of lost property, and the finder is under no obligation to look after it and return it to its owner.

הֶחֱזִירָהּ וּבָרְחָה [5]The Gemara now goes on to consider the next clause of the Mishnah: **"If** the finder **returned** a lost animal to its owner **and it ran away** again, and **he returned it** again to its owner **and** again **it ran away, even** if this happened **four or five times he is obliged to return it** each time; **as it is said: 'You shall surely return them,'** in which a double verb — הָשֵׁב תְּשִׁיבֵם — is used for emphasis." [6]**One of the Rabbis said to Rava:** How does the Mishnah know that the finder is required to return the animal time after time? It is true that the verse repeats the verb and says *"hashev teshivem"* — "you shall surely return them." [7]But maybe we should **say** that the words ***hashev*** **(הָשֵׁב)** ***teshivem*** **(תְּשִׁיבֵם)** **mean: Return it twice!** On what basis does the Mishnah assert that the animal must be returned any number of times?

אֲמַר לֵיהּ [8]Rava **said to him** in reply: The word ***hashev*** alone **means: Return it even a hundred times.** The obligation to restore lost property exists whenever a person is confronted with something that has been lost, and the finder is not considered to have returned it until it is safely in the owner's possession again, even if the finder has to return the animal a hundred times. [9]**With regard to** the seemingly superfluous word ***teshivem,*** I can answer you by saying that it was included in order to teach us another important principle. Without the extra word *teshivem* I would **only know** that a finder **must return** a lost object **to** its owner's **home,**

[1]וְתֵיפּוֹק לֵיהּ מִשּׁוּם אֲבֵידַת גּוּפָהּ, דְּדִלְמָא קָטְלוּ לָהּ! [2]בְּאַתְרָא דְּמַתְרוּ וַהֲדַר קָטְלִי. [3]וְדִלְמָא אַתְרוּ בָּהּ? [4]אִי אַתְרוּ בָּהּ וְלָא אִזְדַּהֲרוּ בָּהּ, וַדַּאי אֲבֵידָה מִדַּעַת הִיא.
[5]"הֶחֱזִירָהּ וּבָרְחָה, הֶחֱזִירָהּ וּבָרְחָה וכו׳". [6]אֲמַר לֵיהּ הַהוּא מִדְּרַבָּנַן לְרָבָא: [7]אֵימָא: "הָשֵׁב" חֲדָא זִמְנָא; "תְּשִׁיבֵם" תְּרֵי זִמְנֵי!
[8]אֲמַר לֵיהּ: "הָשֵׁב" אֲפִילּוּ מֵאָה פְּעָמִים מַשְׁמַע. [9]"תְּשִׁיבֵם" אֵין

LITERAL TRANSLATION

[1]But let him derive it because of the loss of [the animal] itself, for perhaps they will kill it.
[2][It refers] to a place where they warn and then kill.
[3]But perhaps they warned about it?
[4]If they warned about it and they were not careful about it, it is certainly an intentional loss.
[5]"[If] he returned it and it ran away, he returned it and it ran away...." [6]One of the Rabbis said to Rava: [7]Say: *Hashev* [הָשֵׁב — return it] once; *teshivem* [תְּשִׁיבֵם — return it] twice.
[8]He said to him: *Hashev* means: [return it] even a hundred times. [9][Regarding] *teshivem*: I have only [that he

BACKGROUND

וַדַּאי אֲבֵידָה מִדַּעַת הִיא **It is certainly an intentional loss.** Whenever an object is found in a place where it is liable to be damaged and ruined, the finder must take care of it and return it to its owner. However, if the owner shows negligence in tending his object or animal, such an object need not be returned. In certain cases, when an object has been left by its owner in a place where it is likely to be ruined, this can be viewed as a renunciation of ownership, and the object belongs to whoever finds it. However, even if one does not go so far, but merely says that the owner has shown excessive carelessness about his property, a stranger still does not need to take care of an object more conscientiously than does its owner.

NOTES

הָשֵׁב אֲפִילּוּ מֵאָה פְּעָמִים מַשְׁמַע **The word *hashev* (הָשֵׁב) means: return it even a hundred times.** *Rambam,* in his commentary on the Mishnah, explains that the word הָשֵׁב is an infinitive, not an imperative form. The meaning of the infinitive is that of a continuing command that does not distinguish between once and many times. (Compare *Rashi's* commentary on the word זָכוֹר, Exodus 20:8.)

HALAKHAH

הֶחֱזִירָהּ וּבָרְחָה **If he returned it and it ran away.** "If a person returned a lost animal to its owner and it ran away again, he must return it again, even a hundred times." (*Shulḥan Arukh, Ḥoshen Mishpat* 267:2.)

לִי אֶלָּא לְבֵיתוֹ. [1]לְגִינָּתוֹ וּלְחוּרְבָתוֹ מִנַּיִן? [2]תַּלְמוּד לוֹמַר "תְּשִׁיבֵם" — מִכָּל מָקוֹם.
[3]הֵיכִי דָּמֵי? [4]אִי דְּמִינְטְרָא, פְּשִׁיטָא. [5]אִי דְּלָא מִינְטְרָא, אַמַּאי?
[6]לְעוֹלָם דְּמִינְטְרָא, [7]וְהָא קָא מַשְׁמַע לָן: דְּלָא בָּעֵינַן דַּעַת בְּעָלִים, [8]וְכִדְרַבִּי אֶלְעָזָר, דְּאָמַר: [9]הַכֹּל צְרִיכִין דַּעַת בְּעָלִים, חוּץ מֵהֲשָׁבַת אֲבֵידָה, [10]שֶׁהַתּוֹרָה רִיבְּתָה הֲשָׁבוֹת הַרְבֵּה.

LITERAL TRANSLATION

must return it] to his home. [1]From where [do I know that he can return it] to his garden or to his ruin? [2]The verse teaches: *teshivem* — in all cases.
[3]How is it to be visualized (lit., "how is it like")? [4]If it is guarded, it is obvious. [5]If it is not guarded, why [is it permitted]?
[6]In fact, [it means] that it is guarded, [7]and he tells us this: that we do not need the awareness of the owners, [8]and [it is] in accordance with Rabbi Elazar, who said: [9]All require the awareness of the owners, except for the return of lost property, [10]for the Torah included many returnings.

TRANSLATION AND COMMENTARY

and I would assume that only in that way does the finder fulfill the commandment to restore lost property to its owner. [1]**From where do I know that** the finder **can** also **return it to** the owner's **garden or to a ruined** house belonging to the owner, in which he no longer lives? [2]**The verse** therefore **uses** the seemingly superfluous word ***teshivem*** to inform us that **in all cases,** even if the finder returns the animal to the owner's garden or anywhere else belonging to the owner, his act of restoring lost property has been properly fulfilled.

הֵיכִי דָּמֵי [3]The Gemara now asks: **How is** Rava's interpretation **to be visualized?** [4]If Rava means that the finder is permitted to return the lost object to the owner's garden only **if** the garden **is guarded** and is a safe place to leave it, **it is** surely **obvious** that this constitutes an acceptable method of returning lost property and does not need to be specifically mentioned by the Torah. [5]But if Rava means that the finder is permitted to return it there even **if it is not guarded,** and the animal can stray again, **why is this** form of returning lost property **permitted?** How can this be considered a valid method of returning lost property?

לְעוֹלָם דְּמִינְטְרָא [6]The Gemara answers: **In fact,** Rava is referring to a garden that **is guarded,** and, in his opinion, returning an animal to an unprotected garden is not a valid act of returning lost property. [7]However, Rava's ruling is far from obvious, **and** its purpose **is to tell us that we do not insist** that the finder make sure **that the** animal's **owner is aware** that his lost animal has been safely returned. [8]**And this is in accordance with** the ruling of **Rabbi Elazar, who said:** [9]**In every case** where property has to be returned to its owner — for example, where an article entrusted to a bailee or an article stolen by a thief is returned to its owner — **the awareness of the owners is required.** Until the person returning the article has informed the owner that the article has been safely returned, he has not discharged his responsibility and remains liable for any damage that may be caused to the article. This ruling, says Rabbi Elazar, applies to all acts of returning property to its rightful owner **except for the return of lost property,** [10]**because** by using the double verb *hashev teshivem,* as explained above, **the Torah included many** types of **"returning."** In other words, in the case of a lost object, the concept "returning" is to be understood in its most general sense, and the object can be returned to any protected place belonging to its owner, even if the owner is unaware that the object has been returned.

RASHI

לגינתו ולחורבתו מנין — דהוא השבה, ופטור. **דעת בעלים** — לומר לו "שמור פרתך שהחזרתיה לגינתך, שמצאתיה אובדת". **הכל צריך דעת בעלים** — גנב, גזלן, וארבעה שומרים שהשיבו — צריכין להודיעו, ואם לא הודיעו ומתה או נגנבה — חייבים באחריותן, דכיון דידע שאבדה ולא ידע שהושבה — לא נזהר בה, ולא מאכילה.

BACKGROUND

וּלְחוּרְבָתוֹ Or to his ruin. A "ruin" is the remains of someone's private building. It may consist of what is left of a building after its roof has collapsed (in Eretz Israel it was common to roof buildings with wooden beams upon which plaster was spread, and in case of fire the roofs were often destroyed, leaving the rest of the building relatively intact); or else the owner may have built himself a larger house and left the old structure in place, gradually removing building materials from it. In any event, the walls of such a ruin were generally left standing, and an object brought into it would be properly protected.

הַכֹּל צְרִיכִין דַּעַת בְּעָלִים All require the awareness of the owners. This general principle states that whenever a person takes someone else's property, either with the owner's permission (as a bailee or borrower) or without it (as a thief or a robber), he does not fulfill his duty to return the property unless he does so with the owner's knowledge. This is because it can be argued that the presence of the object in the other person's possession (whether with or without permission) has in it a certain element of acquisition. Until the owners *know* that the object has been returned, the element of acquisition by the other person has not been ended, and he remains fully responsible for it. Only when the owners know that the object is once again in their possession do they regain full property rights over it.

NOTES

תְּשִׁיבֵם מִכָּל מָקוֹם You shall return it — in all cases. There is a general dispute in the Talmud as to how to interpret the many double verbs appearing in the Torah. Although the Sages analyzed every word and letter of the Torah, and derived important laws from the slightest case of seeming superfluity, there is an opinion that the use of a double verb is no more than a stylistic matter with no specific Halakhic significance. This opinion is exemplified by the expression

HALAKHAH

הֲשָׁבָה שֶׁלֹּא מִדַּעַת הַבְּעָלִים Returning a lost object without the owner's awareness. "The finder of a lost article must care for it until he returns it to its owner. It is sufficient for him to return it to the owner's garden or ruined house or to any other protected place belonging to the owner, even without informing him that the article has been returned." (Ibid., 267:1.)

הַכֹּל צְרִיכִין דַּעַת בְּעָלִים All things require the awareness

TRANSLATION AND COMMENTARY

שַׁלֵּחַ תְּשַׁלַּח [1]The Gemara now proceeds to bring a long series of examples of interpretations of the use of a double verb in the Torah, similar to the expression *hashev teshivem* on which the discussion up to this point has been focused. When the Torah (Deuteronomy 22:6-7) commands that a mother bird must be sent away before her eggs or chicks can be taken, it used the double verb form: **"You shall surely let it go"** — *shalle'aḥ teshallaḥ* (שַׁלֵּחַ תְּשַׁלַּח).

אֵימָא [2](1) From the use of the double verb the Mishnah (*Ḥullin* 141a) appears to derive the rule that if the mother bird returns to the nest before the person has had time to take the young, she must be sent away again and again, even many times. On this the Gemara asks: It is true that the verse repeats the verb and says *"shalle'aḥ teshallaḥ"* — "you shall surely let it go." But maybe we should **say** that the word ***shalle'aḥ*** (שַׁלֵּחַ) **means "let it go once,"** [3]and the word ***teshallaḥ*** (תְּשַׁלַּח) **means "let it go twice"**? Hence, if the mother bird returns after being sent away once, it must be sent away again, but not if it returns more often. On what basis does the Mishnah in tractate *Ḥullin* assert that the mother bird must be sent away any number of times?

אֲמַר לֵיהּ [4]**The Gemara answers:** The word ***shalle'aḥ*** alone **has the meaning: Let it go even a hundred times,** and the act of letting the mother bird go is only considered to have been properly fulfilled if the mother bird stays away until after the eggs or chicks have been taken, even if this involves sending her away again and again. [5]**With regard to** the seemingly superfluous word ***teshallaḥ,*** it was included in order to teach us another important principle. Without the extra word *teshallaḥ* **I only know that he must let** the mother bird **go** and not take her **when he needs her for an optional matter** — to sell her or use her for food. [6]**From where do I know that he must let** the mother bird **go** and not use her even **if he needs her for the fulfillment of a commandment,** such as the purification of a leper? (See Leviticus 14:4.) [7]**The verse** therefore **uses** the seemingly superfluous word ***teshallaḥ*** to inform us that **in all cases** the mother must be sent away, and may not be used for any purpose.

[1]״שַׁלֵּחַ תְּשַׁלַּח״. [2]אֵימָא: ״שַׁלֵּחַ״ חֲדָא זִימְנָא; [3]״תְּשַׁלַּח״ תְּרֵי זִמְנֵי!
[4]אֲמַר לֵיהּ: ״שַׁלֵּחַ״ אֲפִילּוּ מֵאָה פְּעָמִים מַשְׁמַע. [5]״תְּשַׁלַּח״ אֵין לִי אֶלָּא לִדְבַר הָרְשׁוּת. [6]לִדְבַר מִצְוָה מְנַיִן? [7]תַּלְמוּד לוֹמַר: ״תְּשַׁלַּח״ — מִכָּל מָקוֹם.

LITERAL TRANSLATION

[1]"You shall surely let [it] go" (שַׁלֵּחַ תְּשַׁלַּח). [2]Say: *Shalle'aḥ* [שַׁלֵּחַ — let it go] once; [3]*teshallaḥ* [תְּשַׁלַּח — let it go] twice.
[4]He said to him: *Shalle'aḥ* means: [let it go] even a hundred times. [5][Regarding] *teshallaḥ* I have only [that he must let it go when it is needed] for an optional matter. [6]From where [do I know that he must let it go when it is needed] for the fulfillment of a commandment? [7]The verse teaches: *Teshallaḥ* — in all cases.

RASHI

שלח — לגבי שלוח הקן. **תרתי זמני** — ואנן תנן: שלחה וחזרה, שלחה וחזרה, אפילו ארבע וחמש פעמים חייב. **לדבר הרשות** — שאין צריך לצפור אלא לאוכלה. **לדבר מצוה מנין** — היה צריך לטהר בו את המצורע, מנין שאסור באם על הבנים — **תלמוד לומר "תשלח".**

NOTES

"The Torah spoke in the language of human beings" (see note below, 31b).

The other opinion usually explains the use of the double verb as being an indication that we must broaden our interpretation of the verb in question and apply it to additional cases.

Our Mishnah appears to be expanding the notion of "returning" to include multiple returns, but the Gemara rejects this approach. It looks instead to the standard form of generalization, מִכָּל מָקוֹם — "in all cases." According to this explanation, the use of the double verb tells us that we are not to be restrictive in our interpretation of the verb. Hence, "returning to the owner" means not only returning the found object to the owner's hand or even to his house, but also to any other safe place belonging to him. It is important not to be confused by the word מָקוֹם in this form of exegesis. It should not be understood as meaning "place," and its appearance in the context of a passage seeking to determine to which *place* an object should be returned is purely coincidental, as we see from its repeated use in other contexts below.

שִׁילּוּחַ לִדְבַר מִצְוָה **Letting the mother bird go when she**

HALAKHAH

of the owner. "If the owner of a stolen object is aware that it has been stolen, the thief has not discharged his responsibility to return the object until the owner is aware that it has been returned. The thief need not, however, reveal his identity. If the stolen object is an animal, this rule applies even if the owner is not aware that it has been stolen." (*Shulḥan Arukh, Ḥoshen Mishpat* 395:1-2.)

שִׁלְּחָהּ וְחָזְרָה **If he let her go and she returned.** "If a person finds a mother bird sitting on a nest and he lets her go, in accordance with the Halakhah, and she returns before he can take the young, he must let her go again, even a hundred times." (Ibid., *Yoreh De'ah* 292:5.)

שִׁילּוּחַ הַקֵּן אֲפִילּוּ בִּשְׁעַת מִצְוָה **Letting the mother bird go, even when she is needed for the fulfillment of a**

TRANSLATION AND COMMENTARY

אָמַר לֵיהּ הַהוּא [1](2) The Gemara now brings another example of a similar use in the Torah of a double verb: When the Torah (Leviticus 19:17) commands us to rebuke our fellowman for his sins, it uses the double verb form: "You shall surely rebuke" *hokhe'aḥ tokhi'aḥ* (הוֹכֵחַ תּוֹכִיחַ). The Sifra (*Kedoshim* 43) appears to infer from the use of the double verb that the rebuke must be repeated as often as necessary until it achieves its purpose. Commenting on this passage in the Sifra, **one of the Rabbis said to Rava:** But how does the Sifra know that a person is required to rebuke his fellowman time after time? It is true that the verse repeats the verb and says *"hokhe'aḥ tokhi'aḥ."* [2]**But** maybe we should **say** that the word ***hokhe'aḥ*** (הוֹכֵחַ) **means "Rebuke him once,"** [3]and the word ***tokhi'aḥ*** (תּוֹכִיחַ) **means "Rebuke him twice."** On what basis does the Sifra assert that the rebuke must be administered any number of times?

אָמַר לֵיהּ [4]Rava **said to him** in reply: The word ***hokhe'aḥ*** alone **means: "Rebuke him even a hundred times** if necessary." [5]**With regard to** the seemingly superfluous word ***tokhi'aḥ,*** I can answer you by saying that it was included in order to teach us another important principle. Without the extra word *tokhi'aḥ* **I only know that a teacher must rebuke his pupil.** [6]**From where do I know that a pupil must** also **rebuke his teacher** when the teacher sins? [7]**The verse** therefore **uses** the seemingly superfluous word *tokhi'aḥ* in the expression ***hokhe'aḥ tokhi'aḥ*** to inform us that **in all cases,** even where one might have expected the Torah to distinguish between teacher and pupil, the commandment to rebuke one's fellowman applies.

עָזֹב תַּעֲזֹב עִמּוֹ [8]The Gemara now brings another example of a similar use in the Torah of a double verb: When the Torah (Exodus 23:5) commands us to assist our fellowman in unloading his animal when it collapses under its load, it uses the double verb form: **"You shall surely help with him"** — *azov ta'azov immo* (עָזֹב תַּעֲזֹב עִמּוֹ). [9]From this the Rabbis infer: Without the seemingly superfluous word *ta'azov* **I only know that** the

[1]אָמַר לֵיהּ הַהוּא מֵרַבָּנַן לְרָבָא: [2]וְאֵימָא: ״הוֹכֵחַ״ חֲדָא זִימְנָא; [3]״תּוֹכִיחַ״ תְּרֵי זִמְנֵי! [4]אָמַר לֵיהּ: ״הוֹכֵחַ״ אֲפִילּוּ מֵאָה פְּעָמִים מַשְׁמַע. [5]״תּוֹכִיחַ״ אֵין לִי אֶלָּא הָרַב לְתַלְמִיד. [6]תַּלְמִיד לָרַב מִנַּיִן? [7]תַּלְמוּד לוֹמַר: ״הוֹכֵחַ תּוֹכִיחַ״ — מִכׇּל מָקוֹם. [8]״עָזֹב תַּעֲזֹב עִמּוֹ״. [9]אֵין לִי

LITERAL TRANSLATION

[1]One of the Rabbis said to Rava: [2]But say: *Hokhe'ah* [הוֹכֵחַ — rebuke him] once; [3]*tokhi'aḥ* [תּוֹכִיחַ — rebuke him] twice.

[4]He said to him: *Hokhe'aḥ* means: [rebuke him] even a hundred times. [5][Regarding] *tokhi'aḥ*: I have only [that] the teacher [must rebuke] the pupil. [6]From where [do I know that] a pupil [must rebuke] the teacher? [7]The verse teaches: *Hokhe'aḥ tokhi'aḥ* — in all cases.

[8]"You shall surely help (*azov ta'azov*) with him" (עָזֹב תַּעֲזֹב עִמּוֹ). [9]I have only [that he

RASHI

עזב תעזוב — פריקה.

BACKGROUND

הוֹכֵחַ תּוֹכִיחַ "You shall surely rebuke." There is an explicit commandment in the Torah (Leviticus 19:17) to reprove one's fellowman. This commandment has many detailed applications, but the main point is that one should not harbor a grudge or resentment towards one's fellowman, but should tell him openly in what way he has acted wrongly. This commandment is the Biblical basis for the reproaches of the Prophets and Sages in every generation. Not only is one commanded to reprove, one must also see to it that the reproof is heeded, and that it will not put its object to shame or cause him unnecessary embarrassment. For this reason the Halakhah offers a number of practical guidelines as to whom one may reprove, when, and how.

NOTES

is needed for the fulfillment of a commandment. The Gemara (*Ḥullin* 141a) asks: Why did the Torah need to use the form of a double verb to inform us of this? Why would we imagine that the Torah would allow us to violate the prohibition of taking the mother merely in order to fulfill the commandment of purifying a leper?

The Gemara points to two possible reasons why leper purification should take precedence over sending away the mother bird: (1) Positive commandments generally supersede negative commandments (see note above, 30a). (2) Purifying a leper is an extremely important commandment, because it is needed to maintain domestic harmony in the former leper's family.

הוֹכֵחַ אֲפִילּוּ מֵאָה פְּעָמִים The word (הוֹכֵחַ) means: Rebuke him even a hundred times. The Rishonim ask: In tractate *Arakhin* (16b) the Gemara quotes the Sifra without emendation: "הוֹכֵחַ teaches us to rebuke once, while the extra word תּוֹכִיחַ teaches us to rebuke many times." How is that passage to be reconciled with the Gemara here?

Ramban and *Ran* answer that a distinction is to be made between rebuking a person repeatedly for one sin, and rebuking him for several sins. From the word הוֹכֵחַ alone we can already derive the law that one must rebuke a person repeatedly if he sins repeatedly, but it is only from the double verb that we derive the law that one must rebuke a person repeatedly for the same sin until he repents. They add that both this rule and the rule that a pupil must rebuke his teacher are derived from the double verb. The meaning of the double verb is that the Torah authorizes any kind of rebuke that is appropriate under the circumstances, regardless of who issues the rebuke or how many times it is repeated.

HALAKHAH

commandment. "It is forbidden to take the mother bird together with her young, even if one needs her for the fulfillment of a commandment, such as to purify a leper." (*Rambam, Sefer Kedushah, Hilkhot Sheḥitah* 13:19.)

מִצְוַת תּוֹכֵחָה The duty to rebuke. "If one sees one's fellowman sinning, one must rebuke him. If he accepts the rebuke, it is well. If not, he must be rebuked again, even a hundred times, until the sinner strikes the rebuker and says: 'I do not wish to hear another word.'" (*Rambam, Sefer HaMada, Hilkhot De'ot* 6:7.) "When a pupil sees his

TRANSLATION AND COMMENTARY

passerby **must help** unload the animal **when the owner** unloads together with him. [1]**From where do I know that** the passerby **must help** unload the animal even **when the owner is not** there or is unable to unload together **with him?** [2]**The verse** therefore **uses** the extra word *ta'azov* in the expression ***azov ta'azov*** to inform us that **in all cases,** even when the passerby is called upon to perform the unloading of the animal alone, he is still enjoined to do so.

הָקֵם תָּקִים עִמּוֹ [3](4) Similarly, when the Torah (Deuteronomy 22:4) commands us to assist our fellowman in loading his animal, which has fallen beneath its burden, it uses the double verb form: **"You shall surely lift them up with him"** — *hakem takim immo* (הָקֵם תָּקִים עִמּוֹ). [4]From this the Rabbis infer: Without the seemingly superfluous word *takim* **I only know that** the passerby **must lift** the load **when** the animal's **owner is** lifting together **with him.** [5]**From where do I know that** the passerby **must lift** the load **even when the** animal's **owner is not there,** or is unable to lift together **with him?** [6]**The verse** therefore **uses** the extra word *takim* in the expression ***hakem takim*** to inform us that **in all cases,** even when the passerby is called upon to perform the loading of the animal alone, he is still enjoined to do so.

וְלָמָּה לֵיהּ לְמִכְתַּב [7]The Gemara now asks: **But why does** the Torah **need to** use a seemingly superfluous word to **teach this rule both in connection with unloading and with loading?** Surely the one can be derived from the other.

צְרִיכִי [8]The Gemara answers: **Both** expressions **are needed,** because there is a special factor in each case that renders it unique. [9]**For if the Torah had only written** this rule **in connection with unloading, I might have said** that **there are** two special reasons for the obligation to assist the animal's owner in this case, even if the owner himself is not present: [10](1) The principle of avoiding **inflicting suffering on animals** exists in this case, where the animal has collapsed under its load. (2) The owner may suffer **a loss of money** if the animal is badly hurt. [11]**But in a case of loading, where there is no** problem of avoiding **inflicting suffering on animals, and no loss of money** is involved for the owner, **I might say** that assistance is required of a passerby only if the owner is present and is himself actively involved; but if not, **not.** Therefore, the Torah had to state the rule

אֶלָּא בְּעָלָיו עִמּוֹ. [1]שֶׁאֵין בְּעָלָיו עִמּוֹ מִנַּיִן? [2]תַּלְמוּד לוֹמַר: "עָזֹב תַּעֲזֹב" — מִכָּל מָקוֹם.

[3]"הָקֵם תָּקִים עִמּוֹ." [4]אֵין לִי אֶלָּא בְּעָלָיו עִמּוֹ. [5]שֶׁאֵין בְּעָלָיו עִמּוֹ מִנַּיִן? [6]תַּלְמוּד לוֹמַר: "הָקֵם תָּקִים" — מִכָּל מָקוֹם.

[7]וְלָמָּה לֵיהּ לְמִכְתַּב פְּרִיקָה, וְלָמָּה לֵיהּ לְמִכְתַּב טְעִינָה?

[8]צְרִיכִי. [9]דְּאִי כָּתַב רַחֲמָנָא פְּרִיקָה, הֲוָה אָמִינָא: [10]מִשּׁוּם דְּאִיכָּא צַעַר בַּעֲלֵי חַיִּים, וְאִיכָּא חֶסְרוֹן כִּיס; [11]אֲבָל טְעִינָה, דְּלָאו צַעַר בַּעֲלֵי חַיִּים אִיכָּא, וְלָא חֶסְרוֹן כִּיס אִיכָּא, אֵימָא לָא.

LITERAL TRANSLATION

must help when] its owner is with him. [1]From where [do I know that he must help] when its owner is not with him? [2]The verse teaches: *Azov ta'azov* — in all cases.

[3]"You shall surely lift them up (*hakem takim*) with him" (הָקֵם תָּקִים עִמּוֹ). [4]I have only [that he must lift it when] its owner is with him. [5]From where [do I know that he must help] when its owner is not with him? [6]The verse teaches: *Hakem takim* — in all cases.

[7]But why does it need to write [about] unloading, and why does it need to write [about] loading?

[8]They are needed. [9]For if the Torah had [only] written [about] unloading, I would have said: [10][It is] because there is suffering caused to animals, and there is a loss of money; [11]but [in the case of] loading, where there is no suffering caused to animals, and there is no loss of money, [I would] say not.

RASHI

הקם תקים — טעינה. **חסרון כיס** — שהבהמה מתקלקלת.

NOTES

וְלָמָּה לֵיהּ לְמִכְתַּב פְּרִיקָה, וְלָמָּה לֵיהּ לְמִכְתַּב טְעִינָה But why does it need to write both about unloading and about loading? *Rashi* explains that the question is: Why did the Torah need to write two separate verses? What essential difference is there between loading and unloading? Most Rishonim, however, find this explanation difficult to accept

HALAKHAH

teacher behaving improperly, he must rebuke him in a respectful manner, phrasing his rebuke in such a way that it sounds like an ordinary question." (*Rambam, Sefer HaMada, Hilkhot Talmud Torah* 5:9.)

מִצְוַת פְּרִיקָה וּטְעִינָה The duty to assist one's fellow in unloading and loading his animal. "If a person finds someone else's animal collapsing under its load, or if he finds someone unable to load his animal, he is commanded to assist in the loading or unloading of the animal, as the case may be. Even if the owner is not present, or is present

TRANSLATION AND COMMENTARY

in connection with loading. [1] **And,** on the other hand, **if the Torah had only mentioned** this rule **in connection with loading, I might have said** that there is a special reason for the obligation in this case to assist the owner with his animal, even if the owner himself is not present: **It is because** the passerby **is entitled to be paid** for his assistance in loading the animal. [2] **But in the case of unloading, which** must be done **for nothing, I might say** that assistance is required of a passerby only if the owner is present and is himself actively involved, but if not, **not.** [3] **Therefore, it was necessary** for the Torah to state this rule in both contexts.

וּלְרַבִּי שִׁמְעוֹן דְּאָמַר [4] **But,** asks the Gemara, **according to Rabbi Shimon who said** (below, 32a) **that loading, too,** must be done **for nothing, what is there to say?** Why should the Torah need to state the rule about the passerby's responsibility in both cases? Surely the one can be derived from the other.

לְרַבִּי שִׁמְעוֹן [5] The Gemara answers: **According to Rabbi Shimon, the Torah did not state specifically which verse** refers to loading and which to unloading. Hence, the Torah needed to write the rule in both places, for otherwise we might have taught that it applies only to unloading, because of the previously mentioned factors of (a) avoiding inflicting suffering on animals and (b) financial loss to the owner.

לָמָּה לִי לְמִכְתַּב [6] The Gemara now widens the scope of its inquiry and asks: **Why does** the Torah **need to write about** the responsibility of a passerby to help in **the two cases** of loading and unloading an animal, **as well as about** the responsibility of a person to return **a lost object?** Surely the principle in all these cases is the same: One must assist one's fellowman so that he does not suffer loss to his property.

צְרִיכִי [7] The Gemara answers: **They are** all **needed. For if the Torah had only written about** loading and unloading, [8] **I might have said** that there is an obligation to assist one's fellowman in these cases **because they involve distress for the** animal's **owner, and distress for** the animal itself, until it is loaded or unloaded

[1] וְאִי אַשְׁמְעִינַן טְעִינָה, מִשּׁוּם דְּבְשָׂכָר; [2] אֲבָל פְּרִיקָה, דְּבְחִנָּם אֵימָא לָא. [3] צְרִיכָא.

[4] וּלְרַבִּי שִׁמְעוֹן דְּאָמַר: אַף טְעִינָה בְּחִנָּם, מַאי אִיכָּא לְמֵימַר?

[5] לְרַבִּי שִׁמְעוֹן, לָא מְסַיְּיעֵי קְרָאֵי.

[6] לָמָּה לִי לְמִכְתַּב הָנֵי תַּרְתֵּי, וְלָמָּה לִי לְמִכְתַּב אֲבֵידָה?

[7] צְרִיכִי. דְּאִי כָּתַב רַחֲמָנָא הָנֵי תַּרְתֵּי, [8] מִשּׁוּם דְּצַעֲרָא דְּמָרָהּ אִיתָא, צַעֲרָא דִּידָהּ אִיתָא.

LITERAL TRANSLATION

[1] And if it had [only] taught us loading, [I would have said: It is] because it is for a wage; [2] but [in the case of] unloading, which is for nothing, [I would] say not. [3] [Therefore] it is necessary.

[4] But according to Rabbi Shimon who said [that] loading, too, is for nothing, what is there to say?

[5] According to Rabbi Shimon, the verses are not specific.

[6] Why do I need to write [about] these two, and why do I need to write [about] a lost object?

[7] They are [all] needed. For if the Torah had [only] written [about] these two, [8] [I would have said: It is] because there is distress for its owner, [and] there is distress for it.

RASHI

משום דבשכר — שנותנין לו שכר, דאיכא למאן דאמר לקמן (בבא מציעא לב,ב): טעינה בשכר פריקה בחנם. **לא מסיימי קראי** — הי משמע טעינה והי משמע פריקה, ואי כתב חדא — הוה אמינא לפריקה אתא, אבל טעינה לא, כתב רחמנא אידך לטעינה. **למה לי למכתב אבידה** — השבת אבידה לכתוב או הא או הא וליגמר מניה, דהא כולהו אזהרות ממון ישראל הוא. **צערא דמרה** — הוא העומד שם ואין יכול לטעון לבדו וכן לפרוק.

NOTES

because there are, in fact, several differences between loading and unloading, as the Gemara itself will explain (below, 32a). Our commentary follows *Tosafot* and others, who explain that the question is: Why did the Torah have to double the verb in both verses? Since the rule derived from the double verb is the same in both cases, why was one doubling not sufficient?

צַעֲרָא דִּידָהּ אִיתָא There is distress for the animal. *Ritva* asks: The Gemara appears to contradict itself. First it says that the animal suffers pain only when it needs to be unloaded, but not when it needs to be loaded. Then it says that the animal suffers pain both when it needs to be unloaded *and* when it needs to be loaded, but not when it is lost. Does the loading process involve pain for the animal or not?

He answers that there is a certain amount of pain involved when an animal is being loaded, particularly if the loading is not done properly, such as where there are not enough people to do it. However, the pain suffered by an animal collapsing under a load is much greater.

HALAKHAH

but physically unable to help, the passerby must still load or unload the animal. But if the owner is present and refuses to assist with the loading or the unloading of his own animal, the passerby is exempt." (*Shulḥan Arukh, Ḥoshen Mishpat* 272:7.)

TRANSLATION AND COMMENTARY

properly. [1]**But in the case of a lost object, which** admittedly **does involve distress** for the object's owner, but not for the lost object — because even if the lost object is an animal, it is suffering no pain — [2]**I might say** that the finder is **not** obliged to return the lost object to its owner. Therefore, the Torah had to state the rule in connection with the restoration of lost property. [3]**And,** on the other hand, **if the Torah had only mentioned** the rule **about** returning **a lost article,** [4]I might have said that there is an obligation to save another person's property specifically in this case, **because the owner is not present** where his property has been found, and only the finder can save it for him. [31B] [5]**But in these two cases** of loading and unloading, **where the owner is** normally present **with** his animal, **I might say** that the passerby is under **no** obligation to render assistance, because the owner can hire someone to assist him. [6]**Therefore it was necessary** for the Torah to state the law in all these cases.

מוֹת יוּמַת הַמַּכֶּה [7](5) The Gemara now presents another example of the Torah's use of a double verb: When the Torah (Numbers 35:21) states the law concerning the execution of murderers, it uses the double verb form: **"He that smote him shall surely be put to death"** — *mot yumat hamakkeh* (מוֹת יוּמַת הַמַּכֶּה). [8]From this the Rabbis infer: Were it not for the use of the double verb form I would **only know that** the murderer **is put to death by the** method of **execution prescribed for him** in the Torah, namely, decapitation. [9]**From where do I know that if he cannot be put to death by the** method of **execution prescribed for him** — [10]for example, if he tries to escape and can only be killed by shooting or drowning — **it is permitted to put him to death by any** method of **execution possible?** [11]**The verse uses** the double verb form ***mot yumat*** to inform us that **in all cases** the murderer is to be put to death, even if the method of execution is different from that prescribed in the Torah for this offense.

[1]אֲבָל אֲבֵידָה, דְּצַעֲרָא דְּמָרָהּ אִיתָא, וְצַעֲרָא דִּידָהּ לֵיתָא, [2]אֵימָא לָא. [3]וְאִי אַשְׁמְעִינַן אֲבֵידָה, [4]מִשּׁוּם דְּלֵיתָא לְמָרָהּ בַּהֲדָהּ. [31B] [5]אֲבָל הָנֵי תַּרְתֵּי, דְּאִיתָא לְמָרָהּ בַּהֲדָהּ, אֵימָא לָא. [6]צְרִיכָא.

[7]"מוֹת יוּמַת הַמַּכֶּה". [8]אֵין לִי אֶלָּא בְּמִיתָה הַכְּתוּבָה בּוֹ. [9]מִנַּיִן שֶׁאִם אִי אַתָּה יָכוֹל לַהֲמִיתוֹ בְּמִיתָה הַכְּתוּבָה בּוֹ, [10]שֶׁאַתָּה רַשַּׁאי לַהֲמִיתוֹ בְּכָל מִיתָה שֶׁאַתָּה יָכוֹל לַהֲמִיתוֹ? [11]תַּלְמוּד לוֹמַר: "מוֹת יוּמַת" — מִכָּל מָקוֹם.

LITERAL TRANSLATION

[1]But [in the case of] a lost object, where there is distress for its owner, but there is no distress for it, [2][I would] say not. [3]And if it had [only] taught us [about] a lost object, [4][I would have said: It is] because its owner is not with it. [31B] [5]But [in] these two [cases], where its owner is with it, [I would] say not. [6][Therefore] it is necessary.

[7]"He that smote him shall surely be put to death" (מוֹת יוּמַת הַמַּכֶּה). [8]I have only that he is put to death by the death that is prescribed for him. [9]From where [do I know] that if you cannot put him to death by the death that is prescribed for him, [10]that you are permitted to put him to death by any death by which you can put him to death? [11]The verse teaches: *Mot yumat* — in all cases.

RASHI

דליתא למרה בהדה – שיטרח בהשבתה. **דאיתיה למרה** – דכתיב "עמו", אימא יחזור אחר בני אדם וישכור. **שאם אי אתה יכול להמיתו במיתה הכתובה בו** – והיינו סייף, כגון שהיה בספינה וברח, ואתה יכול לזרוק בו חץ או לטובעו.

BACKGROUND

מוֹת יוּמַת הַמַּכֶּה "He that smote him shall surely be put to death." According to the Halakhah, there are four methods of judicial execution, depending upon the severity of the capital crime. Where the Torah states the means of execution imposed as punishment for the violation of a prohibition, this means of execution must be used. However, from the use of the double verb here we learn that the general obligation to impose the death sentence outweighs the need to carry out the specific details of the sentence. When, for any reason, it is impossible to execute the criminal in the prescribed manner, he is executed by some other method. Greater emphasis is given to murder than to other capital crimes: one must execute a murderer in any event. If he cannot be executed judicially (if, for example, he has fled), then he may be killed in any way by any person.

NOTES

דְּאִיתָא לְמָרָהּ בַּהֲדָהּ Where its owner is with it. The Rishonim ask: The Gemara appears to be contradicting itself. In the previous passage, the Gemara inferred from the use of the double verb that the commandment to assist one's fellow in loading and unloading his animal applies even if the animal's owner is not present, whereas here the Gemara assumes that the owner *is* present.

Tosafot and others answer that in the previous passage the Gemara did not consider the possibility that the owner might not be present to help load or unload the animal. The meaning of that passage is that a passerby is obliged to assist even if the owner is incapable of assisting, so that it is as if he were not present.

Ritva adds that even if the owner is not present, he is surely aware that his animal is carrying a load, and he is therefore quite capable of coming and taking care of it. Hence the Torah needed to tell us that the assistance of passersby is still required.

HALAKHAH

שֶׁאַתָּה רַשַּׁאי לַהֲמִיתוֹ בְּכָל מִיתָה That you are permitted to put him to death by any death. "If a person sentenced to death forcibly resists, so that it is impossible for the court to execute him by the method prescribed by the Torah, he may be executed by any method that is practical. If he is guilty of a crime other than murder, he must be executed by the witnesses; if that becomes physically impossible, he may not be killed at all. But if he is guilty of murder, he may be killed by anyone and by any method." (*Rambam, Sefer Shoftim, Hilkhot Sanhedrin* 14:8.)

LITERAL TRANSLATION

[1]"You shall surely smite" (הַכֵּה תַכֶּה). [2]I have only [that they are put to death] by the blow that is prescribed for them. [3]From where [do I know] that if you cannot put them to death by the blow that is prescribed for them, [4]that you are permitted to smite them with any blow with which you can [smite them]? [5]The verse teaches: *Hakkeh takkeh* — in all cases.

[6]"You shall surely return" (הָשֵׁב תָּשִׁיב). [7]I have only [that it must be returned] where he made him give a pledge with the permission of the court. [8]From where [do I know that he must return it if] he made him give a pledge without the permission of the court? [9]The verse teaches: *Hashev tashiv* — in all cases.

[1]"הַכֵּה תַכֶּה". [2]אֵין לִי אֶלָּא בְּהַכָּאָה הַכְּתוּבָה בָּהֶן. [3]מִנַּיִן שֶׁאִם אִי אַתָּה יָכוֹל לַהֲמִיתָן בַּהַכָּאָה הַכְּתוּבָה בָּהֶן, [4]שֶׁאַתָּה רַשַּׁאי לְהַכּוֹתָן בְּכָל הַכָּאָה שֶׁאַתָּה יָכוֹל? [5]תַּלְמוּד לוֹמַר: "הַכֵּה תַכֶּה" — מִכָּל מָקוֹם.
[6]"הָשֵׁב תָּשִׁיב". [7]אֵין לִי אֶלָּא שֶׁמִּשְׁכְּנוֹ בִּרְשׁוּת בֵּית דִּין. [8]מִשְׁכְּנוֹ שֶׁלֹּא בִּרְשׁוּת בֵּית דִּין מִנַּיִן? [9]תַּלְמוּד לוֹמַר: "הָשֵׁב תָּשִׁיב" — מִכָּל מָקוֹם.

TRANSLATION AND COMMENTARY

הַכֵּה תַכֶּה [1](6) Similarly, when the Torah (Deuteronomy 13:16) states the law concerning the execution of the inhabitants of an entire city convicted of committing idolatry (עִיר הַנִּדַּחַת), it uses the double verb form: **"You shall surely strike"** — *hakkeh takkeh* (הַכֵּה תַכֶּה). [2]From this the Rabbis infer: Without the use of the double verb form I **only know that they are put to death by the blow prescribed for them** in the Torah, namely, decapitation. [3]**From where do I know that if they cannot be put to death by the blow prescribed for them,** [4]**it is permissible to put them to death by any** method of **execution possible?** [5]**The verse uses** the double verb form ***hakkeh takkheh*** to inform us that **in all cases** they are to be put to death, even if the method of execution is different from that prescribed in the Torah for this offense.

הָשֵׁב תָּשִׁיב [6](7) The Gemara now presents another example of the Torah's use of a double verb: When the Torah (Deuteronomy 24:13) commands a creditor to return certain articles taken as pledges from a poor debtor, when the debtor needs them, it uses the double verb form: **"You shall surely return"** — *hashev tashiv* (הָשֵׁב תָּשִׁיב). [7]From this the Rabbis infer: Were it not for the use of the double verb form I would **only know that** the article **must be returned** in a case **where** the creditor **made** the debtor **give** it to him as **a pledge** granted **with the permission of the court,** after the creditor had begun judicial proceedings to collect the debt. [8]**From where do I know that he must return it** even **if he made** the debtor **give** it to him as **a pledge without the permission of the court?** (See note below.) [9]**The verse uses** the double verb form ***hashev tashiv*** to inform us that **in all cases** the pledge must be returned, even if the creditor took it without the permission of the court.

RASHI

הכה תכה — בעיר הנדחת. **אין לי אלא שמשכנו ברשות בית דין** — דצעק עליו בדין, ושלחו שלוחם לתפוס מטלטליו, דקרא דהשבת העבוט עליה כתיב, דכתיב לעיל מיניה "בחוץ תעמוד והאיש", ואמרינן לקמן בפרק "המקבל" (קיג,א) בשליח בית דין הכתוב מדבר. **שלא ברשות בית דין מנין** — דצריך השבה. סתם חבלה על פי בית דין היא, דלא שכיח דחליף איניש ליכנס בבית וליטול מטלטלי שלא ברשות.

NOTES

מַשְׁכּוֹן A pledge. There are two possible situations in which a creditor may demand collateral from a debtor: (1) מַשְׁכּוֹן בִּשְׁעַת הַלְוָאָה — a pledge demanded as a precondition when the terms of a loan are being negotiated, and (2) מַשְׁכּוֹן שֶׁלֹּא בִּשְׁעַת הַלְוָאָה — a pledge seized at a later date, after it becomes clear that the debtor will not be able to pay his debt on time as promised. In general, the Halakhah views the first situation as a private arrangement between creditor and debtor; and provided no other law — such as the law prohibiting interest — is violated, the Halakhah does not regulate this practice. All the laws of the Torah regarding pledges apply to the second situation, and whenever the Gemara mentions the word מַשְׁכּוֹן, it may be assumed that it is referring to the second situation, unless the context indicates otherwise.

When a creditor receives a pledge from a debtor who is unable to repay his debt, he is actually already receiving a form of payment, albeit in kind. He has no right simply to seize the pledge. He must appeal to the court, as is the case with any other form of forced payment. The court has then to assess the value of the article to be seized and collect it. The Torah requires the court's representative to show respect and to stand outside the debtor's home and ask him to produce the article. The Torah also limits the kinds of articles that can be seized, as well as the kinds of debtors from whom a pledge can be seized. Moreover, where certain articles, such as clothing, are allowed to be taken, they must be returned to the debtor every morning or every evening so that he may use them.

מִשְׁכְּנוֹ שֶׁלֹּא בִּרְשׁוּת If he made him give a pledge without

HALAKHAH

הֲשָׁבַת מַשְׁכּוֹן Returning a pledge. "A creditor who takes a pledge from a poor debtor, whether with the permission of the court or with the debtor's permission, or with no one's permission, must return it to the debtor when he

TRANSLATION AND COMMENTARY

חָבֹל תַּחְבֹּל [1] (8) Similarly, when the Torah (Exodus 22:25) commands a creditor to return a garment taken from a poor debtor as a pledge, it uses the double verb form: **"If you surely take as a pledge"** — *im ḥavol taḥbol* (אִם חָבֹל תַּחְבֹּל). [2] From this the Rabbis infer: Were it not for the use of the double verb form **I** would **only know that** the garment **must be returned** where the creditor **made** the debtor **give** it to him as **a pledge with the permission** of the court, after the creditor had appealed to the court to assist him in collecting the debt. [3] **From where do I know that he must return it** even **if he made** the debtor **give** it to him as **a pledge without the permission** of the court? [4] **The verse uses** the double verb form ***ḥavol taḥbol*** to inform us that **in all cases** the pledge must be returned, even if the creditor took it without the permission of the court.

וְהָנֵי תְּרֵי קְרָאֵי לָמָּה לִי [5] **But,** asks the Gemara, **why do we need both of these verses?** Surely they both teach essentially the same law.

חַד לִכְסוּת יוֹם [6] The Gemara answers: We need **one** verse to inform us that **a garment worn during the day** must be returned by early morning, in time for the debtor to be able to wear it during the day, **and** we need **the other** verse to inform us that **a garment worn during the night** must be returned by early evening, in time for the debtor to be able to wear it during the night (see below, 114b).

פָּתֹחַ תִּפְתַּח [7] (9) The Gemara now presents further examples of the Torah's use of double verbs: When the Torah (Deuteronomy 15:7-11) commands us to give charity and lend money to the poor, it uses several double verb forms, which the Gemara will now consider. The first double verb the Gemara considers is (Deuteronomy 15:8): **"You shall surely open** your hand" — *pato'aḥ tiftaḥ* (פָּתֹחַ תִּפְתַּח). [8] From this the Rabbis infer: Were it not for the use of the double verb form **I** would **only know that you must give** charity **to the poor of your own city.** [9] **From where do I know that you must** also **give** charity **to the poor of another city?** [10] **The verse uses** the double verb form ***pato'aḥ tiftaḥ*** to inform us that **in all cases** we must be prepared to give charity, without discriminating against the poor of other places.

[1] ״חָבֹל תַּחְבֹּל״. [2] אֵין לִי אֶלָּא שֶׁמַּשְׁכְּנוֹ בִּרְשׁוּת. [3] מַשְׁכְּנוֹ שֶׁלֹּא בִּרְשׁוּת מִנַּיִן? [4] תַּלְמוּד לוֹמַר: ״חָבֹל תַּחְבֹּל״ — מִכָּל מָקוֹם. [5] וְהָנֵי תְּרֵי קְרָאֵי לָמָּה לִי? [6] חַד לִכְסוּת יוֹם וְחַד לִכְסוּת לַיְלָה. [7] ״פָּתֹחַ תִּפְתַּח״. [8] אֵין לִי אֶלָּא לַעֲנִיֵּי עִירְךָ. [9] לַעֲנִיֵּי עִיר אַחֶרֶת מִנַּיִן? [10] תַּלְמוּד לוֹמַר: ״פָּתֹחַ תִּפְתַּח״ — מִכָּל מָקוֹם.

LITERAL TRANSLATION

[1] "[If] you surely take as a pledge" (חָבֹל תַּחְבֹּל). [2] I have only [that it must be returned] where he made him give a pledge with permission. [3] From where [do I know that he must return it if] he made him give a pledge without permission? [4] The verse teaches: *Ḥavol taḥbol* — in all cases.

[5] But why do I need these two verses?

[6] One for a day garment and one for a night garment.

[7] "You shall surely open" (פָּתֹחַ תִּפְתַּח). [8] I have only [that you must give] to the poor of your own city. [9] From where [do I know that you must give] to the poor of another city? [10] The verse teaches: *Pato'aḥ tiftaḥ* — in all cases.

RASHI

חד לכסות יום וחד לכסות לילה — בפרק ״המקבל״ (בבא מציעא קיד,ב) מפרש לקרא הכי.

BACKGROUND

חַד לִכְסוּת יוֹם וְחַד לִכְסוּת לַיְלָה One for a day garment and one for a night garment. The language of the Torah, "For that is his only covering, it is his garment for his skin: in what shall he sleep?" (Exodus 22:26), indicates that it is referring to a creditor who has impounded a garment worn at night, and he must return it by evening so that the debtor will have something in which to sleep. A parallel verse (Deuteronomy 24:13) also implies the same thing. However, the Sages said that the emphasis in the preceding phrase, "before the sun sets you shall return it to him" (Exodus 22:25), implies the duty of returning it during daytime. By extension, then, the same duty also applies to a garment needed by the debtor during the day, and a creditor must return any garment in sufficient time so that the debtor can use it when he needs it.

NOTES

permission. Taking a pledge from a debtor without the court's permission is a crime. In fact, it is a form of theft, and the creditor should be required to return the pledge forthwith. Therefore the Rishonim ask: Why did the Torah need to use a double form of a verb to teach us that such a creditor is also required to return his pledge?

Some Rishonim explain, based on a passage in tractate *Temurah* (4b-6a), that there is a difference of opinion between the Amoraim Rava and Abaye as to whether a Halakhically significant action carried out in violation of Torah law should be considered valid or not. Hence, the Torah is teaching us that in this case the pledge has effectively been seized, albeit illegally, and the regular rules apply (*Ritva*).

Rabbenu Yehonatan and *Meiri* add that since the garment was originally seized illegally, there is every reason to assume that if the creditor follows the Torah's rules and returns it to the debtor in the evening, he will not get it back the next morning. Nevertheless, the Torah tells us that the creditor must still follow the Torah's rules and return the garment.

HALAKHAH

needs it. Thus, if he seized the debtor's pillows, he must return them by the evening, and if he seized the tools of his trade he must return them by morning. When the debtor has finished using the pledge, he must give it back to the creditor until he needs it again. This applies only to a pledge seized after the time the loan was made; a pledge demanded as a precondition at the time the loan was made is not subject to these laws." (*Shulḥan Arukh, Ḥoshen Mishpat* 97:16.)

LITERAL TRANSLATION

[1] "You shall surely give" (נָתוֹן תִּתֵּן). [2] I have only [that you must give] a large gift. [3] From where [do I know that you must give] a small gift? [4] The verse teaches: *Naton titten* — in all cases.

[5] "You shall surely make him a parting gift" (הַעֲנֵיק תַּעֲנִיק). [6] I have only [that] where the house was blessed because of him a parting gift is made. [7] From where [do I know that a parting gift is made to him even if] the house was not blessed because of him? [8] The verse teaches: *Ha'anek ta'anik* — in all cases.

[9] But [according] to Rabbi Elazar ben Azaryah, who said [that if] the house was blessed because of him, a parting gift is made to him, [10] [but if] the house was not blessed because of him, a parting gift is not made [to him], [11] why do I need [the word] *ta'anik*?

[1] "נָתוֹן תִּתֵּן". [2] אֵין לִי אֶלָּא מַתָּנָה מְרוּבָּה. [3] מַתָּנָה מוּעֶטֶת מִנַּיִן? [4] תַּלְמוּד לוֹמַר: "נָתוֹן תִּתֵּן" — מִכׇּל מָקוֹם.

[5] "הַעֲנֵיק תַּעֲנִיק". [6] אֵין לִי אֶלָּא שֶׁנִּתְבָּרֵךְ הַבַּיִת בִּגְלָלוֹ מַעֲנִיקִין. [7] לֹא נִתְבָּרֵךְ הַבַּיִת בִּגְלָלוֹ מִנַּיִן? [8] תַּלְמוּד לוֹמַר: "הַעֲנֵיק תַּעֲנִיק" — מִכׇּל מָקוֹם.

[9] וּלְרַבִּי אֶלְעָזָר בֶּן עֲזַרְיָה, דְּאָמַר: נִתְבָּרֵךְ הַבַּיִת בִּגְלָלוֹ, מַעֲנִיקִין לוֹ, [10] לֹא נִתְבָּרֵךְ הַבַּיִת בִּגְלָלוֹ, אֵין מַעֲנִיקִין, [11] "תַּעֲנִיק" לָמָּה לִי?

RASHI

מתנה מועטת מנין — אם אי אפשר לך ליתן מתנה מרובה. **אין לי אלא שנתברך הבית בגללו** — דהכי כתיב קרא "אשר ברכך ה' אלהיך תתן לו", דר' אלעזר בן עזריה בקדושין (יז,ב).

TRANSLATION AND COMMENTARY

נָתוֹן תִּתֵּן [1] (10) Another double verb used by the Torah in this context is (Deuteronomy 15:10): **"You shall surely give** — *naton titten* (נָתוֹן תִּתֵּן). [2] From this the Rabbis infer: Were it not for the use of the double verb form I would **only know that you must** give charity if you can afford to **give a large gift,** sufficient to solve the recipient's economic problems. [3] **From where do I know that you must give** whatever you can afford, even if it is only **a small gift?** [4] **The verse uses** the double verb form ***naton titten*** to inform us that **in all cases,** even where the amount we can afford to give as charity is small, we must give what we can. (The third double verb in this passage of the Torah dealing with charity will be considered by the Gemara below.)

הַעֲנֵיק תַּעֲנִיק [5] (11) The Gemara now examines another example of the Torah's use of a double verb from a later verse in the same chapter (Deuteronomy 15:14): When a Hebrew slave goes free at the end of his period of service, he must be given a parting gift by his master, and the Torah uses the double verb form to express this: **"You shall surely make him a parting gift"** — *ha'anek ta'anik lo* (הַעֲנֵיק תַּעֲנִיק לוֹ). [6] From this the Rabbis infer: Were it not for the use of the double verb form I would **only know that where the house** of the master **was blessed because of** the conscientiousness and skill of the slave, **a parting gift is made** by the master to the slave when his period of service ends. This is in accordance with the continuation of the verse: "As the Lord your God has blessed you." [7] **From where do I know that a parting gift is made** to the slave **even if the house was not blessed because of him?** [8] **The verse uses** the double verb form ***ha'anek ta'anik*** to inform us that **in all cases,** even if conspicuous benefit has not accrued to the master as a result of the slave's work, a parting gift is nevertheless to be given to every Hebrew slave when his period of service ends.

וּלְרַבִּי אֶלְעָזָר בֶּן עֲזַרְיָה [9] **But,** asks the Gemara, **according to Rabbi Elazar ben Azaryah — who said that** only **if the master's house was blessed because of** the slave, is a parting gift made to him, [10] **but if the house was not blessed because of** the slave, a parting gift is not made to him, [11] **why do we need the** extra **word** ***ta'anik*?** How does Rabbi Elazar ben Azaryah explain this seemingly superfluous word?

BACKGROUND

הַעֲנֵיק תַּעֲנִיק "You shall surely make him a parting gift." This verse deals with the commandment that one must give a male or a female Hebrew slave a special gift when he or she is freed, as the Torah states: "You shall furnish him liberally out of your flock, and out of your threshing floor, and out of your winepress: of that which the Lord your God has blessed you, you shall give to him" (Deuteronomy 15:14). Rabbi Elazar ben Azaryah is of the opinion that the words "of that with which the Lord your God has blessed you" express a condition: If (and only if) the Lord has blessed you, you must give the slave a gift. However, the Sages are of the opinion that this phrase merely provides additional detail about the type of gift to be given. The master should give of the things with which he has been blessed, and this obligation is not dependent on whether or not the labor of the slave has benefited his master's household.

NOTES

מַתָּנָה מוּעֶטֶת מִנַּיִן From where do I know that you must give a small gift? The Rishonim ask: Why is it more obvious that a person should give a large gift than a small one? Surely the opposite is the case.

Our commentary follows *Rashi* and most of the Rishonim, who infer from the language of the verse that the Torah in this instance is primarily addressing the rich, who can afford to give poor people the substantial gifts they really need. Hence the Torah needs to inform us that less wealthy people must also give charity, in accordance with their means (*Ritva, Rabbenu Yehonatan,* and others; see also *Melo HaRo'im*).

Other Rishonim explain that we might have thought that charity should be restricted to the desperately poor, who need a large gift. Hence the Gemara informs us that we must

HALAKHAH

מִצְוַת הַעֲנָקָה The law of making a parting gift. "A Hebrew slave who goes free at the end of his period of service receives a parting gift from his master, consisting of livestock or fruit worth at least thirty sela'im. This applies whether or not the master profited from the work of the slave. If he *did* profit substantially, the parting gift should be increased accordingly. (*Rambam, Sefer Kinyan, Hilkhot Avadim* 3:14.)

[1]דִּבְּרָה תּוֹרָה כִּלְשׁוֹן בְּנֵי אָדָם. [2]״הַעֲבֵט תַּעֲבִיטֶנּוּ״. [3]אֵין לִי אֶלָּא שֶׁאֵין לוֹ וְאֵינוֹ רוֹצֶה לְהִתְפַּרְנֵס. [4]אָמַר רַחֲמָנָא: תֵּן לוֹ דֶּרֶךְ הַלְוָאָה. [5]יֵשׁ לוֹ וְאֵינוֹ רוֹצֶה לְהִתְפַּרְנֵס מִנַּיִן? [6]תַּלְמוּד לוֹמַר: ״תַּעֲבִיטֶנּוּ״ — מִכָּל מָקוֹם.
[7]וּלְרַבִּי שִׁמְעוֹן, דְּאָמַר: יֵשׁ לוֹ וְאֵינוֹ רוֹצֶה לְהִתְפַּרְנֵס, אֵין נִזְקָקִין לוֹ, [8]״תַּעֲבִיטֶנּוּ״ לָמָּה לִי?

LITERAL TRANSLATION

[1]The Torah spoke in the language of people. [2]"You shall surely lend him" (הַעֲבֵט תַּעֲבִיטֶנּוּ). [3]I have only [that he must lend him] where he has nothing and does not wish to support himself [from you. [4]Hence] the Torah said: Give him by way of a loan. [5]From where [do I know that he must be lent money even if] he has [resources of his own] but does not wish to support himself [from them]? [6]The verse teaches: *Ta'avitennu* — in all cases.

[7]But [according] to Rabbi Shimon, who said [that if] he has [resources of his own] and does not wish to support himself [from them], we are not bound to [help] him, [8]why do I need [the word] *ta'avitennu*?

TRANSLATION AND COMMENTARY

דִּבְּרָה תּוֹרָה [1]The Gemara answers: According to Rabbi Elazar ben Azaryah, **the Torah speaks in the** ordinary **language of people,** and the use of the double verb in this case is purely stylistic, with no special Halakhic significance.

הַעֲבֵט תַּעֲבִיטֶנּוּ [2](12) The Gemara now returns to the third double verb used by the Torah in the passage dealing with charity and the giving of loans: When the Torah (Deuteronomy 15:8) commands us to lend money to a poor person, it uses the double verb form **"You shall surely lend him"** — *ha'avet ta'avitennu* (הַעֲבֵט תַּעֲבִיטֶנּוּ). [3]From this the Rabbis infer: Were it not for the use of the double verb form I would **only know that there is an obligation to lend** money to the poor person **where** the latter **has nothing** of his own **and does not wish to support himself from** the money given him as charity. [4]**Hence the Torah said: Give him** the money he needs **in the form of a loan.** [5]**From where do I know that** a person who claims that he needs a loan **must be lent money, even if he has resources of his own but does not wish to support himself from them** and prefers to borrow from others? [6]**The verse uses** the seemingly superfluous word ***ta'avitennu*** in the expression *ha'avet ta'avitennu* to inform us that **in all cases,** even where the person asking for the loan has resources of his own, the loan must be given. If necessary, the debt can be collected later from the debtor's hoarded property.

וּלְרַבִּי שִׁמְעוֹן [7]**But,** asks the Gemara, **according to Rabbi Shimon, who said that if** a person **has resources of his own but does not wish to support himself from them, we are not bound to help him** and lend him money, [8]**why do we need the** extra **word *ta'avitennu*?** What special interpretation does Rabbi Shimon give to this seemingly superfluous word?

RASHI

שאין לו — ממה שיתפרנס. **ואינו רוצה להתפרנס** — משלך במתנה, ואמר רחמנא; **״העבט״** — דרך הלואה. **יש לו ואינו רוצה להתפרנס** — משלו, אלא משלך, מנין שאתה חייב להעביטו, וליפרע ממנו אחר מיתה — תלמוד לומר ״תעביטנו״, והכי מפרש בכתובות פרק ״מציאת האשה״ (סז,ב).

CONCEPTS

דִּבְּרָה תּוֹרָה כִּלְשׁוֹן בְּנֵי אָדָם The Torah spoke in the language of people. Despite its apparently comprehensive wording, this principle has only narrow and specific application. Frequently, double verbs are used in the Torah (e.g., שַׁלֵּחַ תְּשַׁלַּח — "you shall surely release"). According to Rabbi Yishmael and his school, such verbs have no exegetical significance, as the doubling of the verb is simply an ordinary linguistic usage ("the Torah spoke in the language of people"), whereas Rabbi Akiva and his school attempted to draw Halakhic inferences from such verb repetitions. Thus, "the Torah spoke in the language of people" is not a general principle of Biblical exegesis, as its application is limited to cases where a verb form is repeated. Indeed, this formulation of our rule is not found in the Jerusalem Talmud, where the controversy between Rabbi Akiva and Rabbi Yishmael is described thus: לְשׁוֹנוֹת כְּפוּלִין הֵן / לְשׁוֹנוֹת רִיבּוּיִין הֵן — i.e., double verbs are either "repeated expressions" (and hence exegetically insignificant) or "amplificatory expressions" (in other words, exegetically significant).

NOTES

also help people who are not in such desperate straits but still require assistance (*Rosh* and others).

Torat Ḥayyim offers an original interpretation. He explains that the Gemara's question does not center upon the obligation to give, for it is taken for granted that one is obliged to give whatever one can afford. Rather, since the verse (Deuteronomy 15:10) states that "the Lord your God will bless you" for giving charity, the Gemara asks whether God's blessing will also be granted to someone who only gives a small gift.

יֵשׁ לוֹ וְאֵינוֹ רוֹצֶה לְהִתְפַּרְנֵס Even if he has resources of his own but does not wish to support himself from them. The Gemara in tractate *Ketubot* (67b) explains this passage in detail. The Gemara says that if a desperately poor person is too proud to take charity, one should mislead him and give him charity while pretending to be extending him a loan. It is even permitted to demand collateral for the "loan" in order to maintain the pretense. Conversely, according to Rabbi Yehudah, if a person is too miserly to spend his own money and is starving as a result, one is permitted to mislead him and pretend to be giving him charity, while in fact treating the money as a regular loan. In order to maintain the pretense, the loan cannot be collected immediately, but it should be collected eventually — from the miser's estate after his death, if need be. Rabbi Shimon disagrees and says there is no religious duty to assist a miser.

HALAKHAH

יֵשׁ לוֹ וְאֵינוֹ רוֹצֶה לְהִתְפַּרְנֵס If he has resources of his own but does not wish to support himself from them. "A poor person who refuses to take charity should be given money as a loan, the repayment of which may then be waived, where appropriate. By contrast, a rich person who hoards his wealth and starves himself should not be supported, not even by means of a loan." (*Shulḥan Arukh, Yoreh De'ah* 253:9-10.)

TRANSLATION AND COMMENTARY

דִּבְּרָה תּוֹרָה [1]The Gemara answers: According to Rabbi Shimon, **the Torah speaks in the** ordinary **language of people,** and in this case too, the use of the double verb is purely stylistic, with no special Halakhic significance.

הָיָה בָּטֵל מִן הַסֶּלַע [2]The Gemara now goes on to consider the next clause of the Mishnah: **"If** the finder **wasted a sela's worth of his work time** recovering the lost object, he is entitled to compensation from the owner of the object. But **he may not say to** the owner: **'Give me the** full **sela** that I lost as a result of my efforts on your behalf.' **Instead,** the owner **must give him his wages as** if he were **a laborer."** [3]The Gemara notes that there is a parallel passage in a Baraita in which **the Tanna** adds one extra word — "unemployed" — to the wording of our Mishnah and **says:** "The owner must **give him his wages as** if he were **an unemployed laborer."**

מַאי כְּפוֹעֵל בָּטֵל [4]Regarding this the Gemara asks: **What does** the expression, **"as an unemployed laborer," mean** in this context? It usually means the amount of money that would induce a person to leave his job and do nothing. But this cannot be its meaning here, for in our case, far from doing nothing, the finder exerts himself on the owner's behalf, and may well be working almost as hard as he does in his regular job.

[1]דִּבְּרָה תּוֹרָה כִּלְשׁוֹן בְּנֵי אָדָם. [2]״הָיָה בָּטֵל מִן הַסֶּלַע, לֹא יֹאמַר לוֹ: ׳תֵּן לִי סֶלַע׳, אֶלָּא נוֹתֵן לוֹ שְׂכָרוֹ כְּפוֹעֵל״. [3]תָּנָא: ״נוֹתֵן לוֹ שְׂכָרוֹ כְּפוֹעֵל בָּטֵל״. [4]מַאי ״כְּפוֹעֵל בָּטֵל״?

LITERAL TRANSLATION

[1]The Torah spoke in the language of people. [2]"[If] he wasted [time worth] a sela, he may not say to him: 'Give me a sela,' but he gives him his wages as a laborer." [3]He taught: "He gives him his wages as an unemployed laborer." [4]What is "as an unemployed laborer"?

RASHI

מאי כפועל בטל – והלא אינו בטל שהרי טורח בהשבתה, ומתמיהין תני נותנין לו כשיעור שירצה פועל ליטול להתרפות ממלאכה ולישב בטל.

NOTES

דִּבְּרָה תּוֹרָה כִּלְשׁוֹן בְּנֵי אָדָם The Torah speaks in the ordinary language of people. In medieval Jewish philosophical literature, this statement is utilized for a different purpose — to explain that some of the difficult passages in the Torah, especially the use of anthropomorphisms, are examples of "the ordinary language of people" in which the Torah speaks. Hence, it is important to note that in the Gemara this statement is *never* used to make a general judgment on the Torah's style. As used in the Gemara, it refers only to the Torah's use of double verbs, and occasionally to double pronouns.

There is a Tannaitic dispute as to whether the use of double verbs was intended to convey additional Halakhic information, informing us of a case that we might otherwise not have included, or whether it has no Halakhic significance and was used merely for stylistic reasons, just as "in the ordinary language of people" double verbs are frequently used for stylistic reasons. (Indeed, double verbs are frequently used in the Aramaic of the Gemara for stylistic reasons.)

Several Tannaim are described, in different contexts, as maintaining that "the Torah speaks in the ordinary language of people," and at first glance their positions are not always consistent. Our Gemara, in particular, attributes this opinion to Rabbi Shimon and to Rabbi Elazar ben Azaryah. However, as *Tosafot* and other Rishonim point out, in other passages Rabbi Shimon is known to derive Halakhic information from the use of double verbs. How then can the Gemara here attribute to him the view that "the Torah speaks in the ordinary language of people"?

Tosafot answers that even according to this opinion, we do normally derive information from the use of double verbs. It is only when some other feature of the verse makes such a derivation difficult that we invoke the principle that "the Torah speaks in the ordinary language of people." Thus, in the two instances considered here, the Gemara interprets the double verb to include cases that the Torah appears to have explicitly excluded: namely, the slave who brought no blessing to the house (whereas the verse says "as the Lord your God has blessed you"), and the miser who lacks nothing but is still suffering (whereas the verse says "that which he lacks").

Other Rishonim accept *Tosafot*'s answer regarding Rabbi Shimon, but insist that Rabbi Elazar ben Azaryah never derives any information from the Torah's use of double verbs (*Ritva*). Still others maintain that Rabbi Shimon also never derives any information from the Torah's use of double verbs, and they find answers for the passages quoted by *Tosafot* (*Ramban*).

Torat Ḥayyim has an original explanation, according to which the expression "the Torah speaks in the ordinary language of people" has an unusual meaning: Even those Tannaim who normally derive information from the Torah's use of double verbs may not do so in the case of the slave and that of the miser, since a financial loss is involved. The meaning of the expression, "the Torah speaks in the ordinary language of people," is this: Just as people repeat a command a number of times to emphasize its importance and to make sure it is obeyed, so too did the Torah need to stress the importance of fulfilling these religious duties because of the financial loss involved. Hence, no further Halakhic information can be inferred from these cases.

נוֹתֵן לוֹ שְׂכָרוֹ כְּפוֹעֵל בָּטֵל He gives him his wages as an unemployed laborer. The Rishonim ask: Why must a person who returns a lost object be compensated? The law is that someone who drives away a dangerous animal which might otherwise have done damage to someone else's property, and even someone who voluntarily pays a debt for someone else, does not need to be reimbursed. Why is the person who returns a lost object treated differently?

Ramban and *Rashba* give two separate answers: (1) We must distinguish between cases where a person voluntarily goes beyond the call of duty as a favor to another person, and the returning of a lost object, which one is obliged to

¹אֲמַר אַבַּיֵי: כְּפוֹעֵל בָּטֵל שֶׁל אוֹתָהּ מְלָאכָה דְּבָטֵל מִינָּהּ. ²״אִם יֵשׁ שָׁם בֵּית דִּין, מַתְנֶה בִּפְנֵיהֶם״. ³אִיסּוּר וְרַב סָפְרָא עֲבֵיד עִיסְקָא בַּהֲדֵי הֲדָדֵי. ⁴אֲזַל רַב סָפְרָא פְּלָג לֵיהּ, בְּלָא דַּעֲתֵיהּ דְּאִיסּוּר, בְּאַפֵּי בֵּי תְרֵי. ⁵אֲתָא לְקַמֵּיהּ דְּרַבָּה בַּר רַב הוּנָא. אֲמַר לֵיהּ: ״זִיל אַיְיתִי תְּלָתָא דִּפְלַגְתְּ קַמַּיְיהוּ;

LITERAL TRANSLATION

[1]Abaye said: As a laborer unemployed from that work from which he is unemployed.

[2]"If there is a court there, he may stipulate before them." [3]Issur and Rav Safra did some business together. [4]Rav Safra went [and] divided it up, without the knowledge of Issur, in the presence of two people. [5]He came before Rabbah bar Rav Huna. He said to him: "Go [and] bring the three people before whom you divided it;

TRANSLATION AND COMMENTARY

אֲמַר אַבַּיֵי [1]**Abaye said**: The meaning of the expression here is as follows: He is paid the wages appropriate to **a laborer who stops working in one occupation** but continues in another, inferior occupation. I.e., we pay him the amount of money that would induce him to leave his regular, difficult job in order to perform the relatively easy task of returning a lost object. Thus, the amount received by the finder for his efforts in restoring lost property to its rightful owner takes into account both the difficulty of his regular work and the wage he normally earns.

אִם יֵשׁ שָׁם בֵּית דִּין [2]The Gemara now considers the next clause of the Mishnah: **"If there are** three people **present** who could constitute **a court, he may stipulate before the court** that he is recovering the object on condition that he be compensated in full for his lost time." [3]The Gemara illustrates the ruling with a story: **Issur and Rav Safra did some business together** and formed a partnership. [4]When the time came to dissolve the partnership, **Rav Safra went and divided up** the merchandise belonging to the partnership. The division was performed unilaterally by Rav Safra, **without the knowledge of Issur.** But it was done **in the presence of two** witnesses, who could testify that the division was performed equitably. [5]For some reason Issur was dissatisfied with the way the division had been performed, and the matter **came before Rabbah bar Rav Huna** for judgment. Rabbah bar Rav Huna **said to** Rav Safra: **"Go and bring the three people** — i.e., the court — **before whom you**

RASHI

כפועל בטל של אותה מלאכה דבטל מינה – כמה אדם רוצה ליטול ולפחות משכרו ליבטל ממלאכה זו כבדה שהוא עוסק בה ולעסוק במלאכה קלה כזו, הכל לפי כובד המלאכה וריבוי שכר, יש מלאכה שטורחה קל ושכרה רב, או חילוף. **פלג** – בסחורה, ולא היו מעות, אלא דבר הצריך שומא.

BACKGROUND

אִיסּוּר Issur. The Issur mentioned here appears to be the person known elsewhere in the Talmud as Issur Giyora — "Issur the Convert" — a convert to Judaism who married Raḥel, the daughter of the great Sage Shmuel. Their son was one of the Sages of the following generation: Rav Mari bar Raḥel.

We know little about Issur's life. He apparently came from the city of Neharde'a and was engaged in commerce. Issur had contact with the Jewish Sages of that period, both as a business partner (as is the case here with Rav Safra) and in other commercial dealings involving large sums of money.

NOTES

do by Torah law. (2) We must distinguish between cases where the service is intangible — such as driving away a dangerous animal which one fears may eventually cause damage, or persuading a creditor to waive a debt — and the returning of a lost object, which can be considered a tangible improvement to the owner's financial circumstances.

כְּפוֹעֵל בָּטֵל שֶׁל אוֹתָהּ מְלָאכָה As a laborer unemployed from that work. Abaye's language is somewhat cryptic here, and it may be interpreted in several ways. Our commentary follows *Rashi*. The difficulty with this explanation is that the finder is being paid for returning the object, and not just for his lost time. According to other Rishonim, Abaye answers as follows: The person returning the lost property is reimbursed as if he were a laborer no longer employed in his usual job. These Rishonim understand this answer to mean that the person returning the lost property receives the utility value of his job, the usual meaning of the expression (*Ritva, Rambam*).

Still other Rishonim suggest that the compensation received by the finder is not based on utility value at all. Instead, the finder is entitled to his full salary, but at its lowest assessment. Thus, the term "unemployed laborer" refers to a situation where workers are virtually unemployed, and, as a result, wages and prices are reduced to attract customers. Hence, Abaye is telling us that even if the object is found at a time when business is thriving, the finder is entitled only to such compensation as would be appropriate for a period of recession (*Rabbenu Ḥananel* and others).

HALAKHAH

שְׂכַר הֲשָׁבַת אֲבֵידָה Payment for returning a lost object. "If a person sees a lost object at a time when he is not working, he is obliged to return it without compensation. If he is working at the time and will suffer a loss in wages if he returns the object, he may refuse to return it, as his own loss takes precedence. If he does return the object, he may demand, as compensation for his lost wages, the utility value of his work in the occupation in which he was employed, regardless of whether the effort involved in returning the object was great or little," following *Rambam*'s interpretation of our Gemara in which "unemployed laborer" has its usual meaning. (*Shulḥan Arukh, Ḥoshen Mishpat* 265:1.) *Rema* quotes *Rashi*'s opinion, that we take into consideration the amount of effort involved in returning the object. Accordingly, the finder receives the amount he would be prepared to accept to leave his well-paid but difficult job and engage instead in the easier work of returning the lost object. *Shakh* rules, following *Rabbenu Ḥananel,* that he be paid the lowest wage that he would accept for his regular work — namely, the wage paid when business is slack and he is inactive most of the time, and prices are cut to attract customers. He is paid this even if he found the object during the peak business season.

LITERAL TRANSLATION

[1] or alternatively, [32A] two out of the three; [2] or alternatively, two witnesses that you divided [it] in the presence of three [people]."

[3] He said to him: "From where do you know this?"

[4] He said to him: "Because we have learned: 'If there is a court there, he may stipulate before them. [5] [If] there is no court there, before whom shall he stipulate? [6] His own takes precedence.'"

[7] He said to him: "Is it comparable? [8] There, since he is taking money from this one and giving [it] to that one, we require a court. [9] But here, I took my own. It is merely a revealing of the matter. [10] [The presence] of two is sufficient for it.

[1] אִי נַמִי [32A] תְּרֵי מִגּוֹ תְּלָתָא; [2] וְאִי נַמִי, תְּרֵי סַהֲדֵי דִּפְלַגְתְּ בְּאַפֵּי בֵּי תְּלָתָא״.

[3] אֲמַר לֵיהּ: ״מְנָא לָךְ הָא?״

[4] אֲמַר לֵיהּ: ״דִּתְנַן: ׳אִם יֵשׁ שָׁם בֵּית דִּין, מַתְנֶה בִּפְנֵיהֶם. [5] אֵין שָׁם בֵּית דִּין, בִּפְנֵי מִי יַתְנֶה? [6] שֶׁלּוֹ קוֹדֵם.׳״

[7] אֲמַר לֵיהּ: ״מִי דָּמֵי? [8] הָתָם, דְּמַפֵּיק מָמוֹנָא מֵהַאי וּמוֹתֵיב לְהַאי, בָּעֵינַן בֵּית דִּין. [9] אֲבָל הָכָא, דִּידִי שָׁקְלִי. גִּילּוּי מִילְּתָא בְּעָלְמָא הוּא. [10] בִּתְרֵי סַגֵּי לֵיהּ.

RASHI

תרי מגו תלתא — שנים מן השלשה יבואו ויעידו לומר שלשה היינו. **אם יש שם בית דין** — וסתם בית דין שלשה, אלמא אין כח להפקיר ממון זה אלא זה בפחות משלשה. **גילוי מילתא** — שידעו שחלקתי בשוה.

TRANSLATION AND COMMENTARY

divided the merchandise, [1] **or, alternatively,** [32A] if for some reason you cannot bring them all, bring **two out of the three** judges, and these two can testify that there was a court of three present when the merchandise was divided; [2] **or alternatively,** if this is impossible, bring **two** independent **witnesses** who can testify **that you divided it in the presence of three people.** You must follow one of these three suggestions, because a unilateral division of property by one of two partners is legally effective only if performed in the presence of a court."

אֲמַר לֵיהּ [3] When Rav Safra heard this decision, **he said to** Rabbah bar Rav Huna: **"From where do you derive this** ruling that a unilateral division must be performed in the presence of a court, and that the presence of two witnesses is not sufficient?"

אֲמַר לֵיהּ [4] Rabbah bar Rav Huna **said to** Rav Safra in reply: "**Because we have learned** in the Mishnah (above, 30b): **'If there are** three people **there** who could constitute **a court,** the finder of lost property **may stipulate before the court** that he insists on being compensated in full for his lost time. [5] **But if there is no court there, before whom can he stipulate?** What course of action should he take? [6] **His own** interests **take precedence,** and if the standard compensation is too little, he need not pick up the object.' The implication of this Mishnah is that the finder is not permitted to demand his own rate of compensation unilaterally, even in front of witnesses, because it is not possible to impose a financial obligation on another person without the express consent of the party involved, except by the authority of a court. In the same way, Rav Safra, you cannot decide unilaterally which merchandise should be yours and which should be Issur's, even if two witnesses are present when the merchandise is divided. You need a court of three people."

אֲמַר לֵיהּ [7] Rav Safra **said to** Rabbah bar Rav Huna: "**Are** the Mishnah and my case really **comparable?** [8] **There,** in the Mishnah, the purpose is **to take money from** the owner of the lost object **and give it to** the finder, as compensation for the time he has to spend in returning the object. For this, **we require a court** of three people to authorize the compensation. [9] **But here, I took what** in principle already **belonged to me** — my share of the merchandise. The presence of other people when I divided the merchandise was in order to publicize the fact that the division was performed equitably. [10] Surely, **the presence of two witnesses is sufficient for** this purpose."

TERMINOLOGY

מִי דָּמֵי Is it comparable? i.e., can the two cases be compared, when they are in fact different? Usually, having laid down the basis for rejecting a suggested analogy, the Talmud continues by explaining the difference between the two cases: ...הָתָם ...הָכָא — "There [in the first case], the situation is as follows, while here [in the second case], the situation is different...."

HALAKHAH

דִּפְלַגְתְּ בְּאַפֵּי בֵּי תְּלָתָא That you divided it in the presence of three people. "Partners who have not set a time when their partnership will end, or for whom the time set has past, must divide the shared property at the demand of either partner. If one partner is not available, the division may be performed by the other unilaterally, provided it is done in the presence of three people who form a court. These three people can be completely unlearned in Rabbinic law, provided they are trustworthy and understand property assessment. The above applies to merchandise and the like, but if there is only money to be divided, and if there is no difference in the nature or quality of the various coins, the division may be performed unilaterally, even without the presence of a court." (*Shulḥan Arukh, Ḥoshen Mishpat* 176:18.)

TRANSLATION AND COMMENTARY

[1] Rav Safra now goes on to strengthen his argument: "I can prove to you **that this is true,** and that in cases like mine a court is not necessary, for we have learned in the following Mishnah (*Ketubot* 97a): **'A widow** whose husband died leaving young children and who is being maintained from their property, **may** unilaterally **sell property** from her late husband's estate belonging to the orphans, in order to provide for her maintenance, as required by law. Moreover, she may do this even **without the presence of a court,** provided that two witnesses are present to see that the sale was performed honestly and for a fair price.' From this Mishnah we see that a person does not need the presence of a court to take property that belongs to him!"

אָמַר לֵיהּ אַבַּיֵי [2] **Abaye said to** Rav Safra: **"But was not the following** authoritative interpretation **given to** that Mishnah: **Rav Yosef bar Manyumi said in the name of Rav Naḥman:** [3] It is true that **a widow does not need a court of three experts** to be present when she sells property belonging to orphans to provide for her maintenance from her late husband's estate. **But she does** at least **need a court of** three **laymen** who are capable of assessing the property being sold and protecting the interests of the orphans. This is also the case when one partner acts on his own to dissolve a partnership. A court of three assessors must be present to protect the interests of the absent partner." From this answer of Abaye we see that in Rav Safra's case the presence of two witnesses was not sufficient. Rav Safra's action was therefore invalid.

MISHNAH מָצָאָה בָּרֶפֶת [4] **If** a person **finds** an animal **in a cattle shed, he is not responsible for** looking after **it** and is under no obligation to return it to its owner. [5] But if he finds it **in the public domain, he is responsible for** looking after **it,** and must return it to its owner. The Gemara will explain below what this section of the Mishnah adds to our understanding of the laws of restoring lost property.

[1] תֵּדַע, דִּתְנַן: ׳אַלְמָנָה מוֹכֶרֶת שֶׁלֹּא בִּפְנֵי בֵּית דִּין׳״.
[2] אָמַר לֵיהּ אַבַּיֵי: ״וְלָאו מִי אִתְּמַר עֲלַהּ: אָמַר רַב יוֹסֵף בַּר מַנְיוּמֵי אָמַר רַב נַחְמָן: [3] אַלְמָנָה אֵינָהּ צְרִיכָה בֵּית דִּין שֶׁל מוּמְחִין, אֲבָל צְרִיכָה בֵּית דִּין שֶׁל הֶדְיוֹטוֹת״.
משנה [4] מְצָאָהּ בָּרֶפֶת, אֵין חַיָּיב בָּהּ. [5] בִּרְשׁוּת הָרַבִּים, חַיָּיב בָּהּ.

LITERAL TRANSLATION

[1] Know [that this is so], for we have learned: 'A widow may sell [property] not in the presence of a court.'"

[2] Abaye said to him: "But was not [the following] said about it: Rav Yosef bar Manyumi said in the name of Rav Naḥman: [3] A widow does not need a court of experts, but she does need a court of laymen."

MISHNAH [4] [If] he found it in a cattle shed, he is not responsible for it. [5] In the public domain, he is responsible for it.

RASHI

אלמנה — הניזונת מנכסי יתומים מוכרת למזונות. **שלא בבית דין** — ובלבד שירלו שניס שלא תמכור בזול.

משנה מצאה ברפת — בגמרא מפרש מאי קאמר. היתה בבית הקברות — והוא כהן. או שאמר לו אל תחזיר — והוא במקום שהוא מותר לילך שם.

SAGES

רַב יוֹסֵף בַּר מַנְיוּמֵי **Rav Yosef bar Manyumi.** A Babylonian Amora of the third generation. He was a disciple of Rav Naḥman, and frequently quotes teachings in his name, and in that of Rav Sheshet.

BACKGROUND

בֵּית דִּין שֶׁל מוּמְחִין **A court of experts.** The beginning of tractate *Sanhedrin* contains an extensive discussion of the Jewish judicial system, from the Great Sanhedrin of seventy-one judges, which dealt with major public issues, to the courts permitted to try capital crimes.

Regarding civil suits, Rabbinic courts fall into two categories. Some civil matters involve fines — monetary punishments imposed by the court for the violation of Torah law. Cases of this kind must be tried before courts consisting only of experts — Sages properly ordained by other Sages, who have authority from the Torah to try all kinds of cases. By contrast, civil matters involving monetary disputes need not be adjudicated by experts, and three reputable laymen have the authority to form a court and pass judgment in ordinary civil suits. However, there is a difference between expert and lay courts: If an error was committed by a court of laymen, the person who was improperly judged may sue the court for damages caused by its erroneous decision.

NOTES

אַלְמָנָה מוֹכֶרֶת **A widow may sell.** The Rishonim ask: It is clear from the Gemara (*Ketubot* 97a) that a widow's right to sell the property of her late husband's estate without a court being present was granted for reasons relevant to her personal situation. How then can Rav Safra bring this Mishnah in support of his actions, where the issue is the division of property held in partnership?

The Rishonim answer: The special reasons listed in tractate *Ketubot* are necessary only because the widow has no proprietary interest in her late husband's property. Because of her special situation, the Rabbis were ready to overlook this fact and treat her as though she were a partner. A regular partner, by contrast, should be allowed to take his share by right, even without a court being present, and he does not need special dispensation (*Tosafot, Rosh, Ramban,* and others).

בֵּית דִּין שֶׁל הֶדְיוֹטוֹת **A court of laymen.** The implication of the Gemara here is that for monetary cases other than partnerships and widows' rights, a court of three experts is needed. Now, the normal meaning of the term "expert" in the Gemara is a Rabbi who has received full Rabbinical ordination and is authorized to serve as a judge by the competent authorities. Hence the Rishonim ask: The law is that in monetary cases involving debts and the like (דִּינֵי מָמוֹנוֹת) there is no need for experts, and even laymen can serve on a court. What then is special about partnerships and widows' rights?

Ramban answers that for cases involving ordinary debts

HALAKHAH

אַלְמָנָה מוֹכֶרֶת שֶׁלֹּא בִּפְנֵי בֵּית דִּין **A widow may sell property not in the presence of a court.** "A widow may take an oath and sell her late husband's real estate in order to recover the sum mentioned in her ketubah. She must do this in the presence of a court, but the court may be composed of laymen, provided they are trustworthy and understand property assessment." (*Rambam, Sefer Nashim, Hilkhot Ishut* 17:13.)

LITERAL TRANSLATION

[1] But if it was in a cemetery, he must not make himself ritually impure for it. [2] If his father said to him: "Make yourself ritually impure," or said to him: "Do not return [it]," [3] he must not listen to him.

[4] [If] he unloaded and loaded, unloaded and loaded, even four or five times, he is [still] obliged, as it is said: "You shall surely help."

[5] [If the owner] went and sat down and said: "Since the commandment is upon you, if it is your wish to unload, unload," he is exempt, as it is said: "With him." [6] If he was an elder or sick, he is obliged.

[7] It is a commandment from the Torah to unload, but not to load. [8] Rabbi Shimon says: Also to load.

[1] וְאִם הָיְתָה בְּבֵית הַקְּבָרוֹת, לֹא יִטַּמֵּא לָהּ. [2] אִם אָמַר לוֹ אָבִיו: "הִיטַּמֵּא", אוֹ שֶׁאָמַר לוֹ: "אַל תַּחֲזִיר", [3] לֹא יִשְׁמַע לוֹ.

[4] פָּרַק וְטָעַן, פָּרַק וְטָעַן, אֲפִילּוּ אַרְבָּעָה וַחֲמִישָּׁה פְּעָמִים, חַיָּיב, שֶׁנֶּאֱמַר: "עָזֹב תַּעֲזֹב".

[5] הָלַךְ וְיָשַׁב לוֹ וְאָמַר: "הוֹאִיל וְעָלֶיךָ מִצְוָה, אִם רְצוֹנְךָ לִפְרוֹק, פְּרוֹק", פָּטוּר, שֶׁנֶּאֱמַר: "עִמּוֹ". [6] אִם הָיָה זָקֵן אוֹ חוֹלֶה, חַיָּיב.

[7] מִצְוָה מִן הַתּוֹרָה לִפְרוֹק, אֲבָל לֹא לִטְעוֹן. [8] רַבִּי שִׁמְעוֹן אוֹמֵר: אַף לִטְעוֹן.

RASHI

הלך וישב לו — הבעלים. **אבל לא לטעון** — בגמרא מפרש.

TRANSLATION AND COMMENTARY

וְאִם הָיְתָה בְּבֵית הַקְּבָרוֹת [1] Turning to a new topic, the Mishnah says: **But if** a lost object **was** lying **in a cemetery,** and the person who noticed it from a distance was a priest, **he must not make himself ritually impure** by entering the cemetery to pick it up, because he is forbidden by Torah law (Leviticus 21:1) from coming into contact with corpses or being in their proximity. This prohibition, says the Mishnah, cannot be set aside in order to return a lost object to its owner. [2] **If** the priest's **father said to him:** "Go into the cemetery and **make yourself ritually impure** in order to recover the lost object and restore it to its owner," **or if** he (or a non-priest) saw the lost object in a place where a priest is permitted to pick it up and his father **said to him:** "Do not return it," [3] in such cases the son **must not listen to** his father, because it is not permitted to violate other commandments of the Torah in order to obey the commandment of honoring one's father.

פָּרַק וְטָעַן [4] Turning to a new topic, the Mishnah says: If a person discovers an animal fallen under its load, he must assist with the unloading or the loading, as the case may be. **Even if he has** already **had to unload and reload** the animal **four or five times, he is still obliged** to continue to help its owner, **as it is said** in the verse (Exodus 23:5): **"You shall surely help" — even a hundred times.**

הָלַךְ וְיָשַׁב לוֹ [5] The law requires a passerby to help load or unload a fallen animal only if the owner of the animal is himself sharing in the work. But **if the owner goes and sits down and says: "Since the commandment** to help load or unload the animal **is** incumbent **upon you, if it is your wish to unload,** by all means **unload,"** the passerby **is exempt** from doing so, **as it is said** in the same verse: "You shall surely help ***with him.***" The inclusion of the expression "with him" (עמו) emphasizes that the passerby's obligation only applies if the owner is also taking part. This exemption applies only if the owner willfully refuses to take part in loading or unloading his animal. [6] But **if** the owner **is an elder,** who would not normally be expected to involve himself in so menial a task, **or** if the owner **is sick** and thus unable to help himself, then the passerby **is obliged** to assist and even to complete the entire loading or unloading by himself.

מִצְוָה מִן הַתּוֹרָה לִפְרוֹק [7] The Mishnah now turns to another topic related to the commandment to help load or unload a fallen animal: **It is a commandment from the Torah to unload** such an animal, **but not to load it.** [8] **Rabbi Shimon says:** It is **also** a commandment **to load it.** These statements require clarification, and will be explained below in the Gemara.

NOTES

true experts are not required, but it is essential that the judges be well versed in the law. In this instance, by contrast, three laymen with no special knowledge of the law are sufficient, provided they have enough basic commercial experience to see that the widow's sale or the partner's division of assets is carried out equitably.

HALAKHAH

מִצְוַת פְּרִיקָה וּטְעִינָה **The commandment to unload and load an animal.** "If a passerby sees an animal that has fallen under its burden, and whose owner needs help in unloading or loading it, he must give the owner the assistance he requires, even if he has to do so several times. But if the owner of the animal refuses to take part in the work himself, the passerby need not assist him. If the owner is an elder or sick or otherwise physically incapable of helping himself, the passerby must do the loading or unloading by himself." (*Shulḥan Arukh, Ḥoshen Mishpat* 272:4,7.)

BACKGROUND

יָתֵר עַל מַשָּׂאוֹ More than its burden. The Sages set the limits of a normal burden which an animal can be expected to bear. Overloading an animal is considered criminal neglect. Rabbi Yose HaGelili maintains that when someone has overloaded an animal, he has deliberately acted improperly. Bystanders thus have no obligation to help him, because his negligence frees others from all responsibility and places the onus on him alone.

SAGES

רַבִּי יוֹסֵי הַגְּלִילִי Rabbi Yose HaGelili. He was a Tanna of the generation following the destruction of the Second Temple, and is not to be confused with Rabbi Yose (ben Ḥalafta), a distinguished scholar of the following generation. We do not know who the teachers of Rabbi Yose HaGelili were, but when he arrived at Yavneh he was already an important Sage. We find him in the company of Rabbi Akiva, Rabbi Tarfon, and Rabbi Elazar ben Azaryah. On several occasions he disagrees with Rabbi Akiva, who treated him with respect. Rabbi Akiva's students also regarded Rabbi Yose HaGelili as a great man capable of disagreeing with Rabbi Akiva on Halakhic matters. He applied special exegetical methods to the study of Halakhah. These methods were not unanimously accepted, but his views were followed where he lived. Most of the teachings cited in his name are Halakhic, but he was also the author of many Aggadic teachings. The Talmud in several places speaks of his virtues, especially in his relations with his fellowman, and also of his great righteousness.
Two of his sons, Rabbi Elazar and Rabbi Ḥanina, were important Sages in the following generation.

TRANSLATION AND COMMENTARY

רַבִּי יוֹסֵי הַגְּלִילִי אוֹמֵר [1]**Rabbi Yose HaGelili says:** Sometimes the owner of an animal is himself responsible for making it collapse under its load, and in such cases a passerby need not help. **If** the animal **was bearing more than its** normal **load,** then the passerby **is under no obligation towards** the owner to get involved with it, as the problem has been caused by the owner's own negligence, [2]**as it is said** in the same verse that the animal must be **"lying under *its* burden."** This means that the passerby need only assist with the loading and unloading of **a burden that** the animal **can bear,** but not where the load is excessive.

GEMARA אָמַר רָבָא [3]The Gemara begins its analysis of the Mishnah by considering the first clause: **Rava said: The cattle shed that is spoken of** in the Mishnah is a rudimentary one. It **does not cause the animal to stray, but** also **does not protect** it from straying. [4]Rava goes on to explain: We know that **it does not cause the animal to stray, from the fact that the Mishnah says** that the finder **is not responsible for** looking after **it,** which implies that there is no absolute certainty that the animal will stray. [5]**And** we know that **it does not** completely **protect** the animal from straying, **from the fact that** the Mishnah **needed to say** that the finder **is not responsible for** looking after **it.** [6]**For if it should enter your mind** to think **that this** cattle shed **is** capable of **protecting** the animal from straying, the whole clause would be superfluous, as we have already established (above, 31a) that [7]**if he were to find** a lost animal **outside** a secure cattle shed he would fulfill his obligation to its owner by **bringing it inside,** since a person who finds a lost object does not need to inform the owner that he has returned it; it is sufficient for him merely to bring it to the owner's garden or, by extension, to his cattle shed. [8]Hence, **if he finds** the animal ***inside*** the owner's secure cattle shed, **is it necessary** for the Mishnah **to say that he is not responsible for it?** Obviously he has no obligation, and indeed no business meddling with it. [9]Thus, we can **conclude from this** argument **that** we are dealing here with a rudimentary kind of shed — one that **does not protect** animals from straying — and the Mishnah is informing us that even so the finder has no obligation to look after an animal he finds in such a shed. [10]The Gemara completes the argument by saying: **We may indeed so conclude.**

מְצָאָהּ בָּרֶפֶת [11]The Gemara now considers another aspect of this clause of the Mishnah. The Mishnah states: "If a person **finds** an animal **in a cattle shed, he is not responsible for** looking after **it,** and is under no obligation

[1]רַבִּי יוֹסֵי הַגְּלִילִי אוֹמֵר: אִם הָיָה עָלָיו יָתֵר עַל מַשָּׂאוֹ, אֵין זָקוּק לוֹ, [2]שֶׁנֶּאֱמַר: ״תַּחַת מַשָּׂאוֹ״, מַשּׂאוּי שֶׁיָּכוֹל לַעֲמוֹד בּוֹ.

גמרא [3]אָמַר רָבָא: רֶפֶת שֶׁאָמְרוּ אֵינָהּ מַתְעָה וְאֵינָהּ מְשַׁמֶּרֶת. [4]אֵינָהּ מַתְעָה, מִדְּקָתָנֵי: ״אֵינוֹ חַיָּיב בָּהּ״. [5]וְאֵינָהּ מְשַׁמֶּרֶת, מִדְּאִיצְטְרִיךְ לְמִיתְנֵי: ״אֵינוֹ חַיָּיב בָּהּ״. [6]דְּאִי סָלְקָא דַּעְתָּךְ מְשַׁמֶּרֶת, [7]הָשְׁתָּא מַשְׁכַּח לָהּ אַבְּרָאֵי, מְעַיֵּיל לָהּ לְגַוָּאֵי, [8]מַשְׁכַּח לָהּ מִגַּוָּאֵי, מִבַּעְיָא!? [9]אֶלָּא, שְׁמַע מִינָּהּ: אֵינָהּ מְשַׁמֶּרֶת. [10]שְׁמַע מִינָּהּ.

[11]״מְצָאָהּ בָּרֶפֶת, אֵינוֹ חַיָּיב״.

LITERAL TRANSLATION

[1]Rabbi Yose HaGelili says: If there was on it more than its burden, he is under no obligation towards him, [2]as it is said: "Under *its* burden," a burden that it can bear.

GEMARA [3]Rava said: The cattle shed that they spoke of does not cause [the animal] to stray, but does not guard. [4]It does not cause [the animal] to stray, from [the fact] that it is taught: "He is not responsible for it." [5]And it does not guard, from [the fact] that it needed to teach: "He is not responsible for it." [6]For if it should enter your mind [that it] guards, [7]now [if] he finds it outside, he brings it inside, [8][if] he finds it inside, is it necessary [to say that he is not responsible for it]? [9]Rather, conclude from this [that] it does not guard. [10]Conclude from it.

[11]"[If] he found it in a cattle shed, he is not responsible [for it]."

RASHI

גמרא רפת שאמרו – שנינו במשנתנו, עסקינן כשאינה מתעה את הבהמה שבתוכה להיות בורחת ויוצאת. ואינה משתמרת – שאינה נעולה, ואם באת לצאת – יוצאה. מעייל לגואי – כדאמרינן לעיל (לא,א): לגינתו ולחורבתו מנין.

NOTES

אֵינָהּ מַתְעָה וְאֵינָהּ מְשַׁמֶּרֶת It does not cause the animal to stray, but it does not guard. *Meiri* explains this phrase as follows: The animal cannot escape from the shed easily, but it can escape with a little effort. *Ritva,* elaborating on *Rashi,* explains that there is nothing preventing the animal from wandering away or being stolen, but there is sufficient food in the shed to make it unlikely that the animal will stray.

TRANSLATION AND COMMENTARY

to return it." [1]Commenting on this clause, **Rabbi Yitzḥak said: This** law **applies provided that** the cattle shed **is standing within the city limits,** because the whole environment is protective. But if the cattle shed was outside the city limits, the finder would have to return the animal, because the environment is not protective. [2]On this the Gemara remarks: **This** statement of Rabbi Yitzḥak **proves by implication that** if the animal is found **in the public domain** and not in a cattle shed, then **even** if the animal is **within the city limits,** the finder **is also obliged** to look after it and return it as, according to Rabbi Yitzḥak, the reason why the Mishnah mentioned the case of the cattle shed was to distinguish between the private domain and the public domain in the city.

אִיכָּא דְּמַתְנֵי לָהּ אַסֵּיפָא [3]The Gemara now notes that **there are some** authorities **who transmit** Rabbi Yitzḥak's statement **in connection with the latter clause** of the Mishnah, leading us to conclude that the distinction made by the Mishnah between a cattle shed and the public domain applies specifically *outside* the city. In the latter clause the Mishnah states: "But if he finds the animal **in the public domain, he is responsible for** looking after **it** and returning it to its owner." [4]Commenting on this clause, **Rabbi Yitzḥak said: This** law **applies provided that** the animal **is standing** on a main road **outside the city limits,** implying that if the animal was found in a city street, the finder would not have to return it. [5]On this the Gemara remarks: **This** statement of Rabbi Yitzḥak **proves by implication that** if the animal is found **in a cattle shed** and not in the public domain, then **even if** the cattle shed **is standing outside the city limits,** the finder **is also not responsible for** looking after the animal and returning **it**.

בְּבֵית הַקְּבָרוֹת לֹא יִטַּמֵּא לָהּ [6]The Gemara now considers the next clause of the Mishnah: **"If** a lost object **was** lying **in a cemetery,** a priest **must not make himself ritually impure** by entering the cemetery to pick it up." [7]**Our Sages taught** the following Baraita, which elaborates on the law of the Mishnah and provides sources in the Torah for it: **"From where do we know that if** the priest's **father said to him:** 'Go into the cemetery and **make yourself ritually impure,** in order to recover the lost object and restore it to its owner, or in general if his father **said to him**: **'Do not return it,' that** in such cases the son **must not listen to** his

[1]אָמַר רַבִּי יִצְחָק: וְהוּא שֶׁעוֹמֶדֶת תּוֹךְ לַתְּחוּם. [2]מִכְּלָל דִּבִרְשׁוּת הָרַבִּים, וַאֲפִילּוּ בְּתוֹךְ הַתְּחוּם, נַמִי חַיָּיב.
[3]אִיכָּא דְּמַתְנֵי לָהּ אַסֵּיפָא: "בִּרְשׁוּת הָרַבִּים חַיָּיב בָּהּ". [4]אָמַר רַבִּי יִצְחָק: וְהוּא שֶׁעוֹמֶדֶת חוּץ לַתְּחוּם. [5]מִכְּלָל דְּבָרֶפֶת, אֲפִילּוּ עוֹמֶדֶת חוּץ לַתְּחוּם, נַמִי אֵינוֹ חַיָּיב בָּהּ.
[6]"בְּבֵית הַקְּבָרוֹת לֹא יִטַּמֵּא לָהּ". [7]תָּנוּ רַבָּנַן: "מִנַּיִן שֶׁאִם אָמַר לוֹ אָבִיו: 'הִיטַּמֵּא', אוֹ שֶׁאָמַר לוֹ: 'אַל תַּחֲזִיר', שֶׁלֹּא

LITERAL TRANSLATION

[1]Rabbi Yitzḥak said: And this is [provided] that it is standing within the city limits. [2][This proves] by implication that in the public domain, even within the city limits, he is also obliged.

[3]There are [some] who teach it about the latter clause: "In the public domain, he is responsible for it." [4]Rabbi Yitzḥak said: And this is [provided] that it is standing outside the city limits. [5][This proves] by implication that in a cattle shed, even if it is standing outside the city limits, he is also not responsible for it.

[6]"[If it was] in a cemetery, he may not make himself ritually impure for it." [7]Our Sages taught: "From where [do I know] that if his father said to him: 'Make yourself ritually impure,' or said to him: 'Do not return [it],' that he must not

RASHI

ברישא גרסינן — והוא שעומדת בתוך לתחום, בסיפא גרסינן: והוא שעומדת חוץ לתחום.

NOTES

אָמַר לוֹ אָבִיו: 'הִיטַּמֵּא' If his father said to him: "Make yourself ritually impure." The Rishonim ask: Honoring one's parents means taking care of their needs: cooking for them, dressing them, etc. It does not mean obeying

HALAKHAH

מְצִיאַת פָּרָה Finding a cow. If a person finds a cow on the public highway outside the boundary of a city, he is obliged to return it. If he finds it grazing in a cattle shed within the boundary of a city — even if the shed would not prevent the cow from escaping if it wished, provided that it does not actually cause the animal to stray — he should not meddle with it. If the shed is outside the boundary of the city, the *Shulḥan Arukh* rules that he should not meddle with it there either, following the latter version of Rabbi Yitzḥak's teaching. *Rema* rules that he should return it, following *Rosh* who rules in favor of the stricter first version of Rabbi Yitzḥak's statement. But *Rema* concludes that in practice there is very little difference between the two rulings, as circumstances must be given overriding consideration; if the animal appears lost, it should be returned even in a city. If it is obviously not lost, it should be left alone even outside a city. (*Shulḥan Arukh, Ḥoshen Mishpat* 261:3.)

אָמַר לוֹ אָבִיו לַעֲבוֹר עַל דִּבְרֵי תוֹרָה If his father told him to

יִשְׁמַע לוֹ? [1]שֶׁנֶּאֱמַר: ׳אִישׁ אִמּוֹ וְאָבִיו תִּירָאוּ, וְאֶת שַׁבְּתוֹתַי תִּשְׁמֹרוּ; אֲנִי ה׳׳ — כּוּלְּכֶם חַיָּיבִין בִּכְבוֹדִי״.

[2]טַעְמָא דִּכְתַב רַחֲמָנָא: ״אֶת שַׁבְּתוֹתַי תִּשְׁמֹרוּ״. [3]הָא לָאו הָכִי, הֲוָה אָמִינָא: צַיְיתָא לֵיהּ. [4]וְאַמַּאי? הַאי עֲשֵׂה וְהַאי לֹא תַעֲשֶׂה וַעֲשֵׂה, [5]וְלֹא אָתֵי עֲשֵׂה וְדָחֵי אֶת לֹא תַעֲשֶׂה וַעֲשֵׂה!

TRANSLATION AND COMMENTARY

father?" [1]The Baraita answers: "There is a source for this law in the Torah, **as it is said** (Leviticus 19:3): **'You shall fear every man his mother and his father, and you shall keep my Sabbaths, I am the Lord.'** The additional emphasis at the end of the verse — 'I am the Lord' - means that **all of you are obliged,** before *any* other duty, **to honor Me;** any respect you may owe each other must be subordinated to My commands."

טַעְמָא דִּכְתַב רַחֲמָנָא [2]The Gemara now asks: It is apparent from this Baraita that **the reason** for the rule that the observance of other commandments supersedes the commandment to honor one's parents **is that the Torah wrote** the expression: **"You shall keep my Sabbaths"** in juxtaposition to the expression: "You shall fear every man his mother and his father." [3]Thus, argues the Gemara, it follows that **if it had not been for this** verse, **I would have said** in the case where the father instructs his son not to return a lost object: **Obey** your father and refrain from returning the lost object. [4]**But why,** asks the Gemara, should we think in such a way? Surely, obedience to one's father **is a** single **positive commandment,** whereas returning a lost object **is both a negative and a positive commandment** (see above, 26b), [5]**and** we know (see above, 30a) that **a positive commandment does not supersede** a law supported by both a negative and a positive commandment! In other words, even without the juxtaposition of the commandent to observe the Sabbath next to the commandment to fear and respect one's parents, we would already know that the son is enjoined to disregard his father's instructions not to return a lost object to its owner.

LITERAL TRANSLATION

listen to him? [1]As it is said: 'You shall fear every man his mother and his father, and you shall keep My Sabbaths; I am the Lord' — all of you are obliged to honor Me."

[2]The reason is that the Torah wrote: "You shall keep My Sabbaths." [3]But [if it had] not [been for] this, I would have said: Obey him. [4]But why? This is a positive commandment and that is [both] a negative commandment and a positive commandment, [5]and a positive commandment does not come and supersede a negative commandment and a positive commandment!

RASHI

אני ה׳ — אף על פי שאמרתי לך ירא את אביך — אני אדון לשניכם ואם אמר לך אביך ״עבור על דברי לחלל שבת״ — אל תשמע לו. הוה אמינא צייתא ליה — דאתי עשה דכיבוד ודחי לא תעשה ד״לא תוכל להתעלם״. אבידה עשה ולא תעשה היא — ״השב תשיבם״ ״לא תוכל להתעלם״.

NOTES

commands that have nothing to do with their personal requirements. Hence, why should one imagine that the son might have to obey a parental command to make himself ritually impure?

The Rishonim answer that, in the case referred to, the father had some personal interest in the cemetery — perhaps the object there was one the father wanted. Similarly, when the father tells the son not to return a lost object, we have to assume that he wants the son to do something else instead (*Ramban, Rashba,* and others).

וְאֶת שַׁבְּתוֹתַי תִּשְׁמֹרוּ **And you shall keep My Sabbaths.** The Rishonim ask: The verse states that one must both honor one's parents and observe the Sabbath. How do we know which takes precedence? Perhaps the Torah is telling us not to observe the Sabbath if that interferes with one's filial responsibilities!

They explain that the answer is to be found in the last phrase in the verse — "I am the Lord" — which teaches us that God's commands must be paramount.

Nevertheless, there is still room to ask: How can we be sure that this latter phrase is intended to emphasize the importance of Sabbath observance? Perhaps it is intended to emphasize the importance of honoring one's parents, which is also a Divine command! (It is possible to prove from a parallel verse [Leviticus 19:30], comparing reverence for the Temple and Sabbath observance, that the order of the phrases is immaterial.)

Rosh answers that it is observance of the Sabbath, and not any other commandment, however important, that is the symbol of the honor and reverence due to God, since the Sabbath was instituted to remind us of God's creation of the world.

עֲשֵׂה וְלֹא תַעֲשֶׂה וַעֲשֵׂה **A positive commandment versus a negative and a positive commandment.** Our commentary follows *Rashi*, who explains that it is the returning of a lost object that is described as being both a positive and a negative commandment.

Rashba objects to this explanation, as the positive

HALAKHAH

violate the laws of the Torah. "If a person's father told him to violate a law of the Torah, whether the law in question was a positive commandment or a negative commandment, or even a Rabbinic commandment, he must not obey him." (*Shulḥan Arukh, Yoreh De'ah* 240:15.)

[1] אִיצְטְרִיךְ, סָלְקָא דַּעְתָּךְ אָמִינָא: הוֹאִיל וְהוּקַּשׁ כִּיבּוּד אָב וָאֵם לִכְבוֹדוֹ שֶׁל מָקוֹם — [2] שֶׁנֶּאֱמַר כָּאן: ״כַּבֵּד אֶת אָבִיךָ וְאֶת אִמֶּךָ״, וְנֶאֱמַר לְהַלָּן: ״כַּבֵּד אֶת ה׳ מֵהוֹנֶךָ״ — [3] הִלְכָּךְ, לְצַיֵּית לֵיהּ. [4] קָא מַשְׁמַע לָן דְּלָא לִשְׁמַע לֵיהּ.

[5] ״מִצְוָה מִן הַתּוֹרָה לִפְרוֹק, אֲבָל לֹא לִטְעוֹן״. [6] מַאי ״אֲבָל לֹא לִטְעוֹן״? [7] אִילֵימָא ״אֲבָל לֹא לִטְעוֹן כְּלָל״, מַאי שְׁנָא פְּרִיקָה? דִּכְתִיב: ״עָזֹב תַּעֲזֹב עִמּוֹ״? [8] טְעִינָה נַמִּי, הָכְתִיב: ״הָקֵם תָּקִים עִמּוֹ״!

LITERAL TRANSLATION

[1] It was necessary, [otherwise] it might have entered your mind to say: Since the honoring of [one's] father and mother was compared to the honoring of God (lit., "Place") — [2] for it is said here: "Honor your father and your mother," and it is said there: "Honor the Lord with your substance" — [3] therefore, he must obey him. [4] [Hence] it tells us that he must not listen to him.

[5] "It is a commandment from the Torah to unload, but not to load." [6] What [does] "but not to load" [mean]? [7] If we say "but not to load at all," what is different about unloading? Because it is written: "You shall surely help with him"? [8] [With regard to] loading also, surely it is written: "You shall surely lift them up with him"!

RASHI

הוקש כבודם — בגזירה שוה, ״כבד את אביך״ ״כבד את ה׳ מהונך״.

TRANSLATION AND COMMENTARY

אִיצְטְרִיךְ [1] The Gemara answers: The special verse was still **necessary for otherwise it might have entered your mind to say: Since the honoring of one's father and mother was compared** by Scripture **to the honoring of God** — [2] **for in one place** a verse **says** (Exodus 20:12): **"Honor your father and your mother,"** and **in another place** a verse **says** (Proverbs 3:9): **"Honor the Lord with your substance,"** using the same word "honor" (כַּבֵּד) in both places to emphasize that one must honor both God and one's parents — [3] **therefore** I might perhaps have drawn the mistaken conclusion that the son **must obey** his father even when instructed to commit a transgression. [4] **Hence,** concludes the Gemara, the juxtaposition in the verse from Leviticus (19:3) is needed to **inform us that** the son **must not heed** his father when he instructs him to violate a commandment of the Torah.

מִצְוָה מִן הַתּוֹרָה לִפְרוֹק [5] The Gemara now considers a later clause of the Mishnah: **"It is a commandment from the Torah to unload a fallen animal, but not to load it."** [6] The Gemara asks: **What does** the Mishnah **mean** by the expression **"but not to load"**? [7] **If we say** that it means what it appears to mean — "there is a commandment to unload, **but** there is **no** commandment **at all to load"** — this is impossible. After all, **what is different about** the case of **unloading, about which the verse says** (Exodus 23:5): **"You shall surely help with him"** to unload his fallen animal? [8] **With regard to loading, also, the verse says** (Deuteronomy 22:4): **"You shall surely lift them up with him"!** From this verse we clearly see that the Torah imposes an obligation to load as well as to unload, so the Mishnah cannot be understood in the way suggested above!

BACKGROUND

כִּיבּוּד אָב וָאֵם The honoring of one's father and mother. The duty to honor one's father and mother is one of the Ten Commandments and one of the most important laws in the Torah. The Sages said that a person has three partners in his creation: his father, his mother, and the Holy One, blessed be He. Therefore he has the duty to honor them all. Or, as the medieval Rabbinic scholar Abraham Ibn Ezra says, a man is obliged to honor the source and root of his creation. Thus the equation of honoring parents and honoring God is based not only on the words of Scripture but also on an essential aspect common to these duties.

NOTES

commandment does not apply until the finder actually takes possession of the lost article (see above, 26b), and this will never occur if the son obeys his father and ignores the object. *Rashba* explains instead that the statement here refers to the prohibition against a priest contracting ritual impurity from contact with a dead body.

Rosh objects to *Rashba*'s explanation as well, since it is by no means clear that the priestly obligations are to be treated like regular positive and negative commandments. *Rosh* explains instead that the statement about "a positive and a negative commandment" refers to the observance of the Sabbath.

הוּקַּשׁ כִּיבּוּד אָב וָאֵם לִכְבוֹדוֹ שֶׁל מָקוֹם The honoring of one's father and mother was compared to the honoring of God. The Rishonim ask: Even if we were to equate the honor due to one's parents to that due to God, how could it ever enter our minds that the former could supersede the latter?

Rav Yosef of Jerusalem explains that one might indeed have the option of choosing between the two (quoted by *Ritva* and others).

Rosh states that since honoring one's parents is a commandment, it also possesses a dimension of honoring God. Therefore, one might assume that it could be given priority in practice, even if it were only equal in theory. He also quotes the Jerusalem Talmud (*Pe'ah* 1:1), which states that in a certain sense honoring one's parents is greater than honoring God.

כַּבֵּד אֶת ה׳ מֵהוֹנֶךָ Honor the Lord with your substance. Generally, the Talmud finds it preferable to provide support for a concept by a reference from the Torah itself, rather than from the other books of the Bible. Nevertheless, this verse from Proverbs was chosen — although there are verses from the Torah itself that establish a comparison between fear of God and fear of one's parents — because the Gemara preferred to refer to the concept of honor rather than to that of fear, as the commandment to honor one's parents is stated in the Ten Commandments themselves (*Rosh*).

[1]אֶלָּא, מִצְוָה מִן הַתּוֹרָה לִפְרוֹק בְּחִנָּם, וְלֹא לִטְעוֹן בְּחִנָּם, אֶלָּא בְּשָׂכָר. [2]רַבִּי שִׁמְעוֹן אוֹמֵר: אַף לִטְעוֹן בְּחִנָּם.

[3]תָּנֵינָא לְהָא דְּתָנוּ רַבָּנַן: "פְּרִיקָה בְּחִנָּם; טְעִינָה בְּשָׂכָר. [4]רַבִּי שִׁמְעוֹן אוֹמֵר: זוֹ וָזוֹ בְּחִנָּם".

[5]מַאי טַעֲמַיְיהוּ דְּרַבָּנַן? [6]דְּאִי סָלְקָא דַּעְתָּךְ כְּרַבִּי שִׁמְעוֹן, לִכְתּוֹב רַחֲמָנָא טְעִינָה, וְלָא בָּעֵי פְּרִיקָה, [7]וַאֲנָא אָמֵינָא: וּמַה טְעִינָה, דְּלֵית בָּהּ צַעַר בַּעֲלֵי חַיִּים וְלֵיכָּא חֶסְרוֹן כִּיס, חַיָּיב, [8]פְּרִיקָה, דְּאִית בָּהּ צַעַר בַּעֲלֵי חַיִּים וְחֶסְרוֹן כִּיס, לֹא כָּל שֶׁכֵּן! [9]אֶלָּא, לְמַאי הִלְכְתָא כְּתָבֵיהּ רַחֲמָנָא? [10]לוֹמַר לָךְ: פְּרִיקָה, בְּחִנָּם; טְעִינָה, בְּשָׂכָר. [11]וְרַבִּי שִׁמְעוֹן, מַאי טַעְמָא?

LITERAL TRANSLATION

[1]Rather, it is a commandment of the Torah to unload for nothing but not to load for nothing, but for a wage. [2]Rabbi Shimon says: Loading, too, [must be done] for nothing.

[3]We have learned this, as our Sages taught: "Unloading [must be done] for nothing; loading, for a wage. [4]Rabbi Shimon says: 'This and this' [must be done] for nothing."

[5]What is the reason of the Rabbis?

[6]Because if it entered your mind [to think that it is] as Rabbi Shimon [maintains], let the Torah write [about] loading, and it does not need unloading, [7]and I would say: If [in the case of] loading, in which there is no suffering caused to animals and there is no loss of money, he is obliged [to do it], [8]unloading, in which there is suffering caused to animals and loss of money, how much more so! [9]But, for what law did the Torah write it? [10]To say to you: Unloading [must be done] for nothing; loading, for a wage.

[11]And Rabbi Shimon, what is [his] reason?

TRANSLATION AND COMMENTARY

אֶלָּא [1]**Rather,** answers the Gemara, this is how the Mishnah should be understood: **It is a commandment of the Torah to unload** a fallen animal **without charge, but** there is **no** obligation **to load** the animal **without charge;** even though the Torah requires the passerby to help load the animal, the loading may be done **for a fee.** The passerby can demand to be reimbursed for his time. [2]**Rabbi Shimon** disagrees and **says: Loading, too, must be done without charge.**

תָּנֵינָא לְהָא דְּתָנוּ רַבָּנַן [3]On this the Gemara remarks: **We have learned** in our Mishnah a law that **our Sages taught** explicitly in the following Baraita: **"Unloading** a fallen animal **must be done without charge; loading** may be done **for a fee.** [4]**Rabbi Shimon says: Both** unloading and loading **must be done without charge."**

מַאי טַעֲמַיְיהוּ דְּרַבָּנַן [5]The Gemara now asks: **What is the reasoning of the Rabbis** who disagree with Rabbi Shimon and distinguish between loading and unloading?

דְּאִי סָלְקָא דַּעְתָּךְ [6]The Gemara answers: Their reasoning is as follows: **If it entered your mind to think that** the law **is as Rabbi Shimon maintains,** i.e., that loading and unloading have the same status and must both be performed without charge, **the Torah needed only to write about loading and** then **it would not have needed** to write about **unloading,** and we could have inferred the one from the other. [7]For even if the Torah had written nothing about unloading, **I would have said: If in the case of loading** a fallen animal, **where there is no suffering** being **caused to the animal and there is no financial loss** to the owner, the passerby **is obliged** to help, [8]in the case of **unloading** an animal, where the animal *is* suffering and there is a possibility of financial loss if the animal is injured, **how much more so** is the passerby obliged to help! [9]This being the case, **for** what special purpose — to teach **what** particular **law — did the Torah write** explicitly about unloading? [10]To teach us that there is a difference between the laws, namely, **to say to us: Unloading must be done without charge,** but **loading** may be done **for a fee.**

וְרַבִּי שִׁמְעוֹן, מַאי טַעְמָא [11]The Gemara now turns to the viewpoint of Rabbi Shimon and asks: **What is Rabbi Shimon's reasoning?** Surely, from his point of view, the Torah could have stated only the law concerning loading, and we could have inferred the law concerning unloading from it!

RASHI

דלית ביה חסרון כיס – אם לא יטעון. **פריקה אית בה חסרון כיס** – שהבהמה נשברת תחת משאה. **לומר לך פריקה בחנם** – אבל טעינה לא נצטוית אלא בשכר, הלכך, אי לא כתב פריקה ואתיא מקל וחומר מטעינה, הוה אמינא: דיו לבא מן הדין להיות כנדון, מה טעינה בשכר – אף פריקה בשכר.

HALAKHAH

פְּרִיקָה בְּחִנָּם טְעִינָה בְּשָׂכָר Unloading must be done for nothing. Loading may be done for a wage. "The Torah requires that the unloading of an animal be done without charge, but for loading an animal a reasonable fee may be charged," following the view of the Sages. (*Shulḥan Arukh, Ḥoshen Mishpat* 272:6.)

TRANSLATION AND COMMENTARY

מִשּׁוּם דְּלָא מְסַיְּימֵי קְרָאֵי [1]The Gemara answers: Rabbi Shimon does not agree that the Torah could have stated the law concerning loading alone, **because the verses are not explicit,** and it is impossible to tell which verse refers to loading and which to unloading. Hence, if the Torah had only stated the one verse, I might have assumed that it was referring to unloading, where the animal is suffering and there may be financial loss to the owner. It is only the presence of both verses that enables me to establish that there is an obligation to load as well as to unload.

וְרַבָּנַן [2]The Gemara now asks: In the light of this answer, what do **the Rabbis** say?

אַמַּאי לָא מְסַיְּימֵי קְרָאֵי [3]The Gemara answers: **Why** should you say that **the verses are not explicit?** From the context it is quite obvious which verse refers to unloading and which to loading. [4]**Here,** in Exodus, the Torah **uses the expression** "lying under its burden," implying that the load is on the animal, that it is collapsing under it, and that help is needed to unload it. [5]Whereas **there,** in Deuteronomy, the Torah **uses the expression "falling down by the way," implying that both** the animals **and their burdens are thrown on the road,** and that help is needed to reload them.

וְרַבִּי שִׁמְעוֹן [6]The Gemara now asks: In the light of this answer, what does **Rabbi Shimon** say?

נוֹפְלִין בַּדֶּרֶךְ [7]The Gemara answers: The expression **"falling down by the way"** does not mean that the animals have become separated from their burdens. It **means that** the animals **have fallen with their burdens still on them,** so that help is needed to unload them.

אָמַר רָבָא [8]The Gemara now begins a discussion of a subject that was raised in passing in the previous passage — suffering caused to animals (צַעַר בַּעֲלֵי חַיִּים). Is the obligation to refrain from causing suffering to animals a commandment laid down in the Torah or is it merely of Rabbinic authority? A series of suggested proofs is now brought by the Gemara, some arguing that causing suffering to animals is a Biblical prohibition, and others arguing that it is a Rabbinic prohibition. (1) **Rava said:** [32B] [9]Despite the difference of opinion between Rabbi Shimon and the first Tanna, they both clearly agree that one's obligation to help *unload* a fallen animal is greater than one's obligation to help load it. Taking this as our starting point, **we can learn from the statements of both** Rabbi Shimon and the first Tanna **that the obligation to prevent suffering to animals is a Torah law,** since the main difference between unloading and loading is that unloading is more important for the animal itself. With reference to the first Tanna, Rava's argument is straightforward, because the first Tanna rules that unloading must be done for nothing, whereas loading may be done for a wage.

[1]מִשּׁוּם דְּלָא מְסַיְּימֵי קְרָאֵי. [2]וְרַבָּנַן? [3]אַמַּאי לָא מְסַיְּימֵי קְרָאֵי? [4]הָכָא כְּתִיב: "רֹבֵץ תַּחַת מַשָּׂאוֹ", [5]הָתָם כְּתִיב: "נוֹפְלִין בַּדֶּרֶךְ", דְּרָמוּ אִינְהוּ וּטְעוּנַיְיהוּ בְּאוֹרְחָא מַשְׁמַע. [6]וְרַבִּי שִׁמְעוֹן? [7]"נוֹפְלִין בַּדֶּרֶךְ" אִינְהוּ וּטְעוּנַיְיהוּ עִלָּוַיְיהוּ מַשְׁמַע. [8]אָמַר רָבָא: [32B] [9]מִדִּבְרֵי שְׁנֵיהֶם נִלְמַד: צַעַר בַּעֲלֵי חַיִּים דְּאוֹרַיְיתָא.

LITERAL TRANSLATION

[1]Because the verses are not explicit.

[2]And the Rabbis?

[3]Why are the verses not explicit? [4]Here it is written: "Lying under its burden," [5][and] there it is written: "Falling down by the way," meaning that [both] they and their burdens are thrown on the road.

[6]And Rabbi Shimon?

[7]"Falling down by the way" means [that] they [have fallen] with their burdens [still] on them.

[8]Rava said: [32B] [9]From the words of both of them we can learn [that the obligation to prevent] suffering to animals is a Torah law.

RASHI

לא מסיימי קראי — למשמעות טעינה, הלכך, אי כתיב חד — הוה אמינא: לפריקה אתא. **רובץ תחת משאו** — משמע שצריך לפרוק. **דרמו אינהו וטעונייהו באורחא** — אף המשא מוטל על הקרקע שצריך לטעון. **מדברי שניהם** — מדקאמרי תרווייהו פריקה עדיפא.

BACKGROUND

צַעַר בַּעֲלֵי חַיִּים **Suffering caused to animals.** Although this passage presents a difference of opinion regarding the source and authority of the prohibition against causing unnecessary suffering to animals — as to whether it derives from the Torah or from the rulings of the Sages — no one denies that cruelty to animals is prohibited.

The Torah states explicitly that the first man was given dominion over all the creatures of the world, including permission to use them for his needs, though he was not given the right to kill them for food or for any other reason. That right was given later to Noah and his sons (Genesis 9:3). Nevertheless, the Torah does not say that man has the right to cause suffering to animals. Cruelty to animals is a vice which a person must shun.

Although this prohibition was not explicitly stated in the Torah, several rulings which do appear in the Torah may be viewed as the source for it. For example, there is a prohibition (which also applies to non-Jews, the descendants of Noah) against eating the flesh of a living animal, and there is also the prohibition against muzzling an ox while it is threshing, etc. For this reason the Sages disapproved of blood sports such as hunting and bullfighting.

Thus permission to use animals and eat them is restricted by the prohibition against causing them unnecessary suffering. One may do only what is absolutely necessary for man's benefit, and not cause suffering to animals if one can avoid it.

NOTES

לָא מְסַיְּימֵי קְרָאֵי **The verses are not explicit.** According to some Rishonim, followed by our commentary, Rabbi Shimon does not dispute the fact that the verse in Exodus clearly refers to unloading. His doubts relate only to the verse in Deuteronomy, which may indeed refer to loading but can equally well be interpreted as referring to unloading (*Tosefot Sens;* but see *Tosafot* 31a).

צַעַר בַּעֲלֵי חַיִּים **Suffering caused to animals.** The commentators ask: If this prohibition is indeed a Torah law, what is its Scriptural source? *Meiri* points to the commandment: "You shall not muzzle an ox when it treads out the corn" (Deuteronomy 25:4), and draws a general conclusion from it that one must not make animals suffer. *Ḥatam Sofer* points to the verse: "the Lord is good to all: and His tender mercies are over all his work" (Psalm 145:9). *Ḥatam Sofer* further notes that even according to the opinion that the obligation not to cause suffering to an animal is a Torah law, this obligation applies only to "unnecessary" suffering, i.e., causing suffering to an animal without bringing any benefit to man. But if man can benefit, he is allowed to

BACKGROUND

חֶסְרוֹן כִּיס A loss to the pocket. Consideration of monetary loss suffered by another person is in fact part of the general commandment to return lost property, and it is possible to view the commandment to unload as an aspect of that general commandment. While the animal remains lying on the ground under its burden, it may be injured or die, causing monetary loss to its owner. Moreover, the language of the verse "you shall surely help with him" — seems to relate mainly to the animal's owner, who needs help in unloading it. Therefore one can understand this commandment without reference to the principle of avoiding cruelty to animals.

TRANSLATION AND COMMENTARY

[1]But regarding Rabbi Shimon, Rava felt the need to elaborate: **Even Rabbi Shimon,** who ruled that there is no difference in law between loading and unloading, **only said** that a special verse was needed to teach us the law in the case of unloading **because the verses are not explicit,** and we do not know which of them refers to loading. [2]**But if the verses were explicit, we would** be able to **make** use of **the** ***kal vaḥomer*** (*a fortiori*) **argument** used by the first Tanna and apply it to the viewpoint of Rabbi Shimon to show that the law of unloading can be inferred from the law of loading. Hence, it is clear that the obligation to unload is greater than the obligation to load. [3]Rava continues his argument: Now, **on what** would that *kal vaḥomer* argument **be based? Would we not base the** *kal vaḥomer* **argument on the obligation to prevent suffering to animals,** which is a factor in unloading but not in loading? The argument would run as follows: If in the case of loading a fallen animal, where no suffering is being caused to the animal, the passerby is obliged to help, in the case of unloading an animal, where the animal *is* being caused suffering, how much more so is the passerby obliged to help! Thus, says Rava, we can infer from the statements of both the first Tanna and Rabbi Shimon that the obligation to prevent suffering to animals is a Torah law.

דִּלְמָא [4]The Gemara refutes this argument: It is possible that the obligation to prevent pain to animals is not of Torah origin, and the reason why we treat unloading an animal differently from loading it **is perhaps because** the owner may suffer **financial loss** if the animal is hurt. [5]The *kal vaḥomer* argument is thus different from the one previously suggested, **and this is how it is to be understood: If in the case of loading** a fallen animal, **where there is no financial loss** to the owner if the loading is delayed, the passerby **is obliged to help,** [6]then in the case of **unloading** an animal, **where there is** a possibility of **financial loss** to the owner if the animal is injured, **how much more so** is the passerby obliged to help!

וּטְעִינָה [7]**But,** asks the Gemara, **does** delay in **loading** a fallen animal **not involve a financial loss?** [8]**Could we not be dealing with a situation where in the meantime,** while the animal is lying in the road waiting to be picked up and loaded, and the goods that the owner was planning to sell in the market are lying in the road together with the fallen animal, the owner **is prevented from doing what he was planning to do in the market?** Hence, failure to assist the owner with loading the animal could cost him a great deal of money. [9]**Or alternatively,**

[1]וַאֲפִילּוּ רַבִּי שִׁמְעוֹן לָא קָאָמַר אֶלָּא מִשּׁוּם דְּלָא מְסַיְּימִי קְרָאֵי. [2]אֲבָל מְסַיְּימִי קְרָאֵי, דָּרְשִׁינַן קַל וָחוֹמֶר. [3]מִשּׁוּם מַאי? לָאו מִשּׁוּם צַעַר בַּעֲלֵי חַיִּים דָּרְשִׁינַן? [4]דִּלְמָא מִשּׁוּם דְּאִיכָּא חֶסְרוֹן כִּיס, [5]וְהָכִי קָאָמַר: וּמַה טְּעִינָה, דְּלֵית בָּהּ חֶסְרוֹן כִּיס, חַיָּיב, [6]פְּרִיקָה, דְּאִית בָּהּ חֶסְרוֹן כִּיס, לֹא כׇּל שֶׁכֵּן! [7]וּטְעִינָה, אֵין בָּהּ חֶסְרוֹן כִּיס? [8]מִי לָא עָסְקִינַן דְּאַדְּהָכִי וְהָכִי בָּטֵיל מִשּׁוּקֵיהּ, [9]אִי נַמִי,

LITERAL TRANSLATION

[1]And even Rabbi Shimon only said [what he said] because the verses are not explicit. [2]But [if] the verses were explicit, we would make a *kal vaḥomer* inference.

[3]Because of what? Is it not because of [the obligation to prevent] suffering to animals that we make the inference? [4]Perhaps it is because there is a loss to the pocket, [5]and this is what it is saying: If [in the case of] loading, in which there is no loss to the pocket, he is obliged [to help], [6]unloading, in which there is a loss to the pocket, how much more so!

[7]But loading, is there not in it a loss to the pocket? [8]Are we not dealing [with a situation] where in the meantime he is kept idle from his market, [9]or alternatively,

RASHI

ואפילו רבי שמעון לא קאמר – דאצטריך למכתב פריקה. **אלא משום דלא מסיימי קראי** – לטעינה. **לאו משום צער בעלי חיים** – והכי יליף: מה טעינה דליכא צער בעלי חיים – חייב, פריקה דאיכא צער בעלי חיים – לא כל שכן. **מי לא עסקינן** – וכי אין המקרא מדבר אף בהולך לסחורה, דאדהכי בטיל משוקיה.

NOTES

employ animals for his purposes, as the Torah states (Genesis 1:28): "And you shall have dominion over the fish of the sea, and over the fowl of the air, and over every living thing that moves upon the earth." Accordingly, man may slaughter animals for food and use them to fulfill his needs, but may not cause an animal suffering or discomfort without productive intent.

צַעַר בַּעֲלֵי חַיִּים Suffering caused to animals and the obligation to unload a fallen animal. The Rishonim ask: We have already established (above, 30a) that an elder for whom loading or unloading an animal would be considered undignified is exempt from this obligation. But if the obligation to prevent suffering to animals is a Torah law, how can considerations of personal dignity outweigh it?

Ramban answers that honoring a Sage is a clear, positive command of the Torah which outweighs causing suffering to animals. *Mordekhai* answers that the exemptions from the obligation to help unload a fallen animal apply only

TRANSLATION AND COMMENTARY

we must also consider the possibility that if the animal is not loaded promptly, while the goods are lying on the ground next to it, **thieves may come and take everything that he has with him.** Hence, financial loss cannot be the basis of the *kal vaḥomer* argument, and Rava appears to be correct in his analysis.

תֵּדַע דְּצַעַר בַּעֲלֵי חַיִּים [1]The Gemara now cites our Mishnah to support Rava's argument that the first Tanna and Rabbi Shimon agree that the obligation to prevent suffering to animals is of Biblical authority: **Know that the obligation to prevent suffering to animals is a Torah law, because the last clause of the Mishnah says:** [2]**"Rabbi Yose HaGelili says: If** the fallen animal **had on it more than its** normal **load,** then the passerby **is under no obligation towards** the owner to get involved with it, as the problem has been caused by the owner's own negligence, **as it is said** in the verse (Exodus 23:5) that the animal must be 'lying **under *its* burden,'** which means that the passerby need only assist with **a burden that** the animal **can bear,** but not where the load was excessive." [3]Now, argues the Gemara, **does this not prove by implication that the first Tanna** and Rabbi Shimon **are** both **of the opinion that** the passerby **is under an obligation** to help the owner even if the animal was overloaded? [4]**What could possibly be the reason** for this? Surely from the expression quoted by Rabbi Yose it is clear that there is no obligation to assist an owner who has overloaded his own animal! **Is not** the reason, therefore, why the first Tanna and Rabbi Shimon make no distinction between a normal and an excessive load, and require the passerby to help in all cases, **because the obligation to prevent suffering to animals is a Torah law?**

דִּלְמָא בְּתַחַת מַשָּׂאוֹ פְּלִיגִי [5]The Gemara answers: This argument is not convincing. The first Tanna and Rabbi Shimon may agree with Rabbi Yose that there is no Torah obligation to concern oneself with the animal's welfare. But **perhaps they disagree** with his interpretation of the expression **"under its burden."** [6]**For Rabbi Yose is of the opinion that we** must **interpret "under its burden,"** stressing the seemingly superfluous word "its," **to mean a burden that** the animal **can bear.** [7]**Whereas the Sages are of the opinion that we do not interpret "under its burden" in this way,** and apply the obligation to help irrespective of the weight of the load under which the animal collapsed. Thus our Mishnah would provide no proof for Rava's contention that the obligation to prevent suffering to animals is a Torah law.

אָתוּ גַּנָּבֵי וְשָׁקְלֵי כָּל מַה דְּאִיכָּא בַּהֲדֵיהּ?

[1]תֵּדַע דְּצַעַר בַּעֲלֵי חַיִּים דְּאוֹרַיְיתָא, דְּקָתָנֵי סֵיפָא: [2]״רַבִּי יוֹסֵי הַגְּלִילִי אוֹמֵר: אִם הָיָה עָלָיו יָתֵר עַל מַשָּׂאוֹ, אֵין זָקוּק לוֹ, שֶׁנֶּאֱמַר: ׳תַּחַת מַשָּׂאוֹ׳, מַשּׂאוֹי שֶׁיָּכוֹל לַעֲמוֹד בּוֹ״. [3]לָאו מִכְּלָל דְּתַנָּא קַמָּא סָבַר זָקוּק לוֹ? מַאי טַעְמָא? [4]לָאו מִשּׁוּם דְּצַעַר בַּעֲלֵי חַיִּים דְּאוֹרַיְיתָא?

[5]דִּלְמָא בְּ״תַחַת מַשָּׂאוֹ״ פְּלִיגִי. [6]דְּרַבִּי יוֹסֵי סָבַר: דָּרְשִׁינַן ״תַּחַת מַשָּׂאוֹ״ מַשּׂאוֹי שֶׁיָּכוֹל לַעֲמוֹד בּוֹ, [7]וְרַבָּנַן סָבְרִי: לָא דָּרְשִׁינַן ״תַּחַת מַשָּׂאוֹ״.

LITERAL TRANSLATION

thieves may come and take everything that he has with him?

[1]Know that [the obligation to prevent] suffering to animals is a Torah law, for the last clause [of the Mishnah] teaches: [2]"Rabbi Yose HaGelili says: If there was on it more than its burden, he is under no obligation towards him, as it is said: 'Under *its* burden,' a burden that it can bear." [3][Does this] not [prove] by implication that the first Tanna is of the opinion [that] he is under an obligation towards him? [4]What is the reason? Is it not because [the obligation to prevent] suffering to animals is a Torah law?

[5]Perhaps they disagree about "under its burden." [6]For Rabbi Yose is of the opinion [that] we interpret "under its burden" [as] a burden that it can bear, [7]and the Sages are of the opinion [that] we do not interpret "under its burden" [in this way].

RASHI

תדע — דלרבנן דפליגי עליה דרבי שמעון, ולרבי שמעון — לער בעלי חיים דאורייתא. **מכלל דתנא קמא** — דרבי יוסי הגלילי, רבנן ורבי שמעון. **זקוק לו** — ואמאי זקוק לו, אי משום מלות "עזב תעזב" — הא כתיב משאו הראוי לו, אלא משום לער בעלי חיים. **לא דרשינן משאו** — למשא הראוי לו, דמשאו — כל משא שעליו משמע.

NOTES

when other people are available to do the work. But if no one else is there, even a person who would otherwise be exempt is obliged to help, in order to relieve the suffering of the animal.

HALAKHAH

יָתֵר עַל מַשָּׂאוֹ More than its burden. "The passerby is obliged to assist with the fallen animal regardless of the size of the burden under which it collapsed. Even if the animal was incapable of bearing such a burden, the passerby must still assist," following the anonymous opinion in our Mishnah, and contrary to the minority opinion of Rabbi Yose HaGelili. (*Shulhan Arukh, Ḥoshen Mishpat* 272:1.)

TRANSLATION AND COMMENTARY

תֵּדַע דְּצַעַר בַּעֲלֵי חַיִּים [1]The Gemara now goes further and seeks to prove from our Mishnah that not only is there no proof for Rava's contention, but it is in fact incorrect: **Know that the obligation to prevent suffering to animals is not a Torah law, because an earlier clause of the Mishnah says:** [2]**"If the owner** of the animal **goes and sits down and says to** the passerby: **'Since the commandment to** help load or **unload** the animal **is** incumbent **upon you,** by all means go ahead and **unload** by yourself,' in such a case the passerby **is exempt** from doing so, **as it is said** in the verse: 'You shall surely help **with him,'** and not on your own." [3]The Gemara explains: **But if it entered your mind** to imagine **that the obligation to prevent suffering to animals is a Torah law,** [4]**what difference does it make to me whether** the animal's selfish **master is there** working together **with him or not?** In either case, the animal's suffering is the same! In other words, if the question of the animal's suffering were the main issue, the non-participation of its owner would not release the passerby from the obligation to help the animal. The fact that the non-participation of the owner *does* release the passerby is surely a clear indication that the obligation to prevent suffering to animals is not a Torah law!

לְעוֹלָם צַעַר בַּעֲלֵי חַיִּים [5]The Gemara answers: **In fact, the obligation to prevent suffering to animals** may be a Torah law, as Rava claims, and the proof just brought from the earlier part of the Mishnah may not be conclusive. [6]**Do you think** that the word **"exempt"** used by the Mishnah necessarily **means entirely exempt,** and that the passerby has no obligation whatever to help the fallen animal? [7]**Perhaps** it means that in a case where the owner is unwilling to participate, the passerby **is exempt** from his normal obligation **to unload for nothing, but he** nevertheless remains **obligated to unload for a fee!** [8]Perhaps **this is what** the verse in **the Torah is saying: When the** fallen animal's **master is** working together **with him,** then the passerby must **work for him for nothing; but if** the animal's **master is not** working together **with him,** then the passerby must work for him because of his obligation to prevent suffering to the animal, but **he works for him for a fee.** And he is entitled to collect that fee whether the owner agrees or not. [9]Thus Rava may be correct, and **in fact the obligation to prevent suffering to animals is a Torah** law.

בהמ״ת בהמ״ת [10]The Gemara now continues its effort to decide whether the obligation to prevent suffering to animals is a Torah law or of Rabbinic authority by citing a series of Tannaitic sources. The sequence of cases mentioned is summarized by the following **mnemonic:** בהמ״ת בהמ״ת אוה״ב שונ״א רבצ״ן. These abbreviations are the first (or key) words in each of the sources to be cited.

[1]תֵּדַע דְּצַעַר בַּעֲלֵי חַיִּים לָאו דְּאוֹרַיְיתָא, דְּקָתָנֵי רֵישָׁא: [2]״הָלַךְ וְיָשַׁב לוֹ וְאָמַר לוֹ: ׳הוֹאִיל וְעָלֶיךָ מִצְוָה לִפְרוֹק, פְּרוֹק׳, פָּטוּר. שֶׁנֶּאֱמַר: ׳עִמּוֹ׳״. [3]וְאִי סָלְקָא דַּעְתָּךְ צַעַר בַּעֲלֵי חַיִּים דְּאוֹרַיְיתָא, [4]מָה לִי אִיתֵיהּ לְמָרֵיהּ בַּהֲדֵיהּ, וּמָה לִי כִּי לֵיתֵיהּ לְמָרֵיהּ בַּהֲדֵיהּ? [5]לְעוֹלָם צַעַר בַּעֲלֵי חַיִּים דְּאוֹרַיְיתָא. [6]מִי סָבְרַתְּ ״פָּטוּר״ פָּטוּר לְגַמְרֵי? [7]וְדִלְמָא פָּטוּר בְּחִנָּם, וְחַיָּיב בְּשָׂכָר. [8]וְהָכִי קָאָמַר רַחֲמָנָא: כִּי אִיתֵיהּ לְמָרֵיהּ בַּהֲדֵיהּ, עָבֵד גַּבֵּיהּ בְּחִנָּם, וְכִי לֵיתֵיהּ לְמָרֵיהּ בַּהֲדֵיהּ, עָבֵד גַּבֵּיהּ בְּשָׂכָר. [9]וּלְעוֹלָם צַעַר בַּעֲלֵי חַיִּים דְּאוֹרַיְיתָא.

[10](סִימָ״ן: בהמ״ת בהמ״ת אוה״ב שונ״א רבצ״ן)

LITERAL TRANSLATION

[1]Know that [the obligation to prevent] suffering to animals is not a Torah law, for the earlier clause [of the Mishnah] teaches: [2]"[If the owner] went and sat down and said to him: 'Since the commandment to unload is upon you, unload,' he is exempt, as it is said: 'With him.' [3]But if it entered your mind [that the obligation to prevent] suffering to animals is a Torah law, [4]what [does it matter] to me [whether] its master is there with him, and what [does it matter] to me if its master is not there with him?

[5]In fact, [the obligation to prevent] suffering to animals is a Torah law. [6]Do you think "exempt" [means] entirely exempt? [7]But perhaps he is exempt [from unloading] for nothing, but he is obliged [to unload] for a wage. [8]And this is what the Torah is saying: When its master is with him, he works for him for nothing, but when its master is not with him, he works for him for a wage. [9]But in fact, [the obligation to prevent] suffering to animals is a Torah law.

[10]Mnemonic: בהמ״ת בהמ״ת אוה״ב שונ״א רבצ״ן

RASHI

ותדע – דהכי הוא כדדחינא לך, דצער בעלי חיים לאו דאורייתא.
עביד גביה – משום צער בעלי חיים, ועל כורחו יטול שכר.

[1]לֵימָא מְסַיַּיע לֵיהּ: ״בֶּהֱמַת נָכְרִי מְטַפֵּל בָּהּ כְּבֶהֱמַת יִשְׂרָאֵל״. [2]אִי אָמְרַתְּ בִּשְׁלָמָא צַעַר בַּעֲלֵי חַיִּים דְּאוֹרַיְיתָא — [3]מִשּׁוּם הָכִי מְטַפֵּל בָּהּ כְּבֶהֱמַת יִשְׂרָאֵל. [4]אֶלָּא אִי אָמְרַתְּ צַעַר בַּעֲלֵי חַיִּים לָאו דְּאוֹרַיְיתָא, [5]אַמַּאי מְטַפֵּל בָּהּ כְּבֶהֱמַת יִשְׂרָאֵל?

[6]הָתָם מִשּׁוּם אֵיבָה.

[7]הָכִי נַמִי מִסְתַּבְּרָא, דְּקָתָנֵי: ״אִם הָיְתָה טְעוּנָה יֵין נֶסֶךְ, אֵין זָקוּק לָהּ״. [8]אִי אָמְרַתְּ בִּשְׁלָמָא לָאו דְּאוֹרַיְיתָא — [9]מִשּׁוּם הָכִי אֵין זָקוּק לָהּ. [10]אֶלָּא אִי אָמְרַתְּ דְּאוֹרַיְיתָא, [11]אַמַּאי אֵין זָקוּק לָהּ?

LITERAL TRANSLATION

[1]Shall we say that [the following Baraita] supports him: "One must look after the animal of a non-Jew like the animal of a Jew." [2]It is well if you say [that the obligation to prevent] suffering to animals is a Torah law — [3][it is] because of this [that] he looks after it like the animal of a Jew. [4]But if you say [that the obligation to prevent] suffering to animals is not a Torah law, [5]why does he look after it like the animal of a Jew?

[6]There it is because of enmity.

[7]So, too, it is reasonable, for it teaches: "If it was laden with libation wine, he has no obligation towards it." [8]It is well if you say it is not a Torah law — [9]because of this he has no obligation towards it. [10]But if you say it is a Torah law, [11]why does he have no obligation towards it?

TRANSLATION AND COMMENTARY

לֵימָא מְסַיַּיע לֵיהּ [1](2) The Gemara first seeks to bring a proof from a Baraita that preventing suffering to animals is a Torah law: **Shall we say that the following Baraita supports** Rava's position: "If a person sees an animal collapsed under its load he must go to its assistance irrespective of who its owner is. **He must look after the animal of a non-Jew like** the animal of a Jew." The assumption of the Gemara is that the duty of a Jew to assist his fellowman in need applies specifically to Jews and not to non-Jews (see note). Hence, if the Baraita rules that there is an obligation to help an animal owned by a non-Jew, it cannot be for the sake of the non-Jew himself, but must be for the sake of his animal. [2]Now, the Gemara explains, the Baraita **is understandable if you say that the obligation to prevent suffering to animals is a Torah law.** [3]In that case I would say that it is **for this reason,** namely the pain suffered by the animal, **that** the passerby must **look after** a non-Jew's animal **like the animal of a Jew.** [4]**But if you say that the obligation to prevent suffering to animals is not a Torah law,** [5]**why does he** have to **look after** a non-Jew's animal **like the animal of a Jew?**

הָתָם מִשּׁוּם אֵיבָה [6]The Gemara answers: Even if the Torah does not require us to prevent suffering to animals, we still have to assist non-Jews when they need help, **because of** the necessity to avoid **enmity** and promote better relations with non-Jews. Hence, Jews must help non-Jews unload their animals, even though this act is technically not a fulfillment of the commandment to unload a fallen animal.

הָכִי נַמִי מִסְתַּבְּרָא [7]The Gemara remarks: This explanation is not merely a satisfactory answer to the objection posed above, **it is also** the most **reasonable** way of explaining the Baraita, **for** the Baraita goes on to **say: "If** the non-Jew's animal **was laden with libation wine,** from which Jews are forbidden to derive any benefit, then the passerby **has no obligation towards it,** and need not assist the non-Jew in reloading the animal." [8]Now, explains the Gemara, this clause **is understandable if you say** that preventing suffering to animals **is not a Torah law,** and the assistance is rendered to the non-Jew simply to prevent "enmity." [9]In that case, I would say that **it is for the** following **reason that he has no obligation towards it** — because he can say to the non-Jew that it is forbidden by Jewish law for him to handle libation wine, and thus his unwillingness to help will not lead to strained relations between Jews and non-Jews. [10]**But if you say that** preventing suffering to animals **is a Torah law,** then this consideration should apply both to animals belonging to Jews and to animals belonging to non-Jews. [11]**Why,** then, **does** the passerby **not have an obligation towards** the non-Jew's animal? It seems to be clear that the reasoning of the Baraita is based solely on considerations of preventing "enmity" and not on preventing suffering to animals, which shows that there is no obligation in Torah law to prevent such suffering.

RASHI

לימא מסייע ליה — לרבא, דאמר לעיל: צער בעלי חיים דאורייתא. **מטפל בה** — לפרוק משאה. **אי אמרת לאו דאורייתא** — וטעמא משום איבה הוא — משום הכי אין זקוק לה, שיכול להשמט, ולומר: דבר איסור הוא לנו.

NOTES

נָכְרִי וְיִשְׂרָאֵל Non-Jew and Jew. The underlying assumption behind this entire passage of the Gemara is that the duty to assist one's fellowman applies specifically to Jews and not to non-Jews. Whenever the Torah uses a word like "neighbor" or "brother" or "fellow," Talmudic tradition understands the commandment in question to apply

TERMINOLOGY

לֵימָא מְסַיַּיע לֵיהּ Shall we say that it supports him? The Talmud uses this expression to suggest that a Mishnah or a Baraita supports a particular Amora's view. Suggestions introduced in this way are usually rejected later in the discussion.

BACKGROUND

אֵיבָה Enmity. The avoidance of hostility among people is a consideraton in various areas of the Halakhah, the ideal being the creation and fostering of peaceful and tranquil relations. This consideraton is found mainly in the area of relations between Jews and non-Jews, in situations where insisting on the strict letter of the law and on scrupulous protection of a person's rights could result in misunderstanding and even hatred. In such cases a person is commanded to demand far less than his due (לִפְנִים מִשּׁוּרַת הַדִּין) and, in some cases, even to perform certain actions which by right he ought not to do, in order to avoid damaging the general fabric of relations. The Sages spoke often in praise of peace. For the sake of peace and to avoid hatred and envy, they even advocated altering the truth and helping someone whom one is not legally obligated to help.

יֵין נֶסֶךְ Libation wine. Libation wine, like other things used in idol worship, is forbidden to Jews. They may not derive any benefit from it, and must distance themselves from it. If it comes into their possession, they must destroy it. Furthermore, the Torah forbids idol worship not only to Jews but to all human beings. Hence Jews are commanded not to help in any matter connected with idol worship.

TRANSLATION AND COMMENTARY

הָכִי קָאָמַר [1]The Gemara answers: This argument is not conclusive, as the precise language of the Baraita is not established, and **this is what** the Baraita **may be saying: "But** if the passerby was asked **to load** — rather than to unload as in the previous version of the Baraita — the non-Jew's animal **with libation wine,** then the passerby **has no obligation towards it."** The passerby is exempt from involvement because the animal is not suffering, and the commandment to assist the owner to reload a fallen animal does not apply to a non-Jew's animal. Similarly the argument of "enmity" does not apply to libation wine. Thus this Baraita in its emended form can support Rava's opinion that the obligation to prevent suffering to animals is a Torah law.

תָּא שְׁמַע [2](3) The Gemara now seeks to bring a proof from another Baraita that preventing suffering to animals is not a Torah law: **Come and hear:** "If **the animal** lying collapsed under its load **belongs to a non-Jew, and the load belongs to a Jew,** then the passerby can apply the rule hinted at in the verse (Exodus 23:5): **'And you may forbear,'** and he need not assist in the unloading of the animal." [3]This Baraita seems to show that the Torah does not command us to assist a non-Jew to unload his animal. Thus, the question may be asked: **If you say that the obligation to prevent suffering to animals is a Torah law** which applies equally to all animals, **why does** the expression **"and you may forbear" apply?** [4]The Baraita **should have said** that the passerby is obliged to help the suffering animal irrespective of who its owner is, and it should have quoted the expression from the same verse: **"You shall surely help"!**

לְעוֹלָם צַעַר בַּעֲלֵי חַיִּים [5]The Gemara answers: **In fact the obligation to prevent suffering to animals is a Torah law,** and as to your question why the Baraita used the expression "and you may forbear," I can answer that the Baraita **is referring** specifically **to loading,** refraining from which does not cause the animal suffering.

אִי הָכִי [6]On this the Gemara asks: If this is so, and the Baraita is referring to a case of loading, **consider the latter clause** of the Baraita: "If **the animal belongs to a Jew and the load belongs to a non-Jew,** then the passerby must apply the rule found in the same verse: **'You shall surely help,'** and he must assist the animal." From this clause in the Baraita it would seem that the Torah commands us to assist a non-Jew with his load. [7]Thus the question may be asked: **If** the Baraita **is referring** specifically **to loading, why does** the expression **"You shall surely help" apply?** Surely there is no question here of suffering being caused to the animal!

[1]הָכִי קָאָמַר: ״וּלְהַטְעִינָהּ יֵין נֶסֶךְ, אֵין זָקוּק לָהּ״. [2]תָּא שְׁמַע: ״בֶּהֱמַת נָכְרִי וּמַשּׂאוֹי יִשְׂרָאֵל — ׳וְחָדַלְתָּ׳״. [3]וְאִי אָמְרַתְּ צַעַר בַּעֲלֵי חַיִּים דְּאוֹרַיְיתָא, אַמַּאי ״וְחָדַלְתָּ״? [4]״עָזֹב תַּעֲזֹב״ מִבָּעֵי לֵיהּ! [5]לְעוֹלָם צַעַר בַּעֲלֵי חַיִּים דְּאוֹרַיְיתָא, הָתָם בִּטְעִינָה. [6]אִי הָכִי, אֵימָא סֵיפָא: ״בֶּהֱמַת יִשְׂרָאֵל וּמַשּׂאוֹי נָכְרִי — ׳עָזֹב תַּעֲזֹב׳״. [7]וְאִי בִּטְעִינָה, אַמַּאי ״עָזֹב תַּעֲזֹב״?

LITERAL TRANSLATION

[1]This is what it says: "But to load it with libation wine, he has no obligation towards it."

[2]Come [and] hear: "An animal of a non-Jew and a burden of a Jew — 'and you may forbear.'" [3]But if you say [that the obligation to prevent] suffering to animals is a Torah law, why [does it say]: "And you may forbear"? [4]It should have [said]: "You shall surely help"!

[5]In fact, [the obligation to prevent] suffering to animals is a Torah law, [and] there [it is referring] to loading.

[6]If so, consider (lit., "say") the latter clause: "An animal of a Jew and a burden of a non-Jew — 'You shall surely help.'" [7]But if [it is referring] to loading, why [does it say]: "You shall surely help"?

RASHI

הכי קאמר ולהטעינה — ולעולם דאורייתא, ורישא תנא מטפל בה בין בפריקה בין בטעינה, פריקה — משום צער בעלי חיים, וטעינה — משום איבה ולהטעינה יין אסור, דלאו צערא איכא ולאו איבה איכא — אין זקוק לה. **התם בטעינה** — לקמיה פריך: הא בפריקה כתיב.

NOTES

specifically to fellow Jews (and, to a certain extent, to non-Jews who have abandoned idolatry and accepted the seven Noahide laws). Non-Jews (i.e., idol-worshippers) are excluded. In practice, however, the rule excluding non-Jews has so many qualifications that it is hardly ever applicable.

HALAKHAH

בֶּהֱמַת נָכְרִי וּמַשּׂאוֹי יִשְׂרָאֵל An animal of a non-Jew and a burden of a Jew. "If the fallen animal belongs to a non-Jew and the load belongs to a Jew, and the non-Jew was driving the animal, the passerby need not assist with loading. (According to *Sma,* even considerations of "enmity" do not apply in this case. For unloading, see below.) If a Jew is accompanying the animal, the passerby is required to assist with loading and unloading, because of the distress suffered by the Jew. If the animal belongs to the Jewish driver and the load to a non-Jew, the passerby must assist with the

TRANSLATION AND COMMENTARY

מִשּׁוּם צַעֲרָא דְּיִשְׂרָאֵל [1]The Gemara answers: The reason why the Baraita commands the passerby to assist in loading the animal may be **because of the distress of the Jew,** who must take care of his fallen animal and is being delayed in going about his business.

אִי הָכִי [2]But, the Gemara asks, **if** this is **so,** and we are concerned about the distress of the Jew, **the same thing should be said even in the first clause, too,** where it is the Jew who owns the load! Surely in this case, too, the Jew is suffering distress! The passerby should be required to assist him, so that he is not forced to lift the load by himself!

רֵישָׁא בְּחַמָּר נָכְרִי [3]The Gemara answers: The situations in the two clauses of the Baraita are different. **The first clause is referring to** a situation where **the driver of the ass is a non-Jew,** and the Jewish owner of the load is not present, whereas **the latter clause is referring to** a situation where **the driver of the ass is a Jew.** There is no need to render assistance in the first case, as the driver is a non-Jew, and the suffering of the animal is not a consideration in loading, whereas in the second case assistance must be rendered to prevent distress to the Jew who would otherwise have to reload the animal by himself and is being delayed in going about his business.

מַאי פָּסְקַתְּ [4]The Gemara asks: **Why have you** arbitrarily **decided in this way** that if the animal is owned by a non-Jew it will be driven by a non-Jew, and if it is owned by a Jew it will be driven by a Jew?

סְתָמָא דְּמִלְּתָא [5]The Gemara answers: **Ordinarily a person walks behind his own ass,** and we may assume that the ass is accompanied and driven by its owner.

וְהָא וְחָדַלְתָּ [6]Up to this point the Gemara has assumed that the Baraita is referring to a case of loading, but now it challenges this assumption: **But surely** the Biblical quotations used by the Baraita — **"and you may forbear" and "you shall surely help"** — are both taken from the same verse in Exodus (23:5), and they **are written in the context of unloading!** If the Baraita is referring specifically to unloading, why is the ownership of the animal decisive, and not its suffering? Clearly, because preventing suffering to animals is not a Torah law!

אֶלָּא הָא מַנִּי [7]The Gemara answers: I accept that the Baraita can only be understood according to the viewpoint that the obligation to prevent pain to animals is *not* a Torah law. **But whose opinion does this** Baraita reflect? [8]It reflects the opinion of **Rabbi Yose HaGelili, who** indeed **said that the obligation to prevent suffering to animals is not a Torah law,** when he ruled that owners who overload their animals need not be assisted. Hence, the author of the Baraita may indeed maintain that the Torah does not oblige us to prevent suffering to animals, but this may still not be the normative Halakhah.

[1]מִשּׁוּם צַעֲרָא דְּיִשְׂרָאֵל. [2]אִי הָכִי, אֲפִילּוּ רֵישָׁא נַמִי! [3]רֵישָׁא בְּחַמָּר נָכְרִי, סֵיפָא בְּחַמָּר יִשְׂרָאֵל. [4]מַאי פָּסְקַתְּ? [5]סְתָמָא דְּמִלְּתָא, אִינִישׁ בָּתַר חֲמָרֵיהּ אָזֵיל. [6]וְהָא "וְחָדַלְתָּ" וְ"עָזֹב תַּעֲזֹב" בִּפְרִיקָה הוּא דִּכְתִיבִי! [7]אֶלָּא הָא מַנִּי? [8]רַבִּי יוֹסֵי הַגְּלִילִי הִיא, דְּאָמַר: צַעַר בַּעֲלֵי חַיִּים לָאו דְּאוֹרַיְיתָא.

LITERAL TRANSLATION

[1]Because of the distress of the Jew.

[2]If so, even the first clause, too, [should say the same]!

[3]The first clause [refers] to a non-Jewish ass-driver, the latter clause [refers] to a Jewish ass-driver.

[4]Why have you decided [in this way]?

[5]Ordinarily, a person walks behind his own ass.

[6]But surely "and you may forbear" and "you shall surely help" are written in [the context of] unloading!

[7]Rather, whose [opinion] is this? [8]It is Rabbi Yose HaGelili's, who said [that the obligation to prevent] suffering to animals is not a Torah law.

RASHI

משום צערא דישראל — שצריך להשהות שם. **בחמר נכרי** — ואין בעל המשא שם, ועל הנכרי לטעון. **מאי פסקת** — וכי פסקת הדבר כן דכל בהמת נכרי הוי חמר נכרי, וכל בהמת ישראל הוי חמר ישראל?

BACKGROUND

אִינִישׁ בָּתַר חֲמָרֵיהּ אָזֵיל A person walks behind his own ass. In antiquity, animals were the most common means of transporting goods, and there were professional donkey drivers and camel drivers employed in transportation. Furthermore, the owners of animals preferred to drive them themselves, so as to be certain that the animals were properly fed and cared for.

HALAKHAH

loading and unloading, because of the distress suffered by the Jew. But if both the animal and the load belong to a non-Jew, the passerby need not assist with loading, except where considerations of avoiding enmity and improving relations with non-Jews apply." (*Shulḥan Arukh, Ḥoshen Mishpat* 272:8-9.) If the non-Jew's animal requires unloading, *Rema* rules that the passerby should assist the non-Jew, because of the obligation to prevent suffering to animals.

צַעַר בַּעֲלֵי חַיִּים Causing suffering to animals. *Rema* rules, following *Rashba* and *Rosh,* that the law preventing suffering to animals is a Torah law. (*Shulḥan Arukh, Hoshen Mishpat* 272:9.) *Sma* writes, following *Kesef Mishneh,* that *Rambam,* whose language is followed by the *Shulḥan Arukh,* also shares this position, since in connection with the laws of the Sabbath he rules that consideration for the suffering of animals overrides Rabbinic prohibitions. Nevertheless, *Gra* and other Aḥaronim maintain that, according to *Rambam,* consideration for animals is only a Rabbinic concern. (Ibid.; see *Shulḥan Arukh, Oraḥ Ḥayyim* 305:18-20.)

TRANSLATION AND COMMENTARY

תָּא שְׁמַע [1](4) The Gemara now seeks to bring a proof from a Tosefta (*Bava Metzia* 2:26) that preventing suffering to animals is not a Torah law: **Come and hear: "If** a passerby finds himself in a situation where **his friend needs help to unload** a fallen animal, **and his enemy needs help to load** an animal, and he does not know whom to help first, **his** first **obligation is to** load the animal of **his enemy, in order to subdue his own evil inclination** and uproot sinful hatred from his heart." [2]**But,** asks the Gemara, **if it were to enter your mind that the obligation to prevent suffering to animals is a Torah law, surely the unloading** of his friend's animal should take precedence!

אֲפִילּוּ הָכִי [3]The Gemara answers: Even though, in general, preventing suffering to animals is a major consideration and a Torah law, **nevertheless, subduing one's evil inclination** and diminishing hatred and animosity **take precedence** even over relieving the pain of animals.

[1]תָּא שְׁמַע: ״אוֹהֵב לִפְרוֹק, וְשׂוֹנֵא לִטְעוֹן, מִצְוָה בְּשׂוֹנֵא כְּדֵי לָכוֹף אֶת יִצְרוֹ״. [2]וְאִי סָלְקָא דַּעְתָּךְ צַעַר בַּעֲלֵי חַיִּים דְּאוֹרָיְיתָא, הָא עָדִיף לֵיהּ! [3]אֲפִילּוּ הָכִי, ״כְּדֵי לָכוֹף אֶת יִצְרוֹ״ עָדִיף.

LITERAL TRANSLATION

[1]Come [and] hear: "[If] a friend [needs help] to unload, and an enemy [needs help] to load, the obligation (lit., 'commandment') is [to do it] for the enemy, in order to subdue one's [evil] inclination."

[2]But if it entered your mind [that the obligation to prevent] suffering to animals is a Torah law, [surely] this [the unloading] takes precedence for him!

[3]Even so, "in order to subdue one's [evil] inclination" takes precedence.

NOTES

אוֹהֵב וְשׂוֹנֵא A friend and an enemy. The simple meaning of the verse, "If you see the ass of him that hates you lying under its burden" (Exodus 23:5), is that a person is obliged to assist a fellow Jew whose animal is in distress, even if he is an enemy. On this the Gemara (*Pesaḥim* 113b) asks: Since it is forbidden to hate one's fellow Jew (Leviticus 19:17), how can the person in need be one's enemy? Obviously, the fact that someone hates another person against the express prohibition of the Torah cannot possibly relieve him of his responsibilities towards that person. Why, then, did the Torah need to instruct us to assist even our enemies?

The Gemara there replies that the Torah is referring to a situation where the passerby is allowed and indeed commanded to hate the person in need. Perhaps, for example, the passerby had previously seen the person who is now in need violating the Torah in a serious manner Since on that occasion he was the only witness, he could not correct or punish the other person's violation of the Torah, but he is allowed, indeed commanded, to hate him because of his sin. Nevertheless, when the sinner's animal falls under its burden, the Torah commands the witness to render assistance.

The Rishonim ask: It would appear that the Gemara here contradicts the Gemara in tractate *Pesaḥim,* because the Gemara here rules that the commandment to assist our fellow Jews applies especially when our fellow Jew is our enemy — "in order to subdue our evil inclination." Surely there is no reason to suppress one's justified hatred of sinners!

Many Rishonim answer that the word "enemy" has different meanings in different contexts. The "enemy" mentioned in the verse is indeed the one described in the passage in tractate *Pesaḥim,* but in the Gemara here the word "enemy" is to be understood in the simple sense of the word, because the passage here is not explaining the verse, but rather the Halakhah. The point of our Gemara is simply that it is important to take advantage of the opportunity afforded by a fallen animal to overcome one's hatred for one's enemies, and the use of the word "enemy" must be understood in that context (*Tosafot, Ramban,* and others).

Other Rishonim suggest that the Gemara here may even be referring to the wicked enemy mentioned in tractate *Pesaḥim.* They explain that since the passerby there hates the person in need, albeit with justification, the person in need probably responds in kind and hates the passerby, without justification. Hence, the Torah tells the passerby to make a special point of assisting his enemy, so that the enemy will be encouraged to conquer *his* hatred and repent (*Rosh* and others).

Ritva suggests that the person who violated the Torah, as described in tractate *Pesaḥim,* may not be the owner of the animal, but rather the passerby. The person who witnessed the passerby's transgression (and is therefore, an enemy of the passerby) has an animal that needs to be loaded, while a friend of the passerby has an animal that needs to be unloaded. The Gemara here tells us that it is especially important for the passerby to load the animal of the person who justifiably hates him, in order to conquer his evil inclination.

לָכוֹף אֶת יִצְרוֹ עָדִיף To overcome one's evil inclination takes precedence. *Minḥat Ḥinnukh* explains that even

HALAKHAH

אוֹהֵב לִפְרוֹק וְשׂוֹנֵא לִטְעוֹן If a friend needs help to unload, and an enemy needs help to load. "Generally, if two animals need assistance, one to be loaded and the other to be unloaded, unloading takes priority over loading, because of the animal's suffering. But an animal belonging to an enemy of the passerby must always be given priority over an animal belonging to a friend, whether it needs loading or unloading, so that the passerby can use the opportunity to subdue his evil inclination." *Rema,* however, rules, following *Nimmukei Yosef,* that there is no obligation to grant priority to a person whom one justifiably hates because of his evil ways. (*Shulḥan Arukh, Ḥoshen Mishpat* 272:10.)

TRANSLATION AND COMMENTARY

תָּא שְׁמַע [1](5) The Gemara now seeks to bring a proof from the continuation of the Tosefta quoted above (*Bava Metzia* 2:26) that preventing suffering to animals is not a Torah law: **Come and hear: "The 'enemy' referred to** in the Torah in the expression (Exodus 23:5): 'If you see the ass of him who hates you (your enemy) lying under its burden' **is a Jewish enemy, but not a non-Jewish enemy."** Thus there is no specific commandment in the Torah to assist in the unloading of an animal belonging to a non-Jew. [2]Now, the Gemara asks, **if you say that the obligation to prevent suffering to animals is a Torah law,** [3]**what does it matter to me whether or not the enemy is Jewish?** In either case, an animal is suffering! The distinction made by the Tosefta between Jew and non-Jew thus indicates that the obligation to prevent suffering to animals is not a Torah law!

מִי סָבְרַתְּ [4]The Gemara answers: **Do you think that** this Tosefta **is referring to the "enemy" mentioned in the verse** in Exodus? This is not so. In fact, **it is referring to the "enemy"** mentioned in the previous clause **of the Tosefta,** which ruled that the obligation to load an enemy's animal takes precedence over the obligation to unload a friend's. The latter clause of the Tosefta is thus to be understood as follows: The enemy referred to in the previous clause of the Tosefta specifically means a Jewish enemy of the passerby, and not a non-Jewish enemy of the passerby. It is still possible to maintain that the obligation to prevent suffering to animals is a Torah law. But this aspect has no relevance here, because the case is one of *loading* a fallen animal, and in the case of delay in loading, no suffering to the animal is involved.

תָּא שְׁמַע [5](6) The Gemara now seeks to bring a proof from a Baraita (Mekhilta, *Mishpatim* 20) that preventing suffering to animals is not a Torah law: **Come and hear:** [33A] [6]"From the verse (Exodus 23:5) in the Torah describing the commandment to help pick up a fallen animal — 'If you see the donkey of him that hates you lying under its burden' — it is possible to make a number of deductions: (1) The verse says that the animal is **'lying,'** implying that this situation has occurred only on this one occasion, **but** if the animal is **one that habitually lies down,** the passerby is **not** required to assist. [7](2) The verse says that the animal must be **'lying,'** implying that the obligation to assist does **not** apply as long as it is still **standing.** [8](3) The verse says that the animal must be lying ***'under* its burden,'** implying that if the animal is already **unloaded** and only needs reloading, the passerby is **not** required to assist. (This will be explained below.) [9](4) The verse says that the animal must be lying 'under *its* burden,' meaning, under **a burden that it can bear,** but if the owner overloaded the animal beyond its capacity, the passerby is not required to assist."

[1]תָּא שְׁמַע: ״שׂוֹנֵא שֶׁאָמְרוּ שׂוֹנֵא יִשְׂרָאֵל, וְלֹא שׂוֹנֵא נָכְרִי״. [2]אִי אָמְרַתְּ צַעַר בַּעֲלֵי חַיִּים דְּאוֹרַיְיתָא, [3]מַה לִּי שׂוֹנֵא יִשְׂרָאֵל, וּמַה לִּי שׂוֹנֵא נָכְרִי? [4]מִי סָבְרַתְּ אַשּׂוֹנֵא דִּקְרָא קָאֵי? אַשּׂוֹנֵא דְּמַתְנִיתָא קָאֵי.
[5]תָּא שְׁמַע: [33A] [6]״׳רֹבֵץ׳ — וְלֹא רַבְצָן. [7]׳רֹבֵץ׳ — וְלֹא עוֹמֵד. [8]׳תַּחַת מַשָּׂאוֹ׳ — וְלֹא מְפוּרָק. [9]׳תַּחַת מַשָּׂאוֹ׳ — מַשּׂאוֹי שֶׁיָּכוֹל לַעֲמוֹד בּוֹ״.

LITERAL TRANSLATION

[1]Come [and] hear: "The 'enemy' they referred to (lit., 'said') is a Jewish enemy, but not a non-Jewish enemy." [2][But] if you say [that the obligation to prevent] suffering to animals is a Torah law, [3]what [does it matter] to me [if] the enemy is Jewish, and what [does it matter] to me [if] the enemy is non-Jewish?

[4]Do you think [that] it refers to the "enemy" of Scripture? It refers to the "enemy" of the Tosefta.

[5]Come [and] hear: [33A] [6]"'Lying' — but not one that habitually lies down. [7]'Lying' — but not standing. [8]'Under its burden' — but not unloaded. [9]'Under its burden' — a burden that it can bear."

RASHI

שונא שאמרו — הא קא סלקא דעתך שונא שאמרו אשונא דקרא קאי, דמשתעי בפריקה ״כי תראה חמור שונאך רובץ״ וגומר. **אשונא דמתניתין קאי** — אהך מתניתא דלעיל, דשונא לטעון הוא. **רובץ** — מקרה הוא לו שרובץ תחת משאו בפעם הזאת. **ולא רבצן** — הרגיל בכך. **ולא מפורק** — והוא צריך טעינה, ולקמן פריך: הכתיב ״הקם תקים״.

BACKGROUND

שׂוֹנֵא שֶׁאָמְרוּ The "enemy" they referred to. The discussion here is based on the stylistic difference between the two verses in which the commandments to help unload and load are stated. One verse says explicitly: "You shall not see your brother's ass" (Deuteronomy 22:4), indicating specifically that the animal belongs to a Jew. By contrast, the other verse, "If you see the ass of him that hates you" (Exodus 23:5), does not state explicitly who the enemy is. However, the context of these verses shows that they refer to relations among Jews, and that this is not a more general principle.

NOTES

though the obligation to avoid cruelty to animals is a Torah law, it is superseded by considerations of the passerby's moral development, because only unnecessary cruelty to animals is forbidden (see note above). It is permitted to cause suffering to animals if such an action is essential for human needs. Therefore, just as the passerby can use the animal for materialistic purposes, so too he can and should use it for purposes associated with his spiritual growth.

רֹבֵץ וְלֹא רַבְצָן Lying, but not one that habitually lies down. The Jerusalem Talmud asks: Does this Baraita not contradict the Mishnah (above, 32a), which rules that we are obliged to unload and load an animal repeatedly, as often as is necessary? It answers that that Mishnah is referring to an animal which repeatedly collapses because of its load, whereas the Baraita is referring to an animal which intentionally lies down out of stubbornness or laziness.

TRANSLATION AND COMMENTARY

[1]On this Baraita the Gemara asks: **But if you say that the obligation to prevent suffering to animals is a Torah law,** [2]**what does it matter to me if** the animal **is lying** down under its burden for the first time, **or if it** is an animal that **habitually lies down** under its burden, **or if it is standing?** In all three cases the animal is suffering, and the fact that the Baraita does not take this factor into consideration is an indication that the obligation to prevent suffering to animals is not a Torah law.

הָא מַנִּי [3]The Gemara answers: I accept that this Baraita cannot be reconciled with the viewpoint that the obligation to prevent pain to animals is a Torah law. But **whose teaching does this** Baraita reflect? [4]**That of Rabbi Yose HaGelili, who said that the obligation to prevent suffering to animals is not a Torah law.** Thus, even though the author of the Baraita may indeed maintain that preventing suffering to animals is not a Torah law, the normative Halakhah is not decided on the basis of this minority opinion.

הָכִי נַמִּי מִסְתַּבְּרָא [5]The Gemara now brings a proof that its ascription of the Baraita to the minority viewpoint of Rabbi Yose HaGelili is correct: **This** explanation **is also** the only **reasonable** and logical way to explain the Baraita, **for** the Baraita **says** that the expression in the verse **"under its burden"** means under a burden that it can bear. [6]Now, asks the Gemara, **which Sage have we found expressing such an opinion?** The answer has to be **Rabbi Yose HaGelili,** who expressed precisely this opinion in the last clause of our Mishnah (above, 32a). [7]Thus, you can **conclude from this** argument that the explanation of the Baraita given above is correct, and the author of the Baraita can only be Rabbi Yose HaGelili. Hence, the Baraita proves nothing about the normative Halakhah.

וּמִי מָצֵית מוֹקְמַתְּ לַהּ [8]**But,** asks the Gemara, how **can you explain** this Baraita **as** being **the opinion of Rabbi Yose HaGelili?** [9]**Surely, the third clause** of the Baraita **says:** "The verse says that the animal must be lying **'under its burden,'** implying that if the animal is already **unloaded** and only needs reloading, the passerby is **not** required to assist." [10]Now, **what does** the Baraita **mean** when it says that the passerby need **not** assist if the animal is already **unloaded?** [11]**If we say that** it means that if the animal is **unloaded there is no obligation** on the passerby to assist **at all,** this cannot be correct. **Surely** there **is** a specific commandment **written** in the Torah (Deuteronomy 22:4): **"You shall surely lift them up again with him."** Thus it is clear from this verse that the Torah does indeed command us to assist with the loading of animals. [12]**Rather,** explains the Gemara, **it is obvious that** the Baraita **means** that if the animal is **unloaded** and needs loading, **there is no obligation** on the passerby **to help** load the animal **for nothing, but rather,** even though he must assist, he is entitled to do so **for a fee.** In other words, the Baraita is entirely consistent with the viewpoint that a person helping to unload a fallen animal must do so without charge, whereas a person helping to load an animal is entitled to charge for his assistance. [13]Now, asks the Gemara, **whom did you hear** expressing **this opinion?** Surely it precisely reflects the viewpoint of **the Sages** mentioned in our Mishnah, as interpreted later by the Gemara (above, 32a end). Hence it follows that the opinion expressed in this Baraita is that of the Sages, and not that of Rabbi Yose, as we explained previously.

[1]וְאִי אָמְרַתְּ צַעַר בַּעֲלֵי חַיִּים דְּאוֹרַיְיתָא, [2]מַה לִּי רוֹבֵץ, וּמַה לִּי רַבְצָן, וּמַה לִּי עוֹמֵד? [3]הָא מַנִּי? [4]רַבִּי יוֹסֵי הַגְּלִילִי הִיא, דְּאָמַר צַעַר בַּעֲלֵי חַיִּים דְּרַבָּנַן.

[5]הָכִי נַמִּי מִסְתַּבְּרָא, דְּקָתָנֵי: "'תַּחַת מַשָּׂאוֹ' — מַשָּׂאוֹי שֶׁיָּכוֹל לַעֲמוֹד בּוֹ". [6]מַאן שָׁמְעַתְּ לֵיהּ דְּאִית לֵיהּ הַאי סְבָרָא? רַבִּי יוֹסֵי הַגְּלִילִי. [7]שְׁמַע מִינָּהּ.

[8]וּמִי מָצֵית מוֹקְמַתְּ לַהּ כְּרַבִּי יוֹסֵי הַגְּלִילִי? [9]וְהָא קָתָנֵי סֵיפָא: "'תַּחַת מַשָּׂאוֹ' — וְלֹא מְפוֹרָק". [10]מַאי "לֹא מְפוֹרָק"? [11]אִילֵימָא לֹא מְפוֹרָק כְּלָל, הָא כְּתִיב: "הָקֵם תָּקִים עִמּוֹ". [12]אֶלָּא, פְּשִׁיטָא: לֹא מְפוֹרָק בְּחִנָּם, אֶלָּא בְּשָׂכָר. [13]מַאן שָׁמְעַתְּ לֵיהּ דְּאִית לֵיהּ הַאי סְבָרָא? רַבָּנַן!

LITERAL TRANSLATION

[1]But if you say [that the obligation to prevent] suffering to animals is a Torah law, [2]what [does it matter] to me [if] it is lying, and what [does it matter] to me [if] it habitually lies down, and what [does it matter] to me [if] it is standing?

[3]Whose is this? [4]It is Rabbi Yose HaGelili, who said [that the obligation to prevent] suffering to animals is not a Torah law.

[5]So, too, it is reasonable, for it teaches: "'Under its burden' — a burden that it can bear." [6]Of whom did you hear that he has this opinion? Rabbi Yose HaGelili. [7]Conclude from this.

[8]But can you establish it as [the opinion of] Rabbi Yose HaGelili? [9]But surely the latter clause teaches: "'Under its burden' — but not unloaded." [10]What [does] "not unloaded" [mean]? [11]If we say [that] unloaded, there is no [obligation] at all, surely it is written: "You shall surely lift them up with him"? [12]Rather, it is obvious [that it means]: Unloaded, there is no [obligation to help] for nothing, but rather for a wage. [13]Of whom did you hear that he has this opinion? The Sages.

TRANSLATION AND COMMENTARY

לְעוֹלָם [1]The Gemara answers: This proof is not conclusive. **In fact, it is** quite possible that the Baraita reflects **the viewpoint of Rabbi Yose HaGelili,** as was argued previously. However, it is possible that **concerning** the right of the passerby to charge a fee for helping in **loading** an animal, **he is of the same opinion as the Sages** in their difference of opinion with Rabbi Shimon. In other words, the dispute between Rabbi Shimon and the Sages about charging for loading is completely independent of the dispute between Rabbi Yose and the Sages about preventing pain to animals.

At this point the Gemara's discussion of the obligation to prevent pain to animals comes to an end. Despite six attempts to prove that the obligation is of Torah origin, the discussion here ends inconclusively.

תָּנוּ רַבָּנַן [2]**Our Sages taught** the following Baraita: "The verse (Exodus 23:5) says: **'If you see** the donkey of him that hates you lying under its burden....' What does the term 'see' mean? [3]**I might have thought that it means** that the passerby must go to the trouble of helping **even** if he sees the fallen animal **from far away.** [4]**Therefore,** to avoid this erroneous impression, the previous verse in **the Torah** (Exodus 23:4) **says: 'If you meet** your enemy's ox or his donkey going astray...,' implying that the various commandments to assist one's neighbor all apply only if one is nearby. [5]But **if the verse** in the Torah had only **said:** 'If you meet...,' **I might have thought that it means** that the obligation to help applies only where the passerby **actually meets** the animal in distress, and that he has no obligation to help unless he is right next to the animal at the moment it needs help. [6]**Therefore,** to avoid this impression, the next verse in **the Torah** (Exodus 23:5) **says, 'If you see,'** implying that the various commandments to assist one's neighbor apply as soon as one sees that he is in distress." Hence, the Baraita is describing an intermediate situation, something between "actually meeting" the animal in distress and merely "seeing it from a distance." [7]The Baraita now asks rhetorically: **"But what** definition of **'seeing' is there that has in it** the idea of 'meeting'?" [8]The Baraita answers: **"The Sages calculated** it as being a situation where the passerby is standing at a distance of **one out of seven-and-a-half** parts (i.e., two-fifteenths) **of a *mil*** (2,000 cubits, approximately a kilometer) **and this** 266-cubit (approximately 150-meter) measure of distance **is called a *ris*."** From this Baraita we learn that the maximum distance at which a passerby witnessing an animal in distress is obliged to come to its assistance is approximately 150 meters.

[1]לְעוֹלָם, רַבִּי יוֹסֵי הַגְּלִילִי הִיא, וּבִטְעִינָה סָבַר לָהּ כְּרַבָּנַן. [2]תָּנוּ רַבָּנַן: "׳כִּי תִרְאֶה׳. [3]יָכוֹל אֲפִילּוּ מֵרָחוֹק. [4]תַּלְמוּד לוֹמַר: ׳כִּי תִפְגַּע׳. [5]אִי ׳כִּי תִפְגַּע׳ יָכוֹל פְּגִיעָה מַמָּשׁ. [6]תַּלְמוּד לוֹמַר: ׳כִּי תִרְאֶה׳. [7]וְאֵיזוֹ הִיא רְאִיָּה שֶׁיֵּשׁ בָּהּ פְּגִיעָה? [8]שִׁיעֲרוּ חֲכָמִים אֶחָד מִשֶּׁבַע וּמֶחֱצָה בְּמִיל, וְזֶה הוּא רִיס".

LITERAL TRANSLATION

[1]In fact, it is [the opinion of] Rabbi Yose HaGelili, and concerning loading he is of the same opinion as the Sages.

[2]Our Sages taught: "'If you see....' [3]I might have thought [that this means] even from far away. [4]Therefore the Torah says: 'If you meet....' [5]If [the verse says]: 'If you meet...,' I might have thought [that this means] actually meeting. [6]Therefore, the Torah says: 'If you see....' [7]But what 'seeing' is there that has in it [the idea of] 'meeting'? [8]The Sages calculated: One out of seven-and-a-half of a *mil*, and this is a *ris*."

RASHI

יכול מרחוק – והטיל עליו שילך שם.

BACKGROUND

רִיס ***Ris.*** This word is apparently a shortened form of the Persian *aspris*, meaning a racecourse or stadium.

The length of the *ris* is estimated in various sources (see *Arukh*) as a bowshot, which is 266 cubits, about a seventh of a Roman mile (2,000 cubits), or, in today's measurements, approximately 150 meters. According to an ancient etymological Midrash it was also called a רוס, the numerical value of the letters of which (266) is equal to the number of cubits in a *ris*.

NOTES

כִּי תִרְאֶה...כִּי תִפְגַּע **"If you see... if you meet...."** The Rishonim ask: The two verses refer to two different commandments: "If you see" refers to unloading a fallen animal, and "if you meet" refers to returning a lost animal. How can the Gemara link the two? Perhaps the law is that we must help unload a fallen animal if we see it even from afar, whereas we need not concern ourselves with caring for a stray animal unless we actually come across it.

Ritva explains that since there is a certain similarity between the two commandments, an association can be established between them. Alternatively, since the two verses follow one another in the Torah, they are intended to be linked to each other.

Gra suggests a textual emendation, substituting the verse "You shall not see" (Deuteronomy 22:1) in place of the verse "if you see" (Exodus 23:5), because the verse in

HALAKHAH

כִּי תִרְאֶה...כִּי תִפְגַּע **"If you see... if you meet...."** "From what distance is the passerby required to render assistance? When he sees the animal from a distance that is a combination of 'seeing' and 'meeting.' The Sages fixed this distance at a *ris*, which is 2/15 of a *mil* or just over 266 cubits. If the fallen animal is further away than this, the passerby is not obliged to help with it." (*Shulḥan Arukh, Ḥoshen Mishpat* 272:5.)

TRANSLATION AND COMMENTARY

תָּנָא [1]The Gemara now quotes another Baraita, in which a Tanna taught the following law: "After the passerby has helped reload the animal, **he must accompany** the animal together **with** its owner **up to** a distance of **a parasang** (four *mil,* or approximately four kilometers), to ensure that the animal is now steady on its feet and is not liable to collapse a second time." [2]Commenting on this Baraita, **Rabbah bar Bar Ḥanah** said: The passerby is permitted to **take a fee** for this service, since it is not an essential part of the commandment.

MISHNAH אֲבֵדָתוֹ וַאֲבֵדַת אָבִיו [3]If a person finds two lost objects, one **his own lost object and** the other **a lost object belonging to his father,** and the circumstances are such that he cannot take care of both at the same time and must decide which one to deal with first, **his own lost object takes precedence.**

אֲבֵדָתוֹ וַאֲבֵדַת רַבּוֹ [4]If the choice is between recovering **his own lost object and his teacher's lost object, his own** lost object **takes precedence.**

אֲבֵדַת אָבִיו [5]If the choice is between recovering **his father's lost object and his teacher's lost object, his teacher's takes precedence.** [6]The reason why the respect due to his teacher is in general greater than that due to his father is **because his father** only **brought him into this world,** and gave him physical life, [7]**whereas his teacher who taught him wisdom** and was responsible for developing his spiritual life **brings him into the life of the world to come.** [8]**But if his father is** himself **a Sage,** and must also be respected for his Torah knowledge even though he is not his son's teacher, then **the father's** lost object **takes precedence** over that of the teacher.

[1]תָּנָא: ״וּמְדַדֶּה עִמּוֹ עַד פַּרְסָה״. [2]אָמַר רַבָּה בַּר בַּר חָנָה: וְנוֹטֵל שָׂכָר.

משנה [3]אֲבֵדָתוֹ וַאֲבֵדַת אָבִיו — אֲבֵדָתוֹ קוֹדֶמֶת. [4]אֲבֵדָתוֹ וַאֲבֵדַת רַבּוֹ — שֶׁלּוֹ קוֹדֵם. [5]אֲבֵדַת אָבִיו וַאֲבֵדַת רַבּוֹ — שֶׁל רַבּוֹ קוֹדֶמֶת, [6]שֶׁאָבִיו הֱבִיאוֹ לָעוֹלָם הַזֶּה, [7]וְרַבּוֹ, שֶׁלִּמְּדוֹ חָכְמָה, מְבִיאוֹ לְחַיֵּי הָעוֹלָם הַבָּא. [8]וְאִם אָבִיו חָכָם, שֶׁל אָבִיו קוֹדֶמֶת.

LITERAL TRANSLATION

[1][A Tanna] taught: "And he leads [it] with him up to a parasang." [2]Rabbah bar Bar Ḥanah said: And he takes a wage.

MISHNAH [3]His own lost object and his father's lost object — his own lost object takes precedence.

[4]His own lost object and his teacher's lost object — his own takes precedence.

[5]His father's lost object and his teacher's lost object — his teacher's takes precedence, [6]because his father brought him into this world, [7]but his teacher, who taught him wisdom, brings him into the life of the world to come. [8]But if his father is a Sage, his father's takes precedence.

RASHI

מדדה עמו — לאחר שהטעינו, שמא יחזור ויפול.

BACKGROUND

וּמְדַדֶּה עִמּוֹ And he leads it with him. The word מְדַדֶּה signifies a way of walking that includes both holding and helping along. The verb is also used in connection with helping toddlers to walk. Here it indicates that since the donkey has fallen several times, it is no longer steady on its legs, and must be accompanied over a certain distance and helped so that it does not fall again. The Sages estimated that if it was accompanied in this way for a parasang and did not fall, then it had certainly recovered its strength and could safely continue on its way.

LANGUAGE

פַּרְסָה Parasang. A unit of length of Persian origin. The term derives from the middle-Persian *frasang,* which is *farsang* in modern Persian. The word was borrowed by Semitic languages (in Syrian **פרסחא**, *parsaha*) and by Greek (παρασάγγης, *parasanges*). A פַּרְסָה is approximately four kilometers.

NOTES

Deuteronomy, like the verse "if you meet" (Exodus 23:4), also deals with the returning of a stray animal. But this suggestion had already been rejected by the Rishonim, since, in its amended form, the Baraita would not be dealing at all with assisting a fallen animal, and there would be no reason for the Gemara to quote it in the present context (*Shittah Mekubbetzet*).

HALAKHAH

מְדַדֶּה וְנוֹטֵל שָׂכָר He accompanies the animal, but he may charge a wage for this service. "After the passerby has helped to unload and reload the animal, he must continue to walk with it for a distance of a parasang (four *mil* or 8,000 cubits), so that he is available to render assistance if necessary. He may charge for this service," following the Gemara. (*Shulḥan Arukh, Ḥoshen Mishpat* 272:4.)

אֲבֵדָתוֹ קוֹדֶמֶת His own lost object takes precedence. "If two people lose objects, and one of them finds both objects, he must recover both of them, where that is possible. If it is impossible to recover both of them, the finder's lost object takes precedence over that of any other person, even that of his father or teacher. Nevertheless, a person should go beyond the strict letter of the law and should not put his own personal interests first, except when confronted with the possibility of serious loss. A person who cares only about himself will find himself neglecting the obligation to perform deeds of kindness, and in the end will find himself in need of the assistance of others," following the Mishnah and Gemara. (Ibid., 264:1.)

אֲבֵדַת אָבִיו וַאֲבֵדַת רַבּוֹ His father's lost object and his teacher's lost object. "If a person finds two objects, one lost by his father, and the other lost by his teacher, his teacher's takes precedence, unless his father is also a Torah scholar of the same stature as his teacher. But this law applies only to a teacher from whom the disciple has gained most of his knowledge." (Ibid., 264:2.)

TRANSLATION AND COMMENTARY

הָיָה אָבִיו וְרַבּוֹ נוֹשְׂאִין מַשּׂאוֹי [1]**If his father and his teacher are each carrying a burden,** and both of them need help in unloading what they are carrying, [2]**he must** first unload and **put down his teacher's** burden, **and** only **afterwards** unload and **put down his father's**, for the same reason as mentioned above.

הָיָה אָבִיו וְרַבּוֹ בְּבֵית הַשֶּׁבִי [3]**If his father and his teacher have been taken captive,** and their captors are demanding for their release a ransom beyond the power of the son and disciple to pay, [4]**he must** first **redeem his teacher, and** only **afterwards redeem his father.** [5]**But** here, too, as in the case of a lost object mentioned above, **if his father is** himself **a Sage,** [6]the son **must** first **redeem his father, and** only **afterwards must he redeem his teacher.**

[1]הָיָה אָבִיו וְרַבּוֹ נוֹשְׂאִין מַשּׂאוֹי, [2]מַנִּיחַ אֶת שֶׁל רַבּוֹ, וְאַחַר כָּךְ מַנִּיחַ אֶת שֶׁל אָבִיו. [3]הָיָה אָבִיו וְרַבּוֹ בְּבֵית הַשֶּׁבִי, [4]פּוֹדֶה אֶת רַבּוֹ, וְאַחַר כָּךְ פּוֹדֶה אֶת אָבִיו. [5]וְאִם אָבִיו חָכָם, [6]פּוֹדֶה אֶת אָבִיו, וְאַחַר כָּךְ פּוֹדֶה אֶת רַבּוֹ.

גמרא [7]מְנָא הָנֵי מִילֵּי? [8]אָמַר רַב יְהוּדָה אָמַר רַב: אָמַר קְרָא: ״אֶפֶס כִּי לֹא יִהְיֶה בְּךָ אֶבְיוֹן״ — [9]שֶׁלְּךָ קוֹדֵם לְשֶׁל כָּל אָדָם.

LITERAL TRANSLATION

[1][If] his father and his teacher were [each] carrying a burden, [2]he puts down his teacher's, and afterwards he puts down his father's.

[3][If] his father and his teacher were in captivity, [4]he redeems his teacher, and afterwards he redeems his father. [5]But if his father is a Sage, [6]he redeems his father, and afterwards he redeems his teacher.

GEMARA [7]From where are these things [derived]?

[8]Rav Yehudah said in the name of Rav: The verse says: "Except that there shall be no poor among you" — [9]yours comes before that of every man.

RASHI

גמרא מנא הני מילי — דשלו קודם. **לא יהיה בך אביון** — הזהר מן עניות.

GEMARA מְנָא הָנֵי מִילֵּי [7]The Gemara begins its analysis of the Mishnah by questioning the source for the series of rulings at the beginning of the Mishnah that a person's own interests always take priority, even over the interests of people towards whom he is duty-bound to show respect. **From where** in the Torah, asks the Gemara, **are these rulings derived?**

אָמַר רַב יְהוּדָה [8]**Rav Yehudah said** in reply **in the name of Rav: The verse** (Deuteronomy 15:4) that **says: "Except that there shall be no poor among you."** The word בְּךָ — "in you," "among you" — appears superfluous in this sentence, and Rav uses it as the source for his ruling that we have a responsibility to see to it that we do not ourselves become paupers. [9]Hence, says Rav, **your** financial needs **come before those of all other men.**

NOTES

אָבִיו וְרַבּוֹ His father versus his teacher. Many Rishonim have a different version of the clause of the Mishnah dealing with lost objects. Their text reads as follows: "If his father is equivalent in stature to his teacher, his father takes precedence." But their version of the clause dealing with redemption from captivity is the same as ours: "If his father is a Sage, he redeems his father, and afterwards he redeems his teacher." Thus, according to these Rishonim, the father takes precedence over the teacher in being redeemed from captivity, even if he is not of the same scholarly stature as the teacher, provided that he is a Torah scholar; but in the case of returning lost objects, the teacher always takes precedence, unless the father is of the same scholarly stature (*Rif* and others).

The Rishonim explain the difference between the clauses as follows: With regard to a lost object, since all that is involved is financial loss, more consideration is given to one's teacher. But with regard to redemption from captivity, which is a positive expression of the commandment to honor, more consideration is given to one's father, since he is also a Sage and must be honored for two reasons (*Ritva, Rosh*).

The Aḥaronim offer additional resolutions. Noting a subtle discrepancy between the clauses in the Mishnah — the fact that in the earlier clause "his teacher takes precedence," whereas in the later clause "he redeems his teacher and afterwards he redeems his father" — *Rashash* maintains that the teacher is given priority in regard to redemption from captivity only if it is possible to redeem both individuals; otherwise, the father alone is to be redeemed. But with regard to lost objects, the teacher always takes precedence.

Leḥem Mishneh notes the same subtle discrepancy, and rules that the law is the same regarding both redemption and the returning of a lost object: If the father is a scholar, albeit not of the stature of the teacher, he must be redeemed

HALAKHAH

פִּדְיוֹן אָבִיו וְרַבּוֹ Redeeming his father and his teacher. "If a person's father and teacher are both taken captive, he must first redeem his teacher, and only afterwards redeem his father. Similarly, if a person's father and teacher both need assistance with the burdens they are carrying, he must first unload his teacher's burden and only afterwards his father's. *Rema* adds that if his father is a Torah scholar, even if he is not a scholar of the stature of his teacher, his father takes precedence, unlike the rule in the case of a lost object." (*Shulḥan Arukh, Yoreh De'ah* 242:34.)

BACKGROUND

וְרַבּוֹ, שֶׁלִּמְּדוֹ חָכְמָה **But his teacher, who taught him wisdom.** As explained below in the Gemara, the word חָכְמָה — "wisdom" — is not narrowly defined here. However, it needed to be used here because the honorific title רַבּוֹ — "his master" — can also be applied to teachers in fields other than Torah. Therefore the Talmud had to emphasize that it was not referring to just any sort of teacher, but rather to one who taught his student wisdom.

אֲפִילּוּ לֹא הֵאִיר עֵינָיו **Even if he enlightened his eyes....** A similar teaching is found in the *Ethics of the Fathers* (6:2): "One who learns one chapter or one Halakhah or one verse or one saying or even one word from his fellow must honor him. For we have found that David, King of Israel, learned only two things from Aḥitofel, and he called him his master, lord and familiar."

TRANSLATION AND COMMENTARY

וְאָמַר רַב יְהוּדָה [1]Commenting on this ruling, **Rav Yehudah further said in the name of Rav:** Even though this rule is the Halakhah, and we are exempt from helping others at our own expense, it should not be applied in practice except to avoid serious and certain loss. In all other circumstances we should go beyond the strict letter of the law and expend money to give charity and help others. For **whoever** literally **fulfills this** ruling on his own behalf, and constantly thinks of himself first, **will** ultimately **come to** suffer the fate described in the verse. He will himself become poor, and other people in their turn will not help him — out of concern for their own interests.

הָיָה אָבִיו וְרַבּוֹ [2]The Gemara now considers a later clause of the Mishnah: **"If his father and his teacher are each carrying a burden,** he must first unload and put down his teacher's burden." [3]**Our Sages taught** the following Baraita which gives the opinions of various Tannaitic scholars as to the correct definition of "teacher" in our Mishnah: **'The expression, 'his teacher,' which was used** by the Mishnah, **refers** specifically **to a teacher who taught him the wisdom** of the Talmud, i.e., profound analysis of Torah and Mishnah, and the study of the principles underlying the laws contained in them, **but not to a teacher who** only **taught him Scripture or Mishnah,** i.e., the memorization of Halakhic rulings without the understanding required to delve into their underlying principles. [4]**These are the words of Rabbi Meir.** Thus, according to Rabbi Meir, the elevated status accorded in our Mishnah to a person's teacher refers to someone who imparted not only Torah knowledge but also the ability to analyze and provide answers to actual Halakhic problems. [5]**Rabbi Yehudah says:** In its use of the word 'teacher' the Mishnah **means anyone from whom** the student **has learned most of his wisdom,** whether that consists of Scripture, Mishnah or Talmud. [6]**Rabbi Yose says: Even if** a certain person **enlightened** the student by clarifying his understanding of **only one Mishnah, he is 'the teacher'** referred to in our Mishnah."

[1]וְאָמַר רַב יְהוּדָה אָמַר רַב: כָּל הַמְקַיֵּים בְּעַצְמוֹ כָּךְ סוֹף בָּא לִידֵי כָּךְ.

[2]"הָיָה אָבִיו וְרַבּוֹ נוֹשְׂאִין מַשּׂאוֹי וכו׳". [3]תָּנוּ רַבָּנַן: "'רַבּוֹ' שֶׁאָמְרוּ — רַבּוֹ שֶׁלִּמְּדוֹ חָכְמָה, וְלֹא רַבּוֹ שֶׁלִּמְּדוֹ מִקְרָא וּמִשְׁנָה. [4]דִּבְרֵי רַבִּי מֵאִיר. [5]רַבִּי יְהוּדָה אוֹמֵר: כָּל שֶׁרוֹב חָכְמָתוֹ הֵימֶנּוּ. [6]רַבִּי יוֹסֵי אוֹמֵר: אֲפִילּוּ לֹא הֵאִיר עֵינָיו אֶלָּא בְּמִשְׁנָה אַחַת, זֶה הוּא רַבּוֹ".

LITERAL TRANSLATION

[1]And Rav Yehudah [further] said in the name of Rav: Whoever fulfills this on himself ultimately comes to this.

[2]"[If] his father and his teacher were [each] carrying a burden, etc." [3]Our Sages taught: "[The expression] 'his teacher,' which they said, [means] his teacher who taught him wisdom, but not his teacher who taught him Bible or Mishnah. [4][These are] the words of Rabbi Meir. [5]Rabbi Yehudah says: [It means] anyone from whom [he has learned] most of his wisdom. [6]Rabbi Yose says: Even [if] he enlightened his eyes about only one Mishnah, this is his teacher."

RASHI

כל המקיים בעצמו כך — אף על פי שלא הטילו עליו הכתוב יש לאדם ליכנס לפנים משורת הדין ולא לדקדק שלי קודם, אם לא בהפסד מוכיח, ואם תמיד מדקדק — פורק מעליו עול גמילות חסדים ולדקה וסוף שילטרך לבריות. **שלמדו חכמה** — סברת טעמי המשנה ולהבין שלא יהו סותרות זו את זו, וטעמי איסור והיתר והחיוב והפטור, והוא נקרא גמרא. **מקרא** — תורה נביאים וכתובים. **משנה** — כמו שהן שנויות, ואין טעמן מפורש בהן. **כל שרוב חכמתו הימנו** — אם מקרא אם משנה אם גמרא. **האיר עיניו** — שהודיעו טעם משנה אחת שלא יכול להבין.

NOTES

before the teacher, if it is possible to redeem both. But if it is impossible to redeem both, the teacher comes first, unless the father is a scholar of equal stature.

Concerning the question of the priority of the teacher over the father, *Sefer Ḥasidim* (quoted by *Rema*) rules that if a person's father paid for his Torah education, he is given priority in all cases.

HALAKHAH

מִי הוּא הַנִּקְרָא רַבּוֹ **Who is considered to be a person's teacher?** "The rule that a person must hold his teacher in the utmost reverence applies specifically to the teacher from whom he has learned most of his wisdom. *Rema* (following *Maharik*) explains that this means the teacher who taught him to understand the concepts underlying the practical application of Torah law. Other teachers who taught him Torah must also be shown respect: he must stand when they pass within four cubits in front of him, and he must mourn their death by rending his garments, but the extreme respect displayed towards the teacher from whom he has learned most of his wisdom need not be displayed towards them." (*Shulḥan Arukh, Yoreh De'ah* 242:30.)

[1]אֲמַר רָבָא: כְּגוֹן רַב סְחוֹרָה, דְּאַסְבְּרָן זוּהֲמָא לִיסְטְרוֹן. [2]שְׁמוּאֵל קְרַע מָאנֵיהּ עֲלֵיהּ הַהוּא מֵרַבָּנַן דְּאַסְבְּרֵיהּ: [3]״אֶחָד יוֹרֵד לְאַמַּת הַשֶּׁחִי, וְאֶחָד פּוֹתֵחַ כֵּיוָן״.

[4]אָמַר עוּלָּא: תַּלְמִידֵי חֲכָמִים שֶׁבְּבָבֶל עוֹמְדִין זֶה מִפְּנֵי זֶה, וְקוֹרְעִין זֶה עַל זֶה. [5]וּלְעִנְיַן אֲבֵדָה בִּמְקוֹם אָבִיו, [6]אֵינָן חוֹזְרִין אֶלָּא לְרַבּוֹ מוּבְהָק.

LITERAL TRANSLATION

[1]Rava said: Like Rav Seḥorah, who explained to me *zuhama listron.*

[2]Shmuel rent his garments over a certain Rabbi who explained to him: [3]"One goes down to the armpit, and one opens directly."

[4]Ulla said: The scholars in Babylonia stand one before the other, and they rend their garments one over the other. [5]But with regard to the matter of a [teacher's] lost object in place of one's father's, [6]they do not return except to one's foremost teacher.

TRANSLATION AND COMMENTARY

אֲמַר רָבָא [1]To illustrate Rabbi Yose's opinion, **Rava said: For example,** I must treat **Rav Seḥorah** as my teacher, even though in my entire life he **explained** only one concept **to me**, namely, the meaning of the term ***zuhama listron,*** which appears in the Mishnah (*Kelim* 13:2). (It is a utensil which combines a fork and a spoon, and is used to scrape leftover food from a pot.)

שְׁמוּאֵל קְרַע מָאנֵיהּ [2]The Gemara further illustrates this point with a story: **Shmuel rent his garments** in mourning **over** the death of **a certain Rabbi who explained to him** only one concept in his entire life, namely, the meaning of the line in the Mishnah (*Tamid* 3:6): [3]**"With one he reaches down to his armpit and with one he opens directly."** This expression describes the way in which the priests opened the gates to the Temple each morning: Two locks had to be opened. The first could be opened only by inserting one's entire arm through a hole by the side of the gate and opening the lock from the inside, while the second opened normally. Even though this Rabbi explained nothing else to Shmuel, the latter still regarded him as his teacher, and rent his garments when he died.

אָמַר עוּלָּא [4]**Ulla,** a Sage who frequently travelled between Eretz Israel and Babylonia, now describes the respect with which the Sages in Babylonia treated each other. He **said: The scholars in Babylonia stand in deference to each other** in the same way as a disciple rises in the presence of his teacher, **and they rend their garments** in mourning **over** the death of **another scholar.** These acts of deference were displayed because in Babylonia, in contrast to the practice in Eretz Israel (see "background" note), it was not customary for students to have one particular teacher. Rather, students would study together and learn from each other. Accordingly, each considered the other to be, in a sense, his teacher. [5]**But,** continues Ulla, their practice is different **with regard to the matter of** granting priority to returning **a teacher's lost object before** returning the lost object of **one's father.** [6]In such a situation a Babylonian scholar **does not** give precedence to **returning** the lost property of his colleagues, or of Rabbis from whom he has learned a few concepts. He gives such precedence **only** to returning a lost object **to his foremost teacher,** from whom he has learned most of his wisdom, in accordance with the opinion of Rabbi Yehudah in our Mishnah.

RASHI

דאסברן זוהמא ליסטרון – בסדר טהרות (כלים, פרק יג משנה ב, ופרק כה משנה ג) היא שנויה, ולא הייתי יודע מה כלי הוא, ולמדני שהוא כף גדולה שמסלקין בו זוהם הקדירה והקלחת לצדדין. **קרע מאניה** – קרע שאין מתאחה, כדין תלמיד על הרב. **אחד יורד לאמת השחי** – משנה היא במסכת תמיד (פרק ג משנה ו), אצל הנכנסים שחרית לפתוח דלתות ההיכל: מי שזכה בדישון מזבח הפנימי כו׳, ושני מפתחות בידו, אחד יורד לאמת השחי ואחד פותח כיון, אחד מן המפתחות הללו פותח פשפש הצפוני שאצל פתח ההיכל בקרן מזרחית צפונית של אולם והיכל, כדתנן התם: שני פשפשים היה לו לשער הגדול, אחד לצפון ההיכל והאולם ואחד לדרומו, ואותו שבדרום לא נכנס בו אדם מעולם, כדמפרש התם, ואותו פשפש שבצפון, והוא לפתח שבזוית האולם, שאצל חמש אמות של כותל ההיכל שבצפון פתח ההיכל, ודלת סובבת בו, ואותו מפתח של אותו הפתח יורד לאמת השחי. **פשפשים** – פתחים קטנים, כמין ציפות קטנות, ארכו כעובי רוחב הכותל ודלת סובבת בו *פוסטי״ר בלעז, אחד יורד לאמת השחי, הבא לפתוח בו שחרית [פשפש שבזוית האולם] עומד מבחוץ בתוך האולם, ומכניס ידו בחור שבכותל עד בית שחיו, ופותח. **ואחד פותח כיון** – לאחר שנכנס בזה ובא לו לתא אשר על פני אחת עשרה אמה של אולם וקלת מן ההיכל, ופותח במפתח שני דלת אחד שמן התא להיכל מהר בלא טורח כשאר פתחים, ונכנס להיכל לפתוח דלתות ההיכל. **כיון** – כמו (פסחים לז,א) יעשנה בדפוס ויקבענה כיון, מהר בלא טורח, והאי שער הגדול הוא פתח ההיכל שבין אולם להיכל. **עומדין זה מפני זה** – כדין תלמיד לרב, לפי שהיו יושבין תמיד בבית המדרש יחד ומקשין ומפרקין, וכולם למדים זה מזה. **לרבו מובהק** – שרוב חכמתו ממנו, כר׳ יהודה.

NOTES

רַב סְחוֹרָה דְּאַסְבְּרָן זוּהֲמָא לִיסְטְרוֹן Rav Seḥorah who explained to me *zuhama listron.* *Tosafot* (*Yevamot* 106a, *Sanhedrin* 49b, *Avodah Zarah* 19a) raises the question that there are *many* instances in the Talmud where Rava quotes a Halakhah in the name of Rav Seḥorah. Among the answers he gives are: (1) We should amend the text to read "Rabbah"

LANGUAGE

זוּהֲמָא לִיסְטְרוֹן Zuhama listron. This word, meaning soup-spoon, derives from the Greek, apparently combining the word ζωμός, *zomos,* meaning "soup," with μύστρον, *mustron,* meaning "spoon." According to the sources, this was a metal utensil which had a spoon at one end and a fork at the other.

LANGUAGE (RASHI)

פושטי״ר* Perhaps from the Old French *posterne,* meaning "a small gate."

BACKGROUND

תַּלְמִידֵי חֲכָמִים שֶׁבְּבָבֶל The scholars in Babylonia. Originally there was a marked difference between the organization of study in Babylonia and in Eretz Israel. In Eretz Israel, where the House of Study was close to the Great Sanhedrin and was directly influenced by it, a precise hierarchical order was preserved for many generations. Study took place under the direction of the head of the yeshivah in the House of Study. However, in Babylonia, the head of the yeshivah did not originally have such far-reaching authority, and the majority of the students came only during the special study sessions held twice a year and lasting one month (יַרְחֵי כַּלָּה). Hence the main study was done in small groups, and all the Sages of Babylonia used to derive their knowledge and wisdom as much (if not more) from each other as from the head of the yeshivah.

וְקוֹרְעִין זֶה עַל זֶה And they rend their garments one over the other. Tearing one's garment is a sign of mourning, and one is obliged to tear one's garment upon the death of any of one's immediate family (parents, siblings, children or spouse). Similarly, one tears one's garment upon the death of one's teacher, for he is like one's spiritual father. *Tosafot* comments that the Sages said that one is commanded to tear one's garment upon the death of any upright person, and not necessarily one's teacher. But there is a

[1] קָבָּעֵי מִינֵּיהּ רַב חִסְדָּא מֵרַב הוּנָא: ״תַּלְמִיד וְצָרִיךְ לוֹ רַבּוֹ מַאי״? [2] אֲמַר לֵיהּ: ״חִסְדָּא, חִסְדָּא, לָא צְרִיכְנָא לָךְ. אַתְּ צְרִיכַתְּ לִי עַד אַרְבְּעִין שְׁנִין״. [3] אִיקְפְּדִי אַהֲדָדֵי וְלָא עָיְילֵי לְגַבֵּי הֲדָדֵי. [4] יְתֵיב רַב חִיסְדָּא אַרְבְּעִין תַּעֲנִיתָא מִשּׁוּם דַּחֲלַשׁ דַּעְתֵּיהּ דְּרַב הוּנָא. [5] יְתֵיב רַב הוּנָא אַרְבְּעִין תַּעֲנִיתָא מִשּׁוּם דְּחַשְׁדֵיהּ לְרַב חִסְדָּא.

[6] אִיתְּמַר, רַב יִצְחָק בַּר יוֹסֵף אָמַר רַבִּי יוֹחָנָן: הֲלָכָה כְּרַבִּי יְהוּדָה. [7] רַב אַחָא בַּר רַב הוּנָא אָמַר רַב שֵׁשֶׁת: הֲלָכָה כְּרַבִּי יוֹסֵי.

LITERAL TRANSLATION

[1] Rav Ḥisda asked a question of Rav Huna: "What is [the law regarding] a disciple whose teacher needs him?" [2] He said to him: "Ḥisda, Ḥisda, I do not need you. You will need me up to forty years." [3] They were angry with each other and did not visit each other. [4] Rav Ḥisda sat forty fasts because Rav Huna had felt insulted. [5] Rav Huna sat forty fasts because he had suspected Rav Ḥisda.

[6] It was said: Rav Yitzḥak bar Yosef said in the name of Rabbi Yoḥanan: The Halakhah is in accordance with Rabbi Yehudah. [7] Rav Aḥa bar Rav Huna said in the name of Rav Sheshet: The Halakhah is in accordance with Rabbi Yose.

TRANSLATION AND COMMENTARY

קָבָּעֵי מִינֵּיהּ רַב חִסְדָּא [1] The Gemara now illustrates the relationships between the scholars of Babylonia with the following story: **Rav Ḥisda,** who was the disciple and colleague of Rav Huna, **asked Rav Huna** for the solution to **the following problem: "What is the law regarding a disciple whose teacher is dependent on him** for knowledge of traditions and rulings that the disciple has heard from other teachers?" With this question Rav Ḥisda touched on a sensitive point. Though Rav Huna was recognized by them both as Rav Ḥisda's teacher, Rav Ḥisda was Rav Huna's primary disciple and colleague. Rav Huna thought that Rav Hisda's question implied that Rav Huna was dependent on him. [2] Rav Huna **said to him** in reply: **"Ḥisda, Ḥisda, I am not dependent on you.** But **you will be dependent on me for forty years.** (See note.) [3] The story concludes: From the time of this incident **they were angry with each other, and** as a result **they did not visit each other.** Ultimately they realized that their estrangement had been due to a misunderstanding, and they were reconciled. [4] **Rav Ḥisda took upon himself forty fast days** to atone for the fact that **Rav Huna had felt insulted** by the innocent question he had thoughtlessly asked. [5] **Rav Huna took upon himself forty fast days because he had** wrongly **suspected Rav Ḥisda** of referring to their unique relationship, when in fact he had merely been asking a theoretical question.

אִיתְּמַר [6] **It was said** that there was a dispute between Amoraim as to which opinion in the Baraita mentioned above is accepted as the normative Halakhah: **Rav Yitzḥak bar Yosef said in the name of Rabbi Yoḥanan: The Halakhah is in accordance with Rabbi Yehudah,** who said that the word "teacher" in our Mishnah refers to the teacher from whom a student learned most of his knowledge. [7] **Rav Aḥa bar Rav Huna said in the name of Rav Sheshet: The Halakhah is in accordance with Rabbi Yose,** who said that the word "teacher" in our Mishnah refers to anyone from whom the student learned to understand even a single Mishnah.

RASHI

וצריך לו רבו – ששמע שמועות שיש בידו מפי אחרים. **מאי** – כלומר, קודם לאביו לענין אבדה.

NOTES

instead of "Rava." (2) Everything else that Rava learned from Rav Seḥorah was learned only after Rava made this statement. (3) Everything else that Rava learned from Rav Seḥorah had previously been stated by someone else, and this was the only original explanation Rav Seḥorah ever gave Rava. (4) Rava meant to say that even if his teacher Rav Seḥorah had taught him only this one Halakhah, it would have been sufficient.

עַד אַרְבְּעִין שְׁנִין For forty years. The Gemara elsewhere (*Avodah Zarah* 5b) says: It is only after forty years have passed that a person comprehends his teacher's intentions. This concept is derived from Moses' statement to the Israelites at the end of forty years in the wilderness (Deuteronomy 29:3): "The Lord has not given you a heart to perceive, and eyes to see, and ears to hear, until this day." Hence the Rishonim explain that Rav Huna was reminding Rav Ḥisda that much time had still to pass before he could master everything he had been taught (*Rabbenu Ḥananel* and others).

Maharsha offers an original interpretation based on a different punctuation of the passage: The passage can be read: "For forty years they were angry with each other." Thus the Gemara is implying that Rav Huna's reprimand was so severe that it required forty years to be corrected, as did the sin of the Jews in the wilderness, which also involved a revolt of disciples against their teachers. This would also explain the forty fasts.

distinction, in that in most instances, after one has torn one's garment as a sign of mourning, one may later mend it so that the tear is no longer visible. However, one is forbidden ever to completely mend a garment which one has torn on account of the death of a parent or a teacher.

BACKGROUND

אַרְבְּעִין תַּעֲנִיתָא Forty fasts. The number "forty" appears in other Talmudic passages describing people who fasted as an act of repentance, and the Sages wrote that this number refers to a number of contexts mentioned in the Bible and in the works of the Sages regarding the spiritual level of total self-correction. Here the forty fasts have additional meaning in that Rav Huna mentioned the number forty in his rejoinder.

מִשּׁוּם דְּחַשְׁדֵיהּ לְרַב חִסְדָּא Because he had suspected Rav Ḥisda. The Sages frequently said that a person must always attempt to judge his fellowman positively, for even when someone appears to be sinning, his actions should if possible be given another interpretation, so as to avoid condemning him. The Sages also said (*Yoma* 19a) that someone who suspects the innocent should be lashed: This is the reason why Rav Huna was so remorseful at having wrongly suspected Rav Ḥisda.

SAGES

רַב הוּנָא Rav Huna. A Babylonian Amora of the second generation. See *Bava Metzia*, Part I, p. 52.

רַב חִסְדָּא Rav Ḥisda. One of the greatest Babylonian Amoraim of the second generation, Rav Ḥisda, a priest, was one of Rav's younger students. After Rav's death he remained a colleague and student of Rav's student, Rav Huna. Throughout his life he displayed strong affection for the words of his teacher, Rav, and he tried to add to his knowledge of Rav's teachings. Though he was poor as a youth, he became wealthy and lived most of his life in comfort. He was affable towards his fellowmen, and devoted to his students, to his

TRANSLATION AND COMMENTARY

וּמִי אֲמַר רַבִּי יוֹחָנָן הָכִי [1]The Gemara now asks: **But did Rabbi Yoḥanan** in fact **make such a statement?** [2]**Surely Rabbi Yoḥanan** is the author of the following important rule in Halakhic decision-making: **The Halakhah is** always **in accordance with** the anonymous opinion in the **Mishnah.** [3]And our Mishnah, which contains no Tannaitic disputes and is therefore entirely written by "the anonymous opinion," defines **"teacher"** as the person **who taught his disciple "wisdom."** This presumably means the wisdom of the Talmud, which is Rabbi Meir's and not Rabbi Yehudah's view.

מַאי חָכְמָה [4]The Gemara responds by asking: **What is** meant by the word **"wisdom"** as used in our Mishnah? It answers: Not necessarily "the wisdom of the Talmud," but rather **"most of his wisdom"** — whether it be in Scripture, Mishnah or Talmud — as Rabbi Yehudah ruled in the Baraita. Thus there is no contradiction between Rabbi Yoḥanan's two statements.

תָּנוּ רַבָּנַן [5]The previous discussion as to who should be considered a person's teacher now leads the Gemara to a general statement about the different fields of Torah study. **Our Sages taught** the following Baraita: "It may be said about **those** students **who occupy themselves with** studying **the Bible** alone, to the exclusion of Mishnah and Talmud, that their specialization **is a good way** of studying, [6]**but it is not** as **good** a **way** as they could have found, because the other fields of Torah study are superior to it. [7]It may be said about those students who occupy themselves **with** studying **Mishnah** but not Talmud, that their specialization **is a good way** of studying, **and they** are destined to **receive a reward** from God **for** their efforts. [8]It may be said about those who occupy themselves **with** studying **Talmud**, that **there is no greater way** of studying **than this.** [9]**But** although there is no better way of occupying oneself than studying Talmud, **always run to the Mishnah more than to the Talmud."** [10]Concerning this Baraita the Gemara now asks: **This** Baraita **is difficult** in **itself,** because it seems to be self-contradictory. [11]On the one hand, the Baraita **says** that, for those who occupy themselves **with** studying **Talmud there is no greater way** of studying **than this;** [12]**and then**, in the very next clause, the Baraita **says: "But always run to the Mishnah more than to the Talmud,"** meaning that it is nevertheless better to study Mishnah than it is to study Talmud. How is this contradiction to be resolved?

[1]וּמִי אֲמַר רַבִּי יוֹחָנָן הָכִי? [2]וְהָאָמַר רַבִּי יוֹחָנָן: הֲלָכָה כִּסְתָם מִשְׁנָה, [3]וּתְנַן: "רַבּוֹ שֶׁלִּמְּדוֹ חָכְמָה"!

[4]מַאי חָכְמָה? רוֹב חָכְמָתוֹ.

[5]תָּנוּ רַבָּנַן: "הָעוֹסְקִין בְּמִקְרָא — מִדָּה, [6]וְאֵינָהּ מִדָּה. [7]בְּמִשְׁנָה — מִדָּה, וְנוֹטְלִין עָלֶיהָ שָׂכָר. [8]בְּתַלְמוּד — אֵין לְךָ מִדָּה גְּדוֹלָה מִזּוֹ. [9]וּלְעוֹלָם הֱוֵי רָץ לְמִשְׁנָה יוֹתֵר מִן הַתַּלְמוּד". [10]הָא גוּפָא קַשְׁיָא. [11]אָמְרַתְּ: "בְּתַלְמוּד אֵין לְךָ מִדָּה גְּדוֹלָה מִזּוֹ", [12]וַהֲדַר אָמְרַתְּ: "וּלְעוֹלָם הֱוֵי רָץ לְמִשְׁנָה יוֹתֵר מִן הַתַּלְמוּד"!

LITERAL TRANSLATION

[1]But did Rabbi Yoḥanan say this? [2]But surely Rabbi Yoḥanan said: The Halakhah is in accordance with an anonymous Mishnah, [3]and we have learned: "His teacher who taught him wisdom."

[4]What is "wisdom"? Most of his wisdom.

[5]Our Sages taught: "Those who occupy themselves with the Bible — it is a virtue, [6]but it is not a virtue. [7]With Mishnah — it is a virtue, and they receive a reward for it. [8]With Talmud — there is no greater virtue than this. [9]But always run to the Mishnah more than [to] the Talmud." [10]This itself is difficult. [11]You said: "With Talmud — there is no greater virtue than this," [12]and then you said: "But always run to the Mishnah more than [to] the Talmud"!

RASHI

ותנן רבו שלמדו חכמה — סתמא כרבי מאיר. **רוב חכמתו** — אם מקרא — מקרא, אם משנה — משנה. **מדה** — היא קצת. **ואינה מדה** — שהמשנה ותלמוד יפים ממנה מפני שתלוין בגירסא ומשתכחים, שבימיהם לא היה גמרא בכתב, וגם לא היה ניתן לכתוב, אלא לפי שנתמעטו הלבבות התחילו דורות [אחרונים] לכתבו. **תלמוד** — כבר פירשתי למעלה שהוא לתת לב להבין סתימות טעמי המשנה מה הם, וכששתים סותרות זו את זו יבין לתרץ שיהיו שתיהן קיימות, או לדעת דברי התנאים החלוקים בדבר, ונימא: הא מני — פלוני חכם הוא.

NOTES

מִדָּה וְאֵינָהּ מִדָּה It is a virtue, but it is not a virtue. The Rishonim explain that the Gemara is not attempting to assess the relative importance of the different branches of Torah study, but rather the character of the people who study them. *Rashi* explains that the assessment is based on the amount of effort involved. Scripture can be studied with

HALAKHAH

אֵין לְךָ מִדָּה גְּדוֹלָה מִזּוֹ There is no greater way than this. "A person must divide his study time into three equal parts: One for the study of Scripture; one for Mishnah, which in this case includes all the formal texts of the Oral Law, including the commentaries on Scripture; and one for Talmud, which means in-depth study of the reasoning of the

sons, and to his daughters, guiding them along the right path in worldly matters as well.

Rav Ḥisda is regarded as one of the most sharp-witted and profound thinkers of his generation, while his friend and colleague, Rav Sheshet, was known for his wide knowledge.

Rav Ḥisda served as a judge in Sura for many years, together with Rav Huna, and both of them continued the tradition of Rav's school. After Rav Huna's death, Rav Ḥisda took his place as the head of the Sura Yeshivah. Much is told of his deeds of charity.

He lived to the age of ninety-two. Many of the Sages of the following generation were his students, and he had many sons who became Sages: Rav Ḥanan bar Rav Ḥisda, Mar Yenuka and Mar Keshisha, Rav Mari, Rav Pineḥas, and Rav Taḥlifa. However, Rav Ḥisda used to say that he preferred his daughters to his sons, because they married the greatest Sages of the generation, Mar Ukva bar Ḥama and his brother, Rami bar Ḥama. The daughter, referred to as "the daughter of Rav Ḥisda," who married Rami bar Ḥama, later married Rava.

BACKGROUND

מִדָּה וְאֵינָהּ מִדָּה It is a virtue, but it is not a virtue. *Rashi* explains here that Bible study "is a virtue which is not a virtue," because at that time the Mishnah (and of course the Talmud) had to be learned by heart, which meant that a person had to devote most or all of his time to it. In addition to its importance and depth, this study also demands constant review in order to be retained. This, however, is not true of the Bible, the text of which is widely available. Indeed, from other sources we see that the Sages did not approve of spending all one's time studying Scripture, because the words of Scripture can be understood in various ways, and a person may misinterpret them and fall into error.

תַּלְמוּד Talmud. Although the Talmud did not exist as an edited text at that time, the study of Torah using the methods of the Talmud was

[1]אָמַר רַבִּי יוֹחָנָן: [33B] בִּימֵי רַבִּי נִשְׁנֵית מִשְׁנָה זוֹ. [2]שָׁבְקוּ כּוּלָּא עָלְמָא מַתְנִיתִין וְאָזְלוּ בָּתַר תַּלְמוּדָא. [3]הֲדַר דְּרַשׁ לְהוּ: ״וּלְעוֹלָם הֱוֵי רָץ לְמִשְׁנָה יוֹתֵר מִן הַתַּלְמוּד״.
[4]מַאי דְּרוּשׁ?
[5]כִּדְדָרֵישׁ רַבִּי יְהוּדָה בְּרַבִּי אִלְעַאי: מַאי דִּכְתִיב: ״הַגֵּד

LITERAL TRANSLATION

[1]Rabbi Yoḥanan said: [33B] This teaching was taught during the days of Rabbi [Yehudah HaNasi]. [2]Everyone abandoned the Mishnah and went after the Talmud. [3]Then he expounded to them: "But always run to the Mishnah more than [to] the Talmud." [4]What did he expound? [5]As Rabbi Yehudah the son of Rabbi Il'ai expounded: What is [it] that is written: "Tell

TRANSLATION AND COMMENTARY

אָמַר רַבִּי יוֹחָנָן [1]**Rabbi Yohanan said** in reply: [33B] There is no contradiction between the two parts of the Baraita. **The one statement** — that the best way of studying is to study Talmud — was made during the days of Rabbi Yehudah HaNasi, and its purpose was to emphasize the importance of profound and searching analysis of Torah law. [2]But as a result of this statement **everyone abandoned** the study of **the Mishnah and** specialized in the analytical study of **the Talmud.** [3]As a result, **he then expounded to them** that they should **always run to the Mishnah more than to the Talmud,** for unless a person has a sound basis of formal Halakhic knowledge, he cannot advance to deeper study. Thus the two seemingly contradictory clauses in the Baraita reflect the attitudes of Rabbi Yehudah HaNasi at two different periods.

מַאי דְּרוּשׁ [4]But, asks the Gemara, **what** verse **did** Rabbi Yehudah HaNasi **expound** when he made his first statement? On what Biblical source did he rely when he said that Talmud study is more important than Mishnah study?

כִּדְדָרֵישׁ [5]The Gemara answers: Rabbi Yehudah HaNasi's statement was based on a verse that had previously been **expounded by Rabbi Yehudah the son of Rabbi Il'ai: What is** the meaning of the verse in the Bible (Isaiah 58:1) in which **it is written: "Tell My**

RASHI

בימי רבי נשנית משנה זו — הא דקתני תלמוד אין לך מדה גדולה מזו, לפי שמשרבו תלמידי שמאי והלל, שהיו לפניו שלשה דורות, רבו מחלוקות בתורה ונעשית כשתי תורות, מתוך עול שעבוד מלכיות וגזירות שהיו גוזרין עליהן, ומתוך כך לא היו יכולים לתת לב לברר דברי החולקים עד ימיו של רבי, שנתן הקדוש ברוך הוא לו חן בעיני אנטונינוס מלך רומי, כדאמרינן בעבודה זרה (י,ב), ונחו מצרה, ושלח וקבץ כל תלמידי ארץ ישראל, ועד ימיו לא היו מסכתות סדורות, אלא כל תלמיד ששמע דבר מפי גדול הימנו גרסה, ונתן סימנים: הלכה פלונית ופלונית שמעתי משם פלוני וכשנתקבצו אמר כל אחד מה ששמע ונתנו לב לברר טעמי המחלוקת, דברי מי ראוין לקיים, וסידרו המסכתות; דברי נזיקין לבדם, ודברי יבמות לבדם, ודברי קדשים לבדם, וסתם נמי במשנה דברי יחידים שראה רבי את דבריהם ושנאן סתם כדי לקבוע הלכה כמותם, לפיכך אמרו בגמרא: אין לך מדה גדולה מזו, שיתנו לב לטעמי המשנה. **שבקו כולי עלמא מתניתין** — מלחזור על גרסת משנתם. **ואזלו בתר תלמודא** — לחשוב בסברא. **הדר דרש להו הוי רץ למשנה** — לפי שירא פן ישתכחו המשניות, ויחליפו שמות החכמים, ובמקום חיוב יאמרו פטור ובמקום אסור יאמרו מותר. **מאי דרוש** — מתחילה כשדרש שתלמוד גדול.

NOTES

relatively little effort, as it is written down. Mishnah is conceptually simple but technically difficult, because in Talmudic times it was studied orally. Talmud is the most difficult, because it requires careful reasoning. Other Rishonim emphasized the practical value of the various areas of study in terms of religious observance: Clearly, Talmud study is Halakhically more relevant than Mishnah study, whereas study of Scripture alone has almost no Halakhic relevance (*Rabbenu Ḥananel*).

בִּימֵי רַבִּי נִשְׁנֵית **This teaching was taught during the days of Rabbi Yehudah HaNasi.** Our commentary follows *Rashi*, who explains that, in order to establish the text of the Mishnah, Rabbi Yehudah HaNasi needed the help of Sages who were specialists in profoundly analyzing the teachings of previous generations, and knew the principles upon which each opinion was based, in order to arrive at Halakhic conclusions. Therefore, he placed emphasis on the study of Talmud. *Rabbenu Tam* (quoted in *Tosafot, Bava Kamma* 94b) adds that Rabbi Yehudah HaNasi never intended this teaching to apply to future generations.

הֱוֵי רָץ לְמִשְׁנָה **Run to the Mishnah.** *Rabbenu Ḥananel* explains that students of Mishnah receive a reward for their studies without having to shoulder the tremendous responsibility of a student of Talmud, whose unwitting sins are considered as willful transgressions.

HALAKHAH

Oral Law and its application to new situations. This division only applies when a person begins to study. As he progresses, he should devote only a small amount of time to reviewing Scripture and Mishnah, so that he does not forget them, and should concentrate all his energies on Talmud study," following *Rambam*. *Rema* rules, following *Rabbenu Tam*, that the Babylonian Talmud contains a mixture of all three disciplines. Hence, through its study alone, it is possible to fulfill this Halakhah. (*Shulḥan Arukh, Yoreh De'ah* 246:4.)

---

an essential part of the Oral Law. The Mishnah, and the early Halakhic teachings that preceded the compilation of the Mishnah, consists mainly of practical Halakhic rulings. The Talmud, however, is concerned with exhaustively clarifying matters, and with understanding the reasons and assumptions behind them. Therefore the Sages said that even issues cited in the name of the later generations of Amoraim had been studied before the Mishnah was written.

BACKGROUND

בִּימֵי רַבִּי נִשְׁנֵית מִשְׁנָה זוֹ **This teaching was taught during the days of Rabbi.** Rabbi Yehudah HaNasi is referred to simply as Rabbi. He edited the version of the Mishnah we now possess. But even before his time there were several different oral compilations of Mishnayot from various schools. Although Rabbi was the final compiler and editor of our Mishnah, it presents the approaches of various other Sages over several generations. The Baraitot — whether those that appear in the great collections such as the Tosefta or the Halakhic Midrashim, or those that are cited only in the Talmud — reflect various Halakhic schools, and some derive from generations preceding Rabbi. Therefore it was necessary to state that the Baraita cited came from the time of Rabbi himself.

שָׁבְקוּ כּוּלָּא עָלְמָא מַתְנִיתִין **Everyone abandoned the Mishnah.** *Rashi* explains that, on the one hand, Rabbi wanted to emphasize the importance of theoretical study and profound research, which is the study of the Talmud. But on the other hand, Rabbi's great achievement was the compilation and editing of the Mishnah, and for that purpose he needed many Sages to be engaged in that study, so as to clarify the laws and verify their sources, as well as to quote them correctly.

SAGES

רַבִּי יְהוּדָה בְּרַבִּי אִלְעַאי **Rabbi Yehudah, the son of**

TRANSLATION AND COMMENTARY

people their transgression, and the House of Jacob their sins"? Rabbi Yehudah explains: The verse refers to the two groups of which the Jewish people are composed. [1]The clause, **"Tell My people their transgression," refers to the** Torah **scholars,** who are described as "My people," and **whose unwitting sins are considered as willful transgressions.** This extra severity refers to the possibility that a Torah scholar might give a mistaken Halakhic decision, and thereby cause other people to sin, in which case he would be considered in the eyes of God as having committed a crime. Therefore, a Torah scholar must be extremely careful in his study and teaching of Torah, lest he be judged severely. [2]Rabbi Yehudah goes on to explain that the next clause, **"and the House of Jacob their sins," refers to the ignorant, whose willful transgressions are considered unwitting sins.** Since uneducated people cannot be aware of the full Halakhic significance of their deeds, even their willful transgressions are in a sense unintentional.

וְהַיְינוּ [3]The Gemara now notes that the theme of the previous statement is also to be found in the following Mishnah (*Avot* 4:13), also ascribed to Rabbi Yehudah the son of Rabbi Il'ai, in which **we learn: "Rabbi Yehudah says: Be careful with** your study of **the Talmud, [4]for an unwitting sin committed** because of an error **in Talmud is counted as a willful transgression."**

דָּרַשׁ רַבִּי יְהוּדָה [5]The Talmud concludes the chapter with another teaching of Rabbi Yehudah bar Rabbi Il'ai that relates to the different kinds of Torah scholars: **Rabbi Yehudah the son of Rabbi Il'ai expounded: What is** the meaning of the verse in the Bible (Isaiah 66:5) in which **it is written:** "Hear the word of the Lord, you that tremble at His word: Your brethren, that hate you, that cast you out, said: For my name's sake let the Lord be glorified, and we shall see your rejoicing and they shall be ashamed." [6]Rabbi Yehudah now explains various phrases in the verse: **"Hear the word of the Lord, you that tremble at His word" — this refers to the** Torah **scholars.** [7]**"Your brethren said" — this refers to the masters of Scripture,** who know enough to realize the limitations of their knowledge

לְעַמִּי פִּשְׁעָם, וּלְבֵית יַעֲקֹב חַטֹּאתָם"? [1]"הַגֵּד לְעַמִּי פִּשְׁעָם" — אֵלּוּ תַּלְמִידֵי חֲכָמִים, שֶׁשְּׁגָגוֹת נַעֲשׂוֹת לָהֶם כִּזְדוֹנוֹת. [2]"וּלְבֵית יַעֲקֹב חַטֹּאתָם" — אֵלּוּ עַמֵּי הָאָרֶץ, שֶׁזְּדוֹנוֹת נַעֲשׂוֹת לָהֶם כִּשְׁגָגוֹת. [3]וְהַיְינוּ דִּתְנַן: "רַבִּי יְהוּדָה אוֹמֵר: הֱוֵי זָהִיר בְּתַלְמוּד, [4]שֶׁשִּׁגְגַת תַּלְמוּד עוֹלָה זָדוֹן". [5]דָּרַשׁ רַבִּי יְהוּדָה בְּרַבִּי אִלְעַאי: [6]מַאי דִּכְתִיב: "שִׁמְעוּ דְּבַר ה', הַחֲרֵדִים אֶל דְּבָרוֹ" — אֵלּוּ תַּלְמִידֵי חֲכָמִים. [7]"אָמְרוּ אֲחֵיכֶם" — אֵלּוּ בַּעֲלֵי מִקְרָא.

LITERAL TRANSLATION

My people their transgression, and the House of Jacob their sins"? [1]"Tell My people their transgression" — these are the scholars, whose unwitting sins are considered as willful transgressions.

[2]"And the House of Jacob their sins" — these are the ignorant (lit., "the peoples of the land"), whose willful transgressions are considered as unwitting sins.

[3]And this is what we have learned: "Rabbi Yehudah says: Be careful with the Talmud, [4]for an unwitting sin committed in Talmud is counted as a willful transgression."

[5]Rabbi Yehudah the son of Rabbi Il'ai expounded: What is [it] that is written: [6]"Hear the word of the Lord, you that tremble at His word" — these are the scholars. [7]"Your brethren said" — these are the masters of Scripture.

RASHI

לעמי פשעם — עמי, דהיינו תלמידי חכמים, את חטאתם אני קורא פשע, שהיה להם לתת לב בטעמי משנתם שיבררו להם על העיקר, ולא יורו הלכה מתוך משנה שאינה עיקר. **ולבית יעקב** — שאר העם. **חטאתם** — אפילו פשע שלהם אני קורא חטאת. **הוי זהיר בתלמוד** — בגמרא, שהוא תירוץ [טעמי] המשניות, או אם תשמע דבר משנה מרבך — הזהר לשאול טעמיו ומי שנאה. **ששגגת תלמוד** — אם שגית בהוראה בשגגת תלמודך, שלא ידעת טעם המשנה ונתת בה טעם אחר, ומתוך כך דמית לה דין או הוראה שבא לידך ולמדת הימנה שלא כדת, שאין הטעם כמו שהיית סבור, שאילו ידעת טעם המשנה — לא דמית לה מעשה הבא לידך. **עולה זדון** — ענוש אתה עליה כמזיד, שזדון הוא בידך, שלא שאלת טעם מרבך. **אלו תלמידי חכמים** — ששימשו חכמים הרבה ללמדם טעמי משנתם, זה בזו וזה בזו, שאין הכל בקיאין בשוין.

NOTES

הַגֵּד לְעַמִּי פִּשְׁעָם "Tell My people their transgression." The expression "*My* people" implies a close connection between God and the Jewish people. It is therefore considered to be a reference to the Sages. The verse is saying that Torah scholars commit only willful transgressions, not unwitting sins; hence the idea that for a Torah scholar even an unwitting sin is considered a willful transgression (*Rashi*).

שֶׁשִּׁגְגַת תַּלְמוּד עוֹלָה זָדוֹן For an unwitting sin committed in Talmud study is counted as a willful transgression. Our translation follows *Rashi*, who explains that if a Torah Sage errs in his decision and permits a forbidden action, he is held responsible, as though he had willfully transgressed. This is because a Torah Sage is expected to be careful, and to ask his teachers for assistance with matters about which he is not certain.

Rabbenu Ḥananel renders this phrase as "an unwitting sin committed by a Sage," and explains that Torah Sages are judged by a higher standard because of their knowledge.

Rabbi Il'ai. Rabbi Yehudah the son of Rabbi Il'ai is known in the sources simply as Rabbi Yehudah. He was one of the most important Tannaim of the fifth generation. His father, Rabbi Il'ai, had been a student of Rabbi Eliezer ben Hyrcanus. Rabbi Yehudah himself was a leading disciple of Rabbi Akiva, and one of the Sages who continued in his path. However, Rabbi Yehudah also learned Torah from his father, from Rabbi Tarfon, and from other Sages in Yavneh. He seems to have supported himself by manual labor, and although he was extremely poor he accepted his poverty with love. In general he was a cordial person and saw things in a favorable light, so much so that he sought to praise the actions of the Romans, even though he lived at a time of cruel persecution after the suppression of the Bar Kokhba revolt. It is said (*Bava Kamma* 103b) that in many places where a "righteous man" is mentioned with no further qualification, the person intended is Rabbi Yehudah.

When the Sanhedrin convened again after the Bar Kokhba revolt, the Sages assembled at Usha, in Galilee, which was where Rabbi Yehudah lived. He was the "chief speaker," a kind of temporary Nasi of the Sanhedrin. It seems that after Rabban Shimon ben Gamliel, of the House of Hillel, was appointed Nasi, Rabbi Yehudah continued to serve as the mentor of the House of the Nasi.

Rabbi Yehudah's son, Rabbi Yose, was an important Sage in the next generation, and a colleague of Rabbi Yehudah HaNasi.

שֶׁשְּׁגָגוֹת נַעֲשׂוֹת לָהֶם כִּזְדוֹנוֹת Whose unwitting sins are considered as willful transgressions. Torah scholars are expected not only to know the Torah, but also to be scrupulous in the observance of the commandments, and to "beautify" them. Thus the Sages seek in their own lives to fulfill the Halakhah far beyond the strict limits of their minimal obligations. A Torah scholar, even when he is not instructing people in the Halakhah, provides a public example by his behavior — and an error on his part is liable to cause others to transgress. Moreover, God makes exacting demands on Torah scholars in proportion to their eminence and importance, regarding a sin which they might commit by mistake as if they had done it deliberately.

The opposite is true of the ignorant multitude, for, since they do not know the Halakhah and are uncultured and simple people, even if they commit transgressions deliberately they cannot be held fully accountable. Only someone who acts in full knowledge and understanding can be considered to have committed a willful transgression. Since the ignorant do not actually know what they are doing, and do not understand the gravity of their transgression, even though it may be intentional it is regarded as an unintentional sin.

TRANSLATION AND COMMENTARY

and thus give appropriate honor to the Sages. [1] **"That hate you" — this refers to the masters of Mishnah,** who have enough knowledge to consider themselves rivals of the true Sages. [2] **"That cast you out" — this refers to the ignorant,** who out of hatred keep their distance from the Sages. [3] **Lest you say that the hope** of those who are not Torah Sages **has ceased and their prospect is void** — for in its simple meaning the verse appears to be a vehement condemnation of the "brothers," "haters," and "casters out" — [4] **the verse says: "And *we* shall see you rejoicing,"** using the first person plural form of the verb, to include all the people mentioned above in the rejoicing. [5] **Lest you say that Israel will be ashamed, the verse says: "And *they* shall be ashamed."** Only those who cannot be described as "we" will be ashamed. Hence, we may conclude that it is **the non-Jews,** the idol-worshippers, who **will be ashamed,** and it is **Israel** who **will rejoice.**

[1] ״שׂוֹנְאֵיכֶם״ — אֵלּוּ בַּעֲלֵי מִשְׁנָה. [2] ״מְנַדֵּיכֶם״ — אֵלּוּ עַמֵּי הָאָרֶץ. [3] שֶׁמָּא תֹּאמַר פָּסַק סִבְרָם וּבָטַל סִיכּוּיָם, [4] תַּלְמוּד לוֹמַר: ״וְנִרְאֶה בְּשִׂמְחַתְכֶם״. [5] שֶׁמָּא תֹּאמַר יִשְׂרָאֵל יֵבוֹשׁוּ, תַּלְמוּד לוֹמַר: [6] ״וְהֵם יֵבֹשׁוּ״ — נָכְרִים יֵבוֹשׁוּ וְיִשְׂרָאֵל יִשְׂמְחוּ.

הדרן עלך אלו מציאות

LITERAL TRANSLATION

[1] "That hate you" — these are the masters of Mishnah. [2] "That cast you out" — these are the ignorant. [3] Lest you say [that] their hope has ceased and their prospect is void, [4] the verse says: "And *we* shall see your rejoicing." [5] Lest you say [that] Israel will be ashamed, the verse says: [6] "And *they* shall be ashamed" — the non-Jews will be ashamed and Israel will rejoice.

RASHI

שנאיכם אלו בעלי משנה — ששונאין בעלי תלמוד, לפי שבעלי תלמוד אומרים על בעלי משנה שהן מבלי עולם, כדאמרינן במסכת סוטה (כב,א): התנאים מבלי עולם, שמורים הלכה מתוך משנתם. **מנדיכם אלו עמי הארץ** — שתלמידי חכמים שונאין ומתועבין להן כנדה. **שמא תאמר אבד סברם** — של אלו, שהרי כתיב ״למען שמי יכבד ה׳״ דמשמע שהם אומרים, אבל אין הדבר כן. **תלמוד לומר ונראה בשמחתכם** — ולא נאמר ואראה בשמחתכם, כך אמר הנביא: ״אני ואחיכם שונאיכם ומנדיכם״ — כולנו נראה בשמחתכם. **והם יבושו** — אותם שהם נכרים, שאינם ממנו ואינן נקראין על שם ישראל — הם יבושו וישראל ישמחו.

הדרן עלך אלו מציאות

NOTES

עַמֵּי הָאָרֶץ The ignorant. The Talmud provides various definitions of the term עַם הָאָרֶץ, ranging from people who know nothing at all to the opposite extreme — someone who has studied Torah but does not honor scholars. However, in general, an עַם הָאָרֶץ was someone who had not studied at all and who, because of his ignorance, regarded the Sages as arrogant and overbearing. For that reason the ignorant multitude also hated the Sages, although many of them inwardly acknowledged their virtues.

This ambivalent attitude of the ignorant is expressed here in the Midrash on the verse from Isaiah. Although they appear to hate the Sages, the ignorant multitude nevertheless observe the commandments according to their own understanding.

שׂוֹנְאֵיכֶם אֵלּוּ בַּעֲלֵי מִשְׁנָה "That hate you" — these are the masters of Mishnah. The "masters of Mishnah" mentioned here are scholars who study only the Mishnah. Although they considered themselves expert in the Halakhah and viewed themselves as Sages, the Talmudic Sages were contemptuous of them. This was because they taught the Halakhah on the basis of their knowledge of Mishnah, but did not properly understand its fundamental principles, thus rendering incorrect Halakhic decisions. In their turn, these "masters of Mishnah" were hostile to the Sages, who were on a higher level than themselves, although the basis of their studies was also the Mishnah.

וְנִרְאֶה בְּשִׂמְחַתְכֶם "And we shall see your rejoicing." The entire context of this verse in the Bible is a description of the redemption of Israel, and therefore, although there are some Jews who do not "tremble at His word," and sometimes distance themselves from those who do "tremble," and even hate them, nevertheless these are internal conflicts between various groups and have no effect on the general definition of the Jewish people as a single nation. The redemption of the Jews will therefore be redemption of Jews of every kind.

Conclusion to Chapter Two

One of the principal purposes of this chapter is to determine when the original owner of a lost object may be assumed to have given up hope of recovering it. Generally, we assume that the owner of a lost object which bears distinctive identifying marks despairs of recovering it only if it has been left abandoned for an exceptionally long period of time, or if it was lost as the result of a natural disaster or some other *force majeure*. Moreover, even items which do not bear distinctive identification marks can often be identified by their location, size, weight, number of units, etc., and hence it may be assumed that someone who has lost such objects does not give up hope of recovering them.

One of the longest and most important discussions in our chapter is the one dealing with anticipated *ye'ush* (יֵאוּשׁ שֶׁלֹּא מִדַּעַת). Specifically, Abaye's view — that someone who finds a lost object may keep it only if he is certain that the original owner gave up hope of recovering it *before* it was found — is accepted. Thus, "anticipated despair" is not considered valid. In the wake of this discussion, the general issue of the retrospective validity of actions is also discussed.

The Gemara concludes that a person who finds a lost object which he is not allowed to keep (for example, because the original owner has not given up hope of recovering it) may not derive any personal benefit from it, although he may use it in order to preserve and maintain it if necessary. Likewise, someone who finds a lost animal (or other object which requires exceptional care) is only obligated to care for it for a limited period of time. However, the finder is permitted to use money he received from the sale of the lost object, although he is liable for such money (and for the lost object itself) as if he were a paid bailee.

Three commandments apply to the return of a lost object: (1) It is forbidden to "hide oneself" by refusing to pick up the lost object. (2) The finder must do his best to return the lost object to its rightful owner. (3) The finder is not permitted to keep the lost object for himself, if the original owner is still entitled to it (for example, where the owner has not given up hope of recovering it). However, there are certain cases in which these laws do not apply — for example, where picking up the lost object is beneath the finder's dignity, or would entail violation of a Torah prohibition, or financial loss to the finder. Even though the Torah discusses the laws of returning lost items in connection with specific objects (cows, sheep, etc.), this obligation applies to lost items of all kinds, as well as to extending help to others wherever necessary to prevent them from suffering financial loss.

If a person has to return a number of lost items, then objects belonging to his father and teacher take precedence over those belonging to other people. However, his own property takes precedence even over the property of his father or teacher.

Our chapter also discusses at some length the laws about helping another person unload and reload his animal if it is about to collapse (or after it has already collapsed) under its load. In particular, the different views regarding cruelty to animals (צַעַר בַּעֲלֵי חַיִּים) according to the Halakhah are analyzed. In general, the laws about helping another person unload and reload his animals closely resemble those concerning the return of a lost object, except for the fact that one is required to unload another person's animal without remuneration, whereas it is permitted to demand payment for helping to reload an animal.

Introduction to Chapter Three

הַמַּפְקִיד

"If a man shall deliver to his neighbor money or utensils to keep, and it is stolen from the man's house, if the thief is found he shall pay double. If the thief is not found, then the master of the house shall be brought to the judges to see that he has not misappropriated his neighbor's property. For any manner of trespass, for ox, for ass, for sheep, for clothing, or for any lost object of which one says, 'This is it,' the cause of both parties shall come before the judges, and the one whom the judges condemn shall pay double to his neighbor." (Exodus 22:6–8.)

"If a man steals an ox or a sheep, and kills it or sells it, he shall pay five oxen for each ox, and four sheep for each sheep." (Exodus 21:37.)

The Torah states that someone who receives a deposit for safekeeping — the bailee — is required to return it to the depositor. If the deposit is lost or stolen, the bailee is permitted to take an oath that he was not negligent in safeguarding the deposit. He thereby exempts himself from reimbursing the depositor, unless it is proved that he appropriated the deposit for himself.

One of the fundamental issues arising in this connection relates to ownership of a deposit which has been stolen. If the bailee decides to compensate the depositor for the lost item instead of taking an oath that it has been stolen, is he considered its rightful owner? If so, the thief, when caught, returns the deposit to the bailee, together with the additional compensation paid as a fine for stealing. Or does the depositor retain ownership rights over the deposit? If so, he will have to reimburse the bailee if the lost item is found.

Another issue which must be analyzed is the nature of the bailee's obligation to safeguard the deposit. Obviously, he must take reasonable care of it, but the precise limits of this obligation remain to be clarifed. For example, if the bailee notices that the deposit is deteriorating with the passage of time, is he permitted — or obligated — to take measures necessary to preserve it? Or is his obligation to safeguard the deposit limited solely to avoiding misappropriation?

A precise analysis of the nature of the "misappropriation" mentioned by the Torah in connection with bailees is also necessary. Is misappropriation merely a term for theft committed by the bailee, and hence Halakhically equivalent to any other theft? Or is misappropriation a special Halakhic category, whose essence lies in the abuse of the depositor's trust and the bailee's violation of the agreement to safeguard the deposit? If misappropriation is so defined, does the mere intention to steal automatically render the bailee liable, or can such an obligation only be generated by his actions?

The solutions of these problems, and the issues stemming from them, are the predominant theme of this chapter.

[1]אֶצֶל חֲבֵירוֹ בְּהֵמָה אוֹ כֵּלִים, וְנִגְנְבוּ אוֹ שֶׁאָבְדוּ; [2]שִׁילֵּם וְלֹא רָצָה לִישָּׁבַע — שֶׁהֲרֵי אָמְרוּ: שׁוֹמֵר חִנָּם נִשְׁבַּע וְיוֹצֵא — [3]נִמְצָא הַגַּנָּב, מְשַׁלֵּם תַּשְׁלוּמֵי כֵּפֶל. [4]טָבַח וּמָכַר, מְשַׁלֵּם תַּשְׁלוּמֵי אַרְבָּעָה וַחֲמִשָּׁה. [5]לְמִי מְשַׁלֵּם? [6]לְמִי שֶׁהַפִּקָּדוֹן אֶצְלוֹ.

LITERAL TRANSLATION

MISHNAH [1]Someone who deposits an animal or utensils with his fellow, and they were stolen or they were lost; [2][if the bailee] paid and did not want to take an oath — for they [the Sages] said: An unpaid bailee may take an oath and be exempt (lit., "leave") — [3][if] the thief is found, he pays double payment. [4][If] he slaughtered or sold [it], he pays fourfold or fivefold payment. [5]To whom does he pay? [6]To the one with whom the deposit [was left].

TRANSLATION AND COMMENTARY

MISHNAH הַמַּפְקִיד אֶצֶל חֲבֵירוֹ [1]**If someone deposits an animal or utensils with another person,** who has agreed to look after it without accepting payment, **and** if the deposit **is stolen or lost** while in the bailee's care, there are two courses of action open to the bailee. (1) He can take an oath that he has not misappropriated the deposit, and that he has not been negligent in looking after it. If he takes this oath he is exempt from any further responsibility in the matter, because an unpaid bailee is not held responsible for theft or accident, but only for negligence. (2) He may prefer not to take an oath, but rather repay the depositor the value of the deposit and resolve the matter in this way. [2]The Mishnah now analyzes these two courses of action: **If the bailee pays** the depositor **because he does not want to take an oath — for the Sages** have laid down the principle that **an unpaid bailee may take an oath** if he so desires **and be exempt** from paying the depositor — his decision has the following consequences: [3]**If the thief is** later **found** and the stolen article is in his possession, **he** is ordered to **make double payment**, i.e., he must return the stolen object or its equivalent and he must, in addition, pay a fine equivalent to the value of the stolen object, in accordance with the penalty imposed by the Torah (Exodus 22:3) on thieves. [4]Moreover, **if** the deposit was a sheep or an ox, and the thief has **slaughtered or sold it, he** is required to **make a fourfold payment** in the case of a sheep **or a fivefold payment** in the case of an ox, in accordance with the law of the Torah (Exodus 21:37). Normally, this double, fourfold or fivefold payment is made to the person from whom the thief stole — the owner of the object. But in our case the thief stole an object belonging to a depositor from a bailee, and the bailee has already repaid the depositor for his loss. [5]Hence the question arises: **To whom does** the thief **make this** double, fourfold or fivefold payment? [6]The Mishnah answers: **To the person with whom the deposit was left**, namely, the bailee. Once the bailee has compensated the depositor for the deposit, he is treated as its owner, and is therefore entitled to collect any reimbursement subsequently received in connection with the deposit.

RASHI

משנה המפקיד. ולא רצה לישבע — שבועת שומרים, שלא פשע בה ושלא שלח בה יד — שהיה יכול ליפטר בשבועה זו, שהרי אמרו כו׳. **למי שהפקדון אצלו** — דכיון דשילם קנה כל תשלומיה, ובגמרא מפרש טעמא.

NOTES

אוֹ שֶׁאָבְדוּ Or they were lost. *Tosafot* (ד״ה הַמַּפְקִיד) asks: The purpose of the Mishnah is to determine who should receive the double payment — the depositor or the bailee. But double payment is made by thieves. Hence, the law of this Mishnah is relevant only if the deposit was stolen, not if it was lost!

Tosafot answers that the Mishnah is indeed dealing only with theft. But it is expressing the claim of the bailee, who may not know that the deposit has been stolen and may think that it has been lost.

Other commentators explain that the law of our Mishnah is also relevant to a situation where the deposit was lost and not stolen: Just as the bailee is entitled to receive the double payment if he repays the owner the value of the stolen deposit, so too is he entitled to receive any appreciation in value in the lost object. Thus, if the deposit was lost and the bailee paid the depositor for it, and the deposit was later found and was then worth twice as much as when the bailee repaid the owner, the bailee is entitled to keep the deposit and the depositor has no further claims against him (*Ramban, Rashba*).

שֶׁהֲרֵי אָמְרוּ שׁוֹמֵר חִנָּם For the Sages said: An unpaid bailee.... This parenthetical remark, which informs us of the basic law governing unpaid bailees, appears out of place at this point in the Mishnah. In fact, it can easily lead to the mistaken impression that the law of the Mishnah is

HALAKHAH

שׁוֹמֵר חִנָּם An unpaid bailee. "If a deposit is stolen from or lost by an unpaid bailee, he may take an oath that he has not been negligent in looking after it, and he thereby exempts himself from reimbursing the depositor." (*Shulḥan Arukh, Ḥoshen Mishpat* 291:1.)

שׁוֹמֵר הַפִּקָּדוֹן וְהַכֵּפֶל Double payment in the case of a

BACKGROUND

בְּהֵמָה אוֹ כֵּלִים An animal or utensils. The Gemara explains below why this Mishnah uses the example of an animal and utensils, although the same law seems to apply to both. The main reason is the influence of the language of the Torah: "For an ox, for an ass, for a sheep, or for a garment" (Exodus 22:8).

וְלֹא רָצָה לִישָּׁבַע And did not want to take an oath. The fact that a person upon whom an oath is imposed prefers not to take it does not prove that he is guilty. Although it is permitted to take an oath confirming something that is true (and there is even a commandment to that effect in the Torah), the Sages nevertheless stressed the serious nature of oaths, and that a person could be punished by Heaven for swearing falsely even if he did so unintentionally. They also said that only a righteous and upright person can permit himself to swear without fear of divine punishment. Therefore the bailee may well prefer not to take an oath through fear of the gravity of that action, either because he may think that he has been negligent in some way or because for religious reasons he does not wish to swear at all. In such a case he pays in full the value of the article entrusted to him.

CONCEPTS

שְׁבוּעַת הַשּׁוֹמְרִים The oath of the bailees. A bailee who seeks to free himself from liability for something entrusted to him that he cannot return (Exodus 22:9) must support his statement with an oath. The bailee must swear that he is not guilty for the loss of the object (each type of bailee according to the area of his responsibility), and that he is not liable to pay. The Sages added that he must swear two more oaths: (1) That the article is no longer in his possession. (2) That he did not use the object for his own benefit.

כֶּפֶל Double payment. A thief must repay twice the value of a stolen article (Exodus 22:3), i.e., he must restore the article itself to its legal owner and must make

TRANSLATION AND COMMENTARY

נִשְׁבַּע וְלֹא רָצָה לְשַׁלֵּם [1]However, **if the bailee takes an oath** that he has not been negligent **and does not want to pay** the depositor, **and the thief is** later found with the stolen article in his possession, **he** still **makes the double payment.** [2]And **if** the deposit was a sheep or an ox and the thief **slaughtered or sold it, he** must still **make a fourfold payment** in the case of a sheep **or a fivefold payment** in the case of an ox. But in this case the recipient of the payment is different. [3]The Mishnah asks: **To whom does** the thief **make** payment in this case? The Mishnah answers: **To the owner of the deposit**, and not to the bailee, since the bailee absolved himself of all responsibility for the deposit by taking the oath.

GEMARA לָמָּה לֵיהּ לְמִתְנֵי [4]The Gemara asks: **Why does** the Mishnah **need to** bring two examples of different kinds of deposit and **state** both the case of "**an animal**" **and** the case of "**utensils**"? Surely it would have been sufficient merely to state "if someone deposits an object with another person," rather than specifying two particular kinds of deposit.

צְרִיכִי [5]The Gemara answers: The examples were well chosen, and **it was necessary** to mention **both** of them. **For if** the Mishnah **had** only **stated** the example of **an animal, I would have said** that **it is** only **in the case of an animal,** and not in the case of utensils, **that the depositor transfers** his right to receive **the double payment to the bailee** after receiving indemnification for the loss of his animal, [6]**because there is considerable trouble** involved in **bringing** the animal **in and taking it out** in order to care for it. Thus it is reasonable to assume that the owner made a tacit agreement with the bailee at the moment he entrusted the animal to him, that in the event of the animal being stolen and the bailee voluntarily reimbursing the owner for its loss, any compensation later paid by the thief would belong to the bailee. [7]**But in the case of utensils,**

[1]נִשְׁבַּע וְלֹא רָצָה לְשַׁלֵּם, נִמְצָא הַגַּנָּב, מְשַׁלֵּם תַּשְׁלוּמֵי כֶּפֶל. [2]טָבַח וּמָכַר, מְשַׁלֵּם תַּשְׁלוּמֵי אַרְבָּעָה וַחֲמִשָּׁה. [3]לְמִי מְשַׁלֵּם? לְבַעַל הַפִּקָּדוֹן.

גמרא [4]לָמָּה לֵיהּ לְמִתְנֵי "בְּהֵמָה", וְלָמָּה לֵיהּ לְמִתְנֵי "כֵּלִים"?

[5]צְרִיכִי, דְּאִי תָּנָא "בְּהֵמָה", הֲוָה אָמִינָא: בְּהֵמָה הוּא דְּמַקְנֵי לֵיהּ כְּפֵילָא, [6]מִשּׁוּם דִּנְפִישׁ טִירְחָה לְעַיּוּלָה וּלְאַפּוּקָה. [7]אֲבָל כֵּלִים,

LITERAL TRANSLATION

[1][If the bailee] took an oath and did not want to pay, [and] the thief was found, he pays double payment. [2][If] he slaughtered or sold [it], he pays fourfold or fivefold payment. [3]To whom does he pay? To the owner of the deposit.

GEMARA [4]Why does he have to teach "an animal," and why does he have to teach "utensils"? [5]They are [both] necessary, for if he had taught "an animal," I would have said: It is [in the case of] an animal that [the depositor] transfers the double payment to him [the bailee], [6]because the trouble is great to bring it in and take it out. [7]But [in the case of] utensils,

RASHI

גמרא דמקני ליה כפילא – הבעלים מקנין לשומר כפל העתיד להשתלם, כדאמר לקמן שבשעה שמסרה לו לשמור על מנת כן מסרה, שאם תגנב וירלה וישלם – יהא כפל שלו.

an additional payment equal to the value of the article. This obligation is considered a fine (קְנָס). Accordingly, a thief is only required to make this payment if he is apprehended by others. If he voluntarily admits his wrongdoing and desires to restore the stolen article or its value, he does not make the additional payment. Similarly, a person who swears that something placed in his care was stolen is himself obligated to pay כֶּפֶל if the object is found to be still in his possession.

CONCEPTS

אַרְבָּעָה וַחֲמִשָּׁה **Fourfold or fivefold payment.** A person who steals and then sells or slaughters an ox is obligated to reimburse its owner five times the value of the stolen animal. If the stolen animal is a sheep, the restitution is four times the animal's worth (Exodus 21:37). The Sages offered various explanations as to why the thief must pay more for an ox than for a sheep: (1) The theft of an ox causes additional loss to its owners, who cannot use it for work in plowing. (2) Someone who steals a sheep carries it on his shoulders, and at least suffers fatigue while committing the crime. (3) Someone who steals an ox, which is large and difficult to lead away and hide, may be assumed to be a habitual thief.

TERMINOLOGY

לָמָּה לֵיהּ לְמִתְנֵי... וְלָמָּה לֵיהּ לְמִתְנֵי **Why does he have to teach X, and why does he have to teach Y?** When the Gemara, in analyzing a Mishnah, finds an unnecessary repetition of seemingly identical cases, it often asks: "Why does the author of the Mishnah need to teach case X, and why does he then need to teach case Y? Surely one of the cases is superfluous!" The Gemara answers, using the expression צְרִיכָא, showing that the various cases are in fact necessary, and going on to explain why.

NOTES

dependent on the bailee having the legal option to exempt himself from payment by taking an oath. This impression runs counter to the Halakhah (see below, 34a) that even a paid bailee — who is required to compensate the depositor for theft, and cannot exempt himself from payment by taking an oath — is still entitled to receive the double payment.

Ramban explains that the Halakhah below (34a) applies only if the bailee admits some fact that we could not otherwise have determined, and thus forgoes some way of exempting himself even if the only way would have been by taking a false oath. But if there are witnesses who testify that the bailee was negligent, he is forced to pay and cannot exempt himself by taking an oath, true or false. Hence, this clause in the Mishnah implies that in such a case the bailee would not be entitled to receive the double payment.

Rashba, however, disagrees. He cites a source in the Jerusalem Talmud which states that if witnesses testify that the bailee was negligent and the bailee then pays the depositor, he is still entitled to collect the double payment in case of theft. (In our texts of the Jerusalem Talmud, the Gemara does not actually establish this point, but rather leaves it open as a possibility.) Accordingly, *Rashba* explains that this clause is to be accepted as a brief reminder of the basic laws of unpaid bailees, inserted at the beginning of the chapter.

לְמִי מְשַׁלֵּם לְבַעַל הַפִּקָּדוֹן **To whom does he pay? To the owner of the deposit.** At first glance it would appear self-evident that if the bailee absolves himself of responsibility by taking an oath, he has thereby renounced

HALAKHAH

bailee. "If a deposit is stolen from or lost by an unpaid bailee, and he declares that he would rather pay than take an oath, the thief, when caught, must make double (or fourfold or fivefold payment, if the deposit was a sheep or an ox and the thief slaughtered or sold it) to the bailee. But if the bailee took an oath rather than pay, the additional payment (double, fourfold or fivefold) is paid to the depositor," following the Mishnah. (*Rambam, Sefer Mishpatim, Hilkhot She'elah* 8:1.)

TRANSLATION AND COMMENTARY

where the trouble involved in looking after them **is not considerable,** [1]**I would say that** the owner **does not transfer** his right to receive **the double payment to** the bailee after receiving indemnification for the loss of the utensils. Thus it was necessary to add the example of utensils in the Mishnah, to show that this law applies equally to animals and to inanimate objects. [2]**And** on the other hand, **if** the Mishnah **had** only **mentioned** the case of utensils, **I would have said** that **it is** only **in the case of utensils that** the depositor **transfers** his right to receive **the double payment to** the bailee, [3]**because the extra** potential **payment** involved **is not substantial**. For even if the thief is found, the maximum that the depositor will receive is the double payment. [4]**But in the case of an animal, where** the thief may be required to **make fourfold or fivefold payment if he slaughters or sells** a sheep or an ox, [5]**I would say that**, in the light of the large sums potentially involved, the depositor **would not transfer** his right to receive **the double payment** to the bailee. [6]**Therefore it was necessary** for the Mishnah to mention **both** cases, animals and utensils, to establish that the law is the same for all deposits.

מַתְקִיף לָהּ רָמִי בַּר חָמָא [7]**Rami bar Ḥama raised an objection to** the premise underlying the Gemara's explanation thus far: How is it possible that the owner made up his mind at the time he placed the object in the care of the bailee to transfer to the bailee a double payment for which a thief had not yet become liable? [8]For **surely** there is a Halakhic principle that **a person cannot transfer ownership of something that has not yet come into existence**! The right to receive the double payment does not yet exist, because the object has not yet been stolen, the thief has not yet been found, and the obligation to make the double payment has not yet been imposed. Hence this right cannot be transferred to the bailee by the owner!

דְּלָא נָפֵישׁ טִירְחַיְיהוּ, [1]אֵימָא לָא מַקְנֵי לֵיהּ כְּפֵילָא. [2]וְאִי תָּנָא "כֵּלִים", הֲוָה אָמִינָא: כֵּלִים הוּא דְּקָמַקְנֵי לֵיהּ כְּפֵילָא, [3]מִשּׁוּם דְּלָא נָפֵישׁ כִּפְלַיְיהוּ. [4]אֲבָל בְּהֵמָה, דְּכִי טָבַח וּמָכַר מְשַׁלֵּם תַּשְׁלוּמֵי אַרְבָּעָה וַחֲמִשָּׁה, [5]אֵימָא לָא מַקְנֵי לֵיהּ כְּפֵילָא. [6]צְרִיכָא.

[7]מַתְקִיף לָהּ רָמִי בַּר חָמָא: [8]וְהָא אֵין אָדָם מַקְנֶה דָּבָר שֶׁלֹּא בָּא לָעוֹלָם!

LITERAL TRANSLATION

where their trouble is not great, [1]I would say [that] he does not transfer the double payment to him. [2]And if he had taught "utensils," I would have said: It is [in the case of] utensils that he transfers the double payment to him, [3]because their double payment is not great. [4]But [in the case of] an animal, where if he has slaughtered or sold [it] he pays fourfold or fivefold payment, [5]I would say [that] he does not transfer the double payment to him. [6][Therefore both] are necessary.

[7]Rami bar Ḥama objected to this: [8]But surely a person cannot transfer ownership of something that has not yet come into the world!

RASHI

אימר לא מקנה ליה כפילא — לא מסרה לו מתחילה על מנת כן. **דלא נפיש כפלייהו** — שאין באין לידי ארבעה וחמשה, שאינה נוהגת אלא בשור ושה בלבד. **מתקיף לה רמי כו'** — אמתניתין קא מתמה. **והא אין אדם מקנה דבר שלא בא לעולם** — והיאך הקנו לו בעלים כפל זה, שעדיין לא נתחייב בו גנב?

TERMINOLOGY

מַתְקִיף לָהּ He objected to it. This term is used when an Amora objects to a statement of another Amora on logical grounds rather than on the authority of a literary source (e.g., a Mishnah or a Baraita).

SAGES

רָמִי בַּר חָמָא Rami bar Ḥama. A Babylonian Amora of the fourth generation. See *Bava Metzia*, Part I, p. 83.

CONCEPTS

דָּבָר שֶׁלֹּא בָּא לָעוֹלָם Something that has not yet come into the world. This concept has two meanings: (1) Something that has not yet come into existence — for example, a child that has not yet been born or fruit that has not yet grown. (2) Something which, though in existence, is not yet in a person's possession. Generally, a transaction (or transfer of property) involving a דָּבָר שֶׁלֹּא בָּא לָעוֹלָם has no legal validity. It is legally impossible to sell something that has not yet come into existence, or has not yet come into the seller's possession, and it is impossible to sell or give something to someone who has not yet been born. Only in certain pressing circumstances did the Sages grant legal validity to such transactions.

NOTES

any claims he may have to the double payment. Some commentators explain that the Mishnah is referring to a case where the deposit was stolen as a result of the bailee's negligence. By law the bailee should have compensated the depositor, but he chose to take a false oath instead. Thus the Mishnah is telling us that even though this act by the bailee was illegal, it is still effective, and he loses his rights to the double payment (*Shittah Mekubbetzet*).

Other commentators explain that since the person from whom the thief stole, the bailee, and the person who was wronged, the depositor, are two separate legal entities, we might think that the thief could exempt himself entirely from making the double payment. Hence the Mishnah informs us that this is not so, and the thief must pay the depositor (*Pnei Yehoshua*).

מַתְקִיף לָהּ רָמִי בַּר חָמָא Rami bar Ḥama objected to this. According to *Rashi*, Rami bar Ḥama objected to the Mishnah's ruling. Others, however, note that the term used here, מַתְקִיף, always appears in connection with Amoraic statements and never introduces an objection to the Mishnah. Accordingly, other Rishonim, followed by our commentary, say that Rami bar Ḥama was objecting to the assumption underlying the reasoning of the previous passage of the Gemara — namely, that the depositor has voluntarily transferred his rights to the bailee. The Mishnah could have been explained as a special Rabbinic decree

HALAKHAH

דָּבָר שֶׁלֹּא בָּא לָעוֹלָם Something that has not yet come into existence. "It is impossible to transfer to another person, either as a sale or as a gift, or even as a bequest, ownership of an object that does not yet exist. Thus, if a person says: 'The produce that this field will yield is sold to you' (and the like), the sale of the produce does not take effect, and if the transfer is in the form of a gift the donor can retract." (*Shulḥan Arukh, Ḥoshen Mishpat* 290:4.)

LITERAL TRANSLATION

[1] And even according to Rabbi Meir, who says: A person *can* transfer ownership of something that has not yet come into the world, [2] these words [apply], for example, [to] the fruit of a palm tree, which will [naturally] come [into existence], [3] but here [34A], who says that it will be stolen? [4] And if you say that it will be stolen, who says that the thief will be found? [5] And if the thief is found, who says that he will pay? [6] Perhaps he will admit [the theft] and will be exempted.

[7] Rava said: It is as if he said to him:

[1] וַאֲפִילּוּ לְרַבִּי מֵאִיר, דְּאָמַר: אָדָם מַקְנֶה דָּבָר שֶׁלֹּא בָּא לָעוֹלָם, [2] הָנֵי מִילֵּי כְּגוֹן פֵּירוֹת דֶּקֶל, דַּעֲבִידֵי דְּאָתוּ, [3] אֲבָל הָכָא, [34A] מִי יֵימַר דְּמִגַּנְבָא? [4] וְאִם תִּמְצֵי לוֹמַר דְּמִגַּנְבָא, מִי יֵימַר דְּמִשְׁתַּכַּח גַּנָּב? [5] וְאִי מִשְׁתַּכַּח גַּנָּב, מִי יֵימַר דִּמְשַׁלֵּם? [6] דִּלְמָא מוֹדֵי וּמִפַּטַר.

[7] אָמַר רָבָא: נַעֲשָׂה כְּאוֹמֵר לוֹ:

TRANSLATION AND COMMENTARY

וַאֲפִילּוּ לְרַבִּי מֵאִיר [1] Rami bar Ḥama now further develops his objection: It is true that the principle that a person cannot transfer ownership of something that is not yet in existence is the subject of a Tannaitic dispute, but **even according to Rabbi Meir, who says** that as a rule **a person *can* transfer ownership of something that has not yet come into existence**, it is still impossible to explain our Mishnah, [2] because Rabbi Meir's **words apply** only to cases such as, **for example, the** sale of a future year's crop of **fruit of a palm tree which** regularly produces fruit; such fruit **will**, in all probability, **naturally come into existence** in the fullness of time. Thus, according to Rabbi Meir, it is possible to sell a future year's crop in advance. [3] **But here** [34A], where the subject under discussion is the transfer of the right to the double payment from depositor to bailee, there is no reason to assume that this right will ever come into existence, because there are three things that must happen first, all of which are uncertain. (1) **Who says that** the deposit **will be stolen?** [4] (2) **And** even **if you assume that it will be stolen, who says that the thief will be found?** [5] (3) And even if you assume that the deposit will be stolen, **and** even if you assume that **the thief is found, who says that he will pay?** [6] **Perhaps he will admit** to **the theft** before his guilt is proven in court, **and** will thus **be exempted** from the double payment. According to the Halakhah, if the thief comes forward and admits his guilt, he is ordered to return the stolen deposit, but is exempt from paying the equivalent of the value of the object as a fine. Now, since in the case presented above, three uncertain conditions must be met before the right to receive the double payment comes about, how can the depositor transfer this right to the bailee? Thus far the Gemara has presented the objection raised by Rami bar Ḥama.

אָמַר רָבָא [7] **Rava said** in reply: Rami bar Ḥama's objection is based on an incorrect assumption. We are not dealing with the transfer of ownership of a nonexistent right. Rather, the depositor **is** regarded **as if he** had

RASHI

ואפילו לרבי מאיר דאמר — בפרק שליש דקדושין (סג,א): הרי את מקודשת לי על מנת שאתגייר — איכא למיגמר מינה מוכר פירות דקל לחבירו עד שלא באו לעולם, דאפליגו בה רב הונא ורב נחמן לקמן ב״איזהו נשך״ (סו,ב). **דעבידי דאתו** — גרסינן. **מי יימר דמגנבא** — שעתיד להיגנב, דליקני ליה כפל בשעת מסירה, דעל כרחך משעת מסירה בעי לאקנויה, שמשכה ממנו על מנת כן. **נעשה כאומר לו** — בשעה שמסרה לו, דקים להו לרבנן דניחא להו לבעלים שיהא בטוח בקרן על מנת שיהא ספק כפל העתיד לבא של שומר, והרי היא כמסרה לו על מנת כן שאם תיגנב וישלם לו קרן שתהא פרה קנויה לו משעה שמסרה, נמצא למפרע כשגנב הגנב — של שומר היתה, דפרה כבר היא בעולם.

SAGES

רַבִּי מֵאִיר **Rabbi Meir.** A Tanna of the generation before the completion of the Mishnah. See *Bava Metzia*, Part I, pp. 28-29.

רָבָא **Rava.** A Babylonian Amora of the fourth generation. See above, p. 9.

BACKGROUND

דִּלְמָא מוֹדֵי וּמִפַּטַר **Perhaps he will admit the theft and will be exempted.** The double (or fourfold or fivefold) payment made by the thief is not the return of stolen money, but rather a fine imposed upon him by Torah law. The laws governing fines are different in various respects from those governing civil suits: The judges must be experts who are ordained and competent to adjudicate fines, and the legal procedure is also different. In contrast to civil suits, in which the admission of the defendant (הוֹדָאַת בַּעַל דִּין) is sufficient to oblige him to make full payment, this rule does not apply to the imposition of fines. A fine may only be imposed if two witnesses have testified to the misdeed and the accused has denied it. If the accused (in our case, the thief) confesses his guilt, he does not pay a fine, although he must restore the stolen goods.

NOTES

rather than as a voluntary transfer, but the Gemara clearly understood the Mishnah to be based on a voluntary transfer; hence Rami bar Ḥama's objection (*Ritva*).

כְּגוֹן פֵּירוֹת דֶּקֶל **For example, to the fruit of a palm tree.** The Rishonim ask: Rabbi Meir nowhere discusses the transfer of the fruit of palm trees. Moreover, among the cases explicitly discussed by Rabbi Meir are several that are not particularly likely to come about, such as, "I hereby marry you, and our marriage will become effective if and when your husband dies."

Several answers are given by commentators. *Tosafot* (*Yevamot* 93b) distinguishes between objects that are physically nonexistent and those that are merely subject to some legal obstruction. Rabbi Meir's ruling applies only to objects which are physically in existence but which are legally problematic, such as the case of the married woman. On the other hand, it applies irrespective of whether the removal of the legal obstruction is likely or not. The Gemara feels that it can extend Rabbi Meir's ruling to physically nonexistent objects that normally can be expected to come into existence, but not to objects that do not now exist and are not likely to come into existence.

Rosh explains that Rabbi Meir normally maintains that one can sell property which does not at present exist, even if it is not particularly likely to come into existence. But this does not apply in our case, where the likelihood of a double payment being made to the bailee is extremely remote, as the Gemara explains below (34a).

The Rishonim interpret *Rashi* as follows: The position originally set out by Rabbi Meir was taken up by his disciples and remained a school of thought for generations, until it was finally rejected by the normative Halakhah. Thus,

TRANSLATION AND COMMENTARY

made the following **statement to the bailee** when he handed over the deposit to him: [1]**"If** the deposit **is stolen and you prefer to pay me** rather than take an oath exempting yourself from payment, then **my cow is acquired by you** retroactively **from** the moment of its transfer to you **now."** Since his acquisition of the cow takes effect retroactively, the bailee automatically acquires all privileges stemming from ownership. Rava's solution avoids the problem raised by Rami bar Ḥama's objection, because it posits a retroactive sale of an object already in existence — the cow. Such a retroactive sale is perfectly in order, because it amounts to no more than the fulfillment of a condition stipulated at the time the object was handed over to the bailee. Since the depositor is willing to transfer his right to the double payment to the bailee, on condition that the bailee pays the value of the cow to him promptly if it is stolen, the cow is considered to have been sold to the bailee at the moment of its original transfer.

מַתְקִיף לָהּ רַבִּי זֵירָא [2]As we have seen, Rava's answer is based on the premise that the owner of the cow transfers not the double payment, but the cow itself, retroactively to the bailee. **Rabbi Zera objected to this** premise: **If so,** if the cow was acquired by the bailee at the moment it was entrusted to him, the bailee should immediately acquire all the privileges stemming from ownership. Thus, **even** the animal's **shearings and offspring,** which came into the bailee's possession while the animal was in his care, should **also** belong to the bailee, since he is considered to have acquired the animal from the outset. [3]**Why** then **has it been taught** in a Baraita that if the bailee repays the owner the value of his deposit, the bailee becomes entitled to all rights in the animal **"except for its shearings and its offspring"?**

[1]"לִכְשֶׁתִּגָּנֵב וְתִרְצֶה וּתְשַׁלְּמֵנִי, הֲרֵי פָּרָתִי קְנוּיָה לָךְ מֵעַכְשָׁיו". [2]מַתְקִיף לָהּ רַבִּי זֵירָא: אִי הָכִי, אֲפִילּוּ גִּיזּוֹתֶיהָ וּוְלָדוֹתֶיהָ נַמִּי. [3]אַלְמָּה תַּנְיָא: "חוּץ מִגִּיזּוֹתֶיהָ וּוְלָדוֹתֶיהָ"?

LITERAL TRANSLATION

[1]"If it is stolen and you wish to pay me, my cow is acquired by you from now."

[2]Rabbi Zera objected to this: If so, even its shearings and its offspring as well. [3]Why has it been taught: "Except for its shearings and its offspring"?

RASHI

אי הכי — דנמלא שהיתה שלו משעה ראשונה — יזכה אף בגיזות וולדות שהיו לה משבאה לביתו, דכיון דנגנב ורלה ושילם — נמלאת שלו למפרע.

SAGES

רַבִּי זֵירָא **Rabbi Zera.** An Amora of the third generation. See above, p. 45.

NOTES

cases discussed by Rabbi Meir's disciples are also sometimes attributed to him, since they reflect his thinking. Indeed, it is Rav Huna who is the true author of the "palm tree" case, later on in our tractate (66b). (*Rashba* and others.)

הֲרֵי פָּרָתִי קְנוּיָה לָךְ מֵעַכְשָׁיו **My cow is acquired by you as from now.** The Rishonim ask: The owner has no real wish to sell his cow to the bailee. What he really wants to do is transfer his double payment rights to the bailee in the event that the cow is stolen and the bailee reimburses him for its loss. Only the technical difficulties involved in selling a nonexistent object prevent him from effecting this limited transfer of rights directly. Now, there is a form of sale of nonexistent objects, called "selling a tree for its fruits," that is valid according to all authorities. In using this method, the seller sells one of his rights in the tree, namely, the right to collect the following year's crop. Since he is selling a right in an existent tree, rather than a nonexistent crop, the sale is valid. Similarly here, the depositor should simply sell the bailee one of his rights in the cow, namely, the right to collect the double payment in the event of its being stolen. Why then, is it necessary to introduce this legal fiction of a conditional sale of the entire cow, with the technical problems it creates?

The Rishonim point out that in tractate *Gittin* (42b; see also *Tosafot* there), the Sages take up the problem of whether the right to collect a fine is an ownership right that can be sold in this way, but they leave the issue unresolved. As the Gemara notes in our passage, the situations are not strictly analogous, since fruit can ordinarily be expected to appear on a tree, whereas there is no reason to assume that an animal will be stolen and generate a fine. Accordingly, in tractate *Gittin* the Gemara asks whether it is possible to transfer one's potential rights to a fine without transferring the animal itself, in the same way as it is possible to sell "a tree for its fruits," and the Gemara here does not wish to get involved with that unresolved problem (*Ritva*, others).

גִּיזּוֹתֶיהָ וּוְלָדוֹתֶיהָ **Its shearings and its offspring.** The Gemara concludes that the offspring and shearings belong to the depositor. *Maggid Mishneh* explains that there is a dispute among the Rishonim as to how to interpret this ruling. According to some authorities, the Gemara is referring to shearings and offspring produced *before* the theft. These belong to the depositor, since he is considered to have excluded them, using one of the forms of language proposed by the Gemara. But those produced *after* the theft presumably belong to the bailee (*Rashi*, *Rashba*, and others). Other authorities maintain that the Gemara is referring specifically to shearings and offspring produced *after* the theft, which do not belong to the bailee, since they are produced by the animal's body. Those produced *before* the theft are not even at issue, because they obviously belong to the depositor and were never the subject of the Gemara's discussion (*Rambam*).

Shakh disagrees with *Maggid Mishneh*'s explanation. According to *Shakh*, all the Rishonim agree that in his first version Rava awarded *all* the shearings to the bailee, and that Rabbi Zera's objection to Rava's explanation was based

TRANSLATION AND COMMENTARY

אֶלָּא אָמַר רַבִּי זֵירָא [1]**Rather, said Rabbi Zera,** Rava's explanation can be accepted only if it is revised as follows: The depositor **is regarded as if he made the** following **statement to** the bailee when he handed over the animal to him: "The animal is acquired by you retroactively as from the moment of its transfer to you now, **except for its shearings and its offspring.** These are not included in the retroactive sale."

וּמַאי פָּסְקָא [2]The Gemara now asks: **What is the basis for this arbitrary decision** to make a distinction between the owner's willingness to forgo his rights to double, fourfold or fivefold payments on the one hand, and his insistence on retaining his rights to shearings and offspring on the other?

סְתָמָא דְּמִלְּתָא [3]The Gemara answers: **Ordinarily,** in the case of potential or hypothetical **profits from** an **outside** source, such as a fine, **a person is willing** to forgo them and **transfer** them to someone else, since he may never be in a position to receive them. [4]By contrast, in the case of **profits that come from the animal's body** itself, such as shearings or offspring, **a person is not inclined to** forgo them, nor is he likely **to transfer** them to someone else, since he is always confident that he will receive them. Thus the depositor may be willing to transfer rights to a fine that may eventually be paid by a thief, but not to the future shearings and offspring of his own animal.

אִיכָּא דְּאָמְרִי [5]**There are some who say** that the statement quoted above in the name of Rava was made in a slightly different form: Rava said: The depositor **is regarded as if he** had **made the** following **statement to the bailee** when he handed over the deposit to him: [6]"**If** the deposit **is stolen and you prefer to pay me** rather than take an oath exempting yourself from payment, then the animal **is acquired by you** retroactively, but **close to the time of its being stolen,**" i.e., immediately beforehand, and not at the time the animal was first handed over, as in the previous version of Rava's statement. According to both versions, the bailee acquires the animal itself, and not merely the right to the double payment, but in the first version the acquisition takes effect at the moment of transfer, whereas in the second it takes effect immediately before the theft.

מַאי בֵּינַיְיהוּ [7]The Gemara now asks: **What is the practical difference between** the two versions of Rava's statement?

[1]אֶלָּא אָמַר רַבִּי זֵירָא: נַעֲשָׂה כְּאוֹמֵר לוֹ: "חוּץ מִגִּיזּוֹתֶיהָ וּוְלָדוֹתֶיהָ".
[2]וּמַאי פָּסְקָא?
[3]סְתָמָא דְּמִלְּתָא, שְׁבָחָא דְּאָתָא מֵעָלְמָא עָבֵיד אִינִישׁ דְּמַקְנֵי. [4]שְׁבָחָא דְּמִגּוּפָהּ לָא עָבֵיד אִינִישׁ דְּמַקְנֵי.
[5]אִיכָּא דְּאָמְרִי: אָמַר רָבָא: נַעֲשָׂה כְּאוֹמֵר לוֹ: [6]"לִכְשֶׁתִּגָּנֵב וְתִרְצֶה וּתְשַׁלְּמֵנִי, סָמוּךְ לִגְנֵיבָתָהּ קְנוּיָה לָךְ".
[7]מַאי בֵּינַיְיהוּ?

LITERAL TRANSLATION

[1]Rather, Rabbi Zera said: It is as if he said to him: "Except for its shearings and its offspring."

[2]But why [this arbitrary] decision?

[3]Ordinarily, profit that comes from the outside a person transfers, [4][but] profit that is from [the animal's] body a person does not transfer.

[5]There are [some] who say: Rava said: It is as if he said to him: [6]"If it is stolen and you wish to pay me, it is acquired by you close to [the time of] its being stolen."

[7]What is [the difference] between them?

RASHI

פסקא – פסקת הדבר בכל אדם שדעתו להקנות כפל אם יבא לכך, ואין דעתו להקנות הולדות. **נעשה כאומר לו** – בשעה שמסרה לו. **לכשתגנב ותרצה ותשלמני** – אם תשלם לי הקרן. **סמוך לגניבתה קנויה לך** – שעה אחת לפני גניבתה תהא הפרה קנויה לך, והיא כבר היתה בעולם.

TERMINOLOGY

מַאי פָּסְקָא Why the unqualified statement? Sometimes the Talmud interprets a Mishnah (or a Biblical verse) as applying only under particular circumstances, though they are not specified in the text itself. In such cases, the Talmud may ask: "Why the unqualified, categorical, statement?" i.e., how can you interpret the Mishnah (or Biblical verse) as applying only under the conditions cited above, if this is not explicitly stated in the text?

אִיכָּא דְּאָמְרִי There are some who say. This expression introduces an alternative version of the previous statement or passage.

מַאי בֵּינַיְיהוּ What is the difference between them? Where the Gemara records a difference of opinion regarding the reason for a law or about the definition of a legal concept, it often asks: "What practical difference is there between the different reasons or definitions cited in the previous passage?" The answer to this question is introduced by the expression אִיכָּא בֵּינַיְיהוּ — "There is a difference between them...."

BACKGROUND

שְׁבָחָא דְּאָתָא מֵעָלְמָא Profit that comes from the outside. Profit that a person does not earn from his property appears to be a kind of windfall profit. He cannot be sure he will ever receive it, and does not pin his hopes on doing so. Hence it is a simple matter to waive rights to such unexpected profits. This is not the case with regard to profit earned from the property itself. Not only are such profits more certain, but the property owner also feels he has a full right to them, for a considerable part of his initial investment was motivated by the expectation of receiving these profits. Therefore he does not readily concede rights to profits of this kind to someone else.

NOTES

only on the shearings produced *before* the theft. Moreover, all the Rishonim also agree that the Halakhah is in accordance with Rabbi Zera's revised version of Rava's explanation, according to which the depositor specifically excluded all the shearings from the sale, including shearings produced after the theft.

HALAKHAH

חוּץ מִגִּיזּוֹתֶיהָ וּוְלָדוֹתֶיהָ Except for its shearings and its offspring. "If someone deposits an animal with another person and the deposit is stolen, and the bailee pays the depositor rather than taking an oath, the thief, if caught, makes the double payment to the bailee, but the animal itself returns to the depositor, together with all its shearings and offspring. For the bailee only acquires profits coming from elsewhere, not profits deriving from the animal's body." *Maggid Mishneh* points out that, according to *Rambam*, it would appear that all shearings and offspring, whether produced before or after the theft, belong to the depositor. But other commentators appear to make a distinction between shearings and offspring produced before the theft, which go to the depositor, and those produced after the theft, which go to the bailee. (*Rambam, Sefer Mishpatim, Hilkhot She'elah* 8:1.)

TRANSLATION AND COMMENTARY

אִיכָּא בֵּינַיְיהוּ [1]The Gemara answers: **There are** two practical **differences between them.** The first is **Rabbi Zera's objection** regarding the bailee's right to shearings and offspring, which can be made to the first version of Rava's statement but not to the second. [2]**Alternatively,** there is another practical difference between the two versions: **if** the animal happened to be **standing in an** ownerless **marsh** just before it was stolen. In such a situation, since the animal was not in the bailee's courtyard at the time when, according to the second version, he was supposed to have acquired it, the transfer of ownership by means of his courtyard (קִנְיַן חָצֵר) does not take place, and thus the bailee is not entitled to the double payment. According to the first version, the place where the animal is standing immediately before the theft is irrelevant because the bailee acquired it when it was first entrusted to him.

שִׁילֵּם וְלֹא רָצָה לִישָּׁבַע [3]The Gemara now considers another aspect of the first sentence of our Mishnah, in which we are informed: "**If the bailee paid and did not want to take an oath**," then the double payment belongs to him. [4]**Rabbi Ḥiyya bar Abba said in the name of Rabbi Yoḥanan:** When the Mishnah uses the expression "**he paid**," it **does not** necessarily **mean that the bailee** actually paid. [5]**Rather, the law applies once he says**: "**I am ready to pay**," and he thereby acquires the right to the double payment from the thief, **even if he did not** actually **pay** the owner the value of the deposit before the thief was found. Thus, according to Rabbi Yoḥanan, the commitment expressed by the bailee to compensate the owner for the loss of his deposit has the legal force of an actual payment, and from that moment the bailee is entitled to any payments made by the thief in restitution.

תְּנַן [6]The Gemara now objects that the language of the Mishnah does not support this interpretation: But **we have learned** in our Mishnah: "**If the bailee paid and did not want to take an oath.**" [7]This plainly says that **if** the bailee actually **paid**, he **indeed** acquires the double payment, but **if he did not pay**, even if he said that he was prepared to pay, he does **not** acquire the double payment! This surely contradicts Rabbi Yoḥanan's statement.

אֵימָא סֵיפָא [8]The Gemara answers: **Consider the last clause** of the Mishnah: "**If he took an oath and did not want to pay.**" [9]Following the reasoning used by the objector above, we must conclude from the language of this clause that **the reason** the bailee is not entitled to the double payment in this case **is that he did not want to pay, but if he had wanted to pay, the law would apply even if he had not** yet actually **paid**, and he would be entitled to the double payment. Thus, the two inferences drawn from our Mishnah contradict each other! [10]**Rather**, concludes the Gemara, **it is impossible to infer anything** from this linguistic argument, since the two inferences are mutually contradictory. At least one of the two clauses cannot be interpreted strictly, according to the logic used above, and thus no conclusion can be drawn from either of them about whether actual payment is necessary.

[1]אִיכָּא בֵּינַיְיהוּ קוּשְׁיָא דְּרַבִּי זֵירָא. [2]אִי נַמִּי, דְּקַיְימָא בַּאֲגָם. [3]״שִׁילֵּם וְלֹא רָצָה לִישָּׁבַע [וכו׳]״. [4]אָמַר רַבִּי חִיָּיא בַּר אַבָּא אָמַר רַבִּי יוֹחָנָן: לֹא ״שִׁילֵּם״ שִׁילֵּם מַמָּשׁ, [5]אֶלָּא כֵּיוָן שֶׁאָמַר: ״הֲרֵינִי מְשַׁלֵּם״, אַף עַל פִּי שֶׁלֹּא שִׁילֵּם.

[6]תְּנַן: ״שִׁילֵּם וְלֹא רָצָה לִישָּׁבַע״. [7]שִׁילֵּם — אִין. לֹא שִׁילֵּם — לָא.

[8]אֵימָא סֵיפָא: ״נִשְׁבַּע וְלֹא רָצָה לְשַׁלֵּם״. [9]טַעְמָא דְּלֹא רָצָה, הָא רָצָה, אַף עַל פִּי שֶׁלֹּא שִׁילֵּם. [10]אֶלָּא מֵהָא לֵיכָּא לְמִשְׁמַע מִינָּהּ.

LITERAL TRANSLATION

[1]There is [a difference] between them: Rabbi Zera's objection, [2]or also where it was standing in a marsh.

[3]"[If] he paid and did not want to take an oath...."

[4]Rabbi Ḥiyya bar Abba said in the name of Rabbi Yoḥanan: "He paid" [does] not [mean that] he actually paid. [5]Rather, once he said: "I will pay," even if he did not pay, [the law applies].

[6]We have learned: "[If] he paid and did not want to take an oath." [7][If] he paid — yes. [If] he did not pay — no.

[8]Say the last clause: "[If] he took an oath and did not want to pay." [9]The reason is that he did not want [to pay], but [if] he did want [to pay], [the law would apply] even if he did not pay. [10]Rather, from this, one cannot infer.

RASHI

קושיא דרבי זירא — ללישנא בתרא ליכא לאקשויי גיזות וולדות, דהא סמוך לגניבתה הוא דאקנייה. **אי נמי דהוה קיימא באגם** — כשגנבה גנב, ללישנא בתרא לא קני כפילא, דהא סמוך לגניבתה לא היתה בחצירו שתהא חצירו קונה לו, ומשיכה ההוא שעתה לא הואי, ובמאי נקני? ואם תאמר: תקני לו משיכה ראשונה שמשכה לו על מנת לקנותה שעה הסמוכה לגניבתה, הא אמרינן בכתובות ב״האשה שנפלו לה נכסים״ (פב,א): האומר לחבירו משוך פרה זו ולא תיקני לך אלא לאחר שלשים — לא קנה.

BACKGROUND

דְּקַיְימָא בַּאֲגָם Where it was standing in a marsh. When the owner transfers ownership of the animal to the bailee "close to the time it was stolen," the latter has to acquire it through one of the standard means of acquisition. If the animal is standing in the bailee's courtyard, the bailee can be said to acquire it through "courtyard-acquisition." However, the marsh (or meadow) does not belong to a specific person, since it is either public domain or unowned property. Therefore, the bailee cannot acquire the animal while it is there.

SAGES

רַבִּי חִיָּיא בַּר אַבָּא Rabbi Ḥiyya bar Abba. An Amora of the third generation, Rabbi Ḥiyya bar Abba was born in Babylonia and immigrated to Eretz Israel in his youth. He began his studies under the first generation of Amoraim in Eretz Israel: Rabbi Ḥanina and Rabbi Yehoshua ben Levi. However, he was mainly a student of Rabbi Yoḥanan. Rabbi Zera says of him that he was precise in reporting his teacher's rulings. After the death of Rabbi Yoḥanan, he studied with Rabbi Elazar. Among his colleagues were Rabbi Abbahu, Rabbi Ammi and Rabbi Assi. His sons also became Sages, the most prominent being Rabbi Abba.

רַבִּי יוֹחָנָן Rabbi Yoḥanan (bar Nappaḥa). A Palestinian Amora of the second generation. See *Bava Metzia*, Part I, pp. 19–20.

TERMINOLOGY

אֶלָּא מֵהָא לֵיכָּא לְמִשְׁמַע מִינָּהּ Rather, from this, one cannot infer. See above, p. 93.

TERMINOLOGY

...תַּנְיָא כְּוָתֵיהּ דְּרַבִּי It was taught in accordance with Rabbi X, i.e., the Baraita that follows supports the view of Rabbi X, an Amora whose view has previously been stated and is the subject of disagreement.

SAGES

רַב פַּפָּא Rav Pappa. A Babylonian Amora of the fifth generation. See *Bava Metzia*, Part I, p. 131.

רַב זְבִיד Rav Zevid. A Babylonian Amora of the fifth generation. See *Bava Metzia*, Part I, p. 201.

TRANSLATION AND COMMENTARY

תַּנְיָא כְּוָתֵיהּ דְּרַבִּי יוֹחָנָן [1]The Gemara notes: The following Baraita **has been taught in accordance with** the viewpoint of **Rabbi Yoḥanan**: "If **someone hires a cow from another person and it is stolen, and the** hirer **says, 'I am ready to pay and I will not take an oath,' and later the thief is found,** [2]**he makes the double payment to the** person who **hired** the animal." Thus, from this Baraita it does indeed appear that the bailee acquires the right to the double payment merely by agreeing to pay the depositor.

אָמַר רַב פַּפָּא [3]Continuing the previous discussion, the Gemara considers another aspect of the first clause of the Mishnah. The Mishnah refers explicitly only to an unpaid bailee who could have exempted himself by taking an oath, but chose instead to pay. We have just seen from Rabbi Yoḥanan's statement and the Baraita cited in support of it that the law of the Mishnah also applies even if the bailee has not yet paid, provided that he has expressed willingness to pay. However, two questions remain: (1) The depositor is transferring the double payment to the bailee because he is satisfied to be guaranteed the safe return of the value of the deposit, and this appears reasonable in cases where the bailee was not liable to pay the depositor, but chose to do so out of an exceptional sense of responsibility. But what is the law if the unpaid bailee admitted he had been responsible for the article's loss, and therefore was by law required to reimburse the owner? On this point, **Rav Pappa said: Once an unpaid bailee admits:** "The theft occurred because **I was negligent,"** thereby placing himself under an obligation to reimburse the depositor, **the depositor** immediately **transfers** his right to receive **the double payment to** the bailee if the thief is found. [4]**For** even though the bailee had no lawful alternative but to reimburse the depositor, nevertheless, **if he had wished to, he could have exempted himself** from payment **with a** fraudulent **claim** that the deposit had been **stolen** without any contributory negligence on his part. The fact that he refrained from making this claim is sufficient reason for the depositor to transfer the double payment to him.

שׁוֹמֵר שָׂכָר [5]This leads to the second question: What is the law regarding other bailees? An unpaid bailee is free from liability for any loss or damage to the deposit unless it was caused by his negligence. A paid bailee and a hirer are liable for all losses — even for theft — unless the damage or loss was caused by forces completely beyond their control. A borrower is liable for all losses, even for those caused by forces beyond his control, except for damage to the borrowed item in the ordinary course of the work for which it was borrowed. Now, if a deposit was stolen from the custody of one of these three other bailees — the paid bailee, the hirer, or the borrower — are they too entitled to the double payment if they repay the depositor for his loss before the thief is found? And what is the law if they agreed to pay but have not yet done so? On this point, Rav Pappa said: **Once a paid bailee says:** "The deposit **was stolen,"** thereby placing himself under the obligation to reimburse the depositor, the depositor immediately **transfers** his right to receive **the double payment to** the bailee if the thief is eventually found. [6]**For** even though a paid bailee has no lawful alternative

[1]תַּנְיָא כְּוָתֵיהּ דְּרַבִּי יוֹחָנָן: "הַשּׂוֹכֵר פָּרָה מֵחֲבֵירוֹ וְנִגְנְבָה, וְאָמַר הַלָּה: 'הֲרֵינִי מְשַׁלֵּם וְאֵינִי נִשְׁבָּע', וְאַחַר כָּךְ נִמְצָא הַגַּנָּב, [2]מְשַׁלֵּם תַּשְׁלוּמֵי כֵפֶל לַשּׂוֹכֵר". [3]אָמַר רַב פַּפָּא: שׁוֹמֵר חִנָּם, כֵּיוָן שֶׁאָמַר: "פָּשַׁעְתִּי", מַקְנֶה לֵיהּ כְּפֵילָא, [4]דְּאִי בָּעֵי, פָּטַר נַפְשֵׁיהּ בִּגְנֵיבָה. [5]שׁוֹמֵר שָׂכָר, כֵּיוָן שֶׁאָמַר: "נִגְנְבָה", מַקְנֶה לֵיהּ כְּפֵילָא, [6]דְּאִי בָּעֵי, פָּטַר נַפְשֵׁיהּ

LITERAL TRANSLATION

[1]It has been taught in accordance with Rabbi Yoḥanan: "One who hires a cow from his fellow and it is stolen, and the other says: 'I will pay and I will not take an oath,' and later the thief is found, [2]he pays the double payment to the hirer."

[3]Rav Pappa said: Once an unpaid bailee says: "I was negligent," [the depositor] transfers the double payment to him, [4]for if he wished, he could have exempted himself with [a claim of] theft. [5]Once a paid bailee says: "It was stolen," he transfers the double payment to him, [6]for if he wished, he could have exempted himself with

RASHI

השוכר פרה ונגנבה כו׳ — אף על פי שהשוכר חייב בגניבה ואבידה, מכל מקום אם רוצה לשקר ולישבע שנאנסה — היה נפטר בשבועה, הלכך, כי אמר נגנבה וחייב עצמו בקרן — נקנה לו הכפל. **מקנה ליה כפילא** — נקנה לו הכפל, כל חיובי ופטורי דארבעה שומרין ילפינן מקרא, לקמן בפרק "השואל" (צד,ב): שומר חנם ישבע על הכל אם לא פשע, והשואל משלם את הכל, נושא שכר והשוכר פטורין מן האונסין וחייבין בגניבה ואבידה, שואל פטור במתה מחמת מלאכה הראויה לה, דאמר ליה להכי אושלת לי, ולא לאוקמה בכילתא.

HALAKHAH

וְאָמַר הַלָּה הֲרֵינִי מְשַׁלֵּם And the other says: I will pay. "If a deposit is stolen from a paid or an unpaid bailee, or from a hirer, the double (or fourfold or fivefold) payment made by the thief goes to the bailee, even if he has not yet paid the depositor, provided that he has declared his willingness to pay," following R. Yoḥanan. (*Rambam, Sefer Mishpatim, Hilkhot She'elah* 8:1.)

שׁוֹמֵר חִנָּם כֵּיוָן שֶׁאָמַר פָּשַׁעְתִּי Once an unpaid bailee says:

TRANSLATION AND COMMENTARY

to reimbursing the depositor for the theft of the deposit, nevertheless, **if** he had **wished** to, **he could have exempted himself** from payment **with a** fraudulent **claim that the animal had been hurt or died** in circumstances beyond his control. The fact that the paid bailee refrained from making this claim is sufficient reason for the depositor to transfer the right to the double payment to him. [1]On the other hand, continues Rav Pappa, the case of **a borrower who says: "I am ready to pay,"** is different. Here the depositor **does not transfer the** right to the **double payment to him** when he makes his admission of liability. [2]For **how could** the borrower **have exempted himself** from payment, even fraudulently? [3]Only by making **a claim that the animal died as a result of** ordinary **work!** [4]**But it is not common that an animal dies as a result of** ordinary **work,** and a borrower would not usually dare make such a claim fraudulently. Hence, the fact that the borrower refrained from making this fraudulent claim is not sufficient cause for the lender to transfer the right to the double payment to him. It is thus clear that, according to this statement of Rav Pappa, a borrower cannot acquire the right to the double payment merely by agreeing to pay. But, at this stage, the question as to whether Rav Pappa would maintain that a borrower can acquire this right by actually paying is left open.

אִיכָּא דְּאָמְרִי [5]With regard to the case of the borrower, **there are some who give** another version of Rav Pappa's statement. In this version, **Rav Pappa said: Even in the case of a borrower, once he says:** [6]**"I am ready to pay,"** the depositor **transfers** his right to receive **the double payment to** the bailee. [7]**For if** the borrower had **wished, he could have** effectively **exempted himself** from payment **with a** fraudulent **claim that the animal died as a result of** ordinary **work.**

אֲמַר לֵיהּ רַב זְבִיד [8]**Rav Zevid said to** Rav Pappa: I agree with you that even a borrower can acquire the right to the double payment, but I cannot accept that mere willingness to pay is sufficient to convey this right. For **Abaye said as follows: A borrower does not acquire** the right to **the double payment until he** actually **pays.** [9]On this point Rav Zevid asks rhetorically: **What is the reason** for this distinction between borrowers and other bailees? [10]He answers: All the other bailees are performing a service for the depositor, for which he is presumably grateful. A borrower, by contrast, **has all the benefit** from the borrowed object, for he is permitted to use it without paying for it. Hence, the depositor has no reason for gratitude towards him, and

בִּשְׁבוּרָה וּמֵתָה. [1]שׁוֹאֵל שֶׁאוֹמֵר: ״הֲרֵינִי מְשַׁלֵּם״, לָא מַקְנֵי לֵיהּ כְּפֵילָא. [2]בְּמַאי הֲוָה לֵיהּ לְמִפְטַר נַפְשֵׁיהּ? [3]בְּמֵתָה מֵחֲמַת מְלָאכָה? [4]מֵתָה מֵחֲמַת מְלָאכָה לָא שְׁכִיחַ.

[5]אִיכָּא דְּאָמְרִי: אָמַר רַב פַּפָּא: שׁוֹאֵל נַמִי, כֵּיוָן שֶׁאָמַר: [6]״הֲרֵינִי מְשַׁלֵּם״, מַקְנֵי לֵיהּ כְּפֵילָא, [7]דְּאִי בָּעֵי, פָּטַר נַפְשֵׁיהּ בְּמֵתָה מֵחֲמַת מְלָאכָה.

[8]אֲמַר לֵיהּ רַב זְבִיד: הָכִי אֲמַר אַבַּיֵי: שׁוֹאֵל עַד שֶׁיְּשַׁלֵּם. [9]מַאי טַעְמָא? [10]הוֹאִיל וְכָל הֲנָאָה שֶׁלּוֹ, בְּדִיבּוּרָא לָא מַקְנֵי לֵיהּ כְּפֵילָא.

LITERAL TRANSLATION

[a claim that the animal] had been hurt or died. [1]A borrower who says: "I will pay," he does not transfer the double payment to him. [2]With what could he have exempted himself? [3]With [a claim that the animal] died because of work? [4][But] it is not common that [an animal] dies because of work.

[5]There are [some] who say: Rav Pappa said: Also a borrower, once he says: [6]"I will pay," he transfers the double payment to him, for if he wished, [7]he could have exempted himself with [a claim that the animal] died because of work.

[8]Rav Zevid said to him: Abaye said as follows: A borrower [does not acquire the double payment] until he pays. [9]What is the reason? [10]Since all the benefit is his, by [mere] speech he does not transfer the double payment to him.

RASHI

וכל הנאה שלו — שהיה עושה בה מלאכתו בלא שום שכר. **בדיבורא** — דהריני משלם. **לא מקני ליה** — הבעלים כפל, שאין זו שום טובה, מוטל היה עליו להניח דעתו, שהשאילה לו חנם.

NOTES

מֵתָה מֵחֲמַת מְלָאכָה לָא שְׁכִיחַ **It is not common that an animal dies because of work.** Our commentary follows *Ritva*, who explains that even though the borrower could have exempted himself from payment by making this claim,

HALAKHAH

I was negligent. "An unpaid bailee acquires the right to the double, fourfold, or fivefold payment as soon as he admits that he was negligent, even before he pays. Similarly, a paid bailee and a hirer acquire this right as soon as they declare that the article in their care was stolen. However, a borrower does not acquire the double payment merely by admitting liability. He has actually to reimburse the lender of his own volition," following Rav Pappa and Abaye with regard to a borrower. (Ibid., 8:2.)

TRANSLATION AND COMMENTARY

does not transfer the double payment to him on the basis of mere **words**. He only transfers the right to the double payment to the borrower if the latter actually pays.

תַּנְיָא כְּוָותֵיהּ דְּרַב זְבִיד [1]The Gemara notes: The following Baraita **was taught in accordance with** the viewpoint of **Rav Zevid: "If someone borrows a cow from another person and it is stolen, and the borrower takes the initiative and pays** the lender before the case comes to court, **and later the thief is found,** [2]in such a case the thief **makes the double payment to the borrower."** Thus, it would appear that if the borrower has actually paid the depositor, he is entitled to the double payment if the thief is found, but if he merely announces his intention to pay, he is not entitled to the double payment. Presumably this is because, as Rav Zevid said in the name of Abaye, a mere declaration of intent is insufficient in this case.

לְלִישָּׁנָא קַמָּא [3]The Gemara notes: The fact that **this** Baraita grants the borrower the double payment if he actually reimburses the depositor **is certainly no refutation of the first version of Rav Pappa's** statement, which asserted that a borrower does not acquire the right to the double payment merely by refraining from claiming that the animal died of ordinary work. The question of whether or not the borrower can acquire this right by actually paying was left open by Rav Pappa; he could certainly argue that the borrower *is* entitled to the double payment if he reimburses the owner. [4]But **shall we say that** this Baraita **refutes the latter version** of Rav Pappa's statement, according to which the borrower can acquire this right merely by admitting liability?

אָמַר לָךְ רַב פַּפָּא [5]The Gemara answers: **Rav Pappa can say to you: Is** the language of the Baraita **stronger than** that of **our Mishnah, which** uses the expression **"he paid," and we interpreted it as applying** even **where he** merely **said** that he would pay? [6]**Here, too, we can interpret** the Baraita **as** referring even to a case where **he said** that he would pay, but has not yet done so.

מִי דָּמֵי [7]The Gemara objects: **Can** the Mishnah be **compared** to the Baraita? The Mishnah **does not say "he anticipated** and paid," and it can therefore be interpreted as meaning that the bailee merely declared his willingness to pay. **But** the Baraita specifically **says "he anticipated** and paid," clearly implying that the bailee actually paid. Thus the objection against the second version of Rav Pappa's statement still stands.

[1]תַּנְיָא כְּוָותֵיהּ דְּרַב זְבִיד: ״הַשּׁוֹאֵל פָּרָה מֵחֲבֵירוֹ וְנִגְנְבָה, וְקִידֵּם הַשּׁוֹאֵל וְשִׁילֵּם, וְאַחַר כָּךְ נִמְצָא הַגַּנָּב, [2]מְשַׁלֵּם תַּשְׁלוּמֵי כֶפֶל לַשּׁוֹאֵל״.

[3]לְלִישָּׁנָא קַמָּא דְּרַב פַּפָּא וַדַּאי לָא הָוְיָא תְּיוּבְתָּא. [4]לְלִישָּׁנָא בַּתְרָא לֵימָא תֶּיהֱוֵי תְּיוּבְתֵּיהּ? [5]אָמַר לָךְ רַב פַּפָּא: מִי אַלִּימָא מִמַּתְנִיתִין, דְּקָתָנֵי ״שִׁילֵּם״, וְאוֹקִימְנָא בְּ״אָמַר״? [6]הָכָא נַמִּי בְּ״אָמַר״.

[7]מִי דָּמֵי? הָתָם לָא קָתָנֵי ״קִידֵּם״, הָכָא קָתָנֵי ״קִידֵּם״.

LITERAL TRANSLATION

[1]It was taught in accordance with Rav Zevid: "One who borrows a cow from his fellow and it is stolen, and the borrower has anticipated and paid, and later the thief is found, [2]he pays the double payment to the borrower."

[3]To the first version of Rav Pappa this is certainly no refutation. [4]To the latter version, shall we say that it is its refutation?

[5]Rav Pappa can say to you: Is it stronger than our Mishnah, which teaches "he paid," and we interpreted it as "he said"? [6]Here too [we can interpret it] as "he said."

[7]Is it comparable? There it does not teach "he anticipated," [but] here it teaches "he anticipated."

RASHI

ללישנא קמא דרב פפא — ודאי לא הוי תיובתא דנימא כיון דטעמא דרב פפא משום דלא הוה למפטר נפשיה, דהא מתה מחמת מלאכה לא שכיחא, אפילו קדם ושילם נמי אית ליה לרב פפא דלא קני ליה כפילא, ומיקשי ליה, הא ודאי ליכא לאותובי, דמצי אמר לך: אנא אף על פי שאמר הריני משלם אמרי, ולא אמרי אף על פי ששילם. **נימא תיהוי תיובתא — מי נימא דשילם דוקא קאמר תנא דברייתא.**

TERMINOLOGY

מִי דָּמֵי Is it comparable? I.e., can the two cases be compared, when they are in fact different? Usually, having laid down the basis for rejecting a suggested analogy, the Talmud continues by explaining the difference between the two cases: ...הָתָם...הָכָא — "There [in the first case], the situation is as follows, while here [in the second case], the situation is different...."

NOTES

he is unlikely to do so. He would be afraid to make such a claim, because people would not believe him.

Rabbenu Hananel apparently had a different reading in the Gemara here: He explains that a borrower must produce the body of the animal in order to claim that it died while working, and in our case this cannot be done, because in fact the animal was stolen and did not die. According to this interpretation, the Baraita, which grants the borrower the double payment only if he actually reimburses the lender, is more a refutation of the first version of Rav Pappa's statement than of the second. Accordingly, *Rabbenu Hananel* amends the Gemara to read: "To the first version of Rav Pappa, this is certainly a refutation" (rather than "is certainly not)."

מִי אַלִּימָא מִמַּתְנִיתִין Is it stronger than our Mishnah? Since, in general, the Mishnah was worded very precisely, inferences may be drawn from it regarding cases not explicitly discussed in it. Baraitot, however, may not be used in this way, for they were not worded so accurately. Nevertheless, in cases where the Mishnah need not be interpreted literally, we are also permitted to interpret the Baraita more freely.

TRANSLATION AND COMMENTARY

מַאי קִידֵּם [1]The Gemara answers: **What does "he anticipated" mean?** Only that **he took the initiative and said** that he was willing to pay, not that he actually paid before the thief was found!

הָא מִדְּקָתָנֵי [2]The Gemara objects: **But surely since** the Baraita quoted earlier in support of Rabbi Yoḥanan **uses the expression "and he said** that he would pay," **regarding a hirer, and** this Baraita quoted in support of Rav Zevid uses the expression **"he anticipated** and paid," **regarding a borrower,** [3]we can **infer from this that** our Baraita **means exactly what it says,** and the expression "anticipated" means "anticipated and paid." Thus the objection against the second version of Rav Pappa's statement still stands.

מִידֵּי גַּבֵּי הֲדָדֵי תַּנְיָא [4]The Gemara answers that no proof can be adduced from here. It asks rhetorically: **Were the** two **Baraitot taught together**, as part of a single, longer Baraita, so that inferences can legitimately be drawn from the wording of one to the other? Perhaps there is no connection between them, and the linguistic differences between them merely reflect the styles of their respective authors!

שַׁיְילִינְהוּ [5]In conclusion the Gemara notes: The Sages **asked the** experts on the text of Baraitot, **the Tannaim** (the reciters of Baraitot) **of the school of Rabbi Ḥiyya and of the school of Rabbi Oshaya,** whether these two Baraitot were separate rulings or part of one integral ruling of a single authority. [6]**And** the Tannaim **said** that the Baraitot **were** indeed **taught together.** Hence we may draw inferences from the one regarding the other, and the second version of Rav Pappa's statement is refuted by this Baraita.

פְּשִׁיטָא [7]The Gemara now lays the groundwork for presenting a series of problems by stating an accepted law: **It is obvious that if** the bailee initially **said, "I will not pay," and then said, "I am ready to pay** rather than take an oath," and before he had time to pay, the thief was found, he is entitled to the double payment from the thief. [8]**Surely he did say, "I shall pay,"** and we attach no importance to his earlier refusal. Having stated the law in this straightforward case, the Gemara now presents a series of situations where a decision as to the allocation of the double payment is far less clearcut: (1) The ruling in the case mentioned above is uncontroversial, [9]**but** a question arises **if** the bailee initially **said** to the court, **"I am ready to pay,"**

[1]מַאי ״קִידֵּם״? קִידֵּם וְאָמַר.
[2]הָא מִדְּקָתָנֵי גַּבֵּי שׂוֹכֵר ״וְאָמַר״, וְגַבֵּי שׁוֹאֵל ״קִידֵּם״, [3]שְׁמַע מִינָּהּ דַּוְקָא קָתָנֵי.
[4]מִידֵּי גַּבֵּי הֲדָדֵי תַּנְיָא?
[5]שַׁיְילִינְהוּ לְתַנָּאֵי דְּבֵי רַבִּי חִיָּיא וּדְבֵי רַבִּי אוֹשַׁעְיָא, [6]וְאָמְרִי: גַּבֵּי הֲדָדֵי תַּנְיָין.
[7]פְּשִׁיטָא, אָמַר: ״אֵינִי מְשַׁלֵּם״, וְחָזַר וְאָמַר: ״הֲרֵינִי מְשַׁלֵּם״, [8]הָא קָאָמַר: ״הֲרֵינִי מְשַׁלֵּם״. [9]אֶלָּא אָמַר ״הֲרֵינִי מְשַׁלֵּם״,

LITERAL TRANSLATION

[1]What [does] "he anticipated" [mean]? He anticipated and said.
[2][But] surely since it teaches "and he said" regarding a hirer, and "he anticipated" regarding a borrower, [3]conclude from this [that] it teaches exactly [what it says].
[4]Were they taught next to each other?
[5]They asked the Tannaim of the school of Rabbi Ḥiyya and the school of Rabbi Oshaya, [6]and they said: They were taught next to each other.
[7]It is obvious [that if] he said: "I will not pay," and then he said: "I will pay," [8]surely he said: "I will pay." [9]But [if] he said: "I will pay,"

RASHI

והא מדקתני — תנא דברייתא גבי שוכר ואמר כדאמרינן לעיל תניא כוותיה דרבי יוחנן, וגבי שואל ושילם, בהך דתניא כוותיה דרב זביד. **שיילינהו** — בני הישיבה. **לתנאי** — שהיו שונין תוספתא דרבי חייא ותוספתא דרבי אושעיא, שהם עיקר, כדאמרינן בעלמא (חולין קמא,א): כל מתניתא דלא מיתניא בי רבי אושעיא ורבי חייא לא תותבוה בי מדרשא.

NOTES

מִידֵּי גַּבֵּי הֲדָדֵי תַּנְיָא Were they taught next to each other. The text of the Baraitot (the name literally means "external Mishnayot") was not standardized like that of the Mishnah. The Baraitot were not written down. Moreover, they were not studied together as complete tractates. Indeed, most Baraitot were entirely separate entities. To be sure, certain Baraitot (e.g., the Tosefta) were arranged like the Mishnah, with the different Baraitot grouped in sequence. Only these Baraitot — the Baraitot studied by the Baraita-reciters (the "Tannaim") of the schools of Rabbi Ḥiyya and of Rabbi Oshaya — were considered authoritative. Moreover, only in such ordered compilations may we infer that a different wording implies a different Halakhic ruling.

HALAKHAH

אָמַר אֵינִי מְשַׁלֵּם וְחָזַר וְאָמַר הֲרֵינִי מְשַׁלֵּם If he said: I will not pay, and then he said: I will pay. "If the bailee initially says 'I will not pay,' and later retracts, declaring that he is willing to pay, he acquires the right to the double payment, provided that he retracts before the thief is caught." (*Rambam, Sefer Mishpatim, Hilkhot She'elah* 8:4.)

TERMINOLOGY

מִידֵּי גַּבֵּי הֲדָדֵי תַּנְיָא Were they taught next to each other? Sometimes Baraitot seem to deal with similar subjects but are worded differently. The Gemara infers from these differences in phraseology that the Baraitot disagree (or that some other distinction must be drawn between them). However, the Gemara often rejects this inference by asking: "Were they [i.e., the two Baraitot] taught next to each other?" Perhaps the different wording does not indicate substantive disagreement, but rather shows that the Baraitot derive from different compilations, such as those of Rabbi Hiyya, Rabbi Oshaya, etc.

פְּשִׁיטָא It is obvious. Sometimes פְּשִׁיטָא is used at the beginning of a sentence to introduce a question, first indicating what issues have obvious answers and then setting out those which must be resolved: "It is obvious what the law is in case A; but what about case B?"

BACKGROUND

שַׁיְילִינְהוּ לְתַנָּאֵי דְּבֵי רַבִּי חִיָּיא They asked the Tannaim of the school of Rabbi Ḥiyya.... In Talmudic times many collections of Baraitot existed. They were not in written form, but were memorized. However, many of these collections were imperfectly retained in the memories of professional reciters (תַּנָּאִים). In some cases only part of a Baraita would be remembered, or conversely, sources which did not in fact belong together would mistakenly be combined. However, in the school of Rabbi Hiyya and Rabbi Oshaya, who were students of Rabbi Yehudah HaNasi, the collections of Baraitot were known to be accurate (indeed, some authorities believe that the Tosefta — an extant written compilation of Baraitot — derives from their collections). One could be certain that a Baraita reported by them was cited in proper order, and contained no extraneous material.

TRANSLATION AND COMMENTARY

[34B] **and then said: "I will not pay.** I will take an oath instead and be exempt from payment." The thief was then found. [1]**What is the law** in such a case? To whom is the double payment made? [2]**Do we say that he has retracted** his promise to pay, and therefore is not entitled to the double payment? [3]**Or perhaps he intends to keep his word** to pay, **and he is** merely **putting** the depositor **off** in an attempt to delay payment, and this should not affect his right to receive the double payment.

אָמַר: הֲרֵינִי מְשַׁלֵּם [4](2) Similarly, if the bailee **said: "I am ready to pay," and he died** before he had the opportunity to do so, **and his sons** then **said: "We will not pay,"** and later the thief was found, [5]**what is the law?** To whom is the double payment made? [6]**Do we say that they** have **retracted** their father's promise to pay? [7]**Or perhaps they stand by their father's promise, and they are** merely **putting** the depositor **off** in an attempt to delay payment until they are ready, and are thus entitled to the double payment.

שִׁלְּמוּ בָּנִים מַאי [8](3) The Gemara continues its series of questions: If the bailee died before he was able to make his intentions clear, and **his sons paid** the depositor, and later the thief was found, **what is the law?** [9]**Can** the depositor **say to them: "If I had transferred the double payment,** [10]**I would have done so to your father, because he** was a friend of mine and **did me favors** on many occasions, but I certainly did **not** transfer it **to you"?** [11]**Or perhaps there is no difference** whether the father pays or the sons pay, and whoever pays acquires the double payment.

שִׁילֵּם לְבָנִים מַאי [12](4) Conversely, **if,** after entrusting his animal to a bailee the depositor died, the animal was then stolen and the bailee **paid** the depositor's **sons** the value of the deposit, and later the thief was found, **what is the law?** To whom is the double payment made? [13]**Can** the sons of the depositor **say to** the

[34B] וְחָזַר וְאָמַר: ״אֵינִי מְשַׁלֵּם״, [1]מַאי? [2]מִי אָמְרִינַן: מְהַדַּר קָא הָדַר בֵּיהּ, [3]אוֹ דִּלְמָא בְּמִלְּתֵיהּ קָאֵי, וְדַחוּיֵי הוּא דְּקָא מְדַחֵי לֵיהּ?

[4]אָמַר: ״הֲרֵינִי מְשַׁלֵּם״, וּמֵת וְאָמְרוּ בָּנָיו: ״אֵין אָנוּ מְשַׁלְּמִין״, [5]מַאי? [6]מִי אָמְרִינַן: מְהַדַּר קָא הָדְרִי בְּהוּ, [7]אוֹ דִּלְמָא בְּמִלְּתָא דַּאֲבוּהוֹן קַיְימִי, וְדַחוּיֵי הוּא דְּקָא מְדַחוּ לֵיהּ?

[8]שִׁלְּמוּ בָּנִים, מַאי? [9]מָצֵי אָמַר לְהוּ: ״כִּי אַקְנַאי כְּפֵילָא, לַאֲבוּכוֹן, [10]דַּעֲבַד לִי נַיְיח נַפְשַׁאי, לְדִידְכוּ לָא״? [11]אוֹ דִּלְמָא לָא שְׁנָא?

[12]שִׁילֵּם לְבָנִים, מַאי? [13]מָצוּ אָמְרִי לֵיהּ: ״כִּי אַקְנֵי לָךְ אֲבוּנָא

LITERAL TRANSLATION

[34B] and then he said: "I will not pay," [1]what [is the law]? [2]Do we say he has retracted, [3]or perhaps he stands by his word, and he is putting him off?

[4][If] he said: "I will pay," and he died, and his sons said: "We will not pay," [5]what [is the law]? [6]Do we say they have retracted, [7]or perhaps they stand by their father's word, and they are putting him off?

[8][If] the sons paid, what [is the law]? [9]Can he say to them: "If I transferred the double payment, [10][I did so] to your father, because he did me a favor (lit., 'made for me pleasure for my soul'), not to you"? [11]Or perhaps there is no difference?

[12][If] he paid the sons, what [is the law]? [13]Can they say to him: "If our father transferred the

RASHI

ואמרו בנים אין אנו משלמין – לא הספיק לשלם עד שמת. **שלמו בנים** – והאב לא הספיק לומר הריני משלם עד שמת. **דעבד לי נייח נפשאי** – פעמים רבות עשה לי קורת רוח. **שילם לבנים** – מתו הבעלים ונגנבה ואמר השומר לבנים: הריני משלם, או שילם, מהו?

BACKGROUND

וְדַחוּיֵי הוּא דְּקָא מְדַחֵי לֵיהּ And he is putting him off. When someone refuses to pay (and sometimes when he denies that he owes money at all), this may not be an absolute refusal or denial, but rather a way of postponing payment. Sometimes a person who does not yet have enough money to discharge his debt prefers to declare absolutely that he will not pay it rather than enter into detailed discussions as to why he wishes to postpone payment. Since acquisition of the double payment by the bailee depends both upon the transfer of the right by the owner of the deposit and upon the agreement of the bailee to reimburse the owner in the event of loss, inner intention (גְּמִירַת הַדַּעַת) is clearly an important element in determining the Halakhah.

שִׁילֵּם לְבָנִים If he paid the sons. *Tosafot* (ד״ה הֲרֵינִי מְשַׁלֵּם) asks: The double payment is a fine (see above, 34a), and the Gemara (*Ketubot* 41b-43a) rules that "fines cannot be bequeathed to one's sons," meaning that if a person is owed a fine and dies, the obligation to pay the fine is cancelled. Why, then, does the thief have to make the double payment at all, since the original owner of the stolen object is dead?

The answers given by the Rishonim depend on their interpretation of the discussion in *Ketubot*. Some explain that the only fine that cannot be bequeathed is the one imposed by the Torah (Exodus 22:17; Deuteronomy 22:29) upon a seducer or rapist. (*Rashba* and others.) *Rashba* explains that other fines are treated like ordinary debts, but this particular fine must be paid specifically to the victim's father, and the father's heirs are not her father.

Other Rishonim disagree with this interpretation of the Gemara in tractate *Ketubot*, and say that no fines can be inherited. They explain that our Gemara can be referring only to a case where the depositor died *after* the thief was ordered to pay the fine, thus transforming it into an ordinary debt (*Ritva* and others).

NOTES

דַּעֲבַד לִי נַיְיח נַפְשַׁאי Because he did me a favor. The Gemara does not refer to favors such as the bailee's agreeing to look after the deposit, or to his agreement to pay the depositor instead of exempting himself with an oath. These favors would presumably apply equally to the heirs. Rather, the Gemara assumes that the depositor would not have deposited his property with the bailee in the first place unless they were on good terms, the bailee having done favors for the depositor on previous occasions. (*Rashi*).

שִׁילֵּם לְבָנִים If he paid the sons. It is not clear from the Gemara's description whether the depositor died before or after the animal was stolen, or indeed whether the order of events matters, and this question is the subject of a dispute among the Rishonim.

Ra'avad argues that the Gemara must be referring to a case where the depositor died *after* the animal was stolen,

HALAKHAH

אָמַר הֲרֵינִי מְשַׁלֵּם וְחָזַר וְאָמַר אֵינִי מְשַׁלֵּם If he said: "I will pay," and then he said: "I will not pay." "If the bailee declares in court that he is willing to pay, and then retracts, stating that he is not willing to pay, his retraction does not exempt him from compensating the depositor, although it is not certain whether he receives the double payment if the thief is found." For the procedure to be followed in practice, see next entry. (*Tur, Ḥoshen Mishpat* 295.)

TRANSLATION AND COMMENTARY

bailee: **"If our father had transferred the double** payment **to you,** [1]**it would have been because you** were a friend of his, and **did him favors** on many occasions, **but you have not done us any favors,** and we have no intention of transferring the right to the double payment to you." [2]**Or perhaps there is no difference** whether the bailee reimbursed the depositor or his sons, and in both cases the bailee is entitled to the double payment.

שִׁלְּמוּ בָּנִים לְבָנִים מַאי [3](5) Similarly, if neither of the two friends were still alive at the time the deposit was stolen, and **the** bailee's **sons paid the** depositor's **sons,** and later the thief was found, **what is the law?**

שִׁילֵּם מֶחֱצָה מַאי [4](6) The Gemara continues its series of questions: **If the bailee paid half** the value of the deposit and refused to pay more, and later the thief was found, **what is the law?** Has the depositor transferred to the bailee the right to half of the double payment, or has he transferred no right at all?

שָׁאַל שְׁתֵּי פָּרוֹת [5](7) Similarly, **if** a person **borrowed two cows** and they were later stolen **and** the borrower **paid for one of them** but refused to pay for the other, and later the thief was found, **what is the law?** Is the borrower entitled to the double payment for one cow, or is he entitled to nothing?

שָׁאַל מִן הַשּׁוּתָּפִין [6](8) Similarly, **if** a person **borrowed** an object owned jointly by two **partners**, and the object was then stolen, **and he paid one of them** his share in the value of the object, and later the thief was found, **what is the law?** Is the borrower entitled to that part of the double payment which would otherwise go to the partner he reimbursed, or is he entitled to nothing?

שׁוּתָּפִין שֶׁשָּׁאֲלוּ [7](9) Conversely, if two **partners borrowed** an object from a lender and it was stolen, **and one of them paid** his half of the value of the object, **what is the law?** Is he entitled to half the double payment because he has discharged his responsibility in full, or is he entitled to nothing?

כְּפֵילָא, [1]דְּעָבְדַתְּ לֵיהּ נְיַיח נַפְשֵׁיהּ, אֲבָל אֲנַן לְדִידָן לָא״?
[2]אוֹ דִלְמָא לָא שְׁנָא?
[3]שִׁלְּמוּ בָּנִים לְבָנִים, מַאי?
[4]שִׁילֵּם מֶחֱצָה, מַאי?
[5]שָׁאַל שְׁתֵּי פָּרוֹת וְשִׁילֵּם אַחַת מֵהֶן, מַאי?
[6]שָׁאַל מִן הַשּׁוּתָּפִין וְשִׁילֵּם לְאֶחָד מֵהֶן, מַאי?
[7]שׁוּתָּפִין שֶׁשָּׁאֲלוּ וְשִׁילֵּם אֶחָד מֵהֶן, מַאי?

LITERAL TRANSLATION

double payment to you, [1][it was] because you did him a favor, but [you did] not [do] *us* [a favor]"? [2]Or perhaps there is no difference?

[3][If] the sons paid the sons, what [is the law]?

[4][If] he paid half, what [is the law]?

[5][If] he borrowed two cows and paid [for] one of them, what [is the law]?

[6][If] he borrowed from partners and paid one of them, what [is the law]?

[7][If] partners borrowed and one of them paid, what [is the law]?

RASHI

שלמו בנים לבנים מהו – דליכא שום צד נייחא נפשא באלו שהם קיימים, שלא הם ולא אביהם עשו קורת רוח לאלו, ולא אביהם של אלו קיבל קורת רוח מבני השומר. **או דלמא** – כיון שאביהם הראשונים הוה להו נייחא נפשא בהדדי קנו כפילא אף בנים מן הבנים. **שילם מחצה** – מתחילתו אמר: הריני משלם מחצה ולא יותר. **מהו** – לקנות חצי הכפל. **שאל שתי פרות** – אם תימצי לומר לא קני מחצה, שאל שתי פרות ונגנבו, ואמר הריני משלם אחת, ולא אמר מתה מחמת מלאכה. **מהו** – לקנות כפל שלה, מי אמרינן: כיון דפרה שלימה שילם – קנה, או דלמא: כיון דתרווייהו חד פקדון הוו, ואינו משלם את שתיהם – לא אקני ליה כפילא, שהרי הוא נפסד על ידו. **ושילם לאחד מהם** – חלקו, חצי דמיה שעליו, מהו לקנות חלקו המגיעו, מי אמרינן: כל הקרן שלו שילם, או דלמא בעינן עד שישלם כל הפרה. **ושילם אחד מהם** – חצי דמיו שעליו. **מהו** – שיקנה חצי הכפל, מי אמרינן: הרי שילם כל המוטל עליו.

NOTES

for the following reason: We have already established, according to the second version of Rava's statement (above, 34a) that the depositor is considered to have transferred his animal to the bailee immediately before the theft. Hence, if the depositor died *before* the theft, there was no one to effect this transfer.

Rashi, however, explains that the depositor died *before* the animal was stolen, and the Gemara's question is whether or not the heirs of the depositor are also considered to have been willing to transfer the animal.

There is a dispute among the Rishonim as to how *Rashi* would rule in the situation described by *Ra'avad*, where the depositor dies *after* the theft. *Ritva* says that, according to *Rashi*, the Gemara's question applies equally to both cases. *Rashba* says that, according to *Rashi*, the Gemara's question does not apply to *Ra'avad*'s case at all. In such a case, the double payment would simply go to the bailee, as the depositor would have already transferred his rights, and his heirs would have no standing in the matter.

With regard to the Gemara's previous question about the *bailee* dying, both *Rashi* and *Ra'avad* agree that it applies primarily to a situation where he died *after* the theft, but they concur that it might also apply even if he died *before* the theft.

שׁוּתָּפִין שֶׁשָּׁאֲלוּ וְשִׁילֵּם אֶחָד מֵהֶן If partners borrowed and one of them paid. *Rashi* explains that the partner paid only his own share, and the question revolves around his half of the double payment. Most commentators seem to agree. However, some seek to prove from the language of *Rambam* that the question revolves around the entire sum, it being assumed that the one partner paid both shares (*Mirkevet HaMishneh*).

LITERAL TRANSLATION

[1] [If] he borrowed from a woman and paid her husband, what [is the law]?

[2] [If] a woman borrowed and her husband paid, what [is the law]?

[3] Let [the questions] stand.

[4] Rav Huna said: We make him take an oath that [the deposit] is not in his possession. [5] What is the reason? [6] We are concerned that he might have cast his eyes on it.

[1] שָׁאַל מִן הָאִשָּׁה וְשִׁילֵּם לְבַעְלָהּ, מַאי? [2] אִשָּׁה שֶׁשָּׁאֲלָה וְשִׁילֵּם בַּעְלָהּ, מַאי? [3] תֵּיקוּ. [4] אָמַר רַב הוּנָא: מַשְׁבִּיעִין אוֹתוֹ שְׁבוּעָה שֶׁאֵינָהּ בִּרְשׁוּתוֹ. [5] מַאי טַעְמָא? [6] חָיְישִׁינַן שֶׁמָּא עֵינָיו נָתַן בָּהּ.

TRANSLATION AND COMMENTARY

שָׁאַל מִן הָאִשָּׁה [1] (10) The Gemara continues its series of questions: **If** a person **borrowed** an animal **from a** married **woman,** and the animal was her property and her husband's rights in it were restricted to the usufruct, **and** after the animal was stolen the borrower **paid her husband** its value, **what is the law?** Is the husband considered to have a proprietary interest in the animal, in which case the borrower is entitled to the double payment? Or is the husband considered an outsider who has no authority to transfer the right to the double payment to the borrower?

אִשָּׁה שֶׁשָּׁאֲלָה [2] (11) Conversely, **if a** married **woman borrowed** an animal to work her land, **and** after the animal was stolen **her husband paid** the owner its value, **what is the law?** Is the wife entitled to the double payment, since her husband reimbursed the lender? Or is the lender entitled to the double payment because he lent the husband nothing?

תֵּיקוּ [3] After this series of questions the Gemara concludes: **Let the questions stand.** No answers can be provided for any of them (see Halakhah).

אָמַר רַב הוּנָא [4] The Gemara now considers another aspect of the first clause of the Mishnah, in which the bailee prefers to reimburse the depositor rather than take an oath exempting himself from payment. **Rav Huna said:** Even if the bailee says that rather than take the regular oath, he prefers to reimburse the depositor, this does not totally absolve him of the need to take an oath. **We** (the court) **make him take a** different **oath,** in which he swears **that the deposit is not in his possession** but was lost or stolen, as he claims. [5] **What is the reason** for this oath? [6] It is because **we are concerned that** the deposit may not have been lost or stolen at all. The bailee **may have cast his eyes on** the deposit, with the intention of keeping it for himself. Knowing that the depositor will not sell it to him, he seeks to achieve his purpose by claiming that it has been stolen and offering to pay for it. To prevent this, the court makes him swear that the deposit is not in his possession. Only after taking this oath, says Rav Huna, is the bailee allowed to reimburse the depositor for the loss of his property.

RASHI

שאל מן האשה – פרה של נכסי מלוג, שהקרן שלה והפירות לבעל. **ושילם** – הפרה לבעל. **מהו** – לקנות הכפל, מי אמרינן: כיון דקרן לאו דבעל הוא – לאו תשלומין מעליא נינהו, ולא קני כפילא, או דלמא: כיון דאפוטרופוס הוא על הנכסים ואוכל הפירות – בעלים הוי עלייהו, ותשלומין הן. **אשה ששאלה** – לצורך קרקע מלוג שלה. **משביעין אותו** – אמתניתין קאי, אף על פי שהוא משלם, כדקתני: שילם ולא רצה לישבע – משביעין אותו שבועה שאינה ברשותו.

NOTES

מַשְׁבִּיעִין אוֹתוֹ שְׁבוּעָה שֶׁאֵינָהּ בִּרְשׁוּתוֹ **We make him take an oath that the deposit is not in his possession.** Some Rishonim maintain that this oath is of Rabbinic origin, though it must be taken with a solemnity appropriate to Torah oaths, and while holding a sacred object (*Rambam).* Other Rishonim, however, maintain that this oath is required by Torah law (*Rabbenu Hai Gaon,* quoted by *Ritva* and *Meiri*). Even though there is no specific verse in the Torah requiring this oath, these authorities argue that it is included, together with the other oaths imposed on bailees, in the Torah's command that a bailee who does not want to pay must respond to the depositor's claim by taking an oath.

HALAKHAH

מַאי... תֵּיקוּ **What is the law?...Let the questions stand.** All the questions raised in this passage remain unresolved. Normally, when the Gemara fails to resolve a problem involving conflicting monetary claims, the money remains with the party in possession of it at the time, in accordance with the principle that the burden of proof falls upon the party who seeks to take the money away (הַמּוֹצִיא מֵחֲבֵירוֹ עָלָיו הָרְאָיָה). However, in these cases the money is at present in the possession of a thief, and the question is to whom he should pay it. Accordingly, *Rif* and *Rambam* rule that neither the bailee nor the depositor is considered to be in possession of the deposit, and they must divide the double payment, or any increase in the deposit's value, equally. But if one of them seizes the payment before the case is settled by the court, he becomes the person in possession, and the other litigant may not take it away from him. *Ri* and *Rosh* disagree, ruling that the depositor is considered to be in possession, since he is the original owner. Thus, in the absence of a resolution of the Gemara's problems, the bailee is not entitled to any share of the double payment or in the increase of the deposit's value. (*Tur, Ḥoshen Mishpat* 295.)

מַשְׁבִּיעִין אוֹתוֹ שְׁבוּעָה שֶׁאֵינָהּ בִּרְשׁוּתוֹ **We make him take an**

SAGES

רַב הוּנָא **Rav Huna.** A Babylonian Amora of the second generation. See *Bava Metzia,* Part I, p. 52.

BACKGROUND

מַשְׁבִּיעִין אוֹתוֹ **We make him take an oath.** At first sight this requirement may seem strange, as a person who offers to pay for a lost or a stolen deposit can only be doing so because he is sensitive to the property rights of others, and such a person would never steal. Why then is the bailee required to take this oath?

Ran explains that even though the bailee would never steal, he might violate the prohibition against coveting (see above, 5b), since people do not necessarily realize that this prohibition applies even if they pay for the object coveted, if it is extorted from its original owner.

שֶׁמָּא עֵינָיו נָתַן בָּהּ **That he may have cast his eyes on it.** If someone "casts his eyes" on an object and takes it from its owner against his will, even if he pays the full value of the object, to the owner he is not a robber (גַּזְלָן) but an extortionist (חַמְסָן). An extortionist has violated the Tenth Commandment ("You shall not covet"), the meaning of which is that a person is forbidden to do anything to force someone else to part with property, even though his actions fall short of theft or robbery. Even if he later pays the value of the object, the extortioner has committed a transgression for which he must be punished, and every effort is made to remove from his possession the property he extorted.

תֵּיקוּ **Let the questions stand.** When a series of questions — or even two consecutive questions — is found in the Talmud, and a separate answer is not given to each question, this is an indication that they all have the same answer. Sometimes the answer takes the form of an absolute proof resolving all the questions, but sometimes the result is inconclusive — an admission that the questions cannot be resolved.

The series of questions here moves from topic to topic, and in a certain sense it

LITERAL TRANSLATION

[1] [The Sages] raised an objection: "Someone who lends to his fellow against a pledge, and the pledge was lost, [2] and he said to him: 'I lent you a sela against it, [and] it was worth a shekel,' [3] and the other says: 'Not so. Rather, you lent me a sela against it, [and] it was worth a sela,' [4] he is exempt. [5] 'I lent you a sela against it, [and] it was worth a shekel,' [6] and the other says: 'Not so. Rather, you lent me a sela against it, [and] it was worth three dinarim,'

[1] מֵיתִיבֵי: ״הַמַּלְוֶה אֶת חֲבֵירוֹ עַל הַמַּשְׁכּוֹן וְאָבַד הַמַּשְׁכּוֹן, [2] וְאָמַר לוֹ: ׳סֶלַע הִלְוִיתִיךָ עָלָיו, שֶׁקֶל הָיָה שָׁוֶה׳, [3] וְהַלָּה אוֹמֵר: ׳לֹא כִּי. אֶלָּא סֶלַע הִלְוִיתָנִי עָלָיו, סֶלַע הָיָה שָׁוֶה׳, [4] פָּטוּר. [5] ׳סֶלַע הִלְוִיתִיךָ עָלָיו, שֶׁקֶל הָיָה שָׁוֶה׳, [6] וְהַלָּה אוֹמֵר: ׳לֹא כִּי. אֶלָּא סֶלַע הִלְוִיתָנִי עָלָיו, שְׁלֹשָׁה דִּינָרִים הָיָה שָׁוֶה׳,

RASHI

שקל – חצי סלע. **פטור** – הלוה מן השבועה, שאין כאן הודאה במקצת.

TRANSLATION AND COMMENTARY

מֵיתִיבֵי [1] **The Sages raised an objection** to Rav Huna's view from a Mishnah in tractate *Shevuot* (43a) and the ensuing discussion in the Gemara there. The Mishnah is as follows: **"If someone lends money to another person against a pledge** deposited with the lender by the borrower as security for the loan, **and the pledge is lost,** then the lender and the borrower owe each other money. Obviously, if the value of the pledge is equal to the amount of the loan, the case presents no difficulty as the claims cancel each other out. But there are other possibilites, and these are now analyzed by the Mishnah under four headings. The first two relate to a situation in which the lender is the claimant. The last two relate to a situation in which the borrower is the claimant. [2] (1) The lender **says to** the borrower: **'I lent you a sela** (two shekalim or four dinarim) **against** the lost pledge, **and** the pledge **was worth** only one **shekel**. Thus you owe me one shekel.' [3] But the borrower **says: 'Not so.** I agree that **you lent me a sela against** the pledge, **but** the pledge **was worth a sela,** and thus our counterclaims cancel each other out and I owe you nothing.' In such a case the borrower's claim is accepted, in the absence of any evidence in support of the lender's claim. [4] The borrower **is exempt** from payment, and he does not even have to take an oath in support of his claim, in accordance with the law that a person who denies all liability (כּוֹפֵר בַּכֹּל) need not take an oath in support of his claim. [5] (2) The lender claims: **'I lent you a sela against** the lost pledge, **and** the pledge **was worth** only one **shekel**. Thus you owe me one shekel.' [6] But the borrower **says: 'Not so.** I agree that **you lent me a sela against** the pledge, **but** the pledge **was worth three dinarim** (three-fourths of a sela or one-and-a-half shekalim), and

NOTES

Even though in this case the bailee *does* want to pay, and so is not taking the other oaths normally imposed on bailees, he must still take this oath, just as when the plaintiff wishes to include a series of other claims in an oath (גִּלְגּוּל שְׁבוּעָה) the defendant cannot release himself from these additional oaths by paying the claim that gave rise to the original oath.

Meiri explains that the practical difference between a Torah oath and a Rabbinic oath taken with full solemnity is in the procedure if the defendant refuses to take the oath: Refusal to take a Torah oath generates an enforceable debt, and establishes a lien on the defendant's property, whereas refusal to take a Rabbinic oath renders the defendant liable to the penalty of ostracism (נִידּוּי), but does not create a lien on his property.

HALAKHAH

oath that the deposit is not in his possession. "If the bailee states that he is willing to pay for the deposit rather than swear that it was lost or stolen, he may do so. If the deposit was an item that can easily be obtained, he does not have to take any oath (*Rambam*). However, if it was something unusual, the bailee is required to take an oath that the deposit is no longer in his possession. The oath is of the highest degree of solemnity, and is taken by the bailee while holding something sacred in his hand. The reason he must take this oath, even though he is paying for the deposit, is because we fear that he may have a strong desire to own this particular object, and may be using this procedure as a way of getting the true owner to sell it to him against his will," following the view of Rav Huna. (*Shulḥan Arukh, Ḥoshen Mishpat* 295:1.)

סֶלַע הִלְוִיתִיךָ עָלָיו, שֶׁקֶל הָיָה שָׁוֶה I lent you a sela against it, and it was worth a shekel. "If a lender lends money to a borrower against a pledge, and the pledge is lost or stolen, and the lender claims that the value of the loan was more than the value of the pledge, the following rules apply: First, the lender must take the bailee's oath of Rav Huna, affirming that the pledge is not in his possession. Then, if the borrower maintains that the loan and pledge were equal in value, he must take the special oath (שְׁבוּעַת הֶסֵּת) that the Rabbis imposed on all defendants who deny liability without proof, to affirm that the pledge was indeed worth as much as the loan, after which he is exempt from paying the lender anything. However, if the borrower admits that the pledge was worth less than the loan, yet maintains that it was worth more than the lender claims, then the borrower must take a Torah oath, like anyone else who admits to part of a claim, before paying the sum he admits owing." (*Shulḥan Arukh, Ḥoshen Mishpat* 72:9-10.)

passes from simpler questions, which appear to have a positive answer, to more complex questions based on the earlier, simpler ones.

The first problem was to clarify whether the bailee's declaration — "I will not pay" — annuls his earlier promise or merely postpones its fulfillment. Then, if we say that it postpones it, the same question arises with reference to the bailee's sons: Which is more likely, that they have changed their minds, or that the father's agreement obligates them and they too are merely postponing payment? The Gemara then moves on to the general issue of sons, in which the question is whether the willingness to transfer the double payment is a personal agreement between two people which does not devolve upon their heirs, or whether it is a regular monetary agreement.

The next basic problem involves partial payment, and is here discussed from several angles. First, the simple case is brought of a bailee who paid back only part of the value of the deposit. Then the more complex question is considered of someone who borrowed two cows, each of which may be regarded as a separate loan. Is payment for one of them considered partial payment for both? Then we turn to another aspect of partial payment, where there is not a single lender but partners, and the borrower pays only one of them. Is that considered partial payment of the debt? Then, from the question of a partnership we turn to a more complex question: the relationship between a man and his wife. To what degree can they be seen as partners regarding property which they both acquire?

TERMINOLOGY

אַהַיָּיא To what does this refer? Sometimes, when a concluding sentence in a Mishnah, Baraita or Amoraic statement refers to or differs from an earlier statement in the same source, it is not clear to which of the previous statements it is referring. In such cases, the Talmud may ask: "To which statement does this sentence refer?"

TRANSLATION AND COMMENTARY

thus I owe you only half a shekel (or one dinar).' [1]In such a case the borrower **is obliged to take an oath,** in accordance with the law that a person who admits part of a claim (מוֹדֶה בְּמִקְצָת) must take an oath regarding the part he denies. After taking this oath he fulfills his obligation by paying half a shekel to the lender. [2](3) The borrower claims: **'You lent me a sela against** the lost pledge, **and** the pledge **was worth two** sela'im. Thus you owe me one sela.' [3]**But the** lender **says: 'Not so.** I agree that **I lent you a sela against** the pledge, **but** the pledge **was worth** only one **sela,** and thus our counter-claims cancel each other out and I owe you nothing.' In such a case the lender's claim is accepted, in the absence of any evidence in support of the borrower's claim. [4]The lender **is exempt** from payment, and does not even have to take an oath in support of his claim, in accordance with the law applying to a person who denies all liability (כּוֹפֵר בַּכֹּל). [5](4) The borrower claims: **'You lent me a sela against** the lost pledge, **and** the pledge **was worth two** sela'im. Thus you owe me one sela.' [6]**But the** lender **says: 'Not so.** I agree that **I lent you a sela against** the pledge, **but** the pledge **was** actually **worth five** dinarim, and thus I owe you only one dinar (a quarter of a sela).' [7]In such a case the lender **is obliged to take an oath** in accordance with the law applying to a person who admits part of a claim (מוֹדֶה בְּמִקְצָת). After taking this oath he fulfills his obligation by paying the dinar to the borrower."

מִי נִשְׁבַּע [8]The Mishnah now asks rhetorically: **"Who takes the oath** about the value of the pledge?" The Mishnah answers: **"The one who had the deposit with him,** i.e., the lender. [9]The reason why the lender must take the oath is to prevent a situation in which the borrower **takes an oath** regarding the value of the pledge, and the lender then announces that **the deposit** was not in fact lost and **takes it out,** revealing its true value and exposing the borrower as a perjurer, thus disqualifying him from being a witness or taking an oath." In principle, the Sages are reluctant to impose oaths whose truth or falsehood are liable to be immediately revealed (see note). Therefore the lender, who was in possession of the pledge, is required to take the oath, because if the pledge was not lost, no one else can produce it.

אַהַיָּיא [10]Before going on to describe the problem that this Mishnah poses to the ruling of Rav Huna, the Gemara quotes part of the discussion of the Gemara in tractate *Shevuot*, where the Gemara clarifies a difficult point in the Mishnah, asking: **To which clause**, i.e., to which of the four cases mentioned in the Mishnah is the final remark in the Mishnah **referring**, when it says that the oath imposed by the court is transferred from the borrower to the lender, to prevent the lender from possibly exposing the borrower as a liar?

[1]חַיָּיב. [2]'סֶלַע הִלְוִיתָנִי עָלָיו, שְׁנַיִם הָיָה שָׁוֶה', [3]וְהַלָּה אוֹמֵר: 'לֹא כִּי. אֶלָּא סֶלַע הִלְוִיתִיךָ עָלָיו, סֶלַע הָיָה שָׁוֶה', [4]פָּטוּר. [5]'סֶלַע הִלְוִיתָנִי עָלָיו, שְׁנַיִם הָיָה שָׁוֶה', [6]וְהַלָּה אוֹמֵר: 'לֹא כִּי. אֶלָּא סֶלַע הִלְוִיתִיךָ עָלָיו, חֲמִשָּׁה דִּינָרִים הָיָה שָׁוֶה', [7]חַיָּיב.
[8]מִי נִשְׁבַּע? מִי שֶׁהַפִּקָּדוֹן אֶצְלוֹ, [9]שֶׁמָּא יִשָּׁבַע זֶה וְיוֹצִיא הַלָּה אֶת הַפִּקָּדוֹן". [10]אַהַיָּיא?

LITERAL TRANSLATION

[1]he is obliged. [2]'You lent me a sela against it, [and] it was worth two,' [3]and the other says: 'Not so. Rather I lent you a sela against it, and it was worth a sela,' [4]he is exempt. [5]'You lent me a sela against it, [and] it was worth two,' [6]and the other says: 'Not so. Rather, I lent you a sela against it, [and] it was worth five dinarim,' he is [7]obliged.

[8]Who swears? The one with whom the deposit is, [9]in case this one swears and the other one takes out the deposit."

[10]To which [clause] does this refer?

RASHI

חייב – לישבע שכך היה שוה, ומשלם לו דינר שהודה לו. **ושתים היה שוה** – והלוה תובע את המלוה את יתר דמיו, וקא סבר האי תנא: המלוה על המשכון – שומר שכר הוא. **פטור** – מן השבועה, שאין כאן הודאה שחייב לו כלום. **ויוציא הלה כו'** – ויפסלנו. **אהייא** – קאי "מי נשבע" דקתני בהך?

NOTES

שֶׁמָּא יִשָּׁבַע זֶה In case this one swears. It is clear from the Mishnah in tractate *Shevuot* that in principle the Sages are reluctant to impose oaths that can immediately be verified or proved false, but it is not clear why. *Rif* simply says that such an oath would be a desecration of God's name, but does not elaborate. *Rashi*, followed in the commentary here, explains that if the lender produces the deposit, and thus exposes the borrower's false oath, the borrower will be

HALAKHAH

סֶלַע הִלְוִיתָנִי עָלָיו, שְׁנַיִם הָיָה שָׁוֶה You lent me a sela against it and it was worth two. "If a lender gives money to a borrower against a pledge, and the pledge is lost or stolen, and the borrower claims that the pledge was worth more than the loan, then the following rules apply: If the lender maintains that the loan and the pledge were equal in value, then, if it is certain that the pledge is indeed lost — for example, where the borrower trusts the lender not to lie

TRANSLATION AND COMMENTARY

[1]**If** we **say** that it is referring **to the last clause** of the Mishnah, case (4), where the borrower claims that the pledge was worth more than the debt and wants the lender to pay the difference, but the lender admits only part of the borrower's claim, such a remark is not needed. [2]We do not need the Mishnah's ruling to **derive the fact that the oath is imposed on the lender** and not on the borrower, as this oath is imposed on the lender by Torah law, [3]**because it is he who admits to part of the claim,** and according to Torah law a person who admits to part of a claim is required to take an oath exempting himself from paying the rest! Thus, the question remains: To which of the cases mentioned in the Mishnah does its final remark refer?

אֶלָּא אָמַר שְׁמוּאֵל [4]**Shmuel said** in reply: The final remark of the Mishnah **refers to the first clause** of the Mishnah.

מַאי אַרֵישָׁא [5]At first glance, Shmuel's remark is ambiguous, because the first clause of the Mishnah describes two cases, in the first of which no oath is imposed. Thus the Gemara immediately asks: **What is** meant by the expression **"to the first clause"** in Shmuel's reply? [6]The Gemara answers: Shmuel's reply is referring **to the last part of the first clause,** case (2), where the lender says to the borrower: **"I lent you a sela against** the lost pledge, **and** the pledge **was worth** only one **shekel,"** [7]**and the** borrower **says: "Not so.** [8]I agree that **you lent me a sela against it, but it was worth three dinarim."** [9]In this case the Mishnah at first seems to mean that the borrower **is obliged to take the oath,** for normally [10]**the oath would be imposed on the borrower,** since he was sued by the lender and admits to part of the claim. [11]**Nevertheless,** in the last remark in the Mishnah **the Rabbis said:** In such a situation **let the lender take the oath** instead, to confirm his claim that the

[1]אִילֵימָא אַסֵּיפָא, [2]וְתִיפּוֹק לֵיהּ דִּשְׁבוּעָה גַּבֵּי מַלְוֶה הִיא, [3]דְּהָא קָא מוֹדֵי מִקְצָת הַטַּעֲנָה!
[4]אֶלָּא אָמַר שְׁמוּאֵל: אַרֵישָׁא.
[5]מַאי ״אַרֵישָׁא״? [6]אַסֵּיפָא דְּרֵישָׁא: ״׳סֶלַע הִלְוִיתִיךָ עָלָיו, שֶׁקֶל הָיָה שָׁוֶה׳, [7]וְהַלָּה אוֹמֵר: ׳לֹא כִּי. [8]אֶלָּא סֶלַע הִלְוִיתָנִי עָלָיו, שְׁלֹשָׁה דִּינָרִין הָיָה שָׁוֶה׳, [9]חַיָּיב״. [10]דִּשְׁבוּעָה גַּבֵּי לֹוֶה הוּא, [11]וַאֲמוּר רַבָּנַן:

LITERAL TRANSLATION

[1]If we say: To the last clause, [2]let him derive [the fact] that the oath is [imposed] on the creditor, [3]because [it is] he [who] admits to part of the claim! [4]Rather, Shmuel said: [It refers to] the first clause.

[5]What is "to the first clause"? [6]To the last part of the first clause: "'I lent you a sela against it, [and] it was worth a shekel,' [7]and the other says: 'Not so. [8]Rather, you lent me a sela against it, [and] it was worth three dinarim,' [9]he is obliged." [10]For the oath is [imposed] on the borrower, [11]but the Rabbis said:

RASHI

אילימא אסיפא – אחיוב דסיפא. **תיפוק ליה כו׳** – ולמה ליה למתלי טעמא בשמא יוציא הפקדון ויפסלנו לעדות ולשבועה? **מאי ארישא** – הא רישא פטור קתני. **אסיפא דרישא** – אחיוב דקתני ברישא קאי.

SAGES

שְׁמוּאֵל **Shmuel.** A Babylonian Amora of the first generation. See above, p. 48.

NOTES

disqualified from taking oaths and from giving testimony in the future.

Tosafot (ד״ה שֶׁמָּא) and other Rishonim object: Why should we be reluctant to disqualify a perjurer? Let him tell the truth under oath, and then he will not be disqualified! If anything, the fear of immediate exposure can only strengthen the resolve of the borrower to tell the truth!

To answer this objection, *Rashba* and others quote *Rashi* on the parallel passage in tractate *Shevuot* (43a). There he elaborates somewhat on his explanation here and says: We are concerned in case the borrower makes an honest mistake about the facts, and inadvertently swears to an untruth. Such behavior, while improper, is not grounds for disqualification, but if the borrower is exposed immediately, it is likely that he will be treated as a brazen perjurer.

Many Rishonim, however, follow the explanation of *Rabbenu Ḥananel*: Even if the bailee swears truthfully, his oath is unnecessary if the object can be produced and its value made manifest, and the Torah commands us not to take unnecessary oaths (שְׁבוּעַת שָׁוְא).

HALAKHAH

about such matters, or where witnesses testify that the pledge is lost — the lender must take the special oath (שְׁבוּעַת הֶסֵּת) that the Rabbis imposed on all defendants who deny any liability without proof, to affirm that the loan was indeed worth as much as the pledge, after which he is exempt from paying the borrower anything. If the borrower is not fully satisfied that the pledge is lost, the lender must take the bailee's oath of Rav Huna, affirming that the pledge is not in his possession, and must include in this oath (גִּלְגּוּל שְׁבוּעָה) an affirmation that the loan was worth as much as the pledge. However, if the lender admits that the pledge was worth more than the loan, but maintains that it was worth less than the borrower claims, then the lender must take a Torah oath, like anyone else who admits to part of a claim, and must include in his oath the bailee's oath of Rav Huna, before paying the sum he admits owing," following the Gemara's conclusion below. (*Shulḥan Arukh, Ḥoshen Mishpat* 72:12.)

לִשְׁתַּבַּע מַלְוֶה, [1]שֶׁמָּא יִשָּׁבַע זֶה וְיוֹצִיא הַלָּה אֶת הַפִּקָּדוֹן.
[2]וְאִם [35A] אִיתָא לִדְרַב הוּנָא, כֵּיוָן דְּמִשְׁתַּבַּע מַלְוֶה שֶׁאֵינָהּ בִּרְשׁוּתוֹ, [3]הֵיכִי מָצֵי מַפֵּיק לָהּ?
[4]אָמַר רָבָא: שֶׁיֵּשׁ עֵדִים שֶׁנִּשְׂרְפָה.
[5]אִי הָכִי, מֵהֵיכָא מַיְיתֵי לָהּ?
[6]אֶלָּא אָמַר רַב יוֹסֵף: שֶׁיֵּשׁ עֵדִים שֶׁנִּגְנְבָה.
[7]סוֹף סוֹף, מֵהֵיכָא מַיְיתֵי לָהּ?
[8]דְּטָרַח וּמַיְיתֵי לָהּ.

LITERAL TRANSLATION

Let the lender swear, [1]in case this one swears and the other one takes out the deposit.
[2]But if [35A] Rav Huna['s statement] is [correct], since the lender swears that it [the pledge] is not in his possession, [3]how can he produce it?
[4]Rava said: Where there are witnesses that it was burnt.
[5]If so, from where does he bring it?
[6]Rather, Rav Yosef said: Where there are witnesses that it was stolen.
[7]In the end, from where does he bring it?
[8]He makes an effort and brings it.

RASHI

לשתבע מלוה — שלא היתה שוה אלא שקל, ויטול שקל, דכיון דאיכא שבועה על הלוה מן התורה אי אתה יכול לפוטרו בולא כלום, ומשום תיקון עולם שלא יפסל ישראל שקלוה לשבועה מיניה ושדיוה אמלוה. **ואם איתא לדרב הונא** — שהשומר המשלם דמים נשבע שאינה ברשותו, אמאי חיישינן לשמא יוציא, הא אשתבע. **שיש עדים שנשרפה** — דהשתא לא אשבעינהו, שהרי הביא עדים. **טרח ומייתי לה** — מחזר ושואל אחר הנכנסים בביתו, וימצא הגנב.

TRANSLATION AND COMMENTARY

pledge was worth only one shekel, and let him then receive the money he claims — the other shekel — from the borrower without further ado. This procedure, whereby the requirement to take an oath is transferred from the defendant to the plaintiff, is applied by the Rabbis in cases where a defendant cannot be exempted from payment without an oath, but the oath cannot be taken for other reasons. [1]In our case, as the Mishnah explains in its final remark, we cannot allow the borrower to take the oath he is theoretically obliged to take, **in case he takes the oath and the** lender **takes out the deposit**, thus exposing the borrower as a perjurer. To avoid such a situation, we make the lender take the oath.

וְאִם אִיתָא לִדְרַב הוּנָא [2]Having concluded its analysis of this Mishnah and the Gemara's discussion of it in tractate *Shevuot*, the Gemara now proceeds to explain the objection to Rav Huna's ruling that, where the bailee is prepared to reimburse the depositor rather than take an oath exempting himself from payment, he must nevertheless take an oath that the deposit is not in his possession: **But if** [35A] Rav Huna's statement is correct, the lender in the case in tractate *Shevuot* is himself a bailee. He was entrusted by the borrower with looking after a pledge, and now claims it is lost. He, too, according to Rav Huna's statement, should have to **take an oath that the pledge is not in his possession.** [3]**How can he** later **produce** the pledge after swearing that he does not have it, and thus prove the borrower to be a liar? He will be proving *himself* a liar by so doing! Now, since the Mishnah in tractate *Shevuot* prevents the borrower from taking an oath as to the value of the pledge, for fear that the lender will produce it and expose the borrower as a liar, we must assume that the lender is *not* required to take an oath that the pledge is not in his possession. This, argues the Gemara, is a contradiction of Rav Huna's statement.

אָמַר רָבָא [4]The Gemara now brings a series of answers to this question, given by different Amoraim: (1) **Rava said** in reply: It is true that in general a bailee is required to take an oath that the object that was in his care is not now in his possession. But the Mishnah in tractate *Shevuot* is referring to a case **where there are witnesses that** the pledge **was burnt.** Accordingly, the lender was not required to take Rav Huna's oath.

אִי הָכִי [5]The Gemara objects: **If so,** if the pledge was destroyed, the question returns in a different form: Since we know that the pledge was burnt, why should we be concerned about the possibility that the lender will later produce it? **From where can** the lender **bring it?** Thus, we should require the borrower to take an oath as to its value.

אֶלָּא [6]**Rather,** we must reject Rava's reply and look for another answer to our question. (2) **Rav Yosef said:** Rav Huna's oath is not imposed on the lender in the case described in the Mishnah in tractate *Shevuot*, because the Mishnah there is referring to a situation **where there are witnesses that** the pledge **was stolen.** The lender was thus not required to take Rav Huna's oath because it was known to the court that the pledge was not in his possession.

סוֹף סוֹף [7]**At all events,** objects the Gemara, even if the pledge was not burnt, it *was* stolen, and is not in the lender's possession. How can we suspect him of waiting to produce it at the right moment? **From where can** he **bring it** to prove the borrower a liar?

דְּטָרַח וּמַיְיתֵי לָהּ [8]The Gemara answers: The pledge still exists, and **the** lender can **make an effort and bring** it **back** from the thief in order to prove that the borrower swore falsely. This, as we have seen, is precisely the situation the Mishnah wished to avoid.

TRANSLATION AND COMMENTARY

אִי הָכִי [1]The Gemara objects: **If** this is the situation, the Mishnah's solution — transferring the oath as to the pledge's value to the lender — solves nothing. For **even when the** lender **takes the oath** as to the pledge's value, the same problem exists in reverse. [2]It is possible that **the borrower may make an effort and bring** back the pledge, and prove the *lender* is lying!

בִּשְׁלָמָא מַלְוֶה [3]The Gemara answers: **Granted that the lender,** from whom the pledge was stolen, **knows who enters and leaves his house,** and may well have an idea who the thief is. Hence, **he can go and make an effort and bring** back the pledge. [4]**But does the borrower know who enters and leaves the lender's house?** How can the borrower know where to find the stolen pledge? Thus, there is no reason to be concerned that the borrower will produce the pledge. Hence, if we know that the pledge was stolen, we need not impose Rav Huna's oath on the lender. Instead, we make him take the borrower's oath as to the pledge's value.

אַבַּיֵי אוֹמֵר [5]The two previously suggested answers to the objection to Rav Huna's statement assume that the lender does not take the oath that the pledge is not in his possession, because there are witnesses to the fact. (3) **Abaye** suggested another answer to our original question, and **said:** Even though the lender is, in fact, required to take an oath that the pledge is not in his possession, we are still concerned in case he produces the pledge and exposes the borrower as a perjurer. For this reason, the Sages decided upon **a preventive measure** — that the lender, and not the borrower, should take an oath as to the pledge's value, [6]**so as to avoid** a situation in which the lender produces the pledge at a later stage, **claiming** that the borrower's valuation is incorrect, **and says to** the borrower: **"I found it after** I took Rav Huna's **oath."** Thus, according to Abaye's answer, Rav Huna's oath is administered even in the case described in the Mishnah in tractate *Shevuot.*

רַב אַשִׁי אָמַר [7](4) **Rav Ashi** suggested another, more radical, answer to our original question and **said:** In fact, the Mishnah does not order the lender to take the borrower's oath as to the pledge's value. Rather, what the Mishnah is saying is that the lender **takes** one **oath and** the borrower **takes** another **oath**. [8]Rav Ashi goes on to explain: The lender **takes an oath that** the pledge **is not in his possession,** as Rav Huna requires, **and** the borrower **takes an oath** as to **how much** the pledge **is worth**, since he has already admitted part of the lender's claim. [9]**And the** clause of the **Mishnah** that appears to be telling us to transfer the latter oath from the borrower to the lender **is** actually **saying as follows: Which** of the two parties **takes** his **oath first?** [10]And the Mishnah answers: **First the lender takes** Rav Huna's **oath** that the pledge is not in his possession, **so as to avoid** a situation in which the borrower first **takes** his **oath** as to the pledge's value **and** then **the** lender **takes out the deposit** and exposes the borrower as a liar. This concludes the discussion of the objection to Rav Huna's statement raised above from the Mishnah in tractate *Shevuot.*

[1]אִי הָכִי, כִּי מִשְׁתַּבַּע מַלְוֶה נַמִי, [2]לִטְרַח לֹוֶה וְלֵיתֵי! [3]בִּשְׁלָמָא מַלְוֶה, יָדַע מַאן קָא עָיֵיל וְנָפֵק בְּבֵיתֵיהּ, וְאָזֵיל וְטָרַח וּמַיְיתֵי לַהּ. [4]אֶלָּא לֹוֶה, מִי יָדַע מַאן עָיֵיל וְנָפֵיק בְּבֵיתֵיהּ דְּמַלְוֶה? [5]אַבַּיֵי אוֹמֵר: גְּזֵירָה, [6]שֶׁמָּא יִטְעוֹן וְיֹאמַר לוֹ: "אַחַר שְׁבוּעָה מְצָאתִיהָ". [7]רַב אַשִׁי אָמַר: זֶה נִשְׁבָּע וְזֶה נִשְׁבָּע. [8]זֶה נִשְׁבָּע שֶׁאֵינָהּ בִּרְשׁוּתוֹ, וְזֶה נִשְׁבָּע כַּמָּה הָיָה שָׁוֶה. [9]וְהָכִי קָאָמַר: מִי נִשְׁבָּע תְּחִילָּה? [10]מַלְוֶה נִשְׁבָּע תְּחִילָּה, שֶׁמָּא יִשָּׁבַע זֶה וְיוֹצִיא הַלָּה אֶת הַפִּקָּדוֹן.

LITERAL TRANSLATION

[1]If so, even when the lender swears, [2]the borrower may make an effort and bring it! [3]Granted [that] the lender knows who enters and leaves his house, and he goes and makes an effort and brings it. [4]But does the borrower know who enters and leaves the lender's house?

[5]Abaye says: [It is] a preventive measure, [6]in case he claims and says to him: "I found it after the oath."

[7]Rav Ashi said: This one swears and that one swears. [8]This one swears that it is not in his possession, and that one swears how much it was worth. [9]And [the Mishnah] is saying as follows: Which one swears first? [10]The lender swears first, lest this one swear and the other one takes out the deposit.

RASHI

וזה נשבע — הלוה, שהשבועה עליו נשבע כמה שוה. **מלוה נשבע תחילה** — שאינה ברשותו.

BACKGROUND

וְאָזֵיל וְטָרַח וּמַיְיתֵי לַהּ And he goes and makes an effort and brings it. Since a thief usually steals things to sell rather than for his own use, stolen objects ultimately find their way onto the market. If the owner seeks diligently, he has a good chance of finding the stolen object. Naturally, if a person suspects that one of the people who frequent his home stole the object, it is easier for him to identify the thief and find the stolen property.

וְיוֹצִיא הַלָּה אֶת הַפִּקָּדוֹן And the other one takes out the deposit. If it turns out that the borrower did not state the correct price, his oath becomes a false one, and even if the price he stated is correct, he has still sworn in vain.

NOTES

גְּזֵירָה שֶׁמָּא יִטְעוֹן וְיֹאמַר לוֹ אַחַר שְׁבוּעָה מְצָאתִיהָ It is a preventive measure, in case he claims and says to him: "I found it after the oath." *Rosh* asks: According to *Rabbenu Ḥananel* (see note above, 34b), the reason the Mishnah in tractate *Shevuot* transferred the borrower's oath as to the pledge's value to the lender was to avoid the taking of an unnecessary oath. But if our concern is that the lender may find the pledge after taking Rav Huna's oath, then

רַב הוּנָא בַּר תַּחֲלִיפָא מִשְּׁמֵיהּ[1] דְּרָבָא אֲמַר: רֵישָׁא דְּסֵיפָא תְּיוּבְתָּא לְרַב הוּנָא: "סֶלַע[2] הִלְוִיתָנִי עָלָיו, שְׁתַּיִם הָיָה שָׁוֶה', וְהַלָּה אוֹמֵר: 'לֹא כִּי.[3] אֶלָּא סֶלַע הִלְוִיתִיךָ עָלָיו, סֶלַע הָיָה שָׁוֶה', פָּטוּר". וְאִם אִיתָא[4] לִדְרַב הוּנָא, מִגּוֹ דְּמִשְׁתַּבַּע מַלְוֶה שֶׁאֵינָהּ בִּרְשׁוּתוֹ, לִישְׁתַּבַּע נַמִי אַגִּילְגּוּל שְׁבוּעָה[5] כַּמָּה הָיָה שָׁוֶה!

אֲמַר רַב אַשִׁי: אָמְרִיתָהּ[6] לִשְׁמַעֲתָא קַמֵּיהּ דְּרַב כָּהֲנָא, וַאֲמַר לִי: תְּהֵא בְּמַאֲמִינוֹ.[7]

LITERAL TRANSLATION

[1] Rav Huna bar Taḥlifa said in the name of Rava: The first part of the last clause is a refutation of Rav Huna: [2] "'You lent me a sela against it, [and] it was worth two,' [3] and the other says: 'Not so. Rather, I lent you a sela against it, [and] it was worth a sela,' he is exempt." [4] But if Rav Huna['s statement] is [correct], since the lender swears that it is not in his possession, [5] let him also swear, by means of the addition (lit., "rolling on") of an oath, how much it was worth!

[6] Rav Ashi said: I said this argument before Rav Kahana, [7] and he said to me: Let it be [understood as applying] where he trusts him.

TRANSLATION AND COMMENTARY

רַב הוּנָא בַּר תַּחֲלִיפָא [1] The Gemara now brings another objection to Rav Huna's statement from the same Mishnah: **Rav Huna bar Taḥlifa said in the name of Rava: The first part of the last clause** of the Mishnah from tractate *Shevuot* — case (3) — **is a refutation of Rav Huna.** [2] For that case states that if the borrower, the owner of the pledge, claims: **"You lent me a sela against** the lost pledge, **and** the pledge **was worth two** selaim," [3] **and the** lender **says: "Not so.** I agree that **I lent you a sela against it, but it was worth** only one **sela,"** the lender **is exempt**, since he denies the entire claim, and a defendant who denies a claim entirely is not required to take an oath. [4] **But if Rav Huna's statement is correct** that a bailee (in this case, the lender) must take an oath that the deposit (in this case, the pledge) is not in his possession, then **since the** lender is already **taking** Rav Huna's **oath** that the pledge **is not in his possession,** [5] **he should** also be required to **take** an **additional oath, affirming how much** the pledge **was worth.** The law is that whenever a defendant is required to take an oath to deny one of a plaintiff's claims, the plaintiff can insist that the defendant include in his oath (גִּילְגּוּל שְׁבוּעָה) a denial of other claims he may have against him, even if the other claims would not ordinarily be grounds for imposing an oath. Thus, in our case, if the lender were obliged to take Rav Huna's oath, he should also be required to include a declaration that the value of the pledge was no more than the amount of the loan, even though his total denial of the borrower's claim would normally exempt him from taking such an oath. But this contradicts the third clause of the Mishnah, which states that no oath is imposed on the lender! Hence, it would appear that Rav Huna's statement is incorrect.

אֲמַר רַב אַשִׁי [6] **Rav Ashi said: I presented this question before Rav Kahana,** [7] **and he said to me:** The ruling of the Mishnah that no oath is imposed on the lender **applies** only **where** the borrower **trusts** the lender and accepts his claim that the pledge is no longer in his possession. In such a situation, the Mishnah informs us, the lender is entirely exempt. As he need not take Rav Huna's oath that the pledge is not in his possession, there is no opportunity for another oath to be added to refute the borrower's claim that the value of the pledge was twice that of the loan.

RASHI

רישא דסיפא — היא תיובתא לרב הונא, רישא תביעת מלוה, סיפא תביעת לוה, רישא דסיפא — דקתני: פטור בתביעת לוה. **אגילגול שבועה** — דטענה שאין בה שבועה עם טענה שיש בה שבועה מגלגלין עליו שבועה לישבע על שתיהן וגילגול שבועה דאורייתא היא בקדושין (כז,ב). **תהא במאמינו** — הא דקתני פטור — במאמינו לוה למלוה שאינה ברשותו.

NOTES

regardless of whether the oath as to the pledge's value is taken by the borrower or the lender, someone will have taken an unnecessary oath!

Rosh answers that while both oaths are unnecessary if the pledge is found, the problem is greater with the borrower's oath, as the purpose of Rav Huna's oath is precisely to enable the lender to affirm that he cannot at the moment produce the pledge. Thus, technically speaking, if the pledge is lost somewhere in his house and the creditor cannot find it after a reasonable search, this oath is appropriate. Hence, if the lender must take both oaths, he will search with extra care so as not to take two possibly unnecessary oaths. But if the lender were to take only Rav Huna's oath, and the borrower were to take the other oath, the lender might be satisfied with a cursory check before taking Rav Huna's oath, and after the borrower takes the other oath, he might still find the pledge, thus rendering both oaths unnecessary.

תְּהֵא בְּמַאֲמִינוֹ Let it be understood as applying where he trusts him. The Rishonim ask: This answer reported by Rav Ashi in the name of Rav Kahana to Rav Huna bar Taḥlifa's question would appear to be a good answer to the Gemara's first question as well: If the borrower trusts the lender and does not demand that he take Rav Huna's oath, there is still room for concern in case the lender later produces the pledge. Hence the Mishnah's ruling that the lender take the borrower's oath. But Rav Ashi, who is here conveying the

SAGES

רַב הוּנָא בַּר תַּחֲלִיפָא Rav Huna bar Taḥlifa. A Babylonian Amora of the fifth generation, Rav Huna bar Taḥlifa was a disciple of Rava, whom he quotes on a number of occasions in the Talmud.

רַב כָּהֲנָא Rav Kahana. There were many Sages of this name during different periods, and it is not always clear which was the author of any given statement. In the present context, however, it seems clear that the Rav Kahana quoted was the teacher of Rav Ashi.

This particular Rav Kahana was a Babylonian Amora of the fifth generation. He came from the city of Pum Nahara, and was head of the Pumbedita Yeshivah for twenty years.

His most important student was Rav Ashi, who speaks often in the Talmud about his studies in the home of Rav Kahana. Apparently, despite Rav Ashi's youth, Rav Kahana greatly respected him and sometimes dignified him with the title *Mar* (מָר) — "master."

CONCEPTS

גִּלְגּוּל שְׁבוּעָה The rolling on of an oath, the imposition of an additional oath. When a defendant is obliged to take an oath in order to free himself from liability, the plaintiff has the right to require him to include in this oath an affirmation that he is not liable for other claims the plaintiff has against him — claims which would not in themselves require the defendant to take an oath.

The law of גִּלְגּוּל שְׁבוּעָה is of Torah authority. The Torah states that a woman suspected of adultery (סוֹטָה) must answer "Amen, Amen," to the oath administered to her by the priest (Numbers 5:22). The Mishnah explains that this reply implies both acceptance of the oath with regard to the man with whom she is suspected of committing adultery, and also acceptance of the oath with regard to other men (*Sotah* 2:5).

[1] וְנֶהֱמְנֵיהּ לֹוֶה לַמַּלְוֶה נַמִי בְּהָא — כַּמָּה הֲוָה שָׁוֶה! [2] לָא קִים לֵיהּ בְּגַוֵּיהּ. [3] וְנֶהֱמְנֵיהּ מַלְוֶה לַלֹּוֶה, דְּקִים לֵיהּ בְּגַוֵּיהּ! [4] לָא מְהֵימַן לֵיהּ. [5] וּמַאי שְׁנָא לֹוֶה דִּמְהֵימַן לֵיהּ לַמַּלְוֶה, [6] וּמַאי שְׁנָא מַלְוֶה דְּלָא מְהֵימַן לֵיהּ לַלֹּוֶה? [7] לֹוֶה מְקַיֵּים בֵּיהּ בַּמַּלְוֶה ״תֻּמַּת יְשָׁרִים תַּנְחֵם״. [8] מַלְוֶה מְקַיֵּים בֵּיהּ בַּלֹּוֶה ״וְסֶלֶף בֹּגְדִים יְשָׁדֵּם״.

LITERAL TRANSLATION

[1] But let the borrower also trust the lender in this — how much it was worth!

[2] He is not familiar with it.

[3] But let the lender trust the borrower, because he is familiar with it!

[4] He does not trust him.

[5] But what is different [about] the borrower that he trusts the lender, [6] and what is different [about] the lender that he does not trust the borrower?

[7] The borrower applies to the lender "the integrity of the upright shall guide them." [8] The lender applies to the borrower "but the perverseness of the faithless shall destroy them."

TRANSLATION AND COMMENTARY

וְנֶהֱמְנֵיהּ לֹוֶה לַמַּלְוֶה [1] The Gemara objects: **But** if **the borrower** trusts the lender when he claims the pledge has been lost, **let him also trust the lender regarding how much** the pledge **was worth.**

לָא קִים לֵיהּ בְּגַוֵּיהּ [2] The Gemara answers: The problem is not that the borrower suspects the lender of deliberately lying, but rather that he feels the lender **is not familiar with** how much the pledge is worth, since the pledge was not the lender's property and was only in his possession for a short period.

וְנֶהֱמְנֵיהּ מַלְוֶה לַלֹּוֶה [3] **But**, the Gemara objects, if we base our understanding of the Mishnah on the assumption that the borrower trusts the lender when the latter asserts that the pledge is not in his possession, why do we not assume that **the lender trusts the borrower, who is familiar with** his own pledge and surely knows how much it is worth?

לָא מְהֵימַן לֵיהּ [4] The Gemara answers: The case in the Mishnah assumes that the lender **does not trust** the borrower at all.

וּמַאי שְׁנָא לֹוֶה [5] The Gemara asks: But why should we interpret the Mishnah in this way? **What is different about the borrower, that he trusts the** lender when the latter claims the pledge is not in his possession, [6] **whereas the lender does not trust the borrower** at all?

לֹוֶה מְקַיֵּים בֵּיהּ בַּמַּלְוֶה [7] The Gemara answers: The distinction between the trust shown by the borrower towards the lender and the distrust shown by the lender towards the borrower is not an arbitrary one. It is rooted in the basic attitudes of the parties involved. **The borrower** trusts the lender because he **applies to the lender** the Biblical verse (Proverbs 11:3): **"The integrity of the upright shall guide them."** It is the honesty and trustworthiness of people, according to this verse, that brings them material success. Thus the fact that God saw fit to make the lender wealthy and generous enough to lend money to others is, in the eyes of the borrower, testimony to the lender's honesty. [8] By contrast, **the lender** mistrusts the borrower, because he **applies to the borrower** the latter part of the same verse: **"The perverseness of the faithless shall destroy them."** The fact that God saw fit to impoverish the borrower to the point where he needs to borrow from others is reason enough, in the eyes of the lender, to doubt the borrower's honesty. This concludes the Gemara's extended discussion of Rav Huna's ruling that a bailee must take a special oath that the object he claims was stolen or lost is not in his possession.

RASHI

לא קים ליה בגויה — מימר אמר לוה לא קים למלוה בגויה דמשכון, דלא נתן דעתו עליו לדעת דמיו. **מאי שנא כו׳** — דנקט תנא למלתיה בהכי, שזה נאמן על זה וזה אינו נאמן על זה. **לוה מקיים במלוה** — מקרא זה ״תומת ישרים תנחם״, אם לא שאדם נאמן וישר הוא — לא היו מעשרין אותו מן השמים, שנאמר ״תומת ישרים תנחם״.

BACKGROUND

תֻּמַּת יְשָׁרִים תַּנְחֵם "The integrity of the upright shall guide them." It must be remembered that loans were given without interest, so that the lender was actually being kind to the borrower by advancing money for his needs. In any event, a lender is to be regarded as an honest person, whereas a borrower, though not necessarily wicked, must frequently make a considerable effort to remain a decent person. Therefore it is reasonable to assume that in relations between them the borrower tends to trust the lender more than the lender trusts the borrower.

NOTES

idea that the borrower trusts the lender, himself gave a different answer to the first question!

Ritva suggests that this may indeed be a better answer to the first question, and that Rav Ashi may not have heard of it when he gave his original answer. Several Rishonim suggest that it is only in the third case of the Mishnah — the subject of Rav Huna bar Taḥlifa's question — that the borrower trusts the lender, but in the second case — the subject of the Gemara's first question — the lender is imposing an oath on the borrower, effectively calling him a liar, and the borrower is not likely to forgo imposing an oath on the lender in return (*Rashba* and others).

The Rishonim also point out that, according to *Rabbenu Ḥananel* (see note above, 34b), the goal is to prevent unnecessary, rather than false, oaths. Hence, whether or not Rav Huna's oath is imposed does not depend on the attitude of the borrower. Even if the borrower were to trust the lender, the latter would still not be exempt from taking Rav Huna's oath, if taking it would prevent the danger of an unnecessary oath (*Rashba* and others).

וְנֶהֱמְנֵיהּ לֹוֶה לַמַּלְוֶה נַמִי בְּהָא But let the borrower also trust the lender in this. The Gemara assumes that if the borrower believes the lender when he claims the pledge is lost, he should also believe the lender's assessment of its

LANGUAGE

כֵּיפֵי Jewels. The main meaning of this word seems to be rocks or stones, and it was used in Aramaic (as happens in other languages also) to refer to precious stones. By extension it also means valuable jewelry set with precious stones, as we see here from the debtor's need to sell his house in order to pay his debt.

אַפַּדְנָא House. Derived from the Old Persian *apadana,* meaning "large house, palace," this expression is attested later as a loan-word in the Semitic languages, and even appears in the Book of Daniel (11:45).

[1] הַהוּא גַּבְרָא דְּאַפְקֵיד כֵּיפֵי גַּבֵּיהּ חַבְרֵיהּ. [2] אֲמַר לֵיהּ: ״הַב לִי כֵּיפַי״. [3] אֲמַר לֵיהּ: ״לָא יָדַעְנָא הֵיכָא אוֹתְבִינְהוּ״. [4] אֲתָא לְקַמֵּיהּ דְּרַב נַחְמָן. [5] אֲמַר לֵיהּ: ״כָּל ׳לָא יָדַעְנָא׳ פְּשִׁיעוּתָא הִיא. זִיל שַׁלֵּים״. [6] לָא שַׁלֵּים. אֲזַל רַב נַחְמָן אַגְבְּיֵיהּ לְאַפַּדְנֵיהּ מִינֵּיהּ. [7] לְסוֹף אִישְׁתַּכַּח כֵּיפֵי, וְאַיַּיקוּר. [8] אֲמַר רַב נַחְמָן: הָדְרֵי כֵּיפֵי לְמָרַיְיהוּ, וְהַדְרָא אַפַּדְנָא לְמָרָהּ.

LITERAL TRANSLATION

[1] A certain man deposited jewels with his fellow. [2] He said to him: "Give me the jewels." [3] He said to him: "I do not know where I put them." [4] [The case] came before Rav Naḥman. [5] He said to him: "Every 'I do not know' is negligence. Go [and] pay." [6] He did not pay. Rav Naḥman went [and] caused his house to be seized from him. [7] In the end the jewels were found, and they had increased in value. [8] Rav Naḥman said: The jewels return to their owner, and the house returns to its owner.

RASHI

כיפי – נזמים. ואייקור – יתר על הדמים שפרע לבעלים.

TRANSLATION AND COMMENTARY

הַהוּא גַּבְרָא [1] The Gemara now moves on to a different topic in its analysis of our Mishnah, and begins by describing an actual incident and its legal consequences: **There was a certain man who deposited jewels with someone.** [2] Later the depositor **said to** the bailee: **"Give me back my jewels."** [3] The bailee **said to** the depositor: **"I do not know where I put them."** [4] **The case came before Rav Naḥman** for decision, [5] and **he said to** the bailee: **"Any** bailee who claims, **'I do not know** what happened to the deposit,' **is** considered to have been **negligent** in looking after it. **Go pay** the value of the jewels to the depositor." [6] Despite the court ruling, the bailee **did not pay**. The depositor then returned to Rav Naḥman to demand that his previous ruling be enforced. **Rav Naḥman went and had** the bailee's **house seized and** transferred to the ownership of the depositor, to compensate him for the loss of the jewels. [7] **Eventually the jewels were found, but** in the meantime **they had increased in value.** The depositor again went to Rav Naḥman and demanded the return of the jewels in exchange for returning the bailee's house. The bailee claimed that once he had recompensed the depositor for the value of the jewels, the jewels belonged to him if they were found, and any increase in their value took place once they were his. [8] In giving his decision **Rav Naḥman said: The jewels return to their** original **owner,** the depositor, **and the house returns to its owner**, the bailee. The bailee is not entitled to benefit from the increase in the jewels' value.

NOTES

value. *Pnei Yehoshua* quotes *Kikayon DeYonah,* who asks: The two claims are quite different. The borrower does not know whether or not the pledge is lost, and thus is willing to believe the lender on this point. But why should he believe him with regard to the pledge's value, since he, the borrower, is in the best position to know how much it is really worth?

Pnei Yehoshua answers: If the borrower were certain that the lender was lying about the pledge's value, he would surely no longer trust him about its being lost. Hence, since the borrower believes the lender's claim that the pledge has been lost, he cannot himself be certain about its value. Therefore the Gemara answers that he is certain about the pledge's value; he does not suspect the lender of lying, but of making a mistake.

Other commentators suggest that the Gemara assumes that the borrower does not suspect the lender of deliberately lying about the pledge's value. However, the Gemara finds it difficult to accept the obvious alternative that he suspects him of making a mistake, as it would appear that an oath is not an effective way of dealing with such a suspicion, because the lender can only swear to the truth as he knows it. According to this interpretation, the answer of the Gemara is that the imposition of an oath is an effective way of dealing with honest mistakes, because the lender will not take an oath regarding the pledge's value unless he is certain about the matter (*Maḥazeh Avraham*).

כָּל ״לָא יָדַעְנָא״ פְּשִׁיעוּתָא הִיא Every "I do not know" is negligence. The commentators are troubled by some inconsistencies in relation to this position. If a depositor claims that part of his deposit is missing and must have been stolen, and the bailee replies that he does not know how much there originally was in the deposit, the bailee is not considered negligent and need not pay (see *Shulḥan Arukh, Ḥoshen Mishpat* 298:2). Why, then, is the bailee considered negligent in our case?

Some commentators explain that lack of knowledge *per se* is not considered negligence. But if the bailee does not know where the deposit is, he cannot take an oath that he has not been negligent, and since he cannot take an oath he is required to pay (see *Terumat HaDeshen, Darkhei Moshe, Sma* and *Netivot* 291:7, and the objections of *Mishmerot Kehunah*).

HALAKHAH

כָּל ״לָא יָדַעְנָא״ פְּשִׁיעוּתָא הִיא Every "I do not know" is negligence. "A bailee who says he does not remember where he put — or buried — a deposit is considered negligent. He must pay for the lost object immediately, and may not demand that the depositor wait while he makes further searches." (*Shulḥan Arukh, Ḥoshen Mishpat* 291:7.)

TRANSLATION AND COMMENTARY

אָמַר רָבָא [1]In relation to this story **Rava said: I was sitting** as a student **before Rav Naḥman** when he made this ruling, **and the chapter** of Mishnah we were studying at the time **was** this third chapter of tractate *Bava Metzia*, *HaMafkid*, [2]**and I said to** Rav Naḥman: But surely our Mishnah, the first Mishnah of the chapter, states that, "**if** the bailee **paid and did not want to take an oath,**" he acquires the rights to the double payment. Moreover, we established above (34a) that not only the rights to the double payment, but also all benefits from the deposit, are transferred to the bailee as soon as he pays. Why then should the bailee not be entitled to the increase in the value of the jewels, since he reimbursed the depositor for them?

וְלָא אַהֲדַר לִי [3]Rava continues his story: Rav Naḥman **did not respond to** my objection, [4]**and he did well not to respond**, because I should have realized that my question was not worthy of a response. [5]Rava goes on to explain: **What is the reason** for the difference between the case of the Mishnah and that of Rav Naḥman? [6]It is because **there**, in the Mishnah, where the bailee voluntarily paid the depositor the value of his deposit, he **did not trouble** the depositor by making him **go to court.** For this reason, the double payment, any increase in price, and all similar benefits were willingly transferred by the depositor to the bailee. [7]**Here**, however, in the case of Rav Naḥman, the bailee **troubled** the depositor by making **him go to court.** He then refused to pay, and ultimately only did so under compulsion. The bailee's behavior was such that the depositor did not transfer to him any rights whatsoever in the deposit. Thus, says Rava, there is no contradiction between the ruling of Rav Naḥman and that of our Mishnah.

לְמֵימְרָא דְּסָבַר רַב נַחְמָן [8]The Gemara now analyzes Rav Naḥman's ruling more closely and asks: **Does** Rav Naḥman's ruling in this case **mean that Rav Naḥman maintains that** where an insolvent debtor's property is **appraised**, confiscated and given to the creditor as payment for a debt, it must be **returned** to the debtor on demand if and when he finds the means to repay the debt, just as Rav Naḥman returned the house to the bailee in exchange for the return of the jewels to the depositor?

LITERAL TRANSLATION

[1]Rava said: I was sitting before Rav Naḥman, and our chapter was *HaMafkid*, [2]and I said to him: "[If] he paid and did not want to take an oath," [3]and he did not respond to me. [4]And he did well that he did not respond to me. [5]What is the reason? [6]There he did not trouble him [to go] to court. [7]Here he troubled him [to go] to court.

[8][Do you mean] to say that Rav Naḥman maintains that a valuation returns?

[1]אֲמַר רָבָא: הֲוָה יָתֵיבְנָא קַמֵּיהּ דְּרַב נַחְמָן, וּפִרְקִין "הַמַּפְקִיד" הֲוָה, [2]וַאֲמַרִי לֵיהּ: "שִׁילֵּם וְלֹא רָצָה לִישָּׁבַע", [3]וְלָא אַהֲדַר לִי. [4]וְשַׁפִּיר עֲבַד דְּלָא אַהֲדַר לִי. [5]מַאי טַעְמָא? [6]הָתָם לָא אַטְרַחֵיהּ לְבֵי דִינָא. [7]הָכָא אַטְרַחֵיהּ לְבֵי דִינָא. [8]לְמֵימְרָא דְּסָבַר רַב נַחְמָן דְּשׁוּמָא הֲדַר?

RASHI

הוה יתיבנא – כשדן דין זה. **ופרקין המפקיד הוה** – ובפרק זה היינו עוסקין. **ואמרי ליה שילם ולא רצה לישבע** – קתני מתניתין דקני כפילא והאי נמי שילם, וליקני רווחא דאייקור! **דשומא הדר** – נכסי לוה ששמו בית דין לבעל חוב חוזרין אליו אם נותן מעות לבעל חוב, כי הכא דהדר אפדנא למריה.

BACKGROUND

הֲוָה יָתֵיבְנָא קַמֵּיהּ דְּרַב נַחְמָן I was sitting before Rav Naḥman. Usually when a judge tried a case (even when judging alone), some of his students would be present in the courtroom, since to observe Halakhic decision-making in the course of an actual trial is in itself an important way of learning. It is instructive regarding not only theoretical procedures but also their practical application. The students who sat in the courtroom were permitted to intervene in the proceedings and make comments, and sometimes might change the course of the trial.

וּפִרְקִין "הַמַּפְקִיד" הֲוָה And our chapter was *HaMafkid*. This illustrates that even in the time of the Talmud the chapters of the Mishnah were referred to by names similar to those we use today, generally based on the first word of the chapter. The name is especially appropriate here because the chapter is devoted to the subject of articles on deposit.

וְלָא אַהֲדַר לִי And he did not respond to me. A Sage would usually be scrupulous about answering questions and responding to problems raised by his students. However, a Sage would occasionally not answer a question because it seemed trivial to him, thus forcing the student to think about the subject again and find the answer by himself.

NOTES

וּפִרְקִין "הַמַּפְקִיד" הֲוָה And our chapter was *HaMafkid*. Rava mentioned this point in order to explain why he formulated his objection so concisely: Since this was the subject under discussion at the time, there was no need to elaborate (*Torat Ḥayyim*).

לְמֵימְרָא דְּסָבַר רַב נַחְמָן דְּשׁוּמָא הֲדַר Do you mean to say that Rav Naḥman maintains that an appraisal returns? *Ramban* suggests that this assumption may be based on a kind of *a fortiori* inference: If the owner of the house, who does not want it returned to him because he would prefer to keep the jewels, which have appreciated in value, still receives it back, then confiscations where the principle of "and you shall do that which is upright and good" applies should certainly be returned.

HALAKHAH

אַטְרַחֵיהּ לְבֵי דִינָא He troubled him to go to court. "If a deposit is lost or stolen in a manner that renders the bailee liable, but the bailee refuses to reimburse the depositor until he is compelled to do so by the court, the bailee is not entitled to the double payment or to any appreciation in the value of the deposit if and when the thief is caught or the deposit found. Rather, the deposit must be returned to the depositor, together with any additional payments made by the thief, and the depositor must reimburse the bailee for what he paid. 'Court compulsion' here refers only to cases where the court actually compelled the bailee to pay the depositor. If the bailee took an oath to exempt himself from payment, and subsequently decided to reimburse the depositor anyway, he is entitled to the double payment, even if the court forced him to take the oath." (*Tur, Ḥoshen Mishpat* 295.)

TRANSLATION AND COMMENTARY

שָׁאנֵי הָתָם [1]The Gemara answers that Rav Naḥman's ruling in the case of the jewels proves nothing as to what his ruling would be in an ordinary case of appraisal and confiscation. The case of the jewels **is different** from an ordinary case of appraisal and confiscation. In an ordinary case, the only way for the creditor to recover his debt is to have the debtor's property appraised and confiscated. It is only later that the debtor finds the means to repay the debt. Hence the appraisal and confiscation may well be considered by Rav Naḥman to be a final settlement, and no more capable of being reversed than a sale. But in the case of the jewels, **the appraisal** and confiscation **was made in error, for the jewels were there** in the possession of the bailee **from the outset**, waiting to be returned to their proper owner. The bailee simply misplaced them.

אָמְרִי נְהַרְדְּעֵי [2]Rav Naḥman's opinion on the question of whether an ordinary debtor's appraised and confiscated property must be returned on demand has not been established. The Gemara now proceeds to clarify the issue by quoting statements of other Sages on the subject: **The Neharde'ans** said: **Appraised** and confiscated property must be **returned** to the debtor if he repays the debt **before twelve months have passed** from the time of the appraisal. Once a year has elapsed, the debtor no longer has any right to reclaim the confiscated property. [3]On this statement made by the Sages of Neharde'a, **Amemar said: I am from Neharde'a, but** nevertheless **I maintain that appraised** and confiscated property must be **returned forever.** Thus, irrespective of how long after the appraisal the debt is repaid, the debtor is entitled to receive his property back. [4]The Gemara now summarizes the final Halakhah on this point: **The law is: Appraised** and confiscated property must, on repayment of the debt, be **returned forever, as it is said** in the Torah (Deuteronomy 6:18): **"And you shall do that which is right and good."** Even though technically a confiscation based on a court appraisal is as final as a sale and should not be reversible on demand, in human terms the two transactions are quite different. A person who sells his property has voluntarily decided to exchange it for money. Conversely, the person who buys the property does so only because he prefers the property over the purchase price. But in the case of appraisal and confiscation, the debtor undoubtedly wants to keep his property, and the creditor originally wanted nothing more than his money back. The property came to him as a second choice in place of the money, which he would have preferred. Hence, the proper thing for the creditor to do ("that which is right and good") is to return the property to the debtor whenever the latter is able to repay.

[1]שָׁאנֵי הָתָם, דְּשׁוּמָא בְּטָעוּת הֲוָה, דְּקָא הֲוָה כֵּיפֵי מֵעִיקָּרָא. [2]אָמְרִי נְהַרְדְּעֵי: שׁוּמָא הָדַר עַד תְּרֵיסַר יַרְחֵי שַׁתָּא. [3]וַאֲמַר אַמֵימָר: אֲנָא מִנְּהַרְדְּעָא אֲנָא, וּסְבִירָא לִי שׁוּמָא הָדַר לְעוֹלָם. [4]וְהִלְכְתָא: שׁוּמָא הָדַר לְעוֹלָם, מִשּׁוּם שֶׁנֶּאֱמַר: "וְעָשִׂיתָ הַיָּשָׁר וְהַטּוֹב".

LITERAL TRANSLATION

[1]It is different there, because the valuation was [made] in error, for the jewels were [there] from the outset.

[2]The Neharde'ans said: A valuation returns until [the end of] the twelve months of the year. [3]Amemar said: I am from Neharde'a, but I maintain [that] a valuation returns forever. [4]And the law is: A valuation always returns, as it is said: "And you shall do that which is right and good."

RASHI

דשומא בטעות הוה – דסבור היה שאבדו הנזמים, והרי לא אבדו. **דהא הוו כיפי מעיקרא** – שהרי בתחילת השומא היו הנזמים בידו ולא היה יודע, דאילו היה יודע שכן – לא שמו לו הטרקלין, אבל שומא שבית דין שמין על שאין לו מעות והוא חייב לו, הרי הוא כמכר גמור, ואינה חוזרת.

SAGES

אָמְרִי נְהַרְדְּעֵי The Neharde'ans say. Although this expression is a general one and refers to the Sages of the city of Neharde'a, nevertheless the Sages in the Talmud (*Sanhedrin* 17b) use it to refer to one particular Sage, Rav Ḥama, who was one of the most important Rabbis of that city. Occasionally this expression is used because the opinion expressed is not only Rav Ḥama's personal view, but also reflects the approach taken by all the Sages of Neharde'a.

אַמֵימָר Amemar. One of the greatest Babylonian Amoraim of the fifth and sixth generations, Amemar was born in Neharde'a and was one of its chief Sages. He studied under Rav Zevid and Rav Dimi of Neharde'a, and also studied with the elders of Pumbedita. He cites the teachings of Rava, Rav Pappa and others. He was head of the yeshivah in his city. On several occasions he is found in the company of Mar Zutra and Rav Ashi. Rav Aḥa bar Rava and Rav Gamda were among his most prominent students. He had a son, also a Sage, who was known as Mar.

BACKGROUND

וְעָשִׂיתָ הַיָּשָׁר וְהַטּוֹב "And you shall do that which is right and good." This verse from the Torah expresses an injunction that is not specifically defined. In general, it is a commandment to do things in a way that will encourage others to act morally and will also be beneficial to them. In the present instance we assume that a person's possessions have not only monetary but also sentimental value. Therefore, when someone is forced to sell something against his will (under a court order or the like), it is "right and good" to restore the property to its original owner, once the buyer is fully compensated for the money he paid.

NOTES

דְּשׁוּמָא בְּטָעוּת הֲוָה Because the appraisal was made in error. Our translation and commentary follows *Rashi,* who explains that it became apparent that there had never been a need for the appraisal and confiscation, because the jewels were never lost. *Ramban* and *Rambam,* however, have a different version in their texts, in which the phrase "for the jewels were there from the outset" does not appear. They maintain that the appraisal and confiscation would be cancelled retroactively even if the jewels had indeed been lost or stolen and were subsequently recovered. The depositor never had a monetary claim against the bailee. He simply wanted his deposit back. Hence, the moment he receives it, all claims against the bailee are cancelled retroactively.

HALAKHAH

שׁוּמָא הָדַר לְעוֹלָם An appraisal returns forever. "If property belonging to a debtor is confiscated by the court and handed over to a creditor, and the debtor later finds the means to repay the debt, the creditor must accept the money and return the property, even if many years have passed since the property was handed over to him. If the property had previously been sold to an innocent third party, and the creditor collected it on the basis of a prior lien, there

TRANSLATION AND COMMENTARY

פְּשִׁיטָא [1]The Gemara now proceeds to examine a series of cases related to the returning of confiscated property. First the Gemara notes those cases the resolutions of which are not in dispute: **It is obvious**, says the Gemara, **that if the court appraised** and confiscated a debtor's **property** and awarded it **to the creditor, and** later the creditor himself **went and allowed** this same property **to be appraised** and confiscated from him and awarded **to his own creditor**, to whom he owed money, and later the first debtor approached his creditor's creditor with money to repay the original debt and demanded the return of his confiscated property, [2]**we say to** the creditor's creditor: **"You are no better than the person from whom you came."** I.e., you have no more rights vis-a-vis the original owner of this property than does the first creditor, from whom you confiscated it. Just as he would have been required (on the basis of "and you shall do that which is right and good") to return it to the original owner on demand, you too are required to return it directly to the owner if he is prepared to repay the debt, and you cannot avoid returning it merely because you did not obtain it directly from him.

זַבְּנָהּ אוֹרְתָהּ וִיהַבָהּ בְּמַתָּנָה [3]The Gemara now examines other cases that are not in dispute: **If** a creditor received property from his debtor as a result of court appraisal and confiscation, and then **sold it, bequeathed it, or gave it as a gift**, then the debtor cannot demand that the buyer, heir or recipient return the property to him in exchange for money. Unlike the creditor, who originally received the property as a second choice in place of the repayment of a debt, [4]the buyer, heir or recipient **certainly took possession** of the property **with the intention of receiving land,** [5]**and not with the intention of** accepting **money.** Therefore, the ethical considerations that require the creditor to return confiscated property do not apply to these third parties; they are entitled to demand the strict letter of the law, according to which the confiscation was final and irreversible.

[1]פְּשִׁיטָא, שָׁמוּ לֵיהּ לְבַעַל חוֹב, וַאֲזַל אִיהוּ וְשָׁמָהּ לְבַעַל חוֹב דִּידֵיהּ, [2]אָמְרִינַן לֵיהּ: ״לָא עָדִיף אַתְּ מִגַּבְרָא דְּאָתֵית מִינֵּיהּ״.

[3]זַבְּנָהּ, אוֹרְתָהּ, וִיהַבָהּ בְּמַתָּנָה, [4]וַדַּאי הָנֵי מֵעִיקָּרָא אַדַּעְתָּא דְּאַרְעָא נְחוּת, [5]וְלָאו אַדַּעְתָּא דְּזוּזֵי נְחוּת.

LITERAL TRANSLATION

[1]It is obvious [that if] they appraised [property] for a creditor, and he went and appraised it for *his* creditor, [2]we say to him: "You are not better than the person from whom you came."

[3][If] he sold it, bequeathed it, or gave it as a gift, [4]they certainly took possession (lit., "went down") initially with the intention of [accepting] land, [5]and they did not take possession with the intention of [accepting] money.

RASHI

אמרינן – לבעל חוב שני. **לא עדיפת** – מבעל חוב ראשון שבאת מכחו, כשם שהוא מחזירה ויטול מעותיו משום "ועשית הישר והטוב" – אף אתה קבל מעותיך מבעלים הראשונים משום "ועשית הישר והטוב". **זבנה אורתה כו׳** – בעל חוב ששמו לו קרקע, ומכרה או שנתנה או הוריש. **הני** – אחרונים, או לוקח או יורש או מקבל מתנה. **אדעתא דארעא נחות** – שיהא קרקע שלהם ולא שיקבלו מעות, דאילו בעל חוב אית ביה משום "ועשית הישר והטוב", דאמרינן: לא היה לך עליו אלא מעות והרי הן לך, אבל אלו – קרקע קנו.

NOTES

אוֹרְתָהּ **Bequeathed it.** The Gemara rules that an heir need not return property confiscated by the court and handed over to his father in repayment of a debt. The Rishonim ask: Later on, the Gemara rules that a husband need not return property confiscated and handed over to his wife, because he is considered a buyer, and not an heir. But here the Gemara rules that heirs, too, need not return confiscated property!

Some Rishonim answer: In fact, the husband would not have been required to return the confiscated property even if he had been an heir, and the only reason the Gemara emphasized his status as a buyer was to explain why he has no right to demand that property confiscated from his wife be returned to him (*Tosafot* and others).

Ramban and *Rashba* suggest, as an alternative to *Tosafot*'s explanation, that "he bequeathed it" may mean that the creditor gave the settlement as a gift while on his deathbed. However, if a recipient inherits confiscated property under normal circumstances, he may in fact be required to return it, since he cannot be described as having initially taken possession "with the intention of accepting land," as the land came to him with no effort on his part at all.

HALAKHAH

...וְשָׁמָהּ לְבַעַל חוֹב דִּידֵיהּ... זַבְּנָהּ **And appraised it for his creditor.... If he sold it....** "If a creditor transfers to his own creditor property that he has received as a result of appraisal and confiscation, the original debtor retains the right to demand its return in exchange for repayment of the

is a difference of opinion as to whether the buyer can demand that the creditor return the property to him in exchange for money. *Shulḥan Arukh* rules that he can, while *Rema* rules that he cannot." (*Shulḥan Arukh, Ḥoshen Mishpat* 103:9.)

LITERAL TRANSLATION

[1]If they appraised [property] for a woman and she married, [2]or they appraised [property] from a woman and she married and died, [3]the husband is [considered] as a buyer of his wife's property. [4]He does not return [it], and we do not return [it] to him. [5]For Rabbi Yose bar Ḥanina said: In Usha they enacted: [6]A woman who sold part of her usufruct property in her husband's lifetime and died, [7]the husband may take [it] out from the hand of the buyers.

[1]שָׁמוּ לָהּ לְאִשָּׁה וְאִינְסִיבָא, [2]אוֹ שָׁמוּ מִינָּהּ דְּאִשָּׁה וְאִינְסִיבָא וּמֵתָה, [3]בַּעַל בְּנִכְסֵי אִשְׁתּוֹ לוֹקֵחַ הָוֵי. [4]לָא מִיהֲדַר, וְלָא מְהַדְּרִינַן לֵיהּ. [5]דַּאֲמַר רַבִּי יוֹסֵי בַּר חֲנִינָא: בְּאוּשָׁא הִתְקִינוּ: [6]הָאִשָּׁה שֶׁמָּכְרָה בְּנִכְסֵי מְלוֹג בְּחַיֵּי בַּעְלָהּ וּמֵתָה, [7]הַבַּעַל מוֹצִיא מִיַּד הַלָּקוֹחוֹת.

TRANSLATION AND COMMENTARY

שָׁמוּ לָהּ [1]The Gemara now moves on to other cases that are not in dispute: **If the court appraised and** confiscated **property** from a debtor and awarded it to his creditor, who was **a woman, and she then married** and subsequently died, and her property was inherited by her husband, [2]**or** vice versa, if the court **appraised** and confiscated **a woman** debtor's **property and she then married and** subsequently **died,** and her husband as her heir demands the right to receive the confiscated property back by repaying the money owed, [3]the law is that **the husband is** considered **as if he had bought his wife's property.** [4]**Hence,** if she was the creditor and her husband inherited the confiscated property, **he need not return it** at the demand of her debtor, in accordance with the Gemara's ruling in the previous case, where the creditor sold the confiscated property to a third party. **Nor,** if the wife was the debtor, **does** her creditor have to **return it to** her husband when he demands it. The husband does not inherit his late wife's right to demand special consideration on ethical grounds, since in this respect he is considered a stranger who bought his wife's property, and not an heir. [5]**For Rabbi Yose bar Ḥanina said: In Usha the Sages enacted** that a husband who inherits his wife's property is considered to have bought it at the time of their marriage. [6]Thus, if a **woman sold part of her own usufruct property** (see note) **in her husband's lifetime** on condition that her husband retain the right to the usufruct during her lifetime, and that the principal and the right to the usufruct should pass to the buyer on her death, **and** she subsequently **died,** [7]**the husband may take it away from the buyers,** without even returning them their purchase money, since he is considered not as having inherited the property but as having bought it before they did. By contrast, ordinary heirs have no lien on property they expect to inherit. If, for example, a father sells his property and then dies, his sons have no claim against the buyers. Thus we see that as far as his wife's property is concerned, a husband is considered a buyer and not an heir.

RASHI

ואנסיבא — אפילו לא שמאתן לבעלה בכתובתה להיות נכסי צאן ברזל, שהן קויין לבעל, אלא עיכבתן לעצמה להיות נכסי מלוג, הקרן שלה והבעל אוכל פירות. **בעל** — בנכסי מלוג של אשתו. **לוקח הוי** — דין לוקח נתנו בו חכמים, הלכך לא מיהדר היכא דשמו לה ואינסיבא ומתה וירשה בעלה, כדאמרינן: זבנה אדעתא דארעא נחות. **ולא מהדרינן ליה** — היכא דשמו מינה ואינסיבא ומתה וירשה בעלה, ובא להחזיר החוב וליטול הקרקע, לא מצי למימר "יורשה אני", דכלוקח שוייה רבנן ולא כיורש. **האשה שמכרה בנכסי מלוג** — להיות הבעל אוכל פירות בחייה וגוף הקרקע יהיה ללוקח לכשתמות, ומתה. **בעל מוציא** — גוף הקרקע מיד הלקוחות, והכי מוקי לה בפרק "האשה" בכתובות (עח,ב), תקנת אושא בגופה של קרקע לאחר מיתה, אלמא כלוקח שויוהו רבנן, ואומר לו: אני לקחתי ראשון, דאי כשאר יורש שויוהו רבנן — יורש שמכר אביו נכסיו בחייו אין לו ירושה בהן. **באושא התקינו** — כשהיתה סנהדרין באושא, שגלתה וישבה שם סנהדרי גדולה כדאמרינן בראש השנה (לא,א) גבי עשרה מסעות.

BACKGROUND

בְּאוּשָׁא הִתְקִינוּ In Usha they enacted. After the Sanhedrin was forced to move from Yavneh, the town of Usha (in Galilee) served as a center for Torah scholars. Numerous decrees were enacted there, primarily with regard to monetary matters within the family. The decrees of Usha were not included in the Mishnah, but were accepted in the Amoraic period. Rabbi Yose bar Ḥanina was considered a great expert regarding these decrees.

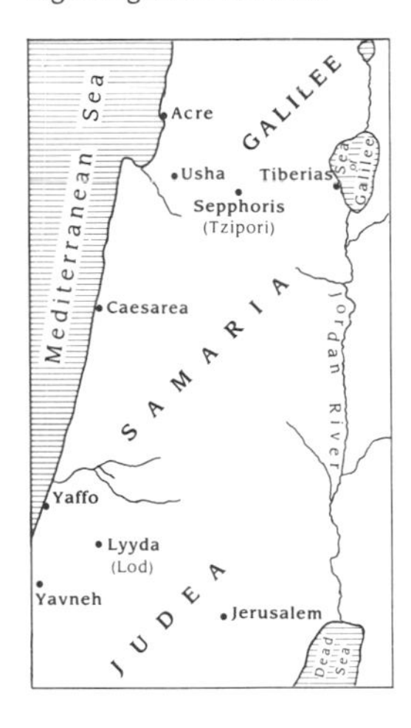

נִכְסֵי מְלוֹג Usufruct property. Most of the property brought by a wife into her marriage falls into the category of נִכְסֵי מְלוֹג. Unless the couple have made an agreement to the contrary, the property itself belongs to the wife, but the husband manages it, and the income derived from it belongs to him. The wife may not, therefore, sell this property against her husband's will during his lifetime, for she would be depriving him of the income from it. However, since this property also belongs to her, she can sell it in such a way that the purchaser is paying for the possibility that she will outlive her husband, at which point the sale will become valid. The question arises as to what is to be done if the woman dies first and her husband inherits her property. Is the husband regarded as an heir, who has no right to property previously sold by its late owner, or is he regarded as a purchaser, since, at the time of his marriage, he acquired certain rights to the property itself?

NOTES

הָאִשָּׁה שֶׁמָּכְרָה בְּנִכְסֵי מְלוֹג A woman who sold part of her usufruct property. When a woman gets married, her property is divided into two categories: נִכְסֵי צֹאן בַּרְזֶל — communal property (lit., "iron sheep property"), which is listed in the ketubah; and נִכְסֵי מְלוֹג — usufruct property (lit., "plucked property"), which is not listed in the ketubah. Communal property is treated for all intents and purposes as the husband's private property. His only duty to his

HALAKHAH

debt. However, if the first creditor sold the property, or gave it away as a gift, or bequeathed it to others, the debtor may not demand its return," following the Gemara. (*Shulḥan Arukh, Ḥoshen Mishpat* 103:10.) Some authorities (*Rema* following *Rosh*) maintain that property bequeathed to others does not return to the original owner only if there are several heirs; if there is a single heir, it does return to the original owner. (Ibid.)

שָׁמוּ לָהּ מֵאִשָּׁה וּלְאִשָּׁה Property appraised and confiscated from or for a woman. "If a woman's property is appraised and confiscated, or if a woman is awarded confiscated property in payment of a debt and later marries, her husband has the status of a buyer with regard to her property. Accordingly, he cannot demand its return in the first case, nor does he need to accept a demand for its return in the second case." (Ibid.) Some authorities maintain that this applies only after the woman has died. (*Rema*, following *Rashi, Rosh* and others; ibid.)

אִשָּׁה שֶׁמָּכְרָה בְּנִכְסֵי מְלוֹג A woman who sold part of her usufruct property. "If a woman sells her usufruct property

TRANSLATION AND COMMENTARY

אַגְבֵּיהּ אִיהוּ בְּחוֹבוֹ [35B] [1]Up to this point the Gemara has examined a series of problems related to the issue of returning confiscated property. In all these cases the defendant did not pay his debt at the time agreed, the plaintiff sued, and the defendant was forced by court order to hand over land in repayment of the debt. The Halakhic rulings in these cases have not been in dispute. The Gemara now examines another problem on this subject whose resolution *is* in dispute: What is the law **if the debtor** sees that he has not got the money when the time for repaying his debt arrives, and **himself offers** land to the creditor in repayment **of his debt,** without having been compelled to do so by the court, and later finds the means to repay the debt and proceeds to demand his land back? Does the fact that the debtor voluntarily handed over the land to the creditor make a difference in this case? **Rav Aḥa and Ravina disagreed about** this problem. [2]**One said:** In this case, too, the creditor must release the confiscated property, and it **returns** to its original owner whenever he finds the means to pay his debt; whereas **the other** Sage **said:** In this case the confiscated property **does not return.**

מַאן דְּאָמַר [3]The Gemara now explains the two conflicting viewpoints: **The** Sage **who says** that the land **does not return maintains** that, in this case, the voluntary transfer of property by the debtor to the creditor was **a valid sale,** [4]**since** the debtor **offered it of his own free will,** without external compulsion. Hence, it is reasonable to assume that he made up his mind to transfer the land without reservation, and cannot later demand his property back.

וּמַאן דְּאָמַר [5]On the other hand, the Sage **who said that** the confiscated property **returns** to the debtor **maintains** that in this case, too, the surrender of property by the debtor **was not a valid sale,** [6]**and the** sole **reason why** the debtor **offered it** to the creditor **of his free will and did not go to court** [7]**was because he was embarrassed** at the prospect of being humiliated in public, **as he** knew that in the end the court would confiscate it from him. This was the reason **he offered** the property to the creditor, and in no sense can this be described as a voluntary decision.

[35B] [1]אַגְבֵּיהּ אִיהוּ בְּחוֹבוֹ, פְּלִיגִי בָּהּ רַב אַחָא וְרָבִינָא. [2]חַד אָמַר: הָדְרָה, וְחַד אָמַר: לָא הָדְרָה.
[3]מַאן דְּאָמַר לָא הָדְרָה סָבַר: הַאי זְבִינֵי מְעַלְּיָא הִיא, [4]דְּהָא מִדַּעְתָּא דְּנַפְשֵׁיהּ אַגְבֵּיהּ.
[5]וּמַאן דְּאָמַר הָדְרָה סָבַר: לָא זְבִינֵי מְעַלְּיָא הוּא, [6]וְהַאי דְּאַגְבְּיֵהּ מִדַּעְתֵּיהּ וְלָא אֲתָא לְדִינָא — [7]מֵחֲמַת כִּיסוּפָא הוּא דְּאַגְבְּיֵהּ.

LITERAL TRANSLATION

[35B] [1][If the debtor] himself offered it for his debt, Rav Aḥa and Ravina disagree about it. [2]One says: It returns, and one says: It does not return.

[3]The one who says it does not return maintains: This is a valid sale, [4]since of his own free will he offered it.

[5]And the one who says it returns maintains: It is not a valid sale, [6]and the [reason] why he offered it voluntarily and did not go to court — [7]it was through embarrassment that he offered it.

RASHI

אגביה איהו בחובו — לעיל מיהדר גבי שומא, כלומר, אם לא שמוהו בית דין למלוה על כרחו של לוה, וקם ליה מעלמו, ולא הטריחו לדין, ואמר לו: טול קרקע זה בחובך.

SAGES

רַב אַחָא Rav Aḥa. This is Rav Aḥa the son of Rava (see above, 22b), a Babylonian Amora of the sixth generation. He was a disciple of Rav Kahana, and a colleague of Ravina and Rav Ashi. He was head of the Pumbedita Yeshivah for five years.

רָבִינָא Ravina. A Babylonian Amora of the fifth and sixth generations. See above, p. 71.

BACKGROUND

זְבִינֵי מְעַלְּיָא הִיא This is a valid sale. The reason why there is a possibility that confiscated property may revert to its owner is because the sale was executed under coercion by the court, and the seller did not truly wish to sell the property. The question here is whether the debtor's willingly making the property available to the creditor shows his full agreement, in which case the transfer should be irrevocable, or whether, being under the pressure of a debt which he could not repay, he was forced to surrender the property rather than enter into litigation with his creditor, in which case he did not truly wish to sell. Hence, if he later gives the creditor the money he may regain possession of the property.

NOTES

wife with regard to this property is to repay its original assessed value as stipulated in the ketubah, should she become widowed or divorced. Usufruct property remains the property of the wife, but the husband has a lifetime's interest in it. As long as the marriage lasts, the husband may use such property as he sees fit, though he may not sell it without the wife's consent. If the wife dies, the property passes entirely to the husband. If the wife is widowed or divorced, the property reverts entirely to her.

A wife has the right to sell her usufruct property. However, the sale has no practical effect as long as the marriage lasts, because she cannot sell her husband's rights without his permission. And, as our Gemara explains, the sale also has no effect if she dies, as her husband is then considered to have bought the property at the time of marriage and he may take it away from the buyers without payment. The sale takes effect only if she is widowed or divorced, at which point the property, instead of reverting to her, is transferred directly to the buyers. (See *Rambam, Sefer Nashim, Hilkhot Ishut* 16:1, 22:7.)

HALAKHAH

after she marries, the husband continues to have exclusive use of it as long as his wife is alive, even though he has no rights to the property itself during her lifetime. If she dies, her husband acquires full rights to the property, but if he dies in her lifetime, or if he divorces her, the buyers acquire the property." (*Rambam, Sefer Nashim, Hilkhot Ishut* 22:7.)

אַגְבֵּיהּ אִיהוּ בְּחוֹבוֹ If the debtor himself offered it to the creditor for his debt. "If a debtor voluntarily gives his creditor land in payment of a debt, and does not trouble him to go to court, the creditor need not return the land if the debtor later wishes to repay the debt. This is the view of the majority of Rishonim, and follows one of the two Amoraim in our Gemara." (*Shulḥan Arukh, Ḥoshen Mishpat* 103:10.)

[1]וּמֵאֵימַת אָכֵיל פֵּירֵי? [2]רַבָּה אָמַר: מִכִּי מָטְיָא אַדְרַכְתָּא לִידֵיהּ. [3]אַבַּיֵי אָמַר: עֵדָיו בַּחֲתוּמָיו זָכִין לוֹ. [4]רָבָא אָמַר: מִכִּי שְׁלִימוּ יְמֵי אַכְרַזְתָּא.

TRANSLATION AND COMMENTARY

וּמֵאֵימַת אָכֵיל פֵּירֵי [1]The Gemara now examines a different aspect of the question of confiscated property. We have seen that confiscated land does not become the creditor's property in all respects, because a possibility exists that the debtor will eventually find the means to repay his debt and demand the restoration of his property. However, at some point the land does become the creditor's property, in the sense that he has the right to use it as he sees fit and to reap all the profits from it. On this point the Gemara asks: **From when** is the creditor entitled to treat the property as his own and **eat** its **fruit?**

רַבָּה אָמַר [2]The Gemara gives three answers to this question in the names of three different Amoraim: (1) **Rabbah said** in reply: The creditor is entitled to the usufruct of the property **from** the time **when the writ authorizing seizure** prepared by the court — stating that the creditor may collect the debt from the debtor's property, wherever it may be — **reaches** the creditor's **hands.** This document is drawn up by the court no less than ninety days after the verdict, and shortly thereafter — when the document reaches the creditor — he is entitled to the usufruct of the property that will later be formally transferred to him. Thus, according to Rabbah, even while the land is still formally in the possession of the debtor, once the creditor has received the document of authorization, he is entitled to make use of the property.

אַבַּיֵי אָמַר [3](2) **Abaye said** in reply: The creditor does not have to wait until he actually receives the document of authorization. As soon as the document of authorization has been drawn up by the court, the creditor is entitled to the usufruct of that part of the debtor's property that will eventually be allocated formally to the creditor. This is in accordance with Abaye's view (see above, 13a) that all **rights** conveyed by a document **are transferred** to the document's recipient upon **the signature of the witnesses** in court, even before the document is actually delivered. Both Rabbah and Abaye agree that the key is the document of authorization. They merely disagree about the moment when it becomes effective.

רָבָא אָמַר [4](3) But the third Amora, **Rava, said** in reply: The document of authorization is not sufficient. The property becomes the creditor's only **from when the days of announcement are completed**, and the debtor's property is publicly allocated to the creditor. Even after the creditor has waited ninety days following the court's decision for the document of authorization to be drawn up, and has spent more time searching for appropriate property, he may still not treat the property he discovers as his own. The court must send assessors to value the land to be confiscated. The property must then be offered ("announced") to the public, to ensure that no one else is willing to pay more for it than the court's evaluation — a procedure which takes a further thirty days. Only after no other potential buyer offers more than the court's evaluation is the creditor permitted to make use of the property.

LITERAL TRANSLATION

[1]And from when does he eat the fruit?

[2]Rabbah said: From when the writ authorizing seizure reaches his hands.

[3]Abaye said: His witnesses acquire the right for him by their signatures.

[4]Rava said: From when the days of announcement are completed.

RASHI

מאימתי אוכל פירות — מי ששמו לו בית דין קרקע בחובו מאימת היא קנויה לו לאכול פירות? **אדרכתא** — לאחר תשעים יום שנפסק הדין, דאמרינן בפרק קמא (טו) דבית דין כותבין אדרכתא, שטר פסק דין אנכסי לוה, שבכל מקום שימצאם משלו יקחם, ומוסרין לו השטר. **עדיו בחתומיו** — מיום שנחתם שטר האדרכתא בבית דין, אף על פי שלא בא לידו. **מכי שלמו ימי אכרזתא** — אף על פי שבאה אדרכתא לידו ולא מצא נכסים ללוה עד לאחר זמן, וכשמצא הוזקק לבא לבית דין, ומכריזין שיש כאן קרקע למכור, כדאמרינן בערכין (כא,ב), ואם בא זה וקיבלה ביותר ממה ששמוה אחרים — מוסרין אותה בידו לאחר שכלו ימי הכרזה, ובמסכת ערכין מפרש כמה ימים מכריזין, בפרק ״שום היתומים״ (שם), ועד דשלמו הנך יומי — הוי פירי דלוה.

NOTES

עֵדָיו בַּחֲתוּמָיו זָכִין לוֹ His witnesses acquire the right for him by their signatures. This expression is not intended to be understood literally in this context. Under ordinary circumstances a document is an instrument whereby rights are voluntarily transferred, and, according to Abaye, the document takes effect upon being authenticated by the

HALAKHAH

וּמֵאֵימַת אָכֵיל פֵּירֵי And from when does he eat the fruit? "If a creditor seizes a field in payment of a debt, he may not benefit from its produce until after the period of proclamation is over," following the opinion of Rava. *Maggid Mishneh* explains that in a dispute between Amoraim, we follow the later opinion. In this case, Abaye and Rava were

CONCEPTS

אַדְרַכְתָּא An authorization. A legal document drawn up by a court authorizing a creditor to seek out and take possession of property belonging to his debtor, as a means of recovering the debt.

BACKGROUND

אַכְרַזְתָּא Announcement. When property was offered for sale as the result of a court order, this sale would be announced over a period of thirty days so as to attract the best possible offer. In certain cases (with consecrated property), this period was extended to sixty days. Conversely, in times of urgent need (for the payment of living expenses which the claimants needed immediately) or for other reasons (such as the sale of slaves who might run away), the sale was made with no prior announcement. But it was customary to wait until the announcement period was over before concluding the sale.

TRANSLATION AND COMMENTARY

MISHNAH הַשּׂוֹכֵר פָּרָה מֵחֲבֵירוֹ [1]If **someone** hires **a cow from another person and** then, with the permission of the owner, **lends it to someone else, and** the animal dies **naturally** while in the borrower's care, [2]**the hirer** of the cow **must take an oath** before the owner to affirm **that it died naturally,** since a hirer is not liable if the animal died or was harmed by forces beyond his control, **and the borrower must pay the hirer** the value of the cow, since a borrower is liable even if the object borrowed died or was damaged by accident, and must reimburse the person from whom he borrowed it.

אָמַר רַבִּי יוֹסֵי [3]**Rabbi Yose** disagreed with this opinion and **said: How can** the hirer **do business with another person's cow,** and make a profit from it? If the first opinion is correct, a very strange situation is being created whereby the owner of the cow receives no compensation for its loss, and the hirer, who does not own it and whose right to its use is limited, receives full compensation for its loss! [4]**Rather,** says Rabbi Yose, the owner is allowed to deal directly with the borrower; the borrower does not reimburse the hirer, but **must return the** value of the **cow** directly **to its owner.**

משנה [1]הַשּׂוֹכֵר פָּרָה מֵחֲבֵירוֹ, וְהִשְׁאִילָהּ לְאַחֵר, וּמֵתָה כְּדַרְכָּהּ, [2]יִשָּׁבַע הַשּׂוֹכֵר שֶׁמֵּתָה כְּדַרְכָּהּ, וְהַשּׁוֹאֵל יְשַׁלֵּם לַשּׂוֹכֵר.

[3]אָמַר רַבִּי יוֹסֵי: כֵּיצַד הַלָּה עוֹשֶׂה סְחוֹרָה בְּפָרָתוֹ שֶׁל חֲבֵירוֹ? [4]אֶלָּא, תַּחֲזוֹר פָּרָה לַבְּעָלִים.

LITERAL TRANSLATION

MISHNAH [1]Someone who hires a cow from his fellow, and he lent it to someone else, and it died naturally, [2]the hirer must swear that it died naturally, and the borrower must pay the hirer.

[3]Rabbi Yose said: How can that [person] do business with his fellow's cow? [4]Rather, the cow returns to the owner.

RASHI

משנה השוכר פרה מחבירו – ועמד שוכר והשאילה לאחר לעשות בה ימי שכירותו. ישבע השוכר – למשכיר. שמתה כדרכה – ופטור, שהשוכר אינו חייב באונסין. והשואל – שהוא חייב באונסין משלם לשוכר.

BACKGROUND

וּמֵתָה כְּדַרְכָּהּ **And it died naturally.** It makes no difference whether the death resulted from natural causes or from an accident, for in either case the death is regarded as being beyond the hirer's control, and hirers are exempt from damage caused by circumstances beyond their control. But it was nevertheless necessary to emphasize that the death was natural, for the hirer might have mistreated the animal and caused it to die. This would be criminal negligence, and the hirer would have to pay.

SAGES

רַבִּי יוֹסֵי **Rabbi Yose (ben Ḥalafta).** A Tanna of the generation before the completion of the Mishnah. See *Bava Metzia,* Part I, pp. 21-22.

NOTES

signature of witnesses. Here, however, the witnesses' signatures do not in themselves give the document validity, since a document of authorization is not a private document but rather a proclamation of the court's ruling. However, according to Abaye, the court's ruling takes effect as soon as the document has been drawn up and signed (*Ritva*).

הַשּׂוֹכֵר פָּרָה **Someone who hires a cow.** The Rishonim ask: Why does the Mishnah single out a hirer rather than speak of bailees in general? *Ritva* explains that other bailees are not allowed to use the objects entrusted to them. Hence, they are certainly not allowed to lend them to others. A hirer, by contrast, hires an object with the express intention of using it.

The Aḥaronim also discuss this problem. *Rashash* points out that the Gemara uses the term "acquisition" (קָנֵי) to describe the hirer's exemption from repaying the owner for his cow. In our commentary we have interpreted this term as meaning "acquiring rights in the cow," but *Rashash* argues that the term should be interpreted literally and that the hirer, actually *acquires* the dead cow. Noting the strangeness of the idea of acquiring something that is no longer alive, and the difficulty in the concept that an animal's death, or even a bailee's oath, could be an act of acquisition, *Rashash* argues that the acquisition actually took place when the animal was first handed over to the hirer, in a manner similar to that in which a bailee acquires the double payment, described in the first Mishnah (above, 33b). The Gemara (below, 56b) notes that hiring is actually a form of purchase for a limited time. Hence, it can be argued that the first Tanna in our Mishnah is of the opinion that a hirer does indeed acquire the animal outright, on condition that it later dies naturally (or the hirer takes the bailee's oath). However, the same reasoning does not apply to other bailees, and accordingly the first Tanna's ruling does not apply to them.

יִשָּׁבַע הַשּׂוֹכֵר **The hirer must swear.** This ruling of the Mishnah applies if the hirer personally knows how the animal died, e.g., if he was present when it died. If he was not present, he must bring two witnesses to testify that the animal died naturally. The borrower himself can serve as one of these witnesses, since he has no personal interest in the dispute between hirer and owner, and in any case is required to pay for the cow. There is a difference of opinion among the Rishonim as to what the law is when the borrower is the only witness available: *Ra'avad* rules that the hirer must pay. *Ramban* rules that the hirer can swear that he does not know precisely how the animal died. *Rosh* argues that the testimony of a single witness is sufficient to exempt from an oath any person who would ordinarily have to take one, and the borrower's testimony is thus sufficient to exempt the hirer (see *Ritva*).

אָמַר רַבִּי יוֹסֵי: כֵּיצַד הַלָּה עוֹשֶׂה סְחוֹרָה **Rabbi Yose said: How can that person do business....** The Gemara does not explicitly explain the reasoning of Rabbi Yose, even though the Halakhah is in accordance with his ruling. The Rishonim offer two major interpretations.

(1) *Tosafot* and others explain: Rabbi Yose agrees with the opinion expressed by Rav Idi bar Avin in the Gemara that

HALAKHAH

a generation after Rabbah. Moreover, in a dispute between Abaye and Rava we generally follow Rava. (*Rambam, Sefer Mishpatim, Hilkhot Malveh VeLoveh* 22:12.)

הַשּׂוֹכֵר פָּרָה מֵחֲבֵירוֹ וְהִשְׁאִילָהּ לְאַחֵר **Someone who hires a cow from his fellow and he lent it to someone else.** "If someone hires a cow and then lends it to someone else, and the animal dies or is destroyed by forces beyond the borrower's control, the borrower must reimburse the

גמרא ¹אָמַר לֵיהּ רַב אִידִי בַּר אָבִין לְאַבַּיֵי: מִכְּדִי, שׂוֹכֵר בְּמַאי קָנֵי לְהַאי פָּרָה? ²בִּשְׁבוּעָה. ³וְנֵימָא לֵיהּ מַשְׂכִּיר לַשּׂוֹכֵר: ״דַּל אַנְתְּ וְדַל שְׁבוּעֲתָךְ, ⁴וַאֲנָא מִשְׁתָּעֵינָא דִּינָא בַּהֲדֵי שׁוֹאֵל״.

⁵אֲמַר לֵיהּ: מִי סָבְרַתְּ שׂוֹכֵר בִּשְׁבוּעָה הוּא דְּקָא קָנֵי לָהּ? ⁶מִשְּׁעַת מִיתָה הוּא דְּקָנֵי, ⁷וּשְׁבוּעָה כְּדֵי לְהָפִיס דַּעְתּוֹ שֶׁל בַּעַל הַבַּיִת.

⁸אָמַר רַבִּי זֵירָא: פְּעָמִים שֶׁהַבְּעָלִים מְשַׁלְּמִין כַּמָּה פָּרוֹת לַשּׂוֹכֵר.

LITERAL TRANSLATION

GEMARA [1]Rav Idi bar Avin said to Abaye: Now, with what does the hirer acquire the cow? [2]With an oath. [3]But let the owner say to the hirer: "Take yourself away and take your oath away, [4]and I will take legal action against (lit., 'talk law with') the borrower."

[5]He said to him: Do you think it is with an oath that the hirer acquires it? [6]It is from the time of death that he acquires [it], [7]and the oath is in order to placate the owner.

[8]Rabbi Zera said: [There are] times when the owner pays several cows to the hirer.

TRANSLATION AND COMMENTARY

GEMARA אָמַר לֵיהּ [1]**Rav Idi bar Avin said to Abaye:** I have difficulty in understanding the point of view of the first Tanna in our Mishnah for the following reason: **How does the hirer acquire** rights to the owner's **cow** so that he has no responsibility to reimburse the owner for its loss, and is in turn entitled to full compensation from the borrower? [2]Clearly, **by taking the oath**, in which he affirms that the cow died naturally. Only after taking this oath is he exempt from responsibility. Thus, says Rav Idi bar Avin, the first Tanna in the Mishnah seems to be asserting that once the hirer has taken the oath and relieved himself of his responsibilities to the owner, the owner has no more claims against him and hence cannot make any claims through him against the borrower. [3]**But** if this analysis is correct, the following problem arises: Since the oath is only imposed on the hirer at the owner's demand, and since the hirer's acquisition of rights to the cow is contingent on the oath, **let** the animal's owner, **who** rented **it out** to the hirer, **say to the hirer: "Take yourself away and take your oath away,** as I do not wish to take legal proceedings against you. [4]Instead, **I will** take legal action against **the borrower**, and obtain payment for the animal directly from him."

אָמַר לֵיהּ [5]Abaye **said** in reply **to** Rav Idi bar Avin: **Do you think that** the hirer **acquires** his rights in the dead cow **by taking the oath**? That is not the case. [6]In fact, the hirer **acquires** rights in the cow **from the time of its death** while in the borrower's care, and these rights are not dependent on the oath he will need to take later. What, then, asks Abaye, is the purpose of the oath? [7]He answers: **The oath is** required only **in order to placate the owner**, and to reassure him that the hirer was not negligent in looking after his animal. But, says Abaye, regardless of whether or not the owner chooses to exercise his prerogative to impose an oath on the hirer, the latter owes him nothing if the animal in fact died naturally, whether while in his care or while in the care of the borrower. Hence, the first Tanna rules that the owner cannot make any claims through the hirer against the borrower.

אָמַר רַבִּי זֵירָא [8]**Rabbi Zera said:** If we apply the logic of the first Tanna in the Mishnah, it may **sometimes** happen that **the owner** will be ordered to **give several cows to the hirer** in place of the one cow he rented out

RASHI

גמרא בשבועה – שהוא נשבע למשכיר. **להפיס דעתו** – שלא יאמר "פשעת בה". **פעמים שהבעלים** – המשכירין הראשונים. **משלמין** – לשוכר זה כמה פרות על פרה זו, לפי דברי משנתנו, יש שיהו כולם שלו, ויש שיעשה בהם ימי שכירותו ויחזירם.

NOTES

the hirer acquires the cow by taking the oath. According to this interpretation, the point of Rav Idi's question is precisely to show that Rabbi Yose's reasoning is so compelling that there is no room for a dissenting opinion, and the point of Abaye's answer is to show that the first Tanna's reasoning can also be defended. According to this view, there are a number of circumstances under which Rabbi Yose's reasoning would not apply — such as the case described by Rabbi Zera, where the owner himself was the borrower in whose custody the animal died, and there was thus no need for the hirer to take an oath. In those cases, Rabbi Yose would agree that the borrower pays the hirer.

(2) Several Rishonim explain that when the hirer lends the animal out, he is effectively acting as the owner's agent, and the borrower thus has a direct relationship with the owner (*Tosefot Sens; Rif, Rambam* and most of the Rishonim hold similar views). According to this interpretation, the Halakhah follows Rabbi Yose in all cases, and the case described by Rabbi Zera is of only academic interest since it can never apply according to Rabbi Yose.

HALAKHAH

original owner for the animal's value," following the conclusion of the Gemara, which rules in accordance with Rabbi Yose. (*Shulḥan Arukh, Ḥoshen Mishpat* 307:5.)

פְּעָמִים שֶׁהַבְּעָלִים מְשַׁלְּמִין There are times when the owner pays.... "If the owner of the animal permitted the hirer to lend it to others, explicitly stipulating that the hirer deal with

SAGES

רַב אִידִי בַּר אָבִין Rav Idi bar Avin. A Babylonian Amora of the third and fourth generations. See *Bava Metzia*, Part I, p. 160.

BACKGROUND

וּשְׁבוּעָה כְּדֵי לְהָפִיס דַּעְתּוֹ שֶׁל בַּעַל־הַבַּיִת And the oath is in order to placate the owner. The owner of the cow cannot sue the hirer, since the death of the animal was completely accidental, and the hirer is not responsible for it. However, since the owner has suffered a loss, he may suspect that the hirer did not act correctly, and that he was in some way responsible for the death of the animal (especially in the case under discussion here, in which the hirer lent the cow to someone else). For that reason the Sages ordained that the hirer take an oath, so that the owner will feel that the renter has acted properly, and will not harbor resentment against him.

[1]הֵיכִי דָּמֵי? [2]אַגְרָהּ מִינֵּיהּ מְאָה יוֹמֵי, וַהֲדַר שַׁיְילָהּ מִינֵּיהּ תִּשְׁעִין יוֹמֵי, [3]הֲדַר אַגְרָהּ מִינֵּיהּ תְּמַנָן יוֹמֵי, וַהֲדַר שַׁיְילָהּ מִינֵּיהּ שִׁבְעִין יוֹמֵי, [4]וּמֵתָה בְּתוֹךְ יְמֵי שְׁאֵלָתָהּ. [5]דְּאַכָּל שְׁאֵלָה וּשְׁאֵלָה מִיחַיַּיב חֲדָא פָּרָה.

[6]אֲמַר לֵיהּ רַב אַחָא מִדִּיפְתִּי לְרָבִינָא: מִכְּדִי, חֲדָא פָּרָה הִיא.

LITERAL TRANSLATION

[1]How so (lit., "how is it like")? [2]If he hired it from him [for] one hundred days, and then he borrowed it from him [for] ninety days, [3][and] then he hired it from him [for] eighty days, and then he borrowed it from him [for] seventy days, [4]and it died during the days of its being borrowed, [5]since for each borrowing he is liable [to pay] one cow.

[6]Rav Aḥa of Difti said to Ravina: Now, it is one cow.

TRANSLATION AND COMMENTARY

to him. Some of this payment will be monetary compensation for the death of his own animal, and some will be replacements which the hirer will be entitled to use and then return to the owner. [1]**How**, asks Rabbi Zera, **is this** paradoxical outcome **possible?** [2]He answers: It could occur in the following way: A person **hired** a cow **from** its owner **for one hundred days, and then,** almost immediately, the owner himself **borrowed it from** the hirer **for ninety** of those one hundred **days,** promising to return it to the hirer for the remaining ten days of rental, [3]**and then** the hirer **hired it** a second time **from** the owner **for eighty days** and paid the owner a second rental fee, **and then** the owner **borrowed it** yet again **from** the hirer **for seventy** of those eighty **days,** [4]**and it died during the** seventy-day **period when it was in the custody of the owner-borrower.** By applying the logic of the first Tanna, says Rabbi Zera, we reach a situation in which even though the borrower is the owner himself, he must pay the hirer for his own dead cow, as would any other borrower. [5]Moreover, **since** the owner borrowed the cow twice from the hirer in two entirely separate transactions, he is considered as if he had borrowed two separate cows, and **is liable to pay** the hirer the value of **one cow for each borrowing,** i.e., twice the value of his own cow. Moreover, the owner has an additional, entirely separate obligation to honor his rental contract with the hirer and make available to him an additional cow for each of the two ten-day periods during which he promised to return it. Thus, the owner must make available to the hirer two cows as replacement, in addition to the value of two cows that he must pay him as a borrower.

אֲמַר לֵיהּ רַב אַחָא מִדִּיפְתִּי [6]**Rav Aḥa of Difti** questioned this line of reasoning. He **said to Ravina:** All the transactions described by Rabbi Zera revolve around **one cow,** whose legal status keeps changing as a result

RASHI

כיצד אגרה מיניה מאה יומי והדר שיילה מינה תשעין יומי וכו׳ — ראובן שסכר פרה משמעון שיעשה בה מלאכה מאה יום, וחזר שמעון ואמר לו ״עשה עמי טובה והשאילני אותה תשעים יום מן המאה ששכרת, ולאחר תשעים אחזירנה לך לעשות אצלך עשרה ימים להשלים המאה״, וכן עשה, יש כאן דין משנתנו דתנן: השוכר פרה מחבירו והשאילה לאחר בתוך ימי שכירותה, דמה לי בעלים ומה לי אחר? אם מתה אצל שואל הרי שוכר פטור בשבועה והשואל משלם לשוכר. חזר ראובן ובא אצלו ואמר לו ״השכירנה לי מתשעים יום שהיא שאולה בידך ממני ואשתעבד בה שמונים יום וטול שכרך״, וכן עשה — הרי היא בחזקת שאילתו על שמעון כאילו השכירה לאחר, שהרי נוטל שכרו וכל הנאה שלו, ואם היתה מתה אצל ראובן — היה ראובן פטור בשבועה, ושמעון משלם לו פרה אחת ששאל ממנו והוא חייב באונסים, ופרה אחרת לעשות אצלו עשרה ימים להשלים המאה. חזר שמעון ושאלה ממנו שבעים יום מן השמונים ששכרה ממנו, על מנת שיחזירנה לו, ויעשה בה עשרה ימים להשלים השמונים של שכירות השני, ואם היתה מתה בתוך שבעים יום הללו — הרי יש כאן דין השני כדין הראשון וישבע ראובן שמתה כדרכה ושמעון השואל משלם לו ארבע פרות; שתים נחלטות לו בשביל שתי פרות שאולות שהשאילו ראובן, ובפעם זה כאילו מתו שתיהן, שהרי אין פרתו בעין שהשאילו בראשון דנימא הרי החזיר לו פרתו, וזו שהוא משלם לו עכשיו — בתורת תשלומין באה לידו והרי יש לו עליו שתי תביעות על שתי שאילות, ושתי תביעות על שתי שכירות לעשות אצלו עשרים יום.

BACKGROUND

פְּעָמִים שֶׁהַבְּעָלִים מְשַׁלְּמִין There are times when the owner pays.... The construction of this unusual case is meant to emphasize Rabbi Zera's approach. For that reason it has certain innovative aspects, both because in this instance the owner must pay the hirer for his *own* dead cow, and also because he must provide *several* cows in payment for the one dead cow.

מְשַׁלְּמִין כַּמָּה פָּרוֹת Several cows. Rabbi Zera discusses this problem in an entirely formalistic fashion. According to his approach, we do not consider the actual cow, but rather the laws of contract. Since there were two separate contracts for borrowing the animal, the borrower must pay for the cow he has borrowed. With respect to the agreements it makes no difference whether it was the very same cow, or whether there were two different cows which he borrowed at separate times. By contrast, Rav Aḥa of Difti discusses the matter from an entirely practical point of view: In the end, only one cow was lost, and when the borrower gives back one cow, he has righted the wrong, so the agreement can be carried out in full in that way. Ravina may not accept the entire formal approach of Rabbi Zera, but he nevertheless argues that since the same cow no longer exists, we are forced to discuss the laws of contractual obligations, and not an actual animal.

SAGES

רַב אַחָא מִדִּיפְתִּי Rav Aḥa of Difti. A Babylonian Amora of the sixth and seventh generations. See *Bava Metzia,* Part I, p. 56.

NOTES

מִכְּדִי, חֲדָא פָּרָה הִיא Now, it is one cow. Rav Aḥa of Difti clearly disagrees with Rabbi Zera's view that the owner must pay the hirer the value of one cow for each borrowing period, but it is not clear what his own position is. *Rashi,* followed in our commentary, explains that Rav Aḥa's position is identical to that of Mar bar Rav Ashi — that the owner must pay the hirer the value of one cow under the category of borrowing, and make one cow available to him to complete his contract of hire.

Shittah Mekubbetzet explains that according to Rav Aḥa,

HALAKHAH

the borrower, then the borrower is responsible to the hirer and not to the owner. Hence, if the animal was destroyed by forces beyond the borrower's control, the borrower must pay the hirer, and the hirer may take an oath to the owner and keep the borrower's payment. Even if the borrower is the owner himself, this rule applies. Thus, if the owner borrows the animal for part of the period of hire and the animal dies, the owner must pay the hirer for the dead animal, and must also provide him with a second animal to complete the period of hire. Even if the owner borrows the animal more than once, this is the maximum payment he must make," following *Rosh,* who rules in accordance with Mar bar Rav Ashi. (Ibid.)

TRANSLATION AND COMMENTARY

of decisions taken by the owner and the hirer. [1]The owner put it **into** one legal status **and** then **brought** it **out** into a different legal status. First of all he transferred it into the care of the hirer. [2]**He** then **took it out from** the status of **being hired, and brought it into** the status of **being borrowed.** [3]**He** then **took it out from** the status of **being borrowed and brought it into** the status of **being hired.** Thus, the two cows are the most that the owner should be required to pay the hirer: the value of one cow as restitution for the loss of the animal he had twice borrowed from the hirer, and a second cow to be used by the hirer for the twenty days' hire of the animal still owed to him by the owner.

אֲמַר לֵיהּ [4]Ravina **said to** Rav Aḥa in reply: If **the cow were** alive and **available, we could say to** the hirer: Here is your cow, and the owner would be completely exempt from payment. All he would have to do is hand over the animal to the hirer for the twenty days' hire to which he is entitled. But since the owner cannot return the cow to the hirer, and must repay him instead, we have to count the number of obligations entered into by the owner, and thus the owner must repay the hirer the value of two cows, because he borrowed twice, and must make two cows available to the hirer to complete the two hiring agreements with him.

מָר בַּר רַב אַשִׁי [5]**Mar bar Rav Ashi** disagreed with the argument used by Ravina in his answer to Rav Aḥa of Difti, and **said** in support of the latter: The hirer's **only claim against** the owner **is for two cows, one as a result of** the **borrowing** agreements **and one as a result of** the **hiring** agreements. [6]The two claims resulting from the two acts of borrowing come under **the single category of borrowing**, and there is no basis for treating the borrower as if he had borrowed two separate cows. [7]The two claims resulting from the two acts of hiring come under **the single category of hiring.** [8]The hirer **acquires the** value of the **borrowed** cow **completely,** [9]whereas **he works with the** replacement for the **hired** cow **for** whatever time is required to complete **the days of its hiring, and he** then **returns it to its owner.**

The statement of Mar bar Rav Ashi concludes this passage of the Gemara. It should be noted that the whole discussion thus far has been based on the line of reasoning adopted by the first Tanna in our Mishnah. We will see below (36b–37a) how the Gemara relates to the point of view of Rabbi Yose in our Mishnah, and how the Halakhah is ultimately decided.

אָמַר רַבִּי יִרְמְיָה [10]The Gemara now moves on to discuss the nature of the oath imposed in our Mishnah, and other aspects of the cases discussed there: When someone swears falsely and afterwards admits to having done so, he is required to bring a sacrifice in atonement. The Torah distinguishes between a false oath taken

[1]עַיְילָהּ וְאַפְּקָהּ. [2]אַפְּקָהּ מִשְּׂכִירוּת וְעַיְילָהּ לִשְׁאִילָה. [3]אַפְּקָהּ מִשְּׁאִילָה וְעַיְילָהּ לִשְׂכִירוּת.

[4]אֲמַר לֵיהּ: וּמִי אִיתָא לְפָרָה בְּעֵינָא, דְּנֵימָא לֵיהּ הָכִי?

[5]מָר בַּר רַב אַשִׁי אֲמַר: אֵין לוֹ עֲלֵיהֶן אֶלָּא שְׁתֵּי פָּרוֹת, חֲדָא דִּשְׁאֵלָה וַחֲדָא דִּשְׂכִירוּת. [6]שׁוּם שְׁאֵלָה אַחַת הִיא, [7]וְשׁוּם שְׂכִירוּת אַחַת הִיא. [8]דִּשְׁאֵלָה קָנֵי לְגַמְרֵי; [9]דִּשְׂכִירוּת — עָבֵד בָּהּ יְמֵי שְׂכִירוּתֵיהּ, וּמִיהֲדַר לֵיהּ לְמָרָהּ.

[10]אָמַר רַבִּי יִרְמְיָה: פְּעָמִים

LITERAL TRANSLATION

[1]He brought it in and took it out. [2]He took it out from hiring and brought it in to borrowing. [3]He took it out from borrowing and brought it in to hiring.

[4]He said to him: And is the cow in existence, that we should say this to him?

[5]Mar bar Rav Ashi said: He has only [a claim] against them [for] two cows, one for borrowing and one for hiring. [6]The category (lit., "name") of borrowing is one, [7]and the category of hiring is one. [8]The one under [the category of] borrowing he acquires completely; [9]the one under [the category of] hiring — he works with it [for] the days of its hiring, and he returns it to its owner.

[10]Rabbi Yirmeyah said: [There are] times when both of them

RASHI

מכדי חדא פרה הואי כו׳ — ולענין תשלומין נמי לשלם ליה פרה אחת, ותעמוד במקום הראשונה תחת שתי השאילות ותהא שלו, ואחת ימסור לו לעשות בה עשרים יום. **מי איתא לפרה בעינא דנימא הכי** — אילו היתה קיימת היה פטור לגמרי, אלא שיעשה בה עשרים יום, עכשיו שמתה — בא עליו בתורת תשלומין שואל לשוכר על שתי תביעות. **מר בר רב אשי** — סבירא ליה כאתקפתא דרב אחא מדפתי. **שום שאלה אחת היא** — דכיון דחדא פרה הואי אלא שמתחת שוכר שהשאיל הוא בא עליו, שני שאילות פרה אחת אינן אלא אחת.

SAGES

מָר בַּר רַב אַשִׁי Mar bar Rav Ashi. A Babylonian Amora of the seventh generation, Mar bar Rav Ashi was the son of the famous Amora, Rav Ashi. His personal name was Tavyumi. He studied under his father, succeeding to his father's position as head of the Mata Meḥasya Yeshivah twenty four years after his father's death. He held this position for thirteen years.

רַבִּי יִרְמְיָה Rabbi Yirmeyah. A Palestinian Amora of the third and fourth generations. See above, p. 5.

NOTES

one and only one cow need be paid. According to this interpretation, Rav Aḥa views the requirement to pay not as an abstract obligation, but as an obligation to replace the cow itself. Having repaid the full value of the cow with the first payment, the owner's obligation has been fulfilled, and there is no more need to pay than there would have been had the cow not died.

TRANSLATION AND COMMENTARY

to avoid paying money — for which the penalty is a guilt-offering "for robbery" (אֲשַׁם גְּזֵילוֹת; Leviticus 5:20-26) — and an ordinary oath, called "an oath as a result of a statement" (שְׁבוּעַת בִּיטּוּי), for which the penalty is a special sliding-scale sin-offering (קָרְבָּן עוֹלֶה וְיוֹרֵד; Leviticus 5:4-6). (See notes below.) Thus, the sacrifice required as atonement for taking an oath depends on whether the oath was intended to have an effect on the swearer's financial obligations. On this subject **Rabbi Yirmeyah said:** If both the borrower and the hirer swore falsely, they must each bring a sacrifice. **Sometimes both of them must bring a sin-offering,** if the false oath had no effect on either of their respective financial obligations. [36A] [1]**Sometimes both of them must bring a guilt-offering,** if the false oath affected both of their respective financial obligations. [2]**Sometimes the hirer must bring a sin-offering and the borrower a guilt-offering.** [3]**Sometimes the hirer must bring a guilt-offering and the borrower a sin-offering.** [4]Rabbi Yirmeyah goes on to explain the principle involved: **How so?** How do these different situations arise? [5]The underlying principle is as follows: A person who takes an oath in which he **denies** owing **money** which he really does owe, must **bring a guilt-offering,** [6]whereas a person who takes a false oath which has no effect on his financial obligations must bring a **sin-offering.**

LITERAL TRANSLATION

[are liable] for a sin-offering. [36A] [1][There are] times when both of them [are liable] for a guilt-offering. [2][There are] times when the hirer [is liable] for a sin-offering and the borrower for a guilt-offering. [3][There are] times when the hirer [is liable] for a guilt-offering and the borrower for a sin-offering. [4]How so? [5][For] denial of money [one incurs] a guilt-offering; [6][for] a false oath (lit., "an utterance of lips"), a sin-offering.

שֶׁשְּׁנֵיהֶם בְּחַטָּאת. [36A] [1]פְּעָמִים שֶׁשְּׁנֵיהֶם בְּאָשָׁם. [2]פְּעָמִים שֶׁהַשּׂוֹכֵר בְּחַטָּאת וְהַשּׁוֹאֵל בְּאָשָׁם. [3]פְּעָמִים שֶׁהַשּׂוֹכֵר בְּאָשָׁם וְהַשּׁוֹאֵל בְּחַטָּאת. [4]הָא כֵּיצַד? [5]כְּפִירַת מָמוֹן, אָשָׁם; [6]בִּיטּוּי שְׂפָתַיִם, חַטָּאת.

RASHI

פעמים ששניהם בחטאת — אמתניתין קאי, השוכר והשואל נשבעו לשקר ולא כפרו ממון, והרי הן בשבועות ביטוי, וקרבן שלו חטאת, כדכתיב בויקרא "או נפש כי תשבע וגו'". **שניהם באשם** — אם נשבעו לשקר והיו נשכרים בשבועתם להקל פרעון מעליהם, כפירת ממון היא זו, וקרבן שבועה שלהם אשם, איל בן שתי שנים, דכתיב (ויקרא ה) "והביא את אשמו איל תמים בערכך כסף (שני) שקלים", והוא אשם גזילות.

NOTES

חַטָּאת וְאָשָׁם Sin-offerings and guilt-offerings. The prohibition against taking a false (or vain) oath is extremely severe. Anyone who swears falsely violates one of the Ten Commandments: "You shall not take the name of the Lord your God in vain" (Exodus 20:7). However, there are many laws governing the penalties imposed on perjurers, and there are technical circumstances under which no penalty is imposed. The details of these laws are discussed in tractate *Shevuot.*

In general, when a person inadvertently takes a false oath, he is required to bring a sacrifice in atonement. (In certain cases, this law applies even if he took a false oath deliberately.) The Torah distinguishes between three kinds of false oaths: (1) A false oath taken by a witness to the effect that he knows nothing about a plaintiff's claim, and cannot testify on his behalf (שְׁבוּעַת הָעֵדוּת). For this offence, the perjurer must bring a special sin-offering called קָרְבָּן עוֹלֶה וְיוֹרֵד (Leviticus 5:1) whether the false oath was intentional or inadvertent. (2) A false oath taken by a defendant to the effect that he owes nothing (שְׁבוּעַת הַפִּיקָּדוֹן). For this offence, the perjurer must bring "a guilt-offering for robbery" (אֲשַׁם גְּזֵילוֹת, Leviticus 5:20-26) whether the false oath was intentional or inadvertent. (3) All other false oaths, called "oaths of utterance" (שְׁבוּעַת בִּיטּוּי). In these cases the perjurer must also bring the special קָרְבָּן עוֹלֶה וְיוֹרֵד — sin-offering (Leviticus 5:4-6) — provided the perjury was inadvertent. If it was intentional, he is subject to the punishment of lashes.

The "oath of utterance" (שְׁבוּעַת בִּיטּוּי) refers primarily to a false oath taken to confirm or deny that certain events have occurred, or to impose an obligation upon oneself, but not to a false oath the purpose of which is to achieve financial gain or avoid financial loss. Someone who inadvertently takes a false oath of this type must confess his sin and bring a special sin-offering (קָרְבָּן עוֹלֶה וְיוֹרֵד), the value of which is assessed on a sliding scale, depending on the

HALAKHAH

כְּפִירַת מָמוֹן אָשָׁם For denial of money one incurs a guilt-offering. "If a person swears falsely that he does not owe money to another person, he must repay the other person the principal, plus an additional fifth (actually 25%). As atonement he must bring a guilt-offering, whether he perjured himself intentionally or inadvertently." (*Rambam, Sefer Hafla'ah, Hilkhot Shevuot* 1:8-9.)

בִּיטּוּי שְׂפָתַיִם חַטָּאת For a false oath, a sin-offering. "A person who swore falsely about a past event, or who swore to perform some task in the future and failed to do so, must bring a sliding-scale sin-offering (קָרְבָּן עוֹלֶה וְיוֹרֵד), in which the type of offering required varies depending on the sinner's financial situation. The sacrifice is brought only if the false oath was taken inadvertently; if it was taken intentionally, the penalty is lashes." (Ibid., 1:2-3.)

BACKGROUND

אָשָׁם Guilt-offering. One of the categories of sacrifices. There are six sub-categories of the אָשָׁם sacrifice: (1) אֲשַׁם גְּזֵילוֹת — a sacrifice brought by a person who denied a debt, swore an oath that he was not liable, and later admitted that he *was* liable and had sworn falsely. This is the category referred to in the Gemara here. (2) אֲשַׁם מְעִילוֹת — a sacrifice brought as atonement for מְעִילָה, the misuse of sacred articles. (3) אֲשַׁם שִׁפְחָה חֲרוּפָה — a sacrifice brought as atonement for relations with a partially non-Jewish maidservant designated to be the wife of a Hebrew slave. (4) אֲשַׁם נָזִיר — a sacrifice brought as part of the purification process of a Nazirite who had become ritually impure. (5) אֲשַׁם מְצוֹרָע — a sacrifice brought as part of the purification process of a leper. (6) אָשָׁם תָּלוּי — a sacrifice brought as atonement when a person is unsure whether or not he committed a sin which requires the bringing of a sin-offering.

חַטָּאת A sin-offering. The laws governing sin-offerings are found in several places in the Torah. The principal laws are found in Leviticus, Chapters 4-5 and in Numbers, Chapter 15. However, additional details are found elsewhere. There are several types of sin-offering, and they may be categorized in various ways. In general, certain sin-offerings are brought as public sacrifices at the various Festivals, but not as atonement for specific sins.

Other sin-offerings are not explicitly intended to atone for transgressions, but are part of the process of ritual purification of those with genital discharges, women who have recently given birth, lepers and Nazirites.

Some of the sin-offerings brought to atone for transgressions are brought as a result of serious sins committed inadvertently, and these are divided hierarchically according to the rank of the sinner (court, High Priest, king, an ordinary person) and also according to

[1] "פְּעָמִים שֶׁשְּׁנֵיהֶם בְּחַטָּאת" — [2] כְּגוֹן שֶׁמֵּתָה כְּדַרְכָּהּ, וְאָמְרוּ נֶאֱנְסָה. [3] שׂוֹכֵר, דְּבֵין כָּךְ וּבֵין כָּךְ מִיפְּטַר פָּטוּר, בְּחַטָּאת. [4] שׁוֹאֵל, דְּבֵין כָּךְ וּבֵין כָּךְ חִיּוּבֵי מִיחַיֵּיב, [5] בְּחַטָּאת.

[6] "פְּעָמִים שֶׁשְּׁנֵיהֶם בְּאָשָׁם" — [7] כְּגוֹן שֶׁנִּגְנְבָה, וְאָמְרוּ מֵתָה מֵחֲמַת מְלָאכָה. [8] דְּתַרְוַיְיהוּ קָא כָּפְרִי מָמוֹנָא — דְּהָא מִיחַיְּיבִי — [9] וְקָא פָּטְרִי נַפְשַׁיְיהוּ.

[10] "שׂוֹכֵר בְּחַטָּאת וְשׁוֹאֵל בְּאָשָׁם" — [11] כְּגוֹן שֶׁמֵּתָה כְּדַרְכָּהּ, וְאָמְרוּ מֵתָה מֵחֲמַת מְלָאכָה. [12] שׂוֹכֵר, דְּבֵין כָּךְ וּבֵין כָּךְ מִיפְּטַר פָּטוּר, חַיָּיב בְּחַטָּאת.

LITERAL TRANSLATION

[1] "[There are] times when both of them [are liable] for a sin-offering" — [2] for example, where it died naturally, and they said it was the victim of violence. [3] The hirer, who in any case is exempt, [is liable] for a sin-offering. [4] The borrower, who in any case is liable, [5] [is liable] for a sin-offering.

[6] "[There are] times when both of them [are liable] for a guilt-offering" — [7] for example, where it was stolen, and they said it died because of work. [8] For both of them deny [owing] money — for they are obliged [to pay] — [9] and they exempt themselves [from paying].

[10] "The hirer [is liable] for a sin-offering and the borrower for a guilt-offering" — [11] for example, where it died naturally, and they said it died because of work. [12] The hirer, who in any case is exempt, is liable for a sin-offering.

TRANSLATION AND COMMENTARY

פְּעָמִים שֶׁשְּׁנֵיהֶם בְּחַטָּאת [1] Rabbi Yirmeyah now explains each situation in detail: (1) **"Sometimes both of them must bring a sin-offering."** [2] This can happen, **for example,** in a case where the animal **died naturally, and** the borrower and hirer both falsely **said it was the victim of violence** — i.e., was carried off forcibly by robbers — and took an oath to that effect. [3] Now, in such a situation **the hirer is exempt** from payment **in any case;** he does not have to pay whether he swears truthfully that the animal died naturally or swears falsely that it was the victim of violence. Thus the oath taken by the hirer is a false oath (שְׁבוּעַת בִּיטּוּי). Hence, he **must bring a sin-offering,** since his false oath would not have spared him from monetary loss. [4] On the other hand, **the borrower is liable** for the loss of the animal **in any case,** whether it died naturally or was the victim of violence. [5] Since by his false oath he was not absolving himself from financial responsibility, he too **must bring a sin-offering.**

פְּעָמִים שֶׁשְּׁנֵיהֶם בְּאָשָׁם [6] (2) **"Sometimes both of them must bring a guilt-offering."** [7] This can happen, **for example, where** the animal **was stolen** from the borrower **and** the borrower and hirer both falsely **said it died because of work,** and took an oath to that effect. [8] In this case **both of them** are effectively **denying owing money** that they really do owe, **inasmuch as** both a hirer and a borrower **are obliged to pay** compensation if an animal in their care is stolen. [9] By taking false oaths, the borrower and the hirer are thus attempting to **exempt themselves from repaying** the owner, and must therefore both bring guilt-offerings.

שׂוֹכֵר בְּחַטָּאת [10] (3) **"The hirer must bring a sin-offering and the borrower a guilt-offering."** [11] This can happen, **for example, where** the animal **died naturally, and** the borrower and the hirer both falsely **said** it **died because of work,** and took an oath to that effect. [12] In such a situation **the hirer is exempt** from paying **in any case,** since he is not liable if the animal died from natural causes. Hence, **he is obliged to bring a sin-offering,**

RASHI

נאנסה — על ידי לסטים, ונשבעו שכך אף על פי שהשואל משלם אונסין, משביעין אותו כדרב הונא, שבועה שאינה ברשותו, דחיישינן שמא נתן עיניו בה ונשבע שנאנסה ואינה ברשותו. **שוכר דבין כך ובין כך מיפטר** — מתשלומין, קאי בחטאת. **בין כך ובין כך** — בין שנשבע באמת שמתה כדרכה, בין שנשבע לשקר שנאנסה, פטר עצמו מלשלם, הלכך אין בשקר זה כפירת ממון, דהא אם הודה על האמת היה פטור, שבועת ביטוי היא, ובחטאת. **שואל דבין כך ובין כך חייב לשלם** — נמצא שלא כפר ממון בשיקור שבועתו, ושבועת ביטוי קאי בחטאת. **כגון שנגנבה** — והשוכר חייב לשלם לבעלים, והשואל ישלם לשוכר. **ואמרו מתה מחמת מלאכה** — ופטר שואל עצמו בשקר מלשלם לשוכר, והשוכר מלשלם לבעלים. **שמתה כדרכה** — ואם הודו על האמת — שוכר פטור ושואל חייב.

NOTES

penitent perjurer's financial situation. A wealthy man must bring the regular sin-offering of a female lamb or kid; a poor man can instead bring two doves; a very poor man must bring a meal offering (Leviticus 20:5-13).

Another law applies to false oaths taken to evade financial obligations. Anyone taking a false oath of this type, whether intentionally or inadvertently, must return the money, pay the injured party an additional fifth of the sum, and offer a sacrifice of a ram (Leviticus 5:24-25). This sacrifice is called "a guilt-offering for robbery" (אֲשַׁם גְּזֵילוֹת).

שֶׁמֵּתָה כְּדַרְכָּהּ וְאָמְרוּ מֵתָה מֵחֲמַת מְלָאכָה Where it died naturally, and they said it died because of work. *Rosh* asks: To whom is the borrower swearing that the animal died because of work? The owner has no claim against him, even if he admits that it died naturally, as the animal was originally hired out, and a hirer need not pay if an animal dies naturally. The hirer likewise has no claim against him, as the hirer is prepared to swear that the animal

the transgression.

In addition, there is a type of sin-offering which the Rabbis call קָרְבָּן עוֹלֶה וְיוֹרֵד — "an ascending and descending (i.e., variable) sacrifice" — because these sacrifices vary according to the sinner's wealth. These particular sin-offerings atone for three types of transgression: (1) The taking of a false oath to evade giving testimony. (2) The entering of the Temple or partaking of sacrifices while ritually impure. (3) Perjury, not keeping one's oath, or swearing in vain.

BACKGROUND

כְּגוֹן שֶׁמֵּתָה כְּדַרְכָּהּ... For example, where it died naturally.... If a bailee perjures himself in order to avoid responsibility, it is clear why he has done so. However, there seems to be no reason for a person to perjure himself without deriving any benefit (in cases where he was either exempt or obliged to pay in any event). An analysis of the cases shows that both claimants are attempting to adopt a consistent position and give an account of the events which, in certain instances, could bring financial benefit to one of them. Moreover, the claims they advance, even if they bring no financial benefit, certainly put them in a more advantageous position with regard to the owner. Whenever an animal dies a natural death, suspicion arises that this may have occurred through the bailee's negligence. But when they claim that the death was caused by forces beyond their control, or that it died while being worked, and that they treated it properly, they place themselves in a more advantageous position. This applies especially to a stolen animal, where some negligence on the part of the bailees is implied. They prefer to claim that the theft was committed by force, even if that claim has no financial significance, in order to absolve themselves of all guilt.

LITERAL TRANSLATION

[1] The borrower, who is liable where it died naturally but exempts himself [by claiming] it died because of work, [2] [is liable] for a guilt-offering. [3] "The hirer [is liable] for a guilt-offering and the borrower for a sin-offering" — [4] for example, where it was stolen, and they said it died naturally. [5] The hirer is he who is liable for theft and loss, and he exempts himself [with a claim] that it died naturally — [6] [hence he is liable] for a guilt-offering. [7] The borrower, who in any case is liable, [8] [is liable] for a sin-offering.

[9] What is he telling us?

[10] To exclude [the view] of Rabbi Ammi, who said: Any oath which the judges make [people] swear, they are not liable on its account because of an oath of utterance, [11] as it is said:

[1] שׁוֹאֵל, דְּמִיחַיַּיב בְּמֵתָה כְּדַרְכָּהּ וְקָא פָּטַר נַפְשֵׁיהּ בְּמֵתָה מֵחֲמַת מְלָאכָה, [2] בְּאָשָׁם.

[3] "שׂוֹכֵר בְּאָשָׁם וְשׁוֹאֵל בְּחַטָּאת" — [4] כְּגוֹן שֶׁנִּגְנְבָה, וְאָמְרוּ מֵתָה כְּדַרְכָּהּ. [5] שׂוֹכֵר הוּא דְּמִיחַיַּיב בִּגְנֵיבָה וַאֲבֵידָה, וְקָא פָּטַר נַפְשֵׁיהּ בְּמֵתָה כְּדַרְכָּהּ — [6] בְּאָשָׁם. [7] שׁוֹאֵל, דְּבֵין כָּךְ וּבֵין כָּךְ חִיּוּבֵי מִיחַיַּיב, [8] בְּחַטָּאת.

[9] מַאי קָא מַשְׁמַע לָן?

[10] לְאַפּוּקֵי מִדְּרַבִּי אַמִי, דְּאָמַר: כָּל שְׁבוּעָה שֶׁהַדַּיָּינִים מַשְׁבִּיעִים אוֹתָהּ, אֵין חַיָּיבִין עָלֶיהָ מִשּׁוּם שְׁבוּעַת בִּיטּוּי, [11] שֶׁנֶּאֱמַר:

TRANSLATION AND COMMENTARY

since his false oath would not have saved him from monetary loss. [1] **The borrower**, on the other hand, **is liable** in a case **where** the animal **died naturally, but** attempted to **exempt himself** illegally **by claiming that** the animal **died because of work.** [2] Hence, since his false oath would have saved him from financial loss, **he must bring a guilt-offering.**

שׂוֹכֵר בְּאָשָׁם [3] (4) "**The hirer must bring a guilt-offering and the borrower a sin-offering.**" [4] This can happen, **for example,** in a case **where** the animal **was stolen, and they** both falsely **said it died naturally**, and took an oath to that effect. [5] **The hirer is liable for theft and loss, but** attempted to **exempt himself** illegally **with the claim that** the animal **died naturally.** [6] Hence, **he must bring a guilt-offering,** since his false oath would have saved him from financial loss. [7] **The borrower,** on the other hand, **is liable in any case,** since he must pay compensation even if the animal died naturally. [8] Hence, **he must bring a sin-offering,** since his false oath would not have saved him from paying compensation.

מַאי קָא מַשְׁמַע לָן [9] The Gemara now asks: **What is Rabbi Yirmeyah telling us** by this series of rulings? They seem self-evident in the light of the known rules regarding sin- and guilt-offerings laid down in a Mishnah in tractate *Shevuot* (49b).

לְאַפּוּקֵי מִדְּרַבִּי אַמִי [10] The Gemara answers: Rabbi Yirmeyah's purpose was **to exclude the view of Rabbi Ammi, who said: Any oath** not taken voluntarily by a litigant but **imposed** on him **by judges does not render him liable** under the category of "an oath of utterance." In other words, Rabbi Ammi argues that the obligation to bring a sin-offering as atonement for a false oath can only come about if a person took the oath voluntarily. [11] Rabbi Ammi derives this principle from the following interpretation of a Biblical verse:

RASHI

שנגנבה — ושניהם חיידין. **ואמרו מתה כדרכה** — השוכר פוטר עלמו בשקר, אבל השואל לא נפטר בכך מלשלם. **חיובי מיחייב** — לשלם, קאי על שבועתו בחטאת. **מאי קא משמע לן** — רבי ירמיה, משניות שלימות הן בשבועות: המשנה מחובה לחובה, ומפטור לפטור, ומפטור לחובה — פטור מאשם גזילות, מחובה לפטור — חייב.

TERMINOLOGY

לְאַפּוּקֵי מִדְּרַבִּי פְּלוֹנִי To exclude the view of Rabbi X. Sometimes the Talmud explains that a source was worded in a particular way in order "to exclude Rabbi X's viewpoint."

BACKGROUND

כָּל שְׁבוּעָה שֶׁהַדַּיָּינִים מַשְׁבִּיעִים Any oath which the judges make people swear. The distinction made by Rabbi Yirmeyah is a simple one: In his opinion, a person who commits perjury for financial gain must bring a guilt-offering for his false oath, whereas anyone who perjures himself for any other reason must bring a sin-offering. By contrast, it seems that Rabbi Ammi draws a distinction between an oath taken by a person at his own initiative and one imposed on him by the court. For perjury in the former case he must bring a sin-offering, whereas for perjury in the latter case he can only bring a guilt-offering. Thus if an oath is imposed on someone by the court and he commits perjury for financial gain, he must bring a guilt-offering, but if he is not required to bring a guilt-offering, he is not obliged to bring any sacrifice at all.

NOTES

died of work. Hence he admits the fact, and can demand no oath from the borrower. Thus the borrower's false oath seems to be entirely gratuitous, and should not render him liable to a guilt-offering.

Rosh answers that the Gemara is not referring to a single case where both parties take false oaths. Rabbi Yirmeyah is merely showing that the same false oath can demand different sacrifices from the borrower or hirer, depending on the circumstances. Thus, if the animal died naturally and the hirer swore it died because of work, he would have to bring a sin-offering, whereas if it was the borrower who swore, he would have to bring a guilt-offering.

כָּל שְׁבוּעָה שֶׁהַדַּיָּינִים מַשְׁבִּיעִים אוֹתָהּ Any oath which the judges make people swear. The commentators object: In the first and fourth cases, the borrower takes an oath that the animal died naturally or was the victim of violence. But a borrower must pay under such circumstances anyway. Why, then, would a court impose an irrelevant oath?

Rashi explains that the court imposed only Rav Huna's oath (see above, 34b) on the borrower — that the object was no longer in his possession. But in the course of taking this oath, the borrower swore falsely that the animal in fact

HALAKHAH

לְאַפּוּקֵי מִדְּרַבִּי אַמִי To exclude the view of Rabbi Ammi. "A bailee who was sued in court and took a false oath from which he could not gain any financial benefit is liable for having taken a false oath, and must bring a sin-offering." (*Rambam, Sefer Hafla'ah, Hilkhot Shevuot* 8:5-6.)

"אוֹ נֶפֶשׁ כִּי תִשָּׁבַע לְבַטֵּא בִשְׂפָתַיִם". [1]"כִּי תִשָּׁבַע" מֵעַצְמָהּ. [2]קָא מַשְׁמַע לָן דְּלָא כְּרַבִּי אַמִי.

[3]אִתְּמַר: שׁוֹמֵר שֶׁמָּסַר לְשׁוֹמֵר — [4]רַב אָמַר: פָּטוּר, [5]וְרַבִּי יוֹחָנָן אָמַר: חַיָּיב.

[6]אָמַר אַבַּיֵי: לְטַעְמֵיהּ דְּרַב, לָא מִבָּעֲיָא שׁוֹמֵר חִנָּם שֶׁמָּסַר לְשׁוֹמֵר שָׂכָר, [7]דְּעַלּוּיֵי עַלְּיֵיהּ לִשְׁמִירָתוֹ. [8]אֶלָּא אֲפִילּוּ שׁוֹמֵר שָׂכָר שֶׁמָּסַר לְשׁוֹמֵר חִנָּם, [9]דְּגַרוּעֵי גָּרְעָהּ לִשְׁמִירָתוֹ, פָּטוּר. [10]מַאי טַעְמָא? דְּהָא מְסָרָהּ לְבֶן דַּעַת.

LITERAL TRANSLATION

"Or a soul who swears to utter something with his lips." [1]"Who swears" [means] voluntarily. [2]He is telling us that [the law] is not like Rabbi Ammi.

[3]It was said: A bailee who handed over [a deposit] to [another] bailee — [4]Rav said: He is exempt, [5]and Rabbi Yoḥanan said: He is liable.

[6]Abaye said: According to Rav's reasoning, there is no need [to state this regarding] an unpaid bailee who handed over [the deposit] to a paid bailee, [7]where he improved its care. [8]But even a paid bailee who handed over [a deposit] to an unpaid bailee, [9]where he made its care worse, is exempt. [10]What is the reason? Because he handed it over to a mentally competent person.

TRANSLATION AND COMMENTARY

As the verse says, when it defines the oath called "an utterance of the lips" (Leviticus 5:4): **"Or a soul who swears to utter something with his lips."** [1]Rabbi Ammi interprets the words **"who swears" as meaning** "if a person swears **voluntarily,**" without being compelled by others as in the case of a court-imposed oath. Thus, according to Rabbi Ammi, the laws governing "an oath of utterance" can never apply to a bailee, because all oaths taken by bailees are court-imposed oaths. [2]Hence Rabbi Yirmeyah's statement is intended to **teach us that the law is not in accordance with Rabbi Ammi,** and even a false oath taken under court compulsion can come under the category of "an oath of utterance," and can obligate the person who swore it to bring a sin-offering.

אִתְּמַר [3]In our analysis of the Mishnah so far we have been discussing a situation in which a hirer lent the animal he had hired to someone else with the permission of the animal's owner. The Gemara now considers a more general question: What is the law where one bailee hands over to another bailee something with which he has been entrusted, but does so without the permission of the owner? **It was said** that there is a difference of opinion between Amoraim on the following matter: If **a bailee hands over a deposit** entrusted to his care **to another bailee,** without the permission of the owner, and the deposit is destroyed while in the care of the second bailee, [4]**Rav said:** The first bailee **is exempt** under all circumstances in which he would have been exempt had the deposit been destroyed in his care, [5]whereas **Rabbi Yoḥanan said:** The first bailee **is liable** by virtue of the fact that he transferred the deposit to another person without permission. Even if the deposit was destroyed by forces beyond the control of the second bailee, the first is still responsible.

אָמַר אַבַּיֵי [6]**Abaye said: According to Rav's reasoning,** the exemption of the first bailee from responsibility **applies not only to an unpaid bailee who** handed over **a deposit to a paid bailee** — [7]thereby **improving its security,** since a paid bailee is expected to look after a deposit more carefully than an unpaid bailee — [8]**but it even** applies to **a paid bailee who** handed over **a deposit to an unpaid bailee,** [9]thereby **reducing its security.** Even in such a case, the first bailee is **exempt** if the deposit was destroyed by forces beyond the second bailee's control. The owner of the deposit cannot claim that the first bailee was negligent in handing over the deposit to the second. [10]**What is the reason? Because** handing over a deposit **to** another **person** is considered acceptable care, provided the latter is a **mentally competent** person.

RASHI

רב אמר פטור – מכל מה שהיה נפטר, אם שמרה הוא עצמו. **חייב** – אפילו באונסין. **ולא מיבעיא כו'** – דפטור מן האונסין, ואין לך לומר פשיעה היא זו שמסרה לאחר.

NOTES

died naturally or was the victim of violence. Hence, the entire oath is considered to have been court-imposed and, according to Rabbi Ammi, does not require a sin-offering.

עלויי עלייה לשמירתו Where he improved its care. At first glance, this clause would appear to be referring to the fact that a paid bailee is liable in circumstances under which an unpaid bailee is exempt. Thus, by handing over the deposit to a paid bailee, the first bailee improves its care, as it is now insured against theft and loss.

However, the Rishonim reject this explanation as it cannot be applied to the other clause, in which a paid bailee reduces the security of a deposit by leaving it with an unpaid bailee, because even after the deposit is handed over the paid bailee remains liable for theft or loss. Hence, he has not really reduced its security at all.

The Rishonim explain instead that a paid bailee's care is normally superior to that of an unpaid bailee, because a paid bailee is afraid that the deposit may be lost or stolen, whereas an unpaid bailee knows he is exempt in such cases. Hence, we might have thought that the owner would feel more secure if his deposit was in the hands of a paid bailee (*Ritva* and others).

SAGES

רב Rav. This is Rav Abba bar Aivo, the greatest of the first generation of Babylonian Amoraim. Rav was born in Babylonia to a prominent family which had produced many Jewish Sages and was descended from King David. He immigrated to Eretz Israel with the family of his uncle, Rabbi Ḥiyya, and studied Torah there, mainly from Rabbi Yehudah HaNasi. Rav was appointed to Rabbi Yehudah's court and remained in Eretz Israel for some time before returning to Babylonia, where he settled. Though there had been Torah centers in Babylonia before his time (in Hutzal and in Neharde'a), Rav founded the great yeshivah in Sura, raising the level of Torah study in Babylonia to that of Eretz Israel. After some time he was acknowledged as the chief Torah Sage in Eretz Israel as well.

Since Rav discussed Halakhic questions with the last of the Tannaim, a principle was stated in the Talmud according to which Rav's authority is equal to that of the Tannaim; a Baraita cannot be used to challenge his teachings, since he too is a Tanna. Indeed, according to a Geonic tradition, when "Rav (or Rabbi) Abba" is quoted in a Baraita, the reference is to Rav. Three places in the Talmud refer to Rabbi Abba, the Tanna.

Rav's closest friend and his opponent in Halakhic discussions was Shmuel, and their controversies are recorded throughout the Talmud. In matters of ritual law the Halakhah follows Rav, and in civil matters it follows Shmuel.

Rav lived to a ripe old age and had many disciples. In fact, all the Sages of the following generation were his students, and teachings cited in his name comprise a significant part of the Babylonian Talmud. The most famous of his students were Rav Huna, Rav Yehudah, Rav Ḥisda and Rav Hamnuna. Rav had at least two sons, Aivo and Ḥiyya. Ḥiyya bar Rav was a Sage, and Rav's grandson, Shimi bar Ḥiyya, was also an important Sage, who had the opportunity of studying with his grandfather. Rav married into the family of the Exilarch, and

TRANSLATION AND COMMENTARY

וּלְטַעְמֵיהּ דְּרַבִּי יוֹחָנָן [1]Having analyzed Rav's point of view, Abaye turns to that of Rabbi Yoḥanan: **According to Rabbi Yoḥanan's reasoning,** the accountability of the first bailee **applies not only to a paid bailee who** handed over **a deposit to an unpaid bailee,** [2]thereby **reducing** the deposit's **security,** since a paid bailee is expected to look after a deposit more carefully than an unpaid bailee. [3]**But it even** applies to **an unpaid bailee who** handed over **a deposit to a paid bailee,** [4]thereby **improving its security.** Even in such a case the first bailee remains **liable,** even if the deposit was destroyed by forces beyond the control of the second bailee, because the first bailee's very act of handing over the deposit to the second bailee can be considered negligence. [5]**For** the owner of the deposit **can say to** the first bailee: **"I do not wish my deposit to be in the hands of** any **other person,** as I trust you and no one else."

אָמַר רַב חִסְדָּא [6]**Rav Ḥisda said: This ruling** cited in **Rav's** name **was not stated** by him **explicitly, but was learned by implication.** In fact, the supposed difference of opinion between Rav and Rabbi Yoḥanan could have been the result of a misunderstanding. [7]Rav's students inferred from the following incident that Rav disagreed with Rabbi Yoḥanan, but, as we shall see, their inference was mistaken: There were **certain gardeners who used to deposit their spades every day with a certain old woman** when they finished work. [8]**One day they deposited** the spades **with one of** the gardeners **themselves.** [9]Later, that gardener **heard the sounds of** celebration coming from **a wedding-hall.** [10]**He went out** to join the party. As for the spades, **he went and deposited them with the same old woman.** [11]**While he was away** at the wedding, **the spades were stolen.** Now, both the gardener and the old woman were unpaid bailees, who are normally not responsible for theft. However, the other gardeners claimed that the gardener was liable for their loss, because he negligently transferred the spades placed in his care to another person. [12]The gardener **came before Rav** for a decision,

[1]וּלְטַעְמֵיהּ דְּרַבִּי יוֹחָנָן, לָא מִיבַּעְיָא שׁוֹמֵר שָׂכָר שֶׁמָּסַר לְשׁוֹמֵר חִנָּם, [2]דְּגָרוּעֵי גָּרְעָה לִשְׁמִירָתוֹ. [3]אֶלָּא אֲפִילּוּ שׁוֹמֵר חִנָּם שֶׁמָּסַר לְשׁוֹמֵר שָׂכָר, [4]דְּעַלּוּיֵי עַלְּיֵיהּ לִשְׁמִירָתוֹ, חַיָּיב. דְּאָמַר לֵיהּ: "אֵין רְצוֹנִי שֶׁיְּהֵא פִּקְדּוֹנִי בְּיַד אַחֵר". [6]אָמַר רַב חִסְדָּא: הָא דְּרַב לָאו בְּפֵירוּשׁ אִתְּמַר, אֶלָּא מִכְּלָלָא. [7]דְּהָנְהוּ גִּינָּאֵי, דְּכָל יוֹמָא הָווּ מַפְקְדֵי מָרָיְיהוּ גַּבָּהּ דְּהַהִיא סָבְתָא, [8]יוֹמָא חַד אַפְקְדִינְהוּ לְגַבֵּי חַד מִינַּיְיהוּ. [9]שְׁמַע קָלָא בֵּי הִלּוּלָא, [10]נְפַק, אֲזַל, אַפְקְדִינְהוּ לְגַבָּהּ דְּהַהִיא סָבְתָא. [11]אַדַּאֲזַל וַאֲתָא, אִגְּנוּב מָרָיְיהוּ. [12]אֲתָא לְקַמֵּיהּ דְּרַב, וּפַטְרֵיהּ.

LITERAL TRANSLATION

[1]And according to Rabbi Yoḥanan's reasoning, there is no need [to state this regarding] a paid bailee who handed over [a deposit] to an unpaid bailee, [2]where he made its care worse. [3]But even an unpaid bailee who handed over [a deposit] to a paid bailee, [4]where he improved its care, is liable. [5]For he can say to him: "I do not wish that my deposit should be in the hands of another [person]."

[6]Rav Ḥisda said: This [ruling] of Rav's was not said explicitly, but [was learned] by implication. [7]For certain gardeners, who used to deposit their spades every day with a certain old woman, [8]one day deposited them with one of themselves. [9]He heard the sound of a wedding-hall, [10]left, went and deposited them with that old woman. [11]While he was going and coming [back], their spades were stolen. [12]He came before Rav, and he exempted him.

RASHI

מריוהו — *פושוי״ר בלעז.

Rabbana Neḥemyah and Rabbana Ukva, Sages descended from the Exilarch, were Rav's grandsons by his daughter.

רַב חִסְדָּא Rav Ḥisda. a Babylonian Amora. See above, p. 198.

BACKGROUND

גִּינָּאֵי Gardeners. From the context it seems that the gardens tended by these people were not in the city itself but at a distance from it. In the city itself (either a walled city or a large village), there were mainly dwellings; the gardens there were small and ornamental, or for the private use of the owner of the courtyard. The gardens where vegetables were grown for sale in the market were at some distance from the city, and the grainfields and vineyards were even further away. Since vegetables grow quickly and require almost daily care, the gardeners used to go out to the fields every day, and stored their tools in isolated outbuildings near the garden plots.

LANGUAGE

מָרָיְיהוּ Their spades. This word is derived from the Latin *marra,* meaning "spade" or "rake."

בֵּי הִלּוּלָא A wedding-hall. The root of הִלּוּלָא is closely related to the Hebrew root הלל, "to sing." However, the Aramaic word refers mainly to epithalamia (wedding songs), and it came to mean a wedding banquet.

LANGUAGE (RASHI)

פושוי״ר* From the Old French *posoir,* meaning "spade" or "hoe."

NOTES

אֵין רְצוֹנִי שֶׁיְּהֵא פִּקְדּוֹנִי בְּיַד אַחֵר I do not want my deposit to be in the hands of another person. The Rishonim are troubled by this idea. Granted that the bailee should not have given the deposit to someone else without asking permission — but why should he be considered negligent in its care merely for so doing?

Some Rishonim explain that a bailee who entrusts a deposit to someone else is Halakhically not merely negligent, but is acting as if he were taking the deposit for his own use (שְׁלִיחוּת יָד). Such a bailee is considered a robber, and is liable for any damage that may thereafter be incurred, whatever the cause (*Rashba*).

The difficulty with this explanation is that it would appear from the Gemara that under certain circumstances, where there is no question of negligence, the bailee is exempt, whereas a robber is never exempt. *Tosafot* explains that the owner is considered to have made a stipulation that if the bailee hands over the deposit to any unauthorized person, he will be deemed to have been negligent. Hence the bailee is exempt only if the damage is manifestly totally unrelated to the negligence. Otherwise, he is liable.

Ra'avad explains that certain people have bad luck and are known to be accident-prone. Therefore, the depositor insists that his property not be given to such people. If the bailee disobeys his wishes, he is considered to have been negligent.

[1]מַאן דַּחֲזָא סָבַר מִשּׁוּם שׁוֹמֵר שֶׁמָּסַר לְשׁוֹמֵר פָּטוּר. [2]וְלָא הִיא. [3]שָׁאנֵי הָתָם, [4]דְּכָל יוֹמָא נַמִי אִינְהוּ גּוּפַיְיהוּ גַּבָּהּ דְּהַהִיא סַבְתָּא הָווּ מַפְקְדֵי לְהוּ.

[5]יָתֵיב רַבִּי אַמִּי וְקָאָמַר לַהּ לְהָא שְׁמַעְתָּא. [6]אֵיתִיבֵיהּ רַבִּי אַבָּא בַּר מֶמֶל לְרַבִּי אַמִּי: [7]״הַשּׂוֹכֵר פָּרָה מֵחֲבֵירוֹ, וְהִשְׁאִילָהּ לְאַחֵר, וּמֵתָה כְּדַרְכָּהּ, [8]יִשָּׁבַע הַשּׂוֹכֵר שֶׁמֵּתָה כְּדַרְכָּהּ, וְהַשּׁוֹאֵל מְשַׁלֵּם לַשּׂוֹכֵר״. [9]וְאִם אִיתָא, לֵימָא לֵיהּ: [10]״אֵין רְצוֹנִי שֶׁיְּהֵא פִּקְדוֹנִי בְּיַד אַחֵר״.

[11]אֲמַר לֵיהּ: הָכָא בְּמַאי עָסְקִינַן? [12]בְּשֶׁנָּתְנוּ לוֹ הַבְּעָלִים רְשׁוּת לְהַשְׁאִיל.

[13]אִי הָכִי, לַבְּעָלִים בָּעֵי לְשַׁלּוּמֵי.

[14]דְּאָמְרוּ לֵיהּ: ״לְדַעְתְּךָ״.

LITERAL TRANSLATION

[1]Those who saw [this] thought [that it was] because a bailee who handed over a [deposit] to a bailee is exempt. [2]But this is not so. [3]It is different there, [4]for every day they themselves also used to deposit them with that old woman.

[5]Rabbi Ammi sat and recited this tradition. [6]Rabbi Abba bar Memel raised an objection to Rabbi Ammi: [7]"Someone who hires a cow from his fellow, and lent it to someone else, and it died naturally, [8]the hirer must swear that it died naturally, and the borrower must pay the hirer." [9]But if this is so, let him [the owner] say to him [the hirer]: [10]"I do not wish that my deposit should be in the hands of another [person]."

[11]He said to him: With what are we dealing here? [12]Where the owner gave him permission to lend it.

[13]If so, [it is] to the owner [that] he should pay.

[14]Where he said to him: "At your [own] discretion."

TRANSLATION AND COMMENTARY

and he exempted him from payment. [1]Rav's students, **who saw** what had happened, **thought** Rav had exempted the gardener **because** he maintained that every **bailee who** hands over **a deposit to another bailee is exempt.** [2]**But this was not** the reason for Rav's ruling. In fact, it is not possible to use this case to prove that in Rav's opinion a bailee who entrusts a deposit to another bailee is exempt. It is possible that Rav agrees with the viewpoint of Rabbi Yoḥanan that the first bailee *is* liable in such a case. [3]The real reason for Rav's ruling in the case of the gardeners was as follows: The case of the gardeners **was different** from the standard case of a bailee handing over a deposit to another bailee. [4]The gardener acted exactly as the other gardeners usually did, **for every day they themselves also used to deposit** their spades **with that same old woman.** Hence, they could not claim that they did not trust her, and this is why Rav exempted the gardener.

יָתֵיב רַבִּי אַמִּי [5]The Gemara now relates: **Rabbi Ammi sat and recited the tradition** that a bailee who entrusts a deposit to another bailee is liable, in accordance with the ruling of his teacher, Rabbi Yoḥanan. [6]**Rabbi Abba bar Memel raised an objection to Rabbi Ammi** from the first clause of our Mishnah, which states: [7]"If **someone hires a cow from another person and** then **lends it to someone else, and it dies naturally** while in the borrower's care, [8]**the hirer must take an oath that it died naturally,** thereby exempting himself from liability, **and the borrower must pay the hirer."** [9]**But,** asks Rabbi Abba bar Memel, **if** the Halakhah is in accordance with Rabbi Yoḥanan's ruling, why is the hirer exempt from payment if he takes an oath? **Let** the owner **say to** him: [10]**"I did not wish my deposit to be in the hands of another person.** You should never have lent it to him, and since you violated my wishes, you are liable!" The fact, says Rabbi Abba bar Memel, that the Mishnah exempts the hirer from payment surely indicates that the Halakhah is not in accordance with Rabbi Yoḥanan's ruling.

אֲמַר לֵיהּ [11]Rabbi Ammi **said to** Rabbi Abba bar Memel in reply: **With what are we dealing here** in the Mishnah? [12]With a case **where the owner gave** the hirer **permission to lend** the deposit to someone else. Thus, the owner cannot claim that he did not want his deposit to be in anyone else's care.

אִי הָכִי [13]Rabbi Abba bar Memel objected again: **If so** — if the cow was lent with the permission of its owner — why does the Mishnah rule that the borrower must pay the hirer? **It is the owner that** the borrower **must pay,** since it was the owner who really lent him the cow; the hirer was no more than the owner's agent. Why should the hirer be reimbursed?

דְּאָמְרוּ לֵיהּ [14]Rabbi Ammi replied: The Mishnah is dealing with a case **where** the owner **said to** the hirer: "I give you permission to lend the deposit out. I will not interfere with your decision as to whether or not to lend it, or to whom. Act **at your own discretion."** Thus the decision to lend the animal was taken by the hirer, but the owner cannot claim that he did not want the animal to be in anyone else's care.

RASHI

מאן דחזא — אחד מן התלמידים ששמע מפיו דפטריה סבר שומר שמסר לשומר כו׳. **הוו מפקדי לה** — דלא מצו אמרי ליה אין רצוננו שיהא בידה. **להא שמעתא** — דרבי יוחנן רביה. **אי הכי לבעלים בעי לשלומי** — שואל, שהם השאילוה לו. **דאמרי ליה** — בעלים לשוכר. **לדעתך** — כרצונך, אם תרצה להשאילה לו ימי שכירותך — אין אנו מקפידין, הלכך הוא השאילה, והבעלים אין יכולין לומר אין רצוננו.

SAGES

רַבִּי אַבָּא בַּר מֶמֶל Rabbi Abba bar Memel. A Palestinian Amora of the second and third generations. See *Bava Metzia*, Part I, p. 229.

[1]מְתִיב רָמִי בַּר חָמָא: ״הַמַּפְקִיד מָעוֹת אֵצֶל חֲבֵירוֹ, צְרָרָן וְהִפְשִׁילָן לַאֲחוֹרָיו, [2]מְסָרָן לִבְנוֹ וּבִתּוֹ הַקְּטַנִּים וְנָעַל בִּפְנֵיהֶם שֶׁלֹּא כָּרָאוּי, [3]חַיָּיב, שֶׁלֹּא שָׁמַר כְּדֶרֶךְ הַשּׁוֹמְרִים.״ [4]טַעְמָא דִּקְטַנִּים, [5]הָא גְּדוֹלִים, פָּטוּר. [6]אַמַּאי? [7]נֵימָא לֵיהּ: ״אֵין רְצוֹנִי שֶׁיְּהֵא פִּקְדוֹנִי בְּיַד אַחֵר.״ [8]אָמַר רָבָא: כָּל הַמַּפְקִיד [36B] עַל דַּעַת אִשְׁתּוֹ וּבָנָיו הוּא מַפְקִיד.

[9]אָמְרִי נְהַרְדְּעֵי: ״דַּיְקָא נַמִי,

LITERAL TRANSLATION

[1]Rami bar Ḥama raised an objection: "Someone who deposits money with his fellow, [if] he bundled it up and threw it behind him, [2][or] gave it to his minor son or daughter and locked [the door] in front of them inadequately, [3]he is liable, since he did not safeguard it in the manner of bailees." [4]The reason is that [they were] minors, [5]but [if they were] adults, he is exempt. [6]Why? [7]Let him say to him: "I do not wish that my deposit should be in the hands of another [person]."

[8]Rava said: Whoever deposits, [36B] deposits on the assumption [that it may be given to] his [the bailee's] wife and sons.

[9]The Nehardeʼans say: It is also precise,

TRANSLATION AND COMMENTARY

מְתִיב רָמִי בַּר חָמָא [1]**Rami bar Ḥama raised** another **objection** to Rabbi Yoḥanan's ruling from a Mishnah (below, 42a): "If **someone deposited money with another person**, and the bailee **bundled it up and threw it over his shoulder**, and on his way home the money was lost, [2]**or** if the bailee **gave** the money **to his minor son or daughter** to look after, and **locked the door in front of them inadequately**, [3]in either case the bailee **is liable** if the money was lost or stolen, **since he** was negligent and **did not look after** it **in the manner** expected of **bailees.**" [4]From the second case, Rami bar Ḥama makes the following deduction: **The reason** the bailee is liable is because he was negligent in entrusting the deposit to his children, and this negligence stems from the fact **that they were minors.** [5]**But if they had been adults, he would have been exempt** — presumably because he fulfilled his duty by handing over the deposit to a competent person. [6]But **why?** asks Rami bar Ḥama. [7]**Surely** the depositor can **say to him,** in the words of Rabbi Yoḥanan: **"I did not wish my deposit to be in the hands of another person.** You acted negligently in entrusting the money to your adult children." Thus the inference drawn by Rami bar Ḥama from this Mishnah appears to contradict the ruling of Rabbi Yoḥanan, and it would seem that the Halakhah is not in accordance with it.

אָמַר רָבָא [8]**Rava said** in reply: No objection can be raised from this case, as it is clear that **whoever deposits** [36B] something with a bailee **does so on the assumption that** the bailee **may give** the deposit **to his wife and sons** for safekeeping, rather than look after it himself the entire time. Thus, according to Rava, this Mishnah poses no contradiction to the ruling of Rabbi Yoḥanan, because even Rabbi Yoḥanan would agree that in circumstances such as those described in the Mishnah, a bailee who hands over a deposit to another bailee is exempt.

אָמְרִי נְהַרְדְּעֵי [9]**The Nehardeʼans say:** Not only does the Mishnah not contradict the ruling of Rabbi Yoḥanan, it in fact supports him! A **precise** analysis of the language of the Mishnah shows that it corresponds completely

RASHI

מסרן לבנו כו׳ — או שמסרן לבנו ולבתו הקטנים. **בפניהם** — בפני אותם הקטנים, שלא יצאו לחוץ ויאבדו המעות. **על דעת אשתו ובניו** — על דעת שהנפקד מוסרו לאשתו ובניו הגדולים, ואין יכולין לומר ״אין רצוננו כו׳״. **דיקא נמי** — דהאי דגדולים פטורין דוקא בניו נקט, ולא אחרים.

NOTES

על דַּעַת אִשְׁתּוֹ וּבָנָיו הוּא מַפְקִיד Deposits on the assumption that it may be given to his wife and sons. The bailee undoubtedly gives his own property to his wife and children for safekeeping. Hence, there is no reason to expect him to be stricter about the depositor's property than about his own (*Rabbenu Ḥananel*).

HALAKHAH

צְרָרָן וְהִפְשִׁילָן לַאֲחוֹרָיו If he bundled it up and threw it over his shoulder. "If a bailee has to take a deposit of money with him while traveling, he must bundle it up and hold it in his hands, or tie it in front of him where he can see it. If he does not do so, he is liable even if the money was lost under circumstances beyond his control, since the loss was caused by his initial negligence." (*Shulḥan Arukh, Ḥoshen Mishpat* 292:20.)

עַל דַּעַת אִשְׁתּוֹ וּבָנָיו הוּא מַפְקִיד Depositing on the assumption that the deposit may be given to the bailee's wife and children. "Anyone who deposits an object expects the bailee to give it to his wife or to other adult members of his household for safekeeping. But if the bailee gives it to a minor, even his own son, or to his non-Jewish (*Sma*) slave, or to family members who do not live with him and are not dependent on him for support, it is as though he gave it to a stranger. Hence, if the deposit is damaged in such circumstances, the bailee is liable." (Ibid., 291:21.)

BACKGROUND

צְרָרָן וְהִפְשִׁילָן לַאֲחוֹרָיו He bundled it up and threw it behind him. Coins were usually kept in a purse (כִּיס) or tied together in a cloth. The purse or pouch was generally hung from a person's belt in front of him, so that it could be kept in view. If the purse was allowed to hang over a person's shoulder, this indicated that it was not properly tended, for it might become detached from his belt, or thieves might snatch it.

קְטַנִּים Minors. Minor children (girls younger than twelve, boys younger than thirteen) are not regarded as mentally competent in most areas of the Halakhah. Therefore, even according to the opinion that anyone mentally competent may be a bailee, children are not included.

וְנָעַל בִּפְנֵיהֶם שֶׁלֹּא כָּרָאוּי And he locked the door in front of them inadequately. There is a detailed discussion below (42a) of the proper way to look after money. If the money is kept in a closed building, the children cannot lose it while it is in the house. But this only obtains when the building is locked — when the children cannot leave or take the money out, and no one else can enter and steal it. But when the building is not properly locked, and the children can go out or open the doors, this means that the money has been left with someone who is not Halakhically competent, which is criminal negligence, and the bailee must pay if the money is lost or stolen.

עַל דַּעַת אִשְׁתּוֹ וּבָנָיו On the assumption that it may be given to the bailee's wife and sons. Usually, when someone deposits an article with the head of a family, he assumes that the bailee will not conceal the article from his family and that they too will participate in looking after it. Hence it is as if he had entrusted the article to every member of the bailee's family, and he only demands that the bailee leave the article in the care of someone competent to look after it.

TERMINOLOGY

דִּיקָא נַמִּי, דְּקָתָנֵי Lit., **It is also precise, for it teaches....** An expression introducing a proof in support of the view previously stated, based on an examination of the precise wording of a Mishnah or a Baraita.

...מִכְּלָל דְּ [This proves] by implication that.... When the Gemara presents an argument for a Halakhic ruling based on an authoritative source (either a Biblical text, a Tannaitic statement, an accepted tradition, or an established legal principle), it often introduces the inference with this expression.

TRANSLATION AND COMMENTARY

with Rabbi Yoḥanan's ruling, **for it states: "If the** bailee **gave** the deposit **to his minor son or daughter** to look after, **he is liable."** [1]**Thus** we can infer that **if he gave it to his adult son or daughter, he is exempt.** [2]Now, since the Mishnah speaks only of a bailee giving the deposit to his own children, **this proves by implication that if** the bailee **gave the deposit to others, he is** always **liable,** [3]and **it makes no difference whether they are adults or minors.** [4]Thus the Mishnah is in complete agreement with the ruling of Rabbi Yoḥanan that a bailee who hands over a deposit to another bailee **is liable.** [5]**For if** this is not what the Mishnah meant, and a bailee is exempt even if he hands over the deposit to a stranger, so long as he is an adult, the Mishnah **should simply have said:** "If he gave it to a **minor** for safekeeping, he is liable," without mentioning his children. From the fact that the Mishnah specifically mentioned "his minor children," we may infer that the bailee is only permitted to hand over the deposit to his own children (provided they are adults), and not to anyone else, in accordance with Rabbi Yoḥanan's ruling. [6]The Gemara concludes: We may indeed **conclude from this** that Rava's argument is correct, and depositors *do* allow bailees to entrust deposits to their wives and adult children for safekeeping.

דְּקָתָנֵי: אוֹ שֶׁמְּסָרָן לִבְנוֹ וּבִתּוֹ הַקְּטַנִּים, חַיָּיב״. [1]הָא, לִבְנוֹ וּלְבִתּוֹ הַגְּדוֹלִים, פָּטוּר. [2]מִכְּלָל דְּלַאֲחֵרִים, [3]לָא שְׁנָא גְּדוֹלִים וְלָא שְׁנָא קְטַנִּים, [4]חַיָּיב. [5]דְּאִם כֵּן, לִיתְנֵי ״קְטַנִּים״ סְתָמָא! [6]שְׁמַע מִינָּהּ.

[7]אָמַר רָבָא: הִלְכְתָא: שׁוֹמֵר שֶׁמָּסַר לְשׁוֹמֵר חַיָּיב. [8]לָא מִבָּעֲיָא שׁוֹמֵר שָׂכָר שֶׁמָּסַר לְשׁוֹמֵר חִנָּם, [9]דְּגַרוּעֵי גָּרְעָהּ לִשְׁמִירָתוֹ. [10]אֶלָּא אֲפִילּוּ שׁוֹמֵר חִנָּם שֶׁמָּסַר לְשׁוֹמֵר שָׂכָר חַיָּיב. [11]מַאי טַעְמָא? [12]דְּאָמַר לֵיהּ: ״אַתְּ מְהֵימַנְתְּ לִי בִּשְׁבוּעָה. [13]הָאֵיךְ לָא מְהֵימַן לִי בִּשְׁבוּעָה״.

LITERAL TRANSLATION

for it teaches: "Or if he gave it to his minor son or daughter, he is liable." [1]Thus, [if he gave it] to his adult son or daughter, he is exempt. [2][This proves] by implication, that [if he gave it] to others, [3][it makes] no difference [whether they are] adults and [it makes] no difference [whether they are] minors, [4]he is liable. [5]For if so, let it simply teach "minors"! [6]Conclude from this.

[7]Rava said: The Halakhah is: A bailee who handed over [a deposit] to [another] bailee is liable. [8]There is no need [to state this regarding] a paid bailee who handed over [a deposit] to an unpaid bailee, [9]where he made its care worse. [10]But even an unpaid bailee who handed over [a deposit] to a paid bailee is liable. [11]What is the reason? [12]For he can say to him: "You are trustworthy to me with an oath. [13]That [person] is not trustworthy to me with an oath."

RASHI

דאם כן — דלאחרים נמי גדולים פטור, ליתני: או שמסרן לקטנים סתמא. **בשבועה** — שלא פשע בה. **האיך לא מהימן לי** — ואני אומר שישנה בידו, או אכלה, או פשע בה.

אָמַר רָבָא [7]**Rava said: The Halakhah is** that **a bailee who handed over a deposit to another bailee is liable,** as Rabbi Yoḥanan ruled. [8]**There is no need to state this with regard to a paid bailee who handed over a deposit to an unpaid bailee,** [9]**where he reduced its security.** [10]**But even an unpaid bailee who handed over a deposit to a paid bailee,** and thereby improved the quality of its security, **is liable.** [11]But, says Rava, **what is the reason** for Rabbi Yoḥanan's ruling? [12]It is not the reason suggested previously by Abaye (above, 36a), but it is **because** the depositor **can say to** the bailee: **"I trust you with an oath,** and if you swear that you were not negligent in looking after the deposit, I will accept your statement. [13]But **I do not trust that** other person **with an oath.** I do not want him looking after the deposit, in case he loses it through negligence and swears falsely that he was not negligent." Thus, according to Abaye, a bailee's act of handing over a deposit to anyone else without permission amounts to negligence. By contrast, according to Rava, it depends on whether the second bailee will have to take an oath, and on whether the depositor can claim that he does not trust him to swear truly.

NOTES

הָאֵיךְ לָא מְהֵימַן לִי בִּשְׁבוּעָה That person is not trustworthy to me with an oath. According to Abaye, a bailee's handing over of a deposit to anyone else (except to close adult family members) without permission amounts to negligence. According to Rava, his handing over of the deposit to another bailee does not in itself constitute negligence; it

HALAKHAH

שׁוֹמֵר שֶׁמָּסַר לְשׁוֹמֵר A bailee who handed over a deposit to another bailee. "If a bailee handed over a deposit to someone else, and the deposit was damaged in circumstances under which the first bailee would ordinarily be exempt, the first bailee is liable, since the original owner can claim that he does not trust the second bailee's oath. This

TRANSLATION AND COMMENTARY

אִתְּמַר [1]**It was said** that there is a difference of opinion between Amoraim on the following issue: **If a bailee was negligent** in looking after an animal entrusted to him for safekeeping, **and it** escaped and **went out to a meadow** — an open area of pasture by the river, where there is a serious risk that an unsupervised animal may be stolen or be killed by wild beasts — [2]**and** despite the bailee's negligence it was not attacked, but happened **to die naturally** while in the meadow, what is the law? [3]**Abaye said in the name of Rabbah:** The bailee is **liable.** [4]**Rava said in the name of Rabbah:** The bailee **is exempt.**

אַבַּיֵי מִשְּׁמֵיהּ דְּרַבָּה [5]The Gemara now explains the two positions in greater detail: **Abaye said in the name of Rabbah:** The bailee **is** clearly **liable,** and [6]**any judge who does not judge in accordance with this judgment is no judge,** since it is so obvious what the law is in this case.

[1]אִתְּמַר: פָּשַׁע בָּהּ, [2]וְיָצָאת לָאֲגַם וּמֵתָה כְּדַרְכָּהּ, [3]אַבַּיֵי מִשְּׁמֵיהּ דְּרַבָּה אָמַר: חַיָּיב. [4]רָבָא מִשְּׁמֵיהּ דְּרַבָּה אָמַר: פָּטוּר.
[5]אַבַּיֵי מִשְּׁמֵיהּ דְּרַבָּה אָמַר: חַיָּיב. [6]כָּל דַּיָּינָא דְּלָא דָּאֵין כִּי הַאי דִּינָא לָאו דַּיָּינָא הוּא.

LITERAL TRANSLATION

[1]It was said: [If a bailee] was negligent with it [an animal], [2]and it went out to a meadow and died naturally, [3]Abaye said in the name of Rabbah: He is liable. [4]Rava said in the name of Rabbah: He is exempt.

[5]Abaye said in the name of Rabbah: He is liable. [6]Any judge who does not judge in accordance with this judgment is no judge.

RASHI

פשע בה — שלא נעל בפניה כראוי. ויצאת לאגם — מקום שאינה משתמרת שם אלא זאבים ולא אלא גנבים, ומיהו, לא אכלוה לא זאבים ולא גנבים. ומתה — דהוי תחילתו בפשיעה, שמא יטרפוה זאבים, וסופו לא אבדה באותה פשיעה אלא בדבר שהוא אונס.

NOTES

depends on whether an oath will need to be imposed, and whether or not the depositor trusts the person on whom the oath is imposed. This subtle distinction sometimes makes a difference. Later on in the Gemara, Rava points out that, according to him, if the first bailee is himself in a position to take an oath — as in our Mishnah, for example — the owner cannot object to his having transferred the deposit.

The Rishonim note a number of other practical differences. Among them: (1) If witnesses testify as to how the deposit was lost, so that there is no need for either bailee to take an oath, then, according to Rava, the owner cannot object to the first bailee's having transferred the deposit to someone else (*Tosafot*, *Rif* and others). (2) If the second bailee is known to be as trustworthy as the first, or more so, some Rishonim rule that, according to Rava, the depositor cannot object to the first bailee's having transferred the deposit to him, since the latter's oath is obviously reliable (*Rabbenu Yeruḥam*). *Rosh*, however, rules that the depositor can claim that he personally does not trust the second bailee, even if he is generally considered reliable.

אַבַּיֵי וְרָבָא מִשְּׁמֵיהּ דְּרַבָּה **Abaye and Rava in the name of Rabbah.** Abaye and Rava were both students of Rabbah, and apparently each had a different version of what their teacher had said. This presents a Halakhic problem: We normally rule in favor of Rava in his differences of opinion with Abaye; however, in this case it appears to be a question of determining what in fact Rabbah said, and there is independent evidence to support Abaye's version. *Rabbenu Ḥananel* actually ruled in favor of Abaye in our case, but most Rishonim were reluctant to depart from the normal procedure. Some commentators suggest that Rabbah may have issued both rulings. Initially he was of the opinion attributed to him by Abaye, but later changed his mind and ruled in the way attributed to him by Rava. This explanation can be applied to other, similar controversies in the Gemara (*Ramban*, *Rabbi Ya'akov Emden*).

כָּל דַּיָּינָא דְּלָא דָּאֵין **Any judge who does not judge.** Abaye and Rava maintain that their rulings apply according to both opinions — both the view that initial negligence followed by accident is negligence, and the view that it is not negligence — and not just according to one of these views, which another judge might not accept. Hence they feel confident enough to declare that any judge who does not rule accordingly errs (*Torat Ḥayyim*, *Maharam Schiff*).

HALAKHAH

rule applies even if the second bailee can be expected to provide better care — e.g., where the first bailee was unpaid and the second was paid. It also applies even if the second bailee was known to be more trustworthy than the first. However, if the owner demonstrates that he trusts the second bailee — if, for example, he ordinarily deposits property with him — the first bailee is exempt as long as he did not decrease the security of the deposit. But if the first bailee was paid and the second was unpaid, the first bailee is considered negligent, and is held liable for any damage to the deposit," following Rava's interpretation of Rabbi Yoḥanan's ruling. (*Shulḥan Arukh*, *Ḥoshen Mishpat* 291:26.)

פָּשַׁע בָּהּ וְיָצָאת לָאֲגַם **If a bailee was negligent with it and it went out to a meadow.** "If the bailee was negligent in taking care of the animal, and it escaped into a meadow and died there naturally, he is exempt. Even though the bailee was negligent initially, the animal would presumably have died wherever it was. However, if the escaped animal was stolen from the meadow, the bailee is liable, even if he was an unpaid bailee, since it was his negligence that made the theft possible. This applies even if the animal died naturally while in the thief's possession," following Rava against Abaye. (Ibid., 291:9.)

BACKGROUND

תְּחִילָּתוֹ בִּפְשִׁיעָה וְסוֹפוֹ בְּאוֹנֶס Its beginning was through negligence and its end was through accident. This Halakhic problem is based on the question of whether one views a sequence of events as a single unit or as separate events which happened to occur one after the other. If one treats the whole sequence as a single event, then since the bailee was negligent — and in the case of negligence all bailees are held responsible — one might say that the bailee became responsible from the moment he was negligent. Although the loss of the animal was not causally connected to the negligence, the bailee remained responsible for whatever happened to the animal later. But if one treats the sequence as a series of separate events, then since the animal's death was not connected to the negligence, the negligence was a separate event. Although the bailee acted improperly, he did not cause any damage. The unavoidable event which occurred later remains unconnected with what went before, and the bailee is not responsible for it.

הַבְלָא דְאַגְמָא The air of the meadow. This term refers to the special climatic conditions that exist on the banks of a lake. Since in Babylonia lakes are low-lying places, they are generally hotter than elsewhere, and humid. The combination of heat and humidity can be harmful to an animal, and its death may be attributable to it.

TRANSLATION AND COMMENTARY

[1]**There is no need** even **to state** that the bailee is liable in such a case **according to the** authority **who says** (below, 42a) that any case of a deposit that **was endangered initially through negligence** — for example, where money was stored in a place that was a fire hazard — [2]**and in the end was lost through an accident** unconnected to the original negligence — for example, where the building that was a fire hazard was broken into and the deposit stolen — is treated as a case of negligence, and the bailee **is liable.** According to this view, it is obvious **that** the bailee in our case **is liable**, as the animal was first placed in danger through the bailee's negligence. [3]**But even according to the** authority **who says** (below, 42a) that such a bailee **is exempt, here** where the animal escaped from the bailee's care **he is liable.** [4]**What is the reason?** [5]Abaye goes on to explain: **For we say:** The bailee is exempt only if the accident was totally unconnected with the original negligence. But here, it is possible that **the air of the meadow killed** the animal, and it would not have died anywhere else. Thus the bailee, through his negligence in guarding the animal, may have been directly responsible for its death, and is thus liable for it.

רָבָא מִשְּׁמֵיהּ דְּרַבָּה אָמַר [6]**Rava said in the name of Rabbah:** The bailee **is exempt,** [7]and, according to Rava, **any judge who does not judge in accordance with this judgment is no judge.** [8]**There is no need** even **to state** that the bailee is exempt in our case, **according to the** authority **who says** (below, 42a) that any case of deposit that **was endangered initially through negligence** [9]**and damaged in the end by an accident** unconnected to the original negligence is treated as an accident, and the bailee **is exempt.** [10]According to this view, it is obvious **that** the bailee in our case **is exempt,** as the animal fell victim to an accident, namely natural death, and the possibility that the air of the meadow was a contributing factor is remote. **But even according to the** authority **who says** (below, 42a) that such a bailee **is liable, here he is exempt.**

LITERAL TRANSLATION

[1]There is no need [to state], according to the one who says [that if] its beginning was through negligence [2]and its end was through accident he is liable, that he is liable. [3]But even according to the one who says he is exempt, here he is liable.[4]What is the reason? [5]For we say: The air of the meadow killed it.

[6]Rava said in the name of Rabbah: He is exempt. [7]Any judge who does not judge in accordance with this judgment is no judge. [8]There is no need [to state], according to the one who says [that if] its beginning was through negligence [9]and its end was through accident he is exempt, that he is exempt. [10]But even according to the one who says he is liable, here he is exempt.

[1]לָא מִבָּעֲיָא, לְמַאן דְּאָמַר תְּחִילָּתוֹ בִּפְשִׁיעָה [2]וְסוֹפוֹ בְּאוֹנֶס חַיָּיב, דְּחַיָּיב. [3]אֶלָּא אֲפִילּוּ לְמַאן דְּאָמַר פָּטוּר, הָכָא חַיָּיב. [4]מַאי טַעְמָא? [5]דְּאָמְרִינַן: הַבְלָא דְּאַגְמָא קְטָלָהּ.

[6]רָבָא מִשְּׁמֵיהּ דְּרַבָּה אָמַר: פָּטוּר. [7]כָּל דַּיָּינָא דְּלָא דָּאֵין כִּי הַאי דִּינָא לָאו דַּיָּינָא הוּא. [8]לָא מִיבַּעֲיָא, לְמַאן דְּאָמַר תְּחִילָּתוֹ בִּפְשִׁיעָה [9]וְסוֹפוֹ בְּאוֹנֶס פָּטוּר, דְּפָטוּר. [10]אֶלָּא אֲפִילּוּ לְמַאן דְּאָמַר חַיָּיב, הָכָא פָּטוּר.

RASHI

לא מיבעיא למאן דאמר — לקמן בפרקין (בבא מציעא מב,א) גבי ההוא דאותיב זוזי דפקדון בצריפא דאורבני, דהויא פשיעותא לגבי נורא ונטירותא לענין גנבי, ואיגנוב, וגניבה לגבי שומר חנם אונס הוא. **אלא אפילו למאן דאמר פטור הכא חייב** — דהתם ליכא פשיעותא אלא לענין נורא, אבל הכא, איכא למימר בפשיעה מתה, שאם היתה בבית לא מתה, ויציאתה לאגם היא פשיעת מיתתה, דשמא הבל המצוי באגם קטלה.

NOTES

הַבְלָא דְאַגְמָא The air of the meadow. Rava dismissed this concern as remote, and even Abaye does not consider it to be genuine negligence. Otherwise, any animal dying in a meadow would be considered a case of negligence, even if the bailee brought it there to pasture and guarded it against thieves and wild beasts, whereas Abaye referred only to cases where the bailee initially failed to look after the animal properly, and as a result it escaped. In fact, animals constantly pasture in meadows without being harmed, and Abaye accepts that natural death in a meadow is an example of accident. His ruling is based on the idea that a deposit initially endangered through negligence and ultimately damaged by accident is considered to have been damaged through negligence. According to Abaye, even the opinion that disagrees with this idea does so only when there is no logical connection between the initial negligence and the ultimate damage, but where there is even a remote chance that the original negligence may have been a contributory factor, Abaye is of the opinion that everyone accepts the principle of "initial negligence" (*Rosh* and others).

רָבָא אָמַר Rava said. Our commentary follows one of the

HALAKHAH

תְּחִילָּתוֹ בִּפְשִׁיעָה וְסוֹפוֹ בְּאוֹנֶס Initial negligence followed by accident. "If the bailee was negligent in his care, and afterwards the deposit was damaged as a result of an accident not related to the initial negligence, the bailee is

TRANSLATION AND COMMENTARY

[1] **What is the reason?** Rava goes on to explain: **For we say:** Even according to the viewpoint that the bailee is liable for the accident, this applies only if it can be shown that the deposit would not have been damaged if the bailee had not been negligent. In the previous example, if the bailee had buried the money in the fire hazard, the thieves would not have found it. [2] But here, **what difference does it make to the Angel of Death if the animal is here or there,** since the animal died naturally — in the Gemara's words, at the hands of the Angel of Death — and not because it happened to be in a particular place. Thus, according to Rava, for a bailee to be liable in a case where negligence preceded accidental loss, there must be a direct connection between the negligence and the loss. In our case, even if the bailee had been scrupulous in his care of the animal, it could still have died naturally in a securely locked cattle shed.

וּמוֹדֵי אַבַּיֵּי [3] The Gemara notes: **And Abaye admits that if** the animal **returned** from the meadow **to its owner's house and died** there the bailee **is exempt,** and the owner cannot claim that the animal's health had been weakened by its exposure to the unhealthy air of the meadow. [4] **What is the reason? Since** we see that the animal **returned** safely to its owner's home, [5] **it is not possible to say that the air of the meadow killed it.**

וּמוֹדֵי רָבָא [6] **Rava,** on the other hand, **admits that** the bailee **is liable in any case where** the animal **was stolen in the meadow and died in the thief's house.** [7] **What is the reason? If the Angel of Death had left** the animal **alone,** and it had not died, [8] **it would have been left standing in the thief's house!** Therefore, because the animal was stolen as a direct result of the bailee's negligence, he is liable from the time of the theft.

[1] מַאי טַעְמָא? דְּאָמְרִינַן: מַלְאַךְ הַמָּוֶת [2] מַה לִּי הָכָא וּמַה לִּי הָתָם?

[3] וּמוֹדֵי אַבַּיֵּי דְּאִי הָדְרָא לְבֵי מָרָה וּמֵתָה, דְּפָטוּר. [4] מַאי טַעְמָא? דְּהָא הָדְרָא לָהּ, [5] וְלֵיכָּא לְמֵימַר הַבְלָא דְּאַגְמָא קְטַלָהּ.

[6] וּמוֹדֵי רָבָא כָּל הֵיכָא דְּאִיגְּנְבָהּ גַּנָּב בַּאֲגַם וּמֵתָה כְּדַרְכָּהּ בֵּי גַּנָּב, דְּחַיָּיב. [7] מַאי טַעְמָא? דְּאִי שְׁבַקָהּ מַלְאַךְ הַמָּוֶת, [8] בְּבֵיתֵיהּ דְּגַנָּבָא הֲוָה קַיְימָא.

LITERAL TRANSLATION

[1] What is the reason? For we say: [To] the Angel of Death [2] what difference is there (lit., "what to me") [if the animal is] here or there?

[3] And Abaye admits that if it returned to its owner's house and died, that he is exempt. [4] What is the reason? Because it returned, [5] and it is not [possible] to say that the air of the meadow killed it.

[6] And Rava admits [that] in any [case] where a thief stole it in the meadow and it died naturally in the thief's house, that he [the bailee] is liable. [7] What is the reason? For if the Angel of Death had left it alone, [8] it would have been [left] standing in the thief's house.

RASHI

מה לי הכא כו׳ — אבל התם גבי זוזי, אם שמרם כהלכתם, דקיימא לן (בבא מציעא מב,א): כספים אין להם שמירה אלא בקרקע — לא נגנבו, ואף על גב דקיימא לן בגריפא דאורבני אין דרך גנבים לבקש שם מעות ואונס הוא, מיהו על ידי שלא שמר כדין שמירתם אבדו, אבל פרה זו אם היתה בבית נמי היתה מתה. **דאיגנבה גנב מאגם** — שזהו דבר שהוא פשיעה אצל יציאתה לאגם, אף על פי שסופה מתה בי גנב — חייב, ולא אמר אי הוה בבית שומר נמי הוה מתה. **מאי טעמא** — משעת גניבה היא אבודה מן הבעלים, דאי נמי שבקה מלאך המות, בי גנב הוה קיימא, הלכך החיוב בא לו על שעת הגניבה.

BACKGROUND

מַלְאַךְ הַמָּוֶת The Angel of Death. It appears that the Rabbis distinguished between death resulting from an accident (including death from exposure, for example), and death resulting from internal illness. It is only death resulting from an internal illness without any tangible cause that they attributed to "the Angel of Death." The Rabbis assumed that an animal which had contracted such an illness would probably die no matter where it was, and hence location or physical exertion played only a negligible role in causing its death.

NOTES

explanations given by *Ra'avad*, according to which Rava dismisses Abaye's concern about the meadow's vapors as remote. After all, cows graze in meadows all the time and nothing happens to them. Alternatively, *Ra'avad* suggests that Rava may accept the possibility that the air in a meadow is unhealthy, but denies that it is unhealthy enough to be dangerous. Hence, if the animal died, it can only be because of some already existing disease, and not because of the air in the meadow.

מַלְאַךְ הַמָּוֶת The Angel of Death. The Rishonim ask: The liabilities of the other bailees are logical, but a borrower is liable even if the animal died or was damaged as a result of circumstances beyond his control. The borrower's total responsibility even when a deposit is lost in circumstances beyond his control — in an earthquake, for example — can be explained in the following way: If the animal had not been lent out, it would never have been hurt. But if we accept Rava's argument, why should the borrower be liable for natural death? What difference does it make to the Angel of Death if the animal is in its owner's house or at the borrower's?

Ritva suggests that the borrower's obligations are based on the fact that he expressly accepts liability for any damage, however caused, and thus if the animal happens to die, it is simply his bad luck.

Other Rishonim suggest that there may even be a logical

HALAKHAH

liable." (Ibid., 291:6.) If, however, there was not even a circumstantial connection between the negligence and the eventual damage, the bailee is exempt (*Sma*).

[1]אָמַר לֵיהּ אַבָּיֵי לְרָבָא: לְדִידָךְ, דְּאָמְרַתְּ: [2]מַלְאַךְ הַמָּוֶת מַה לִּי הָכָא וּמַה לִּי הָתָם, [3]הַאי דְּאוֹתְבֵיהּ רַבִּי אַבָּא בַּר מֶמֶל לְרַבִּי אַמִי, [4]וְשַׁנֵּי לֵיהּ: בְּשֶׁנָּתְנוּ לוֹ בְּעָלִים רְשׁוּת לְהַשְׁאִיל. [5]וְלֵימָא לֵיהּ: מַלְאַךְ הַמָּוֶת מַה לִּי הָכָא וּמַה לִּי הָתָם? [6]אֲמַר לֵיהּ: לְדִידְכוּ, דְּמַתְנִיתוּ: [7]"אֵין רְצוֹנִי שֶׁיְּהֵא פִּקְדוֹנִי בְּיַד אַחֵר", אִיכָּא לְאוֹתְבָה לְהַהִיא. [8]לְדִידִי, דְּאָמֵינָא: [9]"אַתְּ מְהֵימַנְתְּ לִי בִּשְׁבוּעָה, [10]וְהָאֵיךְ לָא מְהֵימַן לִי בִּשְׁבוּעָה", [11]לֵיכָּא לְאוֹתְבָה כְּלָל.

LITERAL TRANSLATION

[1]Abaye said to Rava: According to you, who say: [2][To] the Angel of Death what difference is there [if the animal is] here or there, [3][there is a difficulty regarding] that objection which Rabbi Abba bar Memel raised to Rabbi Ammi, [4]and [to which] he answered him: Where the owner gave him permission to lend it. [5]But let him say to him: [To] the Angel of Death what difference is there [if the animal is] here or there?

[6]He said to him: According to you, who teach: [7]"I do not wish that my deposit should be in the hands of another [person]," there is [a possibility] of raising that objection. [8]According to my [opinion], [in] which I say: [9]"You are trustworthy to me with an oath, [10]but he is not trustworthy to me with an oath," [11]there is no [possibility] whatsoever of raising that objection.

TRANSLATION AND COMMENTARY

אָמַר לֵיהּ אַבָּיֵי לְרָבָא [1]Abaye said to Rava: **According to your opinion**, in which **you say:** [2]**What difference does it make to the Angel of Death if the animal is here or there,** [3]how can you account for **the objection which Rabbi Abba bar Memel raised to Rabbi Ammi,** in connection with a bailee who handed over his deposit to another bailee (above, 36a), [4]**and** how do you explain the forced **answer** Rabbi Ammi gave — that the Mishnah applies only **where the owner gave** the hirer **permission to lend** the animal out. [5]Why could Rabbi Ammi not simply **have said to** Rabbi Abba bar Memel: **What difference does it make to the Angel of Death if the animal is here or there?** Since the animal would have died no matter where it was, it makes no difference in whose custody it died! Such an answer would have been far superior to the one given by Rabbi Ammi. Since Rabbi Ammi did not answer in this way, this indicates that your argument is not acceptable, and in all cases of accident after negligence the bailee is liable.

אֲמַר לֵיהּ [6]Rava **said to** Abaye in reply: Rabbi Abba bar Memel, who raised this objection, did so on the basis of your interpretation of Rabbi Yoḥanan's ruling — (above, 36a). Now, **according to your interpretation,** in which **you teach** that a bailee who handed over a deposit to another bailee is liable because the depositor can claim, [7]**"I do not wish my deposit to be in** any unauthorized **person's hand," it is** indeed **possible to raise** Rabbi Abba bar Memel's **objection.** [8]But **according to my interpretation** of Rabbi Yoḥanan's ruling — in which **I say** that a bailee who handed over a deposit to another bailee is liable **only** where the depositor can say: [9]**"You I trust with an oath,** [10]**but that** other person **I do not trust with an oath"** — the first bailee is liable only if the owner is faced with an oath from the second bailee. But our Mishnah explicitly states that it is the first bailee who must swear to the owner. [11]Hence, **there is no possibility whatsoever of raising** Rabbi Abba bar Memel's **objection** in the first place! Accordingly, there is no basis to ask why Rabbi Ammi did not offer a different answer (see note).

RASHI

הא דאותביה רבי אבא — לעיל, מהשוכר פרה והשאילה לאחר, לימא אין רצוני כו׳. **ושני ליה בשנתנו לו הבעלים רשות** — מאי דוחקיה לשנויי הכי נימא ליה: אם אירע בה אונס אחר, דמצינו למימר אם היתה בבית לא נאנסה — היה חייב, אבל זו מתה כדרכה — מלאך המות נמי בבית שוכר קטיל לה ומדלא שני ליה הכי — שמעינן למאן דאמר תחלתו בפשיעה וסופו באונס חייב, לא שנא אונס מלאך המות משאר אונסין. **לדידכו** — דאמריתו טעמא דשומר שמסר לשומר חייב משום "אין רצוני" — איכא לאותובה להאי, ומאי דניחא ליה לרבי אמי שני ליה, אנא לא סבירא לי לא אתקפתא ולא שינויא, דלדידי דאמרי לעיל טעמא משום דלא מהימן ליה בשבועה ליכא לאותובה כלל, שהרי שוכר עצמו נשבע לו, כדתנן: ישבע השוכר שמתה כדרכה.

NOTES

basis for the borrower's liability for natural death. Since the borrower gets all the advantages from borrowing the animal, without any obligations, the animal is effectively his for the period of the loan. Hence, the Torah considered it to be his for bad as well as for good, and if the animal dies during this period, the borrower can no more claim relief than the owner could if it died while in *his* home.

לְדִידְכוּ דְּמַתְנִיתוּ According to your opinion, in which you teach.... Rava's response to Abaye's question raises problems. Abaye never doubted that Rava had a simpler explanation of the Mishnah than his own. Abaye merely sought to prove that Rabbi Abba bar Memel and Rabbi Ammi supported his view, from the fact that Rabbi Ammi resorted to such a forced answer to Rabbi Abba bar Memel's question instead of giving Rava's simple "Angel of Death" reply. But Rava seems to respond by saying that not only

TRANSLATION AND COMMENTARY

מְתִיב רָמִי בַּר חָמָא [1]**Rami bar Ḥama raised an objection** to Abaye's viewpoint on the basis of the following Mishnah (below, 93b), which seeks to define the difference between negligence and accident: "**If** a bailee **took** an animal **up to the cliff tops** to graze, **and it fell** by itself and died, [2]**this is not an accident** but negligence on the part of the bailee **and he is liable,** as animals frequently slip and fall from steep cliffs." [3]**Thus,** the Gemara infers, **if** the animal had not fallen and been killed but **had died naturally** on the cliff top, [4]**this would be** considered **an accident, and** the bailee **would be exempt.** [5]**But why?** If Abaye's viewpoint is correct, **let** the depositor **say to** the bailee that the bailee was responsible for the animal's death, because **the mountain air killed it,** [6]**or alternatively, the exhaustion** caused by **the mountain climb killed it!**

הָכָא בְּמַאי עָסְקִינַן [7]The Gemara answers: **With what are we dealing here?** [8]With a case **where** the bailee **took** the animal **up to rich, good pasture,** to a place where cows customarily graze. The animal died a natural death there, and the bailee was exempt from liability, because he had not been negligent in its care.

אִי הָכִי [9]The Gemara objects: But **if** the bailee took the animal to a fertile pasture, and was not negligent at all, then even if the animal **fell he should also be exempt.** The bailee was behaving properly when he brought the animal to this place, and it died only because it accidentally slipped and fell. Surely this is a case of accident, and he should be exempt!

[1]מְתִיב רָמִי בַּר חָמָא: ״הֶעֱלָה לְרָאשֵׁי צוּקִין וְנָפְלָה, [2]אֵין זֶה אוֹנֶס, וְחַיָּיב״. [3]הָא, מֵתָה כְּדַרְכָּהּ, [4]הֲרֵי זֶה אוֹנֶס, וּפָטוּר. [5]וְאַמַּאי? לֵימָא לֵיהּ: ״אֲוִירָא דְּהַר קְטָלָהּ״, [6]אִי נַמִּי: ״אוּבְצָנָא דְּהַר קְטָלָהּ״. [7]הָכָא בְּמַאי עָסְקִינַן? [8]שֶׁהֶעֱלָהּ לְמִרְעֶה שָׁמֵן וָטוֹב. [9]אִי הָכִי, נָפְלָה נַמִּי.

LITERAL TRANSLATION

[1]Rami bar Ḥama raised an objection: "If he took it up to the tops of cliffs and it fell, [2]this is not an accident, and he is liable." [3]Thus, [if] it died naturally, [4]this is an accident, and he is exempt. [5]But why? Let him say to him: "The air of the mountain killed it," [6]or also: "The exhaustion of the mountain [climb] killed it."

[7]With what are we dealing here? [8]Where he took it up to rich and good pasture.

[9]If so, if it fell, [he should] also [be] exempt.

RASHI

העלה לראשי צוקין — שומר שהעלה לראשי הרים חדים ומשופעים ונפלה. **אין זה אונס** — אלא פשיעה, דדרכה ליפול. **הא מתה כדרכה** — כראש הצוק. **פטור** — דהוי סופו באונס. **אוירא** — ליגה. **אובצנא** — עייפות, טורח המעלה. **למרעה שמן וטוב** — דדרך הרועים להעלות שם בהמות לרעות.

BACKGROUND

אֲוִירָא דְּהַר קְטָלָהּ The air of the mountain killed it. Mountain air can contribute to an animal's death in several ways. On the one hand, mountain air is colder than air at sea level. Moreover, the air pressure is lower, and the air contains less oxygen. The combination of these factors can cause internal bleeding and a shortage of oxygen, which is particularly needed by the body because of the cold.

אוּבְצָנָא דְּהַר The exhaustion of the mountain climb. Climbing a mountain entails strenuous effort, and becomes more difficult because of the lack of oxygen. This effort can be very hard on an animal. Thus, if an animal dies on a mountain, its death can be attributed to the effort it made to climb it.

LANGUAGE

אוּבְצָנָא Exhaustion. The root of this Aramaic word is apparently parallel to the Hebrew root חבץ, meaning to press, and it means fatigue from overwork.

BACKGROUND

לְמִרְעֶה שָׁמֵן וָטוֹב To rich and good pasture. When a person looking after an animal brings it to an appropriate pasture in the mountains, the ascent does not involve excessive strain on the animal, and there are usually well-trodden paths to a permanent pasture. Lush and fine pasture also indicates that the place is neither too high nor too cold.

NOTES

Rabbi Ammi's response, but even Rabbi Abba bar Memel's question, makes sense only according to Abaye's view, and not only Abaye's view regarding the present problem, but even his view regarding the previous one! If anything, Rava has strengthened Abaye's question! How is this a response?

Our commentary follows several Rishonim, including *Rashi*, who explain that Rava had no real answer to Abaye's objection, and conceded that both Rabbi Ammi and Rabbi Abba bar Memel followed Abaye's opinion. According to this explanation, Rava accounted for this by pointing to the fact that it is clear from Rabbi Abba bar Memel's question itself that these two Amoraim followed Abaye's view in the previous problem as well, and presumably represented a different school of thought from that of Rava.

Many Rishonim find this explanation unconvincing. They maintain that Rava conceded that Rabbi Abba bar Memel and Rabbi Ammi followed Abaye's view only in the previous problem, but not in the present one. According to this explanation, there is a fundamental difference between ordinary negligence, such as failing to prevent an animal from escaping, and willful violation of the owner's wishes, such as occurs when a hirer lends an animal to a borrower even though the owner does not wish it to be in anyone else's hands. In the former case, the "Angel of Death" argument applies, but the latter case resembles theft and should at the very least be subject to the liabilities of borrowing. Hence, just as a borrower is responsible even for natural death, so too this willful violator of the owner's wishes is liable even for natural death, even though he would not be had he merely been negligent. Thus Rabbi Ammi could not have responded to Rabbi Abba bar Memel's question with the "Angel of Death" argument. But this only applies if we assume that Rabbi Abba bar Memel and Rabbi Ammi followed Abaye's view in the previous problem, where a bailee is liable for handing over a deposit to another bailee because the owner does not wish his deposit to be in someone else's hands. According to Rava's view there, it is not considered negligence if one person entrusts a deposit to another responsible person. The owner's only demand is that he should not have to accept the second bailee's oath. Hence, Rava's response to Abaye's question *here* depends on his proving that Rabbi Abba bar Memel and Rabbi Ammi specifically followed Abaye's view about a bailee handing over a deposit, and hence could very well agree with Rava about an animal that died naturally after escaping to a meadow (*Rashba*, *Ramban*, *Ran*, and others).

HALAKHAH

הֶעֱלָה לְרָאשֵׁי צוּקִין **If he took it up to the tops of cliffs.** "If a bailee takes an animal entrusted to him to the top of a cliff and it falls, this is not considered an accident and the bailee is liable. But if the animal died there of natural causes, the bailee is exempt, following Rava." (*Shulḥan Arukh, Ḥoshen Mishpat* 291:10.)

TRANSLATION AND COMMENTARY

שֶׁהָיָה לוֹ לְתוֹקְפָהּ [1]The Gemara answers: The Mishnah (below, 93b) is referring to a case **where** the bailee **could have held** the animal **securely** and prevented its fall, as shepherds regularly do. **But he did not hold it securely.** By not doing so he was negligent, and that is why he is liable.

אִי הָכִי [2]The Gemara objects: **If so,** if the bailee should have held the animal securely and prevented it from falling, **consider the first clause** of the same Mishnah: [3]**"If** the animal **went up to the cliff tops** by itself **and fell, this is an accident,** and the bailee is exempt." [4]But according to the explanation suggested above, the bailee **should have held** the animal **securely** to prevent it from going to a dangerous area. If he did not do so, surely he was negligent!

לָא צְרִיכָא [5]The Gemara answers: **No, this clause is necessary** and applicable in a case **where** the animal **overpowered** the bailee, even though he tried to hold on to it, **and went up** to the top of the cliff, [6]and then when the bailee tried to prevent it from falling, it again **overpowered him and** fell **down.** Thus the first clause of that Mishnah is describing a case where the bailee could not prevent the accident and is therefore not liable.

אָמַר רַבִּי יוֹסֵי [7]The Gemara now considers the next clause of the Mishnah: **"Rabbi Yose said: How can** the hirer **do business** and make a profit from **another person's cow?"** [8]**Rav Yehudah said in the name of Shmuel: The Halakhah is in accordance with Rabbi Yose,** and the compensation paid by the borrower for the loss of the animal is returned to its original owner, and not to the hirer.

אֲמַר לֵיהּ רַב שְׁמוּאֵל בַּר יְהוּדָה [9]**Rav Shmuel bar Yehudah said to Rav Yehudah:** You said something on this subject in addition to the statement you made above in Shmuel's name. [10]**You said to us in the name**

[1]שֶׁהָיָה לוֹ לְתוֹקְפָהּ, וְלֹא תְּקָפָהּ. [2]אִי הָכִי, אֵימָא רֵישָׁא: [3]״עָלְתָה לְרָאשֵׁי צוּקִין וְנָפְלָה, הֲרֵי זֶה אוֹנֶס״. [4]אִיבָּעֵי לֵיהּ לְמִיתְקְפָהּ. [5]לָא, צְרִיכָא שֶׁתְּקָפַתּוּ וְעָלְתָה, [6]תְּקָפַתּוּ וְיָרְדָה. [7]״אָמַר רַבִּי יוֹסֵי: כֵּיצַד הַלָּה עוֹשֶׂה סְחוֹרָה בְּפָרָתוֹ כו׳״. [8]אָמַר רַב יְהוּדָה אָמַר שְׁמוּאֵל: הֲלָכָה כְּרַבִּי יוֹסֵי. [9]אֲמַר לֵיהּ רַב שְׁמוּאֵל בַּר יְהוּדָה לְרַב יְהוּדָה: [10]אָמְרַתְּ לָן

LITERAL TRANSLATION

[1]Where he should have held it securely, but he did not hold it securely.

[2]If so, cite the first clause: [3]"[If] it went up to the tops of cliffs and fell, this is an accident." [4]He should have held it securely.

[5]No, it is necessary where it overpowered him and went up, [6]overpowered him and went down.

[7]"Rabbi Yose said: How can that [person] do business with [his fellow's] cow?" [8]Rav Yehudah said in the name of Shmuel: The Halakhah is in accordance with Rabbi Yose.

[9]Rav Shmuel bar Yehudah said to Rav Yehudah: [10]You said to

RASHI

לתוקפה – להחזיק בה, שכן דרך הרועים. **עלתה** – מאליה. **שתקפתו** – על כרחו ועלתה, ולא יכול להחזיק בה, שחזקה היתה ממנו.

SAGES

רַב שְׁמוּאֵל בַּר יְהוּדָה Rav Shmuel bar Yehudah. A Babylonian Amora of the third generation, Rav Shmuel bar Yehudah was a proselyte and a disciple of Rav Yehudah (bar Yeḥezkel). He also studied in Eretz Israel under Rabbi Yoḥanan and Rabbi Elazar, and on his return to Babylonia he transmitted many rulings in the names of these scholars. Abaye was one of his students.

NOTES

שֶׁתְּקָפַתּוּ וְעָלְתָה Where it overpowered him and went up. The Rishonim ask: The bailee is liable if he was able to prevent the animal from falling and failed to do so. It is immaterial how the animal got there — whether the animal dragged him up, ran up by itself, or whether he took it up. Hence, not only this phrase in the Gemara, but even the distinction made by the Mishnah (below, 93b) between an animal going up and being taken up appears superfluous.

Tosafot explains that the Mishnah described the animal as climbing the mountain by itself to indicate that when it fell it was out of control, and its fall was not preventable. On the other hand, when the animal was taken to the mountain top, it was under control, and its fall too could presumably have been prevented.

Ra'avad takes this idea further. He explains that since the animal was able to overpower the bailee and climb up, it was obviously stronger than he, and the bailee was not obligated to endanger himself by struggling with it. Hence, when the animal fell down, the bailee did not try to overpower it, since he was afraid that he might fall with it.

HALAKHAH

עָלְתָה לְרָאשֵׁי צוּקִין If it went up to the tops of cliffs. "If an animal entrusted to a bailee climbed on its own to the top of a cliff and fell down and died, even if the animal did not overpower the bailee, provided that he was not negligent in looking after it (*Sma*), this is considered neither negligence nor accident, but rather an intermediate category similar to theft. Hence an unpaid bailee would be exempt in such a case, but a paid bailee would be liable." This follows most of the Rishonim, who explain that the Gemara's explanation that the animal overpowered the bailee was needed only to explain the Mishnah according to Abaye's view, but not according to the Halakhah, which follows Rava. (Ibid., 292:11.)

מִשְּׁמֵיהּ דִּשְׁמוּאֵל: חָלוּק הָיָה רַבִּי יוֹסֵי [37A] אַף בָּרִאשׁוֹנָה. [1]הֲלָכָה כְּמוֹתוֹ, אוֹ אֵין הֲלָכָה כְּמוֹתוֹ?

[2]אֲמַר לֵיהּ: חָלוּק הָיָה רַבִּי יוֹסֵי אַף בָּרִאשׁוֹנָה, [3]וַהֲלָכָה כְּמוֹתוֹ אַף בָּרִאשׁוֹנָה.

[4]אִתְּמַר נַמִי: אָמַר רַבִּי אֶלְעָזָר: [5]חָלוּק הָיָה רַבִּי יוֹסֵי אַף בָּרִאשׁוֹנָה, [6]וַהֲלָכָה כְּמוֹתוֹ אַף בָּרִאשׁוֹנָה.

[7]וְרַבִּי יוֹחָנָן אָמַר: מוֹדֶה הָיָה רַבִּי יוֹסֵי בָּרִאשׁוֹנָה, [8]שֶׁכְּבָר שִׁילֵּם.

[9]שִׁילֵּם — אִין; [10]לֹא שִׁילֵּם — לֹא? [11]וְהָאָמַר רַבִּי חִיָּיא בַּר אַבָּא אָמַר רַבִּי יוֹחָנָן: לֹא "שִׁילֵּם" שִׁילֵּם מַמָּשׁ. [12]אֶלָּא

LITERAL TRANSLATION

us in the name of Shmuel: Rabbi Yose disagreed [37A] even in the first [Mishnah]. [1]Is the Halakhah in accordance with him, or is the Halakhah not in accordance with him?

[2]He said to him: Rabbi Yose disagreed even in the first [Mishnah], [3]and the Halakhah is in accordance with him even in the first [Mishnah].

[4]It has also been said: Rabbi Elazar said: [5]Rabbi Yose disagreed even in the first [Mishnah], [6]and the Halakhah is in accordance with him even in the first [Mishnah].

[7]But Rabbi Yoḥanan said: Rabbi Yose agreed in the first [Mishnah], [8]for he [the bailee] already paid.

[9]If he paid — yes; [10]if he did not pay — no?! [11]But surely Rabbi Ḥiyya bar Abba said in the name of Rabbi Yoḥanan: "He paid" [does] not [mean that] he actually paid. [12]Rather,

RASHI

אף בראשונה — בשילם ולא רצה לישבע, כילד זה נותן לתוך כיסו כפילו של זה? אלא יחזיר הכפל לבעלים. **שכבר שילם** — קודם שנמצא הגנב, וקנה כפל — כדאמר מעיקרא: אדעתא דהכי אתאי לידיה.

TRANSLATION AND COMMENTARY

of Shmuel: Rabbi Yose disagreed [37A] even **with** the ruling in **the first Mishnah** in this chapter (above, 33b). When you taught us the Mishnah about the hirer and the borrower (above, 35b), you explained that Rabbi Yose not only disagrees with the first Tanna in *this* Mishnah, but with the ruling of the previous Mishnah as well. In fact, you told us that the two Mishnayot should be read as one long Mishnah, in which the first Tanna issues two rulings, and Rabbi Yose exclaims at the end, "How can a bailee do business with the money given in compensation for another person's cow?" In the previous Mishnah, the first Tanna awards the bailee the fine paid by the thief for stealing the owner's cow, and in our Mishnah the first Tanna awards him the compensation paid by the borrower for the loss of the owner's cow. In both cases, Rabbi Yose objects to the bailee enriching himself by taking the payment that should be made to the owner. [1]Now, says Rav Shmuel bar Yehudah to Rav Yehudah, since you have just ruled that the Halakhah is in accordance with Rabbi Yose in our Mishnah, the question arises: **Is the Halakhah in accordance with** Rabbi Yose in the previous Mishnah as well, **or not?**

אֲמַר לֵיהּ [2]Rav Yehudah **said to** Rav Shmuel bar Yehudah in reply: As you pointed out, **Rabbi Yose disagreed even about the first Mishnah,** [3]**and the Halakhah is in accordance with him even in the first Mishnah.** Thus, according to Rav Yehudah, in the case discussed in the first Mishnah, if the bailee prefers to pay for the loss of the deposit rather than take an oath, then if the thief is found he makes the double payment to the owner of the deposit, and not to the bailee.

אִתְּמַר נַמִי [4]**It has also been said** that Palestinian Amoraim disagree about this matter: **Rabbi Elazar said,** as did the Babylonian Amora, Rav Yehudah: [5]**Rabbi Yose disagreed even with** the ruling in **the first Mishnah,** [6]**and the Halakhah is in accordance with him even in the first Mishnah.**

וְרַבִּי יוֹחָנָן אָמַר [7]**But Rabbi Yoḥanan** held a different viewpoint from that of the other Amoraim and **said: Rabbi Yose agreed** with the first Tanna **in the first Mishnah** — that the bailee, not the owner, is entitled to the thief's double payment. Rabbi Yose's reason, says Rabbi Yoḥanan, is as follows: [8]In the case discussed in the first Mishnah, **the bailee** has **already paid** for the animal, and has thereby acquired all subsequent payments resulting from the discovery of the thief. The owner is quite willing to let the bailee take the payment from the thief if he is caught, since he has already been compensated in full.

שִׁילֵּם [9]The Gemara is puzzled by the language in which Rabbi Yoḥanan's ruling is formulated. The implication of Rabbi Yoḥanan's ruling seems to be that only **if** the bailee **paid** the owner the value of his deposit is he entitled to the double payment from the thief, [10]but **if he did not pay** the owner, he is **not** entitled. [11]This, says the Gemara, cannot be correct. **Surely Rabbi Ḥiyya bar Abba said in the name of Rabbi Yoḥanan** himself: When the first Mishnah uses the expression **"he paid,"** it **does not** necessarily **mean that** the bailee **actually paid** the owner the value of the deposit before the thief was found. [12]**Rather,** the law applies

BACKGROUND

חָלוּק הָיָה רַבִּי יוֹסֵי אַף בָּרִאשׁוֹנָה **Rabbi Yose disagreed even in the first Mishnah.** Occasionally the Mishnah presents a differing opinion which relates directly to the statement preceding it, but which seems to express a view that might also apply in earlier instances where it is not stated directly. In such cases it may be argued that the dissenting Sage waited until the other Sages had finished speaking before expressing his own opinion, which disagrees with all the rulings up to that point.

In the present example, Rabbi Yose asks: "How can that person do business with his fellow's cow?" Although this question refers to the present Mishnah, it could also apply to the first Mishnah of the chapter, which discusses a bailee who chooses to pay rather than take an oath, and who therefore receives the double payment made by a thief.

SAGES

רַבִּי אֶלְעָזָר **Rabbi Elazar (ben Pedat).** A Palestinian Amora of the second generation. See *Bava Metzia*, Part I, p. 103.

BACKGROUND

מָנֶה **Maneh.** The maneh was a coin worth a hundred dinarim. In order to estimate the value of a maneh, it should be borne in mind that the average daily wage for a worker was about four dinarim. Hence it would take a worker about a month to earn a maneh.

TRANSLATION AND COMMENTARY

once he says: "I am ready to pay," and he thereby acquires the right to the double payment, [1]**even if he did not** actually **pay** the owner before the thief was found. Thus, according to Rabbi Yoḥanan, the bailee should not actually have to pay in order to receive the double payment. His declaration of intent should be sufficient.

אֵימָא [2]The Gemara answers: It is necessary to amend the new statement attributed to Rabbi Yoḥanan as follows, and **say: Rabbi Yose agreed** with the first Tanna **in the first Mishnah,** [3]**because** the bailee has **already said: "I am ready to pay,"** and this is sufficient to entitle him to the double payment.

MISHNAH אָמַר לִשְׁנַיִם [4]**If someone said to two people: "I robbed one of you of a maneh,** [5]**but I do not know which of you** I robbed, and I want to make restitution to the person I robbed"; [6]**or** if someone said to two people: **"The father of one of you deposited a maneh with me,** [7]**but I do not know which** one it was," and the sons themselves have no knowledge of the matter, the law in both cases is as follows: [8]The robber/bailee must **give a maneh** to each of the two people, since it is otherwise impossible for him to be certain of fulfilling his duty. [9]The Mishnah adds that this law applies specifically **because** the robber/bailee **himself admitted** his liability. (The Gemara will explain below the significance of this clause.)

שְׁנַיִם שֶׁהִפְקִידוּ [10]The Mishnah now describes a somewhat different situation: If **two people deposited money with** a bailee, but **one** deposited a **maneh** (one hundred zuz), whereas **the other one** deposited **two hundred**

כֵּיוָן שֶׁאָמַר: ״הֲרֵינִי מְשַׁלֵּם״, [1]אַף עַל פִּי שֶׁלֹּא שִׁילֵּם.

[2]אֵימָא: מוֹדֶה הָיָה רַבִּי יוֹסֵי בָּרִאשׁוֹנָה, [3]שֶׁכְּבָר אָמַר ״הֲרֵינִי מְשַׁלֵּם״.

מִשְׁנָה [4]אָמַר לִשְׁנַיִם: ״גָּזַלְתִּי לְאֶחָד מִכֶּם מָנֶה, [5]וְאֵינִי יוֹדֵעַ אֵיזֶה מִכֶּם״, [6]אוֹ: ״אָבִיו שֶׁל אֶחָד מִכֶּם הִפְקִיד לִי מָנֶה, [7]וְאֵינִי יוֹדֵעַ אֵיזֶה הוּא״, [8]נוֹתֵן לָזֶה מָנֶה וְלָזֶה מָנֶה, [9]שֶׁהוֹדָה מִפִּי עַצְמוֹ.

[10]שְׁנַיִם שֶׁהִפְקִידוּ אֵצֶל אֶחָד,

LITERAL TRANSLATION

once he said: "I am ready to pay," [1]even if he did not pay, [the law applies].

[2]Say: Rabbi Yose agreed in the first [Mishnah], [3]for he already said: "I am ready to pay."

MISHNAH [4][If someone] said to two [people]: "I robbed one of you [of] a maneh, [5]but I do not know which of you," [6]or: "The father of one of you deposited a maneh with me, [7]but I do not know which one," [8]he gives this one a maneh and that one a maneh, [9]because he himself admitted.

[10]Two [people] who deposited [money] with one [person],

RASHI

משנה שהודה מפי עצמו – הואיל והודה מפי עלמו, ובגמרא מפרש טעמא מה הוא.

NOTES

אָבִיו שֶׁל אֶחָד מִכֶּם **The father of one of you.** The Rishonim ask: Why does the Mishnah speak of "the *father* of one of you" when discussing deposits, and "one of *you*" when discussing robbery?

Rabbenu Yehonatan points out that the Gemara understands the language of the Mishnah to mean that it is referring to a case where the robber/bailee comes forward of his own accord, and the claimants know nothing of the matter. Now, while it is possible for a victim of robbery to be unsure of the identity of the robber, it is unlikely that a depositor would forget the identity of the bailee who has his deposit. Hence, the Mishnah suggested a case where the depositor died without telling his heirs about the deposit.

HALAKHAH

גָּזַלְתִּי לְאֶחָד מִכֶּם מָנֶה וְאֵינִי יוֹדֵעַ אֵיזֶה מִכֶּם **I robbed one of you of a maneh, but I do not know which of you.** "If someone says to two people: 'I robbed one of you of a maneh, but do not know which of you it was,' he may simply put the maneh in front of them and have them divide it. But if he wants to fulfill his obligation towards Heaven and attain full atonement he must pay each of them a maneh. This applies if the two people themselves knew nothing of the matter and did not sue the robber. But if they both sued him, each one claiming that he was the victim, and the robber admits that he robbed someone, but denies that he robbed *both* of them, insisting he cannot recall which of them it was, then each claimant must swear that he was the victim, and the robber must reimburse each of them in full. Similarly, adds *Rema,* if he robbed one person of one maneh and another person of two hundred zuz, and does not remember whom he robbed of which amount, and they both demand two hundred zuz, he must pay each of them two hundred zuz." These rulings do not follow our Mishnah, which is in accordance with Rabbi Tarfon's view, but rather follow Rabbi Akiva, who disagrees with Rabbi Tarfon in *Yevamot* 118b. (*Shulḥan Arukh, Ḥoshen Mishpat* 365:2.)

שְׁנַיִם שֶׁהִפְקִידוּ אֵצֶל אֶחָד **Two people who deposited money with one person.** "If two people deposit money with a bailee, one depositing one maneh, and the other two hundred zuz, and later each one claims to have deposited two hundred zuz, while the bailee himself does not remember who deposited which amount, each depositor must swear that he deposited two hundred zuz, and the bailee must pay each of them in full. Thus, the bailee loses one maneh of his own money, since he was careless in not recording the depositors' names. If the depositors are themselves uncertain as to who deposited the two hundred zuz and who the one maneh, then, according to the letter of the law, the bailee need pay each of them only one maneh, placing the third in escrow — either in his

TRANSLATION AND COMMENTARY

zuz, and the bailee does not remember how much each one deposited, and later, when he wishes to restore the money to the depositors, [1]each **one says: "The two hundred are mine,"** [2]the law is as follows: **The bailee** must **give** one **maneh** to each of the two depositors, since it is clear that they are each entitled to at least that much, [3]**and the rest** — the third maneh which each claims belongs to him — **is left** until the parties come to an agreement, or indefinitely, **until** the Prophet **Elijah comes** and reveals the truth by his prophetic powers. [4]**Rabbi Yose** disagreed with the opinion of the first Tanna, and **said: If** one adopts the position of the first Tanna that each of the depositors receives a maneh, **what has the fraudulent** depositor **lost** by claiming the larger sum? The depositor of the smaller sum has nothing to lose by lying, since in any case he will get back the amount he deposited! This ruling, says Rabbi Yose, encourages dishonest people to claim the property of others in the hope of gaining some of it. [5]**Rather,** says Rabbi Yose, **the whole amount** — the entire three hundred zuz — **should be left** with the depositary (according to other opinions, with the court) **until** the Prophet **Elijah comes.** In this way the dishonest claimant may admit the truth to avoid losing the money that actually belongs to him.

וְכֵן שְׁנֵי כֵלִים [6]**Similarly,** if two people deposited **two utensils** with a bailee, **one worth** a **maneh** (one hundred zuz), and the other **worth a thousand zuz,** and the bailee does not remember which utensil was deposited by

זֶה מָנֶה וְזֶה מָאתַיִם, [1]זֶה אוֹמֵר: ״שֶׁלִּי מָאתַיִם״, וְזֶה אוֹמֵר: ״שֶׁלִּי מָאתַיִם״, [2]נוֹתֵן לָזֶה מָנֶה וְלָזֶה מָנֶה, [3]וְהַשְּׁאָר יְהֵא מוּנָּח עַד שֶׁיָּבֹא אֵלִיָּהוּ. [4]אָמַר רַבִּי יוֹסֵי: אִם כֵּן, מַה הִפְסִיד הָרַמַּאי? [5]אֶלָּא, הַכֹּל יְהֵא מוּנָּח עַד שֶׁיָּבֹא אֵלִיָּהוּ. [6]וְכֵן: שְׁנֵי כֵלִים, אֶחָד יָפֶה מָנֶה, וְאֶחָד יָפֶה אֶלֶף זוּז,

LITERAL TRANSLATION

this one a maneh and that one two hundred [zuz, [1]and] this one says: "The two hundred are mine," and that one says: "The two hundred are mine," [2]he gives this one a maneh and that one a maneh, [3]and the rest is left until Elijah comes. [4]Rabbi Yose said: If so, what has the deceiver lost? [5]Rather, everything should be left until Elijah comes.

[6]And similarly: Two utensils, one worth a maneh, and one worth a thousand zuz,

RASHI

זה אומר מאתים שלי — לאחר זמן, כשבאו ליטול פקדון. **מה הפסיד הרמאי** — אם כן לא יודה לעולם על האמת.

LANGUAGE

זוז Zuz. A zuz was the Hebrew name for the dinar. The source of the word is not clear, though in the Midrash Rabbah (Numbers, Chapter 22) the following explanation is given: "Earlier, they were called zuzim (זוזים), because they move (זָזִים) from one person to another." This may be more than a homily; it could be the source of the word, meaning money which is used in transactions, which passes from hand to hand.

CONCEPTS

עַד שֶׁיָּבֹא אֵלִיָּהוּ Until Elijah comes. The Prophet Malachi (3:23-24) writes that, before the coming of the Messiah, Elijah the Prophet will come and repair what needs to be repaired in the world. The use of the expression, "Until Elijah comes," therefore means that only when a true prophet comes, who will be able to see truths that are hidden from us, will doubt be resolved absolutely. Practically speaking, it means that the decision in the case is postponed indefinitely.

NOTES

נוֹתֵן לָזֶה מָנֶה וְלָזֶה מָנֶה וְהַשְּׁאָר יְהֵא מוּנָּח He gives this one a maneh and that one a maneh, and the rest is left. Since the third maneh's ownership cannot be determined, it is placed in escrow. *Ramban* objects: The two transactions are essentially separate. Each depositor demands two hundred zuz, and to each the bailee admits owing one hundred zuz, and expresses doubt about the remainder. Surely we have here a standard case of "partial admission" (מוֹדֶה בְּמִקְצָת)! Hence, the bailee should be required to take an oath to each depositor that he does not owe him more than one hundred, and since he cannot take such an oath, he should pay each of them in full, in accordance with the general rule that someone who cannot take an oath must pay.

Some Rishonim suggest that this Mishnah may be an illustration of the law of "here it is" (הֵילָךְ) discussed above (4a; see *Rashba*), or of the concept of "a supportive witness" (עד דמסייע) described in a note above (35b; see *Ritva*).

Ramban rejects these answers, and suggests that the rule that a defendant who admits part of a claim must take an oath applies only if it is possible that the disputed money is in his possession, as the oath may frighten him into admitting the truth. But here, the bailee puts all the money he owes on the table and absolutely denies owing any more. Hence, the rule does not apply.

Rashba points to the Gemara's explanation that the Mishnah refers to a situation where the bailee was under no obligation to remember who deposited what. Indeed, the Gemara compares it to a case of partners depositing three hundred zuz in one package. Hence the bailee is entitled to treat the two claims as one, and put the three hundred zuz on the table, refusing to get involved in the depositors' dispute.

HALAKHAH

own custody or, according to an opinion quoted by *Rema,* in the custody of the court. The money must remain in escrow indefinitely, or until the parties come to an agreement. However, if the bailee wishes to fulfill his obligation towards Heaven, he must in this case as well pay each depositor in full. If the two depositors brought their money together, in the same package, and each insists that he deposited two hundred zuz, then, according to the letter of the law, the bailee need only pay each of them one maneh, placing the third maneh in escrow." According to the *Shulḥan Arukh,* this lenient ruling applies even if he wishes to fulfill his obligation towards Heaven. Since the depositors themselves were not particular about keeping their deposits separate, the bailee is under no obligation to be more particular than they. *Rema,* however, quotes *Rosh,* who rules that if the depositors claim to be certain that the bailee owes each of them two hundred zuz, he must pay each of them in full if he wishes to fulfill his obligation towards Heaven. (*Shulḥan Arukh, Ḥoshen Mishpat* 300:1.)

שְׁנֵי כֵלִים, אֶחָד יָפֶה מָנֶה, וְאֶחָד יָפֶה אֶלֶף זוּז Two utensils, one worth a maneh and one worth a thousand zuz. "If two people each deposited a utensil with a bailee, and the

TRANSLATION AND COMMENTARY

which person, and when the depositors come to collect their utensils, [1]each **one says: "The good one** is mine," [2]the law is as follows: The bailee **gives the smaller** utensil **to one of** the depositors, [3]**and from the larger** utensil, which he sells, **he gives the value of the smaller one to the second** depositor (see note), since it is clear that they are each entitled to at least that much, [4]**and the rest** — the other nine hundred zuz — **is left until Elijah comes.** [5]Here, too, **Rabbi Yose** objected to the ruling **and said: If so, what has the fraudulent** depositor **lost** by claiming ownership of the more valuable article? [6]**Rather,** says Rabbi Yose, **everything** — both utensils — **should be left until Elijah comes,** so that the dishonest claimant will thereby be induced to admit the truth.

GEMARA אַלְמָא [7]The Gemara considers the first clause of the Mishnah: The Mishnah ruled that the robber must reimburse each of the two people to be certain of fulfilling his duty. **Thus,** the Gemara infers, we see that in a case of **doubt,** where a person is uncertain as to whom he must make payment, **we take away money** that belongs to him; [8]**we do not say** that he should only pay what he definitely owes — one hundred zuz — and **leave the** other **money in the possession of its**

[1]וְזֶה אוֹמֵר: ״יָפֶה שֶׁלִּי״, וְזֶה אוֹמֵר ״יָפֶה שֶׁלִּי״, [2]נוֹתֵן אֶת הַקָּטָן לְאֶחָד מֵהֶן, [3]וּמִתּוֹךְ הַגָּדוֹל נוֹתֵן דְּמֵי קָטָן לַשֵּׁנִי, [4]וְהַשְּׁאָר יְהֵא מוּנָּח עַד שֶׁיָּבֹא אֵלִיָּהוּ. [5]אָמַר רַבִּי יוֹסֵי: אִם כֵּן, מַה הִפְסִיד הָרַמַּאי? [6]אֶלָּא, הַכֹּל יְהֵא מוּנָּח עַד שֶׁיָּבֹא אֵלִיָּהוּ.

גמרא [7]אַלְמָא, מִסְּפֵיקָא מַפְּקִינַן מָמוֹנָא, [8]וְלָא אָמְרִינַן: אוֹקֵי מָמוֹנָא בְּחֶזְקַת מָרֵיהּ.

LITERAL TRANSLATION

[1]and this one says: "The good one is mine," and that one says: "The good one is mine," [2]he gives the smaller one to one of them, [3]and from out of the larger one he gives the value of the smaller one to the second, [4]and the rest is left until Elijah comes. [5]Rabbi Yose said: If so, what has the deceiver lost? [6]Rather, everything should be left until Elijah comes.

GEMARA [7]Thus, out of doubt we take money away, [8]and we do not say: Let the money stand in the possession of its owner.

RASHI

מתוך הגדול — ישברנו.

גמרא מספיקא מפקינן ממונא — דקתני: נותן לזה מנה ולזה מנה. ולא אמרינן — כשזה תובע וזה אומר ״איני יודע אם לך אם לחברך״, אוקי ממונא בחזקת נתבע זה, שלא נפסידנו ממונו ויהא מונח עד שיבא אליהו.

BACKGROUND

מִסְּפֵיקָא מַפְּקִינַן מָמוֹנָא Out of doubt we take money away. In monetary disputes as in many other legal situations, there is a general rule that one does not force litigants to change the existing situation without convincing reason, and this is the basis of the principle that "someone seeking to remove something from his fellow's possession must bring proof of ownership." In the case discussed in the Mishnah, it is clear that the defendant owes one maneh and no more. Nevertheless, he is ordered to pay a second maneh because he cannot say with certainty that he does not owe money to the second claimant. This seems to imply that whenever a defendant cannot deny a claim with certainty, he must pay.

NOTES

וּמִתּוֹךְ הַגָּדוֹל נוֹתֵן דְּמֵי קָטָן And from out of the larger one, he gives the value of the smaller one. Below (37b), the Gemara describes this ruling as involving the destruction of the larger vessel. Accordingly, *Rashi* explains that the bailee is actually expected to break the larger vessel, giving part of it to one claimant and placing the other part in escrow.

Many Rishonim find this explanation unacceptable. *Rashba* explains that the bailee sells the larger utensil and gives the claimant part of the money obtained, placing the rest in escrow. He explains the Gemara below (37b) as referring to the fact that the owner of the large vessel loses it permanently, and receives only money in return.

Meiri suggests that the vessel should be physically broken, so long as its value is substantially maintained. This applies, for example, where the "vessel" was a length of cloth or a metal bar. However, if it was an ordinary vessel which would be almost totally destroyed if broken, it should be sold as *Rashba* suggested.

אַלְמָא מִסְּפֵיקָא מַפְּקִינַן מָמוֹנָא Thus out of doubt we take money away. The question of the Gemara is presented as a contradiction between two clauses in the Mishnah. *Ramban,* however, points out that the idea of forcing a robber/bailee to pay in order to resolve all doubts is itself problematic, because the Halakhah follows Rabbi Yoḥanan and Rabbi Naḥman, who ruled (*Ketubot* 12b) that "certainty is no better than doubt" (בָּרִי וְשֶׁמָּא לָאו בָּרִי עֲדִיף). Thus if a plaintiff approaches a defendant and claims that he is owed money, bringing no proof, and the defendant declares that he does not know whether or not he owes him money, the defendant is exempt from paying. *Ramban* explains that the Gemara preferred to raise an objection based on a Mishnah rather than on an Amoraic ruling, and in fact all the answers of the Gemara — the fine imposed on the robber, the fine imposed on the careless bailee, and the idea of "fulfilling one's obligation towards Heaven" — treat this case as exceptional, and agree that the normative law is that a defendant need not pay in a case of doubt.

HALAKHAH

two utensils were not equal in value, and later each one claimed to have deposited the more expensive utensil, while the bailee does not remember who deposited which one, each depositor must swear that the more expensive utensil is his, and the bailee must pay each of them in full. He gives the more expensive utensil to one and the value of the more expensive utensil to the other, and keeps or sells the cheap utensil. But if the depositors were not particular and brought the utensils to the bailee in one package, the bailee need not pay them both in full. He gives the cheap utensil to one depositor, and sells the more expensive utensil, using the money to give the value of the cheap utensil to the other depositor. He then places the rest of the money in escrow." (*Shulḥan Arukh, Ḥoshen Mishpat* 300:2.)

TRANSLATION AND COMMENTARY

present **owner,** the robber himself. [1]**But** surely, says the Gemara, this ruling is in striking contradiction to the second case discussed in the same Mishnah. **Consider** the second case, says the Gemara, and **the contradiction** will immediately be apparent. The second case states: "If **two people** both **deposited money with** a bailee, but **one** deposited a **maneh,** [2]whereas **the other one** deposited **two hundred zuz,** and the bailee does not remember how much each one deposited, and later, when he wishes to restore the money to the depositors, [3]each **one says: 'The two hundred are mine,'** [4]the law is that **the bailee** must **give** one **maneh** to each of the two depositors, [5]**and the rest is left until Elijah comes."** From the second case discussed in the Mishnah we see that in a situation where a bailee is not certain whom to pay, we do not insist that he spend his own money. Rather, we allow him to pay only the amount definitely owed to each claimant, and the money in doubt — the third manch — is not paid. Surely this contradicts the first case!

אֲמַר לֵיהּ [6]The other Amoraim **said** in reply **to** the questioner: **Are you** seeking to **present a contradiction between** the second case, which involves **a deposit, and** the first, which involves **robbery?** The two cases cannot be compared. In principle, the court does not oblige a defendant to pay money in a case of doubt, but the Rabbis sometimes punished people for previous misbehavior, and required them to follow a stricter procedure. [7]Thus, **in the** first part of the Mishnah, which deals with a **case of robbery,** the robber had previously **committed a transgression.** [8]Therefore **the Rabbis fined him,** and insisted that he make restitution, even at the cost of spending his own money to repay two people, when he does not remember which of two people he robbed. [9]But **in the** second part of the Mishnah, which deals with a **case of a** bailee receiving a **deposit,** the bailee **did not commit a transgression** of any kind; he simply forgot who gave him which amount of money. [10]Therefore **the Rabbis did not fine him,** and instead applied the letter of the law whereby a court does not have the right to extract money from a defendant in a case where doubt exists.

וּרְמֵי פִּקָּדוֹן אַפִּקָּדוֹן [11]**But,** objects the Gemara, the answer just given is based on the fact that the two cases — robbery and deposit — are essentially different, and thus the laws in the two cases are different. This distinction, says the Gemara, is invalid, as it is possible to **point out** essentially the same **contradiction** using two clauses concerning **deposits,** [12]**and** similarly it is possible to **point out a contradiction** using two clauses concerning **robbery!**

[1]וּרְמִינְהִי: "שְׁנַיִם שֶׁהִפְקִידוּ אֵצֶל אֶחָד, [2]זֶה מָנֶה וְזֶה מָאתַיִם, [3]זֶה אוֹמֵר: 'שֶׁלִּי מָאתַיִם', וְזֶה אוֹמֵר: 'שֶׁלִּי מָאתַיִם', [4]נוֹתֵן לָזֶה מָנֶה וְלָזֶה מָנֶה, [5]וְהַשְּׁאָר יְהֵא מוּנָּח עַד שֶׁיָּבֹא אֵלִיָּהוּ".

[6]אֲמַר לֵיהּ: פִּקָּדוֹן אַגָּזֵל קָא רָמֵית? [7]גָּזֵל, דַּעֲבַד אִיסּוּרָא, [8]קְנָסוּהוּ רַבָּנַן. [9]פִּקָּדוֹן, דְּלָא עֲבַד אִיסּוּרָא, [10]לָא קְנָסוּהוּ רַבָּנַן.

[11]וּרְמֵי פִּקָּדוֹן אַפִּקָּדוֹן, [12]וּרְמֵי גָּזֵל אַגָּזֵל.

LITERAL TRANSLATION

[1]But raise a contradiction (lit., "cast them together"): "Two [people] who deposited [money] with one [person], [2]this one a maneh and that one two hundred [zuz], [3][and] this one says: 'The two hundred are mine,' and that one says: 'The two hundred are mine,' [4]he gives this one a maneh and that one a maneh, [5]and the rest is left until Elijah comes."

[6]He said to him: Are you presenting a contradiction from a deposit to robbery? [7][In the case of] robbery, where he committed a transgression (lit., "prohibition"), [8]the Rabbis fined him. [9][In the case of] a deposit, where he did not commit a transgression, [10]the Rabbis did not fine him.

[11]But raise a contradiction [from] deposit to deposit, [12]and raise a contradiction [from] robbery to robbery.

NOTES

גָּזֵל דַּעֲבַד אִיסּוּרָא קְנָסוּהוּ רַבָּנַן In the case of robbery, where he committed a transgression, the Rabbis fined him. *Rosh* asks: The Rabbis instituted the practice of treating thieves and robbers who wish to return stolen objects leniently, in order to encourage them to repent (תַּקָּנַת הַשָּׁבִים). They certainly never fined them or forced them to go beyond the letter of the law. Why does this practice not apply here?

Rosh answers that the practice of treating thieves leniently applies only to details that are unimportant to the victim, though important to the thief. For example, if it is possible, but difficult, for the thief to return the stolen object itself, we allow him to pay for it instead. However, our primary consideration is the welfare of the victim, and if leniency — or even the letter of the law — may result in his losing out altogether, as is the case in our Mishnah, we order the thief to go beyond the letter of the law. *Rosh* adds that in many texts the words "the Rabbis fined him" are omitted. Hence, it is possible that the practice of leniency would in fact apply here as well, were it not for the fact that the robber is coming forward of his own accord, as the Gemara explains below. But since the robber wants to make full atonement for his sins, he must remove all doubt that he has compensated his victim — not as a fine, but as an act of repentance.

TRANSLATION AND COMMENTARY

פִּקָּדוֹן אַפִּקָּדוֹן [1]The Gemara elaborates: A contradiction can be pointed out between cases involving **deposits as** follows: **The first clause** of our Mishnah **says:** [2]**"Or** if someone said to two people: **'The father of one of you deposited a maneh with me, but I do not know which** one it was,' [3]the bailee must **give a maneh** to each of the two people." This clause in our Mishnah indicates that not only a robber but also a bailee is obliged by the court to pay out of his own pocket, even though he was not guilty of any crime. [4]**But,** continues the Gemara, this stands in **contradiction** to the second clause of the Mishnah, which states: "If **two people deposited money** with a bailee, he pays only one maneh to each of the depositors, **etc."** For, as we have seen above, this clause indicates that the bailee is not obliged by the court to pay both claimants their full claim in a case where doubt exists, but to leave the decision regarding the third maneh in abeyance until the matter can be resolved by mutual agreement, or until the ultimate resolution of the dispute by the Prophet Elijah.

אָמַר רָבָא [5]**Rava said** in reply that the contradiction between the two "deposit" clauses can be resolved as follows: **In the first clause,** while it is true that the bailee was not guilty of a crime, he was guilty of improper behavior in not remembering who the depositor was. Hence, the case **is treated like** one where a bailee **had two amounts deposited with him** by two people **in two** separate **packages,** [6]**so that** the bailee **should have been careful** to record who gave him which package. If such a bailee was careless and failed to record the identity of the depositors, he must accept the consequences. Likewise, in the case described in the first clause, the bailee should surely have remembered the depositor's identity, since he received only one deposit. Hence, he must pay each of the claimants as a penalty for his carelessness. [7]**In the second clause,** by contrast, the case **is treated like** one where **two amounts** were **deposited with** the bailee by two partners **in one package.** [8]Obviously, in such a case, the bailee **did not need to be careful** about the precise ownership of the contents of the package. Likewise, in the case described in the second clause, we may say that the behavior of the depositors was such that the bailee was entitled not to be careful. [9]Thus, the situation may have been, **for example, that the two** depositors in the Mishnah **together deposited** the respective sums of money with the bailee **at the same time.** [10]Hence, the bailee **can say to them: "You yourselves were not particular about each other.** You deposited your money in each other's presence, and evidently trusted each other. [11]**Should I have been** more **particular** and less trusting than you were? I did not try to remember who deposited which sum, as I assumed that I could always ask you to identify your respective deposits." Therefore no penalty is imposed in this case, and the bailee is entitled to rely on the letter of the law; he is not required to pay more than he actually owes merely to fulfill his duty to both depositors. Thus there is no contradiction between the two "deposit" cases.

[1]פִּקָּדוֹן אַפִּקָּדוֹן, דְּקָתָנֵי רֵישָׁא: [2]״אוֹ: ׳אָבִיו שֶׁל אֶחָד מִכֶּם הִפְקִיד אֶצְלִי מָנֶה, וְאֵינִי יוֹדֵעַ אֵיזֶה הוּא׳, [3]נוֹתֵן לָזֶה מָנֶה וְלָזֶה מָנֶה״. [4]וּרְמִינְהִי: ״שְׁנַיִם שֶׁהִפְקִידוּ וכו׳״.

[5]אָמַר רָבָא: רֵישָׁא, נַעֲשָׂה כְּמִי שֶׁהִפְקִידוּ לוֹ בִּשְׁנֵי כְּרִיכוֹת, [6]דַּהֲוָה לֵיהּ לְמֵידַק. [7]סֵיפָא, נַעֲשָׂה כְּמִי שֶׁהִפְקִידוּ לוֹ בְּכֶרֶךְ אֶחָד, [8]דְּלָא הֲוָה לֵיהּ לְמֵידַק. [9]כְּגוֹן דְּאַפְקִידוּ תַּרְוַיְיהוּ בַּהֲדֵי הֲדָדֵי בְּחַד זִימְנָא, [10]דְּאָמַר לְהוּ: ״אַנְתְּ גּוּפַיְיכוּ לָא קְפַדִיתוּ אַהֲדָדֵי. [11]אֲנָא קְפֵידְנָא?״

LITERAL TRANSLATION

[1][From] deposit to deposit, as the first clause teaches: [2]"Or: 'the father of one of you deposited a maneh with me, but I do not know which one,' [3]he gives this one a maneh and that one a maneh." [4]But raise a contradiction: "Two [people] who deposited, etc."

[5]Rava said: [In the] first clause, it is treated as if they deposited with him in two packages, [6]so that he should have been careful. [7][In the] last clause, it is treated as if they deposited with him in one package, [8]so that he did not need to be careful. [9]For example, where the two of them deposited together at the same time, [10]so that he can say to them: "You yourselves were not particular about each other. [11]Should I have been particular?"

RASHI

רישא — דחד גברא הפקיד אצלו, והוה ליה כשנים שהפקידו אצלו בשני כריכות, כלומר, זה שלא בפני זה, דהוה ליה למידק מי הפקיד אצלו מנה, ומי מאתים. סיפא — שהפקידו לו שניהם זה בפני זה — הוה ליה כמי שנאמנים זה על זה להפקיד שני פקדונותם בצרור אחד, דלית ליה למידק מה יש לזה בתוכו ומה יש לחבירו, ואף על גב דלא כרך אחד הוה, מיהו כיון שהפקידו זה בפני זה — גילו דעתן שלא חשדו זה את זה, לומר שמא חבירו יתבע המאתים.

TRANSLATION AND COMMENTARY

וּרְמֵי גָּזֵל אַגָּזֵל [1]**But,** argues the Gemara, it is possible to **present** essentially the same **contradiction** between two laws involving **robbery: Here the Mishnah states:** [2]**"If someone said to two people: 'I robbed one of you of a maneh, but I do not know which of you** I robbed,' [3]**or** if someone said to two people: **'The father of one of you deposited a maneh with me, but I do not know which one** it was,' [4]the robber/bailee must **give a maneh** to each of the two people." This clause in our Mishnah indicates that the robber is obliged to spend his own money to be certain of fulfilling his duty to the true owner. [5]**But,** continues the Gemara, this **stands in contradiction** to the following Mishnah (*Yevamot* 118b): **"If someone robbed one of five people, and does not know which** of the five **he robbed,** [6]and **this one says: 'He robbed me,' and that one says 'He robbed me,'** [7]the robber may simply **leave the object between them and depart,** letting the claimants settle the matter among themselves. [8]**These are the words of Rabbi Tarfon,** but Rabbi Akiva disagrees." [9]**Thus,** argues the Gemara, we see that, according to Rabbi Tarfon, in a case where **doubt** exists, where a robber is not certain whom to pay, [10]**we do not take** his **money away,** insisting that he fulfill his duty at all costs, **and** in fact **we say** that he should pay only what he definitely owes; and we **leave the money** claimed by the other parties **in the possession of its** present **owner,** the robber. Does this not contradict our Mishnah?

וּמִמַּאי דְּמַתְנִיתִין [11]In presenting this contradiction, the Gemara has assumed that our Mishnah follows the view expressed by Rabbi Tarfon in *Yevamot*. The Gemara now challenges this assumption: **But from where do we know that our Mishnah here is in accordance with** the viewpoint of **Rabbi Tarfon?** Perhaps it is in accordance with that of Rabbi Akiva, who disagrees with Rabbi Tarfon in the Mishnah in tractate *Yevamot*, and is of the opinion that the robber must make restitution to each of the five claimants! Thus it is possible that the contradiction between the two Mishnayot is no more than a reflection of the difference of opinion between Rabbi Akiva and Rabbi Tarfon, with our Mishnah reflecting the opinion of Rabbi Akiva.

[1]וּרְמֵי גָּזֵל אַגָּזֵל: קָתָנֵי הָכָא: [2]"אָמַר לִשְׁנַיִם: 'גָּזַלְתִּי לְאֶחָד מִכֶּם מָנֶה, וְאֵינִי יוֹדֵעַ אֵיזֶה מִכֶּם', [3]אוֹ: 'אָבִיו שֶׁל אֶחָד מִכֶּם הִפְקִיד לִי מָנֶה, וְאֵינִי יוֹדֵעַ אֵיזֶה הוּא', [4]נוֹתֵן לָזֶה מָנֶה וְלָזֶה מָנֶה". [5]וּרְמִינְהִי: "גָּזַל אֶחָד מֵחֲמִשָּׁה, וְאֵינוֹ יוֹדֵעַ אֵיזֶה מֵהֶן גָּזַל, [6]זֶה אוֹמֵר: 'אוֹתִי גָּזַל', וְזֶה אוֹמֵר 'אוֹתִי גָּזַל', [7]מַנִּיחַ גְּזֵילָה בֵּינֵיהֶם וּמִסְתַּלֵּק. [8]דִּבְרֵי רַבִּי טַרְפוֹן". [9]אַלְמָא, מִסְּפֵקָא לָא מַפְּקִינַן מָמוֹנָא, [10]וְאָמְרִינַן: אוֹקִים מָמוֹנָא בְּחֶזְקַת מָרֵיהּ.
[11]וּמִמַּאי דְּמַתְנִיתִין דְּהָכָא רַבִּי טַרְפוֹן הִיא?

LITERAL TRANSLATION

[1]And raise a contradiction [from] robbery to robbery: Here it teaches: [2]"[If someone] said to two [people]: 'I robbed one of you [of] a maneh, but I do not know which of you,' [3]or: 'The father of one of you deposited a maneh with me, but I do not know which one,' [4]he gives this one a maneh and that one a maneh." [5]But raise a contradiction: "[If someone] robbed one of five [people], and he does not know which of them he robbed, [6][and] this one says: 'He robbed me,' and that one says: 'He robbed me,' [7]he leaves the robbed object between them and departs. [8]These are the words of Rabbi Tarfon." [9]Thus, out of doubt we do not take money away, [10]and we say: Let the money stand in the possession of its owner.

[11]But from where [do we know] that our Mishnah here is [in accordance with] Rabbi Tarfon?

RASHI

ומתניתין דהכא ממאי דרבי טרפון היא — דמקשי לך, דלמא רבי עקיבא היא, דפליג נמי בההיא ואומר: לא זו הדרך מוציאתו מידי עבירה עד שישלם גזילה לכל אחד ואחד.

BACKGROUND

גָּזַלְתִּי לְאֶחָד מִכֶּם מָנֶה I robbed one of you of a maneh. Such a mistake could arise in several ways: The robber may vaguely remember the victim's appearance, and then may find two people similar to the one he robbed, so that he is unable to determine which is the right one. Or the robber may have come upon two people walking together and taken property from them without knowing which of the two was its owner. This could also explain how he may have robbed one out of five people — where he came upon a group of people and took whatever he could.

SAGES

רַבִּי טַרְפוֹן Rabbi Tarfon. He was a priest who served in the Temple at the end of the Second Temple period. However, his main period of activity came later, to a large extent in association with Rabbi Eliezer and Rabbi Yehoshua. Rabbi Tarfon was wealthy and extremely generous. He seems to have been one of the first Sages to acknowledge the greatness of Rabbi Akiva. Although he was initially superior to the latter in wisdom and was probably older, he came to consider himself Rabbi Akiva's disciple. Rabbi Tarfon also trained a number of disciples, and we know that Rabbi Yehudah bar Il'ai was one of his students. His grandson was a Sage during the time of Rabbi Yehudah HaNasi.

NOTES

וּרְמֵי גָּזֵל אַגָּזֵל And raise a contradiction from robbery to robbery. The Jerusalem Talmud notes the same contradiction, and offers several other solutions. Among them: The Mishnah here is referring only to a case where the robber/bailee took a false oath that he did not steal anything. The law is that a perjurer of this type must repay the money he owes, add a fifth, and then bring a guilt-offering. But the robber/bailee does not know whom to pay. Hence, he must pay everyone before he can bring his sacrifice. But if the robber/bailee had not sworn falsely, Rabbi Tarfon would not have required him to pay out of his own pocket merely in order to resolve his doubt.

A second answer given by the Jerusalem Talmud is that in one of the two cases there were witnesses who testified that the robber robbed one of the claimants, without specifying which one. *Pnei Moshe* explains that there were witnesses in our case. Hence, the robber must pay both claimants, as each one has witnesses who lend a degree of support to his claim. *Korban HaEdah* explains that there were witnesses in the case in tractate *Yevamot*, and the robber was forced to surrender the object against his will, whereas in our case the robber confessed on his own to each of the claimants, and so generated a personal obligation to each of them.

[1]דְּקָתָנֵי עֲלָהּ דְּהַהִיא: ״מוֹדֶה רַבִּי טַרְפוֹן בְּאוֹמֵר לִשְׁנַיִם: [2]׳גָּזַלְתִּי לְאֶחָד מִכֶּם מָנֶה, וְאֵינִי יוֹדֵעַ אֵיזֶה מִכֶּם׳, [3]שֶׁנּוֹתֵן לָזֶה מָנֶה וְלָזֶה מָנֶה״.

[4]הָתָם דְּקָא תָּבְעֵי לֵיהּ; [5]הָכָא בְּבָא לָצֵאת יְדֵי שָׁמַיִם.

[6]דַּיְקָא נַמִי, דְּקָתָנֵי: ״שֶׁהוֹדָה מִפִּי עַצְמוֹ״. [7]שְׁמַע מִינָּהּ.

[8]אָמַר מָר: ״הָתָם דְּקָא תָּבְעֵי לֵיהּ״. [9]וְהַלָּה מַה טּוֹעֵן?

[10]רַב יְהוּדָה אָמַר רַב: הַלָּה שׁוֹתֵק. [11]רַב מַתְּנָה אָמַר רַב: הַלָּה [37B] צוֹוֵחַ.

[12]מַאן דְּאָמַר הַלָּה צוֹוֵחַ — אֲבָל שְׁתִיקָה כְּהוֹדָאָה.

LITERAL TRANSLATION

[1]Because it teaches in connection with that [Mishnah]: "Rabbi Tarfon admits [that] where [someone] says to two [people]: [2]'I robbed one of you [of] a maneh, but I do not know which of you,' [3]that he gives this one a maneh and that one a maneh."

[4]There [it refers to] where they claim from him; [5]here [it refers] to him coming to fulfill his obligation towards Heaven.

[6]It is also precise, for it teaches: "Because he himself admitted." [7]Conclude from it.

[8]The master said: "There [it refers to] where they claim from him." [9]And what does the other one claim?

[10]Rav Yehudah said in the name of Rav: The other one is silent. [11]Rav Matenah said in the name of Rav: The other one [37B] cries out.

[12][According to] the one who says [that] he cries out — but silence is like admission.

TRANSLATION AND COMMENTARY

דְּקָתָנֵי עֲלָהּ דְּהַהִיא [1]The Gemara answers: We must assume that our Mishnah is in accordance with Rabbi Tarfon, **because a Baraita** elaborating **on that Mishnah** in tractate *Yevamot* **says: "Rabbi Tarfon admits that where someone says to two people: [2]'I robbed one of you of a maneh, but I do not know which of you** it was,' [3]**he must give a maneh to each of the two people."** This is precisely the case described in our Mishnah, and thus there is a contradiction between the two rulings of Rabbi Tarfon.

הָתָם דְּקָא תָּבְעֵי לֵיהּ [4]The Gemara answers: There is a fundamental difference between the two cases. In the Mishnah in tractate *Yevamot,* **it refers to** a case **where** all five people **are claiming** money **from** the robber. Hence the burden of proof is upon the claimants, and the robber need pay only one maneh, according to the letter of the law. [5]But our Mishnah **here refers to** a case where the robber **is coming** forward of his own volition, and admitting what he has done, in order **to fulfill his obligation towards Heaven** to atone for his crime. Thus, he must be stricter with himself than the letter of the law and the rules of evidence require, in order to make sure that the person robbed is fully compensated.

דַּיְקָא נַמִי דְּקָתָנֵי [6]The Gemara notes: **The wording** of our Mishnah **also proves that this** is the correct explanation. **For** the Mishnah **states** that the robber must pay out of his own pocket **"because he** himself **admitted** his crime," and his purpose is to repent and make full restitution. [7]The Gemara concludes: It is indeed logical to **conclude from** the Mishnah's language that the explanation suggested above is correct, and the contradiction is satisfactorily reconciled.

אָמַר מָר [8]The Gemara now returns to one of the points mentioned in the previous passage in order to analyze it in greater detail: **The Sage** who answered the previous question **said** that the Mishnah in tractate *Yevamot* **refers to** a case **where** all five people **are claiming** property **from** the robber. [9]On this point the Gemara asks: **And what does the** robber **claim** in response, as a result of which the Mishnah decides that he must leave the object he took between the various claimants and depart?

רַב יְהוּדָה אָמַר רַב [10]**Rav Yehudah said in the name of Rav: The** robber **is silent.** [11]**Rav Matenah said in the name of Rav: The** robber [37B] **cries out,** protesting to each one: "I have never seen you before, and your claim has no basis."

מַאן דְּאָמַר [12]The Gemara notes: **According to** Rav Matenah, **who says that** the robber **cried out** in protest, Rabbi Tarfon's ruling applies only if he cried out; **but** if he had been silent, as Rav Yehudah suggested, he

RASHI

דקתני עלה דההיא כו׳ — אלמא: מודה רבי טרפון בהא, ומה שנא? ומשנינן **התם דקתבעי ליה** — והוא אין חפץ ליתן אלא מן הדין, ומספיקא לית לן לחיוביה לכל חד וחד. **הבא בבא לצאת ידי שמים** — מאליו בא לימלך מה יעשה ולא יענש, דהשתא ודאי אמרינן ידי שמים לא יצא עד שתתן לשניהם, שאם תהא מונחת עד שיבא אליהו — נמצא הנגזל מפסיד על ידך. **דיקא נמי** — דטעמא דמתניתין בבא לצאת ידי שמים, מן העונש, ולא מן הדין, מדתלי טעמא בהודה מפי עצמו, שלא היה אדם תובעו כלום, משמע שהוא בא לימלך. **הלה מה טוען** — לכל אחד, דקתני: מניח גזילה ביניהם ומסתלק. **צווח** — אמר לכל אחד: איני מכירך.

NOTES

שְׁתִיקָה כְּהוֹדָאָה **Silence is like admission.** The Rishonim note that even if silence is *like* admission, it is not exactly the same, and if a person who was initially silent later explains that he was silent because he was considering what

BACKGROUND

הָכָא בְּבָא לָצֵאת יְדֵי שָׁמַיִם **Here it refers to him coming to fulfill his obligation towards Heaven.** In order to repent fully for a robbery, it is not sufficient for the robber to give up what he has taken. He must seek out his victim (even traveling a considerable distance to do so) and place the goods in his hands. As long as the robber has not done this, he is not completely purified of the sin of robbery.

צוֹוֵחַ **He cries out.** Since we are discussing a case where two people demand the return of stolen goods, and nothing is said of the reaction of the person returning them, it is appropriate to clarify whether he is making a counter-claim (צוֹוֵחַ), or whether he has no need at all to make a claim.

שְׁתִיקָה כְּהוֹדָאָה **Silence is like admission.** Whenever a claim is advanced and someone who has an interest in the matter keeps silent, his silence is interpreted as acceptance of what has been said. This is not only true with regard to civil law, but also applies when someone hears remarks, such as insults to a third person, without contradicting them or protesting. In such a case he is regarded as agreeing with what has been said. Moreover, in cases where the claimant would have to prove his claim if the defendant denied it, if the defendant remains silent his silence is regarded as an admission; and in monetary matters the admission of a litigant is stronger than any other proof.

TERMINOLOGY

אָמַר מָר **It was said above** (lit., "the master said"). A term used to cite a passage from a Mishnah or a Baraita previously mentioned, which will now be elucidated at greater length by the Talmud (usually as a continuation of the previous discussion).

TRANSLATION AND COMMENTARY

would have had to reimburse all of them, as **silence** on his part would have been interpreted **as an admission** of the justice of all the claims made against him. [1]But **according to** Rav Yehudah, **who says that** Rabbi Tarfon's ruling applies even if the thief was **silent,** it is clear that **silence in this case is not** interpreted **as an admission** of guilt. The reason for the exceptional ruling is as follows: [2]It is **because** the robber **can say to** each of the claimants: "The reason **that I was silent** and did not react **to** the claims made by **each** of you was not because I admit your claims. It **was because I said** to myself: [3]**Perhaps this** particular claimant **is the** one whom I robbed. After all, I admit robbing one of you. I simply do not remember which of you it was! That is why I hesitated and remained silent."

אָמַר מָר [4]The Gemara now turns to another point mentioned in the previous passage in order to analyze it in greater detail: **It was stated above** in the quotation from the Mishnah in tractate *Yevamot*: "If someone robbed one of five people and does not know which one, he may simply **leave the robbed object** between the five claimants **and depart.**" [5]On this point the Gemara asks: **But** only one of the claimants is the true owner; the others are making false claims. If the robber simply abandons the object and leaves the claimants to divide it up, **they will each take** a share, **and leave** the true owner with no hope of recovering all his property! [6]**Surely** this is not even an acceptable way of returning a *lost* object, let alone a *stolen* one, as **Rabbi Abba bar Zavda said in the name of Rav** (above, 25b): [7]**In every case where** someone finds an unmarked object, and **we are in doubt** as to whether it was deliberately **placed** where it was found or was lost by its owner, **in the first instance** the finder **should not take** the object at all. It is preferable that he leave it where he found it, giving the owner the opportunity to recover it for himself. [8]**But if** the finder **did take it** for himself, **he should not return it** to anyone. In the absence of identifying marks on the object, its finder must hold on to it indefinitely, until someone produces witnesses that it belongs to him. Now, argues the Gemara, since a robber's responsibilities are no less than those of such a finder of an unmarked object, the robber should also retain the object until he receives clear proof of the rightful owner's identity.

[1]וּמַאן דְּאָמַר הַלָּה שׁוֹתֵק, שְׁתִיקָה דְּהָכָא לָאו כְּהוֹדָאָה הוּא. [2]מָצֵי אָמַר לֵיהּ: "הַאי דִּשְׁתִיקִי לְכָל חַד וְחַד דְּאָמִינָא: [3]דִּלְמָא הַאי הוּא".

[4]אָמַר מָר: "מַנִּיחַ גְּזֵילָה בֵּינֵיהֶם וּמִסְתַּלֵּק". [5]וְשָׁקְלִי לָהּ כּוּלְּהוּ וְאָזְלֵי? [6]וְהָאָמַר רַבִּי אַבָּא בַּר זַבְדָּא אָמַר רַב: [7]כָּל סָפֵק הִינּוּחַ, לְכַתְּחִילָּה לֹא יִטּוֹל, [8]וְאִם נָטַל, לֹא יַחֲזִיר.

LITERAL TRANSLATION

[1][According to] the one who says he is silent, silence here is not like admission. [2][For] he can say to him: "The [reason] that I was silent to each one [is] because I said: [3]Perhaps this is the one."

[4]The master said: "He leaves the robbed object between them and departs." [5]But do they all take it and leave? [6]But surely Rabbi Abba bar Zavda said in the name of Rav: [7][In] every [case of] doubtful placing, in the first instance he should not take [it], [8]but if he took [it], he should not return it.

RASHI

ושקלי ליה כולהו ואזלי — נמצא זה מוציא מידו כדי להפסיד הנגזל עולמית. **והאמר רבי אבא בר זבדא ספק הינוח** — מצא דבר שאין בו סימן בצד מקום שמשתמר קצת, דלא שכיחי אינשי דאזלי, ויש לספוקי שמא מדעת הונח שם לגניזה. **לכתחלה לא יטלנו** — המוצאו, שכשיבא בעליו לא ימצאנו וסימן אין בו שיכריז, לפיכך יניחנו זה ובעליו יבא ויטלנו, וכל שכן לודאי הינוח, כדתנן (בבא מציעא כה,ב): מצא כלי באשפה, מכוסה — לא יגע בו. **ואם נטל לא יחזיר** — ואם בא אחר ואמר "שלי הוא", וסימן אינו נותן בו — לא יחזירנו, שמא אינו שלו וסוף הבעלים לבוא ויביא עדים שהניחו שם, לפיכך יהא מונח ביד זה עד שיבא אליהו, דהאי "לא יחזיר" — לא שיהא שלו קאמר, דהא מעיקרא באיסורא אתא לידיה, אם הינוח הוא, אלמא: מידי דמספקא לן דמאן ניהו — צריך להניחו בידו מי שהוא עד שיתברר הדבר.

SAGES

רַבִּי אַבָּא בַּר זַבְדָּא Rabbi Abba bar Zavda. A Palestinian Amora of the second and third generations. See *Bava Metzia*, Part I, p. 192.

NOTES

response to give, we must accept his claim. What, then, is the basis of Rav Matenah's view that if the robber remains silent, he is considered to have made an admission?

Rosh answers that the difference of opinion between Rav Matenah and Rav Yehudah concerns a case where the robber remained silent and did not offer any explanation for his behavior. Rav Yehudah argues that, under the circumstances, we should interpret his silence as deliberation rather than admission, while Rav Matenah argues that we should not make such a claim on the robber's behalf, and in the absence of an express explanation of the silence, it must be considered an admission.

סָפֵק הִינּוּחַ Doubtful placing. Doubt as to whether an object was purposely placed where it was found is a subject that properly belongs in the laws of lost objects. If someone finds an object which may either be lost or purposely left where it was found, he is forbidden to take it. For if it was purposely left there and has no identifying mark, the person who left it will be unable to identify it if it is moved. However, if the finder *does* take it, either accidentally or purposely, he need not return it to that place, since it is not certain whether the object was left there deliberately or

BACKGROUND

נָפַל הַבַּיִת עָלָיו If the house fell upon him. Here we are considering the case of a widow or a divorcee with property of her own who had a childless son. According to the laws of inheritance, if the mother dies before her son, he inherits her property, and if he later dies childless, his paternal relatives inherit any property he owned, including the mother's property which he previously inherited. However, if the son dies before his mother, and she later dies without any other issue, her father's family inherits her estate. It makes no difference how little time passes between the death of the person bequeathing the estate and that of the heir. Even if the latter outlives the former by only a moment, the estate passes to the latter. In the present instance there is doubt as to who died first. Hence both the son's heirs and the mother's heirs advance claims to the mother's property.

LITERAL TRANSLATION

[1]Rav Safra said: [It means] "And he shall leave it." [2]Abaye said to Rava: Did Rabbi Akiva say: [3]"This way does not clear him of transgression until he repays the [value of the] robbed article to each and every one," [4]thus [implying that] out of doubt we take money away, [5]and we do not say: Let the money stand in the possession of its owner? [6]But raise a contradiction: [7]"[If] the house fell upon him

[1]אָמַר רַב סָפְרָא: ״וְיַנִּיחַ״. [2]אֲמַר לֵיהּ אַבַּיֵי לְרָבָא: מִי אָמַר רַבִּי עֲקִיבָא: [3]״לֹא זוֹ הַדֶּרֶךְ מוֹצִיאָתוֹ מִידֵי עֲבֵירָה עַד שֶׁיְּשַׁלֵּם גְּזֵילָה לְכָל חַד וְחַד״, [4]אַלְמָא מִסְּפֵיקָא מַפְּקִינַן מָמוֹנָא, [5]וְלָא אָמְרִינַן: אוֹקִים מָמוֹנָא בְּחֶזְקַת מָרֵיהּ? [6]וּרְמִינְהִי: [7]״נָפַל הַבַּיִת עָלָיו

RASHI

אמר רב ספרא ויניח — הא דקתני ״מסתלק״ — לאו דלישקלו אינהו וליזלו, ולא שיוליאנה מידו, אלא תהא מונחת בידו עד שיתברר הדבר, והאי ״מסתלק״ — סילוק הדין הוא ויניח גזילה בפניהם בבית דין, ויאמר: ברור של מי הוא, ויטול, ומסתלק מן הדין, והגזילה יניח בידו עד שיבא אליהו. **לא זו הדרך** — סיפא דגזל אחד מחמשה הוא ביבמות (קיח,ב). **נפל הבית עליו ועל אמו** — ואין ידוע איזה מת ראשון, והיו לאמו נכסים מבית אביה.

TRANSLATION AND COMMENTARY

אָמַר רַב סָפְרָא [1]**Rav Safra said** in reply: When Rabbi Tarfon ruled in the Mishnah that the robber may leave the object and "depart," he did not mean that he could leave the object in front of the claimants and simply walk away. Rather the Mishnah **means** that the robber **must leave** the stolen goods in the custody of the court and say: "I have returned the stolen item, and whoever can prove that it belongs to him may keep it." He may then "depart," as it were, and walk away from the case. He will have discharged his duty, since he does not know who the rightful owner is.

אֲמַר לֵיהּ אַבַּיֵי לְרָבָא [2]Up to this point in its discussion of the Mishnah in tractate *Yevamot*, the Gemara has focused its attention on the viewpoint of Rabbi Tarfon. It now moves on to discuss the viewpoint of Rabbi Akiva, who disagrees with Rabbi Tarfon in that Mishnah. Rabbi Akiva maintains that the robber must pay *each* of the claimants the amount he admits having stolen from *one* of them. On this point **Abaye said to Rava: Did Rabbi Akiva** really **say,** at the end of that Mishnah (*Yevamot* 118b): [3]**"The way** suggested by Rabbi Tarfon **does not clear** the robber **of transgression until he returns the** robbed article or makes payment according to **its worth to each and every one** of the five claimants"? [4]Surely this **implies that,** according to Rabbi Akiva, in a case where **doubt exists we take money away** from a defendant, [5]**and we do not say:** Let **the money,** the ownership of which is in doubt, **remain in the possession of its** present **owner,** the robber! [6]If this is indeed Rabbi Akiva's opinion, says Abaye, **it stands in** total **contradiction** to another ruling by Rabbi Akiva in a Mishnah (*Bava Batra* 158b). That Mishnah deals with a number of cases of doubtful inheritance, where two relatives are killed together, and the rights of the respective heirs depend upon who died first. In all these cases, Bet Shammai ruled that the two sets of heirs should divide the estate, as it is impossible to determine who died first, whereas Bet Hillel awarded the estate to the heirs of the party that was its original owner, as a doubtful claim cannot override their presumptive rights. [7]Abaye's objection is based on the last Mishnah in this series, which says: "If a **house fell upon** a man **and upon his mother,** and it is not clear who died first, a question arises regarding the mother's property; the son's property presents no difficulty, as a mother does not inherit her son's estate. If the mother died first, then her son automatically

NOTES

was lost; so once he has taken it, it is his property until proven otherwise.

Although the Halakhah here is dealing with a different subject, the basic assumption in the laws of lost objects can also be applied: If a person is not certain whether property belongs to him, he may not take it. Thus, since none of the claimants can prove that what was returned indeed belongs to him, all of them are forbidden to take the object, and are not permitted to divide it among themselves.

וְיַנִּיחַ And he shall leave it. In the case of a deposit, described in the Mishnah, there is a dispute among the Rishonim as to whether a deposit placed in escrow should be retained by the bailee himself or delivered to the court. In the case of theft, however, most Rishonim agree that the thief must deliver the stolen object to the court, since as long as the object is in his possession he has not fulfilled his obligation to return it (*Ra'avad*). *Rashi*, however, maintains that in this case as well, the thief retains the object in his custody.

מִי אָמַר רַבִּי עֲקִיבָא Did Rabbi Akiva say? Commenting on the Mishnah in tractate *Yevamot*, the Tosefta quotes two opinions: (1) Rabbi Shimon ben Elazar explains that Rabbi Akiva agrees with Rabbi Tarfon about the letter of the law, but argues that, with respect to fines, robbers should be treated more strictly. (2) The other opinion explains that Rabbi Akiva even disagreed with Rabbi Tarfon about the

HALAKHAH

נָפַל הַבַּיִת עָלָיו וְעַל אִמּוֹ If the house fell upon him and upon his mother. "If a house fell upon a man and upon his mother: If the mother died first, the son's heirs inherit everything, but if the son died first, the son's heirs only

TRANSLATION AND COMMENTARY

inherited all her property, and when he died a moment later, he in turn passed it on to *his* heirs on his father's side. On the other hand, if the son died first, then when his mother died a moment later, her property passed to *her* heirs on her father's side. [1]If it is impossible to determine who died first, **and the son's heirs say: 'The mother died first,** and her son inherited her property and we are his heirs,' [2]**and the mother's heirs say: 'The son died first.** He did not inherit her property, and it therefore belongs to us,' [3]the law is as follows: Both Bet Shammai **and** Bet Hillel, who disagree about the procedure to follow in the other cases, **agree that** in this case the two sets of heirs **divide** the disputed estate in accordance with Bet Shammai's rulings in the other cases. [4]**But Rabbi Akiva said:** Not so. Even **I admit in this case that the property** should not be divided, but should **remain in the possession of** the heirs of its original **owner**, as Bet Hillel ruled in the other cases." Thus we see that, according to Rabbi Akiva, money cannot be taken away from someone on the basis of a doubtful claim, and this surely contradicts his ruling in the Mishnah in tractate *Yevamot*!

אֲמַר לֵיהּ [5]Rava **said to** Abaye in reply: The rulings by Rabbi Akiva in the two Mishnayot do not contradict each other, because the cases are not comparable: **There**, in the case of the fallen house, **it is a case of** doubtful claims — **"perhaps versus perhaps,"** in Talmudic terminology. Neither of the two sets of heirs can claim any certainty about what actually happened. Their claims are strictly hypothetical ("maybe he died first"). Hence Rabbi Akiva sees no grounds for taking money away from its presumptive owner. [6]But **where a person robbed one of five people, it is a case of "certain versus perhaps"** — a definite claim opposed by a doubtful denial. Even though the robber is uncertain as to whom to repay, the five "victims" each claim to be certain that they were robbed! Four of them, of course, are lying, but from the robber's point of view, he is facing five independent, definite claims to which he has only doubtful answers. Hence Rabbi Akiva insists that he pay each one.

וְעַל אִמּוֹ, [1]יוֹרְשֵׁי הַבֵּן אוֹמְרִים: ׳הָאֵם מֵתָה רִאשׁוֹנָה׳, [2]וְיוֹרְשֵׁי הָאֵם אוֹמְרִים: ׳הַבֵּן מֵת רִאשׁוֹן׳, [3]אֵלּוּ וְאֵלּוּ מוֹדִים שֶׁיַּחֲלוֹקוּ. [4]וְאָמַר רַבִּי עֲקִיבָא: מוֹדֶה אֲנִי בְּזוֹ שֶׁהַנְּכָסִים בְּחֶזְקָתָן״.
[5]אֲמַר לֵיהּ: הָתָם שְׁמָא וְשֶׁמָּא.
[6]גָּזַל אֶחָד מֵחֲמִשָּׁה, בָּרִי וְשֶׁמָּא.

LITERAL TRANSLATION

and upon his mother, [1][and] the son's heirs say: 'The mother died first,' [2]and the mother's heirs say: 'The son died first,' [3]these and those agree that they divide. [4]And Rabbi Akiva said: I admit in this [case] that the property remains in its [presumptive] ownership."

[5]He said to him: There [it is a case of] "perhaps and perhaps."

[6][Where] a person robbed one of five [people], [it is a case of] "certain and perhaps."

RASHI

יורשי האם — משפחת בית אביה אומרים לקרובי הבן ממשפחת אביו, הבאים לירש את הבן. **הבן מת ראשון** — ולא ירש את אמו להוריש אתכם נכסים, אלא הבן מת ראשון, ואחר כך מתה אמו ואנו יורשים אותה (נכסיה). **ויורשי הבן אומרים האם מתה ראשונה** — וירשה בנה, ואחריה מת הבן, ואנו יורשין אותו. **אלו ואלו** — בית שמאי ובית הלל שנחלקו בנפילות אחרות בפרק ״מי שמת״, שבית שמאי אומרים: יחלוקו, ובית הלל אומרים: נכסים בחזקתן, כאן מודים שיחלוקו. **אמר רבי עקיבא מודה אני בזה** — אף על פי שאני משל בית שמאי, ואומר בשאר הנפילות יחלוקו — בזו אני מודה לבית הלל שהנכסים בחזקתן, ופליגי אמוראי בחזקת מי, והתם מפרש טעמא. **שמא ושמא** — שניהם מכח שמא באים, הלכך נכסים בחזקתן. **הכא ברי ושמא** — כל אחד ואחד אומר ״אותי גזל״, היינו טענת ודאי, וזה אומר ״איני יודע״, וברי עדיף משמא.

BACKGROUND

שֶׁהַנְּכָסִים בְּחֶזְקָתָן That the property remains in its presumptive ownership. In tractate *Bava Batra* (158b), where the main discussion of this ruling is found, the Amoraim are divided regarding the Halakhic significance of the expression בְּחֶזְקָתָן — "in its presumptive ownership" — for it appears that there is no presumptive owner of this property. Some authorities take the position (which is followed by the Halakhah) that the property is regarded as being in the mother's possession. Since there was no proof that her son outlived her to inherit it, and during the mother's lifetime this property belonged to her tribe's lands (and its members are her legal heirs), the property is not removed from their possession. Others argue that the property is presumed to belong to the son's heirs, because while he and his mother were both alive, he was the heir whose rights preceded all others, and that situation has not been altered. Therefore *his* heirs should inherit the property.

בָּרִי וְשֶׁמָּא Certain and perhaps. The Halakhah distinguishes between two kinds of claims: The first is טַעֲנַת בָּרִי — a "certain" claim — in which it is clear to the claimant that the situation is as he represents it. The other type of claim is טַעֲנַת שֶׁמָּא — a "perhaps" claim — in which the claimant states that the case *may* be as he represents it. A "perhaps" claim is one advanced by a claimant in his own favor, although he is not entirely certain that the situation is as he represents it. Halakhically, in the absence of other proof, a "certain" claim is superior to other types of claim. For, although it does not have a greater power of proof, since the claimant may be lying, in any event the claim has not been refuted. Therefore preference should be given to a "certain" claim. On the other hand, when we have two conflicting "perhaps" claims, in which both litigants advance arguments in their own favor, although neither can state his case with certainty, neither claim has a prima facie advantage over the other.

NOTES

letter of the law. According to this interpretation of Rabbi Akiva, a buyer, for example, who does not remember from whom he bought an item, must also pay all the claimants. Now, from the fact that Abaye and Rava are comparing Rabbi Akiva's ruling about a robber to his ruling about inheritance, it is clear that they follow the second opinion in the Tosefta, since according to Rabbi Shimon the case of robbery is unique. Hence, since many Rishonim rule like Rabbi Shimon, this entire passage of the Gemara may have no Halakhic significance (*Ramban*, *Rashba*).

בָּרִי וְשֶׁמָּא Certain and perhaps. The Rishonim ask: The distinction between "certain" and "perhaps" is obvious. How then could Abaye compare the Mishnah in tractate *Yevamot* with that in tractate *Bava Batra*?

Rashba answers that Abaye's question about the Mishnah in *Yevamot* was merely leading up to his real question, from our Mishnah.

מוֹדֶה אֲנִי I admit. Since Rabbi Akiva's ruling in favor of Bet Hillel is called an "admission," it would appear that in other cases he ruled in accordance with Bet Shammai. *Rashi*

HALAKHAH

inherit his property, while the mother's heirs inherit her property. If it is impossible to determine who died first, and the son's heirs claim that the mother died first, while the mother's heirs claim that the son died first, the mother's estate goes entirely to her heirs, as the mother's family and tribe are deemed to have a presumptive right to her property until proven otherwise," following the ruling of Rabbi Akiva and the conclusion of the Gemara in *Bava Batra*. (*Shulḥan Arukh*, *Ḥoshen Mishpat* 280:10.)

TRANSLATION AND COMMENTARY

וְהָא מַתְנִיתִין [1]Abaye objects: According to the answer you have just given, Rabbi Akiva maintains that where the case is one of conflicting doubtful claims, the money claimed is left in the possession of the defendant. **But surely our Mishnah here says: "If someone said to two people: 'I robbed one of you of a maneh.'"** [2]Now the case in our Mishnah, when the robber does not know whom he has robbed and each of the two people addressed by the robber does not know whether he was the robber's victim, **is a case of "perhaps versus perhaps,"** just like the Mishnah in tractate *Bava Batra.* [3]And nevertheless the Mishnah **says: "He gives a maneh to each of them."** Hence we see that in a case of doubt Rabbi Akiva *does* take money away from its owner, even where it is a case of "perhaps versus perhaps"!

[1]וְהָא מַתְנִיתִין דְּהָכָא: ״אָמַר לִשְׁנַיִם: ׳גָּזַלְתִּי לְאֶחָד מִכֶּם מָנֶה״, [2]דְּשֶׁמָּא וְשֶׁמָּא הוּא, [3]וְקָתָנֵי: ״נוֹתֵן לָזֶה מָנֶה וְלָזֶה מָנֶה״!

[4]וּמִמַּאי דְּרַבִּי עֲקִיבָא הִיא? [5]דְּקָתָנֵי עֲלָהּ דְּהַהִיא: ״מוֹדֶה רַבִּי טַרְפוֹן בְּאוֹמֵר לִשְׁנַיִם: [6]׳גָּזַלְתִּי לְאֶחָד מִכֶּם מָנֶה וְאֵינִי יוֹדֵעַ אֵיזֶה מִכֶּם׳ כו׳״. [7]לְמַאן מוֹדֶה? לָאו לְרַבִּי עֲקִיבָא בַּר פְּלוּגְתֵּיהּ?

[8]וּמִמַּאי דְּשֶׁמָּא וְשֶׁמָּא הוּא? [9]חֲדָא, דְּלָא קָתָנֵי: ״תּוֹבְעִין אוֹתוֹ״.

LITERAL TRANSLATION

[1]But surely our Mishnah here [says]: "[If someone] said to two [people]: 'I robbed one of you [of] a maneh,'" [2]which is [a case of] "perhaps and perhaps," [3]and it teaches: "He gives this one a maneh and that one a maneh"!

[4]And from where [do we know] that it is Rabbi Akiva?

[5]For it teaches in connection with that [Mishnah]: "Rabbi Tarfon admits [that] where [someone] says to two [people]: [6]'I robbed one of you [of] a maneh, but I do not know which of you,' etc." [7]To whom does he admit? Is it not to Rabbi Akiva, his disputant?

[8]And from where [do we know] that it is [a case of] "perhaps and perhaps"?

[9]One, because it does not teach: "They claim [money from] him."

RASHI

עלה דההיא — דגזל אחד מחמשה.

חדא דלא קתני — מתניתין "תובעין אותו", דלא קתני "אותי גזל".

וּמִמַּאי דְּרַבִּי עֲקִיבָא הִיא [4]Abaye's objection is based on two assumptions: (1) that our Mishnah reflects the viewpoint of Rabbi Akiva, and (2) that the claims of the two sides to the dispute — the robber and the robbed — are both doubtful. The Gemara will now challenge and justify these two assumptions: **But,** the Gemara asks, **from where do we know that** our Mishnah reflects the viewpoint of **Rabbi Akiva?**

דְּקָתָנֵי עֲלָהּ דְּהַהִיא [5]The Gemara answers: **Because a Baraita** elaborating **on that Mishnah** in tractate *Yevamot* **says: "Rabbi Tarfon admits that where someone says to two people: [6]'I robbed one of you of a maneh, but I do not know which of you it was,'** he must pay both of them," and this is precisely the case described in our Mishnah. [7]Now, **to whom does** Rabbi Tarfon **admit?** Is it **not to Rabbi Akiva, his opponent** on this question? Hence, it is clear that our Mishnah reflects the viewpoint of Rabbi Akiva, and it must, therefore, be compatible with Rabbi Akiva's ruling in tractate *Bava Batra.* We thus see that the first assumption underlying Abaye's objection is justified.

וּמִמַּאי דְּשֶׁמָּא וְשֶׁמָּא הוּא [8]The other assumption underlying Abaye's objection is that our Mishnah is dealing only with doubtful claims. **But,** asks the Gemara, **from where do we know that** our Mishnah is referring to **a case of "perhaps versus perhaps,"** in which the claims of both sides to the dispute are doubtful? Is it not possible that we are dealing with a case where the "victims" claim to be certain that they were robbed by the robber, and this is the reason he is obliged to reimburse them both!

חֲדָא, דְּלָא קָתָנֵי [9]The Gemara now gives two reasons why the assumption that our Mishnah is dealing with hypothetical claims is correct: (1) **Firstly, because the Mishnah does not say** that the two victims are **claiming money from** the robber. On the contrary, it says that the robber came forward on his own. This

NOTES

explains that Rabbi Akiva was of the school of Bet Shammai. The Rishonim object, noting that from many sources it is clear that Rabbi Akiva was a follower of Bet Hillel. They explain that Rabbi Akiva normally ruled in accordance with Bet Hillel, but in the "fallen house" cases he ruled in accordance with Bet Shammai. Alternatively, it is possible that the word "admit" should not be taken literally here, and was used for stylistic reasons, since the previous line of the Mishnah says "Bet Hillel admitted to Bet Shammai." According to this explanation, Rabbi Akiva was simply stating that the Halakhah follows Bet Hillel in this case as in the other cases (*Tosafot, Rosh,* and others).

[1]וְעוֹד: הָא תָּנֵי רַבִּי חִיָּיא: [2]״זֶה אוֹמֵר: ׳אֵינִי יוֹדֵעַ׳, [3]וְזֶה אוֹמֵר: ׳אֵינִי יוֹדֵעַ׳״.

[4]הָא אוֹקִימְנָא לָהּ בְּבָא לָצֵאת יְדֵי שָׁמַיִם.

[5]אֲמַר לֵיהּ רָבִינָא לְרַב אַשִׁי: [6]וּמִי אָמַר רָבָא כָּל בִּשְׁתֵּי כְרִיכוּת הֲוָה לֵיהּ לְמֵידַק? [7]וְהָאָמַר רָבָא — וְאִי תֵּימָא רַב פַּפָּא — [8]הַכֹּל מוֹדִים בִּשְׁנַיִם שֶׁהִפְקִידוּ אֵצֶל רוֹעֶה, [9]שֶׁמַּנִּיחַ רוֹעֶה בֵּינֵיהֶן וּמִסְתַּלֵּק.

LITERAL TRANSLATION

[1]And furthermore: Surely Rabbi Ḥiyya taught: [2]"This one says: 'I do not know,' [3]and that one says: 'I do not know.'"

[4]Surely we explained it [as referring] to [someone] coming to fulfill his obligation towards Heaven.

[5]Ravina said to Rav Ashi: [6]But did Rava say that [in] any [case of] two packages he must be careful? [7]But surely Rava — and some say Rav Pappa — said: [8]All agree in [a case where] two [people] deposited [lambs] with a shepherd, [9]that the shepherd leaves [the lambs] between them and departs.

TRANSLATION AND COMMENTARY

suggests that the victims themselves were not certain about the matter. [1](2) **Furthermore: Surely Rabbi Ḥiyya quoted** the following authoritative **Baraita** explaining our Mishnah: [2]"**If** a robber said to two people: 'I robbed one of you but I do not remember which one,' [3]and in response both victims **said: 'I do not know** if I was the one whom you robbed or not,' the robber must pay both of them." Thus the Baraita, and by implication our Mishnah, is clearly referring to a case where both parties to the dispute are uncertain about their claims, and therefore Abaye's objection is well founded. How, then, are we to reconcile the ruling of Rabbi Akiva in our Mishnah with his ruling in the Mishnah in tractate *Bava Batra* — that property is not taken from its present owner to satisfy a doubtful claim?

הָא אוֹקִימְנָא לָהּ [4]The Gemara answers: **Surely we** have already **explained,** when discussing Rabbi Tarfon's view (above, 37a), that our Mishnah **is referring to** a case where the robber **is coming** forward voluntarily **to fulfill his obligation towards Heaven,** and this explanation can be applied to Rabbi Akiva's viewpoint as well. Thus, even according to Rabbi Akiva, a robber need not pay both claimants according to the letter of the law unless they make a definite claim. (According to Rabbi Tarfon, he need not pay even then.) However, if a robber wants to fulfill his duty towards Heaven, both Rabbi Akiva and Rabbi Tarfon agree that he must repay both parties, even if they do not know for certain that they are entitled to be repaid.

אֲמַר לֵיהּ רָבִינָא [5]The Gemara now reconsiders a point mentioned previously (above, 37a): Rava explained there that when two people deposit two different sums of money in two separate packages, the bailee must take care to remember who deposited which package; if he forgets, he is considered negligent, and must pay both depositors the larger amount, providing the additional sum out of his own pocket. On this point **Ravina said to Rav Ashi:** [6]**But did Rava say** that a bailee **must be careful in any case** where deposits were handed over in **two** separate **packages?** [7]**But surely Rava — and some say Rav Pappa — said** (*Bekhorot* 18b): [8]**Both** Rabbi Tarfon and Rabbi Akiva **agree** that **in a case where two people deposit lambs with a shepherd,** one depositing one lamb and the other depositing two, and later the shepherd cannot remember which lambs belong to which depositor, and the owners each claim that they deposited two, [9]**the shepherd may** simply **leave** the three lambs **between** the two claimants **and depart,** as it is not his responsibility to determine ownership! Why should this not be considered a case of "separate packages" (see note), and the shepherd be required to give two lambs to each claimant?

RASHI

הכי גרסינן: ועוד הא תני רבי חייא זה אומר איני יודע וזה אומר איני יודע — ולא גרסינן: יחלוקו, והכי פירושו: ועוד, הא תני רבי חייא להך מתניתא ד״גזלתי את אחד מכם״ בתוספתא דיליה, ותני לה הכי: אמר לשנים גזלתי אחד מכם ואיני יודע איזהו, זה אומר איני יודע וזה אומר איני יודע — נותן לזה מנה כו׳, כדקתני במתניתין, אלמא: בשמא ושמא עסקינן. **הכל מודים בשנים שהפקידו כו׳** — גבי פלוגתא דרבי טרפון ורבי עקיבא איתמר, במסכת בכורות (יח,ב): שנים שהפקידו זה טלה אחד וזה שנים, זה אומר שנים שלי, וזה אומר שנים שלי, והתם שתי כריכות נינהו, ואפילו הפקידו זה בפני זה — דבר הנראה הוא מי מביא אחד ומי מביא שנים, דבשלמא גבי כריכות מעות, הואיל דאלו ואלו צרורין — הוא שוכח מי הפקיד אצלו צרור גדול ומי צרור קטן, הואיל והפקידו אצלו יחד אבל גבי טלאים — מילתא מוכחת טפי.

NOTES

בִּשְׁנַיִם שֶׁהִפְקִידוּ אֵצֶל רוֹעֶה **In a case where two deposited lambs with a shepherd.** Our commentary follows *Rashi,* who explains that the case of the shepherd is exactly parallel to the case of the three manehs in our Mishnah: One person

HALAKHAH

בִּשְׁנַיִם שֶׁהִפְקִידוּ אֵצֶל רוֹעֶה **In a case where two people deposited lambs with a shepherd.** "If two people each deposited an animal with the same shepherd and one of the animals died, and the shepherd does not remember whose

BACKGROUND

כְּשֶׁהִפְקִידוּ בְּעֶדְרוֹ שֶׁל רוֹעֶה שֶׁלֹּא מִדַּעְתּוֹ **Where people deposited the lambs in the shepherd's flock without his knowledge.** Naturally the Gemara is not referring to people who have brought animals to a shepherd entirely without his knowledge and consent, for in such a case he would not even be regarded as an unpaid bailee. The case here is of a shepherd, hired by the townspeople, whose job was to pasture the animals belonging to them all. The shepherd leads the flock outside the town and tends it there, bringing the animals back to town in the evening. Once in town, each animal returns to its owner by itself. In the case under discussion, two townsmen brought their animals to the pasture without telling the shepherd they had done so. Hence the shepherd has no obligation to ascertain which of the two men's animals died, or which owner brought him two animals.

TERMINOLOGY

צְרִיכָא **It is necessary.** The placing of this term at the end of a sentence indicates the end of an explanation or hypothesis intended to show why it was necessary to mention two different instances when they express the same principle. If the explanation is satisfactory, the Gemara concludes by saying צְרִיכָא, meaning it was indeed necessary to state both cases.

LITERAL TRANSLATION

[1]He said to him: There [it refers to a case] where [people] deposited [the lambs] in the shepherd's flock without his knowledge.

[2]"And similarly: Two utensils, one worth a maneh and one worth a thousand zuz, etc." [3]And it is necessary [to state both]. [4]For if he had [only] taught us that first [case], [5][we might have thought that] the Sages stated [their ruling] in that [case] because there is no loss. [6]But in this [case], where there is a loss for [the owner of] the bigger [utensil], [7]say: They agree with Rabbi Yose.

[1]אָמַר לֵיהּ: הָתָם כְּשֶׁהִפְקִידוּ בְּעֶדְרוֹ שֶׁל רוֹעֶה שֶׁלֹּא מִדַּעְתּוֹ.

[2]"וְכֵן: שְׁנֵי כֵלִים, אֶחָד יָפֶה מָנֶה, וְאֶחָד יָפֶה אֶלֶף זוּז, כו'".

[3]וּצְרִיכָא. [4]דְּאִי אַשְׁמוּעִינַן הָךְ קַמַּיְיתָא, [5]בְּהַהִיא קָאָמְרִי רַבָּנַן מִשּׁוּם דְּלֵיכָּא פְּסֵידָא. [6]אֲבָל בְּהָא, דְּאִיכָּא פְּסֵידָא דְּגָדוֹל, [7]אֵימָא: מוֹדוּ לֵיהּ לְרַבִּי יוֹסֵי.

RASHI

פסידא דגדול — של כלי גדול שמשברוהו, וכשיבא אליהו ויאמר של מי הוא — נמצא מפסיד בשבירתו.

TRANSLATION AND COMMENTARY

אָמַר לֵיהּ [1]Rav Ashi said to Ravina in reply: Rava (or Rav Pappa) understands **the case there** to be **referring** to a situation **where people deposited the lambs in the shepherd's flock without his knowledge.** Only because the circumstances were such is the shepherd not obliged to determine who the depositors were and how much they deposited.

וְכֵן שְׁנֵי כֵלִים [2]The Gemara now considers the next clause of the Mishnah: "**And similarly** if two people deposited **two utensils** of differing value with a bailee, **one worth a maneh and the other worth a thousand zuz,** the law is the same as in the previous clause, which dealt with deposits of money." [3]The Gemara notes: **It was necessary to state both** these clauses, even though the principle involved is identical. [4]**For if the Mishnah had** only **taught us** the difference of opinion between the Sages and Rabbi Yose in **the first case,** about money, [5]**we might have thought that** it was only **in that case** that **the Sages stated their ruling** that the bailee pays each depositor one maneh and places the third in escrow, **because** the true owner of the larger deposit suffers **no** irreparable **loss;** the third maneh is safe in the bailee's hands, and will remain there until the identity of its owner is established. [6]**But in the case** of the utensils, the true **owner of the more valuable utensil** suffers an irreparable **loss** if we apply the principle of the "three manehs," since it is impossible to give each depositor the value of the less valuable utensil without breaking, or at least selling, the more valuable one. [7]Therefore, we might have **said** that in this latter case the Sages **agree with Rabbi Yose**, and both utensils should be placed in escrow until Elijah comes.

NOTES

gave the shepherd one lamb, and the other gave him two lambs, and later the shepherd forgot who gave him one and who two. In such a case, even if the two people approached the shepherd at the same time, the shepherd had no excuse for not noticing who brought what, as the difference between two lambs and one is obvious and unmistakable. Hence the Gemara's suggestion that Rava's lenient ruling about lambs contradicts his strict ruling about money.

The Rishonim found this explanation unsatisfactory, because there is no indication, either in our Gemara or in tractate *Bekhorot*, that Rava is referring specifically to such a case. All Rava says is "two people who deposited with a shepherd," and there are many situations fitting that description which would not contradict Rava's ruling here. In fact, *Rashi* himself, in *Bekhorot* 18b, explains that Rava is referring to a case where each depositor deposited only one animal, and then one of the animals died. According to that explanation — by far the best in the context of the passage in *Bekhorot* — it was quite reasonable for the shepherd not to know whose lamb died, as lambs look very much alike. Hence, it is not at all clear why our Gemara should consider the case of the lambs to be a case of two packages.

Accordingly, *Tosafot* and *Ramban* explain that every shepherd is considered to be like a bailee who has received two packages, regardless of how the animals were actually delivered, for the following reasons: It is quite difficult to tell animals apart, yet the difference in value between two similar-looking animals is frequently significant. Moreover, it is not uncommon for an animal to die, and shepherds must be prepared for such a contingency. Also, sheep are pastured in the open, not locked away out of sight. Hence the owner can assume that everyone knows his sheep were left with this particular shepherd. Thus his willingness to deposit his animals at the same time as someone else can in no way be interpreted as showing trust. Therefore, a shepherd who fails to note from the outset which animal belongs to which owner has no more excuse for his negligence than does a bailee who fails to identify the owners of two deposits left in two packages.

HALAKHAH

animal it was, he must reimburse both owners. (The same law applies if the animals were worth different amounts and the shepherd did not remember to whom to return which animal — *Sma.*) If the deposit was made without the shepherd's knowledge, he may leave the remaining animal in front of the depositors and depart. The animal remains there until one of the depositors admits it was not his, or until they both agree to divide it," following Rava's opinion according to the conclusion of the Gemara. (*Shulḥan Arukh, Ḥoshen Mishpat* 300:4.)

TRANSLATION AND COMMENTARY

[1]Conversely, if the difference of opinion between the Sages and Rabbi Yose **had been stated in the case** of utensils alone, [2]**we might have thought that Rabbi Yose stated his ruling** only **in that case,** so as to avoid irreparable loss to the true owner, [3]**but in the** "money" **case** we might have **said** that **he agrees with the Sages,** and is of the opinion that the bailee must pay each depositor one maneh. [4]**Therefore it was necessary to state both** rulings in order to tell us that irreparable loss is not the consideration in this matter, and the argument applies equally to utensils and to money.

[38A] וְהָא טַעְמָא דְּרַבִּי יוֹסֵי

[5]**But,** the Gemara asks, **surely the reason for Rabbi Yose's ruling** is expressly stated in the Mishnah: **It is because** Rabbi Yose wants to cause **the** fraudulent depositor **a loss,** so as to encourage him to abandon his claim! Since this is Rabbi Yose's reason, what difference is there between the case of the utensils and the case of the money? Why should we imagine that Rabbi Yose would agree with the Sages' ruling in the case of money? It is still necessary to place *all* the money in escrow to deter fraudulent claims. Thus the case of the money is superfluous both according to the Sages and to Rabbi Yose. According to the Sages, it can be inferred *a fortiori* from the case of utensils. According to Rabbi Yose, the argument that applies to utensils also applies to money.

אֶלָּא [6]**Rather,** says the Gemara, we must explain the repetition in the Mishnah in a different way: **Both** clauses **are needed** in order to clarify the position of **the Sages**: The second clause is needed for the reason explained above, [7]and the first clause was included because **the Mishnah** was written in the style called **"not only this but also this"** — a stylistic convention used frequently in the Mishnah. Using this style, a Mishnah often begins by mentioning a simple, relatively obvious matter, and from there proceeds to a more complicated subject. Since the second law is an elaboration of the first, it is pointless to ask what is the need for the first law in the light of the second. Thus, having first told us that the Sages reject Rabbi Yose's argument and insist that the bailee pay the depositors whatever he can, it still needs to tell us that they apply this argument even to cases involving irreparable damage to the deposit.

MISHNAH הַמַּפְקִיד פֵּירוֹת [8]**If someone deposits fruit with another person,** the bailee has no right to take the fruit for any reason whatsoever. **Even if** the fruits **are becoming ruined** because of decomposition or vermin, [9]the bailee must **not touch them** or sell them without the owner's express permission.

[1]וְאִי אִתְּמַר בְּהָא, [2]בְּהָא קָאָמַר רַבִּי יוֹסֵי, [3]אֲבָל בְּהַךְ אֵימָא: מוֹדֵי לְהוּ לְרַבָּנַן. [4]צְרִיכָא.

[38A] [5]וְהָא טַעְמָא דְּרַבִּי יוֹסֵי מִשּׁוּם הֶפְסֵד הָרַמַּאי הוּא.

[6]אֶלָּא, תַּרְוַיְיהוּ לְרַבָּנַן אִיצְטְרִיךְ, [7]וְ״לֹא זוֹ אַף זוֹ״ קָתָנֵי.

משנה [8]הַמַּפְקִיד פֵּירוֹת אֵצֶל חֲבֵירוֹ, אֲפִילּוּ הֵן אֲבוּדִין, [9]לֹא יִגַּע בָּהֶן.

LITERAL TRANSLATION

[1]And if [the ruling] had been stated in this [case], [2][we might have thought that] Rabbi Yose stated [his ruling] in this [case], [3]but in that [case], say: He agrees with the Sages. [4][Therefore] it is necessary [to state both].

[38A] [5]But surely the reason of Rabbi Yose is because of the loss to the deceiver.

[6]Rather, both of them are necessary for the Sages, [7]and [the Mishnah] teaches "not [only] this, [but] also this."

MISHNAH [8]Someone who deposits fruit with his fellow, even if they are [becoming] ruined, [9]he must not touch them.

RASHI

בהא קאמר רבי יוסי — משום פסידא דגדול. **והא טעמא דרבי יוסי משום הפסד הרמאי הוא** — וכיון דטעמא בהכי מה לי כלי מה לי מעות? והיכי תיסק אדעתין למימר דבמעות מודה להו לרבנן, ואמאי אצטריך למתנייה? **לרבנן איצטריך** — לאשמועינן מילתא דרבנן תננהו לתרוייהו, ואי תנא כליס ברישא — הכי נמי דלא אצטריך תו למתני מעות, אבל השתא דתני מעות ברישא — תני כליס, למימר: לא זו בלבד דליכא פסידא דשבירת כלי, אלא אף זו דאיכא פסידא דגדול, אמרינן הכי.

משנה אבודין — על ידי עכברים או ריקבון. **לא יגע בהן** — למוכרן, וטעמא מפרש בגמרא.

BACKGROUND

תַּרְוַיְיהוּ לְרַבָּנַן אִיצְטְרִיךְ Both of them are necessary for the Sages. The argument used above tried to prove that both of the cases mentioned in the Mishnah were needed, since neither could be derived from the other. Now that the explanation regarding a possible controversy with Rabbi Yose has been rejected, this argument is no longer valid. Although we have already explained what was innovative about the second Halakhah regarding larger and smaller vessels, we have not been able to explain why the first Halakhah is needed regarding various sums of money. The Gemara therefore does not explain this repetition logically, but stylistically.

לֹא יִגַּע בָּהֶן He must not touch them. This is a hyperbolic expression meaning that he does not need to be concerned about the produce by selling it to other people. Rather, he should leave it where it is, and its owner must take care of it.

TERMINOLOGY

לֹא זוֹ אַף זוֹ קָתָנֵי It teaches "not only this, but also this." Sometimes the Mishnah cites a series of cases, the first of which seems superfluous. In such instances, the Talmud may explain the inclusion of the seemingly superfluous case on stylistic grounds: The Mishnah began by mentioning a simple, relatively obvious, matter, and from there proceeded to a more complicated subject. The expression used in such cases is: "The Mishnah follows the stylistic principle of teaching not only the simple case [לא זו] but also the more complicated case [אף זו]."

NOTES

אֲפִילּוּ הֵן אֲבוּדִין Even if they are becoming ruined. The Mishnah uses the word "even" because there are other situations in which the bailee may not touch the deposit — for example, if its value increased substantially. Even if the sale of the deposit would result in a substantial gain for the depositor, the bailee is not allowed to touch it (*Ḥaver ben Ḥayyim*).

HALAKHAH

פֵּירוֹת פִּקָּדוֹן שֶׁחָסְרוּ Deposited fruit which began to deteriorate. "If someone deposits fruit with another person and it begins to deteriorate, the bailee may not touch it. This applies only where the fruit's deterioration occurs at the normal rate. But if the deterioration is faster than normal, the bailee should notify the depositor if he is

SAGES

רַב כָּהֲנָא Rav Kahana. There were four Babylonian Amoraim bearing this name. It seems likely that the reference here is to Rav Kahana III, an Amora of the fourth generation who was a disciple of Rabbah and a colleague of Rav Safra.

רַב נַחְמָן בַּר יִצְחָק Rav Naḥman bar Yitzḥak. One of the leading Babylonian Amoraim of the fourth generation. Rav Naḥman bar Yitzḥak was born in Sura. His mother was the sister of Rav Aḥa bar Yosef. His principal teacher was Rav Naḥman bar Ya'akov, but he also studied under Rav Ḥisda. After the death of Rava, Rav Naḥman bar Yitzḥak was appointed head of the Pumbedita Yeshivah.

TRANSLATION AND COMMENTARY

רַבָּן שִׁמְעוֹן בֶּן גַּמְלִיאֵל אוֹמֵר [1]By contrast, **Rabban Shimon ben Gamliel says:** Under such circumstances, the bailee **should sell** the fruit and look after the money he receives from the sale. To protect the owner's interest, says Rabban Shimon ben Gamliel, it is sufficient to sell **them** under the supervision of **a court.** [2]The bailee has the authority to sell the fruit, even though it is not his, **because he is** considered **like someone who returns a lost object to** its **owner.** By selling produce which would otherwise be ruined, the bailee spares the depositor from suffering loss.

GEMARA מַאי טַעְמָא [3]The Gemara begins its analysis of the Mishnah by asking: **What is the reason** why the first Tanna forbids selling the fruit?

אָמַר רַב כָּהֲנָא [4]Two answers by two Amoraim are given. **Rav Kahana said:** The first Tanna applied the following general principle: **A person prefers one** ***kav*** (a measure) of his own fruit **to nine** ***kavs*** **of another person's. People sometimes develop a sentimental attachment to the fruits of their own labor, to the point** where they will not exchange them for other property worth many times more. The bailee must, therefore, assume that the owner does not want his property sold, even if the sale would be very profitable to him. [5]**But Rav Naḥman bar Yitzḥak said:** There is another reason for forbidding the bailee from selling the depositor's fruit. The Mishnah is referring specifically to produce of Eretz Israel, from which terumah — the portion of the crop given to the priests — and tithe must be separated before it can be eaten. Now, if the deposit was an untithed box of figs, for example, and the depositor had nine other boxes of figs somewhere else, he would be fully entitled to designate the box in the bailee's care as the tithe for all his produce (see note). But terumah may not be eaten by anyone except the priest and his household. [6]Hence, says Rav Naḥman bar Yitzḥak, the first Tanna does not allow the bailee to sell the deposit because **we are afraid in case the depositor made** the fruit in the bailee's custody **terumah or tithe for produce in another place;** if we allow the bailee to sell the fruit, it may come into the hands of people who are forbidden to eat it.

[1]רַבָּן שִׁמְעוֹן בֶּן גַּמְלִיאֵל אוֹמֵר: מוֹכְרָן בִּפְנֵי בֵּית דִּין, [2]מִפְּנֵי שֶׁהוּא כְּמֵשִׁיב אֲבֵידָה לַבְּעָלִים.

גמרא [3]מַאי טַעְמָא? [4]אָמַר רַב כָּהֲנָא: אָדָם רוֹצֶה בְּקַב שֶׁלּוֹ מִתִּשְׁעָה קַבִּים שֶׁל חֲבֵירוֹ. [5]וְרַב נַחְמָן בַּר יִצְחָק אָמַר: [6]חָיְישִׁינַן שֶׁמָּא עֲשָׂאָן הַמַּפְקִיד תְּרוּמָה וּמַעֲשֵׂר עַל מָקוֹם אַחֵר.

LITERAL TRANSLATION

[1]Rabban Shimon ben Gamliel says: He sells them before a court, [2]because he is like someone who returns a lost object to the owner.

GEMARA [3]What is the reason?

[4]Rav Kahana said: A person prefers a *kav* of his own to nine *kavs* of his fellow. [5]But Rav Naḥman bar Yitzḥak said: [6]We are concerned in case the depositor made them terumah or tithe for [produce in] another place.

RASHI

גמרא קב שלו – חביבה עליו על ידי שעמל בהן, וקב שישאר לו מהם הוא רוצה מתשעה קבין של אחרים, שיקח בדמיהן אם ימכרם. חיישינן כו' – ואסור להאכילו לזרים.

NOTES

אָדָם רוֹצֶה בְּקַב שֶׁלּוֹ A person prefers a *kav* of his own. Our commentary follows *Rashi* and other Rishonim, who explain that people develop a sentimental attachment to the fruits of their own labor. *Rashash* raises the question as to whether or not it makes a difference, according to this interpretation, if the owner did not grow the fruit himself, but purchased it in the market, and concludes that the ruling of the Mishnah applies specifically to produce grown by the depositor.

רַב נַחְמָן בַּר יִצְחָק אָמַר Rav Nahman bar Yitzḥak said. Our commentary follows *Ran*, who explains that, according to Rav Naḥman bar Yitzḥak, the Mishnah's prohibition against selling the depositor's rotting fruit applies only when there is some danger that the fruit may have been used for tithing purposes, but non-tithable perishables or produce that the bailee knows has already been tithed may be sold if the court considers it to be in the depositor's interest.

Several Rishonim, however, follow *Tosafot*, who suggests that this may not be so. Throughout the passage the Gemara appears to assume that there is no dispute between Rav Kahana and Rav Naḥman bar Yitzḥak over the kinds of fruit included in the Mishnah's prohibition. Indeed, the Gemara specifically refers to honey, which is not tithable. Moreover, the Gemara also assumes that Rav Naḥman bar Yitzḥak is always less willing to allow the bailee to sell the produce than is Rav Kahana. Therefore, *Tosafot* suggests that Rav Naḥman accepts Rav Kahana's argument, and will not allow a bailee to sell any produce of the depositor, because a person prefers one *kav* of his own, etc. However, Rav Naḥman is also concerned about tithing, and hence does not allow the bailee to sell the produce, even if the rate of deterioration is far greater than normal.

חָיְישִׁינַן שֶׁמָּא עֲשָׂאָן הַמַּפְקִיד תְּרוּמָה In case the depositor made them terumah. Our concern is that the owner may

HALAKHAH

available, and if not, should sell the fruit in court," following the first Tanna's view, and according to Rabbi Yoḥanan's interpretation." (*Shulḥan Arukh, Ḥoshen Mishpat* 292:15.)

TRANSLATION AND COMMENTARY

מֵיתִיבִי [1]The Rabbis raised an **objection** from a Baraita: "If **someone deposits fruit with another person,** [2]**the bailee may not touch it.** [3]**Therefore, the owner** may assume that his fruit has not been touched, and **may make it terumah or tithe for produce in another place."** [4]Now, this Baraita **poses no problem to Rav Kahana,** who said that a deteriorating deposit may not be sold because of the owner's attachment to his property. According to Rav Kahana's explanation, it is obvious **why the Baraita uses the expression "therefore** the owner may use the deposit for tithing." Since the produce cannot be sold by the bailee, the depositor is entitled to assume it is available for tithing. [5]**But according to Rav Naḥman bar Yitzḥak, why** does the Baraita say **"therefore"**? According to his explanation, this is precisely the reason *why* it is forbidden to sell the fruit. In other words, according to the Baraita, the reason why the owner may use the deposited fruit as terumah or tithe is that the bailee is not permitted to sell it, whereas Rav Naḥman bar Yitzḥak is saying the opposite — the bailee may not sell the fruit because the owner may already have set it aside as terumah or tithe!

הָכִי קָאָמַר [6]The Gemara answers: **This is what** the Baraita **is saying: Now that the Rabbis have said** that the bailee **must not sell** the produce, **for we are afraid** that the owner may have set it aside as terumah or tithe, there is in fact no further objection to his using it in this way. [7]**Therefore,** the Baraita explains, **the owner may make** the fruit **terumah or tithe for produce in another place.**

אָמַר רַבָּה בַּר בַּר חָנָה [8]**Rabbah bar Bar Ḥanah said in the name of Rabbi Yoḥanan: The dispute** in our Mishnah between Rabban Shimon ben Gamliel and the first Tanna **applies** only in a case of normal loss, **where deterioration** in the fruit and depreciation in its value occurred at the normal rate (described in the Mishnah

[1]מֵיתִיבִי: ״הַמַּפְקִיד פֵּירוֹת אֵצֶל חֲבֵירוֹ, [2]הֲרֵי זֶה לֹא יִגַּע בָּהֶן. [3]לְפִיכָךְ בַּעַל הַבַּיִת עוֹשֶׂה אוֹתָן תְּרוּמָה וּמַעֲשֵׂר עַל מָקוֹם אַחֵר״. [4]בִּשְׁלָמָא לְרַב כָּהֲנָא — הַיְינוּ דְּקָתָנֵי ״לְפִיכָךְ״. [5]אֶלָּא לְרַב נַחְמָן בַּר יִצְחָק, מַאי ״לְפִיכָךְ״? [6]הָכִי קָאָמַר: הַשְׁתָּא דַּאֲמוּר רַבָּנַן לָא נְזַבִּין, דְּחָיְישִׁינַן, [7]לְפִיכָךְ בַּעַל הַבַּיִת עוֹשֶׂה אוֹתָן תְּרוּמָה וּמַעֲשֵׂר עַל מָקוֹם אַחֵר. [8]אָמַר רַבָּה בַּר בַּר חָנָה אָמַר רַבִּי יוֹחָנָן: מַחֲלוֹקֶת בִּכְדֵי חֶסְרוֹנָן,

LITERAL TRANSLATION

[1]They objected: "Someone who deposits fruit with his fellow, [2]he [the bailee] must not touch them. [3]Therefore the owner may make them terumah or tithe for [produce in] another place." [4]Granted according to Rav Kahana — this is why it teaches "therefore." [5]But according to Rav Naḥman bar Yitzḥak, what is "therefore"?

[6]This [is what] it says: Now that the Rabbis have said [that] he must not sell, for we are concerned, [7]therefore the owner may make them terumah or tithe for [produce in] another place.

[8]Rabbah bar Bar Ḥanah said in the name of Rabbi Yoḥanan: The dispute is where [their deterioration] is like the [normal] rate of their loss,

RASHI

לפיכך — הואיל ואסור למוכרן משום דרוצה אדם בקב שלו, הרי הן בחזקת קיימים, ומותר בעל הבית לעשותן תרומה ומעשר על פירות שיש לו בביתו. **מאי לפיכך** — איסור מכירה משום הא הוא, והיכי תלי תנא עשייתו באיסור מכירה. **השתא דאמור רבנן לא תזבין דחיישינן** — שמא עשאן המפקיד תרומה, הרי הן בחזקת שלא נמכרו, ועושה אותן בעל הבית כו׳. **מחלוקת** — דמתניתין. **בכדי חסרונן** — כדרך שאר תבואות, כמו שמפורש במשנתינו (בבא מציעא מ,א): לחיטין ולאורז תשעה חצאי קבין לכור.

BACKGROUND

עוֹשֶׂה אוֹתָן תְּרוּמָה May make them terumah. At least according to Rabbinical decree, terumah — the priestly dues — must be separated from almost every type of produce. Terumah is generally two percent of the total crop, and only after it has been separated are the other tithes separated. Produce which has not yet had terumah and tithes separated from it is called טֶבֶל, and the prohibition against eating it is very severe. In principle, one should only take terumah from within the produce, or close to it (מִן הַמּוּקָף). However, in practice a person is permitted to separate terumah from his produce wherever it may be.

בִּכְדֵי חֶסְרוֹנָן Normal deterioration. As explained in the following Mishnah (40a), stored produce generally deteriorates at a fixed rate, and as long as the deterioration occurs at that rate, it may be assumed that the depositor is aware of it, but for some reason is interested in keeping the deposit where it is and is not concerned about the deterioration. Sometimes, however, as a result of special circumstances (vermin, a change in humidity and the like), deterioration takes place at a much faster rate, causing a change in the situation that is unknown to the depositor.

SAGES

רַבָּה בַּר בַּר חָנָה Rabbah bar Bar Ḥanah. An Amora of the third generation. See *Bava Metzia*, Part I, p. 222.

NOTES

sell them to people who are forbidden to eat terumah. The Rishonim ask: Even though by Torah law it is permitted to use fruit in one location as terumah for fruit in another, there is a Rabbinic prohibiton against tithing fruits in this way, and the only proper way is to bring all the produce together in close proximity (מִן הַמּוּקָף). Why, then, should the bailee be afraid to sell the fruit, since the owner cannot use it for tithing without coming first to collect it?

Tosafot answers that there are certain unusual circumstances under which the Rabbis relaxed their prohibition and permitted fruit to be tithed in two different locations. Although these circumstances are so rare that we normally do not take them into consideration, the idea of allowing a bailee to sell the owner's produce is so problematic that this remote concern is sufficient to dissuade us from granting permission.

Ritva explains that the "close proximity" law does not apply to the "tithe of the tithe" (תְּרוּמַת מַעֲשֵׂר) that the Levite separates from the tithe he receives and delivers to the priest. Accordingly, Rav Naḥman bar Yitzḥak may be concerned that the produce may be first tithe, designated to be given to a Levite, and the owner — who may himself be a Levite — may designate it as "tithe of the tithe" for his other Levitical tithes.

The Rishonim also discuss a simpler solution to this problem: Perhaps the owner designated the fruit as tithes *before* depositing them with the bailee. Unfortunately, this proposal presents insurmountable textual problems. Moreover, it is not at all clear why the owner would have deposited his tithes with the bailee and let them deteriorate, rather than give them to a priest or Levite. Hence the Rishonim reject this solution (*Ramban*, *Rashba*, and others).

BACKGROUND

וַדַּאי פְּלִיגָא He certainly disagrees. The Talmud's method is always to seek to limit controversy and harmonize differing approaches (even when they appear contradictory), or at least to reduce the areas of controversy as much as possible. Nevertheless, there are occasions when it is clearly impossible to do this. Rabbi Yoḥanan's teaching cannot be reconciled with Rabbi Naḥman bar Yitzḥak's approach, since it is evident that Rabbi Yoḥanan does not consider the possibility that the object on deposit may not be sold.

גוּזְמָא בְּעָלְמָא Merely an exaggeration. The term גוּזְמָא, the source of which is unclear, refers to the use of exaggerated language or of excessively large and imprecise numbers or quantities in order to express a certain idea. On occasion the Talmud says דִּבְרֵי חֲכָמִים לְשׁוֹן הֲבַאי — "the words of the Sages are an exaggeration" — meaning that they need not be taken at face value. The Geonim write that certain numbers used by the Sages simply mean a very large quantity, and are intended to give only a general impression.

TRANSLATION AND COMMENTARY

below, 40a). [1]**But where the deterioration is greater than normal,** even the first Tanna accepts Rabban Shimon ben Gamliel's argument; so **according to all** opinions the bailee **may sell** the fruit **in court.**

אַדְּרַב נַחְמָן בַּר יִצְחָק [2]On this statement the Gemara remarks: Rabbi Yoḥanan's viewpoint certainly **disagrees with** that of **Rav Naḥman bar Yitzḥak,** for if we are concerned that the fruit may have been set aside as terumah or tithe for other produce, the degree of deterioration should not affect permission to sell it; its sale should still be forbidden. [3]But **are we** forced to **say that** Rabbi Yoḥanan's viewpoint also **disagrees with Rav Kahana?** Even though a person may prefer his own property to someone else's, nevertheless, if it is deteriorating, Rav Kahana may agree with Rabbi Yoḥanan that it is permitted to be sold.

כִּי קָאָמַר רַב כָּהֲנָא [4]The Gemara replies: **When Rav Kahana said** that a person prefers his own property to someone else's, **he was speaking of normal** deterioration, but he would agree with Rabbi Yoḥanan that where deterioration is faster than normal, even the first Tanna would permit the sale of the fruit in court.

וְהָא [5]The Gemara objects: **But surely** Rav Kahana **said:** "A person **prefers a *kav* of his own to nine *kavs* of another person."** Thus if the ratio is literally one to nine, it is obvious that, according to Rav Kahana, a person still prefers his own produce, even in the event of a considerable loss!

גוּזְמָא בְּעָלְמָא [6]The Gemara replies: Rav Kahana did not literally mean one to nine, and his use of that ratio **was merely an exaggeration.** In fact, a person is willing to suffer some loss in order to retain his own property, but not more than the normal deterioration of produce.

מֵיתִיבֵי [7]The Gemara now raises an **objection** to the viewpoint of Rabbi Yoḥanan from the last clause of the Baraita previously quoted, which said: "The bailee may not sell the produce. **Therefore, the owner may** assume that it is still there and **make it terumah or tithe for produce in another place."** [8]**But** if Rabbi Yoḥanan is correct and the bailee is permitted to sell the produce when it deteriorates at more than the normal rate, we must reject the Baraita's argument that the owner is entitled to assume his produce is available for tithing! **Let** the owner **be concerned that,** before he decided to use the deposit for tithing, the produce **may have deteriorated at more than the normal rate, and** as a result the bailee **sold it!** If this did occur, the owner would be designating produce not in his possession as tithes — an invalid procedure. [9]Thus, if Rabbi Yoḥanan is correct, the owner may unwittingly find himself **eating produce** that he *thinks* he tithed but in fact is still **untithed**. This would be a violation of a Torah prohibition (Leviticus 22:15).

[1]אֲבָל יוֹתֵר מִכְּדֵי חֶסְרוֹנָן, דִּבְרֵי הַכֹּל מוֹכְרָן בְּבֵית דִּין. [2]אַדְּרַב נַחְמָן בַּר יִצְחָק וַדַּאי פְּלִיגָא. [3]אַדְּרַב כָּהֲנָא מִי לֵימָא פְּלִיגָא? [4]כִּי קָאָמַר רַב כָּהֲנָא, בִּכְדֵי חֶסְרוֹנָן קָאָמַר. [5]וְהָא "רוֹצֶה בְּקַב שֶׁלּוֹ מִתִּשְׁעָה קַבִּין שֶׁל חֲבֵירוֹ" קָאָמַר. [6]גּוּזְמָא בְּעָלְמָא. [7]מֵיתִיבֵי: "לְפִיכָךְ בַּעַל הַבַּיִת עוֹשֶׂה אוֹתָן תְּרוּמָה וּמַעֲשֵׂר עַל מָקוֹם אַחֵר." [8]וְלֵיחוּשׁ דִּלְמָא הָווּ לְהוּ יוֹתֵר מִכְּדֵי חֶסְרוֹנָן, וְזַבְּנִינְהוּ, [9]וְקָא אָכֵיל טְבָלִים.

LITERAL TRANSLATION

[1]but where it is more than the [normal] rate of their loss, according to all he sells [them] in court.

[2]With Rav Naḥman bar Yitzḥak he certainly disagrees. [3]Shall we say that he disagrees with Rav Kahana?

[4]When Rav Kahana stated [his ruling], he was speaking of normal deterioration.

[5]But surely he said: "[A person] prefers a *kav* of his own to nine *kavs* of his fellow."

[6][That was] merely an exaggeration.

[7]They objected: "Therefore the owner may make them terumah or tithe for [produce in] another place." [8]But let him be concerned [that] perhaps their deterioration was greater than normal, so he [the bailee] sold them, [9]and he [the owner] is eating untithed produce.

RASHI

אבל אם אבודין יותר מכדי חסרונן — אפילו רבנן מודו דימכרם בבית דין. **ודאי פליגא** — הא דרבי יוחנן, דאי איכא למיחש לשמא עשאן בעליהן תרומה, אפילו ביותר מכדי חסרונן נמי אסור לזבנינהו. **מי לימא פליגא** — דקאמר רב כהנא שאדם תשעה קבין הן, נוח לו שיאבדו עד קב, ואל ימכרם דהוה ליה יותר מכדי חסרונן, ופליגא הא דרבי יוחנן עליה, או לאו דוקא תשעה קבין נקט, אלא נוח לו שיהא נפסד קצת ולעולם כדי חסרונן ותו לא. **גוזמא** — שפת יתר. **מיתיבי** — לרבי יוחנן. **וקאכיל** — בעל הבית טבלים, שאין פירותיו מתוקנין שאין אלו קיימין שהוא סומך עליהן.

NOTES

גוּזְמָא בְּעָלְמָא Merely an exaggeration. The expression "nine *kavs* and a *kav*" also appears in other contexts (see, for example, *Kiddushin* 49b, *Sotah* 20a), where it is clearly not intended to be taken literally.

וְלֵיחוּשׁ דִּלְמָא הָווּ לְהוּ יוֹתֵר מִכְּדֵי חֶסְרוֹנָן But let him be concerned that perhaps their deterioration was greater than normal. To understand this passage, it is important to remember that there are two separate problems connected

[1] יוֹתֵר מִכְּדֵי חֶסְרוֹנָן לָא שְׁכִיחַ. [2] וְאִי מִשְׁתַּכְּחִי, מַאי? [3] מְזַבְּנִינַן לְהוּ? [4] וְלֵיחוּשׁ שֶׁמָּא עֲשָׂאָן בַּעַל הַבַּיִת תְּרוּמָה וּמַעֲשֵׂר עַל מָקוֹם אַחֵר.

[5] כִּי מְזַבְּנִינַן נַמִי, לְכֹהֲנִים בִּדְמֵי תְּרוּמָה מְזַבְּנִינַן לְהוּ.

[6] וּלְרַב נַחְמָן בַּר יִצְחָק נַמִי, נְזַבְּנִינְהוּ לְכֹהֲנִים בִּדְמֵי תְּרוּמָה.

LITERAL TRANSLATION

[1] More than their normal deterioration is not common.

[2] But if it happens, what [do we do]? [3] Do we sell them? [4] But let us be concerned in case the owner made them terumah or tithe for [produce in] another place.

[5] Even when we sell them, we sell them to priests at the price of terumah.

[6] But according to Rav Naḥman bar Yitzḥak too, let us sell them to priests at the price of terumah.

TRANSLATION AND COMMENTARY

יוֹתֵר [1] The Gemara answers: There is no need for the owner to be concerned about such a hypothetical possibility when tithing his produce, since produce that **deteriorates faster than the normal** rate **is not common.** Therefore the owner is allowed to designate the produce as tithe on the assumption that it is still there, and the Baraita's statement authorizing such tithing does not contradict Rabbi Yoḥanan.

וְאִי מִשְׁתַּכְּחִי מַאי [2] The Gemara objects again: Granted that the owner need not concern himself with the possibility of such an unlikely occurrence, **but if it** actually **happens,** and the deterioration is indeed greater than normal, **what do we do?** [3] **Do we** permit the bailee to **sell** the deposit, as Rabbi Yoḥanan suggests? [4] **Surely we should be concerned in case the owner has** already **designated** the deposit **terumah or tithe for produce in another place.** If he has done so, the bailee, by selling the produce, will be causing non-priests, who are forbidden to eat terumah, to do so!

כִּי מְזַבְּנִינַן נַמִי [5] The Gemara answers: **Even when** the produce is deteriorating rapidly and, according to Rabbi Yoḥanan, all authorities agree that the bailee is permitted to **sell it, we** only permit him to **sell it to priests,** who are authorized to eat terumah. He must assume that it has been set aside by the owner as terumah, and must sell it **at the price of terumah,** which is considerably less than the price of regular produce. Thus there is no reason for concern, for even if the deposit has been designated as terumah by the owner, there is nothing to prevent the bailee from selling it.

וּלְרַב נַחְמָן בַּר יִצְחָק [6] The Gemara now asks: We stated above that Rabbi Yoḥanan certainly disagrees with Rav Naḥman bar Yitzḥak, and that the latter forbids the bailee to sell the produce even where its deterioration is faster than normal. **But** if Rabbi Yoḥanan is in fact only permitting the bailee to sell the produce to priests at the price of terumah, perhaps we should revise that assessment. For even **according to Rav Naḥman bar Yitzḥak** there should be no objection to **letting** the bailee **sell** the produce **to priests at the price of terumah,** if the produce deteriorates faster than the normal rate, as Rav Naḥman bar Yitzḥak's only concern was the possibility that the owner might have designated the produce as terumah or tithes.

RASHI

לא שכיחי – ואין לחוש בכך. ופרכינן: **ואי משתכחי מי מזבנינן להו** – בתמיה. **ליחוש שמא עשאן כו'** – ונמצא המוכר מאכיל תרומה לזרים. **בדמי תרומה** – בזול, שאין עליה קופצין לקנותה, שאינה נאכלת אלא לכהנים וצריכה שימור בטהרה.

BACKGROUND

לְכֹהֲנִים בִּדְמֵי תְּרוּמָה מְזַבְּנִינַן לְהוּ We sell them to priests at the price of terumah. While terumah given to the priests becomes their property in every sense, it is, however, considered holy. Not only is it strictly forbidden for anyone who is not a priest to eat it, but the priests are warned only to eat it in a state of ritual purity. Since terumah can be used only by a limited number of people, and only at certain times even by them (when they are ritually pure), it is clear that when a priest or an Israelite who has inherited terumah wishes to sell it, its price is considerably lower than that of ordinary produce, which is not bound by the same restrictions.

NOTES

with tithing and produce on deposit: (1) The owner may already have designated the produce as terumah, thus rendering it forbidden to non-priests. This presents a problem for the bailee who wants to sell it. A solution is proposed by the Gemara — namely that the bailee should only sell the deposit to priests at the price of terumah. (2) The owner may in the future wish to designate the produce as terumah, on the assumption that the produce is not deteriorating faster than normal. This second problem has, in turn, two aspects: (A) Regarding the owner: He ought not to use the deposit for tithing, since he must always consider the possibility that it may have been sold. A solution to this problem too is proposed by the Gemara, namely that the bailee may sell the produce only in the unlikely event that it deteriorates faster than normal, and the possibility of this happening is so remote that the owner is entitled to ignore it. (B) Regarding the bailee: He ought not to sell the deposit even if it deteriorates faster than normal, because the owner may wish to use it for tithing. The Gemara does not address this last problem directly.

Tosafot, followed by our commentary, explains that the Gemara is relying on the explanation of the dispute between Rabbi Yoḥanan and Rav Naḥman bar Yitzḥak, which appears a few lines later: According to Rabbi Yoḥanan, greater-than-normal deterioration is not common and takes a long time to develop. Hence, by the time the produce deteriorates to this extent, any tithing the owner planned to do will have been done. Thus, the bailee need not fear that the owner will in the future designate the produce as terumah.

[1]בְּהָא פְּלִיגִי: דְּרַבָּה בַּר בַּר חָנָה סָבַר: [2]יוֹתֵר מִכְּדֵי חֶסְרוֹנָן לָא שְׁכִיחַ מִידֵי, [3]וְכִי מִשְׁתַּכַּח, לְקַמֵּיהּ הוּא דְּהָוְיָא יָתֵיר מִכְּדֵי חֶסְרוֹנָן. [4]אִי עָבֵיד לְהוּ בַּעַל הַבַּיִת תְּרוּמָה וּמַעֲשֵׂר עַל מָקוֹם אַחֵר, [5]מִקַּמֵּיהּ דְּהָווּ לְהוּ יוֹתֵר מִכְּדֵי חֶסְרוֹנָן עָבֵיד לְהוּ. [6]הִלְכָּךְ, כִּי הָווּ לְהוּ יוֹתֵר מִכְּדֵי חֶסְרוֹנָן, [7]נְזַבְּנִינְהוּ לְכֹהֲנִים בִּדְמֵי תְרוּמָה.

[8]וְרַב נַחְמָן בַּר יִצְחָק סָבַר: יָתֵר מִכְּדֵי חֶסְרוֹנָן מִשְׁכַּח שְׁכִיחַ, [9]וְכִי הָווּ לְהוּ, לְאַלְתַּר הוּא דְּהָווּ לְהוּ. [10]וְאִי אָמְרַתְּ נְזַבְּנִינְהוּ, [11]זִימְנִין דְּקָדֵים וּמְזַבֵּין לְהוּ, [12]וְכִי עָבֵיד לְהוּ בַּעַל הַבַּיִת תְּרוּמָה וּמַעֲשֵׂר עַל מָקוֹם אַחֵר, [13]לָא יָדַע דְּזַבְּנָא, וְקָא אָכֵיל טְבָלִים.

[14]מֵיתִיבֵי: ״הַמַּפְקִיד פֵּירוֹת אֵצֶל חֲבֵירוֹ וְהִרְקִיבוּ, [15]יַיִן וְהֶחְמִיץ, שֶׁמֶן וְהִבְאִישׁ, דְּבַשׁ וְהִדְבִּישׁ,

LITERAL TRANSLATION

[1]They disagree about this: Rabbah bar Bar Ḥanah maintains: [2]More than their normal deterioration is not common at all, [3]and when it happens, it will be after a long period (lit., "further") that their deterioration will be greater than normal. [4][Thus], if the owner made them terumah or tithe for [produce in] another place, [5]he did so before their deterioration was greater than normal. [6]Therefore, when their deterioration is greater than normal, [7]we can sell them to priests at the price of terumah.

[8]But Rav Naḥman bar Yitzḥak maintains: More than their normal deterioration is quite common, [9]and when it happens, it happens immediately. [10]And if you say [that] we sell them, [11]sometimes he will anticipate and sell them, [12]and when the owner makes them terumah or tithe for [produce in] another place, [13]he does not know that he sold them, and eats untithed produce.

[14]They objected: "Someone who deposits fruit with his fellow and it rotted, [15][or] wine and it soured, [or] oil and it became rancid, [or] honey and it spoiled,

RASHI

לקמיה הוא דהויא יתר מכדי חסרונן — לזמן מרובה יש באבודן יתר מכדי חסרון. **מקמי דניהוי כו׳** — שאין אדם משהא טבלים כל כך, זמן מרובה כזה, מלתקנן. **והדביש** — יצא טעם דובשנו והחמיץ, *אשמלי״ר בלעז כמו (איוב לא) ״ובכל תבואתי תשרש״ — תעקר שרשיה, וכמו ״עד לא ירתק חבל הכסף״ (קהלת יב) — יפתחו רתוקות עבותיה.

TRANSLATION AND COMMENTARY

בְּהָא פְּלִיגִי [1]The Gemara answers: Rabbi Yoḥanan (as quoted by Rabbah bar Bar Ḥanah) and Rav Naḥman bar Yitzḥak **disagree about** the likelihood of produce deteriorating faster than normal. **Rabbah bar Bar Ḥanah** in the name of Rabbi Yoḥanan **maintains** [2]that produce that deteriorates at **more than the normal** rate **is not a common** occurrence **at all,** [3]**and when it** does **happen, it is** only **after** the produce has been left **for a long period.** Furthermore, produce is supposed to be tithed promptly, and is never left untithed for such a long period. [4]**Thus,** even **if the owner made it terumah or tithe for produce in another place,** [5]**he** presumably did so long **before the deterioration was greater than normal.** [6]**Therefore, when the deterioration is greater than normal,** the bailee is entitled to assume that tithing has already been done, and the only remaining concern is that the produce may have been set aside as terumah long ago. [7]Hence, the bailee **may sell** the deposit **to priests** at **the price of terumah.** Thus, according to Rabbi Yoḥanan, there is no problem in the sale of the produce. On the one hand, if the owner has set aside this produce as terumah or tithe, he will not be eating untithed produce. On the other hand, since the produce is sold to priests, the bailee will prevent non-priests from eating produce forbidden to them.

וְרַב נַחְמָן בַּר יִצְחָק [8]**But Rav Naḥman bar Yitzḥak maintains:** Produce that **deteriorates at more than the normal** rate **is quite a common** occurrence, [9]**and when it happens,** it can **happen immediately** after the produce is placed in the bailee's custody. [10]Therefore, **if you say** that the bailee is permitted to **sell** the produce to priests for the price of terumah, [11]there is still **sometimes** room for concern, as the bailee **may anticipate** the action of the owner **and sell** the produce **first,** before the owner designates it as terumah. [12]**When the owner makes it terumah or tithe for produce in another place,** [13]**he may not know that** the bailee has already **sold it.** As a result, the owner's tithing will be invalid, and he **may** unwittingly find himself **eating untithed produce!** Thus, selling the produce to priests is a solution according to Rabbi Yoḥanan, but not according to Rav Naḥman bar Yitzḥak. Rav Naḥman bar Yitzḥak disagrees with Rabbi Yoḥanan's ruling permitting the bailee to sell the produce if it has deteriorated faster than normal, and forbids the bailee to sell the produce under any circumstances.

מֵיתִיבֵי [14]The Gemara now raises another **objection** to the viewpoint of Rabbi Yoḥanan from the following Baraita: "If **someone deposits fruit with another person and it rots,** [15]**or wine and it becomes sour, or oil and it**

BACKGROUND

שֶׁמֶן וְהִבְאִישׁ Oil and it became rancid. When olives are pressed to extract the oil, other parts of the fruit also come out. Generally, olive oil is refined in order to remove the other materials, which give it an accompanying taste and odor and a cloudy look. However, if the refining process is incomplete, some of these materials remain in the oil, decomposing over time and giving the oil a bad odor and taste, so that it is no longer usable as food.

דְּבַשׁ וְהִדְבִּישׁ Honey and it spoiled. Honey spoils only rarely. However, if it is removed from a honeycomb before it is sufficiently concentrated (especially if it has been stored for long periods at different temperatures), part of the honey may crystallize, while the rest may become sour. It is this partially sour honey which the Gemara calls spoiled.

LANGUAGE (RASHI)

אשמלי״ר* From the Old French *esmeler,* meaning "to spoil" (with respect to honey).

TRANSLATION AND COMMENTARY

becomes rancid, or honey and it becomes spoiled, [1]**the bailee must not touch them** or sell them." [2]This ruling is referred to in the Baraita as **"these are the words of Rabbi Meir,"** and corresponds to the viewpoint of the first Tanna in our Mishnah. [3]The Baraita continues: **"But the Sages say: A remedy can be provided for them by** the bailee **selling them in court."** This ruling corresponds to the viewpoint of Rabban Shimon ben Gamliel in our Mishnah. [4]The Baraita continues by adding a proviso to the Sages' ruling: **"But when** the bailee *does* **sell** the deteriorating produce, **he may sell it to other** people, [5]**but not to himself,** even though he is willing to pay the market price, so that he will not be suspected of having bought the produce at a discount. [6]**Likewise,** for this same reason — to avoid suspicion — the Rabbis also ordained that **when charity collectors have no poor people among whom to distribute the charity** they have collected, [7]**they may change the** small **coins** they have collected for coins of a larger denomination. But the exchange of coins must be done only **with other** people. [8]The charity collectors **may not change the coins** with coins belonging to themselves, so that they are not suspected of benefiting from the proceeds of charity. [9]Likewise, **when collectors for the soup-kitchen have no poor people among whom to distribute the food** they have collected, [10]they may **sell the food to other** people, and use the proceeds to buy fresh food when it is needed, [11]**but** they may **not sell it to themselves."** This concludes the quotation from the Baraita. [12]The Gemara now explains its objection: **At all events the Baraita teaches** that even when the deposited **fruit rots,** it may not be sold. [13]May we **not** assume that **it is referring even to** a situation where **the deterioration** of the fruit **was greater than normal?** And does this not contradict Rabbi Yoḥanan's statement that everyone, including Rabbi Meir, agrees that the fruit should be sold if its deterioration is greater than normal?

[1]הֲרֵי זֶה לֹא יִגַּע בָּהֶן. [2]דִּבְרֵי רַבִּי מֵאִיר. [3]וַחֲכָמִים אוֹמְרִים: עוֹשֶׂה לָהֶם תַּקָּנָה וּמוֹכְרָן בְּבֵית דִּין. [4]וּכְשֶׁהוּא מוֹכְרָן, מוֹכְרָן לַאֲחֵרִים, [5]וְאֵינוֹ מוֹכְרָן לְעַצְמוֹ. [6]כַּיּוֹצֵא בּוֹ, גַּבָּאֵי צְדָקָה, בִּזְמַן שֶׁאֵין לָהֶם עֲנִיִּים לְחַלֵּק, [7]פּוֹרְטִין לַאֲחֵרִים, [8]וְאֵין פּוֹרְטִין לְעַצְמָן. [9]גַּבָּאֵי תַּמְחוּי, בִּזְמַן שֶׁאֵין לָהֶם עֲנִיִּים לְחַלֵּק, [10]מוֹכְרִין לַאֲחֵרִים, [11]וְאֵין מוֹכְרִים לְעַצְמָן". [12]קָתָנֵי מִיהַת: "פֵּירוֹת... וְהִרְקִיבוּ". [13]מַאי לָאו אֲפִילּוּ יָתֵר מִכְּדֵי חֶסְרוֹנָן?

LITERAL TRANSLATION

[1]he [the bailee] must not touch them. [2]These are the words of Rabbi Meir. [3]But the Sages say: He provides a remedy for them and sells them in court. [4]And when he sells them, he must sell them to others, [5]and he may not sell them to himself. [6]Likewise, charity collectors, when they have no poor [among whom] to distribute [charity], [7]may change [the coins] with others, [8]and they may not change [the coins] with themselves. [9]Collectors for the soup-kitchen, when they have no poor [among whom] to distribute [food], [10]must sell [the food] to others, [11]and may not sell [it] to themselves." [12]At all events it teaches: "Fruit... and it rotted." [13]Is it not [referring] even [to] when their deterioration was greater than normal?

RASHI

עושה להם תקנה — לקמיה מפרש מאי תקנה יש עוד, אלא כל קילקול העתיד לבא כבר בא הוא! **ואין מוכרן לעצמו** — שלא יחשדוהו שמא לקחן בזול. **פורטין** — מחליפין פרוטות נחושת בסלעי כסף, מפני שהפרוטות מתעפשות ונפסלות. **תמחוי** — מאכל שגובין מבעלי בתים לחלק לעניים בכל יום. **מאי לאו אפילו יתר מכדי חסרונן** — ואיכא למאן דאמר לא יגע, ואת אמרת דברי הכל מוכרן!

BACKGROUND

פּוֹרְטִין לַאֲחֵרִים They may change the coins with others. Charity collectors receive money in small coins from the community. If they distribute the money immediately, they are making use of the coins as they are given to them. But if they keep the money for some time, it is inconvenient to keep large numbers of small coins, and therefore they prefer to exchange them for larger coins, which are easier to transport and store.

תַּמְחוּי Soup-kitchen. The basic meaning of this word is a large vessel in which the official in charge of charity collected food contributed from meals which people had cooked for themselves. This food was collected and distributed to the needy on the same day. By extension, the word תַּמְחוּי came to mean the institution distributing food to the poor, and the place where such distribution took place.

מוֹכְרִין לַאֲחֵרִים They must sell the food to others. Although official collectors of charity are regarded as reliable, just as the bailee is so regarded by the depositor, nevertheless in many instances the Sages insisted that a person should take care not only to act justly but also to avoid provoking accusations of wrongdoing. For that reason, when a bailee or a charity official sells something, he sells it to someone else and not to himself, so as not to arouse suspicion that he paid less than the proper price.

NOTES

גַּבָּאֵי צְדָקָה... פּוֹרְטִין לַאֲחֵרִים Charity collectors... may change the coins with others. *Rashba* notes that the Baraita instructs the bailee to sell the deposit in court, but it makes no such stipulation about a charity collector changing money. He explains that the reason why a bailee may not sell produce without the assistance of a court is not because he is suspected of making an illicit profit from the sale, but because in principle a bailee has no business selling a deposit at all, since the depositor entrusted it to him to look after, not to sell. A bailee is permitted to sell

HALAKHAH

עוֹשֶׂה לָהֶם תַּקָּנָה He can provide a remedy for them. "If someone deposits fruit with another person, and it rots, or honey, and it spoils, or wine, and it turns sour, the bailee should inform the depositor, if possible. If the depositor is not available, the bailee should remedy the situation by selling the food in court, so that the containers used to store the food will not be ruined," following the view of the Sages in the Baraita. (*Shulḥan Arukh, Ḥoshen Mishpat* 292:16.)

מוֹכְרִין לַאֲחֵרִים וְאֵין מוֹכְרִים לְעַצְמָן They must sell it to others, and they may not sell it to themselves. "Anyone who sells a deposit according to a court order must sell it to others, and not to himself, to avoid suspicion." (Ibid., 292:19.)

גַּבָּאֵי צְדָקָה וְתַמְחוּי Charity collectors and collectors for the soup-kitchen. "Charity collectors who do not find poor people to whom to distribute the copper coins they have

LITERAL TRANSLATION

[1] No, [it is referring to] normal deterioration. [2] But surely [it mentioned] "wine and it soured, oil and it became rancid, honey and it spoiled," [3] which are [cases of] greater-than-normal deterioration!

[4] These are different, [for] once they stand, they stand.

[5] "Oil and it became rancid, honey and it spoiled" — [38B] [6] for what are they fit?

[7] Oil is fit for tanners, [8] honey for bruises on camels.

[9] "But the Sages say: He can provide a remedy for them and sell them in court." [10] What remedy can he provide for them?

[1] לָא, בְּכְדֵי חֶסְרוֹנָן.

[2] וְהָא "יַיִן וְהֶחְמִיץ, שֶׁמֶן וְהִבְאִישׁ, דְּבַשׁ וְהִדְבִּישׁ", [3] דְּיָתֵר מִכְּדֵי חֶסְרוֹנָן נִינְהוּ!

[4] שָׁאנֵי הָנֵי, כֵּיוָן דְּקָם, קָם.

[5] "שֶׁמֶן וְהִבְאִישׁ, דְּבַשׁ וְהִדְבִּישׁ" — [38B] [6] לְמַאי חֲזוּ?

[7] שֶׁמֶן חֲזֵי לְגִלְדָּאֵי, [8] דְּבַשׁ לִכְתִישָׁא דִּגְמַלֵּי.

[9] "וַחֲכָמִים אוֹמְרִים: עוֹשֶׂה לָהֶם תַּקָּנָה וּמוֹכְרָן בְּבֵית דִּין". [10] מַאי תַּקַּנְתָּא עָבֵיד לְהוּ?

RASHI

כיון דקם קם — מאחר שעמדו בקלקולם — הרי כבר עמדו ולא יתקלקלו מעתה יותר, אבל שאר פירות — הולכין ומרקיבין תמיד. למאי חזו — דקתני מוכרן. לגלדאי — לסוך עורות. לכתישא דגמלא — לכתישה שעל הגמל, שגבו כתוש ומסוקב מחמת משאוי, *איישר״א בלעז.

TRANSLATION AND COMMENTARY

לָא [1] The Gemara replies: **No.** Rabbi Meir's statement in the Baraita **is referring** only **to normal deterioration.** Where the deterioration is greater than normal, Rabbi Meir agrees with the Sages that the produce can be sold.

וְהָא [2] The Gemara objects: **But surely** the Baraita **mentioned,** together with the case of rotting fruit, **"wine which has become sour, oil which has become rancid, and honey which has become spoiled,"** [3] and these **are** all **cases of greater-than-normal deterioration**, since there is a substantial difference in price between wine and vinegar, and good oil and rancid oil. Nevertheless, in all these cases Rabbi Meir rules that they may not be sold! Thus Rabbi Yoḥanan's statement that everyone, including Rabbi Meir, agrees that the produce should be sold if its deterioration is greater than normal cannot be correct!

שָׁאנֵי הָנֵי [4] The Gemara replies: When the Baraita mentioned rotting produce, it was referring only to normal deterioration. The cases of wine, oil and honey, which are cases of greater-than-normal deterioration, prove nothing, as **these** substances **are different** from ordinary produce, **for once they undergo the change described, they remain in that condition.** In other words, once wine, oil or honey becomes spoiled, it does not deteriorate further. Therefore, even though the deterioration is greater than normal, there is no reason to hasten to sell, and the law in this case is the same as for fruits that have not deteriorated more than normal. But even Rabbi Meir would agree that fruits that have deteriorated more than normal should be sold.

שֶׁמֶן וְהִבְאִישׁ [5] Having resolved the question against the viewpoint of Rabbi Yoḥanan raised from the Baraita, the Gemara now analyzes the content of the Baraita itself: Granted, vinegar has a market, but **oil that became rancid and honey that became spoiled** are surely completely worthless. [38B] [6] **What can they be used for,** and why do the Sages in the Baraita rule that they should be sold? Surely nobody will be interested in buying them!

שֶׁמֶן חֲזֵי לְגִלְדָּאֵי [7] The Gemara answers: Even rancid **oil is** still **fit for** use by **tanners** to make leather more supple, [8] and spoiled **honey** is still fit **for** use in the treatment of **bruises** on the backs **of camels** caused by the heavy loads they carry.

וַחֲכָמִים אוֹמְרִים [9] The Gemara now proceeds to analyze the next clause of the Baraita: **"But the Sages say: A remedy can be provided for them by** the bailee **selling them in court."** [10] On this point the Gemara asks: **What remedy can he provide for** the oil and the honey? Since their value has already decreased radically, what does the owner gain by having the bailee sell them?

BACKGROUND

שֶׁמֶן חֲזֵי לְגִלְדָּאֵי Oil fit for tanners. The application of oil or fat is a stage in the processing of leather today as it was in antiquity. During the first part of the tanning process, leather loses its natural oils and is liable to dry out and become brittle. Therefore oil is applied to make it soft and flexible again. Since the oil is absorbed by the leather, its quality is not important, so rancid oil is as good as any other kind.

לִכְתִישָׁא דִּגְמַלֵּי For bruises on camels. A heavy burden on the back of a camel, especially when it is not properly secured, can scrape the animal's skin and create a sore. Because of the high sugar content of honey, it can be used to cover the wound and prevent infection because, at that concentration, sugar inhibits the proliferation of germs. Although the honey discussed here is no longer edible, it is still useful for that purpose.

LANGUAGE (RASHI)

איישר״א* From the Old French *redoisedore*, meaning "an injury to an animal caused by rubbing on its back."

NOTES

only in exceptional cases, therefore a court must oversee the procedure. By contrast, a charity collector has discretionary authority over the money in his custody, and is entitled to change it whenever he considers it appropriate. Hence there is no need for a court. The only requirement is that he not exchange the money with money of his own, so as to avoid any suspicion of dishonesty.

HALAKHAH

collected may exchange such coins for silver ones, provided someone else makes the exchange, but not they themselves. Likewise, collectors for the soup-kitchen may sell the food they collect to others if necessary, but not to themselves. The reason for these regulations is to avoid suspicion." (*Rambam, Sefer Zeraim, Hilkhot Mattenot Aniyyim* 9:11.)

TRANSLATION AND COMMENTARY

אָמַר רַב אַשִׁי [1]**Rav Ashi said** in reply: The remedy is with reference **to the containers.** Even though their contents have deteriorated beyond recovery, the containers themselves are still intact. But if the spoiled contents are left in them, they too will be ruined. Therefore, the bailee must sell the contents to tanners and camel drivers in order to salvage the containers.

בְּמַאי קָא מִיפַּלְגִי [2]The Gemara now asks: Since the Sages' reason for permitting the sale of spoiled wine, oil and honey is, as we have just established, to save the containers, why does Rabbi Meir not agree with the course proposed by the Sages? Why does he say that the bailee may not touch them? **About what** issue **do** Rabbi Meir and the Sages **disagree?**

דְּמָר סָבַר [3]The Gemara answers that they disagree about the following issue: **One Sage,** Rabbi Meir, **maintains** that **the Rabbis were concerned about** avoiding **a substantial loss,** [4]but **not about** avoiding **a small loss.** Therefore, once the main deterioration in the value of the produce had taken place, the Rabbis did not expect the bailee to trouble himself to sell the deposit merely to salvage the containers. [5]**But the other Sages maintain** that the Rabbis **were also concerned about a small loss,** and hence the bailee must sell the produce if it becomes spoiled, so that the containers do not become ruined as well.

רַבָּן שִׁמְעוֹן בֶּן גַּמְלִיאֵל [6]The Gemara now goes on to consider the next clause of the Mishnah: **"Rabban Shimon ben Gamliel says:** The bailee **should sell** the fruit under the supervision of **a court, because he is** considered **like someone who returns a lost object to its owner."** [7]**It was said** that there was a dispute between

[1]אָמַר רַב אַשִׁי: לְקַנְקַנִּים. [2]בְּמַאי קָא מִיפַּלְגִי? [3]דְּמָר סָבַר: לְהֶפְסֵד מְרוּבֶּה חָשְׁשׁוּ; [4]לְהֶפְסֵד מוּעָט לֹא חָשְׁשׁוּ. [5]וּמָר סָבַר: אֲפִילּוּ לְהֶפְסֵד מוּעָט נַמִי חָשְׁשׁוּ. [6]״רַבָּן שִׁמְעוֹן בֶּן גַּמְלִיאֵל אוֹמֵר: יִמְכְּרֵם בְּבֵית דִּין, מִפְּנֵי שֶׁהוּא כְּמֵשִׁיב אֲבֵידָה לַבְּעָלִים״. [7]אִתְּמַר: רַבִּי אַבָּא בְּרַבִּי יַעֲקֹב אָמַר רַבִּי יוֹחָנָן:

LITERAL TRANSLATION

[1]Rav Ashi said: For the containers.

[2]About what do they disagree?

[3]One master maintains: They were concerned about a great loss; [4]they were not concerned about a small loss. [5]And the other master maintains: They were also concerned even about a small loss.

[6]"Rabban Shimon ben Gamliel says: He sells them in court, because he is like someone who returns a lost object to the owner." [7]It was said: Rabbi Abba the son of Rabbi Ya'akov said in the name of Rabbi Yoḥanan:

RASHI

לקנקניו – הכלי שהיה בתוכו יתקלקל, אם ישאר בתוכו. **במאי קמיפלגי** – רבי מאיר ורבנן, מאחר שמודה רבי מאיר ביתר מכדי חסרונן. **להפסד מרובה** – כגון יתר מכדי חסרונן. **הפסד מועט** – כגון בכדי חסרון דריקבון פירות וקילקול הקנקן דיין וחומץ.

NOTES

בְּמַאי קָא מִיפַּלְגִי **About what do they disagree?** Our commentary follows most of the Rishonim (*Ramban, Rashba, Ritva, Ran*), who explain that the Gemara's question — "About what do they disagree?" — and the Gemara's answer — that a distinction must be made between major and minor loss — refer only to the selling of sour wine, rancid oil and spoiled honey in order to salvage their containers, but not to the selling of rotting fruit.

On this basis the Rishonim ask: The dispute between Rabbi Meir and the Sages in the Baraita regarding rotting fruit is the same as the dispute between the First Tanna and Rabban Shimon ben Gamliel in our Mishnah. That dispute has already been explained by Rav Kahana as follows: Would the owner approve of the sale of his produce whenever this would be to his financial benefit, or would he prefer his own produce over someone else's, even at a substantial loss? Now, if we have an explanation for the dispute about fruit, why does the Gemara seek a different explanation for the dispute about wine, oil or honey?

Ramban answers: Even if a person prefers his own property over someone else's, this is only so when it bears some resemblance to its original state. But rancid oil, spoiled honey and sour wine, even though they have some value, cannot possibly be used for what the owner intended them. Hence the owner cannot want to keep them because of an attachment to his own property. Therefore even Rabbi Meir, who forbids the selling of rotting fruit, should not object to selling spoiled wine, oil or honey in order to salvage the containers. Having established this, the Gemara asks: Why is the issue in dispute? Why does Rabbi Meir not agree to let the bailee sell the wine, oil or honey? And the Gemara answers: The dispute about wine, oil and honey has nothing to do with the dispute about fruit. The issue in the case of the wine, etc., is whether a great effort should be made for a small return. According to the Sages, the bailee should sell the wine, oil or honey in order to salvage the containers, whereas according to Rabbi Meir the bailee does not need to sell the deposit merely to salvage the containers.

Rashi explains the Gemara's question and answer entirely differently. According to him, the Gemara is referring not only to wine, oil and honey, but to the fruit as well. The Gemara's question is to be understood as follows: Since, according to Rabbah bar Bar Ḥanah, everyone agrees that a bailee is permitted to sell fruit which is deteriorating at a faster than normal rate, why does Rabbi Meir in the Baraita and the first Tanna in our Mishnah not permit the sale to save the owner from a normal loss, or to save his containers? The Gemara answers: When the potential loss is very great, Rabbi Meir permits the bailee to sell the produce, but when it is not so great, he takes into account considerations such as the owner's attachment to his property, and forbids the bailee to sell.

TERMINOLOGY

בְּמַאי קָא מִיפַּלְגִי **About what do they disagree?** When the practical difference between two conflicting points of view is clear, but the theoretical basis of the dispute is not, the Talmud may use this expression to inquire into the theoretical issue at the heart of the dispute.

BACKGROUND

לְהֶפְסֵד מוּעָט לֹא חָשְׁשׁוּ **They were not concerned about a small loss.** Although the return of lost objects is a religious obligation whether or not the object is valuable, in the present case one may say that a great loss has already been incurred in the spoiling of the wine or oil, while the profit to be derived from the prompt sale of the spoiled produce is relatively small. Moreover, the containers are not completely ruined. Their value has merely decreased because they can no longer be used to store edible commodities. These relatively small losses must be balanced against other considerations such as the inconvenience to the bailee and the general principle that the owner of an object on deposit does not wish the bailee to touch it. Moreover, in cases like these, the owner of the article is liable to think that the bailee did not receive a high enough price for it.

SAGES

רַבִּי אַבָּא בְּרַבִּי יַעֲקֹב **Rabbi Abba the son of Rabbi Ya'akov.** A Palestinian Amora of the third generation, he was a disciple of Rabbi Yoḥanan.

TRANSLATION AND COMMENTARY

Amoraim concerning this matter: **Rabbi Abba the son of Rabbi Ya'akov said in the name of Rabbi Yoḥanan:** [1] **The Halakhah is in accordance with Rabbi Shimon ben Gamliel,** and the bailee should sell the deteriorating deposit. [2] On the other hand, **Rava said in the name of Rav Naḥman: The Halakhah is in accordance with the words of the** first **Sage** of the Mishnah, and the bailee may *not* sell the deposit.

וְהָא אֲמָרָהּ רַבִּי יוֹחָנָן [3] The Gemara now considers the ruling issued in the name of Rabbi Yoḥanan and asks: Why did Rabbi Yoḥanan need to give a ruling on the specific dispute recorded in our Mishnah? **Surely Rabbi Yoḥanan has already** issued a general ruling adequately covering this case! [4] **For Rabbah bar Bar Ḥanah said in the name of Rabbi Yoḥanan:** [5] **Wherever Rabban Shimon ben Gamliel gave a ruling in our Mishnah, the Halakhah is in accordance with him,** even where the Sages disagree with him, [6] **except for the** following three cases: The case of "the **guarantor,"** the case of "the divorce in **Tzaidan," and "the latter ruling about proof"** (see note). Since our Mishnah is not one of these three cases, why does Rabbi Yoḥanan need to repeat that the Halakhah is in accordance with Rabbi Shimon ben Gamliel in our Mishnah?

אֲמוֹרָאֵי נִינְהוּ [7] The Gemara answers: The statements of Rabbi Abba the son of Rabbi Ya'akov and Rabbah bar Bar Ḥanah represent **different traditions of Amoraim, each of which claims to represent Rabbi Yoḥanan's** opinion. In other words, Rabbi Yoḥanan's disciples disagreed about precisely what he said. According to Rabbah bar Bar Ḥanah, Rabbi Yoḥanan issued a general ruling that the Halakhah is always (with three exceptions) in accordance with Rabbi Shimon ben Gamliel, whereas according to Rabbi Abba the son of Rabbi Ya'akov, Rabbi Yoḥanan ruled in this way only with regard to specific cases.

[1] הֲלָכָה כְּרַבָּן שִׁמְעוֹן בֶּן גַּמְלִיאֵל. [2] וְרָבָא אָמַר רַב נַחְמָן: הֲלָכָה כְּדִבְרֵי חֲכָמִים.

[3] וְהָא אֲמָרָהּ רַבִּי יוֹחָנָן חֲדָא זִמְנָא. [4] דְּאָמַר רַבָּה בַּר בַּר חָנָה אָמַר רַבִּי יוֹחָנָן: [5] כָּל מָקוֹם שֶׁשָּׁנָה רַבָּן שִׁמְעוֹן בֶּן גַּמְלִיאֵל בְּמִשְׁנָתֵינוּ, הֲלָכָה כְּמוֹתוֹ, [6] חוּץ מֵ״עָרֵב״ וְ״צַיְדָּן״ וּ״רְאָיָה אַחֲרוֹנָה״.

[7] אֲמוֹרָאֵי נִינְהוּ, וְאַלִּיבָּא דְּרַבִּי יוֹחָנָן.

LITERAL TRANSLATION

[1] The Halakhah is in accordance with Rabbi Shimon ben Gamliel. [2] And Rava said in the name of Rav Naḥman: The Halakhah is in accordance with the words of the Sages.

[3] But surely Rabbi Yoḥanan [already] said it once. [4] For Rabbah bar Bar Ḥanah said in the name of Rabbi Yoḥanan: [5] Wherever Rabban Shimon ben Gamliel taught [something] in our Mishnah, the Halakhah is in accordance with him, [6] except for [the cases of] "guarantor," "Tzaidan," and "the latter [ruling about] proof."

[7] They [are different views of] Amoraim, and [both] according to Rabbi Yoḥanan.

RASHI

ערב — ב״גט פשוט״ (בבא בתרא קעג,ב). צידן — במסכת גיטין (עד,א). ראייה — ב״דיני ממונות״ השני (סנהדרין לא,א), שנחלקו בשני מחלוקות; במביא שטר ראיה לסתור את הדין, בראשונה הלכה כמותו, ובאחרונה אין הלכה כמותו. אמוראי נינהו — רבה אמר: בכללא אמר רבי יוחנן, ורבי אבא אמר: לאו בכללא אמר רבי יוחנן, אלא יש מהן שהלכה כמותו.

NOTES

״עָרֵב״ וְ״צַיְדָּן״ וּ״רְאָיָה אַחֲרוֹנָה״ **"Guarantor," "Tzaidan," and "the latter ruling about proof."** The case of the guarantor appears in tractate *Bava Batra* 173a–173b. The Mishnah rules that a guarantor for a loan can be approached for payment only after the creditor has exhausted all possibilities of extracting payment from the debtor. The Gemara describes a special kind of guarantor called a *kablan* (קַבְּלָן), who must pay on the creditor's demand whether or not the debtor is also able to pay. Rabban Shimon ben Gamliel rules that even a *kablan* need not pay if the creditor can easily extract payment from the debtor, but Rabbi Yoḥanan ruled against Rabban Shimon ben Gamliel in this case.

The case of the divorce in Tzaidan appears in tractate *Gittin* 74a–74b. The Mishnah rules that if a husband made a divorce conditional on his wife's paying him a sum of money, the condition is valid, and the divorce cannot take effect unless the wife pays. However, if the condition was that the wife give the husband a specific object, there is a dispute between Rabban Shimon ben Gamliel and the other Sages. If it is impossible for the wife to give her husband the object in question — if, for example, it has been destroyed in a fire — Rabban Shimon ben Gamliel rules that the wife can render the divorce effective by paying her husband the value of the object, whereas the other Sages rule that there is nothing the wife can do to make the divorce effective. To support his ruling, Rabban Shimon ben Gamliel cited a precedent in which a husband divorced his wife in the town of Tzaidan, and made the divorce conditional on his wife giving him a particular cloak. The court ruled in that case that, although the cloak had been destroyed, the wife could satisfy the condition of the divorce by paying her husband its value. Nevertheless, Rabbi Yoḥanan ruled against Rabban Shimon ben Gamliel in this case.

Two rulings concerning "proof" appear in tractate *Sanhedrin* 31a. In the first of these cases, the Mishnah states that a claimant can set a time limit and demand that the other claimant prove his case within thirty days, or forfeit it.

BACKGROUND

כָּל מָקוֹם שֶׁשָּׁנָה רַבָּן שִׁמְעוֹן בֶּן גַּמְלִיאֵל **Wherever Rabban Shimon ben Gamliel taught.** The meaning of this Halakhic ruling is explained in the Jerusalem Talmud (*Bava Batra* 10:8). Although there were other Sages in that generation who may have been greater Halakhic authorities than Rabban Shimon ben Gamliel, he only cited Halakhot which had been clarified and determined by general agreement. For that reason his rulings are more authoritative than those of other Sages. The Jerusalem Talmud emphasizes that this principle was stated specifically with regard to the Mishnah, but does not necessarily apply to the Tosefta or other Baraitot. Apparently, in citing those sources, the Sages did not insist upon citing the Halakhic rulings specifically chosen by Rabban Shimon ben Gamliel. Nevertheless, certain Sages maintained that this principle also applies to other Tannaitic sources. However, this does not appear to be the opinion of the majority of Rishonim and Aḥaronim (see *Yad Malakhi*).

TERMINOLOGY

אֲמוֹרָאֵי נִינְהוּ, וְאַלִּיבָּא דְּרַבִּי... **They are Amoraim, and according to [the viewpoint of] Rabbi X.** Sometimes, when contradictory statements are attributed to a scholar, the Talmud resolves the contradiction by stating that two Amoraim transmitted variant traditions in his name.

LITERAL TRANSLATION

[1] From Rabban Shimon ben Gamliel['s statement] we may infer that we authorize (lit., "bring down") a relative to [administer] a captive's estates.

[2] From the Sages' [statement] we may infer that we do not authorize a relative to [administer] a captive's estates.

[1] מִדְּרַבָּן שִׁמְעוֹן בֶּן גַּמְלִיאֵל נִשְׁמַע דְּמוֹרִידִין קָרוֹב לְנִכְסֵי שָׁבוּי.

[2] מִדְּרַבָּנַן נִשְׁמַע דְּאֵין מוֹרִידִין קָרוֹב לְנִכְסֵי שָׁבוּי.

RASHI

מדרבן שמעון נשמע דמורידין קרוב – הראוי לירש. **בנכסי שבוי** – לקרקעות שבוי, לעובדן ולשומרן, עד שיבאו הבעלים, ולקמן פליגי בה אמוראי.

TRANSLATION AND COMMENTARY

The Gemara now turns to consider another aspect of the dispute between Rabbi Shimon ben Gamliel and the other Sages. Rabbi Shimon ben Gamliel ruled in our Mishnah that a bailee must take the deposit placed in his care and sell it, under the supervision of the court, if such an act would clearly be to its owner's advantage. He based his opinion on the general obligation to save another person's lost property. The Sages opposed extending the concept of lost property in this way, and ruled that a bailee may not interfere with the owner's property without his permission. But the principles involved in this dispute can be applied to areas that have nothing to do with bailees and depositors. For example, in general it is forbidden to farm a field in the absence of its owner. But what is the law if the owner of a field disappeared without leaving any instructions? Should the field be left fallow indefinitely, and perhaps go to ruin? Or should one of the absentee's relatives look after the field and farm it, under the supervision of the court, until the owner returns? Would Rabban Shimon ben Gamliel and the Sages disagree about this case as they did about the bailee and the deposit?

מִדְּרַבָּן שִׁמְעוֹן בֶּן גַּמְלִיאֵל [1] The Gemara suggests: **From Rabban Shimon ben Gamliel's statement** about bailees and deposits, **we may infer that** he is of the opinion that **we authorize a** close **relative to administer the estate** of a person taken **captive** who disappeared without leaving instructions. Since the captive did not appoint anyone to take care of his property, the court must do so until we know whether the captive is alive or dead. The person selected for this position should be that relative who would ordinarily be expected to inherit the field. The relative does not of course actually inherit the field at this time — he may not sell it, for example — as the owner may still be alive.

מִדְּרַבָּנַן [2] The Gemara continues presenting its hypothesis: Likewise, **from the Sages' statement** about bailees and deposits, **we may infer that** they are of the opinion that **we do not authorize a relative to administer a captive's estate.** Since the captive did not himself appoint anyone to take care of his field, no one has the right to interfere with it, not even a relative. Thus, suggests the Gemara, we see that this question, like the question about the bailee and the deposit, is linked to the dispute between Rabban Shimon ben Gamliel and the Sages in our Mishnah.

BACKGROUND

מוֹרִידִין קָרוֹב לְנִכְסֵי שָׁבוּי We authorize a relative to administer the estates of a captive. Appointing a relative to administer a captive's estate entails a number of problems. On the one hand, if the property is not administered, it may lose its value and be ruined for lack of supervision. On the other hand, the appointment of a relative can be problematic: If he believes that the captive is likely to return soon, he is liable to exploit the property for short-term profit, even if this has a deleterious effect on its total value. For example, he may sow it with crops which deplete the soil, without troubling to fertilize and renew it. Moreover, since the administrator is a relative, he may act as though he were the owner of the property and attempt to sell it or take permanent possession of it, infringing upon the rights of other potential heirs (see below, 39a, regarding the appointment of a relative to administer a minor's property).

NOTES

Rabban Shimon ben Gamliel disagrees, and rules that no time limit can be binding, and the Gemara declares that the Halakhah follows his ruling. In the second of these cases, the Mishnah states that if a claimant has admitted that he cannot prove his case and subsequently produces proof, his proof is rejected, as we suspect him of fabrication. Rabban Shimon ben Gamliel disagrees in this "latter case of proof" as well, but this time Rabbi Yoḥanan rules against him.

דְּמוֹרִידִין קָרוֹב לְנִכְסֵי שָׁבוּי That we authorize a relative to administer a captive's estate. It is important to understand that there are two independent issues here: (1) Whether the court should appoint an administrator for a captive's estate. (2) That the administrator, if he is appointed, should be a relative. The debate in the Gemara and the comparison with our Mishnah revolve around the first issue — whether an administrator should be appointed at all. No one disputes that if an administrator *is* to be appointed, he should be a relative.

The Rishonim ask: Why is it so obvious that a relative should be appointed? After all, the Gemara establishes later that if the field's owner returns, the relative takes a share of the crops as though he were a tenant farmer. Why, then, should the field not be leased to a genuine tenant farmer and administered by him?

There are two reasons given by the Rishonim: (1) If we knew that the owner was still alive, we might indeed lease the field to a regular tenant farmer. But in the case we are considering, we do not know whether the owner is alive or dead; if he is dead, the heir is obviously entitled to take possession of the field. It is true that there is a legal presumption that the owner is alive, so we do not allow the heir to take full possession, but since it is quite likely that the

HALAKHAH

מוֹרִידִין קָרוֹב לְנִכְסֵי שָׁבוּי We authorize a relative to administer a captive's estate. "The estate of a captive (or a fugitive who fled because his life was in danger) must be administered under court supervision. The captive's (or fugitive's) movable property is placed in the custody of a trustee, and his land is given to one of his heirs to work until he dies or returns. If the captive (or fugitive) returns, we appraise the value of the relative's profits less his expenses, and the owner and relative divide the difference between them as if the relative were a tenant farmer."

TRANSLATION AND COMMENTARY

וּמְמַּאי [1]The Gemara now rejects the hypothesis that these two issues are connected by showing that the reasoning involved can lead to diametrically opposed conclusions: **From where can you prove** that Rabban Shimon ben Gamliel and the Sages — who disagreed about deposits — would also disagree in the case of a captive's field? [2]**Perhaps Rabban Shimon ben Gamliel only gave his ruling** that the produce should be sold by the bailee **here,** [3]**because** when a deposit of fruit deteriorates, **the principal is** ultimately totally **destroyed.** If the bailee lets the deposit continue to rot, soon there will be nothing left, and the owner will lose everything. [4]**But there,** in the case of a captive's field, the land will still be valuable even if it is not properly cared for, and even Rabban Shimon ben Gamliel would agree with the Sages that **we should indeed not authorize** the appointment of **an administrator.**

וְעַד כָּאן [5]**And,** conversely, perhaps **the Sages only said** that the produce should not be sold by the bailee **here, because** they were not confident that the owner would approve. [6]For, as we have already established, **they ruled either in accordance with Rav Kahana**'s explanation that a person prefers his own property over someone else's even at a substantial loss, [7]**or in accordance with Rav Naḥman bar Yitzḥak**, that we must always consider the possibility that the owner set aside the deposit as terumah for other produce. [8]**But there,** in the case of the captive's field, where these arguments do not apply, the Sages would agree that **we should indeed authorize** the appointment of **an administrator.**

[1]וּמְמַּאי? [2]דִּלְמָא עַד כָּאן לָא קָאָמַר רַבָּן שִׁמְעוֹן בֶּן גַּמְלִיאֵל הָכָא, [3]אֶלָּא מִשּׁוּם דְּקָא כָּלְיָא קַרְנָא, [4]אֲבָל הָתָם הָכִי נַמִּי דְּאֵין מוֹרִידִין.

[5]וְעַד כָּאן לָא קָאָמְרִי רַבָּנַן הָכָא, [6]אֶלָּא אִי כְּרַב כָּהֲנָא, [7]אִי כְּרַב נַחְמָן בַּר יִצְחָק, [8]אֲבָל הָתָם הָכִי נַמִּי דְּמוֹרִידִין.

LITERAL TRANSLATION

[1]And from what [can you prove this]? [2]Perhaps Rabban Shimon ben Gamliel only said this here, [3]because the principal is being consumed, [4]but there we would indeed not authorize [an administrator].

[5]And the Sages only say this here, [6][because they rule] either according to Rav Kahana, [7]or according to Rav Naḥman bar Yitzḥak, [8]but there we would indeed authorize [an administrator].

RASHI

עד כאן לא קאמר רבן שמעון הכא — דמוכרן. **אלא משום דקא כליא קרנא** — אם יניחם שם, אבל גבי קרקעות וכרמים, אף על פי שמתקלקלות קצת, לא כליא קרנא. **אי כרב כהנא** — אם יניחם דאמר לעיל רוצה אדם בקב שלו. **אי כרב נחמן בר יצחק** — דאמר שמא עשאן תרומה ומעשר.

NOTES

heir is in fact the owner of the land, this should at least give him a certain priority over strangers when we lease the field to a tenant farmer (*Rashba, Ramban,* and others). (2) An ordinary tenant farmer has only a short-term interest in the field. He may misuse the land in an effort to make a quick profit. Therefore, it is not to the owner's advantage to lease the field unless he is present to supervise the tenant's behavior. Ideally, it would be best to find a friend to take care of the field without charge, but as the Gemara explains later on, this is not realistic. Accordingly, if the field is to be leased at all, it is leased only to the person who expects to inherit it, for he at least has some long-term interest in its viability (*Ritva*).

דִּלְמָא עַד כָּאן לָא קָאָמַר רַבָּן שִׁמְעוֹן בֶּן גַּמְלִיאֵל **Perhaps Rabban Shimon ben Gamliel only said this here.** The Rishonim ask: How can there be any doubt about the position of Rabban Shimon ben Gamliel? In a few lines the Gemara will quote a Baraita in which Rabban Shimon ben Gamliel says he is of the opinion that we appoint a relative to administer a captive's estate! A similar question can be asked about the Gemara's attempt to prove that the laws authorizing a bailee to sell a deposit, and a relative to administer a captive's estate, are derived from the same chain of reasoning: The proof is based on Shmuel's ruling in favor of both positions. Why does the Gemara not mention that Rabban Shimon ben Gamliel himself expressly maintains both positions?

Tosafot answers that the author of this part of the Gemara's discussion may not have been aware of the Baraita. He also suggests that the Gemara may have been reluctant to rely on a Baraita, and preferred to use a Mishnah, whose language and authority are far more reliable.

כָּלְיָא קַרְנָא **The principal is being consumed.** At first glance, it would appear that the difference between the damage in a case where the principal is consumed and a case where it is not is merely one of degree: If fruit is destroyed, the owner will have nothing left, whereas if land is left untended, the owner will suffer some damage, but will still retain property of considerable value. Hence, Rabban Shimon ben Gamliel was willing to risk permitting the bailee to sell the deposit, even though this might not be in accordance with the owner's wishes, since refusing permission would probably lead to the total loss of the deposit. On the other hand, he might not have been willing to take the risk of permitting a relative to administer the

HALAKHAH

(*Shulḥan Arukh, Ḥoshen Mishpat* 285:2.) *Rema,* however, rules in the name of *Tur* and *Rosh* that this only applies to appreciation in the land's value under the relative's care, and that the relative is entitled to all the crops produced by the land under his care. Both of these rulings follow Shmuel.

LITERAL TRANSLATION

[1]Do you mean to say that they are two reasons? [2]But surely Rav Yehudah said in the name of Shmuel: The Halakhah is in accordance with Rabban Shimon ben Gamliel, [3]and Shmuel said: We authorize a relative to [administer] a captive's estates. [4]Is it not because it is one reason? [5]No, they are two reasons. [6]So, too, it is reasonable, [7]for Rava said in the name of Rav Naḥman: The Halakhah is in accordance with the Sages, [8]and Rav Naḥman said: We authorize a relative to [administer] the estates of a captive. [9]Rather, conclude from here [that] they are two reasons. [10]Conclude from here.

[11]It was said: A captive who was taken captive — [12]Rav said: We do not authorize a relative to [administer] his estates. [13]Shmuel said: We authorize a relative to [administer] his estates.

[1]לְמֵימְרָא דִּתְרֵי טַעֲמֵי נִינְהוּ? [2]וְהָאָמַר רַב יְהוּדָה אָמַר שְׁמוּאֵל: הֲלָכָה כְּרַבָּן שִׁמְעוֹן בֶּן גַּמְלִיאֵל, [3]וְאָמַר שְׁמוּאֵל: מוֹרִידִין קָרוֹב לְנִכְסֵי שָׁבוּי. [4]לָאו מִשּׁוּם דְּחַד טַעְמָא הוּא? [5]לָא, תְּרֵי טַעֲמֵי נִינְהוּ. [6]הָכִי נַמִי מִסְתַּבְּרָא, [7]דְּאָמַר רָבָא אָמַר רַב נַחְמָן: הֲלָכָה כְּדִבְרֵי חֲכָמִים, [8]וְאָמַר רַב נַחְמָן: מוֹרִידִין קָרוֹב לְנִכְסֵי שָׁבוּי. [9]אֶלָּא שְׁמַע מִינַּהּ: תְּרֵי טַעֲמֵי נִינְהוּ. [10]שְׁמַע מִינַּהּ.

[11]אִתְּמַר: שָׁבוּי שֶׁנִּשְׁבָּה — [12]רַב אָמַר: אֵין מוֹרִידִין קָרוֹב לִנְכָסָיו. [13]שְׁמוּאֵל אָמַר: מוֹרִידִין קָרוֹב לִנְכָסָיו.

RASHI

דתרי טעמי נינהו — מתניתין ונכסי שבוי, ואיכא דאית ליה מוכרין פירות האבודין, ולית ליה מורידין. **קרוב** — הראוי ליורשו ואין קרוב ממנו.

TRANSLATION AND COMMENTARY

לְמֵימְרָא דִּתְרֵי טַעֲמֵי נִינְהוּ [1]The Gemara questions these deductions: **Do you mean to suggest that the rulings** in these two cases **are** the result of **two** unconnected chains of **reasoning?** [2]**But surely Rav Yehudah said in the name of Shmuel: The Halakhah is in accordance with Rabban Shimon ben Gamliel** in the case of the bailee and the deteriorating deposit, and we tell the bailee to sell the deposit to save its owner from a loss. [3]**And Shmuel** also **said: We authorize a relative to administer a captive's estate** to save the owner from loss. Are these two rulings similar simply by coincidence? [4]**Is it not** the case that Shmuel ruled in this way **because** his two rulings **are the result of one** chain of **reasoning?**

לָא [5]The Gemara replies: **No,** the rulings in these two cases **are** the result of **two** independent chains of **reasoning.** Thus Shmuel rendered similar decisions in both cases, even though there is no intrinsic connection between them.

הָכִי נַמִי מִסְתַּבְּרָא [6]The Gemara notes: **It also stands to reason** that there is no connection between the question about captives and the dispute about bailees. We can prove they are not connected by citing an authority who, unlike Shmuel, ruled differently in the two cases. [7]**For Rava said in the name of Rav Naḥman: The Halakhah is in accordance with the Sages** in the case of the bailee and the deteriorating deposit, and we do not allow the bailee to sell the deposit to save the owner from loss. [8]**And** yet we know that **Rav Naḥman** also **said: We authorize a relative to administer the estate of a captive,** as we do not want the owner to suffer a loss. Now, if the motive behind both rulings was the overriding commandment to save a person's property from loss, Rav Naḥman's rwo rulings would be contradictory. [9]**Rather,** it is clear that we may **infer from** Rav Naḥman's rulings **that** these laws are the result of **two** independent chains of **reasoning,** and there is no necessary connection between them. [10]The Gemara summarizes: Indeed, we may **infer from here** that this is the case.

אִתְּמַר [11]Having unsuccessfully attempted to prove a connection between the case of our Mishnah and the case of the captive's field, the Gemara now analyzes the latter case. The Gemara relates that **it was said** that there was a difference of opinion between Amoraim regarding someone **who was taken captive:** [12]**Rav said: We do not authorize a relative to administer his estate,** [13]whereas **Shmuel said: We do authorize a relative to administer his estate.**

NOTES

field, without ascertaining the owner's wishes, since there is no danger of total loss if permission is refused (see *Ramban, Rashba* and others).

Some of the Aḥaronim question this interpretation. Why should a difference in degree of damage be so significant? If it is permitted to intervene to prevent total loss, why is it not permitted in the case of partial loss? To answer this problem, these Aḥaronim make a distinction between loss of capital and failure to make a profit. If fruit is allowed to rot, the owner will suffer a loss of capital, whereas if land is untended, the owner will merely lose a certain percentage of his future crops. Perhaps Rabban Shimon ben Gamliel was willing to extend the commandment to return a lost object to a case of preventing a loss of capital, whereas he was not willing to do so in order to save a potential profit (see *Imrei Maharshah, Nefesh Ḥayyah,* and others).

LITERAL TRANSLATION

[1] Where [people] heard about [the captive] that he died, [2] all agree that we authorize [a relative]. [3] Where they disagree is where [people] did not hear about him that he died. [4] Rav said: We do not authorize [him], [because] perhaps he will damage them. [5] But Shmuel said: We authorize [him]. [6] Since the Master said [that] we appraise them as if he were a tenant farmer, [7] he will not damage them.

[8] They objected: "Rabbi Eliezer says: [9] By [logical] deduction from what is said: 'And My wrath will be inflamed and I will kill you,' [10] I know that their wives will be widows and their sons orphans. [11] What then does the verse teach us [by saying]: 'And your wives will be [widows and your sons orphans]'?

[1] בְּשֶׁשָּׁמְעוּ בּוֹ שֶׁמֵּת, [2] כּוּלֵּי עָלְמָא לָא פְּלִיגֵי דְּמוֹרִידִין. [3] כִּי פְּלִיגֵי בְּשֶׁלֹּא שָׁמְעוּ בּוֹ שֶׁמֵּת. [4] רַב אָמַר: אֵין מוֹרִידִין, דִּלְמָא מַפְסִיד לְהוּ. [5] וּשְׁמוּאֵל אָמַר: מוֹרִידִין. [6] כֵּיוָן דְּאָמַר מָר שָׁיְימִינַן לְהוּ כְּאָרִיס, [7] לָא מַפְסִיד לְהוּ.

[8] מֵיתִיבֵי: "רַבִּי אֱלִיעֶזֶר אוֹמֵר: [9] מִמַּשְׁמַע שֶׁנֶּאֱמַר 'וְחָרָה אַפִּי וְהָרַגְתִּי אֶתְכֶם' [10] יוֹדֵעַ אֲנִי שֶׁנְּשׁוֹתֵיהֶם אַלְמָנוֹת וּבְנֵיהֶם יְתוֹמִים. [11] אֶלָּא מַה תַּלְמוּד לוֹמַר 'וְהָיוּ נְשֵׁיכֶם' וגו׳?

TRANSLATION AND COMMENTARY

בְּשֶׁשָּׁמְעוּ בּוֹ שֶׁמֵּת [1] The Gemara now attempts to delimit the dispute: **Where people have heard that the captive** has **died** — in other words, where there was a persistent rumor to that effect, and we are fairly confident, though not completely certain, that it is true — [2] **all agree that we authorize** the appointment of an administrator. Even Rav would agree in this case, because if the rumor is true, the relative is the captive's heir.

כִּי פְּלִיגֵי [3] **Where** Rav and Shmuel **do disagree** is **where people have not heard that** the captive **has died,** and believe he may eventually return. [4] In such a case **Rav said: We do not authorize** the appointment of a relative as an administrator, **because** we are afraid that he **may** do more **damage** than good to the owner's possessions. Since the administrator believes the owner is still alive, and will eventually return and reclaim his property, he may be tempted to ignore the long-term interests of the estate and concentrate on maximizing his immediate profits. [5] **But Shmuel said: We do authorize** the appointment of a relative as an administrator in such a case. [6] There is no cause for concern about a conflict of interest, **since the Master** — the author of the Baraita quoted later in the passage — **said that** if the owner does return, **we appraise** the administrator's labors **as if he were a tenant farmer,** and give him a fair return for his efforts. [7] Therefore the relative **will not damage** the field, since in any case he will be fully reimbursed for his labors.

מֵיתִיבֵי [8] The Gemara now raises an **objection** to Shmuel's view from a Baraita taken from the minor tractate, *Avot DeRabbi Natan* (38:3): **"Rabbi Eliezer says:** The verse (Exodus 22:23) says that if you oppress widows or orphans, 'My wrath will be inflamed and I will kill you by the sword, and your wives will be widows and your sons orphans.' [9] Now, **by logical deduction from** the first part of this **verse — 'My wrath will be inflamed and I will kill you'** — [10] I already **know** the information contained in the second part, **that their wives will be widows and their sons orphans.** It is obvious that the wife of a man who has been killed is a widow and his son an orphan! Why does the Torah need to stress this obvious fact? [11] **Rather,** explains Rabbi Eliezer, **what is the verse teaching us by saying: 'And your wives will be widows and your sons orphans'?**

RASHI

בששמעו בו שמת כולי עלמא לא פליגי דמורידין — דאם יבאו הבעלים קודם שיאכל זה הפירות — יטול זה כשאר אריסין, ויחזיר השאר ואם יבאו עדים שמת — ירש הכל. **מפסיד להו** — ולא יזבל הקרקעות, ויזרעם תמיד ויכחישם. **כיון דאמר מר** — לקמן וכולם שמין להם כאריס, אם יבאו הבעלים שמין לזה חלקו בכל שנה שעבד בה כמנהג אריסי העיר, אם מחצה אם שליש אם רביע.

NOTES

שָׁיְימִינַן לְהוּ כְּאָרִיס We appraise them as if he were a tenant farmer. The contract between the landowner and the tenant farmer includes not only an agreement regarding the percentage of the profits to be retained by the farmer, but also detailed agreements regarding the division of expenses entailed by caring for the soil and the crops, and the division of profits accruing from any increase in the property's value resulting from the tenant's care. Since according to such agreements the tenant is well compensated for his trouble, we may assume that anyone who occupies land, works it, and enjoys these rights will also take proper care of the soil and not occasion losses to its owner.

HALAKHAH

בְּשֶׁשָּׁמְעוּ בּוֹ שֶׁמֵּת Where people heard about the captive that he died. "If there is a reliable rumor that a captive or a fugitive has died, we do not prevent his heirs from taking over his field and dividing it as if it were their own." (*Shulḥan Arukh, Ḥoshen Mishpat* 285:1.) Even if the heirs have heard that the captive is returning to reclaim his

BACKGROUND

שְׁבוּי שֶׁנִּשְׁבָּה A captive who was taken captive. Halakhic problems associated with prisoners and other missing persons arise because of the basic assumption (חֲזָקָה) that a person is living until proven dead. The Halakhah contains no procedure by which a missing person may be declared dead, even though a long time has passed and nothing has been heard of him. This assumption creates serious problems for the missing person's family. His wife is regarded as a married woman, and his children cannot inherit his estate.

אָרִיס A tenant farmer. Frequently the owner of land would not cultivate it himself, but would allow it to be farmed by someone else. Such agreements could be made in various ways, of which the two principal ones were: (1) Rental for a fixed sum either in cash, if the tenant is a קַבְּלָן (contractor), or in a predetermined quantity of produce if the tenant is a חוֹכֵר (lessee). (2) Sharecropping, where the tenant agrees to give the landowner a certain proportion of his crop (half, one-third or one-quarter). Such contracts could be limited to a single year or extend over several years. There were even hereditary lease-holdings (חֲכִירֵי בָּתֵּי אָבוֹת), which families would pass on over generations. Many of the Halakhot connected with tenant farming and leases are found in the ninth chapter of the present tractate.

TERMINOLOGY

מִמַּשְׁמַע שֶׁנֶּאֱמַר... יוֹדֵעַ אֲנִי... אֶלָּא מַה תַּלְמוּד לוֹמַר... By [logical] deduction from the text... I know... What then does the verse teach? This expression is part of Midrashic terminology. The author of the teaching begins with a quotation from a Biblical text and questions it (often on the grounds that part of the text seems superfluous). He then explains and interprets the text, showing the meaning of the apparently superfluous feature: "From the fact that the text says X, is it not obvious that

TRANSLATION AND COMMENTARY

[1]He answers: **It is teaching** us that God will punish the sinners with an additional punishment. Even after the men are killed in captivity, their death will not be known to their next of kin. Thus their wives and sons will be punished with permanent widowhood and orphanhood. The sinners' **wives will wish to remarry, but we will not permit them** to do so, [2]**and their sons will wish to take possession of their father's estate, but we will not permit them** to do so." The Gemara's objection is as follows: According to this Baraita, if a person is taken captive, and it is not known whether he has been killed, his sons must remain in a state of quasi-orphanhood, similar to the state of quasi-widowhood of a woman who does not know if her husband is alive or dead. They can no more inherit their father's property than their mother can remarry. Thus, from this Baraita, it would appear that Rav is correct and we do not appoint a relative to adminster the estate of someone who is not known to be dead! This is surely a refutation of Shmuel's viewpoint.

אָמַר רָבָא [3]**Rava said** in reply: This Baraita cannot be used to prove that relatives are not appointed to administer a captive's estate. It is not saying that sons are totally forbidden to administer their captive father's estate. What **we learn** from this Baraita is that they are forbidden **to take** full **possession** of the property **and sell** it. But they *are* permitted to work their father's estate and protect it from deterioration. Thus the Baraita in no way contradicts the viewpoint of Shmuel.

הֲוָה עוּבְדָא בִּנְהַרְדְּעָא [4]The Gemara now relates a case in which a leading Amora ruled contrary to the interpretation of the Baraita just given by Rava. **There was a case in Neharde'a** where a relative wanted to take possession of a captive's estate and came to Rav Sheshet for advice as to how to act. [5]**Rav Sheshet deduced from the Baraita** cited above that the law is in accordance with the viewpoint of Rav, and that it is forbidden for relatives to take possession of the property of captives.

אֲמַר לֵיהּ רַב עַמְרָם [6]**Rav Amram** then **said to** Rav Sheshet: **Perhaps the Baraita is** only **teaching** that we do not allow the heirs **to take** full **possession** of the estate **and sell** it? This suggestion by Rav Amram is the same as that made by Rava.

אֲמַר לֵיהּ [7]Rav Sheshet **said** sarcastically **to** Rav Amram, using a similar turn of phrase: **Perhaps you are from Pumbedita, where they insert an elephant through the eye of a needle** (i.e., engage in unjustified hairsplitting)?

[1]מְלַמֵּד שֶׁנְּשׁוֹתֵיהֶם מְבַקְּשׁוֹת לִינָּשֵׂא, וְאֵין מַנִּיחִין אוֹתָן, [2]וּבְנֵיהֶן רוֹצִים לֵירֵד לְנִכְסֵי אֲבִיהֶן, וְאֵין מַנִּיחִין אוֹתָן״.
[3]אָמַר רָבָא: ״לֵירֵד וְלִמְכּוֹר״ תְּנַן.
[4]הֲוָה עוּבְדָא בִּנְהַרְדְּעָא, [5]וּפְשָׁטָהּ רַב שֵׁשֶׁת מֵהָא מַתְנִיתָא.
[6]אֲמַר לֵיהּ רַב עַמְרָם: דִּלְמָא ״לֵירֵד וְלִמְכּוֹר״ תְּנַן?
[7]אֲמַר לֵיהּ: דִּלְמָא מִפּוּמְבְּדִיתָא אַתְּ, דִּמְעַיְּילִין פִּילָא בְּקוֹפָא דְּמַחְטָא?

LITERAL TRANSLATION

[1]It teaches that their wives wish to get married, but we do not permit them, [2]and their sons wish to take possession of (lit., 'go down to') their father's estates, but we do not permit them."

[3]Rava said: We learned: "To take possession and sell."

[4]There was a case in Neharde'a, [5]and Rav Sheshet solved it from this Baraita.

[6]Rav Amram said to him: Perhaps we learned: "to take possession and to sell"?

[7]He said to him: Perhaps you are from Pumbedita, where they insert an elephant through the eye of a needle?

RASHI

אלא מלמד שנשיהם מבקשות לינשא כו׳ — שילכו בשבי ולא ידעו בניהם אם חיים אם מתים, ויהיו נשיהם אלמנות לעולם, שאין בית דין מניחין אותן לינשא, ובניהם כיתומים, שלא ירשו נכסיהם, ושתי קללות הן, אחת של חרב ואחת של שבי, שמע מינה: אין מורידין. **הוה עובדא בנהרדעא** — בשבוי שירד יורשו לנכסיו. **ופשטה רב ששת מהא מתניתא** — דאין מורידין. **אמר ליה רב עמרם דלמא לירד ולמכור תנן** — [קתני] תנא דאין מניחין, אבל לעשות ולאכול וליטול כארים — שפיר דמי. **דמעיילין פילא כו׳** — ומשני שנויא דחיקא, כמבקש להכניס פיל, שהוא חיה גדולה, בנקב מחט.

Y is the case? Why, then, did the text say Y? In order to teach us...."

SAGES

רַב שֵׁשֶׁת Rav Sheshet. A Babylonian Amora of the second and third generations. See *Bava Metzia*, Part I, p. 37.

רַב עַמְרָם Rav Amram. A Babylonian Amora of the second and third generations, Rav Amram transmitted rulings in the names of several scholars, including Rav, Rav Naḥman, Rav Ḥisda, and Rav Sheshet.

BACKGROUND

פִּילָא בְּקוֹפָא דְּמַחְטָא An elephant through the eye of a needle. This is a Talmudic expression for something inconceivable. Here it has an additional meaning, for Rav Sheshet believes that Rav Amram is attempting to stretch the words of the Baraita beyond their literal meaning. Hence he is "pushing an elephant through the eye of a needle" — forcing the text to perform an impossible task.

דִּלְמָא מִפּוּמְבְּדִיתָא Perhaps you are from Pumbedita. During the first generations of Amoraim, two central yeshivot emerged in Babylonia — in Sura and in Pumbedita. Even though there were short periods when these yeshivot split or were dismantled, they continued to flourish for hundreds of years.

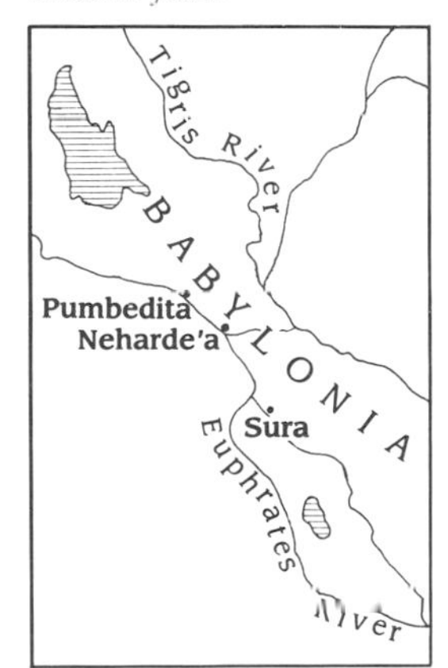

It would appear that from the very outset the Sura Yeshivah's approach to Torah study was closer to that used by the scholars of Eretz Israel

HALAKHAH

property, and they hasten to eat the produce of the estate, we do not take anything back from them (*Netivot*). On the other hand, *Rema* rules in the name of *Rosh* that they are not entitled to reimbursement for any investment they may have made. Rather, whatever they have spent is spent, and whatever they have consumed is consumed.

TRANSLATION AND COMMENTARY

[1]The Baraita, argues Rav Sheshet, does support Rav's position. For **surely it teaches** that the expression **"their sons"** in the verse quoted is meant to **parallel** the expression **"their wives."** [2]**Just as** the wives of captives may **not** remarry **at all,** [3]**so too** the sons of captives may **not** take possession of their fathers' estates **at all.** Thus the verse is describing a situation in which the sons are forced to remain in a state of quasi-orphanhood, comparable to the state of quasi-widowhood of a woman who does not know if her husband is alive or dead. Such a situation is possible only if Rav's opinion is correct and relatives are *not* permitted to administer a captive's estate.

ומורידין קרוב לנכסי שבוי [4]The Gemara now notes: Even though Rav's position has support from the Baraita in *Avot DeRabbi Natan,* Shmuel's position is not necessarily to be rejected, as the question of **whether** it is permitted to **authorize a relative to administer a captive's estate is** actually **the subject of a Tannaitic controversy,** with one Tanna taking Rav's position and the other Shmuel's, [5]**as the** following Tosefta (*Ketubot* 8:3) **teaches.** The Tosefta distinguishes among three cases. The Gemara's argument is based on the second case, as will be explained below: (1) "If a relative **takes possession of a captive's estate, we do not take it away from him.** [6]**Not only** do we not take it away from him, **but even if** the relative **heard that the owner of the field was approaching,** [7]**and he anticipated** the latter's arrival **and picked and ate** all the **fruit** growing in the field, he has not acted wrongly. [8]Indeed, **he is rewarded** for his initiative. [9]**And the following is** the definition of the expression **'a captive's estates':** [10]It refers to a situation **where** the relative's **father or brother or one of the people whose** property he can expect **to inherit went overseas,** [11]**and** later **a report arrived that he had died."** Thus, in the first case it considers, the Tosefta tells us that if the owner of property goes abroad without giving instructions as to what should be done with his estate, and if his closest relative administers the estate in his absence, and then a report arrives that the owner has died, his heir is allowed to retain possession of his estate according to everyone. [12](2) "If a relative **takes possession of an abandoned estate, we take it away from him.** [13]**And the following is** the definition of **'an abandoned estate':** [14]It refers to a situation **where** the relative's **father or brother or one of the people whose** property he can expect **to inherit went overseas,** [15]**and no report arrived that he had died.**

[1]וְהָא דּוּמְיָא דִּנְשׁוֹתֵיהֶם קָתָנֵי. [2]מַה הָתָם, כְּלָל לָא, [3]אַף הָכָא נַמִי, כְּלָל לָא.

[4]וּמוֹרִידִין קָרוֹב לְנִכְסֵי שָׁבוּי תַּנָּאֵי הִיא. [5]דְּתַנְיָא: ״הַיּוֹרֵד לְנִכְסֵי שָׁבוּי — אֵין מוֹצִיאִין אוֹתוֹ מִיָּדוֹ. [6]וְלֹא עוֹד, אֶלָּא אֲפִילּוּ שָׁמַע שֶׁמְּמַשְׁמְשִׁין וּבָאִין, [7]וְקָדַם וְתָלַשׁ וְאָכַל, [8]הֲרֵי זֶה זָרִיז וְנִשְׂכָּר. [9]וְאֵלּוּ הֵן ׳נִכְסֵי שְׁבוּיִין׳: [10]הֲרֵי שֶׁהָיָה אָבִיו אוֹ אָחִיו אוֹ אֶחָד מִן הַמּוֹרִישִׁין הָלְכוּ לָהֶם לִמְדִינַת הַיָּם, [11]וְשָׁמְעוּ בָּהֶן שֶׁמֵּת. [12]הַיּוֹרֵד לְנִכְסֵי נְטוּשִׁים — מוֹצִיאִין אוֹתוֹ מִיָּדוֹ. [13]וְאֵלּוּ הֵן ׳נִכְסֵי נְטוּשִׁים׳: [14]הֲרֵי שֶׁהָיָה אָבִיו אוֹ אָחִיו אוֹ אֶחָד מִן הַמּוֹרִישִׁין, הָלְכוּ לָהֶם לִמְדִינַת הַיָּם, [15]וְלֹא שָׁמְעוּ בָּהֶם שֶׁמֵּת.

LITERAL TRANSLATION

[1]But surely it teaches [their sons] like their wives. [2]Just as there, not at all, [3]so too here, not at all.

[4]And [whether] we authorize a relative to [administer] a captive's estates is a Tannaitic [controversy]. [5]For it has been taught: "Someone who takes possession of (lit., 'goes down to') a captive's estates — we do not take it out of his hand. [6]And not only [this], but even if he heard that [the owner of the field] is approaching, [7]and he anticipated and picked [fruit] and ate [it], [8]this [person] is quick and is rewarded. [9]And these are 'captives' estates': [10]If his father or his brother or one of those who cause him to inherit went to a country overseas, [11]and they heard that he died. [12]Someone who takes possession of abandoned estates — we take it out of his hand. [13]And these are 'abandoned estates': [14]If his father or his brother or one of those who cause him to inherit went to a country overseas, [15]and they did not hear that he died.

RASHI

ותלש — פירות שנה זו. **הרי זה זריז** — מהיר לזכות בשלו בטרם יפסיד, ונשכר בזריזותו. **ואלו הן נכסי שבויין** — דאמר אין מוציאין אותם מידו.

and breadth of knowledge (from the Bible to the Tannaitic sources) was emphasized. Rav Sheshet was a distinguished scholar of this yeshivah.

The Pumbedita Yeshivah was more "Babylonian," and its method of study involved more dialectical argument and casuistry. Rav Amram was a disciple of Rav Sheshet, and Rav Sheshet knew him well. The question, "Perhaps you are from Pumbedita?," is thus ironic, reflecting Rav Sheshet's attitude to the method of study employed in the Pumbedita Yeshivah.

TERMINOLOGY

תַּנָּאֵי הִיא It is a Tannaitic controversy, i.e., the matter under discussion by Amoraim is in fact the subject of a Tannaitic controversy.

BACKGROUND

הֲרֵי זֶה זָרִיז וְנִשְׂכָּר This person is quick and is rewarded. This expression is found in several passages as a generalization regarding the result of prompt action. The Talmud not only mentions cases in which promptness brings people profit. It also mentions those in which promptness leads to loss. In the present instance, the person administering the land profits by taking the produce promptly, for he will not be held to account if his profits are greater than he would have received as a tenant farmer.

מְדִינַת הַיָּם A country overseas. The primary meaning of this expression is "overseas," and in most sources the sea in question is the Mediterranean. In ancient times, since ships had no compasses and used fixed sails, they had to hug the coasts, which meant it took quite a long time to cover even short distances. Moreover, since ships were relatively scarce, communications overseas were sporadic and difficult. When someone journeyed overseas, there was no way of keeping track of him. In certain cases the expression מְדִינַת הַיָּם was extended to include any distant place with which no permanent communication or transport routes were maintained.

HALAKHAH

נִכְסֵי נְטוּשִׁים Abandoned estates. "If there is no reason to assume that a captive or a fugitive is dead, the court appoints one of his heirs to administer the field until his return. *Rema* suggests that an heir who has experience in farming should be appointed. He is treated as if he were a tenant farmer," following Rabban Shimon ben Gamliel and Shmuel. (*Shulḥan Arukh, Ḥoshen Mishpat* 285:2.)

[1]וְאָמַר רַבָּן שִׁמְעוֹן בֶּן גַּמְלִיאֵל: שָׁמַעְתִּי שֶׁהַנְּטוּשִׁים כִּשְׁבוּיִין. [2]הַיּוֹרֵד לְנִכְסֵי רְטוּשִׁים — מוֹצִיאִין אוֹתוֹ מִיָּדוֹ. [3]וְאֵלּוּ הֵן ׳נִכְסֵי רְטוּשִׁים׳: [4]הֲרֵי שֶׁהָיָה אָבִיו אוֹ אָחִיו אוֹ אֶחָד מִן הַמּוֹרִישִׁין כָּאן, [5]וְאֵינוֹ יוֹדֵעַ לְהֵיכָן הָלְכוּ״.

[6]מַאי שְׁנָא הָנָךְ דְּקָרוּ לְהוּ ״נְטוּשִׁים״, [7]וּמַאי שְׁנָא הָנֵי דְּקָרוּ לְהוּ ״רְטוּשִׁים״?

[39A] [8]״נְטוּשִׁים״ דִּבְעַל כָּרְחָן, [9]דִּכְתִיב: ״וְהַשְּׁבִיעִת תִּשְׁמְטֶנָּה וּנְטַשְׁתָּהּ״ — [10]אַפְקַעְתָּא דְּמַלְכָּא.

LITERAL TRANSLATION

[1]But Rabban Shimon ben Gamliel said: I heard that abandoned [estates] are like [estates of] captives. [2]Someone who takes possession of unoccupied estates — we take it out of his hand. [3]And these are 'unoccupied estates': [4]If his father or his brother or one of those who cause him to inherit was here, [5]and [the relative] does not know where they went."

[6]What is the difference that they called these "abandoned," [7]and what is the difference that they called those "unoccupied." [39A] [8]"Abandoned" [means] "against their will," [9]as it is written: "But the seventh year you shall let it rest and abandon it" — [10]expropriation by the [divine] King.

TRANSLATION AND COMMENTARY

[1]**But Rabban Shimon ben Gamliel** disagreed with this position. He **said: I heard that abandoned property is** considered **like property of captives,** and we allow the relative to continue to administer it." Thus, in the second case it considers, the Tosefta tells us that if there is no reason to assume that an absentee owner has died, the Tannaim disagree as to whether his heirs may take possession of his estate. The Gemara above stated that this is the case about which Rav and Shmuel disagree. [2](3) "If a relative **takes possession of an unoccupied estate, we take it away from him.** [3]**And the following is** the definition of **'an unoccupied estate'**: [4]It refers to a situation where the relative's **father or brother or one of the people whose** property he can expect **to inherit was here** previously and then disappeared, [5]**and the relative does not know where he went.** In this case, all agree that the relative is not permitted to enter the field." Thus, in the third case it considers, the Baraita tells us that there is a special kind of absentee owner whose heirs may not take over his estate according to everyone.

מַאי שְׁנָא [6]The Gemara now seeks to define some of the terms used in this Tosefta, and asks: **What is the difference** between **properties called "abandoned,"** which are subject to a dispute between Rabban Shimon ben Gamliel and the other Tanna, [7]**and properties called "unoccupied,"** which according to all opinions may not be given to an administrator? The two terms seem to mean the same thing.

נְטוּשִׁים דִּבְעַל כָּרְחָן [39A] [8]The Gemara answers: When the Baraita uses the term **"abandoned"** (case 2), it **means** "property abandoned **against** its owner's **will,**" — for example, where the owner was taken captive. [9]The Gemara brings Scriptural support for this usage from a verse (Exodus 23:11) which employs the same term, though in a different context: **It is written:** "But **the seventh year, you shall** let the land rest **and abandon it** (וּנְטַשְׁתָּהּ)." When the Torah ordered us to leave our fields fallow during the seventh year, it used the verb לִנְטוֹשׁ — "to abandon" — the same verb used by the Baraita in the case of "abandoned property" (נְטוּשִׁים). [10]The abandoning of fields during the seventh year is a classic example of **expropriation by** order of **the divine King.** We are not merely urged to leave our land fallow, we are ordered to do so by the force of divine law. Hence, since the same Hebrew verb — לִנְטוֹשׁ — is used both in this verse and in our Baraita, the Gemara infers that in the Baraita as well, the "abandoned" property was abandoned against its owner's will.

RASHI

שהנטושים כשבוין — ואין מוציאין מידו. **נכסי נטושין** — שהנכסים נטושין. **נכסי רטושין** — שהנכסים רטושים. ולקמן מפרש להו, רטושין משמע שעזבום בעלים מדעתם והלכו להם, דכיון דהיה לו לצוות: הורידו יורשיי לנכסי, ולא צוה — שמע מינה לא ניחא ליה, ונטושים — שנטשום בעליהם בעל כרחן, כגון שנשבו. והיינו תנאי, דרבן שמעון סבר: מורידין, ורבנן סברי: אין מורידין. הכי גרסינן: נטושים על כרחן דכתיב ״והשביעית תשמטנה ונטשתה״ — היינו על כרחו. **אפקעתא דמלכא** — מצות המלך.

HALAKHAH

נִכְסֵי רְטוּשִׁים Unoccupied property. "If a person travels abroad for personal reasons and leaves no instructions about his property, and there is no reason to assume that he is dead, the court does not appoint a relative to administer his estate. Moreover, even if a relative wishes to take over the administration of the estate on his own initiative, we do not permit it. All the property must be left as it is, since we treat such a case as if it were an intentional loss." (Ibid., 285:4.)

BACKGROUND

נִכְסֵי נְטוּשִׁים וְנִכְסֵי רְטוּשִׁים Abandoned estates and unoccupied estates. These two terms, as explained below (39a), distinguish between property abandoned against the owner's will (for example, if he was taken into captivity or forced to leave his home for some other reason and is unable to return within a short time) and property from which the owner is voluntarily absent. When an owner is unable to return home, there is reason for the court to seek a way of maintaining his family and preserving the value of his property. However, when the owner is voluntarily absent because of financial pressure or for another reason, the court need not interfere in his private affairs or do anything which the absent person has not expressed an interest in having done.

אַפְקַעְתָּא דְּמַלְכָּא Expropriation by the divine King. Both in Jewish law and in the laws of other cultures the king had the right to confiscate property for public use. Such confiscations were by royal fiat, and the owner of the property was unable to oppose them. Moreover, once property was confiscated, the owner had no further rights to it. Even if the king were to return it, this would be a gift and not a restoration of the previous situation. These definitions bear upon the juridical significance of the Sabbatical Year and the Jubilee Year.

The Gemara uses the phrase אַפְקַעְתָּא דְּמַלְכָּא twice in connection with the laws of the Sabbatical Year (below, 106a and 109a). In the first passage, the Gemara explains that for the purpose of interpreting rental contracts, the Sabbatical Year should not be compared to a year in which farmers find it difficult to farm, but rather to a year in which farming is Halakhically forbidden, since the land may not be farmed during the Sabbatical Year "by decree of the divine King." In the second passage the Gemara rules that the laws governing the return of property in the Jubilee Year cannot

[1]״רְטוּשִׁים״ דְּמִדַּעְתָּן, [2]דִּכְתִיב: ״אֵם עַל בָּנִים רֻטָּשָׁה״. [3]תָּנָא: ״וְכוּלָּם שָׁמִין לָהֶם כְּאָרִיס״.

LITERAL TRANSLATION

[1]"Unoccupied" [means] "voluntarily," [2]as it is written: "A mother was forsaken with her sons." [3][A Tanna] taught: "And we appraise all of them like a tenant farmer."

TRANSLATION AND COMMENTARY

רְטוּשִׁים [1]The Gemara continues its answer: On the other hand, when the Baraita uses the term **"unoccupied"** (case 3), it **means** property whose owner **voluntarily** left it untended for some reason. [2]The Gemara brings Scriptural support for this interpretation from a verse (Hosea 10:14) which employs the same term, though again in a completely different context: **It is written: "A mother was forsaken with her sons."** The Gemara explains this passage as meaning that the soldiers will panic and flee, leaving their wives and children behind. When the prophet describes this "leaving" he uses the verb לְרַטֵּשׁ — "to forsake" — the same verb as that used by the Baraita in the case of "unoccupied property" (רְטוּשִׁים). Hence the Gemara infers that, as in the verse in Hosea, in the Baraita too the "unoccupied" property was left because the owner chose to leave his property in haste for some personal reason.

The Tosefta has now been fully explained. Case 1: If the owner was taken captive and there is a reliable rumor that he has died, we permit a relative to take over the field, and even if the owner returns, the relative may consume the produce until the moment of his arrival. Case 2: If the owner was taken captive and there is no reason to assume that he has died, the first Tanna rules that we do not permit a relative to take over the field, whereas Rabban Shimon ben Gamliel rules that we do. Thus the first Tanna sets out the position previously attributed to Rav, whereas Rabban Shimon ben Gamliel sets out the position attributed to Shmuel, and it had been the Gemara's purpose to establish this relationship between the positions of the Tannaim and the Amoraim when it first quoted this Tosefta. Case 3: If the owner was not taken captive, but simply left his property unoccupied for some reason, everyone agrees that we do not permit a relative to take over the field.

תָּנָא [3]Up to this point, the Gemara has been considering the third Baraita of the eighth chapter of the Tosefta of tractate *Ketubot*. The Gemara now considers the next Baraita in the Tosefta (*Ketubot* 8:4), which continues the theme of the previous one: **It was taught in a Baraita: "We appraise all** the people we allow to administer their relative's fields **as if they were tenant farmers."** Thus, if the owner returns, he and the administrator divide the crops produced by the field, as well as any improvement in its capital value, in accordance with the local custom for tenant farmers (sharecroppers).

RASHI

רטושים מדעתן דכתיב אם על בנים רוטשה — היינו מדעתו. ולא שביה, דכתיב רישיה דקרא ״וקם שאון בעמך״, היו יראים שלא יבאו אויבים עליהם ״וכל מבצריך יושד״ — יגלו בגולה מאליהן, וישארו העיירות שדודין מאין איש ״כשוד שלמן בית ארבאל ביום מלחמה״ — כשודדין הבאין למלחמה על ידי מארב על עם היושב בשלום, שלא נזהרו בהם לברוח מפניהם, ושודדים את הכל, וכמוהו (ירמיהו יג) ״הגלת יהודה כולה הגלת שלומים״ — מתוך ישיבת שלום באין מחריד הגלם נבוכדנצר. ״בית ארבאל״ תרגם יהונתן בית מארב. אל״ף למ״ד יתריס בו, כמו (הושע ב) ״יענו את יזרעאל״ שהוא לשון זריעה, ולא לשון עיר, ומדקא אמר ״יושד כשוד שלמן בית ארבאל״ — מכלל דההוא יומא לאו בית ארבאל ביום מלחמה הוה, אלא מורך בא בלבם, והמה עוזבים אם על בנים והולכים להם מדאגת האויב שמא יבא עליהם. **רוטשה** — נעזבה. **וכולן** — מפרש לקמיה אהייא קאי וכללא לאתויי מאי. **שמין להם באריס** — אם יבאו הבעלים — יטלו אלו בשבח קרקעות ופירות כמנהג אריסי המקום.

be compared to the laws of rental, because a sale until the Jubilee is not a long-term rental but rather a full-fledged sale which is then abrogated "by decree of the divine King." The Aharonim adduced an additional regulation from this phrase — that the laws of the Sabbatical Year apply regardless of the attitude of the farmer. Thus crops that grow during this year may be taken by anyone, whether or not the farmer agrees to declare them ownerless (see *Pe'at HaShulhan* and *Hazon Ish*). However, the relevance of this phrase in our passage is not obvious. In our commentary we have explained it as though "expropriation by the divine King" means simply "against one's will." Thus, just as the laws of the Sabbatical Year, which are described in the Torah by the word "abandon," apply even against the farmer's will, so too the "abandoned property" of the Baraita must have been abandoned against its owner's will. Support for this interpretation can be found in the version of *Rashi* appearing alongside the text of *Rif*. But if this phrase means no more than "against one's will," then not only is the Sabbatical Year a "decree of the divine King," but all the Torah's commands are "decrees of the divine King." Hence, the use of this phrase here is unlike its use in the other passages, where it is actually teaching us something about the laws of the Sabbatical Year. Indeed, there are many versions of this passage in which the phrase "expropriation by the divine King" does not appear.

LANGUAGE

רְטוּשִׁים Unoccupied. The interpretation given here to the verse אֵם עַל בָּנִים רֻטָּשָׁה is not the one given by most interpreters of the Bible. Beginning with the Aramaic translation of Yonatan ben Uziel and including *Rashi*, who presents the interpretation given in the Gemara as an alternative, they all explain that רֻטָּשָׁה means "killed, torn to shreds."

The interpretation given by the Gemara here must be viewed as homiletic; the meaning of the term רְטוּשִׁים

NOTES

וְכוּלָּם שָׁמִין לָהֶם כְּאָרִיס And we appraise all of them like a tenant farmer. Among the many different interpretations of this statement found in the Rishonim, *Rashi* explains that the relative of the captive thought to be alive is literally a tenant farmer. Just as a tenant farmer meets with the owner once a year and accounts for his expenses, his consumption, the value of the crops produced, and any increase in the value of the land, and then takes a fixed share for himself — varying between one-quarter and half, according to local custom — so too must the relative administering the captive's land meet with the court once a year and make a similar accounting. He then takes his share and transfers the owner's share to the court for safekeeping.

Ramban disagrees with *Rashi* about the annual accounting. According to *Ramban*, the relative is allowed to treat the field as his own until the owner returns. But once

HALAKHAH

וְכוּלָּם שָׁמִין לָהֶם כְּאָרִיס And we appraise all of them like a tenant farmer. "If an estate has been abandoned by a captive or a fugitive, a relative is appointed to administer it and to till the land. If the captive returns, the relative is entitled to the share of the produce and of the appreciation in the land's value that he would receive if he were a tenant farmer," following *Rambam* and *Ramban*. (*Shulhan Arukh, Hoshen Mishpat* 275:2.) *Rema*, following *Tosafot* and *Rosh*, writes that only the appreciation is appraised as if the relative were a tenant farmer, but he is not required to compensate the owner for produce that he ate.

According to both these views, no attempt is made to

TRANSLATION AND COMMENTARY

אַהַיָּיא [1]The Gemara asks: **To which** of the three **cases** mentioned in the previous Baraita **does this** Baraita **refer?** [2]**If we say** that it refers **to** the first case — the estate of **a captive** rumored to have died — it is not providing us with any new information. [3]For concerning the captive who was rumored to have died, the Baraita **says** that if he returns and his relative picks all the fruit before he arrives, the relative **"is quick and is rewarded"**! [4]Since the relative is permitted to eat as much fruit as he wishes, **is it necessary to state** that he is entitled to the share due to a tenant farmer for **the improvements** he has made in the field?

אֶלָּא אַרְטוּשִׁים [5]**But**, continues the Gemara, **if we say that** the Baraita **is referring to** the third case — the **unoccupied property** of a person who disappeared for personal reasons — this too cannot be correct. [6]For **surely** the Baraita **states** that if someone disappeared for personal reasons, and a relative of his tries to take over the property and administer it, **"we take it away from him."** Hence it is obvious that in such a case the relative is not entitled to the share of a tenant farmer.

אֶלָּא אַנְטוּשִׁים [7]**Rather,** concludes the Gemara, we must explain that the Baraita **is referring to** the second case — the **abandoned property** of a captive thought to be alive. The Baraita is telling us that in such a case we appoint a relative to administer the property, and grant him the share of a tenant farmer.

לְמַאן [8]The Gemara questions further: It is still not clear how the Baraita can be referring even to the second case. For there are two conflicting opinions mentioned in connection with the second case — the opinion of the first Tanna and the opinion of Rabban Shimon ben Gamliel. **According to** which opinion is this Baraita stating that we appoint an administrator and grant him the share of a tenant farmer? [9]**If we say** that the Baraita is **in accordance with the** first **Sage's** opinion, this cannot be correct. [10]For **surely** the first Sage **says** that if the captive is thought to be alive, and a relative tries to take over the property and administer it, **"we take it away from him."** Hence, it is obvious that in such a case the relative is not entitled to the share of a tenant farmer. [11]On the other hand, **if** we **say** the Baraita follows **Rabban Shimon ben Gamliel,** this also seems incorrect. [12]For **surely** Rabban Shimon ben Gamliel **said** about this case: **"I heard that abandoned property is** considered **like the property of captives** rumored to have died" (the first case), and thus the relative should be permitted to eat as much fruit as he wants, like the relative of a captive who is rumored to have died. How then can the Baraita say that the relative receives only the share of a tenant farmer?

[1]אַהַיָּיא? [2]אִילֵימָא אַשְּׁבוּיִין, [3]הָשְׁתָּא זָרִיז וְנִשְׂכָּר הָוֵה, [4]מַאי דְּאַשְׁבַּח מִיבָּעֲיָא? [5]אֶלָּא אַרְטוּשִׁים, [6]וְהָא "מוֹצִיאִין אוֹתָן מִיָּדוֹ" קָתָנֵי! [7]אֶלָּא אַנְטוּשִׁים. [8]לְמַאן? [9]אִילֵימָא לְרַבָּנַן, [10]הָא אָמְרִי: "מוֹצִיאִין אוֹתוֹ מִיָּדוֹ"! [11]אִי רַבָּן שִׁמְעוֹן בֶּן גַּמְלִיאֵל, [12]הָא אָמַר: "שָׁמַעְתִּי שֶׁהַנְּטוּשִׁים כִּשְׁבוּיִין"!

LITERAL TRANSLATION

[1]To which [case does this refer]? [2]If we say to captives, [3]now [that it says]: "he is quick and is rewarded," [4]is it necessary [to say this] about what he improved?

[5]But [if we say that it refers] to unoccupied [property], [6]surely it states: "We take them out of his hand"!

[7]Rather, [it refers] to abandoned [property].

[8]According to whom? [9]If we say according to the Sages, [10]surely they say: "We take it out of his hand"! [11]If [we say] Rabban Shimon ben Gamliel, [12]surely he said: "I heard that abandoned [estates] are like [estates of] captives"!

RASHI

השתא זריז ונשכר הוי — ויטול הכל. דאילו התם זריז ונשכר — דכיון ששמעו בו שמת, כי נחת לה — אדעתא דכולהו פירי נחת, אבל הכא, דלא שמעו שמת — לאו אדעתא דכולה נחית, אלא ליטול כארים בכל שנה, ושאר פירות יהא מונחין.

as used in the Baraita is derived from its use in Aramaic. In several passages in the Aramaic translations of the Bible we find the Hebrew נטש rendered as רטש. The shift from 'n' to 'r' is common in Hebrew and other languages. Consequently, in order to differentiate between different kinds of abandoned property, the Sages used the Hebrew verb נטש in contrast with the verb רטש, which is derived from a related Aramaic root. Other authorities have raised the possibility that the verb רטש is connected with the Latin *restitutio,* meaning the returning of property to its owner.

NOTES

the owner returns, the relative must account for his expenses and consumption, for the value of the remaining crops, and for any improvement in land value for the entire period of his administration. Afterwards, payment must be made in one direction or the other, so that the relative receives the share due a tenant farmer. Our commentary follows this interpretation.

זָרִיז וְנִשְׂכָּר **He is quick and is rewarded.** The Rishonim ask: Why should the rights of the administrator of the estate of a captive thought to be dead depend on his speed in seizing the crops?

Rashi explains that the status of the administrator is never changed retroactively. Thus, since the relative is awarded the field as an inheritance, he may take all the crops he

HALAKHAH

appraise the value of the appreciation or the crops, until the owner returns. However, *Tur* quotes *Rashi* as saying that the appraisal is performed even before the owner returns: Once a year, the courts make an assessment of the value of the land improvement and the crops, and award the relative his share as if he were a tenant farmer. The owner's share is placed in the custody of the court until it is determined whether he is alive or dead.

TRANSLATION AND COMMENTARY

כִּשְׁבוּיִין [1]The Gemara answers: The Baraita is indeed referring to the second case — "abandoned property" of captives thought to be alive — and the Baraita can be explained in accordance with the view of Rabban Shimon ben Gamliel. For when Rabban Shimon ben Gamliel said that "abandoned property **is** considered **like the property of captives,"** he did **not** mean to imply that "abandoned" property is *completely* like **the property of captives.** [2]The Gemara explains: According to Rabban Shimon ben Gamliel, "abandoned property" **is like the property of captives in that** if a relative wishes to administer it, **we do not take it away from him.** [3]**But it is not** wholly like **the property of captives, because** in the case of a captive's property the relative who took over the field is entitled to all the fruit, and even if he picked it a moment before the owner's return, **he is rewarded** for being so **quick.** [4]**Whereas** in the case of "abandoned property," according to Rabban Shimon ben Gamliel, we allow a relative to administer the property, but we do not let him take all the fruit. Instead, **we appraise the property for him** and award him a share **as if he were a tenant farmer.**

וּמַאי שְׁנָא מֵהָא דִּתְנַן [5]The Gemara now considers another aspect of the second Baraita ("we treat the relative like a tenant farmer"): We have explained it as referring to the administrator of the estate of a captive thought to be alive. **But,** the Gemara asks, why should such an administrator be treated like a tenant farmer? **In what** way **is** this case **different from** the case about which **we have learned** in the following Mishnah (*Ketubot* 79b), which also deals with a person administering a relative's property, but does not make such an arrangement: [6]"If a husband **spends money on his wife's** personal **property** and then divorces her or dies, he or his heirs are not entitled to any compensation for his expenses." Under Jewish law, a wife's property falls into two categories: (1) Communal property (נִכְסֵי צֹאן בַּרְזֶל), which is considered to belong to the husband for the duration of the marriage, and (2) personal property (נִכְסֵי מְלוֹג) which remains the property of the wife but is administered by the husband. The Mishnah in tractate *Ketubot* is dealing with the second category. While administering his wife's personal property, the husband will both incur expenses and derive financial benefit. Nevertheless, the Mishnah rules that if he divorces his wife, or dies, no attempt is made to assess his profits and losses. [7]"Thus," the Mishnah continues, **"whether he spent a great deal and consumed little, or spent little**

[1]כִּשְׁבוּיִין, וְלֹא שְׁבוּיִין. [2]כִּשְׁבוּיִין, דְּאֵין מוֹצִיאִין אוֹתָן מִיָּדוֹ. [3]וְלֹא שְׁבוּיִין, דְּאִילּוּ הָתָם זָרִיז וְנִשְׂכָּר, [4]וְאִילּוּ הָכָא שָׁיְימִינַן לֵיהּ כְּאָרִיס. [5]וּמַאי שְׁנָא מֵהָא דִּתְנַן: [6]"הַמּוֹצִיא הוֹצָאוֹת עַל נִכְסֵי אִשְׁתּוֹ, [7]הוֹצִיא הַרְבֵּה וְאָכַל קִימְעָא, קִימְעָא וְאָכַל הַרְבֵּה,

LITERAL TRANSLATION

[1]Like [estates of] captives, but not [estates of] captives. [2]Like [estates of] captives, because we do not take them out of his hand. [3]But not [estates of] captives, because there he was quick and is rewarded, [4]whereas here we appraise [the property] for him as if he were a tenant farmer.

[5]And [in] what is it different from what we learned: [6]"Someone who spends expenses on his wife's property, [7][whether] he spent much and consumed little, [or spent] little and consumed much,

RASHI

נכסי אשתו — נכסי מלוג, שהוא אוכל פירות, והקרן שלה. **הוציא הרבה ואכל פירות קימעא** — קודם שמת או שגירשה.

BACKGROUND

הַמּוֹצִיא הוֹצָאוֹת עַל נִכְסֵי אִשְׁתּוֹ Someone who spends money on his wife's property. There are various aspects of a husband's status regarding his wife's personal property (נִכְסֵי מְלוֹג). The property itself does not belong to the husband, but to his wife. However, by virtue of the marriage agreement, the husband has the right to manage the property and benefit from profits it earns. If the wife dies, the husband inherits this property. The ordinances of Usha support the view that the husband is a kind of buyer, though his acquisition is incomplete, for during his wife's lifetime he only has the right to the profits of the property, but not to the principal. It follows, therefore, that if he is regarded as a buyer, the expenses he incurs or the income he derives from the property are not subject to an accounting between the two parties, for everything he does is done on his own responsibility.

NOTES

wants, until the moment the owner reclaims his field. On the other hand, the relative of the captive thought to be alive has the status of a tenant farmer from the first moment. Hence his rights are fixed, and are not affected by his speed in picking the produce.

Most Rishonim reject *Rashi*'s interpretation, possibly because they disagree with his ruling that the relative of the living captive is a tenant farmer from the first moment. *Ramban* and *Rashba* argue that a specific Rabbinic enactment permits the relative of a supposedly dead captive to take as much as he likes until the moment the owner returns. This enactment is meant to encourage him to invest in the field without fear that he may not reap its profits. The Rabbis made this arrangement for estates of captives thought to be dead, but not for the "abandoned" property of captives thought to be alive, because the former are most unlikely to return and the relative may be tempted to administer the estate irresponsibly.

HALAKHAH

הַמּוֹצִיא הוֹצָאוֹת עַל נִכְסֵי אִשְׁתּוֹ Someone who spends money on his wife's property. "If a husband spends money on his wife's personal property (נִכְסֵי מְלוֹג) and subsequently divorces her or dies, he (or his heirs) may not demand reimbursement for his expenses, even if he did not consume as much as he invested. Rather, what he spent is considered spent, and what he consumed is considered consumed. This law applies only if he did consume

TRANSLATION AND COMMENTARY

and consumed a great deal, [1]**what he spent** is considered **spent, and what he consumed** is considered **consumed."** Thus the wife's personal property reverts to her in its condition at the time of the divorce or the husband's death, and neither side can demand compensation for expenses or profits. But, argues the Gemara, were we to follow the principle established in the case of "abandoned property," we should treat the husband like a tenant farmer and assess his expenses and income accordingly!

הָא לָא דָּמְיָא [2]The Gemara answers: There is a fundamental difference between the case of the relative administering a captive's property and that of a husband managing his wife's property: A husband managing his wife's property does not assume that he will divorce her, whereas a relative administering a captive's property realizes that the owner of the field could return at any moment. This distinction is crucial, as the Gemara will explain below. Now, if we wish to compare a captive's property to a wife's personal property, it can **only be compared to** the case of a man married to a girl who is still a minor, about which **we have learned** in the following Mishnah (*Ketubot* 80a; in our editions of the Talmud it is actually an Amoraic statement): [3]"If a husband **spends money on his wife's property while she is** still **a minor,** he **is like someone who spends money on the property of another** person who is not his wife." In other words, he is treated like a person who has temporarily administered a relative's property, and he is entitled to the share of a tenant farmer. The reason for the distinction between a minor and an adult woman is that the marriage of a minor whose father has died has no validity under Torah law, but is a Rabbinic institution. (By contrast, if a father arranges the marriage of his daughter while she is a minor the marriage is unconditionally valid. But this is not the case being discussed here.) Moreover, the Rabbis also instituted that a girl married in this way by her mother or brothers can dissolve the marriage at any time until she reaches adult status at the age of twelve by simply announcing that she does not wish the marriage to continue. A divorce is not required. Hence, the husband's situation is comparable to that of a relative administering the captive's property. Just as the captive may return and reclaim his property at any time, so too may the wife dissolve the marriage and reclaim her property at any time. If she does dissolve the marriage in this way, her ex-husband is entitled to the share of a tenant farmer.

אַלְמָא [4]The Gemara now explains why the Rabbis granted the share of a tenant farmer to the husband of a minor but not to the husband of an adult: **Since** the husband of the minor **lacks confidence that he will retain** his wife's **property** in his possession long enough to make a profit from it in the ordinary way, he may be tempted to misuse it by overfarming it and avoiding long-term investment in it, in an effort to profit from it quickly. [5]Therefore, **the Sages instituted an enactment for him** — that he be treated like a tenant farmer and receive a share in any improvement in the field's value as a result of his investment — [6]**so that he should**

[1]מַה שֶׁהוֹצִיא הוֹצִיא, וּמַה שֶׁאָכַל אָכַל״.
[2]הָא לָא דָּמְיָא אֶלָּא לְהָא דִּתְנַן: [3]״הַמּוֹצִיא הוֹצָאוֹת עַל נִכְסֵי אִשְׁתּוֹ קְטַנָּה כְּמוֹצִיא עַל נִכְסֵי אַחֵר דָּמֵי״.
[4]אַלְמָא, כֵּיוָן דְּלָא סָמְכָא דַּעְתֵּיהּ, [5]תַּקִּינוּ לֵיהּ רַבָּנַן, [6]כִּי הֵיכִי דְּלָא לִפְסַדִינְהוּ.

LITERAL TRANSLATION

[1]what he spent he spent, and what he consumed he consumed."

[2]This is only comparable to that which we have learned: [3]"Someone who spends expenses on his wife's property [while she is] a minor is like one who spends [money] on the property of a stranger."

[4]Thus, since his mind does not rely [on receiving the property], [5]the Sages made an enactment for him, [6]so that he should not damage it.

RASHI

הא לא דמיא – תרוייהו הוא: הא דנכסי שבויין להא דאשתו קטנה דמי. **קטנה** – שהיא יתומה שהשיאוה אמה ואחיה, ואין קידושין תופסין בה מן התורה אלא מדברי סופרים, לפיכך יוצאה במיאון בלא כרחו, אם תמאן. **כמוציא על נכסי אחר דמי** – ואם הוציא ולא אכל כדי הוצאתו, שמין לו כאריס. **דלא סמכא דעתיה** – שיהא מוחזק בידו, דדואג שמא תמאן בו. **תקינו ליה רבנן** – ליטול כאריס. **כי היכי דלא ניפסדינהו** – שלא יקלקל הקרקעות לזורען תמיד, ולא יעבוד ולא יעדור כרמים.

TERMINOLOGY

...הָא לָא דָּמְיָא אֶלָּא לְהָא **This is only comparable to...** This expression is used by the Gemara to introduce an argument based on the similarity between two cases, seeking to prove that the law applying to one should likewise apply to the other.

BACKGROUND

אִשְׁתּוֹ קְטַנָּה **His wife while she is a minor.** The Sages ordained that a fatherless minor girl may be married off by her relatives. This ordinance was mainly instituted for the benefit of the minor girl, for when she is under a husband's protection she has someone to watch over her and her property. However, a marriage of this kind is not considered a complete marriage, and can be dissolved by מֵיאוּן — "refusal" — if while the girl is still a minor she declares that she does not desire the marriage. In such a case, not only does she not need a bill of divorce, but the Halakhah regards her as if she never married at all. Since we are dealing with a young girl who could easily be swayed by relatives or by a trivial quarrel, this marriage bond is extremely fragile.

HALAKHAH

something, even if it was as little as one fig. But if he consumed absolutely nothing, he is entitled to reimbursement for his expenses or for the increased value of the field, whichever is less." (*Shulḥan Arukh, Even HaEzer* 88:7.)

נִכְסֵי אִשְׁתּוֹ קְטַנָּה **His wife's property while she is a minor.** "If a young girl's father dies, she may be married off by her mother or brothers before she attains adult status at the age of twelve. This marriage is valid only by Rabbinic decree, and can be dissolved by a declaration on the part of the wife while she is still a minor. Therefore, if she does dissolve the marriage in this way, her husband is treated as if he had been a tenant farmer tending her property. We appraise how much he consumed, how much the field improved, and how

¹הָכָא נַמִי, תַּקִּינוּ לֵיהּ רַבָּנַן, ²כִּי הֵיכִי דְּלָא לַפְסְדִינְהוּ.
³״וְכוּלָּן שָׁמִין לָהֶם כְּאָרִיס״.
⁴״וְכוּלָּן״ לְאִיתוּיֵי מַאי?
⁵לְאִיתוּיֵי הָא דְּאָמַר רַב נַחְמָן אָמַר שְׁמוּאֵל: ⁶שָׁבוּי שֶׁנִּשְׁבָּה — מוֹרִידִין קָרוֹב לִנְכָסָיו. ⁷יָצָא לְדַעַת, אֵין מוֹרִידִין קָרוֹב לִנְכָסָיו. ⁸וְרַב נַחְמָן דִּידֵיהּ אָמַר: בּוֹרֵחַ הֲרֵי הוּא כְּשָׁבוּי.
⁹בּוֹרֵחַ מֵחֲמַת מַאי? ¹⁰אִילֵימָא מֵחֲמַת כַּרְגָּא, ¹¹הַיְינוּ לְדַעַת.
¹²אֶלָּא, בּוֹרֵחַ מֵחֲמַת מְרָדִין.

LITERAL TRANSLATION

[1] Here, too, the Sages made an enactment for him, [2] so that he should not damage it.
[3] "And we appraise all of them like a tenant farmer."
[4] What does "all of them" [come] to include?
[5] To include what Rav Naḥman said in the name of Shmuel: [6] A captive who was taken captive — we authorize a relative to [administer] his property. [7] [If] he left voluntarily, we do not authorize a relative to [administer] his property. [8] And Rav Naḥman [gave] his own [opinion and] said: A fugitive is like a captive.
[9] A fugitive because of what? [10] If we say, because of poll tax, [11] this is the same as "voluntarily."
[12] Rather, a fugitive because [he was accused] of bloodshed.

TRANSLATION AND COMMENTARY

not damage the property. [1] The Gemara concludes: **Here too,** in the case of the captive's property, the administrator has no confidence that the property will remain in his hands. Therefore, **the Sages instituted** a similar **enactment for him** — that he be treated like a tenant farmer — [2] **so that he should not** be tempted to **damage** the property.

וְכוּלָּן שָׁמִין לָהֶם כְּאָרִיס [3] The Gemara now considers another aspect of the second Baraita from Tosefta *Ketubot* quoted earlier. That Baraita says: **"And we appraise all of** these cases **as if he were a tenant farmer."** Now, we have already established that this Baraita is referring only to the second case of the previous Baraita — that is, to a captive thought to be alive, and in accordance with the viewpoint of Rabban Shimon ben Gamliel. [4] Hence the Gemara asks: **What** does the expression, **"all of these** cases," implying more than one case, **come to include?** To what case does this law apply, other than that of a person taken captive?

לְאִיתוּיֵי [5] The Gemara answers : **It comes to include the** case considered at the end of the following statement **that Rav Naḥman made in the name of Shmuel:** [6] If someone **was taken captive, we authorize a relative to administer his property.** This is consistent with Shmuel's ruling (above, 38b) which follows that of Rabban Shimon ben Gamliel. [7] On the other hand, **if** the field's owner **left voluntarily,** everyone agrees that **we do not authorize a relative to administer his property.** The above rulings of Rav Naḥman were quoted in the name of Shmuel. [8] **Rav Naḥman** then **gave his own opinion and said: A fugitive is like a captive,** and Shmuel's ruling in favor of authorizing a relative to administer a captive's estate applies equally to a fugitive. Even though the fugitive was not taken away by force, his departure was not voluntary. Thus, the Baraita's use of the expression "all of these cases" was intended to include both the case of the captive and that of the fugitive.

בּוֹרֵחַ מֵחֲמַת מַאי [9] The Gemara asks: Is every fugitive considered to have fled against his will? Surely it depends on how urgent and how serious was the threat! Thus we may ask: **What** threat is considered so serious that **a fugitive** who flees **because of** it is considered to have fled against his will? [10] **If we say:** A fugitive who fled **because** he was unable or unwilling to pay the **poll tax** is considered to have fled against his will, this cannot be correct, [11] because fleeing a financial obligation of any kind **is the same as** fleeing **"voluntarily,"** and the fugitive would always have enough time to leave instructions about his property before the tax becomes due.

אֶלָּא [12] **Rather,** says the Gemara, Rav Naḥman can only have been referring to **a fugitive** who fled **because** the government **accused him of bloodshed** and is likely to execute him if he is captured. Only a fugitive of this type is like a captive, because he has no choice but to flee, and has no time to leave instructions.

RASHI

לאיתויי הא דרב נחמן — בורח מחמת מרדין. **יצא לדעת אין מורידין** — דכיון שהיה שפוי בדעתו, ולא צוהו בלכתו לירד לנכסיו — שמע מינה לא ניחא ליה. **בורח הרי הוא כשבוי** — שאין דעתו מיושבת עליו, מחמת שהוא בהול. **מחמת כרגא** — שאין לו ממה לפרוע כסף גולגלתו למלך, ובורח לפני בוא הזמן. **היינו יוצא לדעת** — שאין כאן בהלה. **מחמת מרדין** — שהרג את הנפש, ופרסאי הורגין על שפיכות דמים, כדאמרינן בבבא קמא (קיז,א), מרדין היא רציחה בלשון פרסי, וכן מפורש בשערים דרב האי גאון (שער מ).

LANGUAGE

כַּרְגָּא **Poll-tax.** This word apparently stems from the ancient Persian *charak*, meaning "land tax."

מְרָדִין **Bloodshed.** This word is apparently of Persian origin. Some scholars maintain that it is derived from *murdan*, meaning "death," while others maintain that it refers to duels (and thus the Gemara is referring to a fugitive who fled after being challenged to a duel).

BACKGROUND

בּוֹרֵחַ מֵחֲמַת כַּרְגָּא **A fugitive because of poll tax.** The poll tax (כַּרְגָּא) was one about which, especially under Persian rule, the authorities were particularly severe, since it was the most dependable financial foundation of the government. By failing to pay this tax, a subject could incur severe penalties, ranging from corporal punishment to the confiscation of his property. Nevertheless, since this tax was collected at set dates, someone forced to flee because he could not pay the tax could plan his actions in advance. If he believed he would be absent for a long time, he could organize his affairs in suitable fashion, and was not viewed as having left his property against his will.

בּוֹרֵחַ מֵחֲמַת מְרָדִין **A fugitive because of bloodshed.** As explained in the Talmud, this refers mainly to the period (from 226 C.E.) of Sassanian rule in the Persian Empire (which included the area of Jewish settlement in Galilee). Unlike their Parthian predecessors, who had been more tolerant and flexible, the Sassanian authorities were extremely strict regarding accusations of murder, and were generally swift in carrying out death sentences. The ability of the accused to defend himself or put off the trial was very limited — so if a person was accused, he was forced to flee if he wished to remain alive.

HALAKHAH

much he spent, and we award him his share." (*Shulḥan Arukh, Even HaEzer* 88:10.) However, if the husband dies or divorces his wife in the usual way, he is not entitled to this special arrangement, and the law is the same as for a marriage between adults (*Tur*).

בּוֹרֵחַ מֵחֲמַת מְרָדִין **A fugitive because he was accused of bloodshed.** "If someone flees his place of residence because his life has been endangered, his property is treated like that of a captive." (*Shulḥan Arukh, Ḥoshen Mishpat* 285:2.)

TRANSLATION AND COMMENTARY

אָמַר רַב יְהוּדָה אָמַר שְׁמוּאֵל [1]Having concluded its consideration of the Baraitot in Tosefta *Ketubot*, the Gemara now considers another statement of Shmuel about the administration of captives' property. **Rav Yehudah said in the name of Shmuel**: [2]If someone **was taken captive, and left standing corn** in his field **to be reaped,** [3]**grapes to be harvested, dates to be cut, or olives to be picked,** [4]**the court** enters **his estate and appoints a guardian** for it, [5]**and he reaps, harvests, cuts and picks** the ripe produce, and deposits it in the custody of the court. The produce is then sold and the proceeds are retained by the court until the captive returns. The guardian performs this service without charge. [6]Only **afterwards** does the court authorize **a relative to administer** the captive's **estate,** and the relative tills the fields as a tenant farmer.

וְלוֹקִים אַפּוֹטְרוֹפָּא לְעוֹלָם [7]The Gemara objects: **But** if it is possible to administer the captive's estate by appointing a guardian who works for no charge, **let** the court **appoint a permanent guardian** for the estate. Why should a relative be appointed as administrator and be granted the share of a tenant farmer, when a guardian is ready to perform the same service as a good deed, without charge?

אַפּוֹטְרוֹפָּא לְדִיקְנָנֵי לָא מוֹקְמִינַן [8]The Gemara answers: **We do not appoint a** permanent **guardian for adult** (lit., "bearded") **men.** It is not reasonable to expect people to act as guardians for the property of adults without charge. It is only out of sympathy for the plight of orphan children that people are ready to put themselves out this way, because the Torah frequently emphasizes the importance of caring for orphans.

[1]אָמַר רַב יְהוּדָה אָמַר שְׁמוּאֵל: [2]שָׁבוּי שֶׁנִּשְׁבָּה וְהִנִּיחַ קָמָה לִקְצוֹר, [3]עֲנָבִים לִבְצוֹר, תְּמָרִים לִגְדּוֹר, זֵיתִים לִמְסוֹק — [4]בֵּית דִּין יוֹרְדִין לִנְכָסָיו וּמַעֲמִידִין אַפּוֹטְרוֹפּוֹס, [5]וְקוֹצֵר, וּבוֹצֵר, וְגוֹדֵר, וּמוֹסֵק, [6]וְאַחַר כָּךְ מוֹרִידִין קָרוֹב לִנְכָסָיו.
[7]וְלוֹקִים אַפּוֹטְרוֹפָּא לְעוֹלָם.
[8]אַפּוֹטְרוֹפָּא לְדִיקְנָנֵי לָא מוֹקְמִינַן.

LITERAL TRANSLATION

[1]Rav Yehudah said in the name of Shmuel: [2]A captive who was taken captive and left standing corn to be reaped, [3]grapes to be harvested, dates to be cut, [or] olives to be picked — [4]the court enters his estate and appoints a guardian, [5]and he reaps, and harvests, and cuts, and picks, [6]and afterwards they authorize a relative to [administer] his estate.

[7]But let them appoint a guardian permanently.

[8]We do not appoint a guardian for adults (lit., "bearded men").

RASHI

מעמידין אפוטרופוס — להכניס דבר המוכן, ויהא שמור לבעלים, ואחר כך מורידין קרוב להשביח וליטול כאריס. **ולוקים אפוטרופוס לעולם** — שלא יטול כלום. **אפוטרופא לדיקנני לא מוקמינן** — אין בית דין טורחין לבקש אפוטרופוס לאנשים גדולים שנתמלא זקנם, לפי שלא ימלאוהו, דבשלמא ליתמי — איכא דשמע להו והוי אפוטרופוס לדבר מצוה, אבל לדיקני לא שמעי להו.

LANGUAGE

אַפּוֹטְרוֹפּוֹס Guardian. This word is derived from the Greek ἐπίτροπος, *epitropos*, meaning "guardian" or "trustee."

BACKGROUND

אַפּוֹטְרוֹפּוֹס Guardian. Although this term sometimes refers to an official who is appointed to administer property, and receives a salary for doing so, in this case the term refers to someone who takes it upon himself to look after someone else's property without receiving any fee. Occasionally a guardian was appointed by the court, or by the father of orphaned children in his will. Although it was an honor to be appointed guardian, and a guardian had broad discretionary powers over the property entrusted to him, it was unlikely that someone would assume this responsibility without some special reason, either friendship with the orphans' father or respect for the court. There was great reluctance to accept a guardianship for an extended period, or without some particular reason for doing so.

NOTES

אַפּוֹטְרוֹפָּא לְדִיקְנָנֵי A guardian for bearded men. Our commentary follows *Rashi* and most of the Rishonim, who explain that guardians cannot generally be found for adults, since people will not ordinarily put themselves out to such an extent for any length of time, except out of sympathy for orphans, because assisting orphans is a very great religious responsibility.

Ritva suggests another reason: A guardian for younger children knows when his term of duty will end — as soon as the children reach maturity. Hence his appointment is temporary, and it is possible to find people willing to act as guardians for a limited period of time. However, there is no limit to the period of guardianship of a captive's property, and people are not willing to accept responsibility for an unlimited period.

HALAKHAH

נִכְסֵי שָׁבוּי A captive's estate. "If a captive (or a fugitive who fled because his life was endangered) left produce to be harvested, the court takes custody of the estate and appoints a guardian to harvest the produce and sell it. The profits are left in the court's custody, together with the missing person's other movable property. The court also appoints someone to manage those of the missing person's possessions that do not require special care (e.g., courtyards to be rented out and the like). This guardian collects the necessary payments and deposits them in court, until the status of the missing person becomes clear. A relative is then appointed to administer those of the missing person's possessions that do require special care (fields and the like). The relative has the status of a tenant farmer, and is entitled to a tenant farmer's share in the profits of the field," following Shmuel. (Ibid., *Shulḥan Arukh, Ḥoshen Mishpat* 285:3.)

אַפּוֹטְרוֹפָּא לְדִיקְנָנֵי A guardian for bearded men. "Since people are usually not willing to serve as guardians for adults, the courts do not attempt to appoint a guardian over an adult's estate for an unlimited period of time. *Rema* observes that if someone nevertheless wished to serve as a guardian under such circumstances, he is welcome to do so. However, there is a dispute as to whether we may accept this unusual offer over the protests of the relatives: Some (*Rosh*) say that the next of kin can demand the right to administer the estate as a tenant farmer, and refuse permission to appoint the guardian, whereas others (*Mordekhai*) say that the next of kin cannot veto the appointment of a disinterested guardian, if one is available." (Ibid., 285:2.)

[1] אָמַר רַב הוּנָא: [2] אֵין מוֹרִידִין קָטָן לְנִכְסֵי שָׁבוּי, [3] וְלֹא קָרוֹב לְנִכְסֵי קָטָן, [4] וְלֹא קָרוֹב מֵחֲמַת קָרוֹב לְנִכְסֵי קָטָן.

[5] ״אֵין מוֹרִידִין קָטָן לְנִכְסֵי שָׁבוּי״ — [6] דִּלְמָא מַפְסִיד לְהוּ.

[7] ״וְלֹא קָרוֹב מֵחֲמַת קָרוֹב לְנִכְסֵי קָטָן״ — [8] בְּאַחֵי מֵאִימָּא.

[9] וְלֹא קָרוֹב לְנִכְסֵי קָטָן — [10] כֵּיוָן דְּלָא מָחֵי, [11] אָתֵי לְאַחֲזוּקֵי בֵּיהּ.

LITERAL TRANSLATION

[1] Rav Huna said: [2] We do not authorize a minor to [administer] the estate of a captive, [3] nor a relative to [administer] the estate of a minor, [4] nor a relative's relative (lit., "a relative because of a relative") to [administer] the estate of a minor.

[5] "We do not authorize a minor to [administer] the estate of a captive" — [6] in case he damages it.

[7] "Nor a relative's relative to [administer] the estate of a minor" — [8] [this refers] to brothers on the mother's side.

[9] "Nor a relative to [administer] the estate of a minor" [10] since he [the minor] does not protest, [11] he [the relative] may come to take possession of it.

TRANSLATION AND COMMENTARY

אָמַר רַב הוּנָא [1] The Gemara now considers special cases in which a relative is *not* authorized to administer an estate: **Rav Huna said:** (1) Even though in general the Halakhah is in accordance with Shmuel's ruling that we appoint a relative to administer the estate of a captive, nevertheless, [2] if the captive's heir is **a minor** — a child who has not yet reached the age of thirteen — **we do not authorize him to administer the captive's estate.** [3] (2) If the owner of the estate is himself **a minor,** we do **not** appoint **a relative** — anyone who could possibly claim to have inherited the property — **to administer** his **estate.** [4] (3) Moreover, if the owner is **a minor,** we do **not** even appoint **a relative's relative to administer** his **estate.**

אֵין מוֹרִידִין קָטָן [5] The Gemara now explains these rulings, though not in the order in which they were stated above: (1) **"We do not** authorize **a minor to administer the estate of a captive,"** [6] because we are concerned **in case he damages it.** Since a minor does not know how to care for the property properly, it is better for the court to appoint an unrelated adult to administer the estate.

וְלֹא קָרוֹב מֵחֲמַת קָרוֹב [7] (3) "We do **not** appoint **a relative's relative to administer the estate of a minor."** [8] The term "relative's relative" **refers to brothers on the mother's side.** The Gemara explains that if the minor has a half-brother on his father's side, and this half-brother in turn has a half-brother on his mother's side, the half-brother of the minor's half-brother is not permitted to administer the minor's estate. Even though the half-brother's half-brother is not related to the minor, he might conceivably act in the interests of his half-brother, who *is* related.

וְלֹא קָרוֹב לְנִכְסֵי קָטָן [9] (2) "We do **not** appoint, **to administer a minor's estate,** any **relative** who could conceivably claim to have inherited it." [10] **Since the minor does not** have the legal capacity or knowledge to **protest** that the property belongs to him, [11] **the relative may come to take possession of it.** In order to avoid such a situation, we do not allow anyone who could possibly claim to have inherited the minor's field to serve as administrator of it, and we seek out an unrelated person to act in this capacity.

RASHI

אין מורידין קטן לנכסי שבוי – ואפילו הוא ראוי ליורשו, דקא מפסיד להו, ומוטב שיורידו להם איש נכרי. **ולא קרוב** – הראוי לירש בנכסי קטן לעשות ולאכול, כדמפרש טעמיה, דכיון דקטן לא ידע למחויי – אתא האי קרוב לאחזוקי בהן, ולומר לחלק ירושתו בא, וטוב להם להוריד איש נכרי, דלא מצי למטען בהו ירושה. **ולא קרוב מחמת קרוב לנכסי קטן** – כגון קטן שיש לו אח מאב, ואותו אח מאב יש לו אח מאם, דאיש נכרי הוא אצל קטן – אין מורידין אותו אח מאם לנכסי קטן מחמת קורבת אחיו של זה שהוא אח של קטן, דאתי לאחזוקי בהו לצורך אחיו, ויאמר: נכסים הללו של אחי מאמי הם, שנפלו לו מאביו, ואלו לחלקו באו. **באחי מאימא** – כדפרישית, שזה אח מן האם לאחיו של קטן מן האב.

NOTES

וְלֹא קָרוֹב לְנִכְסֵי קָטָן Nor a relative to administer the estate of a minor. In our version of the text of the Gemara, it says that we may not appoint a relative to administer a minor's estate because the minor may not realize that he must protest, and thus the relative may succeed in establishing presumptive ownership. The Rishonim ask: The Gemara will shortly establish that, according to Rav Huna, it is impossible to acquire presumptive ownership of a minor's estate. What, then, is the danger in appointing a relative to administer it?

Tosafot explains that the rule that it is impossible to establish presumptive ownership of a minor's estate applies equally to a relative and to a non-relative, and thus there is no time limit on the right of the minor to contest his

HALAKHAH

קָרוֹב לְנִכְסֵי קָטָן A relative in a minor's estate. "If an estate belongs to a minor, his relatives may not be appointed to administer it in case they later claim it is theirs. We may not even appoint a relative on his mother's side, who cannot possibly inherit property from the minor's father, or even a relative of a relative, who is not directly related to the minor at all, as the Rabbis were particularly careful to protect the rights of minors." (*Shulḥan Arukh, Ḥoshen Mishpat* 285:7.)

LITERAL TRANSLATION

[1] Rava said: Infer from Rav Huna's [statement]: [2] [People] do not have presumptive ownership of a minor's estate [39B] even if he has grown up.

[3] And we only say this regarding brothers on the father's [side],

[1] אֲמַר רָבָא: שְׁמַע מִינַּהּ מִדְּרַב הוּנָא: [2] אֵין מַחֲזִיקִין בְּנִכְסֵי קָטָן, [39B] וַאֲפִילּוּ הִגְדִּיל. [3] וְלָא אֲמָרַן אֶלָּא בְּאַחֵי דְאַבָּא,

RASHI

שמע מינה מרב הונא — דאמר אין מורידין קרוב לנכסי קטן שמא יחזיק בהם מחמת ירושה, אבל אחר שאין לו טענת ירושה, מורידין, ולא חיישינן שמא יטעון: אביו של קטן מכרם לי, ואכלתים שני חזקה. שמע מינה: אין מחזיקין בנכסי קטן, אם לא אכל בפני האב שלש שנים — אין שלש שנים שאכלן בפני הקטן חזקה. **ואפילו הגדיל** — הקטן משירד לתוכו, ואכלו שלוש שנים בפניו משהגדיל — לא הויא חזקה, דהואיל ותחילת ירידתו לתוכו הוה קטן, לא ידע כשהגדיל שהן של אביו, ולפיכך לא מיחה, דאי סבירא ליה לרב הונא דמחזיקין בהן משהגדיל — היכי מחתינן נכרי לנכסי קטן? שמא יהא בידו משיגדיל, ויטעון: אתה מכרת לי משגדלת, ואכלתים שני חזקה. **ולא אמרן** — דאין מורידין קרוב לנכסי קטן. **אלא באחי דאבא** — אחיו מאביו, שיטעון בהן צד ירושה.

TRANSLATION AND COMMENTARY

אֲמַר רָבָא [1] **Rava said:** We can **infer from** the second part of **Rav Huna's statement** — [2] that we do not allow a relative to administer a minor's estate, and instead seek out an unrelated person to administer it — that a person who occupies a minor's property and enjoys undisturbed possession for three years **is not granted presumptive ownership of the minor's estate.** The law is that if a person has been in uncontested physical possession of a piece of property for a period of three full years, his claim that the property is his by purchase or gift is accepted, even when not supported by documentary proof, and the burden of proof rests on the person who contests the occupant's claim. This three-year occupation grants the occupier a "presumption of ownership" (חֲזָקָה). Now, if the law of presumptive ownership were to apply to the property of a minor, it would make no difference whether a relative or a non-relative was administering the estate. Just as a relative could claim that the field was his all along by inheritance, the non-relative could claim that the field was his because he had acquired it from the minor's father. And just as the minor might not feel certain enough of the facts to contest his relative's claim, so too he might not be able to contest the non-relative's claim. But since Rav Huna *did* make a distinction between relatives and non-relatives — which shows that he was not concerned about the possibility of a non-relative claiming presumptive ownership of a minor's property — we must conclude that the law of presumptive ownership does not apply to the property of minors. A person claiming to have acquired property that would otherwise belong to a minor must prove his claim, unless he has evidence that he had enjoyed undisturbed possession of the property for three years during the lifetime of the minor's father. [39B] Moreover, says Rava, the law of presumptive ownership does not apply to the property of a minor **even after** the minor **has grown up.** Even if an administrator unrelated to the heir remains in uncontested possession of the field for three full years after the minor has attained majority, his claim to the field — supported by his three years of undisputed possession — is not accepted. Since he occupied the field before the minor attained majority, the latter may not have known that the field belonged to his father, and this is why he did not protest the non-relative's occupation after he attained majority.

וְלָא אֲמָרַן אֶלָּא בְּאַחֵי דְאַבָּא [3] The Gemara now returns to Rav Huna's statement and proceeds to limit its application: When Rav Huna **said** that we do not appoint a relative to administer a minor's estate, he was referring **only to brothers** on **the father's side,** and other relatives who could claim to have inherited the estate,

NOTES

relative's claim. But in the case of a relative, the minor may never realize that he ought to protest, since he may sincerely believe that his relative's claim is justified.

Rashba adds that the neighbors will notice if the occupant of the estate is not an heir of the previous owner, and will inform the minor that he should reclaim his property. However, if the occupant of the estate is himself an heir, the neighbors will think that nothing is amiss, and the minor will never learn that the field is really his.

וַאֲפִילּוּ הִגְדִּיל **Even if he has grown up.** Our commentary follows *Rashi* and the majority of the Rishonim, who rule that even if the guardian was in possession of the estate for three years *after* the minor attained majority, we will not entertain a claim of presumptive ownership by the guardian if he first took possession of the field while the owner was still a minor. Since the owner was a minor when the

HALAKHAH

אֵין מַחֲזִיקִין בְּנִכְסֵי קָטָן **People do not have presumptive ownership of a minor's estate.** "If someone had custody of a minor's estate for three years, or even for one year before he reached maturity and two years after he reached maturity, such custody does not confer presumptive ownership. However, a full three years' custody of the property after the owner has reached maturity is sufficient to confer presumptive ownership." (Ibid., 149:19.) *Rema* disagrees with this last point. He writes that if custody of the estate began while the owner was still a minor, the

LANGUAGE

עִיטְדָא Deed of division. This is the reading of the word given by *Rashi,* who derives it from an Aramaic root meaning "to turn." The term refers to a deed of allocation giving every party a specific part of an estate. Most manuscripts give the reading as עִטְרָא or אִיטְרָא, and the source of the word may be the root עטר, meaning to surround with a fence, to guard something. Hence it is applied to a document intended to define and divide an estate.

BACKGROUND

עִיטְדָא קָלָא אִית לָהּ A deed of division becomes known. To be a valid legal instrument a document must be signed before witnesses. Therefore, by its nature, it is a public document whose contents are widely known. Indeed, it is intended to be publicly known, for the presence of witnesses has the effect of publicizing its contents. Thus, if a deed has been written to divide a field, one may assume that it is known publicly that a certain part of the field belongs to the minor, and that he will have been notified if his part has been taken.

TRANSLATION AND COMMENTARY

[1]**but we have no** objection to appointing **brothers** on **the mother's side,** who cannot possibly claim to have inherited it. By Torah law, inheritance passes through the male line. The only exception is that when a man dies without sons, his daughters inherit his property. Thus, if a man (or a woman) dies without issue, the property passes to his (or her) nearest relative on his (or her) father's side (the father himself, a brother on the father's side, the sons or daughters of the brother on the father's side, an uncle on the father's side, etc.). It is impossible for a mother, or for anyone related only through the mother, to inherit her children's property.

וְאָחֵי דְאַבָּא נַמִי [2]The Gemara now places another limitation on Rav Huna's statement: **Even in the case of brothers** on **the father's side, we only say** that they may not act as administrators **of land,** [3]**but we have no** objection to appointing a relative to administer **a house** belonging to a minor. We need not fear that the relative will claim to be the rightful heir, because the neighbors can testify that the house is part of the minor's share in his late father's estate.

וּבְאַרְעָתָא נַמִי [4]The Gemara now places a third limitation on Rav Huna's statement: **Even regarding land, we only say** that a relative may not administer it **if** the father of the minor **did not draw up a** formal **deed of** division, allocating his property among his heirs and expressly designating this particular piece of land as the property of the minor. [5]**But if he did draw up a deed of** division, **it will have become known** which field belongs to which brother, and there is no danger that the relative will claim to be the rightful heir of the field.

וְלָא הִיא [6]**But,** declares the Gemara, according to the Halakhah **this is not so**. None of the distinctions advanced above, though reasonable in theory, apply in practice. [7]In practice **it makes no difference if** the relatives **are brothers** on **the father's side or** on **the mother's side;** [8]**it makes no difference if** the estate consists

[1]אֲבָל בְּאַחֵי דְאִמָּא, לֵית לָן בָּהּ. [2]וְאָחֵי דְאַבָּא נַמִי, לָא אֲמָרַן אֶלָּא בְּאַרְעָתָא, [3]אֲבָל בְּבָתֵּי לֵית לָן בָּהּ.
[4]וּבְאַרְעָתָא נַמִי, לָא אֲמָרַן אֶלָּא דְּלָא עָבֵיד עִיטְדָא, [5]אֲבָל עָבֵיד עִיטְדָא, קָלָא אִית לָהּ.
[6]וְלָא הִיא. [7]לָא שְׁנָא אַחֵי דְאַבָּא וְלָא שְׁנָא אַחֵי דְאִמָּא; [8]לָא שְׁנָא אַרְעָתָא וְלָא שְׁנָא בָּתֵּי;

LITERAL TRANSLATION

[1]but regarding brothers on the mother's [side], we have no [problem] with it.

[2]And even in [the case of] brothers on the father's [side], we only say [this] regarding land, [3]but regarding houses we have no [problem] with it.

[4]And even regarding land, we only say this where he did not make a deed of division, [5]but [where] he made a deed of division, it becomes known (lit., "has a voice").

[6]But this is not so. [7]There is no difference [if they are] brothers on the father's side and there is no difference [if they are] brothers on the mother's side; [8]there is no difference [if it is] land and there is no difference [if it is] houses;

RASHI

ארעתא – שדות. **אבל בבתי לית לן בה** – שהשכנים מעידין עליהם שבאו לחלקו של קטן. **עיטדא** – שטר חלוקה, כשחלקו מתחילה (מלכים ב׳ יב) ״רק הבמות לא סרו״ מתרגמינן ״במתא לא עטדו״ – לא הפליגו מהם. **לא שנא אחי דאמא** – פן יאמר: של אמי היו נכסי מלוג, ואביו של קטן, בעל אמי היה מוחזק בהן מחמת שהוא אוכל פירות, והוא מת קודם לאמי ולא ירשה, ואני יורש הליין מחמת אמי.

NOTES

guardian first took possession of the field, he may not have been aware at the time that the property belonged to him, and it never occurred to him to protest later.

Rambam, however, disagrees. He rules that the period when the owner was a minor does not count towards the three years needed to establish presumptive ownership, and if the guardian held the field for one year while the owner was a minor and for two years after he attained majority, he cannot make a claim of presumptive ownership. But if the guardian remains in possession of the field for three full years after the owner has attained majority, he may make such a claim.

וְלָא הִיא But this is not so. At first glance the Gemara's conclusion appears strange: Why does it make no difference if the relatives are on the mother's side, or if the property consists of houses, or if a deed of division has or has not been drawn up? What is the flaw in the Gemara's previous argument?

The Rishonim offer several solutions to these problems. A relative on the mother's side may not be able to claim to have inherited the property from the minor's father, but he may be able to persuade people that the neighbors became confused over time and forgot who was the real owner (*Nimmukei Yosef*). Even if a deed of division

HALAKHAH

custodian does not gain presumptive ownership, even if he maintained custody for three years after the owner reached maturity. This view is accepted by most authorities.

אֵין מוֹרִידִין קָרוֹב לְנִכְסֵי קָטָן We do not authorize relatives to administer a minor's estate. "A relative may never be appointed to administer a minor's estate, even if the relative is only a brother on the minor's mother's side, and even if a deed of division is drawn up stating clearly that the field belongs to the minor. Even if the relative offers to sign a document stipulating that he is no more than a tenant, we

TRANSLATION AND COMMENTARY

of **land or houses;** [1]**and it makes no difference if** the minor's father **drew up a deed of** division **or not.** [2]**We do not authorize** a relative to administer a minor's estate under any circumstances, because the possibility always exists that the administrator will make claims to the property that the minor will have difficulty rebutting.

הַהִיא סַבְתָּא [3]On the basis of its discussion of the laws regarding the appointment of a relative to administer the property of a captive or a minor, the Gemara now tells us of two actual cases and the legal principles involved in their solution. The first case concerns **a certain old woman who had three daughters.** [4]**She and one daughter were taken captive,** [5]and of **the other two daughters,** [6]**one died and left a child.** The old woman and one of her daughters had disappeared, leaving an estate to be administered. The question was: to whom should the estate be entrusted? The case came for decision before the court headed by Abaye.

אָמַר אַבַּיֵי [7]**Abaye said: How should we act** in this case? [8]Should we place **the estate in the possession of the** third **sister?** [9]This would be incorrect, **for perhaps the old woman** has **died, and** the minor son of her deceased daughter has inherited either **one**-third of her estate (if the captive sister is still alive) or half of her estate (if the captive sister is dead), and the third sister — the minor's aunt — is not permitted to administer his part of the estate, [10]as **we do not authorize a relative to administer a minor's estate.** [11]On the other hand, **should we place his part of the estate in the hands of the child** himself? [12]This too would be incorrect, for **perhaps the old woman** has **not died and** the estate still belongs to her, [13]and the law is that **we do not authorize a minor to administer the estate of a captive.**

[1]וְלָא שְׁנָא עָבֵיד עִיטְדָא לָא שְׁנָא לָא עָבֵיד עִיטְדָא — [2]לָא מַחְתִּינַן.

[3]הַהִיא סַבְתָּא דַּהֲוָיָא לַהּ תְּלָת בְּנָתָא. [4]אִישְׁתְּבַאי אִיהִי וַחֲדָא בְּרַתָּא. [5]אִידָךְ תַּרְתֵּי בְּנָתָא, [6]שְׁכִיבָא חֲדָא מִינַּיְיהוּ וְשָׁבְקָה יָנוֹקָא.

[7]אָמַר אַבַּיֵי: הֵיכִי נַעֲבֵיד? [8]לוֹקְמִינְהוּ לְנִכְסֵי בִּידָא דַּאֲחָתָא? [9]דִּלְמָא שְׁכִיבָא סַבְתָּא, [10]וְאֵין מוֹרִידִין קָרוֹב לְנִכְסֵי קָטָן. [11]נוֹקְמִינְהוּ לְנִכְסֵיהּ בִּידָא דְּיָנוֹקָא? [12]דִּלְמָא לָא שְׁכִיבָא סַבְתָּא, [13]וְאֵין מוֹרִידִין קָטָן לְנִכְסֵי שָׁבוּי.

LITERAL TRANSLATION

[1]and there is no difference [if] he made a deed of division [and] there is no difference [if] he did not make a deed of division — [2]we do not authorize [them].

[3]A certain old woman had three daughters. [4]She and one daughter were taken captive. [5][Of] the other two daughters, [6]one of them died and left a child.

[7]Abaye said: How should we act? [8]Shall we place the estate in the hand of the sister? [9]Perhaps the old woman has died, [10]and we do not authorize a relative to [administer] the estate of a minor! [11]Shall we place his [part of the] estate in the hands of the child? [12]Perhaps the old woman has not died, [13]and we do not authorize a minor to [administer] the estate of a captive.

RASHI

היכי ליעבד — בנכסי דסבתא, שאין אנו יודעין אם קיימת אם מתה. **בידא דאחתא** — דהילכתא כרבן שמעון בן גמליאל, דקס ליה שמואל כוותיה. **דלמא שכיבא סבתא** — ויש לקטן חלק בהן שהס שלו מחמת אמו, או שמא חלק שלו, שמא מתו שתי השבויות. **לוקמינהו לפלגא דנכסי בידא דינוקא** — איכא למיחש דלמא לא שכיבא סבתא, ואין לו חלק בהן, ואין מורידין קטן לנכסי שבוי.

TERMINOLOGY

הֵיכִי נַעֲבֵיד How should we act? The Gemara asks this question when confronting a choice between two possible courses of action, both of which are liable to be dangerous or unpleasant. It then suggests that both are to be avoided.

NOTES

was drawn up, it may have been lost (*Rabbenu Yehonatan*) or people may have forgotten about it (*Rashba*). However, it is also possible that there is no flaw in the previous argument, and the Gemara's conclusion merely reflects the Sages' punctiliousness on questions relating to the welfare of orphans (*Tosafot, Rosh*; see also *Rambam*).

דִּלְמָא שְׁכִיבָא סַבְתָּא Perhaps the old woman has died. The Rishonim ask: There is a legal principle that we do not assume that someone has died (אֵין חוֹשְׁשִׁין לְמִיתָה). In other words, if a Halakhic decision depends on whether or not a certain person is still alive, we assume he is alive, until proven otherwise. Why, then, are we concerned about the

HALAKHAH

do not allow it. *Rema* writes, following *Ra'avad* and others, that this applies only if the brothers have already divided the estate; but if they have not yet divided the estate, one of them may administer it all, even though a portion is owned by a minor. *Rema* also writes that some authorities rule that all this applies only if the relative insists on taking the share of a tenant farmer; but if the relative is willing to serve as guardian without charge, he may be appointed to administer the estate. Similarly, if the minor acquired the property by some means other than inheritance, a relative may administer it, following the Gemara's conclusion." (*Shulḥan Arukh, Ḥoshen Mishpat* 285:7.)

הַהִיא סַבְתָּא The story of the old woman. An old woman once had three daughters, and she and one of her daughters were taken captive, while another daughter died, leaving a son who had not yet attained majority. The Rabbis ruled that

BACKGROUND

דְּמוֹקְמִינַן אַפּוֹטְרוֹפָּא Since we appoint a guardian. Rava's explanation is that, since one is obliged to appoint a guardian for some of the property, it would be better not to award any of it to someone with only a doubtful claim (for in any event there is doubt as to whether the owner of the property is actually dead). Therefore he ruled that the court should appoint a guardian to oversee all the property of doubtful status. For that reason he believes it preferable to place that part of the estate regarding which there is doubt as to who is entitled to inherit it under the care of a guardian. This will prevent dispute if the owner appears and it turns out that the property has been allocated against his wishes.

[1]אֲמַר אַבַּיֵי: הִלְכָּךְ, פַּלְגָא יָהֲבֵינָא לָהּ לַאֲחָתָא, [2]וְאִידָךְ פַּלְגָא, [3]מוֹקְמִינַן לֵיהּ אַפּוֹטְרוֹפָּא לְיָנוֹקָא.

[4]רָבָא אֲמַר: מִגּוֹ דְּמוֹקְמִינַן אַפּוֹטְרוֹפָּא לְפַלְגָא, [5]מוֹקְמִינַן לֵיהּ אַפּוֹטְרוֹפָּא לְאִידָךְ פַּלְגָא.

[6]לְסוֹף שְׁמַעוּ דִּשְׁכִיבָא סַבְתָּא. [7]אֲמַר אַבַּיֵי: תִּילְתָּא יָהֲבִינַן לָהּ לַאֲחָתָא, [8]וְתִילְתָּא יָהֲבִינַן לֵיהּ לְיָנוֹקָא. [9]וְאִידָךְ תִּילְתָּא,

LITERAL TRANSLATION

[1]Abaye said: Therefore, we give half to the sister, [2]and [as for] the other half, [3]we appoint a guardian for the child.

[4]Rava said: Since we appoint a guardian for [one] half, [5]we appoint a guardian for the other half.

[6]Ultimately [people] heard that the old woman had died. [7]Abaye said: We give one-third to the sister, [8]and we give one-third to the child. [9]And [as for] the other third,

RASHI

פלגא יהבינן לאחתא — ממה נפשך; אם מתו שתי השבויות — הרי זו יורשת חציין, ואם לאו — מורידין קרוב לנכסי שבוי. **מוקמינן אפוטרופוס** — ולא מחתינן קטן לגוייהו, דלמא לא שכיבא, ואין מורידין קטן לנכסי שבוי. **שמעו דשכיבא סבתא** — לסוף שמעו שמתה הזקנה, ועל הבת שנשבית לא שמעו. **תילתא יהבינן כו'** — דהא ודאי שליש הנכסים לזו, ושליש לקטן.

TRANSLATION AND COMMENTARY

אֲמַר אַבַּיֵי [1]**Therefore, Abaye said, we give half** of the estate **to the sister,** for (a) if both captives have died, the surviving sister inherited half of her mother's property, and (b) if both captives are alive, the sister is qualified to administer her captive mother's estate, and (c) if the old woman has died and the captive sister has not, the two living sisters have each inherited one-third of the property, and the free sister is qualified to administer the captive sister's third as well as her own. Thus, whichever of the above three possibilities has occurred, the third sister is entitled to administer at least half of the property. [2]**As for the other half,** we cannot appoint the third sister to administer it in case her mother is dead and the child is heir to part or all of it, since a relative is not authorized to administer a minor's estate. On the other hand, the child cannot be appointed to administer it either, in case his grandmother is alive, and a minor is not authorized to administer a captive's estate. [3]The only possibility left, says Abaye, is that **we appoint a guardian for the child,** and the guardian will look after this half of the estate until the fate of the captives becomes known.

רָבָא אֲמַר [4]**Rava** disagreed and **said: Since we** appoint **a guardian for one half,** [5]**we** appoint **a guardian for the other half** as well, and all the property remains in the guardian's custody until we learn what has happened to the captives.

לְסוֹף שְׁמַעוּ דִּשְׁכִיבָא סַבְתָּא [6]The Gemara continues the story: **Ultimately people heard that the old woman had died.** They did not, however, hear what had happened to the other captive, the old woman's daughter. [7]The case again came before Abaye for review. **Abaye said: We give one-third** of the estate **to the sister** — her share in the old woman's inheritance — [8]**and we give one-third to the child** — since he inherits his dead mother's third of his grandmother's estate. [9]**And as for the remaining third,** which belongs to the captive sister,

NOTES

possibility that the old woman has died? Why do we not assume that she is still alive, and allow her daughter to administer the entire estate?

Tosafot points out that the Gemara (*Gittin* 28a) rules that if someone is over eighty, we do not assume he is still alive, and it is possible that the old woman was in her eighties. But this explanation is difficult, because later on the Gemara considers the possibility that the captive daughter may also have died. *Tosafot* then suggests that the rule that we assume a person is alive may not apply in every case. In particular, it may not apply where the welfare of orphans is involved. Alternatively, *Tosafot* suggests that the reason we cannot assume that the old woman is alive is because she was taken captive, and the life expectancy of captives is very short.

וְתִילְתָּא יָהֲבִינַן לֵיהּ לְיָנוֹקָא And we give one-third to the child. The Rishonim ask: Why is part of the estate given to the child? Throughout the Talmud we find that guardians are appointed to care for the property of minors. Why do we not appoint a guardian to administer the child's third as well?

They answer that the child in our story was already mature enough to care for his own property, even though

HALAKHAH

since a minor may not be appointed administrator of a captive's estate, and a relative may not be appointed administrator of a minor's estate, a guardian is appointed for all the property (following Rava's view against that of Abaye). Later, after it was heard that the woman had died, it was decided that the remaining daughter should take possession of one-third of the estate, the minor take possession of another third, and a guardian be appointed for the remaining third — the property of the captive sister — because we do not know if she is still alive, and if she has died, the minor is entitled to half of it," following Rava. (*Shulḥan Arukh, Ḥoshen Mishpat* 285:9.)

[1]יָהֲבִינַן דַּנְקָא לְאַחְתָּא, [2]וְאִידָךְ דַּנְקָא, [3]מוֹקְמִינַן לֵיהּ אַפּוֹטְרוֹפָּא לְיָנוֹקָא.

[4]רָבָא אֲמַר: מִגּוֹ דְּמוֹקֵים אַפּוֹטְרוֹפָּא לְדַנְקָא, [5]מוֹקְמִינַן נַמִי אַפּוֹטְרוֹפָּא לְאִידָךְ דַּנְקָא.

[6]מָרִי בַּר אִיסַק אֲתָא לֵיהּ אַחָא מִבֵּי חוֹזַאי. [7]אֲמַר לֵיהּ: ״פְּלוֹג לִי״. [8]אֲמַר לֵיהּ: ״לָא יָדַעְנָא לָךְ״.

LITERAL TRANSLATION

[1]we give one-sixth to the sister, [2]and [as for] the other sixth, [3]we appoint a guardian for the child.

[4]Rava said: Since we appoint a guardian for [one] sixth, [5]we also appoint a guardian for the other sixth.

[6]Mari bar Isak's brother came to him from Bei Ḥoza'i. [7]He said to him: "Divide [the estate] with me." [8]He said to him: "I do not know you."

RASHI

דנקא — שתות, חצי השליש. **יהבינן לאחתא** — ממה נפשך; אם מתה האחות — הרי חצי חלקה לזו, ואם לאו — מורידין קרוב לנכסי שבוי. **ואידך דנקא** — לא יהבינן לה שמא של קטן הם, ואין מורידין קרוב לנכסי קטן. **אתא ליה אחא מבי חוזאי** — שהלך אביו לבי חוזאי ונשא שם אשה, וילדה לו את זה, וחזר מרי לכאן וירד לנכסי אביו, ובא זה אחריו לזמן מרובה ותבע חלקו.

TRANSLATION AND COMMENTARY

whose fate is unknown, [1]**we give one-sixth** — half of the third — **to the sister,** for if the captive sister is dead, it belongs to the surviving sister, and if the captive sister is alive, the sister is qualified to administer it. [2]**And as for the remaining sixth** — which belongs either to the captive sister if she is alive, or to the child if the captive sister is dead — [3]**we appoint a guardian for the child,** just as we did with half of the property in the first part of the story. For if the captive sister is alive, the child may not administer her property, and if she is dead and the property belongs to the child, the other sister may not administer his property. Hence, we appoint an unrelated guardian to represent the child, and he administers the property for the child until the fate of the child's captive aunt becomes known.

רָבָא אֲמַר [4]However, in this case as well **Rava** disagreed and **said: Since we appoint a guardian for one-sixth,** [5]**we also appoint a guardian for the other sixth** until we learn what has happened to the captive sister.

מָרִי בַּר אִיסַק [6]The Gemara now tells of another actual case: **Mari bar Isak had** a stranger **come to him from Bei Ḥoza'i** — a distant region — claiming to be his **brother.** [7]The stranger **said to** Mari: **"Divide the estate** you inherited from our father **with me,** since I am your brother." [8]Mari **said to him** in reply: **"I do not know you!** Why should I accept your claim that you are my brother?"

NOTES

he had not yet reached the age of majority. Hence there was no objection to giving him his own property. But he could not be authorized to administer property that did not belong to him (*Rashba*, *Ran*).

מָרִי בַּר אִיסַק אֲתָא לֵיהּ אַחָא מִבֵּי חוֹזַאי Mari bar Isak's brother came to him from Bei Ḥoza'i. This entire passage presents a number of difficulties. The Rishonim agree that it is obvious that a stranger who suddenly appears and claims to be a rich man's brother is not to be believed without conclusive proof, and even if the rich man is known to be violent, his basic right to protection against baseless claims is inalienable. Why, then, did Rav Ḥisda need to seek Scriptural justification for Mari's denial? Even if the brother had had a beard, Mari should still have been believed if he claimed not to know him, as the burden of proof was on the brother.

There are two principal explanations given by the Rishonim: *Tosafot*, and apparently *Rashi*, explain that Mari did not deny the brother's story. On the contrary, he tended to believe it, as he knew that he indeed had a long-lost brother. In the parallel passage in tractate *Ketubot* (27b), both *Rashi* and *Tosafot* suggest that the brother may have been born in Babylonia and taken by his father to Bei Ḥoza'i while still an infant. Here *Rashi* suggests that the entire family may have moved to Bei Ḥoza'i, where the father married a second wife and had this infant son. Mari returned home upon his father's death, whereas the infant brother remained with his mother and only appeared in Babylonia after many years. According to both suggestions, Mari was fully aware of the existence of a brother in Bei Ḥoza'i. Nevertheless, even though he admitted that this stranger might be his brother, Mari claimed not to be able to recognize him and demanded conclusive proof. Now, ordinarily, Mari's claim would be suspicious: If the stranger was not his brother, why did Mari not say so in so many words? Nevertheless, Rav Ḥisda ruled that his claim was reasonable, as he had last seen his brother when he was an infant, and could not be expected to recognize him now. The difficulty with this explanation is that Abaye asks a rhetorical question later (below, 40a): "Did the older brother know that the younger brother existed, and did he waive his rights in advance to compensation for his labor in improving the field?" Apparently, it was obvious to Abaye that Mari did not know of his brother's existence.

Rashba suggests that Mari may have thought that his brother was dead, or may have forgotten about him. *Rosh* suggests that Mari may have been under the impression that his brother had received his share in his father's estate in Bei Ḥoza'i. Alternatively, Abaye may not have been referring to the case of Mari bar Isak, but to a similar case that came before Rabbah in which the older brother had no knowledge of the younger brother's existence (see note below, 40a).

To avoid this objection, some Rishonim explain that Mari was indeed denying the brother's claim entirely, and his denial was acceptable even without Scriptural justification. However, Rav Ḥisda was not trying to justify Mari, but trying to reassure his brother, who was frightened and upset, by explaining to him that Mari was not necessarily being deliberately obstructive, and that he might have made an honest mistake (see *Rashba*, *Ritva*, *Rabbenu Yehonatan*).

LANGUAGE

דַּנְקָא A sixth. A danka is a type of Persian coin. In Middle and Modern Persian, *dang* means a grain. The Hebrew term paralleling danka is מעה, ma'ah, and since a ma'ah is worth one-sixth of a dinar (the standard unit of currency in the Talmud), the word danka was used to denote one-sixth of anything.

REALIA

בֵּי חוֹזַאי Bei Ḥoza'i.

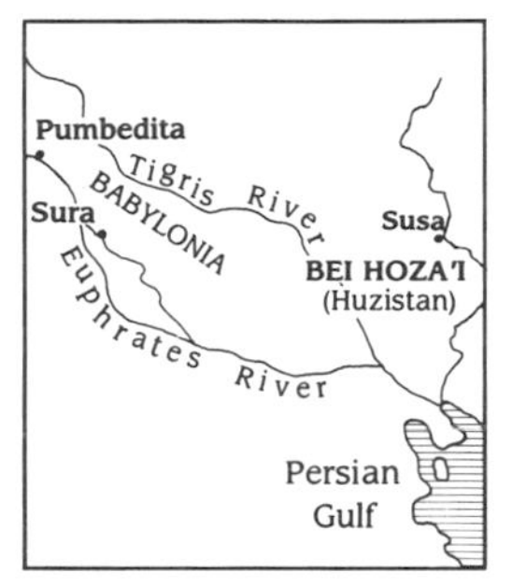

During the Talmudic period, the Persian kingdom was ruled by the Sassanid dynasty, and it was divided into large units similar to independent states. Bei Ḥoza'i refers to the area near the Persian Gulf, far from the centers of Jewish settlement in Babylonia. This area is known to this day as Huzistan — the Persian form of the name Bei Ḥoza'i.

BACKGROUND

אַלִּימָא Violent. This is an Aramaic word also used in Hebrew, meaning aggressive, strong or violent. Sometimes it can also mean large or coarse. A man who is אַלִּים is one who uses his strength — whether it be physical or the power of wealth or political connections — in order to obtain things or to insist upon his rights. A person who is אַלִּים is not necessarily someone who acts unlawfully, but because of his power, people do not want to quarrel with him, and he causes them to waive their rights or to act unlawfully.

TRANSLATION AND COMMENTARY

אֲתָא לְקַמֵּיהּ דְּרַב חִסְדָּא [1]**The case came before Rav Ḥisda** for judgment, [2]and **he said to** the claimant: **"What Mari said to you was reasonable.** It is quite likely that he does not recognize you because even according to your own story a very long time has passed since you were together. [3]I can illustrate this from an incident in the Torah, where **it is said** (Genesis 42:8) about a similar situation: **'And Joseph recognized his brothers, but they did not recognize him.'"** [4]Rav Ḥisda then quoted the traditional explanation of this verse: **"This** verse **teaches** us **that** Joseph **departed without** any **sign of a beard,** as he was only seventeen (Genesis 37:2) when he was sold by his brothers into slavery, [5]**and he came** before his brothers as the viceroy of Egypt at the age of thirty-nine **with the signs of a beard.** On the other hand, the other brothers were older, and had already grown beards when Joseph was sold. Therefore, Joseph had no difficulty in recognizing them, but they did not recognize him. Thus we see that it is possible that your brother may not recognize you with the passage of time, particularly if he last saw you, as you claim, when you were a child."

אֲמַר לֵיהּ [6]Rav Ḥisda then **said to** the claimant: **"Go and bring witnesses that you are his brother."** [7]**He said to** Rav Ḥisda in reply: **"I have witnesses, but they are afraid** that Mari may hurt them if they testify on my behalf, **because he is a violent man."**

אֲמַר לֵיהּ לְדִידֵיהּ [8]Rav Ḥisda then turned **to Mari himself** and **said: "You go and bring those witnesses** that the person claiming to be your brother has brought, and we will see if they testify **that he is not your brother.** Or bring other witnesses of your own."

אֲמַר לֵיהּ [9]Mari then **said to** Rav Ḥisda: **"Is this the law?!** [10]Surely the law is that whoever **seeks to take something away from another person, the burden of proof falls upon** the plaintiff! Thus the burden of proof should fall upon the claimant, not upon me!"

[1]אֲתָא לְקַמֵּיהּ דְּרַב חִסְדָּא. [2]אֲמַר לֵיהּ: ״שַׁפִּיר קָאָמַר לָךְ, [3]שֶׁנֶּאֱמַר: ׳וַיַּכֵּר יוֹסֵף אֶת אֶחָיו, וְהֵם לֹא הִכִּרֻהוּ׳. [4]מְלַמֵּד שֶׁיָּצָא בְּלֹא חֲתִימַת זָקָן, [5]וּבָא בַּחֲתִימַת זָקָן״.

[6]אֲמַר לֵיהּ: ״זִיל, אַיְיתִי סַהֲדֵי דְּאָחוּהּ אַתְּ״. [7]אֲמַר לֵיהּ: ״אִית לִי סַהֲדֵי, וְדָחֲלֵי מִינֵּיהּ, דְּגַבְרָא אַלִּימָא הוּא״.

[8]אֲמַר לֵיהּ לְדִידֵיהּ: ״זִיל אַנְתְּ אַיְיתִי סַהֲדֵי דְּלָאו אָחוּךְ הוּא״.

[9]אֲמַר לֵיהּ: ״דִּינָא הָכִי? [10]הַמּוֹצִיא מֵחֲבֵירוֹ עָלָיו הָרְאָיָה!״

LITERAL TRANSLATION

[1][The case] came before Rav Ḥisda. [2]He said to him: "He spoke well to you, [3]as it is said: 'And Joseph knew his brothers, but they did not know him.' [4][This] teaches that he departed without the sign of a beard, [5]and he came with the sign of a beard."

[6]He said to him: "Go, bring witnesses that you are his brother." [7]He said to him: "I have witnesses, but they are afraid of him, because he is a violent man."

[8]He said to [Mari] himself: "You go [and] bring witnesses that he is not your brother."

[9]He said to him: "Is this the law? [10]Whoever seeks to take [something] away from his fellow, upon him is the [burden of] proof!"

RASHI

שפיר קאמר לך — שאינו מכירך, ואין זה רמאות, שכשיצא מאצלך לא היה לך חתימת זקן ועכשיו באת בחתימת זקן. **ויכר יוסף את אחיו** — שכשיצא מהם היו כולם חתומי זקן, ״והם לא הכירוהו״ — שיצא מאצלם בלא חתימת זקן ובא בחתימת זקן. **דלאו אחוך הוא** — אותם עדים שיש לו לזה, שבאו אצם ומכירין בו מי הוא, הביאם אתה ויעידו שאינו בן אביך, או בקש עדים אחרים.

NOTES

זִיל אַנְתְּ אַיְיתִי סַהֲדֵי You go and bring witnesses. At first sight it is not clear which witnesses are being referred to. The Rishonim agree that even a violent person is not considered guilty without proof, so Rav Ḥisda could not have been ordering Mari to disprove his brother's assertion by bringing witnesses of his own. Rather, Mari was ordered to bring the witnesses named by his purported brother who were allegedly afraid to come forward on their own (*Rashba, Tosafot,* and others; see also *Rashi* on whom our commentary is based).

HALAKHAH

אָח שֶׁבָּא מִמָּקוֹם רָחוֹק A brother who came from a distant country. "If a stranger appears and claims that he is someone's brother and hence entitled to part of his property, and the defendant claims that he does not recognize him, the stranger receives nothing until he proves his claim, even if people have heard that the defendant had a brother who lived abroad." (*Shulḥan Arukh, Ḥoshen Mishpat* 280:6.)

בַּעַל דִּין אַלִּים A violent litigant. "If the court knows (based on positive proof — *Rema,* and see *Sma*) that one of the litigants is a violent person, and the other litigant maintains that he has witnesses to support his claim, but that they are afraid of the violent litigant, the court compels the violent litigant to bring the witnesses himself, following Rav Ḥisda's ruling here." (Ibid., 28:5.)

¹אֲמַר לֵיהּ: ״הָכִי דָּיְינִינָא לָךְ וּלְכָל אַלִּימֵי דְּחַבְרָךְ״. ²אֲמַר לֵיהּ: ״סוֹף סוֹף, אָתוּ סָהֲדֵי וְלָא מַסְהֲדִי!״ ³אֲמַר לֵיהּ: ״תַּרְתֵּי לָא עָבְדִי״. ⁴לְסוֹף אָתוּ סָהֲדֵי דְּאָחוּהָ הוּא. ⁵אֲמַר לֵיהּ: ״לִפְלוֹג לִי נַמִי מִפַּרְדֵּיסֵי וּבוּסְתָּנֵי דִּשְׁתַל״. ⁶אֲמַר לֵיהּ: ״שַׁפִּיר קָאָמַר לָךְ, ⁷דִּתְנַן: ׳הִנִּיחַ בָּנִים גְּדוֹלִים וּקְטַנִּים, ⁸וְהִשְׁבִּיחוּ גְּדוֹלִים אֶת הַנְּכָסִים, ⁹הִשְׁבִּיחוּ לָאֶמְצַע׳״.

LITERAL TRANSLATION

¹He said to him: "This is how I judge you and all your violent friends."

²He said to him: In the end, witnesses will come and they will not testify!"

³He said to him: "Two [evil] things they will not do."

⁴Ultimately, witnesses came [and testified] that he was his brother. ⁵He said to him: "Let him also divide with me from the gardens and orchards that he planted."

⁶He said to him: "He spoke well to you, ⁷for we have learned: '[If] he left sons, adults and minors, ⁸and the adults improved the property, ⁹they improved [it] for all (lit., "for the middle").'"

TRANSLATION AND COMMENTARY

אֲמַר לֵיהּ ¹Rav Ḥisda **said to him** in reply: **"This is the way** I propose to **judge you and all your violent friends.** Since you are known to be violent, I am ordering *you* to bring the witnesses."

אֲמַר לֵיהּ ²Mari **said to** Rav Ḥisda: "But if you are so concerned about his witnesses being frightened of me, what good will it do for me to bring them? Even if **the witnesses come, in the end they will not testify** on the claimant's behalf, but on my behalf instead!"

אֲמַר לֵיהּ ³Rav Ḥisda **said** to Mari in reply: "I am not afraid that you will influence the witnesses to lie in court, as witnesses may do one forbidden thing — refuse to give evidence — out of fear, but they **will not do two** — refrain from telling the truth, and also testify falsely."

לְסוֹף אָתוּ סָהֲדֵי ⁴**Ultimately witnesses came and testified that** the claimant **was** indeed Mari's **brother,** and Mari proceeded to transfer ownership of half of his late father's estate to him, under the supervision of Rav Ḥisda's court. ⁵Mari's brother then **said to** Rav Ḥisda: **"Let Mari also give me half of the gardens and orchards that he planted** after our father's death, as I am entitled to them."

אֲמַר לֵיהּ ⁶Mari objected, as these gardens and orchards were not part of their father's estate, but were added afterwards by Mari himself. Nevertheless, Rav Ḥisda **said to Mari: "What** your brother **said is reasonable.** ⁷He is indeed entitled to his share of the gardens and orchards, **for we have learned** in a Mishnah (*Bava Batra* 143b): **'If** a man died, **leaving** several **sons,** some of whom were **adults** at the time, while the others were **minors,** ⁸then if **the adult** sons **improved the property** before dividing it between the heirs, ⁹**they improved the property for all** the heirs, and they divide the profits equally with their younger brothers.' They cannot claim to be entitled to all the profits because they did all the work. You too must give your younger brother an equal share in the gardens and orchards you developed, and you must do so without charge."

RASHI

אמר ליה — מרי לרב חסדא: אי מיגלי דחלי מה מועלת. **סוף סוף אתו סהדי ולא מסהדי** — אלא כמותי, ולא כמותך. **תרתי לא עבדי** — מיראתך יעשו אחת שישתקו, אבל שתים לא יעשו, לא דיין שישתקו ולא יעידו האמת אלא גם שיעידו שקר. **אמר ליה** — ההוא אחא לרב חסדא. **לפלוג לי מפרדיסי** — כרמים. **ובוסתני** — ביתן של אילנות. **דשתל** — איהו והשביחן, ויתן לי חלק כמו שהן משובחין.

NOTES

בָּנִים גְּדוֹלִים וּקְטַנִּים Adult and minor sons. The Mishnah in tractate *Bava Batra* (143b) deals with an estate that has not yet been divided among the heirs. The Mishnah considers only one specific case: If one of the heirs is a minor who cannot be expected to do his share of the work involved in the upkeep of the estate, are the adult heirs entitled to compensation for their extra effort? The Mishnah rules that they are not entitled to such compensation. However, the Mishnah does not consider other related cases of undivided estates, and these are left for later authorities.

One related case is described in the parallel Tosefta: If the adult brothers make an advance stipulation in court that their labors must be compensated, the law of the Mishnah does not apply. Another related case is described in the Gemara: Rava ruled that the Mishnah applies only if the adult brothers spent no money of their own to improve the field, but used the assets of the estate. In that case, the adult brothers cannot demand compensation for their labor

HALAKHAH

מִי שֶׁהִנִּיחַ בָּנִים גְּדוֹלִים וּקְטַנִּים A man who left adult and minor sons. If a man died and left sons, some of whom were adults and some minors, and the adult sons improved the property before dividing it, all profits resulting from the improvement are divided equally among all the brothers. The adult brothers may not take more than the minors, and are not even entitled to payment for their labor." (Ibid., 287:1.)

BACKGROUND

הָכִי דָּיְינִינָא לָךְ וּלְכָל אַלִּימֵי דְּחַבְרָךְ This is how I judge you and all your violent friends. Although there are fixed legal procedures, the court is nevertheless empowered to alter them when it has reason for so doing. For example, when one litigant's oath cannot be trusted, the court "overturns" the oath (הוֹפְכִים אֶת הַשְּׁבוּעָה) and permits the other litigants to give sworn testimony, though this is not the ordinary procedure. Rav Ḥisda therefore exercised his right as a judge to alter the standard procedure for presenting evidence, in order to clarify the situation. Moreover, this action also penalizes a person known to be violent. Although he cannot be punished for his violence, since his actions are not necessarily illegal, nevertheless the court is concerned to prevent systematic violence, and therefore uses its power in order to punish a person whose behavior is unacceptable.

תַּרְתֵּי לָא עָבְדִי Two evil things they will not do. Although in some circumstances refusing to testify is a criminal act (in certain instances it is a transgression requiring the witnesses to bring atonement offerings, as explained in Leviticus 5:1), it is relatively easy for a person to avoid doing what is incumbent upon him, and he can readily find an excuse for not submitting to a situation where his testimony will lead to confrontation with a violent person. However, we do not suspect that the witnesses will actually commit perjury, which is an act of commission rather than omission.

LANGUAGE

וּבוּסְתָּנֵי And orchards. This term is derived from the Persian *bostan* (lit., "fragrant place"), which means orchard or garden.

[40A] ¹וְכֵן אָמַר רַבָּה: הִשְׁבִּיחוּ לָאֶמְצַע.
²אֲמַר לֵיהּ אַבַּיֵי: מִי דָּמֵי? ³הָתָם, גְּדוֹלִים גַּבֵּי קְטַנִּים יָדְעִי וְקָא מָחֲלִי. ⁴הָכָא, מִי יָדַע דְּלֵיחֵיל?
⁵אִגַּלְגַּל מִלְּתָא וּמְטָא לְקַמֵּיהּ דְּרַבִּי אַמִי. ⁶אֲמַר לְהוּ: גְּדוֹלָה מִזּוֹ אָמְרוּ: ⁷"שָׁמִין לָהֶם כְּאָרִיס". ⁸הָשְׁתָּא, דִּידֵיהּ לָא יָהֲבִינַן לֵיהּ?

LITERAL TRANSLATION

[1] [40A] And likewise Rabbah said: They improved [it] for all.

[2] Abaye said to him: Is it comparable? [3] There, the adults know about the minors and forgo [their rights]. [4] Here, did he know, that he would forgo [his rights]?

[5] The matter rolled on and came before Rabbi Ammi. [6] He told them: They said [something even] greater than this: [7] "We appraise them like a tenant farmer." [8] Now, shall we not give him his own?

TRANSLATION AND COMMENTARY

וְכֵן אָמַר רַבָּה [1] [40A] The Gemara now relates that, a generation later, a **similar** case came before **Rabbah. He** too **said:** The adult sons **improved** the property **for all** the heirs, so they divide the profits equally with their younger brothers.

אָמַר לֵיהּ אַבָּיֵי [2] **Abaye,** who was a disciple of Rabbah, **said to him: Is** the case of the missing brother **comparable** to the case of the Mishnah in *Bava Batra*? [3] **There,** in *Bava Batra*, where all the brothers knew about each other and inherited their father's property together, **the adult** brothers **knew about the minors** from the outset, **and** if they chose to improve the estate before dividing it up, they effectively **waived their rights** to demand compensation for their efforts. [4] But **here, did** the older brother **know,** while he was planting those gardens and orchards, **that he was** effectively **waiving his rights** in favor of a long-lost younger brother?

אִגַּלְגַּל מִלְּתָא [5] The Gemara does not record what answer Rabbah gave to Abaye's objection. Instead, it returns to the original story of Mari bar Isak in the court of Rav Hisda: **The case took a new turn and came** from Babylonia **before Rabbi Ammi** in Eretz Israel. [6] When Rabbi Ammi was told of Rav Ḥisda's ruling, **he said to** the messengers: Rav Ḥisda's ruling is mistaken, for surely the Rabbis **said something even greater than this** — an extreme and far-reaching ruling about such cases — namely: [7] **"We appraise** improvements made by a relative administering the estate of a captive **as if he were a tenant farmer."** Thus we see that even people who look after and improve property that is not theirs are entitled to generous compensation for their efforts! [8] **Now, should we not give** Mari compensation for looking after and improving **what is his?** Mari bar Isak should be entitled to a tenant farmer's share in his brother's half of the garden he planted!

RASHI

וכן אמר רבה השביחו לאמצע — לא גרסינן, שאין זה לשון גמרא להביא דברי האמוראים סיוע למשנה. ועוד: רבה תלמידיה דרב חסדא הוה, והיכי אמר רב חסדא שמעתא משמיה? ולא גרס ליה — וכן אמר רב גרסינן, שהיה רבו של רב חסדא. משום דאיכא למאן דאמר בבבא בתרא (קמג,ב): לא שנו אלא ששבחו נכסים מחמת נכסים, אבל שבחו מחמת עצמן של אחים — השביחו לעצמן, אמרה רב חסדא להא דרב הכא, למימר דלית לן ההיא שמעתא, אלא אפילו השביחו מחמת טורחן של משביחין, כי הכא דשתל פרדס — השביחו לאמצע. **ידעו** — אלו שיטלו חלקם. **מי ידע** — שיש לו אחים. **גדולה מזו** — קרוב היורד לנכסי שבוי שאם יבאו הבעלים יטלו שלהם. **אמרו שמין להם באריס הכא דידיה לא יהבינן ליה** — בתמיה, זה שעשה והשביחן לדעת עצמו לא יהבינן ליה כאריס בחלק השני?

NOTES

However, if they have invested their own money in the operation, they are entitled to compensation even if they did not so stipulate in advance.

A further case on the same subject is discussed by the Rishonim, a case where all the heirs are adults, but one of them did not do his share of the work for some reason — for example, he was away at the time. *Tosafot* (*Bava Batra* 143b) rules that there is no difference between adult and minor brothers, and any improvement in the value of the estate must be divided equally, unless the working brothers stipulated otherwise. This position is supported by most Rishonim, including *Rambam*, *Rashba* and *Ramban*. *Ra'avad*, however, disagrees, and rules that an adult brother who does not do his share of the work has the same status as a captive, and the working brothers are entitled to the share of a tenant farmer in his part of the estate.

וְכֵן אָמַר רַבָּה And similarly Rabbah said. Rabbah's comment and Abaye's unanswered objection appear to interrupt the flow of the story. They also pose the following difficulties to the Rishonim: Rav Ḥisda appears to be quoting the Amora Rabbah to support a Mishnah, which is a highly unusual procedure. Moreover, Rabbah was a disciple of Rav Ḥisda, and not an earlier authority whose views Rav Ḥisda might have quoted. In addition, Abaye was a disciple of Rabbah, so was probably much too young to have taken part in a discussion between Rav Ḥisda and Rabbi Ammi. Finally, Abaye appears to assume that the older brother did not know of the existence of the younger brother, whereas

HALAKHAH

שָׁמִין לָהֶם כְּאָרִיס We appraise them like a tenant farmer. "If someone inherits his father's estate and improves the property, and then a long-lost brother appears and demands his rightful share in the property, then, if the long-lost brother was an adult at the time the father died, we appraise the amount the estate has appreciated and award the original heir the share of a tenant farmer in the portion that he must turn over to his brother, since he did

BACKGROUND

אִגַּלְגַּל מִלְּתָא The matter rolled on. This expression indicates that the question was not asked directly of Rabbi Ammi, since Rav Ḥisda had given his ruling, and Mari bar Isak probably acted accordingly. However, this subject, being an interesting Halakhic problem, was brought to Rabbi Ammi in Eretz Israel by emissaries who used to travel between Eretz Israel and Babylonia, conveying teachings from one center to the other. It could also be that Mari bar Isak was not content with the ruling, and therefore tried bringing the case to another court. Since there was no court in Babylonia more important than Rav Ḥisda's, he may have tried to transfer the matter to Eretz Israel, where the courts had higher authority. The question was thus brought before Rabbi Ammi.

SAGES

רַבִּי אַמִי Rabbi Ammi. A Palestinian Amora of the third generation, Rabbi Ammi (bar Natan) was a priest and a close friend of Rabbi Assi. They studied with the greatest Sages of Eretz Israel and were especially close disciples of Rabbi Yoḥanan. Rabbi Ammi also studied with Rabbi Yoḥanan's greatest students. In the Jerusalem Talmud he is commonly known as Rabbi Immi.

After Rabbi Yoḥanan's death Rabbi Ammi was appointed head of the Tiberias Yeshiva in his place. The Sages of Babylonia also consulted him about Halakhic problems. He is widely quoted in both the Babylonian and Jerusalem Talmuds, not only in transmitting statements by his teachers but also in debate with Rabbi Assi and with other Sages of the generation. Most of the Palestinian Amoraim of the following generation received and transmitted his teachings. He and Rabbi Assi were known as "the distinguished priests of Eretz Israel," and stories are told of their righteousness and holiness. Rabbi Ammi seems to have lived to a great age, and even the Sages of the fourth generation in Babylonia used to send him their questions.

[1] אֲהַדְרוּהּ הָא לְקַמֵּיהּ דְּרַב חִסְדָּא. [2] אֲמַר לְהוּ: מִי דָּמֵי? [3] הָתָם, בִּרְשׁוּת נָחֵית. [4] הָכָא, לָאו בִּרְשׁוּת נָחֵית. [5] וְעוֹד, קָטָן הוּא, [6] וְאֵין מוֹרִידִין קָרוֹב לְנִכְסֵי קָטָן.

[7] אֲהַדְרוּהּ לְקַמֵּיהּ דְּרַבִּי אַמִּי. [8] אֲמַר לְהוּ: לָא סַיְּימוּהָ קַמֵּי דְּקָטָן הוּא.

משנה [9] הַמַּפְקִיד פֵּירוֹת אֵצֶל חֲבֵירוֹ, [10] הֲרֵי זֶה יוֹצִיא לוֹ חֶסְרוֹנוֹת.

LITERAL TRANSLATION

[1] They brought this [statement] back before Rav Ḥisda. [2] He said to them: Is it comparable? [3] There, he went down with permission. [4] Here, he went down without permission. [5] Moreover, he was a [6] minor, and we do not authorize a relative to [administer] the estate of a minor.

[7] They brought this [reply] back before Rabbi Ammi. [8] He said to them: They did not finish [the story] before me that he was a minor.

MISHNAH [9] Someone who deposits produce with his fellow, [10] this [bailee] deducts losses.

TRANSLATION AND COMMENTARY

אֲהַדְרוּהּ הָא לְקַמֵּיהּ דְּרַב חִסְדָּא [1] The messengers then **brought** Rabbi Ammi's **statement back to Rav Ḥisda.** [2] **He said to them: Is** the case of Mari's brother **comparable** to the case of a relative administering a captive's estate? [3] **There,** in the case of the captive's estate, the relative **went down** and took possession of the property with permission. [4] **Here,** in the case of the missing brother, Mari **went down** and took possession of his brother's property without permission. [5] **Moreover,** even if Mari had asked for it, permission would not have been granted. For the brother **was a minor** at the time Mari took over the property, [6] **and we do not authorize a relative to administer the estate of a minor.** Thus Mari did not act properly in administering his brother's estate, and has no right to be compensated like a tenant farmer.

אֲהַדְרוּהּ לְקַמֵּיהּ דְּרַבִּי אַמִּי [7] The messengers **brought** Rav Ḥisda's **reply back to Rabbi Ammi, and he said to them:** Rav Ḥisda is quite right. [8] The messengers **did not finish** telling me **the story, and** did not inform me that the brother **was a minor** at the time Mari took possession of their late father's estate. Now that I have heard the entire story, I agree with Rav Ḥisda that Mari must give his brother a full share in the gardens and the orchards he planted.

MISHNAH הַמַּפְקִיד פֵּירוֹת אֵצֶל חֲבֵירוֹ [9] If **someone deposits produce with another person,** and the bailee mixes the deposit with produce of his own, so that he cannot be certain precisely which fruits are his and which belong to the depositor, he must return a quantity equivalent to that originally deposited. But a problem can arise if the produce deteriorates during storage. What must the bailee do in such circumstances? [10] The Mishnah tells us that **the bailee** may **deduct** a certain percentage to cover the **depreciation.** But what if the bailee is not certain how much the produce has deteriorated? The Mishnah tells us that the bailee may assume that the produce deteriorated at a normal rate, and make his deduction accordingly.

RASHI

ברשות בית דין נחתי – דמורידין קרוב לנכסי שבוי. **הכא לא ברשות נחית** – כשירד זה לתוכו לא נמלך בבית דין. **ועוד** – אם בא לימלך לא היו מורידין אותו, דהא אחיו קטן הוא, ואין מורידין קרוב לנכסי קטן.

משנה הרי זה יוציא לו חסרונות – כשיחזירם לו יפחות כמה הם רגילים לחסור, ובגמרא מוקי לה בשעירבן עם פירותיו.

NOTES

Rav Ḥisda compares Mari bar Isak to Joseph's brothers, who knew he existed but did not recognize him after many years' separation.

Accordingly, *Rashi* removed the entire passage involving Rabbah and Abaye from his text of the Gemara. Alternatively, he suggested an emendation whereby Rav, Rav Ḥisda's teacher, rather than Rabbah is the Amora quoted.

Tosafot suggests that it may have been the editor of the Gemara, and not Rav Ḥisda, who quoted Rabbah and Abaye. Their arguments were mentioned parenthetically in the middle of the story, even though they did not actually deal with the case of Mari bar Isak, because they considered a similar case in a later generation and arrived at a similar conclusion. Our commentary follows this explanation.

הָכָא, לָאו בִּרְשׁוּת נָחֵית Here, he went down without permission. Rav Ḥisda's distinction is problematic. What difference would it have made if Mari had requested permission from the court? In every case where we allow a relative to administer an absentee's estate, we compensate him for his labors even if he failed to request permission, and in every case where we do not allow it, it makes no difference if he asked permission.

Rashba suggests that the text should be emended to remove the word "moreover." Thus Rav Ḥisda was simply arguing that Mari had no permission to administer the field because his brother was a minor.

HALAKHAH

not know that this brother existed. However, if the long-lost brother was a minor when the father died, the increment is divided equally, and the original heir is not entitled to compensation for improving his brother's share of the property," following the conclusion of the Gemara. (*Shulḥan Arukh, Ḥoshen Mishpat* 287:3.)

LITERAL TRANSLATION

[1] For wheat and for rice, nine half-*kavs* per *kor;* [2] for barley and for millet, nine *kavs* per *kor;* [3] for spelt and for linseed, three *se'ahs* per *kor.* [4] Everything according to the quantity, and everything according to the time.

[5] Rabbi Yoḥanan ben Nuri said: But what do the mice care? [6] Do they not eat [the same amount] whether from a lot or from a little? [7] Rather, he deducts losses for one kor alone.

[8] Rabbi Yehudah says: If there was a large quantity, [9] he does not deduct losses, because it increases.

[1] לְחִטִּים וּלְאוֹרֶז, תִּשְׁעָה חֲצָאֵי קַבִּין לַכּוֹר; [2] לִשְׂעוֹרִין וּלְדוֹחַן, תִּשְׁעָה קַבִּין לַכּוֹר; [3] לְכוּסְמִין וּלְזֶרַע פִּשְׁתָּן, שָׁלֹשׁ סְאִין לַכּוֹר. [4] הַכֹּל לְפִי הַמִּדָּה, וְהַכֹּל לְפִי הַזְּמַן.

[5] אָמַר רַבִּי יוֹחָנָן בֶּן נוּרִי: וְכִי מָה אִכְפַּת לָהֶן לַעֲכְבָּרִין? [6] וַהֲלֹא אוֹכְלוֹת בֵּין מֵהַרְבֵּה וּבֵין מִקְּמְעָא? [7] אֶלָּא, אֵינוֹ מוֹצִיא לוֹ חֶסְרוֹנוֹת אֶלָּא לְכוֹר אֶחָד בִּלְבָד.

[8] רַבִּי יְהוּדָה אוֹמֵר: אִם הָיְתָה מִדָּה מְרוּבָּה, [9] אֵינוֹ מוֹצִיא לוֹ חֶסְרוֹנוֹת, מִפְּנֵי שֶׁמּוֹתִירוֹת.

RASHI

אורז — *מי״ל. דוחן — **פטי״ל, ודומה לאורז. הכל לפי המדה — וכן לכל כור וכור. הכל לפי הזמן — שהניחן בידו, לכל שנה ושנה יניח לו כך. רבי יוחנן בן נורי אמר — א״הכל לפי המדה״ פליג. אם היתה מדה מרובה — שהפקיד אצלו הרבה, ובגמרא מפרש עשרה כורים, לא יוציא לו חסרונות, מפני שהם מותירות. שבימות הגורן כשמפקיד — החיטין יבשין, ובימות הגשמים כשמחזיר — נופחות, ובאכילת עכברים אינן נחסרים כל כך לכל כור וכור, דכולי האי לא אכלי עכברים מעשרה כורין, הלכך, נפיחתו משלמת חסרון המגיע לשני כורים או שלשה שהעכברים אוכלין.

TRANSLATION AND COMMENTARY

[1] Specifically: **For wheat and rice,** the bailee may deduct **nine half-*kavs*** per ***kor*** (2.5%); [2] **for barley and millet, nine *kavs*** per ***kor*** (5%); [3] **for spelt and linseed, three *se'ahs*** per ***kor*** (10%). One *kor* equals thirty *se'ahs*; one *se'ah* equals six *kavs*; one *kav* is approximately equal to two liters. The Mishnah's calculation is made on the basis of a deposit of one *kor* left in the bailee's care for one year. [4] However, the actual figures in any individual case vary proportionally **according to the quantity** of produce actually delivered to the bailee, **and according to the** length of **time** the produce was in his care.

אָמַר רַבִּי יוֹחָנָן בֶּן נוּרִי [5] **Rabbi Yoḥanan ben Nuri** disagreed with the provision in the last clause of the Mishnah, which stipulated that the depreciation increases in proportion to the quantity of produce. He **said: What do the mice** who attack stored produce **care** how much produce there is in storage? [6] **Do they not eat the same amount, whether** they take it **from a lot** of produce **or from a little?** [7] **Rather,** says Rabbi Yoḥanan ben Nuri, the formula for calculating normal depreciation does not vary with the quantity of produce in storage, and the bailee **may only deduct depreciation for one *kor* alone,** regardless of how many *kors* of produce were actually in storage, since the mice would not eat more even if more were available.

רַבִּי יְהוּדָה אוֹמֵר [8] **Rabbi Yehudah** also rejects the idea that the deduction is proportional to the quantity of produce in the deposit. He **says: If** the depositor deposited a **large quantity,** [9] the bailee **does not deduct** anything at all for **depreciation, because** the expected losses due to mice will be offset by an increase in the volume of the produce, since large quantities of **produce** tend to absorb moisture and swell when kept in storage. Thus the bailee must return the same quantity as was deposited, and we assume that any depreciation was offset by **an increase in quantity** due to swelling.

BACKGROUND

כּוֹר, סְאָה, קַב ***Kor, se'ah* and *kav*.** A *kor* is the largest dry measure used by the Sages. A *kor* contained thirty *se'ah*, and each *se'ah* contained six *kabim*. There is some disagreement regarding the modern equivalent of these measurements. According to the lowest estimates, a *kor* contained approximately 250 liters.

חֶסְרוֹנוֹת Losses. Stored foodstuffs naturally suffer decrease, mainly from vermin such as worms, beetles, mice and rats. The Geonim wrote that the rates of decrease stated here are not absolute, but are applicable to a specific time and place. Hence "normal" decrease attributable to natural causes must be determined according to local conditions.

LANGUAGE (RASHI)

***מי״ל** From the Old French *mil*, meaning "millet."

****פטי״ל** From the Old French *panil*, meaning a kind of millet.

NOTES

אוֹרֶז Rice. Our translation follows *Tosafot* (*Berakhot* 37a), and is the generally accepted translation of this term. *Rashi*, however, translates אוֹרֶז as millet, and דוֹחַן as a strain of millet called *panil* in Old French.

תִּשְׁעָה חֲצָאֵי קַבִּין Nine half-*kavs*. The Mishnah used this expression rather than the more common "four-and-a-half *kavs*" because it fits better with the next figure given in the Mishnah — "nine *kavs*" (*Ritva*).

HALAKHAH

חֶסְרוֹנוֹת מִפִּקָּדוֹן Depreciation of a deposit. "If a bailee receives a deposit of produce from another person, he may not mix it with his own produce without permission. If he was scrupulous about this law and kept the depositor's produce separate, he simply returns it to him at the end of the period of deposit without any need to account for depreciation, and without any need to take an oath (*Sma*). But if he violated this law and mixed the produce with his own, and the quantity decreased over time, the bailee must calculate what percentage of the produce in storage was his and what percentage the depositor's, and how much of the decrease should come out of each share. He must then swear to the facts upon which he based his calculations, and return to the depositor his share.

"If the bailee consumed some of the mixed produce over the course of time, and lost track of how much he used, he can no longer make a calculation based upon the percentage of the produce that was his and the percentage

TRANSLATION AND COMMENTARY

GEMARA אוֹרֶז טוּבָא חָסֵר [1]The Gemara begins its analysis of the Mishnah by querying the Mishnah's specified rate of depreciation of rice: Does rice depreciate so little? Surely, in the course of a year, the volume of **rice decreases substantially more** than the 2.5% specified in the Mishnah!

אָמַר רַבָּה בַּר בַּר חָנָה [2]**Rabbah bar Bar Ḥanah said in the name of Rabbi Yoḥanan: The Mishnah was referring to peeled rice,** losses for which are only 2.5% per annum. Unpeeled rice, however, decreases in volume at a higher rate.

לְכוּסְמִין וּלְזֶרַע פִּשְׁתָּן [3]The Gemara now examines another rate of depreciation specified in the Mishnah: **"For spelt and for linseed, three *se'ahs* per *kor*,** etc." [4]On this clause in the Mishnah, **Rabbi Yoḥanan said in the name of Rabbi Ḥiyya: The Mishnah,** which says that flax decreases in volume at an annual rate of 10%, **was referring to linseed in pods,** but cleaned linseed does not deteriorate to such an extent. [5]The Gemara now quotes a Tannaitic source supporting both statements of Rabbi Yoḥanan just quoted: **A Baraita also taught this: "For spelt, for linseed in pods and for unpeeled rice,** [6]the bailee may deduct **three *se'ahs* per *kor*,** or 10%." Thus we see that it is only peeled rice that deteriorates slowly, whereas unpeeled rice decreases in volume as rapidly as unpeeled linseed. Unpeeled produce shrinks rapidly because the outer husks constitute a substantial part of the total volume, and they tend to shrivel up and fall away.

הַכֹּל לְפִי הַמִּדָּה [7]The Gemara now examines the next clause of the Mishnah — **"everything according to the quantity, etc."** [8]Explaining this Mishnah, **a Tanna taught** the following Baraita: **"Similarly for each and every *kor*, and similarly for each and every year."** In other words, the percentages mentioned in the Mishnah were given per *kor* and per **annum,** and vary proportionally with quantity and time.

אָמַר רַבִּי יוֹחָנָן [9]The Gemara now examines the next clause of the Mishnah: **"Rabbi Yoḥanan ben Nuri said:** What do the mice care, **etc."** [10]A Baraita **was taught** in which the other Sages replied to Rabbi Yoḥanan ben Nuri's argument that deduction for depreciation is made for no more than one *kor* of produce: "The Sages **said to Rabbi Yoḥanan** ben Nuri: [11]Not only do mice eat the produce, but **much of** the produce **is lost** and **much is scattered** as a result of damage caused by mice, and thus the losses should be assessed on a proportional basis regardless of how large the deposit was."

גמרא [1]אוֹרֶז טוּבָא חָסֵר. [2]אָמַר רַבָּה בַּר בַּר חָנָה אָמַר רַבִּי יוֹחָנָן: בְּאוֹרֶז קָלוּף שָׁנוּ. [3]״לְכוּסְמִין וּלְזֶרַע פִּשְׁתָּן, שְׁלֹשָׁה סְאִין לַכּוֹר, וכו׳״. [4]אָמַר רַבִּי יוֹחָנָן אָמַר רַבִּי חִיָּיא: זֶרַע פִּשְׁתָּן בְּגִבְעוֹלִין שָׁנוּ. [5]תַּנְיָא נַמִי הָכִי: ״לְכוּסְמִין וּלְזֶרַע פִּשְׁתָּן בְּגִבְעוֹלִין וּלְאוֹרֶז שֶׁאֵינוֹ קָלוּף, [6]שְׁלֹשָׁה סְאִין לַכּוֹר״. [7]״הַכֹּל לְפִי הַמִּדָּה וכו׳״. [8]תָּנָא: ״כֵּן לְכָל כּוֹר וָכוֹר, וְכֵן לְכָל שָׁנָה וְשָׁנָה״. [9]״אָמַר רַבִּי יוֹחָנָן בֶּן נוּרִי וכו׳״. [10]תַּנְיָא: ״אָמְרוּ לוֹ לְרַבִּי יוֹחָנָן: [11]הַרְבֵּה אוֹבְדוֹת מֵהֶן; הַרְבֵּה מִתְפַּזְּרוֹת מֵהֶן״.

LITERAL TRANSLATION

GEMARA [1]Rice decreases much more!

[2]Rabbah bar Bar Ḥanah said in the name of Rabbi Yoḥanan: They taught concerning peeled rice.

[3]"For spelt and for linseed, three *se'ahs* per *kor*, etc."

[4]Rabbi Yoḥanan said in the name of Rabbi Ḥiyya: They taught [concerning] linseed in pods. [5]It was also taught thus: "For spelt and for linseed in pods, and for rice which was not peeled, [6]three *se'ahs* per *kor*."

[7]"Everything according to the quantity, etc." [8][A Tanna] taught: "Similarly for each and every *kor*, and similarly for each and every year."

[9]"Rabbi Yoḥanan be Nuri said, etc." [10]It was taught: "They said to Rabbi Yoḥanan: [11]Much of it is lost; much of it is scattered."

RASHI

גמרא זרע פשתן בגבעולין – חסר כל כך, לפי שהגבעולין מתייבשין ונופלים והרוח מנשבתן, אבל זרע פשתן נקי אינו חסר כל כך. לכל כור וכור – פירוש דמתניתין הוא.

BACKGROUND

לְזֶרַע פִּשְׁתָּן בְּגִבְעוֹלִין Linseed in pods. Even though flax is generally grown for the fibers in its pods, the seeds are also useful, as oil is derived from them and the husks are used for animal food.

Linseed is found in round capsules of seed enclosed in a sticky substance. The seeds themselves are liable to fall off while in their capsules, and the resulting loss can be substantial.

SAGES

רַבִּי יוֹחָנָן בֶּן נוּרִי Rabbi Yoḥanan ben Nuri. One of the most important Tannaim of the third generation, Rabbi Yoḥanan ben Nuri was also apprently one of the youngest. His Halakhic differences of opinion are mainly with Rabbi Akiva and his contemporaries.

Rabbi Yoḥanan ben Nuri lived in Lower Galilee (in Ginegar or Bet She'arim), and maintained close ties with the Sages of Galilee (Abba Ḥalafta, the father of Rabbi Yose, and others). His closest students were also among the Sages of Galilee (Rabbi Yose and Rabbi Yehoshua ben Korḥa).

Very little is known about his private life. It is told that he was extremely poor and supported himself by gleaning in fields. The Sage Issi ben Yehudah called him "the peddler's box" because he was expert in every area of the Torah and was held up as a model of piety.

NOTES

הַרְבֵּה אוֹבְדוֹת מֵהֶן Much of it is lost. The Gemara quotes this Baraita as a response to Rabbi Yoḥanan ben Nuri's argument that mice will eat the same amount regardless of the size of the deposit. The Sages' response is that losses are

HALAKHAH

that was the depositor's. He must instead return the quantity he received, after deducting a fixed percentage for normal loss. For wheat and peeled rice (following Rabbi Yoḥanan), he may deduct four-and-one-half *kavs* per *kor* per annum (2.5%); for barley and millet, nine *kavs* per *kor* per annum (5%); for spelt, linseed in its pods, and unpeeled rice, three *se'ahs* per *kor* per annum (10%). These measures are calculated per *kor* per annum, and increase proportionately for increased quantity or time," following the anonymous first Tanna of the Mishnah. (*Shulḥan Arukh, Ḥoshen Mishpat* 292:10,11.)

TRANSLATION AND COMMENTARY

תָּנָא [1]The Gemara now quotes another Tannaitic source explaining our Mishnah: **A Tanna taught** the following Baraita: **"In what circumstances does** the Mishnah's ruling **apply** regarding how much produce may be deducted? [2]**Where** the bailee **mixed** the depositor's produce **with his own produce,** and does not know what belongs to the depositor and what to himself. [3]**But if** the bailee **designated a** specific **corner for** the storage of a depositor's produce, [4]**he may say to** the depositor: **'Look, your** produce stands **before you,'** and return it to him as it is, regardless of how much or how little it has deteriorated."

וְכִי עֵירְבָן עִם פֵּירוֹתָיו [5]The Gemara now examines this Baraita and asks: **But** even **if** the bailee **mixed** the depositor's produce **with his** own **produce, what of it?** Why should he base his assessment of depreciation on the average figures given in the Mishnah? There is a more accurate way to calculate the loss. [6]**Let him see how much** of **his own produce** there **was** originally, and how much there was in the deposit. If, for example, one-third of the produce was his own and two-thirds was the depositor's, let him return two-thirds of the remaining produce to the depositor, regardless of how much deterioration there has been.

בְּמִסְתַּפֵּק מֵהֶם [7]The Gemara answers: The Mishnah's ruling applies **where** the bailee **made use of** the combined produce from time to time, and cannot now determine what proportion is his and what proportion the depositor's.

וְלֵיחֲזֵי כַּמָּה אִסְתַּפֵּק [8]The Gemara asks: **But let** the bailee **see how much he made use of** for his personal needs, and, having deducted this amount, make the appropriate calculations.

דְּלָא יָדַע כַּמָּה אִסְתַּפֵּק [9]The Gemara answers: The Mishnah's ruling applies **where** the bailee **does not know how much** he **used,** as he did not keep a record. Hence, the only basis for the calculation is the original quantity of the deposit, and the bailee must estimate its depreciation using the Mishnah's figures.

רַבִּי יְהוּדָה אוֹמֵר [10]The Gemara now considers the next clause of the Mishnah: **"Rabbi Yehudah says: If** the depositor deposited a large quantity, the bailee may not deduct anything at all for depreciation, etc." [11]The Gemara asks: **How much is a large quantity** in this context?

אָמַר רַבָּה בַּר בַּר חָנָה [12]**Rabbah bar Bar Ḥanah replied in the name of Rabbi Yoḥanan: Ten** ***kors.*** [13]The Gemara now cites a Tannaitic source supporting this statement: **A Baraita also taught this: "How much is a large quantity? Ten** ***kors."***

[1]תָּנָא: ״בַּמֶּה דְּבָרִים אֲמוּרִים? [2]שֶׁעֵירְבָן עִם פֵּירוֹתָיו. [3]אֲבָל יִחֵד לוֹ קֶרֶן זָוִית, [4]אוֹמֵר לוֹ: ׳הֲרֵי שֶׁלְּךָ לְפָנֶיךָ׳״. [5]וְכִי עֵירְבָן עִם פֵּירוֹתָיו, [6]מַאי הָוֵי? לֵיחֲזֵי לְדִידֵיהּ כַּמָּה הָוְיָין. [7]בְּמִסְתַּפֵּק מֵהֶם. [8]וְלֵיחֲזֵי כַּמָּה אִסְתַּפֵּק. [9]דְּלָא יָדַע כַּמָּה אִסְתַּפֵּק. [10]״רַבִּי יְהוּדָה אוֹמֵר: אִם הָיְתָה וכו׳״. [11]כַּמָּה מִדָּה מְרוּבָּה? [12]אָמַר רַבָּה בַּר בַּר חָנָה אָמַר רַבִּי יוֹחָנָן: עֲשָׂרָה כּוֹרִין. [13]תַּנְיָא נַמִי הָכִי: ״כַּמָּה מִדָּה מְרוּבָּה? עֲשָׂרָה כּוֹרִין״.

LITERAL TRANSLATION

[1][A Tanna] taught: "In what case are these things said? [2]Where he mixed it with his own produce. [3]But [if] he designated a corner for it, [4]he may say to him: 'Behold, yours is before you.'"

[5]But if he mixed it with his own produce, what of it? [6]Let him see how much his own [produce] is.

[7]Where he made use of it.

[8]But let him see how much he made use of.

[9]Where he does not know how much he used.

[10]"Rabbi Yehudah says: If there was, etc." [11]How much is a large quantity?

[12]Rabbah bar Bar Ḥanah said in the name of Rabbi Yoḥanan: Ten *kors*. [13]It was also taught thus: "How much is a large quantity? Ten *kors*."

RASHI

ליחזי דידיה כמה הוו כו׳ – וידלה כמה חסרו, ויטול על של חברו כפי חשבון.

NOTES

caused not only by mice but by other factors as well. The Jerusalem Talmud gives a different response to Rabbi Yoḥanan ben Nuri: Mice attract other mice; the more produce there is, the more mice attack it.

The Rishonim suggest various ways of resolving the difference between the two Talmuds (see *Tosafot* and *Ritva*).

כַּמָּה מִדָּה מְרוּבָּה How much is a large quantity? Our commentary follows *Rashi*, who explains that Rabbi Yehudah is referring specifically to a deposit that was delivered during the dry season and returned during the rainy season. According to this interpretation, Rabbi Yehudah's reasoning is the same as that of the Baraita quoted by the Gemara — namely, that produce swells during the rainy season.

There are two difficulties with this explanation. Firstly, it is not clear why the swelling should be affected by the size of the deposit. If a deposit swells during the rainy season, it will do so regardless of whether it is big or small. *Tosafot* suggests that Rabbi Yehudah may mean that ten *kors*

TRANSLATION AND COMMENTARY

תָּנֵי תַּנָּא קַמֵּיהּ דְּרַב נַחְמָן [1] **A Tanna** — a reciter of Baraitot who specialized in precise recollection of the text of Baraitot — **recited** the following **Baraita before Rav Naḥman: "In what circumstances does** the ruling of the Mishnah **apply?** [2] **Where** the depositor **measured out** the produce **for** the bailee **from his granary, and** the bailee **returned it to** the depositor **from his granary,** using the set of measures customarily used in a granary. [3] **But if** the depositor **measured out** the produce **for** the bailee **from his granary and** the bailee **returned it to** the depositor **from his house,** [4] using the set of measures customarily used in the house, the bailee may **not deduct** anything for **depreciation, because** a quantity first measured in a granary **increases** when it is measured in a house, since the measure used in the granary is slightly larger than that used in the house." Thus, a *kor* that was measured in a granary, and has deteriorated over time, will still appear to be a *kor* when measured in the house, for the discrepancy between the two measures makes up for any natural depreciation of the produce. Thus the Baraita recited by the Tanna before Rav Naḥman lays down the principle that for the deduction of depreciation to apply, it is necessary to use the same system of measurement at the time of returning the deposit as used at the time of deposit.

אָמַר לֵיהּ [5] Rav Naḥman found the Baraita as cited to be unintelligible. He **said to** the Baraita-reciter: **Are we dealing with fools, who give with a large measure and take** back **with a small measure?** Obviously, if the depositor measured the produce with a measure from the granary before handing it to the bailee, he will expect the same measure to be used in returning him the produce! [6] Accordingly, Rav Naḥman suggested an emendation in the text of the Baraita: **Perhaps** the text of this Baraita is incorrect, and what you should have **said** was not "from his granary," but **"during the granary season"** (the harvest season). [7] Accordingly, the amended Baraita would read as follows: **"In what circumstances does** the ruling of the Mishnah **apply?** [8] **Where** the depositor **measured out** the produce **for** the bailee **during the granary season and** the bailee **returned**

[1] תָּנֵי תַּנָּא קַמֵּיהּ דְּרַב נַחְמָן: "בַּמֶּה דְּבָרִים אֲמוּרִים? [2] שֶׁמָּדַד לוֹ מִתּוֹךְ גּוֹרְנוֹ וְהֶחֱזִיר לוֹ מִתּוֹךְ גּוֹרְנוֹ. [3] אֲבָל מָדַד לוֹ מִתּוֹךְ גּוֹרְנוֹ וְהֶחֱזִיר לוֹ מִתּוֹךְ בֵּיתוֹ, [4] אֵינוֹ יוֹצִיא לוֹ חֶסְרוֹנוֹת, מִפְּנֵי שֶׁמּוֹתִירוֹת".

[5] אָמַר לֵיהּ: וְכִי בְּשׁוּפְטָנֵי עָסְקִינַן, דְּיָהֲבִי בְּכַיְילָא רַבָּא וְשָׁקְלִי בְּכַיְילָא זוּטָא? [6] דִּלְמָא "בִּימוֹת הַגּוֹרֶן" קָאָמְרַתְּ. [7] "בַּמֶּה דְּבָרִים אֲמוּרִים? [8] שֶׁמָּדַד לוֹ בִּימוֹת הַגּוֹרֶן וְהֶחֱזִיר לוֹ בִּימוֹת

LITERAL TRANSLATION

[1] A Tanna taught [a Baraita] before Rav Naḥman: "In what case are these things said? [2] Where he measured [it] for him from his granary and returned [it] to him from his granary. [3] But [if] he measured [it] for him from his granary and returned [it] to him from his house, [4] he does not deduct losses, because it increases."

[5] [Rav Naḥman] said to him: Are we dealing with fools, who give with a large measure and take with a small measure? [6] Perhaps you [meant to] say: "During the granary season." [7] "In what case are these things said? [8] Where he measured [it] for him during the granary season and returned [it] to him during the granary

RASHI

מדת הגורן — היתה יתירה על של בתים. **בשופטני** — שוטים. **בכיילא** — במדה. **בימות הגורן** — סמוך ליובשן, שנתייבשו בחמה.

LANGUAGE

בְּשׁוּפְטָנֵי With fools. There are differences of opinion regarding the source of the word **שׁוּפְטָנֵי**. Some authorities maintain that it comes from the Persian *seftan,* meaning frightened or confused. Other authorities believe it is the Aramaic word **טַפְשָׁנָא** with the letters reversed. In the language of the Sages, it means an unintelligent person who acts foolishly.

NOTES

swell enough to offset the losses caused by mice to one *kor,* and that the effect on other quantities must be calculated accordingly. *Rosh* adds that it is possible that Rabbi Yehudah agrees with Rabbi Yoḥanan ben Nuri that mice attack only the first *kor.* This idea also finds support in the language of the Baraita (see *Rashba*).

There is a second difficulty with *Rashi*'s explanation. According to *Rashi*, the Baraita's distinction between the dry season and the rainy season is valid only according to Rabbi Yehudah, but not according to the Sages, according to whom the Halakhah is decided. *Ran* explains that it is possible that the Sages do not disagree with Rabbi Yehudah, even though the language of the Baraita does not support this position, as there is some indication that our Gemara did not consider the language of the Baraita reliable.

Meiri suggests that the Baraita is arguing that produce of any quantity swells during the rainy season, but Rabbi Yehudah goes beyond the Baraita and argues that even produce returned during the same season swells if it is a large enough quantity. Thus, it is possible to accept the Baraita's ruling without accepting Rabbi Yehudah's extension.

Ra'avad suggests an interpretation of Rabbi Yehudah's statement that is not based on the Baraita at all. According to *Ra'avad*, a large deposit does not swell more than a small one. However, measuring out a large deposit takes a long time and tends to be done hastily. As a result, measures tend to be less than full, and the amount appears larger than it actually is.

HALAKHAH

כְּשֶׁמּוֹדֵד וּמַחֲזִיר בְּאוֹתָהּ עוֹנָה Measuring produce and returning it during the same season. "The bailee is entitled to make a deduction for depreciation only if he received and returned the produce during the same season. But if he

BACKGROUND

בִּימוֹת הַגּוֹרֶן וּבִימוֹת הַגְּשָׁמִים **The granary season and the rainy season.** During the granary season (the summer), the air is dry, and kernels of grain dry up and shrink. However, during the rainy season the air is very humid and the kernels absorb moisture from the atmosphere; therefore their volume is somewhat greater. When kernels absorb moisture directly they swell considerably, begin to sprout and cease to be edible. Even the relatively moist air of the rainy season is sufficient to cause the kernels to swell slightly.

לִפְקַע כַּדָּא **The container should burst.** A jar generally has a rounded bottom and rises to a narrow neck. If the kernels of grain inside it swell considerably, they do so within the lower, wide part of the vessel, but do not usually rise above it. However, if the vessel was completely full the pitcher would burst from the pressure of the expanding kernels.

מִשּׁוּם אִיצְצָא **Because of pressure.** The assumption here is that if the kernels are placed in a pitcher under great pressure, when they begin to expand the upper level effectively seals the vessel so that no more air can enter, and the rest of the kernels will not expand.

שְׁתוּת לַיַּיִן **A sixth for wine.** Wine is lost at this high rate for two reasons. Firstly, the earthenware vessel absorbs some of the liquid, and wine can also seep through the sides (which is why the inside of the vessel was coated with a sealant such as pitch or wax). Secondly, the alcohol in wine, as well as the water, tends to evaporate over time, adding to the loss.

בֶּלַע **Absorption.** In Talmudic times, jars and barrels were made of earthenware. All earthenware is slightly porous and absorbs some of the liquid stored in it. The rate of absorption depends on the quality of the clay from which the vessel was made and on its coating, as well as on the viscosity of the liquid being stored.

TRANSLATION AND COMMENTARY

it to him during the granary season. [1]But if the depositor **measured it out during the** dry **granary season and** the bailee **returned it to** the depositor **during the rainy season,** [2]the bailee may **not deduct** anything for **depreciation, because** the produce **increases** in volume during the rainy season, offsetting any loss due to mice. Thus a *kor* of produce originally measured during the dry season, even though some has been eaten by mice, will still be a *kor* when measured during the rainy season.

אֲמַר לֵיהּ רַב פַּפָּא לְאַבַּיֵי [3]**Rav Pappa said to Abaye:** If you assume that the volume of produce increases during the rainy season, surely every sealed **container** of produce **should burst** during the rainy season!

הֲוָה עוּבְדָא [4]The Gemara gives two answers to this question: (1) **There was** such **a case, and the container** did indeed **burst.**

אִיבָּעֵית אֵימָא [5](2) **If you wish,** you can **say** that produce in a sealed container does not swell in the rainy season like other produce, **because of the pressure** of the produce in the container. The fact that the produce is tightly packed prevents it from absorbing moisture and swelling.

MISHNAH יוֹצִיא לוֹ שְׁתוּת לַיַּיִן [6]If the deposit consists of wine or oil, and the bailee mixed it with his own wine or oil, then when he returns the deposit he may deduct a certain percentage to cover absorption by the walls of the barrel and sediment that settled at the bottom. In the case of **wine, he may deduct one-sixth. Rabbi Yehudah** disagrees and **says:** He may deduct **one-fifth.**

יוֹצִיא לוֹ שְׁלֹשָׁה לוּגִּין [7]In the case of **oil, he may deduct three *logs* per hundred —** [8]**one-and-a-half *logs* for sediment** that settled at the bottom of the barrel, [9]and **one-and-a-half *logs* for** oil **absorbed** by the walls of the barrel. [10]**If** the oil **was refined oil, he may not deduct** anything for **sediment,** because when oil reached the bailee the sediment had already been removed. Thus he may only deduct 1.5% to cover absorption. [11]Likewise, **if the containers were old** and could no longer absorb any oil, the bailee may **not deduct** anything for **absorption,** and may only deduct 1.5% to cover the loss due to sediment.

הַגּוֹרֶן. [1]אֲבָל מָדַד לוֹ בִּימוֹת הַגּוֹרֶן וְהֶחֱזִיר לוֹ בִּימוֹת הַגְּשָׁמִים, [2]אֵינוֹ יוֹצִיא לוֹ חִסָּרוֹן, מִפְּנֵי שֶׁמּוֹתִירוֹת".

[3]אֲמַר לֵיהּ רַב פַּפָּא לְאַבַּיֵי: אִם כֵּן, לִפְקַע כַּדָּא.

[4]הֲוָה עוּבְדָא, וּפְקַע כַּדָּא.

[5]אִיבָּעֵית אֵימָא: מִשּׁוּם אִיצְצָא.

מִשְׁנָה [6]יוֹצִיא לוֹ שְׁתוּת לַיַּיִן. רַבִּי יְהוּדָה אוֹמֵר: חוֹמֶשׁ. [7]יוֹצִיא לוֹ שְׁלֹשָׁה לוּגִּין שֶׁמֶן לְמֵאָה — [8]לוֹג וּמֶחֱצָה שְׁמָרִים, [9]לוֹג וּמֶחֱצָה בֶּלַע. [10]אִם הָיָה שֶׁמֶן מְזוּקָק, אֵינוֹ מוֹצִיא לוֹ שְׁמָרִים. [11]אִם הָיוּ קַנְקַנִּים יְשָׁנִים, אֵינוֹ מוֹצִיא לוֹ בֶּלַע.

LITERAL TRANSLATION

season. [1]But [if] he measured [it] for him during the granary season and returned [it] to him during the rainy season, [2]he does not deduct the loss, because it increases."

[3]Rav Pappa said to Abaye: If so, the container should burst.

[4]There was a case, and the container burst.

[5]If you wish, say: Because of pressure.

MISHNAH [6]He deducts one-sixth for wine. Rabbi Yehudah says: One-fifth.

[7]He deducts three *logs* of oil per hundred — [8]one-and-a-half *logs* [for] sediment, [9]one-and-a-half *logs* [for] absorption. [10]If it was refined oil, he does not deduct [for] sediment. [11]If the containers were old, he does not deduct [for] absorption.

RASHI

והחזיר לו בימות הגשמים — חזרו ונתפחו מלחלוחית הגשם והקור. **אם כן** — שדרכו לתפוח. **לפקע כדא** — כשממלאין כד חיטין או שעורין בימות הגורן, וגפין את הכד — יפקע בימות הגשמים מחמת תפיחת התבואה. **איצצא** — דוחק, מתוך שהם במקום צר נדחקו יחד ואין תפוחין.

משנה **ליין** — אם הפקיד אצלו יין ועירבו עם יינו, הקנקנים בולעין שתות.

HALAKHAH

received produce during the harvest season and returned it during the rainy season, he may not deduct for depreciation, since moisture will have caused the produce to swell, thereby compensating for any depreciation." (*Shulḥan Arukh, Ḥoshen Mishpat* 292:12.)

פִּקְדוֹנוֹת שֶׁל יַיִן וְשֶׁמֶן **Deposits of wine and oil.** "If the deposit consisted of wine or oil (and the bailee mixed the deposit with his own wine or oil and used it — *Sma*), the bailee may deduct one-sixth of the wine to cover absorption by the barrel and sediment, and three *logs* per hundred of the oil — one-and-a-half to cover absorption and one-and-a-half for sediment. If the oil was refined, he may not deduct for sediment, and if the containers were old and used, he may not deduct for absorption," following the Mishnah. (Ibid., 292:13.)

[1] רַבִּי יְהוּדָה אוֹמֵר: אַף הַמּוֹכֵר שֶׁמֶן מְזוּקָּק לַחֲבֵירוֹ כָּל יְמוֹת הַשָּׁנָה, [2] הֲרֵי זֶה מְקַבֵּל עָלָיו לוֹג וּמֶחֱצָה שְׁמָרִים לְמֵאָה.

גמרא [3] וְלָא פְּלִיגִי: מָר כִּי אַתְרֵיהּ, וּמָר כִּי אַתְרֵיהּ. [4] בְּאַתְרֵיהּ דְּמָר, חָפוּ בְּקִירָא, וְלָא מָיֵיץ טְפֵי; [5] בְּאַתְרֵיהּ דְּמָר, חָפוּ בְּכוּפְרָא, וּמָיֵיץ טְפֵי. [6] אִיבָּעֵית אֵימָא: מִשּׁוּם גַּרְגִּישְׁתָּא. [7] הָא מַיְיצָא טְפֵי, וְהָא לָא מַיְיצָא טְפֵי. [8] בְּאַתְרֵיהּ דְּרַב יְהוּדָה, רָמוּ אַרְבָּעִים וּתְמָנֵי כוּזֵי בְּדַנָּא. [9] אָזֵיל דַּנָּא בְּשִׁיתָּא זוּזֵי. [10] פָּרֵיס רַב יְהוּדָה שִׁיתָּא בְּזוּזָא.

LITERAL TRANSLATION

[1] Rabbi Yehudah says: Even someone who sells refined oil to his fellow all the days of the year, [2] this [buyer] accepts upon himself one-and-a-half *logs* of sediment per hundred.

GEMARA [3] And they do not disagree: [One] Sage [rules] in accordance with his place, and [the other] Sage in accordance with his place. [4] In the place of [the first] Sage, they line with wax, and it does not absorb much; [5] in the place of [the other] Sage, they line with pitch, and it absorbs more.

[6] If you wish, say: Because of the clay. [7] This [kind] absorbs a lot, and that [kind] does not absorb a lot.

[8] In Rav Yehudah's place, they put (lit., "cast") forty-eight jugfuls in a barrel. [9] A barrel went for six zuz. [10] Rav Yehudah sold (lit., "divided") six [jugfuls] for a zuz.

TRANSLATION AND COMMENTARY

רַבִּי יְהוּדָה אוֹמֵר [1] **Rabbi Yehudah** extends the principle that a bailee may deduct a certain percentage for sediment when he returns a deposit of oil placed in his care, and applies it to a case of buying and selling. He **says: Even someone who sells refined** oil in small quantities from his own barrels **to another person** on a regular basis **throughout the year** is entitled to deduct a percentage for sediment. [2] Thus, says Rabbi Yehudah, **the buyer** must **accept** a deduction of **one-and-a-half *logs* for sediment per hundred** *logs*, since this is the usual amount of sediment found in oil. Thus, if the seller deals in refined oil, he may insist that the buyer take only 98.5% of the quantity to which he would ordinarily be entitled.

GEMARA וְלָא פְּלִיגִי [3] The Gemara notes: The anonymous first Tanna in the Mishnah, who said that the bailee may deduct only one-sixth for wine, and Rabbi Yehudah, who said that he may deduct one-fifth, **do not disagree** about the Halakhah. Rather, each **Sage was ruling in accordance with** the practice in **his place.** [4] The Gemara goes on to explain: **In the place of the first Sage, they lined** the inside of barrels **with wax, and they did not absorb much** wine. Therefore the practice in that place was to allow a deduction of only one-sixth. [5] On the other hand, **in the place of the other Sage,** Rabbi Yehudah, **they** lined the inside of barrels **with pitch, and they absorbed more** than one-sixth of the wine. Therefore, the practice there was to allow a deduction of one-fifth.

אִיבָּעֵית אֵימָא [6] The Gemara now offers an alternative explanation: **If you wish,** you can **say** that the difference in the rates of absorption was due not to the substance with which the barrels were lined, but to the construction of the barrels themselves. The barrels absorbed at different rates **because of the** different types of **clay** used to make barrels in each place. [7] **One** kind of clay **absorbs a lot, and the other does not.**

בְּאַתְרֵיהּ דְּרַב יְהוּדָה [8] The Gemara now relates a story concerning the Babylonian Amora, Rav Yehudah, to illustrate problems of absorption and sediment: **In Rav Yehudah's place, they would fill a** standard **barrel with forty-eight jugfuls** of wine, [9] and in that town **a barrel** of wine could be purchased wholesale **for six zuz.** [10] **Rav Yehudah,** who was a retail merchant, purchased such a barrel for six zuz, sold it in units of **six jugfuls,** and charged **a zuz** for each unit.

RASHI

אף המוכר כו׳ — כשם שאמרו במפקיד כן אמרו במוכר, שהמוכר שמן לחבירו ונותן לו מתוך חביותיו כשהוא מספק תמיד והוא מזוקק — הרי הלוקח מקבל עליו לפחות לו לוג ומחצה מחמת שמרים. **למאה** — למאה לוג.

גמרא חפו בקירא — טחו החביות מבפנים בשעוה, כדרך שעושין אנו בזפת. **כופרא** — זפת. **גרגישתא** — קרקע שעושין ממנה החביות *ארזיל״א בלעז. **הא** — באתריה דר׳ יהודה מייץ טפי מההיא דאתריה דתנא קמא. **באתריה דרב יהודה** — מילתא באפי נפשיה היא, ולאו אמתניתין קאי. **רמו ארבעין ותמניא כוזי בדנא** — מדה קטנה היתה במקומו שארבעים ושמונה ממלאין את החבית. **אזיל דנא בשיתא** — בששה זוזים היתה נמכרת ביחד בימות הבציר. **פריס ליה רב יהודה שיתא בזוזא** — נעשה רב יהודה חנווני והיה מוכרן שש כוזי בזוז.

BACKGROUND

חָפוּ בְּכוּפְרָא They line with pitch. The pitch mentioned here was generally produced from a distillation of wood. It was quite soft and filled some of the pores in the clay. However, since the pitch itself seeped into the container, the seal was only partial. In contrast, coating the inside of a vessel with wax made it totally impervious to liquids, almost completely preventing loss due to evaporation or seepage.

LANGUAGE

קִירָא Wax. This word is derived from the Greek κηρός, *keros,* meaning "beeswax."

גַּרְגִּישְׁתָּא Clay. The source of this word is Semitic, meaning a kind of soft earth used to seal vessels and the like.

כּוּזֵי Jugfuls. This word is derived from the Persian *koz,* meaning a pitcher.

דַּנָּא Barrel. This word is derived from the Akkadian *dannu,* from which it was borrowed by Aramaic and other Semitic languages. It means a pitcher, especially an earthenware pitcher.

LANGUAGE (RASHI)

ארדלי״א* (ארזיל״א) From the Old French *arzile,* a kind of clay used as a sealant.

NOTES

אַף הַמּוֹכֵר שֶׁמֶן מְזוּקָּק Even someone who sells refined oil. *Ra'avad* explains that this applies only if the purchaser did not specify that he wanted refined oil. In such a case, if the merchant gave him refined oil, he is entitled to insist on including in the sale a percentage for sediment. But if the buyer stipulated that he was interested only in refined oil, even Rabbi Yehudah would agree that it is permitted to charge him the full price of refined oil.

TRANSLATION AND COMMENTARY

דַּל תְּלָתִין [40B] [1]The Gemara now determines how much profit Rav Yehudah made from his sale: From the forty-eight jugfuls of wine in the barrel, **subtract thirty-six** jugfuls **sold for** a total of **six zuz.** [2]Thus after selling thirty-six out of forty-eight jugfuls in the barrel, Rav Yehudah had recovered his expenses, **leaving twelve** jugfuls as profit. However, not all the remaining twelve jugfuls were usable. Some were no doubt absorbed by the barrel. [3]**Subtract eight** jugfuls from the twelve to allow for absorption, for we learned previously that **one-sixth** of the wine is absorbed by its container, and one-sixth of the original forty-eight jugfuls is eight. [4]Accordingly, **four** jugfuls **were left,** and Rav Yehudah made a profit of four out of forty-eight, or 8.3% on the transaction.

וְהָאָמַר שְׁמוּאֵל [5]The Gemara now objects: **But surely Shmuel said: Someone who profits** must **not profit more than one-sixth,** as that is a reasonable profit on food and other essential items. Why, then, did Rav Yehudah sell the wine so cheaply that his profit was well below the permitted sixth?

אִיכָּא [6]The Gemara answers: In calculating Rav Yehudah's profit, we must also take into consideration the value of **the container and the sediment,** which belonged to Rav Yehudah, since they were included in the original cost of the barrel. These, then, increased the profit made by Rav Yehudah.

אִי הָכִי [7]The Gemara objects: **If** we include the resale value of the barrel and the sediment in Rav Yehudah's profit, then **more than one-sixth is left.** How could Rav Yehudah have allowed himself *more* than the permitted profit?

אִיכָּא טַרְחֵיהּ [8]The Gemara replies: We must also take into consideration certain expenses Rav Yehudah incurred: Firstly, **his labor** costs in transporting, measuring and distributing the wine. Secondly, we must consider **the cost of drilling a hole** in the wine barrel. Because of the difficulty involved in drilling such a hole, Rav Yehuda had to hire a skilled worker to drill it. Rav Yehudah's remaining profit after deduction of these expenses was thus no more than one-sixth.

[40B] [1]דַּל תְּלָתִין וְשִׁיתָּא בְּשִׁיתָּא. [2]פָּשׁוּ לֵיהּ תְּרֵיסַר. [3]דַּל תְּמַנְיָא שְׁתוּתֵי. [4]פָּשׁוּ לְהוּ אַרְבָּעָה.

[5]וְהָאָמַר שְׁמוּאֵל: הַמִּשְׂתַּכֵּר אַל יִשְׂתַּכֵּר יוֹתֵר עַל שְׁתוּת.

[6]אִיכָּא גּוּלְפֵי וּשְׁמָרַיָּא.

[7]אִי הָכִי, נָפֵישׁ לֵיהּ טְפֵי מִשְּׁתוּת.

[8]אִיכָּא טַרְחֵיהּ, וּדְמֵי בַּרְזַנְיָיתָא.

LITERAL TRANSLATION

[40B] [1]Subtract thirty-six [jugfuls sold] for six [zuz]. [2]Twelve are left. [3]Subtract eight sixths. [4]Four are left. [5]But surely Shmuel said: Someone who profits must not profit more than one-sixth.

[6]There are the containers and the sediment.

[7]If so, more than one-sixth is left.

[8]There is his labor, and the cost of making the hole.

RASHI

דל תלתין ושיתא – כוזי, בשיתא זוזי שקנאה, פשו תריסר. **דל תמניא שתותי** – של ארבעים ושמונה, שדרך הוא לחסר בבליעת הקנקן כדתנן: "יוציא לו שתות ליין", פשו לו לשכרו ארבע. **והאמר שמואל המשתכר** – בדברים שיש בהם חיי נפש. **אל ישתכר יותר על השתות** – הא שתות – ישתכר, ולמה לא ישתכר רב יהודה עד שתות? **איכא גולפי ושמריא** – משתכר הוא הקנקן והשמרים, שלקח הכל בששה זוז. **דמי ברזנייתא** – שנותן דמים לחנווני למוכרן, ומוציאן ומכריז עליו בחוצות. ברזנייתא – לשון כרזא. לשון אחר, אומנות יש בנקיבת ברזא בחבית של חרס, וצריך ליתן שכר.

BACKGROUND

דְּמֵי בַּרְזַנְיָיתָא The cost of making the hole. In order to empty a barrel of all its contents at one time, its seal would be opened and the wine or oil poured out. If, however, one wanted to remove the contents gradually, a hole would be made in the side of the barrel, which would be opened periodically (or else a spout would be attached to it). Since during the Talmudic period barrels were made of earthenware, a specially skilled person was needed to drill such holes so as not to crack the barrel, and he was paid the "cost of drilling holes" mentioned in the Gemara.

NOTES

אַל יִשְׂתַּכֵּר יוֹתֵר עַל שְׁתוּת Must not profit more than one-sixth. Even though Shmuel only set an upper limit on permissible profit, the Gemara assumes that merchants try to make the maximum permissible profit (*Tosafot*). There are also versions of the Gemara in which Shmuel's statement reads "no more and no less" (*Rabbenu Ḥananel*). Thus, the Gemara's question is: Why did Rav Yehudah not seek to make a greater profit?

This question poses some difficulty for the Rishonim: Perhaps Rav Yehudah deliberately chose to sell his wares a little more cheaply than others. *Ritva* points out in reply that a Rabbinic scholar has a special obligation to take full advantage of an opportunity to earn an honest living through his labors, so that he will not need to resort to charity.

Rabbenu Ḥananel and *Ra'avad*, however, have a different interpretation of this passage. According to them, Rav Yehudah was not himself the storekeeper, but was issuing Rabbinic instructions to the local retailers to sell their wine for the prices specified here. According to this explanation, the Gemara's question was: Why did Rav Yehudah restrict their profits more than the Halakhah requires?

דְּמֵי בַּרְזַנְיָיתָא The cost of making the hole. Our translation follows the standard edition of the Talmud, and is in accordance with one of *Rashi*'s explanations. *Rashi* also

HALAKHAH

אַל יִשְׂתַּכֵּר יוֹתֵר עַל שְׁתוּת Must not profit more than one-sixth. "The courts are required to appoint supervisors to oversee prices, to make sure that merchants do not profit more than one-sixth on essential goods (e.g., produce, wine or oil). This rule applies only if the merchant sells his goods in bulk, without investing any special effort in their sale. However, if he sells his goods in small quantities over a period of time, he may include labor and other costs in his

TRANSLATION AND COMMENTARY

אִם הָיָה שֶׁמֶן מְזוּקָק [1]The Gemara now considers the next clause of the Mishnah: **"If the oil was refined, he may not deduct** anything for **sediment,** and if the containers were old, he may not deduct anything for absorption." [2]The Gemara objects to the Mishnah's ruling about old containers: **But surely it is impossible that the container did not absorb** *anything,* even if it was old.

אָמַר רַב נַחְמָן [3]Two answers were given to this objection: (1) **Rav Naḥman said:** The Mishnah **was teaching about** old **containers lined with pitch,** which do not absorb at all.

אַבַּיֵי אָמַר [4](2) **Abaye said: You may even say that** the Mishnah was referring to old containers that **were not lined with pitch,** and there is still no justification for making a deduction for absorption. [5]**Once** a barrel **has absorbed** its fill of oil, it cannot **absorb** any more.

רַבִּי יְהוּדָה אוֹמֵר [6]The Gemara now considers the next clause of the Mishnah: **"Rabbi Yehudah says: Even someone who sells refined oil to another person throughout the year** is entitled to deduct a percentage for sediment. [7]**The buyer** must **accept** a deduction of **one-and-a-half** ***logs*** **of sediment per hundred** *logs*." [8]Concerning this clause **Abaye said: When you probe the matter, you will find it necessary to say that** the basis of Rabbi Yehudah's ruling in our Mishnah is as follows: [9]**According to Rabbi Yehudah, it is permissible** for an oil merchant to stir refined oil so as **to mix the sediment** that collects at the bottom of the container **with the** refined **oil,** in order to increase the volume of saleable oil. [10]Conversely, **according to the Sages,** who disagree with Rabbi Yehudah in our Mishnah, **it is forbidden** for an oil merchant **to mix sediment with** refined **oil** in this way, because the buyer is under the impression that he is receiving refined oil.

[1]״אִם הָיָה שֶׁמֶן מְזוּקָק, אֵינוֹ מוֹצִיא לוֹ שְׁמָרִים וכו׳״. [2]וְהָא אִי אֶפְשָׁר דְּלָא בָּלַע.
[3]אָמַר רַב נַחְמָן: בִּמְזוּפָּפִין שָׁנוּ.
[4]אַבַּיֵי אָמַר: אֲפִילּוּ תֵּימָא שֶׁלֹּא בִּמְזוּפָּפִין. [5]כֵּיוָן דִּטְעוּן, טְעוּן.
[6]״רַבִּי יְהוּדָה אוֹמֵר: אַף הַמּוֹכֵר שֶׁמֶן מְזוּקָק לַחֲבֵירוֹ כָּל יְמוֹת הַשָּׁנָה, [7]הֲרֵי זֶה מְקַבֵּל עָלָיו לוֹג וּמֶחֱצָה שְׁמָרִים לְמֵאָה״. [8]אָמַר אַבַּיֵי: כְּשֶׁתִּמְצָא לוֹמַר [9]לְדִבְרֵי רַבִּי יְהוּדָה מוּתָּר לְעָרֵב שְׁמָרִים; [10]לְדִבְרֵי חֲכָמִים, אָסוּר לְעָרֵב שְׁמָרִים.

LITERAL TRANSLATION

[1]"If it was refined oil, he does not deduct [for] sediment, etc." [2]But surely it is impossible that it not absorb.

[3]Rav Naḥman said: They were teaching about [containers] lined with pitch.

[4]Abaye said: You may even say that they were not lined with pitch. [5]Once they absorbed, they absorbed.

[6]"Rabbi Yehudah says: Even someone who sells refined oil to his fellow all the days of the year, [7]this [buyer] accepts upon himself one-and-a-half *log*s of sediment per hundred." [8]Abaye said: When you probe [the matter, you will find it necessary] to say [that] [9]according to the words of Rabbi Yehudah, it is permissible to mix sediment [with the oil]; [10]according to the words of the Sages, it is forbidden to mix sediment [with the oil].

RASHI

במזופפין — דכיון דישנים הם ונתבלעו בלעותם, תו לא בלעי. **כיון דטעון טעון** — תו לא בלע. **כשתמצא לומר** — כשתדקדק ותדע מילוי הדברים. **מותר לערב שמרים** — המוכר שמן לחבירו סתם, בעת שהוא מזוקק, ששקעו ושקטו שמריו — מותר לו לערב ולבלבל שמרים המשוקעות שיחזרו ויתערבו, וילאו עם השמן בתוך המדה. **אסור לערב שמרים** — שבחזקת מזוקק לוקחו ממנו, וזה מקלקלו.

LANGUAGE

כְּשֶׁתִּמְצָא לוֹמַר **When you probe the matter.** Our translation and commentary follows *Rashi,* who understands the word תִּמְצָא to be derived from the root לְמַצּוֹת, meaning "to squeeze" or "to exhaust." Elsewhere, though, he interprets this expression as though the word תִּמְצָא was derived from the root לִמְצוֹא, meaning "to find."

NOTES

suggested another reading — כָּרוֹזְנִיָּיתָא — meaning "announcer." According to this reading, the extra expense is the cost of hiring someone to advertise that the merchant has wine to sell.

בִּמְזוּפָּפִין **Containers lined with pitch.** *Tosafot* asks: Earlier in the passage, the Gemara said that barrels lined with pitch tend to absorb relatively more than other barrels. How can Rav Naḥman claim that they do not absorb at all?

Tosafot answers that the Gemara was speaking about wine, but oil is not absorbed by barrels lined with pitch. Alternatively, new barrels lined with pitch absorb a lot, but old barrels lined with pitch do not absorb at all.

מוּתָּר לְעָרֵב שְׁמָרִים **It is permissible to mix sediment with the oil.** The Gemara is referring only to stirring a barrel so that sediment that has sunk to the bottom will be mixed up again. According to Abaye, Rabbi Yehudah permits such stirring and the Sages prohibit it. However, everyone agrees that it is forbidden to add sediment to a barrel of clear oil, as this tends to spoil the oil. (*Ritva.*)

מוּתָּר/אָסוּר לְעָרֵב שְׁמָרִים **It is permitted/forbidden to mix in sediment.** According to Abaye, Rabbi Yehudah maintains that it is permitted to mix in sediment and the Sages forbid it. According to Rav Pappa (below), the opposite is the case. The Rishonim ask: Since the dispute between Rabbi Yehudah

HALAKHAH

base price, and only then add one-sixth for profit. These laws apply only where the court oversees prices. But if the other merchants do not follow these rules, one is not required to sell for less than they do." (*Shulḥan Arukh, Ḥoshen Mishpat* 231:20.)

TRANSLATION AND COMMENTARY

לְדִבְרֵי רַבִּי יְהוּדָה [1]Abaye now explains his reasoning in detail: **According to Rabbi Yehudah, it is permissible to mix sediment** with the refined oil, [2]**and the reason** Rabbi Yehudah rules in our Mishnah that if the merchant did not mix in the sediment, and sold the buyer pure oil, the buyer must **accept** a reduction of 1.5 percent in the quantity of sediment-free oil he receives, [3]**is because** the seller **can say to him,** if he protests: **"If I** had **wanted to mix** sediment with the refined oil, **could I not have** done so? [4]**Now** that I have given you refined oil, you must **also accept** a reduction of 1.5 percent in the amount you receive, or take this percentage of sediment."

וְלֵימָא לֵיהּ [5]Before continuing with Abaye's explanation of the Sages' view, the Gemara objects to his explanation of the viewpoint of Rabbi Yehudah: **But let** the buyer **say to** the seller: "I would have accepted oil mixed with sediment, but I cannot accept unmixed sediment. For **if you had mixed** the sediment with the oil, **I could** myself **have sold** the sediment together with the oil. [6]**Now what can I do with** the sediment? **I cannot sell it by itself!** Hence, I cannot accept the sediment without suffering a loss."

בְּבַעַל הַבַּיִת עָסְקִינַן [7]The Gemara replies: **We are dealing** here **with a** case where the buyer was not a retail merchant but rather a **private person, who** needed the oil for his personal consumption. Such a buyer always **prefers clear oil,** even at a premium. Hence, it is worth his while to accept slightly less than the total quantity of oil in order not to have sediment mixed with it.

וְלֵימָא לֵיהּ [8]Again the Gemara objects: **But let** the buyer **say to** the seller: "It is true that you could have mixed the sediment with the oil, but **since you did not mix it in, you** effectively renounced **to me** your right to reduce the amount of oil by 1.5 percent."

רַבִּי יְהוּדָה לְטַעְמֵיהּ [9]The Gemara answers: When **Rabbi Yehudah** ruled that the buyer cannot claim that the seller renounced his right to deduct a certain percentage of oil in place of sediment, he was **following his own opinion**, which he expressed elsewhere. [10]**For** Rabbi Yehudah **does not accept** the concept of **renunciation** in a purchase or sale, unless the parties to the transaction make it clear that such is their intention. [11]**For we have learned** in the following Mishnah (*Bava Batra* 77b): "If someone wishes to purchase a yoke of

[1]לְדִבְרֵי רַבִּי יְהוּדָה, מוּתָּר לְעָרֵב שְׁמָרִים, [2]וְהַיְינוּ טַעְמָא דִּמְקַבֵּל, [3]דְּאָמַר לֵיהּ: ״אִי בְּעֵי לְעָרוּבֵי לָךְ, מִי לָא עָרְבִי לָךְ, [4]הָשְׁתָּא נַמִי, קַבֵּיל״.

[5]וְלֵימָא לֵיהּ: ״אִי עֵרַבְתְּ לֵיהּ, הֲוָה מִזְדַּבַּן לִי. [6]הָשְׁתָּא מַאי אַעֲבֵיד לֵיהּ? לְחוּדֵיהּ לָא מִזְדַּבַּן לִי״.

[7]בְּבַעַל הַבַּיִת עָסְקִינַן, דְּנִיחָא לֵיהּ בְּצִילָּא.

[8]וְלֵימָא לֵיהּ: ״מִדְּלָא עַרְבִית לִי, אַחוּלֵי אַחַלְתְּ לִי״.

[9]רַבִּי יְהוּדָה לְטַעְמֵיהּ. [10]דְּלֵית לֵיהּ מְחִילָה, [11]דִּתְנַן: ״מָכַר לוֹ

LITERAL TRANSLATION

[1]According to the words of Rabbi Yehudah, it is permissible to mix sediment, [2]and this is the reason that he accepts, [3]because he can say to him: "If I had wanted to mix [it in] for you, could I not have mixed [it in] for you? [4]Now too, accept."

[5]But let him say to him: "If you had mixed it in, I could have sold it. [6]Now what can I do with it? I cannot sell it by itself."

[7]We are dealing with a private person, who prefers clear [oil].

[8]But let him say to him: "Since you did not mix [it in] for me, you renounced [it] to me."

[9]Rabbi Yehudah [goes] according to his [own] opinion. [10]For he does not accept [the concept of] renunciation, [11]as we have learned: "[If] he sold

RASHI

והיינו טעמא דמקבל עליו – לוקח לוג ומחלה שמרים בשלא ערבו ונתנו לו מזוקק. **דאמר ליה** – מוכר ״אי בעי לערובי״ כו׳. **הוה מזדבן** – כשהייתי מוכרו בחנות היה נמכר שמרים עם השמן. **בבעל הבית עסקינן** – שהלוקח בעל הבית הוא, ולקחו למאכל ביתו. **צמד** – העול שהוא מוטל על שני השוורים ומלמידם.

BACKGROUND

מְחִילָה **Renunciation.** The renunciation about which Rabbi Yehudah and the Sages disagreed is not an explicit act in which a person states that he renounces a certain debt owing to him, for everyone is agreed that any mentally competent person may renounce a debt or give whatever he wishes to whomever he wishes. The disagreement concerns implicit renunciation of a debt. That is to say, can it be assumed that a person is willing to forgo something owed him, and to forbear from insisting on his rights? In Rabbi Yehudah's opinion, as long as the creditor has not explicitly stated that he has waived a debt, one must assume that he has not done so, and he retains the right to collect it in full. However, in the opinion of the Sages, it is common for people to waive debts to each other, and silent assent is as valid as explicit renunciation.

NOTES

and the Sages about the concept of renunciation is an essential element in the reasoning of both Abaye and Rav Pappa, why is it necessary for them to explain our Mishnah differently? Let them say that both Rabbi Yehudah and the Sages agree that it is permitted to mix in sediment, and let them explain Rabbi Yehudah's position as did Abaye, and the Sages' as did Rav Pappa. Thus, Rabbi Yehudah permits the seller to deduct 1.5% for sediment because he could have mixed it in anyway, whereas the Sages forbid him to do so because the seller waived his rights when he failed to mix the sediment in. Why does Abaye look for a different explanation of the Sages' view, and Rav Pappa for a different explanation of Rabbi Yehudah's?

Tosafot and others suggest that the Mishnah may be referring to a case where the buyer bought oil from the seller bit by bit over the course of a year. At the end of the year, when the seller reached the bottom of the barrel, he insisted that the buyer take the sediment. According to Abaye, even the Sages would agree that this is not a case of renunciation, since it is no longer possible to mix the sediment with the oil. But according to Rav Pappa, this too is a case of renunciation, since the seller chose to sell the oil unmixed every time he sold part of it. Moreover, Rav Pappa maintains that even Rabbi Yehudah may accept the idea of renunciation in this case, since he rejected this concept only because "the price makes the parties' intention known," and the difference in price between pure oil and mixed oil is not nearly as significant as that between a yoke and cattle.

LITERAL TRANSLATION

him the yoke, he did not sell him the cattle. [1] [If] he sold him the cattle, he did not sell him the yoke. [2] Rabbi Yehudah says: The price makes it known. [3] How so? [If] he said to him: 'Sell me your yoke for two hundred zuz,' [4] the matter is known that the yoke [does] not [cost] two hundred zuz. [5] But the Sages say: The price is no proof."

[6] According to the words of the Sages, it is forbidden to mix sediment [with the oil], [7] and this is the reason that he does not [need to] accept [sediment]. [8] For he can say to him: "If you had wished to mix in [the sediment], would it have been permitted to you? [9] Now, too, I do not accept [it]."

אֶת הַצֶּמֶד, לֹא מָכַר לוֹ אֶת הַבָּקָר. [1] מָכַר לוֹ אֶת הַבָּקָר, לֹא מָכַר לוֹ אֶת הַצֶּמֶד. [2] רַבִּי יְהוּדָה אוֹמֵר: הַדָּמִים מוֹדִיעִין. [3] כֵּיצַד? אָמַר לוֹ: 'מְכוֹר לִי צִמְדְּךָ בְּמָאתַיִם זוּז', [4] הַדָּבָר יָדוּעַ שֶׁאֵין הַצֶּמֶד בְּמָאתַיִם זוּז. [5] וַחֲכָמִים אוֹמְרִים: אֵין הַדָּמִים רְאָיָה".

[6] לְדִבְרֵי חֲכָמִים, אָסוּר לְעָרֵב שְׁמָרִים, [7] וְהַיְינוּ טַעְמָא דְּלָא מְקַבֵּל. [8] דְּאָמַר לֵיהּ: "אִי בָּעֵית לְעָרוּבֵי, מִי הֲוָה שָׁרֵי לָךְ? [9] הַשְׁתָּא נַמִי, לָא מְקַבֵּילְנָא".

RASHI

הדבר ידוע — שאין צמד נמכר במאתים זוז, אלא כמות שהוא עם הבקר מכרו לו. **וחכמים אומרים אין הדמים ראיה** — אף על גב דלא שוה כולי האי — אחולי אחליה לוקח זה יתר הדמים, ורבי יהודה לית ליה שיהא מוחל מן הסתם, אלא אם כן פירש.

LANGUAGE

צֶמֶד Yoke. In Biblical Hebrew the word צֶמֶד — yoke — refers to a pair of animals (such as cows or donkeys), whereas in Rabbinic Hebrew the term צֶמֶד refers to the physical yoke that attaches the two animals together. A similar semantic development has taken place in other languages, though often in the opposite direction, cf. the Greek ζυγόν, *zugon*, meaning a yoke or a pair.

TRANSLATION AND COMMENTARY

cattle from someone else, he must specify that he wishes to buy both the yoke and the cattle. **If** the seller says only that **he is selling the yoke,** the buyer **cannot** claim that **he** also **sold him the cattle."** The term "yoke" (צֶמֶד) literally means the implement used to link a pair of animals together for plowing, but it can sometimes refer to the pair of animals together with the yoke they are wearing. Now, the general rule is that whenever doubt arises about the meaning of a term used during the course of a sale, we always assume that the seller intended the more restrictive meaning to apply. Accordingly, the Sages ruled that if a seller stated that he was selling a "yoke," only the yoke itself was intended, not the pair of animals. [1] The Mishnah continues: "Conversely, **if** the seller says only that **he is selling the cattle,** the buyer **cannot** claim that **he** also **sold him the yoke."** Here too, the seller's specifications are interpreted restrictively. Thus far, the Mishnah represents the viewpoint of the Sages. [2] It continues: "But **Rabbi Yehudah says:** We do not need to apply the regular rule here, for **the price** agreed upon **makes the parties' intention known,** and we can determine what was included in the sale by an examination of the price. [3] **How so? If,** for example, the buyer **said to** the seller, **'Sell me your yoke for two-hundred zuz,'** and the seller agreed to the terms, [4] **it is known that a yoke** does **not cost two-hundred zuz,** and thus the seller must have agreed to include the cattle in the sale." According to Rabbi Yehudah, if a buyer agrees to pay a sum that is obviously far too high, or a seller agrees to accept a sum that is obviously far too low, we may not simply assume that the buyer or the seller is renouncing the difference (unless, of course, they so stipulated expressly). Thus we see that Rabbi Yehudah does not accept the concept of implied renunciation. [5] The Mishnah continues: **"But the Sages say: The price** agreed upon **is no proof."** It is possible that the buyer simply renounced the additional money to the seller, and bought a cheap item for a high price. Thus, since Rabbi Yehudah does not accept the concept of implied renunciation, the Gemara's objection to Abaye's explanation is removed.

לְדִבְרֵי חֲכָמִים [6] Abaye now resumes his explanation of our Mishnah. Having established that the reason Rabbi Yehudah allows merchants to charge customers for sediment is because he permits them to mix their oil, Abaye now turns to the argument of the Sages who disagree with Rabbi Yehudah: **According to the Sages, it is forbidden to mix sediment with the oil,** [7] **and the reason** why, where the merchant sold the buyer pure oil, **the buyer** can demand all the sediment-free oil he paid for, and **need not accept** a deduction of 1.5 percent for **sediment, is** [8] **because** the buyer **can say to** the seller: **"If you had wished to mix in the sediment, would you have been permitted to** do so? You would not have been permitted. [9] **Now, too, I do not accept it."**

HALAKHAH

מְכִירַת צֶמֶד בָּקָר **Selling yokes and cattle.** "If someone stipulates that he is selling a yoke, cattle are not included in the sale. Likewise, if he states that he is selling cattle, the yoke is not included in the sale, even if some people call a yoke of cattle "cattle." The above rule applies even if the price paid would seem to indicate that the parties intended to include the cattle with the yoke or vice versa, for we do not ordinarily base our determination of what is included in a sale on the price," following the view of the Sages. *Rema* adds in the name of *Tur* that if the yoke and animals were tied together, we do consider the price to be an indication, and both the yoke and the animals are included in the sale. (*Shulhan Arukh, Hoshen Mishpat* 220:4,8.)

מְחִילָה **Renunciation.** "If someone buys a yoke, and claims

TRANSLATION AND COMMENTARY

אֲמַר לֵיהּ רַב פַּפָּא לְאַבַּיֵי [1]**Rav Pappa said to Abaye:** Your explanation of the difference of opinion between the Sages and Rabbi Yehudah in our Mishnah is flawed. **On the contrary, the opposite stands to reason!** [2]For we can argue that, **according to the Sages, it is permitted to mix sediment with the oil,** [3]**and the reason why** they maintain that if the seller did not mix in the sediment and sold the buyer pure oil **the buyer need not accept** any deduction for **sediment is** [4]**because** the buyer **can say to** the seller: "It is true that you could have mixed the sediment with the oil, and I would have had to accept it. But **since you did not mix it in you** renounced **to me** your right to reduce the amount of oil by 1.5%." It is clear, says Rav Pappa, that the Sages accept the concept of renunciation, as we have seen from their opinion concerning the yoke in tractate *Bava Batra*.

[1]אֲמַר לֵיהּ רַב פַּפָּא לְאַבַּיֵי: אַדְּרַבָּה, אִיפְּכָא מִסְתַּבְּרָא. [2]לְדִבְרֵי חֲכָמִים, מוּתָּר לְעָרֵב שְׁמָרִים, [3]וְהַיְינוּ טַעְמָא דְּלָא מְקַבֵּל, [4]דְּאָמַר לֵיהּ: "מִדְּלָא עֵרַבְתְּ לִי, אַחוּלֵי אַחֲלִית לִי". [5]לְדִבְרֵי רַבִּי יְהוּדָה, אָסוּר לְעָרֵב שְׁמָרִים, [6]וְהַיְינוּ טַעְמָא דִּמְקַבֵּל, [7]דְּאָמַר לֵיהּ: "אִי בְּעִי לְעָרוּבֵי, לָא שָׁרֵי לִי לְעָרוּבֵי לָךְ. [8]קַבּוּלֵי לָא מְקַבְּלַתְּ. [9]זְבוּן וְזַבֵּין תַּגָּרָא אִיקְּרֵי"?

LITERAL TRANSLATION

[1]Rav Pappa said to Abaye: On the contrary, the opposite is more reasonable. [2]According to the words of the Sages, it is permissible to mix sediment [with the oil], [3]and this is the reason that he does not [need to] accept [it], [4]because he can say to him: "Since you did not mix [it in] for me, you renounced [it] to me." [5]According to the words of Rabbi Yehudah, it is forbidden to mix in sediment, [6]and this is the reason that he accepts [it], [7]because he can say to him: "If I had wanted to mix [it in], it would not have been permitted to me to mix [it in] for you. [8]You do not accept [it]. [9]Is buying and selling called [being] a merchant?"

RASHI

קבולי נמי לא מקבלת – עלך חסרון השמרים, אם כן מה משתכר הרי השכר כולו בשמרים. **זבון וזבין תגרא איקרי** – בתמיה, משל הוא לאמר לשוטה: לקח בדמים וחזור ומכור בלא שכר, ותיקרי תגר.

לְדִבְרֵי רַבִּי יְהוּדָה [5]Having explained the Sages' view from this new perspective, Rav Pappa continues with his explanation of Rabbi Yehudah: **According to Rabbi Yehudah, it is forbidden to mix in sediment,** [6]**and the reason why the buyer must accept** a deduction of 1.5% for **sediment** [7]**is because** the seller **can say to him: "If I** had **wanted to mix** the sediment **in, I would not have been permitted to** do so. [8]Now, if **you do not accept** the deduction of 1.5% for sediment, I will not earn anything from the sale, [9]and I am not such a proverbial fool as to **'buy and sell** at the same price, just for the privilege of being **called a merchant.'** I am certainly entitled to some profit, and if I must take a 1.5% loss for the sediment, that will remove my profit entirely." Thus, says Rav Pappa, we see that it is possible to explain our Mishnah in precisely the opposite way from that used by Abaye.

NOTES

אִי בְּעִי לְעָרוּבֵי, לָא שָׁרֵי לִי If I had wanted to mix it in, it would not have been permitted to me. *Ritva* objects: It is true that the seller could not have mixed this oil up, but he could have sold him other, less pure oil. *Ritva* answers: The buyer pointed to the oil he wanted to buy. Alternatively, the seller had no mixed oil available, and is not permitted to buy mixed oil in order to substitute it for his own.

HALAKHAH

that he thought he was buying the animals as well, and the sum of money he paid was too much for a yoke alone, we reject his claim to the animals and treat his case as though it were a claim of fraud. Thus, if the difference in price was moderate — within the range that it is possible for a buyer to have overpaid by mistake — we consider this a case of fraud, and the seller must return the difference (if the difference was 20%), or cancel the sale (if the difference was more than 20%). However, if the difference was so great that it is impossible for the buyer to have overpaid by mistake, we do not even accept a claim of fraud. Rather, we assume that the extra money was a gift to the seller," following the Sages. (*Shulḥan Arukh, Ḥoshen Mishpat* 220:8.)

תַּעֲרוֹבֶת שְׁמָרִים Mixing in sediment. "It is forbidden for a merchant to mix any sediment in with his wine or oil. Someone who stipulates that he is buying pure oil does not need to accept any sediment at all, but if he simply agrees to buy oil, without stipulating that it must be pure, he must accept a deduction of 1.5% for sediment," following *Rambam* who apparently rules in favor of Rabbi Yehudah as explained by Rav Pappa because Rav Pappa is a later authority than Abaye (but see *Sma*). *Rema*, however, rules that the merchant is permitted to stir his wine or oil and mix in the sediment. However, if he did not do so, he cannot demand that the buyer accept a deduction of 1.5% for sediment, as he is considered to have renounced his right to mix in the sediment, following *Rosh* who rules in favor of the Sages as explained by Rav Pappa. (Ibid., 228:19,20.)

TRANSLATION AND COMMENTARY

תָּנָא [1]A new subject is now introduced: **A Tanna taught** the following Baraita: **"The law with regard to scum** — the remains of seeds floating on top of oil — **is** the same **both for a buyer and for a depositor."**

מַאי לְפִקְטִים [2]The meaning of this short Baraita is unclear. The Gemara proceeds to analyze it and asks: **What does** the expression "the law is the same **with regard to scum" mean?** Do both the buyer and the depositor accept it, or do they both reject it? [3]**If you say: Just as a buyer does not** need to **accept scum,** [4]**so too a depositor does not** need to **accept scum,** and the bailee must return clear oil, this argument would lead to an absurd conclusion. [5]For the bailee can **say to** the depositor: **"What shall I do with your scum?** After all, the scum is part of the oil you deposited with me. I did not put it there!"

אֶלָּא [6]**Rather,** suggests the Gemara, the Baraita should be understood as follows: **Just as a depositor** must **accept** a certain accumulation of **scum** when he receives his oil back from the bailee with whom he has left it, [7]**so too** must **a buyer accept** a certain percentage of **scum** in oil he buys.

וּמִי מְקַבֵּל לוֹקֵחַ פִּקְטִים [8]The Gemara objects: **But does a buyer** have to **accept scum?** [9]**Surely it has been taught in** another **Baraita: "Rabbi Yehudah says:** When the Sages discussed **turbid oil,** they decided that **any loss** caused by it **should fall on the seller alone,** [10]**since** a **buyer accepts** a deduction of **a *log* and a half of sediment** for every hundred *logs* of oil he receives, and is entitled to receive the remaining ninety-eight-and-a-half *logs* as pure oil **without scum."** From this second Baraita it seems clear that a buyer and a depositor are not treated in the same way with regard to scum floating on top of oil. A depositor has to accept the scum when the oil is returned to him by a bailee, whereas a buyer is under no such obligation.

[1]תָּנָא: ״אֶחָד הַלּוֹקֵחַ וְאֶחָד הַמַּפְקִיד לְפִקְטִים״.
[2]מַאי לְפִקְטִים? [3]אִילֵימָא: כִּי הֵיכִי דְּלוֹקֵחַ לָא מְקַבֵּל פִּקְטִים, [4]מַפְקִיד נַמִי לָא מְקַבֵּל פִּקְטִים, [5]וְלֵימָא לֵיהּ: ״פִּקְטָךְ מַאי אִיעֲבִיד לְהוּ״?
[6]אֶלָּא, כִּי הֵיכִי דְּמַפְקִיד מְקַבֵּל פִּקְטִים, [7]לוֹקֵחַ נַמִי מְקַבֵּל פִּקְטִים.
[8]וּמִי מְקַבֵּל לוֹקֵחַ פִּקְטִים? [9]וְהָתַנְיָא: ״רַבִּי יְהוּדָה אוֹמֵר: לֹא אָמְרוּ שֶׁמֶן עָכוּר אֶלָּא לַמּוֹכֵר בִּלְבַד, [10]שֶׁהֲרֵי לוֹקֵחַ מְקַבֵּל עָלָיו לוֹג וּמֶחֱצָה שְׁמָרִים בְּלֹא פִּקְטִים״.

LITERAL TRANSLATION

[1][A Tanna] taught: "Both the buyer and the depositor [are alike] with regard to scum."

[2]What does "with regard to scum" [mean]? [3]If you say: Just as a buyer does not accept scum, [4]so too a depositor does not accept scum, [5]then let him say to him: "What shall I do with your scum?"

[6]Rather, just as a depositor accepts scum, [7]so too a buyer accepts scum.

[8]But does a buyer accept scum? [9]But surely it has been taught: "Rabbi Yehudah says: They only said turbid oil for the seller alone, [10]since a buyer accepts upon himself one-and-a-half *logs* of sediment without scum."

RASHI

אחד הלוקח ואחד המפקיד לפקטים – לוקח ומפקיד אחד הן לענין פקטים, תורה אחת לשניהם. **פקטים** – פסולת הגרעינים הצפין על פני השמן. **לוקח מקבל פקטים** – אם מכר לו שמן סתם – יקבל ממנו שמן עם פקטים. **לא אמרו שמן עכור אלא למוכר** – לא אמרו הפסד עכירת השמן אלא למוכר. **שהרי הלוקח מקבל עליו** – לפחות ממאה לוגין לוג ומחצה מחמת שמרים, לפיכך צריך ליתן לו שמן מזוקק בלא פקטים.

LANGUAGE

פִּקְטִים Scum. This word is derived from the Greek πηκτός, *piktos*, which in one of its senses means "congealed matter," or "sediment."

BACKGROUND

פִּקְטִים Scum. In the normal commercial process, oil was obtained by having olives pressed and milled. In this process, fibers from the fruit and particles from the crushed seeds are also removed. Some of these particles remain suspended in the oil, making it cloudy, and others, the "scum," float on top. For certain purposes, such as use in the Temple, a special grade of lightly pressed oil was used (שֶׁמֶן כָּתִית). Today, too, edible olive oil is a mixture of the pure oil from the first, light pressing of the olives, and oil removed by heavy pressing which is then purified by a special process.

NOTES

פִּקְטִים Scum. Our translation follows *Rashi*. *Rambam* explains this word as turbid oil that floats to the surface. *Ra'avad* explains it as turbid oil near the sediment.

לֹא אָמְרוּ שֶׁמֶן עָכוּר אֶלָּא לַמּוֹכֵר בִּלְבַד They only said turbid oil for the seller alone. Our commentary follows *Rashi*, who explains that when the Baraita used this expression, it meant: "When the Sages discussed turbid oil, they decided that the seller alone must accept the loss, and not the buyer." This is a most unusual use of this wording.

Ra'avad suggests that the comparison being drawn may be between a seller and a depositor rather than between a seller and a buyer. Thus, the Baraita should read as follows: "When the Sages decided that the recipient of oil could refuse to accept turbid oil, they were referring only to the case of a seller and a buyer, but not to the case of a depositor and a bailee." *Ra'avad* also reports a tradition that the Baraita should be read as follows: "When the Sages decided that turbid oil does not come under the category of oil, they were referring only to a case of buying and selling; but for the purpose of tithing, for example, turbid oil does come under the category of oil."

HALAKHAH

שֶׁמֶן עָכוּר Turbid oil. "The buyer must accept the amount of turbid oil that is normal in that type of oil, if he purchased oil using the slightly larger "Tishri measure." But if he purchased oil using the smaller "Nisan measure," he need not accept any turbid oil." (Ibid., 228:20.)

LITERAL TRANSLATION

[1] There is no difficulty. [2] This [applies] where he gave him money in Tishri, [3] and received [his oil] from him in Nisan according to the price (lit., "measure") of Tishri. [4] That [applies] where he gave him money in Nisan, [5] and received [his oil] from him in Nisan according to the price of Nisan.

MISHNAH [6] Someone who deposits a barrel with his fellow, and the owner did not designate a place for it, and he [the bailee] moved it and it broke; [7] if it broke while in his hand, [8] for his [own] need — he is liable, [9] for its need he is exempt.

[1] לָא קַשְׁיָא. [2] הָא דְּיָהֵיב לֵיהּ זוּזֵי בְּתִשְׁרֵי, [3] וְקָא שָׁקֵיל מִינֵּיהּ בְּנִיסָן כִּי מִדָּה דְּתִשְׁרֵי. [4] הָא דְּיָהֵיב לֵיהּ זוּזֵי בְּנִיסָן, [5] וְקָא שָׁקֵיל מִינֵּיהּ בְּנִיסָן כִּי מִדָּה דְּנִיסָן.

משנה [6] הַמַּפְקִיד חָבִית אֵצֶל חֲבֵירוֹ, וְלֹא יִחֲדוּ לָהּ בְּעָלִים מָקוֹם, וְטִלְטְלָהּ וְנִשְׁתַּבְּרָה; [7] אִם מִתּוֹךְ יָדוֹ נִשְׁבְּרָה, [8] לְצוֹרְכּוֹ, חַיָּיב, [9] לְצוֹרְכָּהּ, פָּטוּר.

RASHI

כי מדה דתשרי — כשער הדמים של תשרי שהוא בזול, ושמן שמנים עכורים, וקיבל עליו פקטים. **הא דשקל מיניה בניסן כשער של ניסן** — ביוקר, דדרך כל השמנים להיות מזוקקין בניסן, והלוקח סתם והמוכר סתם אין מוכר אלא מזוקק.

משנה לא יחדו לו הבעלים מקום — בבית שומר, לאמר לו "זוית זו השאילני". **לצורכו** — להשתמש בה. **לצורכה** — שהיתה במקום התורפה וקרובה להשתבר.

TRANSLATION AND COMMENTARY

לָא קַשְׁיָא [1] The Gemara answers: The meaning of the first Baraita is as we have explained, and the second Baraita poses **no difficulty.** [2] The first Baraita, which rules that a buyer must accept scum, **applies** specifically **where** the buyer **gave** the seller **money in Tishri,** when olives are picked, [3] **and received his oil from** the seller six months later **in Nisan, according to the price in Tishri.** In Tishri, oil is cloudy and turbid and the price is low. Hence, since the buyer paid a Tishri price, he must accept a Tishri oil, including the scum. [4] The second Baraita, which entitles the buyer to refuse scum, **applies** specifically **where** the buyer **gave** the seller **money in Nisan,** [5] **and received his oil from** the seller **in Nisan according to the price in Nisan.** In Nisan, when oil has been standing for six months, the sediment and scum have become separated from it, and the oil is pure. Thus the price of oil rises in Nisan, and since the buyer pays this slightly higher price he may insist upon pure oil.

MISHNAH הַמַּפְקִיד חָבִית אֵצֶל חֲבֵירוֹ [6] The remaining Mishnayot in this chapter deal with another aspect of the laws of bailees and deposits. If a bailee accepts a deposit, he must look after it properly. The degree of responsibility varies among the different kinds of bailees, but even an unpaid bailee who is looking after a deposit purely as a favor may not act negligently towards the deposit (פְּשִׁיעָה), nor may he misappropriate it for his own use (שְׁלִיחוּת יָד). If he does either of these things, he must pay for the deposit if it is damaged (see Exodus 22:7-8).

There is, however, an important distinction between an obligation arising from negligence and one arising from misappropriation. If the bailee was negligent, and as a result the object was damaged, even if the damage itself was accidental, the bailee is liable if the damage can be attributed in some way to his negligence. On the other hand, if the bailee misappropriated the deposit for his own use, the law is much stricter, as the Torah treats such a bailee as a robber (see below, 43a). Now, the law is that a robber is considered to have "acquired" the object he stole, until he returns it to its owner. In practice this means that if, for any reason whatsoever, the robber cannot return the object, he must pay for it. Thus, if a bailee misappropriates a deposit for his own use, and it is damaged before he returns it, even if the damage is in no way connected with the misappropriation, the bailee is liable.

The Mishnah rules: If **someone deposits a barrel** of wine or oil **with another person, and the owner has not designated a particular place** in the bailee's house **for it** to be kept, then if the bailee **moves** the barrel **and it breaks,** we must distinguish between four possible situations: [7] (1) **If it breaks while in the bailee's hand,** [8] and the reason he moved it was to make use of it **for his own sake,** he **is liable,** and must reimburse the owner for the damage, even if the damage was completely accidental, because his action in moving it was a form of misappropriation. [9] But (2) **if he moves it for its sake** — for example, because he wants to remove it from an unsafe place — then even if it breaks while in his hand **he is exempt,** provided he has taken proper

NOTES

מִדַּת תִּשְׁרֵי וּמִדַּת נִיסָן **The Tishri price and the Nisan price.** Our commentary follows *Rashi,* who explains that the measures in Tishri and Nisan were the same size, but the price of a measure of oil in Tishri was slightly less than in Nisan. *Rambam,* however, explains that the measures in Tishri were a little larger than those in Nisan, to allow for the turbid oil.

לְצוֹרְכּוֹ/לְצוֹרְכָּהּ **For his sake, for its sake.** There is one other situation to consider: If the bailee moved the barrel because he wanted to use the place where the barrel was

TRANSLATION AND COMMENTARY

care and did not cause the damage through any negligence. On the other hand, [1](3) **if** a deposit **breaks after** the bailee **has put it down** undamaged and returned it to its proper place, [2]then even if **he** initially **moved it for his own sake** and was guilty of misappropriation, he is exempt, because he has fulfilled his duty to return the "stolen" object to its owner. Likewise, (4) if a deposit breaks after the bailee has put it down and the bailee was not guilty of misappropriation, but rather had initially moved the deposit **for its own sake,** [3]**he is exempt.**

יִחֲדוּ לָהּ הַבְּעָלִים מָקוֹם [4]The Mishnah now considers another case: **If the owner has designated a place for** the deposit to be kept, **and the bailee moves it** from that place **and it breaks,** [5]then it makes no difference **whether** it broke **while in his hand or after he put it down** — in either case, [6]**if he** initially **moved it for his own sake** (examples 1 and 3 above), **he is liable,** since he is guilty of misappropriation, and putting the object down is not a fulfillment of his duty to return the object to its owner. [7]On the other hand, **if he** initially **moved** the deposit **for its sake** (examples 2 and 4), **he is exempt** — provided of course that the object was not damaged because of negligence on his part.

[1]אִם מִשֶּׁהֱנִיחָהּ נִשְׁבְּרָה, [2]בֵּין לְצוֹרְכּוֹ בֵּין לְצוֹרְכָּהּ, [3]פָּטוּר. [4]יִחֲדוּ לָהּ הַבְּעָלִים מָקוֹם, וְטִלְטְלָהּ וְנִשְׁבְּרָה, [5]בֵּין מִתּוֹךְ יָדוֹ וּבֵין מִשֶּׁהֱנִיחָהּ, [6]לְצוֹרְכּוֹ, חַיָּיב, [7]לְצוֹרְכָּהּ, פָּטוּר.

גמרא [8]הָא מַנִּי? [9]רַבִּי יִשְׁמָעֵאל הִיא, דְּאָמַר: לָא בָּעֵינַן דַּעַת בְּעָלִים, [10]דְּתַנְיָא: ״הַגּוֹנֵב טָלֶה מִן הָעֵדֶר וְסֶלַע מִן הַכִּיס,

LITERAL TRANSLATION

[1]If it broke after he put it down, [2]whether for his need or for its need, [3]he is exempt.

[4]If the owner designated a place for it, and he [the bailee] moved it and it broke, [5]whether in his hand or after he put it down, [6]for his need — he is liable, [7]for its need — he is exempt.

GEMARA [8]Whose is this? [9]It is Rabbi Yishmael, who said: We do not need the owner's knowledge, [10]as it has been taught: "Someone who steals a lamb from a flock or a sela from a moneybag

RASHI

אם משהניחה — שכלה תשמישו, הושיבה במקום משתמר, בין שטלטלה מתחלה לצורכה, בין שטלטלה לצורכו — פטור. ובגמרא פריך: מאי שנא לא יחדו מיחדו.

גמרא מני — הא דקתני רישא דאם משהניחה נשברה, אף על פי שלצורכו נטלה מתחלה פטור, דאמר משהחזירה הרי היא ברשות הבעלים כבתחלה ואינו עליה אלא כשומר חנם, ופטור על אונסיה, ואף על פי שלא הודיע לבעלים לומר ״נטלתיה והחזרתיה״ — הויא השבה, רבי ישמעאל היא כו׳.

GEMARA הָא מַנִּי [8]The Gemara now compares the two halves of this Mishnah. The only difference between them concerns the third of the four situations: If the bailee initially moved the deposit for his own sake and thus misappropriated it, and then returned it to its place, the first half of the Mishnah — which deals with a case where the owner did not designate any particular place for the deposit to be kept — rules that the bailee is exempt, whereas the second half — which deals with a case where the owner *did* designate a particular place for the deposit to be kept — rules that the bailee is liable. The Gemara assumes that in both halves of the Mishnah, when the bailee put the deposit back, he put it back in its original place. Nevertheless, the first half of the Mishnah rules that putting the deposit back is a fulfillment of the bailee's duty to return the misappropriated deposit, whereas the second half rules that it is not. Hence, the Gemara asks: **Who is the** author of the first half of **this Mishnah?** [9]The Gemara answers: **It is Rabbi Yishmael, who said:** When someone returns something he stole to its owner, he **does not need the owner's knowledge** to fulfill his obligation. In other words, a robber need not inform his victim that he has returned the stolen object, provided he puts it back in the place where it is supposed to be. So, too, in the first half of our Mishnah, when the bailee fulfills his obligation by returning the misappropriated deposit to it place, he reverts to being an unpaid bailee and is no longer liable for any accident that may befall the deposit. [10]The Gemara now quotes the source for Rabbi Yishmael's view: **It has been taught** in the following Baraita: **"Someone who steals a lamb from a flock**

NOTES

resting. *Yad Ramah* rules that such movement is considered negligence, not misappropriation. Thus, if the barrel was damaged as a result of the movement, the bailee is liable; but if it was damaged by an unconnected accident, he is exempt (see *Tur, Ḥoshen Mishpat* 292).

הַגּוֹנֵב טָלֶה Someone who steals a lamb. This Baraita is discussed in detail in tractate *Bava Kamma* (118b). The Mishnah there (118a) rules that a thief who returns a stolen object without informing the owner remains liable for any accidents that may befall it. However, the Mishnah also rules that as soon as the owner counts his flock and notices that the stolen animal is present, the thief is absolved from any further liability. There is a dispute among the Amoraim as to whether "counting" absolves the thief of liability in all cases, or whether a distinction is to be made between a case where the owner knew that the lamb had been stolen, and a case where he did not know. The Halakhah follows Rav Ḥisda, who rules that counting the flock is sufficient only

TERMINOLOGY

הָא מַנִּי Whose is this? I.e., in accordance with whose viewpoint is this Mishnah or Baraita? This question is often asked in order to clarify the approach taken by the Mishnah, for by identifying the Tanna whose opinion is presented, one can understand the ruling more clearly. Occasionally this inquiry also has Halakhic significance, for a Mishnah which is an individual opinion with which many Sages disagree is rejected by the Halakhah. In the present case this question is actually a preliminary step in examining the Mishnah as a whole, for by means of it our Mishnah is seen to contain an internal Halakhic contradiction.

SAGES

רַבִּי יִשְׁמָעֵאל Rabbi Yishmael. One of the leading Tannaim of the fourth generation, Rabbi Yishmael (ben Elisha) was taken in captivity to Rome as a child, and was rescued by Rabbi Yehoshua. The latter was convinced of the child's intellectual potential and became Rabbi Yishmael's first teacher. Other Sages under whom Rabbi Yishmael studied were Rabbi Eliezer and Rabbi Neḥunya ben HaKanah.

Rabbi Yishmael's main colleague and friend was Rabbi Akiva, and the Tannaitic literature contains many examples of their differences of opinion. Rabbi Yishmael developed a comprehensive system of Biblical interpretation based on commonsense understanding of the text and established hermeneutical principles. Of the Halakhic Midrashim, the Mekhilta, the Sifrei on Numbers and part of the Sifrei on Deuteronomy represent his school of thought, and he is frequently quoted in them.

Rabbi Yishmael's home town was Kfar Aziz in southern Judea. Little is known of his personal life, other than that his two sons died during his lifetime. According to Aggadic Midrashim, Rabbi Yishmael, like Rabbi Akiva, died as a martyr at the hands of the Romans.

SAGES

רַבִּי עֲקִיבָא **Rabbi Akiva.** The greatest of the Tannaim, Rabbi Akiva (ben Yosef) belonged to the fourth generation. He began his Torah education when already an adult, and studied under Rabbi Eliezer and Rabbi Yehoshua for many years. Many stories are told in Rabbinic literature of his devotion to Torah study, of the loyalty of his wife and of the financial difficulties they had to overcome.

Rabbi Akiva was responsible for the first systematic arrangement and division of the Oral Law. This work was carried on by his disciple Rabbi Meir, and formed the basis of the Mishnah as finally edited by Rabbi Yehudah HaNasi. Rabbi Akiva was also the founder of a new school of Biblical interpretation, according to which almost all the regulations of the Oral Law are found to have their basis in the text of the Bible. Rabbi Akiva was active in the period between the destruction of the Second Temple and the Bar Kokhba revolt, in the preparations for which he took an active part. He met his death as a martyr at the hands of the Romans.

TERMINOLOGY

לָא מִיבָּעֲיָא קָאָמַר, לָא מִיבָּעֲיָא...אֶלָּא אֲפִילּוּ **It is speaking [in the style of] "there is no need." There is no need [to state A,] but even [B].** An expression used to explain the inclusion of a seemingly superfluous case in the Mishnah (or the Baraita) on stylistic grounds: First the Tanna began with an obvious case (a case there is "no need to state"), and from there proceeded to a more unexpected case.

TRANSLATION AND COMMENTARY

entrusted to his care **or a sela from a moneybag** entrusted to his care **must return it to the place from where he stole it,** and need not inform the owner. [1]**This is the opinion of Rabbi Yishmael."** The Baraita continues with an opposing view: [2]**"Rabbi Akiva says:** [41A] [3]For a bailee to fulfill his obligation to return an object he has stolen, **the owner's knowledge is necessary."** Hence, the bailee is liable for any accident affecting the lamb or sela he has stolen, until he informs the owner that he has taken and returned it. So, too, in the case described in the first half of our Mishnah, Rabbi Akiva would disagree and insist that the bailee cannot absolve himself of liability in case of accident merely by putting the barrel back in its place. He must inform the owner of what he has done.

לְמָקוֹם שֶׁגָּנַב יַחֲזִיר. [1]דִּבְרֵי רַבִּי יִשְׁמָעֵאל. [2]רַבִּי עֲקִיבָא אוֹמֵר: [41A] [3]צָרִיךְ דַּעַת בְּעָלִים.

[4]אִי רַבִּי יִשְׁמָעֵאל, מַאי אִירְיָא "לֹא יִחֲדוּ"? [5]אֲפִילּוּ יִחֲדוּ נַמִי. [6]לָא. מִיבָּעֲיָא קָאָמַר. [7]לָא מִיבָּעֲיָא יִחֲדוּ, דִּמְקוֹמָהּ הוּא.

LITERAL TRANSLATION

must return [it] to the place [from] where he stole [it]. [1]These are the words of Rabbi Yishmael. [2]Rabbi Akiva says: [41A] [3]The owner's knowledge is necessary."

[4]If [it is] Rabbi Yishmael, why specify "he did not designate"? [5]Even [if] he designated also. [6]It is speaking [in the style of] "there is no need." [7]There is no need [to state the case where] he designated [a place], for it is its place.

RASHI

צריך דעת בעלים — ואם לא הודיעם חייב באחריותם אם מת או נגנב, דמדשקליה קם ליה ברשותיה. והשבה בלא ידיעה לאו השבה היא. **דמקומה היא** — וכיון דבאותו מקום החזירה — חזרה גמורה היא.

אִי רַבִּי יִשְׁמָעֵאל [4]The Gemara objects : **If** the first half of our Mishnah reflects the viewpoint of **Rabbi Yishmael,** and the bailee is exempt because he returned the misappropriated barrel to its proper place, **why** did **the Mishnah** specify **that** the bailee is exempt because the owner **"did not** initially **designate** a place where he wanted the barrel kept"? [5]Surely, says the Gemara, **even if** the owner **did designate a place,** the same rule **should also** apply; the bailee should be exempt, according to Rabbi Yishmael, if he returned the barrel to its designated place without informing the owner.

לָא מִיבָּעֲיָא קָאָמַר [6]The Gemara answers: The Mishnah **was written in the style called "there is no need."** In this style, the Mishnah stipulates that it is dealing with the more unusual of two cases, and expects the reader to understand that "there is no need" to mention that the same law applies to the more usual case. [7]The Gemara elaborates: Our Mishnah is to be read as follows: **There is no need** to mention that **if** the owner has **designated a place** for the barrel to be kept, the bailee can absolve himself of liability by simply returning it to its place. **For** the bailee is returning it to **its place,** where the owner himself put it, and, according to Rabbi Yishmael, a bailee who has misappropriated an object needs to do no more than this to absolve himself of

NOTES

if the owner knew that the lamb had been stolen; but if the owner did not know, the thief cannot absolve himself of liability without expressly informing him that the lamb has been stolen and returned.

The Gemara objects, quoting the Baraita in which Rabbi Yishmael and Rabbi Akiva disagree as to whether a thief need inform the owner. Now, since the Halakhah follows Rabbi Akiva, and since one of the cases in the Baraita concerns a stolen coin, of whose absence the owner cannot fail to be aware (see above, 21b), it would appear that counting alone is never sufficient to absolve a thief of liability, and it is always necessary for the thief to inform the owner. But this contradicts the Mishnah and the Halakhah, which is in accordance with Rav Ḥisda.

This objection leads the Gemara to explain that the Baraita is referring specifically to a case where the flock of sheep or bag of money was in the custody of a bailee. The bailee then stole the lamb or the coin and later returned it. According to Rabbi Yishmael, once the bailee returns the stolen object to its proper place, he once again becomes a bailee, and is absolved from liability for accidents, even if the owner knows nothing about the incident; whereas according to Rabbi Akiva the bailee ceases to be a bailee from the moment he steals the lamb or coin, and remains liable for accidents, like any other thief, until the owner is informed.

HALAKHAH

הַגּוֹנֵב טָלֶה מִן הָעֵדֶר **Someone who steals a lamb from the flock.** "A shepherd who steals a lamb from a flock entrusted to his care, or a bailee who steals a coin from a moneybag that was deposited with him, becomes liable for any accident that may befall the stolen lamb or coin, just like any other thief. He cannot absolve himself of liability by simply returning the lamb or the coin to its place. He remains liable until he informs the owner," following Rabbi Akiva. (*Shulḥan Arukh, Ḥoshen Mishpat* 355:3.)

TRANSLATION AND COMMENTARY

liability if it is accidentally damaged after he returns it. [1]**But even if** the owner **did not designate** any particular **place** for the barrel to be kept, the bailee can still fulfill his obligations by putting it back, even though he is **not** exactly returning it to **its place,** [2]because according to Rabbi Yishmael a thief **does not need the owner's knowledge** to return a stolen item; so once the bailee puts the barrel back where it belongs, he is absolved from liability for accidental damage to it. Thus, according to Rabbi Yishmael, the bailee has no obligation to inform the owner that he has returned the object he misappropriated, irrespective of whether the owner designated a specific place for it.

אֵימָא סֵיפָא [3]On this point the Gemara objects: But **consider the last clause** of the Mishnah: **"If the owner has designated a place for** the barrel, **and the bailee moves it and it breaks,** [4]then it makes no difference **whether** it broke **while in his hand or after he put it down;** [5]in either case, **if he** initially **moved it for his own sake, he is liable,** but **if he moved it for its sake, he is exempt."** Now, the author of the last half of the Mishnah is clearly of the opinion that a bailee who returns a misappropriated barrel to its place has not absolved himself of his obligation. This half of the Mishnah contradicts the viewpoint of Rabbi Yishmael, according to whom returning the barrel to its place — even without informing the owner — is sufficient to absolve the bailee from responsibility if the barrel is later accidentally damaged.

אֲתָאן לְרַבִּי עֲקִיבָא [6]Rather, says the Gemara, **we** must **come to the** conclusion that the second half of the Mishnah reflects the **viewpoint of Rabbi Akiva, who said that** a thief **needs the owner's knowledge** before he can fulfill his obligation to return a stolen object. Since the bailee has not informed the depositor that he has taken and returned the barrel, he remains liable for it, even though he has returned it to its proper place.

אִי רַבִּי עֲקִיבָא [7]Here, too, the Gemara objects: **If** the last half of our Mishnah reflects the viewpoint of **Rabbi Akiva**, and the reason the bailee is liable is because he failed to inform the owner that he had returned the barrel, then it should say so. **Why did the Mishnah specify that** the reason the bailee cannot fulfill his obligation by returning the barrel to its place is because the owner **"designated** a place where he wanted it kept"? [8]Surely, says the Gemara, **even if** the owner **did not designate a place**, Rabbi Akiva's rule should **also** apply: The bailee did not inform the owner that he had returned the barrel, and informing the owner is an indispensable precondition before a thief can be absolved of further liability.

לָא מִיבָּעֲיָא קָאָמַר [9]The Gemara answers: This half of the Mishnah **was** also **written in the style called "there is no need."** [10]The Gemara elaborates: The Mishnah is to be read as follows: **There is no need** to mention that **where** the owner **did not designate a** particular **place** for the barrel to be kept the bailee cannot absolve himself of liability merely by returning it to the place from which he took it. **For** the bailee is **not** really returning the barrel to an agreed, predetermined **place** at all, and it is obvious that according to Rabbi Akiva he must tell the owner where the barrel is in order to be absolved of further liability if it is accidentally damaged after he returns it. [11]**But even if** the owner **did designate a place** for the barrel to be kept, and the bailee returned it there, he has still not fulfilled his obligation, even though he returned it to **its place,** [12]because according to Rabbi Akiva a thief **needs the owner's knowledge** to return a stolen item; merely returning the barrel to its place is not sufficient to absolve the bailee of his responsibility for it.

[1]אֶלָּא אֲפִילּוּ לֹא יִחֲדוּ, דְּלָאו מְקוֹמָהּ הוּא, [2]לָא בָּעֵינַן דַּעַת בְּעָלִים.
[3]אֵימָא סֵיפָא: "יִחֲדוּ לָהּ הַבְּעָלִים מָקוֹם, וְטִלְטְלָהּ וְנִשְׁבְּרָה, [4]בֵּין מִתּוֹךְ יָדוֹ בֵּין מִשֶּׁהִנִּיחָהּ, [5]לְצָרְכּוֹ, חַיָּיב, לְצָרְכָּהּ, פָּטוּר".
[6]אֲתָאן לְרַבִּי עֲקִיבָא, דְּאָמַר בָּעֵינַן דַּעַת בְּעָלִים.
[7]אִי רַבִּי עֲקִיבָא, מַאי אִירְיָא "יִחֲדוּ"? [8]אֲפִילּוּ לֹא יִחֲדוּ נַמִי.
[9]לָא מִיבָּעֲיָא קָאָמַר. [10]לָא מִיבָּעֲיָא לֹא יִחֲדוּ, דְּלָאו מְקוֹמָהּ הוּא. [11]אֶלָּא אֲפִילּוּ יִחֲדוּ נַמִי, דִּמְקוֹמָהּ הוּא, [12]בָּעֵינַן דַּעַת בְּעָלִים.

LITERAL TRANSLATION

[1]But even [if] he did not designate [a place], so that it is not its place, [2]we do not need the owner's knowledge.

[3]Say the last [clause]: "If the owner designated a place for it, and he moved it and it broke, [4]whether in his hand or after he put it down — for his need, [5]he is liable, for its need, he is exempt."

[6]We have come to [the viewpoint of] Rabbi Akiva, who said [that] we need the owner's knowledge.

[7]If [it is] Rabbi Akiva, why specify "he designated"? [8]Even [if] he did not designate also.

[9]It is speaking [in the style of] "there is no need." [10]There is no need [to state the case where] he did not designate, for it is not its place. [11]But even [if] he designated [a place] also, so that it is its place, [12]we need the owner's knowledge.

RASHI

אתאן לרבי עקיבא — מילתא היא.

רֵישָׁא רַבִּי יִשְׁמָעֵאל וְסֵיפָא רַבִּי עֲקִיבָא!? אִין, דְּאָמַר רַבִּי יוֹחָנָן: מַאן דִּמְתַרְגֵּם לִי "חָבִית" אַלִּיבָּא דְּחַד תַּנָּא, מוֹבַלְנָא מָאנֵיהּ בַּתְרֵיהּ לְבֵי מַסּוּתָא. תִּרְגְּמָהּ רַב יַעֲקֹב בַּר אַבָּא קַמֵּיהּ דְּרַב: שֶׁנְּטָלָהּ עַל מְנַת לְגוֹזְלָהּ.

LITERAL TRANSLATION

[1] The first [clause] is Rabbi Yishmael and the last [clause] Rabbi Akiva?!

[2] Yes, for Rabbi Yohanan said: [3] [If] anyone can explain to me [the Mishnah about] "a barrel" according to one Tanna, [4] I will carry his clothing after him to the bathhouse.

[5] Rav Ya'akov bar Abba explained it before Rav: Where he took it in order to rob [the owner of] it.

TRANSLATION AND COMMENTARY

רֵישָׁא רַבִּי יִשְׁמָעֵאל [1] The Gemara now objects: According to this interpretation, the two halves of the Mishnah reflect two differing schools of thought, with **the first half following Rabbi Yishmael and the last half** following **Rabbi Akiva.** Surely this solution is unacceptable!

אִין [2] The Gemara answers: **Yes,** it is indeed the case that the Mishnah is internally inconsistent, and its two halves reflect the views of different Tannaim. **For Rabbi Yoḥanan,** when analyzing this Mishnah, **said:** [3] "If **anyone can explain to me the Mishnah about a barrel** (i.e., our Mishnah) in such a way that it can possibly have been written **according to one Tanna,** and not two differing Tannaim, [4] **I will** honor him by treating him as a disciple treats his teacher, by **carrying his clothing after him to the bathhouse.**" Much as Rabbi Yoḥanan valued an internally consistent interpretation, he felt forced to admit that it was not possible in this case.

תִּרְגְּמָהּ [5] The Gemara now relates three alternative ways of explaining the Mishnah so that it remains internally consistent. According to all of them, the Mishnah is in accordance with the viewpoint of Rabbi Yishmael. The differences between them lie in their interpretations of the circumstances in the two halves of the Mishnah.

The first explanation: **Rav Ya'akov bar Abba explained** the Mishnah **before Rav** as referring to a case **where** the bailee **took** the deposit **in order to rob the owner of it,** but then thought better of it and put it back in another place. According to Rav Ya'akov bar Abba, this is the meaning of the expression "he moved it for his own sake" in the Mishnah. Now, even according to Rabbi Yishmael, a robber cannot absolve himself of liability without returning the object. Hence, in the first half of the Mishnah — where the owner left the precise location of the barrel to the bailee's discretion — the bailee can fulfill his obligation by putting it back anywhere in his house. But in the second half of the Mishnah — where the owner specified that the barrel be kept in a particular location — the bailee cannot fulfill his obligation, even according to Rabbi Yishmael, unless he returns the barrel to the precise spot from which he took it.

RASHI

תרגמה רבי יעקב — דתיקו כולה כחד תנא ובתרי טעמי; רישא שהחזירה למקומה, דכל מקום שהחזירה מקומה היא, דהא לא יחדו לה מקום, וסיפא — שהחזירה למקום שאינה מקומה, כדמסיים במסקנא, דהא דמסקינן בסיומא "וסיפא שהניחה במקום שאינה מקומה" — אתלתא דכולהו קאי, אדרבי יעקב ואדרבי נתן ואדרב ששת. ומשום דהניחה חוץ למקומה לא הויא חזרה, וכגון שנטלו מתחלה על מנת לגוזלה — והיינו "לצרכו" דמתניתין. דאילו לשאלה בעלמא ולתשמיש, כיון דלאו גזילה הוא — סגי לה בהשבה כל דהו, וכל מקום שהניחה פטור באונסין. אבל משום דגזולה הואי, ובגזילה כתיב "והשיב", וזה שהניחה למקום שלא יחדו לה בעלים — לא הויא השבה.

NOTES

מוֹבַלְנָא מָאנֵיהּ בַּתְרֵיהּ **I will carry his clothing after him.** The meaning of this expression is: "I will recognize the greatness of the person who answers this question, and treat him as a disciple treats his teacher." Interestingly, the Sages considered carrying clothes to the bathhouse to be a particularly humiliating task. Accordingly, it is forbidden for a master to have his Hebrew slave carry his clothes in this way. However, it is permitted for a master to order his Canaanite slave to carry his clothes to the bathhouse, and it is also permitted for a free person to agree voluntarily to perform this service (see *Rambam*, *Sefer Kinyan*, *Hilkhot Avadim* 1:7). Hence, when Rabbi Yoḥanan said he would carry clothes to the bathhouse, he was illustrating the principle (*Ketubot* 96a) that any service which a slave performs for his master, a disciple should also perform for his teacher.

HALAKHAH

חָבִית פִּקָּדוֹן שֶׁנִּשְׁבְּרָה **A deposited barrel that broke.** "If a depositor leaves a barrel with a bailee, and the bailee moves it from its place for his own sake, the bailee is considered to have misappropriated the barrel and is liable for any subsequent accidents that may befall it. This law applies regardless of whether or not the depositor specified a particular place for the deposit, and regardless of whether the accident occurred while the bailee was moving the barrel or afterwards, and regardless of whether the bailee put it back in its original place or in some other place. On the other hand, if the bailee moves the barrel for *its* sake, he is exempt under all circumstances. *Rema* adds that even though the bailee is not guilty of misappropriation, his moving of the barrel may still be considered negligent.

TERMINOLOGY

רֵישָׁא ר׳ פְּלוֹנִי וְסֵיפָא ר׳ פְּלוֹנִי **Is the first clause Rabbi A and the last clause Rabbi B?** A formula used to point out an apparent internal contradiction in an anonymous Mishnah, the first clause of which seems to follow one view, while its last clause seems to follow a contrary one.

אַלִּיבָּא דְּחַד תַּנָּא **According to [the viewpoint] of one Tanna.** The Talmud uses this expression to explain that two parts of a Mishnah or two Mishnayot represent a single viewpoint, but apply to two different sets of circumstances.

LANGUAGE

בֵּי מַסּוּתָא **Bathhouse.** The original word is actually בֵּי מַסְחוּתָא, meaning a bathhouse, derived from the root סחא — to wash. However, both in Babylonia and in Galilee, guttural letters were not pronounced clearly and disappeared entirely from many words, leaving only the vowels.

BACKGROUND

תִּרְגְּמָהּ רַב יַעֲקֹב בַּר אַבָּא קַמֵּיהּ דְּרַב **Rav Ya'akov bar Abba explained it before Rav.** The use of the word תִּרְגְּמָהּ (lit., "he translated it") refers to an explanation rather than a translation, particularly the placement of a case described in the Mishnah or the Baraita within a specific context. When some matter is explained in this fashion to an important Sage, this is generally done by a student of his who has already attained an important status and may propose interpretations and explanations of his own. The student offers the explanation to his teacher in order to have him confirm it.

SAGES

רַב יַעֲקֹב בַּר אַבָּא **Rav Ya'akov bar Abba.** A Babylonian Amora of the second generation, Rav Ya'akov bar Abba was a disciple of Rav.

¹תִּרְגְּמָהּ רַב נָתָן בַּר אַבָּא קַמֵּיהּ דְּרַב: שֶׁנְּטָלָהּ עַל מְנָת לִשְׁלוֹחַ בָּהּ יָד.
²בְּמַאי קָמִיפַּלְגִי?
³בִּשְׁלִיחוּת יָד צְרִיכָה חִסָּרוֹן.
⁴מַאן דְּאָמַר "לְגוֹזְלָהּ" קָסָבַר: שְׁלִיחוּת יָד צְרִיכָה חִסָּרוֹן.
⁵וּמַאן דְּאָמַר "לִשְׁלוֹחַ בָּהּ יָד" קָסָבַר: ⁶שְׁלִיחוּת יָד אֵינָהּ צְרִיכָה חִסְרוֹן.

LITERAL TRANSLATION

[1] Rav Natan bar Abba explained it before Rav: Where he took it in order to misappropriate it.
[2] About what do they disagree?
[3] About [whether] misappropriation requires loss.
[4] The one who said "to rob [the owner of] it" maintains: Misappropriation requires loss.
[5] And the one who said "to misappropriate it" maintains: [6] Misappropriation does not require loss.

RASHI

ורבי נתן תרגמה — דאפילו לא נטלה על מנת לגוזלה כו' אלא על מנת לשלוח בה יד וליטול מקצתה, ולא נטל — אפילו הכי קמה ליה ברשותיה כולה, והויא לה גזילה ובעיא השבה, ובמקום שאינו מקומה לאו השבה היא. ורב ששת לא שביק דליסיימו לתירוצייהו, ואתקיף: מידי נטלה קתני כו', ומיהו, סיומא דמילתא דמסקנא "וסיפא שהניחה במקום שאינו מקומה" — אכולהו קאי. שליחות יד — שחייבו הכתוב עליו אפילו נאנסה, דכתיב (שמות כב) "ומת או נשבר או נשבה [וגו'] שבועת ה' תהיה בין שניהם אם לא שלח ידו וגו'", דמשמע הא שלח — נתחייב שוב במיתתה ובשבייתה. צריכה חסרון — לא הוי שליחות יד להעמידה ברשותו אלא אם כן חסרה.

TRANSLATION AND COMMENTARY

תִּרְגְּמָהּ [1] The second explanation: **Rav Natan bar Abba explained** the Mishnah **before Rav** as referring to a case **where** the bailee **took** the deposit **in order to misappropriate it** by taking some of the contents for himself, but changed his mind and put the barrel back in another place.

בְּמַאי קָמִיפַּלְגִי [2] The Gemara now asks: **About what do** Rav Ya'akov bar Abba and Rav Natan bar Abba **disagree?** Their explanations are almost identical. The only difference between them is that, according to Rav Ya'akov bar Abba, the bailee intended to rob the owner of the entire barrel and then changed his mind, whereas according to Rav Natan bar Abba, he merely picked it up with the intention of misappropriating it, and then changed his mind.

בִּשְׁלִיחוּת יָד צְרִיכָה חִסָּרוֹן [3] The Gemara answers: The difference between the two Amoraim is **about whether misappropriation requires loss,** i.e., whether to be liable for misappropriation, a bailee has to cause actual loss or damage to the object he has misappropriated. The Torah declares that a bailee who misappropriates a deposit is liable, and comes under the category of a robber. (Exodus 22:7.) The question is: What constitutes misappropriation? Is the bailee considered to have misappropriated an object simply by moving it? Or is he not liable until he actually takes something away from the deposit? [4] Rav Ya'akov bar Abba, **who said** that the Mishnah is referring to a case where the bailee intended **"to rob the owner of** the barrel," **maintains:** [6] **Misappropriation,** unlike robbery, **requires an** actual **loss,** so the bailee is not viewed as a robber unless he causes such loss. Therefore the only way in which Rav Ya'akov bar Abba can explain the second half of the Mishnah — in which the bailee is held responsible although no loss has been caused to the barrel — is to say that the bailee's intention was to commit an act of robbery. [5] On the other hand, Rav Natan bar Abba, **who said** that the Mishnah is referring to a case where the bailee merely intended **"to misappropriate** the barrel," **maintains:** [6] **Misappropriation,** like actual robbery, **does not require a loss;** from the moment the bailee picks up the barrel with the intent of misappropriating part of it, he cannot absolve himself of liability without returning it to its proper place.

NOTES

שְׁלִיחוּת יָד **Misappropriation.** *Tosafot* and others explain that misappropriation differs from robbery in that a robber is responsible only for what he takes, but a bailee who misappropriates part of a deposit immediately assumes liability for any accidents that may damage any part of the deposit.

Ba'al HaMa'or and *Ra'avad* argue that misappropriation is similar to borrowing without permission (שְׁאֵלָה שֶׁלֹּא מִדַּעַת)

HALAKHAH

Hence, if the barrel breaks while still in the bailee's hand as a result of being moved, the bailee is liable for negligence. However, if the barrel breaks after the bailee puts it down, then, if the bailee put it back in the place designated by the owner, or if the owner did not designate any particular place for the bailee to keep the barrel, the bailee is exempt. However, if the owner designated a particular place to keep the barrel and the bailee put it in another place and the barrel later broke by accident, the bailee is liable, since his negligence in putting the barrel in the wrong place may have been a contributing factor." (*Shulḥan Arukh, Ḥoshen Mishpat* 292:6.)

חִסָּרוֹן בִּשְׁלִיחוּת יָד **Loss in a case of misappropriation.** "A bailee is strictly forbidden to misappropriate a deposit for his own use. Misappropriation applies whenever the bailee picks up a deposit with the intention of stealing it or making use of it in a manner that will cause it damage, however slight. It is not necessary for the bailee to *do* damage. From the moment the bailee picks up the deposit, he becomes liable for any accidents that may subsequently befall it, even

SAGES

רַב נָתָן בַּר אַבָּא **Rav Natan bar Abba.** A Babylonian Amora of the second generation, Rav Natan bar Abba was a disciple of Rav and Shmuel.

BACKGROUND

שְׁלִיחוּת יָד וְחִסָּרוֹן **Misappropriation and loss.** From the legal point of view, the definitions of theft and robbery are quite simple. These acts are considered to have occurred when a person removes an object from its owner's possession and transfers it to his own possession with the intention of keeping it for himself. Misappropriation, however, is a category that applies only to a bailee, where the object is already in his possession. Very clear distinctions must be drawn in order to determine when a certain act constitutes misappropriation. As explained below (43b), some Sages argued that misappropriation is solely a matter of intention, i.e., the bailee's intention to take the object for himself, and according to the Halakhah there can be no misappropriation without an act of acquisition. Nevertheless this definition is not always adequate. "Pulling" (מְשִׁיכָה) — a primary act of acquisition — can be effected by merely moving an object from its place, and the bailee may do this in all innocence, so that the act itself cannot be proof of misappropriation. Therefore it was proposed that misappropriation be connected with the removal of part of the object on deposit, making it clear that misappropriation has taken place. However, those who argue that misappropriation need not include removal of part of the deposit maintain that an act similar to an act of acquisition — one which expresses the bailee's intention of taking the object for himself — already constitutes misappropriation.

TRANSLATION AND COMMENTARY

מַתְקִיף לָהּ רַב שֵׁשֶׁת [1]**Rav Sheshet** strongly **objected to** both explanations: **Does** the Mishnah **say** anything about the bailee actually **taking** the deposit, either in whole or in part? [2]Surely the Mishnah **says:** "The bailee **moved** the barrel for his own sake." This does not necessarily mean he wanted its contents for himself!

אֶלָּא אֲמַר רַב שֵׁשֶׁת [3]**Rather, Rav Sheshet said**, there is a third explanation: **With what are we dealing here?** [4]**Where, for example,** the bailee **moved** the barrel **to bring** down some **young birds** from a dove cote, **while standing upon it.** He had no intention of taking the barrel's contents, but merely wished to borrow it to stand on temporarily. [5]Rav Sheshet **maintains** that **someone who borrows** property **without** its **owner's knowledge is considered a robber,** even though he has every intention of returning it after he has finished using it. Such a borrower is liable for any accident suffered by the borrowed object, until he returns it to its place. Hence, in our case as well, if a bailee borrows the barrel to stand on, without asking permission of its owner, he is deemed a robber, and cannot absolve himself of liability without returning the barrel to its proper place.

[1]מַתְקִיף לָהּ רַב שֵׁשֶׁת: מִידֵּי "נְטָלָהּ" קָתָנֵי? [2]"טִלְטְלָהּ" קָתָנֵי.

[3]אֶלָּא אֲמַר רַב שֵׁשֶׁת: הָכָא בְּמַאי עָסְקִינַן? [4]כְּגוֹן שֶׁטִּלְטְלָהּ לְהָבִיא עָלֶיהָ גּוֹזָלוֹת. [5]וְקָא סָבַר: שׁוֹאֵל שֶׁלֹּא מִדַּעַת גַּזְלָן הָוֵי.

LITERAL TRANSLATION

[1]Rav Sheshet strongly objected to this: Does it teach "he took it"? [2]It teaches "he moved it."

[3]Rather, Rav Sheshet said: With what are we dealing here? [4]Where, for example, he moved it to bring [down] young birds [while standing] upon it. [5]And he maintains: Someone who borrows without [the owner's] knowledge is [considered] a robber.

RASHI

מידי נטלה קתני — דמשמע שנטלה לעצמו. **טלטלה קתני** — לתשמיש בעלמא, משמע "לצרכו" דמתניתין. **אלא כגון שטלטלה להביא עליה גוזלות** — לעלות עליה כדרך סולם ליטול גוזלות מקן גבוה, ואפילו הכי הויא גזילה למיקם ברשותיה עד דעביד השבה, דקסבר: שואל שלא מדעת בעלים גזלן הוא.

NOTES

in that the bailee does not intend to keep any part of the deposit permanently, but rather to borrow it and return it later. Even so, the Torah considers this the equivalent of robbery, and the bailee becomes liable for any accidents that may befall the deposit (see also following note).

Ramban suggests that misappropriation is taking all or part of a deposit with the intention of paying for it.

Rosh says that misappropriation applies even when the use the bailee made of the deposit was so insignificant that the owner would not have objected. Even so, the Torah decreed that a bailee who derives any personal benefit whatsoever from the deposit is considered a robber, and must pay for any subsequent accident that may befall the deposit.

שׁוֹאֵל שֶׁלֹּא מִדַּעַת Someone who borrows without the owner's knowledge. In our commentary we have followed *Rashi* and other Rishonim, who explain that Rav Sheshet was referring to the law that borrowing without permission is equivalent to robbery. Under this law, it makes no difference if the borrower was a bailee or a stranger. Thus, the bailee who borrows a barrel to climb on is not guilty of misappropriation, but is guilty of robbery in that he borrowed the barrel without permission.

Rashi asks: Later on, the Gemara considers a case where a shepherd uses the owner's animal to carry his bag for him. The Gemara states that, according to the opinion that misappropriation requires loss, the shepherd should not be liable unless he physically mistreats the animal. But even if the shepherd is not guilty of misappropriation, he should be considered a robber for borrowing the animal without permission. What is the difference between borrowing without permission and misappropriating without causing a loss?

Rashi answers that the concept of borrowing without permission cannot be applied to shepherds and the like. Since animals can be injured if they are worked, wherever a bailee borrows an animal without permission, he is misappropriating it. This leads to the conclusion that if no injury is caused, the shepherd is guilty neither of misappropriation nor of borrowing without permission.

The Rishonim object to this answer. Why should a bailee be exempt from the law that anyone who borrows without

HALAKHAH

if he immediately returns the deposit to its place without having damaged it in any way (following Rav against Levi). But if the bailee picked up the deposit to use it for some purpose that will not cause it any damage — for example, if he borrowed a barrel of wine to climb on — he is not guilty of misappropriation. He is, however, guilty of borrowing an object without its owner's permission — a law which applies to bailees and non-bailees alike. Hence, he is not liable for damage until he actually uses the deposit. Regarding the question of whether we view a "borrower without permission" as a borrower or a robber, *Shulḥan Arukh* rules that he is a robber and is liable, even after he returns the deposit, until he informs the owner. *Rema* points out that under certain circumstances (see *Sma* and *Shakh*) he is considered a borrower, and is exempt from liability for subsequent accidents as soon as he puts the deposit down." (*Shulḥan Arukh, Ḥoshen Mishpat* 292:1.)

TRANSLATION AND COMMENTARY

וְכוּלָּהּ רַבִּי יִשְׁמָעֵאל הִיא [1]The Gemara now summarizes the three explanations of our Mishnah just given: According to all three, **the entire Mishnah** is in accordance with the viewpoint of **Rabbi Yishmael,** [2]**and the last half** refers to a case **where** the bailee **put** the deposit back **in a place that was not its** original **place.** Hence, since the owner specified that the deposit could not be kept anywhere else, the bailee cannot be considered to have returned the misappropriated object, even according to Rabbi Yishmael, and until he does so he remains responsible for it.

וְרַבִּי יוֹחָנָן [3]The Gemara now asks: **And** what about **Rabbi Yoḥanan,** who declared that it is impossible to explain this Mishnah according to the view of a single Tanna? Why does he not accept one of these three explanations, and say that the bailee put the barrel back in a different place from that stipulated by its owner?

"הִנִּיחָהּ" בִּמְקוֹמָהּ מַשְׁמַע [4]The Gemara answers: According to Rabbi Yoḥanan, the expression "he **put it down" means** "he put it down **in the place** from which he took it." But if the bailee put the barrel back in its place, Rabbi Yishmael would certainly consider him to have returned it. Hence Rabbi Yoḥanan maintains that it is impossible to explain the second half of the Mishnah according to Rabbi Yishmael, and ascribes the second half to Rabbi Akiva.

אִיתְּמַר רַב וְלֵוִי [5]The Gemara now considers a question mentioned in passing in the previous passage: **It was stated that there was a dispute** about the following issue **between Rav and Levi.** [6]**One** of them **said: Misappropriation requires loss,** so a bailee is not considered guilty of misappropriation (and thus liable in the case of accidental damage) until he actually causes a loss to the deposit. [7]**And** the other **one said: Misappropriation does not require loss,** so a bailee is guilty of misappropriation from the moment he picks up the deposit with the intention of using it for himself.

[1]וְכוּלָּהּ רַבִּי יִשְׁמָעֵאל הִיא, [2]וְסֵיפָא שֶׁהִנִּיחָהּ בְּמָקוֹם שֶׁאֵינָהּ מְקוֹמָהּ.
[3]וְרַבִּי יוֹחָנָן?
[4]"הִנִּיחָהּ" בִּמְקוֹמָהּ מַשְׁמַע.
[5]אִיתְּמַר רַב וְלֵוִי. [6]חַד אָמַר: שְׁלִיחוּת יָד צְרִיכָה חִסָּרוֹן.
[7]וְחַד אָמַר: שְׁלִיחוּת יָד אֵינָהּ צְרִיכָה חִסָּרוֹן.

LITERAL TRANSLATION

[1]And all of it [the Mishnah] is Rabbi Yishmael, [2]and the last [clause] is where he put it in a place that was not its place.

[3]And Rabbi Yoḥanan?

[4]"He put it down" means in its place.

[5]It was said [that] Rav and Levi [disagreed]. [6]One said: Misappropriation requires loss. [7]And one said: Misappropriation does not require loss.

RASHI

וכולה רבי ישמעאל היא – אשינויא דכולהו קאי, אדרבי יעקב ואדרבי נתן ואדרב ששת. **וסיפא שהניחה במקום שאינה מקומה** – אבל רישא, כל מקום שהניחה מקומה היא. **ורבי יוחנן** – דאמר לעיל "מאן דמתרגם לי" כו'. **הניחה במקומה משמע** – הלכך לא מיתוקמא כרבי ישמעאל. **שליחות יד** – שחייבו הכתוב עליו ואפילו נאנסה כדכתיב "או נשבר או נשבה וגו' שבועת ה' תהיה אם לא שלח", דמשמע הא אם שלח – נתחייב שוב במיתתה ובשבייתה. **צריכה חסרון** – וכל זמן שלא חסרה לא קמה ברשותיה להתחייב באונסיה.

SAGES

לֵוִי Levi. Levi ben Sisi was a Palestinian Sage of the transitional generation between the Tannaitic and Amoraic periods. He was the outstanding student of Rabbi Yehudah HaNasi, editor of the Mishnah. He would sit before Rabbi Yehudah HaNasi and discuss the Halakhah with his other great students. Rabbi Yehudah HaNasi held him in great esteem, and sent him to be chief judge and preacher in the town of Simonia. He said of him that he was "a man like myself." In several sources it is told that he acquired a limp while trying to show Rabbi Yehudah HaNasi how the High Priest used to prostrate himself on Yom Kippur. It is also explained that this was a punishment for having reproached the Almighty in his prayers.

Towards the end of his life, he went to Babylonia, where he renewed his close bonds with Rav, with whom he had studied under Rabbi Yehudah HaNasi, and became a close friend of Abba bar Abba, Shmuel's father. Shmuel was his student and colleague.

Rambam decided Halakhic rulings in accordance with Levi, against Rav and Shmuel, for in his opinion Levi was their superior. It is not clear whether Levi had sons or who they were. Some authorities believe that Bar Liva'i, who is mentioned in the Talmud, was his son. Others believe that Rabbi Yehoshua ben Levi, the famous Amora, was his son. These conjectures, however, have not been proven.

NOTES

permission is a robber merely because the borrowed animal did not get hurt?

Rosh suggests that a stranger who places a bag on an animal is not considered to be borrowing without permission, because the owner is not likely to object to such an insignificant liberty. However, when the Torah forbade misappropriating a deposit, it made no distinction between major and minor liberties. Thus, a shepherd who places his bag on an animal is guilty of misappropriation even if the owner would not object, provided there is some loss to the deposit, according to Rav Ya'akov bar Abba, and even if there is no loss, according to Rav Natan bar Abba.

Because of the question raised by *Rashi*, some Rishonim suggest that Rav Sheshet was not referring to the law that someone who borrows without permission is a robber, but was enunciating a special law that applies only to bailees. Rav Sheshet agreed with Rav Natan bar Abba that misappropriation does not require loss. He went further and ruled that it is not even necessary for the bailee to *intend* to cause a loss — it is sufficient for him to borrow the deposit without permission. According to this interpretation, the bailee who borrowed the barrel to climb on was indeed guilty of misappropriation. For a bailee, "borrowing without permission" and "misappropriation without causing loss" are to all intents and purposes identical terms (*Ra'avad, Ba'al HaMa'or*).

"הִנִּיחָהּ" בִּמְקוֹמָהּ מַשְׁמַע "He put it down" means in its place. On the surface, it would appear that the only reason Rabbi Yoḥanan rejected the explanations offered by Rav Ya'akov bar Abba, Rav Natan bar Abba and Rav Sheshet was because he did not accept their translation of the word "to put down." However, the Rishonim note that the problem is not quite that simple. According to all three explanations, the bailee put the barrel back in an unsuitable place. But in the first half of the Mishnah, any place in the house is a suitable place, because the owner did not designate any particular spot. Hence, the real distinction between the first and second halves of the Mishnah is the fact that the bailee put the barrel in the right place in the first half, and in the wrong place in the second half, and the distinction the Mishnah purports to be making — between different orders given by the depositor — is of

TERMINOLOGY

תִּסְתַּיֵּים Conclude. Sometimes the Talmud notes that there was a controversy between two scholars concerning a certain issue, but it is not clear which scholar took what position. In such cases the Talmud's initial attempt to attribute the views is often introduced by the expression תִּסְתַּיֵּים דְּר׳ פְּלוֹנִי הוּא דְּאָמַר — "Conclude that it was Rabbi X who said... [and that Rabbi B holds the other view]." If this suggestion is confirmed later on in the discussion, the Talmud may close the discussion with the remark תִּסְתַּיֵּים — "Conclude [that the suggested identification was indeed correct]."

BACKGROUND

וּבָא זְאֵב וְטָרַף, וּבָא אֲרִי וְדָרַס And a wolf came and preyed upon an animal, or a lion came and mauled it. The different verbs used here describe different ways predators kill their prey. A wolf attacks an animal and bites it, usually in the neck, until it dies. This method of attack is known as טָרַף in the narrow meaning of the word (to tear). In contrast, a lion generally fells its prey by delivering a blow to its backbone, and the precise verb used for this action is דָּרַס. Lions existed in Eretz Israel as late as the Middle Ages, and only became extinct in the region in modern times. Wolves are still found in various parts of the country.

תַּרְמִיל Bag. This word refers to the rather large sack, generally made of leather, which is used by shepherds for their food and other belongings. Since a shepherd is away from home all day long and occasionally for several days at a time, he uses a large, strong sack to contain all the food he will need.

LITERAL TRANSLATION

[1] Conclude that it was Rav who said [that] misappropriation does not require loss, [2] for it has been taught: "A shepherd who was shepherding his flock, [3] and left his flock and went to town, and a wolf came and preyed upon [an animal], or a lion came and mauled [it], [4] he is exempt. [5] [If] he placed his staff or his bag upon it, he is liable."

[6] And we were discussing this: [7] Because he placed his staff or his bag on it he is liable? [8] Surely he took them away!

[1] תִּסְתַּיֵּים דְּרַב הוּא דְּאָמַר שְׁלִיחוּת יָד אֵינָהּ צְרִיכָה חִסָּרוֹן, [2] דְּתַנְיָא: "רוֹעֶה שֶׁהָיָה רוֹעֶה עֶדְרוֹ, [3] וְהִנִּיחַ עֶדְרוֹ וּבָא לָעִיר, וּבָא זְאֵב וְטָרַף, וּבָא אֲרִי וְדָרַס, [4] פָּטוּר. [5] הִנִּיחַ מַקְלוֹ וְתַרְמִילוֹ עָלֶיהָ, חַיָּיב".

[6] וְהָוֵינַן בָּהּ: [7] מִשּׁוּם דְּהִנִּיחַ מַקְלוֹ וְתַרְמִילוֹ עָלֶיהָ חַיָּיב? [8] הָא שָׁקְלִינְהוּ!

RASHI

זאב — טורף נושא הטרף לחורו. **ארי** — אינו טורפה אלא דורסה במקומה ואוכלה. **פטור** — דאונסין נינהו, ואי משום דהניח עדרו, ופשיעה היא — מוקמינן לה דעל בעידנא דעיילי אינשי כדאמרינן ב״השוכר את הפועלים״ (בבא מציעא צג,ב), אי נמי: דשמע קול אריה ועל. **הא שקלינהו** — ואי נמי שליחות יד הויא, הא הדר אהדרה כשנטלו הימנו, ואנן מוקמינן לעיל סתם מתניתין כרבי ישמעאל דאין צריך דעת בעלים.

TRANSLATION AND COMMENTARY

תִּסְתַּיֵּים [1] As stated, it is not clear which of the two Amoraim, Rav or Levi, was of the opinion that misappropriation requires loss, and which was of the opinion that it does not. Therefore the Gemara now examines other rulings of Rav to see which of the two opinions is consistent with his general approach. The Gemara suggests: It is reasonable to **conclude that it was Rav who said** that **misappropriation does not require loss, for** Rav is known to have made a comment on the following Baraita, which may shed light on his viewpoint. [2] **The Baraita teaches:** "**A shepherd who was** paid to look after other people's sheep was **herding his flock.** [3] **He left his flock and went to town, and a wolf came and preyed upon one of the animals, or a lion came and mauled it.** [4] In such a case, the shepherd **is exempt,** since the attack of the wolf or the lion could not have been prevented even if the shepherd had stayed with his flock, and a paid bailee is exempt in cases of accident. [5] However, if the shepherd **placed his staff or his bag upon** an animal that was subsequently attacked, **he is liable** for any damage caused to it by the wolf or the lion, since he was guilty of misappropriation when he used the animal to carry his belongings, and a bailee who misappropriates a deposit is liable for any subsequent accidental damage it may suffer."

וְהָוֵינַן בָּהּ [6] The Gemara now continues: **And** while **we** were discussing **this** Baraita the following question was raised about its second half: [7] Why should the shepherd **be liable** in the case of accident merely **because he placed his** staff or his **bag upon** the animal? [8] **Surely, he had** already **taken them away** when he came to town! Even if we accept that the shepherd committed an act of misappropriation by leaving his staff or his bag on the sheep, once he took them off he rectified his misdemeanor and ceased to be liable for misappropriation. (The Gemara is assuming that this Baraita follows the opinion of Rabbi Yishmael above, who said that a bailee who returns a misappropriated deposit to its proper place undamaged absolves himself of further liability, even without informing the owner.)

NOTES

only marginal significance. Moreover, the word "to put down" must be explained differently in the two halves of the Mishnah, which is almost as unsatisfactory as saying that the Mishnah reflects the viewpoints of two different Tannaim (*Ritva*).

Resolving an apparent contradiction within a single Mishnah is a common problem in the Gemara. Usually the Gemara finds an internally consistent way to explain the Mishnah, though sometimes this involves a certain amount of textual emendation. In those rare cases where this is impossible, there remain only two possibilities, both unsatisfactory. One called תְּרֵי טַעְמֵי, is to say that similar words in the different parts of the Mishnah are to be interpreted differently. This was the approach adopted by the three explanations of our Mishnah. The other possibility, called תְּרֵי תַּנָּאֵי, involves accepting the internal contradiction as a fact, and explaining the Mishnah as reflecting two differing schools of thought. This was the approach adopted by Rabbi Yoḥanan. The Gemara in tractate *Sanhedrin* (62b) notes that Rabbi Yoḥanan in general preferred the תְּרֵי תַּנָּאֵי approach over the תְּרֵי טַעְמֵי approach. This played a major role in his rejection of the three explanations in our Gemara (see *Talmid Rabbenu Peretz* and others).

הָא שָׁקְלִינְהוּ Surely he took them away. Our commentary follows *Rashi* and *Tosafot,* who explain that the Gemara understands this Baraita as being in accordance with the view of Rabbi Yishmael who ruled (above, 40b) that a bailee who misappropriates a deposit need only return it to its proper place to absolve himself of further liability. Hence, even though the shepherd misappropriated the animal when he placed his staff and bag on it, he rectified his misdemeanor by removing them.

Ra'avad, however, objects to this explanation, as the Halakhah is in accordance with Rabbi Akiva, who disagrees with Rabbi Yishmael and rules that the bailee must inform the owner to absolve himself of further liability. Accordingly, *Ra'avad* explains that occasionally placing a staff or bag on an animal is not misappropriation at all, since such behavior

[1]אָמַר רַב נַחְמָן אָמַר רַבָּה בַּר אֲבוּהּ אָמַר רַב: [2]בְּעוֹדָן עָלֶיהָ.
[3]וְכִי עוֹדָן עָלֶיהָ, מַאי הָוֵי? [4]הָא לָא מְשָׁכָהּ!
[5]וְאָמַר רַב שְׁמוּאֵל בַּר רַב יִצְחָק אָמַר רַב: [6]שֶׁהִכִּישָׁהּ בְּמַקֵּל וְרָצְתָה לְפָנָיו.
[7]וְהָא לָא חִסְּרָהּ! [8]אֶלָּא לָאו שְׁמַע מִינָּהּ קָסָבַר: [9]שְׁלִיחוּת יָד אֵינָהּ צְרִיכָה חִסָּרוֹן?
[10]אֵימָא: שֶׁהִכְחִישָׁהּ בְּמַקֵּל.

LITERAL TRANSLATION

[1]Rav Naḥman said in the name of Rabbah bar Avuha in the name of Rav: [2]While they were still on it.
[3]And if they are still on it, what of it? [4]Surely he did not pull it!
[5]And Rav Shmuel bar Rav Yitzḥak said in the name of Rav: [6]Where he struck it with a staff and it ran before him.
[7]But surely he caused it no loss! [8]Rather [should one] not conclude from this [that Rav] maintains [9][that] misappropriation does not require loss?
[10]Say: Where he weakened it with a staff.

TRANSLATION AND COMMENTARY

אָמַר רַב נַחְמָן [1]The Gemara now reports Rav's answer to the question just raised concerning this Baraita. It is this answer that the Gemara wishes to use to prove that Rav maintains that misappropriation does not require loss. **Rav Naḥman said in the name of Rabbah bar Avuha in the name of Rav:** [2]The Baraita is referring to a case where the shepherd did not remove his staff or bag from the animal when he returned to town, and the lion or wolf attacked it **while** the staff or bag **were still on it.** Hence, the shepherd had not yet rectified his misappropriation, and remained liable for the damage caused to the animal.

וְכִי עוֹדָן עָלֶיהָ [3]Before explaining how Rav's answer indicates his opinion about whether or not misappropriation requires loss, the Gemara asks: Even **if** the staff or bag **were still on** the animal when the wolf or lion attacked it, as Rav suggested, **what of it?** [4]**Surely** the shepherd **did not pull** the animal, and since he did not pull it, he did not acquire it! Even according to those who maintain that misappropriation does not require loss, it is not sufficient for the bailee merely to plan to misappropriate the deposit; he must take some action that indicates that he is taking the deposit for himself. He must perform an act of acquisition. Now, the normal act of acquisition for an animal is to pull it. Hence, if the shepherd had placed his bag on the animal and pulled it, he would have taken it for himself, and would be guilty of misappropriation. But since he did not pull the animal, his placing of the bag on it is not sufficient to render him liable.

וְאָמַר רַב שְׁמוּאֵל [5]In response to this objection **Rav Shmuel bar Rav Yitzḥak said in the name of Rav:** [6]The Baraita refers to a case **where** the shepherd **struck** the animal **with a stick** while his staff and bag were still on it, **and** so caused **it to run before him.** Causing an animal to run is Halakhically equivalent to pulling. The shepherd acquired the animal by doing that, and thereafter became responsible for any accident that might befall it.

וְהָא לָא חִסְּרָהּ [7]Having completed its analysis of the Baraita, the Gemara now presents its proof that Rav is of the opinion that misappropriation does not require loss: Rav has explained that the shepherd misappropriated the animal by leaving his staff or bag on it and going to town. **But surely he caused it no loss** by leaving his staff or bag on it! [8]**Rather, is it not correct to conclude from here that Rav maintains** [9]**that misappropriation does not require loss?**

אֵימָא [10]The Gemara rejects this proof: It is possible to **say** that Rav did not mean that a shepherd misappropriates an animal merely by leaving his staff or bag on it. Rather, the Baraita is referring to a case **where the shepherd weakened** the sheep when he made it carry his bag for him, by striking **it with** his **staff.** Thus the shepherd is not liable merely because the animal ran before him with his bag on it, but rather

RASHI

הא לא משכה — בשליחות יד כדי לקנותה, ומטלטלין אין נקנין אלא במשיכה, לא במקח, ולא לענין גזל, ולא לענין שליחות יד, כדתנן במתניתין (בבא מציעא מג,ב): הטה את החבית ונטל ממנה רביעית יין — אין משלם אלא רביעית, אלמא בעינן דליקנייה כו׳. **ואמר רב שמואל** — גרסינן. **שהכישה במקל** — כשנתנו עליה ורצתה — זו היא משיכה, משעקרה יד ורגל על ידו. **והא לא חסרה** — לאו פירכא היא, אלא מסקנא וסיומא הוא למילתיה, דאמר: תסתיים דרב הוא דאמר אין צריכה חסרון. מדשני רב למתניתין משום דהכישה ורצתה לפניו. ואי קשיא דלמא הא דהניח מקלו ותרמילו חיוביה לאו משום שליחות יד הוא דליבעי חסרון, אלא משום שואל שלא מדעת הוא, כי ההוא דלעיל דחבית? לא היא, דכי אמרינן בשומרין שאלה שלא מדעת — בדבר שאינו כיחש וחיסר מחמת מלאכה, אבל בעלי חיים המכחישים מחמת מלאכה — תחלתו שליחות יד היא. **שהכחישה** — בהכאתו, דהיינו חסרון.

SAGES

רַב שְׁמוּאֵל בַּר רַב יִצְחָק Rav Shmuel bar Rav Yitzḥak. A Babylonian Amora of the third generation, Rav Shmuel bar Rav Yitzḥak was apparently one of Rav's younger students. He later became a disciple of Rav Huna. Like many of Rav Huna's students, he immigrated to Eretz Israel, and seems to have been of middle age at the time. Though we do not find teachings of his in the name of Rabbi Yoḥanan, we do find him in discussion with Rabbi Yoḥanan's students, some of whom quote him. Rav Shmuel bar Rav Yitzḥak's Aggadic and Halakhic teachings are found in both the Babylonian and Jerusalem Talmuds. We do not know what he did for a living, but we know he had a daughter who was married to Rabbi Hoshaya.

Rav Shmuel bar Rav Yitzḥak behaved with humility, and deferred to those younger than himself. He was accustomed to dance before brides, as we learn from tractate *Ketubot* in the Babylonian Talmud, and from tractate *Pe'ah* in the Jerusalem Talmud.

NOTES

is appropriate for a shepherd, and is not objectionable to the owner. However, regularly placing a staff or a bag on a certain animal is objectionable. Hence, when the Baraita said that the shepherd placed his staff or his bag on an animal, the Gemara remarked that "surely he took them away" shortly thereafter, and the action was unobjectionable. The Gemara then explained that "they were still on it," meaning that the shepherd did not remove his staff and his bag from the animal, and was thus guilty of misappropriation.

SAGES

רַבִּי יוֹסֵי בֶּן נְהוֹרַאי Rabbi Yose ben Nehorai. A Palestinian Amora of the first generation, Rabbi Yose ben Nehorai was a colleague of Rabbi Yehoshua ben Levi. Rabbi Yoḥanan was his main disciple.

TRANSLATION AND COMMENTARY

because he caused its value to decrease somewhat by striking it.

דַּיְקָא נַמִי, דְּקָתָנֵי [1]The Gemara notes: **This** explanation **also** conforms to the **precise** language used by Rav. **For the** statement reported above in Rav's name by Rav Shmuel bar Rav Yitzḥak **uses the expression "where he struck it with a staff."** If all that Rav had wished to say was that the shepherd misappropriated the animal by causing it to run before him with the bag on its back, why was it necessary that he strike it with a staff? The same effect would have been achieved if he had called or whistled or clapped his hands! It is therefore clear that the blow of the stick was significant. Hence we must conclude that, according to Rav, a shepherd is not guilty of misappropriation unless he hurts an animal by striking it with his stick in order to get it to carry his bag for him. This is presumably because misappropriation requires loss. [2]Thus, concludes the Gemara, we can **infer from here** that it is Rav who maintains that misappropriation requires loss.

וּמִדְּרַב סָבַר [3]The Gemara continues: Now, **since** we have proven that **Rav maintains that misappropriation requires loss,** [4]we may infer that it is **Levi** who **maintains** that **misappropriation does not require loss.** [5]The Gemara now asks: **What is Levi's reason** for ruling that misappropriation does not require loss?

אָמַר רַבִּי יוֹחָנָן [6]In answer to this question, **Rabbi Yoḥanan said in the name of Rabbi Yose ben Nehorai:** Levi had a Scriptural source for his opinion. The Torah mentions the law of misappropriation twice — once in connection with the unpaid bailee (Exodus 22:7), and once in connection with the paid bailee (Exodus 22:10). [7]However, **the misappropriation mentioned in connection with a paid bailee is different from the misappropriation mentioned in connection with an unpaid bailee.** In other words, the law of misappropriation mentioned in connection with the paid bailee is not mere repetition. It comes to teach us something new — namely, that misappropriation does not require loss. [41B] Levi's reasoning is in accordance with Rabbi Yose ben Nehorai's exegesis, and the repetition of the law of misappropriation teaches us that misappropriation does not require loss. [8]**But,** continues Rabbi Yoḥanan, **I say** that the two mentions of misappropriation in the Torah **are not different.** It was necessary for the Torah to mention the law of misappropriation in connection with both bailees so that we should know it applies to both. Accordingly, I also disagree with Levi, and maintain, like Rav, that misappropriation requires loss.

[1]דַּיְקָא נַמִי, דְּקָתָנֵי: ״שֶׁהִכִּישָׁהּ בְּמַקֵּל״. [2]שְׁמַע מִינָּהּ.

[3]וּמִדְּרַב סָבַר שְׁלִיחוּת יָד צְרִיכָה חִסָּרוֹן, [4]לֵוִי סָבַר שְׁלִיחוּת יָד אֵינָהּ צְרִיכָה חִסָּרוֹן. [5]מַאי טַעְמָא דְּלֵוִי?

[6]אָמַר רַבִּי יוֹחָנָן מִשּׁוּם רַבִּי יוֹסֵי בֶּן נְהוֹרַאי: [7]מְשׁוּנָּה שְׁלִיחוּת יָד הָאֲמוּרָה בְּשׁוֹמֵר שָׂכָר מִשְּׁלִיחוּת יָד הָאֲמוּרָה בְּשׁוֹמֵר חִנָּם. [41B] [8]וַאֲנִי אוֹמֵר: אֵינָהּ מְשׁוּנָּה.

LITERAL TRANSLATION

[1]It is also precise, for it teaches: "Where he struck it with a staff." [2]Conclude from this.

[3]And since Rav maintains [that] misappropriation requires loss, [4]Levi maintains [that] misappropriation does not require loss. [5]What is Levi's reason?

[6]Rabbi Yoḥanan said in the name of Rabbi Yose ben Nehorai: [7]The misappropriation mentioned in connection with a paid bailee is different from the misappropriation mentioned in connection with an unpaid bailee. [41B] [8]But I say: It is not different.

RASHI

דיקא נמי — דהכחישה קאמר רב, מדנקט הכשת מקל, דמכה חזקה היא. **ומדרב סבר צריכה חסרון** — דהא דייקינן מדנקט מקל. **לוי** — בר פלוגתיה, סבר: אין צריכה חסרון. **משונה שליחות יד כו'** — כלומר, אינה דומה לזו, שזו נאמרה לצורך, ולא משתמע אלא בחסרון. אבל של שומר שכר נאמרה שלא לצורך משמעות שבה, אלא לדרשה, וללמד שאינה צריכה חסרון. **ואני אומר** — רבי יוחנן פליג אדרבי יוסי בן נהוראי רביה, ואמר: אף היא לצורך נאמרה. ולוי סבירא ליה כרבי יוסי בן נהוראי, למידרש מיניה דאין צריכה חסרון. דאי מקרא קמא — לא תיסק אדעתין לחיוביה עד דמחסר ליה. בשומר חנם נאמר "ונקרב בעל הבית וגו'", בשומר שכר כתיב "שבועת ה' תהיה וגו'", ואמרינן ב"השואל" (בבא מציעא לד,ב): פרשה ראשונה נאמרה בשומר חנם, שניה בשומר שכר, וכתיב בתרוייהו "אם לא שלח", הא אם שלח — נתחייב בדברים שהוא פטור עליהם. כגון שומר חנם בין בגנבה בין באונסין, דמשלח בה יד — קנאה, וקמה ברשותו, ושומר שכר פטור במת או נשבר או נשבה דהיינו אונסין.

NOTES

מְשׁוּנָּה שְׁלִיחוּת יָד Misappropriation is different. As the Gemara will explain, Rabbi Yose ben Nehorai's point is that the second mention of the law of misappropriation appears superfluous, and can only have been included to teach us some regulation which we would otherwise not have known — namely, that misappropriation does not require loss. The use of the term מְשׁוּנָּה — "different" — to convey this idea is somewhat unusual. The Rishonim explain that it has two connotations: (1) that the second mention of misappropriation is not needed to teach us the law taught by the first, and (2) that the second mention of misappropriation teaches us a new law not taught by the first — namely, that misappropriation does not require loss (see *Rashi* and others).

TRANSLATION AND COMMENTARY

וּמַאי מְשׁוּנָּה [1]The Gemara now goes on to explain in detail the two approaches to the Torah's repetition of the law regarding misappropriation. First, Rabbi Yose ben Nehorai explained that the second mention of misappropriation is not merely a repetition, but serves a different purpose. The Gemara asks: **In what way is it different?**

לֹא תֵּאָמֵר שְׁלִיחוּת יָד [2]The Gemara answers: If the two mentions of misappropriation are the same, why is the repetition needed? **The Torah need not have mentioned** the law of **misappropriation in connection with a paid bailee**, [3]**since it could have been inferred** through a *kal vaḥomer* argument **from the case of an unpaid bailee.** [4]The Gemara elaborates: **If an unpaid bailee is liable for misappropriation,** even though **he is exempt from liability for theft and loss,** [5]**how much more so** should **a paid bailee** be liable for misappropriation, since **he *is* liable for theft and loss.** Because an unpaid bailee has a lower degree of responsibility than a paid bailee, he must compensate the owner only for losses caused by his negligence, and not for losses caused by theft or loss. In contrast, a paid bailee must compensate the owner for any losses unless due to circumstances completely beyond his control. Nevertheless, the Torah tells us that once an unpaid bailee has misappropriated a deposit, he becomes liable for any accidents it may suffer, however caused. Surely, then, there is no need for the Torah to tell us that the same is true of a paid bailee who misappropriates a deposit. [6]Since the law of misappropriation in the case of a paid bailee could have been inferred from the case of the unpaid bailee, **what law** was **the Torah** seeking to teach us when it **wrote** the law of misappropriation in both contexts? [7]The Gemara answers: The Torah repeated the law of misappropriation **to teach you** an additional law — that **misappropriation does not require loss,** so once a bailee picks up a deposit with the intention of taking some of it, he is liable for any accidental damage it may subsequently suffer.

וַאֲנִי אוֹמֵר [8]Having explained the reasoning of Rabbi Yose ben Nehorai, the Gemara now turns to Rabbi Yoḥanan's dissenting view. Rabbi Yoḥanan said: "But I **say** that the two mentions of misappropriation in the Torah **are not different.** It was necessary for the Torah to mention the law of misappropriation in connection with both bailees, so that we should know it applies to both." [9]On this point the Gemara observes: The point of view expressed by Rabbi Yoḥanan is **in accordance with** the opinion of **Rabbi Elazar, who said:** [10]**This and that** — the two mentions of misappropriation — **are the same.** They were both needed in their own contexts, and thus present no opportunity for additional Halakhic derivations.

מַאי דָּא וְדָא אַחַת [11]The Gemara assumes that the reason Rabbi Elazar and Rabbi Yoḥanan are of the opinion that the two mentions of misappropriation are needed in their respective contexts is that they found a flaw in the *kal vaḥomer* argument presented above. Hence, the Gemara asks: **What does "this and that are**

[1]וּמַאי מְשׁוּנָּה? [2]לֹא תֵּאָמֵר שְׁלִיחוּת יָד בְּשׁוֹמֵר שָׂכָר, [3]וְתֵיתֵי מִשּׁוֹמֵר חִנָּם: [4]וּמַה שׁוֹמֵר חִנָּם, שֶׁפָּטוּר בִּגְנֵבָה וַאֲבֵדָה, שָׁלַח בָּהּ יָד חַיָּיב, [5]שׁוֹמֵר שָׂכָר, שֶׁחַיָּיב בִּגְנֵבָה וַאֲבֵידָה, לֹא כׇּל שֶׁכֵּן. [6]לְמַאי הִלְכְתָא כָּתְבִינְהוּ רַחֲמָנָא? [7]לוֹמַר לָךְ: שְׁלִיחוּת יָד אֵינָהּ צְרִיכָה חִסָּרוֹן.

[8]״וַאֲנִי אוֹמֵר: אֵינָהּ מְשׁוּנָּה״. [9]כְּרַבִּי אֶלְעָזָר, דְּאָמַר: [10]דָּא וְדָא אַחַת הִיא.

[11]מַאי ״דָּא וְדָא אַחַת״?

LITERAL TRANSLATION

[1]And [in] what [way] is it different?

[2]Let misappropriation not be stated in connection with a paid bailee, [3]and it may be inferred (lit., "it will come") from [the case of] an unpaid bailee: [4]If an unpaid bailee, who is exempt [from liability] for theft and loss, is liable [if] he misappropriated it, [5]a paid bailee, who is liable for theft and loss, how much more so. [6]For what reason (lit., "law") did the Torah (lit., "the Merciful One") write them? [7]To tell you: Misappropriation does not require loss.

[8]"But I say: It is not different." [9]In accordance with Rabbi Elazar, who said: [10]This and that are the same.

[11]What [does] "this and that are the same" [mean]?

RASHI

שומר חנם שפטור — כל זמן שלא שלח בה יד, כדכתיב ״אם לא ימצא הגנב ונקרב בעל הבית״, דנשבע שלא שלח בה יד, ולא פשע בשמירתו, ופטור. כדאמרינן לקמן בשמעתין דהאי ״ונקרב״ שבועה הוא. **שומר שכר שחייב בגנבה ואבדה** — דפרשה שניה בו נאמרה, וכתיב בה ״אם גנב יגנב כו׳״. **לא כל שכן** — שאם שלח בה יד חייב באונסין. **דא ודא אחת היא** — כמשמעה של זו כך משמעה של זו, לפי ששתיהן הוצרכו, ואין כאן מקרא יתר. **מאי דא ודא אחת היא** — למה שתיהן שוות, הלא לא הוצרכה השניה.

HALAKHAH

שׁוֹמֵר חִנָּם, שֶׁפָּטוּר בִּגְנֵבָה וַאֲבֵדָה An unpaid bailee who is exempt from liability for theft or loss. "If a deposit is lost or stolen from the custody of an unpaid bailee, he must take an oath that he did not misappropriate it, or cause its loss through negligence. If he is able to take the oath, he is exempt from paying for the loss. If not, he must pay." (*Shulḥan Arukh, Ḥoshen Mishpat* 291:1.)

¹מִשּׁוּם דְּאִיכָּא לְמִפְרַךְ: ²מַה לְשׁוֹמֵר חִנָּם שֶׁכֵּן מְשַׁלֵּם תַּשְׁלוּמֵי כֵפֶל בְּטוֹעֵן טַעֲנַת גַּנָּב. ³וּמַאן דְּלָא פָּרֵיךְ סָבַר: ⁴קַרְנָא בְּלָא שְׁבוּעָה עֲדִיפָא מִכְּפֵילָא בִּשְׁבוּעָה.

LITERAL TRANSLATION

[1]Because it is possible to refute [the previous argument]: [2]What is [special] about an unpaid bailee is that he pays the double payment where he claims a claim of a thief.

[3]And the one who does not refute [it] maintains: [4]The principal without an oath is better than the double payment with an oath.

TRANSLATION AND COMMENTARY

the same" mean? What is the flaw in the *kal vahomer* argument?

מִשּׁוּם דְּאִיכָּא לְמִפְרַךְ [1]The Gemara answers: The reason why Rabbi Elazar maintains that the two mentions of misappropriation are needed in their respective contexts is **because it is possible to refute the previous** *kal vahomer* **argument** as follows: The entire argument was based on the assumption that the responsibilities of a paid bailee are greater than those of an unpaid bailee. But there is an aspect of the laws of bailees in which the unpaid bailee has a greater responsibility than the paid bailee. [2]**What is special about an unpaid bailee is that he has to make the double payment when he** falsely **claims** on oath that the object in his care has been **stolen.** If an unpaid bailee swears that the deposit in his care has been stolen, he need not pay the owner for it. However, if witnesses subsequently prove that the deposit was not stolen, and that the bailee was using this false claim in order to keep the deposit for himself, then the bailee must make the double payment to the owner. This penalty applies only if the unpaid bailee took an oath in court that the deposit was stolen. By contrast, a paid bailee cannot exempt himself from responsibility by claiming theft. Hence, it is impossible for a paid bailee to deprive the owner of his deposit by swearing falsely that it was stolen. Consequently, a paid bailee can never become liable for the double payment for theft. As there are circumstances under which a paid bailee is less liable than an unpaid bailee, the assumption which formed the basis of the *kal vahomer* argument is refuted. Thus, if the Torah had mentioned misappropriation only in connection with the unpaid bailee, we might have thought that this rule, like the rule of the double payment for theft, does not apply to paid bailees. Therefore the Torah had to repeat the law about misappropriation — not to teach us anything new, but to clarify that it applies to all bailees equally.

וּמַאן דְּלָא פָּרֵיךְ סָבַר [3]Having explained the view of Rabbi Yohanan and Rabbi Elazar, the Gemara returns to the view of Rabbi Yose ben Nehorai and Levi. How do they respond to this refutation of the *kal vahomer* argument? The Gemara answers: Rabbi Yose ben Nehorai, **who does not accept the refutation** of the *kal vahomer* argument, **maintains:** [4]**The principal**, which the paid bailee is obliged to pay even **without** taking **an oath, is a more serious** penalty **than the double payment** that the unpaid bailee is obliged to make if witnesses prove he has taken **a** false **oath.** The double payment is imposed for swearing falsely that the deposit was stolen. The only reason the paid bailee is not subject to this penalty is because we do not give him the opportunity to exempt himself from payment by swearing that the deposit was stolen. Thus, the real difference

RASHI

שומר חנם שפוטר עצמו בטענת גנב — כלומר, גנב גנבה ממני, ובאו עדים שהיא אצלו — משלם תשלומי כפל, דכתיב "אם לא ימצא הגנב וגו'" ודרשינן בבבא קמא (סג,ב): "אם לא ימצא" כמה שאמר, אלא שהוא עצמו גנבו, מה כתיב אחריו "אשר ירשיעון אלהים ישלם שנים". אבל שומר שכר אינו משלם כפל, שאם טען נגנבה — משלם קרן, שהרי הוא חייב בגניבה, וטענה אחרת אינה מביאה אותו לידי כפל. **קרנא בלא שבועה עדיפא מכפילא בשבועה** — חמור שומר שכר שחייב בקרן עד שלא נשבע לשקר, במקום ששומר חנם פטור, דהיינו גניבה ואבידה, משומר חנם שמשלם כפל, ומדה זו אינה אלא לאחר שנשבע לשקר שנגנבה, ובאו עדים שהוא גנבה, דכי אתרבי כפל בטוען טענת גנב — לאחר שבועה אתרבי, כדלקמן בשמעתין.

BACKGROUND

קַרְנָא בְּלָא שְׁבוּעָה... The principal without an oath.... The differences of opinion regarding this question are connected to differences in approach regarding how it is possible to refute an *a fortiori* deduction (קַל וָחוֹמֶר).

The approach taken by Rabbi Yohanan and Rabbi Elazar is a formal one: Since we have found a stringency connected with the less serious of the two cases (the קַל) which is not mentioned in connection with the more serious one (the חוֹמֶר — in the present case, the double payment when the bailee advances the claim of theft), it is impossible to use this method of deduction.

In contrast, the other approach maintains that one must analyze the source of the stringency regarding an unpaid bailee. Upon doing so, one discovers that the source of the stringency was not some quality inherent in the status of the unpaid bailee, but rather in the leniency available to him, that he is permitted "to advance the claim of a theft."

Nevertheless, one can also understand the position of those who argue that this is not a refutation of the formal argument. Since we are attempting to evaluate the severity of the two cases, it can be said that the certain payment of the sum deposited, without the defendant's resorting to taking an oath or a proof of fraud being advanced by the claimant, is a more serious penalty than the double payment, which is not at all certain (see earlier in this chapter with regard to the thief's double payment).

NOTES

קַרְנָא בְּלָא שְׁבוּעָה The principal without an oath. *Rashi* in tractate *Bava Kamma* (57b) explains that the double payment penalty is imposed on the unpaid bailee for swearing falsely, and does not really reflect on the degree of his liability vis-à-vis the depositor. *Rashi* here emphasizes a slightly different point. The original *kal vahomer* argument dealt with a bailee who claimed that the deposit had been stolen. In such a case, an unpaid bailee is exempt upon taking an oath, whereas a paid bailee is liable. This is the basis of the *kal vahomer* argument. The objection to this *kal vahomer* argument is that in this case, where the bailee claims the deposit has been stolen, the unpaid bailee may be forced to make the double payment, whereas the paid bailee pays only once. The response to the objection is that the double-payment penalty is imposed only if the deposit was not really stolen, and the bailee ought to have paid for it but instead swore falsely to exempt himself.

עֲדִיפָא מִכְּפֵילָא בִּשְׁבוּעָה Is more serious than the double

HALAKHAH

מְשַׁלֵּם תַּשְׁלוּמֵי כֵפֶל בְּטוֹעֵן טַעֲנַת גַּנָּב He pays the double payment where he claims a claim of a thief. "If an unpaid bailee takes an oath that a deposit has been stolen, and witnesses testify that the oath was false and that the bailee

TRANSLATION AND COMMENTARY

between the bailees is that a paid bailee must pay for theft, whereas an unpaid bailee can exempt himself with an oath. Hence, the fact that the unpaid bailee may ultimately have to make the double payment does not change the fact that the paid bailee is always held more responsible than the unpaid bailee, and therefore the *kal vahomer* argument is valid.

רָבָא אָמַר [1]**Rava said:** Even according to the viewpoint of Rabbi Elazar, who is of the opinion that the law with regard to misappropriation in the case of a paid bailee cannot be deduced from the law with regard to misappropriation mentioned in the case of an unpaid bailee, it is still possible to derive from the text that misappropriation does not require loss. Neither in the case of the unpaid bailee nor in that of the paid bailee is it necessary for the Torah to state the law with regard to misappropriation. Rava explains: The Torah **need not have mentioned** the law of **misappropriation** at all, [2]**neither in connection with an unpaid bailee, nor in connection with a paid bailee,** [3]**for** this law **could have been inferred** through a *kal vahomer* argument **from the case of a borrower.** A borrower is liable for any accidents that the borrowed item suffers while it is in his possession, however caused. Hence, his degree of liability is the same as that of a bailee who has misappropriated a deposit. Now, a bailee who misappropriates a deposit is also in a sense borrowing it. The main difference between someone who borrows an object and someone who misappropriates it is that the borrower has the permission of the owner, whereas the person who misappropriates it does not. But surely this is no cause for leniency with the person who misappropriates it! [4]Hence, we may argue as follows: **If a borrower, who acts with the owner's consent, is** nevertheless **liable for** accidental losses incurred subsequent to his **making use of** the borrowed object, [5]**how much more so should an unpaid bailee and a paid bailee,** who were not authorized to use the deposit, be liable for making use of the deposit and misappropriating it! Thus even Rabbi Elazar should accept Rava's reasoning

[1]רָבָא אָמַר: לֹא תֵּאָמֵר שְׁלִיחוּת יָד, [2]לֹא בְּשׁוֹמֵר חִנָּם וְלֹא בְּשׁוֹמֵר שָׂכָר, [3]וְתֵיתֵי מִשּׁוֹאֵל: [4]וּמַה שׁוֹאֵל, דִּלְדַעַת בְּעָלִים קָא עָבֵיד, שָׁלַח בָּהּ יָד חַיָּיב, [5]שׁוֹמֵר חִנָּם וְשׁוֹמֵר שָׂכָר לֹא כָּל שֶׁכֵּן.

LITERAL TRANSLATION

[1]Rava said: Let misappropriation not be stated, [2]neither in connection with an unpaid bailee nor in connection with a paid bailee, [3]and it may be inferred from [the case of] a borrower: [4]If a borrower, who acts with the owner's consent, is liable [if] he misappropriates it, [5]an unpaid bailee and a paid bailee how much more so.

RASHI

רבא אמר – אפילו לרבי אלעזר נמי אתיא, דלא תימא כו׳. **ותיתי משואל** – שחייבו הכתוב באונסין בשביל שכל הנאה שלו, ושולח יד נמי כל הנאה שלו. **(ומה שואל) שלדעת בעלים** – שלח בה יד לעשות מלאכתו חייב באונסין. **שומר חנם ושומר שכר** – השולחין יד, שעושין מלאכתן שלא לדעת בעלים, לא כל שכן דחייב שוב באונסיה.

NOTES

payment with an oath. The Gemara explains below (94b) that the Torah describes two different sets of laws regarding bailees (Exodus 22:6-8 and Exodus 22:9-12), without specifying which applies to paid bailees and which to unpaid bailees. It seems obvious that the more lenient laws should deal with an unpaid bailee and the more strict with a paid bailee. But each set of laws has an element of strictness and an element of leniency. In one set, the bailee is exempt from paying for theft, but is subject to the penalty of the double payment if he swears falsely, whereas in the other set of laws, the bailee must pay for theft, but need not make the double payment. Hence the Gemara asks: How do we know which set of laws applies to which bailee? And the Gemara answers: Having to pay the principal without taking an oath is more serious than having to make the double payment after swearing falsely.

On this point the Rishonim ask: We see that this argument is basic to our understanding of the laws of bailees. How then can it be the subject of a dispute between Rabbi Yoḥanan and Rabbi Yose ben Nehorai?

Tosafot offers two answers: In the first, in the name of *Rashbam*, he argues that Rabbi Yoḥanan is of the opinion that the imposition of the double payment after the oath is more severe than the immediate payment of the principal, and that the language of the verses already suggests that the first set of laws deals with an unpaid bailee and the second with a paid bailee.

Most Rishonim follow the second explanation of *Tosafot*. According to this view, even Rabbi Yoḥanan would agree that paying the principal without an oath is more severe than making the double payment after an oath. However, a *kal vahomer* argument must be logically flawless, and Rabbi Yoḥanan was of the opinion that the presence of a strict element in the laws of unpaid bailees is sufficient to refute the argument, even though it is obvious that the laws of paid bailees are on the whole much stricter than those of unpaid bailees (see *Ramban*, *Rashba*, and others).

וְתֵיתֵי מִשּׁוֹאֵל And it may be inferred from the case of a borrower. Our commentary follows *Rashi* and most Rishonim, who explain that the *kal vahomer* inference

HALAKHAH

himself has taken the deposit, the bailee is subject to all the penalties that apply to thieves. Thus, he must return the deposit and pay a double payment, and if the deposit was a sheep or an ox, and the bailee sold it or slaughtered it, he must pay fourfold or fivefold compensation. This penalty applies only if the bailee took an oath that the deposit was stolen. If he took a false oath that it was seized by a robber, or was lost, or died, or if he did not take an oath at all but merely made a false claim in court, he need only pay for the deposit once, and is not subject to the double payment." (*Rambam, Sefer Nezikin, Hilkhot Genevah* 4:1,3.)

TRANSLATION AND COMMENTARY

and derive all the laws of misappropriation from the laws of borrowers.

לָמָּה נֶאֱמַר [1]But if so, **why was** the law of misappropriation **said** in the Torah at all? It was surely superfluous both in the context of the unpaid bailee and in the context of the paid bailee!

חֲדָא [2]Rava answers: The law of misappropriation was mentioned **once, in order to teach us that misappropriation does not require loss.** [3]**And the other** mention was needed **so that we should not say** that since we are deriving this law from a *kal vaḥomer* inference, [4]**it is sufficient for what is deduced to be like what it is deduced from.** In other words, the law derived by *kal vaḥomer* inference cannot have a more severe application than the original law from which it was derived. In our case, if we were to derive the laws of misappropriation by unpaid and paid bailees from the laws governing borrowers, the bailee would not be liable if he misappropriated the deposit in circumstances where the borrower would be exempt. Specifically, a person who borrows an article from an employee is exempt from liability (Exodus 22:14). This is called "borrowing an object in the owner's presence" (see below, 94a). But if we were to derive the laws of misappropriation by unpaid and paid bailees from the laws governing borrowers, we would say: [5]**Just as a borrower in the owner's presence is exempt,** [6]**so too an unpaid bailee and a paid bailee** who misappropriate an object **in the owner's presence** should be **exempt,** and thus an employer who agrees to look after his employee's property and then misappropriates it would not be liable for subsequent accidental damage to it. Therefore the Torah mentioned the law of misappropriation a second time, so that we would understand that there is no such exemption, and employers are as liable as anyone else for misappropriation. Thus, the Torah mentioned misappropriation twice to teach us two details that we could not have derived from the laws of borrowers: (1) that misappropriation does not require loss, and (2) that it applies even when the bailee is the depositor's employer.

וּלְמַאן דְּאָמַר [7]Having explained the Torah's repetition of the law of misappropriation according to the viewpoint of Rabbi Yose ben Nehorai, who maintains that misappropriation does not require loss, Rava now explains it according to the viewpoint of Rabbi Yoḥanan and Rav. **According to** Rabbi Yoḥanan, **who says** that **misappropriation requires loss,** [8]**why do we need these two mentions of misappropriation** in the Torah? Why not derive this law from the law of borrowers, using a *kal vaḥomer* argument?

[1]לָמָּה נֶאֱמַר? [2]חֲדָא, לוֹמַר לָךְ שְׁלִיחוּת יָד אֵין צְרִיכָה חִסָּרוֹן. [3]וְאִידָךְ: שֶׁלֹּא תֹּאמַר: [4]דַּיּוֹ לַבָּא מִן הַדִּין לִהְיוֹת כַּנִּידּוֹן: [5]מַה שּׁוֹאֵל בִּבְעָלִים פָּטוּר, [6]אַף שׁוֹמֵר חִנָּם וְשׁוֹמֵר שָׂכָר בִּבְעָלִים פָּטוּר. [7]וּלְמַאן דְּאָמַר: שְׁלִיחוּת יָד צְרִיכָה חִסָּרוֹן, [8]הָנֵי תַּרְתֵּי שְׁלִיחוּת יָד לָמָּה לִי?

LITERAL TRANSLATION

[1]Why was it said?

[2]One, to tell you [that] misappropriation does not require loss. [3]And the other: So that you should not say: [4]It is sufficient for the conclusion inferred to be like the source of the inference: [5]Just as a borrower in the owner['s presence] is exempt, [6]so too an unpaid bailee and a paid bailee in the owner['s presence] is exempt.

[7]And according to the one who says: Misappropriation requires loss, [8]why do I need these two [mentions of] misappropriation?

RASHI

למה נאמרה — בשתיהן. **חדא לומר לך שליחות יד אינה צריכה חסרון ואידך** — האמורה בשומר שכר. **שלא תאמר דיו לבא כו׳** — אם לא נאמרה בשאר שומרין, ולמדה משואל, הייתי אומר: דיו לשליחות יד דשומרין, שבא מדין שואל, להיות כנדון. **מה שואל** — אם בעליו עמו כתיב "לא ישלם" אונסין, אף שומרין ששלחו יד אם בעליו עמו יפטר, כתב קרא יתירא לחייבו אפילו בבעלים, וגלי רחמנא בחדא, והוא הדין בכולהו.

BACKGROUND

דַּיּוֹ לַבָּא מִן הַדִּין It is sufficient for the conclusion inferred. This principle of Halakhic Midrash is one of the most basic, for it defines and delimits the applicability of the *a fortiori* approach, which is one of the most widely accepted hermeneutical principles. The דַּיּוֹ rule is so basic that the Sages found explicit proof of its use in the Torah itself, where we find both the use of *a fortiori* argument and its restriction, applying the principle of דַּיּוֹ (see the lengthy discussion in *Bava Kamma,* 25a).

The דַּיּוֹ rule states that if a certain stringent law is found in case A, and a *kal vaḥomer* is drawn from case A to a more stringent case B, then we may not be more stringent in case B with regard to this law than we are in case A, even though case B is usually stricter than case A. In other words, the stringency of case A is the maximum stringency in respect to this law.

NOTES

proceeds from the law of a borrower to the case of misappropriation. The basis of the argument is that misappropriation is a special case of borrowing without permission. Thus its liability cannot be any less than that of a borrower *with* permission, who is liable even for damage due to circumstances beyond his control.

Ra'avad points out that this passage supports his contention that for a bailee misappropriation and borrowing without permission are one and the same.

Rabbenu Ḥananel has a different interpretation, according to which the inference is from a case of misappropriation by a borrower. The concept of misappropriation does not actually appear in the Torah verses dealing with borrowers (Exodus 22:13-14). It is derived from the laws of paid and unpaid bailees. According to *Rabbenu Ḥananel,* Rava's argument is: "Why did the Torah need to write the law of misappropriation in the case of paid and unpaid bailees? It should rather have written it in the case of the borrower, and we would then apply a *kal vaḥomer* argument to deduce that it applies to the other bailees as well."

TRANSLATION AND COMMENTARY

חֲדָא שֶׁלֹּא תֹאמַר [1]Rava answers: The law of misappropriation was mentioned **once so that we should not say:** [2]**It is sufficient for what is deduced to be like** what **it is deduced from.** We must not conclude that the exemption applying to someone who borrows something in its owner's presence applies also to a paid or unpaid bailee who misappropriated his employee's deposit. [3]**And the other** mention of misappropriation was necessary to teach us the law **that** is taught in **the** following **Baraita:** The Baraita comments on the verse dealing with the case of the unpaid bailee (Exodus 22:7): [4]"'**And the master of the house** (the unpaid bailee) **shall be brought to the judges** to see whether he has misappropriated his neighbor's goods.' The expression 'shall be brought to the judges' refers to the imposition by the judges **of an oath.**" [5]The Baraita now supports this explanation: "**You say** that the bailee is brought to the judges **'for an oath.'** [6]**But might** the verse **not mean** that the bailee is brought to the judges **for judgment?**" In other words, do the laws prescribed in this passage — the unpaid bailee's exemption from liability for theft and loss, and the double payment prescribed in verse 8 where witnesses testify against him — apply only after the bailee swears falsely, or do they apply even if he lies in court and is contradicted by witnesses without swearing falsely? [7]The Baraita reasons as follows: "The law of **misappropriation is mentioned below,** in verse 10, **and** the law of **misappropriation is mentioned above,** in verse 7. [8]**Just as** in verse 10 **the Torah refers** explicitly **to an oath** — 'an oath of the Lord shall be between them both' — [9]**so too here,** in verse 7, **it refers to an oath,** and not just to judgment." The Baraita is applying an exegetical rule called *gezerah shavah*. According to this rule, if the same word appears in two different verses, the same law may be applied in both cases. Specifically, the procedure regarding paid and unpaid bailees is the same, and both must take an oath to be subject to their respective exemptions and penalties. Thus we see that the Torah needed to write the law of misappropriation a second time so that we could use a *gezerah shavah* to infer: (1) that an unpaid bailee makes the double payment only if he has sworn falsely that the deposit has been stolen and then witnesses testify that the deposit is still in his possession, and (2) that if an unpaid bailee takes an oath that the deposit has been stolen or lost, and no witnesses contradict him, he is exempt from payment.

[1]חֲדָא, שֶׁלֹּא תֹאמַר: [2]דַּיּוֹ לַבָּא מִן הַדִּין לִהְיוֹת כַּנִּדּוֹן. [3]וְאִידָךְ, לִכְדְתַנְיָא: [4]"'וְנִקְרַב בַּעַל הַבַּיִת אֶל הָאֱלֹהִים' לִשְׁבוּעָה. [5]אַתָּה אוֹמֵר 'לִשְׁבוּעָה', [6]אוֹ אֵינוֹ אֶלָּא לְדִין? [7]נֶאֶמְרָה שְׁלִיחוּת יָד לְמַטָּה, וְנֶאֶמְרָה שְׁלִיחוּת יָד לְמַעְלָה. [8]מַה לְּהַלָּן לִשְׁבוּעָה, [9]אַף כָּאן לִשְׁבוּעָה".

LITERAL TRANSLATION

[1]One, so that you should not say: [2]It is sufficient for the conclusion inferred to be like the source of inference. [3]And the other, for that which was taught: [4]"'And the master of the house shall be brought to the judges' for an oath. [5]You say 'for an oath,' [6]but might it not be for judgment? [7]Misappropriation is mentioned below, and misappropriation is mentioned above. [8]Just as below [the Torah refers] to an oath, [9]so too here [it refers] to an oath."

RASHI

לשבועה – והכי קאמר. אם לא ימצא כמה שאמר שנגנבה אלא הוא גנבה, והוא כבר נקרב אל הדיינין לשבועה ונשבע לשקר, ואחר כך באו עדים, אשר ירשיעון הדיינין, ישלם כפל. **אתה אומר** – קריבה לשבועה, או אינו אלא קריבה לדין, שמשעה שטען בבית דין נגנבה, אף על פי שלא נשבע ישלם כפל אם באו עדים. **נאמר שליחות יד למטה** – אצל שומר שכר "שבועת ה' תהיה בין שניהם אם לא שלח". **ונאמר שליחות יד למעלה** – "ונקרב בעל הבית אל האלהים אם לא שלח". **אף כאן לשבועה** – למדנו שאין משלמין כפל על ידי טענת גנב אלא לאחר שבועה, וגם למדנו שנפטר מגנבה ואבדה בשבועה.

NOTES

וְאִידָךְ לִכְדְתַנְיָא And the other for that which was taught. The Baraita itself is not in dispute, and is accepted by both Rabbi Yoḥanan and Rabbi Yose ben Nehorai. It is based on an exegetical rule of verbal analogy called *gezerah shavah*, according to which two passages containing the same word are understood to be subject to the same laws. This form of exegesis is not based on logic and can be applied only when there is a tradition that the words in question are to be used to form a *gezerah shavah*. Nevertheless, even when there is such a tradition, it is normally required that the words in question be "available," i.e., apparently superfluous and not used for any other exegetical purpose.

Hence *Tosafot* asks: One of the two references to misappropriation is not "available" according to either Rabbi Yose ben Nehorai or Rabbi Yoḥanan. It is needed to teach us that "we do not say in this context that it is sufficient for what is deduced to be like what it is deduced from." Moreover, according to Rabbi Yose ben Nehorai, who maintains that misappropriation does not require loss, we need both references to misappropriation — one to teach us not to say "It is sufficient...," and one to teach us that misappropriation does not require loss. How then can a *gezerah shavah* be constructed here?

Tosafot answers that the precise repetition of all six words in each of the two references to misappropriation is sufficiently striking to form the basis of a *gezerah shavah* argument. *Ritva*, however, suggests that when there is a strong tradition that a *gezerah shavah* argument is applied, it is not absolutely necessary for there to be superfluous words "available" for such exegesis.

BACKGROUND

שֶׁלֹּא שִׁימֵּר כְּדֶרֶךְ הַשּׁוֹמְרִים **Since he did not safeguard it in the manner of bailees.** When an object is deposited with a bailee — even a paid bailee — one does not expect him to keep it under special surveillance, or to remain awake constantly in order to watch over it. One assumes that the bailee will look after the deposit in a reasonable fashion according to its nature and value. If he does so, this is sufficient. However, if the care exercised by the bailee was insufficient or inappropriate (depending on the deposit's nature: an animal must be tended so that it will not run away, precious objects must be kept in a safe place so they will not be stolen, etc.), this constitutes negligence on his part, and even an unpaid bailee becomes liable.

יְהִיוּ בְּיָדְךָ **It should be in your hand.** This stipulation applies to money, which is valuable and relatively easy to steal. When a person lets a purse full of money hang down behind his back, thieves can approach him and find an opportunity to cut the strap and steal the purse or open it and remove the money. Therefore the only proper way of guarding money is by keeping it in one's hands.

SAGES

רַבִּי יִצְחָק **Rabbi Yitzhak.** A Palestinian Amora of the second and third generations. See above, pp. 4-5.

TRANSLATION AND COMMENTARY

[42A] **MISHNAH** הַמַּפְקִיד מָעוֹת אֵצֶל חֲבֵרוֹ [1]If **someone deposited money with another person, and** the bailee **bundled it up** in a piece of cloth **and threw** the bundle **over his shoulder,** and on his way home the money was lost, [2]**or** if the bailee **gave** the money **to his minor son or daughter** to look after, and **locked the door in front of them insecurely,** [3]in either case the bailee **is liable** if the money was lost or stolen, **since he** was negligent and **did not look after it in the manner** expected **of bailees.** [4]**But if he looked after** the money **in the manner** expected **of bailees,** and it was nevertheless lost or stolen, **he is exempt,** because an unpaid bailee need not reimburse a depositor for damage caused by theft or loss unless his own negligence was a contributory factor.

GEMARA בִּשְׁלָמָא כּוּלְּהוּ [5]The Gemara asks: **All of the cases** described in the Mishnah **are reasonable, because** it is clear that the bailee **did not** look after the deposit **in the manner** expected **of bailees.** [6]**But where** the bailee **bundled up** the money **and threw it over his shoulder, what** more **should he have done?** He had to carry it somehow while taking it home!

אָמַר רָבָא אָמַר רַבִּי יִצְחָק [7]In reply, **Rava said in the name of Rabbi Yitzhak:** [8]**The verse** (Deuteronomy 14:25) **says** with reference to money used to redeem second-tithe produce that must be brought to Jerusalem: **"And you shall bind up the money in your hand."** [9]From here we may infer that when circumstances demand that you carry money with you, **even though** you make sure that **it is bound** securely, **it should be in your hand** or bound in front of you, and nowhere else. Thus the way the bailee carried the money — slung over his shoulder — was in itself negligent, and he must bear responsibility if the money was stolen or lost.

[42A] **משנה** [1]הַמַּפְקִיד מָעוֹת אֵצֶל חֲבֵרוֹ, צְרָרָן וְהִפְשִׁילָן לַאֲחוֹרָיו, [2]אוֹ שֶׁמְּסָרָם לִבְנוֹ וּלְבִתּוֹ הַקְּטַנִּים וְנָעַל בִּפְנֵיהֶם שֶׁלֹּא כָּרָאוּי, [3]חַיָּיב, שֶׁלֹּא שִׁימֵּר כְּדֶרֶךְ הַשּׁוֹמְרִים, [4]וְאִם שִׁימֵּר כְּדֶרֶךְ הַשּׁוֹמְרִים, פָּטוּר.

גמרא [5]בִּשְׁלָמָא כּוּלְּהוּ, שֶׁלֹּא שִׁימֵּר כְּדֶרֶךְ הַשּׁוֹמְרִים. [6]אֶלָּא צְרָרָן וְהִפְשִׁילָן לַאֲחוֹרָיו, מַאי הֲוָה לֵיהּ לְמֶיעֱבַד?

[7]אָמַר רָבָא אָמַר רַבִּי יִצְחָק: [8]אָמַר קְרָא: ״וְצַרְתָּ הַכֶּסֶף בְּיָדְךָ״. [9]אַף עַל פִּי שֶׁצְּרוּרִין, יְהִיוּ בְּיָדְךָ.

LITERAL TRANSLATION

[42A] **MISHNAH** [1]Someone who deposits money with his fellow, [if] he bundled it up and threw it behind him, [2][or] if he gave it to his minor son or daughter and locked [the door] in front of them inadequately, [3]he is liable, since he did not safeguard [it] in the manner of bailees. [4]But if he safeguarded [it] in the manner of bailees, he is exempt.

GEMARA [5]Granted [in] all of them, for he did not safeguard [it] in the manner of bailees. [6]But [if] he bundled it up and threw it behind him, what [else] should he have done?

[7]Rava said in the name of Rabbi Yitzhak: [8]The verse says: "And you shall bind up the money in your hand." [9]Even though it is bound, it should be in your hand.

RASHI

משנה צררן — בסודרו, והפשילן לאחוריו.

גמרא מאי הוה ליה למיעבד — הרי צררן.

NOTES

וְנָעַל בִּפְנֵיהֶם **And locked the door in front of them.** Our commentary follows *Rashi,* who explains that the case of the unlocked door and the case of the minor children are one and the same. According to this interpretation, the bailee can fulfill his obligations by leaving the money in a properly locked house, with minor children standing guard to raise the alarm if thieves break in. However, if the bailee left the children to stand guard without locking the door properly, or if he locked the door and did not leave anyone in the house, he would be liable.

Rif and other Rishonim have a reading in the Mishnah which says "or locked the door," implying that the case of the unlocked door is distinct from the case of the minor children. This explanation also finds support in the Jerusalem Talmud. The difficulty is that this interpretation implies that if the money was left unguarded in the house and the house was locked properly, the bailee would be exempt. But the Gemara later rules that money must be buried in the ground or in a wall, and not merely left in a locked house. To answer this objection, *Rosh* suggests that the Mishnah is

HALAKHAH

שְׁמִירַת כְּסָפִים בְּדֶרֶךְ **Safeguarding money while traveling.** "A bailee who accepts a deposit of money from another person, and needs to carry it home with him, must bundle it up and carry it in his hand, or tie the bundle in front of him in such a way that he can see it. If he does not do this and the money is lost — even if the money was not stolen but was lost as a result of forces beyond his control — he is liable, as his initial action amounted to negligence," following the Mishnah. (*Shulhan Arukh, Hoshen Mishpat* 291:20.)

אוֹ שֶׁמְּסָרָם לִבְנוֹ וּלְבִתּוֹ הַקְּטַנִּים **Or if he gave it to his minor son or daughter.** "If the bailee gave the deposit to his minor sons or daughters to guard, he is liable for any damage that may befall it." (Ibid., 291:21.)

TRANSLATION AND COMMENTARY

וְאָמַר רַבִּי יִצְחָק [1]Having opened the discussion with one statement by Rabbi Yitzḥak, the Gemara now proceeds to cite a series of his statements on related topics: **Rabbi Yitzḥak also said: A person's money should always be ready at hand.** He should not deposit all his money with other people and thus leave himself without ready cash. Rabbi Yitzḥak points out that an allusion to this piece of advice may be found in the verse quoted above, [2]**in which it is said: "And you shall bind up the money in your hand,"** which can be taken to mean that a person's money should always be readily available to him.

וְאָמַר רַבִּי יִצְחָק [3]**Rabbi Yitzḥak also said:** It is a good idea for **a person always to divide his money into three parts:** [4]**One-third** should be invested **in land,** which is a safe form of investment. [5]**One-third** should be invested **in business,** which is often profitable but carries a higher risk. [6]And **one-third** should be kept **in hand,** to take advantage of an unforeseen business opportunity or in case of emergency.

וְאָמַר רַבִּי יִצְחָק [7]**Rabbi Yitzḥak also said:** God's special **blessing is found only in a thing that is hidden from the eye** — i.e., in something that is unseen and unpredictable — [8]**as it is said** in the Torah (Deuteronomy 28:8): **"The Lord will command His blessing upon you in your storehouses."** Rabbi Yitzḥak is making a play on the word "storehouses" (אֲסָמֶיךָ), as if the word meant "hidden things," from the root סמה — "to hide."

תָּנָא דְּבֵי רַבִּי יִשְׁמָעֵאל [9]The Gemara now quotes a slightly different version of the idea expressed by Rabbi Yitzḥak, in which the Scriptural derivation is based on the literal meaning of the word. A Baraita from **the school of Rabbi Yishmael taught: Blessing is found only in a thing that is not exposed** to public view, [10]**as it is said** (ibid.): **"The Lord will command His blessing upon you in your storehouses."** The fact that a person keeps his produce in storehouses will be a source of blessing to him, for such produce is not exposed to public view.

[1]וְאָמַר רַבִּי יִצְחָק: לְעוֹלָם יְהֵא כַּסְפּוֹ שֶׁל אָדָם מָצוּי בְּיָדוֹ, [2]שֶׁנֶּאֱמַר: "וְצַרְתָּ הַכֶּסֶף בְּיָדְךָ". [3]וְאָמַר רַבִּי יִצְחָק: לְעוֹלָם יְשַׁלִּישׁ אָדָם אֶת מָעוֹתָיו: [4]שְׁלִישׁ בְּקַרְקַע, [5]וּשְׁלִישׁ בִּפְרַקְמַטְיָא, [6]וּשְׁלִישׁ תַּחַת יָדוֹ. [7]וְאָמַר רַבִּי יִצְחָק: אֵין הַבְּרָכָה מְצוּיָה אֶלָּא בְּדָבָר הַסָּמוּי מִן הָעַיִן, [8]שֶׁנֶּאֱמַר: "יְצַו ה׳ אִתְּךָ אֶת הַבְּרָכָה בַּאֲסָמֶיךָ". [9]תָּנָא דְּבֵי רַבִּי יִשְׁמָעֵאל: אֵין הַבְּרָכָה מְצוּיָה אֶלָּא בְּדָבָר שֶׁאֵין הָעַיִן שׁוֹלֶטֶת בּוֹ, [10]שֶׁנֶּאֱמַר: "יְצַו ה׳ אִתְּךָ אֶת הַבְּרָכָה בַּאֲסָמֶיךָ".

LITERAL TRANSLATION

[1]And Rabbi Yitzḥak said: A person's money should always be ready in his hand, [2]as it is said: "And you shall bind up the money in your hand."

[3]And Rabbi Yitzḥak said: A person should always divide his money into three parts: [4]one-third in land, [5]one-third in business, [6]and one-third under his hand.

[7]And Rabbi Yitzḥak said: Blessing is found only in a thing that is hidden from the eye, [8]as it is said: "The Lord will command the blessing upon you in your storehouses."

[9]The School of Rabbi Yishmael taught: Blessing is found only in a thing which the eye does not command, [10]as it is said: "The Lord will command the blessing upon you in your storehouses."

RASHI

מצוי בידו – לא יפקידנו לאחרים במקום אחר, שאם תזדמן לו סחורה לשכר יהא מזומן לו. תחת ידו – להיות מזומן לו לצורך ריוח הבא פתאום. אין הברכה – שמתברך ורבה מאליו, *פויישו"ן בלעז. באסמיך – דריש ליה לשון דבר הסמוי מן העין. שאין העין שולטת בו – שנאמר "באסמיך" לשון גנזים.

BAKGROUND

לְעוֹלָם יְשַׁלִּישׁ אָדָם אֶת מָעוֹתָיו **A person should always divide his money into three parts.** The Talmud contains many similar examples of practical advice offered by the Sages. This particular counsel is intended for people of property, and Rabbi Yitzḥak is advising them to diversify their interests so as to make profitable investments and avoid excessive losses. In modern terms this advice means that one should place part of one's capital in low-risk investments such as real estate, although this may not be highly profitable; another part should be invested in more profitable but riskier commercial ventures (even in Talmudic times profits from commerce far exceeded those from agriculture); and a certain percentage should be retained as liquid assets, so that in the event of financial pressure one will not be forced to sell one's property at a loss.

LANGUAGE

פְּרַקְמַטְיָא **Business.** This word is derived from the Greek πραγματεία, *pragmateia*, meaning "business" or "commerce."

LANGUAGE (RASHI)

פויישו"ן* From the Old French *foison*, meaning "increase" or "abundance."

NOTES

referring to a situation where it was impossible to bury the money, such as on the Sabbath. *Rashba* suggests that in the days of the Mishnah, thieves may not have been so prevalent as in the days of the Gemara, and it may have been considered reasonable to leave money in a locked house.

לְעוֹלָם יְשַׁלִּישׁ אָדָם **A person should always divide his money into three parts.** There is a verse which suggests this idea (Deuteronomy 28:8): "The Lord will command the blessing upon you in your storehouses, and in all that you set your hand to, and He will bless you in the land": "In your storehouses" — the money you keep in hand; "in all that you set your hand to" — the money you invest in business; "in the land" — the money you keep in the land. *Maharsha*, followed in our commentary, adds that money "in the land" means money invested in real estate and similar low-risk investments.

שֶׁאֵין הָעַיִן שׁוֹלֶטֶת בּוֹ **Which the eye does not command.** It is not clear if there is any substantial difference in meaning between Rabbi Yitzḥak's version ("hidden from the eye") and the version of the School of Rabbi Yishmael ("which the eye does not command"); *Maharsha* in fact explains that they really mean the same thing. Nevertheless, regarding merchandise that is not exposed to public view, *Rosh* points out that it is considered unwise to do business with large objects such as barrels, since such merchandise attracts too much attention. *Torat Ḥayyim* adds that miracles are normally performed secretly, as it is not

BACKGROUND

תְּפִילַּת שָׁוְא A vain prayer. In tractate *Berakhot* it is explained that anyone who prays for a change in something that has already happened is uttering a vain prayer, for one cannot expect the nature of the world to change for one's sake. Such a prayer is meaningless (שָׁוְא), and can only encourage false hopes.

TRANSLATION AND COMMENTARY

תָּנוּ רַבָּנַן [1]On the same theme of blessings in hidden places, the Gemara quotes another statement of the Sages: **Our Rabbis taught** the following Baraita: **Someone who goes to measure produce in his granary** before separating his tithes **may say** the following prayer: [2]**"May it be Your will, O Lord our God, that You send blessing upon the work of our hands."** [3]**After he has begun to measure, he may say: "Blessed is He who sends blessing upon this pile."** [4]But **if he** has already **measured the produce,** it is too late to recite a blessing along these lines **afterwards, and** if he did **recite** such a **blessing, it is a vain prayer,** [5]**because blessing is not found in something weighed,** [6]**nor in something measured, nor in something counted.** [7]It is only found **in something that is hidden from the eye,** [8]**as it is said** in the verse quoted above: **"The Lord will command His blessing upon you in your storehouses."**

אָמַר שְׁמוּאֵל [9]The Gemara now returns to its analysis of the Mishnah. **Shmuel said: Money can only be looked after** properly by being buried **in the ground.** Hence, if a bailee fails to bury money deposited with him, and the money is then stolen, he is considered negligent.

[1]תָּנוּ רַבָּנַן: הַהוֹלֵךְ לָמוֹד אֶת גּוֹרְנוֹ אוֹמֵר: [2]״יְהִי רָצוֹן מִלְּפָנֶיךָ, ה׳ אֱלֹהֵינוּ, שֶׁתִּשְׁלַח בְּרָכָה בְּמַעֲשֵׂה יָדֵינוּ״. [3]הִתְחִיל לָמוֹד, אוֹמֵר: ״בָּרוּךְ הַשּׁוֹלֵחַ בְּרָכָה בַּכְּרִי הַזֶּה״. [4]מָדַד וְאַחַר כָּךְ בֵּירַךְ, הֲרֵי זֶה תְּפִילַּת שָׁוְא, [5]לְפִי שֶׁאֵין הַבְּרָכָה מְצוּיָה, לֹא בְּדָבָר הַשָּׁקוּל, [6]וְלֹא בְּדָבָר הַמָּדוּד, וְלֹא בְּדָבָר הַמָּנוּי, [7]אֶלָּא בְּדָבָר הַסָּמוּי מִן הָעַיִן, [8]שֶׁנֶּאֱמַר: ״יְצַו ה׳ אִתְּךָ אֶת הַבְּרָכָה בַּאֲסָמֶיךָ״. [9]אָמַר שְׁמוּאֵל: כְּסָפִים אֵין לָהֶם שְׁמִירָה אֶלָּא בַּקַּרְקַע.

LITERAL TRANSLATION

[1]Our Rabbis taught: Someone who goes to measure [produce in] his granary says: [2]"May it be Your will, O Lord our God, that You send blessing upon the work of our hands." [3][After] he has begun to measure, he says: "Blessed is He who sends blessing upon this pile." [4][If] he measured [the produce] and afterwards said a blessing, this is a vain prayer, [5]because blessing is not found, neither in something that is weighed, [6]nor in something that is measured, nor in something that is counted, [7]but [only] in something that is hidden from the eye, [8]as it is said: "The Lord will command the blessing upon you in your storehouses."

[9]Shmuel said: Money has no guarding except in the ground.

RASHI

אין להם שמירה כו׳ — דאם לא טמנן ונגנבו — פשיעה היא.

NOTES

considered appropriate to God's honor for uninvolved bystanders to observe their occurrence. (See, for example, II Kings 4:4.)

הַהוֹלֵךְ לָמוֹד אֶת גּוֹרְנוֹ Someone who goes to measure produce in his granary says.... *Ritva* explains that the blessings prescribed here are recited with the full formula, "Blessed are You, O Lord our God, King of the Universe, etc." The difficulty with this explanation is that formal blessings are normally recited only in relation to definite occurrences, whereas in this case the farmer is praying for special, divine assistance. To resolve this problem, *Ritva* quotes *Ramban*, who explains that this blessing is to be recited only when the farmer is measuring his produce to determine the quantity of tithes to separate, because God promised a blessing to a farmer who tithes his crops (Malachi 3:10).

כְּסָפִים אֵין לָהֶם שְׁמִירָה אֶלָּא בַּקַּרְקַע Money can only be guarded in the ground. The reason for this rule is that money is far more likely to be stolen than other deposits, and can be kept in the ground without danger of corrosion (*Rosh*). Many Rishonim agree with the explanation of *Ri ben Reuven* from Barcelona, based on the Jerusalem Talmud, that this rule depends on the circumstances, and that an unpaid bailee must keep a deposit in the way that most responsible people keep their own valuables (*Rashba, Ramban, Ran, Meiri*). *Meiri* adds that Shmuel may also have been referring to a depositor who was trying to hide his valuables from the authorities, and therefore insisted that they be hidden in a place where they could not be found.

HALAKHAH

תְּפִילָּה לִפְנֵי מְדִידָה Blessings to be recited before measuring produce. "When a person is about to measure the produce in his granary, he should say: 'May it be Your will that You send a blessing on this pile of produce.' Likewise, while actually measuring, he may also recite a blessing: 'Blessed be He who sends a blessing upon this pile of produce.' But if he has completed the measurement, he may no longer recite a blessing. If he does so, it is a vain prayer," following the Gemara. (*Shulḥan Arukh, Oraḥ Ḥayyim* 230:2.)

שְׁמִירַת כְּסָפִים Safeguarding money. "Money and similar valuables can only be looked after properly by burying them in the ground. They must be buried at least one handbreadth (about three-and-a-half inches) in the ground," following the ruling of Rafram, later in the Gemara. "Alternatively, the deposit may be buried one handbreadth deep in a wall, but only in the top handbreadth of the wall next to the ceiling, or in the bottom handbreadth of the wall next to the ground," following the conclusion of the Gemara. (*Shulḥan Arukh, Ḥoshen Mishpat* 291:15.)

LITERAL TRANSLATION

[1]Rava said: And Shmuel agrees regarding the eve of the Sabbath at twilight, [2]that the Rabbis did not trouble him. [3]But if he waited after the end of the Sabbath long enough to bury it and did not bury it, he is liable. [4]But if he [the depositor] was a scholar, [5]he [the bailee] thinks: Perhaps he needs the money for havdalah. [6]But now that money-diviners are common, [7]it can only be guarded in roof beams. [8]And now that roof-breakers are common, [9]it can only be guarded between bricks.

[1]אֲמַר רָבָא: וּמוֹדֵי שְׁמוּאֵל בְּעֶרֶב שַׁבָּת בֵּין הַשְּׁמָשׁוֹת, [2]דְּלָא אַטְרַחוּהוּ רַבָּנַן. [3]וְאִי שְׁהָא לְמוֹצָאֵי שַׁבָּת שִׁיעוּר לְמִקְבְּרִינְהוּ וְלָא קֲבַרִינְהוּ, מִחַיֵּיב. [4]וְאִי צוּרְבָא מֵרַבָּנַן הוּא, [5]סָבַר: דִּלְמָא מִיבָּעֵי לֵיהּ זוּזֵי לְאַבְדַּלְתָּא.
[6]וְהָאִידָּנָא דִּשְׁכִיחִי גְּשׁוּשָׁאֵי, [7]אֵין לָהֶן שְׁמִירָה אֶלָּא בִּשְׁמֵי קוֹרָה.
[8]וְהָאִידָּנָא דִּשְׁכִיחִי פְּרוּמָאֵי, [9]אֵין לָהֶם שְׁמִירָה אֶלָּא בֵּינֵי אוּרְבֵּי.

RASHI

ואם צורבא מרבנן הוא — המפקיד, שהוא חרד על מצות הבדלה על הכוס, אמר השומר דלמא מיבעי ליה זוזי לאבדלתא להכי לא קברינהו ופטור. **גשושאי** — מגששין בקרקע בשפודין של ברזל להכיר מקום שתחתיו חלל. **בשמי קורה** — בגג מתחתיו. **פרומאי** — שוברי התקרה. **ביני אורבי** — בין שורות הבנין בכותל.

TRANSLATION AND COMMENTARY

אֲמַר רָבָא [1]The Gemara now proceeds to qualify Shmuel's ruling: **Rava said: Shmuel agrees that** if a bailee receives money for safekeeping on **the eve of the Sabbath at twilight,** [2]**the Rabbis do not trouble him** to bury the money in the ground immediately. The Sabbath begins at sunset on Friday afternoon. On the Sabbath it is forbidden to dig holes in the ground or to handle money. Thus if a bailee receives money only a few minutes before the Sabbath begins, he cannot be expected to bury it until immediately after the Sabbath, and if the money is stolen during the Sabbath the fact that the bailee did not have time to bury it before the Sabbath is not considered negligence. [3]**But** if the bailee **waits after the end of the Sabbath long enough to bury** the money **and does not bury it,** and the money is then stolen, **he is liable** for negligence. [4]**But if the depositor is a scholar, the bailee** is permitted to wait a while after the Sabbath before burying the money, [5]for he may **think: It is possible** that the depositor **will need the money for the havdalah service.** At the close of the Sabbath, blessings are recited over wine, fragrant spices and the flame of a candle. The scholar who deposited the money just before the Sabbath may need it immediately after the Sabbath to buy wine or a candle. Therefore the bailee is entitled to wait a while after the Sabbath before burying the money.

וְהָאִידָּנָא דִּשְׁכִיחִי גְּשׁוּשָׁאֵי [6]Rava's qualification of Shmuel's ruling is now qualified further: **Nowadays, money-diviners** — thieves who use divining rods to search for money buried in the ground — **are common.** [7]Hence, money **can be kept safe only in** the **roof beams** of a house.

וְהָאִידָּנָא דִּשְׁכִיחִי פְּרוּמָאֵי [8]The Gemara adds a further qualification: **Nowadays, roof-breakers** — thieves who break into roofs to search for objects hidden there — **are common.** [9]Hence, money **can be kept safe only** if it is placed in the space **between bricks** in the wall of a house.

LANGUAGE

צוּרְבָא מֵרַבָּנַן **A Rabbinical scholar.** This is a common term for a scholar (usually a young scholar) in the Talmud, though its source and precise significance are not clear. Some suggest that it derives from the root צרב, meaning something hot, burning with the fire of Torah. Others suggest that it is derived from an Arabic word meaning hard or strong, for indeed a צוּרְבָא מֵרַבָּנַן has a sharp and powerful mind (*Rav Hai Gaon*).

NOTES

דִּלְמָא מִיבָּעֵי לֵיהּ זוּזֵי לְאַבְדַּלְתָּא **Perhaps he needs the money for havdalah.** *Rashi* explains that a scholar is likely to be scrupulous about performing this ritual. The difficulty with this explanation is that the havdalah service is by no means restricted to Talmudic scholars or to individuals of exceptional piety. On the contrary, it is an obligation that is binding on every Jew. *Maggid Mishneh* explains that the Gemara is referring to a place where wine was expensive, so the havdalah service was recited publicly in the synagogue to save money. Nevertheless, a scrupulously pious person might well prefer to recite it over his own cup of wine.

Ra'avad explains that it is the bailee, not the depositor, who is the Rabbinic scholar. Thus the Gemara is ruling that though it is technically permissible to bury money immediately after the Sabbath — even before performing the havdalah service — it is not reasonable to expect this of a Rabbinic scholar. Therefore, if the bailee is a scholar he is not expected to bury the deposit until after he has had time to complete havdalah. Unfortunately, it appears impossible to reconcile *Ra'avad*'s explanation with our texts of the Gemara that speak of the scholar needing the money to perform the service. Hence the Aḥaronim suggest that *Ra'avad* may have had a different reading, though there is no indication what it was (*Leḥem Mishneh*, *Gra*).

HALAKHAH

הַמַּפְקִיד סָמוּךְ לְשַׁבָּת **A deposit made immediately before the Sabbath.** "If a bailee receives a deposit of money immediately before the Sabbath, he is not required to bury it until after the Sabbath. But if he fails to bury it immediately after the end of the Sabbath, he is liable if it is stolen in the meantime. However, if the depositor is a Talmudic scholar (according to the *Rema* in the name of *Tur* and *Ra'avad,* also if the bailee is a Talmudic scholar),

BACKGROUND

רַב אַחָא בְּרֵיהּ דְּרַב יוֹסֵף **Rav Aḥa the son of Rav Yosef.** A Babylonian Amora of the sixth generation, Rav Aḥa, the son of Rav Yosef, was closely associated with Rav Ashi. He frequently asks questions of Rav Ashi, but sometimes supports Rav Ashi's arguments and proofs from the teachings of other Amoraim.

הֲרֵי הוּא כִּמְבוֹעָר **Is considered as if it has been removed.** Before Passover a Jew must remove (לְבָעֵר) all leavened products in his possession. Certain Tannaitic Sages said the only way to remove leaven was to burn it, but other Sages (and this is also the Halakhah) maintained that any method that renders the leavened products impossible to use is sufficient. Therefore they said that if a wall has collapsed on some leavened product, although it may still exist physically, one need take no further action in order to remove it since it cannot actually be used.

TRANSLATION AND COMMENTARY

אָמַר רָבָא [1]The Gemara now returns to Rava's qualification of Shmuel's ruling: **Rava said: Shmuel agrees that** money **can** also **be** adequately **guarded** if it is buried **in a wall,** [2]**or alternatively in the corners** of the house.

וְהָאִידָּנָא דִּשְׁכִיחִי טַפּוּחָאֵי [3]The Gemara now adds a further qualification: **Nowadays, wall-rappers** — thieves who knock on walls to discover if anything has been hidden there — **are common.** [4]Hence, money **can be** kept safe **only in the handbreadth** of the wall closest **to the ground,** where it is impossible to discover hidden objects by knocking, [5]**or in the handbreadth** closest **to the roof beams.**

אֲמַר לֵיהּ רַב אַחָא [6]The Gemara now considers another aspect of Shmuel's ruling that money must be buried in the ground. How deep must it be buried? In order to answer this question the Gemara examines another instance in which the term "buried" appears. **Rav Aḥa, the son of Rav Yosef, said to Rav Ashi:** [7]**We have learned** in a Mishnah in tractate *Pesaḥim* (31b) dealing with the law requiring Jews to remove all ḥametz (leaven) in their possession before the Passover Festival: **"Ḥametz upon which debris has fallen is considered as if it has** already **been removed,** so there is no need to remove it from under the debris. [8]**Rabban Shimon ben Gamliel says: Whatever a dog cannot search for** is considered as if it has been removed." Thus, if ḥametz is buried so deep that a dog cannot find it, it is considered to have been removed. [9]Now, concerning this Mishnah, **a Tanna taught** the following Baraita: **"To what depth does a dog search? Three handbreadths."** [10]Having cited the Mishnah and the Baraita on the subject of ḥametz, Rav Aḥa the son of Rav Yosef now asks: **What is the law** here regarding bailees? [11]**Do they need** to dig to a depth of **three handbreadths** when safeguarding a deposit of money **or not?** Perhaps a depth of less than three handbreadths is sufficient?

אֲמַר לֵיהּ [12]In reply, Rav Ashi **said to** Rav Aḥa, the son of Rav Yosef: The law regarding buried money is not the same as that concerning buried ḥametz. For ḥametz to be considered removed, **it needs** to be buried at least **three handbreadths** deep, **because** otherwise a dog will be attracted by **the odor** of the ḥametz and will dig for it. [13]But a bailee who buries money does so **in order to conceal it from the eye.** [14]Hence **we do not need** to bury it **three handbreadths** deep; a more shallow hole will suffice.

[1]אָמַר רָבָא: וּמוֹדֶה שְׁמוּאֵל בְּכוֹתֶל, [2]אִי נַמִּי בֵּין הַקְּרָנוֹת. [3]וְהָאִידָּנָא דִּשְׁכִיחִי טַפּוּחָאֵי, [4]אֵין לָהֶן שְׁמִירָה אֶלָּא בְּטֶפַח הַסָּמוּךְ לַקַּרְקַע, [5]אוֹ בְּטֶפַח הַסָּמוּךְ לִשְׁמֵי קוֹרָה.

[6]אֲמַר לֵיהּ רַב אַחָא בְּרֵיהּ דְּרַב יוֹסֵף לְרַב אַשִׁי: [7]הָתָם תְּנַן: "חָמֵץ שֶׁנָּפְלָה עָלָיו מַפּוֹלֶת הֲרֵי הוּא כִּמְבוֹעָר. [8]רַבָּן שִׁמְעוֹן בֶּן גַּמְלִיאֵל אוֹמֵר: כָּל שֶׁאֵין הַכֶּלֶב יָכוֹל לְחַפֵּשׂ אַחֲרָיו". [9]וְתָנָא: "כַּמָּה חֲפִישַׂת הַכֶּלֶב? שְׁלֹשָׁה טְפָחִים". [10]הָכָא מַאי? [11]מִי בָּעֵינַן שְׁלֹשָׁה טְפָחִים אוֹ לָא? [12]אֲמַר לֵיהּ: הָתָם, מִשּׁוּם רֵיחָא, בָּעֵינַן שְׁלֹשָׁה טְפָחִים. [13]הָכָא, מִשּׁוּם אִיכַּסּוּיֵי מֵעֵינָא, [14]לָא בָּעֵינַן שְׁלֹשָׁה טְפָחִים.

LITERAL TRANSLATION

[1]Rava said: And Shmuel agrees [that it can be guarded] in a wall, [2]or also in the corners.

[3]But now that wall-rappers are common, [4]it can only be guarded in the handbreadth closest to the ground, [5]or in the handbreadth closest to the roof beams.

[6]Rav Aḥa, the son of Rav Yosef, said to Rav Ashi: [7]We learned there: "Ḥametz upon which debris fell is [considered] as if [it has been] removed. [8]Rabban Shimon ben Gamliel says: Whatever a dog cannot search for." [9]And [a Tanna] taught: "How much is a dog's searching? Three handbreadths." [10]What [is the law] here? [11]Do we need three handbreadths or not?

[12]He said to him: There, because of the odor, we need three handbreadths. [13]Here, in order to conceal [it] from the eye, [14]we do not need three handbreadths.

RASHI

טפוחאי – מטפחים בכותל לידע אם יש שם חלל. **או בטפח הסמוך כו'** – וכולן בכותל. **הרי הוא כמבוער** – ואין צריך לבערו, דאין כאן עוד "בל יראה". **הכא מאי** – לענין שמירת כספים. **משום ריחא** – שהכלב מריח וחופש אחריו, והרי הוא מוציאו, ונראה.

HALAKHAH

the bailee is entitled to take sufficient time to recite havdalah before burying the deposit. (*Shulḥan Arukh, Ḥoshen Mishpat* 291:16.)

חָמֵץ שֶׁנָּפְלָה עָלָיו מַפּוֹלֶת **Ḥametz upon which debris fell.** "It is not required to search under a pile of debris for possible ḥametz, because the risk of getting hurt in the process outweighs the possible benefit. However, if it is known that a piece of ḥametz is buried under debris, it is required to clear the debris away and remove the ḥametz unless it is buried at least three handbreadths deep, in which case it is sufficient to annul it or declare it ownerless," following Rabban Shimon ben Gamliel. (*Shulḥan Arukh, Oraḥ Ḥayyim* 433.8.)

TRANSLATION AND COMMENTARY

וְכַמָּה [1]The Gemara asks: **But how deep** must money be buried for a bailee to have fulfilled his responsibility in looking after it?

אֲמַר רַפְרָם מִסִּיכְרָא [2]**Rafram of Sikhra said** in reply: **One handbreadth** — about eight centimeters or a little over three inches — is sufficient.

הַהוּא גַּבְרָא [3]The Gemara now considers a series of illustrative incidents bearing on the question of negligence in looking after deposits: **A certain man deposited money with someone else,** and the latter accepted responsibility as an unpaid bailee. [4]Now, by law the bailee should have buried the money in the ground as Shmuel ruled, but instead **he put it in a hut made of willows and it was stolen.** The problem in this case is that from one point of view nobody leaves anything of value in a hut made of willows, because such a hut can easily catch fire. On the other hand, it is a place that could reasonably be assumed to be safe from thieves, since it would not normally occur to a thief to look for valuables in such a place. Thus the question arose: Since the bailee was undoubtedly negligent in leaving the money in a fire-trap, should he be liable for the theft? Or do we say that since he actually took very good care that it not be stolen, he should be exempt? The case came before Rav Yosef, and there are two versions of his ruling. [5]In the first version, **Rav Yosef said: Even though** placing money in a hut made of willows **is a proper** method of **protecting** it **against thieves,** [6]**it is** nevertheless considered an act of **negligence with regard to fire,** since the hut does not provide protection against fire. [7]Accordingly, we have **a case the beginning of which** occurred **through negligence and the end of which** occurred **through** unavoidable **accident.** If a bailee (even an unpaid bailee) is negligent and the deposit is damaged as a direct result of his negligence — to use the present example, if the hut catches fire — the bailee is certainly liable, even though the fire itself was obviously an accident. On the other hand, if the bailee's negligence is not the direct cause of the damage, he may well be exempt. In a case where the beginning occurred through negligence and the end through accident, the action of the bailee played some role in causing the damage but was not specifically responsible for the damage that occurred. In other words, if the bailee had not placed the money in the hut, the thief would not have found it. His negligence was with regard to something else — fire — which did not in fact take place. [8]According to this first version of the text, Rav Yosef ruled that **the bailee is liable** in such a case.

וְאִיכָּא דְּאָמְרִי [9]On the other hand, **there are some who say** that Rav Yosef ruled in the opposite way. According to this version, Rav Yosef said: **Even though** placing money in a hut made of willows **is considered** an act of **negligence with regard to fire,** [10]**it is** nevertheless a **proper** method of **protecting** it **against thieves.** [11]And in **a case the beginning of which** occurred **through negligence and the end of which** occurred **through accident,** the rule is that **the bailee is exempt.**

[1]וְכַמָּה? [2]אֲמַר רַפְרָם מִסִּיכְרָא: טֶפַח. [3]הַהוּא גַּבְרָא דְּאַפְקֵיד זוּזֵי גַּבֵּי חַבְרֵיהּ. [4]אוֹתְבִינְהוּ בִּצְרִיפָא דְאוּרְבָּנֵי. אִיגְּנוּב. [5]אֲמַר רַב יוֹסֵף: אַף עַל גַּב דִּלְעִנְיַן גַּנָּבֵי נְטִירוּתָא הִיא, [6]לְעִנְיַן נוּרָא פְּשִׁיעוּתָא הִיא. [7]הֲוָה תְּחִילָּתוֹ בִּפְשִׁיעָה וְסוֹפוֹ בְּאוֹנֶס, [8]חַיָּיב. [9]וְאִיכָּא דְּאָמְרִי: אַף עַל גַּב דִּלְעִנְיַן נוּרָא פְּשִׁיעוּתָא הִיא, [10]לְעִנְיַן גַּנָּבֵי נְטִירוּתָא הִיא, [11]וּתְחִלָּתוֹ בִּפְשִׁיעָה וְסוֹפוֹ בְּאוֹנֶס, פָּטוּר.

LITERAL TRANSLATION

[1]And how much?

[2]Rafram of Sikhra said: One handbreadth.

[3]A certain man deposited money with his fellow. [4]He put it in a hut [made] of willows. It was stolen.

[5]Rav Yosef said: Even though with regard to thieves it is guarding, [6]with regard to fire it is negligence. [7]Its beginning was through negligence and its end was through accident, [8][so the bailee is] liable.

[9]And there are [some] who say: Even though with regard to fire it is negligence, [10]with regard to thieves it is guarding, [11]and [where] its beginning was through negligence and its end was through accident, he is exempt.

RASHI

מסיכרא — שם מקום. **צריפא דאורבני** — בית קטן עגול כמין כובע שעושין ציידי עופות לארוב. **דאורבני** — של ערבה היה. **אף על גב דלענין גנבי נטירותא היא** — אפילו בלא קבורה, שאין גנבים הולכין שם לגנוב, שאין ממון מצוי שם. **תחלתו בפשיעה** — שמא תפול שם דליקה, ונמצא פשע שלא קברן. **וסופו באונס** — שהרי נגנבו, וגניבה לשומר חנם אונס הוא.

BACKGROUND

בִּצְרִיפָא דְאוּרְבָּנֵי In a hut made of willows. This refers to a small structure in the form of a cone which was woven from willow branches (this is the basic meaning of the Hebrew word צְרִיף). Hunters hid in structures of this kind to wait for their prey. The huts could be strongly built (to afford protection against wild animals), but because they were made of willow branches, they were highly flammable.

SAGES

רַפְרָם מִסִּיכְרָא Rafram of Sikhra. According to a Geonic tradition, this is an abbreviation of Rav Efraim. In a parallel version of this text (*Pesaḥim* 31b), the Sage in question is referred to as Rafram bar Pappa — an Amora of the fourth generation. Sikhra was a town on the Tigris River near Meḥoza.

HALAKHAH

תְּחִילָּתוֹ בִּפְשִׁיעָה וְסוֹפוֹ בְּאוֹנֶס Where its beginning was through negligence and its end was through accident. "If a bailee was negligent and failed to safeguard a deposit from one kind of danger, even if that particular danger never materialized, and the deposit was damaged by some other, unrelated accident that could not have been prevented, he is nevertheless considered to have been negligent, and must pay for the damage. For example, if the bailee left a deposit

LANGUAGE

קַרְטַלִיתָא **Basket.** This word is the Aramaic diminutive of the Greek κάρταλλος, *kartallos*, meaning "a basket with a pointed bottom."

LANGUAGE (RASHI)

אשקר״א* (אשקרי״ן) From the Old French *escrin*, meaning "chest" or "box."

TRANSLATION AND COMMENTARY

וְהִילְכְתָא [1]The Gemara concludes: **The** actual **Halakhah** regarding this question **is** as Rav Yosef ruled according to the first version: **Wherever the beginning occurred through negligence and the end through** accident, the bailee **is liable.**

הַהוּא גַּבְרָא [2]The Gemara now relates another incident: **A certain man deposited money with someone else.** [3]The depositor later **said to** the bailee: **"Give me my money."** [4]The bailee **said to him** in reply: **"I do not know where I put it."** [5]**The case came before Rava,** [6]and he **said to** the bailee: **"Any** bailee who says **'I do not know' is** considered **negligent.** [7]**Go and pay."**

הַהוּא גַּבְרָא [8]The Gemara further relates: **A certain man deposited money with someone else.** [9]The bailee **entrusted** the money **to his mother, and she put it in a** basket, **and it was stolen.** [10]The case came before Rava. **Rava said: How should the judges judge this case,** since it is not clear who is responsible? [11]**Shall we say to the bailee himself: "Go and pay,** because you are a bailee who handed over what was entrusted to you to another bailee, and are therefore liable"? [12]If we do so, **he can say:** [42B] "Surely anyone **who deposits** something with a bailee **does so on the assumption** that the bailee **may give** the deposit **to his wife and sons** for safekeeping rather than look after it himself the entire time." This argument was used by Rava himself (above, 36a/b), and there is nothing wrong with a bailee delegating his responsibilities to a trustworthy adult member of his household. Therefore the bailee can claim that he did not act improperly by handing the

[1]וְהִילְכְתָא: תְּחִילָּתוֹ בִּפְשִׁיעָה וְסוֹפוֹ בְּאוֹנֶס, חַיָּיב.

[2]הַהוּא גַּבְרָא דְּאַפְקֵיד זוּזֵי גַּבֵּי חַבְרֵיהּ. [3]אֲמַר לֵיהּ: ״הַב לִי זוּזַאי״. [4]אֲמַר לֵיהּ: ״לָא יָדַעְנָא הֵיכָא אוֹתְבִינְהוּ״. [5]אֲתָא לְקַמֵּיהּ דְּרָבָא. [6]אֲמַר לֵיהּ: ״כָּל ׳לָא יָדַעְנָא׳ פְּשִׁיעוּתָא הִיא. [7]זִיל שַׁלֵּם״.

[8]הַהוּא גַּבְרָא דְּאַפְקֵיד זוּזֵי גַּבֵּי חַבְרֵיהּ. [9]אַשְׁלְמִינְהוּ לְאִימֵּיהּ, וְאוֹתְבִינְהוּ בְּקַרְטַלִיתָא, וְאִיגְּנוּב. [10]אֲמַר רָבָא: הֵיכִי נְדַיְינוּ דַּיָּינֵי לְהַאי דִּינָא? [11]נֵימָא לֵיהּ לְדִידֵיהּ: ״זִיל שַׁלֵּם״? [12]אָמַר: [42B] ״כָּל הַמַּפְקִיד, עַל דַּעַת אִשְׁתּוֹ וּבָנָיו הוּא מַפְקִיד״.

LITERAL TRANSLATION

[1]And the Halakhah is: [Where] its beginning was through negligence and its end was through accident, he is liable.

[2]A certain man deposited money with his fellow. [3]He said to him: "Give me my money." [4]He said to him: "I do not know where I put it." [5][The case] came before Rava. [6]He said to him: "Every 'I do not know' is negligence. [7]Go [and] pay."

[8]A certain man deposited money with his fellow. [9]He entrusted it to his mother, and she put it in a basket, and it was stolen. [10]Rava said: How shall the judges judge this case? [11]Shall we say to [the bailee] himself: "Go [and] pay"? [12]He can say: [42B] "Whoever deposits, deposits on the assumption [that it may be given to] his [the bailee's] wife and sons."

RASHI

אשלמינהו — מסרן לאמו. **קרטליתא** — ארגז, *אשקר״א בלעז. **נימא ליה לדידיה [זיל] שלים** — דשומר שמסר לשומר חייב. **כל המפקיד כו׳** — על דעת שלא יהא שומר נמנע מלמוסרן לאנשי ביתו הגדולים ונאמנים לו הוא דמפקיד. **נימא לה לאימיה** — שתשלם בשביל שלא קברתו.

NOTES

כָּל ״לָא יָדַעְנָא״ פְּשִׁיעוּתָא הִיא **Every "I do not know" is negligence.** The bailee is considered negligent even if he is certain that he will eventually find the deposit, as the depositor cannot be expected to wait indefinitely while the bailee searches for it (*Rabbenu Yehonatan*).

Ritva asks: The unpaid bailee is exempt for damage caused by theft or loss. Now, if he does not know where the deposit is, it must either have been stolen or lost. Why then does Rava rule that he is liable?

Ra'avad maintains that an unpaid bailee is exempt in cases of loss only if an animal he was responsible for strayed away after all normal precautions were taken, or if the deposit consisted of money and the like and the bailee knows precisely where he put it, but it is not there now. But if the bailee does not remember where he left the deposit, he is negligent.

HALAKHAH

of money in a wall made of wood, and the money was stolen, even though the bailee's action was unobjectionable vis-à-vis theft, nevertheless, since the deposit was in great danger of being destroyed by fire, he is liable." (*Shulḥan Arukh, Ḥoshen Mishpat* 291:6.)

כָּל ״לָא יָדַעְנָא״ פְּשִׁיעוּתָא הִיא **Every "I do not know" is negligence.** "A bailee who does not recall where he placed a deposit is considered negligent, and must pay immediately. He cannot demand that the depositor wait until he searches his house," following Rava. (Ibid., 291:7.)

TRANSLATION AND COMMENTARY

deposit to his mother. [1]On the other hand, Rava continues, **shall we say to** the bailee's **mother:** "You were negligent in not burying the deposit, so you must **go** and **pay"?** [2]This, too, is untenable, for **she can say:** "My son **did not tell me that** the money **was not his.** If he had done **so, I would have buried it,** since burial is the best way to guard a deposit. But since he did not do so, I was not negligent in putting it where I always put his money when he gives it to me." [3]On the other hand, continues Rava, **shall we say to** the bailee: **"Why did you not tell** your mother that the money was not yours? That oversight on your part amounts to negligence." [4]This, too, is untenable, for the bailee **can say: "By telling her that it was mine** I assumed that **she would be all the more careful with it."**

אֶלָּא אָמַר רָבָא [5]Having analyzed the alternative courses of action open to the court and the difficulties involved in each, **Rava said** that the court should rule as follows: The bailee **must take an oath that he entrusted the** depositor's money **to his mother,** [6]**and his mother must take an oath that she put this money in a basket, and** that **it was stolen.** On the basis of these oaths we accept that neither the son nor the mother were negligent, [7]**and they are** both **exempt** from paying compensation for the theft.

הַהוּא אַפּוֹטְרוֹפָּא [8]The Gemara relates another incident: **There was a certain guardian** who was appointed by the court to look after the interests **of** some **orphans. He** used some of the orphans' money, **bought an ox for the orphans** as an investment, **and handed it over to a herdsman** to look after. [9]Unfortunately, neither the guardian nor the herdsman noticed that the ox **did not have molars or front teeth with which to eat, and** since it was not given special food, **it died** while in the herdsman's care, and the orphans lost their investment. [10]The case came before **Rami bar Ḥama,** who **said: How shall the judges judge this case?** [11]**Shall we say to the guardian: "Go and pay** for the ox, because you were negligent in buying an ox with no teeth"? [12]This is untenable, for **he can say:** "I know nothing about oxen. **I gave it to the herdsman,** and I relied on him to take care of it properly." [13]On the other hand, continues Rami bar Ḥama, **shall we say**

[1]נֵימָא לָהּ לְאִימֵּיהּ: ״זִילִי שַׁלֵּימִי״? [2]אָמְרָה: ״לָא אֲמַר לִי דְּלָאו דִּידֵיהּ נִינְהוּ, דְּאַקְבְּרִינְהוּ״. [3]נֵימָא לֵיהּ: ״אַמַּאי לָא אָמְרַתְּ לָהּ?״ [4]אָמַר: ״כׇּל שֶׁכֵּן דְּכִי אָמֵינָא לָהּ דִּידִי נִינְהוּ, טְפֵי מִזְדַּהֲרָא בְּהוּ״.

[5]אֶלָּא אָמַר רָבָא: מִשְׁתַּבַּע אִיהוּ דְּהָנְהוּ זוּזֵי אַשְׁלְמִינְהוּ לְאִימֵּיהּ, [6]וּמִשְׁתַּבְּעָא אִימֵּיהּ דְּהָנְהוּ זוּזֵי אוֹתְבִינְהוּ בְּקַרְטַלִּיתָא וְאִיגְּנוּב, [7]וּפָטוּר.

[8]הַהוּא אַפּוֹטְרוֹפָּא דְּיַתְמֵי דִּזְבַן לְהוּ תּוֹרָא לְיַתְמֵי, וּמְסַרֵיהּ לְבַקָּרָא. [9]לָא הֲווּ לֵיהּ כָּכֵי וְשִׁינֵּי לְמֵיכַל, וּמִית. [10]אֲמַר רָמִי בַּר חָמָא: הֵיכִי נְדַיְּינוּ דַּיָּינֵי לְהַאי דִּינָא? [11]נֵימָא לֵיהּ לְאַפּוֹטְרוֹפָּא: ״זִיל שַׁלֵּים״? [12]אָמַר: ״אֲנָא לְבַקָּרָא מְסַרְתֵּיהּ״. [13]נֵימָא לֵיהּ

LITERAL TRANSLATION

[1]Shall we say to his mother: "Go [and] pay"? [2]She can say: "He did not tell me that it was not his, so that I should bury it." [3]Shall we say to him: "Why did you not tell her?" [4]He can say: "How much more so if I say to her that it is mine, she is more careful with it."

[5]Rather, Rava said: He swears that he entrusted this money to his mother, [6]and his mother swears that she put this money in a basket and [that] it was stolen, [7]and he is exempt.

[8][There was] a certain guardian of orphans who bought an ox for the orphans and handed it over to a herdsman. [9]It did not have molars or [front] teeth [with which] to eat, and died. [10]Rami bar Ḥama said: How shall the judges judge this case? [11]Shall we say to the guardian: "Go [and] pay"? [12]He can say: "I handed it over to the herdsman." [13]Shall we say to

RASHI

לבקרא מסרתיה — היה לו להודיעני שאינו אוכל.

NOTES

לָא הֲווּ לֵיהּ כָּכֵי וְשִׁינֵּי לְמֵיכַל **It did not have molars or front teeth to eat.** Our commentary follows *Rabbenu Ḥananel,* who explains that even a toothless ox could have

כָּכֵי **Molars.** Our commentary follows *Tosafot* (*Avodah Zarah* 28a). *Rashi,* however, explains that the word refers to the ox's gums (ibid.).

HALAKHAH

נִפְקָד שֶׁמָּסַר לְאִמּוֹ **A bailee who hands a deposit over to his mother.** "There was once a bailee who received a deposit of money and handed it to his mother for safekeeping without telling her it was a deposit. She hid the money in a reasonably safe place, but did not bury it, and the money was stolen. The Sages said: The bailee need not pay, because he handed the money over to his mother, a member of his household. The mother also need not pay, because she was not told that the money was a deposit. Instead, the bailee must swear that the money

TRANSLATION AND COMMENTARY

to the herdsman: "Go and pay because you should have noticed that the ox was not eating and drawn the guardian's attention to it"? [1]This, too, is untenable, for **he can say: "I put** the orphans' ox **together with** my **other oxen,** and no one told me to give it special treatment. [2]**I placed food before it** in the same way as I do for all my oxen. [3]**I did not know that it was not eating.** How can I be held responsible for what happened?"

מִכְּדִי [4]The Gemara objects: **But, since the herdsman is a paid bailee for the orphans,** and is only exempt if the damage was caused by forces beyond his control, [5]surely **he should have checked** whether or not the ox was eating! Since he did not do so, he should be held responsible.

אִי אִיכָּא [6]The Gemara answers: **If** the death of the ox **had** caused **a loss to the orphans, this would indeed have been so,** and the herdsman would have been held responsible. [7]**But with what** situation **was** Rami bar Ḥama **dealing here?** [8]With a case **where there was no loss for the orphans,** [9]**because they found the ox's owner, and the orphans took** their **money** back **from him.** The original transaction was invalid, because the orphans had no intention of buying a toothless ox. Thus the orphans got their money back, and had no further legal claims.

אֶלָּא מַאן קָא טָעֵין [10]**But, asks** the Gemara, if the orphans were satisfied, **who made the claim** in Rami bar Ḥama's court?

מָרֵיהּ דְּתוֹרָא קָטָעֵין [11]The Gemara answers: **The** original **owner of the ox made a claim** against the guardian and the herdsman, for the guardian or the herdsman **should have informed** the owner that the ox was toothless, so that he could slaughter the animal and sell the meat. For this loss to the owner, the guardian and the herdsman should be liable.

לְבַקָּרָא: ״זִיל שַׁלֵּים״? [1]אָמַר: ״אֲנָא בַּהֲדֵי תּוֹרֵי אוֹקִימְתֵּיהּ, [2]אוּכְלָא שְׁדַאי לֵיהּ. [3]לָא הֲוָה יָדְעִינַן דְּלָא אָכַל״. [4]מִכְּדִי בַּקָּרָא שׁוֹמֵר שָׂכָר דְּיַתְמֵי הוּא, [5]אִיבָּעֵי לֵיהּ לְעַיּוּנֵי. [6]אִי אִיכָּא פְּסֵידָא דְּיַתְמֵי, הָכִי נַמִי. [7]וְהָכָא בְּמַאי עָסְקִינַן? [8]דְּלֵיכָּא פְּסֵידָא דְּיַתְמֵי, דְּאַשְׁכַּחוּהוּ לְמָרֵיהּ דְּתוֹרָא, [9]וּשְׁקוּל יַתְמֵי זוּזֵי מִינֵּיהּ. [10]אֶלָּא מַאן קָא טָעֵין? [11]מָרֵיהּ דְּתוֹרָא קָטָעֵין: ״אִיבָּעֵי לֵיהּ לְאוֹדוּעַן״.

LITERAL TRANSLATION

the herdsman: "Go [and] pay"? [1]He can say: "I put it together with [other] oxen, [2][and] I placed food before it. [3]I did not know that it was not eating." [4][But] since the herdsman is a paid bailee for the orphans, [5]he should have checked. [6]If there had been a loss for the orphans, this would indeed have been so. [7][But] with what are we dealing here? [8]Where there is no loss for the orphans, [9]because they found the ox's owner, and the orphans took the money from him. [10]Then who is claiming? [11]The owner of the ox is claiming: "He should have informed me."

RASHI

איבעי ליה לעיוני – אם אוכל אם לאו. **אי איכא פסידא ליתמי כו׳** – תירוצא הוא. **דאשכחיה למריה דתורא** – המוכר. **ושקול דמייהו** – דאמרי ליה: מקח טעות הוא. **אלא מאן טעין** – מי תובע כלום דקאמר (רבא) היכי נידייננו. **מריה דתורא טעין** – ושואל שמתה בהמתו אצלך, ותובע את האפוטרופוס.

NOTES

been maintained with proper care and appropriate feeding. *Tosafot,* however, explains that the proper thing to have done was to slaughter the ox immediately, before it died of starvation.

HALAKHAH

he gave his mother was the deposit money, and the mother must swear that she hid that money and it was stolen, and they are both exempt. *Rema* adds in the name of *Maggid Mishneh, Ran* and *Nimukei Yosef* that if the deposit consisted of a valuable article but not money, the bailee need not swear that he gave it to his mother, since there is no reason to suspect that he had another similar article of his own and gave that article to his mother instead of the deposit." (*Shulḥan Arukh, Ḥoshen Mishpat* 291:23.)

מִקָּח שֶׁיֵּשׁ בּוֹ פְּסוּל **Defective merchandise.** "If a person sells defective merchandise to someone else, and the defect is not obvious, and the merchandise is destroyed because of the defect, the seller must return to the buyer the money he paid. For example, if a man bought an ox with no teeth and placed it with his other cattle, and it died, he may return the carcass to the seller and demand his money back. But if the seller also did not know that the merchandise was defective — for example, where the seller was a middleman who bought and sold merchandise on the spot — the seller need only swear the Rabbinic 'oath of inducement' (שְׁבוּעַת הֶיסֵּת) that he did not know of the defect, and he need not return the purchase money to the buyer, since it was the buyer's responsibility to check the merchandise for defects," following *Rambam. Rema* disagrees, and rules in the name of *Maggid Mishneh* and *Tur* that even if the seller was only a middleman, he must still refund the purchase price. *Shakh* and *Gra* rule, in the name of *Baḥ,* that there is, in fact, no argument between

TRANSLATION AND COMMENTARY

מַאי מוֹדְעִינַן לֵיהּ [1]The Gemara objects: **What** should the guardian **have informed** the owner about? It was the owner who defrauded the guardian, not the other way round. Surely the owner **knew that the sale was in error,** i.e., made under false pretenses!

בְּסַפְסִירָא [2]The Gemara answers: **We are dealing with** a case where the person who sold the ox to the guardian was **a middleman who buys** oxen **from here and sells** them elsewhere, and hence he may well not have known that this particular ox was toothless, and it was the duty of the guardian to inform him. [3]**Therefore,** concludes the Gemara, the middleman has a case against the guardian, and the guardian against the herdsman. [4]The herdsman, being a paid bailee, is liable. Hence, the middleman **swears that he did not know** that the ox was unable to eat normally, **and the herdsman pays** the middleman for the dead ox. However, in view of the circumstances, the herdsman pays only **the value of the meat at a lower price,** i.e., two-thirds of the market price of the meat, rather than the full value of the ox.

[1]מַאי מוֹדְעִינַן לֵיהּ? מֵידַע יָדַע דְּמִקַּח טָעוּת הָוֵי! [2]בְּסַפְסִירָא, דְּזָבֵן מֵהָכָא וּמְזַבֵּין לְהָכָא. [3]הִלְכָּךְ, מִישְׁתַּבַּע אִיהוּ דְּלָא הֲוָה יָדַע, [4]וּמְשַׁלֵּם בַּקָּרָא דְּמֵי בָשָׂר בְּזוֹל.

LITERAL TRANSLATION

[1]What should he have informed him? He knows that it was a sale in error!

[2][We are dealing] with a middleman, who buys from here and sells to there. [3]Therefore, he swears that he did not know, [4]and the herdsman pays the value of the meat at a low [price].

RASHI

ספסירא — קונה ומוכר בהמות בשוק, ביום שקונה מוכר. **משתבע ספסירא** — דלא הוה ידע. **ומשלם בקרא דמי בשר בזול** — ותמיה אני: מנין לרמי בר חמא דין זה? מה לו לספסירא עם הרועה, לא שומר שלו הוא! ונראה לי דממתניתין (בבא מציעא לה,ב) דהשוכר הפרה לחבירו והשאילה לאחר ומתה כדרכה דקאמר רבי יוסי יחזיר פרה לבעלים, ואוקימנא הלכה כרבי יוסי, אלמא: אף על פי שאין הבעלים בעלי דברים של שואל, והשוכר שהוא לו בעל דברים אינו חסר כלום, שהרי פטור באונסין, אפילו הכי, הואיל ויש לו דין על השואל לגבות — יעמדו הבעלים הראשונים במקומו, וגובין מן השואל. הכי נמי, הואיל ויש ליתומים לגבות מן הרועה, שהוא שומר שכר שלהם — יעמדו בעלים במקום היתומים וגובין. ומיהו, אי הוה מפסדי יתומים — לא היה עושה פשרה בממון יתומים לשלם בזול דיתמי לאו בני מחילה נינהו, אבל עכשיו, שהוא מגבה לבעלים, וכאן אין פשיעה כל כך דאמר בהדי תורא אוקימתיה כו׳. הטיל פשרה ביניהם, ולא ישלם כל דמי השור כמות שהוא חי, אלא העור יחזיר לבעלים והבשר שמין וישלם שני שלישים, דהיכא דאמרינן בגמרא משלם בזול כל זוזא שהוא שש מעה כסף חשבינן בארבעה דנקי, בפרק "מי שמת" (בבא בתרא קמו,ג).

CONCEPTS

מִקַּח טָעוּת A sale in error. A transaction in which one of the participants was under a false impression regarding its terms. Such a transaction is considered a mistake, and the injured party can invalidate it. For example, if someone buys an animal and discovers it to be diseased, he can invalidate the sale. A related concept is בִּיטּוּל מִקָּח — "the invalidation of a transaction." If an object is overpriced or underpriced by more than one-sixth, the sale is invalid and either party can retract. Similarly, if a man marries and subsequently discovers that his wife has serious physical defects of which he was unaware at the time of the marriage, he can divorce her and not pay her marriage settlement.

LANGUAGE

סַפְסִירָא A middleman. This word is derived from the Middle Persian *sasper*, meaning "an intermediary, one who buys and sells goods."

NOTES

מִישְׁתַּבַּע אִיהוּ He swears. It is not clear why the middleman needs to swear. After all, he is not a bailee, he is the claimant. *Rosh* explains that the oath here is not the bailee's oath with which we have been dealing until now, but an oath of Rabbinic origin called שְׁבוּעַת הֶיסֵּת — "an oath of inducement." This oath, which was instituted during the Amoraic period, can be imposed whenever a claimant insists that he is in the right but cannot prove his case. Thus, in our case, the herdsman insists that the middleman *did* know the ox was toothless. However, since the burden of proof falls on him, he must pay the middleman. Nevertheless, he is entitled to demand that the middleman take this Rabbinic oath.

The difficulty with this explanation is that the "oath of inducement" can only be imposed if the claimant says he is absolutely certain that his opponent is lying, and in our case there is no way for the herdsman to know one way or the other. Nevertheless, *Rosh* argues that the possibility that the middleman did not know the ox was toothless is so remote that the herdsman is entitled to declare himself certain and demand an oath.

וּמְשַׁלֵּם בַּקָּרָא And the herdsman pays. This ruling should be understood in the light of the Mishnah above (35b). That Mishnah deals with a case where a person hired a cow and lent it to a third party with the tacit approval of the owner. The cow then died. Now, the law is that a borrower is liable for natural death and a hirer is not. Hence, we have a peculiar situation where the owner has no claim against the hirer, but the hirer *does* have a claim against the borrower. The Halakhah follows Rabbi Yose, who rules that in such a case the owner can sue the borrower directly, in place of the hirer.

In our case, the sale of the ox was invalid, so it was up to the guardian to return the ox to the middleman who sold it to him and take the orphans' money back. But until he does so, the law is that the guardian has the status of an unpaid bailee (*Ritva*). Hence he is not responsible for any damage to the ox unless caused by his negligence. In the meantime, however, he entrusted the ox to a herdsman, a paid bailee. The herdsman was liable for the death of the ox, since he could have prevented it by paying closer attention. Hence, we have the same peculiar situation as in the Mishnah above, where the middleman has no claim against the guardian and the orphans, but the guardian and the orphans *do* have a claim against the herdsman. In the light of Rabbi Yose's ruling, the middleman may sue the herdsman directly (*Rashi*).

דְּמֵי בָשָׂר בְּזוֹל The value of cheap meat. Our commentary follows *Rashi,* who explains that Rami bar Ḥama's ruling was a compromise. Technically speaking, the herdsman was

HALAKHAH

Rambam and *Maggid Mishneh.* Rather, *Maggid Mishneh*'s ruling applies only if the buyer was unable to check the merchandise for defects; but if he was able to check, *Rambam*'s ruling applies, and the seller need not refund the purchase money, since the buyer is responsible for his own loss. (Ibid., 232:18.)

BACKGROUND

כְּשׁוּתָא Hops.

The Aramaic word כְּשׁוּתָא refers to hops, *humulus lupulus* — a rough twining species of the hemp family (*Cannabinaceae*) that is a dioecious, perennial climbing plant with branches reaching a length of 8-10 m. Its flowers are similar to pine cones, and contain a high percentage of resins, alkaloides and oils. These flowers are used in the beer industry to give the drink its typical taste and aroma, and as a preservative.

The use of hops in manufacturing beer reached Europe after Talmudic times, but from the evidence here in the Talmud it appears that the plant had already been used for this purpose for many generations.

When the hops are of poor quality, or when weeds are mixed with the climbing plant, they can give the finished beverage a bad aftertaste.

LANGUAGE

סָרְסֵיהּ His steward. This expression refers to a steward or someone responsible for a household. The source of the word is not certain. Some authorities derive it from סָרִיס — "eunuch" — for the meaning of that term had already been expanded in Biblical times to refer to someone who looked after other people's needs.

LANGUAGE (RASHI)

הומלו״ן* From the Old French *homlon*, meaning "hops."

[1]הַהוּא גַּבְרָא דְּאַפְקֵיד כְּשׁוּתָא גַּבֵּי חַבְרֵיהּ. [2]הֲוָה לֵיהּ לְדִידֵיהּ נַמִי כַּרְיָא דִּכְשׁוּתָא. [3]אֲמַר לֵיהּ לְסָרְסֵיהּ: "מֵהַאי רְמֵי". [4]אֲזַל רְמָא מֵאִידָךְ. [5]אֲמַר רַב עַמְרָם: הֵיכִי נְדַיְינוּ דַּיָּינֵי לְהַאי דִּינָא? [6]נֵימָא לֵיהּ לְדִידֵיהּ: "זִיל שַׁלֵּים"? [7]אֲמַר: "אֲנָא אֲמַרִי לֵיהּ, 'מֵהַאי רְמֵי'". [8]נֵימָא לֵיהּ לְסָרְסֵיהּ: "זִיל שַׁלֵּים"? [9]אָמַר: "לָא אֲמַר לִי, 'מֵהַאי רְמֵי, וּמֵהַאי לָא תִּרְמֵי'".

[10]וְאִי דִּשְׁהָא שִׁיעוּר לְאִיתוּיֵי לֵיהּ וְלָא אַיְיתִי לֵיהּ, [11]גַּלֵּי אַדַּעְתֵּיהּ דְּנִיחָא לֵיהּ.

TRANSLATION AND COMMENTARY

הַהוּא גַּבְרָא [1]The Gemara now relates another incident: **A certain man** had a pile of **hops** — a plant used in making beer. **He deposited** his hops **with someone else** for safekeeping. [2]The bailee **himself also had a pile of hops,** which he was about to use to make beer. [3]The bailee pointed to his own pile and **said to his steward: "Throw** hops **from this pile** into the beer." [4]However, the steward **went and threw** hops into the beer **from the other pile** — the one belonging to the depositor. [5]The case came before **Rav Amram,** who **said: How shall the judges judge this case? [6]Shall we say to the bailee himself: "Go and pay"?** [7]This in untenable, for **he can say:** "I am not responsible for the mistake. I specifically **told** my steward: **'Throw** in hops **from this pile,'** pointing to my own pile." [8]**Shall we say to his steward: "Go and pay"?** [9]This is untenable, for **he can say:** "My employer **did not say to me: 'Throw** hops into the beer **from this pile, but not from that one.'** I thought he was merely making a helpful suggestion, telling me where the nearest pile of hops was. I did not realize that it made any difference which pile I used."

וְאִי דִּשְׁהָא שִׁיעוּר לְאִיתוּיֵי לֵיהּ [10]The Gemara now asks: **But if** the depositor's pile of hops was further away than the bailee's and **the steward delayed long enough to bring** the bailee **his own hops but did not bring** them **to him** — i.e., if the steward took so much time to bring the hops that it was obvious that he had not gone to the nearer of the two piles — the bailee should have realized that a mistake had occurred. [11]Since the bailee paid no attention to the time taken by his steward, **he** thereby **revealed his approval** of his steward's actions. In this he acted negligently, and thus should be held responsible for the depositor's loss.

LITERAL TRANSLATION

[1]A certain man deposited hops with his fellow. [2]He himself also had a pile of hops. [3]He said to his steward: "Throw from this [pile]." [4]He went [and] threw from the other [pile]. [5]Rav Amram said: How shall the judges judge this case? [6]Shall we say to [the bailee] himself: "Go [and] pay"? [7]He can say: "I said to him, 'Throw from this [pile].'" [8]Shall we say to his steward: "Go [and] pay"? [9]He can say: "He did not say to me, 'Throw from this [pile], but do not throw from that [one].'"

[10]But if he [the steward] delayed long enough to bring him [his own hops] but did not bring [them] to him, [11]he [the bailee] revealed his mind that he was pleased.

RASHI

כשותא – *הומלו״ן שמטילין לתוך השכר. **כריא** – כרי. **אמר ליה** – בעל הבית. **לסרסיה** – לאשר על ביתו, העושה שכר שלו. **מהא רמי** – הראהו הכרי שלו, ואמר לו: מזה תטיל לשכר. **מאידך** – של פקדון. **ואי דשהא שיעור כו׳** – גמרא פריך: אם היה כרי שלו קרוב, ושל פקדון רחוק, ושהא השליח שיעור מהלך דרך הקרוב, ולא אייתי. **גלי דעתיה** – דבעל הבית דניחא ליה, שהרי ידע שמשל פקדון הוי, ולא מיחה בידו.

NOTES

fully liable for the damage, and should have compensated the middleman in full (see previous note). However, in view of the circumstances — where the misconduct of the herdsman vis-a-vis the middleman was purely technical, and where the herdsman was really no more guilty than the middleman himself, who also failed to pay attention to the defects in the animal he was selling — Rami bar Ḥama decided that the herdsman should pay only two-thirds of the price the ox would have brought had it been slaughtered for meat.

The difficulty with this explanation is that the Gemara does not explicitly state that Rami bar Ḥama imposed a compromise. Moreover, while there is a Geonic tradition that the price of cheap meat is two-thirds of the regular price, there is no source for this idea in the Gemara itself (*Ramban*). Accordingly, some Rishonim explain that Rami bar Ḥama required the herdsman to pay the full price of the ox. However, since the ox was unhealthy, its meat was probably not worth very much. Hence the "cheap meat" ruling (*Ba'al HaMa'or, Ra'avad*).

Tosafot, Ramban and others explain the Gemara differently. According to this explanation, the only thing to be done with a toothless ox is to slaughter it immediately, before it dies. But because of the laws of supply and demand, an ox that must be slaughtered in haste cannot be sold for its full price. Hence the "cheap meat" ruling.

HALAKHAH

כְּשׁוּת שֶׁל פִּקָּדוֹן A deposit of hops. "If a bailee receives a deposit of hops, and has a supply of his own hops as well, and an employee of his makes a mistake and throws the depositor's hops into his employer's beer, then the bailee must swear to the facts and both the bailee and his employee are exempt from payment. The bailee must, however, pay

LITERAL TRANSLATION

[1] Where he did not delay.

[2] Ultimately, what loss is there? [3] Surely he benefited! [4] Rav Samma, the son of Rava, said: Where the beer became sour.

[5] Rav Ashi said: [We are dealing] with thorns, [43A] and he pays him the value of the thorns.

MISHNAH [6] Someone who deposits coins with a money changer, [7] if they are bound up, he may not use them. [8] Therefore, if they were lost, he is not liable for them.

[1] בְּדְלָא שְׁהָא.
[2] סוֹף סוֹף, מַאי פְּסֵידָא אִיכָּא?
[3] וְהָא קָא מִשְׁתַּרְשֵׁי לֵיהּ!
[4] אֲמַר רַב סַמָּא בְּרֵיהּ דְּרָבָא: דַּהֲוָה שִׁיכְרָא חָלָא.
[5] רַב אַשִׁי אֲמַר: בְּכִיסֵי, [43A] וּמְשַׁלֵּם לֵיהּ דְּמֵי כִיסֵי.
משנה [6] הַמַּפְקִיד מָעוֹת אֵצֶל שׁוּלְחָנִי, [7] אִם צְרוּרִין, לֹא יִשְׁתַּמֵּשׁ בָּהֶן. [8] לְפִיכָךְ, אִם אָבְדוּ, אֵינוֹ חַיָּיב בְּאַחֲרָיוּתָן.

RASHI

והא קמשתרשי ליה — והלא הוא נשכר הכשות של פקדון שהטילו בשכר, ושלו עומד, וישלם משלו. **חלא** — החמיץ. **בכיסי** — שהיתה כישות גרועה, וקוצים מעורבין בה, ולא השביח השכר כרלונו וקשה בעיניו שהטילוהו בתוכו. **ומשלם לו דמי כיסי** — דמי כשות של קוצים, לפי מה שהשביח.

SAGES

רַב סַמָּא בְּרֵיהּ דְּרָבָא Rav Samma the son of Rava. A Babylonian Amora of the seventh generation, Rav Samma the son of Rava served as head of the Pumbedita Yeshivah for twenty years. His name is mentioned only a few times in the Talmud.

TRANSLATION AND COMMENTARY

בְּדְלָא שְׁהָא [1] The Gemara answers: We are referring to a case **where** the steward **did not delay** a long time — i.e., where the two piles were near enough to make it impossible to tell that the steward had gone to the wrong one. Thus, the bailee and the steward can each claim not to be responsible. Hence Rav Amram's difficulty with the case.

סוֹף סוֹף [2] But, the Gemara objects, **ultimately what loss is there** if the bailee does pay? [3] **Surely**, even though it was not the bailee's intention or responsibility that the depositor's hops were put in his beer, the bailee **benefited** from the depositor's hops. Therefore, he should replace them with his own, and this solution should prove satisfactory to all.

אֲמַר רַב סַמָּא בְּרֵיהּ דְּרָבָא [4] The Gemara offers two solutions to this objection: (1) **Rav Samma the son of Rava said:** We are dealing with a case **where the beer became sour** as a result of the addition of the hops, and the bailee gained no benefit from them. Therefore, since the bailee was unpaid and the mistake did not arise through his negligence, he is not liable.

רַב אַשִׁי אֲמַר [5] (2) **Rav Ashi said: We are dealing with** hops mixed with **thorns.** The depositor's hops were of an inferior quality — by no means equivalent to the bailee's hops. Thus, the benefit the bailee derived from the hops was marginal at best. [43A] Nevertheless, in such a case the bailee must still **pay** the depositor **the value of** hops mixed with **thorns**. In other words, he must pay for the benefit he actually derived from the deposit.

MISHNAH הַמַּפְקִיד מָעוֹת אֵצֶל שׁוּלְחָנִי [6] If **someone deposits coins with a money changer,** and the latter agrees to take care of them as an unpaid bailee, is he permitted to use these coins for his own business and return other coins, or must he put the money deposited with him aside and look after it like any other bailee? [7] The Mishnah rules: **If** the deposited coins **were** handed over to the money changer **bound up** in a bundle, **he may not use them**, since the tying up of the money indicates that the depositor expects to receive the same bundle back unopened. [8] **Therefore, if** the money changer took good care of the bundle of coins, and nevertheless the coins **were lost, he is not liable for them**. He has the same status as any other unpaid bailee, and is exempt from liability for robbery or loss.

NOTES

בְּכִיסֵי **With thorns.** Our commentary follows *Rashi,* who explains that, according to Rav Ashi, the hops were of an inferior quality. The difficulty with his explanation is that the bailee is still paying the full value of the admittedly inferior hops. Hence, it is not clear why Rav Ashi found it necessary to stipulate that the hops were inferior, as regardless of their quality the bailee must pay their full value.

Other Rishonim explain that the depositor's hops were perfectly good. However, they were not yet ready to be

HALAKHAH

the value of the benefit he derived from the depositor's hops. Thus, if the beer was spoiled by the hops, he does not pay anything.

"The above applies only if it is possible that the bailee and his employee made an honest mistake — for example, where the two piles of hops were nearby. But if one was near and the other far, the bailee should have noticed that the employee took too much or too little time bringing the hops, and should have questioned him." The *Shulḥan Arukh* also quotes an opinion that this law applies only if the bailee was unpaid. A paid bailee, however, is liable for mistakes of this kind, as he must make certain that his employees do not touch the deposit. (Ibid., 291:25.)

הַמַּפְקִיד מָעוֹת אֵצֶל שׁוּלְחָנִי **Someone who deposits money with a money changer.** "If someone deposits money with a money changer or with a shopkeeper (following Rabbi

LITERAL TRANSLATION

[1] [If] they are loose, he may use them. [2] Therefore, if they were lost, he is liable for them.

[3] [If the coins were deposited] with a private person (lit., "a house-owner"), whether they are bound up or loose, [4] he may not use them. [5] Therefore, if they were lost, he is not liable for them.

[6] A shopkeeper is like a private person. [7] [These are] the words of Rabbi Meir. [8] Rabbi Yehudah says: A shopkeeper is like a money changer.

GEMARA [9] Because they are bound up he may not use them?

[1] מוּתָּרִין, יִשְׁתַּמֵּשׁ בָּהֶן. [2] לְפִיכָךְ, אִם אָבְדוּ, חַיָּיב בְּאַחֲרָיוּתָן. [3] אֵצֶל בַּעַל הַבַּיִת, בֵּין צְרוּרִין וּבֵין מוּתָּרִין, [4] לֹא יִשְׁתַּמֵּשׁ בָּהֶן. [5] לְפִיכָךְ, אִם אָבְדוּ, אֵינוֹ חַיָּיב בְּאַחֲרָיוּתָן. [6] חֶנְוָנִי כְּבַעַל הַבַּיִת. [7] דִּבְרֵי רַבִּי מֵאִיר. [8] רַבִּי יְהוּדָה אוֹמֵר: חֶנְוָנִי כְּשׁוּלְחָנִי.

גמרא [9] מִשּׁוּם דִּצְרוּרִין לֹא יִשְׁתַּמֵּשׁ בָּהֶן?

RASHI

גמרא משום דצרורין לא ישתמש בהן – בתמיה, ומה גילוי דעת יש כאן שאין חפץ שישתמש בהסל מאחר שאם הן מותרין קאמרת ישתמש בהן, דהמפקיד אללו יודע שהוא לריך תדיר למעות – לרורין נמי ישתמש, דדרך כל אדם לצור מעותיו.

TRANSLATION AND COMMENTARY

מוּתָּרִין [1] On the other hand, **if** the coins **were** delivered to the money changer **loose, he may use them,** as the loose delivery of the money indicates that the depositor has no objection to the money changer using the money and returning him other coins of equal value. [2] **Therefore, if** the coins **were lost,** even if the money changer was in no way negligent and did not make use of the money, **he is liable for them.** The right to use the money is a benefit enjoyed by the money changer, so he no longer enjoys the status of an unpaid bailee.

אֵצֶל בַּעַל הַבַּיִת [3] All of the above applies only if the bailee was a professional money changer, but **if the coins were deposited with a private person,** it makes no difference **whether they were bound up or whether they were loose.** [4] In either case the bailee **may not use** the money, since it never occurred to the depositor that the bailee would do so. [5] **Therefore, if** the coins **were lost,** the bailee **is not liable for them,** because he has the status of an unpaid bailee.

חֶנְוָנִי כְּבַעַל הַבַּיִת [6] The Mishnah has so far considered the cases of a professional money changer and of a private person. Intermediate cases are the subject of a difference of opinion between Tannaim. **A shopkeeper is** treated **like a private person** with regard to these laws. He may not use the money, and is not liable if it is lost. [7] **This is the opinion of Rabbi Meir.** [8] But **Rabbi Yehudah says: A shopkeeper is** treated **like a money changer,** and may use the money, provided it was handed to him loose.

GEMARA מִשּׁוּם דִּצְרוּרִין [9] The Gemara begins its analysis of the Mishnah by considering the stipulation that the money must be handed to the money changer loose. The Gemara asks: Since the money changer is permitted to use the coins if they are loose, why should he **not** be permitted to **use them** merely **because they were bound up?** People ordinarily tie up their money, so this does not prove they are unwilling to have it used!

NOTES

added to the beer, because they had not yet been softened properly. Nevertheless, their market value was not affected by this defect, since they could have been prepared for use very quickly. Hence, Rav Ashi's point is that the bailee need pay only for the benefit he derived from the fact that the untreated hops were thrown into his beer, not for the full market value of the hops (*Tosafot, Rif,* and others).

חֶנְוָנִי כְּבַעַל הַבַּיִת **A shopkeeper is like a private person.** In tractate *Kiddushin* (53b), *Rashi* explains that the difference between a money changer and a private person is that the money changer uses money all the time for his business, and hence the depositor naturally expects him to

HALAKHAH

Yehudah against Rabbi Meir), if the money was loose, or even if it was in a bundle, so long as it was not sealed or tied with an unusual knot, the money changer or shopkeeper is allowed to use it. Therefore he is considered to be a paid bailee, and is liable immediately for loss or theft, even if he did not in fact use the money. As soon as he does use the money, he becomes a borrower and is liable even for unavoidable accidents, until he returns an equivalent sum to the depositor (following Rav Naḥman). It is not sufficient in this case to set aside an equivalent sum of money and bury it. It must be returned to the depositor's possession.

"If the money was tied in a bundle and sealed (following Rav Assi), or even if it was not sealed, so long as it was tied with an unusual knot (following the first version of Rav Mari's ruling), the money changer or shopkeeper may not use the deposit. Therefore they remain unpaid bailees, and if the deposit is lost or stolen they are not liable, provided they were not negligent.

"If the money was deposited with a private person, the bailee may not use it regardless of whether it was loose, bound or sealed. Therefore the private person remains an unpaid bailee, and if the deposit is lost or stolen, he is not liable, provided he was not negligent." (*Shulḥan Arukh, Ḥoshen Mishpat* 292:7.)

TRANSLATION AND COMMENTARY

אָמַר רַב אַסִי [1]The Gemara gives two answers to this question: (1) **Rav Assi said in the name of Rav Yehudah: This Mishnah** refers specifically to a case **where the coins were** not only **bound up** but also **sealed,** and it is obvious that the depositor did not want the seal to be broken. But if the coins were simply tied up in an ordinary bundle, they would be treated in the same way as if they had been delivered loose.

רַב מָרִי אָמַר [2](2) **Rav Mari said:** The Mishnah may also be referring to a case where the depositor tied the coins up **with an unusual knot,** even if he did not seal the bundle. An unusual knot is an indication that the depositor does not want the bundle to be opened.

אִיכָּא דְּאָמְרִי [3]**There are some who** report a different version of Rav Mari's statement. In this version **Rav Mari asked: What is the law concerning** coins bound with **an unusual knot?** Is this the equivalent of a seal or not? [4]To this question there was no response, and the Sages **let the question remain undecided.**

מוּתָּרִין יִשְׁתַּמֵּשׁ בָּהֶן [5]The Gemara now considers a different aspect of the Mishnah. The Mishnah said: **"If** the coins **were loose,** the money changer **may use them."** He is thus liable for theft or loss, even if he does not make use of them, because he is no longer an unpaid bailee. Concerning this clause, there was a difference of opinion between Amoraim. [6]**Rav Huna said: This law applies even if** the money **was unavoidably lost** in circumstances beyond the money changer's control. In other words, once the money changer receives permission to use the deposited money, he immediately assumes the status of a borrower. He is liable for any damage to the money, however caused, just as an ordinary borrower is liable for any damage to the borrowed object from the moment he takes possession of it, regardless of whether or not he has yet had the opportunity to use it.

וְהָא אָבְדוּ קָתָנֵי [7]**But,** the Gemara objects, **surely** the Mishnah **states** that the money changer is liable if the coins **"were lost."** Now a borrower is liable for any damage, however caused, whereas a paid bailee is liable for theft and loss, but not for loss in circumstances beyond his control. Does not the Mishnah's choice of words suggest that the money changer has the status of a paid bailee and not that of a borrower?

כְּדְרַבָּה [8]The Gemara answers: This Mishnah must be explained in **accordance** with a statement **Rabbah** made elsewhere (see above, 29b). [9]**For Rabbah said:** Sometimes the expression **"they were stolen,"** appearing in a Mishnah, **means** that they were stolen **by armed robbers,** [10]and likewise the expression **"they were lost" means that his ship sank at sea.** Thus we see that the Mishnah sometimes uses the terms "theft" and "loss" in a wider sense, to include damage beyond the bailee's control. Hence, no objection can be raised against Rav Huna's opinion from the Mishnah's choice of words.

[1]אָמַר רַב אַסִי אָמַר רַב יְהוּדָה: בִּצְרוּרִין וַחֲתוּמִין שָׁנוּ.

[2]רַב מָרִי אָמַר: בְּקֶשֶׁר מְשׁוּנֶּה.

[3]אִיכָּא דְּאָמְרִי: בָּעֵי רַב מָרִי: קֶשֶׁר מְשׁוּנֶּה מַאי? [4]תֵּיקוּ.

[5]"מוּתָּרִין יִשְׁתַּמֵּשׁ בָּהֶן כו'".

[6]אָמַר רַב הוּנָא: וַאֲפִילּוּ נֶאֶנְסוּ.

[7]וְהָא "אָבְדוּ" קָתָנֵי!

[8]כִּדְרַבָּה, [9]דְּאָמַר רַבָּה: "נִגְנְבוּ" בְּלִסְטִין מְזוּיָּין; [10]"אָבְדוּ" שֶׁטָּבְעָה סְפִינָתוֹ בַּיָּם.

LITERAL TRANSLATION

[1]Rav Assi said in the name of Rav Yehudah: They taught [this] concerning [coins that were] bound up and sealed.

[2]Rav Mari said: With an unusual knot.

[3]There are [some] who say: Rav Mari asked: What is [the law concerning] an unusual knot? [4]Let [the question] remain [undecided].

[5]"[If] they are loose, he may use them, etc." [6]Rav Huna said: And even if they were unavoidably lost.

[7]But surely it teaches: "They were lost"!

[8][It is] in accordance with Rabbah, [9]for Rabbah said: "They were stolen" [means stolen] by an armed robber; [10]"they were lost" [means] that his ship sank in the sea.

RASHI

ואפילו נאנסו – קאמר מתניתין דחייב באחריותן, ואפילו לא נשתמש בהן, דמהשתא הוי שואל עלייהו.

BACKGROUND

לִסְטִין מְזוּיָּין **An armed robber.** A thief is someone who steals in secret and does not wish to be seen by anyone. For that reason, normal precautions are useful against his depredations. However, an armed robber (לִסְטִין מְזוּיָּין) does not refrain from violence, and for that reason, when he robs someone, it is regarded as an unavoidable loss.

SAGES

רַב (רַבִּי) אַסִי **Rav (Rabbi) Assi.** A leading Amora of the third generation, Rav Assi was born and brought up in Babylonia, and studied there under Shmuel and Rav Yehudah. He immigrated to Eretz Israel, where his principal teacher was Rabbi Yoḥanan. He was a close colleague and friend of Rabbi Ammi.

רַב מָרִי **Rav Mari.** Of the two Babylonian Amoraim of this name, the one quoted here is more likely to be the first, who belonged to the third generation.

NOTES

use the deposited money as well. By contrast, a private person is not expected to use the deposited money at all. The shopkeeper, however, is difficult to classify. On the one hand, he is a professional, and uses money in his business, just like a money changer. On the other hand, money is not as essential a part of his business as it is for a money changer, since a great deal of the shop's business is based on credit and barter.

בְּקֶשֶׁר מְשׁוּנֶּה **With an unusual knot.** As we know from the laws governing lost property, an unusual knot is an identifying mark, so to tie one's purse with an unusual knot is tantamount to sealing it. On the other hand, the probability exists that the person who tied the knot did not do so for any special purpose, and that this was his regular way of tying knots. For that reason, doubt arises as to whether an unusual knot forbids the recipient of the purse to open it.

TRANSLATION AND COMMENTARY

וְרַב נַחְמָן אָמַר [1]**But Rav Naḥman** disagreed with Rav Huna and **said:** If the coins **were unavoidably lost** in circumstances beyond the money changer's control, the law of the Mishnah does not apply, and **the money changer is not liable.** It is important to note that even Rav Naḥman would agree that once the money changer actually makes use of the money, he must return its value to the depositor, and cannot excuse himself from his obligation by claiming that the money was lost in circumstances beyond his control. The difference of opinion between Rav Huna and Rav Naḥman concerns a money changer who has permission to spend the money but has not yet done so. Rav Huna considers him a borrower already, while Rav Naḥman treats him like a paid bailee.

אֲמַר לֵיהּ רָבָא לְרַב נַחְמָן [2]**Rava said to Rav Naḥman: According to you, who say** [3]that **if** the money **was** unavoidably lost in circumstances beyond the money changer's control, the law of the Mishnah does not apply and **the money changer is not liable,** [4]**we may infer** that the money changer **is not** yet **considered to have borrowed the money,** since a borrower would be liable even for damage due to circumstances beyond his control. [5]But **if he is not** yet **considered a borrower, he** should **also not be considered a paid bailee,** since the remuneration he receives for his service is the right to make use of the money. According to you, he has not yet received this benefit. Why, then, is he liable if the money was lost before he could make use of it? He should be considered an unpaid bailee until he actually makes use of the money.

אֲמַר לֵיהּ [6]In reply, **Rav Naḥman said to** Rava: **On one point I agree with you.** In other words, I accept your reasoning that a change of status occurs from the moment the money changer receives permission to make use of the money, even before he actually does so, since the money changer can no longer claim to be doing a favor for no charge. [7]**For since** the money changer has **benefited** from the depositor's permission to make use of the money, **he must** also **confer benefit** on the depositor by accepting responsibility

[1] וְרַב נַחְמָן אָמַר: נֶאֱנְסוּ לֹא.
[2] אֲמַר לֵיהּ רָבָא לְרַב נַחְמָן: לְדִידָךְ, דְּאָמְרַתְּ: [3] נֶאֱנְסוּ לֹא,
[4] אַלְמָא לָא הָוֵי שׁוֹאֵל עֲלַיְיהוּ.
[5] אִי שׁוֹאֵל לָא הָוֵי, שׁוֹמֵר שָׂכָר נַמִי לָא הָוֵי!
[6] אֲמַר לֵיהּ: בְּהָא מוֹדֵינָא לָךְ, [7] דְּהוֹאִיל וְנֶהֱנֶה מְהַנֶּה.

LITERAL TRANSLATION

[1] But Rav Naḥman said: If they were unavoidably lost, [the bailee is] not [liable].

[2] Rava said to Rav Naḥman: According to you, who say: [3] If they were unavoidably lost, [the bailee is] not [liable], [4] consequently he is not [considered] a borrower with respect to them [the coins]. [5] If he is not [considered] a borrower, he is also not [considered] a paid bailee!

[6] He said to him: In this I agree with you. [7] For since he benefited, he confers benefit.

RASHI

נאנסו לא — כל זמן שלא נשתמש לא הוי שואל. אלא אבדו דוקא חייב, כשומר שכר. **ואי שואל לא הוי שומר שכר נמי לא הוי** — מה שכר נטל על שמירתם? אלא על שסמך עליהם להחליפן ולהשתכר אם יצא לידו אתה מחייבו, ושאלה היא זו, שהרי כל הנאה שלו. **בההיא מודינא** — אף על גב דאמינא לא הוי שואל מהשתא עד שישתמש, מודינא דשומר שכר הוי. **דהואיל ונהנה מהנה** — לבעלים.

NOTES

וְרַב נַחְמָן אָמַר נֶאֱנְסוּ לֹא But Rav Naḥman said: If they were unavoidably lost, the bailee is not liable. According to Rav Naḥman, since the money changer has permission to use the money, he is no longer an unpaid bailee. But he does not become a borrower until he makes use of the money. The Rishonim note: Earlier in the tractate (above, 29a), the Gemara considers the case of a person who finds lost money and takes care of it until he can find its owner. Rabbah is of the opinion that the finder of the money has the status of an unpaid bailee, while Rav Yosef rules that he has the status of a paid bailee. But even Rav Yosef agrees that where the finder is permitted to spend the money and return other money, he has the status of a borrower even before he spends the money. Hence the Rishonim ask: What is the difference, according to Rav Naḥman, between a finder of lost money and a money changer who agrees to safeguard a deposit of loose money? Both are permitted to spend the money in their charge. Why is the finder a borrower from the first moment, whereas the money changer becomes a borrower only when he actually makes use of the money?

Several Rishonim accept the explanation of *Rabbenu Efraim,* who says that a money changer who is not permitted to use money placed in his care is an unpaid bailee. Therefore, in circumstances where he *is* permitted to use the money, he is raised to the level of a paid bailee until he actually uses it, when he becomes a borrower. A finder, however, is already a paid bailee, according to Rav Yosef. Therefore, when he is permitted to use the lost property, he is immediately raised to the level of a borrower, whether or not he actually uses it.

Other Rishonim prefer *Ra'avad*'s interpretation. He argues that a person cannot become a borrower without agreeing to borrow. Hence, a money changer does not become a borrower unless he actually chooses to use the money. If he prefers to keep the money for a while in the expectation that the owner will soon come to collect it, he remains a paid bailee, since permission to use the money is equivalent to remuneration. In the case of a finder, however, the two parties did not agree to anything, since the owner and the finder have had no contact with each other. It was the Sages who assessed the finder's state of mind, and they decided

TRANSLATION AND COMMENTARY

if the money is stolen or lost. [1]Rav Naḥman elaborates: **By virtue of the benefit that** the money changer enjoys — namely, **that if a potentially profitable purchase presents itself,** [2]**he** is permitted to **buy it with** the coins — he can no longer claim to be doing a favor with no personal benefit. [3]Therefore **he is** immediately **considered** to be **a paid bailee with regard** to the money, even though he has not yet made use of it, and must accept the degree of responsibility appropriate to his new status. If and when he actually makes use of the money, his status will change to that of a borrower; he will be fully liable for the money under all circumstances.

אֵיתִיבֵיהּ רַב נַחְמָן לְרַב הוּנָא [4]**Rav Naḥman raised an objection to Rav Huna** from a Baraita similar but not identical to a Mishnah in tractate *Me'ilah* (21b). The subject of this Tannaitic source is the law of inadvertent *me'ilah* (מְעִילָה) — the inadvertent unlawful use of property consecrated to the Temple. The Torah states (Leviticus 5:15-16) that if a person "commmits a trespass and sins through ignorance against the holy things of the Lord," he must pay a fine and bring a guilt-offering.

הַמַּפְקִיד מָעוֹת אֵצֶל שׁוּלְחָנִי [5]The Baraita reads as follows: **"If the Temple treasurer deposited coins with a money changer,** [6]and when the treasurer handed them over **they were bound up** in a bundle, the money changer **may not use them.** [7]**Therefore, if** the money changer **spent** the deposited coins, and later learned that they were Temple funds that the Temple treasurer had mixed up with his own coins and deposited by mistake, [8]**the treasurer** who deposited the coins with the money changer **is not guilty of *me'ilah,*** since he did not give the money changer permission to spend the money. Rather, *me'ilah* was committed by the money changer, who misappropriated a deposit, not realizing that it belonged to the Temple treasury. [9]**But if** the coins **were** delivered by the Temple treasurer to the money changer **loose,** the money changer **may use them,** as the treasurer is considered to have given him permission to do so. [10]**Therefore, if** the money changer **spent** the deposited coins, [11]**the treasurer,** and not the money changer, **is guilty of *me'ilah,*** since he gave the money changer permission to use the money, and the law is that a person who directs another person to commit *me'ilah* is liable."

[1]בְּהַהוּא הֲנָאָה דְּאִי מִיתְרְמֵי לֵיהּ זְבִינָא דְּאִית בָּהּ רַוְוחָא, [2]זָבֵן בְּהוּ, [3]הָוֵי עֲלַיְיהוּ שׁוֹמֵר שָׂכָר.

[4]אֵיתִיבֵיהּ רַב נַחְמָן לְרַב הוּנָא: [5]"הַמַּפְקִיד מָעוֹת אֵצֶל שׁוּלְחָנִי, [6]אִם צְרוּרִין, לֹא יִשְׁתַּמֵּשׁ בָּהֶן. [7]לְפִיכָךְ, אִם הוֹצִיא, [8]לֹא מָעַל הַגִּזְבָּר. [9]וְאִם מוּתָּרִין, יִשְׁתַּמֵּשׁ בָּהֶן. [10]לְפִיכָךְ, אִם הוֹצִיא, [11]מָעַל הַגִּזְבָּר".

LITERAL TRANSLATION

[1]By virtue of that benefit that if a purchase occurs for him in which there is profit, [2]he can buy [it] with them, [3]he is [considered] a paid bailee regarding them.

[4]Rav Naḥman raised an objection to Rav Huna: [5]"[A Temple treasurer] who deposits coins with a money changer, [6]if they are bound up, he may not use them. [7]Therefore, if he spent [them], [8]the treasurer has not committed *me'ilah.* [9]But if they are loose, he may use them. [10]Therefore, if he spent [them], [11]the treasurer has committed *me'ilah.*"

RASHI

המפקיד מעות — גזבר שהפקיד מעות הקדש, כסבור שהן שלו. **לא מעל גזבר** — שהרי לא ברשות הוציאן, ולאו שלוחו. **מותרין** — דהוה ליה כנותן רשות, והוה ליה שלוחו. **לפיכך אם הוציא** — שולחני, מעל גזבר.

CONCEPTS

מְעִילָה *Me'ilah.* The unlawful use of consecrated property. Anyone who benefits from consecrated property or damages it through use is guilty of *me'ilah.* Intentional *me'ilah* is punishable by death at the hand of Heaven, according to some authorities, and by lashes, according to others. One who commits *me'ilah* unintentionally, or even under duress, must repay the Temple for the loss he caused or the benefit he gained, plus a fine of one-fifth of the value of the loss or of the benefit he gained. He must also bring a special sacrifice, **אָשָׁם מְעִילוֹת** — a "guilt-offering for trespass." (See Leviticus 5:15-16.) The laws of *me'ilah* apply to all types of consecrated property, whether sacrifices, money or objects donated to the Temple. *Me'ilah* is a special case in that the principle of אֵין שָׁלִיחַ לִדְבַר עֲבֵירָה — "there is no agent for transgression" — does not apply to it. If someone commits a transgression at the behest of someone else, only the person who actually committed the act is usually liable to punishment, and not the person who sent him. In the case of *me'ilah,* however, if an agent was sent by someone else to make use of consecrated property, the sender is the one who transgressed.

NOTES

that most finders would prefer to borrow the money and treat it as their own, rather than keep it indefinitely in a safe place. Hence the finder is bound by this assessment, even if he feels otherwise and chooses not to use the money.

מְעִילָה *Me'ilah.* The fundamental principle involved in the law of inadvertent *me'ilah* (*me'ilah* committed deliberately is subject to a different and more serious penalty) is as follows: A person is guilty of inadvertent *me'ilah* only if he inadvertently stole or damaged Temple property. To be guilty of inadvertent *me'ilah,* it is sufficient for the transgressor not to realize that the object belongs to the Temple. As soon as a person is guilty of *me'ilah,* the article ceases to be Temple property, and the transgressor must pay its value to the Temple treasury. Where an act of *me'ilah* involves more than one person, it is important to determine at precisely what point the article ceased to be Temple property. It is also important to bear in mind that the normal rule that a person guilty of a misdemeanor cannot excuse himself by claiming to have been following someone else's orders (אֵין שָׁלִיחַ לִדְבַר עֲבֵירָה) does not apply in the case of *me'ilah.* Thus, if someone commits *me'ilah* against Temple property at another person's direction, the one who gives the order — and not the person who carries it out — is guilty.

HALAKHAH

דִּין מְעִילָה בְּפִקָּדוֹן The law of *me'ilah,* as it applies to a deposit. "If the Temple treasurer deposited Temple funds with a private person, thinking they were his own, the bailee has no right to use the money. Therefore, if the bailee did

[1]וְאִי אָמְרַתְּ ״אֲפִילּוּ נֶאֱנְסוּ״, [2]מַאי אִירְיָא ״הוֹצִיא״? [3]אֲפִילּוּ לֹא הוֹצִיא נַמִי!
[4]אֲמַר לֵיהּ: הוּא הַדִּין אַף עַל גַּב דְּלָא הוֹצִיא, [5]וְאַיְּידֵי דְּתָנָא רֵישָׁא ״הוֹצִיא״, [6]תָּנָא סֵיפָא נַמִי ״הוֹצִיא״.

מִשְׁנָה [7]הַשּׁוֹלֵחַ יָד בְּפִקָּדוֹן, [8]בֵּית שַׁמַּאי אוֹמְרִים: יִלְקֶה

LITERAL TRANSLATION

[1]But if you say "even if they were unavoidably lost," [2]why specify "[if] he spent"? [3]Even if he did not spend also!

[4]He said to him: The same law applies even if he did not spend [the money], [5]but since the first clause taught "he spent," [6]the last clause also taught "he spent."

MISHNAH [7]Someone who misappropriates a deposit, [8]Bet Shammai say: He is penalized

TRANSLATION AND COMMENTARY

וְאִי אָמְרַתְּ אֲפִילּוּ נֶאֱנְסוּ [1]Rav Naḥman now explains his objection: **If you**, Rav Huna, **say** that the law of our Mishnah applies **even if** the coins **were unavoidably lost** in circumstances beyond the money changer's control, because the money changer is considered to have borrowed the money from the moment he received it into his care, [2]**why** does the Baraita **specify** in the second clause that the treasurer is guilty of *me'ilah* only **"if** the money changer **spent** the money"? [3]**Even if he did not spend** the money, the law should **also** apply. In the second clause, where the money was deposited loose, the treasurer is considered to have given the money changer permission to spend it, and according to you the treasurer is considered to have lent it to the money changer at the moment he deposited it.

אֲמַר לֵיהּ [4]In reply to this objection, Rav Huna **said to** Rav Naḥman: **The same law applies even if** the money changer **did not spend the money,** for as soon as the money was delivered loose by the treasurer to the money changer, the treasurer is considered to have lent Temple funds to him, and is guilty of *me'ilah,* regardless of any subsequent actions on the part of the money changer. [5]**But since the first clause** of the Baraita **used the expression "he spent,"** because in the first clause the money changer had no permission to spend the money, and no one was guilty of *me'ilah* until the money was spent, [6]therefore **the last clause also used the** same **expression — "he spent"** — even though it is not strictly appropriate. For as soon as the depositor lends the money to the money changer, he has already committed *me'ilah;* it makes no difference what the money changer does with the money afterwards.

MISHNAH הַשּׁוֹלֵחַ יָד בְּפִקָּדוֹן [7]If a bailee **misappropriates a deposit** and takes it for his own use, he must return it to its owner. If, after the bailee has taken it for his own use, it subsequently leaves his possession (e.g., if he sells it, gives it away or destroys it), he must repay its value to the depositor. If the value of the misappropriated article fluctuates over time, the question arises: Should the bailee pay for the deposit according to its value at the time it was misappropriated, or according to its value at the time it left his possession? Or should he pay the amount it would cost to replace the article at the time repayment is demanded by the depositor? On this question, there is a difference of opinion between Tannaim. [8]**Bet Shammai say: The bailee is penalized for** any **decrease** in the deposit's value **and for** any **increase** in the deposit's value.

RASHI

ואי אמרת אפילו נאנסו — תנא מתניתין דחייב שולחני באחריותן, נמצא משעה שהפקידו אצלו יצאו מרשות הקדש ובאו לרשות שולחני, ונעשה כמו שלוה לו. ואין הוצאה גדולה מזו, מאי איריא הוציא? **איידי דתנא רישא הוציא** — לאשמועינן רבותא, דאפילו הוציא לא מעל, תנא סיפא הוציא.

HALAKHAH

misappropriate it and spend it, he is guilty of *me'ilah* and must bring a guilt-offering.

"If the money was deposited with a money changer or a shopkeeper and was tied in a bundle and sealed, or tied in a bundle with an unusual knot, the law is the same as in the case of the private person. If the money was delivered to the money changer or shopkeeper loose, or tied in a bundle with an ordinary knot and unsealed, the money changer or shopkeeper is permitted to use the deposit. Therefore, if the deposit consisted of Temple funds inadvertently deposited as ordinary funds, and the bailee spent the money, neither the depositor nor the bailee is guilty of *me'ilah,* and neither need bring a guilt-offering. The depositor is exempt, because he did not order the bailee to spend the money, and the bailee is exempt, because he had permission to spend the money." (*Rambam, Sefer Avodah, Hilkhot Me'ilah* 7:9-10.)

Rambam's ruling is not consistent with our Gemara. *Kesef Mishneh* explains, in the name of *Ri Korkos,* that *Rambam* rejected the Baraita quoted in our Gemara, because he was of the opinion that, in a case such as ours, *me'ilah* could occur only if the depositor expressly ordered the bailee to spend the money, but not if he merely gave him permission to do so.

הַשּׁוֹלֵחַ יָד בְּפִקָּדוֹן **Misappropriation of a deposit.** "A bailee who misappropriates a deposit has the status of a robber. If he is unable to return the deposit itself to its owner, he must pay the owner its value, in accordance with the laws pertaining to robbers. *Shakh* explains that this means that he must pay what it was worth at the time of the misappropriation, following the view of Bet Hillel." (*Shulḥan Arukh, Ḥoshen Mishpat* 292:5.)

בְּחָסֵר וּבְיָתֵר. [1]וּבֵית הִלֵּל אוֹמְרִים: כִּשְׁעַת הוֹצָאָה. [2]רַבִּי עֲקִיבָא אוֹמֵר: כִּשְׁעַת הַתְּבִיעָה.

גמרא [3]אֲמַר רַבָּה: הַאי מַאן דִּגְזַל חָבִיתָא דְּחַמְרָא מֵחַבְרֵיהּ, [4]מֵעִיקָּרָא שַׁוְיָא זוּזָא, [5]הָשְׁתָּא שַׁוְיָא אַרְבָּעָה, תַּבְרָהּ אוֹ שַׁתְיָיהּ, [6]מְשַׁלֵּם אַרְבָּעָה. [7]אִיתְבַּר מִמֵּילָא, מְשַׁלֵּם זוּזָא. [8]מַאי טַעְמָא? [9]כֵּיוָן דְּאִי אִיתָהּ הָדְרָא לְמָרַהּ בְּעֵינָא, [10]הַהִיא שַׁעְתָּא דְּקָא שָׁתֵי לֵיהּ אוֹ דְּקָא תָּבַר לַהּ קָא גָּזַל מִינֵּיהּ,

LITERAL TRANSLATION

for decrease and for increase. [1]But Bet Hillel say: [He pays] as at the time of taking out. [2]Rabbi Akiva says: As at the time of the claim.

GEMARA [3]Rabbah said: [If] someone robbed his fellow of a barrel of wine, [4][and] originally it was worth a zuz, [5][but] now it is worth four, [and] he broke it or drank it, [6]he pays four. [7][If] it broke on its own, he pays a zuz.

[8]What is the reason? [9]Since, if it is there, it returns to its owner as it is, [10]it is at that hour when he drinks it or breaks it [that] he robs him [of it],

TRANSLATION AND COMMENTARY

In other words, if prices fell between the time he misappropriated it and the time it left his possession, the bailee repays the value of the deposit at the time of the misappropriation. And if prices rose, he pays the value at the time it left his possession. [1]**Bet Hillel say:** The bailee always **pays according to** the deposit's value at **the time of "taking out."** The meaning of this expression will be explained by the Gemara. [2]**Rabbi Akiva says:** The bailee must always reimburse the depositor, **according to** the value of the article **at the time** when **the claim** is made in court.

GEMARA אֲמַר רַבָּה [3]**Rabbah** now describes a case similar to that mentioned in our Mishnah, but involving a robber, not a dishonest bailee. He **said:** If **someone robs another person of a barrel of wine,** he must return it to its owner. If, after the robbery, it leaves the robber's possession or is destroyed, he must repay its value to the owner. [4]Rabbah makes the following distinction: If the barrel of wine **was originally worth one zuz,** [5]but at the time the barrel was destroyed it **was worth four** zuzim, **and** the robber himself **broke** the barrel **or drank** the wine, he cannot simply repay the value of the barrel as it was at the time of the robbery, i.e., one zuz. [6]Rather, **he** must **pay four** zuzim — the value of the barrel at the moment he destroyed it or consumed its contents. [7]On the other hand, **if** the barrel **broke on its own, he pays** only **one zuz** — the value of the barrel of wine at the time of the robbery.

מַאי טַעְמָא [8]The Gemara now explains Rabbah's ruling: **What is the reason** why the robber must pay four zuzim if he himself destroyed the barrel or consumed its contents? [9]The answer is as follows: **If** the barrel **was in existence** at the time the case came to court, **it would return to its owner as** it **is.** In other words, the robber would be obliged to return it intact. Hence, even after the robber took possession of the barrel, the owner still had an interest in it, [10]and **it was** only **at the time when** the robber **drank** the wine **or broke** the barrel **that** the owner was deprived of that interest. Thus, in effect, the robber only **robbed** the owner of the

RASHI

משנה **ילקה בחסר וביתר** — אם חסרו דמיה, שהוזלה בשוק, ישלם דמיה כמו שהיתה שוה בשעה ששלח בה יד, שהיא שעת הגזילה. וכן כל הגזלנין משלמין כשעת הגזילה, וכגון שהוציאה, שאינה בעין. אבל אם ישנה בעין כמות שגזלה, אומר לו: הרי שלך לפניך, כדאמרינן גבי מטבע ונפסל, תרומה ונטמאת, בפרק "הגוזל" [קמא] (בבא קמא לו,ב). **וביתר** — אם שהתה בידו משלח בה יד ונתייקרה, ואחר כך הוציאה — לוקה ביתר דמיה, לשלם כשעת הוצאה. **ובית הלל אומרים כו'** — בגמרא מפרש מאי קאמרי. **בשעת התביעה** — כשעת שיתבעו לדין ובגמרא מפרש טעמא.

גמרא **מעיקרא** — כשגזלה. **ולבסוף** — כשילתה מן העולם. **תברה** — בידים. **או שתייה** — אחר שהוקרה. **דאי איתה** — כאן, בשעת התביעה — הוה מהדרנא בעינא, דכי אמרינן משלם כשעת הגזילה — היכא דליתה בעין, אבל ישנה בעין, בין שהוקרה בין שהוזלה — חוזרת כמות שהיא. הלכך, הואיל ואם תבעה בעודה קיימת לאחר שהוקרה היתה חוזרת בעין, אשתכח דההיא שעתא דקא שתי לה הוא דגזיל לה.

BACKGROUND

יִלְקֶה בְּחָסֵר וּבְיָתֵר He is penalized for decrease and for increase. Unlike Bet Hillel and Rabbi Akiva, who base their rulings on different legal principles in order to determine the moment when the liability of the person who misappropriates an object begins, the approach taken by Bet Shammai involves a form of fine. Since the bailee has violated his trust and misappropriated the deposit, he should be punished in such a way that he can never profit from his action. Therefore what he pays must be neither less than the value of the object at the time of the misappropriation nor less than it is worth at the time of the claim.

NOTES

אִיתְבַּר מִמֵּילָא מְשַׁלֵּם זוּזָא If it broke on its own he pays a zuz. *Ramban* asks: The Gemara (*Sanhedrin*, 72a) compares the cases of a robber and a borrower, and rules that a robber has no more rights in the object he has taken than a borrower has in the object he has borrowed. Now, if someone borrows an object and the object is unavoidably lost, he must pay for it. If the value of the object fluctuated betweeen the time it was borrowed and the time it was destroyed, the borrower must pay what it was worth when it was destroyed. Thus, in a case such as that described by Rabbah, the borrower would pay four zuzim even if the barrel broke by itself. But why should the law

HALAKHAH

הַגּוֹזֵל חֵפֶץ וְהִתְיַיקֵּר Someone who robs another person of an object, and that object thereafter appreciates in value. "A robber has no right at all to any increase in the value of the object after the time of the robbery. Therefore, if he robbed someone of a barrel of wine worth one zuz and it went up in price and became worth four zuzim, he must

BACKGROUND

כָּל הַגַּזְלָנִין מְשַׁלְּמִין כִּשְׁעַת הַגְּזֵילָה All robbers pay as at the time of the robbery. The amount that must be paid by the person who has robbed or stolen or misappropriated an object depends on when he acquired it.

Taking the object from its owners or removing it from their possession deprives them of its use, and the Halakhah no longer regards them as its owners in all respects. Nevertheless, since the Torah requires the robber or thief to return the stolen object, and he is not entitled to pay for it and keep it, only when the object has been destroyed or altered beyond restoration can it be said to have been completely acquired by him. He is then obligated to pay only its value to the former owners.

TRANSLATION AND COMMENTARY

barrel at the time he destroyed it, [1]**and we learned** in a Mishnah (*Bava Kamma* 93b): **"All robbers pay** the value of the object **as** it was **at the time of the robbery."** Therefore, since the barrel of wine was worth four zuzim at the time it was destroyed or consumed by the robber, he must pay four zuzim.

אִיתְבַּר מְמֵּילָא [2]The Gemara now proceeds to explain the second part of Rabbah's statement. **"If the** barrel **broke on its own,** by accident, the robber **pays a** single **zuz** — the value of the barrel at the time of the robbery, and not four zuzim — its value at the time of the accident." [3]**What is the reason** why in this case the robber has to repay the owner of the barrel only one zuz? [4]The answer is as follows: In this case, the robber **did not do any** harm **to** the barrel **now,** at the time it was destroyed, for the loss of the barrel was the result of an accident. [5]So **why do you hold him liable** at all? Clearly, he is liable for the crime he committed at **the time when he robbed** the owner of the barrel. As we have said, a robber must return the article and is liable for any damage to it, however caused. [6]But **at the time** when he committed the robbery, **it was worth** only one **zuz!** Hence, the robber must pay only one zuz — the value of the barrel of wine at the time of the robbery — for we are not charging him with destroying the owner's barrel; we are holding him responsible for having robbed him of it.

תְּנַן [7]The Gemara now compares Rabbah's ruling with the ruling of our Mishnah, on the assumption that there is no difference between the laws applying to a bailee's misappropriation and those applying to robbery: **We have learned** in our Mishnah: **"Bet Hillel say:** The dishonest bailee always pays **as at the time of 'taking out.'"** [8]The Gemara asks: **What does** the expression **"as at the time of 'taking out'" mean?** Does it refer to the time of misappropriation or to the time of destruction?

[1]וּתְנַן: ״כָּל הַגַּזְלָנִין מְשַׁלְּמִין כִּשְׁעַת הַגְּזֵילָה״. [2]״אִיתְבַּר מְמֵּילָא, מְשַׁלֵּם זוּזָא״. [3]מַאי טַעְמָא? [4]הָשְׁתָּא לָא עֲבִיד לַהּ וְלָא מִידֵּי. [5]אַמַּאי קָא מְחַיְּיבַתְּ לֵיהּ? אַהַהִיא שַׁעְתָּא דִּגְזָלָהּ. [6]הַהִיא שַׁעְתָּא זוּזָא הוּא דְּשָׁוְיָא. [7]תְּנַן: ״בֵּית הִלֵּל אוֹמְרִים: כִּשְׁעַת הוֹצָאָה״. [8]מַאי כִּשְׁעַת הוֹצָאָה?

LITERAL TRANSLATION

[1]and we have learned: "All robbers pay as at the time of the robbery."

[2]"[If] it broke on its own, he pays a zuz." [3]What is the reason? [4]He did not do anything to it now. [5]For what do you hold him liable? For the time when he robbed it. [6]At that time it was worth a zuz.

[7]We have learned: "Bet Hillel say: As at the time of taking out." [8]What does "as at the time of taking out" [mean]?

NOTES

applying to a robber be more lenient than that applying to a borrower?

Ramban answers than an object lent to a borrower remains the property of its owner. He can sell it or donate it to the Temple. Conversely, the borrower has no financial obligations towards the lender, so long as nothing has happened to the object. The obligation to pay for the object begins only when the object has been lost. By contrast, the robber takes possession of the object immediately, and its owner cannot sell it or donate it to the Temple. Hence, the financial obligation of the robber is considered to have begun at the moment of robbery, regardless of what happened later. Therefore, the robber pays as at the time of the robbery, and the borrower as at the time the object was unavoidably lost.

כָּל הַגַּזְלָנִין מְשַׁלְּמִין כִּשְׁעַת הַגְּזֵילָה All robbers pay as at the time of the robbery. This quotation from the Mishnah in *Bava Kamma* appears to add nothing to Rabbah's argument. After all, Rabbah's point is precisely that a robber who consumes or deliberately destroys a stolen object does not pay according to the value of the object at the time of the robbery. *Torat Ḥayyim* explains that this clause was included to cover the case where the barrel depreciated in price — a case not specifically mentioned by Rabbah. The law in such a case is that the robber pays the (higher) value — what the goods were worth at the time of the robbery, even if he broke the barrel deliberately. The reason is as follows: If the robber had not broken the barrel, he would have been entitled to return it intact to its owner, even though it had depreciated in value. But if the barrel had broken by accident, he would have been required to pay the original, higher value of the barrel, in accordance with the Mishnah in *Bava Kamma*. Hence, the robber cannot exempt himself from this higher payment merely because he broke the barrel deliberately, rather than by accident.

HALAKHAH

return it as it is. If he broke the barrel, or sold it, or drank the wine, he must repay the higher price, four zuzim. On the other hand, if the barrel broke by accident, he need only pay what it was worth when it was stolen, one zuz," following Rabbah. (*Shulḥan Arukh, Ḥoshen Mishpat* 362:10.)

גַּזְלָנִין מְשַׁלְּמִין כִּשְׁעַת הַגְּזֵילָה Robbers pay as at the time of the robbery. "Property of which a person has been robbed that has undergone no physical change since the robbery must be returned to its owner as it is, even if the owner has already given up hope of recovering it. Even if the robber has died and the property is in the hands of his heirs, it must still be returned. However, if the object underwent a significant physical alteration while in the robber's custody, he need not return the object, but must

TRANSLATION AND COMMENTARY

אִילֵימָא [1]The Gemara now considers each possibility in turn: **If we say** that the expression means that the bailee must repay the value of the deposit **"as it was at the time it was taken out of the world"** — in other words, if we say that Bet Hillel rule that the dishonest bailee always pays what the deposit was worth when it was destroyed or consumed — [2]we have to establish **in which case** Bet Hillel and Bet Shammai **disagree.** [3]**If** we say that they disagree **in the case** where there is a **decrease** in value — where the deposit's value fell between the time it was misappropriated and the time it was destroyed, and Bet Hillel rule that the dishonest bailee need pay only the value of the deposit at the time it was destroyed — [4]**is there anyone who says** that, where the object cannot be restored intact, a robber can repay less than the value of the object at the time of the robbery? [5]**Surely we have learned** in the **Mishnah** (*Bava Kamma* 93b) quoted above: **"All robbers pay** the value of the object **as** it was **at the time of the robbery,"** and the dishonest bailee was guilty of robbery from the moment he misappropriated the deposit! [6]**And if we** say that Bet Hillel and Bet Shammai disagree only in the case of **increase** in value, where the deposit's value rose between the time it was misappropriated and the time it was destroyed, and Bet Hillel rule that the bailee must pay the value of the deposit at the time it was destroyed — [7]surely **this is** precisely **the same as** the view of **Bet Shammai,** with whom Bet Hillel are supposedly in disagreement!

אֶלָּא [43B] [8]**Rather, it is obvious that** the term "as at the time of taking out" **means** that the bailee must repay the value of the deposit **"as it was at the time it was taken out of the owner's house,"** i.e., at the time it was misappropriated. Thus, according to Bet Hillel, the bailee must always repay the value of the deposit as it was at the time of misappropriation, regardless of any subsequent fluctuations in price. If the deposit depreciated in value between the time it was misappropriated and the time it was destroyed, both Bet Hillel and Bet Shammai agree that the bailee must repay the deposit's value at the time it was misappropriated. But Bet Hillel disagree with Bet Shammai if the deposit appreciated in value between the time it was misappropriated and the time it was destroyed. According to Bet Hillel, the bailee need pay only the deposit's value at the time of misappropriation. Bet Shammai, on the other hand, maintain that if the deposit increased in value, and the bailee destroyed or consumed it, he must pay the higher value, just as Rabbah argued above (43a).

לֵימָא רַבָּה דְּאָמַר [9]The Gemara asks: **Shall we say that Rabbah rules in accordance with Bet Shammai** and not in accordance with Bet Hillel, although the Halakhah ordinarily follows Bet Hillel?

[1]אִילֵימָא: כְּשָׁעַת הוֹצָאָה מִן הָעוֹלָם. [2]וּבְמַאי? [3]הַאי בְּחָסֵר, [4]מִי אִיכָּא לְמַאן דְּאָמַר? [5]וְהָא תְּנַן: ״כׇּל הַגַּזְלָנִין מְשַׁלְּמִין כְּשָׁעַת הַגְּזֵילָה״. [6]וְאִי בְּיָתֵר, [7]הַיְינוּ בֵּית שַׁמַּאי! [43B] [8]אֶלָּא פְּשִׁיטָא: כְּשָׁעַת הוֹצָאָה מִבֵּית בְּעָלִים. [9]לֵימָא רַבָּה דַּאֲמַר כְּבֵית שַׁמַּאי?

LITERAL TRANSLATION

[1]If we say: As at the time it was taken out of the world, [2]in what [case do they disagree]? [3]If in [the case of] decrease, [4]is there anyone who says [this]? [5]But surely we have learned: "All robbers pay as at the time of the robbery"! [6]And if in [the case of] increase, [7]this is the same as Bet Shammai! [43B] [8]Rather, it is obvious [that it means]: As at the time of the taking out from the owner's house.

[9]Shall we say that Rabbah says as Bet Shammai?

RASHI

ובמאי — אהייא פליגי בית הלל. **אי בחסר** — כשהוזלה, דקאמרי בית שמאי ילקה לשלם כדמים שהיתה בשעת הגזילה, וקאמרי בית הלל כשעת הוצאה. **ומי איכא למאן דאמר** — היכא דליתיה בעין, דכל הגזלנין לאו כשעת הגזילה משלמין. **אלא פשיטא כשעת הוצאה מבית בעלים** — כשעת הגזילה. וביתר פליגי, דקאמרי בית שמאי: אם הוקרה — ילקה לשלם כשעת הוצאה מן העולם. ובית הלל אמרי: כשעת הוצאה מבית הבעלים.

NOTES

לֵימָא רַבָּה דַּאֲמַר כְּבֵית שַׁמַּאי **Shall we say that Rabbah says as Bet Shammai?** At this stage in its reasoning, the Gemara assumes that Bet Shammai always impose the higher of the two values, whereas Bet Hillel always impose the value as at the time of the robbery. The objection of the Gemara is that Rabbah's ruling appears identical with that of Bet Shammai.

Tosafot asks: Rabbah imposed the higher of the two values only if the robber deliberately broke the barrel. If the barrel broke by accident, he imposed only the value as it was at the time of the robbery. Thus, the Gemara's objection — that Rabbah appears to agree with Bet Shammai — is based on the assumption that Bet Shammai and Bet Hillel are referring specifically to a case where the robber

HALAKHAH

pay for it, in accordance with its value at the time of the robbery. This law applies even if the change occurred before the owner gave up hope of recovering his property." (Ibid., 362:1.)

LITERAL TRANSLATION

[1] Rabbah can say to you: [2] Regarding appreciation everyone does not disagree. [3] Where they disagree is regarding depreciation.

[4] Bet Shammai maintain: Misappropriation does not require loss, [5] and when it depreciates, it depreciates in his own possession.

[1] אָמַר לָךְ רַבָּה: [2] בְּיָתֵר כּוּלֵּי עָלְמָא לָא פְּלִיגִי. [3] כִּי פְּלִיגִי בְּחָסֵר.

[4] בֵּית שַׁמַּאי סָבְרִי: שְׁלִיחוּת יָד אֵינָהּ צְרִיכָה חִסָּרוֹן, [5] וְכִי חָסֵר, בִּרְשׁוּתָא דִּידֵיהּ חָסֵר.

RASHI

כי פליגי בחסר — וקאמרי בית הלל כשעת הוצאה מן העולם. ודקא קשיא לך כל הגזלנין משלמים כשעת הגזילה אי בגזילה ממש דגזלה מעיקרא — הכי נמי, אבל הכא, דבהיתרא אתא לידיה ומשום שליחות יד קמחייבת ליה — בהא פליגי. **בית שמאי סברי שליחות יד אינה צריכה חסרון** — ומשלח בה יד, אף על פי שלא חסרה — הויא גזלה, וקמה ברשותיה. וכשהוזלה — ברשותו הוזלה. ואם היתה בעין — אומר לו: הרי שלך לפניך. עכשיו שהוציאה — משלם כשעת שליחות יד.

TRANSLATION AND COMMENTARY

אָמַר לָךְ [1] The Gemara replies: **Rabbah can say to you:** The laws applying to misappropriation are not identical to the laws applying to robbery. Both Bet Hillel and Bet Shammai would agree that a robber must pay one zuz if the barrel broke by accident and four zuz if he broke it deliberately, as a robber must always pay the object's value at the time of the robbery, and deliberately breaking a barrel finalizes the act of criminal acquisition. But in the case of a bailee, it is not clear when precisely "the time of the robbery" is. Bet Shammai maintain that it is the moment when the bailee first picks up the deposit with the intention of misappropriating it. Hence the situation of the bailee is the same as that of the robber, and Bet Shammai accordingly rule, as did Rabbah in the case of the robber, that the dishonest bailee must pay the higher of the two values if he destroyed or consumed the deposit deliberately. Bet Hillel, however, maintain that, in the case of a bailee, "the time of the robbery" is the moment when the bailee destroyed or consumed the deposit. Therefore, the bailee must always pay the value of the deposit as it was at the time of destruction, regardless of whether that value is greater or less than the value at the time of misappropriation. We can now explain the words of Bet Hillel — "the time of taking out" — to mean "the time of taking out of the world" (i.e., the time of destruction), [2] and say that **everyone** — both Bet Shammai and Bet Hillel — **agrees** that the bailee must pay the higher value if the deposit **appreciated** in value between the time of misappropriation and the time of destruction. [3] **Where they disagree is regarding depreciation** — if the deposit depreciates in value between the time of misappropriation and the time of destruction. Bet Shammai treat this like a case of robbery and apply Rabbah's principle to impose the higher value, whereas Bet Hillel insist that in the case of a bailee the time of robbery is the time of destruction, not the time of misappropriation, and the bailee must never pay more than the deposit's value at the time of destruction.

בֵּית שַׁמַּאי סָבְרִי [4] The Gemara now explains the meaning behind the two positions: **Bet Shammai maintain: Misappropriation,** like robbery, **does not require** the deposit to suffer **loss,** and a dishonest bailee is guilty of misappropriation. He is liable for any subsequent accidents from the moment he picks up a deposit with the intention of taking some of it for himself. [5] Therefore, **when** the value of the deposit **depreciates** after the time of misappropriation, **it** is considered to have **depreciated** after the bailee has taken it **into his own possession,** i.e., after the time of robbery. The laws of robbery apply, and the bailee must pay the higher of the two rates.

NOTES

deliberately destroyed or consumed the deposit. But there is nothing in the language of the Mishnah to support this assumption! It is equally possible to explain the Mishnah as referring to a case where the deposit was destroyed by accident, regarding which Rabbah ruled that the robber pays the value as it was at the time of the robbery. Now, if we explain the Mishnah in this way, Rabbah's ruling would correspond to the view of Bet Hillel, and Bet Shammai would be stricter — imposing the higher payment even when the barrel broke by accident. This reading of the Mishnah removes the basis of the Gemara's objection to Rabbah's ruling. So what are the grounds for the Gemara's objection?

Tosafot answers that Rabbah's reasoning in the case where the barrel broke by accident is so compelling that it appears inconceivable that anyone — even Bet Shammai — could disagree. For it is obvious that if the barrel broke by accident, the only basis for charging the robber can be the original act of robbery. Hence the robber cannot be held accountable for any increase in value after that date.

שְׁלִיחוּת יָד אֵינָהּ צְרִיכָה חִסָּרוֹן Misappropriation does not require loss. The Rishonim ask: In the following Mishnah, Bet Shammai rule that a bailee who decides to

HALAKHAH

שְׁלִיחוּת יָד אֵינָהּ צְרִיכָה חִסָּרוֹן Misappropriation does not require loss. "A bailee who misappropriates a deposit becomes liable for any accidents it may subsequently suffer. This law applies even if he does not intend to keep the deposit permanently, but only to borrow it for a while, because the law is that someone who borrows without

TRANSLATION AND COMMENTARY

וּבֵית הִלֵּל סָבְרִי [1]**But Bet Hillel maintain: Misappropriation,** unlike robbery, **requires** the deposit to suffer **loss,** so a bailee is not liable for accidents suffered by a deposit until he actually destroys or consumes part of it. [2]Therefore, **when** the value of the deposit **depreciates** after the time of misappropriation, **it** is considered to have **depreciated** while still **in its owner's possession,** as the bailee does not become a robber until the time of destruction. The time of robbery in this case is the time of destruction, and the bailee always pays the value of the deposit as it was at the time of destruction. (The question of whether or not misappropriation requires loss is discussed in detail above, 41a.)

[1]וּבֵית הִלֵּל סָבְרִי: שְׁלִיחוּת יָד צְרִיכָה חִסָּרוֹן, [2]וְכִי חָסֵר, בִּרְשׁוּתָא דְּמָרֵיהּ חָסֵר. [3]אֶלָּא הָא דַּאֲמַר רָבָא — שְׁלִיחוּת יָד אֵינָהּ צְרִיכָה חִסָּרוֹן — [4]לֵימָא רָבָא דַּאֲמַר כְּבֵית שַׁמַּאי? [5]אֶלָּא הָכָא בְּמַאי עָסְקִינַן? [6]כְּגוֹן שֶׁטִּלְטְלָהּ לְהָבִיא עָלֶיהָ גּוֹזָלוֹת,

LITERAL TRANSLATION

[1]But Bet Hillel maintain: Misappropriation requires loss, [2]and when it depreciates, it depreciates in its owner's possession.

[3]But regarding that which Rava said — misappropriation does not require loss — [4]shall we say that Rava says as Bet Shammai?

[5]Rather, with what are we dealing here? [6]For example, where he moved it to bring [down] chicks [while standing] upon it,

RASHI

אלא הא דאמר רבא — לעיל בשמעתין (מא,ב). **שליחות יד אינה צריכה חסרון** — דקאמר שלא תאמר שליחות יד כו'.

אֶלָּא הָא דַּאֲמַר רָבָא [3]The Gemara now questions the hypothesis that Bet Shammai and Bet Hillel disagree as to whether or not misappropriation requires loss: **But** in the light of this hypothesis, how can we explain the following ruling **given by Rava** (see above, 41b): The Halakhah is that **misappropriation does not require loss.** We have just postulated that this is the view held by Bet Shammai. [4]**Shall we say that Rava maintains** the same view **as Bet Shammai?** Surely it is unacceptable for an Amora to rule in favor of Bet Shammai and against Bet Hillel!

אֶלָּא הָכָא בְּמַאי עָסְקִינַן [5]**Rather,** we must seek another explanation for the difference of opinion in our Mishnah. In this further attempt to explain the Mishnah, the Gemara argues that the essence of the dispute between Bet Hillel and Bet Shammai remains whether the robbery occurs at the time of misappropriation or the time of destruction. But it proposes a different explanation of the reasoning behind their dispute. The Gemara suggests: **With what are we dealing here?** [6]**For example,** with a case **where** the bailee **moved** the barrel, not to take its contents for himself, but to use it as a ladder **to bring down young birds** from a dovecote **while**

NOTES

misappropriate a deposit immediately becomes liable for any accidents that it may suffer, even if he has not yet taken any action, whereas Bet Hillel rule that he is not liable until he actually misappropriates the object. Ostensibly the two schools disagree as to whether or not misappropriation requires loss. Bet Shammai rule that it does not, and a bailee is liable even for intent, whereas Bet Hillel rule that it does, and a bailee is not liable until he actually causes damage. But according to the Gemara's current interpretation, this is precisely the point of dispute in our Mishnah. What, then, is the difference between these two Mishnayot?

Tosafot points out that the second Mishnah is needed to teach us the full extent of the position of Bet Shammai, as our Mishnah deals with an action — albeit one that does not cause loss — and there is no indication in our Mishnah that Bet Shammai would render a bailee liable for intention alone. Likewise, our Mishnah is needed to teach us the full extent of the position of Bet Hillel, as there is no indication in the following Mishnah that Bet Hillel would not be satisfied with an action that involved no loss, so long as it was not merely an intention. Hence, both Mishnayot are needed.

Rosh and *Ramban* add that "intention" in the following Mishnah refers to a declared intention, not merely to a thought. Hence, were it not for our Mishnah, we might have thought that Bet Shammai would not render a bailee liable for picking up a deposit, even though in the second Mishnah they render him liable for a declared intention to cause damage, since picking up a deposit does not itself cause any damage, and his intention to cause damage is undeclared.

HALAKHAH

permission is considered a robber. The misappropriation does not necessarily have to involve an immediate loss to the deposit. Rather, from the moment the bailee picks up the deposit with the *intention* of causing a loss, he becomes liable for any accidents that may subsequently befall it. If, however, he picks it up with the intention of borrowing it for some use that will not cause any loss, he is not liable until he actually uses it, since the basis of the liability is not the regular rule applicable to misappropriation, but rather the law that someone who borrows without permission is deemed to be a robber," following Rava and the Gemara's conclusion. (*Shulḥan Arukh, Ḥoshen Mishpat* 292:1.)

LITERAL TRANSLATION

[1] and they disagree about someone who borrows without [the owner's] knowledge.

[2] Bet Shammai maintain: Someone who borrows without [the owner's] knowledge is [considered] a robber, [3] and when it depreciates, it depreciates in his own possession.

[4] But Bet Hillel maintain: Someone who borrows without [the owner's] knowledge is [considered] a borrower, [5] and when it depreciates, it depreciates in its owner's possession.

[6] But [regarding] that which Rava said — someone who borrows without [the owner's] knowledge is [considered] a robber according to the Sages — [7] shall we say that Rava says as Bet Shammai?

[8] Rather, they disagree here regarding a gain from a robbed object.

[1] וּבְשׁוֹאֵל שֶׁלֹּא מִדַּעַת קָא מִיפַּלְגִי.

[2] בֵּית שַׁמַּאי סָבְרִי: שׁוֹאֵל שֶׁלֹּא מִדַּעַת גַּזְלָן הָוֵי, [3] וְכִי חָסֵר, בִּרְשׁוּתָא דִּידֵיהּ חָסֵר.

[4] וּבֵית הִלֵּל סָבְרִי: שׁוֹאֵל שֶׁלֹּא מִדַּעַת שׁוֹאֵל הָוֵי, [5] וְכִי חָסֵר, בִּרְשׁוּתָא דְּמָרָהּ חָסֵר.

[6] אֶלָּא הָא דַּאֲמַר רָבָא — שׁוֹאֵל שֶׁלֹּא מִדַּעַת לְרַבָּנַן גַּזְלָן הָוֵי — [7] לֵימָא רָבָא דַּאֲמַר כְּבֵית שַׁמַּאי?

[8] אֶלָּא הָכָא בְּשֶׁבַח שֶׁל גְּזֵילָה

TRANSLATION AND COMMENTARY

standing on it. [1] Thus we are not dealing with a case of misappropriation, but with a bailee **who borrows** a deposit **without the owner's knowledge.** Bet Shammai and Bet Hillel **disagree about** the law in such a case.

בֵּית שַׁמַּאי סָבְרִי [2] **Bet Shammai maintain: Someone who borrows without the owner's knowledge is considered a robber.** Hence, the bailee is guilty of robbery from the moment he picks up the barrel to borrow it. The time of robbery is the time of misappropriation, and the regular rules apply, as explained by Rabbah (above, 43a). [3] Therefore, **when** the value of the deposit **depreciates** after the time of misappropriation, **it** is considered to have **depreciated** after the bailee has already taken it **into his own possession,** i.e., after the time of robbery. The laws of robbery apply, and the bailee must pay the higher of the two rates.

וּבֵית הִלֵּל סָבְרִי [4] **But Bet Hillel maintain: Someone who borrows without the owner's knowledge is considered a borrower,** not a robber. The act of robbery occurred only when the bailee chose to destroy or consume the deposit. [5] Therefore, **when** the value of the deposit **depreciates** after the time of misappropriation, **it** is considered to have **depreciated** while still **in its owner's possession,** as the bailee does not become a robber until the time of destruction. Therefore, the time of robbery in this case is the time of destruction, and the bailee always pays the value of the deposit as it was at the time of destruction. (The question whether someone who borrows an object without permission is considered a borrower or a robber is discussed in detail above, 41a.)

אֶלָּא הָא דַּאֲמַר רָבָא [6] The Gemara now probes the hypothesis that Bet Shammai and Bet Hillel disagree as to whether or not borrowing without the owner's knowledge is equivalent to robbery. **But** how can we explain the following ruling, also **given by Rava** (*Bava Batra* 88a): **"According to the Sages,** who disagree with Rabbi Yehudah in a Mishnah in *Bava Batra* (87b), **someone who borrows without the owner's knowledge is considered a robber"?** Now, the Halakhah normally follows the viewpoint of the Sages, and since Rava said that the Sages were of the opinion that borrowing without the owner's knowledge is equivalent to robbery, it follows that he himself holds the same opinion. But we have just postulated that this is the view held by Bet Shammai [7] **Shall we say that Rava holds** the same view **as Bet Shammai?** Surely, it is unacceptable for an Amora to rule in favor of Bet Shammai and against Bet Hillel!

אֶלָּא הָכָא [8] **Rather,** both of the previous explanations of the logic behind our Mishnah must be rejected, and we must seek another explanation based on entirely different principles. In this third explanation, the term "misappropriation" will be understood in its usual sense, and the expression "the time of taking out" will be

BACKGROUND

שֶׁבַח גְּזֵילָה **Regarding a gain from a robbed object.** When a robber has completely acquired a stolen object after the owner has despaired of recovering it, and has made some irreparable change in it, all authorities agree that the original owner of the object has absolutely no further proprietary rights in it, and can only claim its value. However, before full acquisition has been effected, one may well ask whether the robber owns any part of the thing he has stolen. Although he must return it, perhaps the profits it brings over time do not belong to the owner since, following the robbery, he no longer has full ownership of it. On the other hand, we may perhaps argue (in agreement with Rabbi Meir, and in accordance with the laws of many countries) that the robber is no more than a guardian of the object he has stolen, and that the owner still has full property rights over it.

RASHI

הא דאמר רבא — ב"המוכר את הספינה" (בבא בתרא פח,א). **שואל שלא מדעת לרבנן גזלן הוא** — גבי שולח את בנו אצל חנוני, דפליגי רבנן ורבי יהודה, ואוקי רבא פלוגתייהו בשואל שלא מדעת. ואמר דלרבנן גזלן הוי. ומדאוקי רבא לרבנן בהכי — סבירא ליה לדידיה גזלן הוי, ואהדר לאוקמי מילתיה כרבנן, דהלכתא כרבים. **לימא כבית שמאי** — אמרה. **אלא הכא בשבח גזילה פליגי** — והאי חסר ויתר דמתניתין — לאו ביוקרא וזולא, אלא במאי דחסרה דהיינו גיזות, ובמאי שהותירה כגון אם נתעברה אצלו, דבית שמאי סברי: הכל ישלם, כרבי מאיר דברייתא, ובית הלל כרבי יהודה, כשעת הוצאה מבית הבעלים.

HALAKHAH

שׁוֹאֵל שֶׁלֹּא מִדַּעַת **Someone who borrows without the owner's knowledge.** "A person who borrows an object from its owner without first obtaining his permission is considered a robber, even though he has every intention of returning the object after he has finished with it. All the laws applicable to robbers apply to him." (*Shulḥan Arukh, Ḥoshen Mishpat* 359:5.)

TRANSLATION AND COMMENTARY

interpreted to mean "the time of taking out of the owner's possession," i.e., the time of misappropriation. Bet Hillel and Bet Shammai agree that there is no Halakhic difference between a dishonest bailee and a robber, and both agree that Rabbah's principle applies — a dishonest bailee who consumes a deposit after misappropriating it should be liable for the highest assessable value. However, the dispute between the two schools does not concern fluctuations in price, but rather a physical change in the deposit, and Bet Shammai's ruling that "the bailee is penalized for decrease and increase" does not refer to changes in market price, but to physical changes which occur after the misappropriation or robbery — for example, when an animal is sheared ("decrease") or gives birth ("increase"). Thus, Bet Shammai and Bet Hillel **disagree here about** who is entitled to **gains** from physical changes in **a stolen object.** [1]**Bet Shammai maintain: Gains from a stolen object are the property of the person who was robbed.** [2]**But Bet Hillel maintain: Gains from a stolen object are the property of the robber,** and the robber need only return the stolen object as it was when he took it.

קָמִיפַּלְגִי. [1]בֵּית שַׁמַּאי סָבְרִי: שֶׁבַח גְּזֵילָה דְּנִגְזָל הָוֵי. [2]וּבֵית הִלֵּל סָבְרִי: שֶׁבַח גְּזֵילָה דְּגַזְלָן הָוֵי.

[3]וּבִפְלוּגְתָּא דְּהָנֵי תַּנָּאֵי, [4]דְּתַנְיָא: "הַגּוֹזֵל אֶת הָרָחֵל, [5]גְּזָזָהּ וְיָלְדָה, [6]מְשַׁלֵּם אוֹתָהּ וְאֶת גִּיזּוֹתֶיהָ וְאֶת וְלָדוֹתֶיהָ. [7]דִּבְרֵי רַבִּי מֵאִיר. [8]רַבִּי יְהוּדָה אוֹמֵר: גְּזֵילָה חוֹזֶרֶת בְּעֵינֶיהָ.". [9]דַּיְקָא נַמִי, דְּקָתָנֵי: "בֵּית שַׁמַּאי אוֹמְרִים: [10]יִלְקֶה בְּחָסֵר וּבְיָתֵר. [11]וּבֵית הִלֵּל אוֹמְרִים: כִּשְׁעַת הוֹצָאָה". [12]שְׁמַע מִינָּהּ. [13]"רַבִּי עֲקִיבָא אוֹמֵר: כִּשְׁעַת הַתְּבִיעָה". [14]אָמַר רַב יְהוּדָה אָמַר שְׁמוּאֵל: הֲלָכָה כְּרַבִּי עֲקִיבָא.

LITERAL TRANSLATION

[1]Bet Shammai maintain: A gain from a robbed object is [the property] of the person who was robbed. [2]But Bet Hillel maintain: A gain from a robbed object is [the property] of the robber.

[3]And [they differ] in the dispute between these Tannaim, [4]for it was taught: "Someone who robs [another person of] a ewe, [5][and] sheared it or it gave birth, [6]he pays for it, and for its shearings and for its offspring. [7][These are] the words of Rabbi Meir. [8]Rabbi Yehudah says: The robbed object returns as it is." [9]This is also precise, for it teaches: "Bet Shammai say: [10]He is penalized for decrease and for increase. [11]But Bet Hillel say: [He pays] as at the time of taking out." [12]Conclude from this.

[13]"Rabbi Akiva says: As at the time of the claim." [14]Rav Yehudah said in the name of Shmuel: The Halakhah is in accordance with Rabbi Akiva.

RASHI

דיקא נמי — דבגיזות וולדות פליגי, דקתני לשון חסר ויתר, ולא קתני לשון זול ויוקר.

BACKGROUND

בִּפְלוּגְתָּא דְּהָנֵי תַּנָּאֵי In the dispute between these Tannaim. Sometimes the Talmud compares Tannaitic differences of opinion, suggesting that the subject of one difference (at present under discussion) is also in dispute between a second pair of Tannaim, whose disagreement about another case is based on the same principles.

וּבִפְלוּגְתָּא דְּהָנֵי תַּנָּאֵי [3]The Gemara explains: Bet Hillel and Bet Shammai **differ about the same principle as do the following Tannaim,** with Bet Shammai taking one side, and Bet Hillel the other. [4]**For it was taught** in the following Baraita (*Bava Kamma* 95a): **"Someone robbed another person of an ewe,** [5]**and** while it was in his possession, he **sheared it, or it gave birth.** Later, the robber was caught and returned the ewe to its owner, or paid for it. A question arose, however, about the shearings and the offspring. [6]One Tanna ruled: The robber must **pay for the ewe and for its shearings and for its offspring.** [7]**These were the words of Rabbi Meir.** [8]But **Rabbi Yehudah said: The stolen object returns as it is,** without the shearings or the offspring." Thus Bet Shammai are expressing the opinion held by Rabbi Meir, whereas Bet Hillel are expressing the opinion held by Rabbi Yehudah, and their dispute has no bearing on Rabbah's ruling.

דַּיְקָא נַמִי דְּקָתָנֵי [9]The Gemara notes: **This** last interpretation of our Mishnah to fit Rabbah's ruling **also** reflects the wording of the Mishnah. In other words, it has textual support not connected to Rabbah and his ruling. **For** the Mishnah **teaches: "Bet Shammai say:** [10]**The bailee is penalized for decrease and for increase.** [11]**But Bet Hillel say:** The bailee always **pays according to the time of 'taking out.'"** [12]Now, **from** the fact that the Mishnah uses the unusual terms "decrease and increase" rather than the customary "appreciation and depreciation," we may **conclude** that Bet Shammai were referring to physical changes rather than price fluctuations, and the interpetation offered above of the dispute between Bet Shammai and Bet Hillel is the correct one.

רַבִּי עֲקִיבָא אוֹמֵר [13]Having explained the views of Bet Hillel and Bet Shammai in our Mishnah, the Gemara now considers the view of Rabbi Akiva. The Mishnah states: **"Rabbi Akiva says:** The bailee must always reimburse the depositor **according to the** value of the misappropriated article at the **time of the claim."** [14]**Rav Yehudah said in the name of Shmuel: The Halakhah is in accordance with Rabbi Akiva.**

[1]וּמוֹדֶה רַבִּי עֲקִיבָא בְּמָקוֹם שֶׁיֵּשׁ עֵדִים.

[2]מַאי טַעְמָא? [3]דְּאָמַר קְרָא: ״לַאֲשֶׁר הוּא לוֹ יִתְּנֶנּוּ בְּיוֹם אַשְׁמָתוֹ״, [4]וְכֵיוָן דְּאִיכָּא עֵדִים, [5]מֵהַהוּא שַׁעְתָּא הוּא דְּאִיחַיַּיב לֵיהּ אַשְׁמָה.

[6]אֲמַר לֵיהּ רַב אוֹשַׁעְיָא לְרַב יְהוּדָה: רַבִּי, אַתָּה אוֹמֵר כֵּן? [7]הָכִי אָמַר רַבִּי אַסִי אָמַר רַבִּי יוֹחָנָן: [8]חָלוּק הָיָה רַבִּי עֲקִיבָא אֲפִילּוּ בְּמָקוֹם שֶׁיֵּשׁ עֵדִים.

[9]מַאי טַעְמָא? [10]דְּאָמַר קְרָא: ״לַאֲשֶׁר הוּא לוֹ יִתְּנֶנּוּ בְּיוֹם אַשְׁמָתוֹ״, [11]וּבֵי דִינָא הוּא דְּקָא מְחַיְּיבֵי לֵיהּ אַשְׁמָה.

LITERAL TRANSLATION

[1]And Rabbi Akiva agrees where there are witnesses.

[2]What is the reason? [3]Because the verse says: "To whom it belongs he shall give it on the day of his guilt," [4]and since there are witnesses, [5]it is from that hour that he becomes liable for guilt.

[6]Rav Oshaya said to Rav Yehudah: My teacher, do you say so? [7]Thus said Rabbi Assi in the name of [8]Rabbi Yoḥanan: Rabbi Akiva disagreed even where there are witnesses.

[9]What is the reason? [10]Because the verse says: "To whom it belongs he shall give it on the day of his guilt," [11]and it is the court which renders him liable for guilt.

RASHI

ומודה רבי עקיבא במקום שיש עדים — כמה היתה שוה ביום שגזלה וראו שגזלה הימנו, דמשלם כשעת הגזילה. **מאי טעמא דרבי עקיבא** — דאמר כשעת התביעה. **דאמר קרא ביום אשמתו** — בדמים של אותו יום שהוא מתחייב לו, והיכא דתבעו והודה, דעל פיו הוא מתחייב — העמדתו בדין והודאתו הוא יום אשמתו, אבל אם יש עדים — משעה שראוהו שגזלה הוא אשם לו.

TRANSLATION AND COMMENTARY

[1]**And** Rav Yehudah went on to say that although the Halakhah follows Rabbi Akiva, and the bailee normally pays according to the value of the article at the time of the claim, an exception is made **where there are witnesses** who saw the bailee misappropriate the article, for in such a case **Rabbi Akiva would agree** that the bailee must pay what the deposit was worth at the time he misappropriated it.

מַאי טַעְמָא [2]Rav Yehudah explains: **What is the reason** for this distinction? [3]**Because the verse** (Leviticus 5:24, which deals with a robber who wishes to atone for his sins) **says: "To whom it belongs he shall give it on the day of his guilt."** From the fact that the verse says that he must pay "on the day of his guilt," Rabbi Akiva deduces that the payment must be according to the value of the article on the day of the claim, since the verse is dealing with a robber who was charged in court and admitted his crime, and such a robber is found guilty on the day he makes his admission in court. [4]But if **there were witnesses** to the misappropriation, it is unnecessary for the robber to admit anything, and he can be found guilty on the basis of the witnesses' testimony. [5]Hence, it is **from the time** that the witnesses were in a position to convict him — i.e., from the time of the misappropriation — **that** the bailee **becomes liable,** and that is "the day of **his guilt."** Therefore, if there were witnesses to the misappropriation, Rabbi Akiva would admit that the payment should be based on the deposit's value on the day of misappropriation.

אֲמַר לֵיהּ רַב אוֹשַׁעְיָא [6]**Rav Oshaya said to Rav Yehudah: My teacher, are you** really **saying** that if there are witnesses to the misappropriation Rabbi Akiva agrees that repayment is based on the value of the deposit when it was misappropriated? [7]But surely you know that **Rabbi Assi said in the name of Rabbi Yoḥanan as follows:** [8]**Rabbi Akiva disagrees** with the views of Bet Hillel and Bet Shammai, and maintains that the payment is always based on the deposit's value on the day of the claim, **even where there were witnesses** who testified to the misappropriation!

מַאי טַעְמָא [9]The Gemara explains: **What is the reason** for Rabbi Yoḥanan's statement as reported by Rabbi Assi? [10]It is **because the verse says: "To whom it belongs he** shall **give it on the day of his guilt,"** from which Rabbi Akiva argues that the assessment must be based on the object's value on the day of the claim, [11]**and,** says Rabbi Yoḥanan, **it is** always **the court which renders** the bailee **liable for** his **guilt,** even when its decision is based on the testimony of witnesses.

NOTES

וּמוֹדֶה רַבִּי עֲקִיבָא **And Rabbi Akiva agrees.** From this expression it would appear that Rabbi Akiva differs with Bet Hillel and Bet Shammai when he insists that the assessment is to be based on the value of the deposit at the time of the claim, but agrees with them — at least according to Rav Yehudah — if there are witnesses to the misappropriation. Bet Hillel and Bet Shammai, by contrast, always maintain that the assessment should be based on the value at the time of misappropriation or destruction, not at the time of the claim.

The Rishonim object: In the previous passage, we established that Bet Hillel and Bet Shammai were not discussing price fluctuations at all. Rather, they disagreed about the procedure to be followed if a stolen animal is sheared or gives birth. How then is Rabbi Akiva's ruling related to theirs?

SAGES

רַב אוֹשַׁעְיָא **Rav Oshaya** (or Hoshaya) belonged to the beginning of the third generation of Babylonian Amoraim, and must be distinguished from the Sage known in the Jerusalem Talmud as Rabbi Oshaya Rabbah, a disciple of Rabbi Yehudah HaNasi. While living in Babylonia, Rav Oshaya studied Torah from the greatest of the Amoraim, especially from Rav Yehudah. Some authorities claim that Rav Oshaya and Rav Ḥananyah were brothers of the great Babylonian Amora Rabbah, and like Rabbah were priests who could trace their descent from the Biblical High Priest Eli.

Rav Oshaya and Rav Ḥananyah immigrated to Eretz Israel, where they knew Rabbi Yoḥanan and studied Torah from him. Rav Oshaya married the daughter of the Amora Rabbi Shmuel bar Yitzḥak. The two brothers lived in Tiberias, where they eked out a meager living as cobblers.

In the following generations, Rav Oshaya is mentioned as a model of piety and modesty. Out of respect, the Babylonian Amora Rav Safra calls him "Moses."

TRANSLATION AND COMMENTARY

אֲמַר לֵיהּ רַבִּי זֵירָא [1]Rav Yehudah's statement in Shmuel's name contained two rulings — that the Halakhah is in accordance with Rabbi Akiva, and that Rabbi Akiva agrees with Bet Hillel and Bet Shammai where there are witnesses to the misappropriation. It has just been established that Rabbi Yoḥanan disagreed with Rav Yehudah with regard to the second ruling. The Gemara now turns to Rav Yehudah's first ruling: **Rabbi Zera said to Rabbi Abba bar Pappa:** [2]**When you go** to Eretz Israel, **go around by way of the Ladder of Tyre, and go to Rabbi Ya'akov bar Idi,** [3]**and ask him whether he heard from Rabbi Yoḥanan that the Halakhah is in accordance with Rabbi Akiva or not.**

אֲמַר לֵיהּ [4]Rabbi Abba bar Pappa went to visit Rabbi Ya'akov bar Idi, and asked him Rabbi Zera's question. In reply, Rabbi Ya'akov bar Idi **said to him: Rabbi Yoḥanan said as follows:** [5]**The Halakhah is always in accordance with Rabbi Akiva.**

מַאי לְעוֹלָם [6]The Gemara asks: **What did** Rabbi Yoḥanan **mean** when he used the word **"always"**? The question was about one particular case; clearly Rabbi Yoḥanan was implying that the Halakhah also follows Rabbi Akiva in at least one additional, related case. Which case could it be?

אֲמַר רַב אַשִׁי [7]**Rav Ashi said:** Rabbi Yoḥanan stressed the word "always" **so that you should not say** that **this** ruling — that the Halakhah is in accordance with Rabbi Akiva — **applies** only **where there are no witnesses,** [8]**but** that **where there are witnesses,** the Halakhah is **not** in accordance with him. In other words, Rabbi Ya'akov bar Idi confirmed the previous report of Rabbi Yoḥanan's view — namely, that Rabbi Akiva applies his opinion to all cases, even where there are witnesses, and further states that Rabbi Yoḥanan ruled that the Halakhah follows Rabbi Akiva in this matter.

[1]אֲמַר לֵיהּ רַבִּי זֵירָא לְרַבִּי אַבָּא בַּר פַּפָּא: [2]כִּי אָזְלַתְּ לְהָתָם, אַקִּיף אַסּוּלָּמָא דְּצוֹר, וְעוּל לְגַבֵּיהּ דְּרַבִּי יַעֲקֹב בַּר אִידִי, [3]וּבְעֵי מִינֵּיהּ אִי שְׁמִיעָא לֵיהּ לְרַבִּי יוֹחָנָן הֲלָכָה כְּרַבִּי עֲקִיבָא אוֹ אֵין הֲלָכָה כְּרַבִּי עֲקִיבָא. [4]אֲמַר לֵיהּ: הָכִי אָמַר רַבִּי יוֹחָנָן: [5]הֲלָכָה כְּרַבִּי עֲקִיבָא לְעוֹלָם.

[6]מַאי "לְעוֹלָם"?

[7]אֲמַר רַב אַשִׁי: שֶׁלֹּא תֹּאמַר הָנֵי מִילֵּי הֵיכָא דְּלֵיכָּא עֵדִים, [8]אֲבָל הֵיכָא דְּאִיכָּא עֵדִים, לָא.

LITERAL TRANSLATION

[1]Rabbi Zera said to Rabbi Abba bar Pappa: [2]When you go there, go around by way of the Ladder of Tyre, and go to Rabbi Ya'akov bar Idi, [3]and ask him whether he heard from Rabbi Yoḥanan [that] the Halakhah is in accordance with Rabbi Akiva or [that] the Halakhah is not in accordance with Rabbi Akiva.

[4]He said to him: Thus said Rabbi Yoḥanan: [5]The Halakhah is always in accordance with Rabbi Akiva.

[6]What does "always" [mean]?

[7]Rav Ashi said: That you should not say [that] these words [apply] where there are no witnesses, [8]but where there are witnesses, not.

RASHI

להתם – לארץ ישראל. אקיף – הרבה את הדרך, וסבב דרך ארוכה על דבר זה ללכת, דרך מעלת של הר צור מקום שרבי יעקב שם, ובעי מינה מה שמע מרבי יוחנן רבו על כך. כל מהלך דרך ארוכה במקום שיש קצרה מקיף הוא.

BACKGROUND

אַקִּיף אַסּוּלָּמָא דְּצוֹר **Go around by way of the Ladder of Tyre.**

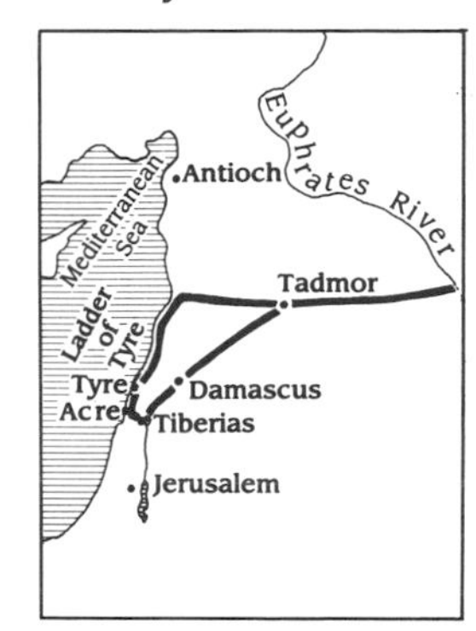

This map shows the various routes by which Rabbi Abba could have reached Eretz Israel. There was a northern route which passed through Tadmor and Damascus. The shortest way to reach Tiberias via Tadmor and Damascus was to cross Golan and lower Galilee. However, there was a longer route, from Tadmor to the Mediterranean Sea and then along the coast to Acre, from which Rabbi Abba would have continued to Tiberias by land. Hence, in order to pass through the "Ladder of Tyre" it was necessary to take a longer, roundabout route to Eretz Israel.

The "Ladder of Tyre" refers in general to the uneven shore-F line of southern Lebanon, as far as the city of Tyre, and in the Talmud it usually refers specifically to the rocky promontory of Rosh HaNikrah, which was then regarded as the northernmost point in Eretz Israel and today marks the northern border of the State of Israel.

SAGES

רַבִּי יַעֲקֹב בַּר אִידִי **Rabbi Ya'akov bar Idi.** A Palestinian Amora of the third generation, Rabbi Ya'akov bar Idi knew the greatest Palestinian Amoraim of the first generation, Rabbi Oshaya, Rabbi Hanina, and Rabbi Yehoshua ben Levi, and studied Torah from them. However, his main teacher was Rabbi Yoḥanan, who was extremely fond of him and used to lean on him while they walked together.

The Sages of the following generation regarded Rabbi Ya'akov bar Idi with great

NOTES

Because of this objection, some Rishonim attempt to explain that Rabbi Akiva is not referring to price fluctuations either, but rather to shearings and offspring (*Ra'avad, Ritva*). Most Rishonim, however, find this explanation difficult to reconcile with the language of our Gemara. *Tosafot* explains that, even according to the conclusion of the previous passage, the Gemara never claimed that Bet Hillel and Bet Shammai were not expressing an opinion about the question of price fluctuations. Rather, because of the considerations raised by Rabbah, the Gemara concluded that Bet Hillel accepted the view of Bet Shammai on this aspect of a more general problem, as we shall now explain. According to *Tosafot*, the Mishnah says that when Bet Shammai ruled that the bailee "is penalized by decrease and increase," they meant that the bailee must always pay the higher assessment, resulting either from physical changes in the misappropriated deposit, or from price fluctuations, as explained by Rabbah. Thus, Bet Shammai are expressly referring to the ruling brought later in the name of Rabbah — that a bailee who misappropriates a deposit and then consumes or destroys it must pay its value either at the time of misappropriation or at the time of destruction, whichever is higher. This was the Gemara's understanding of Bet Shammai from the beginning, and the Gemara never departed from it. The only change in the Gemara's interpretation of the Mishnah concerned Bet Hillel: At first the Gemara thought that Rabbah's ruling was not compatible with the view of Bet Hillel, whereas in the end the Gemara concluded that the point of dispute between Bet Shammai and Bet Hillel concerned only physical changes in the deposit, and that even Bet Hillel could accept Rabbah's ruling regarding fluctuations in price. But even according to the Gemara's conclusion, Bet Shammai (and apparently also Bet Hillel, who agree with Bet Shammai on this point) disagree with Rabbi Akiva, and insist that the assessment must be based on the time of misappropriation and the time of destruction, not on the time of the claim.

respect. Rabbi Zera called him "the greatest of the generation," and his Torah teachings were made known in Babylonia by emissaries from Eretz Israel.
He seems to have lived in the city of Tyre, and the Sages (even Rav Naḥman, the greatest Sage of Babylonia in that generation) used to send questions to him. His teachings are quoted in the Jerusalem Talmud and in the Midrash. Two of his sons were Sages.

BACKGROUND

הֲלָכָה כְּרַבִּי עֲקִיבָא The Halakhah is in accordance with Rabbi Akiva. Since the Halakhah nearly always follows Bet Hillel rather than Bet Shammai (with very few specific exceptions), and since Rabbi Akiva seems to be contributing an independent opinion, a number of factors must be taken into consideration in this Mishnah. On the one hand, Rabbi Akiva's authority is very great, and the Halakhah follows him whenever he is in dispute with other Sages. On the other hand, it is difficult to accept his approach as opposed to that of Bet Hillel, who preceded him in time (generally the Halakhah follows the earlier authority against later authorities, until the middle of the Amoraic period). Thus, despite Shmuel's Halakhic ruling, Rabbi Zera still wished to confirm these matters by basing them on the authority of Rabbi Yoḥanan, whom the Halakhah follows even in opposition to Rav and Shmuel.

TRANSLATION AND COMMENTARY

וְאִי נָמִי [1]**Or alternatively,** Rabbi Yoḥanan, in using the expression "always," may have been **referring to** a different, albeit related, ruling of Rabbi Akiva — namely, **the case where** a dishonest bailee had a change of heart and **returned** a misappropriated deposit **to its place** undamaged, **and** subsequently **it broke** by accident (the case is discussed in detail above, 40b-41a). In that case, Rabbi Yishmael ruled that the bailee is not liable, provided the deposit was not damaged through his negligence, since the bailee returned the deposit to its place and so absolved himself of any liability for misappropriation. Rabbi Akiva, on the other hand, ruled that the bailee cannot absolve himself without informing the owner. [2]Thus in "always" ruling in favor of Rabbi Akiva, Rabbi Yoḥanan's purpose is **to exclude** (i.e., rule against) **the view of Rabbi Yishmael, who said** that the bailee **does not need the owner's knowledge** that he has returned the article to absolve himself of liability for misappropriation. [3]**Therefore** Rabbi Yoḥanan **informs us that we do need the owner's knowledge,** as the Halakhah also follows Rabbi Akiva in this case.

וְרָבָא אָמַר [4]Until now, the Gemara has been assuming that the Halakhah follows Rabbi Akiva in our Mishnah. The only question has been whether Rabbi Akiva himself would agree that his ruling does not apply where there are witnesses. **But Rava said: The Halakhah is** in fact **in accordance with Bet Hillel,** and the bailee must pay in accordance with the value of the object at the time of misappropriation.

MISHNAH הַחוֹשֵׁב לִשְׁלוֹחַ יָד בַּפִּקָּדוֹן [5]If a bailee, in the presence of witnesses, expressed an **intention to misappropriate a deposit,** but the deposit was destroyed before he could carry out his plan, the law is the subject of a Tannaitic dispute. [6]**Bet Shammai say:** From the moment the bailee announces his intention to misappropriate the deposit **he is liable** for whatever happens to it subsequently. Even if the deposit is destroyed by forces beyond his control, he is liable as though he had actually misappropriated it. [7]**But Bet Hillel say: He is not liable until he** actually **misappropriates** the deposit, [8]**as it is said in** the verse (Exodus 22:7): "Then the master of the house (the bailee) shall be brought to the judge to determine **whether he has not put his hand to** [i.e., misappropriated] **his neighbor's goods,"** implying that the bailee is liable only if he actually misappropriates the deposit.

[1]וְאִי נָמִי, דְּאַהַדְרָהּ לְדוּכְתָּהּ וְאִיתַּבְרָא, [2]לְאַפּוּקֵי מִדְּרַבִּי יִשְׁמָעֵאל דְּאָמַר לָא בָּעֵינַן דַּעַת בְּעָלִים. [3]קָא מַשְׁמַע לַן דְּבָעֵינַן דַּעַת בְּעָלִים.

[4]וְרָבָא אָמַר: הֲלָכָה כְּבֵית הִלֵּל.

מִשְׁנָה [5]הַחוֹשֵׁב לִשְׁלוֹחַ יָד בַּפִּקָּדוֹן, [6]בֵּית שַׁמַּאי אוֹמְרִים: חַיָּיב. [7]וּבֵית הִלֵּל אוֹמְרִים: אֵינוֹ חַיָּיב עַד שֶׁיִּשְׁלַח בּוֹ יָד, [8]שֶׁנֶּאֱמַר: "אִם לֹא שָׁלַח יָדוֹ בִּמְלֶאכֶת רֵעֵהוּ".

LITERAL TRANSLATION

[1]Or also [it may refer to] where he returned it to its place and it broke, [2]to exclude [the views] of Rabbi Yishmael, who said: We do not need the owner's knowledge. [3][Therefore] it tells us that we do need the owner's knowledge.

[4]But Rava said: The Halakhah is in accordance with Bet Hillel.

MISHNAH [5]Someone who intends to misappropriate a deposit, [6]Bet Shammai say: He is liable. [7]But Bet Hillel say: He is not liable until he misappropriates it, [8]as it is said: "Whether he has not put his hand to his neighbor's goods."

RASHI

אי נמי דהדרה לדוכתה – להכי אשמועינן "לעולם", לומר שאם החזירה למקומה לאחר ששלח בה יד, ונשברה באונס – אף בזו הלכה כרבי עקיבא, דאמר לעיל גבי גנב טלה מן העדר – צריך דעת בעלים. **ורבא אמר הלכה כבית הלל** – כשעת גזילה, ואנן כרבא עבדינן, דהוה ליה בתרא.

משנה החושב לשלוח יד – אמר בפני עדים: אטול פקדונו של פלוני לעצמי. **חייב** – באונסים, מהיום והלאה, אם נאנס – חייב באחריות.

NOTES

מַחְשָׁבָה בְּפִקָּדוֹן **Intent to misappropriate a deposit.** Our commentary follows *Rashi*, who explains that even according to Bet Shammai, intent to misappropriate a deposit is effective only if expressed in the presence of witnesses. Support for this interpretation can be found in the Scriptural source (Exodus 22:8) for Bet Shammai's opinion — "for every *word* of trespass" (עַל כָּל דְּבַר פֶּשַׁע). The difficulty with this explanation is that the Mishnah uses the word חוֹשֵׁב — from the verb "to think" — to describe the dishonest bailee's crime.

Tosafot points out that in other places also, speech is referred to as thought (see, for example, *Pesaḥim* 63a). *Ramban* suggests that the word "to think" may not mean "to think" as opposed to "to speak." Rather, it may mean "to intend" or "to plan." *Torat Ḥayyim* adds that mere words without deliberate intent are not to be taken seriously, and cannot render a bailee liable for the crime of misappropriation.

Ritva agrees with *Rashi* that, to be liable, the bailee must

HALAKHAH

הַחוֹשֵׁב לִשְׁלוֹחַ יָד בַּפִּקָּדוֹן **Someone who intends to misappropriate a deposit.** "Mere intent to commit misappropriation is not sufficient to render a bailee liable. Even if the bailee announces his intention in the presence

LITERAL TRANSLATION

[1] [If] he tilted the barrel and took a *revi'it* from it and it broke, [2] he pays only a *revi'it*. [3] [If] he lifted it and took a *revi'it* from it and it broke, [4] he pays the value of all of it.

[44A] **GEMARA** [5] From where are these things [derived]?

[6] As our Rabbis taught: "'For any word of trespass,' [7] Bet Shammai say: It teaches that he is liable for intention as [for] action. [8] But Bet Hillel say: He is not liable until he misappropriates it, [9] as it is said: 'Whether he has not put his hand to his neighbor's goods.' [10] Bet Shammai said to Bet Hillel:

[1] הִטָּה אֶת הֶחָבִית וְנָטַל הֵימֶנָּה רְבִיעִית וְנִשְׁבְּרָה, [2] אֵינוֹ מְשַׁלֵּם אֶלָּא רְבִיעִית. [3] הִגְבִּיהָהּ וְנָטַל הֵימֶנָּה רְבִיעִית וְנִשְׁבְּרָה, [4] מְשַׁלֵּם דְּמֵי כּוּלָּהּ.

[44A] **גמרא** [5] מְנָהָנֵי מִילֵּי? [6] דְּתָנוּ רַבָּנַן: "'עַל כָּל דְּבַר פֶּשַׁע', [7] בֵּית שַׁמַּאי אוֹמְרִים: מְלַמֵּד שֶׁחַיָּיב עַל הַמַּחְשָׁבָה כְּמַעֲשֶׂה. [8] וּבֵית הִלֵּל אוֹמְרִים: אֵינוֹ חַיָּיב עַד שֶׁיִּשְׁלַח בּוֹ יָד, [9] שֶׁנֶּאֱמַר: 'אִם לֹא שָׁלַח יָדוֹ בִּמְלֶאכֶת רֵעֵהוּ'. [10] אָמְרוּ לָהֶן בֵּית שַׁמַּאי לְבֵית הִלֵּל:

RASHI

הטה את החבית — מלתא באנפי נפשה היא. **ונשברה** — לאחר זמן. **אינו משלם אלא רביעית** — דשליחות יד אינו מתחייב באונסין עד שימשוך או יגביה, דהוי קנייה. **הגביהה ונטל** — דהוי קנייה בהגבהתה, וחסרון מנטילת רביעית, חייב באונסיה.

TERMINOLOGY

מְנָהָנֵי מִילֵּי From where are these things derived? I.e., what verse in the Torah is the source of the statement just made? This question by the Gemara is usually followed either by a specific Biblical text or by a Midrashic interpretation of Biblical verses from which the Halakhic ruling is derived.

TRANSLATION AND COMMENTARY

הִטָּה אֶת הֶחָבִית [1] The Mishnah now considers a case not directly related to the dispute between Bet Shammai and Bet Hillel. Misappropriation, like robbery, can only take effect if a dishonest bailee illicitly takes possesssion of a deposit for himself. To be sure, the bailee does not legally acquire the deposit. He merely becomes liable for any damage it may subsequently suffer. Nevertheless, the bailee (or robber) must perform "an act of acquisition" before he can be considered to have taken the deposit into his possession. Accordingly, the Mishnah rules: **If** a bailee **tilted a barrel** deposited with him **and took from it a *revi'it*** (a measure approximately equal to half a measuring cup) of wine for himself, **and** later the barrel accidentally **broke,** [2] **he only pays for a *revi'it*,** since that is all that he took. Tilting the barrel is not an "act of acqusition" for the purposes of misappropriation. Hence, the bailee is liable for the *revi'it* he took, but not for the rest of the barrel. [3] On the other hand, **if** the bailee **lifted** the barrel — a recognized "act of acquisition" for the purposes of misappropriation — **and took from it a *revi'it*** of wine for himself, **and** later the barrel accidentally **broke,** [4] the bailee must **pay** the full **value of the entire** barrel, since he misappropriated the entire barrel by lifting it for the purpose of taking some of it, and a bailee who misappropriates a deposit is liable even for damage caused by forces beyond his control.

[44A] **GEMARA** מְנָהָנֵי מִילֵּי [5] The Gemara considers the difference of opinion in the Mishnah between Bet Hillel and Bet Shammai, and asks: **From where do** Bet Hillel and Bet Shammai **derive** their rulings concerning a bailee who expresses the intention to misappropriate property?

דְּתָנוּ רַבָּנַן [6] The Gemara replies: From the verse cited in the following Baraita which **our Rabbis taught:** "Regarding the laws of misappropriation, the verse (Exodus 22:8) says: **'For any matter of trespass**...he shall pay.' Now, the Hebrew word דְּבַר, which we have translated as 'matter,' literally means 'word.' [7] Hence **Bet Shammai say:** This verse **teaches that** a bailee **is liable for** expressed **intention** just **as** he is **for action.** Since the verse speaks of 'any *word* of trespass.' it implies that the person is liable even if he expressed in words the intention of committing misappropriation but did not actually carry it out. [8] On the other hand, **Bet Hillel say:** A bailee **is not liable until he** actually **misappropriates** a deposit. The source for this view is also Scriptural, [9] **as the verse** (ibid., 22:7) **says:** 'Then the master of the house (the bailee) shall be brought to the judges to determine **whether he has not put his hand to** (i.e., misappropriated) **his neighbor's goods,'** implying that the bailee is liable only if he actually misappropriates the deposit. [10] **Bet Shammai said to Bet Hillel:**

NOTES

express his intent in words, but suggests that it may be sufficient for the bailee to have expressed this intent privately, rather than in front of witnesses. According to *Ritva*, this is why the Mishnah refers to such speech as "thought."

Other Rishonim, however, insist that the language of the Mishnah should be interpreted literally (*Rosh* in the name of *Rabbenu Barukh* and others). *Rashi* himself, in tractate *Kiddushin* (42b), appears to follow this opinion. According to this view, a bailee who decides to misappropriate a deposit is liable for any accidents that may subsequently befall it, according to Bet Shammai, even if he said nothing at all about his intention. These Rishonim also reinterpret the passages cited by *Tosafot*. They claim that the Talmud uses the terms "thought" and "speech" interchangeably, because whenever one is required, the other will suffice.

HALAKHAH

of witnesses, he is still exempt if the deposit is damaged by accident before he has an opportunity to carry out his plans," following Bet Hillel. (*Shulhan Arukh, Hoshen Mishpat* 292:4.)

[1]וַהֲלֹא כְּבָר נֶאֱמַר: ׳עַל כָּל דְּבַר פֶּשַׁע׳? [2]אָמְרוּ לָהֶן בֵּית הִלֵּל לְבֵית שַׁמַּאי: וַהֲלֹא כְּבָר נֶאֱמַר: [3]׳אִם לֹא שָׁלַח יָדוֹ בִּמְלֶאכֶת רֵעֵהוּ׳? [4]אִם כֵּן, מַה תַּלְמוּד לוֹמַר: ׳עַל כָּל דְּבַר פֶּשַׁע׳? [5]שֶׁיָּכוֹל אֵין לִי אֶלָּא הוּא. [6]אָמַר לְעַבְדּוֹ וְלִשְׁלוּחוֹ מִנַּיִן? [7]תַּלְמוּד לוֹמַר: ׳עַל כָּל דְּבַר פֶּשַׁע׳״.

TRANSLATION AND COMMENTARY

[1]**But has the verse not already said: 'For any *word* of trespass'?** Surely this implies that expressed intent is sufficient to make the bailee liable for misappropriation! [2]**Bet Hillel said to Bet Shammai: But has the verse not already said:** [3]**'Whether he has not *put his hand* to his neighbor's goods'?** Surely this implies that expressed intent is not sufficient, and that only action constitutes misappropriation! [4]Bet Shammai asked Bet Hillel: **If so,** if you are correct in maintaining that to be liable for misappropriation the bailee must actually take possession of the deposit, **what is the Torah teaching us by saying: 'For any word of trespass'?** [5]Bet Hillel replied: This expression is needed **because** if it had not been included, **I might have thought that I have learned** that the bailee is **only** liable for misappropriation which he **himself** committed with his own hand. [6]**From where do I learn that the law is the same if** the bailee misappropriated the deposit by words alone? For example, if the bailee **told his servant or his agent** to misappropriate some wine from the barrel, how do we know that he is liable for their actions? [7]It was to teach us this law that **the Torah states: 'For any word of trespass,'** to teach us that in this case the bailee is liable for his words, and this is an exception to the general principle that an agent (rather than the person he represents) is responsible for misdeeds he commits as an agent."

LITERAL TRANSLATION

[1]But has it not already been said: 'For any word of trespass'? [2]Bet Hillel said to Bet Shammai: But has it not already been said: [3]'Whether he has not put his hand to his neighbor's goods'? [4]If so, why does the Torah state: 'For any word of trespass'? [5]Because I might have thought [that] I have only [learned about] him [the bailee]. [6]From where [do I learn that the law is the same if] he said to his servant or his agent? [7]The Torah states: 'For any word of trespass.'"

RASHI

גמרא אמר לעבדו — שישלח יד, וכן עשה. מנין — שהוא חייב.

NOTES

וַהֲלֹא כְּבָר נֶאֱמַר ׳אִם לֹא שָׁלַח יָדוֹ׳ But has it not already been said: "Whether he has not put his hand." The Gemara does not tell us what explanation, if any, Bet Shammai had for the verse quoted by Bet Hillel, and the Aḥaronim suggest several possibilities.

Some say that Bet Shammai learn from this verse that a person who intends to misappropriate *part* of a deposit is not liable unless he actually takes it, but a person who intends to misappropriate an *entire* deposit is liable from the moment he expresses the intent (*Agudat Ezov*). Others suggest that, even according to Bet Shammai, a bailee is not liable for mere intent without action, as the verse cited by Bet Hillel rules out such a possibility. Rather, according to Bet Shammai, the Halakhah is a combination of the two verses: Because of Bet Hillel's verse, the bailee is not liable without action, but because of the "word-of-trespass" verse, the bailee is liable from the moment he expresses his intent. Thus, if the bailee takes action to carry out his intent, he becomes liable retroactively, from the moment his intent was expressed in words (*Meshekh Ḥokhmah*).

אָמַר לְעַבְדּוֹ וְלִשְׁלוּחוֹ If he said to his servant or his agent. *Meiri* points out that since the bailee is liable because the agent carried out his orders, it is not important whether the bailee himself benefited from the misappropriation. Even if the bailee told his servant to take deposited fruit and eat it, the bailee would still be liable, since the bailee's words amount to making a gift of the deposit, and this too is misappropriation.

אָמַר לְעַבְדּוֹ וְלִשְׁלוּחוֹ If he said to his servant or his agent. As noted in the commentary, this law is an exception to the rule that a person violating a law cannot absolve himself by claiming to have been following someone else's orders (אֵין שָׁלִיחַ לִדְבַר עֲבֵירָה — lit., "there is no agent for transgression").

There are a number of exceptions to this rule — our case here, and the case of *me'ilah* (מְעִילָה) discussed above (43a) are two of them — and it is interesting to note that in these cases the agent has no way of knowing that his act is illegal. In our case, the agent has no way of knowing that the object the bailee asked him to bring was a deposit, and in the case of *me'ilah* the money changer has no way of knowing that the money being deposited with him was taken out of the Temple treasury by mistake. The Aḥaronim discuss the significance of this point, and suggest that this characteristic of misappropriation and *me'ilah* may be the reason for the Torah's decree that the ordinary rules are suspended in such cases. Accordingly, some Aḥaronim suggest that it is possible that the law of Bet Hillel may only apply if the agent was indeed unaware of the object's status. But if the agent

HALAKHAH

שְׁלִיחוּת יָד עַל יְדֵי שָׁלִיחַ Misappropriation through an agent. "A bailee who asks another person to misappropriate a deposit in his care is liable for any subsequent accidental damage to the deposit as though he himself had taken it, following Bet Hillel. *Sma* adds that this applies only if the agent is not aware that the object is a deposit. If the agent *was* aware, and consciously agreed to assist the bailee in his crime, the agent and not the bailee is liable for robbery." (*Shulḥan Arukh, Ḥoshen Mishpat* 292.)

TRANSLATION AND COMMENTARY

הִטָּה אֶת הֶחָבִית כו׳ [1]The Gemara now considers the next clause of the Mishnah. The Mishnah states: **"If he tilted the barrel,"** he is only liable for what he actually took, because tilting is not in itself a valid act of acquisition. [2]**Rabbah said:** The Mishnah **only taught this** law exempting the bailee from payment for the entire barrel in a case **where** the barrel later **broke** by accident. In this case the bailee is not guilty of misappropriating the entire barrel, since the barrel did not break because it had been tilted. [3]**But if** the barrel did not break, but the wine in the barrel **turned sour,** the bailee must **pay** for **all of** the contents of the barrel, since the souring of the wine can be attributed to a negligent action on his part.

מַאי טַעְמָא [4]The Gemara explains: **What is the reason** why the bailee is considered negligent? [5]The Gemara answers: **It was his arrows that affected it.** In other words, his actions caused the damage. Thus, even if the bailee was not guilty of misappropriation, he was guilty of negligence. For as the Gemara will explain below, wine has a tendency to sour if not kept in a full barrel. By removing a *revi'it* of wine, the bailee precipitated the souring process. He is considered negligent, and is liable.

הִגְבִּיהָהּ וְנָטַל הֵימֶנָּה כו׳ [6]The Gemara now considers the next clause of the Mishnah: **"If** the bailee **lifted** up the barrel **and took** out a *revi'it* of wine **from it,** he must pay the full value of the entire barrel," as lifting the barrel is considered a valid act of acquisition. [7]**Shmuel said:** The expression **"took"** in this Mishnah **does not** necessarily **mean** that **he actually took** wine from the barrel. [8]The law of the Mishnah applies **once** the bailee **has lifted** the barrel in order **to take** something out of it, **even though he has not** yet actually **taken** anything. Thus, according to Shmuel, if the bailee lifts a barrel in order to take wine out of it, and then for some reason puts it down and then, before he has a chance to pick it up again to take the wine, the barrel breaks by accident, the bailee is liable.

[1]"הִטָּה אֶת הֶחָבִית כו׳". [2]אָמַר רַבָּה: לֹא שָׁנוּ אֶלָּא נִשְׁבְּרָה, [3]אֲבָל הֶחֱמִיצָה, מְשַׁלֵּם אֶת כּוּלָּהּ.

[4]מַאי טַעְמָא? [5]גִּירֵי דִּידֵיהּ הוּא דְּאַהֲנוּ לַהּ.

[6]"הִגְבִּיהָהּ וְנָטַל הֵימֶנָּה כו׳". [7]אָמַר שְׁמוּאֵל: לֹא "נָטַל" נָטַל מַמָּשׁ. [8]אֶלָּא כֵּיוָן שֶׁהִגְבִּיהָהּ לִיטּוֹל, אַף עַל פִּי שֶׁלֹּא נָטַל.

LITERAL TRANSLATION

[1]"[If] he tilted the barrel, etc." [2]Rabbah said: They only taught [this where] it broke, [3]but [if] it turned sour, he pays all of it.

[4]What is the reason? [5]It was his arrows that affected it.

[6]"[If] he lifted it and took from it, etc." [7]Shmuel said: "He took" [does] not [mean] he actually took. [8]But once he has lifted it to take [he is liable], even though he has not taken.

RASHI

לא שנו — דהיכא דנטל ולא הגביה כל החבית — פטור. **אלא נשברה** — דאונס הוא, והרי לא קנאה שיתחייב באונסין. **אבל החמיצה** — פשיעה היא ומזיק בידים הוא, דבשביל שחסרה החמילה, שכן דרך יין להחמיץ בכלי חסר. **גירי דידיה אהנו לה** — חציס שלו גרמו לה להחמיץ.

BACKGROUND

הֶחֱמִיצָה It turned sour. In early times, it was extremely difficult to prevent wine from turning sour. Pressing the grapes without properly straining or purifying the juice left much foreign matter in it, as well as the micro-organisms that caused it to ferment. After the fermentation process had produced alcohol, the yeasts would soon turn the wine into vinegar — either partially, giving it an acid taste, or completely.

One way of preventing wine from going sour was to store it in sealed barrels. Lack of oxygen would inhibit the action of the yeasts and prevent the formation of vinegar. When wine was not stored in a sealed barrel, or was exposed to the air, it quickly turned sour. Opening a barrel and removing some wine also allowed air to enter, introducing microbes and the oxygen they need to make the wine sour. Moreover, simply shaking a barrel could spread the small amount of air left inside, aerate the wine, and thus increase the activity of the microbes.

גִּירֵי דִּידֵיהּ His arrows. The judicial concept of "arrows" (חִיצִּים) is discussed at length in tractate *Bava Kamma*, which deals with the laws of damage. This term refers to any damage where the person causing it has no direct contact with the object damaged. Shooting arrows is the primary example of this type of damage, for although it is not the person himself who causes the damage, he is fully responsible for any damage his arrows cause. With regard to wine, although the person who took some of it from the barrel did not touch the rest, his action allowed air to enter the barrel; or he shook the wine, and this caused it to spoil.

NOTES

knew the object was a deposit, then he, and not the bailee, would be liable, because the regular rule that a person cannot absolve himself by claiming to have been following orders would again apply (see *Sma* and *Shakh — Shulḥan Arukh, Ḥoshen Mishpat* 292:5).

גִּירֵי דִּידֵיהּ His arrows. Our commentary follows *Rashi,* who connects the comment of Rabbah with the comment of Shmuel a few lines later — that wine is best kept with other wine. According to this interpretation, Rabbah is arguing that emptying out some of the wine may hasten the souring process by exposing the rest to the air. Other Rishonim, however, suggest that it was the shaking of the barrel that stimulated the souring. According to their interpretation, the bailee would be liable for the wine's turning sour even if he tilted the barrel to remove some wine, but then refrained from doing so (*Ra'avad*).

HALAKHAH

הִטָּה אֶת הֶחָבִית If he tilted the barrel. "If a bailee tilts a barrel without actually picking it up, and takes a small quantity of wine, he is liable for misappropriation only for the wine he took. Thus, if the barrel subsequently breaks by accident, the bailee is not liable. However, if the wine turned sour, the bailee is liable for the entire barrel. This is because the removal of some of the wine may have precipitated the souring. This law applies only to wine, but not to other produce, which does not tend to spoil more rapidly when some is removed." (Ibid., 292:2,3.)

הִגְבִּיהָהּ If he lifted it. "If the bailee picked up the barrel in order to take a small quantity of wine, he is liable for misappropriation even before he actually takes the wine out of the barrel. Thus, if the barrel breaks by accident, he must pay for it, following Shmuel. This law applies only to wine (according to *Tosafot*), or possibly also to other liquids (according to the *Shulḥan Arukh*). But if the deposit consisted of a wallet full of coins, and the bailee picked it up in order to remove one coin, it is doubtful whether he is liable for misappropriation of the entire wallet, following Rav Ashi, whose question remained unresolved." (Ibid., 292:2.)

TRANSLATION AND COMMENTARY

לֵימָא קָא סָבַר שְׁמוּאֵל [1]The Gemara asks: **Shall we say that Shmuel maintains that misappropriation does not require loss?** This concept was described in detail above (41a). According to the opinion that misappropriation does not require loss, a bailee who picks up a deposit with the intention of misappropriating some of it is liable for the entire deposit, even if the deposit was destroyed by forces beyond his control before he had a chance to carry out his intention. It would appear from Shmuel's statement here that this is his opinion as well.

אָמְרִי [2]The Gemara rejects this suggestion: **We can say: No.** Shmuel's ruling here tells us nothing about his opinion regarding the general question of whether misappropriation requires loss, because it is possible that the law regarding wine **is different** from that regarding other kinds of deposits. In the case dealt with in our Mishnah, even though the bailee only wants to take a *revi'it* of wine for himself, [3]**he is pleased that the entire barrel should** serve as **a base** (a container) **for this *revi'it,*** since a small quantity of wine left by itself tends to turn sour. Hence the bailee would prefer to leave the *revi'it* in the barrel until he is ready to drink it. Therefore, when he picks up the barrel with the intention of misappropriating a *revi'it,* he is considered to be taking the entire barrel into his possession. He is misappropriating part of the wine and borrowing the rest without permission, to help preserve "his" *revi'it.* Therefore he is liable for misappropriating the entire barrel, even according to the opinion that misappropriation requires loss.

[1]לֵימָא קָא סָבַר שְׁמוּאֵל שְׁלִיחוּת יָד אֵינָהּ צְרִיכָה חִסָּרוֹן? [2]אָמְרִי: לָא. שָׁאנֵי הָכָא, [3]דְּנִיחָא לֵיהּ דְּתֶיהֱוֵי הָא חָבִית כּוּלָּהּ בָּסִיס לְהָא רְבִיעִית.

LITERAL TRANSLATION

[1]Shall we say [that] Shmuel maintains [that] misappropriation does not require loss?

[2]We can say: No. It is different here, [3]because he is pleased that this entire barrel should be a base for this *revi'it.*

RASHI

דניחא ליה דתיהוי כולה חבית בסיס להאי רביעית — שתשמר אותה רביעית ולא תחמיץ, ולעולם שליחות יד בדבר אחר צריכה חסרון והנוטל פקדון ומגביהו על מנת לשלוח בו יד, כל זמן שלא חסרו — אינו מתחייב בהגבהתו, הואיל ולא נטלו על מנת לגזול את כולו, אלא לשלוח בו יד ושליחות יד בלא חסרון ליתיה, אבל יין שאינו משתמר אלא בכלי מלא — הוה ליה כמי שנטל והניחו עם השאר להשתמר, ונעשה שואל על כל שאר החבית.

NOTES

דְּנִיחָא לֵיהּ דְּתֶיהֱוֵי הָא חָבִית כּוּלָּהּ בָּסִיס לְהָא רְבִיעִית Because he is pleased that this entire barrel should be a base for this *revi'it.* Our commentary follows *Rashi,* who explains that the bailee is liable for the whole barrel because he is considered to have taken it into his possession in its entirety — one *revi'it* to drink, and the rest to safeguard this *revi'it.* According to this interpretation, the bailee is liable for the rest of the barrel as a borrower, not as a robber.

Ritva, however, explains that Shmuel's reasoning is based not on the liability of a borrower, but on the idea that in the specific case of wine, misappropriation does not require loss. Thus the bailee is liable for having picked up the barrel with the intention of taking some of the wine for himself because, with respect to wine, misappropriation does not require loss. This is true even according to the Gemara's conclusion that Shmuel maintains that misappropriation ordinarily *does* require loss: When the Gemara declared that wine was different from other deposits, it was considering the special properties of wine, not the logic of liability for misappropriation without loss. It meant that in the case of wine, everyone would agree that misappropriation does not require loss. Misappropriation of other kinds of deposits may ordinarily require loss, because the bailee demonstrates, by not actually taking the object he desires, that he is still hesitating and may yet change his mind. But in the case of wine, the only reason the bailee did not remove the wine he wanted is because it keeps better in the barrel. Hence, everyone would agree that in the case of wine, misappropriation does not require loss.

Both these interpretations imply that this passage is relevant only according to the opinion that misappropriation requires loss. But according to the Halakhah, which follows the opinion that misappropriation does not require loss, it makes no difference whether the deposit was a barrel of wine, a wallet full of money, or anything else, since a bailee who picks up any deposit with the intention of stealing part of it is immediately guilty of misappropriating it in its entirety.

Rambam, however, rules that the distinction between wine and other deposits is relevant even according to the opinion that misappropriation does not require loss. *Maggid Mishneh* explains that, according to *Rambam,* Shmuel's main point was that the bailee is liable for misappropriating the entire barrel even though he never intended to take more than one *revi'it,* and the question about misappropriation requiring loss was parenthetical. Interpreted in this way, the Gemara would be distinguishing between deposits that can readily be separated from each other, such as fruit, and deposits that can only be kept properly when intact, such as wine. Rav Ashi's question may also be explained in the same way: Is a wallet full of money a single unit or a number of smaller units that can easily be separated? According to this interpretation, the passage has Halakhic relevance, as it limits the application of the law that misappropriating part of a deposit renders a bailee liable for all of it. This law applies only if the deposit must be kept intact, but not if it is readily divisible.

TRANSLATION AND COMMENTARY

בָּעֵי רַב אַשִׁי [1]**Rav Ashi asked:** According to this view, if a bailee lits up a barrel with the intention of misappropriating some of its contents, he is considered to have misappropriated the entire barrel, because wine keeps best in a full barrel. But what is the law in the case of other deposits? For example, **if** a bailee **lifted up a wallet** deposited with him, with the intention of **taking** one **dinar from it,** and for some reason did not actually remove the dinar, and afterwards the entire wallet was accidentally lost, **what is the law?** Is the bailee considered to have misappropriated the entire wallet or only the one dinar?

חַמְרָא הוּא [2]The basis of the question is as follows: Does Shmuel's ruling apply only in the case of a barrel of wine, because **wine can only be safeguarded together with** other **wine,** [3]**but** not to a coin, because **a coin can be safeguarded** by itself without causing it any harm? If so, the case of the wallet would not be analogous to the case of the barrel, and a bailee who picks up a wallet to take only one coin would not be viewed as having borrowed the entire wallet. Consequently he would not be liable for misappropriation until he actually removed the coin from the wallet. [4]**Or perhaps** Shmuel's ruling applies even to a coin, because **the safeguarding of a wallet differs from the safeguarding of a dinar,** since it is easier to keep a whole wallet safely than an individual coin, as coins tend to get lost. If so, the case of the wallet would be precisely parallel to the case of the barrel, and a bailee who picks up a wallet to misappropriate one coin would be considered as having taken the entire wallet — part of it to spend, and the rest of it to safeguard the dinar he wishes to misappropriate.

תֵּיקוּ [5]The Gemara concludes: **Let** Rav Ashi's **question stand unanswered.**

[1]בָּעֵי רַב אַשִׁי: הִגְבִּיהַּ אַרְנָקִי לִיטּוֹל הֵימֶנָּה דִּינָר, מַהוּ? [2]חַמְרָא הוּא דְּלָא מִינְטַר אֶלָּא אַגַּב חַמְרָא, [3]אֲבָל זוּזָא מִינְטַר? [4]אוֹ דִּלְמָא, שָׁאנֵי נְטִירוּתָא דְּאַרְנָקִי מִנְּטִירוּתָא דְּדִינָר? [5]תֵּיקוּ.

הדרן עלך המפקיד

LITERAL TRANSLATION

[1]Rav Ashi asked: [If] he lifted a wallet to take a dinar from it, what [is the law]?

[2]Is it wine that is not guarded except by wine, [3]whereas a coin is guarded? [4]Or perhaps, guarding a wallet differs from guarding a dinar?

[5]Let [the question] stand [unsolved].

RASHI

הגביה ארנקי ליטול דינר — ולא נטל, לשמואל מהו? **אבל זוזא מינטר** — לבדו, ולא ניחא ליה דלהוי איך בכיס להאי, ולא הוי כנוטל ומניח. **שאני נטירותא דארנקי** — כיס מלא נראה ומשתמר, ואין נוח להיות נאבד כדינר יחידי.

הדרן עלך המפקיד

Conclusion to Chapter Three

In this chapter we learn that if a deposit is stolen from a bailee, and the bailee undertakes to reimburse the depositor, he acquires ownership of the property. (Legally speaking, such ownership rights are treated as if they had been included in the original conditions of the deposit.) Accordingly, the bailee does not need to make any monetary payment in order to acquire the deposit; he acquires it merely by waiving his right to take an oath exempting him from payment. However, the bailee acquires the deposit only if he fulfills its initial conditions. Accordingly, if he transferred the deposit to someone else without the depositor's permission, he does not acquire it.

Even if the bailee reimburses the depositor, he is still obliged to take an oath affirming that the deposit is no longer in his possession. He is required to swear that he cared for the deposit in the way people normally do — as a rule, a bailee must look after a deposit entrusted to him in the same way he cares for his own property in his own house (although extra caution is necessary when looking after money).

The bailee is not liable for reasonable, natural losses to the deposit, and examples of the exact quantities considered reasonable are given in the Mishnah. If the bailee notices that the loss is exceeding these specified quantities, he must inform the depositor. If this is not possible, he must make sure that the deposit is sold, so the depositor will not suffer a total loss. This responsibility is part of safeguarding an object, and is tantamount to returning a lost item to its rightful owner.

Misappropriation is defined as a violation of the special relationship between depositor and bailee. Therefore a bailee who misappropriates property is required to compensate the depositor for the loss, beginning from the time he derived the slightest forbidden benefit from the deposit, even if this did not damage it. Even so, one is not liable for mere intention (even if the intention was expressed in words), but only for action. In certain respects, an object which has been misappropriated is treated as if the bailee has robbed the depositor of it, and all responsibility for it (or for changes in its value) devolves upon the bailee from the time it was misappropriated, as for any other act of robbery.

List of Sources

Agudat Ezov, novellae on the Talmud by Rabbi Moshe Ze'ev (Wolf), Lithuania (d. 1830).

Aḥaronim, lit., "the last," meaning Rabbinical authorities from the time of the publication of Rabbi Yosef Caro's code of Halakhah, *Shulḥan Arukh* (1555).

Arukh, Talmudic dictionary, by Rabbi Natan of Rome, 11th century.

Arukh HaShulḥan, commentary on *Shulḥan Arukh* by Rabbi Yeḥiel Mikhel Epstein, Byelorussia (1829–1908).

Ba'al HaMa'or, Rabbi Zeraḥyah ben Yitzḥak HaLevi, Spain, 12th century. *HaMa'or*, Halakhic commentary on *Hilkhot HaRif.*

Baḥ (Bayit Ḥadash), commentary on *Tur* by Rabbi Yoel Sirkes, Poland (1561–1640).

Be'er HaGolah, commentary on unusual Aggadic passages in the Talmud by Rabbi Yehudah Loew ben Betzalel of Prague (see *Maharal*) (1525–1609).

Bertinoro, Ovadyah, 15th-century Italian commentator on the Mishnah.

Bet Shmuel, commentary on *Shulḥan Arukh, Even HaEzer*, by Rabbi Shmuel ben Uri Shraga, Poland, second half of the 17th century.

Darkhei Moshe, commentary on *Tur* by Rabbi Moshe ben Yisrael Isserles, Poland (1525–1572).

Even HaAzel, novellae on *Mishneh Torah* by Rabbi Isser Zalman Meltzer, Lithuania and Eretz Israel (1870–1953).

Even HaEzer, section of *Shulḥan Arukh* dealing with marriage, divorce, and related topics.

Geonim, heads of the academies of Sura and Pumbedita in Babylonia from the late 6th century to the mid-11th century.

Gra, Rabbi Eliyahu ben Shlomo Zalman (1720–1797), the Gaon of Vilna. Novellae on the Talmud and *Shulḥan Arukh*.

Hagahot Maimoniyot, commentary on *Mishneh Torah* by Rabbi Meir HaKohen, Germany, 14th century (see *Ramakh*).

Ḥatam Sofer, responsa literature and novellae on the Talmud by Rabbi Moshe Sofer (Schreiber), Pressburg (1763–1839).

Ḥaver ben Ḥayyim, novellae on the Talmud by Rabbi Ḥizkiyah Ḥayyim Ploit, Lithuania, 19th century.

Ḥazon Ish, Rabbi A. I. Karelitz, Halakhist, Lithuania and Eretz Israel (1878–1953).

Ḥokhmat Manoaḥ, commentary on the Talmud by Rabbi Manoaḥ ben Shemaryah, Poland, 16th century.

Ḥoshen Mishpat, section of *Shulḥan Arukh* dealing with civil and criminal law.

Imrei Maharshaḥ, novellae on *Bava Metzia* by Rabbi Simḥah ben Aryeh Naftali.

Kesef Mishneh, commentary on *Mishneh Torah* by Rabbi Yosef Caro, author of the *Shulḥan Arukh.*

Ketzot HaḤoshen, novellae on *Shulḥan Arukh, Ḥoshen Mishpat* by Rabbi Aryeh Leib Heller, Galicia (1754?–1813).

Kikayon DeYonah, novellae on the Talmud by Rabbi Yonah Te'omim, Bohemia and Germany, 19th century.

Korban HaEdah, commentary on the Jerusalem Talmud by Rabbi David ben Naftali Frankel, Germany (1707–1762).

Leḥem Mishneh, commentary on *Mishneh Torah* by Rabbi Avraham di Boton, Salonica (1560–1609).

Magen Avraham, commentary on *Shulḥan Arukh* by Rabbi Avraham HaLevi Gombiner, Poland (d. 1683).

Maggid Mishneh, commentary on *Mishneh Torah* by Rabbi Vidal de Tolosa, Spain, 14th century.

Maharal, Rabbi Yehudah Loew ben Betzalel of Prague (1525–1609). Novellae on the Talmud.

Maharam Schiff, novellae on the Talmud by Rabbi Meir ben Ya'akov HaKohen Schiff (1605–1641), Frankfurt, Germany.

Maharik, Rabbi Yosef Kolon, France and Italy (c. 1420–1480). Responsa literature.

Maharsha, Rabbi Shmuel Eliezer ben Yehudah HaLevi Edels, Poland (1555–1631). Novellae on the Talmud.

Maharshal, Rabbi Shlomo ben Yeḥiel Luria, Poland (1510–1573). Novellae on the Talmud.

Maḥazeh Avraham, novellae on the Talmud by Rabbi Avraham Yaffe, Lithuania, 19th century.

Mat'amei Yitzḥak, novellae on the Talmud by Rabbi Yitzḥak HaLevi Horowitz, Germany (1715–1767).

Meiri, commentary on the Talmud (called *Bet HaBeḥirah*) by Rabbi Menaḥem ben Shlomo, Provence (1249–1316).

Melo HaRo'im, commentary on the Talmud by Rabbi Ya'akov Tzvi Yolles, Poland (c. 1778–1825).

Meshekh Ḥokhmah, commentary on the Torah by Rabbi Meir Simḥah HaKohen of Dvinsk, Latvia (1843–1926).

Minḥat Ḥinnukh, commentary on *Sefer HaḤinnukh* by Rabbi Yosef Babad, Poland (1800–1874/5).

Mirkevet HaMishneh, novellae on *Mishneh Torah* by Rabbi Shlomo ben Moshe of Chelm, Poland, 18th century.

Mishmerot Kehunah, novellae on the Talmud by Rabbi Avraham ben Yitzḥak HaKohen (Yitzḥaki), Lithuania, 19th century.

Mordekhai, compendium of Halakhic decisions by Rabbi

Mordekhai ben Hillel HaKohen, Germany (1240?-1298).

Nefesh Ḥayyah, novellae on *Bava Metzia* by Rabbi Moshe Betzalel Luria, Poland, 19th century.

Netivot, short title of *Netivot Hamishpat*, commentary on *Shulḥan Arukh, Ḥoshen Mishpat*, by Rabbi Ya'akov Lorberboim of Lissa, Poland (1760-1832).

Nimmukei Yosef, commentary on *Hilkhot HaRif* by Rabbi Yosef Ḥaviva, Spain, early 15th century.

Or Same'aḥ, novellae on *Mishneh Torah* by Rabbi Meir Simḥah HaKohen of Dvinsk, Latvia (1843-1926).

Oraḥ Ḥayyim, section of *Shulḥan Arukh* dealing with daily religious observances, prayers, and the laws of the Sabbath and Festivals.

Pe'at HaShulḥan, laws relating to Eretz Israel, by Rabbi Yisrael of Shklov, Lithuania and Eretz Israel (1770-1839).

Pnei Yehoshua, novellae on the Talmud by Rabbi Ya'akov Yehoshua Falk, Poland and Germany (1680-1756).

Ra'avad, Rabbi Avraham ben David, commentator and Halakhic authority. Wrote comments on *Mishneh Torah*. Provence (c. 1125-1198?).

Rabbenu Efraim, Efraim Ibn Avi Alragan, Halakhist, North Africa, late 11th-early 12th century.

Rabbenu Ḥananel (ben Ḥushiel), commentator on Talmud, North Africa (990-1055).

Rabbenu Tam, commentator on Talmud, Tosafist, France (1100-1171).

Rabbenu Yehonatan, Yehonatan ben David HaKohen of Lunel, Provence, Talmudic scholar (c. 1135-after 1210).

Rabbenu Yeruḥam, Rabbi Yeruḥam ben Meshullam, Halakhist, Spain, 14th century. Author of *Toledot Adam VeḤavah*.

Rabbi Ya'akov Emden, Talmudist and Halakhic authority, Germany (1697-1776).

Rabbi Zvi Ḥayyot (Chajes), Galician Rabbi, 19th century.

Radbaz, Rabbi David ben Shlomo Avi Zimra, Spain, Egypt, Eretz Israel and North Africa (1479-1589). Commentary on *Mishneh Torah*.

Ramakh, Rabbi Meir HaKohen of Rothenburg, Germany (14th century). Author of *Hagahot Maimoniyot* (commentary on *Mishneh Torah*).

Rambam, Rabbi Moshe ben Maimon, Rabbi and philosopher, known also as Maimonides. Author of *Mishneh Torah*, Spain and Egypt (1135-1204).

Ramban, Rabbi Moshe ben Naḥman, commentator on Bible and Talmud, known also as Naḥmanides, Spain and Eretz Israel (1194-1270).

Ran, Rabbi Nissim ben Reuven Gerondi, Spanish Talmudist (1310?-1375?).

Rash, Rabbi Shimshon ben Avraham, Tosafist, commentator on the Mishnah, Sens (late 12th-early 13th century).

Rash Vidash, Rabbi Shmuel Vidash, Spain and Eretz Israel, 15th century.

Rashash, Rabbi Shmuel ben Yosef Shtrashun, Lithuanian Talmud scholar (1794-1872).

Rashba, Rabbi Shlomo ben Avraham Adret, Spanish Rabbi famous for his commentaries on the Talmud and his responsa (c. 1235-c. 1314).

Rashbam, Rabbi Shmuel ben Meir, commentator on the Talmud (1085-1158).

Rashi, Rabbi Shlomo b. Yitzḥak, the paramount commentator on the Bible and the Talmud, France (1040-1105).

Rav Hai Gaon, Babylonian Rabbi, head of Pumbedita Yeshivah, 10th century.

Rav Yehudai Gaon, Gaon of Sura, 8th century.

Rema, Rabbi Moshe ben Yisrael Isserles, Halakhic authority, Poland (1525-1572).

Ri, Rabbi Yitzḥak ben Shmuel of Dampierre, Tosafist, France (died c. 1185).

Ri Korkos, Rabbi Yosef Korkos, Spain, 15th-16th century. Responsa literature.

Rid, see *Tosefot Rid*.

Rif, Rabbi Yitzḥak Alfasi, Halakhist, author of *Hilkhot HaRif*, North Africa (1013-1103).

Rishonim, lit., "the first," meaning Rabbinical authorities active between the end of the Geonic period (mid-11th century) and the publication of the *Shulḥan Arukh* (1555).

Ritva, novellae and commentary on the Talmud by Rabbi Yom Tov ben Avraham Ishbili, Spain (c. 1250-1330).

Rivash, Rabbi Yitzḥak ben Sheshet, Spain and North Africa (1326-1408). Novellae on the Talmud by *Rivash* mentioned in *Shittah Mekubbetzet*.

Rivmatz, Rabbi Yitzḥak ben Malkitzedek of Siponto, Italy, 12th century. Commentary on the first order of the Mishnah, *Zeraim*.

Rosh, Rabbi Asher ben Yeḥiel, also known as Asheri, commentator and Halakhist, Germany and Spain (c. 1250-1327).

Sefer HaOrah, compendium of Halakhic decisions attributed to *Rashi*.

Sefer Ḥasidim, a major work on ethics. Tradition attributes authorship of the work to Rabbi Yehudah of Regensburg (d. 1217).

Sefer HaTerumot, Halakhic work by Rabbi Shmuel ben Yitzḥak Sardi, Spain (1185-1255).

Shakh (Siftei Kohen), commentary on *Shulḥan Arukh* by Rabbi Shabbetai ben Meir HaKohen, Lithuania (1621-1662).

Shittah Mekubbetzet, a collection of commentaries on the Talmud by Rabbi Betzalel ben Avraham Ashkenazi of Safed (c. 1520-1591).

Shulḥan Arukh, code of Halakhah by Rabbi Yosef Caro, b. Spain, active in Eretz Israel (1488-1575).

Sma (Sefer Meirat Einayim), commentary on *Shulḥan Arukh, Ḥoshen Mishpat*, by Rabbi Yehoshua Falk Katz, Poland (c. 1550-1614).

Talmidei Rabbenu Yonah, commentary on *Hilkhot HaRif*, by the school of Rabbi Yonah of Gerondi, Spain (c. 1190-1263).

Taz, abbreviation for *Turei Zahav*. See below, *Turei Zahav*.

Terumot HaDeshen, responsa literature and Halakhic decisions by Rabbi Yisrael Isserlin, Germany (15th century).

Torat Ḥayyim, novellae on the Talmud by Rabbi Avraham Ḥayyim Shor, Galicia (d. 1632).

Tosafot, collection of commentaries and novellae on the Talmud, expanding on Rashi's commentary, by the French-German

Tosafists (12th-13th centuries).

Tosefot HaRosh, an edition based on *Tosefot Sens* by the *Rosh*, Rabbi Asher ben Yeḥiel, Germany and Spain (c. 1250-1327).

Tosefot Rid, commentary on the Talmud by Rabbi Yeshayahu ben Mali di Trani, Italian Halakhist (c. 1200-before 1260).

Tosefot Sens, the first important collection of Tosafot, by Rabbi Shimshon of Sens (late 12th-early 13th century).

Tur, abbreviation of *Arba'ah Turim*, Halakhic code by Rabbi Ya'akov ben Asher, b. Germany, active in Spain (c.1270-1343).

Turei Zahav, commentary on *Shulḥan Arukh* by Rabbi David ben Shmuel HaLevi, Poland (c. 1586-1667).

Yad Malakhi, a work on Talmudic and Halakhic methodology, by Rabbi Malakhi ben Ya'akov HaKohen, Italy (died c. 1785).

Yad Ramah, novellae on the Talmud by Rabbi Meir ben Todros HaLevi Abulafiya, Spain (c. 1170-1244).

Yoreh De'ah, section of *Shulḥan Arukh* dealing with dietary laws, interest, ritual purity, and mourning.

D0687818

INSECTOS FASCINANTES

Los ciempiés

John Willis

SPANISH & ENGLISH eBOOKS
AV2 BY WEIGL™
ADDED VALUE • AUDIO VISUAL

www.av2books.com

Visita nuestro sitio www.av2books.com e ingresa el código único del libro.
Go to www.av2books.com, and enter this book's unique code.

CÓDIGO DEL LIBRO
BOOK CODE

K729828

AV² de Weigl te ofrece enriquecidos libros electrónicos que favorecen el aprendizaje activo.
AV² by Weigl brings you media enhanced books that support active learning.

El enriquecido libro electrónico AV² te ofrece una experiencia bilingüe completa entre el inglés y el español para aprender el vocabulario de los dos idiomas.
This AV² media enhanced book gives you a fully bilingual experience between English and Spanish to learn the vocabulary of both languages.

Spanish

English

Navegación bilingüe AV²
AV² Bilingual Navigation

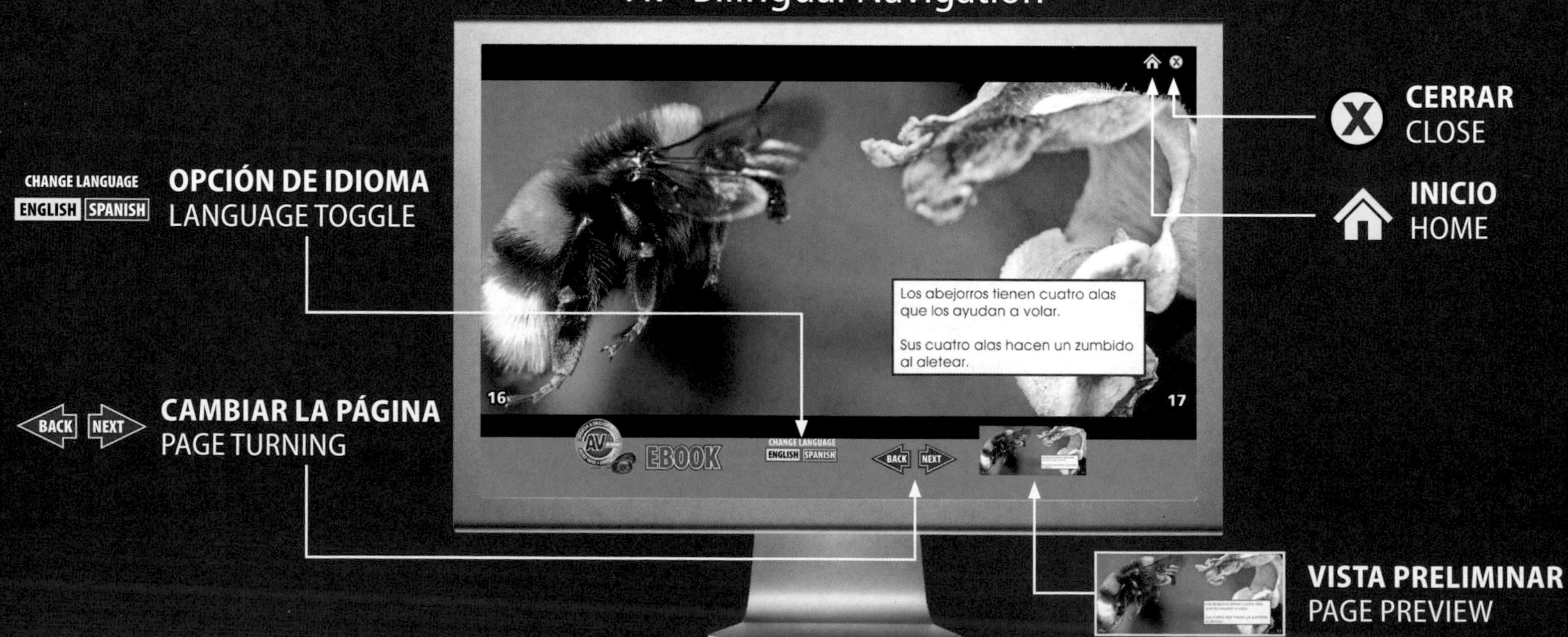

Los ciempiés

ÍNDICE

Este es el ciempiés.

Los ciempiés son animales pequeños. Tienen el cuerpo largo y delgado.

Hay ciempiés en todas partes
del mundo.

En todas partes del mundo, los
ciempiés viven en lugares húmedos.

7

Algunos ciempiés envuelven su cuerpo alrededor de sus huevos.

Envolviendo su cuerpo
alrededor de sus huevos, los
ciempiés los mantienen seguros.

Los ciempiés nacen cuando salen de los huevos.

Cuando salen de los huevos, algunos ciempiés tienen menos patas que los adultos.

Los ciempiés pueden tener muchas patas.

Con tantas patas, los ciempiés pueden moverse muy rápido.

Los ciempiés tienen dos antenas en la cabeza.

Con esas dos antenas, los ciempiés pueden encontrar su alimento en la oscuridad.

16

Los ciempiés tienen uñas filosas.

Las uñas filosas los ayudan a atrapar su comida y defenderse.

Los ciempiés comen
insectos pequeños y arañas.

Comiendo insectos y arañas, los ciempiés tienen todo lo que necesitan para estar sanos.

Los ciempiés son importantes en la naturaleza.

En la naturaleza, los ciempiés ayudan a controlar las plagas.

21

DATOS SOBRE LOS CIEMPIÉS

Estas páginas contienen más detalles sobre los interesantes datos de este libro. Están dirigidas a los adultos, como soporte, para que ayuden a los jóvenes lectores a redondear sus conocimientos sobre cada criatura presentada en la serie *Insectos fascinantes.*

Páginas 4–5

4
Este es el ciempiés.
5
Los ciempiés son animales pequeños. Tienen el cuerpo largo y delgado.

Los ciempiés son animales pequeños. Pertenecen a un grupo de animales llamados artrópodos. Al igual que los insectos, los artrópodos no tienen un esqueleto interno. En su lugar, los ciempiés tienen una coraza externa dura conocida como exoesqueleto, que los protege. El exoesqueleto no crece. Por eso, el ciempiés debe mudar, o cambiar el exoesqueleto regularmente por otro nuevo.

Páginas 6–7

6
Hay ciempiés en todas partes del mundo.
En todas partes del mundo, los ciempiés viven en lugares húmedos.
7

Hay ciempiés en todas partes del mundo. Viven en casi todos los continentes. Su población se extiende hasta el Círculo Ártico. El ciempiés más largo puede llegar a medir más de 10 pulgadas (26 centímetros) de largo. A diferencia de los insectos y arácnidos, los ciempiés no tienen una capa impermeable en su exoesqueleto. Por eso, los ciempiés tienden a vivir en áreas más húmedas para no secarse.

Páginas 8–9

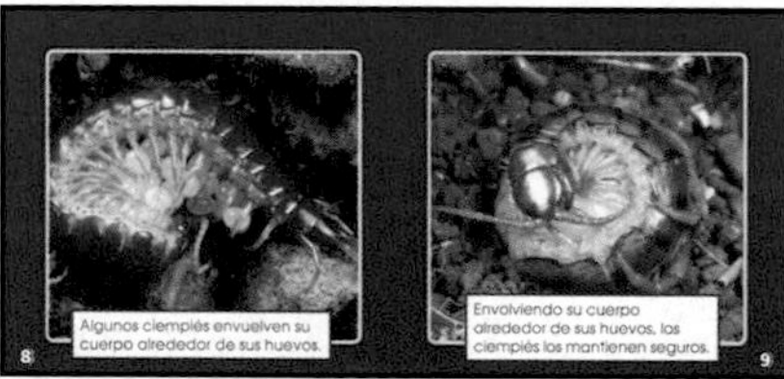
8
Algunos ciempiés envuelven su cuerpo alrededor de sus huevos.
9
Envolviendo su cuerpo alrededor de sus huevos, los ciempiés los mantienen seguros.

Algunos ciempiés envuelven su cuerpo alrededor de sus huevos. El conjunto de huevos del ciempiés se llama nidada. Envolviéndose alrededor de la nidada, el ciempiés puede proteger a sus huevos de los depredadores. Cuando los huevos eclosionan, algunas hembras se quedan junto a los bebés ciempiés hasta que estén listos para cazar. Algunas especies de ciempiés no ponen huevos en una nidada sino que ponen huevos individuales en agujeros que hacen en el suelo.

Páginas 10–11

10
Los ciempiés nacen cuando salen de los huevos.
11
Cuando salen de los huevos, algunos ciempiés tienen menos patas que los adultos.

Los ciempiés nacen cuando salen de los huevos. Al nacer, se parecen a sus padres en miniatura. Pero, algunos ciempiés nacen con menos segmentos corporales y menos patas que un adulto. Durante las mudas, los ciempiés crecen y desarrollan nuevos segmentos, alcanzando la cantidad total con el tiempo. Para ser artrópodo, el ciempiés tiene una larga vida. Algunas especies llegan a vivir hasta seis años.

Páginas 12–13

Los ciempiés pueden tener muchas patas. Si bien la palabra ciempiés significa "que tiene cien patas", no hay ninguna especie de ciempiés que tenga exactamente 100 patas. Esto se debe a que cada ciempiés tiene un número impar de pares de patas. La cantidad de pares de patas va desde menos de 20 hasta más de 150, dependiendo de la especie. Cada segmento del cuerpo puede tener solo un par de patas. Algunos ciempiés pueden separar sus extremidades del cuerpo para distraer a los depredadores. Luego, les vuelven a crecer.

Páginas 14–15

Los ciempiés tienen dos antenas en la cabeza. Usan estas antenas para oler y sentir lo que tienen delante. Algunas especies de ciempiés no tienen ojos. Por eso, deben confiar en sus otros sentidos para poder cazar. Las antenas pueden ayudarlos a encontrar a su presa. Los ciempiés suelen ser más activos por las noches, cuando salen a cazar.

Páginas 16–17

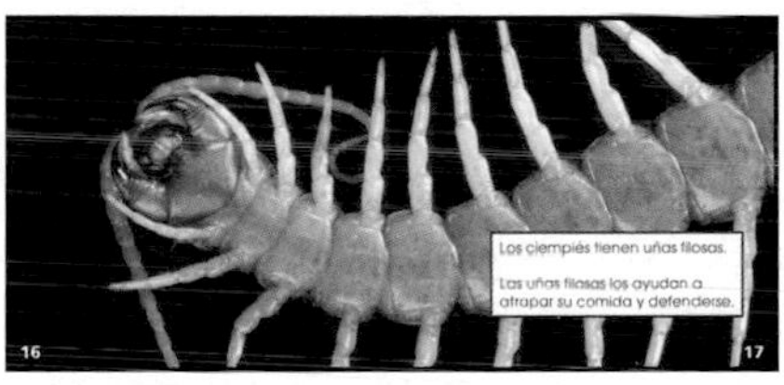

Los ciempiés tienen uñas filosas. El par de patas delanteras del ciempiés tiene unas uñas especiales llamadas forcípulas. El ciempiés es el único tipo de animal que tiene esta clase de patas. Cuando un ciempiés se encuentra con su presa, utiliza estas uñas filosas para inyectarle veneno. Aunque la picadura de la mayoría de los ciempiés no provoca síntomas graves, algunas pueden ser peligrosas para las personas alérgicas al veneno del ciempiés.

Páginas 18–19

Los ciempiés comen insectos pequeños y arañas. Los ciempiés son carnívoros, es decir, comen mayormente a otros animales. Si bien suelen cazar a otros artrópodos, algunas especies más grandes comen reptiles, anfibios e incluso mamíferos. Una especie, el ciempiés gigante del Amazonas, se cuelga del techo de las cuevas y atrapa a los murciélagos en pleno vuelo.

Páginas 20–21

Los ciempiés son importantes en la naturaleza. Una de las especies de ciempiés más comunes de América del Norte es el ciempiés doméstico. Se lo suele considerar una plaga por su gran velocidad y aspecto desagradable. Sin embargo, el ciempiés doméstico es en realidad un animal beneficioso, ya que consume varias plagas destructivas o dañinas, como las polillas y las cucarachas.

¡Visita www.av2books.com para disfrutar de tu libro interactivo de inglés y español!

Check out www.av2books.com for your interactive English and Spanish ebook!

1 Entra en www.av2books.com
Go to www.av2books.com

2 Ingresa tu código
Enter book code

K729828

3 ¡Alimenta tu imaginación en línea!
Fuel your imagination online!

www.av2books.com

Published by AV² by Weigl
350 5th Avenue, 59th Floor New York, NY 10118
Website: www.av2books.com

Library of Congress Control Number: 2016956044

ISBN 978-1-4896-5583-7 (hardcover)
ISBN 978-1-4896-5584-4 (multi-user eBook)

Printed in the United States of America in Brainerd, Minnesota
1 2 3 4 5 6 7 8 9 0 20 19 18 17 16

112016
103116

Weigl acknowledges Getty Images, Alamy, and Corbis as the primary image suppliers for this title.

Project Coordinator: Jared Siemens
Spanish Editor: Translation Cloud LLC
Designer: Terry Paulhus

Author:
Ian Graham studied applied physics at City University in London, England. He then received a postgraduate degree in journalism, specializing in science and technology. Since becoming a freelance author and journalist, he has written more than one hundred children's nonfiction books.

Artist:
David Antram was born in Brighton, England, in 1958. He studied at Eastbourne College of Art and then worked in advertising for 15 years before becoming a full-time artist. He has illustrated many children's nonfiction books.

Series creator:
David Salariya was born in Dundee, Scotland. He has illustrated a wide range of books and has created and designed many new series for publishers in the UK and overseas. David established The Salariya Book Company in 1989. He lives in Brighton with his wife, illustrator Shirley Willis, and their son, Jonathan.

Editor: Jamie Pitman

Editorial Assistant: Mark Williams

Published in Great Britain in 2009 by
The Salariya Book Company Ltd
25 Marlborough Place, Brighton BN1 1UB

ISBN-13: 978-0-531-21326-1 (lib. bdg.) 978-0-531-20517-4 (pbk.)
ISBN-10: 0-531-21326-9 (lib. bdg.) 0-531-20517-7 (pbk.)

Published in 2010 in the United States
by Franklin Watts
An imprint of Scholastic Inc.
Published simultaneously in Canada.

A CIP catalog record for this book is available from the Library of Congress.

Printed and bound in China.
Printed on paper from sustainable sources.

You Wouldn't Want to Be a World War II Pilot!

Written by
Ian Graham

Illustrated by
David Antram

Created and designed by
David Salariya

Air Battles You Might Not Survive

Franklin Watts®
An Imprint of Scholastic Inc.
NEW YORK TORONTO LONDON AUCKLAND SYDNEY
MEXICO CITY NEW DELHI HONG KONG
DANBURY, CONNECTICUT

Contents

Introduction

You are 16. Home is San Antonio, Texas. The year is 1934. You're crazy about aircraft and flying. Your room is filled with models and posters of airplanes. You go to your local airfield, Stinson Field, to study pilots and their planes at every opportunity. The airfield's name recently changed to Windburn Field, but everybody still calls it Stinson Field.

The pilots there tell you about Charles Lindbergh. He was the first person to make a solo, nonstop flight across the Atlantic Ocean. Before he became world famous, he did his military flight training in San Antonio and kept a plane of his own at Stinson Field.

Watching the planes pitch and swoop through the sky, you realize that flying a plane is very tricky, and that proper training is crucial to develop the skills you'll need to survive. Who knows? In a few years, you may really need to know how to keep your plane in the sky!

YOU GET A JOB at the airfield cleaning small private planes and helping the mechanics. You hang out with the pilots and talk to them about flying. One way or another, you're going to be a pilot too.

Learning to Fly

You are paid for your work with flying lessons. Experienced pilots teach you how to hold a plane level in the air, how to turn, and eventually how to take off and land. After you receive your pilot's license, you get a job flying a crop duster, dropping pesticides on local farms. You use the money to buy an old biplane of your own.

On weekends, you fly the biplane at air fairs. People flock to see pilots perform stunts with their planes. A favorite with the crowds is wing-walking. While you fly your plane, a friend stands on the top wing and waves to the crowd below. It's a spectacular but very risky trick.

Flying Solo

EVERY STUDENT PILOT has to make a successful flight alone before being awarded a pilot's license. It's called "going solo." You go solo a week after your 17th birthday.

**slang for "pilot"*

Air Shows

STUNT FLYING at air fairs in fragile 1930s planes can be very dangerous. A pilot can find himself hurtling toward the ground if a stunt goes wrong.

AIR RACES are popular in the 1930s. Crowds of spectators watch the planes race each other around a course marked by towers called pylons.

YOU GIVE FLYING LESSONS and take people on sightseeing flights to help pay for your plane. People are very eager to get a taste of flying.

Squawk!
Handy Hint
Remember to fasten your safety harness!
Looks like someone couldn't wait until lunchtime!

Joining Up

In the 1930s, the newspapers are full of stories about the coming war in Europe. In 1933, Adolf Hitler's sinister Nazi party comes to power in Germany. Then in 1939, Nazi Germany invades Poland. As a result, Britain and France declare war on Germany. World War II, the long, bitter war between the Axis powers and the Allied nations,* has begun.

You learn that the British Royal Air Force (RAF) is recruiting American pilots. The thought of flying fantastic modern fighters like the Hurricane and Spitfire—while helping the British fight the Nazis—is very exciting. You apply to join the RAF, eager to start your training.

**The Axis powers included Germany, Japan, Italy, and several other countries. Great Britain, France, and Poland were among the major Allied nations at the start of the war. In 1941, the U.S. and the Soviet Union joined the Allies.*

THE RAF ISN'T LOOKING for just any old pilot. You have to be able to say "yes" to a list of requirements:

- Are you between 20 and 31 years old?
- Do you have a pilot's license?
- Do you have 300 flying hours?
- Do you have good eyesight?

You don't need any military experience. That's a relief!

Handy Hint

Pay attention in class, or you'll never be a fighter pilot.

PILOTS HAVE TO LEARN Morse code. That's a way of sending messages as a stream of short bleeps (dots) and long bleeps (dashes). Each letter of the alphabet is made up of a different set of dots and dashes.

Dot-dot-dot-dash*

**Morse code for the letter "V," meaning "victory"*

BEFORE YOU CAN GO to Britain, you must complete an RAF training course in the United States. You wave one last good-bye to your family and set off for the nearest training center.

IT'S BEEN QUITE A WHILE since you were in school, and you struggle to keep up with some of the classes.

YOU DO YOUR FLIGHT TRAINING in a Stearman PT-17 biplane. It handles like your own biplane, so it's easy to learn how to fly it. Most pilots go solo within 12 hours.

Fighter Training

Language Barrier

YOU CAN'T UNDERSTAND what your officers and mechanics are saying in their strange-sounding British accents.

*Be quiet!

**a pilot fresh from training

YOUR TEXAN DRAWL sounds just like a foreign language to British ears.

You arrive in Britain after a nerve-racking voyage across the Atlantic Ocean. As the passengers know very well, ships are at constant risk of attack by German submarines called U-boats. You begin to realize how much danger you are in. In London, you sign the official papers that make you an RAF officer and receive your uniform.

Your next stop is an Operational Training Unit (OTU), where you will be trained to fly a fighter. You meet Polish pilots who have also come to aid Britain's war effort. The Poles form a Polish Air Force in Britain and fight courageously alongside the RAF.

Tight Squeeze!

THE SPITFIRE'S COCKPIT is so cramped that the pilot needs help to get strapped in. Mechanics help the pilot and then give the windshield a final wipe before takeoff.

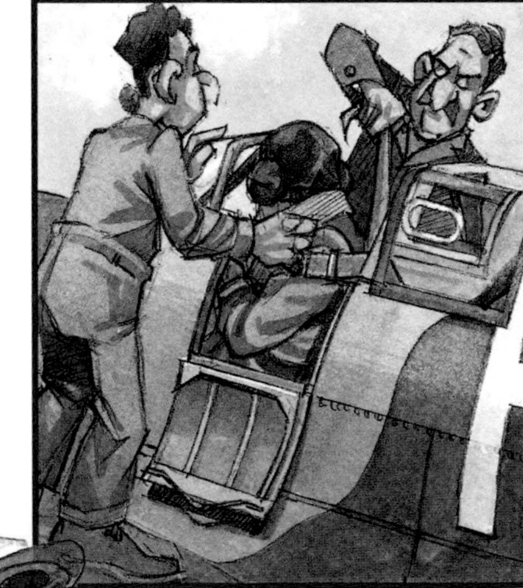

GUNNERY PRACTICE involves firing your guns at a windsock (called a drogue) that's towed behind another plane.

Leather helmet
Oxygen mask
Earphones
Life jacket
(called a "Mae West" after a film star of the same name)
Leather gloves
Parachute
Sheepskin-lined boots
Looking good, huh?
Handy Hint
Keep an eye on your altitude gauge!
SNIP!
SNAP!
Censored
YOUR LETTERS HOME arrive with holes in them because an official called a censor cuts out anything that he thinks might be useful to the enemy.
SNIP!

The Spitfire

The Spitfire is the leading British fighter at the beginning of World War II. It's a small, fast, and heavily armed plane. Its main job is to attack enemy aircraft and protect Allied bombers from enemy fighters. It can also strike at targets on the ground. The Spitfire proves to be such a good all-around aircraft that it is built in greater numbers than any other Allied fighter.

R. J. Mitchell

THE SPITFIRE was designed by R. J. Mitchell, the leading British aircraft designer of the 1930s. Sadly, Mitchell never saw its success because he died in 1937 when he was only 42.

Propeller

*SPITFIRE Mk Vb**

Engine: 1,440 horsepower Rolls-Royce Merlin
Length: 29 ft., 10 in. (9.1 m)
Wingspan: 36 ft., 10 in. (11.2 m)
Top speed: 375 mph (603 kmh)
Weapons: two 20mm cannons and four Browning machine guns
Maximum altitude: 37,000 ft. (11,277 m)
Manufacturer: Supermarine Aviation Works

Wing cannon

Landing gear

*pronounced "Mark Five B"

The Spitfire does not stay the same all through the war. There will be more than 20 different types of Spitfires, with different wings, guns, engines, and propellers. There is a naval version, too, called the Seafire.

THE SPITFIRE'S COCKPIT (left) is just big enough for the pilot to squeeze into. The canopy (below) slides back to make more room for the pilot to climb into the cockpit.

BELTS OF AMMUNITION are loaded into the guns from underneath the wings.

THE GROUND CREW swarms all over a Spitfire as soon as it lands. They refuel it and re-arm it for the next mission.

First Post

You arrive at an air base to join your fighter squadron. It's one of three RAF squadrons of American pilots, called Eagle Squadrons. You are replacing a pilot who was KIA*—a young American just like yourself. It's yet another reminder of the dangers you face.

For every pilot, there are up to ten men and women working on the ground to keep the planes repaired and ready for action. Each plane has its own crew chief and assistant. Together they look after the plane, giving work to other members of the ground crew when necessary.

WHEN YOU'RE ON cockpit alert, you have to sit in your plane for two hours, ready to go in case of an attack. If you see a bright flare bursting in the sky above you, you'd better scramble** because enemy aircraft are about to arrive.

SMALL SWASTIKAS (Nazi symbols) are sometimes painted on the side of a plane to show how many enemy aircraft the pilot has shot down. Each swastika represents one aircraft.

*killed in action
**take off as quickly as possible

KA-POW!
Handy Hint
A good landing is one you can walk away from.
Listen up! I'm only going to say this once...
Major Tom? Come in, Major Tom!
BEFORE EACH PLANNED MISSION, all the pilots who will take part attend a briefing to learn the details.
GROUND CONTROLLERS plot the positions of Allied planes and Axis planes on a map. They talk with the Allied pilots by radio.

Combat

It isn't long before you get your first taste of combat. It's exciting, but the odds aren't great. A new fighter pilot in World War II has only a 50/50 chance of surviving his first five combat missions. Your first mission is to escort B-17 bombers attacking a factory in Germany. During the briefing, you begin to feel nervous. All the training is over and it's for real now. Lives will depend on what you do. The B-17 bombers have their own guns and gunners, but they can't maneuver quickly, which makes them easy targets for enemy fighters. You take off and join the bombers. On the way across the North Sea, you spot enemy fighters coming toward you!

Women at War

WHEN PLANES ARE LOST in combat, new planes are delivered by ferry pilots, many of whom are women.

PLANES OFTEN RETURN with battle damage. There might be bullet holes or part of a wing shot away. The ground crew has to repair the damage as fast as possible.

THE SOVIET UNION has regiments of women pilots. Pilots in the 588th Night Bomber Regiment are known as the Night Witches.

The Night Witches fly old-fashioned Polikarpov Po-2 biplanes. They are slow, but they can turn quickly to escape an attack from an enemy fighter.

Allied and German fighters chase each other through the sky, twisting and turning to try to get each other's planes in their gun sights without leaving themselves exposed to enemy fire. Bursts of gunfire tear through the air.

The German fighters, out of ammunition, disappear as quickly as they arrived. You are relieved to have survived your first combat mission, but afterward you realize how terrifying it was.

Handy Hint

Keep looking around—enemy fighters can come from any direction.

*enemy fighter

Passing Time

Fighter pilots don't fly all day, every day, even in wartime. Sometimes they have time off. Or they may be on standby, waiting for the signal to dash to their planes and take off. They also have to wait around if the weather is bad, if planes are out of service, or if the airfield is closed for repairs after an air raid.

Pilots pass the time reading, writing letters home, or playing games. If they're lucky, they get weekend leave—permission to be off duty all weekend! Off-duty pilots in southern England head for London.

Off Duty in London

CITIES IN THE U.S. are brightly lit at night, but in London and other British cities, there's a blackout. No one is allowed to show any light at all. That way, German pilots won't know where to drop their bombs. People have to cover their windows with thick curtains to make sure that no light leaks outside. If any light gets out, you're in trouble!

AIR-RAID PRECAUTIONS (ARP) wardens patrol the streets and make sure that no one shows any light at night.

WATCHING A FILM or a stage show is a favorite night out in London, but be prepared for it to be spoiled by an air raid.

THE WAILING SOUND of air-raid sirens warns everyone that enemy bombers are on the way and bombs will start falling soon.

LONDONERS WAIT OUT the bombing in private air-raid shelters, public shelters, or underground subway stations.

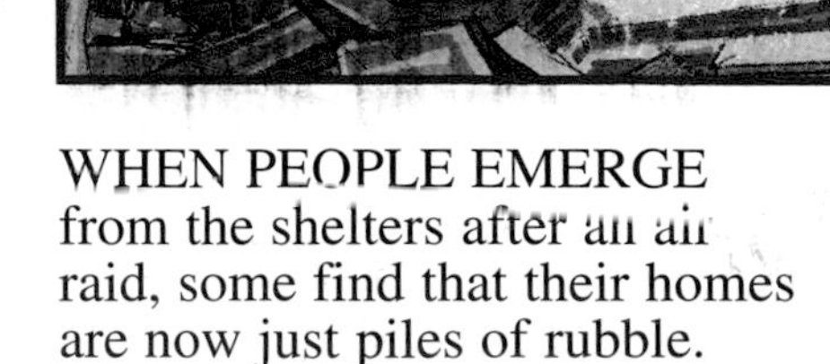

WHEN PEOPLE EMERGE from the shelters after an air raid, some find that their homes are now just piles of rubble.

Bailing Out

You wear a parachute, but it's not on your back. You sit on it! The parachute and a life raft double as a seat cushion. You hope you'll never need them.

One day, you are taken by surprise by a Messerschmitt Bf-109. The 109 is the leading German fighter—and you're in its gun sights! As its pilot opens fire, bullets slam into the armor plate behind your head and shatter the cockpit canopy. Oil sprays out of bullet holes in your engine. You'll have to bail out!

YOU PUT ON YOUR PARACHUTE, slide the shattered canopy back, and climb out of the cockpit into the cold air outside.

AS YOU TUMBLE THROUGH THE AIR, you pull the rip-cord handle, and your parachute billows open above you.

Handy Hint

Remember how you were taught to roll when you land by parachute.

SPLISH!

Survival

IF YOU LAND IN THE SEA, your life raft will keep you afloat while you wait for a ship to pick you up.

IF YOU HAVE TO WAIT to be picked up, or if you land behind enemy lines, you'll need your survival kit. It contains maps, money, a knife, matches, and a compass.

attacked by surprise

Pearl Harbor

On December 7, 1941, Japanese forces launch a surprise attack on the U.S. Pacific Fleet at Pearl Harbor, Hawai'i. More than 350 Japanese fighters, bombers, and torpedo planes attack in two waves. Five midget submarines join the attack. Americans, who have not suffered a major attack on their home territory in living memory, are shocked. The next day, the United States declares war on Japan. Germany and Italy respond by declaring war on the United States. Now the United States will join the war in Europe as well as the war in the Pacific.

U.S. PRESIDENT FRANKLIN D. ROOSEVELT gives one of the most famous speeches of the 20th century on the day after the attack.

SOME AMERICAN PILOTS in the RAF ask the U.S. Embassy to transfer them to U.S. forces. They will get their wish, but not for another year.

AMERICAN FAMILIES hear their president describe the attack on the radio. The speech clearly signaled America's entrance into the war.

Pacific Fighters

Some of your friends became pilots in the U.S. Navy. Now they are fighting the Japanese in the Pacific. Navy pilots are based on flat-decked warships called aircraft carriers. The pilots have to take off from, and land on, a heaving deck that looks the size of a postage stamp from the air. If they miss their ship, they're swimming home!

The most successful U.S. Navy fighter is the Grumman F6F-5 Hellcat. The leading Japanese navy fighter is the Mitsubishi A6M2. The Allies call it the Zero.

Japanese A6M2 Zero fighter

SHORT NEWS FILMS called newsreels keep you informed about the Pacific war. They are shown in movie theaters before the feature films.

**8 a.m.: pronounced "oh-eight-hundred"*

GRUMMAN F6F-5 HELLCAT (USA)

Engine: 2,000 horsepower Pratt & Whitney R-2800-10W
Wingspan: 42 ft., 10 in. (13.1 m)
Top speed: 380 mph (610 kmh)
Weapons: a variety of cannons, machine guns, rockets, bombs, and torpedoes
Maximum altitude: 37,300 ft. (11,370 m)

AS THE ALLIES ADVANCE across the Pacific, Japan uses a terrifying method of attack as a desperate last resort—kamikaze. Kamikaze pilots deliberately crash their planes onto Allied warships.

MITSUBISHI A6M2 ZERO (Japan)

Engine: 950 horsepower Nakajima Sakae 12
Wingspan: 39 ft., 4 in. (12 m)
Top speed: 331 mph (533 kmh)
Weapons: two 20mm cannons, two machine guns, and two bombs
Maximum altitude: 33,790 ft. (10,300 m)

**anti-aircraft fire*

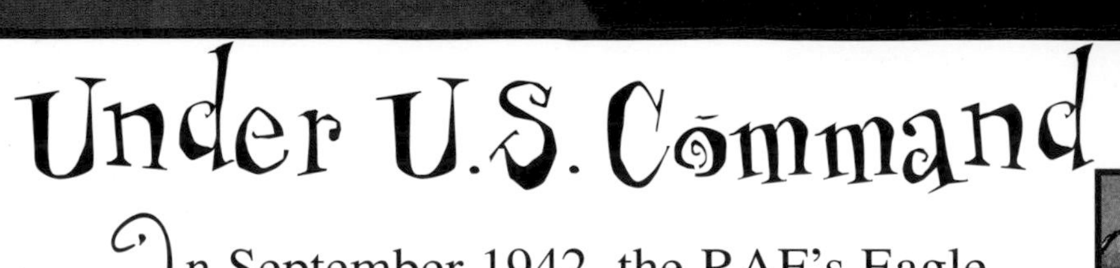

Under U.S. Command

In September 1942, the RAF's Eagle Squadrons, manned by U.S. pilots, are transferred to the U.S. Army Air Forces (USAAF). They become the 4th Fighter Group of the 8th Air Force. All the pilots hand back their blue RAF uniforms and get olive USAAF uniforms. They continue to fly Spitfires until American Thunderbolt fighters arrive.

NOW THAT YOU'RE UNDER U.S. COMMAND, you get U.S. rations. It's great to eat pancakes, burgers, and cookies again.

I wouldn't like to be struck by this Thunderbolt!

Flying in a Steel Jug

THE P-47D THUNDERBOLT is known by its pilots as the "Jug." Jug is short for "Juggernaut"—meaning an unstoppable force—because the Thunderbolt is such a big, heavy, and powerful aircraft. It is the biggest single-seat fighter of its day.

IT'S A SAD DAY when your Spitfire is taken back by the RAF because you'll no longer get to fly in one.

Handy Hint

Don't fire too soon—wait until your target is within the range of your guns.

P-47D Thunderbolt

P-47D THUNDERBOLT

Engine: 2,535 horsepower Pratt & Whitney R-2800
Wingspan: 40 ft., 9 in. (12.4 m)
Top speed: 433 mph (697 kmh)
Weapons: eight Browning machine guns and two bombs or ten rockets
Maximum altitude: 42,000 ft. (12,800 m)

ON YOUR LAST DAY under British command, you receive a medal to mark your service in one of the RAF's famous Eagle Squadrons.

Peace at Last

Germany surrenders on May 7, 1945. The war in Europe is over, though the war in the Pacific will continue for another three months. You are on leave in London when you hear the good news. You've survived, and soon it will be time to go home to the U.S.A.! You join thousands upon thousands of people in front of Buckingham Palace, the official home of the British royal family. When the royal family and Prime Minister Winston Churchill come out onto the palace's balcony, the crowd goes wild. Soldiers, sailors, and airmen throw their hats into the air. One woman, a Wren (a member of the Women's Royal Naval Service) named Kitty Cardle, loses her hat. When she goes on duty without it the next day, her superiors charge her with being improperly dressed!*

*The Wren, Kitty Cardle, is the author's mother.

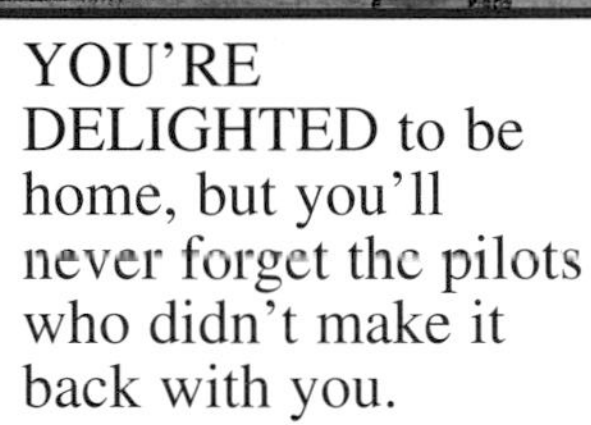

YOU'RE DELIGHTED to be home, but you'll never forget the pilots who didn't make it back with you.

ONE OF THE FIRST THINGS you do is have a meal—steak and french fries, and as much as you can eat. You're lucky, because food is still scarce back in Britain.

AT THE AIRFIELD where you learned to fly a biplane, a youngster admires your medals...

Glossary

Air fair A day or more of flying displays and competitions to entertain spectators.

Allies The countries that joined forces during World War II to fight against Germany, Italy, and Japan, which were known as the Axis powers.

Altitude Height above sea level.

Biplane A plane with two main wings, one above the other.

Briefing A meeting held before a mission to give pilots their instructions.

Canopy The transparent cover over a plane's cockpit.

Cockpit The part of a plane where the pilot sits.

Drogue A small parachute or windsock towed behind a plane and used as a practice target by fighter pilots.

Eagle Squadrons The three squadrons of American pilots in the RAF.

Ferry pilots Pilots who delivered new planes to RAF squadrons during World War II.

Fuselage The main body of an aircraft.

Going solo Flying a plane alone, without an instructor, for the first time.

Ground controllers A team of people who communicate with aircraft and keep track of their positions.

Ground crew The people who repair fighters and bombers, and keep them flying.

Gunnery practice Learning to use guns.

Kamikaze A Japanese word meaning "divine wind." It was the name for suicide attacks on Allied warships by Japanese pilots toward the end of the war.

Landing gear The wheels that support a plane while it is on the ground.

Mission A military operation such as an air attack or bombing raid. A mission or attack by one aircraft is also called a *sortie*.

Morse code A method of sending messages as a series of long and short sounds or visual marks.

Nazi Party The political party that ruled Germany from 1933 to 1945; led by dictator Adolf Hitler, it tried to exterminate certain ethnic groups, especially Jews.

Newsreel A short film showing events in the news.

Night Witches A regiment of all-women pilots in the Soviet Air Forces during World War II.

Pesticides Chemicals which are sprayed on crops to eliminate pests.

Pylon One of the towers that mark out the course for an air race.

RAF The British Royal Air Force.

Rip cord The cord that, when pulled, releases a parachute.

Scramble To get a plane into the air as quickly as possible.

Stunt An aerobatic maneuver made by a pilot to impress or entertain spectators.

U-boat The English term for a German submarine.

Wingspan The width of a plane from one wingtip to the other.

Wren A member of the Women's Royal Naval Service—the female branch of the British Royal Navy.

Index